AN ANNOTATED
SECONDARY BIBLIOGRAPHY SERIES
ON ENGLISH LITERATURE
IN TRANSITION
1880–1920

HELMUT E. GERBER
GENERAL EDITOR

W. SOMERSET MAUGHAM
JOSEPH CONRAD
THOMAS HARDY
E. M. FORSTER
JOHN GALSWORTHY
GEORGE GISSING
D. H. LAWRENCE
H. G. WELLS

THE CONTRIBUTORS

PAUL BEAM
University of Waterloo

HELMUT E. GERBER
Northern Illinois University

PAUL GOETSCH
University of Köln

LAWRENCE GRAVER
Williams College

CHARLES H. GREEN
University of Texas at Arlington

JOHN LESTER
Haverford College

ELEANOR MANHEIM
Hartford, Connecticut

MARION C. MICHAEL
Auburn University

HAROLD F. MOSHER
University of Nice

THOMAS SCHULTHEISS
Arlington, Virginia

EARL E. STEVENS
Rhode Island College

H. RAY STEVENS
Western Maryland College

BRUCE E. TEETS
Central Washington State College

Joseph Conrad

AN ANNOTATED BIBLIOGRAPHY OF WRITINGS ABOUT HIM

COMPILED AND EDITED BY
BRUCE E. TEETS
AND
HELMUT E. GERBER

NORTHERN ILLINOIS UNIVERSITY PRESS
DE KALB, ILLINOIS

Bruce E. Teets is a professor of English at Central Washington State College, Ellensburg.
Helmut E. Gerber is a professor of English and director of Graduate Studies in English at Northern Illinois University, DeKalb.

       Library of Congress Cataloging in Publication Data
       Teets, Bruce E   1914-
         Joseph Conrad: an annotated bibliography about him.
         (An Annotated secondary bibliography series on English literature in transition, 1880-1920)
         1.   Conrad, Joseph, 1857-1924—Bibliography.
       I.   Gerber, Helmut E., 1920-   joint author.
       II.   Title.   III.   Series.
       Z8189.7.T4   016.823'9'12   70-146639
       ISBN 0-87580-020-3

Copyright © 1971 by Northern Illinois University Press
Published by the Northern Illinois University Press, DeKalb, Illinois 60115
Manufactured in the United States of America
All Rights Reserved
Design by John B. Goetz

Preface

Without omitting any accessible important works, we have tried to compile a bibliography as broadly representative of writings on Joseph Conrad as possible. The 1,977 entries, dated between 1895 and 1966, include abstracts of writings in about fourteen languages and publications of all kinds: reviews, general appreciations, bibliographies, biographies, critical books, documented articles, chapters in books, scattered references in books and articles, Ph.D. dissertations, letters to the editors of major newspapers and journals, introductions to editions of Conrad's works, and explications in anthologies and "case books." We include at least a sampling of trivia and nonsense as well as more nearly definitive, highly perceptive, clearly important writings on Conrad. We have tried to include abstracts of some writings published in obscure periodicals and newspapers and little-known books.

We aimed for the ideal of completeness, but, not unexpectedly, fell short of it. Our hope is that eventually we can come closer to our ideal in a supplementary volume which will continue this one beyond 1966 and which will include earlier important items we were regrettably unable to include, or only to include without abstracts in this volume. It is difficult enough to compile lists of very nearly everything that has ever been written on Conrad, as Kenneth A. Lohf and Eugene P. Sheehy; in JOSEPH CONRAD AT MID-CENTURY (1957), and Theodore G. Ehrsam, in A BIBLIOGRAPHY OF JOSEPH CONRAD (1969), came near to doing. It is far more difficult, however, to locate every item in a library and to find a qualified abstracter with access to a particular library. Many items we are certain exist could not be located; some could not be photographed or borrowed; many foreign-language items, especially those in Polish and Russian, were inaccessible or could not be read or abstracted, even over the course of ten years, for lack of a sufficient number of competent readers in those languages to give the necessary time and energy to such a project.

Lacking major funding for our project and lacking a sufficient number of competent researchers in all the right places at the right time, we have reluctantly resigned ourselves to a number of specific limitations and have simply tried to do our human best. We have tried to provide as many meaningful abstracts as possible and, in most instances, bracketed critical comments on the entry; we have tried to correct the inaccuracies of others and not to add to the myriad of errors that already plague the Conrad researcher; in the abstracts, we have tried to represent the original author's voice as honestly as abstracts, paraphrases, selected quotations, and human nature allow; we have tried to include all major work on Conrad (we have not consciously excluded any major work that was accessible to us); and we have tried to give a reasonably thorough sampling of minor and even, admittedly, trivial material. We believe that there is some value in including poor stuff and labeling it for what it is.

We have, insofar as it was possible, placed entries under date of first publication and there provided data on reprintings and later revisions or translations. We have avoided, wherever it was possible, listings under different dates of essentially the same items, a difficult thing to do with such writers on Conrad as Georges Jean-Aubry, Richard Curle, and even Morton Dauwen Zabel. To give this book maximum usefulness for a variety of research purposes, we have provided five different indexes. So much for our affirmations and good intentions. Something remains to be said of what we chose not to do and what, for various reasons, we could not do.

We chose not to include reviews of secondary works, for in most instances, the abstracter has provided a comment on the value of the secondary work, or its value is revealed in the abstract; however, we have regarded Mrs. Conrad's books on her husband and some "Life-and-Letters" books by others as partly primary works and have thus included abstracts of reviews of these works. We have also included some comments on the works of Jerry Allen and Norman Sherry because of the controversy which evolved from their publication. We also chose to exclude undergraduate honors theses and M.A. theses.* We have listed Ph.D. dissertations without abstracts but with references to DISSERTATION ABSTRACTS, or similar series, when applicable. Wherever possible, we have provided abstracts for foreign dissertations, since most of them are published in monograph series or as books and since they are generally not abstracted in works like the

---

* Anyone interested in such material has ready access to it in JOSEPH CONRAD: A BIBLIOGRAPHY OF MASTERS' THESES AND DOCTORAL DISSERTATIONS, 1917-1963, compiled by Edmund A. and Henry T. Bojarski (Lexington: University of Kentucky Libraries Occasional Contributions No. 157, 1964), a mimeographed list; reprinted with slight changes and corrections as "Three Hundred and Thirty-Six Unpublished Papers on Joseph Conrad: A Bibliography of Masters Theses and Doctoral Dissertations, 1917-1963," BULLETIN OF BIBLIOGRAPHY, XXVI (July-Sept. 1969), 61-66, 79-83; absorbed and updated in CONRAD IN ACADEME, edited by Edmund Bojarski and H. Ray Stevens (Ann Arbor, Mich.: Pierian Press, 1971), the first volume in the Thesis Bibliography Series.

Preface

American DISSERTATION ABSTRACTS. Although we have listed many Russian language items, generously provided by Julius I. Kagarlitzkii (U. S. S. R. Academy of Science, Moscow), we regretfully were not able to get abstracts for them.† We also very much regret that we could not include a larger number of Polish entries; since so many we know of have been inaccurately listed in Theodore G. Ehrsam's A BIBLIOGRAPHY OF JOSEPH CONRAD and elsewhere, we have not risked even listing them. We hope to be able to include these entries eventually in a supplement, hopefully with abstracts.‡ Also, a number of items in Hungarian came to our attention too late to locate and have abstracts prepared. We also feel certain that there must be some work on Conrad in Japanese and probably in Finnish, but these we were not able to ferret out. Like other writings, these, too, must wait for a supplementary volume.

This is perhaps the proper place to say that we are relieved to have brought much effort on the part of many people over many years to this tentative conclusion. Yet we must add that we would be pleased to hear from students of Conrad who are frustrated by our omissions and our cut-off date. With an adequate number of contributors, particularly readers of Polish, Russian, Hungarian, and Finnish, we could begin work on a supplementary volume almost immediately. By 1974, the fiftieth anniversary of Conrad's death, perhaps we could significantly supplement the beginning.

ACKNOWLEDGMENTS

Besides the co-editors, those who have contributed most heavily to this bibliography during the years it has been in progress are named opposite the title page. Their patience in the face of great mechanical difficulties, long delays during periods when the co-editors changed their academic affiliations, and much uncertainty whether all the effort they had invested would, indeed, ever result in a book warrants more than the minimal reward we are able to bestow. Our contributors have been colleagues in the best and larger sense of the term and many have over the years become our friends. Only their sustained interest has often saved this difficult project from collapse.

In addition, over all the years this bibliography has been in the making, we have benefited from the assistance at critical moments of very nearly a small army of busy people who allowed us to enlist their talents for more

---

† The items in Kagarlitzkii's list, transliterated and translated by Madeline Long (Western Maryland College), have also appeared in CONRADIANA, I (Summer 1968), 61-66.

‡ For the present, Ehrsam's work, despite inaccuracies, is useful.

limited but nonetheless important tasks. Among those gifted with fluency in various foreign languages, we are especially grateful to the following: Rolena Adorno (Ithaca College, Ithaca, N. Y.) for excellent help with Spanish items, Doris R. Asmundsson (Queensborough Community College, Bayside, N. Y.) for help with Swedish writings, Edmund Bojarski (McMurry College, Abilene, Texas) for allowing us to make use of his bibliographies of theses and dissertations and for corrections in some Polish entries, Edward Herbert (Northern Illinois University) for abstracts from Polish, Julius Kagarlitzkii (U. S. S. R. Academy of Science) for allowing us to use his bibliography of Russian studies of Conrad, Lev Soudek (Northern Illinois University) for abstracts of Czech writings and corrections in various Slavic-language entries, Gustaaf van Cromphout (Northern Illinois University) for much help with writings in Dutch and German, Kristina Valaitis (Graduate Student, Northern Illinois University) for help with French and Italian entries far beyond any call of duty, and Ivo Vidan (University of Zagreb) for bibliographical contributions and some abstracts of Slovene and Serbo-Croatian writings.

Among many friends who came to our aid whenever in moments of despair we had to impose on them, we especially wish to thank the following: Joseph Burkhart (Temple University), W. Eugene Davis (Purdue University), Arra Garab (Northern Illinois University), William Halloran (University of Wisconsin at Milwaukee), James G. Kennedy (Northern Illinois University), Robert L. Peters (University of California at Irvine), and Joseph Wolff (Loyola University, Chicago).

Many graduate students with more good cheer than we had cause to expect helped maintain cardfiles, correct bibliographical data, read difficult proofs, and generally kept us all in good humor. We especially want to record our appreciation to several of them for the often unrewarded hours they gave: Dana Arnold and Deanna Rengstorff of Central Washington State College; Charles O'Malley, Dona Ruby, and, again, Kristina Valaitis, all of Northern Illinois University. The arduous task of preparing the final typescript has fallen largely to Mrs. Stephen (Jeanine) Brundage (Northern Illinois University). Bruce Teets is especially indebted to Mrs. Nancy Weed (Central Washington State College) for typing.

The co-editors are also grateful to the librarians and the several English Departments with which they have been affiliated during the past ten years for generous cooperation, various kinds of support, and always encouragement: the librarians of the Otto G. Richter Library, University of Miami (Florida), the Purdue University librarians at the Lafayette and Indianapolis campuses; the librarians of the Victor J. Bouillon Library, Central Washington State College; and the librarians of the Swen Franklin Parson Library, Northern Illinois University. This list could readily be extended to include a hundred or more libraries throughout the United

PREFACE

States and Europe; almost without exception, the editors and contributors enjoyed the benefits of a long tradition of cooperation from the libraries the use of whose facilities we requested. We are grateful to the English Departments of the University of Miami and the Indianapolis Campus of Purdue University for granting Bruce Teets reduced teaching loads; to the Faculty Research Committee of Central Washington State College for providing Bruce Teets with research grants; to the Purdue University Research Foundation for providing summer research grants and to Northern Illinois University for a generous Council of Deans Fund award to H. E. Gerber.

Finally, we owe most to two ladies who have endured the making of this book for ten years and who have managed to endure us even longer, Virginia Teets and Helga Gerber, our wives.

BRUCE E. TEETS
HELMUT E. GERBER

Contents

Preface	v
A Checklist of the Works of Joseph Conrad	3
Introduction	7
The Bibliography	13
Index of Authors	615
Index of Titles of Secondary Works	627
Index of Periodicals and Newspapers	659
Index of Foreign Languages	665
Index of Primary Titles	667

NOTE ON ENTRY STYLE

Titles of Conrad's books appear in italic type; titles of his stories, in roman capitals and lower case with quotation marks. Titles of books by other authors, collections of stories and letters edited by other writers, and names of periodicals and newspapers appear in capitals and small capitals. The translations appearing in parentheses are confined to meanings of the phrases; however, it should be noted that the titles of translations are seldom literal ones.

Joseph Conrad

AN ANNOTATED BIBLIOGRAPHY
OF WRITINGS ABOUT HIM

A Checklist

OF THE WORKS OF JOSEPH CONRAD
CITED IN THIS BIBLIOGRAPHY

I. FICTION
A. Separate Works

Almayer's Folly. Lond. and New York, 1895.

An Outcast of the Islands. Lond. and New York, 1896.

The Nigger of the Narcissus. New York (as *Children of the Sea, A Tale of the Forecastle*) and Lond., 1897.

Tales of Unrest. Lond. and New York, 1898. Contents: "The Idiots," 1896; "Karain," 1897; "The Lagoon," 1897; "An Outpost of Progress," 1897; "The Return," 1898.

Lord Jim, A Tale. Edinburgh and Lond., New York, and Toronto, 1900.

The Inheritors, An Extravagant Story. (With Ford Madox Hueffer) New York and Lond., 1901.

Youth, A Narrative, and Two Other Stories. Edinburgh and Lond., 1902; New York, 1903. Contents: "Youth," 1898; "Heart of Darkness," 1899; "The End of the Tether," 1902.

Typhoon. New York and Lond., 1902.

Typhoon, and Other Stories. Lond., 1903; New York, 1923. Contents: "Amy Foster," 1901; "Typhoon," 1902; "To morrow," 1902; "Falk," 1903.

Romance, A Novel. (With Ford Madox Hueffer) Lond., 1903; New York, 1904.

Nostromo, A Tale of the Seaboard. Lond. and New York, 1904.

The Secret Agent, A Simple Tale. Lond. and New York, 1907.

A Set of Six. Lond., 1908; New York, 1915. Contents: "An Anarchist," 1906; "The Brute," 1906; "Gaspar Ruiz," 1906; "The Informer," 1906; "The Duel," 1908; "Il Conde," 1908.

Under Western Eyes, A Novel. Lond. and New York, 1911.
'Twixt Land and Sea, Tales. Lond. and New York, 1912. Contents: "The Secret Sharer," 1910; "A Smile of Fortune," 1911; "Freya of the Seven Isles," 1912.
Chance, A Tale in Two Parts. Lond. and New York, 1913.
Victory, An Island Tale. New York and Lond., 1915.
Within the Tides, Tales. Lond. and Toronto, 1915; New York, 1916. Contents: "The Partner," 1911; "The Inn of the Two Witches," 1913; "Because of the Dollars," 1914; "The Planter of Malata," 1914.
The Shadow-Line, A Confession. Lond. and Toronto, and New York, 1917.
The Arrow of Gold, A Story Between Two Notes. New York and Lond., 1919.
The Rescue, A Romance of the Shallows. New York, and Lond. and Toronto, 1920.
The Rover. New York and Lond., 1923.
The Nature of a Crime. (With Ford Madox Hueffer) Lond. and New York, 1924.
Suspense, A Napoleonic Novel. New York, and Lond. and Toronto, 1925.
Tales of Hearsay. Lond. and New York, 1925. Contents: "The Black Mate," 1908; "Prince Roman," 1911; "The Tale," 1917; "The Warrior's Soul," 1917.
The Sisters. New York, 1928.

B. COLLECTED EDITIONS

The Works of Joseph Conrad. Lond., 1921-1927. 20 vols.
The Works of Joseph Conrad. The Uniform Edition. Lond. and Toronto, 1923-1928. 22 vols.
Collected Works of Joseph Conrad. The Memorial Edition. New York, 1926. 21 vols. (Several additional sets—Concord, Kent, Canterbury, etc.—are substantially the same.)
Collected Edition of the Works of Joseph Conrad. Lond., 1946-1955. (Reprinted from the Uniform Edition, without the dramas.) 21 vols.

II. ESSAYS AND MEMOIRS (INCLUDED IN THE COLLECTED EDITIONS)

The Mirror of the Sea, Memories and Impressions. Lond. and New York, 1906.
A Personal Record. (Under title, *Some Reminiscences,* New York, 1908, to secure American copyright, probably only six copies printed) Lond. (as *Some Reminiscences*) and New York, 1912.

A CHECKLIST

Notes on Life and Letters. Lond. and Toronto, and New York, 1921. Contents: "Books," 1905; "Henry James," 1905; "Alphonse Daudet," 1898; "Guy de Maupassant," 1914; "Anatole France—I. *Crainquebille,*" 1904; "Anatole France—II. *L'Ile des pingouins,*" 1908; "Turgenev," 1917; "Stephen Crane, A Note Without Dates," 1919; "Tales of the Sea," 1898; "An Observer in Malay," 1898; "A Happy Wanderer," 1910; "The Life Beyond," 1910; "The Ascending Effort," 1910; "The Censor of Plays," 1907; "Autocracy and War," 1905; "The Crime of Partition," 1919; "A Note on the Polish Problem," 1921; "The Shock of War," 1915; "To Poland in War-time," 1915; "The North Sea on the Eve of the War," 1915; "My Return to Cracow," 1915; "Poland Revisited," 1916; "First News," 1918; "Well Done!" 1918; "Tradition," 1918; "Confidence," 1919; "Flight," 1917; "Some Reflections on the Loss of the *Titanic,*" 1912; "Certain Aspects of the Admirable Inquiry into the Loss of the *Titanic,*" 1912; "Protection of Ocean Liners," 1914; "A Friendly Place," 1912.

Last Essays. Lond. and Toronto, and New York, 1926. Contents: "Geography and Some Explorers," 1924; "The 'Torrens,' A Personal Tribute," 1923; "Christmas Day at Sea," 1923; "Ocean Travels," 1923; "Outside Literature," 1922; "Legends," 1924; "The Unlighted Coast," 1925; "The Dover Patrol," 1921; "Memorandum on the Scheme for Fitting Out a Ship," 1926; "The Loss of the 'Dalgonar,'" 1921; "Travel," 1923; "Stephen Crane," 1923; "His War Book," 1925; "John Galsworthy," 1906; "A Glance at Two Books," 1925; "Preface to 'The Shorter Tales of Joseph Conrad,'" 1924; "Cookery," 1923; "The Future of Constantinople," 1912; "The Congo Diary," 1925.

III. DRAMA

A. Separate Works

One Day More, A Play in One Act. (Adaptation of "To-morrow") Lond., ENGLISH REVIEW, 1913.
The Secret Agent, Drama in Four Acts. (Adaptation of the novel) Canterbury, 1921.
Laughing Anne, A Play. (Adaptation of "Because of the Dollars") Lond., 1923.

B. Collected Edition

Three Plays: Laughing Anne; One Day More; and The Secret Agent. Lond., 1934.

IV. LETTERS: MAJOR COLLECTIONS

Five Letters by Joseph Conrad Written to Edward Noble in 1895. Foreword by Edward Noble. Lond., 1925.

Joseph Conrad's Letters to His Wife. Lond., 1927.

Joseph Conrad, Life and Letters. G. Jean-Aubry. 2 vols. New York and Lond., 1927.

Conrad to a Friend, 150 Selected Letters from Joseph Conrad to Richard Curle, ed. by Richard Curle. New York and Lond., 1928.

Letters from Joseph Conrad, 1895-1924, ed. by Edward Garnett. Indianapolis, 1928.

Lettres françaises, ed. by G. Jean-Aubry. Paris, 1930.

Letters of Joseph Conrad to Marguerite Poradowska, 1890-1920, ed. by John A. Gee and Paul J. Sturm. New Haven and Lond., 1940.

Joseph Conrad: Letters to William Blackwood and David S. Meldrum, ed. by William Blackburn. Durham, N. C., 1958.

Conrad's Polish Background: Letters to and from Polish Friends, ed. by Zdzisław Najder. Lond., New York, Toronto, 1964.

Introduction

An account of the secondary material, 1895 through 1966, on Joseph Conrad may be divided, somewhat arbitrarily, into three convenient periods. Attention needs to be given separately to the major theory of Conrad's career as a writer, the achievement-and-decline concept. The first period, 1895 to 1913, includes Conrad's gradual rise to fame from his first published work, *Almayer's Folly,* to *Chance,* the novel which finally brought him both international recognition and financial success. During his earlier years of writing, Conrad was noticed especially for *The Nigger of the Narcissus, Lord Jim,* the volume *Youth, Nostromo, The Mirror of the Sea, The Secret Agent,* the stories in *A Set of Six* and *'Twixt Land and Sea,* and *A Personal Record*. He soon became known as a writer of sea stories and was compared to Loti, Turgenev, Flaubert, and Maupassant. His first novel, like his other works before *Chance,* was at least fairly well received by the reviewers but was practically ignored by the public. *The Nigger of the Narcissus* (1897) was the first book to be widely noticed by the critics, most of whom praised it.

By the time of *Chance,* Conrad, then aged fifty-six and an author for eighteen years, encountered public approval for the first time. This novel almost immediately became a best seller in both the United States and Britain. It was not exactly what the reviewers said about his work that counted, but the amount of space they gave to him. This acclaim provided the occasion for a somewhat lush panorama of his achievement to date in the TIMES LITERARY SUPPLEMENT (London), 15 January 1914, and gained for him a place of honor, along with space, in most of the leading dailies. The commentators still labeled him a writer of sea stories and reflected not very perceptively upon such matters as his attitude toward women and toward life in general.

The second period of writing about Conrad, 1913 to about 1940, includes an increase of popularity followed by a decline in reputation. By 1922, Conrad, the Polish master of English, was one of the best known living authors in Britain and the United States. In 1923, the number of items published about him increased markedly. His death in 1924 was

7

naturally the occasion for a great spate of laudatory statements, obituary notices, memorial tributes, appreciations, reminiscences, nostalgic attempts to assess his life and works, and considerations of his view of women, of his style, of his irony, and of his pessimism. Up to this time, however, the critical appraisals of his work were halting, uncertain, unsophisticated. For several years after his death, though, Conrad still received much attention: *Suspense, Tales of Hearsay,* and *Last Essays,* published posthumously, helped keep him in the minds of readers and critics alike. In 1929, George T. Keating published, while his subject's renown was extensive in the eyes of the public, his A CONRAD MEMORIAL LIBRARY, made up of contributions by many well-known literary figures. These years also saw the appearance of further productions which maintained his reputation, such as it was: typical appreciations like AN APPRECIATION OF JOSEPH CONRAD, by Arthur J. Price (1931); more perceptive insights into Conrad's works; studies of his collaborations with Ford Madox Ford; the appearance of Jean-Aubry's LIFE AND LETTERS (1927); and miscellaneous publications by Richard Curle. Granville Hicks noted, however, in 1930, that Conrad's reputation was declining because he was too long-winded, too philosophical, too pessimistic, and too greatly out of touch with modern life.

Although collections of letters appeared until 1940, interest in Conrad faltered in the 1930s; his work was highly praised, but the public did not respond seriously after its reception of *Chance*. Opinions of his work ranged from the charge of its being unreadable to the declaration of his being the greatest novelist of the twentieth century. Many comments from foreign critics appeared. Altogether, Conrad was recognized as a distinguished foreigner in England. Jessie Conrad's JOSEPH CONRAD AND HIS CIRCLE (1935), appearing eleven years after her husband's death and containing important new material about him, was not very well received, perhaps because of Mrs. Conrad's exaggerated claims for herself. On the whole, of several attempts to assess his works, none was of outstanding quality. In an effort to relate him to other writers, commentators compared him to Hardy, Kipling, Marryat, and Anatole France. In 1936, Edward Crankshaw in JOSEPH CONRAD: SOME ASPECTS OF THE ART OF THE NOVEL tried to reinstate Conrad as a major craftsman in thinking and in writing novels; he championed him when his reputation was low. Although Conrad was out of fashion at this time, indications existed that he would in due time return to favor. There were, for example, serious efforts to understand his techniques, and the 1940s were to bring further developments in the criticism of his works.

The third period of secondary material on Conrad, about 1940 to 1966 (where the present volume ends), begins auspiciously with JOSEPH CONRAD: THE MAKING OF A NOVELIST by John Dozier Gordan (1940), and

INTRODUCTION

inaugurates a revival of interest in him and his achievement. Gordan's factual book was the first detailed scholarly study; it deals with such topics as Conrad's methods of work, his complete dedication to fiction, and his meticulous revision. Published in 1941, M. C. Bradbrook's little volume, JOSEPH CONRAD: POLAND'S ENGLISH GENIUS, was an impressive survey of Conrad's writings which recognized the increasing technical complexity of his accomplishment. During the mid-1940s, the analyses of individual stories became more perceptive and complex. By 1947, Morton Dauwen Zabel was able to edit notably THE PORTABLE CONRAD, with an excellent introduction and a generous sampling of the work; and, in the same year, William York Tindall in FORCES IN MODERN BRITISH LITERATURE recognized forcefully Conrad's tales of empire, his determinism, his idea of nature, his impressionism, and his symbolism.

Several pathbreaking books on Conrad appeared after World War II. The year 1948, for instance, produced THE GREAT TRADITION by F. R. Leavis, who placed Conrad directly in the "great tradition" of the English novel, following Jane Austen, George Eliot, and Henry James. Since this time, the standard of Conrad criticism has remained high.

In 1949, Walter F. Wright's ROMANCE AND TRAGEDY IN JOSEPH CONRAD and Vernon Young's "Joseph Conrad: Outline for a Reconsideration" strengthened Conrad's reputation substantially; and Oliver Warner's JOSEPH CONRAD (1950) provided comparatively early discernments, perceptive and often suggestive of later criticism. In CONRAD: A REASSESSMENT (1952), Douglas Hewitt found that Conrad's greatness lies in the use of a technique which forces the reader to understand the plight of the main characters as only one manifestation of "the working of universal spiritual and moral laws." In 1954, Paul L. Wiley in CONRAD'S MEASURE OF MAN explored the archetypal and emblematic aspects of Conrad's art and thereby continued the course of Conrad's second rise to fame, a parallel to his long writing career which had first reached a climax with *Chance*. During the 1950s, Conrad received increasingly more attention, and the early 1960s may be seen as the time of his greatest recognition. Richard Curle in JOSEPH CONRAD AND HIS CHARACTERS and Robert F. Haugh in JOSEPH CONRAD: DISCOVERY IN DESIGN generated further interest, the latter considering the twelve major works of 1897 to 1917 in a "new critical" analysis of style and structure. The year of their books, 1957, produced also the first major bibliography of Conrad, Kenneth A. Lohf and Eugene P. Sheehy's JOSEPH CONRAD AT MID-CENTURY: EDITIONS AND STUDIES, 1895-1955, which lists 1,008 critical items in addition to many reviews.

A major contribution to studies of Conrad was Thomas Moser's excellent and influential book, JOSEPH CONRAD: ACHIEVEMENT AND DECLINE (1957). By searching psychoanalytically into Conrad's alleged achievement and decline during his years as a writer, Moser continued and developed in greater depth this widely-held opinion and aroused much new interest in Conrad. In 1957, also, Zabel in CRAFT AND CHARACTER IN MODERN FICTION collected four of his earlier essays on Conrad (1940-1957) in their final form. As a result of these many efforts, the Conrad who survived in 1958 as a great novelist was not the romantic, picturesque, and inscrutable exploiter of the sea and the unknown, but the more subtle and profound creator of the works from *Nostromo* through *Chance*. In this year, too, Albert J. Guerard published his seminal book, CONRAD THE NOVELIST, taking into account all the preceding research and using a psychological approach to the writings. His work is perhaps the most significant consideration of Conrad to date, although some of his concepts are currently being somewhat modified. In 1959, Jocelyn Baines published JOSEPH CONRAD: A CRITICAL BIOGRAPHY, which will no doubt remain for some time the definitive biography. The 1950s saw also much Polish activity in Conrad scholarship, and during these years many serious and discerning analyses of the works appeared.

Two centennial symposia of 1960 deserve noting: JOSEPH CONRAD: CENTENNIAL ESSAYS, edited by Ludwik Krzyżanowski, and THE ART OF JOSEPH CONRAD: A CRITICAL SYMPOSIUM, edited by R. W. Stallman, the latter being the fullest and most useful collection of essays to date. In the early 1960s, Bruce Harkness not only broadened the perspectives on Conrad's works but also made some of them readily available for use in college classes with CONRAD'S "HEART OF DARKNESS" AND THE CRITICS (1960) and CONRAD'S "SECRET SHARER" AND THE CRITICS (1962), which contained much of the significant current interpretation of these stories. Frederick R. Karl's A READER'S GUIDE TO JOSEPH CONRAD (1960) included fresh material on Conrad's techniques and new evaluations of several stories and novels. In these years also appeared numerous original views of *Nostromo* and *The Secret Agent,* novels which were being recognized as two of Conrad's greatest achievements. In 1963, Eloise Knapp Hay brought out another excellent study, THE POLITICAL NOVELS OF JOSEPH CONRAD, stressing "Heart of Darkness," *Nostromo, The Secret Agent,* and *Under Western Eyes,* and originating a series of books on Conrad's "political" works; but Mrs. Hay is helpful on Conrad's total oeuvre. Many articles of the 1960s concentrated on "Heart of Darkness," so that the test of a critic on Conrad now is largely determined, or so it often seems, by what he says about this story. *Lord Jim, Under Western Eyes, The Nigger of the Narcissus, The Secret Agent,* and "The Secret Sharer" also received special emphasis. Several other stories and tales as well as *Victory* have been reconsidered. J. I. M. Stewart's EIGHT MODERN WRITERS (1963) contains an important chapter on Conrad, one of the eight authors who appeared to hold an unchallengeable position as outstanding British writers.

INTRODUCTION

In addition to great numbers of studies of individual works by Conrad, many investigations of more general topics helped to clarify his accomplishment: Conrad's themes, his epistemology, his sources (as in Norman Sherry's CONRAD'S EASTERN WORLD [1966]), his symbolism and meaning (as in Ted E. Boyle's SYMBOL AND MEANING IN THE FICTION OF JOSEPH CONRAD [1965]), and his so-called "Polishness" and his relation to his native country, which was the major interest of Andrzej Busza in CONRAD'S POLISH LITERARY BACKGROUND AND SOME ILLUSTRATIONS OF THE INFLUENCE OF POLISH LITERATURE ON HIS WORK (1966). In JOSEPH CONRAD AND THE FICTION OF AUTOBIOGRAPHY (1966), Edward W. Said studied the correlation between Conrad's fiction and his letters, and J. Hillis Miller seems to comprehend Conrad's aesthetic unusually well in POETS OF REALITY: SIX TWENTIETH-CENTURY WRITERS (1965), a refutation of the facile labeling of Conrad as a nihilist. CONRAD: A COLLECTION OF CRITICAL ESSAYS, edited in 1966 by Marvin Mudrick, seems less fresh than the earlier symposium edited by Stallman.

Critical studies of Conrad continue to appear so unceasingly that one is hard pressed to keep abreast of them. Among the notable books published since 1966 are Avrom Fleishman's CONRAD'S POLITICS: COMMUNITY AND ANARCHY IN THE FICTION OF JOSEPH CONRAD (1967), which carries further Mrs. Hay's earlier work on this subject, as does Claire Rosenfield in PARADISE OF SNAKES: AN ARCHETYPAL ANALYSIS OF CONRAD'S POLITICAL NOVELS (1967); Bernard C. Meyer's JOSEPH CONRAD: A PSYCHOANALYTIC BIOGRAPHY (1967); John A. Palmer's JOSEPH CONRAD'S FICTION: A STUDY IN LITERARY GROWTH (1968); Lawrence Graver's CONRAD'S SHORT FICTION (1969); Theodore G. Ehrsam's A BIBLIOGRAPHY OF JOSEPH CONRAD (1969), the only sizable effort of this kind since that of Lohf and Sheehy; and Wilfred S. Dowden's JOSEPH CONRAD: THE IMAGED STYLE (1970). And Norman Sherry's CONRAD'S WESTERN WORLD has been announced by Cambridge University Press for publication in 1971. One periodical, CONRADIANA, is devoted entirely to matters related to Conrad. In addition to the almost innumerable books and articles on Conrad, several conferences at recent meetings of the Modern Language Association also bespeak the current lively interest in him.

A survey of writings about Conrad would be incomplete without some notice of the most widely accepted theory about his writing career, the so-called achievement-and-decline concept, according to which Conrad's creative powers gradually developed to a peak with such works as *Lord Jim, Nostromo,* "The Secret Sharer," and a few others (opinions differ as to the exact location of the greatest accomplishment) and then fell off in imaginative invention in his later efforts, including particularly *Chance, Victory, The Arrow of Gold,* and *The Rover. Victory* has remained a test case of a kind. This principle of rising and falling quality, first suggested in 1927 by John Galsworthy in "Reminiscences of Conrad" in his CASTLES IN SPAIN AND OTHER SCREEDS, was developed in greater detail in 1949 by Vernon Young in "Joseph Conrad: Outline for a Reconsideration." Young anticipated most of the argument, and Douglas Hewitt in CONRAD: A REASSESSMENT (1952) first considered the idea at length. In CONRAD'S MEASURE OF MAN (1954), Paul L. Wiley agreed with the earlier advocates of this position; but Thomas Moser in JOSEPH CONRAD: ACHIEVEMENT AND DECLINE (1957) supplied the greatest impetus while adding a psychoanalytical dimension to Hewitt's version of the thesis. Albert J. Guerard in CONRAD THE NOVELIST (1958) accepted the broad outlines of the Hewitt-Moser view, but his explanation of the "decline" was more cautious. Frederick R. Karl in A READER'S GUIDE TO JOSEPH CONRAD (1960) helped keep the theory before the public. Edward W. Said in JOSEPH CONRAD AND THE FICTION OF AUTOBIOGRAPHY (1966) claimed that the climax of Conrad's letters coincides with the fulfillment of his desire for self-discovery and also with World War I, the period of *Victory,* thus restoring to this novel some of its lost regard. So stood this view in 1966, but in more recent years it has been questioned, notably by John A. Palmer in JOSEPH CONRAD'S FICTION: A STUDY IN LITERARY GROWTH (1968). At present, with the exception of *The Shadow-Line,* which has usually been seen as a masterpiece, *Victory* seems to be regarded as the last example of Conrad's major achievements.

At the present time, Conrad seems to be at the height of his second great period of recognition, and the sheer bulk of writings about him makes him both noticeable and notable. The high quality of many articles and books, however, greatly surpasses the aggregate, and Conrad firmly remains a major modern author who not only is clearly and unmistakably in the "great tradition" of the English novel, where F. R. Leavis first placed him in 1948, but has also been assigned a secure place in world literature.

The Bibliography

1895

1 *"Almayer's Folly:* A Story of an Eastern River," ATHENAEUM, LXVIII (25 May 1895), 671.

In *Almayer's Folly,* JC "break[s] new ground" in presenting unfamiliar pictures "evidently drawn from life." His style suffers from "exuberance" and stifling convolutions, but his characters are effective. His "overloaded" but "powerful" description of the Bornean forest shows the influence of Zola.

2 Noble, James Ashcraft. "New Novels," ACADEMY, XLVII (15 June 1895), 502.

Almayer's Folly has faults [not specified] "thick as blackberries," probably because of JC's inexperience; but the book shows promise (the character of Almayer is "certainly distinct enough") and leaves an impression of "grasp and power." The novelty of setting is attractive.

1896

3 Little, James Stanley. "New Novels," ACADEMY, XLIX (27 June 1896), 525.

An Outcast of the Islands is a masterpiece, a clever psychological study of subtleties and "wayward contradictions" of human nature. The style is "mellow," and the diction "round and picturesque."

4 "New Publications. . . ." NEW YORK TIMES, 23 Sept 1896, p. 10.

In *An Outcast of the Islands,* "Mr. Conrad writes the romance of the furthest East, his special ground being the Malayan Peninsula. . . . His main theme is human degradation. . . . Mr. Conrad writes at a fever heat, and you catch at times a scent of that miasma which is ever lowering over the pestilential swamps of the Sambir country."

5 "New Writers: Mr. Joseph Conrad," BOOKMAN (Lond), X (May 1896), 41.

The background for *Almayer's Folly* and *An Outcast of the Islands* is personal experience; there are parallels to Loti's "exotic romances." *Almayer* is a "remarkable novel where wild nature and strange humanity were so powerfully pourtrayed [sic]."

6 *"An Outcast of the Islands,"* ATHENAEUM, LXIX (18 July 1896), 91.

The promise of *Almayer's Folly* is fulfilled in *An Outcast of the Islands,* one of the "strongest and most original novels of the year." The novel manifests extensive experience, close observation, subtle analysis, and poetic appreciation of nature. The moral atmosphere is "magnificently sordid." Though the "dramatic personae do not reflect much credit on humanity," the book marches inevitably like Greek drama to a close. The "cynical epilogue" is unnecessary. The style is sometimes roughhewn, but the book is brilliant.

1897

7 Dinamov, S. *"Kapriz Olmeira,"* (*Almayer's Folly*), KNIGNOSHA, 8 (1897), 9.
[In Russian.]

8 "Recent Novels," SPECTATOR (Lond), LXXIX (25 Dec 1897), 940.

The Nigger of the Narcissus gives "an extraordinarily vivid picture of life on board of a sailing vessel." JC's choice of themes and "the uncompromising nature of his methods" interfere with his popularity.

1898

9 "Books and Authors," OUTLOOK (NY), LVIII (9 April 1898), 929.

"A true and exact account" of "forecastle life in all its ignorance, wretchedness, courage, endurance, and moral weakness," in "odd contrast" to

1896: 5-6   1897: 7-8   1898: 9-15

William W. Jacobs's "amusing stories of sailors' pranks" "so widely read of late." *The Children of the Sea* [*The Nigger of the Narcissus*] is "not a novel in the ordinary sense; it is romantic only in its treatment of the vast forces of external nature; it is not at all humorous."

10 "Book Reviews," ACADEMY, LIII (5 Feb 1898), 163.

In *The Nigger of the Narcissus,* JC followed in the footsteps of Stephen Crane, the beginner of a new class of descriptive artists who "aspire to make visible the inside of great scenes" in such a way as to make it "look like the truth" [SPEAKER (unlocated)]. JC's style is better than Crane's, though it has the same "jerky and spasmodic" quality and too much minute description [DAILY TELEGRAPH (Lond), 8 Dec 1897, p. 4]. *Nigger* is "oppressively monotonous . . . yet enthralling" [MANCHESTER COURIER, 11 Dec 1897, p. 3]. [A review of reviews on *Nigger*.]

11 "Brown Humanity," OUTLOOK (Lond), I (23 April 1898), 372.

Tales of Unrest is an indication that JC is not bound by his South Seas environment. Two of the best stories are from there, but two other great ones have their settings in West Africa and London. The landscape is even better in these stories than elsewhere. "An Outpost of Progress" and "Karain" are excellent as tales. "The Return" is "Ibsenish" and surprising. The style is occasionally loose and haphazard, but this is a cavil.

12 "Chronicle and Comment," BOOKMAN (NY), VIII (Oct 1898), 91.

Under the title *The Children of the Sea, The Nigger of the Narcissus* received "unanimous praise." The realism of the book resembles that of Marryat and Melville.

13 Crane, Stephen. "Concerning the English 'Academy,' " BOOKMAN (NY), VII (March 1898), 22-24.

The Nigger of the Narcissus is "a marvel of descriptive writing" and the best sea story written by a living author, but in "A Reviewer's Puzzle," the ACADEMY [LIII (1 Jan 1898), Fiction Supplement, 1-2] unfairly judged it to be "too slight and episodic" to be chosen as the best novel of 1897.

14 "From Outlying Stations," LITERARY WORLD (Lond), LVII (10 June 1898), 534.

The five "stories and sketches" in *Tales of Unrest* are "dun-coloured . . . strong grim and relentless," and description is JC's "strong point" in this unsustained production.

15 [Garnett, Edward]. "Mr. Joseph Conrad," ACADEMY, LV (15 Oct 1898), 82-83; rptd enlgd and altered in FRIDAY NIGHTS (Lond: Cape; NY: Knopf, 1922), pp. 83-101.

An artist reveals a glimpse of "a mysterious world behind the apparent"; only the artist causes the life of man to appear "suddenly natural and comprehensible." JC thus breaks through the "blank solid wall of the familiar" to see in everything *"the significant fact"* as only a poet can do. The peculiar quality of his art is to make his readers "perceive men's lives in their natural relation to the seen universe around them" conjoined with "insight into human nature and a power of conceiving character," a quality of poetic realism like that of the great Russian novels. JC is "an artist of artists, his love is for Nature, his sure instinct is for beauty."

16 "Literature: *Tales of Unrest*," CRITIC, XXXII (14 May 1898), 328.

In *Tales of Unrest,* JC is an "impressionistic realist" with great descriptive powers. A sense of dismay in the stories raises the question, "What is Art—and to what end?"

17 "Mr. Conrad's Latest Story," SATURDAY REVIEW (Lond), LXXXV (12 Feb 1898), 211.

In *The Nigger of the Narcissus,* JC "gives us the sea as no other storyteller of our generation has been able to render it." But he "has not realised, as yet, the importance . . . of 'the human interest.'" Singleton and the Captain do not come alive. Donkin "remains shadowy" (in drawing him, JC may have been influenced by "The Ebb Tide"), and the Nigger "wearies the reader from the outset."

18 *"The Nigger of the Narcissus,"* NEW YORK TIMES SATURDAY REVIEW OF BOOKS AND ART, 21 May 1898, p. 344.

The book known as *The Nigger of the Narcissus* in England and published here as *The Children of the Sea* is not a boy's book "but a pre-Raphaelite picture of actual life in the forecastle."

19 "Novel Notes," BOOKMAN (Lond), XIII (Jan 1898), 131.

"[I]n spite of an overminute method" that in *The Nigger of the Narcissus,* where there is little plot to hurry the reader on, might easily become irritating and irksome, Mr. Conrad succeeds in interesting us in no ordinary degree." In *Nigger,* except for Jimmy, the crew is "strikingly true to life."

20 Payn, James. "Our Note Book," ILLUSTRATED LONDON NEWS, CXII (5 Feb 1898), 172.

The Nigger of the Narcissus owes its attraction to the inhabitants of the forecastle of the ship—"dissatisfied, half-mutinous, and quaintly humorous."

21 Payne, William Morton. "Recent Fiction," DIAL (Chicago), XXV (1 Aug 1898), 75-79.

The Children of the Sea [*The Nigger of the Narcissus*] is a searching story of life at sea; its power lies in the "exposition of the psychology of the mutiny, of the storm."

22 "The Rambler," BOOK BUYER (NY), XVI (June 1898), 389-90.

JC's reputation rose rapidly, *Tales of Unrest* having just appeared and *The Nigger of the Narcissus* having been published serially by Henley and in book form in England and America (as *The Children of the Sea*). *The Rescue* is forthcoming in ENGLISH ILLUSTRATED MAGAZINE.

23 "Recent Fiction," ILLUSTRATED LONDON NEWS, CXII (8 Jan 1898), 50.

In *The Nigger of the Narcissus*, JC portrays powerfully "the psychology of the primitive passions of man (as opposed to the opposite sex)." The emotions of the rough crew caused by James Wait's presence on the ship and the fearful storm are "very well done," but "at too great length, and in language too technical."

24 "Recent Fiction," NATION (NY), LXVII (14 July 1898), 54.

There is nothing sensational or exciting in *The Nigger of the Narcissus*, published as *The Children of the Sea,* yet "the narrative makes an indelible impression" because JC appears to know everything about the sea and sailors. JC "has no form; he wanders, he wavers, does not lead, but is driven." [Typically imperceptive, like many early comments on JC's works.]

25 "Recent Fiction," NATION (NY), LXVII (21 July 1898), 54.

All the tales in *Tales of Unrest* are "very tragic," really "quite horrible." "The Idiot" might have been written by Maupassant; but the other stories, although "less impressive," have some power and meaning, "some question about the inscrutable mystery and enduring pain of life."

26 "Recent Fiction," NATION (NY), LXVII (21 July 1898), 54.

The Children of the Sea [*The Nigger of the Narcissus*] shows "an imaginative power which was never let loose in [Conrad's] earlier long-winded tales of South Sea savages and traders." The incidents are ordinary; there is nothing exciting except "a vaguely threatened mutiny and a bad storm, which the *Narcissus* outrode." But a lasting impression is left because the narrator seems to be a seaman who knows all about the sea and ships, and because he has "the poet's trick of heightening and deepening, producing a harmony of untruth which is a powerful representation of truth."

27 "Recent Short Stories," SPECTATOR (Lond), LXXXI (13 Aug 1898), 218-19.

In *Tales of Unrest*, "Karain: A Memory" and "The Lagoon" are "masterpieces of exotic portraiture." JC's European-laid stories are an "experiment" which is "by no means satisfactory." His "white men and women nine times out of ten cut but sorry figures alongside of the dignified, heroic, unhappy Orientals."

28 "Short Stories," ATHENAEUM, LXXI (30 April 1898), 564.

All five tales in *Tales of Unrest* are worth reading. The best, "The Return," is a tale of matrimonial unhappiness. However, JC exceeds "all limit of metaphor" in "The Lagoon" in speaking of "a strange obsession that wound like a black thread" through life. His writing is "occasionally slipshod."

29 Sullivan, T. R. "The Burdens of Restless Lives," BOOK BUYER, XVI (May 1898), 350-52.

The Children of the Sea [*The Nigger of the Narcissus*] seems to be "a chronicle of bitter experience rather than a story." JC's sympathy for his characters shows that he writes out of a first-hand experience. The method "is the modern realistic one, not entirely free from the vice of over-elaboration." While the book "would hardly tempt a schoolboy to ship before the mast," it has beauty. *Tales of Unrest* has a wide range and shows JC's "preference for themes as far removed from commonplaces as one may hope to find upon our planet." His introspective treatment of his tale of London suggests Hawthorne's "Wakefield." Here, however, "the treatment is prolonged, and its first effect is strange in the extreme." "The Return" demonstrates again JC's "power to distinguish himself in an untried field."

30 *"Tales of Unrest,"* REVIEW OF REVIEWS (NY), XVIII (Dec 1898), 729.

JC produces effective variations on two themes: the Sea and Fear. "An Outpost of Progress" and "The Idiots" "create a nightmare in their sheer bald horror."

1899

---

31 Alden, William L. "London Literary Letter," NEW YORK TIMES SATURDAY REVIEW, 17 June 1899, p. 388.

"Heart of Darkness" and *The Nigger of the Narcissus* assure JC of immortality. "Heart of Darkness" is not fiction: "It is literally true in every detail."

32 *"The Nigger of the Narcissus,"* NEW YORK TIMES SATURDAY REVIEW OF BOOKS AND ART, 4 March 1899, p. 136.

[A reader (unsigned) inquires about the availability in print of the title *The Nigger of the Narcissus*. The only previous mention of this title had been in a recent article by a Mr. Alden in this same newspaper. The editor replies that *The Nigger of the Narcissus* is the English title of a book known in this country as *The Children of the Sea*.]

33 "Our Awards for 1898: Mr. Joseph Conrad and *Tales of Unrest*," ACADEMY, LVI (14 Jan 1899), 66-67.

JC has been awarded 50 guineas for *Tales of Unrest*. JC shows the "aloofness" of Turgenev and the irony of Greek drama; he keeps man in his place in the universe (transitory versus permanent forces). He blends nature and man. JC is a poet, able to transfer to paper the very heart of the thing described.

34 Teincey, Jean. "Le roman américain et *'Le Nègre du Narcisse,'* " (The American Novel and *The Nigger of the Narcissus*), REVUE BRITANNIQUE, III (1899), 185-215.

James Wait is a symbol of fatality in whom the crew finds a torturing obsession. [Mostly on a number of American novels in which *The Nigger of the Narcissus* is included. Mostly plot summary.] [In French.]

1900

35 Alden, William L. "London Literary Letter," NEW YORK TIMES SATURDAY REVIEW, 3 March 1900, p. 138.

[A two-paragraph squib or puff remarking on JC's mastery in "Heart of Darkness."]

36 Alden, William L. "London Literary Letter," NEW YORK TIMES SATURDAY REVIEW, 10 Nov 1900, p. 770.

Lord Jim has most recently been published in book form.

37 Alden, William L. "London Literary Letter," NEW YORK TIMES SATURDAY REVIEW, 1 Dec 1900, p. 836.

Lord Jim "is hardly a novel, for it lacks the essential form." It is better than anything else JC has done; it should put him "at the head of English short story writers with the solitary exception of Mr. Kipling."

38 "Fiction," ACADEMY, LIX (10 Nov 1900), 443.

Lord Jim is art, a searching study, a revelation of the East. It is structurally excellent. The characters other than Jim, though fully drawn, have a place solely in relation to Jim. JC is a novelist's novelist. "Blemishes" in his work are slight, but JC's starting Jim as a water clerk and turning the story over to a narrator who would in real life have taken about eleven hours to talk the 99,000 words are objectionable. The narrator's diction is not always really conversational.

39 "Joseph Conrad's *Lord Jim*," NEW YORK TIMES SATURDAY REVIEW, 1 Dec 1900, p. 839.

In reference to *Lord Jim,* there is a similarity between JC's method and Henry James's method—both are involved and intricate.

40 "Tales of Adventure," ATHENAEUM, No. 3810 (3 Nov 1900), 576.

Lord Jim is the best book JC has written so far. He is more successful in his use of materials than in *The Nigger of the Narcissus.* Style, mannerisms, and structure create difficulties. Only a small portion of the book "is free from the inverted comma, and it is essential to right understanding . . . that the distinction between the two portions should be observed." Many found the story easier to read as it appeared serially in BLACKWOOD'S MAGAZINE.

1901

41 "Fiction," ACADEMY, LXI (3 Aug 1901), 93.

The Inheritors is "an allegory, a satire *à clef.*" The characters (Churchill, Duc de Mersch, Polehampton, Gurnard) are probably identifiable as real people. But this novel never lives; it has neither the necessary high-handed gusto of political comedy nor the normal effect of being close to human nature required of satire. It is too allegorical. The character Fox, a "Fourth Dimensionist," is Wellsian, a blot on the book. All is too "ultra-delicate" in expression.

42 "General Gossip of Authors and Writers," CURRENT LITERATURE, XXX (Feb 1901), 222.

Few writers have increased in stature so much recently as JC. *Lord Jim,* expanded to six times the version in BLACKWOOD'S, proves him one of "the ablest and most compelling of living writers about the sea." His "quality is always in keeping with his quantity."

43 "The Inheritors," ATHENAEUM, LXXIV (3 Aug 1901), 151-52.

The Inheritors is astonishingly subtle. Though perhaps pseudo-psychological, it is brilliantly clever. The tension reached is so high that the reader is exhausted by these "emotionless inevitable people of the Fourth Dimension, who are like . . . an unpleasant branch of Nietzsche's 'Overmen.' " An extravaganza, it shows more ability and artistry than "four-fifths of the fiction of the year."

44 "The Inheritors," NEW YORK TIMES SATURDAY REVIEW, 13 July 1901, p. 499.

Enjoyment of *The Inheritors* will depend on the reader's "ability to enjoy satire of a subtle and highly finished order." Although the plot is neither original nor pleasant, the "treatment is fresh and unconventional." JC's power of characterization and "his sensitive appreciation of the conflicting subtleties of human motive and conduct . . . make the story actual and effective." Although the story lacks the emotional power of *Lord Jim,* it is "clean, vigorous, and not machine made."

45 "New Writer: Joseph Conrad," BOOKMAN (Lond), XX (Sept 1901), 173.

A review of JC's background shows that his "life has from the beginning been rich in change" and that his experiences (illness after the journey to the Congo and loss of money in investments) influenced his writing. *Typhoon* is eagerly awaited "in a few weeks."

46 "Novel Notes," BOOKMAN (NY), XIII (April 1901), 187.

Lord Jim is "more than usually serious, more than usually depressing." Although "there is no bad work in it," there is "far too much good." Half of it should have been omitted. The book is "all Jim—there is nothing else in it that counts." Jim "will never face that part of him that made 'the mistake,' but he knows he has to expiate it." Considered as a story, *Jim* "may find various criticism," but judged as a psychological document "it must be acknowledged a masterpiece."

1902

47 Clifford, Hugh. "The Art of Mr. Joseph Conrad," SPECTATOR (Lond), LXXXIX (29 Nov 1902), 827; rptd in LIVING AGE, CCXXXVI (10 Jan 1903), 120-23.

Despite the fact that JC's works are really *"written,"* like "an elaborate piece of mosaic," they make "stiff reading" and demand close attention and reperusal. The style is "occasionally difficult, instinctive, moulded on no ready-made model"; but the matter is of greater significance and higher value. Description is undoubtedly JC's "forte." His realism is "born of sure knowledge." [Gives general comments on each tale in *Youth, A Narrative, and Two Other Stories.*]

48 Garnett, Edward. "Mr. Conrad's New Book: *Youth: A Narrative; and Two Other Stories,*" ACADEMY, LXIII (6 Dec 1902), 606-7; rptd in JOSEPH CONRAD'S "HEART OF DARKNESS": BACKGROUNDS AND CRITICISMS, ed by Leonard F. Dean (Englewood Cliffs, NJ: Prentice-Hall, Spectrum Books, 1960), pp. 145-47.

"Heart of Darkness," the best of the three tales, is "most amazing, a consummate piece of artistic *diablerie,* . . . the high-water mark of the author's talent." The art of the story analyzes in a masterly manner "two Continents in conflict" and displays the "abysmal gulf between the white man's system and the black man's comprehension of its results." "Youth" is "the song of every man's youth," and "The End of the Tether" displays JC's special gift as an artist in his placing a whole scene before the reader so that the details "all fuse in the perfect and dream-like illusion of an unforgettable reality."

49 "Mr. [William L.] Alden's Views," NEW YORK TIMES SATURDAY REVIEW, 13 Dec 1902, p. 898.

"Youth" is a superlative achievement with no plot; it is simply a description of a shipwreck which is wonderfully described. The accomplishment of this story places JC "with the foremost writers of fiction in any language."

50 [Putnam, George Palmer]. "The Story of a Storm," HARPER'S WEEKLY, XLVI (4 Oct 1902), 1412-13.

JC's empirical knowledge of the workings of a ship, his fine sense of humor, and his descriptive style which succeeds in involving the reader in the narrative help make JC a facile storyteller and "Typhoon" a forceful novel. [Mainly plot summary.]

51 "The Quiet Captain," NEW YORK TIMES SATURDAY REVIEW, 20 Sept 1902, p. 626.

" 'Typhoon' is notable not only for its description of a storm but also for the presentation of contrast between the raging elements" and "the cool . . . deliberate efforts of a man, even a commonplace man, to fight . . . against what seems inexorable fate." JC has created a new character in Captain MacWhirr, a man who is "deficient in imagination . . . apparently dull . . . silent because he really has nothing to say." The Captain's main traits are his honesty, his sense of duty, and his humanity.

52 "Short Stories," ATHENAEUM, LXXV (20 Dec 1902), 824.

In *Youth*, JC's scholarly thoroughness, his untiring attempt to be flawless, is extremely praiseworthy. His short stories—really, perhaps, concentrated novels—combine the usually separated categories of movement and adventure with that of characterization and analysis of the human mind. JC is especially good at surrounding a character, by unobtrusive methods, with a distinctive atmosphere inside a few pages. He shows some signs of growing "over subtle in his analysis of moods, temperaments, and mental idiosyncrasies." "Heart of Darkness" is a "big and thoughtful conception, the most important part of the book."

53 *"Youth,"* TIMES LITERARY SUPPLEMENT (Lond), 12 Dec 1902, p. 372; rptd in JOSEPH CONRAD'S "HEART OF DARKNESS": BACKGROUNDS AND CRITICISMS, ed by Leonard F. Dean (Englewood Cliffs, NJ: Prentice-Hall, Spectrum Books, 1960), pp. 147-48.

In *Youth,* JC's method is "a little precious." "Youth" displays, "as in a picture," "the colour, the atmosphere of the East"; the concluding scene of "Heart of Darkness" is one of "picturesque" and "extravagant" horror; and "The End of the Tether," the best of the stories, should have Captain Whalley "in the forefront of the book."

1903

54 Cooper, Frederic Taber. "The Sustained Effort and Some Recent Novels," BOOKMAN (NY), XVIII (Nov 1903), 311.

In *Typhoon, and Other Stories,* "Falk" is the finest of the tales. "Tomorrow" is representative of JC's "grim queerness", and "Amy Foster," "equally simple in structure," is "the story of a mute, inglorious tragedy." "Falk," however, is more than it seems to be at first; on the surface "it gives promise of pure comedy," but underneath is Falk, haunted for six years by the memory of having eaten human flesh and now having his suffering doubled because he has at last found a woman who fascinates him but who probably cannot marry a man guilty of cannibalism.

55 "Fiction," ACADEMY, LXV (31 Oct 1903), 469.

Alone, JC "paints the soul of man and nature," but, in *Romance,* he and Hueffer [Ford Madox Ford] together paint mere outward semblances, which are drowned with elaboration. The plot hangs fire and is not convincing.

56 "Fiction," FORUM, XXXIV (Jan 1903), 400.

In the story "Typhoon," JC gives "less than usual" of a mysterious Eastern atmosphere. His immediate scene is no larger than his freighter. The hero is the ship and Captain MacWhirr is "a man as incapable of harboring a fancy or a novel idea as he was of neglecting a recognized duty." Jukes, the mate, is "the chorus of the sea tragedy." While "Typhoon" resembles Kipling's "The Ship That Found Herself," it "avoids the rather mechanical impersonation of that thrilling tale." JC is "one of the greatest craftsmen in fiction today"; his greatness as an artist will be determined "only when his peculiar kind of impressionism has had a longer test."

57 "Five Novels," NATION (NY), LXXVI (11 June 1903), 477-78.

Youth places JC "unmistakably among the best imaginative writers of his period." The qualities of importance in it are "observation and knowledge of men, of affairs, of places; abundant resources for action and for variety of people to carry it on, and a power of expression so fluent and intense that it often runs into prodigality." "Youth" is "so suffused with emotion that literal account of disaster and failure becomes a lyrical expression of the hope and courage and joy of youth." "Heart of Darkness" is "a dreadful and fascinating tale, full as any of Poe's of mystery and haunting terrors, yet with a substantial basis of reality." "The End of the Tether" contains "no strained heroism, nothing ever so slightly improbable or artificial in the portrait of Capt. Whalley," who is simply "an honest, strong, invincibly proud old man, fighting fate single-handed, and determined to fight to the finish."

> **58** Masefield, John. "Deep Sea Yarns: 'Youth, A Narrative,'" SPEAKER, N.S. VII (31 Jan 1903), 442; rptd in JOSEPH CONRAD'S 'HEART OF DARKNESS': BACKGROUNDS AND CRITICISMS, ed by Leonard F. Dean (Englewood Cliffs, NJ: Prentice-Hall, Spectrum Books, 1960), pp. 148-49.

Both "Youth" and "Heart of Darkness" consist of "page after page of stately and brilliant prose, which is fine writing, good literature, and so forth, but most unconvincing narrative." "Youth" is the best of the three tales; "Heart of Darkness" fails to create its central character; and "The End of the Tether," "a more precise piece of creation," is "a trifle tedious and diffuse." This volume, however, is JC's best work to date.

> **59** "Mr. Conrad's Way," ACADEMY, LXIV (9 May 1903), 463-64.

In *Typhoon and Other Stories,* JC, basically a writer of the sea as seen in "Typhoon," reveals "a consciousness of vastness and of wide and sinister horizons," with characters whose truth the reader never questions: his "psychology has the accuracy of brilliant diagnosis." Indirectness, sudden outside comments, and a "returning upon himself" are part of JC's inherent method designed to heighten effects. "Falk" shows JC as "an interpreter . . . of moods and the human spirit"; "Amy Foster" is "true tragedy—the tragedy of attraction and misunderstanding."

> **60** "New Novels," ATHENAEUM, LXXVI (7 Nov 1903), 610.

Romance suffers from collaboration with Hueffer [Ford Madox Ford]. It is brilliant, but not convincing. The first three parts are too drawn out. JC's talent, complete in itself, is "distinctive, strong, individual."

> **61** Quiller-Couch, A. T. "Four Tales by Mr. Conrad," BOOKMAN (Lond), XXIV (June 1903), 108-9.

In *Typhoon and Other Stories,* JC, like James, is "wonderful" but not in the sense of "wonder which is excited by a touch of genius—in a tale, say, by Mr. Barrie or by Mr. Kipling." The amateur is slightly baffled when faced with the analytic presentation of character in James and JC. "To-morrow" is best for its "objective story-telling." "Typhoon" is admirable for its portrait of MacWhirr; "Amy Foster" is "not worthy" of the writer of "Youth"; "Falk" is "spoilt for me by a natural repugnance." The collection of stories is evidence of JC's ability to work in different veins.

62 "Recent Fiction," NEW YORK TIMES SATURDAY REVIEW, 4 April 1903, p. 224.

The stories in *Youth and Two Other Stories* are of the sea, of strange lands, and "of abnormal human beings developed under abnormal conditions." JC has exceptional power "to portray extraordinary scenery" and "to impress a character upon the credulity of his readers"; he wavers between the "objective and the subjective method," and his philosophizing is wearisome. "The End of the Tether" is the best of the three.

63 "Stories by Conrad," NEW YORK TIMES SATURDAY REVIEW, 24 Oct 1903, p. 756.

In *Typhoon and Other Stories,* "Falk," "Amy Foster," and "To-morrow" prove that JC's genius continues to grow.

64 *"Typhoon,"* ATHENAEUM, LXXVI (2 May 1903), 558-59.

In *Typhoon and Other Stories,* "Typhoon" has the most powerful presentation of a storm in fiction. As in all JC's works, the development and analysis of character are "integral," yet "structure . . . is the typhoon." JC "thinks in pictures" and forces the reader to see in pictures. JC occasionally makes mistakes in language (uses *crimson* as expletive for *bloody;* makes a van *trot* over a bridge; has someone grabbed by "the seat of his inexpressibles")—but these are unimportant in the face of his art.

65 Vorse, M. H. "Books Reviewed—Fact and Fiction," CRITIC, XLIII (Sept 1903), 280.

Although JC's works are well known, inferior books have been much more widely read because JC has not made use of one very powerful form of advertising: "he has neglected to court the interviewer" so the public can know whether he "takes lemon or cream in his tea" and why he left his former profession. But he is, nevertheless, "destined to be one of the best-known writers of this generation." "His analysis of character is penetrating and subtle, and yet it never for a moment checks the current of the story."

1904

66 Alden, William L. "Mr. Alden's Views," NEW YORK TIMES SATURDAY REVIEW, 29 Oct 1904, p. 735.

JC's admirers will be disappointed by *Nostromo*. Although it is his most ambitious effort, "the general verdict will probably be that Mr. Conrad has given us far too much of the San Tome Mine and far too much of the politics of Costaguana." Although the book has superb moments, it is tedious and lacks the focus that *Lord Jim* possesses.

> **67** "The Best Recent Novels," OUTLOOK (NY), LXXVII (18 June 1904), 424-25.

The "common complaint" about JC's works, "lack of story-interest," cannot be made about *Romance,* "and in part the fact may be due to Mr. F. M. Hueffer [Ford Madox Ford]," JC's collaborator. *Romance* contains almost too much "dramatic incident" and "thrill of suspense." But the main idea of the novel seems to be "to show what might be termed the seamy side of 'romance.'" JC keys the work on "one word—anguish." The tale is oppressively powerful; "it is too constantly near the very verge of tragedy to entertain."

> **68** "Books: Novels," SPECTATOR (Lond), XCIII (19 Nov 1904), 800-1.

In reference to *Nostromo,* JC, even with his great talent, does not know "where to begin or to end" the tale of his interesting characters; his novel is therefore "a series of brilliant episodes connected by a trickle of narrative." Toward the end of the novel, Nostromo gradually fades away and serves as a *deus ex machina* of the story of the Occidental Republic. Although the construction of the book is "topsy-turvy," the plot is "of surpassing interest" because of the mystery of the sea and the mountains and the "glamour of romance" of the characters. The greatest achievements are in the minor personages—Decoud, Antonia, Hernandez, Viola, and "the amazing crowd of schemers and swaggerers" who play at politics; but even more important is "the strife of ideals in a sordid warfare." The novel "shows signs of haste both in style and construction"; JC has spoiled his work by "an inability to do the pruning and selecting which his art demands." [Typical of early reactions to *Nostromo.*]

> **69** "Chronicle and Comment," BOOKMAN (NY), XIX (July 1904), 449-50.

[A photograph of JC's home at Pent Farm in "the days of his prosperity" and brief comments on other well-known figures, such as Henry James and Ellen Terry, who lived near JC, provide early examples of interest in the writer's personal life.]

> **70** "Chronicle and Comment," BOOKMAN (NY), XIX (Aug 1904), 544.

It seems that from JC's collaboration with Ford Maddox [sic] Hueffer [Ford] in the writing of *Romance,* JC "will get whatever there is of honour" and Hueffer "whatever there is of blame," or that the two will "be swamped together." It was JC who had asked to be permitted to work with Hueffer. The plot of *Romance* was Hueffer's idea. Hueffer was JC's "literary adviser" and he helped JC in completing the last chapters of his stories, "which Mr. Conrad finds most difficult to write."

71 Clifford, Hugh. "The Genius of Mr. Joseph Conrad," NORTH AMERICAN REVIEW, CLXXVIII (June 1904), 842-52; rptd LITERARY DIGEST, XXIX (2 July 1904), 11-12.

Since JC's books are "peculiarly, arrestingly original," they require some knowledge of his unusual temperament. His "exotic flavor" derives from the circumstances of his "birth, race, experience, training and even tradition," all of which are different from those of any other great English writer. A summary of his life and experiences shows their effects upon his writing: in some of the early works the "marvellous descriptive passages" are mingled with an unsatisfactory psychology of Asiatics. *The Nigger of the Narcissus* was the first example of JC at his best, and it also displays his Slavic mind, "more delicate and more subtle than the mind of the Englishman." *Lord Jim* is the most important of JC's latest books, although "Youth" and "Typhoon" are no less remarkable.

72 "Conrad in a New Field," NEW YORK TIMES SATURDAY REVIEW, 14 May 1904, p. 325.

Romance is a collaboration with F. M. Hueffer [Ford] and is therefore bad. There is little of the psychological insight that one associates with the earlier JC. Except for the old serving man, Tomas Castro, there is no flesh and blood character. The purpose of the book is to write a swashbuckling tale of adventure, and one prefers the earlier JC.

73 Cooper, Frederic Taber. "The Man's Novel and Some Recent Books," BOOKMAN (NY), XX (Nov 1904), 217-19.

In *Nostromo*, JC's style is difficult, and the author seems to refrain from "pouring out all that he knows of strange lands and alien races." His distinction "lies in the power of suggestion, the ability to make you feel that, however much he shows you of life, there is vastly more that he leaves untold." *Nostromo* cannot be easily or briefly "epitomised," as can several of his previous works. In brief, this novel is "a study of the curse which may come from the secret knowledge of a buried treasure."

74 "New Novels," ATHENAEUM, LXXVII (5 Nov 1904), 619.

Nostromo is "an opera in prose." The "sounding music . . . rises and falls, fades and swells . . . to the ordered crash of the finale." Every word seems charged with thought, every sentence "vivid and melodious." The colors are brilliant; the grim, ironic humor hard to match. Though a romantic tale of South American politics, it is primarily a novel of character.

75 *"Nostromo,"* NEW YORK TIMES SATURDAY REVIEW, 31 Dec 1904, p. 944.

Nostromo is more than the "novel of present-day adventure." It uses the typical melodramatic touches but it puts them to serious, psychological use. "Never before . . . have they [the Latin Americans] been analyzed with such brilliant and comprehensive accuracy as in this book." Above all, *Nostromo* was meant "as a parable upon modern conditions," and this meaning has been missed by many. "In Mr. Conrad's story, every one who seems to be working for the benefit of poor Costaguana is really working for himself, to the ultimate ruin both of himself and of the object of his solicitude," as in Carlos Gould's wrong conception of success.

76 Payne, William Morton. "Recent Fiction," DIAL (Chicago), XXXVII (16 July 1904), 37.

Written in collaboration with Ford Madox Hueffer [Ford], *Romance* is "a series of pictures" rather than a coherent novel. JC was probably responsible for the vivid pictures, the strong dramatic qualities of the situations, and the power of characterization of the figures in the story, and Hueffer was represented by "the working-out of the plot and in the swing of the narrative." The book as a whole is disappointing.

77 "Personalities: Joseph Conrad," ACADEMY, LXVI (20 Feb 1904), 198.

In a brief interview, JC shyly regarded the interviewer with "terror" on first meeting him, then thawed out. JC's love of English may be due to his love of the sea: he learned English from an East Coast fisherman.

1905

78 Beerbohm, Max. "Mr. Conrad's Play," SATURDAY REVIEW (Lond), C (8 July 1905), 48-49; rptd in AROUND THEATRES. Two Volumes (NY: Knopf, 1930), II, 495-99; ibid. (Lond: Hart-Davis, 1953; NY: British Book Centre, 1953), II, 384-87.

One Day More is a powerful tragedy in a modern setting. The play is straightforward and well-knit, with no technical blemish. JC is "just the sort of person who ought to be coaxed into writing plays." He has a wide knowledge of varied ways of life, acute vision, human sympathy, and passionate, dramatic imagination.

79 Clifford, Hugh. "Sketch of Joseph Conrad," HARPER'S WEEKLY, XLIX (14 Jan 1905), 59.

What has been called JC's obsession with the sea appeared early in JC's life, when as a restless, patriotic youth, he journeyed to Constantinople to fight for the Turks against the Russians. Unsuccessful in joining this cause, he became a seaman and sailed the world's seas for twenty years without writing a line except in his logbook. During this time, however, he became an omnivorous reader who developed an instinct for style, and his sea experiences became the basis for much of his fiction. During a six-month holiday at the end of his sea career, he began *Almayer's Folly*. Finally, with the publication of *Nostromo*, JC proves that his literary artistry increases with each publication.

    80 Dunbar, O. H. "A Book of Substance and Dignity," CRITIC, XLVI (April 1905), 377.

Nostromo displays "a firmly and richly woven fabric."

    81 Gomulicki, Wiktor. "Polak czy Anglik?" (Pole or Englishman?), ŻYCIE I SZTUKA (Petersburg) [Supplement to KRAJ], No. 1 (1905), np.

[Gomulicki was the first scholar to point out the allegory of *Patna*-Poland.] [In Polish.]

    82 "Literature," INDEPENDENT, LVIII (9 March 1905), 557-58.

JC fascinates a circle of elect, but bores others. *Nostromo* is more of an exposition of a South American republic than of the central character, who is, however, successfully delineated in few words. The moral and psychological issue is as modern as Ibsen.

    83 Payne, William Morton. "Recent Fiction," DIAL (Chicago), XXXVIII (16 Feb 1905), 126.

In *Nostromo*, JC, as usual sets "a very high standard of diction, characterization, and penetrative observation"; but the greatest weakness of the novel is its structure. "The psychological interest predominates over the adventurous or romantic interest," thus justifying the naming of the book after a minor character. The novel is "a very strong one." [Typical of many early reviews of this work.]

    84 Waliszewski, Kazimir [Kazimierz (?)]. "Un cas de naturalisation littéraire: Joseph Conrad" (A Case of Literary Naturalism: Joseph Conrad), REVUE DES REVUES [REVUE MONDIALE], XLVII (15 Dec 1905), 734-48.

"Conrad" is a pseudonym; *Korzeniowski* is a name known as that of a prolific writer, pre-Sienkiewicz era. [Biographical data, with the usual stress on compulsive influence of the sea.] JC forged his English style in less than ten years' familiarity with the language. The "United States of Europe" has produced writers of some value, but not an original one until JC. JC's sailors are usually British, except in "Falk." JC did for the sailors of the United Kingdom what Kipling did for its soldiers—and he isn't even English! JC judges non-whites harshly, but is also severe on whites (e.g., Kurtz in "Heart of Darkness"). JC's pen is "chaste," though he depicts sordid scenes. His work sometimes suffers from monotony of viewpoint (that of the sailor). There is philosophy in JC's work, but his ideas are not easily grasped; he sometimes seems to be groping for clarity himself. JC's style and method are characterized by "meandering" through a plot and mystification. Collaboration with Hueffer brought praise, which JC rejected as not reflecting his own ideas. JC's style is too heady and often incomprehensible. [Surveys works through 1903, including *Romance*.] [In French.]

1906

85 "Comment on Current Books," OUTLOOK (NY), LXXXIV (17 Nov 1906), 678-79.

To his "practical knowledge of seamanship, of lading cargoes, ruling crews, managing and navigating vessels," JC in *The Mirror of the Sea* adds "the vision of a poet" and displays "the witchcraft of a master of style." Although he is "careless of pointing a moral or adorning a tale," his thought leaves a serious impression of "the profound moral meaning" in everything he writes.

86 "Conrad's New Book," NEW YORK TIMES SATURDAY REVIEW, 10 Nov 1906, p. 734.

The Mirror of the Sea is valuable because it will permit the reader to get a clearer idea of JC the man.

87 "From Departure to Landfall," OUTLOOK (Lond), XVIII (13 Oct 1906), 480-81.

In *The Mirror of the Sea,* JC compares favorably to other English sea writers. [Several interesting connections between autobiography and fiction are noted.] JC's ability to describe marine conditions is praiseworthy. There is a powerful subcurrent of fear and respect below JC's love of the sea.

88 "A Guide to the New Books," LITERARY DIGEST, XXXIII (10 Nov 1906), 685.

Nothing finer than the works of JC has appeared since Hugo's THE TOILERS OF THE SEA. In *The Mirror of the Sea,* JC's "high gift of imagination, held in abeyance by a clear, rational perception, has enabled him to impart a vivid idea of the wonder and charm of the Infinite as expressed by its most potent symbol, the ocean."

89 Macy, John. "Joseph Conrad," ATLANTIC MONTHLY, XCVIII (Nov 1906), 697-702; rptd in CURRENT LITERATURE, XLII (Jan 1907), 58-59; and in THE CRITICAL GAME by John Macy (NY: Boni and Liveright, 1922), pp. 105-20.

The Nigger of the Narcissus and "Typhoon" fail in point of view; *Nostromo* "is told forward and backward in the first half of the book, and the preliminary history of the silver mine is out of all proportion to the story of Nostromo." On re-reading *Lord Jim,* the reader no longer finds the novel confusing. JC's shortcomings are emphasized because his involuted ways of telling a story drove off thousands of readers who should have been reading JC because his work is really important. [Comments on JC's ten books from 1895, *Almayer's Folly* to *Nostromo.*]

90 *"The Mirror of the Sea,"* ACADEMY, LXXI (20 Oct 1906), 393-94.

JC's learning English is an advantage over the native-born, who are too fluent and "stand in their own light." JC's prose is neither too prolix nor distorted. His sea language is accurate (anchors are "let go" in JC, never "cast" as in journalese). The title of *The Mirror of the Sea* is justified by flawless prose, accuracy, and reality of pictures. JC is especially good in dealing with the elements, but he "never writes better than he knows." One sees beauty and terror, but is not plagued with mystery.

91 *"The Mirror of the Sea,"* TIMES LITERARY SUPPLEMENT (Lond), 12 Oct 1906, p. 344.

JC is the sea's first critic in the full sense of the word. *The Mirror of the Sea* should have a long life.

92 Moss, Mary. "Notes on New Novels," ATLANTIC MONTHLY, XCVII (Jan 1906), 45-46.

In *Nostromo,* the technique is "involved, the movement seems to go backward; it is clumsy." But this is JC's method, "the most extraordinary blending of mystification and revelation." The reader is "saturated with the place, the people, with the stern, pessimistic morality of the whole."

93 "Our Library Table," ATHENAEUM, No. 4122 (27 Oct 1906), 513.

The Mirror of the Sea, a "pure delight" and modern, shows a perfection of finish that makes skipping impossible. Completely authentic, it is born of a real experience which provides something not even the "most brilliant impressionist" could produce without JC's long apprenticeship to sea life.

94 "Pilgrims' Scrip," SPECTATOR (Lond), XCVII (1 Dec 1906), 888-89.

The Mirror of the Sea is "too subtle, too profound, too exacting" to appeal to the casual reader; but it contains "the whole soul of a man who has known the deeps of sea mysteries, who has sought them as a lover, with joy, and reverence, and fear." The "chief note" of the work is its "sombre passion." JC, a "subjective observer," treats "landfalls and departures and anchorings" as an "allegory of mortal life."

95 "Recent Fiction," NATION (NY), LXXXIII (1 Nov 1906), 374.

The Mirror of the Sea, a "series of impressions and memories," is "the fruit of a real and long sea experience." "Pathetic fallacy or not, ships are persons" to JC, who considers "the last detail of seamanly terminology" of great importance. JC's use of "a pure and vigorous English" achieves effects "which recall Maupassant, or, far oftener, Pierre Loti."

1907

96 "Books: Novels," SPECTATOR (Lond), XCIX (21 Sept 1907), 400-1.

London as a microcosm, especially the "colony of Anarchists and revolutionists," provides the setting for *The Secret Agent,* a "psychological romance of terrorism" subtle and engrossing enough to advance JC's reputation as "a literary sorcerer of the first rank." JC's "penetrating insight" into his enigmatical character is excellent, but unnecessary digressions interrupt the narrative.

97 "Comment on Current Books," OUTLOOK (NY), LXXXVII (12 Oct 1907), 309.

JC's real subject in *The Secret Agent* is not "the plots of the Anarchists, the treachery of a spy among their number, the horror of a premature explosion by which an innocent and half-witted boy is blown to pieces, but rather the fine shades of temperament and intellectual process developed by the actors in these sensational scenes." Although the book is lacking "in [the] narrative and descriptive ability" of some of JC's early works, it contains "notable tragic intensity."

98 "Current Fiction," NATION (NY), LXXXV (26 Sept 1907), 285.

JC's early stories have promised something better than this "coming novelist" has yet supplied. *Nostromo* was "prolix and in construction suggesting Browning's 'The Ring and the Book,'" and *The Secret Agent* is "still less of a story" because the narrative taken as a whole "does not move."

The incidents are "the raw stuff of a shilling shocker." [Obviously, JC's works are not understood.]

99 "Fiction (Division III) / Books by English Novelists," NEW YORK TIMES AUTUMN BOOK NUMBER, 19 Oct 1907, Pt. II, p. 667.
[A "brief-mention" listing of *The Secret Agent*.]

100 "Joseph Conrad's Latest and Best," NEW YORK TIMES SATURDAY REVIEW, 21 Sept 1907, p. 562.
JC is a "specialist in the sombre," as in *The Secret Agent,* his latest and best work.

101 "New Novels," ATHENAEUM, No. 4170 (28 Sept 1907), 361-62.
In *The Secret Agent,* JC's subtleties, keenness, artistry, and disregard of time tend to separate him from the general reading public. JC is too arbitrary, but his novel is still a "diamond lying among shingle."

102 Payne, William Morton. "Recent Fiction," DIAL (Chicago), XLIII (16 Oct 1907), 252.
In *The Secret Agent,* the programme of anarchists "promises lively entertainment, but we get instead JC's interminable descriptions and discussions of motive." The story is smothered by analysis. "We hardly recall an equal disappointment since reading THE PRINCESS CASAMASSIMA."

103 *"The Secret Agent,"* TIMES LITERARY SUPPLEMENT (Lond), 20 Sept 1907, p. 285.
JC is recognized for his profound knowledge of the "nether" world and for his insights into anarchist mentality, especially in his creation of the Professor. *The Secret Agent* is not JC's masterpiece, but it is an advance on *Nostromo,* which contained too crowded a canvas.

1908

104 Bennett, Arnold. "Joseph Conrad and the Athenaeum," NEW AGE, N.S. III (9 May 1908), p. 33; rptd in PERSONS: BEING COMMENTS ON A PAST EPOCH (Lond: Chatto; NY: Doran, 1917).
The review of *A Set of Six* in "Short Stories," ATHENAEUM, No. 4218 (29 Aug 1908), 237, is full of clichés and other nonsense.

105 Cooper, Frederic Taber. "The Romantic Creed and Some Recent Books," BOOKMAN (NY), XXVI (Feb 1908), 669-70.
JC is not romantic but "consistently and effectively realistic." In his plots, which are often "strange" and "startling," a group of people, "exceptional

yet unmistakably living, flesh-and-blood men and women," are placed in "exceptional yet perfectly possible conditions," and the consequences are such as "must logically follow." JC's slight leaning toward romanticism may be detected in "the vague, unspoken sense he conveys, of something unrevealed, some hidden depth behind and below the facts that he has chosen to set forth," a sense of mystery which is "merely a mannerism." *The Secret Agent* is also a good example of his realism: the reader never knows "what is going on inside the brain of Mr. Verloc," but JC shows "how logically and inexorably nature, when not interfered with, can make the punishment fit the crime," without being melodramatic.

106 "Current Fiction," NATION (NY), LXXXVII (15 Oct 1908), 364.

"The Point of Honor: A Military Tale" is "essentially a short story, slightly expanded," which tells about "a long feud between two officers of Napoleon's army." It is "swifter in movement and holds the attention better than *The Secret Agent* or *Nostromo*." The characters are portrayed well, and the style is one "of distinction."

107 "Fiction," A. L. A. BOOKLIST, IV (Dec 1908), 301.
[A thirty-five-word summary of "The Point of Honor."]

108 Galsworthy, John. "Joseph Conrad, A Disquisition," FORTNIGHTLY REVIEW, LXXXIII (Jan-June 1908), 627-33; rptd in LIVING AGE, 7th Series, XXXIX (16 May 1908), 416-20; and as "Joseph Conrad, A Disquisition: 1910," TWO ESSAYS ON CONRAD. WITH A STORY OF A REMARKABLE FRIENDSHIP BY RICHARD CURLE (Freelands: pvtly ptd; Cincinnati: Ebbert & Richardson, 1930), which also includes "Reminiscences of Conrad: 1924," from "Souvenirs sur Conrad," NOUVELLE REVUE FRANÇAISE, XXIII (1 Dec 1924), 458-649. [Also see Richard Curle, "The Story of a Remarkable Friendship" (1930).]

JC had the power of making his reader feel "the inevitable unity of all things that be; of breathing into him a sense of solace that he himself is part of the wonderful unknown." He persuades man to observe at least briefly the "Irony of Things." From *Almayer's Folly* to *The Secret Agent,* JC's work becomes clearer, more subtle, more austere. His greatest defect is to produce a book about the upper classes, but his penetrating diagnosis of the "departmental Briton" is made with a loving eye in terms of his inquiring spirit.

109 "A Hero of the Old Guard," NEW YORK TIMES SATURDAY REVIEW, 24 Oct 1908, p. 612.
[A one-paragraph, pleasantly favorable summary of "The Point of Honor: A Military Tale."]

110 "Literature," INDEPENDENT, LXIV (9 Jan 1908), 105-6.

The Secret Agent, with "its grueling and sanguinary plot," should not be called "A Simple Tale"; but it is "saved by some excellent character sketches." "The descriptions are vivid, and the book works up to a series of climaxes, that would enrich any melodrama."

111 "Literature," INDEPENDENT, LXV (5 Nov 1908), 1066.

[Mainly plot summary of "The Point of Honor."]

112 MacCarthy, Desmond. *"The Secret Agent,"* ALBANY REVIEW (Lond), II (1908), 229-34.

JC's story "is the inner history, perhaps fictitious, perhaps true, perhaps half-true and half-fictitious," of the suicide (1894) of the anarchist Martial Bourdin in Greenwich Park. JC's treatment "is far above the level of sensationalism." He succeeds "in charging the slow and furtive lives" of his characters and their surroundings "with a Balzacian significance, without turning all London into a phantasmagorical city." The details are "definite and real," yet give the sense of being "imagined and then felt, rather than observed."

113 Maurice, Furnley. "Old Ships," SPECTATOR (Lond), CI (7 Nov 1908), 734-35.

[A bad poem addressed to JC.]

114 "Mr. Conrad's New Stories," SPECTATOR (Lond), CI (15 Aug 1908), 237.

The stories in *A Set of Six* are "right good Conrad," but not very fresh JC. The author does not delve deeply enough into the subject of anarchism in "The Informer" and "An Anarchist." "Gaspar Ruiz" contains a "finely subtle reading of a man's heart and character" which no one but JC could have written. "The Duel" includes the most thrilling piece of writing in the book.

115 "On Unbending Over a Novel," ACADEMY, LXXIV (1 Feb 1908), 413-14.

The Secret Agent is "terrible, amusing, convincing." Probability is achieved by "minutest touches." The novel is written objectively: JC does the "telling"; the reader does the "thinking." This is not JC's greatest work, but it is a good story. Friends of the author are annoyed by having lesser works preferred to greater ones.

116 "Recent Fiction and the Critics," CURRENT LITERATURE, XLIV (Feb 1908), 223-24.

Critics who approach *The Secret Agent* and are disappointed because it has nothing to do with the sea are unfair; they "seem to forget that Conrad has always been a psychological as well as a descriptive writer." JC's style, "like that of Henry James, whom he heartily admires, grows more subtle and involved as the years pass."

117 Scott-James, R. A. "The New Romance," MODERNISM AND ROMANCE (Lond: Lane, 1908), pp. 229-35.

The "new" romance seems to be the kind of romance practiced by R. L. Stevenson as distinct from the romance of Scott or Dumas. JC has the ability to produce atmosphere, as in *The Mirror of the Sea,* where there is freedom from plot. JC is no merely descriptive writer; he is "an originator in that he has learnt to apply the modern spirit of self-consciousness to the panorama of nature." [See Arnold T. Schwab, "Joseph Conrad's American Friend: Correspondence with James Huneker" (1955).]

118 "Short Stories," ATHENAEUM, No. 4218 (29 Aug 1908), 237.

Since Meredith and Hardy no longer write novels, no one else gives as much pleasure as JC to those appreciative of fine craftsmanship. "Studiously chiselled and hammered out," his stories in *A Set of Six* are more like novels than short stories in their concentration, analysis, and steady cumulative effect. Though JC produces vivid impressions, his method is not impressionistic. The long military tale, "The Duel," is reminiscent of Turgenev. [See Arnold Bennett, "Joseph Conrad and the Athenaeum" (1908).]

119 White, Stewart Edward. "Mr. Conrad's *The Secret Agent,*" BOOKMAN (NY), XXVI (Jan 1908), 531-32.

The Secret Agent is deficient when compared to JC's earlier works. The "chief fault" is that "the book has to do with anarchists, diplomats, policemen and stodgy middle-class English people," of whom only the Professor "with his n*th* power explosive are [sic] either opéra bouffe or treated as such." JC sketches a half-dozen characters with the sort of contempt that refuses to take seriously "either the motives, temperaments or actions of the specimens at which it laughs." The "disagreeable ending" is not prepared for by "an exact realism" that makes the tragedy inevitable. This novel "seems to have been written from the blind spot of Mr. Conrad's literary vision." [An important review in that it indicates the failure of early critics to see the real value of the novel.]

1909

120 Payne, William Morton. "Recent Fiction," DIAL (Chicago), XLVI (16 April 1909), 263.

The directness of "The Point of Honor" [American title of "The Duel"] excels at the expense of JC's earlier diffuse and indulgently analytical novels.

1910

[No entries for this year.]

1911

121 "Conrad's Latest Novel," NEW YORK TIMES REVIEW OF BOOKS, 10 Dec 1911, p. 818.
Under Western Eyes is a story of revolutionary activity treated psychologically rather than melodramatically. The story excels some of JC's other stories "in searchingness of character study and in its dramatic interpretation."

122 Cooper, Frederic Taber. "The Clothing of Thoughts and Some Recent Novels," BOOKMAN (NY), XXXIV (Dec 1911), 441-42.
The "foreign strain" has never been stronger in JC's writings than in *Under Western Eyes,* but here the author is trying "to reveal and explain the spirit of Russia to Western Europe." The theme—"nihilism, anarchy, torture, exile, and all the nameless things that Siberia stands for"—marks this work as something new for JC, but the method is "unmistakably identical" with that of "Heart of Darkness," *Lord Jim,* and *The Children of the Sea.* JC always has "that same wonderful ability to make us see, that inimitable suggestiveness that shows us a hundred things behind the specific details that he has chosen to mention." This work, a good book, will never rank with *Jim* or one or two other works that represent JC at his very best; but it is "a rather big book and one which no critical estimate of Conrad's life work could afford to ignore."

123 Curran, Edward F. "A Master of Language," CATHOLIC WORLD, XCII (March 1911), 796-805.
JC's language is "pure, idiomatic," and distinctive. Unconventional in his acceptance of convention, JC is not afraid to accept the moral and spiritual teaching of the ages. His books do not offend, morally; he is a good Catholic. JC makes the reader see, feel, and experience sea life as no one else can, and his treatment of exotic Malay and Africa is also realistic. Perhaps only Meredith excels JC in analysis of character. JC avoids pseudo-psychol-

ogy, false motivation. He develops characters fully, though sympathetically, while hiding himself. Every word is functional. The reader is led deftly from place to place without knowing how he got there. "No analysis will make him yield up the secret of his power. Of the short stories, "The Brute" is the best and "is unworthy of him." JC appeals to the cultured mature reader, not to the young. The more he is compared to his contemporaries, the more his superiority will be evident. [Appreciative favorable criticism, occasionally heavily Catholic, of *The Nigger of the Narcissus, Typhoon, Lord Jim, Nostromo, Almayer's Folly, The Secret Agent,* and of several short stories.]

124 "Fiction," ACADEMY, LXXXI (2 Dec 1911), 669-700.

In *Under Western Eyes,* JC displays an "extraordinary subtlety in the portrayal of emotions" and utilizes "marvellous" psychology in his "character-studies"; but he fails to solve the "unfathomable" mystery of the Russian character.

125 "Fiction," A. L. A. BOOKLIST, VIII (Dec 1911), 172-73.

With reference to *Under Western Eyes,* "Review," NATION (Lond), X (21 Oct 1911), 140 [not seen], said: "The artistic intensity of the novel lies . . . less in the remarkable drawing of characteristic Russian types than in the atmospheric effect of the dark national background."

126 Gibbon, Perceval. "Joseph Conrad: An Appreciation," BOOKMAN (Lond), XXXIX (Jan 1911), 177-79.

The key to JC's method is "Imagination, the faculty of whole vision that sees men and women, not as detached and arbitrary figures, but as the product of circumstances, environment, heredity and in relationship to their world and their neighbors." All JC's characters have their *raison d'être,* except a few mystery figures who at first seem unaccountable: Verloc in *The Secret Agent,* Wait in *The Nigger of the Narcissus.* JC's theory of literature is already exemplified in *Almayer's Folly* as is his technique of "rendering the *flavour* of a situation," a faculty at its height in *Lord Jim.* The abandonment of the pilgrim ship is especially well handled. *Nigger* is the only full-scale novel of the sea JC has written, despite reviewers' labels. *Nigger* is praiseworthy for its truthfulness, but also because JC's vision enlarges truth. *Under Western Eyes,* which is appearing periodically, fulfills one's expectations of JC, who is ranked with James and Hardy.

127 Hueffer, Ford Madox. "Joseph Conrad," ENGLISH REVIEW, X (Dec 1911), 66-83.

JC "is the finest of the Elizabethans," having a certain tone because of his Polish origins: Poland preserves "the virtues" it had when it was a great sixteenth-century empire, a nation of Romantic, heroic aristocrats. JC's preoccupations with "death, destiny, . . . the cruel sea, the dark forests of strange worlds or the darker forests, . . . the hearts of our fellow man" resemble Webster, Shakespeare, Marlowe, and Kyd. He shares also their "desperate . . . remorselessness." He differs in his emphasis on points of honor—and here he is a Pole, an aristocrat and an individualist. His central moral is "that when our private and intimate honour is in conflict with the law, we must break the law," that "conventional arrangement of the relations between man and man." As a writer his chief maxim is *"Never state: present."* His stories are, therefore, an "experience" for the reader. His greatness is that we never admire his cleverness at the expense of what we and his characters have undergone.

128 "New Books Reviewed," NORTH AMERICAN REVIEW, CXCIV (Dec 1911), 935-36.

Since fiction must be written "as present-day history," it must, unlike history, allow for "the instinctive thirst for happiness." Even "the intrigues and counter-intrigues of Russia's struggle for self-expression are indications of this thirst." In *Under Western Eyes,* "the picture is too unrelieved for art, and yet is doubtless admirable as history." But JC knows Russia and the Russian people thoroughly, and his novel has "unusual psychologic and subjective qualities," portraying subtly, as it does, "the inversions and perversions" of the revolutionist mind in Russia. His book, "somber as it is," gives "an impressive idea of human nature under terrible conditions."

129 "New Novels," ATHENAEUM, No. 4382 (21 Oct 1911), 483-84.

In *Under Western Eyes,* JC's synthesis of "a mood, a frame of mind of emotional conditions," usually tragic, "is something quite by itself in English fiction" (as also in *Lord Jim, The Nigger of the Narcissus,* and "Heart of Darkness"). The novel, un-English, reads like "a translation from some other tongue, presumably Russian." JC is "reckless" in his form of narrative and leaves a general impression of ineffectiveness, stupidity, and hopelessness seen in the agents of a Cause, of revolutionaries.

1912

130 Beerbohm, Max. "The Feast. BY J*S*PH C*NR*D," A CHRISTMAS GARLAND (Lond: Heinemann, 1912); rptd (1950), pp. 127-34.

[This parody of JC's "The Feast" is a delightful little short story. The subject and style are witty, exaggerated imitations of JC's emphasis on foreign turns of phrase, grammatical convolutions, and so on.]

131 Björkman, Edwin. "Joseph Conrad, A Master of Literary Color," REVIEW OF REVIEWS (NY), XLV (Jan-June 1912), 557-60; rptd as "General Knights of Modern Literature" in VOICES OF TOMORROW (NY and Lond: Mitchell Kennerly, 1913), pp. 240-59.

JC fulfills the true function of an artist—to imitate life—though he "holds a place apart . . . a modern knight of the Holy Graal, seeking . . . beauty, worth, truth . . . in triune radiance." He is "above social purpose." Perhaps self-discipline is the principle that appeared "hallowed" to JC. Each novel stages "elementary passion in many shades and variations." [Broad and general; little analysis of works.]

132 "Books: Fiction," SPECTATOR (Lond), CIX (16 Nov 1912), 815-16.

In *'Twixt Land and Sea,* JC has shaken himself loose from the influence of Henry James as displayed in *The Secret Agent* and returned to his own manner of writing. The stories are filled with the glamor of the tropics. In all three stories both background and drama create "an overwhelming effect." The interest in "A Smile of Fortune" is comic and psychological, and the tragic "Freya of the Seven Isles" is JC's greatest success.

133 "Briefs on New Books," DIAL (Chicago), LII (1 March 1912), 172.

A Personal Record has "enough incident and adventure to form the groundwork of several novels." One of JC's oddities in the use of English idiom is his "fondness for a participial construction where the sense might better require an infinitive."

134 Cooper, Frederic Taber. "Joseph Conrad," SOME ENGLISH STORY TELLERS (NY: Holt, 1912), pp. 1-30.

Although JC is now under attack for his style and diction, a "far heartier recognition" of JC is in order. John A. Macy, in "Joseph Conrad," in ATLANTIC MONTHLY (1906), objects unjustly to JC's being difficult, but Galsworthy's recognition of JC's being the "only writing of the last twelve years that will enrich the English language, to any extent" is praiseworthy. JC measures "man against the universe, foredoomed to defeat . . . yet always the focal point of interest." His method is that of a spider spinning its web, crossing, recrossing, zigzagging, but ultimately creating perfect symmetry, as in *Almayer's Folly* (the story opens when the end is already in sight). JC is enormously compressed, as in *The Nigger of the Narcissus* and "Heart of Darkness." His is not an easy realism.

135 Cooper, Frederic Taber. "Representative English Story Tellers: Joseph Conrad," BOOKMAN (NY), XXXV (March 1912), 61-70.

JC, like James, has been subjected to inadequate, prejudiced, blindly narrow and one-sided consideration. Two reproaches frequently leveled against JC—his zig-zag way of telling a story and his lack of proportion—may be dismissed on the grounds that a genius must work in his own way. The leading part in "Typhoon" is the storm itself, and in *The Nigger of the Narcissus* it is the "treacherous, implacable sea." "Heart of Darkness" is nothing less than "a presentment of the clashing of two continents, a symbolic picture of the inborn antagonism of two races, the white and the black." The true JC is that of the middle period ("Typhoon," "Heart of Darkness," *Nostromo, Lord Jim*). His best work is that about the sea.

136 Curle, Richard. "The Art of Joseph Conrad," EVERYMAN, I (22 Nov 1912), 176.

Being both realistic and romantic, JC is closer to Flaubert and the Russians than to any English novelist; his melancholy, irony, and exuberance make his writing seem alien to "many placid English intelligences." Romance and realism combine in his method of characterization, his ability to create atmosphere, and in his powers of description. His portrayal of Jim, for instance, is actual, "extraordinarily exact," and yet veiled in romance. Melancholy underlies the sense of futility JC conveys in any number of his novels—in *Almayer's Folly,* "where lost hopes of love and wealth break Almayer's heart," as well as in *Nostromo, Lord Jim,* and *Under Western Eyes*. An outgrowth of his pessimism, irony in JC is not merely a literary convention, but rather an integral part of his world view, a comment on the disgusting folly he sees in the world. His exuberance is apparent in his exotic style, his narrative technique, as well as in his characterization (the moving portrait of Winnie Verloc). Part of JC's originality rests on the fact that his powerful personality is impressed on his work; yet, as an artist, like Turgenev and Flaubert, he remains aloof from his creations.

137 Curle, Richard. "Joseph Conrad," RHYTHM (Lond), II (Nov 1912), 242-55.

JC's personality pervades everything he wrote, which in part makes him difficult to assess, although this is not due to mannerism of Meredith's kind. Readers find Hudson's PURPLE LAND easier to grasp than JC's "Youth" because JC "gives only a philosophic dream of what youth ought to be." Although *Under Western Eyes* is unlike CRIME AND PUNISHMENT, JC shares with Dostoevski a divided audience. *Lord Jim* and *Nostromo* may lack structure as *Some Reminiscences* does. His originality is the "striking blend of romance and psychology" in his work. *Nostromo* is one of his most "astonishing achievements." He combines the "melancholy of Turgenev and the compassion of Dostoievsky." *The Nigger of the Narcissus* reveals some influence of Flaubert. In "Typhoon," JC makes a boring man into "an heroic figure"—JC "has an unbounded respect for singleness of heart." He creates "one illusion within another," mundane reality within a larger sense of reality. He "realizes very intensely and very poetically the spirit of places" (the river in *Almayer's Folly* and *Outcast of the Islands;* the tropics in *Jim;* the wilds and the river in "Heart of Darkness"). The sea, too, "has a kind of emblematic influence" ("Typhoon," *Nigger,* "Tomorrow," "The End of the Tether"). Such depictions of places result in graphic depiction of character: they are "thrilling"; atmosphere is "thrilling." [A rambling mélange with an occasional nice, pointed phrase.]

138 "Current Fiction," NATION (NY), XCIV (18 Jan 1912), 60.

In *Under Western Eyes,* JC has "distinction of style."

139 "Fiction," ATHENAEUM, No. 4434 (19 Oct 1912), 446.

In *'Twixt Land and Sea,* JC is able to paint character "in a flash; a word; an act; an idiosyncrasy." He writes at "white heat." His stories are tragic, vivid and penetrating. Sometimes JC, underestimating the reader, explains too much.

140 "General Literature," A. L. A. BOOKLIST, VIII (March 1912), 297.

JC's *A Personal Record* has the "literary quality of his best fiction." Despite scanty biographical material, the work does "present a clear idea of his personality."

141 Gibbon, Perceval. "Conrad," BOOKMAN (Lond), XLII (April 1912), 26-27.

In *Some Reminiscences,* two related memories are especially important, that of JC's first contact with the sea and that of writing his first book. JC possessed Walter Bagehot's requirement for a great experience, "an experiencing nature"; and his experiences included a wide range. In this "vital and individual" book he revealed himself more intimately than he had done in his novels.

142 Huneker, James Gibbons. "A Visit to Joseph Conrad, The Mirror of the Sea," NEW YORK TIMES MAGAZINE SECTION, 17 Nov 1912, p. 4; rptd as "Joseph Conrad: A Pen Portrait," in Alfred A. Knopf, JOSEPH CONRAD; THE ROMANCE OF HIS LIFE AND OF HIS BOOKS (Garden City, NY: Doubleday, Page, 1913), pp. 99-100; ibid. (Garden City, NY: The Country Life P, 1919).

In an interview in his house in Kent, JC proved to be a "simple mannered gentleman" who asked more questions than he answered. His main interest in fiction was the human soul; and in conversation he expressed "boundless sympathy for all things human." Commonly regarded as a writer about the sea, JC really treats the human soul. In doing so, he has a variety of etchings of women whom he always treats in reverent manner rather than portraying them as mere "automatons of passion and intrigue."

143 "Joseph Conrad," SPECTATOR (Lond), CIX (13 July 1912), 60-61.

English as a foreign language forced JC to be perpetually vigilant, but only occasionally does his vigilance slumber. The dominant characteristic of *Some Reminiscences* is "a kind of sustained, yet never hysterical, exaggeration," an ironical mood with "a kind of dull heat" in the irony which suggests more than philosophical observation; in fact, the constant pressure creates a certain monotony. It is JC's "fierce objectivity" which gives its peculiar value to this book; but more than anything else the work leaves one with a strong impression of a wonderfully mature, wise, and charitable mind.

144 "Joseph Conrad's Profession of Artistic Faith," CURRENT LITERATURE, LII (April 1912), 471-72.

Unlike Shaw, Wells, Chesterton, Bennett, and others, JC let his works speak for themselves for fifteen years and offered no explanation. Then in *A Personal Record* he completely answered his critics with a "profession of faith" in which he claims "nothing but a striving for artistic verity"; he desires to be a faithful interpreter of the "gigantic spectacle" of the world, but he believes it cannot be explained in ethical terms. His "subtlety" and "circuitousness almost mischievous" add to the difficulties of the critics, who do not sufficiently consider his emphasis on sobriety for the captain of a ship as well as, by implication, for literature.

145 "Literature," NATION (NY), XCIV (7 March 1912), 238-39.

In the early pages of *A Personal Record,* a "fragmentary narrative," JC is "self-conscious and ill at ease"; but with the beginning of his reminiscences he succeeds in portraying a "vision of a personality." His main purpose is "to account for himself as a man and as a writer." And the book has "a curious completeness" because JC uses the method of the writer of fiction, "a careful choice of telling detail."

146 "Mr. Conrad at His Best," BOOKMAN (Lond), XLIII (Dec 1912), 187.

'Twixt Land and Sea is as good as the best of JC's early works. There is a fine combining of adventure and psychopathology. The stories conceal JC's literary power and thereby heighten it. New impressions and experiences now come to the narrator rather than his having to go on a Pateresque search for them. The stories are less consciously labored and consequently more effective.

147 "Mr. Conrad's Own Story," NEW YORK TIMES SUNDAY REVIEW OF BOOKS, 18 Feb 1912, p. 77.

Among authors, JC is considered "the truest artist and the most splendid and honorable craftsman." *A Personal Record* is valuable for the insight it provides into JC the man.

148 *"Na Vzgliad Zapada"* (*Under Western Eyes*), RUSSKOW BOGATSTVO, No. 9 (1912), 211.
[A review.] [In Russian.]

149 "New Books," CATHOLIC WORLD, XCIV (Jan 1912), 535-36.
Under Western Eyes is "a minute study of Russian character," "a well-proportioned book," and holds the reader's attention by means of "psychological speculation."

150 "New Books Reviewed," NORTH AMERICAN REVIEW, CXCV (April 1912), 569-70.
JC "is a man of the least subjective temperament in the world"; he needs much prodding to be brought to talk about himself, and "he appears as a mere chance and random observer of cosmic affairs." Although he writes about his art, about the sea, and about friends, his "life-story is shut in his own bosom and never will it be revealed except by indirection." Anyone who has loved JC's novels will read this book for the same purpose, "for the dignity and power of words, for the great free sense of the sweeping cosmic forces, and for the penetrating pity, yet stoic and unyielding, with which the evanescent destinies of man are handled."

151 N[ovorusskii], M. *"Na Vzgliad Zapada"* (*Under Western Eyes*), NOVYI ZHURNAL DLIA VSEKH, No. 8 (1912), 128.
[In Russian.]

152 "Our Library Table," ATHENAEUM, No. 4397 (3 Feb 1912), 124.
Some Reminiscences is reminiscent of Sterne "in its indifference to the claims of mere narrative and the subtlety of its touches." [Slight.]

153 *"A Personal Record,"* CATHOLIC WORLD, XCV (May 1912), 254-56.
JC should have written more (his paragraphs could be developed into chapters) and one desires to know more about his creative activity. Avoiding clichés, JC admits criticism as a high adventure and writing as something like a wrestling "with the Lord" [in JC's words], endless work, to the exclusion of "all that makes life really lovable and gentle." [Short favorable appreciation.]

154 "Recent Fiction and the Critics," CURRENT LITERATURE, LII (Feb 1912), 236-37.
What Henry James achieves for the sophisticated English, JC achieves for the sophisticated Russians. *Under Western Eyes* "is a study in remorse,

and, as such, is appropriately keyed in the poignant pitch of personal anguish which made some of Mr. Conrad's earlier volumes so compelling" in their emotional appeal. Though he is frequently compared with Tolstoi, Dostoevski, and Turgenev, he "possesses angles of refraction that are all his own."

155 Reynolds, Stephen. "Joseph Conrad and Sea Fiction," QUARTERLY REVIEW, CCXVII (July 1912), 159-80.

JC is consciously and completely English, and his work begins with that assumption. He is unique in our literary history, and his sea stories are the real basis of his power. He is the first writer to portray the sea from a sailor's view as an end in itself and not just a means from one place to another. All of his great settings and situations are merely backgrounds to his testings of human character. He shows us civilized man in attitudes of isolation and then describes how he disintegrates through small flaws in character. Singleton is his greatest creation because the old sailor embodies all of JC's ideals. Only in paintings have human likenesses been so finely drawn, and criticisms of JC's verbosity miss the point because his many angles to one event develop the definition of the whole; they are not merely repetition. He controls the complete range of sensory description and his strengths are concentration from a single cohesive philosophy, humour, and irony. [Brief descriptions of aspects of *The Secret Agent, Under Western Eyes,* "Heart of Darkness," *An Outcast of the Islands,* and *The Nigger of the Narcissus.*]

156 "Sailor and Author, Too," INDEPENDENT, LXXII (28 March 1912), 678.

JC is naturally reticent, but *A Personal Record* ("this not altogether orderly autobiography") has some exquisite pages.

157 Sanger, Vincent. "Bibliographics of Young Reputations: Joseph Conrad (Korzeniowski)," BOOKMAN (NY), XXXV (March 1912), 70-71.

[Part I lists JC's published works and includes references to reviews; part II lists about twenty appreciations.]

158 Smet, Joseph De. "Joseph Conrad," MERCURE DE FRANCE, XCVII (1 May 1912), 51-75.

JC's experiences as a child, as a sailor and as a naval captain influenced his books (*Almayer's Folly, Lord Jim, The Mirror of the Sea, The Nigger of the Narcissus*). JC's writings are characterized by both vivid imagination and imagery. His desire for perfection of style is reminiscent of Flaubert, who worked to perfect a phrase and to harmonize it artistically with his thoughts. JC reflects on specific moments with great detail. His models include Flaubert, Anatole France, Tristan Bernard, and Charles Dickens. His strong will and persistence make him a master of his language and style. In his first books, JC paints the land, sea, and rivers as he remembers them ("Typhoon," *Mirror*). The mysterious enigma that every man carries within himself preoccupies JC in *Jim*. He explores and analyzes impressions, passions, sentiments, and fate. Very few writers have succeeded in making one feel the inevitable destiny resting on human existence. In *Nigger* and *Folly,* he recounts the history of troubled souls in a splendid universe but who are incapable of controlling fate. Almayer, Jim, Nostromo, Captain Whalley, and Mrs. Verloc—all of them are driven to a tragic end with the logic of fatality that one senses as inevitable at the moment when one definitive act of their career is accomplished. In *Nostromo,* an extraordinary book, JC illustrates that the hero is not merely one man; rather a social grouping (an imaginary republic in Central America), where the people's intrigues and ferociousness evolve around a silver mine, and their destinies reflect a universal economic and social evolution. One can almost read in JC's works, the romantic generalizations of Zola, but JC's form differs in style and color. His simpler works, which are some of his best (*Nigger,* "Youth," "Typhoon"), reflect the same intensity. One can truly *see* in JC's novels—"Il sait voir, il sait imaginer, il sait exprimer." One can speculate that JC is the Rudyard Kipling of the sea although JC's psychology is much more profound. In England, however, the two authors are balanced in their reputations. The results of JC's labors have produced works of magnificent quality. [In French.]

159 Vengerova, Z. *"Na Vzgliad Zapada* (Angliiskii Roman Iz Ruskoi Zhizni)" (*Under Western Eyes* [An English Novel from Russian Life]), Rechi: Biulletenin Lit. I Zhizni, No. 13 (1912), 522-24.

[In Russian.]

1913

160 "Chronicle and Comment," Bookman (NY), XXXVIII (Dec 1913), 352-54.

A young Cambridge man named Jacques, who died not long afterwards, was once asked by the captain (JC) of the sailing ship *Torrens* to read his manuscript of *Almayer's Folly,* which was written, in a desultory manner, over a period of five years.

161 Cooper, Frederick T[aber]. "The New Flamboyance and Some Recent Fiction," Bookman (NY), XXXVII (March 1913), 85.

'Twixt Land and Sea is JC's return to "exotic lands and waters" after writing

about "Nihilism and dynamite." "A Smile of Fortune" is the best of the trio; it is JC's suggestiveness which gives the tale its distinction. JC knows exactly what he wishes to do, and he remains "untouched by the taint of the new flamboyance in fiction."

162 "Current Fiction," NATION (NY), XCVI (10 April 1913), 360-61.

The stories of *'Twixt Land and Sea* have ships as "the background for some of the scenes," but the sea is not the usual one of JC's works; it is only "a broken body of water surrounding various man-infested bodies of land, and subject to indignities." "The odd fascination" of these stories arises from "Mr. Conrad's faculty of creating an atmosphere—the atmosphere of a strange enchantment, or a deadly fear, or an imminent catastrophe."

163 Dawson, Warrington. "Joseph Conrad,/ Hardy, Meredith and Conrad the Great Triumvirate." NEW YORK TIMES REVIEW OF BOOKS, 2 Feb 1913, p. 51.

In *'Twixt Land and Sea,* JC is more than a stylist or a writer of sea stories. His stories, although restricted at times to shipboard, "are symbolic of society at large." "His principle is to unfold a tale to us just as we ourselves might observe it if we were thrown in intimate touch with the characters. He has no use for the straight line which many modern novelists try to impose upon us as the only form of art; he knows that the straight line does not exist in nature." Like Balzac, JC has created a new form. This is a period "when the very existence of novels is threatened by the overdevelopment of sheer technique in rubbishy literature which has rendered the current novel-form odious to a large and discriminating public." The three tales of this book "rank with the most mature and romantic of his work."

164 E[dgett], E[dwin] F[rancis]. "Joseph Conrad," BOSTON EVENING TRANSCRIPT, 29 Jan 1913, p. 22.

The only flaw in three otherwise flawless stories in *'Twixt Land and Sea* is a rather clumsy point of view.

165 "A Few of the Season's Novels," REVIEW OF REVIEWS (NY), XLVII (13 June 1913), 762-63.

The tales in *'Twixt Land and Sea* are in JC's "best, most characteristic vein." His "delicacy and balance" "rivals Dickens and Thackeray."

166 Ficke, Arthur Davison. "Joseph Conrad," CHICAGO EVENING POST, 27 June 1913, p. 8.

JC is no mere writer of sea stories; for him the sea "fades" to a background "against which are silhouetted the haunting figures in which he interprets man's endless struggle." Each of his landscapes is "drenched" with the color of his own mind, and his characters perturb the reader "with their tremendous storms." In *'Twixt Land and Sea,* as in his earlier books, "no one ever fully understands Joseph Conrad's figures and no one fully forgets them."

167 "Fiction," A. L. A. BOOKLIST, IX (March 1913), 298.

The three tales in *'Twixt Land and Sea* "have a literary finish that will delight educated readers." The book is recommended for small libraries and for first purchase.

168 "Joseph Conrad," BOOKMAN (NY), XXXVII (Aug 1913), 594.

The success of many best sellers at a time when JC is "very inadequately rewarded" is resented, but one hopes for his "coming into his own" with the appearance of *Youth* and "The Point of Honour" in new editions.

169 "Literature," AMERICA (NY), VIII (22 March 1913), 571.

JC deserves his vogue if all his tales are as powerfully written as those in *'Twixt Land and Sea,* but Alice, in "A Smile of Fortune," is as "improbable as she is unpleasant." [There are capsule synopses of "The Secret Sharer" and "Freya of the Seven Isles."]

170 "The New Books," OUTLOOK (NY), CIII (15 March 1913), 596.

In *'Twixt Land and Sea,* the three "tales of Eastern lands and waters" are JC's "very best," better even than "the elaborate book-romance in which the author's "tendency to involution" carries him "beyond the limit of the reader's patience." Here, "passion, fate, and character play their parts in human life mercilessly but with exactness of truth."

171 "*'Twixt Land and Sea,*" INDEPENDENT, LXXIV (6 March 1913), 538-39.

[Summary of contents.]

1914

172 Aynard, Joseph. "Le roman du hasard par Joseph Conrad" (The Novel of Chance by Joseph Conrad), JOURNAL DES DÉBATS, CXXVI (9 May 1914), 1-2.

JC's novel of chance is compared with the treatment of this subject by Rudyard Kipling and Thomas Hardy, who both see in chance the potency of gods. Kipling is conservative but not a puritan. Hardy has pity for mankind. JC is neither optimistic nor pessimistic. For him chance may bring a new course into our lives, and often imposes irrational ones in spite of man's rationality. A detailed examination of the story and the interplay of personalities show how each event was produced by chance. [A brief résumé of *Chance* is given.] [In French.]

173 "Books: Fiction," SPECTATOR (Lond), CXII (17 Jan 1914), 101-2.

Although the story of *Chance* is engrossing, it is Marlow's telling of it and his self-revelation in the telling which constitute the "paramount attraction" of the novel, for Marlow is a remarkable person. He is JC's *alter ego*. The portraits of Captain Anthony and Charles Powell are splendid in their "heroic unselfishness and simple loyalty." *Chance* is more of a tragicomedy than a tragedy. The book contains no quotation or literary allusion, and JC's pages are "void of offence" and "unsullied by unnecessary squalors"—two curious points to be noted.

174 Boynton, H. W. "Joseph Conrad," NATION (NY), XCVIII (9 April 1914), 395-97.

JC's position among contemporary English writers is "detached, and a little aloof." His is a name which "stands for fine and strong work." "If there is one element in human life upon which, more than upon any other, Mr. Conrad's fancy habitually plays, it is the element of pure chance." *Chance* is "decidedly the best of the Conrad stories which are not exclusively stories of the sea."

175 Bullis, Helen. "Mr. Conrad's New Field," NEW YORK TIMES REVIEW OF BOOKS, 22 March 1914, pp. 129-30.

"*Chance* is the story of the tragic issues that flow from the destruction of a woman's belief in herself." In construction it is "a model of apparent awkwardness and actual effectiveness." JC has proved again his mastery of "zigzag method."

176 "Chance and Her Victims," ACADEMY, LXXXVI (31 Jan 1914), 145-46.

Parts of *Chance* are intricately woven together. The scene in which the governess turns on Flora is intensely effective. The word "devil" is used so often in the first twenty-five pages as to make it seem that JC regarded it "in the nature of a superlative."

177 Colbron, Grace Isabel. "Joseph Conrad's Women," BOOKMAN (NY), XXXVIII (Jan 1914), 476-79.

JC's women are always passive, not complex, and do not develop. JC succeeds better with primitive women. "Nina, of *Almayer's Folly*, is the most memorable of these women." "The sheltered women of Occidental civilisation, and the woman who was the soul of the savage jungle, meet in the bond of primitive womanhood, which is the one phase of woman's life that seems to hold and interest Mr. Conrad, the one phase that calls out his best work."

178 Cooper, Frederick Taber. "The Accustomed Manner and Some Recent Novels," BOOKMAN (NY), XXXIX (May 1914), 323-24.

Chance is closer in spirit to *Almayer's Folly* and *An Outcast of the Islands* than to JC's more recent work. The typical JC theme concerns his heroes or heroines suffering from "some sort of a soul-scar: they carry the mark of Cain, they are branded upon their conscience." This differentiates JC's hero from his fellows and makes him see life from a peculiar angle and in a more or less distorted form.

179 Cooper, Frederick Taber. "Twenty or More of the Latest Novels," PUBLISHERS' WEEKLY, LXXXV (18 April 1914), 1335-36.

Chance ranks with JC's best, *Nostromo* and *Lord Jim*. JC's method of construction is "the method of the spiderweb: he suddenly shoots downward from some point of departure, apparently with no purpose; he crawls around the new point of arrival, shoots off at a tangent, crossing and recrossing his own trail, pausing to tie mysterious and unmenacing knots in his own narrative—and then, all of a sudden, the significance of it all bursts upon the reader, and the whole intricate design stands revealed in its marvelous and inimitable symmetry."

180 Curle, Richard. "Biographical and Autobiographical. Novels and Stories," BOOKMAN (NY), XXXIX (Aug 1914), 662-68; XL (Sept-Oct 1914), 99-104, 187-201; expanded through many pages in JOSEPH CONRAD: A STUDY (Garden City, NY: Doubleday, Page; Lond: Kegan Paul, 1914); rptd in *A Set of Six* by Joseph Conrad (Garden City, NY: Doubleday, Page, 1916) [eleven unnumbered pages]; ibid. (Garden City, NY: Doubleday, Page, 1919), pp. 105-15; and ibid. (NY: Russell & Russell, 1968).

JC's work through *Chance* marks a new epoch in writing. He is not "sparkling," not a crusader; he is realistic, but has an alien "sort of philosophy"; he is aloof in style, manner, and range of subject, he has the sardonic humor of disillusionment, and an "un-English irony." He approaches human sympathy largely through an "intensely imagined atmosphere." Atmosphere complements the mind in the early works, but in later works atmosphere becomes more impersonal. As a psychologist, JC's method is primarily inductive. Male characters usually have an *idée fixe*—"beneath the usual level of sanity and good will there is an immense under-world of darkness and unrest." Like Dostoevski, he probes the duality of the mind. Usually optimistic in character portrayal, he is often pessimistic about life.

People are victimized by the madness of the world; humanity is the "one sane thing in the universe," while nature is an "incoherent jumble." JC has an aristocratic disregard for universal types. Life is more important than "intellectualism": his finest men have a "rare sensitiveness," and his true seamen are often childish and artless. The hero of *Lord Jim,* who must be viewed as a "passionate and melancholy Pole," illustrates the theme that without honor life is meaningless; Marlow, "one of the few bores in Conrad," is a mistake, even though he adds a colloquial tone; Nostromo is the one "real genius" in JC; and Decoud's death demonstrates the author's great psychological powers in presenting the debilitating effect of silence and insomnia. JC's women have a "subtle femininity"; since his finest are good women, they are not often very exciting. JC is an ironist influenced by Slavonic melancholy. His ironic stance, a philosophic conception as well as an artistic device, gives perspective (in the artistic, emotionless, and impersonal irony of *The Secret Agent*). Melancholic irony sometimes becomes the irony of pity (in the death of Jim). JC's humor is the humor of his "special ironic realism"; his irony is more tragic than comic.

Noteworthy aspects of JC's art are his prose style, his "realism tinged by romance," and a dramatic intensity more tragic than ironic. The dramatic sense is at its best in the contrast of the serenity of nature with the turmoil of human passion (the end of *Nostromo*). JC has "ascetic faithfulness to an ideal, which is the root of artistic morality." He was influenced by Flaubert, and to a lesser degree by Maupassant, Anatole France, Turgenev, and Henry James; and with the help of James he first brought England to the tradition of continental literature. [Curle's early study of JC helped to arouse interest in the serious scholarly discussion of his art. Some sound critical opinions have since become commonplace in JC criticism. Curle's personal prejudices are sometimes based on insufficient critical criteria.]

> **181** Dabrowski, Marian. "Rosmowa z J. Conradem" (Interview with J Conrad), TYGODNIK ILLUSTROWANY, 16 (18 April 1914); trans by Bronislas A. Jezierski as "An Interview with Joseph Conrad," AMERICAN SCHOLAR, XIII (July 1944), 371-75; rptd in SZKICE O CONRADZIE (Warsaw: Państowy Instytut Wydawniczy, 1959); rptd in POLISH AMERICAN STUDIES, XVII (July-Dec 1960), 66-71.

In the first interview that JC ever granted to anyone, his face was noted to be "uncommonly virile," and the great writer had "the glance of a sea-wolf—eyes which had penetrated the depths of the soul of the earth and the sea." He spoke in "perfect Polish" as he gave a brief account of his life, omitting many important events. He explained the inability of English critics to understand his books by the fact that he was a Pole. Although known as a writer, he claimed that he was still a sailor: "C'est mon métier." He disliked the translations of his works into Polish because they were "so careless, so false to the meaning of the text." He claimed that he still loved his fatherland, and that two things filled him with pride: he, a Pole, was a captain in the English Merchant Marine, and he could write "fairly well in English."

182 Edgett, Edwin Francis. "Joseph Conrad's Latest Novel," BOSTON EVENING TRANSCRIPT, 21 March 1914, p. 8.

Chance presents "life itself," but the reader is often entangled in a difficult narrative background.

183 "Fiction," A. L. A. BOOKLIST, X (May 1914), 369.

Chance is recommended for small libraries and for first purchase.

184 "Fiction," ATHENAEUM, No. 4499 (17 Jan 1914), 88-89.

Chance is marred by JC's use of a second narrator occasionally interrupted by the first. The second half of the book is better because it deals with the sea; JC is less at home on land. The tragic experience of the heroine is described with a "wealth of remorseless detail." The story is perilously close to melodrama. The anticlimax is surprising; "verisimilitude" is gained "at the expense of art."

185 "Five Hundred New and Recent Books," NEW YORK TIMES, 5 April 1914, p. 172.

["Brief-listing" of *Chance*.]

186 Huneker, James. "The Genius of Joseph Conrad," NORTH AMERICAN REVIEW, CC (Aug 1914), 270-79; rptd in IVORY APES AND PEACOCKS (NY: Scribner's, 1915), pp. 1-21.

"The figure of Joseph Conrad stands solitary among English novelists as the very ideal of a pure and disinterested artist." JC is primarily a painter of the sea, who has carried the sea-romance of such writers as Smollett, Marryat, and Melville into new territory. He has also revealed "obscure atavisms and the psychology lurking behind the mask of the savage." Realist as JC is, he is also a poet. As a stylist he is unique; "his rhythmic sense is akin to Flaubert's." His invention is second only to his imagination. "His novels are the novels of ideas dear to Balzac—though tinged with romance—a Stendhal of the sea." His characters are never "at rest": they are always transformed as "they grow in evil or wisdom." JC especially loves to explore the soul and the sea, but he recognizes "the relativity of things"; and the "ineluctable vastness and sadness of life oppress him," although his pessimism is implied, not overt.

Naturally, he drew men better than women, but he often makes "life-like sketches" of the latter: in *Chance,* for example, he portrays with sympathy and understanding the soul of an unhappy girl. In *Victory,* where he "deals with elemental causes," JC mingles the romantic and the analytic. "At a period when the distaff of fiction is too often in the hands of men," JC "sounds a dynamic masculine bass amid the shriller choir." [An early appreciation of JC that contains some insight into the works and has helped to establish JC's reputation as a writer of sea stories.]

187 Huneker, James. "The Seven Arts," PUCK, LXXV (2 May 1914), 9, 17.

JC did not look like a sailor and "a less pretentious person I never encountered." *Chance,* despite its critical success, is not likely to be a best seller. JC here carries off narration "to the pitch of polyphonic intricacy." Its moral is that "pairing off is the fate of mankind."

188 Huncker, James. "The Seven Arts," PUCK, LXXVI (25 July 1914), 8, 23.

JC "looms bigger and bigger on the horizon." According to Richard Curle, *Nostromo* is his greatest romance.

189 James, Henry. "The Younger Generation," TIMES LITERARY SUPPLEMENT (Lond), 19 March 1914, pp. 133-34; 2 April 1914, pp. 157-58; rvd and enlgd as "The New Novel," NOTES ON NOVELISTS WITH SOME OTHER NOTES (Lond: Dent, 1914), pp. 249-87.

In *Chance,* JC has achieved in technique the "miracle" of a refinement of design which has been widely recognized even if the success may be questioned. A number of reporters of the basic story, each depending on a preceding one, generates a drama in which JC's "own system and his combined eccentricities of recital represent the protagonist in face of powers leagued against, and of which the dénouement gives us the system fighting in triumph." The only flaw is that the "predicament was not imposed rather than invoked, was not the effect of a challenge from without, but that of a mystic impulse from within." Thus, *Chance* is an example of objectivity, "most precious of aims," seriously compromised because of the "lapse of authenticity," which readers seem not to recognize. But unlike his "fellow fabulists," JC acquits himself "with authority of the structural and compositional office."

190 Middleton, George. "Joseph Conrad's *The Nigger of the Narcissus,*" BOOKMAN (NY), XXXIX (July 1914), 563-65.

JC's publishers are to be commended for restoring the original title to *The Children of the Sea* for a uniform edition of JC's works and also for including a recently written foreword by the author as well as a preface which was suppressed when the novel was first published in book form after its serialization. In *The Nigger of the Narcissus* JC's art is great enough to make the reader believe that "all of life is condensed" into the lives of the few men on the ship. The book is "one of the world's great sea stories, differing from others in that it is psychological as well as external."

191 "The New Books," OUTLOOK (NY), CVII (2 May 1914), 45-46.

There is no humor in *Chance,* but otherwise it contains only excellence.

192 "Nineteen Notable New Novels," REVIEW OF REVIEWS (NY), XLIX (March 1914), 373-74.

Chance is "a brilliant piece of pessimistic puzzling over the apparent disorder of life." JC finds nothing but "accident and blind chance" in human life.

193 "The Novels of Mr. Conrad," TIMES LITERARY SUPPLEMENT (Lond), 15 Jan 1914, pp. 21-22.

The special virtue of JC's writings is found in their "intensely individual point of view, in the manner and method of presentation," rather than in the thing presented. The characters in *Chance,* although not especially complex, are used "kindly, or cruelly, or indifferently, as they use each other." The *dénouement* verges perhaps a little too closely on melodrama. The construction is loose and apparently aimless; JC may have sacrificed art to verisimilitude. At any rate, the dramatist and the novelist in JC are in conflict. Like others of JC's novels, this one contains an awareness of an "enveloping strangeness . . . of significance," as if earthly experience closely resembles a dream. And at times "the sardonic becomes ferocious and macabre, the mocking silent laughter resembles a grin of agony."

194 "Recent Reflections of a Novel-Reader," ATLANTIC MONTHLY, CXIV (Oct 1914), 530.

Chance, in which JC chose a subject "somewhat closer to everyday life," shows how the author, as if in a "laboratory," constructs his works; and it offers "intellectual stimulus rather than emotional relaxation."

195 "Reviews of New Books," LITERARY DIGEST, XLVIII (9 May 1914), 1119.

In *Chance,* JC uses the "zigzag" method of narration. The story "hinges" upon the psychological point that "it is lack of faith in herself that, according to Mr. Conrad, makes a woman a prey to chance and deprives her of the privilege of choice." A "Conrad story always stands for the best in contemporary literature."

196 "A Romance of Chance," INDEPENDENT, LXXVIII (27 April 1914), 173.

In *Chance,* JC is preoccupied with "the symbolism of treachery." A profound novel, *Chance* "deserves to become permanent."

197 Saxton, Eugene F. "The Romantic Story of Joseph Conrad," JOSEPH CONRAD (Garden City, NY: Doubleday, Page, nd [1914, and later revisions]), pp. 3-6; rptd in *A Set of Six,* by Joseph Conrad (Garden City, NY: Doubleday, Page, 1916), p. 4 [appended]; THE COUNTRY LIFE PRESS (Garden City, NY: Doubleday, Page, 1919), pp. 101-4; *"The Duel, A Military Tale,"* by Joseph Conrad (Garden City, NY: Garden City Publishing Co., 1923), p. 119.
[Saxton gives an appreciation of JC's romantic life at sea and lauds his transition to novelist.]

198 Wyzewa, T. de. "Un conteur anglais: M. Joseph Conrad" (An English Story-Teller: Mr. Joseph Conrad), REVUE DES DEUX MONDES, 6ème série, LXXXIV (March-April 1914), 935-46.
Some of the general qualities of JC's works are realism by means of picturesque details, suggestiveness, and musicality. *A Set of Six* reveals his Slavic sensibility. Although the time shift of *Chance* allows the reader to concentrate on character instead of on mere action, this method sometimes destroys suspense. Another fault of *Chance* is that the English characters do not seem to fit their background; they seem to be more Slavic than English. Flaubertian objectivity does not suit JC's Polish temperament. Happily, he abandons this technique in *Chance.* [Flimsy generalizations.] [In French.]

1915

199 "Book Selection Department," WISCONSIN LIBRARY BULLETIN, XI (March 1915), 89.
The stories in *A Set of Six* are "very characteristic, both in style and in their penetrating insight into the springs of human action."

200 "Books: Fiction," SPECTATOR (Lond), CXIV (6 March 1915), 338-39.
In the stories of *Within the Tides,* JC displays "an aristocratic disdain of convention." The tragedies narrated are developed organically and inevitably, and they enhance a belief in "the invincible and indomitable quality of goodness." No one but JC could have created the pathos and impressive themes without degenerating into "mere horror and squalor."

201 Borie, Edith. "Joseph Conrad," NEW REPUBLIC, II (17 April 1915), 647.

JC's stated desire, fondly to believe that the object of creation is "purely spectacular" and his statement that "unwearied self-forgetful attention to every phase of the universe reflected in consciousness may be our appointed task on earth" reveal an objectivity, a "godlike quality," which leaves the reader lonely, sometimes "joyfully, breathlessly so." It is JC's notion that emotions are "our affair," not the objective universe's. His characters are of such "potent spirit, good or bad" as to make his subject really a "state of soul," and incident the stuff of a bad dream (Captain Anthony's power of love and pity in *Chance;* Heyst's "tragic powerlessness to trust in life"). "This inability to trust recklessly to the human heart" must have seemed to JC an evil state of soul characteristic of the "man of the last hour," for doubt is a theme in much of his later work, including *Chance*. JC is sensible to the influence of other artists: an echo of Meredith "being charming" is heard in "The Duel"; a ring of Henry James is often heard in JC; *Almayer's Folly* suggests the eighteenth century being romantic about the Noble Savage. In *Folly,* the "most stifling malodorous heat" of the jungle prevails. JC is able to render physical impressions perfectly. [Review of *Victory* with brief sidelights on *The Secret Agent,* "The Duel," and *Folly*.]

202 Capes, M. Harriet M. (comp). WISDOM AND BEAUTY FROM CONRAD: AN ANTHOLOGY (Lond: Andrew Melrose, 1915; NY: Doubleday, Page, 1923).

JC's quality of wisdom is the outcome of a wide study of human nature. The passages selected show JC's "deep sympathy" for his fellow man. [The collection, made by Capes with JC's approval, consists of 143 pages of quotations, only severally identified, of "wisdom and beauty" gleaned from 16 volumes, and varying in length from one sentence to one page. JC dedicated an edition of *A Set of Six* to Capes.]

203 "Chronicle and Comment," BOOKMAN (NY), XLI (April 1915), 128-30.

A map illustrating the world of JC's novels and tales and an illustration of the *Otago,* JC's first command, made from a drawing by G. F. W. Hope, "an old sea friend," give early background information on JC. Hope reports that in the first days of their friendship soon after JC had left the sea, the future novelist visited the Hope home frequently and read aloud parts of *Almayer's Folly*. He later dedicated *Lord Jim* to Mr. and Mrs. Hope. The *Otago* is very likely the boat that figures in "The Secret Sharer," and readers should compare the first chapter of *The Mirror of the Sea* with this tale.

204 Colbron, Grace Isabel. "Seven Books of the Month," BOOKMAN (NY), XLI (May 1915), 322-23.

The character development, exciting action, and direct style of *Victory* are praiseworthy. "The greater directness of attack may win some friends for this gifted writer who have found him too elusive hitherto."

205 Curle, Richard. "Mr. Joseph Conrad and *Victory*," FORTNIGHTLY REVIEW, XCVIII (Oct 1915), 670-78.

In many novels, JC's "indirect manner [of narration] is merely a search for conciseness in difficult circumstances," but *Victory* is characterized by "austere simplicity of execution." It is a story "of an intolerable situation and of the nemesis of temperament." Heyst cannot bear Lena's suffering, but rescuing her brings disaster because he "cannot face successfully the changes that follow any decisive step." The night of climax "reaches a height of gloomy power hardly overmatched in LEAR itself." JC is a "romantic psychologist." His subjects may be gloomy, "but his belief in simple hearts, in honour, goodness, and pity, sheds a warm glow over all he writes."

206 "Current Fiction," NATION (NY), C (18 Feb 1915), 199.

A Set of Six may be a good introduction to JC's works. "The Duel," which had appeared earlier as "The Point of Honor," however different it may seem from JC's other works, is "a characteristic story"; it is "credible, as well as comic." Otherwise, "The Brute" and "Il Conde" are, "perhaps, the most notable."

207 "Current Fiction," NATION (NY), C (15 April 1915), 416-17.

In *Victory,* JC, "the Polish-Englishman," has a secret kind of art which is not easy to analyze. Perhaps most readily understood is "the unity of the impression produced in spite of the mass of preliminary detail" and his beginning the story in the middle. There is no doubt that JC is "enchanted" with the islands of southeastern Asia, and he "projects the spell so powerfully that the reader emerges from perusal of the story with a numbing sense of being no less bewitched than was Enchanted Heyst." The main purpose of the book is for the reader to become aware of Heyst and Lena. This work takes "its rightful place well up in the first rank" of JC's best productions.

208 [De la Mare, Walter.] "At the World's End," TIMES LITERARY SUPPLEMENT (Lond), 30 Sept 1915, p. 330; rptd in PRIVATE VIEW (Lond: Faber and Faber, 1953), pp. 19-22.

In reading *Victory,* one's "ceaseless search has also for a moment found rest and solace—"in 'truth rendered by beauty,' " as Flaubert wrote.

209 E[dgett], E[dwin] F[rancis]. "Joseph Conrad in the South Seas," BOSTON EVENING TRANSCRIPT, 24 March 1915, p. 24.

Victory is typical of JC's powers and "emphatic in its revelation of his originality."

210 E[dgett], E[dwin] F[rancis]. "Joseph Conrad the Versatile," BOSTON EVENING TRANSCRIPT, 23 Jan 1915, p. 6.

Among the stories of *A Set of Six,* "Il Conde" is especially praiseworthy, for nothing can excel its ingenuity, delicacy, simplicity, and pathos.

211 F., J. H. "Reviews," AMERICA (NY), XIII (1 May 1915), 75-76.

Victory, "not exactly a sea novel," "has all that vividness of characterization" for which JC is known. The story has "mostly villains" and "sordid scenes" and is probably "inferior" among JC's work.

212 F., W. A. "The Defeated Hermit," BOOKMAN (Lond), XLIX (Oct 1915), 21.

In *Victory,* JC's anti-German sentiments and insights into various national characters are praiseworthy. *Victory* and *Lord Jim* are connected through Schomberg. The novel portrays the conflict between "idealistic nihilism" and the "events of life."

213 "Fiction," A. L. A. BOOKLIST, XI (March 1915), 315.

A Set of Six is "well written but unusually distressing and not necessary in a small collection."

214 "Fiction," A. L. A. BOOKLIST, XI (May 1915), 411.

With reference to *Victory,* "Current Fiction," NATION (NY), C (15 April 1915), 416-17, is cited. The book is recommended for small libraries and for first purchase.

215 "Fiction," ATHENAEUM, No. 4558 (6 March 1915), 211.

In *Within the Tides,* JC's stories are good models for other writers to follow. JC avoids sensationalism and harmonizes the grotesque with credibility by employing irony (his treatment of murder-by-descending-bed-canopy in "The Inn of the Two Witches" affords convenient comparison with the methods of, for example, Wilkie Collins). The stories, highly inventive, afford JC a chance to indulge his "taste for arranging into patterns the futility, irony, and melancholy of this limited world." Though savage humor in "The Partner" is dearer to the intellect, "The Planter of Malata" and "Because of the Dollars" are nearer to the heart. "Laughing Anne" affords a vivid contrast to the marble stupefied woman of "The Planter of Malata."

216 "Fiction," ATHENAEUM, No. 4587 (25 Sept 1915), 208.

In *Victory,* Heyst is a kind of "materialized shadow, incapable of passion, capable instead of refinements of appreciation and a sympathy sacrificial of self." The evil partners are humorous and sinister: "Satire cannot easily achieve anything more comic than the junior partner's admirations of his comrade's gentlemanliness." *Victory* is perhaps a fantasy, with a "contagious air of enjoyment," including the "brutal, eccentric, bizarre."

217 Follett, Wilson. Joseph Conrad: A Short Study (Garden City, NY: Doubleday, Page, 1915); rptd (NY: Russell & Russell, 1966).

JC's work evidences the conflict between man and his world. His universe is indifferent as Thomas Hardy's is, but JC, the observer, is not indifferent. He uses the indifference of things to heighten the feeling of disaster, but the mind and will of man remain the hero. JC lets the lesser struggle stand for the greater, as in *Victory*. His transitions from Poland to the west, from the sea to the shore, affected his writings. Perhaps because he was born in an inland nation, JC can write with a blend of intimacy and detachment about the sea, and because he left it early in his life, his stories "consist of something tremendous in the past to which everything leads forward." *The Nigger of the Narcissus* is the record of men drawn by the indifference of the world into closer relationship with people. JC sees man's place among his own to be part of a group, and the supreme tragedy, consequently, is not being part of a group, as in "Typhoon." His vision of man also involves an acknowledgement of racial identities and tragedy in interracial conflicts, as in *Almayer's Folly* or to some extent in "Heart of Darkness." Whereas most of the stories deal with an outcast trying to break barriers, *Nostromo* considers a complete and coherent society, its illusion of order; it is about avarice, a pariah among favorable attributes. The core of JC's work is human solidarity or its lack. JC works as a professional notebook realist, but he does not merely offer his memories as fiction. He reacts against brevity and compression as laws set on the subject from without. He will include much detail, relevant or not, if the whole is effective, if the character can be known intimately. What pulls this together is mood at the risk of distorted chronology, as in *Nostromo, Folly, Under Western Eyes*. He is a master in making the story illustrative of something greater than itself, and his technical development parallels his grasp of this process (which culminates in *Victory*) of recreating life, of snatching "in a moment of courage, from the remorseless rush of time, a passing phase of life."

218 "How I 'Broke Into Print,' III. Joseph Conrad," Strand (NY), L (Aug 1915), 92-93; rptd in Strand (Lond), I, (Nov 1915), 575-76.

JC and Stevenson are bracketed as to style; JC now gets £200 per story. [Reviews the story of how *Almayer's Folly* was written, "discovered," lost, found, and, after five or six years, published. Not by JC.]

219 "Joseph Conrad's Latest Romance," Review of Reviews (NY), LI (June 1915), 761.

JC's "marvelous gift" for producing "enthralling romance and profound and magnificent philosophy inextricably tangled with the mystery and freedom of the sea" is seen best in *Victory*. The symbolism is sublime.

220 "Literature and Art," CURRENT OPINION, LVIII (May 1915), 351.

In *Victory,* Heyst, "a piece of fine analysis," is "a veritable Hamlet of the South Seas, but essentially a Hamlet of our own days." Lena is also a successful creation and "almost equals the Flora de Barral of *Chance.*" Lena "is a woman, but she is also a floating, a permeating essence." [Almost wholly quoted from NEW YORK TIMES review of *Victory.*]

221 Lynd, Robert. "Some of the Fiction That Is Being Read This Spring," PUBLISHERS' WEEKLY, LXXXVII (20 March 1915), 924.

Victory has the "same fantastic, far-removed atmosphere" as Kipling's "The Disturber of Traffic."

222 "The New Books," OUTLOOK (NY), CX (5 May 1915), 44.

Victory "has something Stevensonian in its texture and color." The Swedish fatalist's tragedy is "subtle in its psychology," but "it deals more sharply with incident than is Mr. Conrad's wont."

223 Payne, William Morton. "Recent Fiction," DIAL, LVIII (13 May 1915), 383.

In *Victory,* JC's knowledge of "the flotsam and jetsam of humanity" is especially worthwhile.

224 "Recent Reflections of a Novel-Reader," ATLANTIC MONTHLY, CXVI (Oct 1915), 511.

In *Victory,* JC takes Heyst and Lena, "two negligible folk," and makes "a great drama, charged with pity and terror," of the last few weeks of their lives. "He sees them with crystal clearness, with absolute detachment, yet with a yearning pity, a vast gentleness."

225 "Reviews of New Books," LITERARY DIGEST, L (17 April 1915), 885.

"There is never anything conventional or commonplace about Mr. Conrad's stories." JC uses "themes that are original, a distinctive style, and an exceptional technique." In *Victory,* Heyst is "an enigmatical character."

226 Rider, Fremont. "Novels too Good to Miss . . . . *A Set of Six,*" PUBLISHERS' WEEKLY, LXXXVII (13 Feb 1915), 480.

"Gaspar Ruiz" is better than the other five stories put together.

227 *"A Set of Six,"* CATHOLIC WORLD, C (March 1915), 825.

"The Duel" is the best story; "Gaspar Ruiz" is the next best, but not so gripping all the way through. "The Brute" is uncannily effective. "No author gets inside his character so thoroughly as does Conrad."

228 *"A Set of Six,"* NEW YORK TIMES BOOK REVIEW, 31 Jan 1915, p. 38.

[A brief three-paragraph review of the reprint of *A Set of Six* in a uniform edition.]

229 "A South Sea Hamlet," NEW YORK TIMES BOOK REVIEW, 28 March 1915, pp. 109-10.

In *Victory*, JC has outborrowed Shakespeare by using a noble Swede to write a HAMLET of the South Seas, but it is weaker than *Chance*: "incident and analysis do not blend as they might, and the agents of the final catastrophe are cheap."

230 Symons, Arthur. "Conrad," FORUM, LIII (May 1915), 579-92; rptd in DRAMATIS PERSONAE (Indianapolis: Bobbs-Merrill, 1923), pp. 1-23.

JC's "unexplicable mind" has created its "secret world," hidden from view. From his corner, JC "throws out tentacles into the darkness." At the center of his web is "an elemental sarcasm" calm and cynical. He must make entertainment-seekers uneasy, for he presents "the bare side of every virtue, the hidden heroism of every vice or crime." In all of this "there is no judgment, only an implacable comprehension." He sees through reality "into a realm of illusion of the unknown." No other writer has reached so well the hidden depths of the soul; a brilliant achievement is Lord Jim's death. JC "gives us the soul's own dream of itself, as if a novelist of adventure had turned Neo-Platonist." It is through his men that he best succeeds; his women are definite creatures, "easily indicated." Men fear and hate them as parasites. At his best JC evades definite statement. *Lord Jim* represents the zenith of his genius. He writes without plots, and does not require them. His stories are "a series of studies in temperaments, deduced from slight incidents; studies in emotion, with hardly a rag to hold together the . . . scraps of action."

231 Williams, Michael. "Literature: XIII—Joseph Conrad," AMERICA (NY), XIV (13 Nov 1915), 113-14.

JC made his first deep impression with *The Nigger of the Narcissus* in Henley's NEW REVIEW. Apart from its other qualities (imagination, vision, truth, beauty of style), JC brought "spiritual interest" into the English novel (i.e., the sense of "seriousness of human life"). However different, JC is a serious artist as are Shaw, Wells, and James, Benson, Chesterton, and Belloc. JC is nearer the Catholic rather than the humanist group in his vision of life—in part this is supported by JC's "consistent treatment . . . of the mystery of evil." JC does not explain away evil as lying outside of man, who is then not responsible.

1916

232 "Current Fiction," NATION (NY), CII (10 Feb 1916), 164.
The four tales of *Within the Tides* are "perfectly distinctive of their author," although "The Planter of Malata" is a failure. The other three "show Mr. Conrad at his best as a story-teller pure and simple."

233 D., W. "Reviews," AMERICA (NY), XIV (5 Feb 1916), 403.
Within the Tides reaffirms that JC is "the greatest living writer of descriptive English and one of the greatest psychological novelists of any time." The four tales are powerful.

234 Edgett, Edwin Francis. "Joseph Conrad on Sea and Shore," BOSTON EVENING TRANSCRIPT, 22 Jan 1916, p. 6.
"The Inn of the Two Witches," of *Within the Tides,* has notable parallels with Wilkie Collins's "A Terribly Strange Bed." JC's stories are "of the innermost feelings of mankind."

235 "Fiction," A. L. A. BOOKLIST, XII (March 1916), 288.
Within the Tides has "fascinating, tragic stories written in the author's usual vein."

236 Freeman, John. "Joseph Conrad," THE MODERNS (Lond: Robert Scott, 1916), pp. 5, 216-17, 243-64.
Almayer's Folly has "the strangeness, the passion, the pity, the sadness, as well as the slight exoticism and casual extravagance that mark the whole Conrad line." *Lord Jim* is "the most simply human of all the novels, the most purely Conradian." Jim, cursed with an ever-acute imagination, "meets death proudly, now, the spiritual indignity of that earlier failure forgotten, tranquil in his re-established individuality." The spiritual value of imaginative work is highest in *Lord Jim, Nostromo,* and *Under Western Eyes*. JC gives not only the event and motive, but also the value, "the human effect of the psychology," of the event and motive. He is chiefly fascinated with the "clash of human aspiration with secret falseness." Honor endures in JC's books. His imagination is mythopoetic. "He is obviously a romantic ["in the element of strangeness, of surprising beauty . . . , the apprehension of which is a specially modern quest"], just as obviously as his method is in several books realistic." The later books lean to realism.

237 Hale, Edward E. "Recent Fiction," DIAL, LX (2 March 1916), 216.
[Brief note in general praise of *Within the Tides*.]

238 Lynd, Robert. *"Within the Tides,"* PUBLISHERS' WEEKLY, LXXXIX (19 Feb 1916), 642.

Within the Tides contains one mediocre tale, "The Inn of the Two Witches," and three fine tales: "The Planter of Malata"; "Because of the Dollars," an action yarn; and "The Partner," perhaps "the best tale of the book."

239 "A Master of the Ironic," NEW YORK TIMES BOOK REVIEW, 16 Jan 1916, pp. 17, 22.

Except for "The Partner," *Within the Tides* is not up to JC's best.

240 "The Newest Fiction," REVIEW OF REVIEWS (NY), LIII (March 1916), 377.

Within the Tides contains four "fine tales" which are "the finest of their kind offered today; Conrad is the supreme story-teller of this generation."

241 Phelps, William Lyon. "Conrad, Galsworthy and Others," BOOKMAN (NY), XLIII (May 1916), 297-304; rptd in THE ADVANCE OF THE ENGLISH NOVEL (NY: Dodd, Mead, 1919), pp. 192-231, espec 192-217.

JC, J. M. Barrie, John Galsworthy, May Sinclair, and M. P. Willcocks, among modern novelists have the biggest ideals and "write with soberness of mind." Although JC chose to write in English and although there is little of Poland in his books, his experiences and reflections at sea color his books. His experiences and his "Slav temperament" made him a "grave, steady, reliable" man. *Under Western Eyes* is the "most Slavic of all his novels," unlike *Victory,* "a novel quite unworthy of him." Unlike such sea-story writers as Smollett, Scott, Cooper, Marryat, Russell, and Jack London, but like R. L. Stevenson, JC is noteworthy for his style—he was influenced in this by the English Bible. He is Stevenson's heir. JC "is more sincere than Loti." JC "is the psychologist of sailors; a kind of union of Richardson and Smollett." JC is famous, although he has no public [cites Galsworthy's FORTNIGHTLY REVIEW (1908) comment]—JC "is overcareful for popular taste . . . in minuteness and accuracy of description, . . . in analysis, . . . in the shades of his conversations." *Chance* illustrates his method of construction "at its worst." He can never equal Tolstoi, Turgenev, or Dostoevski, for he lacks their universality or their transparency of style. His is a highly self-conscious style, "never a happy accident." JC's *The Nigger of the Narcissus* is probably his masterpiece and the preface his most noteworthy critical statement. He rejects artistic and philosophical dogmas. New readers should begin with "Typhoon" and then soon go on to *Nigger.* JC "describes fearful storms in nature and frightful passions in man, and with . . . the calm of the observant artist." A comparison between Cooper's Long Tom, in THE PILOT, and Singleton, in JC's *Nigger,* reveals "what mere thoughtfulness has done to the art of fiction."

242 "Stories of Men and the Sea," INDEPENDENT, LXXXVI (10 April 1916), 73.

Within the Tides contains adventure stories with psychological interest which will please the average reader as well as the connoisseur.

243 Sutherland, J. G. AT SEA WITH JOSEPH CONRAD (Lond: Grant Richards; Boston: Houghton, Mifflin, 1922).

In 1916, Captain Sutherland took JC with him on his brigantine, the *Ready,* renamed the *Freya* for JC, for U-boat hunting experiences in the North Sea. JC was extremely alert and knowledgeable about marine affairs and quick to comprehend the fine details of submarine warfare. JC, delighted to be once again on a sailing vessel, eagerly aided the officers in making decisions and joined in the work of the ship. His temperament and nature made him more than a seaman. [This book is padded heavily.]

244 Walpole, Hugh. JOSEPH CONRAD (NY: Holt; Lond: Nisbet, nd. [1916]); rvd (1924).

Three backgrounds, "Poland, the Sea, the inner security and tradition of an English country-side," made JC the artist he was, the creator of novels and tales containing simplicity, fidelity, a healthy hatred of self-assertion and self-satisfaction, sobriety, zest, and vigor. Almost all of his themes are about combats "unequal to his own far-seeing vision, but never to the human souls engaged in them"; and this consciousness "of the blindness that renders men's honesty and heroism of so little account . . . gives occasion for his irony." Most of his heroes are "solid and unimaginative" human beings who have no vision. These men command the author's pity, his reverence, and his tenderness; but at last he admits that they have not won in their struggle. "Typhoon," which contains the very epitome of JC's themes, is "the struggle of M'Whirr [sic] against the storm"; but even if the captain seems to win, the reader hears in the last lines of the book "the storm's confident chuckle of ultimate victory." The "poet" in JC is "lyrical as well as philosophic." The works of his middle period display the finest of his lyrical gifts: the "spontaneous emotion" and "the spirit of the first rapture" were never again quite recaptured after "Typhoon," "Youth," and "Heart of Darkness." His style also is best in his middle period.

JC's "potential qualities . . . of atmosphere" are his "union of Romance and Realism." *Nostromo* is "the supreme example" of his creation of atmosphere because of "the juxtaposition of the lyrical and the realistic." As for JC's philosophy, JC is convinced that "life is too strong, too clever and too remorseless for the sons of men"; and although he admires the simplicity of their faith, his irony "springs from his knowledge of the inevitable end." The qualities in the human soul that he most admires are "blind courage and obedience to duty." For JC, realism alone was not sufficient; he had a poet's mind, a romantic mind, and he therefore "used romance realistically." But in his later works, in *Victory* for example, he did not exert "the discipline and restraint that were once his law." [An early sympathetic assessment of JC and his work to date, but still of value to the student of JC.]

245 *"Within the Tides,"* OPEN SHELF (Cleveland), 16 April 1916, p. 33.

"Conrad's hallmark of atmosphere and soulbaring psychology distinguishes these tales from the usual story of mystery and adventure."

1917

246 "Books: Fiction," SPECTATOR (Lond), CXVIII (31 March 1917), 391-92.

The Shadow-Line is a Conradian version of "The Ancient Mariner," with a young captain who has "courage and nerve." The headstrong captain sometimes seems to be merged in the author and thus to take on "a subtlety and a vision foreign to his normal and somewhat aggressive self-confidence," but the ultimate impression is one of achievement.

247 Boynton, H. W. "Outstanding Novels of the Year," NATION (NY), CV (29 Nov 1917), 600.

The Shadow-Line is a fine story for "the novice seeking initiation into the Conradian mysteries." This book includes "the menace and the glamour of his ocean" and "the humanly strange yet strangely human atoms with which it plays." The voyage of the ship is "morbid, yet somehow sanative."

248 Boynton, H. W. "Some Stories of the Month," BOOKMAN (NY), XLV (July 1917), 536-37.

The Shadow-Line is characteristic, perfectly simple and straightforward and "the more effective for it."

249 "A Conrad Hero's Quest for the Truth," NEW YORK TIMES BOOK REVIEW, 22 April 1917, p. 157.

In reference to *The Shadow-Line,* JC's works are not popular because his "are novels of great quests and of absorbing passions" and the present era is uncongenial. JC's cornerstone of faith is Fidelity. "Through Mr. Conrad's work has always run the feeling that however much his favorite virtue, fidelity, may profit a man's soul, his earthly existence is largely the sport of circumstance."

250 D., W. "Reviews," AMERICA (NY), XVII (19 May 1917), 145-46.

The Shadow-Line is an excellent example of JC's manner and method; it contains less of the indirect narration that made some of his other psychological stories hard to follow.

251 E[dgett], E[dwin] F[rancis]. "Joseph Conrad the Supreme Analyst," BOSTON EVENING TRANSCRIPT, 5 May 1917, p. 6.

The Shadow-Line is the most characteristic of JC's stories, "an epitome of his manner and a summary of his method." It strengthens JC's position as one of the greatest and most substantial of modern writers.

252 Eno, Sara W. "Joseph Conrad: A Contribution Toward a Bibliography," BULLETIN OF BIBLIOGRAPHY (Bryn Mawr College), IX (April 1917), 137-39.

[This "contribution" contains a biographical sketch, lists of novels, short stories, miscellaneous writings, biographies, general criticisms, and magazine portraits.]

253 "Fiction," A. L. A. BOOKLIST, XIII (June 1917), 402.

The Shadow-Line gives a similar "sense of the power of the sea and the wonder of human nature as 'Youth' and 'Typhoon.' "

254 "Fiction," ATHENAEUM, No. 4617 (May 1917), 253.

The Shadow-Line is more of an elaboration of a short story than a novel.

255 Follett, Helen Thomas, and Wilson Follett. "Joseph Conrad," ATLANTIC MONTHLY, CXIX (Feb 1917), 233-43; rptd in SOME MODERN NOVELISTS: APPRECIATIONS AND ESTIMATES (NY: Holt, 1918; Lond: George Allen & Unwin, 1919), pp. 13, 17, 300-309, 312-35, 342, 347.

Although JC may appear at first to be a romancer, he is actually a realist. He effects an awareness of tension between appearance and reality with his verbal irony, reminding us of the contrast between the inner reality of man and the outer surface of his life. He notes well the minutiae of reality, but he uses them as guides to the moral life, being concerned most with character and motive. He has studied man in isolation whether he be cut off by his own actions or, in JC's later works, by his own nature. He is at his best when he discusses not racial differences alone, but rather the variations among individuals. JC studies the solitary man in Captain MacWhirr ("Typhoon"), a man who remains aloof because of his incapacity for fear, in Jim (*Lord Jim*), who is set apart by his self-loathing, as well as in Heyst, Falk, and Captain Whalley. When JC writes about man in isolation, he writes in part about his own life. Details revealed in *A Personal Record* lay in the back of his imagination as he wrote. Losing in effect his first life in Poland and his second life on the sea, JC writes with an awareness of the paradox of physical loss and spiritual retention. In *Victory* and *Nostromo,* JC treats the question raised by the pessimism of Heyst and Martin

Decoud—whether man should strive for brotherhood if indeed there are warring species in Nature and whether he ought not to get as much as he can out of life regardless of others. He answers them in one sense with a dark, negative, non-ethical view of the world purpose. That the world has no meaning does not mean that what man feels about it has no meaning. JC's view of art falls between one which regards art as purely decorative and one which looks upon it as didactic and utilitarian. It hinges on the evocation of a mood and the sacrifice of movement and often chronology in the narrative. In *Chance* the mood of the observer of the story, Marlow, is integrated into the story. JC's main focus is Marlow's interpretation of Fyne's and Powell's summaries of what happened rather than on the love affair itself. *Nostromo* evidences the subordination of chronology for a greater coherence. The technique used in this tale supports only the fact that JC is a great and far-reaching influence on English letters.

256 Glaenzer, Richard Butler. "Snap-Shots of English Authors. Conrad," BOOKMAN (NY), XLV (June 1917), 346.
[This short poem about JC refers satirically to his "vaulting subtleties," a needless device preferred by this "Poet-explorer of all seas, all jungles, / Whether of earth or of the microcosm," to make "through love and loyalty / The landfall, Truth!"]

257 Hall, Leland. "Joseph Conrad [with selections]," THE WARNER LIBRARY (NY: Knickerbocker P, 1917), VII, 3956 a-v; rptd in ENGLISH LITERATURE DURING THE LAST HALF CENTURY, ed by John William Cunliffe (NY: Macmillan, 1919); 2nd ed. (1923), pp. 179-99; and in COLUMBIA UNIVERSITY COURSE IN LITERATURE, BASED ON THE WORLD'S BEST LITERATURE (NY: Columbia U P, 1929), V, 345-56.
The style of JC's early books, obviously based on French novels, is "too consciously sonorous." "The latter works do not contain such conscious profusion of rhythm and regular cadence, though even in *Victory* there is often a suspicion of timbre that is not English." "*Chance* as a whole is a perfectly rounded work of art, art in the abstract sense of form and structure." JC's first four novels deal almost exclusively with life in the eastern archipelagoes, to which the search for profit and gold has brought the white men. *Nostromo* reveals on a "truly colossal" scale the avarice of men. In *Chance* and *Victory,* JC was concerned with the struggle of men and women against the evils of greed. For JC, "evil is that power which turns man against his kind, tearing that bond of fellowship, of solidarity as he called it, in which is man's source of comfort and strength." The victories of *Chance* and *Victory* are in that "two human beings have become united in spite of fate." "The deepest and best" of JC is in *The Shadow-Line*.

258 K., Q. "Conrad's New Story," NEW REPUBLIC, XI (16 June 1917), 194-95.

The Shadow-Line goes "straight through from beginning to end," without any of the typical Conradian zigzagging, which incidentally is wholly admirable as a means of preparing fresh insights, of stalking the human heart. [A plot summary of *The Shadow-Line* is interspersed with appreciative adjectives concerning JC's artistic powers to render scene and character intensely.] JC in the first third of the novel rouses an anticipation of sinister adventure which is not really fulfilled in the "simple beautiful story that follows."

259 Macy, John. "Kipling and Conrad," DIAL, LXII (17 May 1917), 441-43.

In *The Shadow-Line,* JC is a poet of the sea, "the chief figure in contemporaneous English prose." A double review which does not compare Kipling's A DIVERSITY OF CREATURES with JC's work.

260 Mencken, H. L. "Joseph Conrad," A BOOK OF PREFACES (NY: Knopf, 1917), pp. 11-64.

Melancholy and a fascination with the indifference of the universe underscore all of JC's stories. His heroes do not conquer fate, but rather, as Prometheuses, are themselves conquered. JC's resignation cannot be solely a Slavic trademark. Perhaps more than Twain, Hardy, Dreiser, and Crane, JC is concerned about man's inability to make the universe intelligible. He writes of the meaninglessness of life in "Heart of Darkness" and "Falk." JC does not moralize, but rather observes, pities, and is amused by the situation of man. This distance and the resultant quality of irony set him off from other writers. His purpose was to record some part of his wonder of life and the "prodigality of life" as men live it. In doing so, he probes motivations of men. His view of moral systems is that of a skeptic who constantly falls back on his inability to comprehend the universe. His novels do not contain typical "sympathetic" heroines; he shows how little they count in man's struggle. JC's heroes are rarely moved by *amour*.

As a literary artist, JC is known for his involved method of narration—his shifts in narrator, the stories within stories, to the disapproval of orthodox critics who expect an omniscient author. He questions, experiments, and is sometimes perplexed by his characters. In this element of inexplicability lies part of JC's art. JC has a disposition for melodramatic scenes, perhaps like such writers as Dumas and Lew Wallace; but being a supreme artist, he does not use shipwreck and assassination for their own sake; rather he probes motives and the inner workings of the event. Most of his materials reveal "a shop worn shoddiness." In "Youth," an orthodox sea story and in *Nostromo,* O. Henry and Richard Harding Davis character types appear, but JC handles them with extraordinary graphic skill. When *Youth* was published in 1902 the "praise was unanimous," but the mass of novel readers remained unaffected. Even with the publication of *Typhoon* sales of JC's books were small. However, today (1917) he has both a British and an American publisher, and his first editions bring more than those of any other living author. Reading "Youth," or "Heart of Darkness," and then Kipling at his best reveals the difference between "an adroit artisan" and "a first-rate artist."

261 Meredith, Mark. "Joseph Conrad," BOOK NEWS MONTHLY (Philadelphia), XXXV (July 1917), 431.

JC's influence on literature has increased steadily. His first novel, *Almayer's Folly,* so different from the kind of literature then being produced (e.g., James's novels), merited more attention than it received. JC gained a public with *Chance,* and *Victory* confirmed his reputation. In *Lord Jim,* JC carefully analyzes the coward Jim, giving him qualities that interest us and cause us to sympathize with him. In *Jim,* JC's regard for personal honor surfaces. The characters he portrays are vital, unique, sometimes grotesque and exotic. Nature (typhoons, primeval forests, the sea) is as prominent as concern for honor in his narratives.

262 "The New Books," OUTLOOK (NY), CXVI (16 May 1917), 116.

The Shadow-Line is "one of the best and most carefully wrought of Conrad's shorter sea tales." Only JC could have "evolved the situation with such pains and care."

263 "New Books Reviewed," NORTH AMERICAN REVIEW, CCV (June 1917), 949-50.

In *The Shadow-Line,* JC's genius enables him to make "a realistic and tremendously impressive story of the sea" into something much greater than that. The reader is aware of "the outward realities of the story" and also of "its subjective truth." This simple tale of a young man's becoming mature is "as vivid and as haunting as 'The Ancient Mariner.'"

264 "Review," BOOKMAN (Lond), LII (June 1917), 98.

The Shadow-Line is "one of those sombre studies of the individual struggling in the meshes of fate"—it is not as good a novel as *Chance* or "The End of the Tether." It is a sea story as opposed to a psychological analysis. "It is the description of the deadly and ineluctable calm that gives the book its value." The ghostly elements are not terrifying except as they influence the characters of the story.

265 "Reviews of New Books," LITERARY DIGEST, LV (27 Oct 1917), 36.

In reference to *The Shadow-Line:* "Of all modern sea-story writers none has a more indescribable power and charm than Joseph Conrad," who "excels in method, in style, in choice of language, and, under and through all, in spirit."

266 *"The Shadow-Line,"* TIMES LITERARY SUPPLEMENT (Lond), 22 March 1917, p. 138.

In *The Shadow-Line,* the narrative technique is weak, the moral "overbalances the story," and the "serene assurance" of JC's "genius is here broken and uncertain."

267 "A Sinister Voyage," INDEPENDENT, XC (2 June 1917), 437. [Brief review of *The Shadow-Line.*]

268 Squire, J. C. "Mr. Conrad's Masterpiece," LAND AND WATER, LXIX (26 July 1917), 15; rptd in LIFE AND LETTERS (Lond: Heinemann; NY: Doran, 1921), pp. 139-45.

In the light of *Lord Jim,* one wonders why JC was not recognized as the equal of Hardy and Meredith twenty years ago. "As an achievement in construction, it is in the first rank." The digressions and the portraits of minor characters all contribute to the total effect, but Jim "always remains a little vague." In no other book of JC "is a greater variety of scenes so surely sketched. . . . And it is all done in the English of a grave music which, from one to whom our language is not native, is miraculous." Although, like James, JC "scarcely ever preaches," he is "in the best sense a didactic writer." JC's books are admirable *because* they "are an incitement to decent living."

269 "Three Ages of Youth," NATION (NY), CIV (28 June 1917), 760-61.

The Shadow-Line: A Confession seems to be based on "some episode of his [JC's] early experience." The incident is interesting to the author not only for his own sake but "because he sees it as typical of what in some form is bound to happen to every man." The shadow line is that "between dream and waking," and JC is a master in telling such a story.

270 "Two Novels of Distinction," REVIEW OF REVIEWS (NY), LV (June 1917), 663.

The Shadow-Line, JC's "simple story," "expresses to us a message of spiritual discernment from that larger world of which the elements are symbols, and which swings its tides against the shores of the common deeds of our daily lives." It should arouse men to meet their great responsibilities in a time of "world disaster."

271 Walsh, James J., M.D. "Literature and Twaddle," AMERICA (NY), XVII (21 July 1917), 381.

In comparing Jack London and JC, one compares "small things with great."

JC is one of the few serious novelists: he demands thought; London does not. In London's work, "the incidents are everything"; in JC's, "the characters are everything." JC is deeply concerned with "human life in its moral aspects."

272 Ward, Laura A. "The Sea in English Fiction from 1918-1930." Unpublished thesis, University of Pennsylvania, 1917.

1918

273 Baum, Paull Franklin. "A Source," MODERN LANGUAGE NOTES, XXXIII (May 1918), 312-14.

Wilkie Collins's "A Terribly Strange Bed," in AFTER DARK (1856), and JC's "The Inn of the Two Witches," in *Within the Tides* (1915) are similar: "On the whole, I cannot help feeling that the apparent straight-forward simplicity and directness, the air of matter-of-fact truthfulness of the earlier version make it superior to Conrad's as a tale of mystery and horror." The reader finds himself more fascinated with JC's style than with his meaning. The structure of JC's story may be more contemporary, but it "seems a bit thin and diffuse, and gives the impression of a lack of unity."

274 Bendz, Ernst. "Joseph Conrad, Sexagenarian," ENGLISCHE STUDIEN, LI (Jan 1918), 391-406.

No writer of contemporary British fiction can rightly be mentioned before JC because this writer's "interpretation of life is more profound, more embracing, artistically more perfect," than that offered by Kipling, Wells, Galsworthy, or Shaw. *Almayer's Folly* and *An Outcast of the Islands* still retain their "pristine freshness and charm" because they reveal an entire world "non-existent, in a literary sense," to Western minds. JC is an "admirable teller of stories and a shrewd observer of men and things—a romanticist with the backbone of a realist," whose "exquisite genius" is enhanced by an "astonishing gift of visualization, a strong view of philosophy, a sense of humour." For him, the "outward incident" is of value only as it conveys "some sort of spiritual meaning." His art relies for its ultimate effect on "intenseness of soul-matter," and his philosophy is gloomy, containing an "element of tragedy and pathos." JC's humor is not "genial and convivial"; rather, it is "instinct with irony." His style is gifted with "raciness and colour"; he displays extraordinary "subtlety and shrewdness of insight." JC will never become a "popular novelist" because many readers are repelled by his irony and pessimism or by the "ghastliness" of his subjects.

275 "Conrad in Poland," BOOKMAN (NY), XLVI (Feb 1918), 659.

[Speculation on the events surrounding JC's safe return from Poland to Vienna in the months immediately following the outbreak of World War I. The author hopes that JC's experiences will be included in his next book.]

276 "Conrad's Implacable Comprehension Interpreted by Arthur Symons," CURRENT OPINION, LXIV (Jan 1918), 53.

JC writes by instinct, he is not in a strict sense a novelist, and, since he sees through to the unknown, reality is non-existent to him.

277 Cutler, Frances Wentworth. "Why Marlow?" SEWANEE REVIEW, XXVI (Jan 1918), 28-38.

Although Marlow's "knowledge is sometimes in fact impossible, it is seldom in imagination improbable." In contrast to the older novel where there is no appeal from the verdicts already made, the reader enters into the creative process when he reads JC because of the way JC makes use of Marlow.

278 Droz, Juliette. "A propos d'un livre de M. Joseph Conrad" (Concerning a Book by Mr. Joseph Conrad), REVUE HEBDOMADAIRE, XXVII (Sept 1918), 322-27.

The "morbidity" in *Lord Jim* linking JC to Dostoevski and Gorki is recognized by JC in his preface to a 1917 edition in which he refers to a remark by an unknown lady that *Jim* is "morbid." [Analysis of the novel based on JC's preface.] [In French.]

279 "Joseph Conrad's War-time Thoughts of Ships and Sea," CURRENT OPINION, LXV (Nov 1918), 326.

[Extensive quotations from JC's articles in the LONDON CHRONICLE on the ties that bind together men at sea.]

280 "Methods in Fiction," NEW YORK TIMES REVIEW OF BOOKS, 6 Jan 1918, p. 4.

JC confessed that *Lord Jim* was originally a short story. JC's account of writing *Jim* disposes of the idea that writers plan all novels as if they were geometrical problems. *Jim* has a story that surprises all, including its author.

281 Morley, Christopher. "The Skipper (Conrad)," SHANDYGAFF (Garden City, NY: Doubleday, 1918), pp. 238-45.

"No book of memoirs since the synoptic gospels exceeds *A Personal Record*." It is an autobiography "true to the inner secrets of the human soul." [Lyric effusion—pointless.]

282 Pease, Frank. "Joseph Conrad," NATION (NY), CVII (2 Nov 1918), 510-13.

JC's great "subjective adventures of character" are accompanied by intrinsic outer adventures to form a "synchronism" which is "completely satisfying," thus creating a "sustained and secret sympathy between the outer aspect and the inner reality," a reality that is well illustrated in "Heart of Darkness" by "the dark heart of Kurtz [which] is inseparable from the African heart of darkness." This "subtle interweaving of outer and inner worlds" is caused in Captain MacWhirr by the fury of the sea. JC's "thesis that for good or evil literary characters must possess character comes as a veritable Attic rebirth of adventure." His "meditative quality" enabled him to perceive the truth "that all art sooner or later has its influence upon life"; it caused literature to disregard the "lackadaisical conventions" which had overwhelmed it and to recognize again "the everlasting foe of mankind." This foe JC shows well in Donkin's character in *The Nigger of the Narcissus,* but he displays other aspects in such persons as Lord Jim, Charles Gould, and Razumov. His art is both human and "moral." [An early thought-provoking analysis of the significance of JC's works.]

283 Robertson, J. M. "The Novels of Joseph Conrad," NORTH AMERICAN REVIEW, CCVIII (Sept 1918), 439–53.

JC already has "a high repute and a wide audience," as "vogue" existed for authors who were not writing for "the multitude." He has the "double faculty" of an "intense susceptibility to the appeal of environment" and of "a no less intense inner life of imaginative reconstruction"; he displays "in a supreme degree" the two faculties of "perception and conception, vision and reproduction, in a spontaneous union"; and his is "a universal response to all visible phenomena." The artist in JC makes everything alive that he sees; his "very artistic faults are excesses of creative faculty, never the outcome of deficiency." He is a realist in spite of his use of Marlow, who has "no true personality," and Decoud, who unrealistically writes the long letter to his sister. His characters come to be known gradually, as people do in life. The same is true of JC's plots; JC "especially loves . . . to prelude and evolve a great situation," as he does in *Chance* and *The Shadow-Line.* His variety is seen in *Victory* and *Lord Jim.* Without humor, "the ironic and tragic vision" of life "overlaps for him the spirit of comedy, of laughter"; but in him this is not a defect.

The final impression left by JC's art is "that of greatness, of tragic intensity, of vivid realization of life and circumstance." His "Shakespearean realism" imagines events and characters "in terms of true vision," and in that sense he is also an idealist; he "makes the ideal pass as real." His masterpiece is *Jim* rather than *Nostromo;* he has written "no feeble book or story." He is "a great figure in English fiction" who has given a strong "stimulus to a serious handling of that great art." [An early perceptive, if not altogether accurate, appraisal of JC's achievement.]

284 Salmon, Arthur L. "Joseph Conrad: Russian Pole, British Seaman, English Novelist," BOOK NEWS MONTHLY (Philadelphia), XXXVI (Aug 1918), 442-43.

Although JC writes in English, his fiction retains a Slavic note and is cosmopolitan. He is a master of reticence. In *Some Reminiscences* we learn something about his character; we feel that a good deal of JC's fiction is "veiled autobiography." He is at his best when he deals with life at sea or in port, except for "Heart of Darkness" which takes place inland. His writing power lies in his psychology, which exposes character without judgment, and also in his analytic powers. For instance, *Chance* is a patient, detailed psychological study, and JC does not, in general, tell us that his characters are either heroes or villains. In *Victory* and "The End of the Tether" we note, perhaps, an inclination to give a tragic ending when a happy one is equally possible, but we cannot quarrel with this tendency without questioning all JC's work. We can regret "that so ruthless an art is not entirely true to the whole of nature, though infallibly true to a part of it," and can suggest that his method sometimes fails in interest, in writings marked by "an insistent psychology and little else."

285 Voisins, Gilbert de. "Joseph Conrad," REVUE DE PARIS, XXV (1 March 1918), 5-16.

JC is not only a great author of sea stories but is also a perceptive writer about man and his destiny. His descriptions of the sea and ships often dramatize the conflict between man and nature. A full life at sea before his writing career began gave him material for his realistic observations, which avoid excessive romanticism and naturalism. *A Personal Record* is perhaps his most representative work. *Almayer's Folly* for a first novel creates surprisingly convincing characters. *An Outcast of the Islands* dramatizes an important moral problem. JC's power to make the reader enter the skin of his main character is demonstrated by *Lord Jim,* which also creates his best realized female figure. The reader is skillfully manipulated by the point of view in *The Shadow-Line* to sympathize with the sailors. The arrested movement in this novel is JC's symbol of the reluctance of youth to cross the threshold of life. [Suggestive generalizations which are poorly demonstrated.] [In French.]

286 Wells, Carolyn. "Chronicle and Comment," BOOKMAN (NY), XLVI (Feb 1918), 659.

JC was isolated in Poland at the outbreak of World War I, and the ambassador at Vienna finally sent a special messenger into Poland with papers and money which would enable him to return safely at least to Vienna.

287 [Woolf, Virginia]. "Mr. Conrad's Crisis," TIMES LITERARY SUPPLEMENT (Lond), 15 March 1918, p. 126; rptd as "Fifty-Year

Rule," TIMES LITERARY SUPPLEMENT (Lond), 14 March 1968, p. 275.

Whether *Nostromo* is "astonishing" or a "failure," as various critics term it, it is the work of a writer who "has become aware that the world which he writes about has changed its aspect. He has not got used to the new prospect. . . . It is a world of bewildering fullness, fineness, and intricacy" which leaves "a crowding and suffocating superabundance," thus making *Nostromo* a "rare and magnificent wreck," dogged by "the demon of langour, of monotony, of . . . inertness."

1919

288 *"Arrow of Gold,"* OPEN SHELF (Cleveland), Nov 1919, p 106.

[Quotes "Dark Blue and Rose," NATION (NY), CVIII (14 June 1919), 951-52.]

289 "Books: Fiction," SPECTATOR (Lond), CXXIII (27 Sept 1919), 410.

In *The Arrow of Gold,* the story of M. George and Rita is a mystery, and the "fastidious and unerring distinction of the style" is worthy of JC at his best.

290 Colvin, Sir Sidney. *"The Arrow of Gold,"* DAILY TELEGRAM (Lond), 24 Aug 1919, p. 3; rptd in LIVING AGE, CCCII (27 Sept 1919), 792-95; and as "Introduction," *The Arrow of Gold,* Memorial Edition, XVII (Garden City, NY: Doubleday, Page, 1925), pp. vii-xiii.

JC's plot hypnotizes the reader. Doña Rita is the finest of all specimens of the eternal feminine; the inconclusive or disappointing ending springs from autobiographic fact, from life rather than literary invention. Rita's first appearance on the staircase is comparable to Beatrix Esmond's staircase-advent. JC keeps us aware "without crudity or coarseness" of the movements of Rita's heart and blood—"woman to the core," etc. The events "following the critical night" are too hurriedly and slightly told, and the final veil is drawn too suddenly on everybody. Perhaps Rita leaves George because "in her honesty of heart and consciousness of failure she holds herself no fit mate for life."

291 "Conrad Compared with Dostoevski and Other Masters," CURRENT OPINION, LXVII (Dec 1919), 320-21.

[See Edward Moore, "A Note on Mr. Conrad," New Statesman, XIII (13 Sept 1919), 590-92 [not seen], of which this article is a restatement.]

292 Cooper, Frederic Taber. "Notable Novels to Suit Many Tastes/Woman: An Amazing Study," Publishers' Weekly, XCV (19 April 1919), 1129.

The two books that a future historian of English literature cannot overlook in summing up JC are *Lord Jim* and *The Arrow of Gold*. In *Arrow*, JC "has created a haunting, inimitable spirit of womanhood, that truly is a blend of all the women who ever lived, yet with infinite subleties [sic] and reserves that are all her own. Best of all, he has told a love story that is one of the big love stories of the world of books."

293 "Dark Blue and Rose," Nation (NY), CVIII (14 June 1919), 951-52.

The Arrow of Gold seems at first to be "hardly Conrad at all": it lacks a "spectacular universe," "wonderful description of the sea," "sympathy with sailormen," tragedy, remorse, and Marlow. But it is "obviously" by JC: Doña Rita and Monsieur George take the place of the usual elements found in his works. Here he avoids "the possible romance of surrounding or circumstance" for "the one great thing—the passion that unites these two," and their passion replaces the usual elements in his books.

294 Doubleday, Page and Company. The Country Life Press, Garden City, New York (Garden City, NY: Doubleday, Page, 1919), pp. 99-115.

Contents, abstracted separately under year of first publication; James Huneker, "A Visit to Joseph Conrad," New York Times Magazine Section (1912); Eugene F. Saxton, "The Romantic Story of Joseph Conrad" (1914); and Richard Curle, "Biographical and Critical. Novels and Stories" [see Curle, "Biographical and Autobiographical," Bookman (NY), XXXIX (Aug 1914), 662-68; XL (Sept-Oct 1914), 99-104, 187-201.]

295 E[dgett], E[dwin] F[rancis]. "The Strange Case of Joseph Conrad," Boston Evening Transcript, 19 April 1919, p. 8.

JC has brought something new to English fiction, something that is not imitative and cannot be imitated. In *The Arrow of Gold* he "is more emphatically and more distinctly himself than ever." The manner and method make the story wholly unintelligible at points.

296 E[dgett], E[dwin] F[rancis]. "Writers and Books," Boston Evening Transcript, 24 May 1919, p. 11.

According to the Chicago Daily News, *The Arrow of Gold* is "probably Conrad's worst effort" on the grounds that it is "shoddy stuff." Doña Rita is nebulous and unrealized, yet the real reason for the book. M. George's "baffled boobery" is not accounted for.

297 Ellis, Havelock. "Mr. Conrad's World," THE PHILOSOPHY OF CONFLICT AND OTHER ESSAYS IN WAR-TIME, 2d Series (Boston: Houghton, Mifflin, 1919), pp. 246-56.

"The sensation of excitement is produced, not by stating the mystery and then slowly evolving its solution, but by presenting the solution first and then building up the mystery." Novels of sensation like *Under Western Eyes* are in a field where "Dostoevski rules."

298 "Fiction," A. L. A. BOOKLIST, XV (May 1919), 313.

The Arrow of Gold has "an atmosphere of pure romance"; it is "an absorbing story, a less 'difficult' introduction to the reading of Conrad than others."

299 Gerould, Katherine Fullerton. "Eidolons of Ulysses," BOOKMAN (NY), XLIX (May 1919), 368-70.

In *The Arrow of Gold,* JC's achievement is to have "brought the supreme tests of civilization to bear on human problems far removed from civilization's sphere of influence." The sea is only his setting; his dramas are human and universal. *Arrow* is "absorbing," "beautiful and authoritative." M. George is very nearly "an eidolon of Ulysses." [Perceptive for an early review.]

300 Gillet, Louis. "Le nouveau roman de M. Conrad" (The New Novel by Mr. Conrad), REVUE DES DEUX MONDES, 6ème série, LIII (1 Oct 1919), 676-85; rptd as "Joseph Conrad: *La Flèche d'or*" (*The Arrow of Gold*) in Gillet's LECTURES ÉTRANGÈRES 1re série (Paris: Plon, 1924), pp. 1-14.

In much of JC's work, including *The Arrow of Gold,* characters occasionally behave inconsistently as if they were someone different from the person we had grown to know. This fact results from the conflict between their wills and the power of life operating on them. The effect is a tragic one. JC's technique of multiple narrators is particularly suited to his psychological examination of the relativity of viewpoints. He is particularly adept at creating an ambiguous mystery around Doña Rita which haunts us throughout *Arrow*. [Flimsy generalizations.] [In French.]

301 Kinninmont, Kenneth. "A Conrad 'Genesis'; How He Harks Back to His Youth in His Novel *The Arrow of Gold,*" BOOK MONTHLY (Lond), XIV (Nov 1919), 851-55.

The Arrow of Gold parallels the *Tremolino* episode of *The Mirror of the Sea;* the characters of the syndicate of Royalists and the soul of the ship are comparable. [Very impressionistic and favorable review; details the comparison alluded to.]

302 L., P. "Books and Things," NEW REPUBLIC, XIX (10 May 1919), 56.

The Arrow of Gold is less a love story than a portrait of Rita. George's love is believable. Blunt is not quite credible. Rita's cousin is at first sinister, then absurd, a resolution worthy of JC. Rita believably may be questioned by some, but Therese's substantiality, never—she is "simple, sinister, not to be forgotten."

303 Lunn, Arnold [Henry Moore]. LOOSE ENDS (Lond: Hutchinson [1919]), pp. 142-47.

[Contrasts Kipling and JC. No new insight.]

304 Lynd, Robert. "Mr. Joseph Conrad," OLD AND NEW MASTERS (Lond: Unwin; NY: Scribner's, 1919), pp. 212-23.

JC is the only English novelist (1919 vintage) writing with the grand tragic sense of Webster—the tragedy of man's strength with "courage never to yield." He exalts rather than dispirits in his tales of wonder. Like Henry James, JC is a psychologist who discovers "significance in insignificant things." He leaves us wondering where the mystery lies—ships and men are "possessed."

305 M[ansfield], K[atherine]. "A Backward Glance," ATHENAEUM, No. 4658 (8 Aug 1919), 720; rptd in NOVELS AND NOVELISTS, ed by J. M. Murry (NY: Knopf; Lond: Constable, 1930), pp. 60-64; rptd (Boston: Beacon P, 1959), pp. 57-61.

The Arrow of Gold may have been written much earlier than it seems to have been, for it is by no means up to JC's standard in plot, or character, or language. It contains incredible elements. The stereotyped *femme fatale* character of Rita and the jungle of wild but stereotyped language JC uses to describe her are a character and a language which compare so unfavorably with JC's usual economy, spare use of gesture, and power of converging mystery as to make one wonder how he could ever have risen from one to the other. The characters—Blunt, Mills, Rita, Rita's maid—are as preposterous as the descriptions and the plot.

306 "A Master Makes Mistakes," NEW YORK TIMES, 18 April 1919, p. 12.

One of the first sentences in *The Arrow of Gold* ("If I start to tell you I would want you to feel that you have been there yourself.") is appalling. Nevertheless, JC has written "a mighty fine story." He occasionally imitates the Southerners' "like" when he means "as." [Inconsequential letter.]

307 Meldrum, D. S. "The Romance of Mr. Conrad. How, His Genius Has Found Us and How We Have Absorbed It," BOOK MONTHLY (Lond), XIV (Sept 1919), 697-700.

The reader of JC is too busy noting the wonderful developments he brings to the English novel to remember that English is not his native language. [A summary of *The Arrow of Gold* notes its setting, the scanty action and the opening and closing "Notes" which carry almost all the plot; it is "structure with atmosphere."]

308 "Mr. Conrad's New Novel," TIMES LITERARY SUPPLEMENT (Lond), 7 Aug 1919, p. 422.

In *The Arrow of Gold,* the mysterious, elusive, ineffable quality is effective, but ultimately the novel is "in a vital degree fragmentarily and insecurely told."

309 "The New Books," OUTLOOK (NY), CXXII (21 May 1919), 122.

In *The Arrow of Gold,* the Carlist plot of approximately 1875 is "the mere background for a subtle, intensive study of an elusive woman, Doña Rita, and the strange fascination she exercised over more than one admirer."

310 "Novels by Joseph Conrad and Ibañez," NEW YORK TIMES BOOK REVIEW, 13 April 1919, p. 189.

Despite differences in plot, setting, characters, and situation, *The Arrow of Gold* is perhaps nearly related to *Under Western Eyes.*

311 Reilly, Joseph J. "The Short Stories of Joseph Conrad," CATHOLIC WORLD, CIX (May 1919), 163-75; rptd in OF BOOKS AND MEN (NY: Julian Messner, 1942), pp. 79-92.

The finest shorter stories (from 4,000 to 60,000 words) are "The Lagoon," "The Secret Sharer," "Typhoon," "The Smile of Fortune," "Freya of the Seven Isles," "Amy Foster," and possibly "Karain," "To-morrow," and "An Outpost of Progress." The protagonists' concerns are moral and ethical, not physical: in "The Secret Sharer," the conflict is between compassion and responsibility to law; in "Typhoon," the officers react to "justice and compassion" under the circumstances of the storm. JC's characters live because they are human souls who have "fears, longings, hopes" and a "conscience which . . . plays an inescapable role" in their lives. JC is careful and meticulous sometimes to the extent of wearying his readers. "Illusion" is one of JC's most important words and concepts, which he uses to "imply a conception" giving "more joy, hope, serenity or courage than reality warrants." JC's tragic or tragi-comic nature in the best short stories results from the repression following the insurrection of 1863, a racial strain of melancholy, "an imagination shadowed by apprehension and fears," and a usually unhappy "supersensitive nature."

312 "A Selected List of Current Books," WISCONSIN LIBRARY BULLETIN, XV (May 1919), 143.

The Arrow of Gold is told "in such a way that setting, character analysis, and atmosphere play much more important parts than plot."

313 Shanks, Edward. "London, February 20," DIAL, LXVI (19 April 1919), 417-18.

After twenty years "before the public," JC had earned a respectable reputation with men of letters and other novelists. With the publication of *Chance,* JC finally became famous in the mind of the large reading public.

314 Squire, John C. [Solomon Eagle]. "Other Peoples' Books," BOOKS IN GENERAL, BY SOLOMON EAGLE (NY: Knopf, 1919), pp. 183-86.

Almayer's Folly is "absurdly unlike a first book." The structure, the writing, and minor characterization are good. If *Folly* suffers at all, it is from a dull principal character.

315 Wadell, Helen. "Mass-penny," NEW STATESMAN AND NATION, XII (1 Feb 1919), 375-76.

JC has restored the old tale to its proper station—he has reinvigorated it; he has also restored "the villain [Ricardo, Mr. Jones] as distinct from the international spy" to literature. [A rather rambling self-revealing splutter.]

1920

316 Anglin, Norman. "Conrad: From Life to Literature," PAPERS OF THE MANCHESTER LITERARY CLUB, XLVI (1920), 60-75.

JC will be remembered not as a "great stylist" or as a masterful writer of fiction, but as a historian "who will be loved for the wealth of his reminiscences and the touch of his incomparable perceptions; an historian . . . of men's actions . . . aspirations . . . fears . . . and . . . doubts." [A general and sometimes emotional discussion of JC's works.]

317 Bellessort, André. "Le premier roman de Conrad" (Conrad's First Novel), REVUE POLITIQUE ET LITTÉRATAIRE [formerly REVUE BLEUE], LVIII (2 Oct 1920), 599-603.

LA NOUVELLE REVUE FRANÇAISE has begun publication of JC's complete works in French. The latest is JC's first novel, *Almayer's Folly* [trans by Geneviève Séligmann-Lui as *La Folie-Almayer* (1919)], which is superior to Kipling's works, although Kipling has more epic qualities. JC's psychology is profound and he is master of the mood of the East. A little slowness, a little obscurity are the only flaws in JC's first novel. [A detailed analysis of *Almayer* concludes the article.] [In French.]

318 "Bibliographies of Modern Authors: Joseph Conrad," LONDON MERCURY, II (Aug 1920), 476-77.

[A listing of forty-two items, mostly by JC, with very brief descriptions of source, location and date. Includes material like newspaper essays, critical comments and collaboration.]

319 "The Book Table: Devoted to Books and Their Makers," OUTLOOK (NY), CXXV (9 June 1920), 280.

Foremost among recent novels is JC's *The Rescue,* which combines "the lucidity of his earlier work with the subtlety of his later manner." Perhaps less attractive to the average reader than the romance and adventure in the tale is "the deliberate, half-veiled dissection of the conflict of passion, ambition, and duty in the hearts of the man and woman who are overwhelmed and shaken under the hand of relentless fate and the crushing power of untoward circumstances." The "moral complex" of the novel is of the kind that JC likes, and his treatment of it here is "masterly."

320 "Books: Fiction," SPECTATOR (Lond), CXXV (10 July 1920), 52-53.

In *The Rescue,* a change from JC's usual practice appears: the oblique method of narration has been abandoned, and no shadowy principal narrator hovers in the background. Otherwise, the story is "pure Conrad." Although JC has no use for happy endings, there is nothing artificial in his "contrivance of tragic catastrophe."

321 Boynton, H. W. "Conrad the Great," WEEKLY REVIEW (NY), II (16 June 1920), 629.

The Rescue contains "the old magic" of the earlier JC, the spirit and adventure of romance, and magnificent imagery. Here also are JC's more recent ironic vision and the more restrained manner of his later works. The novel exemplifies the "Conradian struggle" between Fate and "the primary valor and fidelity of the human soul."

322 Clarke, Joseph I. C. "The Gossip Shop," BOOKMAN (NY), LI (July 1920), 602.

Lee Forster Hartman, the author of "The Judgement of Vulcan" (HARPERS MAGAZINE, CXL [March 1920], 521 36) was unduly influenced by JC's *Victory* in that he imitates JC's simile of a volcano "puffing" and "glowing" like a lighted cigar. [For a response see F., G. G., ibid., LII (Sept 1920), 93.]

323 Crudgington & Co. [See "The First Edition of *Chance,*" BOOKMAN'S JOURNAL, III (10 Dec 1920), 109-10.]

324 "A Disillusioned Romantic," TIMES LITERARY SUPPLEMENT (Lond), 1 July 1920, p. 419.

In *The Rescue,* JC's conception of theme and brilliance of detail are good, but the way in which the idea worked out, especially in the relationship between Lingard and Mrs. Travers, is weak. JC "has attempted a romantic theme and in the middle his belief in romance has failed him."

325 E[dgett], E[dwin] F[rancis]. "Joseph Conrad Revisits the South Seas," BOSTON EVENING TRANSCRIPT, 26 May 1920, p. 4.

The Rescue is another of JC's typical stories of sea and shore in which an involved narrative technique creates only obscurity.

326 F., G. G. "The Gossip Shop," BOOKMAN (NY), LII (Sept 1920), 93.

Since it is known that JC read French extensively, he may well have taken the basic idea for the volcano simile in *Victory* ("glowing" and "puffing" like a "gigantic cigar") from Théophile Gautier's "Arria Marcella" ("The volcano . . . smoked his pipe peacefully"). [A response to a letter by Joseph I. C. Clarke, ibid., LI (July 1920), 602.]

327 Fairley, Barker. "The New Conrad—and the Old," CANADIAN BOOKMAN, II (Jan 1920), 26-29.

Some of the intricacies of JC are mere confusion or an inability to express ideas. JC's most popular works—*The Nigger of the Narcissus* and "Typhoon"—are not his best. His real work started with *Lord Jim* and *Nostromo.* Serial publication, the complex time sequences and the single fundamental moral dilemma have kept it from being publicly popular. *Nostromo* is a historical novel with a sociological basis which lacks the sincerity and "ghostly envelope" of "Heart of Darkness." *Chance* and *Victory* were successful: *Chance* because it is JC's extension of Jamesian technique to its furthest possible limit, *Victory* because it is his best "narrative" —a story with a plot. *The Rescue* "combines the formal mastery of *Victory* with the fuller reality of Conrad's earlier tales." It is the greatest English novel since Hardy. It makes both *Almayer's Folly* and *An Outcast of the Islands* its sequels. "Of the novel as a whole one can only say that at almost every point it appears to be worthy of its tremendous climax."

328 "Fiction," A. L. A. BOOKLIST, XVI (July 1920), 346.

In *The Rescue,* "a man's endurance is tested to its limit. A characteristic story, one of his [JC's] best."

329 Field, Louise Maunsell. "Conrad's Art Spans Two Decades," NEW YORK TIMES BOOK REVIEW, 23 May 1920, pp. 263-64.

[An overwhelmingly favorable review of *The Rescue.*]

330 "The First Edition of *Chance,*" BOOKMAN'S JOURNAL, III (10 Dec 1920), 109-10.

[Under this heading is printed correspondence from C. S. M., Grant

Richards, Crudgington & Co., and T. B. J., suggesting there were three issues of the first edition. Also see T. J. Wise, "Conrad's *Chance*," BOOKMAN'S JOURNAL, III (31 Dec 1920), 160.]

331 Gwynn, Stephen. "Novels of Joseph Conrad," EDINBURGH REVIEW, CCXXXI (April 1920), 318-39.

JC's fiction deals with people "separated by choice or chance" from their natural surroundings. His "normal home" is the sea. His themes are situations where men are "flung back on their own natures for guidance" and where conventional restraints are lacking. At his best his feeling that the civilized European is "seedy and bankrupt" by comparison with the primitives is subtle and ironic (e.g., in *Almayer's Folly, An Outcast of the Islands,* and *Lord Jim*). JC "abhors emphasis and subtilises to excess"; as a result later books do not present the East-West "clash and struggle" so strongly. His sea stories, in the main, deal with "the psychology of ordinary men under extraordinary but quite simple stress": Captain MacWhirr's lack of imagination and ideas is excessive; and in a curious way he pulls through—perhaps a hero, perhaps not. JC is unequalled in his skill at presenting a character who does not recur and who "yet continues to be felt throughout the whole." The French lieutenant in *Jim* is such a character. JC "remains not cosmopolitan but European; one of the best international interpreters," but not without partialities, particularly against the Russians and the Germans. The Congo is for him a world in which no man can maintain his sanity; he is "too far from his kind, too . . . remote from such human shapes as he encounters." JC is significant for his moral force, the result of his assimilation of a main direction in English literature. With the possible exception of Hardy, no living English novelist is superior to him—he surpasses Stevenson as a creative artist. And "it is for England that Mr. Conrad thinks and speaks; England and not the British Empire."

332 Hueffer, Ford Madox. "Thus To Revisit . . . ," ENGLISH REVIEW, XXXI (July, Aug, Sept 1920), 5-13, 107-17, 209-17; also, in part and with changes, in DIAL, LXIX (July, Aug, Sept 1920), 52-60, 132-41, 239-46; absorbed, with changes, in THUS TO REVISIT (Lond: Chapman & Hall; NY: Dutton, 1921) [a detailed account of correspondences between periodical and book version is given in David Dow Harvey, FORD MADOX FORD 1873-1939, A BIBLIOGRAPHY OF WORKS AND CRITICISM (Princeton, NJ: Princeton U P, 1962), A52, D281, D282].

On W. E. Henley's recommendation, JC wrote to Hueffer for assistance with English prose. JC was always "just 'Marlow,' " the reflective hyperconscientious narrator of "Youth," of "Heart of Darkness," and *Lord Jim*.

In searching for a new form for the English novel, JC proposed that a novel should be a rendering of an affair, "one psychological progression" that produces unity of form.

James Joyce descends from Henry James in his "perception of minute embarrassments" and has carried JC's early searching after "ramified Form" almost as far as it can go.

 333 J., T. B. [See "The First Edition of *Chance*," BOOKMAN'S JOURNAL, III (10 Dec 1920), 109-10.]

 334 "Joseph Conrad's Tribute to Stephen Crane," CURRENT OPINION, LXVIII (April 1920), 537-38.

JC comments on Crane's artistry in impressive terms and gives a keen insight into the personality behind Crane's writing. [Brief personal remarks on JC's friendship with Stephen Crane.]

 335 Kranedonk, A. G. van. "Joseph Conrad," ENGLISH STUDIES, II (Feb 1920), 1-8.

[General survey of titles and themes.]

 336 M., C. S. [See "The First Edition of *Chance*," BOOKMAN'S JOURNAL, III (10 Dec 1920), 109-10.]

 337 M[ansfield], K[atherine]. "Mr. Conrad's New Novel," ATHENAEUM, No. 4705 (2 July 1920), 15; rptd in NOVELS AND NOVELISTS (NY: Knopf; Lond: Constable, 1930), pp. 222-26, ibid. (Boston: Beacon P, 1959), pp. 213-17.

Each new JC novel is a further revelation; JC never repeats or runs dry. The effectiveness of *The Rescue* depends chiefly on a hard-to-define "quality of emotion" in which the novel is steeped, involving a "peculiar responsive sensitiveness to the significance of everything, down to the slightest detail." This heightened state of awareness extracts the last drop of juice from each moment. That JC does not tell us why Lingard, symbol of fidelity, should have come to disaster through his inability to recognize that the white lady is a flower of corruption puts the "seal of greatness" on this story of adventure.

 338 Muddiman, Bernard. THE MEN OF THE NINETIES (Lond: Henry Danielson, 1920), pp. 12, 45, 58, 69.

JC's "The Idiots" is the "only unique feature" in the sixth number of THE SAVOY. JC, like some other writers not connected with the Rhymers' Club, was working out his "own salvation." Before JC and Louis Becke gave "new vistas to our fiction," only Kipling, Crackanthorpe, and, perhaps, Arthur Morrison, Zangwill, and Henry James "resharpened" prose fiction.

339 "New Books," CATHOLIC WORLD, CXII (Dec 1920), 394-95.
A new book by JC is "a literary event of the first significance," and *The Rescue* contains both "the finish and precision of style" of the period of *Chance* and "the opulent glow" of the earlier tropical tales.

340 Putnam, George Palmer. "Conrad in Cracow," OUTLOOK (NY), CXXIV (3 March 1920), 382-83.
On a visit to JC's home in Cracow with a boyhood chum, JC told strange stories "of the sea and ships and far-away countries," "weird and fantastic almost beyond belief."

341 R., C. M. "Joseph Conrad Tells a New Tale," FREEMAN, I (21 July 1920), 454.
The Rescue is disappointing in descriptive detail but massive in final effect. JC's essential gift lies in "his penetration of essential moralities."

342 *"The Rescue,"* OPEN SHELF (Cleveland), Aug 1920, p. 70.
In *The Rescue,* tragedy is "inevitable" and "sweeps over" nearly everyone; this is the stuff of which great stories are made.

343 Richards, Grant. [See "The First Edition of *Chance,*" BOOKMAN'S JOURNAL, III (10 Dec 1920), 109-10.]

344 Roberts, R. Ellis. "Joseph Conrad," BOOKMAN (Lond), LVIII (Aug 1920), 160-62.
On the basis of *The Rescue,* there are connections between Western Christian love for the downtrodden and the English reader's love for suppressed peoples in JC's work—"the people with whom the point of honour is always greater than any other call of duty." Mrs. Travers is a new direction for JC's women: she is not perfect but more human. *Rescue* compared to *Victory* contains "less sharp acrid pain; and to *The Arrow of Gold,* lacks the tapestried colour."

345 Rothenstein, William. TWENTY-FOUR PORTRAITS, WITH CRITICAL APPRECIATIONS BY VARIOUS HANDS, 1st series (Lond: Allen & Unwin, 1920).
[Portrait of JC with a one-page appreciation that emphasizes his "ruthless realism," love of human nature and "his magnificent partiality for the adjective."]

346 "The Run of the Shelves," WEEKLY REVIEW, II (5 June 1920), 604.
The Rescue, representative of JC's "fourth manner," is too difficult even for the "devout Conradian."

347 "The Secret of Joseph Conrad," NATION (NY), CX (12 June 1920), 804-5.

Whereas JC's later works have been marred by "a strain and mannerism" and his autobiographical writings have displayed a "spiritual meagerness," *The Rescue* "takes us back to the golden days" of *Lord Jim,* "Typhoon," and "Youth." But this book is not of the great quality which JC had attained earlier; "the passions are magnificent, the scene is superb, the style is gorgeous, and the story is dull." There is, however, no "intellectual structure" to support the "primitive" tale, the story "has no implications beyond itself," and "actions and passions and the things that belong to human life are engulfed." Even the style sometimes slips into that of a minor French novelist.

348 Seldes, Gilbert. "A Novelist of Courage," DIAL, LXIX (Aug 1920), 191-96.

In *The Rescue,* JC's ability to make a story "move," to write beautiful prose, and to center his chief interest on "the gallant and valorous effort of human beings to solve the notable case of conscience which comes to every man at least once in a lifetime" is notable. JC is a genius and a great novelist.

349 "A Selected List of New Novels and Children's Books," WISCONSIN LIBRARY BULLETIN, XVI (Nov 1920), 193.

The Rescue represents "both the old and the new Conrad." It is the story of a man divided between two loyalties, "between faith to his plighted word and love for a woman." The story, with all the "peculiar Conrad mannerisms," is not easy reading.

350 Stawell, F. Melian. "Conrad," ESSAYS AND STUDIES BY THE ENGLISH ASSOCIATION, VI (1920), 88-111.

JC's place among English novelists "bids fair to be one of the highest." It is not fanciful to suggest that his being non-English helped to keep him from writing "oddly" and experimenting with style as Carlyle, Browning, Meredith, James, and Hardy did. His love for England began early, with a "childhood's delight in Dickens . . . Walter Scott, Thackeray, and Shakespeare." A "sense of conflict must have been strong in him from the first," since this sense is "never absent" from his "feeling for nature." There are connections between his "conflict," learned mainly at sea, and the self-control one finds everywhere in his writing. Another dominant theme is "sympathy for those who have failed, especially if they are natures sensitive, impressionable, quick to feel the sting of shame," as in *Lord Jim.* His sympathy, however, never becomes sentimental. A "penetrating sympathy" also characterizes *Under Western Eyes.* Here it is not only Razumov, the central figure, we find illuminated, but "the whole Russian people." Jim and Razumov represent one important variety of person interesting to JC; he was intrigued equally by "men whose character seems to crumble under the strain of life beyond the possibility of redemption." *Almayer's Folly* deals with such a man. The "wretched nigger on the *Narcissus*" is "a born parasite" who sponges to the last "on men better and braver than himself." Character, then, "is always the supreme thing for Conrad." Some of his characters succeed or fail when confronted with the primitive world; "every book of Conrad vibrates with the conviction that the man who misses his 'chance' when he is called upon to act has been false to life." JC is not a "systematic thinker," and in this "he is representative of his generation." He is baffled by "the majesty and the mystery in things and men."

351 Taylor, W. D. "The Novels of Joseph Conrad," QUEENS QUARTERLY, XXVIII (July 1920), 15-31.

JC's romanticism led him to the sea; his novels differ from typical sea yarns because he understands the sea's moods. In *The Nigger of the Narcissus*, JC is interested in characters, with incidental detail mentioned accidentally. His epic style often begins *in medias res*, and he can keep the past in the present. Marlow fails as a narrator because (1) of the problem of creating "an all wise kind of character"; (2) of many tedious speeches; and (3) of Marlow's taking no real part in the action. JC will be a novelist of stature because of (1) his wealth of sea experience; (2) his ability to give life to nationalities other than English; (3) narrative excitement; (4) the fusion of tropical settings with the sea; and (5) his prose style. [Concludes with a stereotyped view of JC.]

352 Thompson, J. C. "Conrad's *Chance*. The Real First Edition and the 'Fakes,' " BOOKMAN'S JOURNAL, III (26 Nov 1920), 77.

A comparison of some differences between a 1913 and a 1914 issue of *Chance* shows that far more copies exist of the "faked" 1914 issue than of the genuine 1913 one. [See By "A Conrad Collector," ibid. (Dec 1921); "The First Edition of *Chance*," ibid. (10 Dec 1920); T. J. Wise, ibid. (31 Dec 1920).]

353 Williamson, Claude C. H. "Joseph Conrad: Sailor and Novelist," WRITERS OF THREE CENTURIES, 1789-1914 (Lond: Richards, 1920), pp. 391-97.

Both realism and romanticism are inadequate bases to judge a novel. The "crucial test . . . is to ask . . . how far its representation, its imaginative creation of life is true to our own experience of life, how much it illuminates, enlarges, and enriches that experience." JC's method of "indirect narrative" seems clumsy. For JC, defeat is not failure or death but "commerce or compromise with evil or in weak and cowardly surrender." JC's characters are static and do not develop much. His art is limited by his "persistent brooding over life's inequalities." The real unity of *Lord*

Jim is to be found in "Jim and his psychology." [Williamson repeats the error of thinking that JC first thought of writing in French.]

354 Wise, T. J. "Conrad's *Chance*," BOOKMAN'S JOURNAL, III (31 Dec 1920), 160.
[Wise contributes a letter to the editor on the number of issues and "fakes" of *Chance*. Also see "The First Edition of *Chance*," BOOKMAN'S JOURNAL, III (10 Dec 1920), 109-10, for further correspondence.]

1921

355 Aubry, G. Jean-. "Joseph Conrad's Confessions," FORTNIGHTLY REVIEW, CIX (May 1921), 782-90.
The novels are forceful, noble, compassionate. [Review of JC's prefaces to the novels and general survey.]

356 "Briefer Mention," DIAL, LXXI (Sept 1921), 374.
In *Notes on Life and Letters,* the essay on Henry James is "superb."

357 By "A Conrad Collector." "New Discoveries in the Bibliography of *Chance*," BOOKMAN'S JOURNAL, V (Dec 1921), 81-82.
[The writer describes in detail another fake 1913 copy of *Chance* with forged substitutions not previously described; see J. C. Thompson, "Conrad's *Chance*" (1920).]

358 By An Occasional Contributor. "Early Conrad First Editions," BOOKMAN'S JOURNAL, IV (15 July 1921), 189-90.
[The writer traces the rise in value of JC's early books: *Almayer's Folly, An Outcast of the Islands, The Nigger of the Narcissus, Tales of Unrest, Lord Jim, Youth, Typhoon.*]

359 Chevalley, Abel. LE ROMAN ANGLAIS DE NOTRE TEMPS (The English Novel of Our Time) (Lond: Humphrey Milford, 1921), pp. 111, 115-18, 155, 170, 175-84, 193; THE MODERN ENGLISH NOVEL, trans Ben Ray Redman (NY: Knopf, 1927).
The greatest artist among contemporary English novelists, JC lacks their concern with moral and social issues; nor has he the detachment and indifference of the great French writers. His realism groups him, rather, with the Primitives and the Russians. His art conceals art; he makes us "see" without tedious psychological analysis; he succeeds in conveying, with great fidelity, the exact sensation. In his later books JC has advisedly abandoned the circuitous narrative methods and the excesses of sensual richness in his earlier style. [In French.]

360 "Conrad Reveals his Literary Loves and Antipathies," CURRENT OPINION, LXX (June 1921), 819-21.

In *Notes on Life and Letters,* published in newspapers and magazines from 1898 to 1920, we trace "the workings of one of the subtlest and most sophisticated minds of our time." JC's essays on literature are the most impressive. He distrusts "what is generally known as fine writing." He admires a writer's "courage, compassion, self-denial, fidelity to an ideal." He "intimates" that "purely literary gifts . . . are temptations and seductions." He praises Stendhal, Daudet, Turgenev (the latter at the expense of Dostoevski), Stephen Crane, and Cooper. His dislike of hasty political panaceas equals his dislike for literary formulas. His ideas make such good sense because "the draught he offers us" has "stood for a moment in the cool."

361 Cross, Wilbur Lucius. "Some Novels of 1920," YALE REVIEW, N.S. XVII (Jan 1921), 402-3.

JC has reworked the old, complicated romantic epic and made it the background for character study (best illustrated in *The Nigger of the Narcissus*). In relation to the prevailing literary trends of his time, JC has always gone his own way.

362 Field, Louise Maunsell. "Joseph Conrad Critic and Prophet," NEW YORK TIMES BOOK REVIEW AND MAGAZINE, 8 May 1921, p. 10.

In *Notes on Life and Letters,* JC is a critic of letters and of events and a political prophet.

363 [Forster, E. M.]. "The Pride of Mr. Conrad," NATION AND ATHENAEUM, XIX (March 1921), 881-82; rptd as "Joseph Conrad: A Note," in ABINGER HARVEST (NY: Harcourt, Brace, 1936), pp. 136-41.

In *Notes on Life and Letters,* JC's character remains unclear; he cannot have philosophic approval because "he is always promising to make some general philosophic statement about the universe, and then refraining with a gruff disclaimer."

364 Hind, Charles Lewis. "Joseph Conrad," AUTHORS AND I (Lond: Lane, 1921), pp. 61-64.

The reader of JC, a writer's writer, must be patient while JC develops his immensity of background, to which JC adds men who find their places in the immensity. "The art of writing in [JC] is stronger than the art of story telling."

365 Hueffer, Ford Madox. THUS TO REVISIT: SOME REMINISCENCES (NY: Dutton; Lond: Chapman and Hall, 1921), pp. 18,

26-27, 34-35, 39-41, 44, 46, 47, 51-54, 69-70, 71, 72, 79-101, 105, 108, 114, 119, 140, 207, 216.

JC made a study of technique more determined than that of any other writer. France provided an overwhelming influence on style, but JC's point of view toward life is English (not provincial). His works are great because they have universal appeal, and this is "a true smile of fortune—for Anglo-Saxondom!"

366 L., P. "Books and Things," NEW REPUBLIC, XXVII (1 June 1921), 25.

Notes on Life and Letters does not satisfy the reader's curiosity about JC, whose "austere, compassionate, ironic imagination lies high up the mountain slope, in places difficult of access." JC's suspicion of "theories" of fiction; his belief that fiction "stands on firmer ground" than history (a second-hand affair as compared to art's "imaginative effort at finding inspiration from reality of forms and sensations"); his recurrent use of the word "renunciation" of vain sentimentalism, of the desire to reveal all; and his notion of art as a sort of "rescue work carried out in darkness," seizing upon and representing "vanishing phases of turbulence" intrigue the reader but leave him unsatisfied.

367 Larbaud, Valéry. "Les lettres étrangères: lettres Anglaises" (Foreign Letters: English Letters), REVUE DE FRANCE, I (15 May 1921), 423-28.

The publication in the LONDON MERCURY of the prefaces of some of JC's works [e.g., *Notes on My Books* (Garden City, NY: Doubleday, Page; Toronto: Doubleday, Page; Lond: Heinemann, 1921)] is an important event because it is the first time JC has given public expression of his methods of writing. The technique of *Chance* is the most "Conradian" of JC's productions. The prefaces are comparable in importance to those of Dryden. That of *The Secret Agent* might be called "The Role of Intuition in Creative Literature," a work of such subtlety that it defies analysis. After his long sojourn in the Central America [sic] of *Nostromo,* the novelist made London the real subject of *Agent* and displayed the human mystery of London. A study of the prefaces reveals the fact that each of JC's novels and tales is the poetic reconstruction of what Aristotle calls the "exactement" of the continents and cities in the memory of the storyteller, with sometimes a person as a secondary element, like Lena in *Victory*. [In French.]

368 "Literature," A. L. A. BOOKLIST, XVII (May-June 1921), 291.

Notes on Life and Letters is "for all special lovers of Conrad."

369 Lynd, Robert. "Mr. Conrad at Home," NEW STATESMAN, XVI (12 March 1921), 674; rptd in LIVING AGE, CCCIX (23

April 1921), 221-24; and in BOOKS AND AUTHORS (NY: Putnam's, 1923), pp. 196-205.

Essentially, JC, in *A Personal Record, Notes on Life and Letters,* and in other personal statements, seems purposely "to leave us unsatisfied and speculating." He gives "himself away in his admiration for other men," as when he talks of Henry James, Maupassant, or Turgenev. Yet he rejects schools and formulas. JC prefers to portray an author, not "to measure him with a tape"; he is concerned to get at the truth that is in a man, not the absolute truth. Thus, for JC, as for Aristotle and Schopenhauer, fiction "is nearer truth than history" [Lynd disagrees, asserting that "Imagination and the sense of life are as necessary to a good historian as to a good novelist"]. JC "as critic often seems to be defining his own art rather than the art of fiction in general." To some extent he praises other writers for qualities he himself possesses. The essay on Anatole France, in *Notes on Life and Letters,* "reminds us that Mr. Conrad is as impatient of political panaceas as of literary formulas." Both in politics and ships he hates "the blind worship of machinery."

370 McFee, William. "The Artist Philosopher," HARBOURS OF MEMORY (Garden City, NY: Doubleday, Page, 1921), pp. 278-92; rptd as preface in *Lord Jim* (Garden City, NY: Doubleday, Page, 1922), pp. vii-xviii; and in *Youth and Two Other Stories,* Educational Edition (Garden City, NY: Doubleday, Page, 1925), pp. ix-xx.

Seamen reacted favorably to JC: "men reacted in direct ratio to their integrity of character. The cunning, the avaricious, and the ignoble are not admirers of Conrad." The preface to *The Nigger of the Narcissus* is the "confession of faith of a supreme master of prose."

371 McFee, William. "The Sea—and Conrad," BOOKMAN (NY), LIII (March 1921), 102-8; rptd as "The Sea—and Conrad: Revelation and Inspiration in the New Volume *Notes on My Books,*" WORLD'S WORK (NY), XXXVIII (July 1921), 181-86.

JC, unlike most seamen, is speculative. *Nostromo* is a masterpiece; JC's prefaces are masterful, especially the preface to *The Nigger of the Narcissus.* [A writer about the sea himself, McFee records the reactions of sailors to whom he had introduced novels of JC. No new insight.]

372 Macy, John. "A Conrad Miscellany," NEW YORK EVENING POST LITERARY REVIEW, I (4 June 1921), 3; rptd in THE CRITICAL GAME (NY: Boni and Liveright, 1922), pp. 121-32.

JC's "The Return" and "The Idiots" are the only stories that show the influence of Maupassant's "austere fidelity to fact." JC's "fine rhythms" and "essential metaphors" and his honesty and courage are grounds for comparing him to Maupassant. Like Henry James, he "distort[s] life into a new reality," writes a style that is more interesting than the characters are, and by analysis makes a situation "often as static as anything in James." [Review of *Notes on Life and Letters*.]

373 "Mr. Conrad's Miscellanea," SPECTATOR (Lond), CXXVI (14 May 1921), 624-25.

Notes on Life and Letters, a "tidying up" of JC's work, "adds a ray to the light" necessary for the reading of his romances.

374 Moult, Thomas. "Joseph Conrad as Playwright," BOOKMAN'S JOURNAL, VII (Dec 1922), 65-66.

The Secret Agent dramatization is not JC's first attempt at playwriting. "One Day More" (pvtly ptd, Feb 1917) is his first dramatic work and based on his short story "To-morrow" [Moult gives the background of its publication and production]. This was followed by "Laughing Anne," a dramatization of "Because of the Dollars." JC disclaims any connection with the dramatization of *Victory*.

375 "The New Books," OUTLOOK (NY), CXXVIII (15 June 1921), 297.

Notes on Life and Letters contains "bits of journalism," none of which is "trivial." The best is "Poland Revisited," in which JC gives "a delightful and semi-humorous account" of a visit to his childhood home near Cracow. "In some ways this book gets us closer to Mr. Conrad's remarkable personality than anything he has written."

376 Pearson, Hesketh. MODERN MEN AND MUMMERS (Lond: Allen and Unwin, 1921), pp. 201-3; ibid. (NY: Harcourt, Brace, 1922), pp. 189-90.

JC's critical esteem is due to the Englishman's innate preference for the foreign; his popularity is due to his style, which "hints at immensities, at illimitables"—something his urban reader "knows nothing about and therefore dotes upon." [Superficial.]

377 "A Prince of Prose," TIMES LITERARY SUPPLEMENT (Lond), 3 March 1921, p. 141.

In *Notes on Life and Letters,* the essays on James and Daudet are good. JC's art displays sanity, coolness, and control. JC "would be a greater writer if, besides honouring the quiet depths of the heart, he felt also its storms and transciencies, if he were dramatic as well as static, instant and direct as well as composed and compassionate."

378 Redman, Ben Ray. "Creators as Critics," NATION (NY), CXII (29 June 1921), 921.

JC does not reveal as much of himself in *Notes on Life and Letters* as he does in such works as *Nostromo, Lord Jim,* and *Chance.* He expresses the same "artistic creeds" as those in the preface to *The Nigger of the Narcissus,* but uses "a fresh figure" in attempting again to define his art: "The creative art of a writer of fiction may be compared to rescue work," to a "snatching of vanishing phases of turbulence, disguised in fair words, out of the native obscurity into a light where the struggling forms may be seen, seized upon, endowed with the only possible form of permanence in this world of relative values—the permanence of memory."

379 S., G. "Conrad the Statesman," BOOKMAN (Lond), LX (April 1921), 33-34.

JC's appeal to Englishmen is a fad, but his combination of idealism and politics is praiseworthy. His *Notes on Life and Letters* is a probing historical essay—especially on implications of the Russo-Japanese war. The best work in this volume is in politics, not literary theory. The essay has a very Dickensian style.

380 Wise, Thomas J. "Preface," A BIBLIOGRAPHY OF THE WRITINGS OF JOSEPH CONRAD (Lond: pvtly ptd [1921]); 2nd ed, rvd and enlgd [1921], pp. ix-xii; rptd (Lond: Dawson's, 1964).

Some of the pitfalls and complications of the JC bibliography are due to the first editions of several works being American; "the first edition of *The Nigger of the Narcissus* is a pamphlet issued only for the protection of copyright"; "[t]he exposure of the fraudulent reproduction of the '1913' title-page of the first edition of *Chance* causes difficulty." "Many of Conrad's books may, in fact, be studied profitably in three published states: (1) the serial state (England and America), (2) the partly-revised state from the serial (America) and (3) the finally-revised state (England)." [The bibliography is based largely upon the JC collections of Richard Curle and Wise himself.]

1922

381 Aynard, Joseph. "L'exotisme de Joseph Conrad à propos de *Lord Jim*" (The Exoticism of Joseph Conrad in *Lord Jim*), JOURNAL DES DÉBATS, CXXXIV (18 Nov 1922), 3.

LA NOUVELLE REVUE FRANÇAISE, now putting out a complete edition of JC, has published *Lord Jim.* As in JC's other works, exoticism is the background for the story of Jim's moral rehabilitation. The mysteries of the East have never failed to intrigue readers; speculations on the "savages" were raised in the seventeenth and eighteenth centuries, and in our time the soul and mind of the East are being closely studied. JC does not "explain" the natives. He depicts them in action, as he does the whites living anywhere. Through this delineation of their similarities and their differences there pierces the truth common to men of all races—their instincts. JC, overwhelmed by human fragility, experiences a queer dichotomy of outlook: moral nihilism and at the same time a tremendous attachment to duty, to responsibility. A romantic quality emerges. Jim's hiding his shame in a lost village of Malaysians is a Byronic gesture. Moreover, there is something of Shakespeare in the stacking up of enough explosive material in the recesses of the human heart to make one's outer shell crack wide open in one split second. JC's exoticism is magnetic; yet it is not essential to the tale. The breath of humanity palpitates on the page whatever the color of the skin may be. [In French.]

382 Brown, A. J. C. "Iz nove engleske literature. Joseph Conrad" (From Recent English Literature. Joseph Conrad), REVI (Belgrade), 7 Dec 1922, pp. 12-13.

[Earliest comment on JC in Yugoslavia.] [In Serbo-Croatian.]

383 Canby, Henry Seidel. "Conrad and Melville," NEW YORK EVENING POST LITERARY REVIEW, II (4 Feb 1922), 393-94; rptd in DEFINITIONS: ESSAYS IN CONTEMPORARY CRITICISM (NY: Harcourt, Brace, 1922), pp. 257-68; and in MODERN ESSAYS, selected by C. D. Morley, 2nd series (NY: Harcourt, Brace, 1924), pp. 202-14.

One reads JC for his brooding Slavonic tendencies that become thematic necessities. Stories like *Chance* and "Gaspar Ruiz" give "the impression of not caring to understand if only he can fully picture the mind that his brooding imagination draws further and further from its sheath." JC like Melville transcends the sea, sublimating it into a "vapor of pure imagination." Melville, writing at the beginning of the age of science, sees man trying to control the universe, but failing. JC, coming at the height of the age of science, has man conquering nature (typhoons, dangers at sea), learning to "master all but his own heart." "Melville is a moral philosopher, Conrad a speculative psychologist." Melville is centrifugal, JC centripetal. JC is modern because he "transfers wonder from nature to the behavior of man," and he differs from many contemporaries because "he avoids the plain prose of realism and sets his romantic heroes against the great powers of nature."

384 C[larke], G. H. "Book Reviews," SEWANEE REVIEW, XXX (March 1922), 108.

Notes on Life and Letters is a valuable psychological and biographical commentary. "If Conrad is a Pole by nativity, and an Englishman by sympathy and naturalization, he is certainly a Frenchman by understanding."

385 Clarke, George Herbert. "Joseph Conrad and His Art," Sewanee Review, XXX (Summer 1922), 258-76.

JC's greatness will depend on the novels, the best of which are *The Rescue, Lord Jim, Nostromo, Under Western Eyes, Chance,* and *The Nigger of the Narcissus.* Marlow is "among the most memorable of Conrad's creations." JC has an "almost passionate fondness for privatives beginning with in-, im-, il-, and ir-, particularly such as irresistible, incredible, incomprehensible, impenetrable." Of the three novels, *Jim, Nostromo,* and *Rescue,* the last is the best because it is "strong in the development of both character and atmosphere, and in their balanced interrelation." [An introductory appreciation.]

386 Colvin, Sir Sidney. "Some Personal Reflections . . . III- Robert Louis Stevenson," Scribner's Magazine (Lond), LXVII (March 1920), p. 338; rptd in Memories & Notes of Persons & Places, 1852-1912 (NY: Scribner's, 1921), 2nd ed (1922), pp. 149, 151-52.

JC preferred R. L. Stevenson's In the South Seas to Treasure Island because of the portrait of the native king Tembinok.

387 Evans, C. S. "Joseph Conrad," Music Teacher, IX (July 1922), 541.

Though JC's novels command a large reading public, they have little in common with popular fiction. The exciting incidents are only a background against which JC explores "the agony of the human soul, alone and solitary, and because of its very being, at war with the world." [A brief interpretive survey of JC's achievement.]

388 Guedalla, Philip. "Under the Knife IV—Mr. Joseph Conrad," Illustrated London News, CLXI (12 Aug 1922), 240; rptd as "Mr. Joseph Conrad," in A Gallery (Lond: Constable; NY and Lond: Putnam's, 1924), pp. 77-84; rptd in Collected Essays of Philip Guedalla, Four Volumes (Lond: Hodder & Stoughton, 1927), I (Men of Letters), pp. 124-35.

[Writing in a lightly ironic-satiric vein, Guedalla gives the usual view of JC's "strange" background, praises his use of Marlow and conversational manner of narration, has reservations about multiple narrators.] In 1895 the public was ready for a more vivid kind of narrative than was being produced, but JC was not really recognized until *Chance.* After 1913 "he has soared (or sunk) into popularity." JC is at his best as "ironical observer" (e.g., in "The Duel"), but is not good at his most exotic.

389 MacCarthy, Desmond. "Anarchists," New Statesman and Nation, XX (11 Nov 1922), 174-75.

Bourdin, an anarchist who, in 1894, tried to blow up the Observatory is the source for *The Secret Agent* (1907), staged in 1922. JC's book rose above sensationalism—he is a "master of vivid description and the psychology of violent emotion." JC's characters are "steeped in an atmosphere of ignoble futility." Out of this excellent story with all its dramatic potential was made "A complete hash!" [Gives some details about the dramatic performance.]

390 McFee, William. "Great Tales of a Great Victorian," NEW YORK TIMES BOOK REVIEW AND MAGAZINE, 1 Jan 1922, pp. 1, 22.

JC's art is best explained as a species of word painting rather than as various kinds of tales. His treatment of the sea possesses a pictorial quality which holds the subject in the reader's memory. The fiction as a whole presents imperishable pictures of man's spirit struggling with fate and rarely succeeding in the conflict; JC is thus the "biographer of unconquerable souls." [Review of THE WORKS OF JOSEPH CONRAD (Garden City, NY: Doubleday, Page, 1922).]

391 Pierrefeu, Jean de. "Un romancier d'aventures: Joseph Conrad" (A Novelist of Adventure: Joseph Conrad), JOURNAL DES DÉBATS, CXXXIV (24 May 1922), 2.

The Nigger of the Narcissus was the first of JC's novels in a French translation (c 1917). It revealed a strange and tumultuous talent; a gift of divination in soul searching in its innermost recesses along with startling depiction of the unexpected aspects of distant places. Like Kipling, JC intrigues the reader both by psychological analysis and vividness of imagination. [A brief biographical account is given of JC's youth and dreams.] Once on a ship, he found his real *Patrie,* England. He became English on the high seas and in far-off places. His observations written on bits of paper hint at depths found in the writers of Poland. JC is a strange flowering of two literatures. He borrowed Kipling's secret of the art of writing, i.e., the precision of detail which makes an unknown reality plausible: an amputated thumb is more impressive than a high forehead. JC saw the aesthetic value of this method. Like Dostoevski, JC contemplated the unusual, the insane, the abnormal. *Nigger* is a contribution to psychopathology. Other observations of this kind are to be found in *Almayer's Folly* and *Within the Tides* (Stafford is depicted as a degenerate). The unique quality of JC is to be found in his empathic and aesthetic probing of the abnormal in human nature and his rendition of the unconscious acts of man in certain situations regardless of country of origin. [In French.]

392 Rhys, Ernest. "An Interview with Joseph Conrad," BOOKMAN (NY), LVI (Dec 1922), 402-8.

JC opines that some new writers do not keep their readers as fully *engaged* as he himself tries to do. In his own writing, he explains, his psychological aim comes first; then he looks about for some event or personal adventure or catastrophe "to *motiver*" his main characters. But he always keeps his aim in view. A contrast of Stevenson's TREASURE ISLAND and JC's *The Nigger of the Narcissus* reveals that the latter could have been written only by a narrator who had been a seaman and was one still in imagination when he wrote; he made the sea into the "revealer of men and women" and every ship into a "living thing, a personal instrument, an agent of destiny," thus enabling himself to take hold of his public and to keep it fast. [Ernest Rhys and M. Larigot, author of "Les Revenants sans Appel," report on a visit to JC at his home in Kent.]

> **393** Schelling, Felix Emmanuel. "Joseph Conrad on Life and Letters," APPRAISEMENTS AND ASPERITIES AS TO SOME CONTEMPORARY WRITERS (Philadelphia and Lond: Lippincott, 1922), pp. 62-66.

Notes on Life and Letters has "the intimacy of good talk." JC's liberal view is an example of his cosmopolitan spirit, "which has not deprived him either of a fervent love for his mother Poland, nor of devotion to his adopted mother England." Best in the book is the "revelation of a man thinking mainly without prejudice or sophistication, literary or social."

> **394** Stauffer, Ruth M. JOSEPH CONRAD: HIS ROMANTIC-REALISM (Boston: Four Seas, 1922).

JC may be labeled both a Realist and a Romanticist by explaining the meaning of the two concepts, by considering his plot, character development, and setting, and by analyzing his "spirit." In JC there is "almost equal balance" between the two attitudes. The Romantic-Realist "aims to translate into the medium of fiction life as it actually is." JC, with "the poetic imagination of the Romanticist and the minute observation of the Realist," assembles in his works "an impersonal study of motives, conduct, and character" that is at the same time "as restrained and as passionate as life itself." He seldom tells a story in the old "chronological sequence of cause and effect"; since his aim is to make a story known as it would actually be, "it is necessary that the events be retold after they have happened." Many chance remarks of the characters are "symbolic premonitions of events"; some are also ironical. For JC, "character is destiny," and the reader must put together the glimpse he has of a character; and even then some mystery may remain. The epitome of JC's art is "Realistic photographic detail side by side with the Romantic interpretation of the meaning of things and the yearning for beauty." JC is "supreme" as a writer of the seas as well as of the tropics and the jungles, but "the prevailing atmosphere" of his works is used both realistically and romantically. His "dominant strain" is "an abiding realization of the mystery that shrouds life." For him "sincerity, unselfishness, sympathy, love, are the truth of life. Courage, endurance, responsibility, fidelity to duty, are the ethics on which the solidarity of mankind is founded." For everything that concerns Mystery, JC "employs the style of the Romanticist," and in all that he has written "the outlines of his sharply intense Realism are blurred by the softening shades of his Romanticism." [Includes a long but inaccurate and incomplete early bibliography of works about JC.]

395 Whitford, Robert Calvin. "Book Reviews," SOUTH ATLANTIC QUARTERLY, XXI (April 1922), 189-90.

Readers hoping "to find it a full harvest of frank reminiscences will be somewhat disappointed" in *Notes on Life and Letters*.

1923

396 Abbott, L. F. "Joseph Conrad," OUTLOOK (NY), CXXXIV (23 May 1923), 14-15.

[Account of an appearance of JC at a gathering in NY during his American visit.]

397 Adams, Elbridge Lapham. "Joseph Conrad—the Man," OUTLOOK (NY), CXXXIII (18 April 1923), 708-12; rptd in CONRAD: THE MAN. WITH A BURIAL IN KENT, by John Sheridan Zelie (NY: Rudge, 1925).

JC thought *Some Reminiscences* "a faithful record of the feelings and sensations connected with the writing of" his first book. [Based on knowledge of JC from 1916 to 1923.]

398 Aksenov, I. A. *"Prilivy I Otlivy"* (*Within the Tides*), PECHAT I REVOLUTSIA, No. 7 (1923), 268-71.

[A review.] [In Russian.]

399 Armstrong, Martin. "A Romantic Realist," SPECTATOR (Lond), CXXXI (15 Dec 1923), 960-61.

The Rover is a very typical JC novel, but not JC's finest book. The characters are typical, but also individual. JC writes in the familiar convention of boys' stories by G. A. Henty and R. L. Stevenson, but he is better than they are. Both a romantic and a realist, JC is also a psychologist and an "extra-ordinary visualizer." The gradual shaping of events in this novel is too obscurely hinted at.

400 Aubry, G. Jean-. "Joseph Conrad et l'Amérique Latine" (Joseph Conrad and Latin America), REVUE DE L'AMÉRIQUE LATINE, II (April 1923), 290-99; rptd as "Joseph Conrad and Latin America," LIVING AGE, CCCVII (12 May 1923), 350-55.

JC wrote three works, *Romance, Nostromo* and "Gaspar Ruiz," in the settings of South America. Although he "brushed" past these islands in his early sea career, his passages capture the atmosphere of this continent because of his resourcefulness in drawing details from books on South America. JC, after his retirement (1894), drew material for his sea novels from his life experience even though he hardly wrote a word during his career as a seaman. This "second vocation" possessed the same vitality and sensations that he experienced in his sea career. *Romance,* written in collaboration with F. M. Ford, displays JC's acute perception and sensitivity. JC is an imaginative writer with a vast storehouse of picturesque details taken from adventure novels which he avidly read. His enthusiastic reading and yarns heard on voyages gave JC the materials to present such authentic and vibrant scenes. [Biographical sketch.] [In French.]

401 Aubry, Georges Jean-. "Joseph Conrad et la France" (Joseph Conrad and France), FIGARO (Suppl. litt.), No. 211 (21 April 1923), 1; excerpted in CHRONIQUE DES LETTRES FRANÇAISES, I (May-June 1923), 425; rptd in NOUVELLES LITTÉRAIRES, VII (11 Feb 1928), 7.

JC's first efforts as a seaman began in the Port of Marseilles (the scene of *The Arrow of Gold*); he had a fluent knowledge of French, learned as a child; he was widely read in French literature, with which his home is well stocked; he was an avid reader of Flaubert; and he read Hugo's TOILERS OF THE SEA, translated into Polish by his father. During JC's two-year stay in Montpellier, he worked on "The Duel" and part of *The Secret Agent.* During a stay in Brittany, the first pages of *The Nigger of the Narcissus* were begun. [Describes JC's home, work, and family circle in a small village near Canterbury; gives a sketchy biography, highlighting details pertinent to France. Repeats much of what Aubry has said in other places.] [In French.]

402 B., H. I. "Gentlest of Deep-Sea Skippers," NEW YORK TIMES MAGAZINE, 13 May 1923, p. 10.

JC's fiirst efforts as a seaman begin in the Port of Marseilles (the scene of landscape as well as of character and story.

403 Bendz, Ernst. JOSEPH CONRAD: AN APPRECIATION (Gothenburg: Gumbert; NY: H. W. Wilson Co., 1923).

JC shows the influence of his early vocation in both his general outlook and his literary methods. Utilizing the advantages of the exotic milieu, he makes us accept the existence of individuals outside the range of our experience. "An artistically perfect blending . . . of Romance with Reality, the rendering, by the methods of realism, of a unique vision of the universe as reflected in a romantic temperament, is what constitutes the peculiar fascination and power of Conrad's writings." The naturalistic novel offers no lasting attraction to him, except in *The Secret Agent.* "With a detachment perhaps more real than Flaubert's, Conrad has much of the expansive temperament of the talker." This "bent for musing discursiveness" determines the structure of his narratives and serves as a medium for a kind of realism peculiar to him. His spiritualized conception of the universe makes "the purely aesthetic appeal of his stories . . . inseparable from their quality of dreaminess and spiritual suggestiveness." JC is responsive to the mystery of nature and uses natural scenery or disturbances to mirror the crisis in a moral drama or the anguish of a tortured soul. Romance is the very substance of his stories. The love motif is important in *Almayer's Folly, An Outcast of the Islands,* and "Karain"; and *The Nigger of the Narcissus* is a study of collective psychology. *Lord Jim* presents the antagonism between dream and reality in a life-drama of a far more subtle character than *Nigger* and is compared to the more melodramatic *Victory.* While *Nostromo* may come to be regarded as JC's greatest achievement, it lacks a leading character. JC's most intellectual book, *Chance,* deals with the tribulations arising from Anthony's and Flora's slowness in realizing their common destiny. *Agent* appeals by the force of a consistent Russian life and his gift for analyzing cases of moral aberration and the perplexities of passion. The extreme elusiveness and the sophisticated reveries of the far from perfect *The Arrow of Gold* reveal the way JC has travelled from *Outcast* with its fresh sensualism and voluptuous intensity. In all his stories, suffering and pathos are prominent and give his work an impression of sadness. As an analyst of illusions, whose pity is tempered with irony, JC resembles Anatole France. He points the simple truth that in a time of crumbling faiths humanity requires some scheme of practical ethics. JC's style includes an effective use of metaphor and irony, but the foreign flavor of his style is objectionable. [Still important; contains valuable observations on individual novels.]

404 Brock, H. I. "Brewed From the French Revolution by Conrad," NEW YORK TIMES BOOK REVIEW, 2 Dec 1923, pp. 6, 22.

The Rover falls far below JC's very best; the happy ending is labored, oversweet. The logic and art of the story are obviously interfered with "for the sake of an amiable propaganda of mutual esteem between the English and the French." The book is more or less a commercial one.

405 Brock, H. I. "Joseph Conrad, Sculptor of Words," NEW YORK TIMES BOOK REVIEW, 10 June 1923, p. 2.

JC "uses words in his art as Rodin used his clay." The manuscript version is different from the published version of *The Rescue.* "The elimination from the script of *The Rescue* shows that the original trouble was, in fact, the riot of color which with its splendor obscured the form. In fact, in the novel as published, the 'elaborate creation of atmosphere' does still work to 'the detriment of the action.'"

406 C., C. "L'Aristocratisme slave de Conrad" (The Slav Aristocracy of Conrad), Figaro (Suppl. litt.), No. 247 (29 Dec 1923), 3; excerpted in Chronique des Lettres Françaises, II (May-June 1924), 412-14.

There is a Slavic impulse first of all in the decision to turn to writing. The "Slavism" is evident in JC's use of the same amount of energy to re-create his experiences into literature as he had used physically in these experiences. JC's study of the vicissitudes of the human soul and all its motivation is due to this "Slavism." [Works sketchily commented on are: *The Shadow-Line, Lord Jim, The Rover,* "Skimmer of the Sea." The whole article is pretentious and shallow. Brief biographical sketch of JC's early life.] [In French.]

407 "Captain Conrad," Outlook (NY), LXXXIII (16 May 1923), 879-80.

In an interview, JC said that he still held a master's license in the British Merchant Service. Of contemporary writers he said, " 'My mind is not critical' "; " 'I don't read much fiction.' " The order in which to read JC's novels is *The Rescue, Lord Jim, Typhoon, The Nigger of the Narcissus,* and *Almayer's Folly. Nigger,* "his most subtle and strongest work," was first published in the U.S. as *The Children of the Sea,* "through an oversensitive feeling that the original title would not be well received here."

408 Carroll, Sydney Wentworth. "Conrad and the Critics," Some Dramatic Opinions (Lond: F. V. White, [1923]); rptd (Port Washington, NY: Kennikat P, 1968), pp. 171-74.

[General comment on problems of a novelist trying to write for the stage, defending the critic's right to attack a bad play regardless of the writer's stature. Mentions in passing JC's lackluster stage presentation of *The Secret Agent.* Of no critical value.]

409 Colby, Elbridge. "A Sample of Bibliographical Method," Papers of the Bibliographical Society of America, XVI (1923), 118-46.

An examination of some of JC's works in "the usual Doubleday, Page editions" (not the special limited set of 1922) and the "Memorial Edition" of the Plays of Clyde Fitch illustrates the value of examining books for bibliographical information. The different kinds of pagination in a "uniform" edition, variations in the kinds of type used, slight divergences in the number of lines to the page, broken type, and the "signature letters" which appear on the first page of each signature indicate that when Doubleday, Page and Company acquired from McClure, Phillips the copyright and the plates of some of the JC books, they recognized in the Polish novelist "his then unappreciated qualities as a literary genius." Also, "by persistent effort and a sincere faith" in JC and by resorting to devices like using old plates for some of the volumes, they were eventually able to publish his works in a uniform binding, thereby dignifying his name and reputation by issuing a series in a permanent style. Other advantages of the practices revealed by close bibliographical inspection are the use of old plates, which makes possible at low cost uniform editions like those of JC and the volumes in Everyman's Library; a distinct service of publishers who supply many books otherwise unobtainable; the circulation and the dignity deserved by a worthy author; assistance in counteracting the "senseless rage for first editions"; and a gladdening of the heart of the bibliographer.

410 "Conrad For 'Movies' But Can't Sell One," NEW YORK TIMES, 8 May 1923, p. 16.

[Brief account of interview JC gave at Mill Neck, Long Island, 7 May 1923.]

411 "Conrad is 'Gripping,'" GREENSBORO [N.C.] DAILY NEWS, 30 Dec 1923, p. 10.

In *The Rover,* Jean Peyrot [sic] is "as natural as life itself," but the unusual feature of the book is that JC lets his characters lay their souls bare, thus presenting his people in a "strictly objective" manner. The novel is "gripping" mainly because of the Rover's "mind."

412 "Conrad Manuscripts. Notes on Sales," TIMES LITERARY SUPPLEMENT (Lond), 22 Nov 1923, p. 796.

[Notes the John Quinn Library sale. Original MSS and a few of JC's comments are listed.]

413 "Conrad's Treasure Chest of Experience," NEW YORK TIMES BOOK REVIEW, 26 Aug 1923, pp. 9, 22.

[Gives the biographical and geographical origins of many of JC's works.]

414 Constant Reader. "Looking Backward: Joseph Conrad," NEW YORK EVENING POST LITERARY REVIEW, III (28 April 1923), 647.

[Recalls his first reaction to JC.]

415 Curle, Richard. "Conrad in the East," YALE REVIEW, N.S. XII (April 1923), 497-508.

Although JC's evocations of the East are marked by closeness to detail and although his characters suggest some basis in real life, there is also "a touch of the subliminal" and the presence of "imaginative art dealing with human fate and emotions." JC's wanderings in the East took him to Bangkok and to Sumatra (*Almayer's Folly, An Outcast of the Islands,* "Karain," "The Lagoon," *Lord Jim,* "The End of the Tether," "Typhoon," "Falk," "The Secret Sharer," "Freya of the Seven Isles," *Victory, The Shadow-Line,* and *The Rescue*). His absence from the East after 1889 turned his memories into a source of inspiration before he published his first book in

1895, and his descriptions of the East thus have a kind of "symbolic force." Since JC was much more concerned with humanity than with nature, his fatalistic idea of man's relationships is extraordinarily impressive as it is displayed in this fatalistic background. Being a poet, JC has called up "the melancholy and the indifference" of the "teeming East" in the colors of "imaginative realism." His tragic characters cannot escape its clutches. His sense of tragedy is not a sense of pessimism; he believed firmly in "the greatness of courage, faithfulness, endurance, and honor." His elusive romanticism awakens a resonance in the "inward ear," thereby being an "asset of reality."

> **416** [Curle, Richard.] "The History of Mr. Conrad's Books," TIMES LITERARY SUPPLEMENT (Lond), 30 Aug 1923, p. 570; excerpted in NEW YORK TIMES BOOK REVIEW, 26 Aug 1926, pp. 9, 22; pub separately as JOSEPH CONRAD: THE HISTORY OF HIS BOOKS (Lond: Dent, 1924); rptd in JOSEPH CONRAD: INCLUDING AN APPROACH TO HIS WRITINGS (Garden City, NY: Doubleday, Page, 1926), pp. 47-56.

JC transmutes "the particular into the general" through his deep concern with human nature. His books do not "age" because the author's "creation was powerful enough to have at his heart a universal feeling." This "final truth" about JC is the basis of his appeal to many different kinds of people. [Relates, with some details, JC's experiences to several of JC's fictions and begins a minor controversy: for the immediate discussion, also see Sir F. Swettenham's "The Story of *Lord Jim*," ibid., 6 Sept 1923, p. 588; The Writer of the Article, ibid., 13 Sept 1923, p. 604; Swettenham, ibid., 20 Sept 1923, p. 620; and Alfred Holt & Co., ibid., 11 Oct 1923, p. 670; for the controversy revived in 1966, see references listed under "Lord Jim's Line," ibid., 3 Nov 1966, pp. 993-94.]

> **417** Edgett, Edwin Francis. "Joseph Conrad and His Idolaters," BOSTON EVENING TRANSCRIPT, 8 Dec 1923, p. 4.

The state of mind of the "Conrad idolaters" is that they cannot see the works as a whole, their eyes being too filled with details. *The Rover* "is a good story very badly told, and that seems to us to be worse than a bad story well told." After nearly a quarter of a century, JC "has not yet learned the rudiments of his art."

> **418** Fernández, Ramón. "Lettres étrangères," NOUVELLE REVUE FRANÇAISE, X (1 May 1923), 841-43.

In *Lord Jim*, the story of Jim, the man "under a cloud," is the exotic orchestration of a basic problem posed by Rousseau and still unresolved. It reveals a strong relationship between literary technique and morale. In this novel, JC raises exotic literature to the level of eternal literature. [In French.]

419 Herrick, Robert. "Mr. Conrad and Romance," New York Evening Post Literary Review, IV (22 Dec 1923), 387.

With *Lord Jim,* JC started the shift [in readers' expectations] from anticipating "action and atmosphere," to looking for the "cerebral," for inner significance, in a romance. The JC adventure is "fundamentally psychologic." *The Rover,* however, obeys the limitation of the earlier romance of Stevenson, "the mood of youth." This novel is incredible and trite: "coincidences . . . . abound sufficient for a motion picture."

420 Holt, Alfred & Co. "The Story of *Lord Jim,*" Times Literary Supplement (Lond), 11 Oct 1923, p. 670.

[Gives details of the actual pilgrim ship incident used in *Lord Jim*. For the origin of the controversy in 1923, see "The History of Mr. Conrad's Books," ibid., 30 Aug 1923, p. 570; for the controversy revived in 1966, see "Lord Jim's Line," ibid., 3 Nov 1966, pp. 993-94.]

421 Hutchison, Percy Adams. "Joseph Conrad, 'Master in Sail for All Oceans,'" New York Times Book Review, 29 April 1923, p. 6.

Nostromo should not be used as an introduction to JC. "The true course to JC lies through the books which do taste of the salt." JC's chief interest was in the "collective psychology," the uniting of mankind, and his philosophy was the "idealism of service." True reality for JC was in the soul, in things spiritual.

422 Hutchison, Percy A. "Revealing the Soul of a Sea-Rover," Literary Digest International Book Review, II (Dec 1923), 31, 67.

Like JC's masterpiece, *Victory, The Rover* has the sea as "an immutable force." The author's one interest is "the human soul"; his stories are the attrition of soul and soul; or of soul in the struggle of circumstance." From the sea comes Old Peyrol, and into the sea he returns. It is Arlette who dominates the novel, even if she is "felt rather than perceived." Since the method here is simpler than that of *Nostromo* and *Victory,* "something of the Conrad impact has been lost." Only after the book has been laid aside does the reader see its "true grandeur," "its naked fidelity to truth and beauty."

423 "Joseph Conrad," Chronique des Lettres Françaises, I (March-April 1923), 267-70.

JC is being called to the attention of the French public by the translation of some of his major works in a collection gotten out by Nouvelle Revue Française. These works are widely read and appreciated. The critics are comparing him to Kipling and Hardy. JC's slavic background is presumed to account for the multiple beauty of his work. JC, observer of the human soul in exotic surroundings, may be compared to Dostoevski (morbid psychologist of mental adventures). By other critics he is likened to Jack London and Mérimée. [This article seems to be a composite of articles by the following: André Chaumeix, LE GAULOIS (Supp. litt.), 16 Dec 1922; Émile Henriot, LE TEMPS, 4 April 1922; Jean de Pierrefeu, JOURNAL DES DÉBATS, 24 May 1922; Joseph Aynard, JOURNAL DES DÉBATS, 16 Nov 1922. Includes biographical sketch, brief comments on subject matter and style.] [In French.]

    424 "Joseph Conrad: the Gift of Tongues," NATION (NY), CXVI (16 May 1923), 561.

Great is the creative power of JC, one of the major living stylists in English, in a language not "learned at his mother's knee." "A few faint Gallicisms—nothing of a Slavic tinge . . . pursue him."

    425 Kleczkowski, Paul. "Une traduction polonaise des oeuvres de Joseph Conrad" (A Polish Translation of the Works of Joseph Conrad), POLOGNA (Paris), IV (1 March 1923), 256-61.

Polish translations of the works of JC, an "English writer," are to be published by the firm of "Ignis." The first volume, translated by A. Zagorska, is *Almayer's Folly,* with a preface by Z. Zeromski. Why the craze for JC among Poles? JC's great literary value was evidenced by Gide's French translation of *Typhoon.* As to Poles, the answer is simple: JC, a Pole by birth, was at heart still faithful to the land and language of his ancestors. His works show his commiseration with "inferior races." The fate of his own Poland impelled him to sympathize with other small ravaged countries. A. Potocki published (1922) a study on JC which includes many details of his early life and his later visits to his uncle in the Ukraine; in 1914, JC took his two sons to Cracow; in 1908 he wrote a political study, "Autocracy and War"; he revisited Poland in 1915. JC must have thought in Polish for forty years; therefore, in translating these thoughts into another language, the words take on a new significance. His basic English vocabulary is gathered from poorer circles of society; only later did higher circles exert an influence. The *impressions* received at sea were sub-vocally in Polish; later, when written, a certain Polish *tonality* is retained, giving rise to an originality not found in other English authors. [Frequent reliance on such critics as R. Curle, Z. Zeromski, A. Potocki.] [In French.]

    426 Koch [karev], [N. A.]. "Dlia pishchevarenia" (For Digestion), ZORI, No. 7 (1923), 14.

[In Russian.]

    427 L., P. "*The Rover,*" NEW REPUBLIC, XXXVII (26 Dec 1923), 124.

With respect to the genesis of *The Rover,* a passage, JC's preface to *No-*

stromo, in which JC says, discussing his source, that he had no desire to invent details of a robbery he had just read about, and was not interested in transforming the episode into a story until it occurred to him that the thief "need not necessarily be a confirmed rogue," must have come often to JC when his "imagination is beginning to discuss the chief actor in crime . . . or cowardice . . . or heroism." So, in *Rover,* the hero need not be an "ultra patriotic French naval officer," but ironically, perhaps a man "quite unlike this." It would be helpful if we could measure the difference between the order of persons, events, and places as they came to JC's mind and the way they are finally presented.

428 "Letters and Art: Meeting Conrad at the Ship," LITERARY DIGEST, LXXVII (19 May 1923), 27-28.

JC's arrival in America aroused more interest than has been shown in any literary visitor since Henry James returned after twenty-five years in 1906. [Quotations from newspaper articles about JC's reception.]

429 Littell, Robert. "Arriving with Joseph Conrad," NEW REPUBLIC, XXXIV (16 May 1923), 319; rptd in READ AMERICA FIRST (NY: Harcourt, Brace, 1926), pp. 141-45.

[Description of JC's arrival in NY.]

430 Lovett, Robert Morss. "The Realm of Conrad," ASIA, XXIII (May 1923), 325-27, 377-78.

Like Thomas Hardy, JC is a novelist of environment. His favorite approach is that of the "behaviorist psychologist"—to "know men as tested by their surrounding circumstances." *Victory* is perhaps JC's most perfect synthesis of environment and human life. In his great stories, the sea manifests itself in dynamic and naked strength, especially with overpowering rainstorms; yet equally important are the sea's static and enduring moods: tropical darkness becomes a "palpable horror," and the assault of light sometimes is violent. JC seldom creates a "social fabric"—"human contacts are occasional, the result of circumstances. The individual is the measure of humanity." Within this latter context the themes of the beauty of women, the perfect sacrifice maintained with stainless honor against betrayal, and deterioration through environment focus. [Perceptive, anticipating critical perspectives of the 1960s.]

431 M., A. *"Prilivy i Otlivy"* (*Within the Tides*), KNIGONOSHA, No. 23 (1923), 10.

[A review.] [In Russian.]

432 McGoldrick, Rita C. "The Coming of Joseph Conrad," AMERICA (NY), XXIX (26 May 1923), 136-37.

On JC's visit to America, "Davy" Bone was Captain of the ship and

Muirhead Bone, an old cabin mate of JC, was aboard. JC is not popularly read but is a great stylist. "Every character in the stories had its prototype in the pages of his own experience" (e.g., James Wait, in *The Nigger of the Narcissus*). JC's "lyrical prose" is especially praiseworthy.

433 Martin, Dorothy. "Two Aspects of Conrad," FREEMAN, VIII (12 Sept 1923), 10-12.

JC is a psychologist who emphasizes character and the tragedy of human life and a lyric poet who depicts "man's greatness in the face of nature's majesty." Now the psychological gift is more highly valued; one day he may be considered among "the greatest English prose poets."

434 Mégroz, Rodolphe Louis. "The Personality of Joseph Conrad," REVIEW OF REVIEWS (Lond), LXVIII (Sept 1923), 120-22.

[Very general biographical comments and analysis of distinctive elements of JC's art. Stresses JC's emphasis on *The Mirror of the Sea* as his personal statement.]

435 "Mr. Conrad's New Novel," TIMES LITERARY SUPPLEMENT (Lond), 6 Dec 1923, p. 849.

The Rover is not one of JC's best books; yet "it stands out for speed of movement, and . . . for the impress of its truth to human nature."

436 Morley, Christopher. "Conrad and the Reporters," NEW YORK EVENING POST, 3 May 1923, p. 8; 4 May 1923, p. 10; 5 May 1923, p. 10; 7 May 1923, p. 8; 10 May 1923, p. 8; rptd as CONRAD AND THE REPORTERS (Garden City, NY: Doubleday, Page, 1923).

While JC was visiting the United States, reporters printed misinformation. [In a postscript Morley comments on the sale of John Quinn's MSS collection of Conradiana for $110,998. Long digression on reports no longer being "literary."]

437 Mortimer, Raymond. "New Novels," NEW STATESMAN, XXII (15 Dec 1923), 306-7.

The Rover is distinctly below JC's earlier achievements—dark, shady, shadowy throughout, with little vividness of character or scene. "The reader has to construct for himself all the relations between the characters."

438 Osbourne, Maitland LeRoy. "Joseph Conrad—Interpreter of the Sea," NATIONAL MAGAZINE, LII (June 1923), 31-32; rptd in POLAND, V (Feb 1924), 87-89, 114, 116.

[An overdone glimpse of JC during his visit to the United States, e.g., "his spiritual vision overleaps the boundaries of time and space."]

439 Ould, Herman. "Joseph Conrad's First Play," BOOKMAN (NY), LVI (Feb 1923), 739-40.

Despite the report that the dramatization of *The Secret Agent* was a complete failure, "[I was] held and moved by this play as I have not been held and moved by a play for many years." The critics objected to the play because they had first read the book and because the audiences were affected in a way which English audiences dislike—they were made to feel genuine emotion.

440 Overton, Grant. "In the Kingdom of Conrad," BOOKMAN (NY), LVII (May 1923), 275-84; rptd in AMERICAN NIGHTS ENTERTAINMENT (NY: Appleton, 1923), pp. 64-90; in AUTHORS OF THE DAY (NY: George H. Doran, 1924), pp. 32-56.

JC wrestled with the problem of self-knowledge; he has also given us the best definition of the novel: "a conviction of our fellowmen's existence strong enough to take upon itself a form of imagined life clearer than reality." [Overton devotes a sentence or less to the generally accepted comments on various works. Comments presented as though Marlow were writing.]

441 Powys, John Cowper. "Joseph Conrad," SUSPENDED JUDGMENTS: ESSAYS ON BOOKS AND SENSATIONS (NY: G. Arnold Shaw, 1916), pp. 337-64; rptd in ESSAYS ON JOSEPH CONRAD AND OSCAR WILDE (Girard, Kansas: Haldeman-Julius, 1923), pp. 3-28.

JC's "inherent genius" is "that strange margin of our minds, where memories gather which are deeper than memories, and where emotions float by and waver and hover and alight, like wild marsh-birds upon desolate seabanks." JC, uninterested in social problems, is most concerned with relations between men and women; he has achieved for the latter "an extraordinary triumph" by means of "an art of description which by a few fastidious and delicate touches can make the bodily appearance indicative of the hidden soul." His style, "a rare achievement," is the result of his treating the English language "with such scrupulous and austere reverence." In portraying his women, he absolutely eliminates *"the sensual"* from his depiction of each, and he also avoids the sentimental. JC grasped the "psychology" of men and women better than other modern writers. He is best in his "direct uncomplicated scenes" where two "passionate and troubled natures"—men or women or both—"are brought together in direct and tragic conflict," but next best is his "curious and intricate method" of telling his stories. Although JC "finds nothing except meaningless and purposeless chance in the ways of Nature, [he] is inspired by a splendid tenacity of courage in resisting any desperate betrayal of human joy."

442 *"Prilivy i Otlivy"* (*Within the Tides*), KRASNAIA NIVA, No. 37 (1923), 32.

[A review of *Within the Tides*.] [In Russian.]

443 [Quinn, John]. LIBRARY OF JOHN QUINN: PART ONE [A-C] (NY: Anderson Galleries [Sale 1768], 1923), pp. 164-213.
[This catalog contains a three-paragraph biographical sketch; facsimiles of letters and MSS; and items 1780-2010.]

444 "The Secret of Joseph Conrad's Appeal," CURRENT OPINION, LXXIV (June 1923), 677-79.
JC passed from the "collective psychology" of a ship to that of mankind. He was nothing if not a psychologist. [Quotations from Hutchison, "Joseph Conrad 'Master in Sail for All Oceans,'" NEW YORK TIMES BOOK REVIEW, 29 April 1923, p. 6.]

445 Shanks, Edward. FIRST ESSAYS ON LITERATURE (Lond: Collins, 1923), pp. 185, 187.
JC is "the most significant figure in the English novel of to-day." "One might almost say that, instead of the situation being invented to display them [JC's characters], they are invented to support the situation. The centre of gravity of Mr. Conrad's novels lies in action and situation; and here he coincides with a tendency which was already in operation before he began to influence it. The narrative gift, the faculty of telling a story, is taking with renewed importance its place in the development of the novel."

446 Swettenham, Sir Frank. "The Story of *Lord Jim*," TIMES LITERARY SUPPLEMENT (Lond), 6 Sept 1923, p. 588.
The facts of the historical events on which JC based *Lord Jim* left Jim in Singapore "where he found work in a ship's chandler's store, grew fat and prosperous." The real Jim's salvation was not working on Patusan. [For the origin of the controversy in 1923, see references under "The History of Mr. Conrad's Books," ibid., 30 Aug 1923, p. 570; for the controversy revived in 1966, see references listed under "Lord Jim's Line," ibid., 3 Nov 1966, pp. 993-94.]

447 Swettenham, Sir Frank. "The Story of *Lord Jim*," TIMES LITERARY SUPPLEMENT (Lond), 20 Sept 1923, p. 620.
"I questioned whether that part of Conrad's romance which describes how Jim 'worked out his salvation' supports the statement that 'it is this sense of contact with life that gives to his pages the feeling that things happened so and no [sic] otherwise.'" [Reply to "The Story of *Lord Jim*," by The Writer of the Article, ibid., 13 Sept 1923, p. 604, Swettenham restating the position he took in ibid., 6 Sept 1923, p. 588. For the origin of the controversy in 1923, see references listed under "The History of Mr. Conrad's Books," ibid., 30 Aug 1923; for the controversy revived in 1966, see references listed under "Lord Jim's Line," ibid., 3 Nov 1966, pp. 993-94.]

448 Tittle, Walter. "Portraits in Pencil and Pen," CENTURY, CVI (May 1923), 53-61; rptd with pt II, ibid., CVIII (Sept 1924), 641-45, in STRAND MAGAZINE, LXVII (June 1924), 546-50; and POLAND, V (Sept 1924), 141-44, 188-89, 192, 194.

JC "is possessed with a happy cordiality that carries with it the deepest conviction." Among his qualities are alertness, energy, humor, intelligence, and kindness. [JC's house in Bishopshire described; luncheon there with JC, his wife and son, and M. Aubry. JC recounts the actual experience on which "Youth" was based. He also makes complimentary remarks about Henry James, Arnold Bennett, and Chesterton. An artist's conversation with JC as he spent a Sunday sketching him at Bishopshire.]

449 "An Unusual Modern," AMERICA (NY), XXIX (19 May 1923), 111.

JC told interviewers that he put down thoughts, and style took care of itself. Unlike modern writers, JC held an unpublished MS for ten years waiting for inspiration to finish it. JC is visiting America as a guest of a friend and not making a commercial enterprise of the visit.

450 Weygandt, Cornelius. "The Art of Joseph Conrad," SCHELLING ANNIVERSARY PAPERS, compiled by his former students (NY: The Century Co; Phila: University of Pennsylvania P, 1923), pp. 319-41.

Despite adventurers' tales by Sandys, Evelyn, Bruce, Defoe, Smollett, and Melville, English literature had to wait until 1895 for a good travel story, JC's *Almayer's Folly*. JC cannot explain why he began to write. His experience in Malaya must have prompted him to begin the first novel. It evidenced the appearance of a new personality, which pervaded the description, narration of the story, and presentation of character. The writings that made him famous are those that came out of his Malayan experiences, psychological studies of strange people in the manner of Henry James but with JC's Slavic detachment, such as *Folly, An Outcast of the Islands,* "Karain," "Youth," *Lord Jim,* "The Lagoon," "The End of the Tether," "Typhoon," "Falk," "The Secret Sharer," *Victory*. There is brooding romance in these stories which chronicle the vehemence and resignation of broken men, as well as the spell of the East—a hush and an inscrutably dark atmosphere.

Though his early stories are more easily understandable than later ones (*Chance, The Shadow-Line,* and *The Rescue*), *Chance* brought JC to the public eye. Henley's acceptance of *The Nigger of the Narcissus* for the NEW REVIEW was a sign of recognition that a new author had arrived; and with this third book, JC achieved full power. Though Meredith influenced him briefly, it was Henry James whom JC followed for a long time—in character analysis and psychology. Though he read Scott, Dickens, Thackeray, and Trollope, he was little influenced by them; and although he admits obligations to Marryat's and Cooper's sea stories, such an influence is hard to detect. JC also regarded Turgenev highly, but his influence is scant.

With *Jim,* JC became more widely read, perhaps because Jim is such a universal character. "Youth," JC's most praised story, has little characterization, but it conveys with great skill the joy of youth triumphing over all difficulties and misfortunes. Nine years after "Falk," in which a man commits what he considers the unpardonable sin of cannibalism, JC published *'Twixt Land and Sea,* which included "The Secret Sharer" and "Freya of the Seven Isles." Whereas "The Secret Sharer" has a subdued eeriness, "Freya" has a tumult surpassing even *Victory* with its four murders. With "Because of the Dollars," *Shadow-Line, Victory,* and *Rescue,* JC fills out his portrait of Malaya. *Shadow-Line* deals with the same period of life as "Youth" did, the passing of youth into manhood. In *Victory,* JC explains his characters more than in the other novels, and they are understood more easily. Characters sometimes are reduced to their dominant emotion, as Captain Lingard is in *Rescue.* Heyst in *Victory,* however, is a most palpable character. Despite the vivid character portrayal in *Rescue,* it is not considered one of JC's greatest novels. None of the books which deal with Malaya, except *Victory,* can approach *Nostromo, Under Western Eyes,* and *The Arrow of Gold,* which reach into his experiences as a youth in Marseilles, boyhood in Poland, and youth on the Mediterranean respectively. *Nostromo* combines romance with realism expertly. In *Eyes,* JC, knowing well many stories of the tyranny of the Czarist regime, finds it difficult to maintain his reserve, yet in fact sympathizing with strongly centralized authority. *Arrow,* while not as ambitious as *Nostromo,* is perhaps better harmonized than the parts of *Nostromo* could be. Doña Rita ranks with the great women portrayed in literature. Nostromo stands out as an especially vivid and palpable creation of the over thirty characters in JC that provoke discussion. He is a universal character whose self-esteem (which was his undoing) we can understand.

Often JC seems to hold that life is an illusion, yet he believes it is a good thing whether it brings happiness or unhappiness. His books have grown more English with the years. He came to the front by following other ideals of writing than those of Dostoevski and Turgenev, both of whom most other novelists were following. Indeed JC influenced younger English novelists, such as Forster, Lawrence, Beresford, George Swinnerton, Viola Meynell, and Brett Young, according to Walpole, and in America Eugene O'Neill and Hergesheimer.

451 Whiting, George Wesley. "Conrad's Revision of Six of His Short Stories," PMLA, XLVIII (June 1933), 552-57.

JC was indifferent with regard to the American texts of his work [incorrect]. There is no support for JC's statements about the dates of composition of some of his stories. Most of the changes in "An Outpost of Progress" are verbal, there is no extensive revision in "The Lagoon," "Karain" underwent almost no revision, the alterations in "Youth" tend to make the style more idiomatic than it was in the serial version, the revisions in "Heart of Darkness" are mainly in details, and "The End of the Tether" also illustrates JC's "habitual method of revision." JC is therefore careful in making slight revisions, but he conceived no "radical change of conception, no drastic revision," thus displaying his "remarkable word-sense" and justifying his claim that English was his natural medium of expression.

452 [Woolf, Virginia.] "Mr. Conrad: A Conversation," NATION AND ATHENAEUM, 1 Sept 1923, pp. 681-82; rptd in THE CAPTAIN'S DEATH BED (Lond: Hogarth P; NY: Harcourt, Brace, 1950); and COLLECTED ESSAYS (Lond: Hogarth P; NY: Harcourt, Brace, 1966), pp. 309-13.

"There is nothing colloquial in Conrad; nothing intimate; and no humour, at least of the English kind." He is composed of two men: Marlow ("subtle, psychological, loquacious") and the sea captain ("simple, faithful, and obscure"). From this fusion, JC reveals paradoxes and conflicts. Marlow is a man of words, while the sea captain considers words as "no great matter," and it is the sea captain who triumphs. JC's themes bear against falsehood, sentimentality, and slovenliness. JC is a strange combination of artist, aristocrat, and Pole, and the beauty of his novels results from the unlikely fusion of Marlow and the sea captain. *The Arrow of Gold* and *The Rescue* were puzzling after such early works as "Youth," *Lord Jim*, and *The Nigger of the Narcissus*. *Chance* is a great book.

453 Writer of the Article, The. "The Story of *Lord Jim*," TIMES LITERARY SUPPLEMENT (Lond), 13 Sept 1923, p. 604.

Swettenham's account (ibid., 6 Sept 1923, p. 588) of the historical basis of *Lord Jim* does not distract from the assertion that JC's books have a basis in experience. JC's imagination used actual incidents to build on. [For the origin of the controversy in 1923, see references under "The History of Mr. Conrad's Books," ibid., 30 Aug 1923, p. 570; for the controversy revived in 1966, see references listed under "Lord Jim's Line," ibid., 3 Nov 1966, pp. 993-94.]

1924

454 A., C. E. [Aiken, Conrad?]. "Nostr'Omo," NEW REPUBLIC, XL (27 Aug 1924), 391.

JC's *The Secret Agent* was "sadly neglected by the critics." The essence of JC is "a sense of the complexity of human life, of the unpredictability of human motives, of the overwhelming significance of the massive impersonal forces of nature and of civilization moving obscurely in the background." JC's greatness rests "upon the delicate tracery of his lyric poetry and the grand outlines of a cosmic philosophy."

455 Aldington, Richard. "Conrad and Hardy," NEW YORK EVENING POST LITERARY REVIEW, V (6 Sept 1924), 8; rptd in PUBLIC LEDGER LITERARY REVIEW (Phila), 7 Sept 1924, p. 8.

JC is a better "artist in words" than Hardy.

456 Allen, C. K. "Joseph Conrad," CONTEMPORARY REVIEW, CXXV (Jan 1924), 54-62.

JC is an important writer, yet he never produced a single first-rate book; all the major works are flawed by a devious narrative method. *Romance*, though, will endure "when the masterpieces of Scott and Dumas have gone to their unremembered shelves."

457 Armstrong, Martin. "Joseph Conrad," BOOKMAN (Lond), LXV (Feb 1924), 237-39; rptd in LIVING AGE, CCCXX (15 March 1924), 512-16.

JC combines all the stages of literary maturity that a reader experiences: the fairy tale (romantic), the adventure story, and the socio-psychological novel. By means of "sharpness of visualization" he imposes a remarkable sense of actuality on his work. His mind is well stocked with "memories of arduous living" (e.g., in *The Mirror of the Sea*, and *Some Reminiscences*), and he has the artistry to convert experience into art. There is "little or no literary development" from *Almayer's Folly* on. All his works are mature and excellent in their kind, but *Lord Jim* especially stands out, for it has a great degree of "tension" in the action and in the psychology; a similar tension is developed in "The Secret Sharer." But this tension sometimes results in his chief failure, when "tension of action is sustained beyond its elastic limit"; on the psychological plane the result of mismanagement of tension is unjustified mystification. JC has a fine detachment that makes him neither a bitter satirist nor a sentimentalist. JC will always rank high in British literature.

458 Aronsberg, E. "Joseph Conrad," NEW YORK EVENING POST LITERARY REVIEW, IV (16 Aug 1924), 974.

[Letter to the editor emphasizing JC's "all-forgiving generosity."]

459 Aubry, G. Jean-. "Joseph Conrad (6th December, 1857-3rd August, 1924)," FORTNIGHTLY REVIEW, CXXII (Sept 1924), 303-13.

This tribute recognizes in JC "a deep and instinctive faith in the absolute necessity of human solidarity," which is the basis of "the Conradian literary structure." JC's special gift of enlarging any common subject and imparting a certain dignity to it gave his conversation an unforgettable superiority. Absorbed in himself and remaining alone much of the time, JC made others feel the power of his personality and his simplicity. His achievement in writing is "undoubtedly one of the mightiest that we have seen published in our time" because of the "strange power of his imagination, the personal beauty of his style, [and] the range and variety" of his books and characters. Even from the greatest despondency and bitterness which JC sometimes experienced, "there pulsates a deep pity, an infinite commiseration which throws us back into life and heals our thoughts"; JC always maintains the nobility of man. *Nostromo* may be his most successful work [a strong power of perception appears in this early judgment]. Particularly Conradian is the concept of youth which JC depicted in "Youth," *Lord Jim, The Shadow-Line,* and *The Arrow of Gold.*

460 Aubry, G. Jean-. "Joseph Conrad," REVUE HEBDOMADAIRE, XXXIII (Feb 1924), 439-52.

JC's talent was intimately bound to his character. Early influences were Victor Hugo's TOILERS OF THE SEA; experience on French ships; the Carlist incident in Spain which put an end to his French career and diverted him to England. [Reviews genesis of *Almayer's Folly*.] JC was a man of two professions although he never went back to the sea. It is difficult to pinpoint aspects of JC's artistry. His talent aggrandized the themes he used. The finest description of a sea storm ever written is in *The Nigger of the Narcissus,* but the sea is only half his subject matter; the rest is *man,* stripped to his bones and threatened by the sea and death. JC's work has wide scope of background, including English bourgeoisie, Russian circles, South Americans, anarchists in London, a whole country in *Nostromo,* which rivals SALAMMBÔ. JC's style is personal and rich; he was more aware of the force of the English language than any Englishman of his time. JC, nourished by Shakespeare, further enriched by twenty years' contact with realities, created a vocabulary with the force and freshness of the Elizabethans. The grandeur of his vision commanded his style, reflecting a temperament which is an amalgam of a sense of reality and a romantic view of time and life. JC is friend to man; his sense of futility is not bitter.

Nobility lies in the struggle, even when hopeless. [Following this critique, JC's "The End of the Tether" is reprinted, pp. 453ff, translated as "Jusqu'au Bout de la Chaine."] [In French.]

461 Aubry, Georges Jean-. "More about *The Nigger of the Narcissus*," BOOKMAN'S JOURNAL AND PRINT COLLECTOR (Lond), XI (Oct 1924), 7-10.

In a conversation on *Nigger,* JC spoke of its conception, the factual sources for James Wait and the ship *Narcissus,* and the source of the epigraph.

462 Aubry, G. Jean-. "Souvenirs" (Fragments), NOUVELLE REVUE FRANÇAISE, XII (1 Dec 1924), 672-80.

During the last ten years of his life, the principal traits of JC's personality were his power, his simplicity, his courtesy, and his gaiety. Some intellectual traits are the vastness of JC's reading, his superb memory, and his "prodigious" knowledge of French. JC admired Flaubert, Proust, and other French writers. [In French.]

463 Aubry, G. Jean-. "Sur la mort de Joseph Conrad" (On the Death of Joseph Conrad), REVUE DE FRANCE, IV (1 Oct 1924), 616-22.

JC's life, though adventurous, was not lived only for adventure's sake. JC was not only a man of genius but was good, simple, and kind. He kept up with the latest developments of European thought and art. His work dramatizes the struggle between man and his ships with the sea. His sense of duty links him with Vigny, Balzac, Flaubert, and Turgenev. [Conventional appreciation.] [In French.]

464 Aubry, Georges Jean-. "Un récent entretien avec le grand romancier Anglais, Joseph Conrad" (A Recent Interview with the Great English Novelist, Joseph Conrad), NOUVELLES LITTÉRAIRES, III (9 Aug 1924), 1.

The interview revealed the circumstances which led to the novels, particularly *The Arrow of Gold* in Marseilles, *The Nigger of the Narcissus* in the Congo in 1896, "An Outpost of Progress," *The Rescue,* and JC's early married life in England. In *Nigger,* Singleton was actually Sullivan, Wait was the name of a Negro on another ship, but beyond minor changes both actually existed, along with most other crew members. [JC reminisces about his literary debt to Edward Garnett, his first publisher, Heinemann, letters exchanged with Robert d'Humières, his French translator, and his first interview with Henry James. A very laudatory article with high praise for the personality and character of the man. Editor's prefatory note on JC's death gives circustances leading to the interview.] [In French.]

465 Aynard, Joseph. "Joseph Conrad," JOURNAL DES DÉBATS, XXXI (12 Aug 1924), 3.

JC's life was a novel in itself, of which the keynote was the moral experience. He transferred this experience into his writings, using the backdrop of foreign places that he knew so well to enhance the human drama of which he was always aware. [Obit. Good analysis of JC's style and contrast with Kipling.] [In French.]

466 [Bone, Muirhead.] "Conrad Spinning Sea Yarns with Bone," LITERARY DIGEST, LXXXII (27 Sept 1924), 31.

[Essentially cites "The Soul of Conrad. An Artist's Impression," MANCHESTER GUARDIAN, XI (1 Aug 1924), 124, describing a passage to America with JC on the *Tuscania*. A discerning personal tribute.]

467 Bone, Muirhead. "Joseph Conrad—A Modern Ulysses," MANCHESTER GUARDIAN, 26 Aug 1924, p. 5; rptd in LIVING AGE, CCCXXII (13 Sept 1924), 551-54.

[Describes passage with JC to America on the *Tuscania*.]

468 Brewster, Dorothy, and Angus Burrell. *"Nostromo:* Twenty Years After," DEAD RECKONINGS IN FICTION (NY: Longmans Green, 1924); essentially rptd as *"Nostromo:* Thirty Years After" in MODERN FICTION (NY: Columbia U P, 1934), pp. 63-84.

An examination of *Nostromo* shows the "double fascination" of JC; the reader is led through the enchantments of charm, color, sunshine, and shadow to the absorbing mystery of the human heart. *Nostromo* is also "our modern life in miniature," with the economic forces triumphant. JC isolates his characters (Dr. Monygham, Nostromo, Decoud) and studies them "in the manner of Chekhov and Katherine Mansfield." *Nostromo* is dazzling in the splendor of its scenes, but ultimately puzzling. It is a dramatization of JC's notion that the universe is "purely spectacular." But JC has his own illusion, that of beauty, which he communicates to his readers.

469 Bridges, Horace James. "Joseph Conrad: A Memorial Tribute," STANDARD, XI (Nov 1924), 75-82.

JC "is forever disturbing us with the mysterious sense of the permanence of what the fleeting moment reveals, and the tragic significance of what seems trivial." "Gaspar Ruiz" is a miniature of JC's whole method, with General Santierra taking the role that Marlow has in other works. His characters change little, most following the pattern of the titular hero of *Almayer's Folly;* what happens within the character is more important than what happens to him. A storyteller such as Marlow allows for deeper character revelation than one normally expects. JC is a "loving, tenderhearted, seeming pessimist" who is ultimately an optimist. [Commemorates JC's death and comments generally on his work.]

470 Brock, H. I. "Joseph Conrad, Able Seaman," NEW YORK TIMES BOOK REVIEW, 10 Aug 1924, pp. 1, 18.

There is much truth and sincerity in JC and his work.

471 Burt, H. T. "Joseph Conrad: An Appreciation," HIBBERT JOURNAL, XXIII (Oct 1924), 141-57.

JC's style developed from "emotional" to "intellectual," structure is based on "the retrospective method," and JC uses a wide spectrum of nationalities and character types. Hardy's philosophy contrasts with JC's. [Brief biography and chronological listing of major works, essays and autobiography.]

472 Cadby, Carine. "Conrad's Dislike of the Camera, and How it was Conquered by Will Cadby," GRAPHIC, CX (1 Nov 1924), 728.

Despite JC's aversion to being photographed he proved "an heroic sitter" for the GRAPHIC photographer. The photographer's assistant made things easier by commenting on "Typhoon" in a way that pleased JC. Although the day was dark, JC sat long and patiently.

473 Cecchi, Emilio. "Indiscrezioni su J. Conrad (1924)" (Indiscretions on Joseph Conrad [1924]), [unlocated]; rptd in SCRITTORI INGLESI E AMERICANI (English and American Writers) (Milan: Carabba, 1935), pp. 186-91.

Ford's JOSEPH CONRAD: A PERSONAL REMEMBRANCE caused general literary arguments. Jessie Conrad resented the book because it does not show her as having a great influence on her husband's literary career. Although Ford considered JC at best a guest in the English language, JC actually used English beautifully, though he spoke it badly. JC's very sense of imperfection in English was a great source of strength in his use of it. [In Italian.]

474 Cecchi, Emilio. "Joseph Conrad," IL CONVEGNO, V (Aug 1924), 375-94; excerpted in NOUVELLE REVUE FRANÇAISE, XXIII (Dec 1924), 805-6; rptd in SCRITTORI INGLESI E AMERICANI (English and American Writers) (Milan: Carabba, 1935), pp. 162-85.

[Brief biographical survey and general critical comments on major works.] [In Italian.]

475 Chevrillon, André. "Conrad," NOUVELLE REVUE FRANÇAISE, XII (1 Dec 1924), 704-7.

JC is a romantic and mystic realist, like so many Slavic and Anglo-Saxon writers. The romantic in him shows in his visionary quality, his preference for the huge and heroic, and his tendency to melodrama. The realist is seen in his attention to accumulation of detail and his precise recording of the visible world. The Slavic heritage is overlaid by his acquired English traits, such as his devotion to ideals of duty and valor. His typical hero is derived from the Anglo-Saxon side of him—the skipper devoid of nerves and imagination who opposes his stubborn will and experience to the unchained furies of nature. Although some of his work is marred by its *longueurs* and its complicated structure, when he writes of the sea and sailors, his style is always direct, rapid, and grandly evocative. [In French.]

> **476** Clifford, Sir Hugh Charles. "Joseph Conrad: Some Scattered Memories," BOOKMAN'S JOURNAL AND PRINT COLLECTOR, XI (Oct 1924), 3-6.

JC and his work were one, "welded parts of a tremendous whole, and that a miracle." His vital personality, love of the sea, artist's sensitive perceptions, writing in a tongue not his native one, all contributed to his individuality as a writer. [Reminiscence similar to the address (1927) to the Ceylon branch of the English Association. Recalls his introduction to JC's work through *Almayer's Folly* while he was bound for England after having spent twelve years in Malaya, his actual introduction to JC, and their subsequent long acquaintance.]

> **477** Connolly, James B. "Conrad the Writer," COLUMBIA (Dec 1924) [not seen]; rptd in CATHOLIC MIND, XXIII (22 Feb 1925), 61-78.

Lord Jim succeeded because no Englishman could believe an Englishman was all bad; *Nostromo* failed because JC had portraits of two not entirely despicable Catholic priests and the public was angered. JC is a failure at sea narratives. "Conrad must have written that storm thing ["Typhoon"] in many sittings with his thesaurus, his books of synonyms and antonyms handy to him." He never had much ability as a storyteller, and what little he had was killed by Jamesian techniques. He "would also have made a good priest, if started that way in time." JC's early Polish life is a capsule history of persecuted Ireland, and this was an advantage. "The advantage of superior race, the moral balance and open-mindedness which should be every Catholic's, were Conrad's in the beginning." Every great artist was a Catholic, including Shakespeare, and JC might have been greater had he remained in the Church. [No understanding of JC's literary principles or preferences.]

> **478** Connolly, Myles. "Hudson, Conrad, and the Simple Style," AMERICA (NY), XXXI (31 May 1924), 162-63.

Neither the extremes of a bizarrely decorated style nor the thinly simple style is good art, but in a crisis "the work of the laboriously clever man" would be preferable. W. H. Hudson is the best example of "selflessness, of natural simplicity, in English literature of these days." [Ford is cited, in reference to "that greatest of modern tales," *Romance*.] JC struggled to attain his style, "a model of sincere and attractive simplicity" [a curious reversal of the usual comment on JC's difficult style]; by style JC meant "habit of mind" to enable him "to transfer his vision to other men." JC's quest for a style was probably "little more than the discovery of himself."

479 "Conrad and His Fame," NATION (NY), CXIX (13 Aug 1924), 157.

JC pleased many classes by his combination of spirit, subtlety of style and adventure. "It was his fortune either that he had no quarrel with his generation, or at least that the generation did not know that he had." He won't retain preeminence in the minds of the masses, "for though he outdistanced in popular estimation certain other great figures, it was not because of enduring artistry."

480 Conrad, Jessie. "A Blessing in Disguise," BOOKMAN (NY), LIX (July 1924), 533-34.

In 1903, a stranger whose appearance was like the description of Hermann in "Falk" frightened Mrs. Conrad at her home near Hythe by attempting to gain entry into the farmhouse to see JC, who was ill with gout, and then by threatening to shoot him at sight. This man, a mad German named Mee, was later imprisoned for many years for fatally shooting a man who, he thought, was laughing at him.

481 Conrad, Jessie. "Joseph Conrad: A Personal Remembrance," TIMES LITERARY SUPPLEMENT (Lond), 4 Dec 1924, p. 826.

This letter intends to correct "a few of the most fantastic statements" made in Ford Madox Hueffer's JOSEPH CONRAD: A PERSONAL REMEMBRANCE (1924). Hueffer endeavors "on every page to show the vast difference between himself and his friend, and always to the detriment of that friend." JC never "poached on Mr. Hueffer's vast stock of plots and material"; JC's books came from chance phrases from histories, memories or travel books. Hueffer was a mental stimulus to JC in his early writing days, but he was not JC's literary advisor.

482 Conrad, Jessie. PERSONAL RECOLLECTIONS OF JOSEPH CONRAD (Lond: pvtly ptd, 1924). [Incorporated in JOSEPH CONRAD AS I KNEW HIM (1926).]

483 "Conrad Pays Tribute to Mark Twain," MENTOR, XII (May 1924), 45.

"On his recent visit to the United States, Joseph Conrad told THE MENTOR of his admiration for Mark Twain, as a writer and as a man who had earned his bread on the water." The one book of Twain's that came closest to JC's own life was THE MISSISSIPPI PILOT, an early edition, perhaps pirated, of LIFE ON THE MISSISSIPPI. JC's description in "Heart of Darkness" of going up the Congo River and Twain's assertion in LIFE ON THE MISSISSIPPI that he must "learn the shape of the river in all the different ways that could be thought of" mark "a very special feeling of fellow craftsmanship . . . , a role that both had described."

484 "Conrad Supplement," TRANSATLANTIC REVIEW, II (Oct 1924), 325-50.

[Contents, abstracted separately, all under 1924: Ford Madox Ford, "C'est toi qui dors dans l'ombre," continued as "Joseph Conrad: A Portrait" in subsequent issues; H.-R. Lenormand, "Il y a quatre ans, en Corse avec Joseph Conrad, coureur de mers"; Ernest Hemingway's untitled tribute; Robert McAlmon's untitled tribute; Ethel Colburn Mayne's untitled tribute; Antoni Potocki's "Le cas de Joseph Conrad."]

485 Curle, Richard. "La fin de Conrad" (Conrad's Last Days), trans by Isabelle Rivière, NOUVELLE REVUE FRANÇAISE, XII (1 Dec 1924), 681-94.

[An almost hour-by-hour account of the last three days of JC's life, including physical symptoms of illness; comments on JC's kindness, his grandeur of spirit, and the fascination of his conversation.] [In French.]

486 Curle, Richard. "Joseph Conrad's Last Day," JOHN O'LONDON'S WEEKLY, XI (20 and 27 Sept 1924), 813-14, 829, 848-49; rptd as "The Last of Conrad," MENTOR, XIII (March 1925), 13-19; separately, as JOSEPH CONRAD'S LAST DAY (Lond: pvtly ptd [Strangeways], 1924); incorporated in THE LAST TWELVE YEARS OF JOSEPH CONRAD (1928).

On the last day of his life, JC attempted to show Richard Curle the new house he had found, but was overtaken by illness and forced to return home, where he died that night. The formidable person who wrote JC's books had about him "a zest of affectionate playfulness," "perfect in its charm." Although JC was in many ways a mysterious and complex man "whom nobody understood profoundly," when he made a friend "he accepted him once and for all." In him were "deep strata of ironic melancholy, aristocratic contempt, and exasperated disillusionment"; but for the people for whom he cared "he had a simplicity of affection which allowed for everything and overlooked all shortcomings."

487 Davray, Henry D. "Joseph Conrad," MERCURE DE FRANCE, CLXXV (1 Oct 1924), 32-55; digested in CHRONIQUE DES LETTRES FRANÇAISES, III (Jan-Feb 1925), 57-61.

JC is essentially a tragedian and a pessimist. His meaning in the symbol of the sea is as a backdrop for men's actions, with the sailing ship as a microcosm of society. [Impressionistic memories of JC's literary beginnings to his death: Henley's early praise of *The Nigger of the Narcissus,* Davray's meeting with JC in a rural train station, JC's wide knowledge of French literature. A brief but interesting biography which relates the writer to England and the various settings of different books to his life.] [In French.]

488 Dinamov, S. "Freia semi ostrovov" (Freya of the Seven Isles), KNIGONOSHA, No. 31 (1924), 6.

[Review.] [In Russian.]

489 Din[amov], S. "Komissioner Dzhekobus" (Agent Jackobus), KNIGONOSHA, No. 43 (1924), 21.

[In Russian.]

490 Dodd, Lee Wilson. "One of the Masters," SATURDAY REVIEW OF LITERATURE, I (9 Aug 1924), 27.

JC possesses the quality of masters, "his great, hallucinated, and therefore hallucinating imagination." When JC is too difficult, confusing or tedious, it is because of "being too much at ease in some private Zion." His watchwords are irony, pity, and loyalty. Notable are JC's summing up ("always pregnant and grave and wise") and his "sudden strokes of characterization." However, "the construction of his longer tales is sometimes willful" and his women do not always come alive. [Review of the Concord Edition of THE WORKS OF JOSEPH CONRAD.]

491 "Editorial Notes," LONDON MERCURY, X (Sept 1924), 449-51.

[Obituary tribute to JC, especially for his longstanding interest in the LONDON MERCURY.]

492 Estaunié, Édouard. "Hommage" (Homage), NOUVELLE REVUE FRANÇAISE, XII (1 Dec 1924), 703.

JC is praiseworthy for his almost hallucinatory creation of mood and the "interior method" by which his characters are endowed with life. [In French.]

493 Fernández, Ramón. "L'art de Conrad" (The Art of Conrad), NOUVELLE REVUE FRANÇAISE, XII (1 Dec 1924), 730-37; rptd in MESSAGES, PREMIÈRE SÉRIE (Paris: Éditions de la Nouvelle Revue Française, 1926); in MESSAGES, trans by Montgomery Belgion (NY: Harcourt, Brace, 1927), 137-51; trans by Charles Owen in THE ART OF JOSEPH CONRAD: A CRITICAL SYMPOSIUM, ed by Robert Wooster Stallman (East Lansing: Michigan State U P, 1960), pp. 8-13.

JC, in avoiding an intellectual appeal in his work, achieves his effects by overwhelming us with sensations." His impressionism imitates a mind's becoming aware of the meaning of action and people. JC's two manners are his chronological tales and intense action, and his stories told by various narrators and employing time-shift. The latter method gives several viewpoints, juxtaposes the past with the present, creates an illusion of reality, and makes the reader concentrate. In addition, the relativity of viewpoint creates the illusion of life's mysteriousness. JC's observers are active moralists who avoid what to him is man's greatest weakness: to doubt in *"one's ability to conduct one's life."* [In French.]

>**494** Ford, Ford Madox. "C'est toi qui dors dans l'ombre . . ." (It Is You Who Sleeps in the Shadow), TRANSATLANTIC REVIEW, II (Oct 1924), 327-37; continued as "Joseph Conrad: A Portrait," ibid., II (Nov 1924), 454-65; (Dec 1924), 570-82; (Jan 1925), 689-700; rptd in JOSEPH CONRAD: A PERSONAL REMEMBRANCE (1924).

Ford explains in his preface that his book is "a novel, not a monograph." The relationship of the two men while collaborating in writing fiction was "curiously impersonal": not once did they discuss each other's past, their "ethical or religious outlook," or any political matter. Both agreed in their attitudes toward the British novel: the novel "went straight forward, whereas in your gradual making acquaintanceship with your fellows you never do go straight forward." In order, therefore, "to get . . . a man in fiction you could not begin at his beginning and work his life chronologically to the end. You must first get him in with a strong impression, and then work backwards and forwards over his past." To achieve "the general effect that life makes on mankind," certain devices seemed useful: impressionism, selection, a special use of conversations, surprise, style (with the sole purpose of making a work interesting), cadence, "justification" (a sense of inevitability), *progression d'effet,* and the most exact use of language possible. Ford remembers best his friend's fear of being jolted in some manner, perhaps by fate, for his aristocratic but gloomy intellect, and his "alert, dark, extremely polished and tyrannous personality." [This "portrait" is useful for understanding JC and his theories and practices in writing, but one must read it with care in order to equate Ford's "impressions" with the facts.]

>**495** Françillon, Robert. "Conrad, psychologue de l'imagination" (Conrad, Psychologist of the Imagination), NOUVELLE REVUE FRANÇAISE, XII (1 Dec 1924), 724-29.

JC's heroes are driven by their imagination into solitude. Like JC dreaming as a boy of going to sea, his heroes are possessed by their dreams to the extent that the dreams are more real than the external world. Yet the dreams are accompanied by ironic doubts of their value. It is not the conflict between illusion and reality but the doubt as to which is which that concerns JC. [In French.]

496 Franklin, John. "New Novels," NEW STATESMAN, XXIV (25 Oct 1924), 81-82.

The Nature of a Crime reflects, in JC's words, "the crudely materialistic atmosphere of the time of its origin."

497 Galsworthy, John. "Introduction," LAUGHING ANNE & ONE DAY MORE: TWO PLAYS BY JOSEPH CONRAD (Lond: Castle, 1924), pp. 5-15; rptd, with one brief deletion, as "Joseph Conrad, Playwright," NEW YORK HERALD TRIBUNE BOOKS, 3 May 1925, pp. 1-2; revd and condensed as "Preface to Conrad's Plays: 1924," CASTLES IN SPAIN AND OTHER SCREEDS (NY: Scribner's; Lond: Heinemann, 1927); rptd (1928), pp. 173-84; rptd in the condensed version as "Preface to Conrad's Plays," FORSYTES, PENDYCES AND OTHERS, Manaton Edition, Vol. XXX (Lond: Heinemann, 1936), pp. 264-71.

The novel suited JC's nature better than the drama, for the novel permitted the "word painting and the subtler efforts of a psychologist."

498 Galsworthy, John. "Souvenirs sur Conrad" (Reminiscences of Conrad), trans by André Maurois, NOUVELLE REVUE FRANÇAISE, XII (1 Dec 1924), 649-58; trans into German by Max Meyerfeld in DIE LITERATUR, XXVII (5 Dec 1924), 194-201; rvd and enlgd as "Reminiscences of Conrad," SCRIBNER'S MAGAZINE, LXXVII (Jan 1925), 3-10; rptd in the revd version as "Reminiscences of Conrad: 1924," CASTLES IN SPAIN AND OTHER SCREEDS (1927; rptd 1928), pp. 99-126; rptd in LESE ZIRKEL (Zurich), XIV (1928-29), 77; rptd in TWO ESSAYS ON CONRAD, WITH THE STORY OF A REMARKABLE FRIENDSHIP BY RICHARD CURLE (1930); rptd in CANDELABRA (1933); rptd as "Wspomnienie o Conradzie," TWÓRCZOŚĆ, Jan 1947, pp. 59-70.

[Galsworthy knew JC thirty-one years, beginning with a voyage of fifty-six days on the *Torrens,* of which JC was first mate, in 1893. He describes and discusses a variety of aspects of JC's life and work: his poverty, his lack of financial commonsense, his illness, his passion for CARMEN and for Meyerbeer, the ordeal of "blood and tears" which his writing was, his loyalty to friends and to ideas, his dynamic energy, his modesty, his lack of literary influences, his best work having appeared before *Chance,* his hatred of any kind of pretentiousness.] [In French.]

499 Garnett, Edward. "Romantic Biography," NATION AND ATHENAEUM, XXXVI (6 Dec 1924), 366, 368.

Ford was "a biographical romanticist" and his JOSEPH CONRAD: A PERSONAL REMEMBRANCE (1924) is "a fictional biography" with the emphasis on fiction. [Garnett introduced Ford to JC and encouraged Ford's early work.] The book captures aspects of JC's home life and the atmosphere in which he worked, but even this is too highly embellished. Ford distorted the relationship between himself and JC, giving far too much credit to himself for the work on which they collaborated, and making JC seem almost dependent on him [points out several severe errors in biography and many mistakes or wilful misinterpretations in Ford's judgment]. [In all, a serious criticism which makes Ford out to be a blatant liar with an embarrassing need for self-glorification.]

  500 Gide, André. "Joseph Conrad," NOUVELLE REVUE FRANÇAISE, XII (1 Dec 1924), 659-62; rptd separately as JOSEPH CONRAD (Liège: Éditions de la Lampe d'Aladdin, 1927); in FEUILLETS D'AUTOMNE (Paris: Mercure de France, 1949), trans by Elsie Pell as AUTUMN LEAVES (NY: Philosophical Library, 1950), pp. 70-75; trans by Charles Owen, in THE ART OF JOSEPH CONRAD: A CRITICAL SYMPOSIUM, ed by Robert Wooster Stallman (East Lansing: Michigan State U P, 1960), pp. 3-5.

JC's chief characteristics are a native nobility, a largeness of outlook, a certain despair—qualities resembling Lord Jim's. In later life, the sea was for JC like an old mistress whom he had abandoned; his dedication to literature had become total, and the sea was simply raw material for his writing. He had a wide knowledge of French literature, and he hated Dostoevski. [A brief *in memoriam* account of JC, to whose work Gide was introduced by Claudel.] [In French.]

  501 "The Gossip Shop," BOOKMAN (NY), LX (Oct 1924), 247-48.

JC's "work stands as an unforgettable tribute to sailors and the sea, a matchless gift of time." [Obituary.]

  502 Gould, Gerald. THE ENGLISH NOVEL TODAY (Lond: John Castle, 1924), pp. 12, 193-94.

JC ranks near the top of the great short story writers. [Only incidentally on JC.]

  503 Graham, Robert B. Cunninghame. "Inveni Portum; Joseph Conrad," SATURDAY REVIEW (Lond), CXXXVIII (16 Aug 1924), 162-63; rptd separately (Cleveland: The Rowfant Club, 1924); trans into French by G. Jean-Aubry in NOUVELLE REVUE FRANÇAISE, XII (1 Dec 1924), 695-702; rptd in REDEEMED AND OTHER SKETCHES (Lond: Heinemann, 1927), pp. 161-71.

[A moving account, with Edwardian mellowness, of JC's burial in Kent.]

  504 Graham, Stephen. "Dat Ole Davil Sea," SATURDAY REVIEW OF LITERATURE, I (6 Sept 1924), 90; rptd in THE DEATH OF YESTERDAY (Lond: Benn, [1930]), pp. 62-70.

Writers about the sea are "romantics all" even when they use the realistic method. JC alone of contemporaries knows the mood of the sea. He is spell-binding, like Coleridge's ancient mariner; Marlow "out-Conrad's Conrad." JC heightens "suspense with an unconcerned leisureliness." There is little of the Pole in him, and nothing Slav, in *Under Western Eyes*. O'Neill's Emperor Jones is similar to JC's Lord Jim: O'Neill "disenchanted the sea yarn" in presenting a "colored Lord Jim." [Often unsubstantiated generalizations, but provocative.]

505 "The Greatest of Sea Writers: Newspaper Tributes to Joseph Conrad," CURRENT OPINION, LXXVII (Sept 1924), 304, 313.

That JC received tributes from newspapers as well as "highbrow journals" proves his "universal appeal." [Extensive quotations.]

506 Grein, J[ames] T[homas]. "*The Secret Agent*—The Late Alfred Capus, November 18, 1922," THE NEW WORLD OF THE THEATRE, 1923-1924 (Lond: Martin Hopkinson, 1924), pp. 1-5; rptd from ILLUSTRATED LONDON NEWS, probably in a 1923 issue [not seen].

JC's dramatization of *The Secret Agent* fails because he has not mastered "two exigencies of stage projection—distribution and economy," but these defects can be removed with practice.

507 Hemingway, Ernest. "Conrad Supplement," TRANSATLANTIC REVIEW, II (Oct 1924), 341-42.

Most people think of JC as a "bad writer" and of T. S. Eliot as a "good writer," but JC's greatness is evident: "If I knew that by grinding Mr. Eliot into a fine dry powder and sprinkling that powder over Mr. Conrad's grave Mr. Conrad would shortly appear, looking very annoyed at the forced return and commence writing I would leave London early tomorrow morning with a sausage grinder."

508 Hoffmann, Richard. "Proportion and Incident in Joseph Conrad and Arnold Bennett," SEWANEE REVIEW, XXXII (Jan 1924), 79-92.

JC uses trifling incidents to suggest "the truth behind the appearance of our world," but Bennett "is even more concerned . . . with the little things of experience." JC's method "is to convey a moment of fragmentary vision into deeper things." With Bennett, "The value of the incident lies within itself entirely." "Bennett's vividness is achromatic; Conrad's is shot through with color. Both pursue a level, but Bennett's is of the commonplace while Conrad's is of the unusual." JC did not go further "than Bennett in not confining his world to matter. It would be nearer true, perhaps, to say that Bennett has explored beyond material bounds and found there nothing.

Conrad . . . has passed beyond and discovered something so vast as to make any material finity inconsequential,—so mysterious as to make it a futile consideration."

509 "Hommage à Joseph Conrad" (Homage to Joseph Conrad), NOUVELLE REVUE FRANÇAISE, XII (1 Dec 1924), [Special Number].
[Contents, separately abstracted, all under 1924: G. Jean-Aubry, "Souvenirs"; André Chevrillon, "Conrad"; Richard Curle, "La fin de Conrad"; Édouard Estaunié, "Hommage"; Ramón Fernández, "L'art de Conrad"; Robert Françillon, "Conrad, psychologue de l'imagination"; John Galsworthy, "Souvenirs sur Conrad"; André Gide, "Joseph Conrad"; Edmond Jaloux, "Joseph Conrad et le roman d'aventures anglais"; R. B. Cunninghame Graham, "Inveni portum. Joseph Conrad"; J. Kessel, "Conrad slave"; H.-R. Lenormand, "Note sur un séjour de Conrad en Corse"; André Maurois, "En marge des marées"; Albert Saugère, "Quelques recherches dans la conscience des héros de Conrad"; Paul Valéry, "Sujet d'une conversation avec Conrad."] [In French.]

510 Hutchison, P[ercy] A[dam]. "Joseph Conrad—Alchemist of the Sea," LITERARY DIGEST INTERNATIONAL BOOK REVIEW, II (Sept 1924), 713-14; condensed as "Conrad's Greatest Romance—Himself," LITERARY DIGEST, LXXXII (13 Sept 1924), 48.
Especially significant is JC's request to sail through the treacherous Torres Strait to Mauritius, identifying him with great navigators like Torres and James Cook. Both the Torres Strait request and his change to novelist were dictated by an "all-compelling imagination." Necessity for the master mariner to have "omnipotence and . . . unremitting vigilance" led to JC's emphasizing solidarity and unfaltering vigilance. He does not fit into the usual categories of realism, romanticism, sentimentalism, or naturalism because to do so would be to compromise, impossible to do with the sea. "To romance he gave the solid foundation and the dignity of realism; his realism he shot through and irradiated with the color and glow of romance."

511 "The Inspirations of Joseph Conrad: A Literary Journey in Pictures," INDEPENDENT, CXIII (27 Sept 1924), 189-92.
[Pictures and a map of the localities of JC's stories.]

512 "The J. B. Pinker Collection of Conradiana," BOOKMAN'S JOURNAL AND PRINT COLLECTOR (Lond), XI (Jan 1924), 190-91.
[First editions and rare pamphlets in the Pinker collection, presented for sale Dec 15-17, 1924, are listed.]

513 J., H. "Joseph Conrad. Uz nas novi roman" (Joseph Conrad. On Our New Novel), OBZOR (Zagreb), XLV: 309 (1924), 2.

[Slight comments accompanying the beginning of a translation of *The Rover* in installments.] [In Serbo-Croatian.]

514 Jaloux, Edmond. "Joseph Conrad et le roman d'aventure anglais" (Joseph Conrad and the English Adventure Novel), NOUVELLE REVUE FRANÇAISE, XII (1 Dec 1924), 713-19; rptd in FIGURES ÉTRANGÈRES (Foreign Personages) (Paris: Plon, 1925), pp. 202-10; and in LITERARISCHE WELT, II (19 Nov 1926), 4-5.

The hero of adventure novels before JC, from Smollett to R. L. Stevenson, was not psychologically believable nor was he intended to be. He was a "flat" character who existed only in terms of the adventures he was created to encounter. JC's heroes are not made for adventure; typically (Heyst, for example), they are uprooted and classless, often intellectual, and placed in or near the unknown or savage parts of the world. They are often closer to a hero of Dostoevski (as Heyst is alone on his island, so Raskolnikov is alone in the middle of men) or of Gorki than to Stevenson's pirate. Stevenson's interest is adventure itself; JC's interest, like that of all great novelists, is to elucidate human nature. His heroes are not depicted with a rigid psychology—like Proust's; they are in a state of "becoming." [In French.]

515 "Joseph Conrad," INDEPENDENT, CXIII (16 Aug 1924), 86-87.

"No novelist of this time has explored the mystery of the heart of man with surer knowledge or exposed it with more vivid clarity. . . . One of the masters is gone." [Obituary notice.]

516 "Joseph Conrad," NOSOTROS, XLVIII (Dec 1924), 513-14.
[Brief review of the contents of the 1 Dec 1924 special issue of NOUVELLE REVUE FRANÇAISE, abstracted separately under author or title.] [In Spanish.]

517 "Joseph Conrad," OUTLOOK (Lond), LIV (9 Aug 1924), 101.

JC's technique makes him a great English writer, and he wisely deals only with what he knows the sea. He has absolutely no art of narrative. He could not make up his mind how to tell his tale; he wanders and nothing happens. Also, he has no humor. His harsh view of life and tragedian's sense, along with his complexity make him a difficult, and therefore, never popular, writer. But his serious view might make him remembered in the future. [Not a very perceptive or detailed analysis.]

518 "Joseph Conrad," SATURDAY REVIEW (Lond), CXXXVIII (9 Aug 1924), 136.

JC is a master of written English because he wrote not with the ease of a native but conscious that "he is using an artistic medium." He had great appeal for English readers because he told sea stories, colored by the exotic East. He is a great novelist in that he had "no theory as to the purpose of life." What mattered to JC was that his characters "should intensely be themselves in a crisis."

519 "Joseph Conrad," WORLD'S WORK (NY), XLVIII (Sept 1924), 478.

[Very short and sketchy biography.]

520 "Joseph Conrad, Seaman and Novelist," OUTLOOK (NY), CXXXVII (13 Aug 1924), 562.

It requires patience to read JC: his method of "inducting the reader into what he wants to show him" is clumsy and "too much like explanatory remarks from off stage."

521 "Joseph Conrad's Heroic Pessimism: What Life Meant to the Author of 'Youth' and 'Typhoon,'" CURRENT OPINION (NY), LXXVII (Nov 1924), 630-31.

JC does not project the spirit of Roman Catholicism; his Catholic characters are invariably "dull and lifeless," if not "repulsive and degraded." [Quotations from JC, H. L. Mencken, George Sterling, G. Jean-Aubry, and others.]

522 Journeyman, The. "Conrad and Cowes," ADELPHI, II (Sept 1924), 254-58.

The London press's lack of interest in JC's death contrasts with reports of a fashionable week at Cowes; an indifferent England passes by its great artists, as it does men like Singleton, for flashy shows. In later life JC deprecated his many sea stories, but they are a lasting tribute to a way of life which is now forever gone. [A very nostalgic article.]

523 Kessel, J. "Conrad slave" (Conrad the Slav), NOUVELLE REVUE FRANÇAISE, XII (1 Dec 1924), 720-23.

Despite JC's denials, there are strong Slavic elements in his writings: his typical hero is *déclassé;* his characters define themselves by their own words, in long dialogues full of digressions; there are the "infinite stratification of moral nuance" and the "hidden richness of the human soul." Very close similarities, even to identical phrases, exist between *Under Western Eyes* and CRIME AND PUNISHMENT. JC's celebrated aversion to Dostoevski is part of a love-hate feeling of the Polish author for the Russian. [In French.]

524 L., T. "Dzhozef Konrad" (Joseph Conrad), KRASNAIA NIVA, No. 36 (1924), 877.

[In Russian.]

525 Lenormand, H.-R. "Il y a quatre ans, en corse avec Joseph Conrad, coureur de mers" (Four Years in Corsica with Joseph Conrad, the Sea Rover), TRANSATLANTIC REVIEW, II (Oct 1924), 338-40.

[A dramatist who had known JC in Ajaccio four years before the novelist's death praises JC as a person and for his works; but he recognizes the great writer's Polish prejudices—doubtless ethnical—against Russian novelists, even against Dostoevski. Also see Lenormand's "Met den zeevaarder Joseph Conrad op Corsica," WITTE MIER, I (1924), 332-34 (not seen) and his "Note sur un séjour de Conrad en Corse," NOUVELLE REVUE FRANÇAISE, XXIII (1 Dec 1924), 666-71, trans in THE ART OF JOSEPH CONRAD: A CRITICAL SYMPOSIUM, ed by R. W. Stallman (1960).] [In French.]

526 Lenormand, H.-R. "Note sur un séjour de Conrad en Corse" (A Note on Conrad's Sojourn in Corsica), NOUVELLE REVUE FRANÇAISE, XII (1 Dec 1924), 666-71; excerpted in THE ART OF JOSEPH CONRAD: A CRITICAL SYMPOSIUM, ed by Robert Wooster Stallman (East Lansing: Michigan State U P, 1960), pp. 5-8.

While in Ajaccio during the winter of 1921, JC revealed the fact that even with his literary eminence and the popular success he had finally achieved he was beset with doubts, and the act of writing was so exhausting as to reduce him to despair. Questioned about the complexities of meaning in some of his novels, such as the incest theme in *Almayer's Folly,* he was unwilling to explore them and seemed unconscious of the deeper layers which his own unconscious mind had created. As for his attitude toward other writers, he refused to read Freud; he admired Kipling, Hardy, and Bennett; he detested Meredith; he had an aversion to Dostoevski; and he admired Turgenev. [In French.]

527 "Letters and Art: Joseph Conrad," LITERARY DIGEST, LXXXII (23 Aug 1924), 27-28.

JC is unique in having taken up a foreign language and used it "as well as the best." [Quotations from and summaries of newspaper articles about JC. Reproduces a page of JC manuscript.]

528 "Life, Letters, and the Arts: Tributes to Joseph Conrad," LIVING AGE, CCCXXII (20 Sept 1924), 613-14.

[Quotations from articles praising JC, especially those in OUTLOOK and the NEW STATESMAN. Their "honest sincerity" shows how deep an impression JC made on his age.]

529 "The Literary Circle," AMERICA (NY), XXXI (30 Aug 1924), 479.

The Requiem Mass was said in JC's parish, and in one of his last letters JC praised Francis McCullagh's THE BOLSHEVIK PERSECUTION OF CHRISTIANITY. [McCullagh was about to go to America on a lecture tour. A letter to the editor replying to John K. Ryan, "Conrad's Catholicism Questioned," ibid. (19 April 1924), 14.]

530 McAlmon, Robert. "Conrad Supplement," TRANSATLANTIC REVIEW, II (Oct 1924), 343-44.

JC's greatness as a novelist and the "Slavic touch" that he brought to "the psychologic development of his characters and scenes" are worthy of note. In his work there is "a clarity, and directness to his intelligence" that could very well be English even if his style is sometimes difficult to read. His mind was modern, and his "austere fatalism" seldom has "any kind of moralization" in it. JC often wrote "out of sheer will to write." In his works there is "an intelligence which commands respect" as well as "a quality of grandeur" possessed by few other writers of the past generation.

531 MacCarthy, Desmond. "Literary Causerie: To a Distant Friend (VIII)," EMPIRE REVIEW, XL (Sept 1924), 291-99; rptd, trans into French, by Betty Colin, in EUROPE (REVUE MENSUELLE), VI (15 Dec 1924), 470-79.

JC respected originality only if accompanied by an "aesthetic sense," the ability "to write a fine sentence." Influenced profoundly by England and English seamen, JC "remained in temperament a fierce, independent, sensitive, magniloquent Pole, with a far-ranging speculative imagination." *A Personal Record* and *Notes on Life and Letters* offer a better understanding of JC and "the relation in which his way of thinking stood to his work" than anything others have written about him. His constant theme is "the spirit of loyalty in men, struggling, sometimes victoriously, sometimes vainly, either against the forces of nature, or the power of mean persons." A profoundly ethical author writing about an indifferent universe, JC believed that man's glory is to have put justice and honor in that universe. He became a writer "because he had seen so many things in human nature that he did not wish to be forgotten."

532 McFee, William. "Rolling Home," SATURDAY REVIEW OF LITERATURE, I (6 Sept 1924), 89-90; rptd in SWALLOWING THE ANCHOR (Lond: Heinemann; NY: Doubleday, Page, 1925), 107-12.

JC's achievement complements Kipling's. Both brilliant authors write of the East. Kipling insists on "draughtsmanship and the color*est* view of writing," JC captures "the travail of a soul expressing itself as an alien idiom."

533 Malone, Andrew E. "Joseph Conrad: 1857-1924," STUDIES (Dublin), XIII (Sept 1924), 457-66.

JC in describing Marlow as revealing meaning "as a glow brings out a haze" is describing his own method—the meaning envelops a tale but is not seen until a glow illuminates it from within. "All his writing is one long look backward and inward." [Malone reviews JC's early years, the publication of *Almayer's Folly* and *An Outcast of the Islands* (containing some of JC's best work).] *Tales of Unrest* lacks ease and has a rhetorical style which makes it his worst work. *The Nigger of the Narcissus* is his "most perfect work"; *Lord Jim* is fine and JC's most popular work before 1914. After "Youth," "Heart of Darkness," and "Typhoon," "reminiscence ceased to dominate," for *Nostromo* "was deliberate creation." *The Mirror of the Sea* is his "happiest book"—full of "spontaneous lyricism." With *The Secret Agent* (1907) and *Under Western Eyes,* JC began his period of popularity. With *Chance* (1914) and *Victory,* JC had "arrived," but these later works are not his best. In his last book (*The Rover*), JC "reached his highest again." The cause of doom is in each character, not blind destruction as in Hardy. As a stylist he "had few compeers." His "romantic realism" gave the novel new inspiration. [Essentially an obituary appreciation.]

534 "A Master Dies," INDEPENDENT, CXIII (16 Aug 1924), 110-11.

[Inconsequential obituary notice.]

535 Maurois, André. "En marge des marées" (On the Edge of the Tides), NOUVELLE REVUE FRANÇAISE, XII (1 Dec 1924), 708-12.

JC's typical hero is a silent and simple man. To avoid the omniscient point of view, to achieve greater realism, JC selects a vocal and sophisticated narrator to describe the silent man. Often secondary narrators are employed to supply, in a believable manner, other aspects of the narrative than those with which the primary narrator has been established as familiar. When the method succeeds, as it does in JC's best books, when the narrators are drawn direct from JC's own experiences, the advantages gained in credibility are so great that one does not too much miss the clarity and simplicity of direct exposition. The narrator method became a fixed habit to the extent that if JC could not draw on his memory for a narrator, he invented one. These inventions are unsuccessful. JC does not believe in the invented Jones and Ricardo of *Victory* in the way that he believes in the sailors—whom he had actually known—in "Typhoon." JC invariably needed the hint from real life to develop his fictions. His imagination could not operate successfully in a vacuum, and his total inventions remain inventions and unreal. [One wonders if what Maurois is saying about JC could not be said of any writer.] [In French.]

536 Mayne, Ethel Colburn. "Conrad Supplement," TRANSATLANTIC REVIEW, II (Oct 1924), 345-47.

JC's death left the effect of "a light gone out." *Lord Jim* especially caused us "to have stood for judgment on ourselves"; in this book there are greatness, loveliness, and even "heavenliness." JC's books reveal "a passion of fidelity" and the presence of "a conscious artist." His women are remote, except for the girl in *Chance,* and this girl is undoubtedly the reason for the "boom" of that novel. Some of the shorter tales such as "Typhoon" serve best as an introduction to "the heights and depths to which *Lord Jim* will take you."

537 "The Meaning of Conrad," NEW REPUBLIC, XXXIX (20 Aug 1924), 341-42.

JC is at the beginning of a new era in literary history. He describes sensually and subjectively, has verbal beauty and is preoccupied with the unknown. "The theme which [he] presents most constantly is one of affection, devotion, protection, tested by danger, by the fury of nature and by the craft of savage men, calling out courage, loyalty, endurance, sacrifice."

538 Mencken, Henry Louis. "Joseph Conrad," NATION (NY), CXIX (20 Aug 1924), 179.

JC's realism went beyond careful representation; "it struck for the inner reality of things." Only his "thumping good stories" are remembered now. Others are forgotten, for the reader expects an answer in the books, and is asked a question. "More, there is a dismaying tone in the question, as if no answer were really expected." JC expresses the "serene skepticism of a scientist."

539 Moult, Thomas. "Joseph Conrad," BOOKMAN (Lond), LXVI (Sept 1924), 301-4.

JC's work cannot be adequately analysed, and critical attempts have failed. "Essentially it expressed, and continued to express, the pessimistic, harsh, and sinister vision of a Polish aristocrat." JC's work is divided into three periods: (1) *Almayer's Folly* and *An Outcast of the Islands,* where sea experience adds technical terms and some technique; (2) from *Lord Jim* to *Typhoon, and Other Stories,* where the sea becomes the symbol for a philosopher's "given set of circumstances"; and (3) the storyteller period of *Chance* to *The Rover.* [This article seems a bit facile.]

540 Moult, Thomas. "Joseph Conrad," QUARTERLY REVIEW (NY), CCXLII (Oct 1924), 247-61.

JC's death may be equated with the passing of the age of sail which he did so much to record. JC "was the first psychologist of the sea and the sailor" and his "disciplined symbolism" is better in its way than Melville's sea literature or James's character insights. JC's constant search for the chink in human character is essentially sinister and pessimistic, an offshoot of his Polish and Slavic background which he never moves away from. JC as Marlow achieves his best work in indirect narration, and fictional sources may be seen in JC's biography. JC's view of women is incomplete from his long years at sea, but he makes up for this by his reverence. There is an irony in viewing JC's years of literary struggle with poverty. [Cites some humorous domestic incidents between JC, Crane, and Huneker. Notes JC's comparison of himself to Flaubert in the way both had to struggle with their prose.]

541 Muir, Edwin. "A Note on Mr. Conrad," LATITUDES (Lond: Melrose, nd; NY: Huebsch, 1924), pp. 47-56.

That JC, "incomparably the most subtle writer of his age," has no "philosophy" indicates how much lies behind his work. Three outstanding qualities of his novels are the love of beauty, the insight into the human mind, and the sense of character. He shows man in his relation, not to God, but to men and to nature. He is interested essentially in beauty, the mind, and character. In his ethics, reason is moral and the irrational, immoral. His heroes fight to maintain a few truisms: thus, "Man voyages over the devouring waste of existence on nothing more stable than a few concepts, a few platitudes." But only JC's profound mind could have given such fundamental meaning to platitude.

542 "New Novels," TIMES LITERARY SUPPLEMENT (Lond), 2 Oct 1924, p. 610.

In *The Nature of a Crime,* JC is "breathing an atmosphere which did not suit him." But the collaboration with Ford Madox Hueffer [Ford] is not beneath notice; it has some appealing pages.

543 Page, R. Edison. "Recent English Novels," TRANSATLANTIC REVIEW, I (May 1924), 365.

JC's *The Rover* is a dreary, historical romance; "and when Mr. Conrad gets away from the people he has met, he is not at all at his best." [Quite incidental, minimal reference to JC.]

544 "Pictorial Survey of the Literary Life of Joseph Conrad," SATURDAY REVIEW OF LITERATURE, I (18 Oct 1924), 206-7.

[Contains pictures, mostly of settings for JC's work.]

545 Potocki, Antoni. "Le cas de Joseph Conrad" (The Case of Joseph Conrad), TRANSATLANTIC REVIEW, II (Oct 1924), 348-50.

JC's work was to bring into rapport three different races that dominate the earth, the Slavic, the Anglo-Saxon, and the Latin. This he did by means of his art, which reveals the basic meaning of life. His creations are symbolic types *"fidèles à leur propre code d'honneur."* JC introduced into modern English literature "la sublime, la rédemptrice figure de Don Quichotte." [In French.]

546 Rascoe, Burton. "Contemporary Reminiscences: A Remembered Interview with Conrad on the Occasion of His First Visit to America," ARTS AND DECORATION, XXI (Sept 1924), 36, 63, 65.

JC stayed with Frank N. Doubleday while visiting America, but was too ill to travel much. A small group of reporters [including Rascoe] interviewed JC aboard the *Tuscania*. It was a bad interview, the reporters being tongue-tied, JC shy and nervous [several columns of passages from JC are quoted]. Among JC's comments: "Enthusiasm makes life interesting." JC denies having a critical mind or much general culture. [Rascoe's general impression: JC is complex under a simple exterior, a man hard to know, a "rigid disciplinarian" impatient with laziness, a gentle, kind, tender, compassionate man. Essentially an obituary appreciation based on JC's visit to America one year before his death.]

547 Reid, Forrest. "A Conrad Story," NATION AND ATHENAEUM, XXXVI (11 Oct 1924), 58-60.

The Nature of a Crime is "definitely unlike" JC's other works, with nothing present to indicate the scale of moral values. The lack of irony leaves "a slightly sentimental flavour," and any importance in the work lies almost entirely in "the grace of the writing."

548 Roman, F. Vinci. "Popular Fiction and Publishers' Notes: Early Conrad; *The Nature of a Crime* in Format Much Too Flattering," NEW YORK WORLD (Editorial Section), 12 Oct 1924, p. 8E.

The Nature of a Crime shows "an effeminateness of touch, a mincing glorying in detail" not characteristic of the rest of JC's work. This "carefully drawn" "case history," which in places is like the "painstaking analysis of James," should have been left in the TRANSATLANTIC REVIEW (1923).

549 "*Romance:* An Analysis. (I)," TRANSATLANTIC REVIEW, I (Feb 1924), 84-89.

A collaboration between JC and Ford Madox Hueffer, *Romance* was "a friendly . . . contest of wills," so exhausting that in the course of several years, "two definite breakdowns occurred." [A passage from the fifth part of *Romance* is printed. "The writer will give, by way of souvenir, a small prize—say, a copy of *Romance!*—to any reader who shall first identify this sentence—or more properly, this phrase."]

550 Ross, Ernest Carson. "The Development of the English Sea Novel from Defoe to Conrad." Unpublished thesis, University of Virginia, 1924 (Ann Arbor, Mich: Edwards Brothers, 1926). [Mimeographed.]

551 Ryan, John K. "Conrad's Catholicism Questioned," AMERICA (NY), XXXI (19 April 1924), 14.

Although JC is listed in the English Catholic Directory, his "sympathies are anything but orthodox," even in stories set in a Catholic country and among Catholic people (*The Arrow of Gold, Nostromo*). In *Arrow,*

"Catholic" characters (Therese, de Villarel) are "wretched caricatures"; in *Nostromo,* Holroyd's and Decoud's theories have "at least implied approval by their author." [See "The Literary Circle," ibid. (30 Aug 1924), 479 for a reply.]

552 S[argent], G. H. "Conrad Manuscripts in America," BOOKMAN'S JOURNAL, IX (Jan 1924), 137-39.

[This record of the sale of JC MSS and first editions records the name of each item, its sale price, and the person to whom it was sold. The gross for all items was $110,990.]

553 Saugère, Albert. "Quelques recherches dans la conscience des héros de Conrad" (Some Investigations into the Conscience of Conrad's Heroes), NOUVELLE REVUE FRANÇAISE, XII (1 Dec 1924), 738-42.

[Disconnected reflections (a series of *pensées*) on the metaphysic of JC's heroes. They are compared and contrasted to those of Dostoevski. Their relationship to Fate, God, and numerous other abstractions is considered.] [In French.]

554 Sée, Ida R. "Joseph Conrad à Montpellier" (Joseph Conrad at Montpellier), PETIT MÉRIDIONAL (Montpellier), 6 Sept 1924, p. [1].

JC visited (1906-1908) Montpellier with his wife and two small sons because of the city's reputation as a medical center, one of his boys needing treatment. JC was modest; he admired Flaubert above other French writers; loved the old houses and streets of Montpellier, whose horizons rivalled those of Greece or Palestine. He saw in the city "a grand old lady who does not seek to 'impress' because she is *sure* of pleasing the lovers of pure beauty." He brought away from that city the greatest joy of his life—the restored health of his son. [Obit. Mme. Sée served as French teacher.] [In French.]

555 Seligmann, Herbert J. "Suavity and Color," NEW YORK EVENING POST LITERARY REVIEW, V (27 Sept 1924), 4.

The Nature of a Crime, a rediscovered, early bit of collaboration by Ford and JC, is "less an actuality than the construction of two stylish imaginations." In the appended passages from *Romance,* showing parts that each writer contributed, "suavity" predominates in Ford's writing and in JC's.

556 Shand, John. "Some Notes on Joseph Conrad," CRITERION (Lond), III (Oct 1924), 6-14; rptd in THE ART OF JOSEPH CONRAD: A CRITICAL SYMPOSIUM, ed by Robert Wooster Stallman (East Lansing: Michigan State U P, 1960), pp. 13-19.

General reflections on JC's writing include criticism of his digressional methods and too deliberately elaborate prose.

557 Shanks, Edward. "Mr. Joseph Conrad," LONDON MERCURY, IX (March 1924), 502-11; rptd in SECOND ESSAYS ON LITERATURE (Lond: Collins, 1927), pp. 23-40.

Some of JC's great popularity is due to his writing in an age when distant places had great appeal for many Englishmen. In "The Return," JC's strength is as "the novelist of situation and *not* of character." JC's prefaces are remarkable for the views, not always complimentary and sometimes self-contradictory, which they give us of the artist himself. JC was a dramatist in prose, subjecting well-defined characters to the particular event, and making plots a series of emotionally charged crises. *The Arrow of Gold* and the *Tremolino* incident of *The Mirror of the Sea* show how a single incident lingered in the author's memory, and is all that connects the two stories—there is no real thematic unity. The difficulties of JC's narrative method are necessitated by his view of life. [Concludes with a survey of JC's influence on English letters.]

558 Sherman, Stuart P. MEN OF LETTERS OF THE BRITISH ISLES: PORTRAIT MEDALLIONS FROM LIFE. By Theodore Spicer-Simson. With Critical Essays by Stuart P. Sherman (NY: Rudge, 1924), pp. 39-40.

"Two contrasting elements conspire in the work of Conrad for its peculiar distinction and significance: a temperament which responds powerfully to the deduction of the elemental and a character which resists seduction." JC tracked Romance on the sea and found that she was not there. "Though Conrad's vision of Nature is tremendously disillusioned, yet in the midst of his disillusion there gleams again for him, redemptively, the true Romance, the Great Adventure, namely, the discovery of one's own virtue, the maintenance, against the buffeting of the elements, of one's own essence." JC made his voyages into religious symbols; and his heroes, incarnations of a simple, strong, traditional faith.

559 Sholl, Anna McClure. "Joseph Conrad," CATHOLIC WORLD, CXIX (Sept 1924), 799-806.

JC has a "profound and virile understanding of life," "recognition of the value of unmarked and unheralded humanity," and fascination with "the lost causes of this world." [Laudatory obituary emphasizing JC as a writer of sea stories.]

560 Strunsky, Simeon. "About Books, More or Less: Complex or Complicated," NEW YORK TIMES BOOK REVIEW, 17 Aug 1924, p. 4.

JC's method became simpler during the last ten years of his life, "emancipating itself from introspections that were not infrequently longueurs." JC sometimes used refined analysis on very simple problems. Marlow "finds astonishment in everything."

561 Symons, Arthur. "Joseph Conrad: A Personal Impression," QUEEN, CLV (20 Aug 1924), 5.

JC is "one of the most original and sinister and somber personalities of our time." He is a great novelist even though his novels "have no plots" and women are not at the center of them. *Lord Jim* is JC's best novel, illustrating "applauded heroism." "To read Conrad is to shudder on the edge of a gulf, in a silent darkness." He is inscrutable and "almost inhuman" at times; his prose is thus "fantastically inhuman, like fiery ice" with "an almost uncalculable fascination." "When a soul plays Dice with the Devil there is only a second in which to win or lose: but the second may be worth an eternity." [A memorial tribute.]

562 Talbot, Francis X. "Conrad, Seas and Men," AMERICA (NY), XXXI (23 Aug 1924), 452-53.

Although famous at his death, JC is still not popular; he "was too subtly artistic in his stories"; he used Marlow, always "a bore," too much; in *The Rover* he bewilders the reader "by abruptly shifting his time and place"; and he builds no plots. "[P]reeminently he was the historian of the seas and the searcher of souls." His gropings into "the labyrinthine complexities of the souls of his characters" make his portraits memorable as his stories are not. JC "could not write a story unless he had some psychical problem to work out in it." JC's work will live as Shakespeare's does. [Obit.]

563 "This Week's Books," SPECTATOR (Lond), CXXXIII (4 Oct 1924), 472, 474.

The Nature of a Crime seems to be more by Ford Madox Hueffer [Ford] than by JC. JC may possibly have written half of it, but he could not have "interfered much in the progress and air of the story."

564 Tittle, Walter. "Portraits in Pencil and Pen II," CENTURY, CVIII (Sept 1924), 641-45; and see ibid., CVI (May 1923), 53-61 for pt. I and reprinting.

"Frequently in his gayer moments Mr. Conrad indulges in whimsical raillery . . . revealing a quaint imaginative gift for nonsense that rarely appears in his writings. At table he often indulges this lighter mood." [JC mourns the passing of sailing ships and rugged seamen. He comments enthusiastically on Spain and his youthful experiences in Barcelona. Conversation with JC during a one-day sitting for a portrait in Bishopshire, shortly after his return from a month in America.]

565 Townsend, R. D. "The Book Table," OUTLOOK (NY), CXXXVI (9 Jan 1924), 69-70.

Even if *The Nigger of the Narcissus* and *Lord Jim* are likely to be considered JC's masterpieces, *The Rover* is "matchless in the impression it leaves of outstanding characters," especially in that of Peyrol, "a clear, actual, living personality." And "quite minor characters" are "done with a sure touch." It is "a great story . . . sometimes apparently half telling this or that, but always finally bringing out situation and action, and moving on to a heroic and satisfying climax."

> **566** Valéry, Paul. "Sujet d'une conversation avec Conrad" (Subject of a Conversation with Conrad), NOUVELLE REVUE FRANÇAISE, XII (1 Dec 1924), 663-65.

After two meetings, JC seemed "the most affable and agreeable man in the world." In a conversation, JC said that France had never attained supremacy on the seas because, though superior in individual combats with the British, the French fleet in mass engagements, acting upon the orders of Versailles, were always defeated by the British. [Valéry told JC of the great French fleet that Napoleon was having constructed at the time of Waterloo—implying that if it had been completed, France would finally have attained supremacy of the seas.] [In French.]

> **567** Vidaković, Aleksandar. "Josif Conrad" (Joseph Conrad), SRPSKI KNJIZEVNI GLASNIK (Belgrade), N.S. XIII: 2 (1924), 160.

[In Serbo-Croatian.]

> **568** Vinaver, Stanislav. "Smrt Josepha Conrada" (The Death of Joseph Conrad), VREME (Belgrade), No. 949 (11 Aug 1924), 5.

[A personal tribute to JC, stressing the metaphorical unity of his sea imagery and his narrative technique.] [In Serbo-Croatian.]

> **569** W., G. "Conrad, the Man," NEW YORK EVENING POST LITERARY REVIEW, IV (9 Aug 1924), 952.

[Reminiscences of JC, emphasizing shyness and desire for seclusion in his study.]

> **570** W., G. "More About Conrad," NEW YORK EVENING POST LITERARY REVIEW, V (30 Aug 1924), 8.

[Reminiscences.]

> **571** Ward, Alfred C. "Joseph Conrad: 'Typhoon,' " ASPECTS OF THE MODERN SHORT STORY: ENGLISH AND AMERICAN (Lond: University of London P, 1924; Lincoln, Neb: MacVeagh, 1925; NY: Dial P, 1925), pp. 145-57.

JC's view of the world includes both the "hidden unity of human life" and its "infinite diversity." The "Typhoon" volume contains three-dimensional characters created by accumulated evidence drawn from varied sources. JC's purpose in the story is to show Captain MacWhirr, a simple ordinary man, in conflict with the physical forces of nature—and a winner; and in order to do this, he utilizes direct external description, he exhibits the man in action, and he employs the evidence of the shipbuilders. Thus man endures and prevails; JC's view of life, therefore, is not pessimistic.

572 West, H. F. "Joseph Conrad's Funeral," SATURDAY REVIEW OF LITERATURE, I (6 Sept 1924), 96.

[Impressionistic and pictorial reminiscence of the day JC was buried: the countryside, the weather, snippet from the church service, the mourners—Edward Garnett, W. W. Jacobs, Cunninghame Graham, and Richard Curle.] It was striking that such a great man had such a small funeral. "But the really great men, I suppose, die and go to their graves with no pomp and pageantry."

573 Woolf, Leonard. "Joseph Conrad," NATION AND ATHENAEUM, XXXV (9 Aug 1924), 595; rptd in ESSAYS ON LITERATURE, HISTORY, POLITICS . . . (Lond: Hogarth P; NY: Harcourt, Brace, 1927), pp. 57-71.

JC belongs "to the school of the great self-conscious stylists"—a born craftsman and artist as opposed to more cerebral writers—Shaw and Hardy. JC's style is the starting point of criticism about him because he consciously used it as a vehicle of emotive power. JC had no politics, no social axes to grind. He had no plots as such, only incidents. Perfect method was to him a prerequisite to the conveyance of any message. The last novels seem to some readers [Woolf himself] "a kind of tropic calm, a letting down in intensity." He held the honor of his art very high.

574 [Woolf, Virginia.] "Joseph Conrad," TIMES LITERARY SUPPLEMENT (Lond), 14 Aug 1924, pp. 493-94; rptd in THE COMMON READER (Lond: Hogarth P; NY: Harcourt, Brace, 1925); combined edition (1948), pp. 309-18; and in COLLECTED ESSAYS, Four Volumes (Lond: Hogarth P, 1966; NY: Harcourt, Brace, 1967), I, 302-8.

JC was compounded of two men: the sea captain and Marlow. The sea captain dominates the early works; Marlow, the middle works. "After the middle period Conrad never again was able to bring his figures into perfect relation with their background. He never believed in his later and more highly sophisticated characters as he had believed in his early seamen, because when he had to indicate their relation to that other unseen world of the novelists, the world of values and convictions, he was far less sure what those values were."

575 Young, Filson. " 'French Literature' in England," NEW YORK TIMES BOOK REVIEW, 24 Aug 1924, p. 8.

The world of letters sustained an irremediable loss with the death of JC although his death will leave no gap in the social circle, since he preferred to live and work in the bosom of his family. He spoke English with an accent, but was acknowledged a master of English prose. He once told a friend that when writing a novel, "he thought in Polish, arranged his thoughts in French, and expressed them in English."

576 Zelie, John Sheridan. "A Burial in Kent," CHRISTIAN CENTURY, XLI (23 Oct 1924), 1363-64; rptd in Eldridge L. Adams, CONRAD: THE MAN. WITH A BURIAL IN KENT (NY: Rudge, 1925), pp. 55-72.

JC's quiet funeral in St. Thomas's Catholic Church in Canterbury and his burial in the cemetery there provide a strange contrast to "winds and waves and skies" and "the elemental and the universal" with which the great writer was associated during his life.

1925

577 Atteridge, A. H. "Conrad the Catholic," CATHOLIC MIND, XXIII (22 Feb 1925), 78-80; also in COLUMBIA (1925) [not seen].

JC's disavowal of the Catholic faith as an adult may be attributed to his years at sea among morally depraved men. There are no informing Roman Catholic principles in JC's work or any real use of good Catholics in characterization. The family had Catholic rites for JC after his death, but JC did not receive extreme unction. [Also see J. B. Connolly, "Conrad the Writer," COLUMBIA (Dec 1924).]

578 Aubry, G[eorges] Jean-. "The Inner History of Conrad's *Suspense:* Notes & Extracts from Letters," BOOKMAN'S JOURNAL, XII (Oct 1925), 3-10.

The public expected *The Rover* to be a full-scale Napoleonic novel. JC had not planned such a book, but had a notion about dealing with an episode on Elba. In a letter to J. B. Pinker, JC indicated he was working on a Mediterranean novel but needed "to discover the moral pivot." JC interrupted *Chance* to write "The Duel," which covers the Napoleonic period. Aubry gives the background to explain JC's interest in the Napoleonic story and his preparation for it. The subject haunted him longer than any other; he kept putting off the completion of *Suspense*. Letters and other documents give evidence of work on the novel after about summer, 1920. Evidence shows JC's borrowing from life for some characters; Cosmo Latham, however, is "a pure invention." Cosmo is like John Kemp in *Romance* or Mr. George in *The Arrow of Gold*. Thus, *Suspense* is not in JC's later manner. Miscellaneous notes give slight clues to JC's plans for ending *Suspense*.

579 Aubry, Georges Jean-. "Joseph Conrad au Congo: d'après des documents inédits," MERCURE DE FRANCE, CLXXXIII (15 Oct 1925), 289-338; pub separately (Paris: Extrait de *Mercure de France,* 1925); trans as JOSEPH CONRAD IN THE CONGO (Lond: "The Bookman's Journal" Office, 1926).

[Written before Aubry was able to prepare a "full story" of JC's life, this book was intended to show by an example—JC's journey to the Congo in 1890—how his life and work are merged, how one is the result of the other, how experience is responsible for "the stirring illusion of real life which pervades all his work," and how the "magnificent personality" of the man, with his "penetration and depth," has "recreated, enriched and animated his written recollections." Excellent in its time for biographical information, but only slightly critical. Largely incorporated in Aubry's LIFE AND LETTERS (1927).] [In French.]

580 Bone, David. "Memories of Conrad," SATURDAY REVIEW OF LITERATURE, II (7 Nov 1925), 286.

[Letter, written for the Seaman's Church Institute of NY, whose main reading room was dedicated to JC. Recollections of acquaintance with JC.]

581 "Books and Authors," AMERICA (NY), XXXIV (7 Nov 1925), 94.

Suspense might have been JC's "greatest novel"; it is interesting in revealing a JC novel in the making. Regrettably, there is no evidence of JC's Catholicism.

582 "Books in Brief," NATION (NY), CXXI (23 Dec 1925), 738.

Suspense has all of the familiar JC techniques. "It has elaboration and an extraordinary vividness of natural setting and an equally extraordinary dulness of development. . . . As in the other Conrad novels, the mighty initial groundswell does not carry one to the revelation of divine godhead."

583 Brickell, Herschel. "An Armful of Fiction," BOOKMAN (NY), LXII (Nov 1925), 337-38.

Not only is *Suspense* incomplete, the chapters that remain are "in need of file and sandpaper," but the work is "invested with an inevitable fascination" because it marks the close of "a great man's career."

584 Bridges, Horace James. "The Genius of Joseph Conrad," THE GOD OF FUNDAMENTALISM AND OTHER STORIES (Chicago: Pascal Covici, 1925), pp. 297-319.

JC's characters are not self-revealing; we see them "through the eyes of others. The narrator . . . is a device for disclosing to us more of the character than he is himself aware of, and also for conveying the impression he has made upon his fellows." Two of JC's strengths are "his power of analyzing the wounded or bewildered soul" and "his mastery of all the secrets of the sea." A serious weakness of his work is his dialogue, for "he stumbles and stutters" in it.

585 "Briefer Mention," DIAL, LXXIX (Oct 1925), 350.

Tales of Hearsay, "beautifully fitted mosaics," illustrate different periods in JC's work.

586 Budnev, V. *"Na Vzliad Zapada"* (*Under Western Eyes*), KNIGONOSHA, Nos. 15-16 (1925), 24.

[In Russian.]

587 Chadbourne, Marc. "Du nouveau sur la collaboration de Joseph Conrad avec Ford Madox Hueffer" (Another Look at the Collaboration of Joseph Conrad with Ford Madox Hueffer), NOUVELLES LITTÉRAIRES, IV (18 July 1925), 5.

Ford's statements about his and JC's collaboration and their mutual admiration are reliable. Ford and JC loved Flaubert and felt *Romance* had been written by a third person (Flaubert) rather than by either one of them. Ford's JOSEPH CONRAD: A PERSONAL REMEMBRANCE (1924) is an accurate account of a deep and abiding literary friendship. [See Edward Garnett's review in NATION AND ATHENEUM, XXXVI (6 Dec 1924), 366, 368 for a more critical judgment.] [In French.]

588 Chew, Samuel C. "Essays on *Suspense*. I," SATURDAY REVIEW OF LITERATURE, II (14 Nov 1925), 289-90.

JC's trip to Corsica and Elba was not merely to get "local color" for *The Rover,* but for his unfinished romance, *Suspense.* [First-place entry in SRL Conrad contest.]

589 "Conrad Books and Manuscripts," TIMES LITERARY SUPPLEMENT (Lond), 25 Feb 1925, p. 144.

[Sale announcement and partial description of JC's manuscripts, corrected typescripts, proofs, and personal book collection.]

590 "Conrad Fought Death to Finish His Book, Author's Widow Tells of Last Vain Efforts," NEW YORK TIMES, 17 Sept 1925, p. 8.

[Interview with Mrs. Conrad, 16 Sept 1925, on publication of JC's last work, the unfinished *Suspense.*]

591 "Conrad Memories," MENTOR, XIII (March 1925), 3-11.

["Printed for MENTOR readers with Mr. Conrad's Special Consent," this item consists chiefly of JC's own reminiscences.]

592 Conrad, Mrs. Joseph. "Conrad's Share in *The Nature of a Crime* and His Congo Diary," BOOKMAN'S JOURNAL, XII (July 1925), 135-36.

Very little of the "fragment" belongs to JC, who later denied knowing anything about it. Ford should have reprinted the fragment in TRANSATLANTIC REVIEW under Ford's name alone. JC also refused to admit he wrote "Autocracy and War," which he did in 1905. The Congo diary barely missed destruction. [Concludes with general reminiscences about JC's work habits.]

593 Conrad, Mrs. Joseph. "The Romance of *The Rescue*," BOOKMAN'S JOURNAL, XII (April 1925), 19-20.
[Jessie discovers after twenty-eight years a first draft of *The Rescue*, and finds that it differs markedly from the published book. She first began to type *Rescue* April 11, 1896; she persuaded JC not to let Ford assist in finishing *Rescue*.]

594 "Conrad's Last Novel," TIMES LITERARY SUPPLEMENT (Lond), 17 Sept 1925, p. 597.
Suspense is a "romance of physical adventure" marked by JC's diminishing use of lengthy introspection, which gives rise to "a greater simplicity and clarity of style." The heroine of *Suspense* is on a level with those of *The Rescue* and *The Arrow of Gold*. It is impossible to know the fate of JC's "real" and "arresting" characters.

595 "Conrad's *Suspense*," SATURDAY REVIEW OF LITERATURE, I (20 June 1925), 833.
[Announcement of the upcoming serial publication of JC's *Suspense* and subsequent contest of speculation on its probable ending, both in SATURDAY REVIEW OF LITERATURE.]

596 Curle, Richard. "Conrad's Diary," BLUE PETER, V (Oct 1925), 319-21 [not seen]; rptd in YALE REVIEW, N.S. XV (Jan 1926), 254-66; as "Introduction," published separately in JOSEPH CONRAD'S DIARY OF HIS JOURNEY UP THE VALLEY OF THE CONGO IN 1890 (Lond: pvtly ptd by Strangeways, 1926), pp. 5-13.
Passages from "Heart of Darkness" show how closely some of the earlier pages of this story are a recollection of JC's own Congo journey. The notebook helps to prove that "nearly all Conrad's work is founded upon autobiographical remembrance," but in writing "Heart of Darkness" JC had either forgotten the notebook or did not know of its survival, since his "piercing memory for essentials" was sufficient for him to recreate vividly vanished scenes and figures for his work. [Reproduces a part of JC's diary kept in the Congo in 1890 and prints a rough sketch of his journey along the river.]

597 Curle, Richard. "The Personality of Joseph Conrad," EDINBURGH REVIEW, CCXLI (Jan 1925), 126-38; rptd as a pamphlet (Lond: pvtly ptd, 1925); included in Curle's THE LAST TWELVE YEARS OF JOSEPH CONRAD (1928).

A "unique personality," JC "remained enigmatic to the end." He displayed compassion for human weaknesses, but contempt for "calculated betrayals" and expressed his "passionate vitality" in his writings. JC thought *Nostromo* his best novel.

598 Davidson, Donald. "Essays on Conrad's *Suspense*" [IV], SATURDAY REVIEW OF LITERATURE, II (21 Nov 1925), 315.

"The technique of the closing episodes in JC's novels is . . . organic, and at its final growth is the symmetrical, inevitable product of all that has gone before." The solution to the problem of supplying an ending for *Suspense* is "to reduce the book to the simplest possible terms, to find the essential situations which call for resolution in a climax, and to discover the inevitable outcome of forces which the novelist has set in motion." JC can discover nothing so remarkable in man as his fidelity, which lies at the heart of *Suspense.*

599 Davidson, Donald. "Joseph Conrad's Directed Indirections," SEWANEE REVIEW, XXXIII (April 1925), 163-77.

In order to reconcile "melodramatic subject-matter and intellectual content," JC uses five varieties of inverting the natural order: (1) story-within-a-story; (2) the pluperfect summary; (3) parallel narratives; (4) the mystery story; (5) the newspaper report. Except for the collaborations, *Romance* and *The Inheritors,* JC used the "inversive method" in all but three of the twelve novels: viz, *The Nigger of the Narcissus,* "Typhoon," and *The Shadow-Line*. He generally used the inversive method in the short stories. The most complex use of this device is found in *Chance*. [Derived from "The Inversive Method of Narration in the Novels and Short Stories of Joseph Conrad," Master's thesis, Vanderbilt University, 1922.]

600 DeGruyter, J. "A Master of English," ENGLISH STUDIES (Amsterdam), VII (Dec 1925), 169-75.

Suspense, a fragment, is worth reading. [Summarizes JC's themes and interests.]

601 Dinamov, S. *"Taifun" (Typhoon),* KNIGONOSHA, Nos. 15-16 (1925), 24.

[A review.] [In Russian.]

602 "Dzhozef Konrad (Vmesto Nekrologa)" (Joseph Conrad [Instead of an Obituary]), ALMANAKH, No. 1 (1925), 3-5.

[In Russian.]

603 Estaunié, Édouard. "Le roman est-il en danger?" (Is the Novel in Danger?), REVUE HEBDOMADAIRE, XXXIV (14 Feb 1925), 132-50, espec 142-44.

Long before JC wrote *Almayer's Folly,* the appearance of a certain man on the deck of a ship created a moment of shock which obsessively persisted in his memory. [Cites JC on the inception and intention of the novel.] [In French.]

> **604** Estelrich, Juan. "Un caràcter" (A Portrait), [probably published early in 1925 in a Catalonian periodical, unknown]; rptd in Entre la Vida i els Llibres (Between Life and Books) (Barcelona: Llibrería Catalonia, 1926), pp. 275-301.

JC had great sympathy for humanity and a strong curiosity. His adventurers are not the type defined by R. L. Stevenson (medieval knights-errant of Scott or musketeers of Dumas), nor the energetic heroes of Kipling sprung from an imperialistic concept of life; rather, they fall into more realistic categories such as officers of the British merchant marine [some analysis of personality types is given]. JC was much influenced by the Bible and Flaubert. He rejected Dostoevski and Tolstoi and preferred Turgenev. JC was influenced also by Dickens and Meredith (characters), Hardy (poetry), and Henry James (psychological force and method). [JC's adoption of and facility with English are discussed.] [In Spanish.]

> **605** Estelrich, Juan. "José Conrad (1857-1924). El autor y su obra" (Joseph Conrad [1857-1924]. The Writer of the Sea), Cuba Contemporánea, XXXVIII (July 1925), 244-73; rptd in Nosotros (Buenos Aires), XIX (July 1925), 284-316; in Joseph Conrad's *Alma Rusa,* trans by Juan Mateos de Diego (Barcelona: Motaner y Simón, 1925), I, [v]-xlv.

From his birth in the Ukraine and early exile, to his life at sea and the literary creativity of his later years, JC's existence was permeated by an ever-increasing solitude. Stoic in character and strong and modest in personality, he was always reticent to reveal his inner self, even in his memoirs. Fidelity was a central concept in his life: fidelity to his art, to himself, to his friends. His artistic credo rested on the search for truth: the total truth that finds a real and undeniable existence only in the imagination of men. The essence of his works is the greatness of man confronting that of nature. His method consists largely in lightning-flash glimpses of his characters and a narrative form that does not always respect the order of time. The central motive is not the sea, but the struggle that frees men from that element. Unlike the authentic adventurer, his heroes are passive men whose exceptional acts result only from the extraordinary circumstances in which they find themselves. JC's literary preferences included Flaubert, and a curious passion against Dostoevski. He repudiated the "Slavic spirit" as being completely alien to the Polish temperament. His choice of English over Polish and French as a literary vehicle was regarded by him not as a preference but rather as a natural aptitude. [Also see Estelrich, Entre la Vida i els

LLIBRES (Barcelona: Llibrería Catalonia, 1926), pp. 275-314.] [In Spanish.]

606 Estelrich, Juan. "Josep Conrad: La Novella" (Joseph Conrad: The Novel), [probably published early in 1925 in a Catalonian periodical, unlocated]; rptd in ENTRE LA VIDA I ELS LLIBRES (Between Life and Books) (Barcelona: Llibrería Catalonia, 1926), pp. 302-314.

[The essay is chiefly an exposition of JC's artistic principles and methods derived, in the main, from the preface to *The Nigger of the Narcissus*.] [In Spanish.]

607 Ferguson, J. De Lancy. "Essays on Conrad's *Suspense*" [III], SATURDAY REVIEW OF LITERATURE, II (21 Nov 1925), 315.

The formula of a JC story is simple. "Conrad's art consists not in his material but in what he does with it." His major concern is the effect of the action on the souls of the people engaged in it. In his unfinished *Suspense,* JC's familiar dramatic machinery becomes significant "because we see the souls and not merely the bodies, and still more because all these souls are moved by a force greater than themselves—the Man of Elba." Regardless of how the story might materially end, it is *spiritual* success or failure which emerges as the ultimate index of a man's life.

608 "Fiction," A. L. A. BOOKLIST, XXI (April 1925), 274.

All the stories in *Tales of Hearsay* "characteristically involve an implied moral issue."

609 "Fiction," A. L. A. BOOKLIST, XXII (Nov 1925), 72.

In *Suspense,* Cosmo Latham is swept into "active and sympathetic participation" in an unknown Napoleonic intrigue.

610 Frid, Ia. *"Na Vzgliad Zapada"* (*Under Western Eyes*), NOVII MIR, No. 8 (1925), 154-55.

[A review.] [In Russian.]

611 Gardner, Monica M. "Joseph Conrad as a Pole," SPECTATOR (Lond), CXXXV (1 Aug 1925), 190-91.

Although of JC's fiction only "Amy Foster" portrays a Pole, his other examples are set apart from the tradition of English fiction by a "power of reproducing atmosphere" which is "fundamentally Polish," by his portrayal of men "caught into the toils of revolutionary conspiracy" in *The Secret Agent* and *Under Western Eyes,* and by his style: "the richness and redundancy of his language may be traced to his Polish birth."

612 Garnett, Edward. "The Danger of Idols," SATURDAY REVIEW (Lond), CXL (31 Oct 1925), 505.

Gerald Gould [ibid. (24 Oct 1925), 471-72] has "misrepresented my attitude both to Conrad and his critics." P. C. Kennedy's review of *Suspense* ["Current Literature: New Novels," NEW STATESMAN AND NATION, XXV (26 Sept 1925), 665-66] "showed great insensibility to the artistic qualities" of the novel. "I own I wrote chiefly as a propagandist of his [JC's] merits during the first twenty years he was struggling against the British public's indifference to his genius."

613 Garnett, Edward. "Reviews: Conrad's Last Tales," NATION AND ATHENAEUM, XXXVI (21 Feb 1925), 718.

In *Tales of Hearsay*, "The Black Mate" is weak, "The Warrior's Soul" is JC "almost at his best," "Prince Roman" is "a charming souvenir of Conrad's boyhood," and "The Tale" is JC "almost at his finest." In the last story, only JC "could have held the balance with a hand so unerring that the story closes on the note of uncertainty as to whether the *Neutral*'s crew were guilty men or innocent"; in fact, no Englishman could have written so effective a story.

614 Garnett, Edward. *"Tales of Hearsay,"* NEW REPUBLIC, XLII (8 April 1925), 189-90.

JC's art in "The Black Mate," is "buttoned up in a cheap and skimpy suit" —perhaps an attempt to be popular, like W. W. Jacobs. "The Warrior's Soul" (JC "almost at his best") is a story showing JC's "peculiar strength to establish relation between remorseless fact and moral judgment." "Prince Roman" is good, but not so good as "The Tale," a very fine work in which the management of narrative is perfect. The opening scene, the balance, and the uncertainty as to the guilt of the *Neutral*'s crew are typical JC. A temperamentally subtle and delicate chiaroscuro bespeak not an Englishman but a new influence—Slav, continental, cosmopolitan, or all three.

615 Georgin, B. "Une conférence sur Joseph Conrad" (A Lecture on Joseph Conrad), CHRONIQUE DES LETTRES FRANÇAISES, III (Jan-Feb 1925), 55-57.

For the first time since JC's death, G. Jean-Aubry spoke in public on his friend at the University of Strasbourg, 8 Dec 1924. Much moved, Aubry gave many personal details on JC's life and an account of JC's literary achievement. Aubry noted that JC preferred English to French for artistic purposes. [In French.]

616 Gillet, Louis. "Le dernier roman de Conrad" (Conrad's Last Novel), REVUE DES DEUX MONDES, 7ème série, XCV (Nov-Dec 1925), 931-42.

In *Suspense*, JC evokes the power of Napoleon artistically without even bringing him on stage. One of JC's main accomplishments is to dramatize the mystery of life by creating a sense of *déjà vu*. [In French.]

617 Gould, Gerald. "The Danger of Idols," SATURDAY REVIEW (Lond), CXL (24 Oct 1925), 471-72.

Edward Garnett [ibid. (31 Oct 1925), 505] was wrong to attack P. C. Kennedy's criticism of *Suspense* ["Current Literature: New Novels," NEW STATESMAN AND NATION, XXV (26 Sept 1925), 665-66] that " 'it does not come to life at all.' " Garnett has erred in that "he has set up [JC as] an idol in his mind." "He has assumed that to find fault with Conrad, is to do wrong to art."

618 Hagen [Anisimov, I. I.]. "Na Otmeliakh" (In the Shallows), KNIGONOSHA, No. 2 (1925), 18.

[In Russian.]

619 Hartley, L. P. [Review of *Tales of Hearsay*], BOOKMAN (Lond), LXVII (March 1925), 314-15.

There is a connection between JC's experience as a sailor and his characters' attitudes toward the transience of life. His people are heroic in the size of their consciences, "the intense antagonism between reason and action." The characters' highly developed sense of honor is the thing which demands no errors in conduct: "They cannot live after that they have fallen."

620 Hodgson & Company, Auctioneers. A CATALOGUE OF BOOKS, MANUSCRIPTS, AND COLLECTED TYPESCRIPTS FROM THE LIBRARY OF THE LATE JOSEPH CONRAD. TO BE SOLD . . . MARCH 13, 1925 . . . preface by Richard Curle (Lond: Hodgson & Co., 1925).

[The catalogue contains 159 items, the most important ones being the complete holograph MS of "The Tale" in 48 folio sheets in JC's handwriting; and the corrected typescripts of two unpublished articles, "The Unlighted Coast" (16 pp.) and "A Glance at Two Books." In addition to some of JC's volumes were presentation copies by such writers as Crane, James, W. H. Hudson, H. G. Wells, Bennett, and Symons.]

621 [Horvath, Josip]. "Predgovor" (Preface), in JC's *Almayerova Ludnica* (*Almayer's Folly*) (Zagreb, 1925), pp. 5-11.

[A psychological portrait of JC, based on articles published as "Hommage à Joseph Conrad, 1857-1924," NOUVELLE REVUE FRANÇAISE, N.S. XII (Dec 1924), 649-806.] [In Serbo-Croatian.]

622 Hutchison, Percy A. "Conrad's Unfinished Novel Resembles His *Nostromo*," NEW YORK TIMES BOOK REVIEW, 13 Sept 1925, p. 3.

Suspense lacks what is necessary to "carry a reader forward." "The one thing that saves the fragment, the overwhelming sense of destiny so permeatingly present in *Nostromo*, is at least intermittently present." The fragment does not detract from JC's fame, although it has weak joining and absence of effect, which JC would have corrected.

623 Hutchison, Percy A. "*Tales of Hearsay,*" LITERARY DIGEST INTERNATIONAL BOOK REVIEW, III (May 1925), 429, 439.

In *Tales of Hearsay,* three of the stories are excellent. "The Warrior's Soul" demonstrates JC at his best in using nature "to convey the mood," and in it is "the heart of the Conradian philosophy or ethic: Better that a man lose his life than that he lose faith and high courage!" "The Black Mate" shows JC's "struggle at once to embody and to disembody a woman but for whose existence the action would have never taken place." "Prince Romain [sic]" is the only fictional piece in which JC "reveals the Pole" he was. "The Tale" is a great story; two naval officers "seem to slip in and out of the fog," including the fog of "mental perplexity and moral turpitude."

624 "Joseph Conrad: Master Seaman and Master Writer," MENTOR, XIII (March 1925), 1.

JC spent his first twenty years chafing "for the sea and the radiant lands of the South," the next twenty years with "his face . . . turned to the gales of the Seven Seas, and the buffets of men and the elements," and the last twenty years as "the sailor who had brooded on life's mysteries [and had become] the artist-writer."

625 "Joseph Conrad, Personal Memories," MENTOR, XIII (March 1925), 1-26 [Special Number]. [Contents, abstracted separately, all under 1925 unless otherwise noted: "Joseph Conrad: Master Seaman and Master Writer"; "Conrad Memories"; Richard Curle, "The Last of Conrad," from JOHN O'LONDON'S WEEKLY (1924); Rutherford J. Platt, Jr., "How Conrad Came to Write"; and Christopher Morley, "A Word About Joseph Conrad."]

626 "Joseph Conrad's Tales," SPECTATOR (Lond), CXXXIV (7 Feb 1925), 206.

In *Tales of Hearsay,* JC's first story, "The Black Mate," shows many of the faults which JC fought later to overcome, whereas the last one to be written, "The Warrior's Soul," is "perhaps the simplest and most lucid" of them all. "The Tale" is much like most modern short stories. In "Prince Roman," JC gave "free rein" to his Polish feelings. Seldom is such a good volume posthumously published.

627 Kennedy, P. C. "Current Literature: New Novels," NEW STATESMAN AND NATION, XXV (26 Sept 1925), 665-66.

JC was great in two methods: the philosophical romance (*Lord Jim*) and the sublimated detective story (*The Secret Agent*), but his later works "read rather as if they had been written by a student and admirer of the Conrad manner than by the great man himself." Because *The Rover* evidenced a possible new manner, one expected much of *Suspense,* which "does not come to life at all." [See Gerald Gould, "The Danger of Idols,"

Saturday Review (Lond), CXL (24 Oct 1925), 471-72, and Edward Garnett, ibid. (31 Oct 1925), 505.]

628 Krasilnikov, V. "Dzhozef Konrad *Na Vzgliad Zapada*" (Joseph Conrad's *Under Western Eyes*), Rabochii Zhurnal, No. 6 (1925), 138-39.

[In Russian.]

629 Lambuth, David. "Essays on *Suspense* (II)," Saturday Review of Literature, II (14 Nov 1925), 290-91.

Suspense is "a story of divided and tested loyalties complicated by mistakes of the past and by uncontrollable circumstance." An individual must look to his own integrity for life's answers; despair for JC is the final impiety. [Second place essay in contest on *Suspense* sponsored by SRL.]

630 Latorre, Mariano. "José Conrad," Atenea (Santiago de Chile), II (30 Sept 1925), 161-72.

Verisimilitude, "an artistic concept which is expressed with the help of the written word, should be directed to feelings, if its intimate intention is to arrive to the very fountain of our emotions." Adventure in JC's works is only a means to an end. "He does not locate reality in front of man but rather man in front of reality." He conceives life in a Russian manner: his characters are "outside of the law, they are ex-men." But there is an essential difference: these characters always show "an active feeling of sorrow, the result of a firm will." [In Spanish.]

631 Leiteizen, M. *"Na Vzgliad Zapada" (Under Western Eyes),* Pechat i Revolutsia, IV (1925), 285-87.

[In Russian.]

632 Lewis, Sinclair. "Swan Song of Joseph Conrad," New York Evening Post Literary Review, VI (19 Sept 1925), 1-2.

Suspense is "essentially a chart of obscure spiritual wondering."

633 L[ittell], R[obert]. "Recent Fiction," New Republic, XLIV (28 Oct 1925), 263.

Suspense is not JC at his best: it is thin, forced, and bloodless.

634 Littell, Robert. "Shadows of Conrad," New Republic, XLI (4 Feb 1925), 287-88.

Ford's Joseph Conrad: A Personal Remembrance (1924) seems to be "really an excuse made by Mr. Ford for writing about himself," but one can catch snatches and glimpses of JC, despite Ford's presence. *The Nature of a Crime* "is difficult, mannered, obscure, and rather soft stuff, impossible to finish." "Hommage à Joseph Conrad" (1924) ranges from testimonials to criticism. Richard Curle's article "is probably the most moving and unpreoccupied picture of Conrad at close range that we have." JC disdained Freud and said, "I do not want to go to the bottom of things." [Also refers to THE SHORTER TALES OF JOSEPH CONRAD (Garden City, NY: Doubleday, Page, 1924).]

635 Loks, K. " 'Na Otmeliakh,' *Rasskazy o Nepokoe"* (In the Shallows, *Tales of Unrest*), PECHAT I REVOLUTSIA, II 1925), 279-81.
[Review.] [In Russian.]

636 McFee, William. "The Secret of Conrad's Unfinished Romance," LITERARY DIGEST INTERNATIONAL BOOK REVIEW, III (Oct 1925), 705-6.
Suspense, JC's Napoleonic novel, was a legend before his death. Unless he planned a work of great length, he must have intended to revise the part he had written, especially in view of the "vagueness" of plot and characterization. Publication of an unfinished novel is "unnecessary and unwise." *Suspense* will rank with *The Rover, The Rescue,* and *The Arrow of Gold,* "below such bursts of splendor as 'Heart of Darkness' and 'Youth.' " [Gives plot summary.]

637 Mille, Pierre. "Pourquoi Conrad n'a pas écrit en français?" (Why Did Conrad Not Write in French?), NOUVELLES LITTÉRAIRES, IV (17 Jan 1925), p. 1; rptd as "Why Conrad Did Not Write in French" in LIVING AGE, CCCXXIV (14 March 1925), 622-23; excerpted in LITERARY DIGEST, LXXXV (23 May 1925), 28-29.
There are three reasons for JC's choice of nation and language. English offered a possible readership of over 200 million in England, the dominions, and the U. S., while French had a quarter of that number. Most of JC's stories have to do with the sea, which makes them of greater interest to a nation which cherishes its naval tradition. As one can see in the work of Loti, Frenchmen require explanations for the simplest nautical terms. Finally, and most important, JC's Polish origins required a medium where freedom and hatred of things Russian would be accepted. France, as Russia's ally, could not provide an acceptable base for JC's writing. [In many ways an interesting article.] [In French.]

638 Mogilianskii, M. "Avanpost Progressy" (An Outpost of Progress), ZHITTIA REVOLUTSIA, No. 12 (1925), 107-8.
[In Russian.]

639 Morley, Christopher. "Storms and Calms," SATURDAY REVIEW OF LITERATURE, I (25 April 1925), 707; rptd in ROMANY STAIN (NY: Doubleday, Page, 1926), pp. 218-22; in ESSAYS (Garden City, NY: Doubleday, Doran, 1928), pp. 1066-71; and in MORLEY'S VARIETY (NY: World, Forum Books, 1944), pp. 565-67.

Although critics suggest a novice reader begin his study of JC with his " 'storm pieces' " ("Typhoon," *The Nigger of the Narcissus*), *The Shadow-Line* and *'Twixt Land and Sea* are more representative places to begin. One wonders whether "The Secret Sharer" is "a magnificent allegory of the horrors of man's duality" or Jacobus in "A Smile of Fortune" is "a veiled hero or . . . a scoundrel." JC's greatest gift is "that enveloping haze of significance." The simplicity of such stories make "Youth," "Typhoon," and "Heart of Darkness" seem a trifle melodramatic.

640 Morley, Christopher. "A Word About Joseph Conrad," MENTOR, XIII (March 1925), 24-26.

JC had insufficient "general culture" to be a literary critic; his memory "was packed with wisdom of a more elemental sort." He was interested in "the things that lie behind literature," in "the hopes and terrors and wearinesses which all human beings know." He was not a writer of the sea or an ironist or a philosopher; he was a poet, a creator. His English is more "consciously splendid" than that of any native-born writer and sometimes ungrammatical, but it is the thought more than the words that is "vital and durable" in his works.

641 Moult, Thomas. "The Life and Work of Joseph Conrad," YALE REVIEW, N.S. XIV (Jan 1925), 295-308; excerpted in CHRISTIAN SCIENCE MONITOR, 21 Jan 1925, p. 9.

JC expressed "the pessimistic, harsh, and sinister vision of a Polish aristocrat, in whom, somewhere, bone-deep was more than a dash of the Asiatic." His work, dominated by fearless imagination, used "the kink of character and the moment of crisis," exposing man's "infinite littleness." Cause and effect are intricately mingled. He was "the first psychologist among novelists who not only chose the sea deliberately, but was able to use it worthily as a background for what a philosopher would call the 'given set of circumstances.' "

642 *Na Vzgliad Zapada (Under Western Eyes)*, KNIGA I PROFSOIUZY, Nos. 5-6 (1925), 8-9.

[A review of *Under Western Eyes* in COLLECTED WORKS (Moscow: Zif, 1925).] [In Russian.]

643 "New Fiction: *Suspense*," SATURDAY REVIEW (Lond), CXL (3 Oct 1925), 373.

Suspense shows that JC did not need Eastern settings to create his special moral atmosphere. A "sense of obscure peril" is evident throughout the fragment. Latham's decision to go to Elba would have been a fateful one, had JC completed the novel. The book is "among the greatest preludes in our literature." Yet it would have lost much in the completion. As a fragment, *Suspense* has "infinite wealth of suggestion." With the commencement of the drama proper, however, "we should have been in a world in many respects narrower."

644 "New Novels," TIMES LITERARY SUPPLEMENT (Lond), 29 Jan 1925, p. 70.

The stories of *Tales of Hearsay* are characteristic, but they lack JC's "essential magnetism." "The Warrior's Soul" is the best of the group.

645 Noble, Edward (ed). "Foreword," FIVE LETTERS BY JOSEPH CONRAD WRITTEN TO EDWARD NOBLE IN 1895 (Lond: pvtly ptd [Strangeways, printers], 1925), pp. 7-9.

In 1895, soon after *Almayer's Folly* was published, the editor, a sailor like JC, realized that the latter's suggestion that they might collaborate in writing would require the sacrifice for at least one of them of some part of his individuality and that JC's training and genius would add to the difficulty. The two men, then, just "walked and talked" and made no definite decision about the matter.

646 Nusinov, I. *"Pobeda" (Victory)*, KNIGONOSHA, No. 6 (1925), 17.

[A review.] [In Russian.]

647 Pearson, Edmund. "The Book Table," OUTLOOK (NY), CXLI (14 Oct 1925), 243.

The incomplete *Suspense* is still "one of his best" for its mood and characters, "each a finished portrait."

648 Platt, Rutherford H., Jr. "How Conrad Came to Write," MENTOR, XIII (March 1925), 20-23.

When JC, a ship's officer on the *Vidar,* saw a figure emerge from the mist forty miles or so up a river in Borneo, he had met his Almayer. That figure haunted him, "consciously or unconsciously," until it became "the hidden, obscure necessity that drove him to write." Previous to 1889, JC had written nothing but a few letters; but the mist outside his lodgingplace in London then caused him to think of the derelict trader and to begin writing at once. For four years he slowly added new chapters to his first work until, in May 1894, he wrote the last word and sent the manuscript to T. Fisher Unwin, publisher, where Edward Garnett recommended its publication. A year later *Almayer's Folly* appeared, and JC then allowed Garnett to persuade him to write another novel.

649 Preston, John Hyde. *"The Nature of a Crime,"* LITERARY DIGEST INTERNATIONAL BOOK REVIEW, III (Jan 1925), 137-38.

In *The Nature of a Crime,* JC's "sympathetic understanding" and "irony, of which tolerance itself is simply an essence," can be detected as well as certain characteristics of Ford. This story casts "a bit of new light" on JC, even if "the collaboration is not harmonious."

650 Pridorogin, A. *"Rasskazy o Nepokoe"* (*Tales of Unrest*), KNIGONOSHA, No. 21 (1925), 18.

[A review.] [In Russian.]

651 Priestly, J. B. "Joseph Conrad," ENGLISH JOURNAL, XIV (Jan 1925), 13-21; rptd in an abbreviated form in THE ENGLISH NOVEL (Lond: Benn, 1927, 1946).

[Brief survey of life and books.]

652 Prieur, François. "Joseph Conrad et les pilotes de Marseille" (Joseph Conrad and the Pilots of Marseilles), PETIT PROVENÇAL (Marseilles), 15 May 1925, p. 5.

G. Jean-Aubry, translator of JC's *Some Reminiscences* as *Souvenirs,* had first met JC at Marseilles with the pilots of that city. A young man, Solary, put JC in touch with the pilots. JC's acquaintances in the city were M. and Mme. Delestang, a banker and his wife at whose home JC visited frequently. During his first stay (1874), JC spent most of his time with the pilots [his impressions of them are cited]. As other cities boast of their famous visitors, why should not Marseilles inscribe JC as one of its finest eulogizers? [Many citations from Aubry's translation of *Some Reminiscences.*] [In French.]

653 R., A. "Dzhozef Konrad" (Joseph Conrad), LENINGRAD, No. 18 (May 1925), 13.

[In Russian.]

654 Roberts, Cecil. "Joseph Conrad: A Reminiscence," BOOKMAN (NY), LXI (July 1925), 536-42; rptd, with trivial changes, in BOOKMAN (Lond), LXIX (Nov 1925), 95-99; and in LIVING AGE, CCCXXVIII (6 Feb 1926), 308-13.

JC revealed, not the sea captain but the Polish aristocrat, the "personal" JC who does not appear in his books and, most important, his attitude toward his own writing. He considered *Nostromo* his best book.

655 Schriftgiesser, Karl. *"Suspense:* A Napoleonic Chronicle," BOSTON EVENING TRANSCRIPT BOOK SECTION, 19 Sept 1925, p. 5.

JC wanted to write about the "uneasy sentiment of suspense" from the point of view of "the average citizen of the age." Napoleon, who does not enter into the completed book of 274 pages, is felt on every page. *Suspense* is one of the most direct of the longer tales and is JC's best effort in plot development, with more action than usual. It lacks psychological analysis. *Suspense* is only for the "inveterate lover of Conrad, who knows his peaks and valleys of success."

656 "Slaven, engleski pripovjedac Joseph Conrad (Korzeniowski)" (Slav, English Story-Teller. Joseph Conrad [Korzeniowski]), Obzor (Zagreb), LXVI: 188 (1925), 2-3.
[Review of Terkovic's Croatian translation of *Almayer's Folly*.] [In Serbo-Croatian.]

657 *"Suspense,"* Outlook (NY), CXLI (14 Oct 1925), 243.
Suspense, though unfinished, is "one of his [JC's] best" novels.

658 Symons, Arthur. Notes on Joseph Conrad with Some Unpublished Letters (Lond: Myers, 1925), pp. 7-38.
JC was "one of the most original and sinister and sombre personalities of our time, and one of the greatest novelists." One imagines JC "squatting like some Satanical spider in his web, in some corner, stealthily hidden away from view, throwing out—almost like *la Pieuvre*—tentacles into the darkness. At the centre of his web sits an elemental sarcasm discussing human affairs with a cynical ferocity; behind that sarcasm crouches some powerful devil, insidious, poisonous, irresistible, spawning evil for his own delight." JC's novels do not have plots and do not need them. His novels "are a series of studies in temperaments, deducted from slight incidents." [The letters are fragments and are vaguely dated.]

659 *"Tales of Hearsay,"* Open Shelf (Cleveland), July 1925, p. 84.
JC had "style, tone, grace, force of old masters."

660 "This Week's Books," Spectator (Lond), CXXXIV (24 Jan 1925), 121.
[Review of *Tales of Hearsay,* which says nothing of the quality of the short stories. Quotes briefly from R. B. Cunninghame Graham's preface (1925).]

661 Tittle, Walter. "The Conrad Who Sat for Me," Outlook (NY), CXL (1, 8 July 1925), 333-35, 361-62.
JC's "vital personality and abundant nervous energy" are notable. He approached each new work as an experiment. JC thought his portrait showed him "'as the rough old sea-dog that I am.'" He had a strong bias against the cinema. [Remembrance of the JC Tittle came to know when he painted his portrait.]

662 Vaisbrod, A. *"Negr s Nartsissa"* (*The Nigger of the Narcissus*), Molodaia Gvardia, No. 6 (1925), 187-88.
[A review.] [In Russian.]

663 Waldman, Milton. "Fiction," London Mercury, XI (March 1925), 543-44.
JC's Polish origins and Slavic background are reflected in the four stories

of this volume [*Tales of Hearsay*]. Like the great Russian novelists, JC is introspective and highly autobiographical in all his writing. Brooding irony is the dominant trait of this work.

664 Waldman, Milton. "Fiction," LONDON MERCURY, XIII (Nov 1925), 97-98.

There are good indications that *Suspense* might have been as great as *Lord Jim*. Language is increasingly more simple in the later work. [Summarizes extremes of critical reaction to *Suspense*.]

665 Warren, C. Henry. "Conrad's Last Novel," BOOKMAN (Lond), LXIX (Oct 1925), 27-28.

Suspense might have been JC's longest and best novel. It has "greater maturity" and "an unmatched epic dignity." JC developed from the early sensuous romantic style to severe simplicity. He develops especially good settings and atmosphere.

666 W[illard], G[race]. "Conrad in Excelsis," NEW YORK EVENING POST LITERARY REVIEW, V (21 March 1925), 3.

In *Tales of Hearsay,* "Prince Roman," clearly from JC's youth, gives a picture of "autocratic eastern Europe" and shows JC's aristocratic Polish patriotism and hatred of the Russians. Of the other stories, "The Black Mate" is JC's first story, "The Tale" might have been written at the time of *The Arrow of Gold* [1919], and "The Warrior's Song" is his last story.

667 Woolf, Leonard. "The Last Conrad," NATION AND ATHENAEUM, XXXVIII (3 Oct 1925), 18.

The 300 pages of *Suspense* provide enough material for enjoyment and a critical judgment. JC's early work is superior to his later. *Suspense* is not as great as *Lord Jim* although it is closely and well written. "An historical novel of the classic type," it depicts a period which JC found very fascinating, and the intermingling of fictional and historic personages is well done. The book is more adventure-history than psychological insight and as a result the characters remain essentially unreal; like the greater part of the later work, it is "splendid but hollow" after what we have come to expect from the earlier stories. It lacks a central informing idea but has the empty form.

668 Zelie, John Sheridan. "An Evening with Joseph Conrad," CHRISTIAN CENTURY, XLII (19 Feb 1925), 251-53.

A visit to JC in Great Barrington revealed him to be extremely foreign in appearance, to have a close identification with his adopted country, to have practically no theories about his art, to consider writing as being extremely difficult for him, to resent being called a writer of sea stories, and to consider *A Personal Record* his favorite book. [Typical of many similar accounts of JC.]

1926

669 Adams, Elbridge Lapham. "In Memory of Joseph Conrad," NATION (NY), CXXII (30 June 1926), 725.
[Letter soliciting contributions for a village center in Bishopsbourne as a memorial to JC.]

670 Arns, Karl. "Conrad, Joseph: *Jugend. Der Geheimagent. Spiel des Zufalls. Die Schattenlinie.* Romane. S. Fischer, Berlin 1926" (Conrad, Joseph: *Youth. The Secret Agent. Chance. The Shadow-Line.* Novels. S. Fischer, Berlin 1926), GRAL (Munich), XXI (1926-27), 327-28.
[Brief review praising the translations of JC's romantic novels.] [In German.]

671 "As Joseph Conrad Appeared to His Wife/ Jessie Conrad's Memoir of Her Husband Gives a Lively Picture of Genius in Shirtsleeves," NEW YORK TIMES BOOK REVIEW, 26 Sept 1926, pp. 2, 14.
Jessie Conrad's JOSEPH CONRAD AS I KNEW HIM (1926) supplies firsthand anecdotes of JC. In the past there were two notorious martyrs—Job and Jane Welsh Carlyle. Now Mrs. Conrad joins this group.

672 Aseev, N. "Dzhozef Konrad" (Joseph Conrad), 30 DNEI, No. 4 (1926), 85-86.
[In Russian.]

673 Ashton-Gwatkin, W. H. T. "A Conrad Memorial," TIMES LITERARY SUPPLEMENT (Lond), 11 March 1926, p. 182.
Proposal for a local memorial to JC in the village of Bishopsbourne, near Canterbury, where he lived from 1919 until his death. [A bowling green and porch were added to the village hall, "in the construction of which Conrad took great interest."]

674 Atkinson, Mildred. "Conrad's *Suspense,*" TIMES LITERARY SUPPLEMENT (Lond), 25 Feb 1926, p. 142; rptd in SATURDAY REVIEW OF LITERATURE, II (27 March 1926), 666.
[A letter gives many parallels in characters, plot and wording between *Suspense* and MEMOIRS OF THE COUNTESS DE BOIGNE.]

675 Aubry, Georges Jean-. "Introduction," TWENTY LETTERS TO CONRAD (Lond: First Edition Club, Curwen P, 1926).
JC, like most men of the sea, kept few possessions that were not of immediate use. Those retained usually attested to his character and recommended him. Thus JC kept some correspondence by significant men of letters

(Kipling, Gissing, Crane, Edward and Constance Garnett, Galsworthy, Henry James, Lucas, Bennett, Huneker, and Wells) that attested to his ability during the early years of his career as novelist. [The letters, printed separately, are packetted under the names of the various writers and listed separately under the names of their authors (1926).]

676 Aubry, G. Jean-. "Joseph Conrad in the Heart of Darkness," BOOKMAN (NY), LXIII (June 1926), 429-35.

Evidence exists of the authenticity of much of the story in "Heart of Darkness" [gives detailed parallels between the fiction and JC's actual experiences]. If JC decided in 1890 to give up his Congo expedition, he did so partly because of ill health and partly because of Delcommune's refusal to let him have command of the *Florida*. Thereupon, his strength of character gave way, and he left Africa, where he would, in all probability, have died soon had he remained.

677 Bartoszewic, Kazimierz. "Ojciec Conrada" (Conrad's Father), NOWA REFORMA (Cracow), Nos. 91-92 (1926) [not seen]; rptd as "Conrad's Father" in POLAND (NY), VII (July 1926), 414-15.

[A conventional discussion of Apollo Korzeniowski based primarily on surviving letters. One interesting fact given is that Apollo's gravestone is by "the gifted sculptor Gadomski."] [In Polish.]

678 Bennett, Arnold. ARNOLD BENNETT TO JOSEPH CONRAD (Lond: First Edition Club, Curwen P, 1926), text, pp. [1-2]; editor's note, p. [3]. [See Aubry, TWENTY LETTERS TO CONRAD (1926).]

679 "Biography," A. L. A. BOOKLIST, XXIII (Dec 1926), 128.

"One is impressed with the ingenuousness of" Mrs. Conrad's JOSEPH CONRAD AS I KNEW HIM (1926). "The book is, however, the story of a beautiful and successful marriage, all the more beautiful because of the difficulties Mrs. Conrad overcame."

680 "Books in Brief," NATION (NY), CXXIII (13 Oct 1926), 381-82.

In the short critical essay of *Last Essays*, JC reveals "a vapidity rather surprising in the artist who wrote 'Heart of Darkness' and 'The End of the Tether.' " He works best in a restricted area "of concrete situations dealing with the sentiments of esprit de corps, fidelity to one's calling, and stoicism in the face of disaster."

681 Braudo, E. *"Lord Dhim"* (*Lord Jim*), NOVII MIR, No. 7 (1926), 191-92.

[A review.] [In Russian.]

682 Bullett, Gerald William. "Joseph Conrad," MODERN ENGLISH FICTION: A PERSONAL VIEW (Lond: Jenkins, 1926), pp. 54-69.

JC's subject matter is often exotic, fantastic, but his real interest is "the drama in the soul," the mind's response to the storms of life. In times of crisis "the only virtue is fidelity." Loneliness is one of JC's frequent themes, as in "Heart of Darkness," where "we see Kurtz, the idealist, guarding his integrity, a thin bright flame, in the heart of darkness and moral corruption." JC's use of Marlow is effective, especially in *Chance* and *Lord Jim,* which have "a deceptive air of haphazard or hearsay that peculiarly stimulates the reader by seeming to invite his collaboration."

683 Childs, Mary. "Snapshots of the Literary World: Last Essays of Joseph Conrad," LITERARY DIGEST INTERNATIONAL BOOK REVIEW, IV (Aug 1926), 590.

The chief value of *Last Essays* is "in the evidence it adds to our knowledge that Conrad's work was largely autobiographical." "The variety of these essays reflects the versatile richness of the author's mind, the sweep of an observation that, like a powerful searchlight, picks out of the obscurity of the shoreline of humanity unexpected flashes of reality."

684 Chubb, Edwin Watts. "The Romance of Conrad," STORIES OF AUTHORS, BRITISH AND AMERICAN, new ed (NY: Macmillan, 1926), pp. 393-400; rptd (Freeport, NY: Books for Libraries P, 1968).

[Chubb ties together quoted passages from Percy A. Hutchison on JC's transition from seaman to writer, James Norman Hall on JC as stylist in *Lord Jim,* Pierre Mille on his choice of English over French, F. M. Ford on his deliberate selection of words, and other reminiscences by John Galsworthy.]

685 Cobley, W. D. "Joseph Conrad," PAPERS OF THE MANCHESTER LITERARY CLUB, LII (1926), 69-94.

JC is a "singer of sea-sagas," whose collaboration with Hueffer [Ford] was not so disastrous as H. G. Wells had feared. JC's stories are "mostly simple sea yarns"; his message is fidelity, and his characters are "solid, unimaginative": MacWhirr learns nothing, and the storm casts him off with contempt. JC's atmosphere gives to "reality the glow and splendour of romance," turning his "vision of life into poetry." *The Secret Agent* marks a subtle change in JC's manner—after *Agent* he never writes as one "still sailing the seas," even though he wrote repeatedly of the sea. Stylistically, *Almayer's Folly* and *An Outcast of the Islands* have excellent rhythm and meter, with echoes of French phraseology. JC relies too much on the adjective; he does not let the reader get close enough to his characters; his narrative technique resembles the sailor's yarn. JC is especially aware of man's solitary nature: people speaking in the novels often seem to take distinct lines of thought, as though a veil existed between those conversing. [Concludes with general comment on JC's Romance and Realism.]

686 Conrad, Jessie. JOSEPH CONRAD AS I KNEW HIM, with an introduction by Richard Curle (Garden City: Doubleday; Lond: William Heinemann, 1926); incorporates PERSONAL RECOLLECTIONS OF JOSEPH CONRAD (Lond: pvtly ptd, 1924).

JC was of "indifferent health and nervous temperament"; his wife gave him such "constant care" that he was enabled "to produce so fine a volume of work [as] to stand as a perpetual monument to his memory and as a heritage to his sons." She was "able to make those early writing years less trying than they might have been" because she, unlike most people, understood him "sufficiently to be happy in constant contact with a nature so charming, yet often hypersensitive and broodingly reserved." She "never interfered in the slightest with his liberty of thought or action" so that he "grew to depend on [her] much more than he himself was aware." He was often to his wife "a son as well as a husband." Since JC was an artist, his imagination was "far too lively . . . for everyday events"; and "in his later years he carried fastidiousness to a degree that bordered on the fantastic." She acquired a maternal attitude not only toward her husband but also toward his writings. Their trip to Poland (1914) enabled her to understand JC much better than previously. She understood her husband's books as best she could; some parts she thought very beautiful, and some, like "Falk," made her "quite physically sick." JC was not "a practical person—certainly not in domestic matters." Once, when both were "acutely conscious that there was something hidden" between them, Mrs. Conrad wrote articles for the *Daily Mail,* which were published without her husband's knowledge. She concludes that although much will be written about JC in the future, "this is the only book that can be written about his private life; the most human, because the most intimate account of him." [Although poorly written and almost completely uncritical of JC's works, this book contains essential information about JC's domestic affairs and his family. Clearly, Mrs. Conrad, failing to understand her husband, claimed more credit for helping him than she really deserved. Her greatest contribution to our knowledge of JC consists of domestic matters, many of which are unavailable elsewhere.]

687 Conrad, Mrs. Joseph. "Recollections of Stephen Crane," BOOKMAN (NY), LXIII (April 1926), 134-37.

Crane and JC are "on easy terms of complete understanding." [Only sporadically concerned with JC.]

688 "Conrad, the Pole Famous in English Letters," WORLD REVIEW (Chicago), I (1 Feb 1926), 263.

JC "had a sympathy for the mysteriously pictorial in life, whether in a man, an ocean, or a landscape." He believed "it was man's job to confront Nature with a loyal and steady heart."

689 "Conrad's Last Essays," NEW STATESMAN, XXVII (1 May 1926), 84-85.

JC's splendid style in these *Last Essays* is especially to be appreciated.

690 "Conrad's Last Essays," TIMES LITERARY SUPPLEMENT (Lond), 4 March 1926, p. 159.

Of twenty essays in *Last Essays* "some half-dozen are as good as we could hope for." [General summary of contents.]

691 Crane, Stephen. TWO LETTERS FROM STEPHEN CRANE TO JOSEPH CONRAD. (Lond: First Edition Club, Curwen P, 1926), text, pp. 3-4; preface, pp. 1-2.

[See Aubry, TWENTY LETTERS TO CONRAD (1926).]

692 Cross, Wilbur. "Conrad's Last Words," YALE REVIEW, N.S. XVI (Oct 1926), 161-63.

In *Last Essays,* JC's portrait of Stephen Crane is "in mood and phrasing among the rarest literary portraits in our language since Thackeray died." JC seemed to conclude that the life of man "is best expressed as a struggle against the hostile forces that encompass him or as a struggle between conflicting emotions within his mind." [Of little value.]

693 Cuppy, Will. "Here are Essays," BOOKMAN (NY), LXIII (July 1926), 598.

[Summary of the contents of *Last Essays*.]

694 Curle, Richard. "The History of My Conrad Collection," MERMAID (Detroit), Oct 1926 [not seen]; rptd in THE RICHARD CURLE CONRAD COLLECTION. TO BE SOLD THURSDAY APRIL 28, AT 8:15 (NY: American Art Association, 1927).

[Curle explains how he acquired some of the 234 items in the catalogue. Items included a series of MSS, typescripts, and proof sheets; items corrected with JC's autograph (including "Christmas Day at Sea," the original autograph MS); books, mainly first editions; translations of JC's works; works originally appearing in serial form; eleven drawings by JC; and miscellaneous Conradiana.]

695 Curle, Richard. "Objection and Reproof," NEW YORK TIMES BOOK REVIEW, 9 May 1926, p. 25.

JC himself stated that he was not a Jew. [A refutation of Mr. Joseph Pennell's statement in his THE ADVENTURES OF AN ILLUSTRATOR (NY: Little, Brown, 1925) that JC told him he was a Jew (quoted in NEW YORK

TIMES BOOK REVIEW, 27 Dec 1925): JC refutes a similar claim by Frank Harris in a letter in NEW REPUBLIC (NY), 4 Aug 1918.]

696 Dinamov, S. "Pryzhok za Bort" (Jump Overboard), KNIGONOSHA, Nos. 46-47 (1926), 38.

[A review of *Lord Jim,* ed by E. Lann (Moscow and Leningrad, 1926).] [In Russian.]

697 Dinamov, S. "Romanticheskie prikliuchenia Dzhona Kempa" (Romantic Adventures of John Kemp), KNIGONOSHA, Nos. 23-24 (1926), 24.

[Review of *Romance,* trans by P. Rait and N. Volpin (Leningrad: Seiatel, 1926).] [In Russian.]

698 Drew, Elizabeth. "Joseph Conrad," THE MODERN NOVEL (NY: Harcourt Brace, 1926), pp. 221-40.

JC's "great central aim" is to "arrive at the truth," in which, artistically, he succeeds by making his readers hear, feel, and above all, see what he does. Philosophically, if the vision is uncomforting or cruel, the consolation inherent in JC's human truthfulness is durable. His method is to look beneath the surface of commonplace and common emotions. In *Lord Jim,* the hero, whose adventures are intimately, uncomfortably enigmatic, is nevertheless representative of the lives of all men. JC renders ruthlessly the "infinite unimportance and mystery" of human beings, the events that show man's inner fiber, intolerable ironies, and the "indestructable loneliness" of human life. Though success is denied, the struggle for fellowship is the law, as shown in "Heart of Darkness," *Victory,* and *Jim.* JC is not a pessimist in the ordinary sentimental sense; "his care is for life as life, not as an illustration of, or negation of, any moral law." In making us see and experience life he is successful. He is the only modern English writer "who creates large positive characters of the type of Lingard." Lingard, Capt. Anthony, Peyrol, and Marlow are robust and strong; Lingard is especially of "epic quality." In contrast, JC's handling of women is timid: "the only full-length figure, Rita" in *The Arrow of Gold,* is unconvincing. Flora de Barral, Mrs. Gould, Lena, and Mrs. Travers are always sacrificed. JC's verbal picture-making is supreme; his involved narrative method is an effective support of his aim—to get at the truth.

699 Doubleday, Page & Co. JOSEPH CONRAD: INCLUDING AN APPROACH TO HIS WRITINGS (Garden City, NY: Doubleday, Page, 1926).

"Introduction": JC has "genial human qualities," his works have a "matchless style," he has insight "into the tragic human emotions," his artistry is subtle, and his subject matter diverse. "The Approach to Joseph Conrad" [comments by twenty critics not specifically identified]: "Youth" is excellent because of JC's ability "to evoke an emotion without expressing it," "Typhoon" is noteworthy both for its description of a storm and its "human drama," and *The Nigger of the Narcissus* is important mainly because of the artist's creed in the preface. "Joseph Conrad, A Sketch": JC, with Hardy and George Moore, "represented the first definite break away from the manners and mannerisms of the Victorian novel that Dickens and Meredith exemplified." "Bibliography": first editions in England and the U. S., exclusive of magazine articles and translations of JC's books, are listed. [Reprints Richard Curle, "The History of Joseph Conrad's Books" (1923). Similar, on the whole accurate, publisher's brochures were issued at various earlier dates, beginning about 1914.]

700 Galsworthy, John. A LETTER FROM JOHN GALSWORTHY TO JOSEPH CONRAD (Lond: First Edition Club, Curwen P, 1926), text, pp. 5-6; editor's note, p. 3. [See Aubry, TWENTY LETTERS TO CONRAD (1926).]

701 Garnett, Constance. CONSTANCE GARNETT TO JOSEPH CONRAD (Lond: First Edition Club, Curwen P, 1926), text, pp. 2-3; editor's note, p. 1. [See Aubry, TWENTY LETTERS TO CONRAD (1926).]

702 Garnett, Edward. FOUR LETTERS FROM EDWARD GARNETT TO JOSEPH CONRAD (Lond: First Edition Club, Curwen P, 1926), text, pp. 5-11; editor's note, pp. 1-3. [See Aubry, TWENTY LETTERS TO CONRAD (1926).]

703 "The Genius by the Hearth," SPECTATOR (Lond), CXXXVII (11 Sept 1926), 387.

Since Jessie Conrad's JOSEPH CONRAD AS I KNEW HIM (1926) is "a direct and artless personal document by a brave woman and devoted wife," it properly lies outside the realm of criticism. Mrs. Conrad's "gift of spiritual faith and dignity" shines through the pages of this "simple record."

704 Gissing, George. TWO LETTERS FROM GEORGE GISSING TO JOSEPH CONRAD (Lond: First Edition Club, Curwen P, 1926), text, pp. 3-7; editor's note, p. 1. [See Aubry, TWENTY LETTERS TO CONRAD (1926).]

705 "A Great Adventure," NATION AND ATHENAEUM, XL (16 Oct 1926), 90-92.

Jessie Conrad's JOSEPH CONRAD AS I KNEW HIM (1926) indicates it is "very probable" that Mrs. Conrad made possible JC's "massive achievement": she "wived and mothered him for nearly thirty years." Her book reveals much of the real man, but it is "small-scale evidence" of JC, just enough to send the reader quickly from the man to his books.

706 Greene, Graham. "The Domestic Background," SPECTATOR (Lond), CLV (July 1926), 164; rptd in THE LOST CHILDHOOD AND OTHER ESSAYS (Lond: Eyre & Spottiswoode, 1951; NY: Viking P, 1952), 100-1.

Jessie Conrad was apparently too close to her husband to place an accurate perspective in her memories of their relationship. Her book JOSEPH CONRAD AS I KNEW HIM (1926) includes much which is trivial and is full of petty judgments, such as her total misrepresentation of Ford Madox Ford. "Out of a long marriage she has remembered nothing tender, nothing considerate. . . . But there is obviously no conscious dishonesty in the one-sided record. . . . It is simply that her mind is of a kind which harbors slights more than acts of kindness." [A brief yet seemingly comprehensive response to Mrs. Conrad's largely erroneous portrait of JC.]

707 Huneker, James Gibbons. A LETTER FROM JAMES GIBBONS HUNEKER TO JOSEPH CONRAD (Lond: First Edition Club, Curwen P, 1926), text, p. 3; editor's note, p. 1. [See Aubry, TWENTY LETTERS TO CONRAD (1926).]

708 Hunt, Violet. THE FLURRIED YEARS (Lond: Hurst and Blackett, [1926]), pp. 38, 203-4; pub as I HAVE THIS TO SAY (NY: Boni & Liveright [1926]).

Ford Madox Ford "adored Conrad." In response to being "cheeked" as regards Marie Antoinette's being a traitress, JC, flashing eyes, banging his fist, said, "I believe in the Divine Right of Kings."

709 Hutchison, Percy A. "In Conrad's *Last Essays* Is the Key to His Character / Spiritually He Belonged to 'the Company of the Great Navigators,'" NEW YORK TIMES BOOK REVIEW, 28 March 1926, pp. 3, 14.

The opening article of *Last Essays,* "Geography and Some Explorers," contains the master-key to JC. "Conrad is never lonely on the sea, for there he never lacks company, 'the company of the great navigators.'" And it is this spiritual oneness of the seaman-novelist with "the company of the great navigators" which is the master-key to JC.

710 James, Henry. THREE LETTERS FROM HENRY JAMES TO JOSEPH CONRAD (Lond: First Edition Club, Curwen P, 1926), text, pp. 3-8; editor's note, pp. 1-2. [See Aubry, TWENTY LETTERS TO CONRAD (1926).]

711 "Joseph Conrad," SPECTATOR (Lond), CXXXVI (24 April 1926), 765-66.

It is a marvel that a child of a mid-European aristocratic family should have developed such an "exotic genius" as JC's. His hold on English literature "has nothing earthy or rooted about it, but only a sporadic grip, fungoid and wholly inexplicable." The cause of his "spiritual travel" is "one of the greatest enigmas in that eternal mystery, the flood and ebb of human temperament." [Review of *Last Essays*.]

712 "Joseph Conrad," TIMES LITERARY SUPPLEMENT (Lond), 9 Sept 1926, p. 594.
Jessie Conrad's JOSEPH CONRAD AS I KNEW HIM (1926) is not of great literary merit but is interesting and honest enough to win respect.

713 Kalinovich, M. A. "Dzhozef Konrad" (Joseph Conrad), *Avanpost Progressu (An Outpost of Progress)*, trans by C. Vilkhov (Kiev: Slovo, 1926).
[In Ukrainian.]

714 Kashkin, I. *"Ozhidanie" (Suspense)*, WEST AND EAST (Moscow), I-II (1926), 159-60.
[A review.] [In Russian.]

715 Kellett, Ernest Edward. "A Note on Joseph Conrad," LONDON MERCURY, XIII (March 1926), 485-93; rptd in RECONSIDERATIONS; LITERARY ESSAYS (NY: Macmillan, 1928), pp. 243-61.
Critics who argue that JC mastered English prose style, and "wrote like an Englishman" are wrong. JC has genius, but his early work had serious flaws. A selection from "the first three or four chapters of *The Rover*" reveals severe stylistic lapses and errors, some of which impair the meaning of the story. While these lapses affect the work they are not typical, and JC rapidly moved beyond them to more correct forms, but his style is closer to seventeenth-century English than present day style.

716 Kipling, Rudyard. A LETTER FROM RUDYARD KIPLING TO JOSEPH CONRAD (Lond: First Edition Club, Curwen P, 1926), text, p. 3; editor's note, p. 1. [See Aubry, TWENTY LETTERS TO CONRAD (1926).]

717 Lalou, René. PANORAMA DE LA LITTÉRATURE ANGLAISE CONTEMPORAINE (Panorama of Contemporary English Literature) (Paris: Kra, 1926), pp. 8, 206, 208-16, 217, 218, 238.
JC's calm objectivity is a contribution of French classicism to the chaos of the English novel. His impressionism is created by multiple points of view as in a novel like *Nostromo*. In "Youth," JC is a symbolist. "Heart of Darkness," like many of his works, deals with the conflict between savagery and civilized progress. The sea is his favorite vehicle for uniting the human adventure with the cosmic one. Although service and love are two of his most frequent themes, ultimately JC is pessimistic about the outcome of

the struggle between the individual and life. [A general survey.] [In French.]

718 "Literature," A. L. A. BOOKLIST, XXII (July 1926), 409. [Trivial review of *Last Essays*.]

719 Loks, K. "Pryzhok za Bort" (The Jump Overboard), PECHAT I REVOLUTSIA, VII (1926), 216.
[In Russian.]

720 Loks, K. "Romanticheskie prikliuchenie Dzhona Kempa" (Romantic Adventures of John Kemp), PECHAT I REVOLUTSIA, VII (1926), 222.
[A review.] [In Russian.]

721 Lucas, E. V. E. V. LUCAS TO JOSEPH CONRAD (Lond: First Edition Club, Curwen P, 1926), text, pp. 2-3; editor's note, p. 1. [See Aubry, TWENTY LETTERS TO CONRAD (1926).]

722 McFee, William. "Mrs. Conrad Speaks," NEW YORK HERALD TRIBUNE BOOKS, 21 Nov 1926, Sect vii, p. 6.
In JOSEPH CONRAD AS I KNEW HIM (1926), Mrs. Conrad's style is "the worst in the world"; the book reveals her "amazing wifely solicitude," her "indomitable domestic character," and JC's great dependence on her. Whereas Ford's book on JC is art, Mrs. Conrad's book is, in spite of its turgidity, "life."

723 Mann, Thomas. "Vorwort" (Preface); *Der Geheimagent* (*The Secret Agent*) (Berlin: Fischer, [1926]); rptd as "Vorwort zu Joseph Conrads Roman *Der Geheimagent*" (Preface to Joseph Conrad's *The Secret Agent*), DIE FORDERUNG DES TAGES (The Challenge of the Day) (Berlin: Fischer, 1930), pp. 325-40; as "Conrad's *The Secret Agent*," in PAST MASTERS AND OTHER PAPERS, trans by H. T. Lowe-Porter (Lond: Secker; NY: Knopf, 1933), pp. 234-47; in ALTES UND NEUES (Frankfurt: Fischer, 1953), pp. 493-506; and in THE ART OF JOSEPH CONRAD: A CRITICAL SYMPOSIUM, ed by Robert W. Stallman (East Lansing: Michigan State U P, 1960), pp. 227-34.
"[H]is virile talent, his Englishness, his free brow, his clear, steady and humorous eye, his narrative verve, power, and grave-faced whimsicality, show up as well when the author stops on dry ground." The background of *The Secret Agent* is in the whole conflict between British and Russian political ideology. Russia is made to bear the guilt of all the human tragedy which is responsible for his limited reputation in Germany, for Germany chose the East and is now moving back to a central position. Anglo-Saxondom has always excelled, as does JC, in the comic-grotesque. He is

sarcastic of Utopias and of the bourgeois (disregard of art, combined with reverence for utilitarian science); he is not anti-bourgeois, but class-free and objective. JC's objections to Lombroso's science rest "not upon social grounds, but upon profounder, religious ones." Stevie is "far and away the finest figure in the book." Here Russian influence is evident, for "without Dostoevski's Idiot, Stevie is unthinkable. The dominant psychology is "one with religious implications." [In German.]

724 Mégroz, Rodolphe Louis. "Joseph Conrad: Man and Artist," BOOKMAN (Lond), LXX (Aug 1926), 238-41.

An interview with JC on the opening night of *The Secret Agent* [play], which JC was too nervous to attend, revealed JC didn't enjoy drama because "it meant cutting all the flesh off the book. And I realized then, as I had never done, what a gruesome story I had written." G. K. Chesterton's CHARLES DICKENS gives JC's view of that novelist. JC is classified according to Dr. Miller's TYPES OF MIND AND BODY as an "aesthetic introvert." Loyalty, endurance, courage "and the craftsman's conscience" are JC's best traits and the results of his "racial memories." [JC is imagined as Marlow throughout. Similar to conclusions Mégroz has stated in other places.]

725 Mencken, H. L. "Joseph Conrad," PREJUDICES: FIFTH SERIES (NY: Knopf, 1926), pp. 34-41; rptd in SELECTED PREJUDICES (NY: Knopf, 1927), pp. 37-45; and in A MENCKEN CHRESTOMATHY (NY: Knopf, 1949), pp. 518-22.

JC's view of the world order has "an atheistic and demoniacal smack," and the God he visualizes is not "a loving papa in carpet slippers, but a comedian." "Heart of Darkness" is the key to his metaphysical system, and it, "Youth" and "The End of the Tether" comprise the best books of imaginative writing in English literature in the twentieth century. JC's Slavic background is reflected in his language, which has a sharp, exotic flavor. He reworks language in spite of its prohibitions and is not shackled to embalmed ideas. He views English logically, analytically, freshly. JC is a great man, decidedly underestimated, and mistaken for a mere romantic and later as a linguistic marvel because he could write in English though Polish was his native tongue. *Lord Jim* is a human document as well as a work of art, and *Almayer's Folly,* his first work, is a work of genius in its planning and working out.

726 Morris, Lawrence S. "In Praise of Devotion," NEW REPUBLIC, XLVI (12 May 1926), 383.

In *Last Essays,* some of JC's reticence disappears, showing the small Polish boy identifying himself with great explorers loyal to an immaterial purpose and without assurance of a goal. JC's "touchstone of values" is transferred from the sea to literary art. His brief sketches of reminiscence are charming; his literary criticism acute, reasoned. All essays are "unified in the light of Conrad's distinctive vision of life."

727 "Our Own Bookshelf," LIVING AGE, CCCXXIX (5 June 1926), 555.

Though the essay was "not an entirely happy mode of expression" for JC and shows too much his failure to achieve "integration and composure," still it shows the "inalienable distinction" of his mind, and is valuable for his accents of Stephen Crane. [Review of *Last Essays*.]

728 Parton, Ethel. "Betwixt and Between," OUTLOOK (NY), CXLII (28 April 1926), 654.

Last Essays is a small volume of "brief miscellaneous pieces, few of them important"; but each has "a real reason" for being included, "either in their own charm and beauty or for some light they cast upon Conrad's character or career."

729 Perry, F. M. "Joseph Conrad—Master of the Interaction of Natural and Moral Forces," STORY WRITING: LESSONS FROM THE MASTERS (NY: Holt, 1926), pp. 104-39, 179.

The interplay of forces of nature and morality in JC's works is "vital and inevitable." To JC, civilization blurs distinctions that keep men from knowing themselves. Even his treatment of savages shows the "capacity of a man vested with power for unemotional justice." JC's "certain foreign quality" gives "freshness and opulence" to common themes. Cardinal virtues are steadfastness, duty to self, "stiffness to stand alone," and power to "rouse emotional appreciation of experiences that transcend our intimate personal range of experience." In JC's style, the action is not the "form-giving skeleton of the story," but a "central core of light . . . [that brings] out the nature of the enveloping haze." Marlow is a visible projection of the writer. JC's art is elaborate; he does not give a consecutive easily flowing narrative"; rather, the story is "gleaned by bits that come to us, as do things we seem always to have known in life . . . fragments illuminating one another and pointing forward as well as backward." JC does not answer questions before they are asked, but he holds "attention alert for solutions for which reason has been skillfully incited to clamor." Like his sense of chronology, JC's movement in space "attains a certain simultaneousness of impression." [Good insight in a text designed for study by a class in advanced writing.]

730 Randall, John Herman. "Joseph Conrad—His Outlook on Life," UNITY (Chicago), XCVI (18 Jan 1926), 281-86; rptd from JOSEPH CONRAD: HIS OUTLOOK ON LIFE, The Community Series,

VI (NY: The Community Church, 1924-1925) [a pamphlet, not seen].

JC's style changed from an early one, in which "romantic and sonorous passages . . . abound" to a later "more nervous and less poetic manner." The sea "was the first of Conrad's illusions." He later came to see it as it really was. JC's characters are "all supremely individual." His novels are never "based on adventurous incident, but on adventurous personality." JC is not a pessimist, and quite unlike Hardy. In Hardy's novels man and all sentient beings are doomed to suffer in an amoral universe where moral failure has no place. But in JC "tragedy . . . is from first to last human." Essence of JC's tragic irony is illusion, in the sense of covering "all the ends of human action, even when in themselves good." Yet "Fidelity, Sincerity, Humanity and action expressive of these" virtues are not illusions. JC's heroes cannot guess the outcome of their crises, but some know what JC felt was essential for men—*"how to act now."*

731 Read, Herbert. "The Essential Conrad," NATION AND ATHENAEUM, XXXIX (3 April 1926), 20.

Last Essays suggests that JC's strength was not really in the sphere of a novelist, for this writer "did not possess the right kind of imagination for that role; he had, really, no creative imagination whatsoever—only an amazing visual memory for the sensible details of life and a capacity to make use of that memory, to set it working within a formula he got from Turgenev, or Flaubert, or Henry James." JC was most nearly himself in such works as *Last Essays*.

732 "Recent Additions: Essays," ST. LOUIS PUBLIC LIBRARY MONTHLY BULLETIN, N.S. XXIV (Sept 1926), 248.

Last Essays contains all of JC's previously uncollected "important miscellaneous writings."

733 Ruch, Gertrud. "Zeitverlauf und Erzählerstandpunkt in Joseph Conrads Romanen" (Time and Angle of Narration in Joseph Conrad's Novels) (Zurich: pvtly ptd, 1926). Published thesis, University of Zurich, 1926).

Nostromo seems chaotic at first sight and unsatisfactory even after several readings. *Lord Jim* (especially the second half) suffers from Marlow's interruptions, while *Chance,* though achieving a convincing kind of realism, does not quite succeed in solving the problem of the obtrusive Marlow. [This study of JC's handling of time and point of view deals with *Almayer's Folly, Lord Jim,* and *Chance.* Though Ruch acknowledges sincerity and recognizes a few of his intentions, she criticizes his technique strongly.] [In German.]

734 S[chriftgiesser], K[arl]. "Joseph Conrad in the Role of Essayist," BOSTON EVENING TRANSCRIPT BOOK SECTION, 10 April 1926, p. 1.

Like *Notes on Life and Letters, Last Essays* (introduction by Richard Curle) reveals much about JC's philosophy and literary countenance. Certain essays on Crane, Galsworthy, and James are particularly valuable.

735 "Seeing Conrad Plain," SATURDAY REVIEW (Lond), CXLII (11 Sept 1926), 289-90.

Taking JC to be one of those authors whose real self is to be found in his own works, not in works written *about* him, one can appreciate Jessie Conrad's affectionate and skillful view of JC the man, and his eccentricities in JOSEPH CONRAD AS I KNEW HIM (1926). But "what it does for us is only to convince us that Conrad understood himself, knew what in him could be projected into his art."

736 S[karzewski], [Tadeusz] Ż[uk]. "Conradiana," POLAND (NY), Aug 1926, pp. 469-71, 512; Sept 1926, pp. 542-43, 573-74; Oct 1926, pp. 615-16, 637, 640; Nov 1926, pp. 675-77, 700-2, 704; Jan 1927, pp. 22-24, 45-48, 50; Aug 1927, pp. 471-72, 490.

[Żuk Skarzewski is one of Poland's better "fuilletonists" of the twenties, and his series contains some new and interesting material. The description of the scene in which the little JC sees his father peering through the bars of the prison in Warsaw is especially strong. Skarzewski's essays are of biographical rather than critical interest. This comparatively inaccessible journal is available in the Library of Congress.]

737 S[ufflay], M[ilan]. "O Josephu Conradu. Polska i ruska umjetnicka krv" (On Joseph Conrad. Polish and Russian Artistic Blood), OBZOR (Zagreb), LXVII: 341 (1926), 3.

[Review of Jessie Conrad's JOSEPH CONRAD AS I KNEW HIM (1926) and Elbridge Adams's CONRAD THE MAN (1925; see 1923).] [In Serbo-Croatian.]

738 Vidakovic, Aleksandar. "Najnovija dela engleske knijizevnosti" (Recent Works of English Literature), LETOPIS MATICE SRPSKE (Novi Sad), C: 1-2 (1926), 202-10.

[Review, among other current fiction, of *Suspense*.] [In Serbo-Croatian.]

739 Villard, Léonie. "A Conrad Heroine in Real Life," T. P.'s AND CASSELL'S WEEKLY, V (23 Jan 1926), 476; rptd in LIVING AGE, CCCXXVIII (20 March 1926), 637-39.

Adèle d'Osmond is a model for Adèle de Montevesso in *Suspense*.

740 Villard, Léonie. "Joseph Conrad et les mémorialistes (À propos de *Suspense*)" (Joseph Conrad and the Memorialists [With

Reference to *Suspense*]), REVUE ANGLO-AMÉRICAINE, III (April 1926), 313-21.

Although the exoticism of JC's work has often been noticed by critics, his European mentality has not been so frequently appreciated. A brief study of one historical source—MÉMOIRES DE LA COMTESSE DE BOIGNE—reveals not only JC's ability to understand European attitudes but also his artistry in transforming history into psychological drama. The MÉMOIRES provided JC certain episodes of his plot, some of his minor characters, and also the figure of Adèle de Montevesso. The name of Osmond is changed by JC to Armand; the fictional Lady Latham draws some of her characteristics from the historical Lady Legard; Dr. Martel of *Suspense* is suggested by Dr. Marshall of the MÉMOIRES; the interview between Mme de Boigne and Napoleon is changed very little by JC. But a scene which allows one to study JC's artistic use of his historical data is the one in which Adèle de Montevesso reveals her sorrowful life to Cosmo Latham. Although the MÉMOIRES give JC most of the facts of this lady's past, he transforms colorless narration into an emotionally charged atmosphere that serves as the background for psychological drama. [General assertions without much specific analysis of JC's artistic transformations.] [In French.]

> **741** Waldman, Milton. "The Book World: What Britain Is Reading; Huntsman's Book, Hewlett's Letters, Conrad's Essays and 'Rough Justice,'" NEW YORK WORLD (Editorial Section), 11 April 1926, p. 6M.

"Unimportant" to JC the writer, the essays in *Last Essays* give "light" on JC "the mariner and the man."

> **742** Wells, Herbert George. TWO LETTERS FROM H. G. WELLS TO JOSEPH CONRAD (Lond: First Edition Club, Curwen P, 1926), text, pp. 3-6. [See Aubry, TWENTY LETTERS TO CONRAD (1926).]

> **743** Willard, Grace. "Mrs. Conrad's Book About Her Husband: 'Conrad Was an Amateur Husband but Always Remained Great Lover,'" NEW YORK EVENING POST LITERARY REVIEW, VII (9 Oct 1926), 5.

Jessie's forbearance, in JOSEPH CONRAD AS I KNEW HIM (1926), of the sea captain's command against arguments and of his rolling bread pellets at dinner, and her cleverness at typewriting and at putting out bedroom fires is praiseworthy.

> **744** Willard, Grace. "Title is Like a Knell: Conrad's *Last Essays*, Swan Song of Master," NEW YORK EVENING POST LITERARY REVIEW, VI (1 May 1926), 3.

Last Essays contains JC's descriptions of his seagoing and of meeting Stephen Crane, and JC's "The Congo Diary."

1927

745 Arns, Karl. "Conrad, Joseph: *Taifun,* Stuttgart, 1927; *Sieg; Nostromo,* Berlin 1927" (Conrad, Joseph: *Typhoon,* Stuttgart, 1927; *Victory; Nostromo,* Berlin 1927), GRAL (Munich), XXII (1927/28), 465-66.

JC is said to be one of the great writers of life instinct and racial solidarity, a discoverer of the soul, who avoids having recourse to a too complicated psychology. The translations of his works are praiseworthy. [In German.]

746 Aubry, G. Jean-. JOSEPH CONRAD: LIFE AND LETTERS. Two Volumes (Lond: Heinemann; NY: Doubleday, Page, 1927).

[This basic biography of JC, containing many of his letters as well as a detailed account of his life, was a monumental achievement in its time. JC willed his personal papers to his close friend, who tries in this work "to trace every step in that [JC's] strange career," relying not on rumors but on "plain facts." He believes that his plan of "following minutely" the events of JC's life "will show how immense was the transmuting power of his imagination and that nothing happened to him in vain." He assures his readers that in spite of his inability to unravel every puzzle in his friend's life they "will find nothing conjectural in this book, nothing unsupported by documentary evidence." Although Aubry's THE SEA DREAMER (1957) supersedes it, the LIFE AND LETTERS remains *the* indispensable biographical source-book on JC.]

747 Aubry, G. Jean-. "Polska w zyciv i dzielach Josepha Conrada" (Poland in the Life and Work of Joseph Conrad), DROGA, No. 12 (Dec 1927), 18-29; rptd as "La Pologne dans la vie et l'oeuvre de Joseph Conrad," POLOGNE LITTÉRAIRE, VI (15 May 1932), 2.

Critics have not sufficiently examined the influence of Poland on JC. This influence includes JC's life in Poland, Polish literature, and JC's Polish temperament. Except for his romantic heritage from Poland, JC's native country seems to have had more of a negative influence on his character and work. The principal effect is the widespread feeling in his work of solitude, exile, isolation, and alienation among foreign people. That only "Prince Roman" and "Amy Foster" bear the stamp of Poland can be explained by the painfulness and closeness of JC's memories of Poland, which made it nearly impossible for him to write about such experiences. As for JC's general philosophy, his Polish character undoubtedly shaped it; as for his style, a thorough study by Polish linguists would certainly reveal the influence of Polish upon some of the peculiarities of his English.

[Exploratory argument weakened by lack of support and an impression of rationalization.] [In Polish and French.]

748 Blunden, Edmund. "A Conrad Repository," LONDON MERCURY, XVII (Dec 1927), 179-86.

G. Jean-Aubry's LIFE AND LETTERS OF JOSEPH CONRAD (1927) has "no special gleam or force to make one's attention glide on." JC's letters have an indefinite, repetitive style in which is reflected his "uneasiness of spirit" as he strove "to be accepted by the mates and the crew of intellectual action." The letters lack both the "touch of Ariel" and "mild or laughing humour"; their humor "defies augury" and comes from wildness. JC's literary work is "a pathetic triumph," for especially during his devotion to *Nostromo* and afterward, JC stopped "perceiving the outward things" "passing daily in his way."

749 Brickell, Herschel. "The Literary Landscape," NORTH AMERICAN REVIEW, CCXXIV (Nov 1927) [unpaged, among advertisements at beginning of issue].

G. Jean-Aubry's JOSEPH CONRAD: LIFE AND LETTERS (1927) is an "infinitely rich" source for all future biographers of JC.

750 Buenzod, Emmanuel. "Traductions: Joseph Conrad: 'Gaspar Ruiz' (N.R.F.)" (Translations: Joseph Conrad: "Gaspar Ruiz" [N.R.F.], BIBLIOTHÈQUE UNIVERSELLE ET REVUE DE GENÈVE, II (Dec 1927), 796.

In the form of the novella, JC, otherwise so meticulous to limit his subject, fails to keep it within artistic bounds. Though imperfect artistically, stories like "The Duel" reveal, nevertheless, the prodigious imagination of their author. [Review of *A Set of Six*.] [In French.]

751 Church, Richard. "The Life of Joseph Conrad," SPECTATOR (Lond), CXXXIX (12 Nov 1927), 829, 831.

G. Jean-Aubry's JOSEPH CONRAD: LIFE AND LETTERS (1927) is a more "scientific exposition" of the material in JC's *A Personal Record*. JC "lives" in Aubry's pages, which reveal "a thousand and one snapshots" of a genius and offer some clues to the genesis of his disposition and genius.

752 Clifford, Sir Hugh Charles. A TALK ON JOSEPH CONRAD AND HIS WORK (A Lecture delivered to the Ceylon branch of the English Association) (Colombo: H. W. Cave, 1927).

[In an anecdotal reminiscence, Clifford recalls his thirty-one-year long association with JC, focusing largely on his early recognition of JC's genius and his preaching "the Gospel of Conrad, often to indifferent ears." Includes remembrances of his "instant appreciation" of *Almayer's Folly*, his early (late 90s) reviews of JC's early work in the SINGAPORE FREE

PRESS (not seen) at a time when JC was virtually unknown, his help in calling JC's books to the attention of Gordon Bennett. JC had only a superficial acquaintance with Malaysia and its people; however, he captured the charm of this culture imaginatively in his novels. JC wrote English with great skill although it was not his native tongue, and his genius was acclaimed almost as soon as he began to write. Popular acclaim, however, did not follow for nearly twenty years. In general, a very warm, personal, and sympathetic account.]

753 "A Conrad Collection," TIMES LITERARY SUPPLEMENT (Lond), 12 May 1927, p. 340.

[Notes results of April 28, 1927, sale of Richard Curle's collection. Sale catalogue is said to contain bibliographical details which are "almost unknown to biographers."]

754 Conrad, Jessie. "Earlier and Later Days," SATURDAY EVENING POST, CXCVII (13 Sept 1927), 12-13, 212-14.

[Reminiscences about life with JC from marriage to Borys Conrad's return from the army, this material is covered in greater detail in JOSEPH CONRAD AND HIS CIRCLE (1935).]

755 [Conrad (Korzeniowska), Jessie]. "Preface," JOSEPH CONRAD'S LETTERS TO HIS WIFE (Lond: Pvtly ptd, 1927 [Neill & Co., Edinburgh]), pp. 7-8.

[Contains thirty-six letters from JC to his wife, written from 1916 to June 1924. Includes rare photograph of JC while on special service aboard the *Ready* in 1916.]

756 "Conrad Letters," TIMES LITERARY SUPPLEMENT (Lond), 27 Oct 1927, p. 761.

[Review of Aubry's JOSEPH CONRAD: LIFE AND LETTERS (1927). Most of the letters are about "shop and family." Mostly comment on JC as a sea writer; little on letters or on editor's work.]

757 Davray, Henry D. "Lettres anglaises" (English Letters), MERCURE DE FRANCE, CXCIII (1 Jan 1927), 485-91.

The age had a morbid interest in biographic eccentricities from which JC's personal life should be excluded. JC was "a public-private man," keeping a mask for the public world and another personality for his family. Jessie's biography is intimate and charming, "filled with homey insights into a simple and complex personality." Ford's biography isn't strong on facts but portrays the man as he appeared to a friend. JC is "homo europeans sapiens," a kind of Renaissance Englishman like Drake. JC loved self-analysis, and the complexities of his style cut him off from readers who would like the subject matter. [Review of Jessie Conrad's JOSEPH CONRAD AS I KNEW HIM (1926), Ford Madox Ford's JOSEPH CONRAD: A PERsonal Remembrance (1924), and JC's Last Essays, *Nostromo* and *Suspense*. Comments on JC's personal appearance, speech and mannerisms. Reviews of JC's books are brief, usually listing some contents, and very laudatory.] [In French.]

758 Ford, Ford Madox. "The Other House," New York Herald Tribune Books, 2 Oct 1927, Sect vii, p. 2.

Georges Jean-Aubry belongs to the "other house" of the conscientious uninspired. There are serious omissions in Aubry's Joseph Conrad: Life and Letters (1927). JC's interest in Henry James [he thought James his only equal, says Ford] and their correspondence [only two of several scores of letters are represented] are slighted; JC's relationships to and correspondence with Frieger and Marwood are scanted; and JC said that he once served on a French naval vessel (the *Ville d'ompleda*) and that he had been "under fire on service" contrary to Aubry's belief that JC had served only in merchant ships. Even if JC liked to "poetiser un peu," the truth of his romantic emotion was truer than Aubry's facts. [Almost totally negative comment on Aubry's book.]

759 Galsworthy, John. "Six Novelists in Profile: An Address," Castles in Spain and Other Screeds (NY: Scribner's, 1927; rptd 1928), pp. 201-35; rptd in Candelabra (NY: Scribner's, 1933), pp. 133-54.

JC belongs in the company of Dickens, Turgenev, de Maupassant, Tolstoi, and Anatole France; he is the most powerful of English novelists "in word-painting," and his writing is "a singular blending of reality with romance."

760 Gerould, Katherine Fullerton. "Stream of Consciousness," Saturday Review of Literature, IV (22 Oct 1927), 233-35.

People who loved JC's methods before he was critically endorsed were usually "Jacobites," people who already adored Henry James. JC applied James's method, using mental rhythms instead of rhetorical rhythms, to exotic new subjects. JC, though a great writer, was not always a great novelist but *Victory* was a great novel. He became more rhetorical and faced his audience while James became less rhetorical and turned on it. Both used stream of consciousness to determine attitudes; nevertheless, the plot progresses during a character's reflecting. Even in masters like JC and James, the stream of consciousness method is unpopular. The generation of stream of consciousness writers after JC (Dorothy Richardson, Sherwood Anderson, Virginia Woolf, the latest Joseph Hergesheimer, the latest Willa Cather) are "notably unmemorable." Beauty is not their concern—it was the concern of JC and James.

761 Golding, Henry J. "Glimpses of Conrad," Standard, XIV (Nov 1927), 68-75.

JC is especially concerned for "community of experience." *The Mirror of the Sea* is an "exercise in piety . . . a tribute of gratitude and love." By temperament JC is a philosopher, transcending "psychological accuracy and implicit moral judgment" to aim at an interpretation of life; a brooder concerned with the opposition of will to an "insentient world." JC has a "tragic sense of life," the keynote of which is isolation and respect. [Highly laudatory, touching aspects of JC that are now commonplace.]

762 Gorman, Herbert. "The Literary Review: Jean-Aubry's CONRAD: LIFE AND LETTERS; Conrad's Earlier Years and His Later Letters; in the Former, He Lived the Gist of His Romances," NEW YORK EVENING POST, 24 Sept 1927, p. 10.

In LIFE AND LETTERS (1927), Aubry shows that "Conrad saw his own life through a veil of sparkling romance" and that "nearly all of his books were portions of the biography of his days." Volume II is chiefly a "loose-rock formation . . . of reprinted correspondence," which shows "Conrad on semi-parade," but JC is "always either wise, witty, or intensely human."

763 Hansen, Harry. "The Book World: The First Reader; Jean-Aubry's 2-Volume Study Shows Life Was Conrad's Source," NEW YORK WORLD (Editorial Section), 11 Sept 1927, p. 7E.

JC's letters in G. Jean-Aubry's LIFE AND LETTERS give the work value, since they show "superb eloquence" and "humility," "so rarely met with in the egotistical writers of our time."

764 Hopkins, Frederick M. "Curle Sale of Conradiana," PUBLISHERS' WEEKLY, CXI (4 June 1927), 2186-88. [A descriptive list.]

765 Hutchison, Percy. "Conrad's Life Was a Romance / In His Tales He Transmuted Much of His Own Experience," NEW YORK TIMES BOOK REVIEW, 18 Sept 1927, pp. 1, 19, 22.

In G. Jean-Aubry's LIFE AND LETTERS (1927), the coverage of the latter years of JC's life is inadequate. Except for a few instances, "it cannot be said that Jean-Aubry adds greatly to our knowledge of the facts of Conrad's life."

766 Kalinovich, M. A. "Perdmova" (Foreword), *Konets Nevoli* (The End of the Tether) (Kiev: Slovo, 1927), pp. v-x. [In Ukrainian.]

767 Loks, K. "Serdtse Tmy" (Heart of Darkness), PECHAT I REVOLUTSIA, VIII (1927), 207.

[In Russian.]

768 Lubbock, Basil. THE LAST OF THE WINDJAMMERS (Glasgow: Brown, Son & Ferguson, 1927), I, 409-10; 485.

The clipper ship *Otago,* one of the "small fry" among sailing vessels, an iron barque of 367 tons built by Stephen & Sons of Glasgow in 1869, "had the honour of being commanded by Joseph Conrad." In his works, JC gives "ample evidence of his affection for her and he makes her the scene of many of his powerful short stories." Judging from JC's books, the *Otago* appears to have been mostly employed in the Dutch East Indies. [The author gives a description and a brief history of the barque.]

769 [Mackay, W. MacDonald.] "The Bibliography of Joseph Conrad," BOOKMAN'S JOURNAL, XV (1927), 163-64.

A Canadian edition of *Chance* should be noted; Wise is in error as to the number of copies printed of *Almayer's Folly* and of *An Outcast of the Islands.*

770 Morley, Christopher. [Title unknown], SYDNEY BULLETIN (1927) [not seen]; rptd as "Temperamental Writing," in INTERNAL REVENUE (Garden City, NY: Doubleday, Doran, 1933), pp. 185-99.

Ford Madox Ford in his memoirs deals with JC as a professional. He takes him seriously as an artist, as JC regards himself. In his note on JC's *The Sisters,* Ford asserts JC is unable to make his women characters real. However, despite the remarkable collection of JC data and letters by Aubry, no one has yet evaluated the man's greatness.

Chance sold well because of his publisher's efforts, not because of any virtue in the book itself. People "who are interested in literature as a sincere form of trickery" will always find it fascinating. It contains an old plot—The Wife in Name Only—but characters in the story are seen through a double lens: that of a simple observer, in contact with crisis and a subtle commentator not at the crisis, but cognizant of the situations. *The Nigger of the Narcissus* is too great to be considered merely as a work of art; it is grand because it comes from the secret places of the heart; it wrings experience; it creates a microcosm. [Anecdotal; repeats some earlier Morley comments.]

771 Partington, Wilfred. "Joseph Conrad Behind the Scenes: Unpublished Notes on His Dramatisations," BOOKMAN'S JOURNAL, XV: 4 (1927), 179-84.

The editor of BOOKMAN'S JOURNAL had sent JC proofs of an article on JC's theatrical interests; JC returned them heavily corrected—some editorial cuts offended JC. JC's marginal comments on the proofs also indicate he was capable of self-criticism, not nearly so eager to advance a dramatist's career as some supposed, and that he had no wish to dramatize *Almayer's Folly.* A letter from JC indicates his disinclination to discuss his work in public. JC's most detailed comment on "The Secret Sharer" is in a letter to

Galsworthy, quoted by Galsworthy in preface to LAUGHING ANNE AND ONE DAY MORE (1924).

772 Roquette de Fonvielle, A. "Conrad et la Pologne" (Conrad and Poland), ANNALES POLITIQUES ET LITTÉRAIRES, LXXXVIII (15 May 1927), 527.

JC's work reveals his typically Polish nature: moral restraint, spontaneity, reserve, loyalty, and individual responsibility. His novels also deal with the universal problem of the uprooted. [In French.]

773 Safroni-Middleton, A. TROPIC SHADOWS: MEMORIES OF THE SOUTH SEAS, TOGETHER WITH REMINISCENCES OF THE AUTHOR'S SEA MEETINGS WITH JOSEPH CONRAD (Lond: Richards, 1927), pp. 35-59.

[The author recalls various incidents which occurred during meetings with JC in Australia, London, and San Francisco.]

774 Schriftgiesser, Karl. "Joseph Conrad as He Knew Himself," BOSTON EVENING TRANSCRIPT BOOK SECTION, 17 Sept 1927, p. 4.

JC's achievement as an English novelist is great, and G. Jean-Aubry's JOSEPH CONRAD: LIFE AND LETTERS (1927) is objective and straightforward.

775 Shanks, Edward. "Joseph Conrad," SATURDAY REVIEW (Lond), CXLIV (5 Nov 1927), 622.

G. Jean-Aubry's two-volume JOSEPH CONRAD: LIFE AND LETTERS (1927) is "a rambling and unsatisfactory hodge-podge," coming so soon after JC's death that it perhaps could not be done properly or completely—but thereby forestalling the day when the job can be done again. There is some value in Aubry's confirming the fact that much of JC's best work is based closely on his own experience even if JC's life remains in many respects a bewildering enigma.

776 S[malc], M[atevz]. "Joseph Conrad," LJUBLJANSKI ZVON (Ljubljana), XLVII: 4 (1927), 256.

[A note accompanying translation of "The Lagoon."] [In Slovene.]

777 Sper, Felix. "The Cream of Conrad," POET LORE, XXXVIII (Sept 1927), 422-25.

JC has lifted the sea-story "from colorless reporting" to "poetic transcripts of the play of human passion colored with elemental beauty." He is undoubtedly unique, violating the obvious requirement of simple plotting. His clear-cut characters are developed from the inside out. But he can't draw women; "his women are uniformly recaptured dreams or gargoyles." JC will be valued as an "historian of the passing of picturesque savagery slowly murdered by ruthless Western commercialism."

778 Tomlinson, H. M. "Joseph Conrad," SATURDAY REVIEW OF LITERATURE, IV (15 Oct 1927), 191-92.

G. Jean-Aubry's JOSEPH CONRAD: LIFE AND LETTERS (1927) illustrates how JC's proud humility made him feel inferior as a writer of English prose and as an Englishman. He never felt he was treated as a native and "tried too hard" to be English. "The trouble with almost any foreigner who would serve another tradition is that he treats that tradition with greater reverence than they who were born in it." JC's letters "show what a simple and loveable man he was." Aubry has been "a patient but enthusiastic investigator and editor, and the biography in volume one, with its elucidation of people and places in the novels and stories, reads like an elaborate piece of detective work."

779 Zeromski, Stefan. "Joseph Conrad," NINETEENTH CENTURY AND AFTER, CI (March 1927), 406-16.

The Mirror of the Sea is especially good for an adequate understanding of JC himself, and his best works are his sea stories. JC in 1914 was still "a perfect master of our Polish language" and his knowledge of Polish enabled him to add "an altogether new note" to his use of the English language. JC was one of the only two sailors produced by Poland prior to 1927, but the credit for his greatest achievements belongs to his own "hard work and endurance."

1928

780 Al, F. *"Nostromo,"* KNIGA I PROFSOUIUZY, 3 (1928), 32. [A review.] [In Russian.]

781 American Art Association. THE HISTORIC EDWARD GARNETT CONRAD-HUDSON COLLECTION. TO BE SOLD THE EVENINGS OF APRIL 24 & 25, AT 8:15 (NY: American Art Association, 1928). [Lists 254 JC items, consisting of many autograph JC letters, an unpublished translation by JC from the French, and some early editions of JC volumes. The biggest attraction was W. H. Chesson's presentation copy of the copyright issue of *The Nigger of the Narcissus* (one of 7 printed in London by Heinemann in 1897, it sold for $4,900).]

782 Ames, Van Meter. "The Technique of the Novel," AESTHETICS OF THE NOVEL (Chicago: University of Chicago P, 1928), pp. 179-81, 183-84.

In *Almayer's Folly,* JC was the omniscient author. As far as it is told from Almayer's point of view, the reader gets a consistent impression; when the point of view shifts to other characters the unified effect is lost. In contrast to *The Nigger of the Narcissus, Folly* lacks unity because there is no apparent reason why different threads of the yarn should stick to the generalized narrator.

783 Anderson Galleries, Inc. LETTERS TO THE COLVINS (NY: Anderson Galleries, 1928), pp. 18-47.
[Sale catalogue of letters sold by executors of the estate of Sir Sidney Colvin, 7 May 1928, in which JC's letters are items 70-174.]

784 Aubry, Georges Jean-. "Conrad à Marseille" (Conrad at Marseilles), NOUVELLES LITTÉRAIRES, VII (29 Sept 1928), 7.
[An account of JC's stay in Marseilles, his journey from Poland, the early sea experiences, the Mexico expedition compared to *The Arrow of Gold*, and the contraband trips to Spain. Contains few new biographic facts. See, also, Aubry's "Un récent entretien . . . ," ibid., III (9 Aug 1924), 1.] [In French.]

785 Austin, H. P. "Joseph Conrad and the Ironic Attitude," FORTNIGHTLY REVIEW, CXXX (1928), 376-88.
Just as Dickens and Hardy represent an optimistic and pessimistic view of life, JC represents an ironic view as seen in *Nostromo,* "Typhoon," and other works.

786 "Biography," A. L. A. BOOKLIST, XXIV (July 1928), 399.
[Merely gives contents of LETTERS FROM JOSEPH CONRAD, edited by Edward Garnett.]

787 "Books," CHRISTIAN CENTURY, XLV (9 Aug 1928), 980.
The letters in LETTERS FROM JOSEPH CONRAD, 1895-1924, ed by Edward Garnett (1928), reflect JC's struggle "with and for words."

788 Chevrillon, Pierre. "L'homme dans le roman marin de Conrad" (Man in Conrad's Sea Novels), REVUE ANGLO-AMÉRICAINE, V (April 1928), 316-30.
With his intuitive psychology, JC sees the same forces operating in man and in nature, both of which signify a spiritual reality. His characters are less rational beings than creatures of feeling and will, whom he more often than not characterizes indirectly and dramatically rather than directly. His sailors represent a human ideal of simplicity and nobility. Captains like MacWhirr, Allistoun, Beard, and Whalley are ennobled by their determination which usually directs itself to accomplishing a single goal. They also possess the qualities of pragmatism, propriety, fairness, and devotion to duty, a trait especially developed in the deck hands. But JC's world has its dark side also. The sinister forces in nature are found in man as well. The equatorial calms are matched by the crew's lethargy and despondency, for

example, in *The Rescue*. However, in speaking about JC's pessimism, one must remember such triumphs over fatality as MacWhirr's in "Typhoon." [Clear and fairly well supported though somewhat limited.] [In French.]

789 Church, Richard. "Further Thoughts on Joseph Conrad," SPECTATOR (Lond), CXLI (7 July 1928), 23-24.
LETTERS FROM JOSEPH CONRAD, 1895-1924 (1928), edited by Edward Garnett, shows there was never a writer other than JC "so completely and single-mindedly devoted to his craft." Through more than three hundred pages, representing a span of thirty years, the theme is "work, work, work." Others things, such as marriage, are incidentals. JC wrote painfully because he had to contend both with the remoteness of his ideas and with expressing them in a medium that was foreign to him. These published letters, though, show his increasing skill in manipulating English. He displays "a sort of fatalism" which is both "a belief in inspiration and a vague reliance on revelation." His "observant eye" is responsible for the physical side of his work; as for the deeper qualities there are "the inward gaze, the recognition of abysmal horrors, the mitigating beauty and heroism." Here is the JC "whom we reverence—and shrink from."

790 Clifford, Hugh. "Concerning Conrad and his Work," EMPIRE REVIEW, XLVII (May 1928), 287-94.
In *Almayer's Folly*, JC's knowledge of the Malayan people was "superficial and inaccurate in an infuriating degree." JC was his own "harshest and most exacting critic." Though JC later repudiated the statement, he said that his decision to write in English was a conscious choice. JC had an "unreliable memory." [Reprints JC letter concerning Clifford's STUDIES IN BROWN HUMANITY. Anecdotal.]

791 Cross, Wilbur. "The Illusions of Joseph Conrad," YALE REVIEW, N.S. XVII (April 1928), 464-82.
For JC the first essential of a novel was "a good story taken directly from real life and standing in some personal relation with himself." JC has little "psychological discernment" and little imagination, and his use of chronology in his works puts "an undue strain upon the memory and imagination of readers who have little of either." Marlow is really a character through whom JC "could speak in various moods" at different times, but he is an awkward person to manage in works of varying lengths. In JC there is no "easy-going narrative" as in Scott or Defoe; everything is "premeditated in the interest of suspense" that determines character. JC is fascinated by the way in which fear re-shapes itself so it appears to be something else; fear becomes terror, then shock, something much more complex than being afraid. JC was no more a pessimist than Plato: so far as JC worked out his philosophy, it is somewhat like Berkeley's idealism, according to which the

world is "a creation out of the images of the mind." In this sense the world is an illusion: different kinds of people have their own peculiar illusions, with equally different results. The philosophy of illusions in itself is not inherently depressing or gloomy. Most of JC's tales are tragedies or "nondescript tragi-comedies"—tragedies like *Nostromo* and "The End of the Tether" are notable. JC was not concerned with building model worlds; instead, he presented life as he saw it, "within and without." His psychology is best demonstrated in "Youth," "Heart of Darkness," "Typhoon," *The Nigger of the Narcissus,* and *Lord Jim.* [Readers today no doubt wish to include at least *Nostromo.*] The background of the stories is important: "everywhere the scene . . . is a presence to be reckoned with." By a kind of illusion it seems to be "the creation of the characters themselves, so completely is the novelist's imagination fused with theirs." [An interesting early reaction to JC and his works, with some penetrating insights.]

792 Curle, Richard. "Introduction," A CONRAD LIBRARY; A CATALOG OF PRINTED BOOKS, MANUSCRIPTS AND AUTOGRAPH LETTERS BY JOSEPH CONRAD (TEODOR JÓSEF KONRAD KORZENIOWSKI) COLLECTED BY THOMAS JAMES WISE (Lond: Pvtly ptd, 1928), pp. xv-xvii.

[Curle suggests that he may have been responsible for awakening Wise's interest in JC. The JC collection herein described is the finest in England and possibly the finest in the world.]

793 Curle, Richard. "Introduction," CONRAD TO A FRIEND (Lond: Sampson Low, Marston; NY: Doubleday, Doran, 1928), pp. vii-xi.

[Includes 150 letters from JC to Curle, written from 6 Nov 1912 to 31 July 1924. Only ten of the letters included had already been published in Aubry's LIFE AND LETTERS (1927). The inclusive dates make these letters an important supplement to Curle's THE LAST TWELVE YEARS OF JOSEPH CONRAD (1928). The material in the Introduction duplicates Curle's other work on JC.]

794 Curle, Richard. THE LAST TWELVE YEARS OF JOSEPH CONRAD (Lond: Sampson Low, Marston; Garden City, NY: Doubleday, Page, 1928); incorporates JOSEPH CONRAD'S LAST DAY (1924), rptd (NY: Russell & Russell, 1968).

JC had great power of visualization, and in his often cryptic and elusive manner, he was a fine talker, demonstrating shrewdness, a "sort of fatalism," and an "unselfconscious modesty"; and he usually wrote in the morning, a good day's work being 350 words. He did much revising and strove to be historically and geographically accurate. Especially fond of *The Nigger of the Narcissus* and *The Mirror of the Sea,* he thought *Nigger* his most original work and *Nostromo* his principal achievement. To be called a novelist of the sea annoyed him.

JC owed much to the consciousness of his father Apollo's position and to Flaubert. He praised Dickens for his "mastery of crowds," preferred the simplicity and accurate knowledge of Cooper and Marryat to Melville's "portentous" MOBY DICK, disliked Dostoevski because he was the "ultimate force of confusion and insanity," and reread Wallace's MALAY ARCHIPELAGO because of its directness and sincerity. Keats was his favorite poet, but he seldom read poetry, and rarely mentioned Shakespeare. He preferred cinema to stage productions. JC did not care much for social life, preferring the peace of mind he could find at home in his study. He was devoted to Jessie and to his two sons. "No man had a more skeptical view of the value of existence or a more modest conception of his own needs." The report that JC planned to return to Poland was "utter nonsense," because of his idealistic conception of England, his strong sense of reality, and his "philosophic conservatism." Kent, like Poland, was too much a part of JC's intimate life to be used in his work. He was intensely patriotic without being sentimental. JC received a tumultuous reception in the United States in 1923; especially enjoyable was the motor tour of New England; but JC disliked American commercialism and the rushed pace of American life. [Curle closes with a detailed account of JC's death, rptd from JOSEPH CONRAD'S LAST DAY (1924). Curle's book, fluent and quite readable, was obviously written by one who luxuriated in the glow of JC's good will. Some comments and anecdotes are still fresh and interesting, giving insight that only a personal friend can give.]

795 Dawson, Ernest. "Some Recollections of Joseph Conrad," FORTNIGHTLY REVIEW, CXXX (Aug 1928), 203-12.
JC loved his English home, spoke English "with an un-English grace," respected good writing only, and slowly changed in appearance as the years passed. [Of little value.]

796 De Ternant, Andrew. "An Unknown Episode of Conrad's Life," NEW STATESMAN AND NATION, XXXI (28 July 1928), 511.
JC was employed in the early 90s for two months as a translator of Slavonic languages by a translating agency. He reported he had quit. JC showed Polish short stories to Edgar Lee, an editor of ST. STEPHEN'S REVIEW, but he had to return them as too revolutionary. [Letter to editor.]

797 Doubleday, F. N. "Joseph Conrad as a Friend: His Publisher's Memories of the Novelist, Who Was as Shy as He Was Brilliant," WORLD TODAY (Lond), LII (July 1928), 145-47.
JC's shyness made it difficult to become intimate with the well-known

writer, but JC's "perfectly simple and open manner" made him popular with many people, even if his speech was "extremely difficult to understand." A very "dramatic" event in publishing history was the sale of JC's manuscripts for $110,000, for which the novelist received about £10 each. The modest JC refused to accept degrees from universities in England, saying he was "a plain sailorman," and he once rejected a proposal that he be known as Sir Joseph Conrad.

798 Dukes, T. Arch. "Memories of Joseph Conrad," SPECTATOR (Lond), CXLI (20 Oct 1928), 526.

A medical officer aboard "almost the last passenger sailing ship" [?] of which JC was first mate, was asked by JC for help with his written English; JC was careless about his speaking. It is doubtful if JC "cared for the subtle distinctions expressed by English; and supposing that he preferred those words which *sounded* best."

799 Feider, V. *"Nostromo,"* PROSVESHCHENIE, No. 2 (1928), 121.

[A review.] [In Russian.]

800 Follett, Wilson. "Joseph Conrad, 1907—: a Humble Apology," BOOKMAN (NY), LXVII (Aug 1928), 640-47.

[Personal account of how Follett came to read JC under the influence of Copeland at Harvard. General survey of JC's work.]

801 Ford, Ford Madox. "Introduction," *The Sisters* (NY: Crosby Gaige, 1928), pp. 1-16.

The Sisters is an early attempt to treat the theme of incest, already hinted at in the collaboration *Romance*. JC did not learn English from his collaborator. [Ford refused to finish the fragment but agreed to write this introduction.]

802 Ford, Ford Madox. "On Conrad's Vocabulary," BOOKMAN (NY), LXVII (June 1928), 405-8.

The collaborators "worked together during many years with absolute oneness of purpose and with absolute absence of rivalry." JC sought "most of all a new form for the novel," and Ford worked for "a limpidity of expression that should make prose seem like the sound of some one talking in rather a low voice into the ear of a person that he liked." In looking over the manuscript of *The Sisters,* one wonders, "Where *did* Conrad get his English?" He did not get it from Ford, who directed his collaborator mainly toward "an easy use of the vernacular." JC aimed at the dialect of the drawing room or the study, but found it most difficult. The whole secret of JC's attractive style is, though, the "mosaic of little crepitations of surprise," of little jolts, which JC loved.

803 Ford, Ford Madox. "Joseph Conrad and Ford Madox Ford," BOOKMAN (NY), LXVIII (Oct 1928), 217-18.

The Sisters is not "a sketch" for *The Arrow of Gold* and was to be the beginning of a quite different story. [Reply to Shannon, ibid., pp. 216-17.]

804 Ford, Ford Madox. "Tiger, Tiger: Being a Commentary on Conrad's *The Sisters,*" BOOKMAN (NY), LXVI (Jan 1928), 495-98.

JC seemed to regard *The Sisters* [published in this issue of the BOOKMAN] and "The Return" as something "slightly obscene." *The Sisters* and "The Return" indicate JC's gradually weakening desire to be a "straight" writer as opposed to a relatively exotic novelist of the sea. JC wanted most of all to write well about the life of great cities; but urged by Henley and Edward Garnett to continue to write in the spirit of "Heart of Darkness," "An Outpost of Progress," or the Malay tales to meet the demands of the public, he turned from *The Sisters* to *Chance*. Incest was definitely to have been the subject of the abandoned story. [For correspondence in response to Ford's article, see "Joseph Conrad and Ford Madox Ford," ibid. (Oct 1928).]

805 Garnett, Edward. "Introduction," LETTERS FROM JOSEPH CONRAD, 1895-1924, ed, with intro and notes, by Edward Garnett (Lond: Nonesuch P; Indianapolis: Bobbs-Merrill, 1928); rptd (Indianapolis and NY: Bobbs-Merrill, Charter Books, 1962), pp. 1-28.

Fisher Unwin's "reader" noted in *Almayer's Folly* the strangeness of the tropical atmosphere and the poetic "realism" of the romantic narrative. When he met JC in person, he was struck by his masculine keenness and his feminine sensitiveness. JC felt himself "lying under a slight stigma among his contemporaries for having expatriated himself." Intimate as their relationship was, Garnett failed to recognize the poet in JC, but he recognized JC's ironic aspect, from the Korzeniowski parental side, as displayed in *The Secret Agent,* and his "Bobrowski heritage," as seen in *The Mirror of the Sea*. JC's nineteen years of arduous work from 1895 to 1913 failed to bring him real popularity because his productions were too "exotic" for the insular taste of British readers. Garnett worked for some time trying to assuage JC's doubts and fears about his writing powers and to relieve his tension and anxiety about the "salability" of his works. [This "cursory sketch" of JC's life through his struggles with what he then called "The Rescuer" reveals several intimate details of JC's mind and art and indicates the importance of his letters and the variety of subtle tones in them of which the reader must be aware.]

806 Garnett, Edward. "Joseph Conrad," CENTURY MAGAZINE, CXV (Feb, March 1928), 385-92; 593-600.

After reading the manuscript of *Almayer's Folly* in 1894, Garnett encouraged JC to write another book. His relationship with JC was one of admiration for the "romantic magic of his scenes" and an appreciation and criticism of all he wrote, but the depth of JC's "creative vision" eluded him as well as everyone else; the voice of the poet in JC remained unrecognized. There are two natures in JC, one "feminine, affectionate, responsive, clear-eyed," and the other "masculine, formidably critical, fiercely ironical, dominating, intransigent." "The Duel" is the best example of the fusion of the two moods in JC's temperament. His memory contained an "extraordinary wealth of observation to draw on" for his writing, and his faculty of "selecting the telling detail" was acute. Nineteen years of hard work (1895-1913) failed to bring JC into real popularity because his work was too "exotic" for British taste. In his early years of writing, JC suffered the "extraordinary nervous strain and agony" that even Jessie George could not alleviate. Often Garnett encouraged him to continue writing certain works, especially *The Nigger of the Narcissus*. JC did not write by theories and convictions but by intuition, "after a preliminary meditation." He had a "buoyant temperament and resilient moods"; an "uncanny insight"; a "skeptical faith and philosophic irony"; a "charming frankness," "great affectionateness"; "flashing wit"; and "humor, often playful, often fiercely sardonic." [A good account of JC's early years of writing and his long, hard struggle for success.]

807 Gates, Barrington. "Reviews: More News of Conrad," NATION AND ATHENAEUM, XLIII (7 July 1928), 464.

LETTERS FROM JOSEPH CONRAD, edited by Edward Garnett (1928), takes the reader "straight into the difficulties of Conrad's creative mood" when his struggles as a writer were greatest and explains how Garnett befriended JC in every possible manner at a time when the novelist doubted his ability to create anything worthwhile, even if he managed to express "a profound confidence" near the end of *The Nigger of the Narcissus*. There are two natures in JC, one feminine, one masculine. The second half of this correspondence, "spread thinly over the last twenty-five years of Conrad's life," might profitably have been curtailed, although some of the details are "delightful."

808 Grabo, Carl H. "Conrad's Management of the Point of View," THE TECHNIQUE OF THE NOVEL (NY: Scribner's, 1928), pp. 66-71.

JC's kind of point of view opens in the first chapter with the unidentified "I" which is later lost, that is, becomes merely the omniscient author. In *Lord Jim,* Marlow becomes indistinguishable from other minor characters. The point of view in *Chance,* "like viewing a scene through several thicknesses of colored glass," comes from Marlow, Powell, and the narrator.

809 Grabo, Carl H. "Conrad's *The Rover* and Its Structural Method," THE TECHNIQUE OF THE NOVEL (NY: Scribner's, 1928), pp. 171-99.

In *The Rover,* JC introduces characters whose roles in the story are not immediately apparent. The unfolding of Peyrol's story is an example of this method of indirection. JC often interrupts the narration to explore the past events. His characteristic mingling of the past and present, his turning back from effect to cause, is ideal for a novel of character, if not of adventure.

810 Hansen, Harry. "The Book World: The First Reader; Richard Curle's Reminiscences of Joseph Conrad Describe 'The Anguish of the Creative Mind,'" NEW YORK WORLD-TELEGRAM (Editorial Section), 28 Oct 1928, p. 8E; rptd in LOOKOUT (NY), XXV (June 1934), 1-2, 12.

Richard Curle's THE LAST TWELVE YEARS OF JOSEPH CONRAD (1928) "conveys in a number of passages not only Conrad as he must have been but the conviction that he really knew him." Curle shows that JC was complex, cordial, and solitary.

811 Harris, G. W. "The Literary Review: Conrad to Garnett; Conrad as a Letter Writer, The Jean-Aubry 'Life' Is Supplemented, Admirably, With Everything He Wrote to Edward Garnett," NEW YORK EVENING POST, 7 April 1928, p. 12.

LETTERS FROM JOSEPH CONRAD, edited by Edward Garnett (1928), shows JC's genius both for writing and "for friendship." Rarely "bitter," JC's "jabbering" is "always vastly entertaining."

812 Hawk, Affable [pseudonym]. "Books in General," NEW STATESMAN, XXXII (8 Dec 1928), 290.

In one passage of LETTERS TO A FRIEND [CONRAD TO A FRIEND, edited by R. Curle (1928)], JC objects strongly to being typed as a writer of sea stories. In another, he comments perceptively on his technique of *"unconventional grouping* [sequence] *and perspective."*

813 Jézéquel, Roger. "Le sentiment de la destinée chez Joseph Conrad" (The Sense of Destiny in Joseph Conrad), BIBLIOTHÈQUE UNIVERSELLE ET REVUE DE GENÈVE, II (1928), 111-23.

JC believes that destiny is accomplished in the relationship between man and all that is not man. This destiny dictates that man will always be conquered, but he will always express his greatness, his faith, loyalty, and his self-mastery. JC avoids authorial commentary because a character's destiny is so incommunicable and must remain a mystery. JC's heroes are defeated by circumstances which make them act according to their true natures, which represent their destinies. [Unsubstantiated claims.] [In French.]

814 "Joseph Conrad and Ford Madox Ford," BOOKMAN (NY), LXVIII (Oct 1928), 216-18.

This correspondence is in reply to Ford, "Tiger, Tiger," ibid., LXVI (Jan 1928). Homer S. Shannon suggests in a letter to the editor of the BOOKMAN that *The Sisters* is actually a discarded early attempt to write the later novel, *The Arrow of Gold,* and that Ford's comment is therefore mainly irrelevant. Ford replies, denying categorically that the story is "a sketch" for the later novel and asserting that it was to be the beginning of a quite different story.

815 K., E. E. "A Hero-Worshipper," NEW STATESMAN, XXXII (15 Dec 1928), 329-30.

THE LAST TWELVE YEARS OF JOSEPH CONRAD, edited by Richard Curle (1928), an overly adulatory and hastily written book, is of value in supplying first-hand information on the man and his critical opinions, but it consists largely of hasty notes and epistolary ephemera.

816 K[ashk]in, Iv. "Novoe O Konrade" (Something New about Conrad), VESTI INNOSTRANNOI LITERATURY, No. 2 (1928), 144-45.

[Commentary on Aubry's JOSEPH CONRAD: LIFE AND LETTERS (1927) and LETTERS FROM JOSEPH CONRAD, edited by E. Garnett (1928).] [In Russian.]

817 "LETTERS FROM JOSEPH CONRAD," CATHOLIC WORLD, CXXVIII (Nov 1928), 247.

The letters, edited by Edward Garnett, suggest but do not answer questions as to whether JC was a Roman Catholic strayed, never intending to return, or a "self-torturing agnostic," or a "disgruntled esthetic egotist," or a "bitterly ironic skeptic without a sense of humor." JC was paradoxical: "witness his thrust at Christianity" and his "loyalty to traditions of British Merchant Marine . . . , family . . . , [and] native land." Though he was a great literary artist, he was no philosopher. "Thank Heaven, Conrad was accorded the rites of the Church in his burial . . . , also that the Church embodies the truth he vainly pursued."

818 Levinson, André. "Joseph Conrad, est-il un écrivain français?" (Joseph Conrad: Is He a French Writer?), NOUVELLES LITTÉRAIRES, VII (21 July 1928), 8.

Ford's memoir is very fanciful. JC was annoyed about the old myth, which Ford perpetuates, that JC thought out his works in French and then translated them into English. In a letter to Hugh Walpole, 7 June 1918, JC states that he would never have written if he had not learned English. JC came to regret his early connections with sea fiction and his Slavic background as critics began to over-emphasize them. [See also Levinson, "Joseph Conrad, est-il un écrivain polonais?" ibid. (4 Aug 1928), 8.] [In French.]

819 Levinson, André. "Joseph Conrad, est-il un écrivain polonais?" (Joseph Conrad: Is He a Polish Writer?), NOUVELLES LITTÉRAIRES, VII (4 Aug 1928), 8.

A letter [published here] by JC's biographer and translator, G. Jean-Aubry, condemns Ford's biography as a travesty of errors in its argument that JC was essentially "French-thinking." He rejected Polish for the same reason he rejected French. English was the only language in which he had any inclination to write. But a Polish acquaintance of the writer and JC detects Polish "cadences" in JC's work. Aubry's ideas of subconscious influences are foolish; all style is individual while all expression comes from the language used. [A confused article at best, with national feeling playing a larger part than any real criticism.] [See also Levinson, "Joseph Conrad, est-il un écrivain français?" ibid. (21 July 1928), 8.] [In French.]

820 Littell, Robert. "Conrad's Letters to Edward Garnett," BOOKMAN (NY), LXVII (July 1928), xxii-xxiii.

LETTERS FROM JOSEPH CONRAD, 1895-1924, edited by Edward Garnett (1928), is "one of the most interesting documents that exists [sic]."

821 McAlpin, Edwin A. *"Lord Jim*—The Story of a Guilty Conscience," OLD AND NEW BOOKS AS LIFE TEACHERS (Garden City, NY: Doubleday, Doran, 1928), pp. 50-65.

Jim, a strong man who fell in a moment of weakness, is tormented by guilt; thus he is "one of us." [Plot summary and moral instruction.]

822 McFee, William. "Beyond Idolatry," NEW YORK HERALD TRIBUNE BOOKS, 4 Nov 1928, Sect. xi, p. 4.

Most of the letters in Richard Curle's THE LAST TWELVE YEARS OF JOSEPH CONRAD (1928) and CONRAD TO A FRIEND (1928) are slight. Curle is industrious but his picture of JC is deficient, perhaps because he knew JC only at the end of his life. Curle does show JC's detestation of being called a "sea-writer"; his belief that meticulous accuracy in biographical data is unimportant; JC's inability as a letter writer because JC adopted a super-conventional middle-class English vocabulary; and the contrast between the early adventurous JC and the later conventional JC.

823 McFee, William. "Sea Captain and Novelist," NEW YORK HERALD TRIBUNE BOOKS, 1 April 1928, Sect. vii, pp. 1-2.

Edward Garnett's LETTERS FROM JOSEPH CONRAD (1928) is important because it shows not merely the troubled spirit painfully groping but also reveals the great extent to which JC was the creation of a "limited coterie of friends." The world owes JC to Mrs. Conrad and to Edward Garnett, who recommended *Almayer's Folly* for publication and on whom JC laid all his troubles. Other focal points of the book are JC's reaction to Russian writers and his astounding deprivation of himself. The letters show JC's "spiritual travail, his pathetic dependence on a friend, his austere artistic integrity, and his indomitable will."

824 Macy, John. "Conrad: Master on Sea and Land," BOOKMAN (NY), LXVI (Jan 1928), 566-70.

Aubry's LIFE AND LETTERS (1927) shows that JC's letters are even better than one would have expected. JC's main interest is in people. Hardy is the born storyteller; JC is often baffling and indirect. [Discursive survey of life and work; commonplace critique.]

825 Marble, Annie Russell. "Joseph Conrad," A STUDY OF THE MODERN NOVEL BRITISH AND AMERICAN SINCE 1900 (NY: Appleton, 1928), pp. 5-12, 79, 106, 263, 265.

JC, born to landed gentry in Poland, became a storyteller of the sea, an exponent of impressionism, and transgressor of literary standards, went to sea in 1874, became a master seaman and an English citizen in 1885, and met Almayer on whom he based his first novel, *Almayer's Folly*. Edward Garnett first recognized JC's genius and gave him encouragement to write a second book. JC wrote more than two thousand letters, sometimes worked on two novels at once (*The Nigger of the Narcissus* and *The Rescue*), and collaborated with Ford Madox Ford. Among his friends were W. H. Hudson, H. G. Wells, John Galsworthy, Edmund Gosse, Arnold Bennett, Cunninghame-Graham, and Stephen Crane. The strong atmosphere he creates of storms and sea reflect his own keen observations, and he displays haunting realism in character portrayal, such as Tom Lingard and Nostromo. These characters also have an intimate relation with the author's life. The power of the written word to make one feel, hear, and above all to see is found especially in *Nigger*, *Nostromo*, and *Lord Jim*.

826 "More Conrad Letters," TIMES LITERARY SUPPLEMENT (Lond), 23 June 1928, p. 483.

LETTERS FROM JOSEPH CONRAD (1928), edited by Edward Garnett, allows "a peep behind the veil" of JC's mystery and impersonality. Different moods emerge, especially disenchantment and perhaps fear. [Discursive.]

827 Morley, Christopher. "A Note on Conrad," SATURDAY REVIEW OF LITERATURE, IV (14 Jan 1928), 519.

A review of *Youth* by Doubleday notes that JC gives feeling and mood with the story. "Youth," "alone of its kind," has intuition, inspiration. " 'Heart of Darkness' is a very fine piece of descriptive and psychological fiction." [Chatty collection of comments on JC, citing Ford Madox Ford and J. Stewart Doubleday.]

828 Nemerovska, O. "Dzhozef Konrad: Snpoba literaturnovo portretu" (Joseph Conrad: Recollection of a Literary Portrait), CHERVONII SHLIAKH, Nos. 5-6 (1928), 129-39. [In Ukrainian.]

829 Overton, Grant. THE PHILOSOPHY OF FICTION (NY: Appleton, 1928), pp. 161-84.

Nostromo, like *Chance, Under Western Eyes* and *The Rescue,* is one of JC's "difficult" works and one of his principal experiments with the novel (e.g., "The suspended situation"). In *Nostromo,* the experiments "are subordinate to a general scheme and a controlling purpose." JC makes his imaginary country of Costaguana exceptionally real. Avarice on the part of a strong, noble, vain man is the subject of *Nostromo.* Sub-subjects are "the history of Latin America in terms of racial temperament" and "the bondage of material interests." [Gives a lengthy redaction of the story.] The " 'breath of life' is more completely in the people of this book than in any but the few supreme works of fiction." *Nostromo* is only a little less great than WAR AND PEACE. All aspects of the novel are interrelated. JC's "Man of the People typified the fate of the people themselves, of democracy so-called, in political order." His technique provides a sense of reality, drama, and vividness.

830 Rang, Bernhard. "Joseph Conrad," HEFTE FÜR BÜCHEREIWESEN, XII (1928), 277-87.

The Secret Agent is a powerful novel, in some respects reminiscent of Dickens (but JC's view is darker, more bitter, and more abysmal) and Dostoevski (who differs from JC essentially in that he is more interested in the struggle of the soul). Isolation and loneliness were essential traits of JC's being, and these traits explain both his feverish desire to participate in life, to live a life of action, to become part of a group, and his turning away from metaphysical speculation, his horror of death, his unchristian despair. [After a short biographical introduction, Rang summarizes and provides some sketchy comments upon the following works, all of them translated into German: *The Nigger of the Narcissus, Lord Jim, Youth,* "Heart of Darkness," "The End of the Tether," *The Shadow-Line, The Secret Agent, Chance, Nostromo,* and *Victory.*] [In German.]

831 "Richard Curle Recalls Conrad in His Later Years," NEW YORK TIMES BOOK REVIEW, 4 Nov 1928, pp. 2, 10.

"Mr. Curle makes no concealment of the fact that he sought out Conrad, that he hoped to win the novelist's friendship and to install himself in something of the relation of a Boswell." It is perhaps just as well that the volume of letters is published, but "the letters themselves contribute nothing." [Comment on THE LAST TWELVE YEARS OF JOSEPH CONRAD (1928) and CONRAD TO A FRIEND (1928), both edited by Curle.]

832 Rinz, Arthur Friedrich. "Joseph Conrad," ORPLID (Augsburg), IV (Feb-March 1928), 95-97.

JC in wedding the adventure novel with the psychological novel brought the first significant development into the former genre. *Chance* is JC's most characteristic work of the first four volumes in German: complicated, psychologically deeply etched, well structured. The reader is struck by the play of chance, the adventures, the exotic scenes. The setting in "Heart of Darkness" is unforgettable. In *The Secret Agent* a landsman's world is keenly revealed. JC measures up to any contemporary writer as artist. He has lived his world view. [Essentially a review of the first four volumes of the Fischer German editions (*Der Geheimagent, Spiel des Zufalls, Die Schattenlinie, Jugend*).] [In German.]

833 Rops, H. Daniel-. CARTE D'EUROPE (Map of Europe) (Paris: Perrin, 1928), pp. 57-84.

JC's heroes are different from Dostoevski's in that they act with greater willpower. JC's novels do not limit themselves to a realistic description of the surface of life but investigate deep psychological and moral problems. JC uses the adventure novel to explore character. His Polish nature breathes in his heroes who accept conflict though they know that they will be defeated. Thus they refuse to accept a stable life for fear that without challenge their lives will be sterile. A sense of mystery is developed by the multiple narrators who reveal characters by describing only their physical exteriors, not their interiors, and by describing the landscapes that surround them. However, JC intends the reader to understand his characters' interiors. Despite his pessimism, JC believes in humanity and love. [Poorly documented; repeats much hackneyed criticism.] [In French.]

834 Roughead, William. "Conrad on Crime: A Note of Admiration," JURIDICAL REVIEW (Edinburgh), XL (Sept 1928), 250-65; rptd in MALICE DOMESTIC (Edinburgh: W. Green, 1928), pp. 261-78.

[Character study of JC's criminals. Conventional comments, emphasizing the villainies. Originally published in Edinburgh University students' magazine.]

835 S[chriftgiesser], K[arl]. "Letters Written by the Novelist to Edward Garnett," BOSTON EVENING TRANSCRIPT BOOK SECTION, 2 June 1928, p. 1.

LETTERS FROM JOSEPH CONRAD, edited by Edward Garnett (1928), reveals with unusual frankness the many difficulties under which JC wrote. In its account of the relationship of the two men, the introduction is a "genuine contribution to Conradiana."

836 Seldes, Gilbert. "Better than Ecstasy," DIAL, LXXXV (Sept 1928), 249-53.

LETTERS FROM JOSEPH CONRAD, edited by Edward Garnett (1928), is useful because it provides insight into JC's attitude toward his work and toward his public. In his role as JC's most trusted critic, Garnett "did not inspire Conrad, but he gave him intellectual discipline."

837 Shannon, Homer S. "Joseph Conrad and Ford Madox Ford," BOOKMAN (NY), LXVIII (Oct 1928), 216-17.

The Sisters is actually a discarded early attempt to write the later novel, *The Arrow of Gold,* and Ford's comment is therefore mainly irrelevant. [Reply to Ford, "Tiger, Tiger . . . ," ibid., LXVI (Jan 1928), 495-98.]

838 Ward, Alfred Charles. "Joseph Conrad," TWENTIETH-CENTURY LITERATURE (Lond: Methuen, 1928; rptd 1940), pp. 33-43; ibid. (NY: Longmans, 1940), pp. 42-52.

JC's characters are both foreign and universal. As a novelist, he was a practitioner of "romantic realism"; "his actualities and facts become clothed with romantic glamour and adventurous exaltation." A key element in his philosophy is "the keeping of faith between man and man"; thus Razumov is a betrayer; in "The Secret Sharer," the Captain has an acute "sense of solidarity" between himself and Leggatt; in *Lord Jim,* the protagonist "violated 'the solidarity of the craft.' "

1929

839 Aubry, G. Jean-. "Introduction," LETTRES FRANÇAISES DE JOSEPH CONRAD (French Letters of Joseph Conrad) (Paris: Gallimard, 1929), pp. 7-23.

JC spoke and wrote French well but chose English because it seemed more natural for him. There are probably many other French letters which were unaccessible. *Under Western Eyes* is a book in the Russian tone. *The Rescue* is very complicated in technique. The title of *Victory* refers to Lena's death. One letter deals with some textual corrections to *The Secret Agent.* In the letter of 2 April 1902, JC summarizes his intentions in "Typhoon," "Amy Foster," "To-morrow," and "Youth." In the letter of 5 Dec 1903, there is a brief autobiography along with a statement about JC's pride in having been a trusted naval officer and in having accomplished his goals without outside help. His ideals in writing are honesty and sincerity. [The letters provide many insights into JC's intentions.] [In French.]

JOSEPH CONRAD

840 Aubry, Georges Jean-. "*The Rover,*" A CONRAD MEMORIAL LIBRARY: THE COLLECTION OF GEORGE T. KEATING (Garden City, NY: Doubleday, Doran, 1929), pp. 326-36.

JC had great difficulty in writing *The Rover,* which developed from an attempt to compose a short story. From his childhood he had been familiar with the life of Napoleon, and he "felt impassioned" about the naval rivalry between France and England. He indubitably favored the French— a fact to be noted in this novel—but he clearly made in his book "more secret and personal confessions." For the first time in any of his works, the principal character is *"a sailor who longs for rest, who no longer wishes to sail."* Peyrol was born for JC of "an imaginary vision" of a Corsican sailor whom he had known long before, Dominic Cervoni; and Scevola was also based on a real person. Thus, these two characters and "the general trend of the book" can be attributed to particular sentiments and reminiscences of the novelist. Although it is highly improbable that JC had actually seen all the places described in the story, he was remarkably accurate, as Aubry proved by a walking trip over the entire scene of *Rover.* [Contains several important facts about JC and his writing *Rover.*]

841 Aubry, Georges Jean-. "*Suspense,*" A CONRAD MEMORIAL LIBRARY: THE COLLECTION OF GEORGE T. KEATING (Garden City, NY: Doubleday, Doran, 1929), pp. 351-57.

JC was able to call upon many reminiscences from his childhood and early adolescence for use in stories because history and his family chronicles were closely related. A chance meeting with a French artillery officer revived his early recollections so strongly that he read carefully all he could find about Napoleon's stay on the island of Elba. Several years passed before he was able to depict in writing "the state of uncertainty, uneasiness, expectation, hope, and fear which prevailed in the western part of the Mediterranean when Napoleon was at Elba." In working on *Suspense,* he returned also to the companion of his youth, Dominic Cervoni, who appears in the novel as Cosmo Latham. JC turned back to the part of the world that had seen his first adventures, but he also relied on books, taking six of his leading characters from his reading. Evidence exists that most of the text of *Suspense* as JC left it would not have been retained. It is, thus, merely a sketch for a novel.

842 Austin, Mary. "*Typhoon,*" A CONRAD MEMORIAL LIBRARY: THE COLLECTION OF GEORGE T. KEATING (Garden City, NY: Doubleday, Doran, 1929), pp. 103-10.

In America, men instead of women feel an attraction to "the missing fragment by which the pattern of human society had been once for all, rendered intelligible" in the heart of a hurricane in "Typhoon." JC could not understand that "there was as yet no realism in American fiction" to prepare women to understand men who worked alone, with no desire for approval from the opposite sex. [Austin popularized some of JC's works in the U.S.]

843 Babb, James T. "A Check List of Additions to A CONRAD MEMORIAL LIBRARY, 1929-38," YALE UNIVERSITY LIBRARY GAZETTE, XIII (July 1938), 29-40.

[Lists the materials which George T. Keating added to his collection after the publication of his catalogue, annotated items including manuscripts, printed books, and a bronze relief portrait of JC by Theodore Spicer-Simson. With Keating's A CONRAD MEMORIAL LIBRARY (1929), this check list is an excellent early attempt to bring together many important items by and about JC.]

844 Bohnenberger, Carl, and Norman H. Hill. "The Letters of Joseph Conrad to Stephen and Cora Crane," BOOKMAN (NY), LXIX (May, June 1929), 225-35, 367-74.

[Tells the story of their friendship and prints partial text of twenty-eight letters. Affectionate exchange on family affairs, meetings, and friends. Includes a few remarks on Crane's work and his appreciation of JC's fiction; also, JC's defense of Cora and his desire to help when Stephen was in Cuba.]

845 Bone, David W. *"The Shadow-Line,"* A CONRAD MEMORIAL LIBRARY: THE COLLECTION OF GEORGE T. KEATING (Garden City, NY: Doubleday, Doran, 1929), pp. 255-61.

The Shadow-Line is "clear autobiography," JC's recollection of his appointment to command in the barque *Otago,* twenty-seven years before he wrote the story. JC's "profound visual memory recreates the emotion with which he gazed upon his ship as he saw her for the first time." Ransome, "the tragic steward of the *Otago,*" is an unusually believable figure. In fact, the entire tale seems true to one who has "himself crossed that phantom belt at sea." [An early impression of this novel, which has been found to be much more complex than early critics suspected.]

846 Buenzod, Emmanuel "Joseph Conrad: *Entre terre et mer* (N.R.F.)" (Joseph Conrad: *'Twixt Land and Sea* [N.R.F.]), BIBLIOTHÈQUE UNIVERSELLE ET REVUE DE GENÈVE, II (July 1929), 126.

G. Jean-Aubry's biographical introductions show that what might be taken for purely imaginary incidents are usually episodes transposed from JC's life. "A Smile of Fortune" combines humor with a sense of destiny to create a masterly fullness. "The Secret Sharer" examines the image of mocking appearances and the heroic futility of all effort. [In French.]

195

847 Burt, Struthers. *"Within the Tides,"* A CONRAD MEMORIAL LIBRARY: THE COLLECTION OF GEORGE T. KEATING (Garden City, NY: Doubleday, Doran, 1929), pp. 230-39.

JC was mostly interested in tragedy, which proved to him that "the only really important thing" is to be one of the lucky people who always see the world as if it were new. A sense of wonder is necessary if one is not to be conquered by life. JC was fundamentally "a teller of tales . . . par excellence," in an old and honorable tradition. Generally he "could not help making emotion and fate his protagonists, because . . . he knew that emotion and fate ruled the individual life."

848 C., G. "Bibliographie" (Bibliography), REVUE DE L'ENSEIGNEMENT DES LANGUES VIVANTES, XLVI (1929), 71.

Eleven years later is a bit tardy for Tauchnitz to present to its readers *The Shadow-Line,* which is one of JC's most powerful novels because of its evocative magic and odor of the sea. One can hardly say anything original about it now and it would be inexcusable to offer a banal or rehashed criticism. [In French.]

849 Canby, Henry Seidel. *"Under Western Eyes,"* A CONRAD MEMORIAL LIBRARY: THE COLLECTION OF GEORGE T. KEATING (Garden City, NY: Doubleday, Doran, 1929), pp. 187-93.

JC's purpose in *Under Western Eyes* was "to interpret the Russian mind to aliens." JC is "Russia's hereditary enemy writing of a race that no alien friend could understand" so well as he could. Razumov's being forced to be "a spy for autocracy" is "a magnificent situation such as Conrad loved." According to Western eyes, all the heroes in the book are fools, and "the fools are all heroic"; but JC gives even the most minor characters in the story "the full complexity of inconsistent, intensely human man." This novel differs from JC's others in that here "the strange Fate, intangible, and more subjective than objective, which broods over *Nostromo,* "Youth," and *Chance,* is for once externalized and made concrete." JC, "with extraordinary skill of analysis, makes even a Westerner believe in the unity of the Russian soul. . . . The same resignation, the same almost cynical disbelief in happiness and the rewards of virtue," are also characteristic of JC's Slavic soul. He, however, could escape to England and the sea, where he found release from brooding in his books, but his great characters are all "obsessed men," with Slavic souls, Westerners written down and interpreted under Slavic eyes. JC's great contribution to English literature is thus "an extension of the human soul" in new directions.

850 Clifford, Sir Hugh. *"An Outcast of the Islands,"* A CONRAD MEMORIAL LIBRARY: THE COLLECTION OF GEORGE T. KEATING (Garden City, NY: Doubleday, Doran, 1929), pp. 14-21.

Edward Garnett persuaded JC to write a second novel, but JC failed for about fifteen years to win a large audience for his works, partially because several of them were popularly considered as "difficult" reading. *An Outcast of the Islands* has a sentimental interest for the people who knew the struggling author, but it can never be ranked among his best works. Although it belongs to a period when JC had just become a writer, the characters in this novel are "unconvincing."

>**851** Conrad, Jessie. "Joseph Conrad, an Eccentric but Loveable Genius—Described by His Wife," WORLD TODAY (Lond), LIII (May 1929), 582-84.

[Anecdotes about JC's family life.]

>**852** Conrad, Jessie. *"Some Reminiscences,"* A CONRAD MEMORIAL LIBRARY: THE COLLECTION OF GEORGE T. KEATING (Garden City, NY: Doubleday, Doran, 1929), pp. 196-99.

JC was so much "troubled" by the necessity to change the title of this book to *A Personal Record* that he did not write a second volume, "perhaps even more intimate, and recording reminiscences even earlier than these." No doubt his "later associations with his country and countrymen recalled much to his mind that the passage of time had erased from his memory," and the visit to Poland in 1914 would have provided much more material. [Slight, dealing mainly with Mrs. Conrad's helpfulness to her husband and why she sold some of his books.]

>**853** Curle, Richard. *"The Arrow of Gold,"* A CONRAD MEMORIAL LIBRARY: THE COLLECTION OF GEORGE T. KEATING (Garden City, NY: Doubleday, Doran, 1929), pp. 273-77.

This novel is "profoundly autobiographical," "a slice out of Conrad's own past." JC did not make Rita "as marvellous as he wants us to believe," perhaps because "we only see her reflection through his words." There is "a certain obscurity" in the structure of the book. This work is, though, "the most deeply and tenderly reminiscent" of all JC's novels. [Curle, not one of its "fanatical admirers," approves of the symbolic title, which caused JC much difficulty in determining.]

>**854** D., E. "Bibliographie" (Bibliography), REVUE DE L'ENSEIGNEMENT DES LANGUES VIVANTES, XLVI (1929), 71.

In *Typhoon and Other Stories* (Tauchnitz) are found: "Typhoon," which, in about 100 pages, describes a hurricane in the China Sea and in which Captain MacWhirr's obstinate triumphs over the rage of the waves is unforgettable; "Amy Foster," "Falk," and "To-morrow," which are commendable. In all these tales, the intrigue counts for the least, the sea itself, with its environs, counts most. But first place is awarded to the human being, his sensations, his instincts, and his feelings. [In French.]

855 David, Maurice. JOSEPH CONRAD: L'HOMME ET L'OEUVRE (Joseph Conrad: The Man and the Work). Collection des célébrités étrangères, I, 3 (Paris: Editions de la Nouvelle Revue Critique, 1929); absorbs "La psychologie et la morale de Conrad" (The Psychology and Moral Principles of Conrad), NOUVELLE REVUE CRITIQUE, XIII (May 1929), 289-304.

JC chose English in which to write his novels because it is less rigid than French. The most striking feature of his characters is their need to know themselves, and it is through action that they accomplish this need rather than through skeptical withdrawal from life as Decoud does in *Nostromo,* rather than through constant self-analysis as Razumov does in *Under Western Eyes,* or rather than through empty talk or delusive imagination as Jim does in *Lord Jim.* Action leading to self-knowledge results from conflict. Other ideals of the Conradian hero are service to others, generosity, duty, and fidelity to one's calling and one's own morality. One must avoid vanity or else suffer the fate of Kurtz or Nostromo. JC's pessimistic belief that man must struggle against a hostile universe leads in a positive way to his belief that this struggle results in energy and the creation of man's individual morality. For JC, technique is important to reveal a moral truth. He uses setting to develop characters. His gradual revelation of action and character imitates the human perception of them as in reality. Thus we only gradually get to know the whole Kurtz. This slow revelation of character is appropriate to JC's heroes' reluctance to analyze themselves. There is no omniscient comment to break the illusion of reality. His best characters are imagined rather than copied from life. [Clear summary of most French criticism plus some good original insights.] [In French.]

856 Dierlamm, G. "Joseph Conrad," ZEITSCHRIFT FÜR FRANZÖSISCHEN UND ENGLISCHEN UNTERRICHT, XXVIII (1929), 93-102.

The Nigger of the Narcissus, "Youth," "Heart of Darkness," *Lord Jim* and "Typhoon" are JC's best works. JC's power declined after *Chance,* and JC had a colorful and dramatic way of storytelling ("Heart of Darkness," "Typhoon," and "The Secret Sharer"). JC is aware both of the sense of mystery surrounding our lives and the presence of God. [Surveys JC's life; describes his struggles with the English language.] [In German.]

857 Dinamov, S. "Dva zapadnykh khudozhnika upadka" (Two Western Writers of Decadence), REVOLUTSIA I KULTURA, No. 8 (1929), 78-79.

[In Russian.]

858 Douglas, Robin. "My Boyhood with Conrad," CORNHILL MAGAZINE, N.S. LXVI (Jan 1929), 20-28.

[Anecdotes and descriptions of JC at Capel House.]

859 Fabes, Gilbert Henry. MODERN FIRST EDITIONS: POINTS AND VALUES. First Series (Lond: W. and G. Foyle, 1929), pp. 6-10.

Several of JC's first editions are described: *Chance, Notes on Life and Letters, The Arrow of Gold, The Inheritors, The Nigger of the Narcissus, The Secret Agent, 'Twixt Land and Sea, Tales of Unrest,* and *Within the Tides.* [See Fabes, third series (1932), pp. 13-14.]

860 Fernández, Ramón. "Notes," NOUVELLE REVUE FRANÇAISE, XXXIII (Oct 1929), 571-72.

All of JC's method depends on the dichotomy of good and evil as manifested in his image of the ship and its crew. The stories in *Entre Terre et Mer* ['*Twixt Land and Sea*], some of his best, add the two additional elements of land and sea. "The Secret Sharer" is central to an understanding of these tales in its enigma of character and JC's emphasis on paradox. JC seems slightly naive in his insistence on the murderer's justification, but this is a minor flaw in a great work. [In French.]

861 Fisher, Rev. Ernest F. "Joseph Conrad as Novelist," HOLBORN REVIEW, N.S. XX (Oct 1929), 497-510.

Despite JC's love of England, his novels do not have "the stamp of our genius." JC's description of "seafaring Britons" and his delineation of character are praiseworthy, but his characters and his pessimism are not admirable. JC's shortcomings may finally exclude him from the company of Shakespeare, Dickens, and other English "Immortals."

862 Ford, Ford Madox. "*The Inheritors*," A CONRAD MEMORIAL LIBRARY: THE COLLECTION OF GEORGE T. KEATING (Garden City, NY: Doubleday, Doran, 1929), pp. 74-83.

Ford labored as hard over *Romance, Nostromo, The Rescue,* and "The End of the Tether" as over any "relics" of his own included in John Quinn's catalogue. "Getting Conrad afloat" was for many years the main object of his life. He worked especially hard with *The Inheritors.* Keating's collection is "an honest and impressive memorial" to JC, whose works may be forgotten for a time but will eventually be recognized again for their "authenticity, . . . a quality arising from a fierce or as a steadfast determination on the part of the writer to render his world as he sees it." JC's "whole mind, his whole ambition, his whole life, went into his work."

863 Ford, Ford Madox. "In the Last Quarter of a Century," BOOKMAN (NY), LXIX (March 1929), 77-78; rptd in THE ENGLISH NOVEL, FROM THE EARLIEST DAYS TO THE DEATH OF JOSEPH CONRAD (Philadelphia and Lond: Lippincott, 1929), pp. 142-49.

About Henry James, Stephen Crane, and JC there is "a certain oneness of method and even a certain comradeship." All three treated characters with aloofness, kept themselves out of their work, and rendered rather than told.

JC is more poetic and "less remorselessly aloof" than the others, but all three "had before all for their strongest passion the desire to convey vicarious experience to the reader."

> **864** Ford, Ford Madox. "Working with Conrad," YALE REVIEW, N.S. XVIII (June 1929), 699-715; rptd in RETURN TO YESTERDAY (NY: Liveright, 1932), pp. 186-201.

There was never a quarrel in Ford's collaboration with JC nor in their friendship. In publishing three books together, the two writers worked for five years in close intimacy. Ford corrected JC's proofs, wrote from his dictation, suggested words for him to use, and helped him recall forgotten incidents. The strongest bond was the great amount of time spent together and "the same taste in words." The five years of writing *Romance* taught Ford the greatest part of what he knew of the technical side of writing. Ford helped JC with several of his works, including the writing in of several passages of such productions as *Nostromo*, "The End of the Tether," and *The Secret Agent*. Ford also suggested some plots to JC and caused him to write despite his despair and fatigue. He continued his friendship and "common work" until JC's death. In the collaborations, one would write a passage or an entire draft of a book; then the other would make changes or rewrite. Ford wrote all of *Romance* before he met JC, almost all of *The Inheritors,* and much of *The Nature of a Crime*. The two were "writers without envy, jealousy, or any of the petty feelings that writers do not unusually cherish, the one towards the other." [Ford defends himself from attacks by the press and the public; his claims in the collaborative work may be excessive.]

> **865** Galsworthy, John. *"Nostromo,"* A CONRAD MEMORIAL LIBRARY: THE COLLECTION OF GEORGE T. KEATING (Garden City, NY: Doubleday, Doran, 1929), p. 138.

Nostromo seemed to JC "his most considerable book," and it is his "most sheer piece of creation." It is doubtless "a brilliant piece of work," although JC's genius was not so well suited to the long novel as to stories like "Heart of Darkness" and *The Nigger of the Narcissus*. Towards the end, *Nostromo* becomes melodrama, but JC in all probability did not realize this fact. [Galsworthy's insight has been reiterated many times since he wrote this perceptive article.]

> **866** Garnett, Edward. *"Tales of Unrest,"* A CONRAD MEMORIAL LIBRARY: THE COLLECTIONS OF GEORGE T. KEATING (Garden City, NY: Doubleday, Doran, 1929), pp. 50-56.

JC, in 1894-95, wrote such "rotten twaddle," as he called it, as his first short story, "The Idiots." This tale indeed "betrays too openly Maupassant's influence," which appears also in "An Outpost of Progress," but JC's own "subject-matter, environment, and tropical atmosphere" are here. "The Lagoon," "a return to the mood and method" of *An Outcast of the Islands,* is typical of the early JC, but it is "a lyric in prose, the forerunner of the finest piece of poetical ardour, 'Youth,' that Conrad ever penned." "Karain" is "a brilliant piece of work, one of true individual quality; but it has no deep roots under its polished surface." "The Return" is the only "complete failure" JC ever made "at story-telling." [Gives details of composition and publication of each story.]

867 Groom, Bernard. "The Novel," A LITERARY HISTORY OF ENGLAND (Lond: Longmans, Green, 1929), pp. 370-72.

Eccentricities of style are extensions of JC's view of life—"complex and self-contradictory." JC is a realistic writer with poetic powers. Loyalty and duty are his two great principles. [Groom lists several titles and attempts one-line definitions of them.]

868 K., H. F. "Joseph Conrad," EUROPAISCHE REVUE, V (Aug 1929), 359-63.

For JC "England" was not a rainy and fogbound northern island, but a world-wide experience, an oceanic experience. More substantially than anyone else he has recorded the interpenetration of the English and the sea. In German literature the exotic world is usually an unreal or utopian world; in JC the faraway and the exotic are intensely real. Yet for JC the sea is more than experienced reality; it functions as a symbol. On the surface JC's novels are stories of high adventure, but the adventures acquire a fatal significance. The apparently casual concatenation of extraordinary events actually portrays man's fate, and the sea itself is the principal incarnation of Fate, the metaphysical power against which man has to measure himself. At the heart of JC's world one always finds man versus his destiny. The human catastrophes are of the kind one finds in ancient tragedy; essentially they are revelations of Moira, the inescapable fatality of existence. Ultimately, JC's work is mytho-religious in nature: the basic theme is man's being subjected to the severe tests that are inherent in his confrontation with his fate. JC's characters often achieve moral greatness and heroic stature in the course of their struggle with their psychological or metaphysical destiny. Such "heroes" are at the center of his epics. Ancient epic art—with its extraordinary adventures and its myths, with its eternal conflict between darkness and light, with its titanic struggles and heroic defeats—was given new life by JC. [In German.]

869 Keating, George T. (ed). A CONRAD MEMORIAL LIBRARY: THE COLLECTION OF GEORGE T. KEATING (Garden City, NY: Doubleday, Doran, 1929).

[Contents, abstracted separately, all under 1929: George T. Keating,

Joseph Conrad

"Foreword"; H. M. Tomlinson, *"Almayer's Folly:* The Prelude"; Sir Hugh Clifford, *"An Outcast of the Islands";* Christopher Morley, *"The Nigger of the Narcissus";* Edward Garnett, *"Tales of Unrest";* T. F. Powys, *"Lord Jim";* Ford Madox Ford, *"The Inheritors";* Llewelyn Powys, *"Youth";* Mary Austin, *"Typhoon";* William McFee, *"Romance";* John Galsworthy, *"Nostromo";* Felix Riesenberg, *"The Mirror of the Sea";* Hugh Walpole, *"The Secret Agent";* Arthur Symons, *"A Set of Six";* Henry Seidel Canby, *"Under Western Eyes";* Jessie Conrad, *"Some Reminiscences (A Personal Record*); Liam O'Flaherty, *" 'Twixt Land and Sea";* John Cowper Powys, *"Chance";* Struthers Burt, *"Within the Tides";* Arthur Machen, *"Victory";* David W. Bone, *"The Shadow-Line";* Richard Curle, *"The Arrow of Gold";* Neil Munro, *"The Rescue";* George T. Keating, *"Notes on Life and Letters";* G. Jean-Aubry, *"The Rover";* George T. Keating, *"The Nature of a Crime";* G. Jean-Aubry, *"Suspense";* George T. Keating, *"Tales of Hearsay";* George T. Keating, "Last Essays"; George T. Keating, "Personal Documents, Works Biographical, Critical, and Bibliographical, Letters, Etc."]

870 Keating, George T. "Foreword," A Conrad Memorial Library: The Collection of George T. Keating (Garden City, NY: Doubleday, Doran, 1929), pp. vii-viii.

This "library" of JC "speaks for itself" because "completeness, condition, and association interest are present in every item." JC's position in literature is secure, and the "master" himself has had a "sustained interest" in the preparation of this collection.

871 Keating, George T. "Last Essays," A Conrad Memorial Library: The Collection of George T. Keating (Garden City, NY: Doubleday, Doran, 1929), pp. 371-96.

[A bibliographical listing and description of the first editions of Last Essays, with a record of earlier publications of each essay.]

872 Keating, George T. *"The Nature of a Crime,"* A Conrad Memorial Library: The Collection of George T. Keating (Garden City, NY: Doubleday, Doran, 1929), pp. 348-50.

[A bibliographical description of *The Nature of a Crime* in its first editions of 1919 and 1924.]

873 Keating, George T. *"Notes on Life and Letters,"* A Conrad Memorial Library: The Collection of George T. Keating (Garden City, NY: Doubleday, Doran, 1929), pp. 301-25.

[A bibliographical listing and description of the first editions of *Notes on Life and Letters,* with a record of earlier publications of each essay.]

874 Keating, George T. "Personal Documents, Works Biographical, Critical, and Bibliographical, Letters, Etc.," A CONRAD MEMORIAL LIBRARY: THE COLLECTION OF GEORGE T. KEATING (Garden City, NY: Doubleday, Doran, 1929), pp. 397-448.

[Lists and describes books in JC's library, navigation charts, discharges, letters of reference, photographs and portraits, pamphlets, collections of "Wisdom and Beauty from Conrad," prefaces, bibliographies, works, corrected typescripts, presentation copies of books, appreciations of JC, and other relative materials.]

875 Keating, George T. *"Tales of Hearsay,"* A CONRAD MEMORIAL LIBRARY: THE COLLECTION OF GEORGE T. KEATING (Garden City, NY: Doubleday, Doran, 1929), pp. 364-70.

[A bibliographical description of the first editions and the contents of *Tales of Hearsay*.]

876 Kociemski, Leonardo. "Letteratura straniere in Italia" (Foreign Literature in Italy), ITALIA CHE SCRIVE, XII (Jan 1929), 18. Marcellini has translated JC's masterful novel, "The End of the Tether," faithfully as *Fino all'estremo* (Milan: Corticelli, 1928). The novel, which recounts the tragedy of an anguished old captain, impoverished by a swindler and forced to wander again across the seas to help his daughter, is full of humanity and was probably conceived during JC's career as a sea captain. [In Italian.]

877 Kreemers, Raph. "Joseph Conrad. Een bibliographisch argument" (Joseph Conrad. A Bibliographical Argument), BOEKZAAL, No. 17 (1929), 261-62.

Lord Jim and "Heart of Darkness" are especially admirable. [A series of brief statements about such matters as JC's reception in Holland, his growing popularity and world-wide recognition as a major literary figure, the relative significance of various works in the totality of his achievement, and the debate concerning his own favorite among his works. The entire discussion is based on G. Jean-Aubry's "Joseph Conrad au Congo," MERCURE DE FRANCE, XXXVI (15 Oct 1925), 289-338, and the testimony of such persons as Edward Garnett.] [In Dutch.]

878 Lann, E. [also, Land, Eugenivsz.] "Literaturnii zapad sevodnia: Dzhozef Konrad" (Literary West Today: Joseph Conrad), KRASNAIA NIVA, No. 15 (1929), 18 [In Russian.]

879 Leites, A. "Peredmova" (Foreword), *Almerova Primkha. Roman* (*Almayer's Folly*, Novel) trans by M. Lisichenko (Kharkov: Derzh Vid, 1929).

[In Ukrainian.]

880 McFee, William. *"Romance,"* A Conrad Memorial Library: The Collection of George T. Keating (Garden City, NY: Doubleday, Doran, 1929), pp. 120-27.

A group of officers, with some time to spend in Port Tewfik, looked in a bookstore for "a book to read," and one found a copy of *Romance*. From this novel he derived the idea that JC was a great artist, and this "conviction grew with the years." [Slight; the officer probably was McFee.]

881 Machen, Arthur. *"Victory,"* A Conrad Memorial Library: The Collection of George T. Keating (Garden City, NY: Doubleday, Doran, 1929), pp. 245-49.

JC understood alike "the enigmas of both good and evil." Although nobody in *Victory* "begins to know what sort of man Heyst really was," JC understood—or at least knew—him. Schomberg, who could not really know Heyst, created a legend about him and believed in his invention. Nor did Lena know anything about the real man, and Heyst is indeed a paradox to himself.

882 Mille, Pierre. "Sur Joseph Conrad" (On Joseph Conrad), Nouvelles Littéraires, VIII (2 Nov 1929), 1.

JC's style displays a love for words. JC is English in his impetuosity, Polish in his rationality, and Slavic in his dreaming and reflections. Imagination made him a man of action and a writer. He lacked humor because of his Slavic origins. Kipling and JC have made adventure stories of the highest of modern modes of literature. [Praises Maurice David's Joseph Conrad (1929). Over-generalized defense of JC's complex makeup.] [In French.]

883 Morley, Christopher. "Granules from an Hour-glass: The Longest Parenthesis," Saturday Review of Literature, V (11 May 1929), 997.

Chance, published in 1914, is the first of JC's novels to reach a large public, due to the publisher's promotion. Though not a complete success, *Chance* shows JC, the brilliant artist, more than any other book. The novel is remarkable for its narration, a form of distillation, in which "the subtle commentator [Marlow] hands on the story, enriched with his own temperamental comments, to the colorless 'I' who serves merely as a proxy for the public." Everything the reader learns in the novel is colored by at least one hearsay, perhaps even two.

884 Morley, Christopher. *"The Nigger of the Narcissus,"* A Conrad Memorial Library: The Collection of George T. Keating (Garden City, NY: Doubleday, Doran, 1929), pp. 28-31.

The Nigger of the Narcissus is more than a work of art; "It is a rendering of life, a monument of a whole era." Its essence is "the pure poetic gift of informing inanimate things with the emotion of live spirits." JC observes deeply and employs an "exquisite pictorial skill." This romantic novel is "a celibate story, lonely, beautiful, and proud."

885 Munro, Neil. *"The Rescue,"* A CONRAD MEMORIAL LIBRARY: THE COLLECTION OF GEORGE T. KEATING (Garden City, NY: Doubleday, Doran, 1929), pp. 288-93.

JC confided that his morale was shaken by "a public apathy to his books," and that the "skeleton in his cupboard" was the unfinished first draft of *The Rescue*. So serious was his discouragement that he tried to get a command on a ship. Altogether, for almost twenty years he attempted to finish a novel which should have been completed *"au premier coup,"* but when it was published at last in 1920 it betrayed no sign of the author's struggles with it.

886 Nikolskii, A. "Dzhozef Konrad" (Joseph Conrad), KONRAD DZH. TVORI (The Creator: Joseph Conrad) (Cracow: Knigospilka, 1929).

[In Ukrainian.]

887 O'Flaherty, Liam. *" 'Twixt Land and Sea,"* A CONRAD MEMORIAL LIBRARY: THE COLLECTION OF GEORGE T. KEATING (Garden City, NY: Doubleday, Doran, 1929), pp. 207-11.

[The author writes vaguely about the tales in this collection. Very slight.]

888 Palffy, Eleanor. "Drunk on Conrad," FORTNIGHTLY REVIEW, CXXXII (Oct 1929), 534-38.

A ballroom on Fifth Avenue, satirically described, and the fashionable people who "battened on personalities" is the scene for JC's reading from *Victory* in his guttural English. But for some of the listeners the two and a half hours soon passed, and when JC finished with tears in his eyes, all who had followed him were "drunk on Conrad."

889 Powys, John Cowper. *"Chance,"* A CONRAD MEMORIAL LIBRARY: THE COLLECTION OF GEORGE T. KEATING (Garden City, NY: Doubleday, Doran, 1929), pp. 217-22.

"The essential subject" in JC's works is "neither land nor water, but the rooted fidelities and ebbing passions of the frustrated yet invincible heart of man." *Chance* and *The Arrow of Gold* are JC's "finest creations" because of Flora de Barral and Doña Rita. Admirable are Captain Anthony's "archaic chivalry," and the novelist's method of telling his story. JC's "unique charm" lies in a mixture of "cynical worldly wisdom with an incurable boyish zest for grandiose stoical gestures."

890 Powys, T. F. *"Lord Jim,"* A CONRAD MEMORIAL LIBRARY: THE COLLECTION OF GEORGE T. KEATING (Garden City, NY: Doubleday, Doran, 1929), pp. 65-70.

In writing this novel, JC kept by him both women, one the sailor's art and the other Imagination, so he could write down his vision. "Jim himself is the most significant of Conrad's creations." Jim must die because "The deep and silent calm, the everlasting beauty of the sea, together with all its uttermost cruelty, go with Conrad where he goes, and so deep and vast a beauty must lead to death." *Lord Jim* "will not be forgotten" because it delves under the "obscure surface" of the earth and shows "the horror, the hunger, that is in the soul of man."

> **891** Powys, Llewelyn. *"Youth,"* A CONRAD MEMORIAL LIBRARY: THE COLLECTION OF GEORGE T. KEATING (Garden City, NY: Doubleday, Doran, 1929), pp. 88-93.

[Despite the title, the author writes only about "Heart of Darkness."] In this masterpiece JC saw, heard, and smelled Africa. He both understood and expressed the exploitation of Africa by Europeans. He sketched character in a few words, and his style is "incomparable."

> **892** Riesenberg, Felix. *"The Mirror of the Sea,"* A CONRAD MEMORIAL LIBRARY: THE COLLECTION OF GEORGE T. KEATING (Garden City, NY: Doubleday, Doran, 1929), pp. 151-53.

A predominant note in JC's "prose poem," *The Mirror of the Sea,* is "that of a retrospective melancholy, an echo of old longing and sorrow reaching across vast spaces of time and distance." For ages, sailors were "romantic figures," and with the end of sailing vessels "that blue world once so mysterious and symbolic of the greater universe" disappeared. Long voyages gave JC "his perspective and his melancholy, and many of his great qualities of mind and heart," as well as his "profound love" for the sea. *Mirror* reflects "from many sides" the sailors of JC's time.

> **893** Rockwood, Stanley W. "A Comparative Study of the Works of Pierre Loti and Joseph Conrad." Unpublished thesis, University of Wisconsin, 1929.

> **894** Shaw, Roger. "Ports of the Conrad Country," GOLDEN BOOK MAGAZINE (NY), X (Oct 1929), 124.

Some cruises offered by Dollar Lines and Cunard go to places associated with *The Rescue, Chance,* and "Freya of the Seven Isles." [Information based on Mac T. Greene's article in JAPAN OVERSEAS TRAVEL MAGAZINE (not seen).]

> **895** Symons, Arthur. *"A Set of Six,"* A CONRAD MEMORIAL LIBRARY: THE COLLECTION OF GEORGE T. KEATING (Garden City, NY: Doubleday, Doran, 1929), pp. 170-81.

In "Gaspar Ruiz," "Conrad evokes that atmosphere—tragic, deadly, and implacable—where at times a twofold darkness invades the little spaces of light in which, for a moment, we move." "The Informer" is "an ironical tale" with "something in it of the detective spirit in which *The Secret Agent* was written." "An Anarchist" contains in the person of the convict a "wonderful comprehension of the basest of souls, of men's criminal instincts, of their implacable desire for revenge, of their final . . . resignation to their Fate." "The Duel" contains much of JC's "sardonic humour," and "Il Conde" is "one of Conrad's finest stories." JC never admitted that he had taken from Balzac "the method of doubling or trebling the interest by setting action within action."

896 Thiébaut, Marcel. "Chronique Bibliographique: *Entre Terre et Mer,* par Joseph Conrad, traduit par G. J. Aubry" (Bibliographical Chronicle: *'Twixt Land and Sea,* by Joseph Conrad, translated by G. J.-Aubry), REVUE DE PARIS, XXXVI (Sept-Oct 1929), 474-77.

JC has transformed a minor newspaper incident into art in "The Secret Sharer." Atmosphere turns fact into a mysterious design as the captain discovers that his companion is his double. In this story one finds typical Conradian themes and techniques, as in "Freya of the Seven Isles" and "A Smile of Fortune": gratuitous action, youthful desire for adventure, a passion for the sea, and objective rendering of characters. [In French.]

897 Thompson, Alan Reynolds. "The Humanism of Joseph Conrad," SEWANEE REVIEW, XXXVII (April 1929), 204-20.

JC's work is more classic than romantic. Classicism or humanism is that which strives for "control, normality, and unification of experience." Because JC rejected a Wordsworthian interpretation of nature or a religious explanation, he "seems to have been driven by despair of all else to a new humanism, to a revival of interest in mankind not as part of nature—the scientific view—but as separate from and in a way antagonistic to nature. . . . [He] cast off all anthropomorphic illusions about the world and adopted the 'free man's worship'; he sought the solidarity of mankind; isolated from the unregarding flux of the universal machine of which he himself in body was a part, he sought in men and women the consolations of purpose, of justice, of love, and fidelity."

898 Tomlinson, H. M. *"Almayer's Folly:* The Prelude," A CONRAD MEMORIAL LIBRARY: THE COLLECTION OF GEORGE T. KEATING (Garden City, NY: Doubleday, Doran, 1929), pp. 3-7.

"This prelude to Conrad's contribution to English letters is genuinely indicative of what was to follow."

899 Walpole, Hugh. *"The Secret Agent,"* A CONRAD MEMORIAL LIBRARY: THE COLLECTION OF GEORGE T. KEATING (Garden City, NY: Doubleday, Doran, 1929), pp. 159-64.

JC lived in an age when telling a good story was not to be ashamed of (the age of Wells, Q, Weyman, Haggard, and Hope), but to good storytelling he added human beings. He thus "blazed the way for the newer novelists." *The Secret Agent* contains incidents which may seem at first melodramatic —bombs and murder in England. But JC is not melodramatic because he makes no pretense that these incidents are normal. By implicating normal people in abnormal events "he redoubles his dramatic values because he shows us that human nature does not change one jot."

1930

900 Adelgeim, E. "Taifun" (Typhoon), in *Taifun* (*Typhoon*) (Kharkov and Kiev: Knigospilka, 1930), p. xxxii.
[In Ukrainian.]

901 Bennett, Arnold. THE JOURNAL OF ARNOLD BENNETT. Two Volumes (Lond: Cassell, 1930; Garden City, NY: Garden City Publishing Co., 1933), I, 263, 497.
The Secret Agent is a short story stretched to novel length. The domestic scenes are excellent, but after *Nostromo* "the book gives a disappointing effect of slightness." *Chance* "is a discouraging book for a writer, because he damn well knows he can't write as well as this."

902 Conrad, Jessie. "Joseph Conrad and the Congo," LONDON MERCURY, XXII (July 1930), 261-63.
[Jessie Conrad corroborates parts of Lütken's account (ibid., May 1930) and feels all of it is correct. She adds some early biographic details about JC's desire to see central Africa, and substantiates JC's hatred of Belgian officials, both for their exploitation of resources and for their use of uniforms in dealings with him.]

903 Conrad, Jessie. "The Manuscript of *Almayer's Folly*," BOOKMANS JOURNAL, XVIII (1930), 1-3.
Almayer's Folly was not circulated to publishers till it was ragged; a number of incidents delayed publication of some works (e.g., *An Outcast of the Islands,* "The End of the Tether").

904 Cox, Sidney. "Joseph Conrad: The Teacher as Artist," ENGLISH JOURNAL, XIX (Dec 1930), 781-95.
JC is a great teacher because he deals with important problems of character and conduct in his fiction.

905 Cross, Wilbur L. "Joseph Conrad," FOUR CONTEMPORARY NOVELISTS (NY: Macmillan, 1930), pp. 9-60.

The circumstances of JC's life provided both the material and the moral tone of the fiction. Life came to mean "endurance for ideals in the pursuit of which hope might fade but faith was not lost." Ever concerned with technique, JC created Marlow to provide for free expression of various moods. But Marlow proved awkward from the first, and JC had to give him up. JC was essentially an impressionist and a great master of suspense.

906 Curle, Richard. "Conrad and the Younger Generation," NINETEENTH CENTURY, CVII (Jan 1930), 103-12.

The younger generation of writers regards JC "as an exotic 'spirit,' rather than as a serious novelist." The younger writers admire "daring conceptions" and "directness" of expression, and find JC "too involved in his approach, too sumptuous in his language, and, . . . too conventional in his attitude." JC's "atmospheric effects and emotional stress" lead younger English writers to find that he lacks "classicalism," and for American writers, he lacks "matter-of-fact downrightness." JC is said to "walk round his characters," which are not firsthand studies of people, but "romantic figments." Hardy, though Victorian, is preferred as "realistic and direct," whereas JC is held to appeal to "some false need of the [modern] age." JC's eloquence is "bound up with his whole method and personality." He was "concerned with fundamentals"; and though "his attitude was basically simple," the "combined sobriety of his outlook and splendour of his imagination" gave a "rounded harmony" to his whole work. JC appeals to the "inner consciousness" of readers, whether men or women.

907 Curle, Richard. "The Story of a Remarkable Friendship," TWO ESSAYS ON CONRAD, by John Galsworthy (Freelands: pvtly ptd; Cincinnati: Ebbert & Richardson, 1930); rptd in CARAVANSARY AND CONVERSATION: MEMORIES OF PLACES AND PERSONS (NY: Stokes, 1937), pp. 153-63.

The "epic friendship" of thirty-one years between Galsworthy and JC reveals the dissimilar temperaments of the two writers who nonetheless enjoyed an association which permitted no jealousy of change through the years. [Also includes Galsworthy's "Joseph Conrad, A Disquisition," FORTNIGHTLY REVIEW, LXXXIII (Jan-June 1908), 627-33, as "Reminiscences of Conrad: 1924."]

908 Cutler, Bradley Dwayne, and Villa Stiles. "Joseph Conrad: 1857-1924," MODERN BRITISH AUTHORS THEIR FIRST EDITIONS (NY: Greenberg; Lond: Allen & Unwin, 1930), pp. 23-28.
[Checklist of JC's first editions.]

909 Hicks, Granville. "Conrad After Five Years," NEW REPUBLIC, LXI (8 Jan 1930), 192-94.

JC's reputation is perhaps shrinking. Too long-winded for many readers, he is primarily a philosophical novelist—nearest to Hardy, far away from sociological Wells, Bennett, and Galsworthy. His philosophy is pessimistic, as in all his novels from *Almayer's Folly* to *Suspense*, but is linked to admiration for heroic virtues. JC held that intellect interferes with heroic qualities; most of his heroes are stupid. Heyst has to abandon intellectuality; Jim is "sound in his obsessions with his disgrace." F. M. Ford is wrong in wanting Garnett to advise JC to give up his concern with the sea. The ways and problems of seafaring men are perfectly adapted to JC's world view. The sea, like the world, is cruel; one must struggle. JC said that success comes only to the fortunate and the deserving. If fortune fails, then heroic attempt still brings inner victory (Heyst in flames, Jim on Patusan, Peyrol in his tartane). JC's Jamesian "doublings and redoublings" in narration, a technique designed not to thrill but to bring out moral problems, shows too much strain and pressure, "quite unlike the feeling of unlimited resources conveyed by great masters." JC falls short of the first rank in narrative technique, but the strain and struggle showing through is like that of his characters. The current depreciation of JC comes from a belief that his "subject matter is without a true significance," whereas the fact is that JC really "occupies himself with what is central in our civilization" though his subjects are peripheral. His code is "too simple for sophisticates, too barbaric for humanists, not barbaric enough for new primitivists." JC seems out of touch: he ignores modern women (his portraits of women are always weak, his primitive women best); he depreciates intellect in a scientific age, and he ignores involved sex and social reform. [See Don Bregenzer, ibid. (29 Jan 1930), 277, for an attack on Hicks.]

910 Lütken, Otto. "Joseph Conrad in the Congo," LONDON MERCURY, XXII (May 1930), 40-43.

The first part of "Heart of Darkness," through the repair of the steamer, is based on personal experience whereas the rest of the story, "no less excellent as a literary work," is "related from hearsay." JC seems "somewhat less than just" to the Belgians of the Congo and "Heart of Darkness" would have lost no merit by being "more faithful in local colour." [For Jessie Conrad's reply to Captain Lütken, see "Joseph Conrad and the Congo," ibid. (July 1930), 261-63, and Lütken's further comment in ibid. (Aug 1930), 350-51.]

911 Lütken, Otto. "Joseph Conrad in the Congo," LONDON MERCURY, XXII (Aug 1930), 350-51; rptd as "To the Editor of the LONDON MERCURY, August 1930," in JOSEPH CONRAD'S "HEART OF DARKNESS": BACKGROUNDS AND CRITICISMS, ed by Leonard F.

Dean (Englewood Cliffs, NJ: Prentice-Hall, Spectrum Books, 1960), pp. 93-95.

JC's "Heart of Darkness" and "An Outpost of Civilisation" [sic, i.e., Progress] must be considered as "literary, fictional work only and not . . . as colour-true pictures of colonial life of the period"; JC actually made a voyage to Stanley Falls, but not as a captain; and on the river voyage a M. Klein, who had been the Company Agent at Stanley Falls, was aboard and died, apparently supplying the model "in so far as Conrad worked by model," for Kurtz in "Heart of Darkness." [A second reply to Jessie Conrad, "Joseph Conrad and the Congo," ibid. (July 1930).]

912 Mansfield, Katherine. NOVELS AND NOVELISTS (NY: Knopf, 1930), pp. 60-64, 222-26.

In *The Arrow of Gold,* JC is a pioneer looking into his own mind. *The Rescue* has "a responsive sensitiveness to the significance of everything." In *Rescue,* JC ranks fidelity as the greatest of virtues. But JC's novels refuse to give readers "a simple answer to the dilemma of the mind."

913 Morf, Gustav. THE POLISH HERITAGE OF JOSEPH CONRAD (Lond: Sampson Low, Marston; NY: Smith, 1930).

Polish sources reveal new information about JC and some of his works. Although JC revolted against his father's religious faith, father and son had the same kind of temperament, including the same romantic realism. The death of JC's father left the boy with "the awful sensation of the inevitable" which is responsible for his "philosophy of fate, and partly for his pessimism." JC's fits of depression were caused by his being a self-made man who sometimes feared that "the country which he had adopted, might not adopt him." At heart a mystic, he made human destiny the theme of his work. His heroes are "outcasts, living far from their home or in strange surroundings, and there is little or no hope for them ever to return. *If* they return home, it is only to die there." But since "the final tragedy" brings out their best human qualities, "their defeat is really their victory." Although JC had unusually good luck on the sea, his pessimistic strain was "strengthened by the necessity of repressing that Polish part within him, which had to be sacrificed to an English career." [Psychological analyses of some of JC's work are noteworthy.] *Nostromo* is based on JC's Polish past: Antonia is modelled on JC's "first love"; Martin Decoud is JC himself, who does not want to return to his Polish bonds; Don José is based on JC's father and uncle; and Costaguana is Poland, for which Decoud dies. *Lord Jim,* seen according to the ideas of Freud and Jung, shows Jim on Patusan where, "Brown is the embodiment of that unforgettable and unforgiving past which stands up against him in the very moment when he expected it least"; Brown is Jim's other self, or double. Jim therefore "cannot resist the evil" represented by Brown *"because the evil is within himself."* In the last novel (*The Rover*) JC completed, he "fixed a vision which had been the great mission of his boyhood: that of a free Rover going out into the world in search of adventure and glory, fighting his way all over the seas, and finally coming home again, white-haired but still strong, admired but modest, and with a bag of money." Some of Miss Stauffer's explanations in JOSEPH CONRAD: HIS ROMANTIC REALISM (1922) are wrong; "the conscious Conrad was realistic, the unconscious Conrad, ever dissatisfied and unhappy, was incurably romantic," and "that which tortured him could be expressed only in an irrational, symbolic form." [A fascinating psychological study of JC which should be studied, though, with some reservations.]

914 Mouradian, Jacques. "Conrad and Anatole France," TIMES LITERARY SUPPLEMENT (Lond), 30 Oct 1930, p. 890.

A passage in Anatole France's LE LYS ROUGE is similar to one in JC's *The Arrow of Gold,* perhaps being a deliberate allusion, perhaps only a literary reminiscence. [Letter.] [In French.]

915 O'Flaherty, Liam. JOSEPH CONRAD: AN APPRECIATION. Blue Moon Booklets, No. 1 (Lond: E. Lahr [1930]).

JC accepted the "God of the British Empire" as unsurpassable, and all his characters stand "on tiptoe striving to be like that God," who exemplifies all the middle-class virtues. JC is the "prophet" of the "God of romance," a beautiful God, but the author, aware of the cruelty in nature, admires "that man [who] is great [because he] is his own God."

916 Overton, Grant. *"Lord Jim:* Do You Remember It?" MENTOR, XXII (Oct 1930), 34-35.

[Plot summary of *Lord Jim* followed by a biographical sketch of JC. Inconsequential.]

1931

917 Adams, J. Donald. "Introduction," *Lord Jim* (NY: Random House, Modern Library, 1931), pp. v-vii.

Despite its structural flaws, *Lord Jim* is representative of all that JC "stands for in English literature."

918 Bancroft, William Wallace. JOSEPH CONRAD: HIS PHILOSOPHY OF LIFE (Philadelphia: University of Pennsylvania P, 1931; Boston: Stratford, 1933; NY: Haskell House, 1964).

JC, whose philosophy had matured by the time he began writing, is interested in the "moral drama basic to the universal expression of human life," especially of the inner life. His philosophical idealism (originating in his focus on the inner life of man) and his literary realism complement his goal, which is to find the best expression of the "Infinite Individual" and to avoid separation from "Human Solidarity." JC fuses the three concepts of "Cosmos," "Moral Law," and "Human Solidarity."

The cosmos, like the sea, is indifferent and neutral: thus *The Nigger of the Narcissus,* set on the sea, is "concretized in existences" by the crew of the *Narcissus;* or as JC comments in *Chance,* each "of us arranges the world according to his own notion of the fitness of things." The social context of human solidarity emphasizes the need for a cosmic bond, illustrated in *Under Western Eyes, Lord Jim, Nostromo,* and "The Informer." Cruelty that seems to exist in the cosmos is removed through the "transmutation of experience" and the assumption of individual responsibility. Each man thus has his "Secret Sharer," the "created creature of his transmutation." JC treats moral law negatively because it is the "logical, universal correcting force of life." Unselfishness becomes the "absolute tendency and reality." Willems, Razumov, the Planter of Malata, Travers, and Lingard feel the force of moral power. Moral law often warns such characters as Almayer (selfishness vs. conviction of duty), Nostromo (vanity and pride), Razumov (betrayal), Willems (meeting Aïssa), and Renouard (deception). They cannot escape themselves, and become outcasts when separated from "Human Solidarity."

Principle can triumph only under moral stress: thus Kurtz, who violated moral law in Africa while gaining ivory but losing his vision, glimpses the truth of moral law just before his death. JC attacks "settled convictions," defined in *Jim* as "artful dodges to escape the grim shadow of self knowledge": Lingard, believing in the permanence of wealth, is defeated by its presence. Defeated also are Almayer (duty to himslf), Nostromo (pride), Willems (loss of honesty), and de Barral (selfishness). Allied to "settled convictions" are "false adhesion to ideas," secret fears (Razumov, Old Nelson in "Freya of the Seven Isles," and Jim), conceit (Nostromo), and ignorance (Willems). The way out of the chaos of violation of moral will is confession—or "heroism of mind and will." Almayer and the Planter of Malata almost confess; Kurtz, Jim, Arlette, and Razumov do so. As for the importance of human solidarity, in JC's novels, God's will is often judged by the individual's conception of it, but JC does not rebuke any concept of God; rather he emphasizes that moral law (as distinct from an anthropomorphic God) never fails. The *summum bonum* to JC is self realization, or anything that unites man to moral law, which fulfills the "infinite individual." [Bancroft ends with a quotation from JC's introduction to *Chance:* "It may have happened to me to sin against taste now and then, but apparently I have never sinned against the basic feelings and elementary convictions which make life possible to the mass of mankind." Bancroft's book, though in part superseded by studies that examine individual works in greater detail, still has value as one of the first comprehensive overviews of JC's philosophy.]

919 Berkovic, Josip. "Izdanja Tiskovne zadruge u Ljubljani za 1931. god" (Publications of the Printing Co-operative in Ljubljana for 1931), HRVATSKA REVIJA (Zagreb), V: 6 (1932), 401-3.

[Review of books by Fedin and Baroja and of *The Shadow-Line.*] [In Serbo-Croatian.]

920 Blüth, Raphael [also Rafał]. "Joseph Conrad et Dostoievski: le problème du crime et du châtiment" (Joseph Conrad and Dostoevski: The Problem of Crime and Punishment), VIE INTELLECTUELLE, XII (10 May 1931), 320-39.

JC may have been influenced by Dostoevski through reaction against the Russian's ideas, JC being essentially rationalistic and Dostoevski mystical. *Under Western Eyes* is a direct reply to THE POSSESSED. In *Lord Jim,* the protagonist fails to maintain the Conradian ideal of struggle against irrational fears by succumbing to destiny. Although JC is rational in his conception of man, his idea of destiny is mystical as an unexplainable force governing man. The same evasion from the struggle with destiny, irrational passions, and dreams that brings Jim's downfall can be seen in JC's escape from his responsibilities to his homeland in distress. For Dostoevski, on the other hand, failure occurs when man listens too much to his rational intellect. In CRIME AND PUNISHMENT, Raskolnikov is led to murder by his reason. In both novels the heroes' downfalls are a result of disequilibrium between human faculties, but JC's protagonist accepts his responsibility for causing the vengeance of destiny while Dostoevski's does not. [Convincingly argued.] [In French.]

921 Braybrooke, Patrick. "Joseph Conrad: An Appreciation," DUBLIN REVIEW, CLXXXIX (Oct 1931), 318-25.

The symbolism and the desire to expose the purpose behind action "arise consciously or unconsciously from the fact that Conrad was a Catholic novelist." The strength of his prose is in its "fine cadences," but frequently there is too much repetition and color.

922 Coleman, A. P. "Polonisms in the English of Conrad's *Chance,*" MODERN LANGUAGE NOTES, XLVI (Nov 1931), 463-68.

According to Gustav Morf, in THE POLISH HERITAGE OF JOSEPH CONRAD (1930), JC's passionate love of romantic adventure, "instinctive penetration of exotic mentalities," his recurrent use of the figure of the wanderer spiritually exiled (JC himself expiating the "guilt complex of himself as Korzeniowski"), and his use of English all show Polish inheritance or influence. The influence of Polish on JC's English was greater, however, than Morf suspected. *Chance* has the "general characteristic" of JC's work—rich color, lavish use of similes, and a heroine who manifests the "Slavonic defeatism with which all his writing is permeated." The Polish influence appears most "frequently and startlingly" in JC's feeling for English prepositions (for example, in *Chance*). JC also never mastered the English articles, frequently omitting them since there are no articles in Polish. Sometimes he used articles where they were not needed, sometimes using the definite where the indefinite would have been more characteristic of English. Polish has no anticipatory "there," nor any equivalent for the "it" which JC omitted from his "May be that a glimpse . . . is the proper way of seeing." JC also had trouble with tenses, a difficulty arising partly because English is concerned with the time of action rather than with quality. Also the English scheme of tense sequence is derived from Latin, which is strange to Polish. Sometimes his word choice and turn of expression are Polish. His phrase "regretting the girl" involves a use of a Polish verb which can be followed by a *substantive,* whereas in English the substantive following "to regret" implies a verbal idea. Finally, JC's looseness of sentence structure may have been a holdover from highly inflected Polish, in which relationships depend on inflectional endings instead of order. JC's sentence structure and word order, especially in abstract passages, "have all the sonorousness of literary Polish."

923 Conrad, Jessie. "Joseph Conrad's War Service," BLUE PETER, XI (May 1931), 252-55.

JC accepted the Admiralty's invitation to active duty at the end of 1916, devoting time to inspecting ships, anti-aircraft artillery, and (once) mending deep-sea nets. He spent about two weeks off the English coast aboard the HMS *Ready,* which was disguised as a Norwegian timber carrier; becoming ill, he went ashore and was arrested briefly for being on the coast without an official permit. After the *Ready* episode, service was limited to one or two visits to Dover. JC wrote only two or three tales based on his military duty [Jessie quotes from "The Tale" and "The Unlighted Coast"] because the actual experience was "too close and real for so nervous a man to portray." [Jessie, as usual, tends to emphasize her role as concerned wife.]

924 Conrad, Jessie. "Journeys with Joseph Conrad: Poland in the Great War," CHAMBER'S JOURNAL, 7th ser., XXI (11 July 1931), 497-500.

JC's journey to Poland at the outbreak of World War I fills in details not included in *A Personal Record* and contrasts with his cooler appraisal of the same events. [Interesting for details of JC's reactions in Poland and his love for the country.]

925 Ford, Ford Madox. RETURN TO YESTERDAY (Lond: Gollancz, 1931; NY: Liveright, 1932), pp. vii, 31-33, 58-60, 114, 139, 166-67, 181, 186-201 [rpts "Working with Conrad," YALE REVIEW, N.S. XVIII (June 1929), 699-715], 216, 239-44, 279-81.

"Where it has seemed expedient to me I have altered episodes that I witnessed but I have been careful never to distort the character of the episode. The accuracies I deal in are the accuracies of my impressions." [Ford's remarks repeat essentially what he had said in earlier works (see author-title index). He describes how he and JC worked together, how he bolstered JC, how he helped write and rewrite passages, and how he suggested various plots. He repeats the notorious error that JC first showed his manuscript of *Almayer's Folly* to Galsworthy on board the *Torrens*. He claims that after the beginning of his acquaintance with JC, he had at least a subordinate connection with nearly all of JC's work.]

926 Ford, Ford Madox. "Three Americans and a Pole," SCRIBNER'S MAGAZINE, XC (Oct 1931), 379-86.

At the time when JC, with Stephen Crane, W. H. Hudson, and Henry James, lived near Rye, he was a romantic figure, dark, and "passionate in the extreme"; but he could readily be stirred to great fury. He was also "the most marvellous raconteur in the world." His sufferings, which were great both at that time and later, arose mainly from poverty. [Ford's account of four foreigners in England who "changed the course of modern literature" (editor's note) provides a brief but useful portrait of JC.]

927 G[raher]. I[ve]. "Joseph Conrad: *Senčna črta*" (Joseph Conrad: *The Shadow-Line*), MODRA PTICA (Ljubljana), III: 1 (1931-32), 25-26.

[Review of the Slovene translation.] [In Slovene.]

928 Jarc, Miran. "Joseph Conrad: *Senčna črta*" (Joseph Conrad: *The Shadow-Line*), DOM IN SVET (Ljubljana), XLIV: 10 (1931), 516-18.

[Review of the Slovene translation.] [In Slovene.]

929 Knight, Grant C. "Joseph Conrad," THE NOVEL IN ENGLISH (NY: Richard R. Smith, 1931), pp. 305-13, 60, 72, 98, 132, 211, 230, 349, 359.

General, conventional survey of JC's career. *Chance* (1913) established JC's name. In all his novels, JC wrote to inspire. His heroes, though often beaten, go triumphantly to their deaths (*The Nigger of the Narcissus, Lord Jim, Victory*) and show the reader the glory in commitment, in doing one's duty. He arouses sympathy in the reader for these brave, yet pitiful characters. His Slav background caused him to be preoccupied with the significance of life and death, and he emphasized the loneliness of man—many of his characters are isolated from their fellows. Although English was an acquired language, JC is one of the very few to make a lasting contribution to English literature.

930 Lloyd, C. F. "Joseph Conrad," CANADIAN BOOKMAN, XIII (Feb 1931), 29-32.

JC's characters are unable to speak but have tremendous powers of communication. JC does not constantly remind one of a moral. [A light and personal testimonial.]

931 MacCarthy, Desmond. "Conrad," PORTRAITS (Lond and NY: Putnam, 1931; NY: Macmillan, 1932; NY: Oxford U P, 1954), 68-78.

The adventure in JC's stories is always the same: the spirit of loyalty in men, struggling either vainly or victoriously, against the forces of nature or of "mean men." JC is a "profound ethical writer" even if for him the universe is utterly indifferent: in an inscrutable universe without justice and honor, man's glory is to put them there. JC has no "message," and his philosophy of life is not a popular one. His devotion to his work prevented his becoming dehumanized.

932 McDonald, Evelyn. "DAVID COPPERFIELD and *Lord Jim* in the Upper School," SCHOOL (Toronto), XX (Oct, Nov 1931), 167-74, 265-69.

[Discusses a method of teaching *Lord Jim* in high school.]

933 Mégroz, R. L. "Conrad's Craftsmanship," THIS QUARTER (Paris), IV (July, Aug, Sept 1931), 130-40.

JC achieves credibility in his fiction by avoiding all suggestions of supernatural agencies, by his richness of style and his use of description as "an inseparable element of the drama," by his wide range of impressions and his sense of unity achieved by relating his differing characters dramatically to one another, by his innovation of departing from a natural time order as a means of "bounding" the reader into belief, and by "the triumph of dynamic unity achieved through diversity of material."

934 Mégroz, R. L. JOSEPH CONRAD'S MIND AND METHOD: A STUDY OF PERSONALITY IN ART (Lond: Faber & Faber, 1931; NY: Russell & Russell, 1964).

JC's personality had to be expressed "through an endlessly varied presentation of a few simple and profound truths," and Poland supplied most of these: "the virtues of fidelity, loyalty, courage in adversity, and the craftsman's conscience [were] closely interwoven with the aspirations and experiences of the oppressed people whose memories were part of his inmost being." The literary work of JC's father and his father's leadership in the Polish rebellion against Russia in 1863 were "the only link" between JC's boyhood and his career as an English writer; an unhappy boyhood and his father's death made "an indelible impression" upon the boy's mind. Sailing ships and writing books became "a means of externalizing the activity of a mind which had a powerful tendency to introspection at the expense of the practical life." As a result of his need to justify his escape from Poland, "he was never entirely in control of the intellectual activity which accompanied writing."

"Prince Roman" is the only frankly autobiographical story with a Polish setting in JC's works, and the Polish part of JC's life leaves scarcely any obvious evidence of its "factitive influence," although we may suspect a richer Polish influence in those stories where "identification with the author's personal history is less direct." [Mégroz corrects the "possibly undue emphasis" of psychological criticism (like Morf's, 1930) of the personal and Polish elements in JC's works, and finds a "certain doubt" in JC, because the repressed factors appear in *The Secret Agent, Under Western Eyes,* and *The Rover.*] JC "never confused literal truth with imaginative truth." His historical knowledge was deep and wide in range, and his political views were not shallow. As a thinker "capable of a systematic philosophy," he found it necessary "to ally himself morally with England," because as an English writer he had no "national tradition" to use as a background for his philosophical fiction. Both his essays and stories share "a certain manner of perception" that reveals his "romantic feeling for the realities of life and his insistent moral idealism." He was too conscientious a realist to depart from the truth of his own sensations. In *The Mirror of the* Sea he glorified the man of action and found glamor in the technical language of the sea.

JC has a place "among the greatest English prose writers in fiction" because of his "rich and varied" "collection of beautiful long passages, descriptive, essayistic, dramatic," although his writing contains some stylistic faults, the greatest of which is "an occasional failure to join the edges of the poetic passages with connecting sentences of the narrative." The "predominantly fantastic element" in JC's works is closely related to "an interest in human behaviour which springs from moral convictions." In the stories, good and evil are often interchangeable with beauty and ugliness.

Recurring situations in JC's works stem from the author's seamanship as an "escape" from the "oppressive atmosphere" of his Polish childhood and from the unexpected death of his father: old Viola, old Jorgensen, and Dominic Cervoni, who "have served a cause ardently," are strong men who are disappointed. Certain settings also recur: darkness and the thick tropical forest are symbolical of a moral influence, and they too "surround lost men with menace." Indeed, "the material and symbolic images reflect the spiritual condition of the chief characters, held in the toils of an inevitable destiny." Nostromo is "the most complete idealization of [his] hero as a man of action"; this kind of characterization is the expression of JC's "personal fantasy." More clearly than in most fiction, JC's management of plots is "a means of creating atmosphere and giving a sense of depth, that is reality to the characters." "An Anarchist" shows most plainly his commonest system of plot, "mirrors within mirrors, . . . or three circles, the middle of which overlaps those on either side of it." In *Nostromo,* although some chapters are poorly constructed, everything present "will eventually turn and twist back to the main road." *Chance* marks the end of JC's "loosening of the logical time sequence to make room for psychological associations centering around the chief characters," and the "main fantasy—the fairy-tale motive—is unconvincing because it is permeated by "the Marlow-Conrad intellect"; the essayist steps in to "help to keep the fable afloat." The main purpose of Mégroz's book is to show JC's life story as "an extraordinarily apt example of the typical artist's passive resistance to the world." The psychology of the artist explains his "romantic-realism," which Ruth M. Stauffer wrote about (1922). It is JC's "sense of reality" that made him great, not his realism, even if he is notable among impressionists. JC's writings are difficult to analyze because they are well balanced between romanticism and classicism. His "extraordinary creative power" is derived from the strength of his "intellectual control over the primitive forces of fantasy, the double-sidedness of his mind, which enabled him to be both inside the skin of his chief characters and outside gaining the most vivid impressions of their world." His ultimate greatness lies in "the power he exercises of exalting as well as intensifying our consciousness," in his "vision of reality," which is always "a reflection of his own tragic and aspiring self." [Although Mégroz helps to correct the distorted views of such earlier commentators as Stauffer and Morf, he himself seems to be groping for a final explanation of JC's genius; but his book, an important one in its time, is still worth serious consideration by the student of JC.]

935 Oates, David W. "Introduction," AN APPRECIATION OF JOSEPH CONRAD, by Arthur J. Price (Lond: Simpkin Marshall, 1931), pp. 3-6.
[Oates expresses his pleasure in reading this volume reprinting "the series of talks on Joseph Conrad broadcast by Captain A. J. Price." The volume

provides "a valuable guide and companion to the study of Conrad's works." See Arthur J. Price, AN APPRECIATION OF JOSEPH CONRAD (1931).]

936 Price, Arthur J. AN APPRECIATION OF JOSEPH CONRAD (Newport, Monmouthshire: Joyce & Sons; London: Simpkin Marshall, 1931).

JC creates an intensity, "an agreement between himself and the reader," by placing the reader in the position of critic, by achieving a vagueness "both mysterious and fascinating," and by "half explaining a vital incident." He is at his best when dealing with tropical islands and tropical seas, and *Victory* contains all that readers prize most: "characterization, description, atmosphere and teaching." JC's style, although somewhat prolix, is never artificial; his language in general has "dignity, grandeur and conviction." JC is a writer "whose poet-soul is aflame with the glory of nature, and is transported by the majesty of the sea." Readers admire him because of the "sense of adventure in his works"; *Romance,* for example, "is romance in every sense of the word." JC's philosophy of life as revealed in his characters is based most of all on endurance, "an endurance which implies loyalty and heroism" and which comes to a man whose teacher was the sea. The word *clean* best describes his teaching. He is at once a fatalist and a realist. In his short stories, JC is "more Conradesque" than in any of his novels; in these we have all that JC stands for "as a teacher and an artist." [This small book is typical of the many early attempts, perhaps sincere but usually superficial, to assess JC's life and works. See David W. Oates, "Introduction," ibid.]

937 Rothenstein, William. MEN AND MEMORIES. Two Volumes. MEN AND MEMORIES, 1872-1900, Volume I (Lond: Faber; NY: Coward-McCann, 1931); two volumes in one (NY: Tudor, 1934). p. 374.

JC "had conceived one of his odd prejudices against Masefield." [Also see ibid., Volume II: 1900-1922 (1932).]

938 Schwartz, Jacob. 1100 OBSCURE POINTS: THE BIBLIOGRAPHIES OF TWENTY-FIVE ENGLISH AND TWENTY-ONE AMERICAN AUTHORS (Lond: Ulysses Bookshop [1931]), pp. 15-17.

[A descriptive list of first editions of JC's books is provided.]

939 Tonquédec, Joseph de. "Le Message de Conrad" (Conrad's Message), ÉTUDES, REVUE CATHOLIQUE D'INTÉRÊT GÉNÉRAL (Paris), CCVIII (July 1931), 69-77.

Unlike most contemporary heroes, JC's characters are nearly savages in their lack of sophistication, in their intense and adventurous lives, and in their courage, energy, and honor. His novels dramatize the conflict between the individual and the universe and show the value of generosity, service to others, and willpower. Though uncomplicated, his characters are profound and never quite reveal their entire nature. By means of conciseness and precision, JC is able to suggest the mystery that lies beneath the surface of his events. [Convincingly argued though not completely demonstrated.] [In French.]

1932

940 Anthony, Irvin. "The Illusion of Joseph Conrad," BOOKMAN (NY), LXXIV (March 1932), 648-53.
JC was greatly interested in "illusion" as a word and as a literary method, as a dozen instances where word and theme appear in his work indicate.

941 Aubry, Georges Jean-. "Une idylle de Conrad à l'Ile Maurice" (An Idyll of Conrad on the Island of Mauritius), FIGARO, 14 May 1932, p. 5.
The action of "A Smile of Fortune" takes place on the Island of Mauritius, called by JC "The Pearl of the Ocean." At the end of the story, JC himself states that not wishing to return to that island, he had asked to be relieved of his post on the *Otago,* which served as model in *The Shadow-Line,* "Falk," and "The Secret Sharer." A Mr. S. Mérédac of Mauritius, reading Aubry's introduction to the French translation of *'Twixt Land and Sea,* made an investigation there which he published in a literary journal, L'ESSOR, 15 Feb 1931. He stated that JC had sailed on the *Otago* from Australia to Port-Louis, arriving on 30 September and leaving on 22 November 1888. Much of the plot of "A Smile of Fortune," says he, had parallel events and personalities in Port-Louis. Mérédac was able to contact an elderly lady whose family had received JC as a visitor in 1888. Their pastimes included a game of questions to which JC wrote (in English) very revealing answers. After his departure, JC wrote to the brother of the family, asking for his sister's hand in marriage. Response: she was already engaged. JC never returned to Mauritius. [In French.]

942 Austin, Mary. EARTH HORIZON: AUTOBIOGRAPHY (Boston: Houghton Mifflin; NY: Literary Guild, 1932), pp. 312-13, 342, 343.
In 1904, JC, then living at Capel House, was "ill and not very happy," because the returns of his publishers were unsatisfactory. In 1922 he informed Austin that the Fabians were no longer the intellectual leaders. She helped him sell one of his novels to the PICTORIAL REVIEW.

943 Baker, Ernest A., and James Packman (eds). A GUIDE TO THE BEST FICTION, new and enlgd ed (Lond: Routledge, 1932), pp. 110-12.

[Chronological list of JC's works with brief comments on each.]

944 Beach, Joseph Warren. "Impressionism: Conrad," THE TWENTIETH CENTURY NOVELISTS: STUDIES IN TECHNIQUES (NY: Appleton-Century, 1932), pp. 337-65.

JC was experimental, "forever trying out new methods." Though he disliked Dostoevski, he shared his feeling of the mysteriousness of human nature. JC's Slavic and "Oriental" style and his love of Flaubert led him to use too many words in his earlier effort to make the reader "see," but in his later stories he discovered a considerable variety of structural devices to bring his subject into focus. The technique of *Under Western Eyes* is "very special and complicated": the first half is based on Razumov's diary, transposed into the third person, edited and abridged by an English professor and others; the second half is told in the first person by the professor himself. The story is told in large blocks, with everything authenticated by written document. It combines psychology, political intrigue, and mystery in the manner of Dostoevski. In *The Arrow of Gold,* autobiography becomes fiction by means of a manuscript and the third person narrative, which look like fiction becoming autobiography. Four parts of *Arrow* are exposition working up curiosity and suspense; the fifth is climax, presented in a limited point of view, successfully, giving a particular moment sharp isolation. Powell's looking into Captain Anthony's cabin in *Chance* shows JC's use of close-up and his careful control of tempo in which revelation takes place. *The Nigger of the Narcissus* is "the last word in subtlety and sophistication." JC presents his subjects from outside as well as inside, "in every manner known to narrative art," including his "Oriental style." The story begins in the omniscient third person, skips to the first person ("crew" becomes "we" instead of "they"), and then after ten pages returns to the first person. Afterward there is constant alternation between the objective third person and the subjective first, implying participation by various writers. To serve the "advantage of many points of view without losing coherence," JC invented Marlow, who in *Lord Jim* tells the story in an Oriental style, by word-of-mouth, achieving amazing authenticity.

945 Bolander, Louis H. "Joseph Conrad's Last Ship," NEW YORK TIMES MAGAZINE, 17 April 1932, p. 15.

On the *Torrens,* JC carried the first nine chapters of *Almayer's Folly.* A fellow seaman encouraged JC to finish the book. John Galsworthy took passage on the *Torrens* and befriended JC, but was never shown the manuscript of the book.

946 Braybrooke, Patrick. "Joseph Conrad: Master Novelist," SOME VICTORIAN AND GEORGIAN CATHOLICS: THEIR ART AND OUTLOOK (Lond: Burns, Oates & Washbourne, 1932); rptd in Essay Index Reprint Series (Freeport, NY: Books for Libraries P, 1966), pp. 137-68.

"Conrad was a novelist who was not only worthy to be called a Catholic novelist but was also worthy to be considered as a Catholic who was a writer of genius. The combination of genius and Catholicism (always an inspiration and a brake to his work) allowed Conrad to be outstanding." He was lucky in his faith, his art, and his temperament. One disappointment is that "we are not quite intimate enough with his characters."

947 Cadot, Raoul. "Conrad et le Navire" (Conrad and the Ship), REVUE DE L'ENSEIGNEMENT DES LANGUES VIVANTES, XLIX (1932), 390-96, 433-38.

Man's love for the sea is paralleled by his love for the instrument which enables him to conquer it—the ship. It is for him a refuge, an ark, a home. It has a personality, which stands out in relief in JC's tales. The intimate collaboration between pilot and instrument is such that they have the same reflexes, reactions, and even will. In this coordination of effort to conquer the external world (the sea), the two (ship and man) achieve a confluence which causes the personality of the one to merge into that of the other. Sailing vessels, not being as mechanically controlled as are steamers, held a special fascination for JC. They seem to exhibit free will, a style of their own (e.g., the *Tweed* in *The Mirror of the Sea*). A history of the ship named the *Apse Family*, christened *The Brute* (in *A Set of Six*) by the sailors, depicts the personality, even the whims, that a ship may have.

JC once spent 130 days in the Bay of Bengal without once touching land, ship and seamen linked together through fair weather and foul. For the mariner there is but one ship: his own. He endows it with his own unexpressed aspirations toward an ideal. The ship's personality is conceived variously in the minds of different members of its crew: for the old unlettered seaman it is clothed in superstitions; for JC, élite of seamen, it is a being conscious of its own grace; though wary of its behavior, it has the will to brave the sea. JC never tires of describing its beauty in repose or its docile obstinacy in facing dangers (*The Nigger of the Narcissus*). He once tactfully refused to name a defunct ship that had caused disasters, saying, "It has now disappeared." JC loved the old figurehead-bearing ships. The *Hilda* ("A Smile of Fortune"), a ship with the figurehead of a woman in a blue tunic edged with gold, was lost. The old grieved captain would no more replace her than he would remarry. The ship's personality is best revealed after a storm (*Nigger*). "Didn't she do cleverly?" cry the crew. In an approaching storm (*The Shadow-Line*), JC's crew were too ill to move; nevertheless they readied their ship for action.

How account for this emotional tie? For the youth it is adventure, the period of testing and trial, the memory of which often persists into maturity. Experience deepens the affection of the master for his ship: their mutual interdependence, the instrument's challenge to his talents, its witness to his prowess create solid bonds between them, bonds of the most disinterested kind. The cult of the ship is reserved to men. Deprived of the usual domestic situations on shore, the mariner admires the harmonious lines of his instrument. He wants it painted, shining clean. In English the ship is feminine—"the old girl," "she." In "Freya of the Seven Isles" a captain's love for his ship is greater than that for his wife. JC, when he boarded the *Otago* as master for the first time, felt "like a lover awaiting a rendezvous." The English seaman's high evaluation of *duty* greatly appealed to JC. He knew that in certain situations the ship was master to the crew (*Nigger*); it demanded obedience to rule.

The pride of the Apse family was brought low by the *Brute*. Yet it is usually rectitude, honesty, and skill which are demanded of the mariner by his ship. Of all artifacts created by man the ship is the least inclined to yield to a pretender. The captain who is guilty of the sin of egotism or pride is not in the state of grace which alone leads to success. The mariner takes the ship as the symbol of his professional conscience; it is a severe guide to and teacher of virtue. The sea provides no permanent code of morality. Once on land the seaman may discard bourgeois virtues. JC sees the problem of existence as parallel to that of life on board ship: the power of human resistance to its eternal enemies—savage and primitive forces. In *Mirror,* JC pays his debt to the ship which made him a man and a writer. [In French.]

948 Clemens, Cyril. "Introduction," DID JOSEPH CONRAD RETURN AS A SPIRIT? [See Jessie Conrad, DID JOSEPH CONRAD RETURN AS A SPIRIT? (1932).]

949 "Conrad at Thirty-one," LIVING AGE, CCCXLIII (Sept 1932), 82-83.

A letter to Savinen Mérédac from a sugar exporter focuses upon JC's physical appearance and speech. A questionnaire submitted to JC by a ladyfriend indicates that JC thought himself lazy, sought "reality," and lacked self-confidence. [Prints two documents concerning JC when he arrived on the island of Mauritius as captain of the *Otago* in September 1888.]

950 Conrad, Jessie. DID JOSEPH CONRAD RETURN AS A SPIRIT? Intro by Cyril Clemens (Webster Groves, Mo.: International Mark Twain Society, 1932).

[Clemens's brief introduction relates the circumstances of his meeting with Jessie. Jessie's comments discount reports about manifestations of JC's spirit appearing to several people, and of JC wanting to get in touch with her through a medium. Jessie affirms that she has seen JC's form "in complete contour" in his favorite chair. No critical value.]

951 Curle, Richard. A HANDLIST OF THE VARIOUS BOOKS, PAMPHLETS, NOTES, ARTICLES, PREFACES, REVIEWS AND LETTERS WRITTEN ABOUT JOSEPH CONRAD BY RICHARD CURLE 1911-1931 (Brookville, Pa: Pvtly ptd, 1932).

[Lists, with brief comments, his two books, five pamphlets, and sixty-six prefaces, articles and reviews.]

952 Ellis, Havelock. "A Note on Conrad," VIEWS AND REVIEWS: A SELECTION OF UNCOLLECTED ARTICLES, 1884-1932. 1st and 2nd ser (Boston: Houghton Mifflin, 1932), pp. 116-20.

Intuition suggests that JC had "essential and radical qualities of a great writer [but was one] who wrote too much, and often in fields for which his genius had not fitted him." His early short works were written "at the impulse of genius"; genius later degenerated into talent. JC's "unreasoning hatred" of Dostoevski's art resulted from competition with him, as in *Under Western Eyes*.

953 Elphinstone, Petronella. "Miscellany: Tuan Jim," NEW STATESMAN AND NATION, N.S. IV (20 Aug 1932), 203-5.

An allegedly true [?] account of one Andrews, a prosperous ship chandler in Singapore, is taken as the original for the titular hero of *Lord Jim*. Andrews does not jump from his ship, being off-watch and asleep at the time of the other officers' desertion; after help in repairs and assistance from the crew of a passing ship, Andrews brings his vessel safely to Aden.

954 Fabes, Gilbert Henry. MODERN FIRST EDITIONS: POINTS AND VALUES, 3rd ser (Lond: W & G Foyle, 1932), pp. 13-14. [Supplements items in 1st ser (1929).]

955 Grzegorczyk, Piotr. "Jozef Conrad w Polsce. Material bibliograficzne." (Joseph Conrad in Poland. Bibliographic Materials), ROCZNIK LITERACKE (Warsaw, 1932).

[This is the only bibliography of Polish work on JC. It is not available in the U. S. Róża Jabłkowska reported in her JOSEPH CONRAD (1961) that Grzegorczyk was engaged in bringing his bibliography up to date. There have been no reports of progress since that time.] [In Polish.]

956 Heine, Herta. "Joseph Conrad als Dichter des Meeres" (Joseph Conrad as Writer of the Sea). Unpublished thesis, University of Vienna, 1932.
[In German.]

957 Kovarna, Fr. "Conradova *Nahoda*" (Conrad's *Chance*), ROZHLEDY PO LITERATUŘE A UMĚNI (Prague), I (2 Nov 1932), 119-20.

Chance is written with maximal economy of expression and a safe sense for composition. JC was not concerned with the outer reality, outer fates of his heroes. The plot of *Chance* serves only as a thread for stringing pearls. The network of outer reality, the construction of the story is a means for unveiling JC's vision of the world. This vision seems pessimistic at first. And yet it is not mere fatalism but a brave cognizance of human dimensions and limitations. Man is not omnipotent; all he can achieve has its limits, which are not all too wide but wide enough to provide space for human fortitude, increasing or decreasing together with his pain and suffering. This knowledge of human limitations is, paradoxical as it may seem, the beginning and an important source of self-consciousness.

As it was established that Polonisms form an important part of JC's poetic diction, it appears useful to trace Slavic blood also in other means of his expression. In contrast to the Russian novel, French readers especially comprehend the nature of characters in a geometrical way. A character filled with certain attributes passes through the plot without major changes, while in the Russian novel it turns, pauses, and changes. In JC's characters this ungeometrical development occurs quite frequently [illustrative quotations]. Comparative literature might find an interesting if not important stimulus in this aspect of JC's work. [In Czech.]

958 Leavis, Q. D. FICTION AND THE READING PUBLIC (Lond: Chatto and Windus, 1932), pp. 6, 46, 168, 213, 238, 265-68.

JC and Hardy were "the last great novelists known to the nation at large," the former because he told "a story that grips the imagination." JC was popular for superficial reasons; his best work—*The Secret Agent,* "Heart of Darkness"—"is not popular" and the more profound implications of his work were not recognized. Hardy's simpler structure and plainer irony made possible a more correct and immediate assessment of his work.

959 Lovett, Robert Morss, and Helen Sard Hughes. THE HISTORY OF THE NOVEL IN ENGLAND (Boston: Houghton Mifflin, 1932), pp. 401-11.

"Heart of Darkness" is one of JC's "most powerful and characteristic stories." JC commanded "one leading motive of romantic feeling—the lure of the remote." With Henry James, R. L. Stevenson, Galsworthy, and Bennett, JC evidences "the modern attitude toward the novel as a work of art"; he rejects the limitations of dogmatic realism and asserts that realism must be conditioned "by the temperamental handling of personal experience." For JC "the sea was the great school of human character and conduct"; less preoccupied with technical maritime detail than Marryat and Cooper, JC makes atmosphere "an essential element of structure," especially in "Youth" and "Heart of Darkness." He is a psychologist rather than an analyst, "preferring the dramatic and objective method of presentation." "Deterioration of character through environment" is a common theme, as in *Almayer's Folly, An Outcast of the Islands,* "Heart of Darkness," and *Nostromo*. The structure of his novels is perplexing because of JC's devious "search for inner truth," except in such simpler structures as "Youth" and *The Shadow-Line*. JC's complex use of Marlow is effective in *Lord Jim, Chance,* and *Victory,* but in *The Arrow of Gold,* JC attains inadequate perspective. In his precise use of images, JC anticipated the Imagist poets. He was a very conscious stylist. His philosophy is based on the scientific account of the universe. For him, as for Huxley, the world results from "two processes of evolution, one cosmic, the other ethical." For him, as for Hardy, "the supreme tragedy is that of consciousness," but art provides "an alleviation." [Relates JC's art to his personal experiences, his use of atmosphere and his philosophy to Hardy's, his techniques to James's.]

960 Morley, Christopher. "Escaped into Print," Ex LIBRIS CARISSIMIS (Philadelphia: University of Pennsylvania P, 1932), pp. 49-62; excerpted in CATHOLIC WORLD, CXXXV (July 1932), 472-73. JC was detached from Anglo-Saxon ideas as a result of his Polish background and his poetic imagination. "The Secret Sharer" is one of his most profound psychological studies, and parallels R. L. Stevenson's DR. JEKYLL AND MR. HYDE. He didn't always write beautifully, but he always thought beautifully. [Anecdotal.]

961 Newbolt, Sir Henry [John]. "Conrad and Trafalgar," MY WORLD AS IN MY TIME: MEMOIRS OF SIR HENRY NEWBOLT, 1862-1932. Two Volumes (Lond: Faber and Faber, 1932), I, 300-312. JC's character is reflected in his features, as seen from different perspectives. Newbolt with the assistance of William Rothenstein and Edmund Gosse was able to obtain a grant for JC. JC had a "profound imaginative knowledge of human nature," and from the "long and shadowy solitude" of his life he had learned to mistrust people. JC's reply to the gift of Newbolt's THE YEAR OF TRAFALGAR records the origin of the study of Nelson which JC eventually included in *The Mirror of the Sea*.

962 Prezelj, J[eske]. "Dva angleska romana" (Two English Novels), LJUBLJANSKI ZVON (Ljubljana), LII: 5 (1932), 313-17.
[Compares JC's procedure in *The Shadow-Line* and R. L. Stevenson's in KIDNAPPED; gives a sensitive account of JC's method of rendering the essence of life through brief surface descriptions rather than through intellectual analyses.] [In Serbo-Croatian.]

963 Raphael, Alice. "Joseph Conrad's Faust," GOETHE THE CHALLENGER (NY: Jonathan Cape and Robert Ballou, 1932), pp. 39-83.
JC's *Victory* is the FAUST of "our generation": Heyst comes from "the soul of the dying nineteenth century" and is "the incarnation of its sophistications." He is, even on a diminished scale, JC's expression of the ancient problem of good and evil. Heyst's only vice is the negativistic philosophy of his father; without evil, he is also without strength of goodness, and he therefore refuses to accept his "alter ego" when it appears on his island as mysteriously as the traveling scholar appeared to Faust. Mr. Jones is as truly Heyst's other half, which he has rejected, as Mephistopheles is Faust's "other self." Although Heyst has determined against action, he is drawn to participate in life by the very qualities he least suspects in himself. Mr. Jones is a nineteenth-century Mephistopheles, "world-weary," "neurotic," and incapable of action. If Marguerite represents the pure love and the self-surrender of the girl, then Lena, or "Alma," symbolizes the "soul of Woman" and achieves a "triumphant death." The slight story of *Victory* is a criticism of an attitude toward life that was prominent at the close of the nineteenth century and a portrayal of an age that is scarcely past—"an overfastidious, oversensitized era which bore the seeds of catastrophe ever present in its philosophies." Into a world in which nothing is particularly right or wrong, the powers of evil may crash violently, leaving only annihilation. Even if neither Goethe nor JC stated the Faustian problem from the point of view of "Woman," it may be that Woman must lead the way out of "the present cosmic deadlock." "Equipped with knowledge of the forces of good and evil and with a mind 'tempered with forbearance,' it may yet be the willed choice of Woman, as it was the blind fate of Lena . . . to capture the very sting of death in the service of Love."

964 Rothenstein, William. "Genius at the Turn of the Century," ATLANTIC MONTHLY, CXLIX (Feb 1932), 233-43.
JC was an artist, a writer who "wore himself out in his struggle for *le mot juste.*" There was always an element of strain in him, an "excitability" which may have been either individual or Polish. He was by nature an aristocrat. Greatly harassed by expenses and by old debts, and suffering much from gout, he "strained after an unattainable standard of perfection, and the effort to reach it often exhausted him."

965 Rothenstein, William. MEN AND MEMORIES. Two Volumes. II: 1900-1922 (Lond: Faber; NY: Coward-McCann, 1932) 2 Vols. in 1 (NY: Tudor P, 1934), II, 38-44, 60-62, 66, 67, 86, 157-60, 278-79, 350, 370.

[Scattered comments]: "Joseph Conrad had met few painters and was curious about the painter's outlook on life." JC desired "to impress the passion of life on his pages." He "had an aggressive side, which his friends overlooked, because of his obvious genius. Conrad was nervous and sensitive, and could be very irritable." [Prints letters from JC to Rothenstein: 13 Oct 1903; 3 Sept 1904; 18 April 1904; 17 Dec 1909; 20 May 1910; 2 Aug 1913; plus several undated notes. JC and Rothenstein became such fast friends basically as a result of their apparent unity of purpose. A vague tone of pity and respect runs through the account. An intimate, though not very extensive, character portrait of JC.]

966 Sire, P. "Les Livres: 'Au bout du rouleau,' par Joseph Conrad (N.R.F.)" (Books: *The End of the Tether,* by Joseph Conrad [N.R.F.]), CAHIERS DU SUD, XIX (July 1932), 476-79.

JC's hero never avoids life no matter how tragic its experiences may be. In fact, the meaning of life can be found only in pursuing its experiences despite the risks. It is above all in the life of the sea that a man can attain his intuitive dream, his nobility in the face of overwhelming odds. "The End of the Tether" dramatizes the conflict between Captain Whalley and the sea, which no longer plays the game fairly. This unequal struggle gives the book its tragic beauty. [Impressionistic.] [In French.]

967 Wellek, René. "Joseph Conrad," ROZHLEDY PO LITERATUŘE A UMĚNI (Prague), I (22 June 1932), 80-82.

JC is predestined to influence the whole sphere of European culture. His deep humaneness is not bound by mere technique or by contemporary social or political problems. [Biographical sketch.]

As a child he had a French governess and he was fond of French, which was his current language. During his long voyages to Australia and the East Indies, JC acquired a good knowledge of English. He became an Englishman by his own choice. It may well be that for a long time he spoke better French than English. His accent and certain stylistic peculiarities in English bear witness of his foreign origin. But neither French nor Polish ever tempted him to artistic expression. He certainly spoke the truth when he said that he would not have written a single line had he not written in English. Hence, the widespread contention that he wavered between French and English is incorrect. It has been claimed widely that JC is a novelist of the sea, another Jack London. Indeed, he displays a marvellous ability of describing the sea, tropical nature, life on ships, and in harbors. But this localization is only an outer peel, a pretext for his artistic intentions. A ship gives him the advantage of isolating human relations, making them stand out in their pure form. The widely held opinion that JC's psychology shows influences of the great Russian writers is incorrect. He disliked Dostoevski and Tolstoi; the only Russian author he liked was Turgenev. JC is a master of ingenious technique which sometimes is almost in antagonism with his plot which, told briefly and simply, would be just an adventure or even a thriller. But in the end JC's technique is only a means to achieve his aim, which is purely artistic and hence also ethical. [Contents given of *Victory, The Secret Agent, The Rover, Nostromo, Chance;* other works mentioned briefly.] [In Czech.]

1933

968 [Bork-o, Božidar]. "Joseph Conrad in Poljaki" (Joseph Conrad and the Poles), JUTRO (Ljubljana), XIV: 45 (1933), 5-6.
[The biographical comments are based on Jean-Aubry's lecture in the Polish academy of science and literature in Paris, as reported in NOUVELLES LITTÉRAIRES, 18 Feb 1933, and used to introduce Zupancic's translation of *The Shadow-Line*.] [In Slovene.]

969 Cadot, Raoul. "Les traits moraux de la mer dans l'oeuvre de Joseph Conrad" (The Moral Traits of the Sea in Joseph Conrad's Work), REVUE DE L'ENSEIGNEMENT DES LANGUES VIVANTES, L (1933), 399-407.
The sea is inarticulate. JC conveys his love and terror of it through poetic personification. Its storms were "warning whispers" from afar, to become wild and terrifying in the attack. JC, like Baudelaire, contemplated his soul "in the infinite roll of the wave." *The Mirror of the Sea* reveals a mythology of oceans. Two sovereigns rule: the West and East Winds, worthy of an Olympus—the North and South Winds are not dominant. The Trade Winds, blowing toward the equator from either northeast or southeast, are the friends of mankind. Should they blow into a more northerly latitude (where the West Wind is liege) they become treacherous. The West Wind is a terror. JC conveys the ultimate that speech can give in his delineation of these two forces.

The sea—at the mercy of the winds—seems to JC old, never young, like earth in spring. It seems also immortal, created even before light. As for the "moral" traits of the sea, JC finds that for youth it is strong, good, of bewitching breath; full of rewards as vast as itself. But it is also cruelly indifferent, diabolic, one of the forces of Evil. Perhaps, its enormity precludes ordinary virtues. At times it even seems "good," opposing its freshness and purity to the vices of the land. It challenges the seamen to discover their own reality. One cannot be a slacker on the sea. It is a tool of salvation. JC adopts a religious tone. The sea confers upon men the means of whatever redemption they seek—through compliance with its exigencies. The sea is thus a great educator. "Great power, fierce at first but fundamentally divine, therefore a friend," said Michelet. JC shares this view. [Excellent article.] [In French.]

970 Cunliffe, J. W. "Conrad and Galsworthy," NEW YORK TIMES, 6 Feb 1933, p. 14.

JC did not show Galsworthy the manuscript of *Almayer's Folly*. He did show it to H. W. Jacques, another passenger on the *Torrens,* the ship on which JC was the first officer. [Letter in reply to "Galsworthy Dies After Long Illness," ibid., 1 Feb 1933, p. 17.]

971 Cunliffe, J. W. "Joseph Conrad," ENGLISH LITERATURE IN THE TWENTIETH CENTURY (NY: Macmillan, 1933; 1934; 1935; 1939), pp. 125-36.

Conventional, superficial review of JC's life with emphasis on circumstances that bear specifically on his writings. Edward Garnett, reader for Fisher Unwin, encouraged JC to write a second story, *An Outcast of the Islands* (1896). His own experiences were the basis for this story about Malaya and a man who is not loyal to his European tradition and who deals with the natives unfairly. His voyages to Borneo in 1887-88 also served as the basis for *Almayer's Folly,* which recounts the moral disintegration of Almayer. *The Nigger of the Narcissus* evidences JC's romantic tendencies; *Lord Jim* evidences a complex narrative technique in which JC not only shows his characters as they are formed in his imagination but also as they appear to an observer. In *Nostromo,* JC sets out the theme of greed for material things which is a most powerful source of evil. Though his work had been highly praised, the public had not been responding to his novels (e.g., *The Secret Agent, Under Western Eyes*), but *Chance,* despite its sophisticated method, appealed to the public. However, in *The Rescue* JC is at his best. He weaves the tale of Tom Lingard, torn between devotion to friends and passion for an unfaithful woman. The conclusion, which he left unwritten for twenty years, is evidence of his greatest artistry.

972 Cushwa, Frank W. AN INTRODUCTION TO CONRAD (NY: Odyssey P, 1933).

[A mingling of JC's letters and memoirs with fragments of stories and novels makes up an "autobiographical" section of the book occupying three-fifths of the volume. The central premise ("Marlow is really Conrad") prevents an accurate and clear understanding of JC's intention as an artist in fiction. It necessarily lacks evidence based on more recently revealed information about JC's early life in Poland and France and does not distinguish between reminiscences and fiction. [The book is useless for any serious student of JC and confusing to the beginning reader. Reviewed: Raney Stanford, "Conrad: Mixture Warmed Over," ENGLISH LITERATURE IN TRANSITION, VII: 4 (1964), 246.]

  973 Edgar, Pelham. "Joseph Conrad," THE ART OF THE NOVEL (NY: Macmillan, 1933), pp. 184-95.

JC's repudiation of philosophy and science in art in favor of imagination (preface to *The Nigger of the Narcissus*) and his notion of a "purely spectacular universe" (*A Personal Record*), define JC's "impersonal" attitude, setting him apart from many English readers and writers. JC also avoids the indifference of a certain kind of realism. His interlinking of the senses with imagination, together with his conviction of human solidarity, is "almost Wordsworthian." "Actions, incident, scene, setting, words, thoughts, impulse are all coordinated to create a total impression." JC is above race or class; his characters are drawn from everywhere impartially. The early JC is lyrical, passionate ("Youth," "Typhoon," *Nigger*), the later JC is more impersonal (*Nostromo*). Marlow as a device is successful in the first part of *Lord Jim,* not so successful in the last part. *Nostromo* "combines naturalism and romantic-realism of the Russians" and achieves "greater reality than does *Lord Jim*." JC's curious method of "going backwards and forward over the events" interrupts the narrative but lets us realize the characters fully. His involved method "has a sound psychological basis."

  974 Ford, Ford Madox. IT WAS THE NIGHTINGALE (Phila and Lond: Lippincott, 1933), pp. 31, 35, 36, 45, 75, 89, 129, 150, 208, 286, 308-11.

[Scattered reminiscences of JC's bringing Galsworthy to meet Ford, Ford's wanting to clarify the disagreement between JC and James on art, JC's learning English from EAST LYNNE, an incident involving Hall Caine and its connection with "The End of the Tether," JC's futilely trying to make money by writing plays, and, in some detail, JC's relationship with John Quinn.]

  975 Hamilton, Cosmo. "Joseph Conrad: Blown Sand and Foam," PEOPLE WORTH TALKING ABOUT (NY: McBride, 1933), pp. 41-49.
JC is a "man of magnificent courage." [Conventional biographical sketch.]

  976 Holder, Alfred. Beiträge zur Ästhetik des Romans der Ausgehenden Viktorianischen und nach Viktorianischen Periode (Contributions to the Aesthetic of the Novel of the Late Victorian and Post-Victorian Periods) (Wurtemberg: G. Hauser Metzingen,

1933), pp. 33-45. Published thesis, Tübingen University, 1933. [In German.]

977 Hourcade, Pierre. "Les hommes de Conrad" (Conrad's Men), CAHIERS DU SUD, X (Sept 1933), 481-88.

The conception of JC as a writer of adventure stories must yield to that of JC as a psychological author. Adventure serves to reveal character, and it serves to make men act according to their real selves. JC's hero does not adapt to life because his ideals always conflict with society's conventions, and the hero must remain faithful to his ideals. The hero always fails to realize his dream either because of the world's cruelty or because of temptations like love or happiness. As for JC's technique, he is objective and dramatic; he does not moralize nor tell us about his characters, but rather allows us to know them by their actions, words, and thoughts. Yet JC never fails to suggest a theme, to imply an ideal man or an ideal philosophy. Through his sense of humor he both creates a distance between himself and his characters' illusions and distresses and also manages to make the reader sympathize with his characters. By means of entertaining the reader, JC persuades him to infer the book's meaning. [Well argued though not well demonstrated; one of the first French criticisms to recognize the importance of psychology in JC.] [In French.]

978 Jesse, F. Tennyson. "Joseph Conrad," THE POST VICTORIANS, with Introduction by W. R. Inge (Lond: Nicholson & Watson, 1933), pp. 117-28.

Four things make JC's art different from Hardy's and George Moore's: (1) JC's backgrounds were not his own particular ones, but were rather world-wide; (2) JC, unlike Hardy and Moore, accepts intrusive fate as a factor in life (*Victory* depends upon the acceptance of accident); (3) JC stands apart from his contemporaries, especially the masters of style, because he knew the whole of life; and (4) he accepted physical danger as a part of life and not a romantic part. JC's tales may seem to be tales of adventure, but the adventure really takes place in the soul. Although he reveals a delicate critical approach to the art of Cunninghame Graham, Henry James, and Turgenev, JC felt that he could not criticize. He made things difficult for himself, using oblique narration, but he used it masterfully.

979 L., G. A. "Conrad, Joseph: *Mit den Augen des Westens.* Übertragen von E. W. Freissler, Berlin 1933" (Conrad, Joseph: *Under Western Eyes*, trans by E. W. Freissler, Berlin, 1933), GRAL (Munich), XXVIII (Dec 1933), 183-84.

Razumov represents the conflict between Russian irrationalism and Western reason and comprehension. Dostoevski would not have understood the happy ending. [In German.]

980 Lamont, William Hayes Fogg. "A Study of Isolation in the Life of Joseph Conrad." Unpublished thesis, University of Pennsylvania, 1933.

981 M., N. "Joseph Conrad," PRIJATELJ (Zagreb), VII: 6 (1933), 182.

[Conventional information.] [In Serbo-Croatian.]

982 Mackenzie, Compton. "Joseph Conrad," LITERATURE IN MY TIME (Lond: Rich and Cowan, 1933; NY: Museey [?], 1934), pp. 12, 142, 168-74, 175, 186, 190.

JC used the multiple narrator device to avoid having to write English dialogue. He had an amazing vocabulary, but was not a great stylist. Read aloud, his prose sounds "costive and stilted." His "tales of the sea can only be read by landsmen," which suggests "a doubt of the permanence of his reputation." *Lord Jim* is "a great short story ruined by protracted spasms of wearisome psychology." JC has received critical acclaim because the English "delight in the art that does not conceal itself."

983 Morley, Christopher. "The Folder," SATURDAY REVIEW OF LITERATURE, X (19 Aug 1933), 55.

Breakfasting at Bessborough Gardens, London, where he was lodging, JC on impulse ordered his table cleared and "in a seizure that always remained a mystery to himself sat down to begin *Almayer's Folly*." That incident was in September 1889; he finished the novel in 1894. In 1894 JC, in a letter to Fisher Unwin, inquired after his MS of *Folly,* noting "however worthless for the purpose of publication, it is very dear to me." He did not possess another copy of it, written or typed.

984 Parker, W. M. "With Joseph Conrad on the High Seas," BLUE PETER, XIII (May 1933), 221-23.

JC talked to the bookseller on the *Tuscania* (April 1923) about his days at sea and his books. [General comment about JC's personal features and modesty; no critical value.]

985 R[ihtersic], B[oris]. "Josef Conrad" (Joseph Conrad), ZENA IN DOM (Ljubljana), IV: 8 (1933), 291.

[Compares and contrasts JC with Dostoevski.] [In Serbo-Croatian.]

986 Süskind, W. E. *"Mit den Augen des Westens.* Roman. Von Joseph Conrad. Deutsch von Ernst W. Freissler. Berlin 1933, S. Fischer" (*Under Western Eyes*. Novel. By Joseph Conrad. German by Ernst W. Freissler. Berlin 1933, S. Fischer), LITERATUR, XXXVI (Dec 1933), 172-73.

One wonders during what time-span *Under Western Eyes* was produced, for, apart from *The Secret Agent,* it is the only major work in which the sea plays no role. Yet the same reminds one of the Marseilles of *The Arrow of Gold*. It strikes one as a book of background in scene, characters, and problems. It is somewhat deadened and not one of JC's strongest works. Razumov is the most significant figure and belongs among the guilt-ridden heroes such as Lord Jim. The un-Conradian technique at the beginning is not successfully meshed with the complex technique into which the reader is later plunged. [In German.]

1934

987 Carroll, Welsey Barnett. "The Fiction of Joseph Conrad." Unpublished thesis, Cornell University, 1934. [Abstract, Cornell University, Ithaca, NY, 1934.]

988 Cunliffe, John William. "Late Victorian Novelists," LEADERS OF THE VICTORIAN REVOLUTION (NY: Appleton-Century, 1934), pp. 267-301, espec 290-95.

JC's main quality was "the power to make the reader see," supplemented by his broad outlook. "It seems likely that [JC's] permanent fame will rest . . . upon simpler examples [than *Lord Jim* and *Chance*] of romance, fortified by psychological and philosophical thought . . . , in which the reader's interest is maintained by a straightforward story."

989 Curle, Richard. "Joseph Conrad: Ten Years After," VIRGINIA QUARTERLY REVIEW, X (July 1934), 420-35; rptd in FORTNIGHTLY REVIEW, N.S. CXXXVI (Aug 1934), 189-99.

Pessimistic at heart, JC was both simple and highly complex. Many of his works have an autobiographical basis, combining the author's memory and his strong sentiment. His "marked sense of humor" was not always "of the English variety." Although he had an affection for sailing ships, he probably had little affection for the sea; his main concern was with people. His record of "honourable efficiency" at sea he applied to his work as a novelist: he composed very slowly and rewrote carefully. The least egotistic of authors, he did not speak of his work unless the subject was introduced naturally; then he spoke freely, but with restraint and good taste. When angry, he was unapproachable, but basically he was just and magnanimous. Tenacity of purpose was one of his most marked characteristics: he triumphed over poverty and ill-health. [Curle helps to originate the conventional view of JC's political conservatism, which was to remain undisputed until 1967.]

990 Franzen, Erich. "Über Joseph Conrad" (On Joseph Conrad), NEUE RUNDSCHAU (Frankfurt), XLV (Jan 1934), 122-28.

JC never ceased being a Polish patriot. The indifference of the sea symbolized for him, among other things, the barbarian tyranny of Russia. He himself compared Dostoevski's books with the sea and attacked the Russian author's irrationality and mysticism, especially in *Under Western Eyes*. He was deeply aware of the futility of human effort, but depicted man's struggle against nature and his consciousness of defeat. In some ways he was a self-conscious Don Quixote. [Brief introduction mentioning *Eyes, Nostromo,* and *The Nigger of the Narcissus.*] [In German.]

991 Lann, E[ugeniusz]. "Klassik nashevo veka" (A Classic of Our Century), LITERATURANAIA GAZETA, 14 Nov 1934, p. 2.
[In Russian.]

992 Leavis, Q. D. "Fleet Street and Pierian Roses," SCRUTINY, II (March 1934), 387-92.

If Fleet Street's journalistic values are correct values, then JC's are not. Ford Madox Ford, *Nostromo* and "Heart of Darkness" are alien to a world of "saucy, catchy articles" or to "a sonnet for a leader page on a topical subject [written] at a moment's notice."

993 Leslie, Shane. THE PASSING CHAPTER (Lond: Cassell; NY: Scribner's, 1934), p. 141.

JC is a "Slav Captain Marryat. . . . The spice of the East makes up for a queer grammar. He has been called 'the wreck of Henry James floating in the slops of Stevenson.' "

994 "A Sale of Conrad Letters," SATURDAY REVIEW OF LITERATURE, X (3 Feb 1934), 453.

The 105 letters, all but two unpublished, to Madame Poradowska of the REVUE DES DEUX MONDES were sold. According to Sotheby's catalogue, the letters "throw much new light on [JC's] life before he settled as a writer in London."

995 Strawson, H. "Joseph Conrad—Master Mariner and Master Novelist," QUARTERLY REVIEW (Lond), CLIX (July 1934), 315-24.

Having overcome first the sea and then the English language, JC became the greatest novelist of the present century. "Exactitude was his aim and fidelity his creed." [Brief biography, listing some of his readings.] JC's early style was "rich and luxuriant," but "subservient to the characterization, which is always definite and fully conceived." With *Nostromo,* he emerged from a "ten years' novitiate" and joined the company of Meredith and Hardy. The atmosphere of his world is "irony, that flames into contempt, and softens into tender pity. Its morality is faithfulness: faithfulness to duty in the simpler souls, to instinctive feeling in the more complex characters." His aim was to trace action to its source in human character. He is primarily a novelist not of the sea, but of the soul, "usually of the soul isolated by some chance, some frailty, or some fault."

996 Swinnerton, Frank. "Joseph Conrad," THE GEORGIAN SCENE (NY: Farrar & Rinehart, 1934), pp. 146-55; rptd (Lond: J. M. Dent, Everyman's Library, 1938), pp. 109-16.

JC's "two passions were the sea and the human species." [Swinnerton reviews JC's life at sea to the publication of *Almayer's Folly.*] JC's greatest talent was for the long short story centering on a "problem of character or conduct": "An Outpost of Progress," *The Nigger of the Narcissus,* "Youth," "Heart of Darkness," *Lord Jim,* "Typhoon," "Falk." After 1903, "He never . . . wrote anything as fine"; he tried new styles and resorted to the "treacherous craft of collaboration." Swinnerton thought *Nostromo* JC's greatest novel when it first appeared but does not now; it is the first of JC's books "to be built or manufactured." *Nostromo* "is very elaborate; it is as rich as can be in comprehensions and in diverse characters; but its movement is extremely slow, the detail of its intrigue is not always intelligible; and it does not quite escape dullness." For ten years "his fiction was the least interesting part of his writing"; *The Mirror of the Sea* and the early work kept his reputation alive. Bringing "complicated ingenuity to bear upon Terrorism was unfortunate." Then *Chance* created a "furor"; JC returned "to the yarn," his "happiest medium of expression." *Chance* "has charm, fluency, suspense, a few vividly drawn persons. . . ." His return to the Eastern scenes in his next book caused a "further fond blurring of the critical faculty." He may now rouse less enthusiasm than twenty years ago "because the novelty of his manner has gone and because we have not yet had time to rediscover it." *Jim* "loses its authentic quality in the middle and drops to a quality not wholly beyond the range of a lesser writer." Its quality "lies in the curious intricacy and subtlety of the method by which we are made aware of all the circumstances of failure and discovery. . . ." It is told as the Ancient Mariner tells his tale. "What an elastic method!" JC takes Henry James's "method farther." JC's "true gift was for the reproduction of scene and atmosphere, not for analysis." [The chapter has some suggestive insights but is mainly derivative.]

997 Telauer, Frank. "Svět Josepha Conrada" (The World of Joseph Conrad), ROZHLEDY PO LITERATUŘE A UMĚNI (Prague), III (15 Oct 1934), 91-93.

Joseph Conrad

JC's position in English literature has been very specific, overemphasized and underestimated at the same time. He still remains a distinguished foreigner. His feeling of life is different from what is customary in England, and his morals are different—he has none, he does not preach, does not wish to improve things, he is not an optimist. Being fatalistic and pessimistic, he remains a thorough and curious observer, never tired of solving the many conflicting complexities of life.

Although in *Chance* his persons are characterized in a somewhat artificial and simplified way, the play of forces which engulf them is not artificial at all. The contents are marvellously matched with JC's artistic style. The essence and height of his art are manifested in his mastery of complex composition, planned with specific refinement and yet presented in an extremely natural way. In *The Rover* the fundamental tone of JC's fatalism can be heard. This novel, as well as all of his works, could be subtitled *Chance,* as it is chance that directs the fates of his heroes. His chance is not romantic or melodramatic, but an immensely complex kind of causality, sometimes impossible to understand. In *Rover* as well as in JC's other works it is not the novelty of material or the originality of events but the depth and intensity of images that bear witness to the author's great literary mastery. Adventurous and exotic as it is, *Lord Jim* is a fatalistic narrative about the tragic fate of a man who has to pay his whole life for having been born an ill-fated person. The story itself is not a direct epic description, but a complex rearrangement and unveiling, a relativization of the plot through several subjective transcriptions.

JC's early works did not indicate that this Anglicized Pole would become one of the greatest epicists of the sea. *The Secret Agent,* one of his early detective stories, has nothing to do with the sea. It is a rather heterogeneous work, but it bears the heavy mark of JC's fatalism. In contrast to his later novels, *Agent* is written in a technique of quasi-simple objective epics revealing influences and inspiration by realism. But JC's psychology is deeper and sharper than one can find in novels with similar themes and thus the story has a certain force of tragic ominosity.

Out of the whole series of Conrad's works published by Melantrich (Prague), the most typical is *Victory,* a resigned story of passion and crime. Here the author uses sensationally contradicting and effective elements and welds them into an unusual parable of love, sympathy, and instincts with a tragic finale in form of a heroic apotheosis. JC's art of explicit psychic characteristics is manifested here in antagonistic types of nobleness and crime, intellect and passion, cultivated humaneness and ruthless brutality. *Victory* is JC's representative novel because it presents the purest types of his own philosophy of life. This fatalism is a bitter but elating knowledge of the inevitability of a manly fight which always has a tragic end. The only possible victory is that of love, which fights although it cannot escape death. In this finale of JC's epic, one can hear a tone that is not vernacular in England. It is only in this respect that this great artist of the English novel remains a poetic foreigner in England. [In Czech.]

998 Tretiak, Andrzej. "A Note on Joseph Conrad," REVUE ANGLO-AMÉRICAINE, XII (Oct 1934), 46-47.

JC's *A Set of Six* resembles P. de Musset's LA TABLE DE NUIT, a collection of short stories first published in 1832 and reissued in 1884. The support for this assertion is that all except one of Musset's stories are told indirectly through secondary narrators; each collection contains six stories; and the subtitles are identical in form in each collection, that is, "Histoire sentimentale" is like "A Romantic Tale." [The resemblances seem very superficial to justify such a claim.]

999 Whiting, George W. "Conrad's Revision of *Lord Jim*," ENGLISH JOURNAL, XXIII (Dec 1934), 824-32.

A collation of the texts of the BLACKWOOD serial and the novel reveals that all changes are slight (tenses, articles, prepositions) and show JC's "exacting attention to details" and "his extraordinary sense of words."

1000 Wohlfarth, Paul. "Joseph Conrad und die Rahmenerzählung" (Joseph Conrad and the Frame Tale), LITERATUR, XXXVI (June 1934), 507-10.

A work making use of the frame tale must provide an intrinsic basis for the use of the device, for evaluating a work of art is not merely a matter of judging it on its formal aspects. JC, recognized only in recent years in Germany, is the youngest and most persistent practitioner of the form. The construction appears most familiarly in "Freya of the Seven Isles" [story summary], but the simple form is massively elaborated. In *Lord Jim*, the tragedy develops even more complexly [story summary]. Still more intricate is the construction of *Chance* [story summary]. JC's type of the frame story is barely distinguishable from the stories of Conrad Ferdinand Meyer, except that in JC we are concerned with novels with the great style, further implemented by the devices of ramification and "Chinese-boxing" evident in *Jim* and *Chance*. [Reviews, with many quotations from letters, JC's struggle for form.] Because JC apparently could not detach the episodes from chaotic feelings, he presented them in the form of interior narratives. It is, in fact, by means of the frame tale that, in the course of his struggle with form, JC became master over the chaos. In JC's work, three groups of narrations are discernible: (1) In works like *Nostromo* and *The Secret Agent*, the sea is essentially meaningless. In these works, JC's separation or distance from his "life-center" removed the tension in his struggle to give artistic form to experience; these works are further removed from his "tragic zone" than others. The effect of distance on form is evident in the fact that the fate of his characters is plainly narrated, without intrusive letters or reports. (2) In the second group, the only theme is the sea. Here, as in *The Shadow-Line,* JC had to choose first-person narration because he was so united with the sea. (3) In the third group, the sea emphatically provides the background but is not the only theme. At the bases of these works are very powerful personal experiences and memories which gripped JC even after many years and which provided the last cause for the battle with form. This is the case with *The Arrow of Gold,* a frame tale with three intrusive documents. In this novel, the hero-narrator is JC drawing on his own experiences. So, also, *Under Western Eyes* is a frame tale with intrusions and draws on JC's personal experiences. JC could endure some of these powerful memories and turn them into works of art only by objectifying them with the technique of the frame tale. By allowing intrusive letters or reports or objectified narrators to introduce disturbing personal experience, JC was able to release experience from chaos.

Not all JC's works fit neatly into the three groups. In content, *The Rescue* belongs in Group 3, but it is not a frame tale, perhaps because here JC mastered the material without needing the frame device. [Wohlfarth has dealt with the specific types of the frame tale more fully in his "Rahmenerzählung als Kunstform" (Frame Tale as Art Form), LITERARISCHEN ECHO, XXI, p. 1410. The above abstracted piece on JC is suggestive but rather superficially developed.] [In German.]

> **1001** Wollnick, Ludwig. "Joseph Conrad. En kritisk studie" (Joseph Conrad. A Critical Study), EDDA (Oslo), XXXIV (1934), 183-218, 307-26.

JC's melancholy fatalism is believed to be inherent in his Slavic soul, but is probably due partly to childhood experiences in Siberia and partly to his twenty years at sea. His interest in a strong personal morality was based not on Christian or social laws, but on the individual's ideal of himself. Moral or physical isolation was important in his novels.

Influenced by Flaubert, JC shared his taste for orientalism, barbarism and fatalism. After an early period of overwriting, Conrad developed in *Typhoon* a soberer style and was at the height of his craft around 1900. But his plots were too digressive and, like Dostoevski, he is sometimes considered melodramatic, yet he delays his tragedies so long that they seem not banal, but logical. His trademark is the remarkable union of action and atmosphere. Although his characters came from all races, he was most fond of inarticulate seamen, determined and loyal. JC was interested in the psychoanalytic make-up of man, yet his characters have a universal humanity about them which differs from scientific psychology, where the man merely illustrates the theory. His great novels are not pictures of men, but the depiction of their moods. In *Victory, The Rescue,* and the middle part of *Nostromo,* there is little action. Dialogue is restrained; men seem to live in a trance in spiritual isolation. JC was weak in his portrayal of women. At its best his world was a world of men alone.

JC had a weakness for generalizations. He used his characters' thoughts and actions as a springboard for aphoristic observations on human nature. He was a student of the French moral philosophers from Montaigne to Anatole France, but he was not a slave to any one idea. JC is believed to have been influenced by Dostoevski, whom he detested, and there are similarities. Both wrote of declassed men and of similar types of inner conflict.

In his best psychological study, *Lord Jim,* there is the conflict between the predisposition toward passivity and a personal and professional ideal of active life. JC usually isolates his characters in situations where they have only their deepest personal resources to rely on. Loyalty and dedication are the highest ideals and his men are strong individualists. Actions are judged by the superego; moral suffering is settled by the ego. JC's psychological specialty is the negative reaction. The form of expression is not so much anger as self-contempt. The worst crime to a JC character is the loss of value in his own eyes. [In Norwegian.]

1935

1002 "Biography," A. L. A. BOOKLIST, XXXII (Nov 1935), 62-63.

Jessie Conrad's JOSEPH CONRAD AND HIS CIRCLE (1935) is a matter-of-fact account of domestic details. "It is a one-sided picture, not intentionally harsh, but limited in its view."

> **1003** Burkhardt, Johanna. "Das Erlebnis der Wirklichkeit und Seine Künstlerische Gestaltung in Joseph Conrads Werk" (The Experience of Reality and its Artistic Representation in Joseph Conrad's Work). Published thesis, University of Marburg, 1935 (Marburg: Pvtly ptd, 1935).

[This study offers a succinct summary both of JC's views on art and his favorite techniques and concentrates on his experience and analysis of reality. It describes the dangers JC's characters are confronted with and distinguishes between borderline situations such as those created by history (time), death, suffering, the problem of identity. JC is said to discover the meaning of life in the heroic affirmation of one's incomprehensible destiny. Though a somewhat Heideggerian treatment of works as reservoirs of ideas, the best German study of JC in the pre-war period.] [In German.]

1004 Cecil, David. EARLY VICTORIAN NOVELISTS (Indianapolis: Bobbs-Merrill, 1935); rptd as VICTORIAN NOVELISTS: ESSAYS IN REVALUATION (Chicago: University of Chicago P, 1958), pp. 15, 174, 195, 297.

Emily Brontë's WUTHERING HEIGHTS and *Lord Jim* both begin the story in the middle. George Eliot's works are the first examples in English of the novel in its mature form. In JC, Bennett, James, and Wells the novel "structurally comes of age."

1005 Chamberlain, J. "The World in Books," CURRENT HISTORY, XLIII (Nov 1935), xii.

Jessie Conrad's JOSEPH CONRAD AND HIS CIRCLE (1935) shows that JC was a difficult husband.

1006 "Conrad and his Circle," TIMES LITERARY SUPPLEMENT (Lond), 18 July 1935, p. 460.

Jessie Conrad's trivial JOSEPH CONRAD AND HIS CIRCLE (1935) unwittingly presents an unattractive portrait of JC. He appears as the obstinate, irresponsible egotist, "the desperately unreasonable man." But luckily other works on JC remain; more comes from a few paragraphs of Ford's memoirs than from most entire books.

1007 Conrad, Jessie. JOSEPH CONRAD AND HIS CIRCLE (Lond: Jarrolds; NY: Dutton, 1935); 2nd ed (Port Washington, NY: Kennikat P, 1964).

Jessie George met JC in 1893, married him in 1896, and exercised her "motherly instincts" until his death in 1924. Very soon after their marriage, "he became to me as much a son as a husband. And this state of accord lasted all our married life." [Mrs. Conrad tells little about JC other than ordinary outward events. She regarded him as a great writer, but was apparently unable to explain why. Even though he was strange and terrifying to her, she considered it one of her wifely duties to protect him—or over-protect him—against the vexations of everyday life. She makes herself the heroine of every anecdote; she naively reveals more of herself than of her husband. But she is obviously unconscious of any dishonesty. No doubt she suffered bitterly in her marriage, but she has no idea that JC also suffered. With no literary pretensions at all, she succeeds, though, in leaving a valuable factual record of JC's married life and of his "circle" of friends and acquaintances.]

1008 Doran, George Henry. CHRONICLES OF BARABBAS: 1884-1934 (NY: Harcourt, Brace, 1935), pp. 83, 95.

JC owes his fame and popularity to Alfred A. Knopf more than to any other one person. J. B. Pinker, literary agent, financed JC.

1009 Ferguson, J. Delaney. "The Plot of Conrad's 'The Duel,'" MODERN LANGUAGE NOTES, L (June 1935), 385-90.

JC's "The Duel," so far from being largely invented, as the author claims in his preface to *A Set of Six,* is in fact very close in plot, motivation, name of character, and detail to an account in HARPER'S MAGAZINE (obviously a close paraphrase of a French paper) for September 1858. The parallels are so very close that one can conclude only that JC must have read the original in full, then thirty years later read a brief reference to the story, and then must have drawn on his subconscious for details and assumed these details to be his own invention. At the time of writing, JC was under heavy strain, ill, and worried over money, and he may well have forgotten the source of the details.

1010 Ford, Ford Madox. "Conrad and the Sea," AMERICAN MERCURY, XXXV (June 1935), 169-76; rptd in LONDON MERCURY, XXXII (July 1935), 223-31; PORTRAITS FROM LIFE (Boston: Houghton Mifflin, 1937), pp. 57-69; MIGHTIER THAN THE SWORD (Lond: Allen and Unwin, 1938), pp. 83-97; and as "Conrad at Work," JOSEPH CONRAD'S HEART OF DARKNESS, ed by L. F. Dean (Englewood Cliffs, NJ: Prentice-Hall, Spectrum Books, 1960), pp. 128-37.

Although JC protested that he was not a writer of sea stories, the sea plays an important role in the early works. But as JC came "to see life more collectively and less as a matter of Conway-trained and steadfast individuals heroically fighting august northwesters," women, non-seafarers, political intrigues, and careers of republics become more and more prominent. Although JC is enduring "a commercial and fashionable eclipse," he will eventually be considered one of the greats, and his reputation will be built on his land books, *The Nigger of the Narcissus* remaining, however, a masterpiece.

1011 Ford, Ford Madox. "Decennial (It is ten years on the day of writing since the last book of Joseph Conrad's writing was posthumously published in New York)," LONDON MERCURY, XXXII (July 1935), 223-31.

Although JC is in "eclipse" due to current interest in the masses, the "land" books will assure that he remains "great." JC said that "he was not a writer about the sea" and showed that he was conscious of the masses in *Nostromo*. He was "relatively fair" to the political left, though at heart he was "an aristo-royalist apologist" who saw the "salvation of mankind" in the "restoration of the Polish kingdom with its irresponsible . . . nobility." In *The Secret Agent,* JC "really made efforts to get behind the revolutionary mind," and in *Under Western Eyes,* he was "almost kind" to the revolutionaries "who in the end must give Poland her freedom." [Ford identifies himself as the "omniscient friend" to whom JC refers (in his "Preface" to *Agent*) as his source of information about revolutionaires. Ford identifies the Home Secretary in that novel as Sir William Vernon Harcourt.] *Almayer's Folly* exposes Dutch exploitation. JC could see "opposing sides of human characters" even though they were antipathetic to him: so "Heart of Darkness" is "the most impassioned unveiling of the hidden springs of human hypocrisy, greed, and blood-lust—and, of course, heroism." Along with "Youth" and *The Nigger of the Narcissus,* "Heart of Darkness" is JC's "best" and "cleanest work." He showed his "workmanliness" in his devoting three days with Ford to the four sentences ending "Heart of Darkness." JC was living then in Stamford-le-Hope in Essex and had drawn the Director of Companies, the lawyer, and the accountant from counterparts living in the town. JC's workmanship, however, did not save him from "contriving" "any old end" for a book. When it was time, JC said sadly that he "broke the back" of his books. Before all, *The Mirror of the Sea* "affects" Ford most, since JC wrote with "authenticity" and "pathos" about that "malignant and stupid element." *Nigger* is "the only mass-romance of the sea." JC made the sea appear "human-divine," and left women "altogether" out of his sea books (as that "great novelist" Captain Marryat did not). Yet in *Agent,* Mrs. Verloc is the "eternal Mother-Woman"; and in general, JC's "curiosity" made the "human dearer to me than the wealth of the world." [Useful information on JC revising and concerning himself with style.]

1012 Garnett, David. "Current Literature: Books in General," NEW STATESMAN AND NATION, X (20 July 1935), 96.

Jessie Conrad, in JOSEPH CONRAD AND HIS CIRCLE (1935), tells how she, an invalid herself, "bore with" JC's recurrent attacks of gout. Perhaps for this reason her memories are "filled with misfortunes occasioned by the bad behaviour of others," and "life is represented as a series of serious illnesses and minor disasters." Although Mrs. Conrad had a deep respect for her husband's books and for his success, she seemed to have "a tone of contempt" when she referred to that "strange being," her husband, the writer. She had very little in common with JC. Possibly she reveals JC's narrow range as an artist; he seemed obsessed by the subject of betrayal.

1013 Greene, Graham. "The Domestic Background," Spectator (Lond), CLV (26 July 1935), 164.

In Jessie Conrad's Joseph Conrad and His Circle (1935), Mrs. Conrad remembers nothing tender, nothing considerate, out of a long marriage. "She is the heroine of every anecdote." Such a book makes "rather repellent reading." The author is "curiously naive"; she must seem to her readers "either heartless or hypocritical." But there is "obviously no conscious dishonesty in the one-sided record; the writer does not realize how damaging it is." No doubt she suffered bitterly in her marriage, but she had no idea that JC also suffered.

1014 Hartman, Captain Howard. "I Meet Joseph Conrad," The Seas Were Mine (NY: Dodd, Mead, 1935; Lond: Granger & Harrop, 1936), pp. ix, 1, 78-84, 94, 109-21, 122-24, 226-28, 240, 245, 274-76, 282, 330.

A year or two before JC began writing his first novel, the Captain met JC, when both were seeking the same berth on the same ship. In Singapore, Hartman came to know Tom Lingard, whom JC was to "immortalize" in *The Rescue,* and his nephew, Jim Lingard, known as "Tuan Jim," who, Hartman thought, was the original Lord Jim. JC loved a good yarn or tale, discussed the "subject of Yogi" without knowing anything about it, and read widely. Hartman also observed the boisterous episode of Jim Lingard's taking as wife Neola, a dancing girl from Bali. Much later, Hartman learned about JC's command of the *Ortego* [sic] and made a pencil sketch of the vessel shortly after JC had left her. He renewed his friendship with JC when the latter lived in Kent. [According to Norman Sherry, Conrad's Eastern World (1966), Jim Lingard provided the title of *Lord Jim* and probably certain characteristics of Lord Jim, but not all of them, as Hartman supposed.]

1015 "How's Your Wild Man?" Saturday Review of Literature, XII (12 Oct 1935), 12.

Jessie Conrad's Joseph Conrad and His Circle (1935) gives a candid view of courtship, marriage, and domestic life with JC, this "high-strung temperamental man."

1016 Hutchison, Percy. "A Portrait of Conrad As a Husband / His Wife's Book About Him Is a Domestic Rather than a Literary View of Him," New York Times Book Review, 29 Sept 1935, p. 4.

Jessie Conrad's Joseph Conrad and His Circle (1935) seems to be an all but priceless portrait of a loving and lovable, highly irascible genius, one of the world's greatest, who never guessed his own greatness. And in it Mrs. Conrad shows that she also is possessed of no small talent."

1017 "Joseph Conrad and His Circle," Open Shelf (Cleveland), Oct 1935, p. 19.

Jessie Conrad's Joseph Conrad and His Circle (1935) is an intimate picture of an eccentric husband and is in poor taste.

1018 "Kniga o Dzhozefe Konrade" (A Book about Joseph Conrad), Literaturnaia Gazeta, 15 Oct 1935, p. 4.

[A review of Jessie Conrad's Joseph Conrad and His Circle (1935).] [In Russian.]

1019 Lukić, Berislav. "Dzozef Konrad. Pomorac i pisac 'Tajfuna' " (Joseph Conrad, Seaman and Author of "Typhoon"), Jadranska Straza (Split), XIII: 7 (1935), 284-87.

[Review of "Typhoon."] [In Serbo-Croatian.]

1020 Manly, John Matthews, and Edith Rickert. Contemporary British Literature (NY: Harcourt, Brace, 1921); rvd by Manly and Rickert (1928); 3rd rvd and enlgd ed by Fred B. Millett (1935), pp. 16, 19, 21, 30-32, 49, 177-83.

[Brief biographical sketch; "Suggestion for Reading," with allusions to the influence of James and Flaubert, "Bibliography" to date; Millett's third revised and enlarged edition (1935) adds some slight evaluative comments in the preliminary surveys on the novel and vastly expands the bibliographical listings.]

1021 Maurois, André. "Les écrivains anglais contemporains" (Contemporary English Writers), Revue Hebdomadaire, XLIV (April 1935), 52-70 ("I. Joseph Conrad"); 154-66 ("II. Le Marin Moraliste" [II. The Sailor-Moralist]).

JC, admired in France and England by writers like Valéry and Gide, Virginia Woolf and Desmond MacCarthy, as well as by Claudel and a vast number of general readers, not only contributed to his adoptive language, but also expressed better than the British certain Anglo-Saxon ideals. He has the stoic philosophy of the British man of action; he expressed better than Kipling the soul of the Englishman. He proposes an active pessimism in the mode of Chekhov, though perhaps somewhat more romantically.

JC's stories fall into two classes: (1) those in which he has a witness or an actor and (2) those which were recounted to him. The latter give to certain of his works their peculiar and complex form. ["Typhoon," "Youth," *Lord Jim,* and *The Nigger of the Narcissus* are summarized and explicated.] JC did not wish to be known as a writer of sea stories; he had no love for the sea but a love for the struggle against the sea. The core of JC's observation is always man or a group of men. His only tribute to the sea as such is *The Mirror of the Sea,* a boring work. The sea is never viewed as man's friend, but as his enemy. Yet he could love ships, as his ship captains demonstrate. "Youth" depicts the death of a ship, but JC's real interest is man's love for the ship, man's grandeur in the face of the waves. The struggle between the man of action and blind opposing forces is not always hopeless, but uneven, as illustrated by *Almayer's Folly,* "Heart of Darkness," and *Nostromo.* JC believed "mass-man" to be evil. *Jim* suggests that an invisible hand seems to impel our unconscious drives into unsuspected channels.

JC is a pessimist as regards man's actions; an optimist when viewing the qualities developed by man in the performance of these actions, e.g., devotion, loyalty, honor. JC was convinced that the ideal of this temporal world is *fidelity*. Thus, when Jim realizes his honor is gone and that he has lost face with his peers, he can live only to redeem himself. JC subordinates intelligence to moral rectitude in the conduct of living. [Evidence from JC cited.] JC finds the virtues he prizes in sailors rather than in "land crews." The latter have too much security and not enough responsibility. Their boat will never capsize nor will their families be washed away. The seaman, of necessity, learns to do his job in strict obedience to his master (MacWhirr, JC's favorite hero, gives his straightforward advice, "Stand to the wind!"). Like Kipling's, JC's philosophy is aristocratic. It is not that he loves the sailor less, but that he detests the men who rail about their rights with no thought of their obligations. Donkin, in *Nigger,* is the epitome of all he detests in man. JC is also pessimistic about women. The sailor, far from home, tends to idealize women in romantic terms; hence, confronted by "real" women, he is disillusioned and frightened. In his "art," JC is conscientious and aloof from anything but "truth." JC's extremely "complicated" method may be only the reflexes of an honest man, committed to poetic expression of ideals; he is without probable imitators in the near future. [Much extrapolation of Maurois's theories on wars of the future, democracy, etc., often forced into JC's mouth. This double article is a transcript of a lecture delivered to The Lecture Society, probably 13 March 1935 (headnote wrongly says May).] [In French.]

1022 Maurois, André. MAGICIENS ET LOGICIENS (Paris: Grasset, 1935), pp. 179-213. Trans by Hamish Miles as PROPHETS AND POETS (NY: Harper's, 1935), pp. 177-211.

JC's work dramatizes the sailor's love for his ship; the unequal struggle between man and his universe; the evils of the mob acting without a sense of duty or honor; the necessity for endurance and aristocratic devotion and responsibility. JC observes and records carefully and honestly. *Lord Jim* is a good example of his multiple narrator technique. [Not very original.] [In French.]

Joseph Conrad

1023 Mencken, H. L. "Contributions to Martyrology," NATION (NY), CXLI (16 Oct 1935), 444.

"Poor Conrad gets the worst of it" in Jessie Conrad's JOSEPH CONRAD AND HIS CIRCLE (1935): his widow describes him as "a peculiarly flagrant and unappetizing bounder." She seems to think of herself, eleven years after her husband's death, as "a Christian martyr." Although JC, with his Slavic background, was not "a model of placidity" and many of his "friends and acquaintances" were merely nuisances, Mrs. Conrad has chosen her manner of writing her book and she must accept "the consequences that go with it." Nowhere does she display "an adequate understanding of her husband's greatness or of the cruel difficulties that he grappled with."

1024 Mirande, R. "Joseph Conrad, curieux homme" (Joseph Conrad, Unusual Man), ANNALES POLITIQUES ET LITTÉRAIRES, CVI (10 Oct 1935), 368-70.

Jessie Conrad, in JOSEPH CONRAD AND HIS CIRCLE (1935), gives an incomplete though interesting portrait of her husband, who appears as a polite and ceremonious man but who sometimes loses his temper like a spoiled child. Mrs. Conrad's attention to anecdotal detail, though not revealing an appreciation for ideas, goes far in conveying the characters of JC and his friends H. G. Wells, Henry James, and John Galsworthy. [In French.]

1025 Owen, Lyman B. "Adventuring with Joseph Conrad," ENGLISH JOURNAL (High School Edition), XXIV (Sept 1935), 567-71.

[A high school teacher explains how he led a class of senior boys to "discover" JC. His methods are those of a so-called "progressive" school of the 1930s. Of negligible value for the scholar.]

1026 Pritchett, V. S. "Let This Be a Warning to Wives," CHRISTIAN SCIENCE MONITOR WEEKLY MAGAZINE SECTION, 18 Sept 1935, p. 11.

Jessie Conrad's JOSEPH CONRAD AND HIS CIRCLE (1935) belongs to a "greatly increasing group of embarrassing books." Mrs. Conrad "has written a trivial and self-important book about a great subject." The portion dealing with their courtship and marriage is the most readable. The marriage must have been an adventure for JC, who was "an excitable, irritable foreigner," now living "among a cool, suspicious people."

1027 Stillman, Clara Gruening. "From a Wife's Point of View," NEW YORK HERALD TRIBUNE BOOKS, 22 Sept 1935, Sect vii, p. 8.

Jessie Conrad's JOSEPH CONRAD AND HIS CIRCLE (1935) reveals the oft-observed badness of Mrs. Conrad's style and the genteel triteness she used to describe JC and her children.

1028 Wohlfarth, Paul. "Die verbrecherische Persönlichkeit bei Dostojewski und Joseph Conrad" (The Criminal in Dostoevski and Joseph Conrad), Monatsschrift für Kriminalpsychologie, XXVI (1935), 349-57.

JC's treatment of crime is simpler and more uniform than Dostoevski's. Typical of all his criminals is the fact that they are criminals through and through. Examples are the titular character in *The Secret Agent,* the Russian anarchists in *Under Western Eyes,* Heemskirk in "Freya of the Seven Isles," Barral in *Chance,* Mr. Jones and his two accomplices in *Victory.* In *Lord Jim,* we find two characters of this type: the captain of the pilgrim ship and pirate Brown. With the possible exception of *Romance* (written in collaboration with Ford Madox Ford), JC's works are not marred by the simplistic "black-white" contrast to which his creation of uniformly evil characters might easily have led. The significance of his narratives lies not in the contrast between evil and noble characters, but in the fact that his heroes and his villains have one trait in common: boundless isolation and loneliness. This trait is symbolized most effectively by the captain, essentially alone on and with his ship in the immensity of the ocean. JC's obsession with solitude has been superficially explained as due to his life at sea; actually, loneliness was one of the deepest traits of his soul, and it makes more sense to say that he chose his marine profession on account of it. It is not surprising that the greatest of all *isolati,* Napoleon, is the real hero of his unfinished *Suspense.* JC's solitary heroes are often more than just alone. They are outcasts: e.g., Jim, Heyst in *Victory,* Almayer, and, above all, Leggatt in "The Secret Sharer." It is also this outcast state that endows the criminals among his characters with their bitterness, cruelty, and tragic greatness. Dostoevski's criminals are also outcasts, but whereas JC's evil characters are noncomplex, unaffected by moral qualms or religious impulses, and beyond reconciliation with the cruel, evil world they fight, Dostoevski's are more mysterious, less outright criminals; they are men divided against themselves, whose moral darkness and despair are traceable to their basic sin of isolation from the larger world around them, the world of light and faith—a world to which a return through expiation is not impossible. For JC's criminals, who would rather burn outright than smolder expiatively, there is no return of this kind. Their creator, not surprisingly, was little appreciative of Dostoevski's achievement. [In German.]

1029 Wood, Miriam H. "A Source of Conrad's *Suspense,*" Modern Language Notes, L (June 1935), 390-94.

Parallels between JC's unfinished *Suspense* and the Memoirs of the Countess de Boigne (NY, 1908, edited by Charles Nicoullaud) are so striking as to make the latter an obvious source of *Suspense*. The Emperor's questioning of and advice concerning children given to Adèle is the same in MEMOIRS. JC's Dr. Martel is Dr. Marshall; JC's Sir Charles Latham, who marries a Miss Aston, is Sir John Legard (of MEMOIRS), who also marries a Miss Aston, and for the same reason. Some of the descriptive details, particularly of character, are the same in both. Some events are parallel, including the meeting of Adèle and the Count, which has its parallel in Nicoulland's book.

1030 Z[abel], M[orton] D[auwen]. "Books in Brief," NEW REPUBLIC, LXXXV (18 Dec 1935), 180.

In JOSEPH CONRAD AND HIS CIRCLE (1935), Jessie Conrad "succeeds in disclosing the passion and resolution at the center of Conrad's character" in spite of herself, and the book is therefore valuable in spite of itself.

1936

1031 American Art Association, Anderson Galleries. THE LIBRARY OF THE LATE ELBRIDGE L. ADAMS . . . [including] THE EXTRAORDINARY ADAMS COLLECTION OF BOOKS INSCRIBED BY JOSEPH CONRAD. TO BE SOLD 29 JANUARY AT 8:15 (NY: American Art Association, Anderson Galleries, 1936), pp. 50-65.

[Lists fifty items consisting primarily of inscribed first editions and JC letters.]

1032 Bates, H. E. "Thomas Hardy and Joseph Conrad" [sic; reversed in chapter head], THE ENGLISH NOVELISTS, ed by Derek Verschoyle (Lond: Chatto and Windus, 1936), pp. 231-44.

A comparison of Hardy's unreal, dated, Victorian world and JC's unreal but undated, timeless one reveals the latter's advantage. Hardy was a novelist of rural life, JC of the sea. Hardy was provincial, a Victorian moralist; JC was cosmopolitan, universal: "the difference between chalk and cheese . . . between sardonic Englishman and sardonic Pole." JC was adventurous, Hardy a "home-bird"; JC was aristocratic, Hardy, middle-class; JC was a "race-horse," Hardy a "cart-horse." Both, however, were remorseless, both "in heroic mould." Both were masters of atmosphere. Hardy's great "defect" was that he failed to see that morality is "really nothing but a fashion," a "fraud." His plots, emphasizing causality, overburden him; JC placed no emphasis on plot, but on character and atmosphere. JC's "gorgeous verbosity" is sublime; Hardy is long-winded (except in his poetry). JC's first book, *Almayer's Folly,* published in the same year as Hardy's last novel, JUDE THE OBSCURE (1895), marks the end of one era and the beginning of another—the new more allied to painting and less to architecture, brighter, more graceful, of "higher temperature." The best of

Hardy's works are pictorial scenes, like the pig-sticking in JUDE; but the whole emphasis in JC is on the pictorial. There are too many dead words in Hardy prior to his good scene; JC's books themselves are "living scenes."

1033 Bowen, Elizabeth. "Conrad," SPECTATOR (Lond), CLVI (24 April 1936), 758; rptd in COLLECTED IMPRESSIONS (NY: Knopf, 1950), pp. 151-53.

JC is "in abeyance," "suspect for the very magnificence that had us under his spell: we resist verbal magic now," preferring Hemingway's muffled heroics. JC's "dramatic ironic sense of fate" is not in accord with "our fatalism." JC was concerned with the individual; we are not. Edward Crankshaw's JOSEPH CONRAD: SOME ASPECTS OF THE ART OF THE NOVEL (1936) tends to reinstate JC, not merely as a "brilliant phenomenon" but as a real practitioner of the art of the novel, selecting, rejecting, working hard—combining original genius with effort.

1034 Colenutt, Richard. "Joseph Conrad—Twelve Years After," CORNHILL MAGAZINE, CLIV (Aug 1936), 129-40.

Polarity of opinion about JC is due to the uneven quality of his writings caused by ill-health and uncongenial subjects. JC's thoughts and his narratives "begin at a point" and "spread outward in circles." He "ranges back and forth in time and space without any obvious plan, although in the end everything fits together to complete a picture." Sheer massiveness is a barrier for some. The key to JC's greatness is the ability to enter the "minds and hearts of others" and "penetrate the motives of their thoughts and actions."

1035 Crankshaw, Edward. JOSEPH CONRAD: SOME ASPECTS OF THE ART OF THE NOVEL (Lond: Lane, 1936); rptd (NY: Russell & Russell, 1963).

JC's novels are whole artistic unities. JC is highly personal and impressionistic, ironic, subtly fatalistic, and melancholic, with moods of exaltation. He took the world as he found it, preached fidelity, and wanted to touch the souls of his readers.

Two major forces motivate JC's male characters: responsibility and irresponsibility. His good men (Willems, Gould) have in common a sense of responsibility outside themselves; while the evil characters (Ossipon, Schomberg, Mr. Jones) are completely irresponsible, attached only to the "self of the moment." Oppressed by a sense of evil that cannot really be corrected, JC is fascinated by the psychological problems of evil. The moralist in JC is strong, but not at the expense of art; he is more interested in dramatizing motives than in developing an *idée fixe*.

Joseph Conrad

To JC, the artist must "render life accurately according to his vision." His task is "to make you feel—it is, before all, to make you see." His message ". . . is himself," yet he tries to avoid authorial intrusion by using external observation with comments by others in the story to present character. JC was not a psychologist in the sense that James was; he presents characters from the outside in a variety of viewpoints. For this reason, Marlow becomes important along with the elderly teacher of languages, Martin Decoud, and the ironic method of *The Secret Agent*. Marlow's role is to moralize (since JC as novelist could not). A "technical device" and a character in his own right, Marlow shares JC's fundamental outlook on life.

Many of JC's novels come from his life experiences, and often "the actual experience becomes the story itself," as in *Nostromo*. JC's comment in the preface of the volume containing "Heart of Darkness"—"The sustained invention of a really telling lie demands a talent which I do not possess"—points to his lack of invention. Yet he was an excellent analyzer, the "first of two stages of invention," and he is capable of understanding a character subjectively, which is an imaginative process. Since JC could not invent, "his whole magnificent perceptiveness depended absolutely on the senses." JC was "an analytical psychologist of a most distinguished order, but not a creative psychologist at all." Thus Marlow and others could comment on "subjective . . . states of mind which he [JC] could never have rendered objectively because he could not invent." Garnett's comment that JC created Marlow to save trouble is wrong.

The structure of *Chance* is fugal and contrapuntal, both a work of "spiritual significance, and a technical *tour de force." Under Western Eyes* is inferior to *Chance* because the narrator as narrator and the narrator as character are at odds. In *The Arrow of Gold* and *The Shadow-Line*, a diary becomes a technical device to enable the writer to justify the characters' remembering so much detail. On occasion JC's creation of the sense of illusion suffers a lapse (e.g., in *The Nigger of the Narcissus,* it is impossible for the narrator to write knowingly of what happens in the brain of the cook). In *Nostromo,* the third person exterior treatment is effective; and in *Agent,* the author's ironic intent gives multiple and shifting perspective to the narrative.

JC uses time-shift as a device to break down "the forced unnaturalness of the strictly chronological narrative." The broken time and action sequence method in *Chance* and the use of montage in *Nostromo* are effective. JC often rearranges sequences for dramatic effect and rhythm to accelerate or to retard the narrative. (E.g., in *Eyes,* the loose ends are brought together, in the scene between Razumov and Miss Haldin; *Nostromo* closes with an acceleration followed by restrospection, as do "Darkness," *Lord Jim, Agent,* and *The Rover.*)

Atmosphere is the "final key" to the whole of JC's technique to the extent that he often sacrifices "objective precision" to "subjective vision," even changing viewpoint in the course of a single sentence to get new associations. [Crankshaw's perceptive remarks about JC are too often obscured by banalities about art and the role of the artist that are sometimes didactic and condescending. The study, heavily indebted to Percy Lubbock's THE CRAFT OF FICTION (1921), championed JC when his reputation was low, and in effect was prophetic of the critical concern given JC in the 1950s and 1960s.]

1036 Egart, M. "Freia semi ostrovov" (Freya of the Seven Isles), NOVII MIR, No. 3 (1936), 268.
[A review.] [In Russian.]

1037 Garrett, George. "Conrad's *The Nigger of the Narcissus*," ADELPHI, 3rd ser, XII (June 1936), 150-55.
JC does not "portray life whole" because his view of the crew is that of "a conservative-minded ship's officer," Donkin being the "scapegoat" in this novel. [Garrett tries to make a case for Donkin as more to be pitied than censured, JC's bias getting in the way of a just view of Donkin. Donkin is shown to be worked hard by Baker; he is the only one to protest against bad conditions. Having Donkin rob Jimmy's sea chest is poor fictional logic, determined by JC's personal biases.]

1038 "Kipling et Conrad" (Kipling and Conrad), MERCURE DE FRANCE, CCLXVI (15 Feb 1936), 218-19.
JC was ignored initially by all but a faithful few in contrast to Kipling's early lionization. [A brief account of JC's and Kipling's relative fortunes and rises to fame, their mutual regard and meetings, with the publication of a letter from Kipling to JC thanking him for a copy of *The Mirror of the Sea* and praising it highly.] [In French.]

1039 Marquet, Jean. "Sur le traces de Conrad" (In the Footsteps of Conrad), MERCURE DE FRANCE, CCLXXII (1 Dec 1936), 444-47.
There are correspondences between the details of G. Jean-Aubry's biography and JC's fiction, especially in the white woman in Saigon, in the *Otago* and in the dead captain, but by absence of any death record of any English captain in or around Saigon on the dates when JC travelled through there, the incident was probably an invention by the author. [The article is good

for biographic dating for this period, a study of JC's activities in Indo-China by a man who was there at that time. A comparison between JC's biography and the experiences recorded in "Falk," *The Rescue,* "The End of the Tether," and especially *The Shadow-Line.*] [In French.]

1040 Neri, Fernando. "La Persona Velata" (The Veiled Person), Saggi di Letteratura (Essays on Literature) (Napoli: Luigi Loffredo, 1936), pp. 9-17.

In the preface to Some Reminiscences, JC has said that in his work a novelist remains a veiled person whose presence the reader suspects rather than sees. JC's narrative method is one of indirection. His technique shuns the development of a psychological story in the semblance of a thesis so as to better ensnare the story in his passionate resonances and images. Such indirection is employed in portraying the irreparable judgment that Jim bears for his moment of cowardice. It is evident in his casual encounter with the mariner with steel-gray eyes who took part in the rescue of the ship. This episode figures a new type of revelation where the feeling is found in the winding of plot, scattered wherever possible in the aspect of a reflection or judgment.

Romance, written in collaboration with F. M. Ford, is similar in theme to R. L. Stevenson's Treasure Island: the theme of struggle across the seas and also of a human conscience inured to its fate. The theme of struggle is found most notably in those JC narratives dealing with storms ("Typhoon," *The Nigger of the Narcissus*), but it is also present in other adventures which deal with human tempests. JC has a disgust for colonial groups in which a temptation to treachery germinates; however, when he deals with the deserter, the degenerate of the West, he creates an atmosphere of evil few writers have imaged. When we have a story in which the hero confronts danger and evil, we have the simple JC, novelist of sea and adventure, who can evoke agitated scenes and is a master of them. The tragedy begins when the hero is troubled by an intimate, hostile thought, a memory, a discordant image, the sense of having lost time, of having erred once without pardon. *Nostromo* contains a vast picture of a confused world in which rank and intelligence do not prove to suppress the passions. Much of it is revealed through the character of the doctor, Monygham, who always penetrates the condition of others' spirits. We learn he scorns humanity because, as JC indirectly tells us, he did not fulfill his ideal in "a particular circumstance." It is not important for us to know the circumstance. The author alludes briefly to a confession under torture in a time long gone in another revolution. Monygham was returned to the light, after months in prison; and for the remnant of his life the disgrace of that hour of torture could not be absolved. In *The Rover,* the last book composed by JC (*Suspense* was interrupted by his death), there are personal reflections of his life, of the fiber of the ancient mariner. But now we do not look for the biographical elements, the real events of which he writes in the novels, rather for the trace of the spirit that animates and guides them. [In Italian.]

1041 Orwell, George [Eric Blair]. "Recent Novels," NEW ENGLISH WEEKLY, IX (23 July 1936), 294-95.

Since there is almost nothing memorable in *Almayer's Folly,* one wonders why it was chosen by Penguin Books. In 1936, JC was "out of fashion," ostensibly because of "his florid style and redundant adjectives" but perhaps actually because he was a gentleman, "a type hated by the modern intelligentsia." He will certainly come back into favor again.

1042 St. John, William E. "The Conception of the Novel as Presented by the Leading English and American Novelists Since 1800." Unpublished thesis, Southern California University, 1936.

1043 Schieszlová, Olga. "Národnostni bloudění Josefa Conrada" (The National Gropings of Joseph Conrad), ČASOPIS PRO MODERNÍ FILOLOGII (Prague), XXII (June 1936), 338-48.

JC has always vehemently opposed those who tried to find traces of Slavic background in his works. Was this due to his absolute nationalization in England or was it a betrayal of his native country? [Gives a detailed account of JC's childhood.] JC's desire to escape derived from his early reading in Polish and French about countries where one can breathe freely and fight openly, where one need not whisper. When he was sixteen he went to Marseilles, Russia was closed for him, he hated Germany, he was more than indifferent toward Austria, England was too far away, and France always attracted him, a current phenomenon with all educated Poles. At twenty-one, when he first came to England, he could not speak English at all. During his long voyages on British ships, he learned the language and he began to admire the character, qualities, and skills of English seamen. The most valuable documents of that period, JC's letters to his uncle, were destroyed in 1918 when the Communists burned his uncle's estate in the Ukraine.

For a long time his English readers did not care about JC's national background. Much later, when literary critics began to discover real or apparent Slavic elements in his work, he resented it. He argued that everything genuinely personal in his writings is incorrectly ascribed to his race, that Poles actually do not possess those features which the West generally denotes as typically Slavic, that he himself lacks these features and, moreover, hates them. He knew that to a Westerner the term Slav was equivalent to Russian. All his hopes were firmly rooted in England, but he remained faithful to his native country.

Several problems remain open, such as whether JC's exoticism in style, and in character, was a contribution of his race or of his personality. How much did French mean to him? Those who are familiar with the Polish and Russian intellectual milieu of those times will note that JC's lasting affection for French gives evidence that he was a Pole from a territory annexed by Russia, and not a Frenchman. It is the task of comparative stylistics to ascertain the exact contribution of Poland and France to the English work of JC. Although he could have become a writer in three languages and although three nations show jealousy because of him, it was JC's personal irony that he felt lonely during most of his life. [In Czech.]

1044 Sealey, Ethel. "Typhoon," SCHOOL (Toronto), XXIV (Jan 1936), 393-96.

The "haphazard spontaneity" demonstrates JC's control of human life as it is. [A plot summary followed by teaching plans for a high school class. Of no critical value.]

1045 Süskind, W. E. "*Spannung*. Roman. Von Joseph Conrad. Deutsch von E. McCalman. Berlin 1936, S. Fischer" (*Suspense*. By Joseph Conrad. German by E. McCalman. Berlin 1936, S. Fischer), LITERATUR, XXXVIII (June 1936), 436-37.

Much has been speculated about this novel, first published posthumously in 1925. One should not take the Napoleon connection too seriously. It is a fragment in the later intrigue-spinning manner of JC and parallels *The Arrow of Gold*. [In German.]

1046 Wise, Thomas J. THE ASHLEY LIBRARY: A CATALOGUE OF PRINTED BOOKS, MANUSCRIPTS AND AUTOGRAPH LETTERS COLLECTED BY THOMAS J. WISE. Eleven Volumes (Lond: Pvtly ptd, 1936), X, 84-86; XI, 55-56, 138.

[Lists and describes twelve items by and about JC.]

1047 Wohlfarth, Paul. "Der Gattenmord in *Der Geheimagent* von Joseph Conrad" (The Marital Murder in Joseph Conrad's *The Secret Agent*), MONATSSCHRIFT FÜR KRIMINALPSYCHOLOGIE, XXVI (Feb 1936), 523-31.

Winnie Verloc is exceptional among JC's criminals because she has character traits that are far from criminal: when we first meet her she is a good-natured, gentle, quiet housewife whose only passion is her love for her weak-minded brother Stephen. This last trait, however, leads her to the murder of her husband. Her obsessive love for Stephen also induced her to marry Verloc, whom she does not love but who is capable of providing security for her and Stephen. This "ruling passion" sometimes amounts to a virtual identification with her brother. One of Stephen's traits is his morbid excitability when confronted, even if only imaginatively, with the suffering of others. His death is a final illustration, so to speak, of this characteristic: he obeys Verloc's orders to avoid displeasing him, and only he (Stephen) gets killed in the explosion. In a sense Winnie has no real existence apart from being Stephen's sister: her potential for affection and love for other people, in whatever relation they stand to her, is undeveloped. She differs from her brother in that she is mentally healthy, but as far as morbid sensitivity to the suffering of others is concerned, she resembles him. However, she manages to control that sensitivity—except in connection with one person, her brother. This is the reason why her brother's violent death makes her lose control of herself. The little girl who threw the poker at her father to defend her brother, and the mature woman who murders her husband on account of her brother, are one and the same. The knife with which she murders Verloc is the one which Stephen grasped to "kill" the Russian officer about whose cruelty towards a recruit he had read. Brother and sister are united by their outrage at suffering inflicted upon others. [In German.]

>**1048** Wohlfarth, Paul. "War Joseph Conrad ein englischer Dichter?" (Was Joseph Conrad an English Writer?), GERMANO-SLAVICA, IV (1936), 143-51.

When he turned to writing, JC had no overt relationship with his homeland. His works are set in many countries, but only one takes place on Polish soil and deals with a Polish problem, "Prince Roman." JC's Polishness, however, is also evident in various motifs in other works. One is JC's persistently evident hatred for everything Russian, presented in a generally un-English way. (Though exceptions occur in some works by Hugh Walpole and Maurice Baring, Maugham and Kipling, with dry humor, present Russian characters in a more characteristically English manner.) In JC, this hatred for Russians is reflected in *Under Western Eyes, The Secret Agent,* and "The Informer." JC always remembered his youth and always remained a Pole.

Also a reflection of JC's Polishness is the motif of revolutions or uprisings (*Nostromo*, "Gaspar Ruiz," *An Outcast of the Islands, Lord Jim, The Rescue, The Arrow of Gold,* and "The Tremolino"). When a real war becomes the setting, it is not an orderly campaign that is depicted, but the French retreat in Russia in 1812, ending in a disorganized remnant of an army ("The Soul of the Warrior"). Reflecting the Polish experience, JC depicts or alludes to hopeless battles against overwhelming superpowers. Although World War I is dealt with only in "The Tale," no Englishman would have dealt with the pitiless events with such candor as JC did. It is doubtful that one can justifiably declare the sole cause of JC's content and style to be his Polishness; his years at sea are just as good an explanation.

Contrary to Thomas Mann's view in the introduction to *Der Geheimagent* [*The Secret Agent*], little of the characteristic English humor is evident in JC. It is such a lack of English literary characteristics that declares JC not to be an English writer. Unlike English heroes, JC's heroes live alone, isolated, outcasts from the world, for JC's world is a tragic one. Only *Chance* has something like a happy ending. Even some of the short stories ("The Black Mate" and "Falk") that seem like exceptions and appear to have some lighter touches are pierced by strong tragic motifs.

A fundamental contrast to the English character is evident in JC's representation of nature. The Englishman is concerned with particulars, with knowing specific entities of nature. JC is concerned with the whole forest, not single trees. [The conversation on JC in W. S. Maugham's ASHENDEN is cited as a statement of the preceding contrast.] In vivid contrast with such English writers as Galsworthy and Swift, JC seems insensitive to the plight of animals and generally uninterested in them. There is little of the English sense of "togetherness," as exemplified by the family, in JC (as in Galsworthy and Hugh Walpole's Herries books). Except for the Goulds in *Nostromo,* one futilely seeks a family that makes up a home; not even the Hermanns in "Falk," Anthony and Flora in *Chance,* the Fynes, and others do so. Other couples, like the Schombergs and the Verlocs in *Victory* and *Agent,* only arouse horror. Equally dreadful are the marriages in *Almayer's Folly, Outcast,* "Amy Foster," "The Return," and *Suspense.*

Despite all JC's un-Englishness, can one nevertheless claim that he belongs to English literature, as an enricher, as a contributor of new values—encompassed by the bond of JC's adopted language? The contrary evidence goes too deep, even reaching into the most significant aspect of artistic construction—the style. The English style is characterized by clear, economical diction, which may be related to English Puritanism—asceticism is the enemy of wordiness. JC, to the contrary, paints in broad strokes, he lengthily spins out the passionate dialog of his heroes, lets his heroes pour out elementary passions. JC is one of the few great epic writers of the new literature, the magic of whose language derives from foreign sources. [Raises interesting problems but evades attempts to deal with them in real depth.] [In German.]

1937

1049 Becker, May Lamberton. "Joseph Conrad," SCHOLASTIC, XXXI (9 Oct 1937), 22.
[Advice to "young folks" on why to read JC and which works are best to read first. Directed to high school students.]

1050 Britten, Lew. "Conrad," READING AND COLLECTING, II (Dec 1937), 15.
JC's leading theme seems to be the inscrutability of human affairs. [Britten finds his liking for JC inexplainable.]

1051 Clemens, Florence. "Conrad's Malaysian Fiction: A New Study in Sources with an Analysis of Factual Material Involved," ABSTRACTS OF DISSERTATIONS (Ohio State University), N.S. 24 (Spring 1937), 43-52. Unpublished thesis, Ohio State University, 1937.

1052 Garnett, Edward. "Conrad's Place in English Literature," CONRAD'S PREFACES TO HIS WORKS (Lond: Dent, 1937), pp. 3-34.
JC's works represent a bridge between Continental and English spirits. The Continental spirit emerges in JC's mentality, where his "Polish sardonic irony and fine susceptibility to every shade of feeling are mingled." His English spirit emerges in his concern for the English seamen, especially in *The Nigger of the Narcissus*. JC's genius "hangs" upon his power of seizing the essential characteristics and features of an environment and his power of portraying the characters that people "the humble drama he had either met in life or arrived at creating." [Garnett includes running commentary on the major works.]

1053 Greene, Graham. "Remembering Mr. Jones," SPECTATOR (Lond), CLIX (17 Sept 1937), 469-70; rptd in THE LOST CHILDHOOD AND OTHER ESSAYS (Lond: Eyre & Spottiswoode, 1951; NY: Viking P, 1952), pp. 98-99.
CONRAD'S PREFACES TO HIS WORKS, with an introductory essay by Edward Garnett (1937), shows that JC's prefaces, unlike James's, are not "an elaborate reconstruction of technical aims," but are "about life as much as about art." Thus, they appeal more to the general reader than to the practicing novelist.

1054 Müller, Erich. "Joseph Conrad und die Tragik des Westens" (Joseph Conrad and the Tragedy of the West), LITERATUR (Stuttgart), XL (Dec 1937), 161.
Hermann Stresau reveals JC's spiritual conquistadors. [The passage is ap-

parently quoted from a comment on Stresau's JOSEPH CONRAD: DER TRAGIKER DES WESTENS (Joseph Conrad: The Tragedian of the West) and originally appeared in a Berlin newspaper.] [In German.]

1055 Muller, Herbert J. "Joseph Conrad," MODERN FICTION: A STUDY OF VALUES (NY: Funk & Wagnalls, 1937), pp. 244-61.

If JC must be labeled, "impressionist" is the most suitable label. He tried to evoke an enveloping atmosphere. "Hence his concern with point of view and tone, his habit of telling his story at several removes, his avoidance of generalized narrative, his disregard of chronology and of other conventionalizations of perception." His career resembles Proust's and his works suggest Shakespearian tragedies. His world is based on "invincible pessimism" and is completely unintelligible from a rational viewpoint. His heroes are always combating the Dark Powers hopelessly, but did not have the profound compassion that distinguishes much modern tragedy. Although the heroes' struggles are futile, they are not meaningless. He was interested less in effects than causes, in actions than states of mind. His most characteristic theme is "the searing loneliness of all these unfortunates." "For the very reason that he does not scratch the peculiar itches of this generation, and is by it therefore somewhat overlooked, he is in time likely to take an assured place among the great. Meanwhile *Nostromo* is an example of the monumental work that can yet be produced by the modern pessimistic spirit."

1056 Routh, Harold Victor. "Chapter XXII," TOWARDS THE TWENTIETH CENTURY: ESSAYS IN THE SPIRITUAL HISTORY OF THE NINETEENTH (NY: Macmillan, 1937), pp. 331-45, espec pp. 336-39.

JC's experiences as mariner "embraced the epic of modern times"—the exploration and exploitation of savage lands. JC knew well the decivilizing power and danger of Eastern life and had a clear idea of the manhood necessary to subdue it: "responsibility, self-control, self-adaptation, and recognition of what is due to justice, humanity and one's personal dignity." He was at his best when studying "aberrations from the perfect type [of man]." He adopted a "satirically dispassionate attitude" toward his characters. "He experiments with the . . . ignoble strangeness of real life; . . . since he can create no deeper interest, this Olympian aloofness ends in the posing of psychological puzzles."

1057 Whiting, George W. "Conrad's Revision of 'The Lighthouse' in *Nostromo*," PMLA, LII (Dec 1937), 1183-90.

One of JC's main purposes in revision was by additions to clarify and vitalize his narrative. "As a rule, the style of the revision is vital and rich and more subtly modulated." For JC, the typescript of *Nostromo* "was rather a rough draft than a finished work." [Key references to Richard Curle's JOSEPH CONRAD: A STUDY (1914).]

1938

1058 Batho, Edith C., and Bonamy Dobrée. THE VICTORIANS AND AFTER (Lond: Cresset P, 1938); 2nd rvd ed (1950), pp. 76, 94-95, 148, 267, 308, 327.
JC, unlike earlier Victorian novelists, was among those late Victorians who built their novels around a theme. JC is "the only important figure within our period who can claim descent in the legitimate line from James, as a conscious artist." [Scattered conventional remarks; listing in various bibliographical categories.]

1059 Brown, Bob. "Collector's Luck," CORONET, III (Jan 1938), 95-98; excerpted as "Conrad by Chance," LITERARY DIGEST, CXXV (5 Feb 1938), 15.
The writer unwittingly bought the rare first issue, dated 1913, of the first edition of *Chance* for two cents in Argentina and sold it to a book dealer for eight dollars. The dealer then sold it for $2,200. The first edition was interrupted after fifty copies by a binder's strike, and the remainder was printed with a new title page dated 1914.

1060 Fryer, Benjamin N. and James Johnson. BRUCE ROGERS AND THE FIGUREHEAD OF THE *Joseph Conrad* (San Francisco: Windsor P, 1938).
The typographer who had set the type of Elbridge Adams's JOSEPH CONRAD: THE MAN (1925; see 1923) made a "monumental figurehead of JC for the sailing ship *Joseph Conrad,* which was bought in 1934 by Alan Villiers. In many ways, the two artists seem to be alike: each is an exemplar "of industry, of uprightness, a pursuer of an ideal."

1061 Gee, John Archer. "The Conrad Memorial Library of Mr. George T. Keating," YALE UNIVERSITY LIBRARY GAZETTE, XIII (July 1938), 16-28.
Keating's A CONRAD MEMORIAL LIBRARY (1929) and numerous supplementary purchases make "a collection alike distinguished for its richness and for its solidarity." It is scrupulously complete. This collection contains many valuable manuscripts and typescripts as well as some unpublished material, and affords many opportunities for further investigation. [Originally delivered as an address at the opening of the exhibition of the collection at the Sterling Memorial Library, 20 April 1938.]

1062 Gerlach, Richard. "Joseph Conrad, *Zwischen Ebbe und Flut*. Übertragen von E. McCalman" (Joseph Conrad, *Within the Tides*. Trans by E. McCalman), MAGDEBURGISCHE ZEITUNG, 21 Jan 1938; rptd BUCHBESPRECHUNG (Leipzig), II (April 1938), 104-5.

The same major character types appear in the four stories of this collection as in the major novels. [Four stories are summarized: "Der Pflanzer von Malata" (The Planter of Malata), "Der Teilhaber" (The Partner), "Das Gasthaus der beiden Hexen" (The Inn of the Two Witches), and "Wegen der Dollars" (Because of the Dollars).] [In German.]

1063 Gordan, John D. "The Rajah Brooke and Joseph Conrad," STUDIES IN PHILOLOGY, XXXV (Oct 1938), 613-34.

James Brooke, the first white Rajah of Sarawak, Borneo, after much effort, won the love and trust of his people. External evidence is lacking to show that JC was familiar with the character and the adventures of this Englishman, but internal evidence lends credence to the supposition that JC had such knowledge. Several clues appear in *Almayer's Folly, An Outcast of the Islands,* and *The Rescue;* and it is especially surprising to note how much of the characterization in *Rescue* may have been taken from Brooke's life and writings. The clearest evidence, however, is found in the latter part of *Lord Jim,* because much of the background and many specific incidents there suggest Brooke. This investigation gives a glimpse of JC's creative imagination at work. [For external evidence that JC knew of the Brooke family, see John D. Gordan, "The Ranee Brooke and Joseph Conrad," ibid., XXXVII (Jan 1940), 130-32.]

1064 Hoare, Dorothy M. "The Tragic in Hardy and Conrad," SOME STUDIES IN THE MODERN NOVEL (Lond: Chatto and Windus, 1938), pp. 113-32, espec 119-32; rptd (Litchfield, Conn: Prospect P, 1940); rptd (Philadelphia: Dufour, 1953).

JC deflects tragedy from its traditional course by a combination of romanticism and irony. JC, "with whom Hardy has much in common, is impelled . . . to show the tangle, the inexplicable element in life." For this purpose he invents Marlow, who can be compared to James's ideal spectator. "This method of gradual accretion in the mind of one person is useful not only to show the intricacy of problems of behavior but also to give a framework, to detach the problem from immediacy." This technique was especially useful in *Chance,* not so successful in *Lord Jim,* and entirely successful in "Heart of Darkness." JC is master of quiet and straightforward narrative as well, and of "a sort of atmospheric and romantic effect." His concern with the unanalyzable, when not under strict control, led him to pseudo-romanticism, often coexisting with authentic romanticism. His settings are romantic, but in his studies of persons he never strays far from reality. JC is "most romantic in stories whose setting is in the tropics, and most realistic in those where the background is the sea, although sometimes both modes combine in one book." His main characters are usually men, but he can draw "exquisite portraits of women," emotional but not sentimental beings. All the tales are in essence accounts of a single soul's adventures.

1065 McFee, William. "Conrad After Fourteen Years," YALE UNIVERSITY LIBRARY GAZETTE, XIII (July 1938), 3-15.

Outside a small and "extremely literate section of the community," JC was never considered an important writer in England, and in America his fame was "artificially stimulated" among parts of the public who read very few of his books. His books were put aside as incomprehensible. For a time the imaginary JC was "a reincarnation" of Morgan Robertson, Louis Tracy, Robert Louis Stevenson, Jack London, and the early Kipling. His work is unlike the usual conception of a sea story, a story requiring violent and melodramatic action; JC "could invent but he could not imitate." JC was an artist whose function was to give "enchantment" to his readers; he was an entertainer in the most exalted sense, an ironist, neither a romanticist nor a realist, but an impressionist who painted pictures of "something his imagination had conceived." He romanticized his characters. All JC's characters are not Polish in temperament, as Morf maintained in THE POLISH HERITAGE OF JOSEPH CONRAD (1930). Readers should return to the works themselves and to the "intellectual" ironist who cannot be popular as Dickens or Jack London was popular but who painted pictures as Rembrandt painted them, "with brilliant colors and profound shadows." [A good early article.]

1066 Mason, J[ohn] Edward. JOSEPH CONRAD. Makers of Literature, No. 3 (Exeter: A. Wheaton, 1938).

JC's "abiding passion" was a deep, genuine love of the sea. His greatest admiration was for "the way in which the apparently cruel majesty of the sea seemed to bring into strong relief only that which was finest and best in human nature." [This short book consists of a brief survey of JC's life and a few comments on some of his works. It grossly overemphasizes JC as a writer of sea stories and displays practically no critical perception.]

1067 Medanić, Lav. "O Josephu Conradu" (On Joseph Conrad), SAVREMENIK (Zagreb), XXVII: 2 (1938), 829-40.

JC is the modern cosmopolitan, the "fascinating and destructive artist." [Comments on the role of Fate in his works, resonances of contemporary revolutions in *The Rover*, Heyst as the typical Conradian hero.] [In Serbo-Croatian.]

1068 Murdoch, Walter. "The Balfour-Conrad Question," Collected Essays (Lond: Angus and Robertson, 1938), pp. 176-79, 570-75.

Lord Balfour wrote JC's novels. [The essay resulted from an invitation to take part in the Shakespeare-Bacon controversy.]

1069 Murdoch, Walter. "Three Tombstones," Collected Essays (Lond: Angus and Robertson, 1938), pp. 23, 155, 267-68, 318, 540.

[Describes Murdoch's attempt to find JC's grave site at the Roman Catholic cemetery, Canterbury.]

1070 Süskind, W. E. *"Geschichten vom Hörensagen.* Von Joseph Conrad. Deutsch von Richard Kraushaar und Hans Reisiger. Berlin 1938, S. Fischer" (*Tales of Hearsay.* By Joseph Conrad. German by Richard Kraushaar and Hans Reisiger. Berlin 1938, S. Fischer), Literatur, XL (Sept 1938), 754.

Except for the youthful "The Black Mate," the stories in this volume, especially the three most important ("The Warrior's Soul," "Prince Roman," "The Tale"), have a sketch-like quality. The stories are limited, static, and offer little in content, but they are highly interesting in form, for which they warrant close analysis [see Süskind, "Die Seele des Kriegers," Kölnische Zeitung, 23 July 1938, pp. 1-2]. [In German.]

1071 Süskind, W. E. "Die Seele des Kriegers: Anmerkungen zu Joseph Conrad" (The Warrior's Soul: Notes on Joseph Conrad), Kölnische Zeitung, 23 July 1938, pp. 1-2.

Unlike the familiar, often confusing and complex structures of JC's stories, the structure of "The Warrior's Soul" (*Tales of Hearsay*) is simple [detailed synopsis of plot]. Tomassow's unexpected "passive act" has a powerful effect and the narrative takes a wholly new direction into the character's retrospective experience, his first love and his first hero-worship. As the title suggests, JC turns the story inward. "Die Geschichte" ("The Tale") begins in the manner of a folk epic, without a frame tale, but close analysis shows a more complex structure in which form and content become identical, something more memorable than mere craftsmanship. "The Partner" is the most powerful tale in *Within the Tides*. Often JC's complex narrative technique in short stories and novels succeeds because of a simple explosive comment or action in the midst of the narrative maze. [Essentially a defense of JC's narrative technique with particularly high regard for the later work.] [In German.]

1072 Süskind, W. E. [*"Zwischen Ebbe und Flut* von Joseph Conrad. Deutsch von E. McCalman. Berlin 1937" (*Within the Tides.*

By Joseph Conrad. German by E. McCalman. Berlin 1937)], LITERATUR, XL (Jan 1938), 247.

The four stories, written between 1910 and 1913, all deal with criminal plots and their propitiation or frustration, yet they hardly seem to derive from the same period of JC's career. "The Planter of Malata" evolves out of a disorganized prelude and belatedly moves toward a powerful, although too melodramatic, conclusion; thus, it has not translated well. "Because of the Dollars" is suspenseful but crude and conventional. "The Inn of the Two Witches" is a "penny-dreadful"; in content related to Poe's "The Pit and the Pendulum," it is suspenseful but nevertheless a magazine story. "The Partner" is a superb story, a genuine JC story in its form and its pitiless portraiture, but it is uncommonly direct and spare, Kiplingesque in execution; with "Gaspar Ruiz," it is JC's most powerful short fiction. [Part of a review including Hermann Stresau's JOSEPH CONRAD, DER TRAGIKER DES WESTENS (1937).] [In German.]

1073 "Vystavka, posviashchannaia Dzhozefu Konradu v B-ke Ielskovo Un-ta v S. Sh. A" (Exhibition Dedicated to Joseph Conrad in the Library of Yale University), INTERNATIONATIOSIONAL 'NAIA LITERATURA, No. 10 (1938), 236-38.
[In Russian.]

1074 Wittig, Kurt. "Joseph Conrad, *Within the Tides*," ENGLISCHE STUDIEN, LXXIII (Nov 1938), 120-22.

In *Within the Tides,* "The Planter of Malata" is unsuccessful as a study of the inner life—it includes improbabilities and portrays an artificial personality of the planter—but the conclusion is poetic. The other tales are adventure stories, of which "The Partner" is the best; the main figure here comes to life with astonishing genuineness, and the unromantic type of presentation gives the work the impression of reality. The other two tales lack this high artistic worth.

1939

1075 Baker, Ernest A. THE HISTORY OF THE ENGLISH NOVEL. Ten Volumes (NY: Barnes & Noble, 1939); rptd (1960), X, 11-104.

JC as the spinner of yarns culminates in *Lord Jim,* and JC the novelist is represented by *Nostromo, The Secret Agent,* and *Under Western Eyes.* JC was an impressionist, and his method required the reader to enter a character's mind and follow the illogical tangles of mixed emotions and motives.

For JC, life remained an insoluble, complex mystery. In his mature work irony was an integral part of his art, his outlook, and his philosophy.

1076 Clemens, Florence. "Conrad's Favorite Bedside Book," SOUTH ATLANTIC QUARTERLY, XXXVIII (1939), 305-15.

JC's favorite bedside book was Alfred Wallace's MALAY ARCHIPELAGO. A comparative study of Wallace's book with JC's works shows that JC used Wallace's volume extensively. There is a general pervading influence of Wallace in JC's work. Sometimes JC used certain phrases and statements of facts taken from Wallace. He used some of Wallace's experiences for some of his own characters: e.g., Wallace with the butterfly and Stein.

1077 Daiches, David. "Joseph Conrad," THE NOVEL AND THE MODERN WORLD (Chicago: University of Chicago P, 1939), pp. 48-64; revd ed (1960), pp. 25-62.

JC is more interested in the relation of man to environment than of man to man. JC, unlike Austen and Galsworthy, took geography rather than economics as his "interpretative science." He was concerned with the "accidents" in history rather than with the "mainstream of historical causation." Seeking out the isolated, the exotic, the unusual (in Europe as well as in the China seas) is romantic, but JC was also realistic in his "vivid and accurate descriptions of sense impressions." JC "wavers" between two attitudes: indifference and aloofness, "the universe purely spectacular," and a desire for complete sympathy with and understanding of it. This conflict he resolves technically by creating the narrator who can express attitudes without implicating the author at all. However, philosophically, the conflict between the concept of an indifferent, amoral, spectacular universe, pessimism, and the concept of a necessity of interestedness, the need to be "informed by love," is never logically resolved. "Heart of Darkness" leaves the impression that there is no reality outside individual experience. *Nostromo* makes the point that even if political action can never be real, it can never be avoided. JC probes various aspects of the "human dilemma," moving from his knowledge of the sea to find other ways of exploring human paradoxes (*The Secret Agent, Under Western Eyes*). *Victory* ends on a note of triumph, simply out of JC's nonironic "inner conviction of optimism." *Lord Jim* is also romantically optimistic, but the sense that somehow Jim's adventures had been worthwhile is not supported by the facts given. "The reality of experience, for Conrad, was contained in mood, atmosphere emanating from events and setting." JC gives only enough of Almayer's reminiscences to establish the mood of contrast between youthful high hopes and present decay, and all details symbolically serve this end. If JC had appeared at any other period he might have founded a new tradition, a "modification of Stevenson combined with the subtlety of Forster," but now writers are worried about problems which to JC were not problems at all; hence he is an "outsider."

1078 Ehrentreich, Alfred. "Verwendung von Leitmotiven bei Joseph Conrad" (Joseph Conrad's Use of Leitmotifs), NEUPHILOLOGISCHE MONATSSCHRIFT, X (1939), 403-6.

Leitmotifs in "Youth" are "Pass the bottle," "Do or Die," "O youth," and similar terms. These leitmotifs are not used mechanically, but remind the reader of important aspects of the story. The same is true for the "hidden" leitmotifs in "Youth" as well as in "The Tale," that is for the references to odors, the weather, to light and darkness. [In German.]

1079 Hohoff, Curt. "Über Joseph Conrad" (On Joseph Conrad), HOCHLAND (Munich), XXXVI (Aug 1939), 378-88.

JC is the heir of Flaubert, Dostoevski, and the British sea novel, but an original writer nevertheless. He is a romantic whose work is based not so much on his imagination as on experience deeply felt and tortuously meditated upon. Some of his short stories, especially *The Shadow-Line,* "Typhoon," "Youth" (his best work), and the first part of *Lord Jim* deserve the epithet "Dichtung," not so his novels which are pieces of not always successful craftsmanship. Both JC's self-division and self-consciousness make him write a style that veils experience ("Stil der Schleier") and explain his longing for a naïveté which he knew to be impossible in the age of the psychological novel. He was the first to describe uprooted men without faith. His portraits of unbroken heroes (Lingard, Nostromo) are failures. His fame is still uncertain, for he is very much of an outsider in English literature. [In German.]

1080 Łann, E. [Land, E.] "Esse o velikom romantike" (Essay about a Great Romantic), 30 DNEI, No. 2 (1939), 70-77.
[In Russian.]

1081 Las Vergnas, Raymond. JOSEPH CONRAD (Paris: Didier, 1939).

Although drawn to adventure, JC avoids the sensationalism of the adventure story by relying on his accurate memory and on history to create the impression of reality. Yet many of his novels have three qualities of the standard adventure tale: secrecy, plotting, and violence. JC tempers his occasional melodrama and romanticism with realistic action, round characters, and dramatic presentation of character. However, his flaws include verbosity, purple passages, and faulty structure. As a stylist he seems to work more like a sculptor shaping his characters before our eyes and like a musician in his handling of the sounds of words. JC's methods include the time-shift and objectivity. A disadvantage of the time-shift is that in revealing the future it breaks the illusion of reality. A disadvantage of objectivity is that it fails to reveal the characters' interiors. Although not a didactic novelist, JC is a moralist believing in human solidarity and dignity, the necessity of service, the need to fight destiny, in self-sacrifice, fidelity, honor, and simplicity. Other themes include the illusions of youth, hope, money, and love; the relativity of viewpoints; the testing of man. In the end JC is pessimistic and skeptical. [Generally well-documented though occasionally impressionistic.] [In French.]

1082 Partington, Wilfred. FORGING AHEAD: THE TRUE STORY OF THOMAS JAMES WISE . . . (NY: Putnam's, 1939), pp. 85, 86n, 92, 188, 202, 207-9, 211-13, 215-16, 223, 233, 274; rptd as THOMAS WISE IN ORIGINAL CLOTH (Lond: Hale, 1946).

Wise complained of the exploitation of JC after the author's death, but Wise himself exploited JC during his lifetime. Wise got JC to write inscriptions and dictated certificates of genuineness, which JC was totally unqualified to do (e.g., the 1913 "right" edition of *Chance*). Wise also acquired some JC manuscripts and sold them at high prices without JC's knowledge and he produced "highly manufactured association items," probably in larger quantities than certified. Wise also listed unpublished items in his catalogue although he had disposed of them or planned to (e.g., *Laughing Anne*).

1083 Süskind, W. E. "Arbeit und Kunst: Anmerkungen zu Joseph Conrads *Spiegel und See*" (Work and Art: Notes on Joseph Conrad's *The Mirror of the Sea*), KÖLNISCHE ZEITUNG, 20 July 1939, p. 1.

The great JC's works, say what one will about real life, have provided moments of spiritual depth. JC wrote *The Mirror of the Sea* during a pause in his career. He had previously made sparing use of factual reminiscences (e.g., in "Youth" and *The Nigger of the Narcissus*). Even later, he avoids direct self-revelation through the difficult technique of the frame story. Not until *Personal Reminiscences* does JC reveal personal information about his early life. In *Mirror,* one hears him groan at the idea that something personal might be wrung out of him. To avoid this he turns to circumstances one deals with at sea. Out of this effort came an incomparable book, in which subjects evolve organically. In *Mirror,* JC often remarkably joins practical things of the sea with literary art. He often moves from the plainly pictorial to richly profound thought. [Review of the Fischer German edition of *Mirror,* translated by Georg Spervogel.] [In German.]

1084 Visiak, Edward Harold. "Creative Memory. (A Note on Joseph Conrad)," NOTES AND QUERIES, CLXXVII (21 Oct 1939), 292-93.

JC's energetic memory both produces and is knowledge.

1085 Visiak, E. H. "Joseph Conrad," NOTES AND QUERIES, CLXXVII (11 Nov 1939), 349.

The replies of Captain MacWhirr in "Typhoon," scarcely audible in the storm, suggest a reversal of the natural order of things; the storm is "penetrated by shafts of silence." JC believed the "literary creator does not judge life; he enables it to be judged."

1086 Visiak, Edward Harold. "Joseph Conrad, The Evolution of Love," NOTES AND QUERIES, CLXXVII (30 Dec 1939), 473-74.

Most of JC's women, all physically beautiful and almost all young, are creatures of ethereal substance. Mrs. Travers, in *The Rescue,* JC's greatest novel, is the most realistic. The love of JC's women remains personal, not universal, never attaining freedom through its renunciations.

1087 Visiak, Edward Harold. "Joseph Conrad. Tragedy: Sublimity," NOTES AND QUERIES, CLXXVII (2 Dec 1939), 402-3.

JC's style is "the style of sublimity and of tragedy." He is a "tragedian of prose." He attains the sublime by his novels' beginning at the end.

1088 Visiak, E. H. "The Spiritual Fall (A Note on Joseph Conrad's Philosophy)," NOTES AND QUERIES, CLXXVII (12 Aug 1939), 114-16.

The harmony that exists in an individual between soul and body, spirit and matter, is disturbed "with the emergence of the amatory instinct." The "twin-instincts" of egotism and sex are seen in the split in the characters of Falk ["Falk"], Mr. Kurtz ["Heart of Darkness"], and Ortega [*The Arrow of Gold*].

1940

1089 "Books," CHRISTIAN CENTURY, LVII (20 Nov 1940), 1451. THE LETTERS OF JOSEPH CONRAD TO MARGUERITE PORADOWSKA, 1890-1920 (1940) is a "literary treasure."

1090 Clemens, Florence. "Joseph Conrad as a Geographer," SCIENTIFIC MONTHLY, LI (Nov 1940), 460-65.

JC is amazingly accurate both in locations and in description: over one hundred difficult place names are correct to the present day and can be checked. JC subjected accuracy in description to the literary needs but only infrequently. Sea training and great memory account for this. [Clemens compares sources like Sir James Brooke's diaries to JC's descriptions and makes striking parallels. A helpful article for biography and geography for the five novels and twelve short stories set in Malaysia.]

1091 Cooper, F. G. "Some Aspects of Joseph Conrad," MARINER'S MIRROR, XXVII (Jan 1940), 61-78.

JC was not merely a perceptive sea writer: he was a psychologist (*The Nigger of the Narcissus*), a humorist, a master of the English language, and an excellent master mariner. [Conventional and sometimes emotional praise, with frequent quotations, in JC's defense against adverse criticism in the press.]

1092 Cornish, W. Lorne. "Notes and Discussions: Joseph Conrad: 'A Dedicated Soul,'" QUARTERLY REVIEW (Lond), CLXV (Jan 1940), 75-77.

JC remains a "profound mystery"; a definitive study is needed, and it must come soon, for many of his contemporaries are dying. [Brief mention of major works about JC and a thumbnail biography.] JC's goal was that of the mystic: knowledge and peace. The "secret" of his life was his "pious austerity which is the hallmark of every dedicated soul."

1093 Dataller, Roger [pseudonym of A. E. Eagleston]. THE PLAIN MAN AND THE NOVEL (Lond: Nelson, 1940), pp. 65, 121-31.

JC's only able seamen portrayed in detail are depicted "in terms of dispraisement" (e.g., Donkin in *The Nigger of the Narcissus*). Marryat, unlike JC, "was sensitive to the democratic tradition of the navy" and knew "every portion of the vessel." Marryat's style is "bold," JC's "feline"; Marryat's humor "bubbles," JC's is "infrequent and disappointing," yet JC was "hailed as the greatest maritime writer of them all." [Sketch of JC's background to suggest "that his own secretive and explosive nature accounts for the type of character that he delighted to portray."] "Youth," "Typhoon," and *Nigger* are some of his best "sea pieces." The hero of *Lord Jim* "is the Midshipman Uneasy of nautical literature," a figure beyond Marryat. "What Marryat accepted as the perfectly natural thing, Conrad pondered constantly."

1094 Fletcher, James V. "Ethical Symbolism in Conrad," COLLEGE ENGLISH, II (Oct 1940), 19-26.

JC's four "temperamental types" of character are found most clearly in *Lord Jim:* (1) "the egocentric compulsive type," introverted and "driven by a compelling ego fantasy," best represented by Lord Jim; (2) JC's "ideal type of man," motivated by "a set of ideals or symbols, which Conrad calls illusions," but "effectively related to society in their practical activities," portrayed best in Marlow and Stein; (3) "the reliable salt-of-the-earth man," stable and having little imagination, such as the French lieutenant; and (4) JC's movie villains, like Gentleman Brown. As for the relation of these "protopsychological types" to JC's ethics, Lord Jim's type lacks "the elementary virtue of courage to actualize their ideals in crises" and the quality of "solidarity with other human beings"; such "ideal characters" as Stein and Marlow "are prompted by all the Conradian virtues"; the "practical-unimaginative characters possess, above all, the virtue of simple courage"; and the "basely realistic, self-seeking rogues" have only "a kind of foolhardy bravado dimly related to courage." In the fourth type JC shows most clearly his deficiency as a writer of psychological fiction. But many of his characters will not fit readily into this classification— several men and all his women. Such a grouping of characters into ethical types led JC to "a weak and unrealistic psychology" and to the creation of several "flat" characters. Readers should seek in JC's works "a faithful record" of the lost days of British imperialism instead of the "psychological subtlety" of Dostoevski and Proust. [Oversimplified and unfair to JC's power of characterization.]

1095 Gee, John A., and Paul J. Sturm. "Introduction," LETTERS OF JOSEPH CONRAD TO MARGUERITE PORADOWSKA 1890-1920, ed by John A. Gee and Paul J. Sturm (New Haven, Conn: Yale U P; Lond: Oxford U P, 1940), pp. xiii-xix.

The "aunt, a dear enthusiastic soul," who helped Marlow in "Heart of Darkness" "to get a job" was not JC's aunt at all, but the widow of a distant cousin, Marguerite Poradowska, who spent much of her life in Brussels. Through her influential connections there she assisted in securing for JC the post that took him to the Congo. Their relationship, important to JC when he was beginning to write his first novel, was based on the facts that she was no doubt the first published author of fiction whom JC had known, that they had become acquainted under tragic circumstances—at the deathbed of her husband, that she was an unusually beautiful woman, that in her works (of ephemeral interest only) she dealt with people and things related to the memories of his early life, and that to him she seemed to be "a kindred soul." His gratefulness to her, expressed in his letters, was partly due, at least, to the loneliness of the several years preceding his marriage. Their relationship between 1890 and 1895 helped to detract JC somewhat from his "passionate introspection" and left its mark not only on his writings but also on his entire subsequent history.

1096 Gordan, John Dozier. JOSEPH CONRAD: THE MAKING OF A NOVELIST (Cambridge, Mass: Harvard U P, 1940); based on "Joseph Conrad: His Development as a Novelist from Amateur to Professional" [Unpublished thesis, Harvard University, 1939], SUMMARIES OF THESES (Harvard, 1942), 237-39.

JC's career as a seaman casts light upon his career as a writer. The other three main sources of inspiration were observation, hearsay, and reading. Poverty, ill-health, debt, and a lack of privacy and established routine harassed JC while he was writing *Almayer's Folly, The Nigger of the Nar-*

cissus, and *Lord Jim.* A study in the variant stages of the development of these three works reveals much about how JC struggled against his difficulties, became fully dedicated to writing as a way to give meaning to life, and emerged "as one of the great English novelists of his generation." The holograph of *Folly* reflects the haphazard uncertainties of an apprentice novelist. Not until he prepared the story for publication did JC remove the inconsistencies in the presentation of characters and ideas. The heavily revised holograph of *Nigger* marks JC's full dedication to fiction. Some of the revisions run through as many as five stages, revealing "the efforts of the amateur corrected by brilliant strokes into the successes of the professional writer." The pattern of revisions in these three works reflects closely JC's lifelong working habits. In turn, he gave meticulous care to all prepublication states: holograph, typescript, and proofs. When his story had appeared in serial publication, as with *Nigger* and *Jim,* JC would revise the serial printing for the first book form. He then revised the first English book form for the collected edition. [The final chapters of Gordan's study give a history of composition and publication of some of JC's early stories and discuss his reception by the public. An essential study for any JC critic.]

1097 Gordan, John D. "The Ranee Brooke and Joseph Conrad," STUDIES IN PHILOLOGY, XXXVII (Jan 1940), 130-32.

External evidence indicates that JC read widely in the annals of the Brooke family, including MY LIFE IN SARAWAK by the Ranee Margaret Alice de Windt Brooke, published in London in 1913. *The Rescue* appears to owe something to the Ranee Brooke's work. This evidence supports the supposition that JC knew the diaries and letters of James Brooke, the first white Rajah of Sarawak. [See Gordan, "The Rajah Brooke and Joseph Conrad," ibid., XXXV (Oct 1938), 613-34.]

1098 Gray, Hugh. "Conrad's Political Prophecies," LIFE AND LETTERS TODAY, XXIV (Feb 1940), 134-39.

In *A Personal Record,* "Autocracy and War," "The Crime of Partition," and "A Note on the Polish Problem" suggest that JC could have been "a great political or historical writer." "Autocracy and War" foresaw the troubles in Russia and the inevitability of war in Europe, with industrialism and commercialism as the main causes. The "accuracy of his prophecies" about Poland is "uncanny."

1099 R. "Joseph Conrad. Poljak koji je postao glavni engleski moderni knjizevnik" (Joseph Conrad. The Pole Who Became the Chief Modern English Writer), HRVATSKA STRAŽA (Zagreb), XII: 199 (1940), 4.

[Basic biographical facts.] [In Serbo-Croatian.]

1100 Visiak, Edward Harold. "Joseph Conrad. Concluding Remarks," NOTES AND QUERIES, CLXXVII (13 Jan 1940), 25-26.

JC is classical in his preoccupation with destiny and in his suggestions that nature is sympathetic to tragic events. "Conrad is the tropics in human nature apperceived through Polish sensibility, which has known much bitterness of repression." Conscience is "an ethical fastidiousness" to JC.

1101 Zabel, Morton Dauwen. "Conrad: Nel Mezzo de Cammin," NEW REPUBLIC, CIII (23 Dec 1940), 873-74; absorbed in "Conrad in His Age," CRAFT AND CHARACTER (1957).

JC's reputation, now beginning to recover, needs to be established on a firm foundation. "After George Moore pronounced the esthetic veto on his labors (the wreck of Henry James floating on the slops of Robert Louis Stevenson), it needed only the painful sentimentality of William McFee and similar pipe-sucking imitators to demote the author of *Victory* and *Under Western Eyes* from his place of respected fellowship with James, Gide, and Mann to the rank of a somber yea-sayer for the stolider manly virtues and hypnotic moral complacency that readily pass as substitutes for serious thought, tragic insight and human virtue in modern fiction and drama." Two recently published books, LETTERS OF JOSEPH CONRAD TO MARGUERITE PORADOWSKA: 1890-1920 (1940), edited by John A. Gee and Paul J. Sturm, and John Dozier Gordan's THE MAKING OF A NOVELIST (1940), have "special documentary value for criticism." JC's letters to his cousin Mme. Poradowska, his Belgian friend of "Heart of Darkness," reveal his varying mental and physical states, indolence, despair, suspicions, "trussed-up sense of honor"—his "state of soul" out of which his books were written. Gordan's book is factual, never rising to appreciating JC's esthetic psychological significance, but it gives mountains of documentation on JC's early texts, revisions, sources, chronology, history of criticism, geographical location of plots and characters, and so on—all the "dates and facts of his formative years."

1941

1102 Bradbrook, M. C. JOSEPH CONRAD: POLAND'S ENGLISH GENIUS (Cambridge: Cambridge U P, 1941), pp. 62-67; rptd in part as "The Hollow Men: Victory," in THE ART OF JOSEPH CONRAD: A CRITICAL SYMPOSIUM (1960), Robert Wooster Stallman (ed).

JC "published his first novel in the year Hardy published his last, the year before the appearance of A SHROPSHIRE LAD, when the public favourites were Kipling, Rider Haggard, and Conan Doyle; an age of romantic pessimism and flamboyant assurance." Out of this remote period came two great writers, JC the novelist and Yeats the poet. "Their power to write of the great simple heroic themes almost frightens the modern reader." Especially important are JC's politics, which are "apt to the present time"; but JC is also "relevant as an artist." He is "strengthening without being a facile optimist."

JC's productions are divided chronologically and qualitatively into three groups. The early works, "The Wonders of the Deep" (*Almayer's Folly* to *Romance,* 1895-1903), are mostly based on personal reminiscences. JC "discovered his true field" in *The Nigger of the Narcissus* and "his method" in *Lord Jim.* For JC, fidelity is "the virtue of virtues," and betrayal is the "crime of crimes." The works of JC's maturity, "The Hollow Men" (*Nostromo* to *Victory,* 1904-14), reflect "the deepening power" of his subjects, which "become more tragic and more introverted," and also display "the correspondingly deeper powers of technique." All the great figures of this period of work (Nostromo and Monygham, Razumov, Renouard, Flora, and Heyst) "have in common with Lord Jim a profound self-distrust . . . , but they have not lost their beliefs, and so they are tormented by their failure, or what they think their failure, to live up to those principles in which they most deeply believe." Developments in technique include a "new use of a time-shift, and of a consistent irony." "In this period JC's world is almost achingly solid"; yet "somehow there is a curious feeling that all is a shell . . . . It is a more than usual awareness of the world together with a strange feeling of detachment or dissociation from it."

The products of JC's "relaxed old age," his "Recollections in Tranquillity" (*The Shadow-Line* to *Suspense,* 1914-24), are "for the most part sound, careful, but incurably listless works. They are exercises in the manner of Conrad." The five books (*Tales of Hearsay* consists mostly of older uncollected stories) "are reminiscent of Conrad's youth, in a direct, simple way." In JC's best works, "the vision of evil is so strong as to be very nearly omnipotent—but not quite. They show that ability to face the worst that the writer can frankly conceive—not to deal with it, just to face it—which is the distinctive quality of tragedy." [A small book which had much to do with the current revival of interest in JC, this work is still valuable for many of the author's insights.]

 1103 Clemens, Florence. "Conrad's Malaysia," COLLEGE ENGLISH, II (Jan 1941), 338-46.

Although white men and women, far away from their homes, are at the center of JC's Malaysian fiction, "the native life forms the necessary isolating background and is of great importance." In general, JC knew much about Malaysia: his depiction of its geography is almost perfect, his knowledge of the "complicated pattern" of life there is accurate, he understands the influence of Mohammedanism on this life, he includes the important foreign minorities such as the Arabs and the Chinese, and he records accurately the appearance of native scenes and native costumes. But his knowledge of "native psychology" may be doubted; instead of knowing natives intimately, he relied heavily on the works of Alfred Wallace and Sir James Brooke. Thus his portrayal of Malay nature is "not very far wrong" but is "probably never quite right."

>**1104** Dyboski, Roman. "Joseph Conrad," GREAT MEN AND WOMEN OF POLAND, ed by Stephen Paul Mizwa (NY: Macmillan, 1941), pp. 300-12.

The conditions of Poland in the nineteenth century produced a spirit of adventure especially in the border gentry, from which JC descended. Because of his origin, he liked to set his stories in borderlands between two civilizations. "What matters most to JC is . . . man in his sublime solitude," a solitude of heroic struggle. He often chose for his hero a man who had "lost caste." From the middle of his career, he emphasized moral victories and personified evil in a demoniac figure. Poland gave him his "tragic pessimism" and his melancholy.

>**1105** Kerby-Miller, Charles. "Complementary," BOSTON EVENING TRANSCRIPT, 18 Jan 1941, p. 1.

THE LETTERS OF JOSEPH CONRAD TO MARGUERITE PORADOWSKA, 1890-1920, edited by J. A. Gee and Paul J. Sturm (1940), and J. D. Gordan's JOSEPH CONRAD: THE MAKING OF A NOVELIST (1940) are complementary, revealing much about JC's development as a novelist up through *Lord Jim*.

>**1106** Leavis, F[rank] R[aymond]. "Revaluations (XIV): Joseph Conrad," SCRUTINY, X (June and Oct 1941), 22-50, 157-81; rptd in Leavis's THE GREAT TRADITION (NY: George W. Stewart; Lond: Chatto & Windus, 1948); rptd (NY: New York U P, 1963); and in part as "On 'Typhoon' and *The Shadow-Line*," in THE ART OF JOSEPH CONRAD: A CRITICAL SYMPOSIUM, ed by Robert W. Stallman (East Lansing: Michigan State U P, 1960), pp. 191-98.

The Arrow of Gold is one of JC's worst books. *The Rescue* is "boring in its innocence." JC, "for all his sophistication, exhibits a certain simplicity of outlook and attitude. About his attitude toward women there is perceptible, all the way through his literary career, something of the gallant simple sailor. The sailor in him, of course, is rightly held to be a main part of his strength." The strength of "Typhoon" is not so much in the description of the storm, as in the presentation of Captain MacWhirr, Jukes, and Soloman Rout at the opening of the tale. "The distinctive art of a novelist . . . is apparent in the rendering of personality, its reactions and vibrations; the pervasive presence of the crew, delicately particularized, will turn out on analysis to account for the major part of the atmosphere." Nothing is forced or injected in the story. In *The Shadow-Line* the sinister spell over the ship is felt by the contrast with tradition and its values, embodied in the crew. *Lord Jim* is "decidedly thin" as a consequence of eking out a short story to make a novel. Each detail, character and incident of *Nostromo*, one of the great novels in English, bears on the book's themes and motives.

1107 McFee, William. "Conrad's Letters to a Literary Relative," YALE REVIEW, N.S. XXX (March 1941), 606-8.

The importance of the letters in LETTERS OF JOSEPH CONRAD TO MARGUERITE PORADOWSKA, edited by John A. Gee and Paul J. Sturm (1940), lies in their displaying JC's "evolution from a homeless wanderer to an established man of letters in England." The editors managed to retain JC's informal style in their translation from the French.

1108 Monroe, N. Elizabeth. THE NOVEL AND SOCIETY (Chapel Hill: University of North Carolina P, 1941), pp. 169-70.

Lord Jim had to be told by Marlow to become a psychological story. If it had been described from an omniscient viewpoint, it would have been simply an adventure story.

1109 Retinger, Joseph Hieronim. CONRAD AND HIS CONTEMPORARIES: SOUVENIRS (Lond: Minerva; Toronto: Macmillan, 1941; NY: Roy, 1943).

[Personal reminiscences by a countryman of JC describing JC's home life, his return to Poland, his friends, and his opinions of several authors.]

1110 Steegmuller, Francis. "Conradiana," NEW YORK HERALD TRIBUNE BOOKS, 2 Feb 1941, p. 12.

The letters in LETTERS OF JOSEPH CONRAD TO MARGUERITE PORADOWSKA, 1890-1920, edited by John A. Gee and Paul J. Sturm (1940) will be helpful to an understanding of JC's early career; most of the letters are from the period 1890-1895. "Conrad's French, while generally adequate, has none of the beauty of his English as we know it from the novels, and the undistinguished style of the present translation appears to be only appropriate."

1111 Zabel, Morton Dauwen. "Conrad: The Secret Sharer," NEW REPUBLIC, CIV (21 April 1941), 567-68, 570-74; absorbed in "Conrad in His Age," CRAFT AND CHARACTER (1957).

JC's characteristic devices—the shift in time, the plot-inversions and dislocation, the repetition of motifs, the employment of interlocutors and other agencies for observation, the specialized use of indirection—originated in "profoundly habitual, deeply ingrained, almost incurably obsessional tendencies of his character" and in his own experiences. His method of composition was haphazard and precipitous; he wrote each work almost word by word, with great difficulty. For him the act of composition took place between two contradictory impulses, one instinctive, casual, unmethodical; the other cautious, analytical, and calculating; his "congenital impulsiveness" was often checked by "acute principles of honor and sincerity." His leaving Poland caused a sense of guilt which was undoubedly "sublimated into his novels." Thus he was forced, in order to write, to exert "an appalling and heroic exercise of will power"; and he confers his heroism upon his characteristic heroes. He also imposed "the *structure* of the psychic condition and of its moral equivalent upon the dramatic structure of the plot"; he compelled dramatic action to "subserve" the necessities and processes of the moral sensibility while at the same time keeping it essentially dramatic. The devices he used probe the nature of illusion and at last reveal "a hard irreducible center of moral certitude and human conviction." His method of composition is seen at its best in *Under Western Eyes,* which demonstrates that personality can be saved by "the test of experience and the recognition of selfhood" and also that JC included "the rescue of his own character from its defeats and confusions by the ordeal of his art." He believed that it is both impossible and futile for a man to understand or save mankind as a group before he has first learned to know and save himself. [A serious and important article.]

1942

1112 Atkinson, Brooks. "Books That Hold the Harsh Salt of the Sea," NEW YORK TIMES BOOK REVIEW, 13 Sept 1942, p. 2.
JC was a tragic writer who saw man as an intruder on a wild universe; his sailors save from the chaos "the shred of a lost cause." *The Mirror of the Sea* and *A Personal Record* one can read every summer with respect and wonder.

1113 Gee, J. A. "The Final Typescript of Book III of Conrad's *Nostromo,*" YALE UNIVERSITY LIBRARY GAZETTE, XVI (April 1942), 80.
The Yale acquisition of two portions of the final typescript of *Nostromo*

provides a fairly complete sequence of this draft through the first eight chapters of book III of *Nostromo*. The less extensive and at times somewhat "finicky" changes in the final typescript are in some respects the most interesting because they are the "finishing touches" made by such "a master of expression" as JC.

1114 Gerould, Gordon Hall. "Explorers of the Inner Life," THE PATTERNS OF ENGLISH AND AMERICAN FICTION (NY: Little, Brown, 1942), pp. 438-61, espec 447-55.

The shorter fictional forms were better suited to JC's genius in the beginning of his career. Although JC worried that his romantic material might obscure the nature of his writing, his work has value as "romance of adventure." His tales often deal with a man's or a group of men's destiny, in which chance plays a notable but limited role. For JC, composition is a dire struggle to communicate "his imaginative vision."

1115 Hall, James Norman. "My Conrad," ATLANTIC MONTHLY, CLXIX (May 1942), 583-87.

Of JC's books, *Lord Jim, Under Western Eyes,* "Youth," *Victory,* "Typhoon," *Nostromo, Chance,* and *The Nigger of the Narcissus* are prized in that order. "Matured" readers will always realize that JC's works are "of unique Conradian stature." JC often provides digressions from his main narratives which "reveal a creative mind functioning serenely." *Eyes* "engages the interest . . . swiftly" and "holds it . . . relentlessly."

1116 Hall, James Norman. "Tunnelled Pages," UNDER A THATCHED ROOF (Boston: Houghton Mifflin, 1942), pp. 170-87.

JC's value rests in his "unapproachable oneness." *Under Western Eyes* engages and holds one's interest. [Book talk of the informal and general variety.]

1117 Kunitz, Stanley J., and Howard Haycraft (eds). TWENTIETH CENTURY AUTHORS (NY: Wilson, 1942), pp. 307-10.

JC from early youth on was caught between the practical, realistic outlook represented by his uncle Bobrowski and the "extravagant, idealistic" "Korzeniowski strain." He was not primarily a writer of sea stories. "Like Melville's, Conrad's novels are a long confession: they are egocentric." In his greatest books, JC deals with "damaged souls." [On the whole amalgamates fairly well-known, now conventional, views from various sources, but noteworthy for the amount of space given JC in 1942 in such an encyclopedic work.]

1118 Latcham, Ricardo A. "La obra novelesca de Joseph Conrad," NOSOTROS (Buenos Aires), 2nd ser, XIX (Oct 1942), 25-52.

[Relates various experiences in JC's life, beginning with the several times he worked on *Almayer's Folly*. The second part discusses the Spanish translations of JC's works and names Spanish authorities on JC. Further considers reasons why JC wrote in English instead of Polish. The third section comments on the situations in which the protagonists of his novels find themselves.] In almost all cases the protagonist must overcome a physical, environmental force or threat. British authors assumed supremacy with regard to stories which have the sea as their background. [Discusses JC's "aristocracy": loyalty and honor of the individual for great causes.] JC, through his characters, stated he did not believe in the revolutionary way; his characters are loyal to their duties. JC's settings are universal. JC is preoccupied with Central America and Chile. He seems to have painted the feelings and thoughts of these countries. [Repeatedly asserts that "moral health of the characters" is the reason why JC is a superior author.] [In Spanish.]

1119 McFee, William. "Introduction," A CONRAD ARGOSY (Garden City, NY: Doubleday, Doran, 1942), pp. vii-x.

The first readers of JC's works were dazzled by the "glamour of the eastern seas" and swept off their feet by *Victory*. *The Nigger of the Narcissus* and "Typhoon" are "indisputable masterpieces of modern fiction" which do not derive from any previous novelists. Because of his "personal touch," JC left no successors; but he "so enlarged the resources of the English language as a vehicle of imaginative prose" that his influence is one of the greatest of all writers.

1120 "The New Editions," NEW YORK TIMES BOOK REVIEW, 27 Dec 1942, p. 10.

A CONRAD ARGOSY (1942), with an introduction by William McFee, "is irrefutable proof . . . that Joseph Conrad . . . was an artist of supreme originality."

1121 Onofrio, Lilia D'. "El hombre y el mar en la novela de José Conrad" (Man and the Sea in Joseph Conrad's Novels), NUEVE ENSAYOS DE CRITICA LITERARIA (Nine Essays in Literary Criticism) (Buenos Aires: Libreria y Editorial "El Ateneo" [1942], pp. 47-55.

JC brings to the adventure narrative the clearness of direct observation and the depth of psychological analysis. The sea nourished JC's subconscious; therefore the changing tonality and incessant mutations of the states of the ocean are present in his works. His aesthetic consists in the transformation of ephemeral impressions into expressions that concretely create the emotional atmosphere of time and place. This technique is apparent in his evocation of ships as well as of men. Besides producing aesthetic emotion, JC's ships have a precise consciousness of their role in men's missions. JC finds the imperatives of honor and loyalty superior to life itself. He exalts the professional integrity of the old, silent wolves of the sea, and condemns violence. His heroes are ordinary men whom circumstances lead to deeds of heroic magnitude. The sea serves to purify the moral forces of the men that confront it; this is the most personal trait of JC's literary creation. [In Spanish.]

> **1122** Pritchett, V. S. "Books in General," NEW STATESMAN AND NATION, XXIII (10 Jan 1942), 78; rptd with minor changes as "A Pole in the Far East" in THE LIVING NOVEL (Lond: Chatto & Windus, 1946; NY: Reynal & Hitchcock, 1947), pp. 139-44.

A re-reading of some of JC's Malayan stories after a lapse of twenty years leaves the impression that it is difficult to know "what *was* the issue Conrad had in his tentative, evasive, suspicious, and rather exasperated imagination," although this judgment is not true of the best works such as "Youth," "The Secret Sharer," *The Nigger of the Narcissus,* and "Typhoon." In the early works JC's sense of history is derived from his "Slavonic imagination" and turned to the defeated natives of the Eastern islands, who are really "transplantations" from the history of Poland. In his later career, when his early material was exhausted, improvisation supplanted imagination, and JC became a "prophetic" novelist, considering human beings as timeless. His excellence lies not in a "Romantic overworld" but in actual observation. In the "big elaborated books" JC always avoids climaxes, as in *An Outcast of the Islands;* his "eye for the soul, before the soul ran away with him, is tremendous." [Pritchett develops his concept of JC and his works much further in "Conrad," THE LIVING NOVEL AND LATER APPRECIATIONS (NY: Random House, 1964), pp. 190-99.]

> **1123** Raimondi, Giuseppe. "Capitano Conrad," GIORNALE OSSIA TACCUINO 1925-30 (Journal or Notebook [1925-30]), gathered by Giuseppe de Roberts (Firenze: LeMonnier, 1942), pp. 73-78.

Readers of JC who hoped for intimate revelations in *Lettres Françaises,* edited by G. Jean-Aubry (1929), will be disappointed in the work. The letters, notes written in haste, are honest and reveal his doubts and fatigues and also the brief consolations in his artistic life. The letter to his French translators, André Gide and G. Jean-Aubry, treat mainly questions about the translations of JC's works. JC rarely judges or appraises persons in his novels, although there is a strong bond between the author and his characters. In a letter to Philippe Neel, hinting at *Nostromo,* JC remarked about putting invented matter into prose so that the character touched his heart as well as his soul as if the character lived. JC's Slavic heritage is recognizable in his art: the mode of telling the story in which the importance lies in the diverse sentiments of the men who live life rather than in the facts of existence. His characters are also Slavic; they are adrift in life (Jim, Heyst, Almayer) as are those we have encountered in Dostoevski. His characters are those who refute and remove themselves from social bonds. Also, an old Parisian workman in Zola does not speak too differently than does a mariner in Conrad—Naturalism is their bond. We never will know where the literary form of JC's style is rooted. His fantasy was occupied with natural and physical events—storms, rain, the dawn. His sea life introduced him to this sense of space and time, most desolate and dreadful. Perhaps, he is thus interested in man lost in the events of a monstrous and silent solitude. Works like "Typhoon" and *The Nigger of the Narcissus* are works of his period of expressing man's desire for a voice amidst the dumbfoundedness of the cosmic elements. He was a great writer who lost himself in every literature, trusting only to the resources of his own temperament. If anyone thinks JC is an adventure novelist, he will see in *Victory,* "The End of the Tether," *A Set of Six,* and *Tales of Unrest* that he is preoccupied with those who strive to understand and clarify the unknown, the continuous upheaval of the soul from quiet to sorrow, calm to passion. He writes of creatures of passion. [In Italian.]

1124 Schunk, Karl. "Der Zufall bei Joseph Conrad" (Coincidence in Joseph Conrad). Unpublished thesis, Göttingen University, 1942. "Zufälle" are defined as accidents and coincidences which have not been planned by any higher, rational power. JC's attitude towards such accidents prove that he is a Slav. He thinks life is mysterious and irrational and underestimates the importance of reason. Man to him is a creature of his impulses. That is why JC's works often convey the atmosphere of a madhouse. Sometimes he pretends to deal with such matter as a sober Englishman; as a matter of fact, his experience may have sobered him a bit. But on the whole he was most deeply fascinated by the irrationalities of life. One often feels that he views the chain of coincidences as an expression of the supernatural. Though he admires man's heroic struggle against fate, he prefers to describe passive men, as do many Russian writers. Another motif that links his fiction to the Russian novel is that of pity. The opinions JC acquired in the West sometimes serve as an escape from tormenting doubts and feelings of guilt. [In German.]

1125 Temple, Phillips. "The Fatalism of Joseph Conrad," AMERICA (NY), LXVIII (28 Nov 1942), 213-14.
JC, despite his "Catholicism," "thinks far less as a Catholic than as a fatal-

ist." In fact, he is "a pessimistic fatalist rather than a Catholic optimist." [Mencken's "sad litany of Conradian heroes" is cited.] Destruction of self in JC is "a meaningless mockery," but in Graham Greene an "ultimate affirmation." *An Outcast of the Islands* makes "sardonic use of the word 'hope' "; *Victory* makes ironic use of the title; *The Mirror of the Sea* has "uncompromising fatalism." Nevertheless, inconsistently, JC worked out a notion of faith (loyalty could give life meaning), e.g., in *The Nigger of the Narcissus*. JC should be read but not regarded as a Catholic writer—his fatalist attitude that there are no answers to most important questions is not the Catholic tragic view of life.

1126 Vestdijk, S. "Eenige proefjes zout water" (A Few Sips of Salt Water), CRITERIUM (Amsterdam), III (1942), 48-60.

The sea novel has been a moribund genre for some time, because modern technology (speed and radio communications) eliminates a world that is sufficiently isolated to be usable as the setting of a self-contained drama. It is not surprising that he was attracted to the East-Indian archipelago, because the islands themselves, by their very insularity, strengthened the motif of isolation. In general, the only way the sea novel can survive is by becoming either a historical or a psychological novel. JC chose to write novels of the latter type, and his works succeed (or fail) to the extent that they succeed as such. His excursions into psychology often appear forced. He never wrote a "perfect" novel, but some of his short stories come as close to perfection as seems artistically possible. Among his novels, perhaps his best is *Chance,* but this work is only peripherally a sea novel. Although JC's psychological concerns frequently drew him away from the sea, one should nevertheless keep in mind that his interest in psychology often enabled him to strengthen the ties that bind a character to his ship or his island. Obsessions, aspirations, feelings of guilt, struggles of conscience are factors that force JC's characters into a stoical confrontation with themselves. Few environments provide a better symbolic setting for such confrontations than the sea, where the narrow intensity of man's pursuits and passions is accentuated by a contrasting immensity. Not surprisingly, the outcast motif pervades JC's *oeuvre*. In his best works, however (e.g., *Chance,* "A Smile of Fortune"), the outcast motif is complemented by two other motifs: the father-daughter relationship and matchmaking (or its opposite, matchbreaking). Obviously these two are not intrinsically related to sea fiction. Perhaps they should be interpreted as "land" motifs contrapuntally related to the principal, sea-oriented motif, the outcast motif. All three are wonderfully united in *Chance,* where the ship continues De Barral's isolation after his prison term and at the same time provides him with enough freedom to interfere in the lives of his nearest relations, his daughter and son-in-law, the ship's captain. [Reflections on Defoe, Melville, Stevenson, Van Schendel, and JC as novelists of the sea.] [In Dutch.]

1127 Wagenknecht, Edward. " 'Pessimism' in Hardy and Conrad," COLLEGE ENGLISH, III (March 1942), 546-54.

Neither Hardy nor JC can be adequately labeled as a pessimist. Hardy "steers away from pessimism" by means of his "respect for humanity"; JC sees the world as "resting squarely on a few ancient fundamentals, the most important of which was fidelity." Neither one, however, "viewed the world as, in the ordinary sense, friendly to man." JC was almost obsessed with "the subject of the psychic wound," and Jim, Razumov, and Lena, like Christ, paid for their spiritual victories with their lives. The works of these two writers were not based on a philosophical system, nor can such a system be "deduced" from their works. Like Keats, they perceived "that the poet has no opinions but only perceptions." Both were "creational—not scholastic, not dogmatic—in their approach to literature." JC was "the more creational of the two." "He had ideas," but the "unifying principle" in his works should be looked for in his temperament; a writer's metaphysic should simply "serve his own art as a frame of reference."

1128 Wimsatt, W. K., Jr. "When Is Variation 'Elegant'?" COLLEGE ENGLISH, III (Jan 1942), 368-83; rptd in THE VERBAL ICON: STUDIES IN THE MEANING OF POETRY (Lexington, Ky: University of Kentucky P, 1954), pp. 187-99.

With reference to "elegant" variation, JC's description of a French man-of-war's shelling the bush of the African coast in "Heart of Darkness" contains a passage in which "nouns refer to different objects under clearly different aspects, while adjectives refer to the same objects under aspects which approach one another and suggest a single generic aspect—for which perhaps there is no single word." This is "the method of concreteness, of narrative symbol as opposed to abstract science," basically "the way in which the diverse concrete elements of any fiction gain relevance or unity."

1129 Zabel, Morton D. "Conrad in His Age," NEW REPUBLIC, CVII (16 Nov 1942), 644; expanded in CRAFT AND CHARACTER (1957).

William McFee's introduction to A CONRAD ARGOSY (1942) is sophomoric and peppered with "journalistic clichés." The greatness of JC is not well served by this "Argosy." JC is a critic of the ideal who reveals the stress and tension in man's soul. "Heart of Darkness," "The Secret Sharer," *Chance, Nostromo, Victory,* and *Under Western Eyes* are among the greatest books of the century.

1943

1130 Bolles, Edwin Courtlandt. The Literature of Sea Travel since the Introduction of Steam, 1830-1930 (Philadelphia: pvtly ptd, 1943), pp. 36-7, 76-7, 84-5, 109-11, 118-19 [not seen]. Unpublished thesis, University of Pennsylvania, 1943.

1131 Church, Richard. British Authors (Lond and NY: Longmans, Green, 1943); new ed (1948), pp. 28-31.

Two opposed forces characterize JC: "the sea, for light and movement; England for justice and freedom." Galsworthy and Garnett encouraged JC to write; James influenced JC's elaborate technique and made it more difficult for him to find himself. JC's foreignness gave an "overladen quality" to his prose. Marlow, "a symbol and a focus-point," held back JC's "poetic urgency" by providing a disciplining device. JC became popular with *Chance* (1914), lost public interest after 1924, and his work is now acknowledged for its "subtlety of mood, range of knowledge and experience, its poetic richness." JC's temporal world rests on fidelity, "the genius of his work."

1132 Goldring, Douglas. South Lodge: Reminiscences of Violet Hunt, Ford Madox Ford and the English Circle (Lond: Constable, 1943), pp. 165-77.

JC did not outgrow his Flaubertism and except for two or three early books his work is a total loss. JC's prose "seems to be largely pastiche Flaubert translated into English by someone with no great ease in the use of the language." The reception Ford's Joseph Conrad: A Personal Remembrance (1924) received "was characteristic of a period in which London reviewing, much of which had been cornered by commercial gangsters, reached its lowest level." JC "had been accepted by the cliques as a Great Writer, therefore his long connection with that rank outsider, Hueffer, must be explained away or hushed up." There is no reason to question the truth of Ford's account of his relationship with JC as presented in Return to Yesterday [earlier in Yale Review (1929)]. [Goldring's hostility to and criticism of JC and the Edward Garnetts are motivated by his partisanship for Ford.]

1133 Hanley, James. "Minority Report," Fortnightly Review, N.S. CLIII (June 1943), 419-22.

Donkin appears as "Captain Conrad's dodger," the "grumbler," whose place was not "to inform his creator that in keeping himself within the safe boundaries, he was shutting out valuable areas of information." Donkin was a tradition long before JC "decided to take his ticket"; he represents the sailor's right to be suspicious, to complain, to refuse to believe, but he is unable to make a suitable "historic gesture" to solve his problems.

1134 Mélisson-Dubreil, M.-R. LA PERSONNALITÉ DE JOSEPH CONRAD (The Personality of Joseph Conrad) (Paris: Maurice Lavergne, 1943).

The part that JC's Polish personality plays in his work is revealed by a study of his memoirs, his letters, and his fiction. His Polish traits are his affability, sensitivity, impulsiveness, generosity, compulsiveness, anxiety, and moodiness. JC's aesthetic of realism and objectivity comes in part from his Polish love of independence. One reason for his partial failure is his choice of overly complicated narrative technique which clashes with his originally clear and simple vision of his subject. Though JC's understanding of his characters is limited, he is adept at rendering the overwhelming extent of the cosmos in relation to the smallness of man. His work dramatizes the failure of communication, the need for illusions, a mystical belief in the power of feeling and intuition, the necessity for brotherly love, indulgence, courage, responsibility, and fidelity. These virtues reflect the requirement of a Polish temperament subject to the extremes of enthusiasm and pessimism. [Marred by overemphasis on JC's Polish qualities; tends to oversimplify. Originally a University of Paris thesis.] [In French.]

1135 Mélisson-Dubreil, M.-R. LE VOCABULAIRE MARITIME DE JOSEPH CONRAD (The Maritime Vocabulary of Joseph Conrad) (Paris: Maurice Lavergne, 1943).

JC owes his reputation as a great though flawed author to his judicious employment of technical sea terms which checked his tendency toward vagueness and kept him in the realistic world of men and ships. [Wholly unconvincing. University of Paris supplementary thesis.] [In French.]

1136 Sinha, Dr. Murari Shri. "The Craft of Joseph Conrad as a Novelist." Unpublished thesis, Lucknow University, 1943.

1137 Staral, Margarete. "Die Behandlung des Meeres bei Joseph Conrad" (Joseph Conrad's Treatment of the Sea). Unpublished thesis, University of Prague, 1943. [In German.]

1138 Wagenknecht, Edward. "Values and Joseph Conrad," CAVALCADE OF THE ENGLISH NOVEL (NY: Holt, 1943; 1954), pp. 166-67, 243, 372, 390, 423-40, 442, 507, 509, 512, 572, 611-13.

(1) "Conrad's Approach to Fiction": Not being a facile inventor, JC used individual experiences, observation, hearsay, and even reading as a basis for his novels. He was not a reporter of fact, however. (2) "Conrad's Writing Career": JC's first two books *Almayer's Folly* and *An Outcast of the Islands* seem negligible compared to *The Nigger of the Narcissus*. A most

original book, *Nigger* deals with the effect of a dying black sailor on his fellow crew members. JC's next works, *Tales of Unrest, Youth,* and *Typhoon,* have much in common with *Nigger.* JC felt *Nostromo* to be his greatest book, although it was his most neglected. Difficult to read because of its method of narration, *Nostromo* contains a microcosm of the world. *The Secret Agent, Under Western Eyes,* and *Chance,* the most complicated in method of all JC's novels, follow, and then *Victory,* which has just as much, if not more, melodrama as *Chance.* In *The Shadow-Line* he reverts to autobiography, as he does in *The Rescue,* whose last page is a grand example of restraint in expressing powerful emotion. JC died while working on an historical novel, *Suspense,* but he had finished *The Rover,* a novel which had grown out of *Suspense.* (3) "Conrad's Vision of Life": JC felt that art, which should bring to light the truth, can appeal only through the senses—a belief which perhaps explains why he is often called an impressionist. He abhorred overt didacticism in literature, but realized that each subject if treated properly must have a morality of its own. Though nominally a Roman Catholic, he exemplifies little specific Catholic doctrine. He does mention God in terms of "the Most High" and "Infinite Wisdom" in *Folly*. JC saw the world as a spectacle for love, not despair, a world in which one can win a spiritual victory. He finds values in the world at sea where nonessentials disappear and man confronts fundamentals. JC's life must be taken into consideration in appraising the character of his books. He detested autocracy, and he knew that revolution was ineffectual. He could, therefore, never write a "proletarian" novel, and critics of the 1930s took him to task for that. Perhaps, also, if he had not been a sailor, there would not have been so much melodrama in his work. He believed the object of life was the perfection of individual conduct, and he reiterates this theme in all of his books. He employs the theme of the psychic wound in his introspective analysis of individual conduct in "The End of the Tether," *Rover,* and most explicitly in *Lord Jim,* where Jim cannot escape his past. (4) "Conrad's Narrative Method": JC uses various points of view in his narration: direct, objective narration in *Nostromo;* first person in *Shadow-Line* and *The Arrow of Gold;* Marlow, "that preposterous master mariner" in "Youth," "Heart of Darkness," *Jim,* and *Chance.* A single motive seems to apply to JC's use of chronology—he never tells things in the order in which they occurred. Using these different narrators, according to some of JC's critics, lends a plausibility and intensity to characters as they appear to a keen observer; he did not thrust himself into the story directly; he achieves perspective by having it seen through an observer such as Marlow.

JC was not a didacticist, and he did not write allegories like Kafka; however, his interest was always in values and the significance of his tale; and, in this sense, every novel of quality is an allegory. His method is enveloped in mystery; for him human character was the greatest mystery. He never declared that he understood himself or his characters. His method was individual, and consequently even cultivated readers may find it difficult to meet him on his own ground. JC's metaphysic served him as an artist if not in his life. [Selected bibliography included.]

1944

1139 Curle, Richard. "Sea Captain and Novelist: Memories of Joseph Conrad," LISTENER, XXXII (27 July 1944), 102-3.

"Glowing and vital," JC "dominated any company in which he found himself." He preferred peaceful Kent to the splendid places he wrote about. His many-layered mind made him "everlastingly elusive." He valued many writers, but thought MOBY DICK "a portentous fake." Wallace's MALAY ARCHIPELAGO was his favorite book.

1140 Dean, Leonard F. "Tragic Pattern in Conrad's 'The Heart of Darkness,'" COLLEGE ENGLISH, VI (Nov 1944), 100-104.

Published criticism of JC's works finally reaches the question, "Is his best work truly tragic?" "Heart of Darkness" has been found to be both "profoundly affirmative" and belonging to the great tradition of tragedy, but it is lacking when compared to KING LEAR. An analysis of the story shows that "the true philosopher is the one who has seen reality but who then . . . has returned and accepted the illusion which has now become a saving ideal." In Act IV of KING LEAR, Lear and Gloster [sic] reach a point that is similar to the final horror of Kurtz, but the main difference between JC's story and Shakespeare's play is found in their conclusions: in KING LEAR, Lear dies "asserting" his belief in what Cordelia represents; in JC's story, the Intended does not deserve the quality which she is meant "to represent." JC's conclusion was probably invented; JC's inability to invent has been frequently noticed. A "wider explanation" is that Marlow's insight is "an inadequate substitute" for Kurtz's "complete disillusionment." Marlow's approach to the Intended is not Lear's "exhilirating otherworldliness," and Marlow seems to persuade himself that "it is possible to mollify a stern deity by behaving admirably within the illusion," a conclusion obviously lacking "the dynamic quality" of KING LEAR. JC, in intention at least, is important for "a new affirmative myth."

1141 Michael, George. THE BIG FIVE (Lond: The Library of Fighting Poland, November 1944), pp. 18-23.

[A brief biographical vignette of JC.]

1142 Potter, Norris W. "The Critical Theory and Literary Practice of Joseph Conrad." Unpublished thesis, Boston University, 1944.

1143 Roditi, Edouard. "Trick Perspectives," VIRGINIA QUARTERLY REVIEW, XX (Autumn 1944), 545-49.
[Roditi describes meeting JC in 1920 at Elstree school.]

1144 Selle, Cäcilie. "Das Wesen der Schicksalsmacht nach dem Werk Joseph Conrads und ihre Bedeutung für seine Weltbetrachtung" (The Nature of the Power of Fate According to the Work of Joseph Conrad and Its Significance for His World View). Unpublished thesis, University of Marburg, 1944.
The meaning of providence, fate, destiny, chance, and fortune in JC's works is dealt with systematically and the attitudes of the weakling, the scoundrel, the immobile person, the native, and the hero towards fate are described. For JC, man's conflict with fate is a tragic one. From this conflict only his heroes emerge as defeated victors ("besiegte Sieger"), for the meaning of fate is to be discovered in the way the heroes fight against, and bear, defeat. The struggle as such is important, not its moral implications. Because of his heroic code, JC is said to be important for the 1940s. [In German.]

1945

1145 Binsse, Harry Lorin. "Polish Picture," COMMONWEAL, XLII (27 April 1945), 43-45.
In *A Personal Record,* a classic in its "condensed, essentially sinuous style," JC was mainly concerned to explain how he came to write, especially in English, and how he came to go to sea in the British Merchant Marine. In this book, his first novel serves as a leitmotif, binding his reminiscences together as they move now backward, now forward, in time. JC is unable to explain why he was irresistibly drawn toward England and the English, but he may have felt the "insoluble antinomy" existing between the predominant climate of polite Polish society and the Ukrainian or White Russian peasantry in the region of his birth. His account of what happened to Nicholas B. during the uprising of 1863 supplies evidence for this conclusion.

1145 Brown, E. K. "James and Conrad," YALE REVIEW, N.S., XXXV (Dec 1945), 265-85.
In the later fiction of Henry James, such as THE AMBASSADORS, we don't ask questions relating to "the objective theatre" (interpersonal dramatic

contact) but questions relating to "the theatre within—in which a person's essential nature is in development, in which, so to speak, he enters into dramatic contact with himself." JC succeeds where James fails in "the theatre within." JC's "adjectival style" is "admirably suited to convey material impressions . . . , and its best effects hang upon rich accumulations." His approach to "the world within" is "highly peculiar" in most of his novels, especially *Lord Jim, Nostromo,* and *Victory.* In *Jim* he employs the device of "lens-like characters," whereas in *Nostromo* and *Victory* he uses analogy. "In THE AMBASSADORS the world is seen only through the consciousness of a single character; in *Lord Jim, Nostromo,* and *Victory* the central character is seen chiefly by the power of others—lenses or analogues." In THE WINGS OF THE DOVE, James's "reason for obliging us to withdraw to a considerable distance as the crisis approaches is quite unlike Conrad's reason for indirect presentation" in *Jim.* Except in dialogue, James's later manner is "almost always torpid and ruminative, without edge and without color." An extreme in art becomes safe when it has immense vitality. James's final novels lack as much vitality as JC's greatest novels possess.

1147 Webster, H. T. "Joseph Conrad: A Reinterpretation of Five Novels," COLLEGE ENGLISH, VII (Dec 1945), 125-34.

In his preface to *The Nigger of the Narcissus,* JC "means that the personal experience of his characters contains a general human significance" which is "inseparable from the narrative." Thus in this novel, James Wait, "with his pathetic disbelief in his mortal illness," is really "all people who can never reconcile themselves to death and never cope with it." And as "Heart of Darkness" was JC's "emotional reaction to imperialism," so was *Nostromo* "his reasoned interpretation of the same subject." The imperialists in the latter novel are "unequivocally wrong," and JC cannot imagine the active forces of opposition to them as being effectual. The characters of the novel "represent typical reactions to the familiar process of bribery and corruption" by which Costaguana is dominated; and *Nostromo* as a whole is therefore disappointing. *Chance,* on the other hand, is entirely successful. "The story is unfolded like a psychological detective story in which the problem is to catch a motive rather than a murderer," and JC paints his characters "in bold strokes which did not belong to his earlier manner." *Victory,* unlike *Chance,* "is by no means a light or pleasant novel"; it represents "the conflicts between two philosophies," the "passive pessimism" of Heyst and the "active cynicism" of Mr. Jones. Heyst "embodies the resigned acceptance of that profound pessimism which seems to have been latent in the minds of thinking men for the past century," and the three villains "form a perfect microcosm of what later emerged as fascism." Finally, *The Arrow of Gold* is "the story of a love that assumes a temporary importance over all other affairs of life; Rita suffers from an early love experience which she considers "completely sullying and unworthy." This is her relationship in common with most people, "the feeling of guilt for an act inconsistent with the self she later becomes." In sum, JC's characters "include a profusion of races and nationalities all treated in their common dignity as human beings, and his situations are concerned with the universals of human experience." Thus his best productions give him "every claim to belong in the small company of really great writers of prose fiction." [This limited and sometimes wholly doubtful interpretation is somewhat typical of more recent faltering, but gradually more perceptive analysis of JC's works.]

> **1148** Zabel, Morton Dauwen. "Joseph Conrad: Chance and Recognition," SEWANEE REVIEW, LIII (Winter 1945), 1-22; rptd as "Joseph Conrad" in ORIGENES (Havana), II (Oct 1946), 27-41; partly incorporated in "Editor's Introduction," THE PORTABLE CONRAD (1947); rptd in CRITIQUES AND ESSAYS ON MODERN FICTION 1920-1951, ed by John W. Aldridge (1952); in CRAFT AND CHARACTER (1957); and in THE ART OF JOSEPH CONRAD: A CRITICAL SYMPOSIUM, ed by Robert Wooster Stallmann (1960).

The basic theme of JC's fiction is that "his work dramatizes a hostility of forces that exists both in the conditions of practical life and in the moral constitution of man himself." "The crisis in almost every one of Conrad's novels . . . arrives when, by a stroke of accident or by an act of decision or error rising from the secret necessities of temperament, a man finds himself abruptly committed to his destiny . . . . It is the test and opportunity of fundamental selfhood, and there is no escape from it." There are two decisive dates in JC's life: June 18, 1878, when JC arrived in England with "Poland, Marseilles, Carlism, and youth . . . behind him," and 1895, "when he threw up the sea and ventured on a career in literature." JC's dramatizations of "isolation and spiritual recognition" are probably unsurpassed, except possibly by Kafka. The distinguishing characteristic of his contribution to modern fictional method is "his imposition of the processes and structures of psychological experience . . . on the form of the plot." His three most characteristic books are *Lord Jim, Chance,* and *Under Western Eyes.* But "more sheerly creative feasts of dramatization" are *The Secret Agent,* "his highest achievement in tragic irony; *Nostromo,* his most elaborate historical and political canvas; and *Victory,* his most concentrated dramatic narrative."

1946

1149 Aubry, Georges Jean-. "Introduction," *Le Miroir de la Mer* (*The Mirror of the Sea*), trans with an introduction and notes by G. Jean-Aubry (Paris: Gallimard, 1946), pp. 9-17.
[A brief biographical sketch of JC's activities during the composition of *Mirror;* French translations of letters to JC by Kipling, Galsworthy, H. G. Wells, Garnett, and Henry James.]

1150 Cranfield, Lionel. "Books in General," NEW STATESMAN AND NATION, N.S., XXXI (12 Jan 1946), 28.
JC admired and celebrated the Public School tradition. Like Henry James, he placed his highest value on the "peak of silence," the silence of restraint and of suspense. *The Shadow-Line,* a masterpiece as an essay in symbolism, shows his great improvement in style in its "greater ease and fluency, a clearer line, and lack of emphasis which exactly balances character against event in a design of great poetic power."

1151 Hoppé, A. J. "Introduction," THE CONRAD READER, ed by A. J. Hoppé (Lond: Phoenix House, 1946), pp. 1-26; rptd as THE CONRAD COMPANION (1947).
JC disliked being regarded as a "literary freak," a foreigner who knew English well, and herein lay "the complexity of his life and allegiances." Outwardly he resolved his loyalties to two countries "by siding with the normal and traditional in each land and by keeping them in separate compartments." [This introduction to a collection of JC's works consists mainly of "a condensed biography of the man," based on Aubry's LIFE AND LETTERS OF JOSEPH CONRAD (1927). It is of little value.]

1152 H[oppé], A. J. "Joseph Conrad: A Biographical Note," COLLECTED EDITION OF THE WORKS OF JOSEPH CONRAD (Lond: Dent, 1946-50) np, at the end of *Lord Jim* (1946), "Youth," "Heart of Darkness," "The End of the Tether" (1946), *Almayer's Folly* and *Tales of Unrest* (1947), *The Arrow of Gold* (1947), *The Secret Agent* (1947, in abbreviated form), *'Twixt Land and Sea* (1947), *Under Western Eyes* (1947), *Victory* (1948), *Chance* (1949), *Notes on Life and Letters* (1949), *The Rescue* (1949), *The Nigger of the Narcissus* and *Typhoon and Other Stories* (1950, in abbreviated form). [A perceptive and factually reliable two page biographical sketch.]

1153 Johnson, Fred Bates. "Bibliographical Notes: Joseph Conrad. *Suspense,*" PAPERS OF THE BIBLIOGRAPHICAL SOCIETY OF AMERICA, XL (Third Quarter 1946), 237-38.

A comparison of the printed text of a passage from part III, chapter I, first edition, of *Suspense* (Garden City, NY: Doubleday, Page, 1925) and JC's holograph corrected typescript of the same passage shows that the word *moment* in the printed text should have been *monster*.

1154 McCullough, Bruce. "The Impressionist Novel," REPRESENTATIVE ENGLISH NOVELISTS: DEFOE TO CONRAD (NY: Harper, 1946), pp. 336-48.

JC's background, especially the "experience acquired in distant lands and the foreignness of his point of view" provided "an element of strangeness" that appealed to his readers. JC, like James, rejected "a precise and scientifically documented realism"; the artist's task is stated in the preface to *The Nigger of the Narcissus*. Fellowship and its absence are essential motivating elements in JC's fiction. The effect of various barriers that separate people and cause tragedy is illustrated in *Chance, Victory,* and *Lord Jim*. "The inescapable loneliness of the individual is a recurring theme"—secrets and concealment (in "The Secret Sharer") are often the cause of isolation. To convey a sense "of the elusive and inexplicable character of life" JC developed a technique akin to impressionism in art, particularly the method of discontinuity which is evident in all arts and William James's and Bergson's description of the mind. JC, too, "sees his subject as something shifting and somewhat illusory." The technique of presenting life "in isolated and fleeting glimpses" supports JC's view of human life and the artist's role of searcher "for truth in moments of vision." *Jim* illustrates JC's concern with "human truth" beneath circumstance and moral values. JC, unlike James, calls attention to the act of narration; like Defoe, JC "achieves an air of authenticity by making the act of narration itself appear plausible." Marlow is used best when he is most involved in the story; the scenes after Marlow and Jim are separated "are less convincing."

1155 Morris, Robert L. "The Classical Reference in Conrad's Fiction," COLLEGE ENGLISH, VII (March 1946), 312-18.

Current readers of JC's works realize that the existence of heroes like Jim, Kurtz, and Heyst is dependent on the existence of a Marlow or a Davidson and that taken together the two groups constitute the "we," which for JC is to be defined as "the civilized" who "support their unsteady gleaming in a darkness best described as 'barbarism,'" a present barbarism, "a time of war and revolution," reminiscent of that of the ancient past. In *Lord Jim*, "Heart of Darkness," and *Victory*, Jim, Kurtz, and Heyst are "inheritors of romantic illusions"; but Marlow and Davidson in some degree recognize and understand the contrast between these civilized men and "the barbarism that is about and within them." [This article is typical of several attempts to relate JC's work with the turbulence of the twentieth century.]

1156 Routh, H. V. ENGLISH LITERATURE AND IDEAS IN THE TWENTIETH CENTURY (Lond: Methuen, 1946); 2nd ed (Lond: Methuen; NY: Longmans, Green, 1948), pp. 19-25, 43, 45, 69, 91, 147.

After 1906, JC's work became "not less powerful, but less confident, and less inspired by the sea." His twenty years of sea life revealed to him the central problem of human nature, "the tension between our higher and lower selves." JC was aloof and objective in characterizations, making them seem real by placing them against a background "in tune with their behaviorism." JC's mood in writing was so free from illusions that he sometimes appeared disillusioned. "If he relapsed into irony it was as a last resource, because even his best characters disappointed him . . . . That is why [he] could seldom stop at the right place." He tried to include all traits and details, not allowing the reader to contribute to the effect. "Kipling, Conrad, Wells, Shaw, Bennett, de la Mare, Masefield, Forster, and Yeats stand in the forefront of Edwardian literature because they showed the educated reader how to think out his own immediate affairs in terms of other people." Yet these humanists used nineteenth century methods.

1157 T., R. "Notes on Joseph Conrad," NATIONAL EDUCATION (Wellington, New Zealand), XXVIII (April 1946), 120.
[General biographical appreciation.]

1947

1158 Aubry, Georges Jean-. "La jeunesse de Conrad" (Conrad's Youth), REVUE DE PARIS, XLV (May 1947), 92-107.
[This article is nearly the same as chapter II ("Jours de France," pp. 52-71) and chapter III ("Jeunesse," pp. 72-93) of Aubry's VIE DE CONRAD (Paris: Gallimard, 1947). The REVUE DE PARIS version of the two chapters is shorter, the quantity of quotations from JC's letters to his Uncle Thaddeus having been considerably reduced. There are almost no changes in sentences which appear in both versions; there are, however, some changes in paragraphing.] [In French.]

1159 Aubry, Georges Jean-. VIE DE CONRAD (The Life of Conrad) (Paris: Gallimard, 1947); trans by Helen Sebba as THE SEA DREAMER: A DEFINITIVE BIOGRAPHY OF JOSEPH CONRAD (Garden City, NY: Doubleday, Lond: Allen and Unwin, 1947).
[This "definitive" biography of JC attempts to recount "the successive phases" of JC's life "in the precise and detached fashion of a ship's log," to

"set down the indisputable facts" which can be "supported by proof." Aubry believes that the works "show, along with their authenticity, the force and permanence of the impressions that gave birth to them" and that the story of JC's life "casts penetrating light upon the conditions and character of Conrad's artistic creation." Practically no support or source other than JC's own statements is given for many serious conclusions, e.g., that the "facts" recounted in *The Arrow of Gold* "may be considered true." This biography, neither "definitive" nor critical, is now superseded by Jocelyn Baines's JOSEPH CONRAD: A CRITICAL BIOGRAPHY (1959).]

1160 Becker, May Lamberton. "Read This One First," SCHOLASTIC, XXXI (9 Oct 1937), 22.

The narrative of *Lord Jim* is confusing to the beginner; *Nostromo* is more straightforward in plot and thus a better introduction to JC. [Brief and superficial advice to "young folks" on why to read JC and which works to read first.]

1161 Churchill, R. C. "Conrad in School," JOURNAL OF EDUCATION (Lond), LXXIX (March 1947), 130, 132.

JC should be in the English curriculum immediately after Dickens and Shakespeare. His own stories of youthful adventure such as "Youth," "Typhoon" and *The Nigger of the Narcissus* have particular appeal for boys.

1162 Clarke, David Waldo. "Joseph Conrad," MODERN ENGLISH WRITERS (Lond: Longmans, Green, 1947), pp. 18-24.

[General biographical and critical sketch, emphasizing the lonely suffering in JC's works.]

1163 Crankshaw, Edward. "Joseph Conrad and To-day," NATIONAL REVIEW, CXXVIII (March 1947), 224-30.

Since JC's almost forgotten works are being made available again [in 1947], a new generation will be able to read not only the early novels, with all their "embroidery" and "impressions" but also the "supreme specimens" of "elaborate and crowded pictures of the world we inhabit today" (such as *Nostromo, Chance, Under Western Eyes, The Secret Agent, Victory,* and "Heart of Darkness"), a world where man, like many of JC's heroes, finds himself in a "moral jungle," lacking faith to confront a cruel, inimical universe. The long neglect of this novelist who is extremely relevant to modern life is caused by the fact that many readers, intoxicated by the writer's qualities as a virtuoso, have failed to ask what his works are about; to JC's inability to explain clearly his intentions; and to the rootlessness of many of his characters. JC, recalling his origins on the "great Eurasian plain," was forced eventually to employ a new technique for the novel in order to bring "infinity into the streets, the compact and blinkered societies of Western civilization." And in reading his stories, we find no answers to our questions: JC was not a philosopher but "an artist and a novelist." Not knowing himself the answers to the overwhelming situations in which he placed his characters, he evolved "simple principles of conduct in a spirit that was mainly negative." This was only a beginning, but "an all-important beginning, since it is nothing less than the transference of the antinomy of good and evil to the secular level." [Writing before the current revival of interest in JC's works, Crankshaw, along with several wrong and inadequate judgments, goes far in recognizing their real value.]

1164 "Exertions in the Deep," TIME, L (29 Sept 1947), 107-8.
THE PORTABLE CONRAD (1947), edited by Morton Dauwen Zabel, is excellent for its selections and its critical introduction. JC in particular is notable for his simultaneous mastery of the art of fiction and his struggle to tell the truth.

1165 Farrelly, John. "Worth Reprinting," NEW REPUBLIC, CXVII (27 Oct 1947), 31.
In addition to creative works, in THE PORTABLE CONRAD (1947) Zabel has included excerpts from JC's critical writings and selections from the letters. There are copious notes by the editor and an elegiac introduction containing biographical and critical materials. *Almayer's Folly* and *Victory* are also reviewed. The richness of work is not easily estimated.

1166 Follett, Wilson. "Joseph Conrad, Hip-Pocket Size," NEW YORK TIMES BOOK REVIEW, 19 Oct 1947, p. 5.
THE PORTABLE CONRAD (1947), edited by Morton Dauwen Zabel, shows that JC's "special relevance to 1947 is that of a man who never forgot that the values of our organized conspiracy against nature rest ultimately on a few simple ideas—and that none among these is more important than the idea of fidelity. So he asserted outright. By the conditions of his strange personal adventure it was given him to understand, not only the tragic moral history of all infidelity, but also the host of ways in which abiding fidelity and love itself can wear at times the desperate face of betrayal. This also he said; and it is the reason why the stories that he told will always be even greater in their meaning than in their events—the reason of reasons why he cannot be outgrown."

1167 Freund, Philip. HOW TO BECOME A LITERARY CRITIC (NY: Beechurst P, 1947); new rvd ed as THE ART OF READING THE NOVEL (NY: Collier Books, 1965), pp. 33, 47, 51-52, 54-55, 64, 89-100, 101, 103-5, 119, 144, 148, 154, 158, 160, 170-80, 195-99, 214-17, 226-27, 229, 231-34, 248, 250-52, 260, 275, 282, 293-94, 296, 298-99, 311, 317, 319-20, 322-27, 331-33, 345, 397.

JC was often skeptical, but he would not permit in his canon either defeatism or withdrawal although he does come to grips with these themes in *Victory, Lord Jim,* and *Nostromo.* He faced Nature's defects and made them the foundation of beauty. He was a romantic, and yet in "A Smile of Fortune," "Because of the Dollars," "Typhoon," and "Heart of Darkness," he evidences a romanticism tinged with irony. The depth of his irony and the heights of his romantic affirmation are seen in *Victory.* This duality is also seen in the characters of Martin Decoud in *Nostromo* and Jim in *Jim.* His preface to *The Nigger of the Narcissus* is one of the most influential essays on literary craftsmanship; he wanted to find a way of telling a story in which familiarity between author and reader would be diminished but with a technique that would yet be "aimed essentially at the intimacy of personal conduct." In "Youth," "Heart of Darkness," and *Jim,* JC experiments with point of view. He presents characters much more fully than Henry James could with the limited third person point of view. He carried his experiment further in novels after *Jim,* as in *Nostromo,* where he uses a naive narrator, and in *Under Western Eyes,* which is narrated partly in the third person, partly via a diary transposed into third person, and partly through comments of others acquainted with the main character, Razumov. Characters are revealed through a chain of rumors, associations, and impressions in *Chance,* a novel which at last brought him popular success, but which is a lesser work because he pushed his device too far. JC also experimented with time (the unchronological narration). He reveals other pertinent facts bit by bit. Jim then is viewed from different vantage points in time—past, present, and future. He gives *Jim* organic form, first by providing tonal unity through Marlow and then by using mixed chronology which tends to weave the separate parts together.

1168 Guerard, Albert, Jr. "Joseph Conrad," Direction, I (1947), 7-92; pub separately (NY: New Directions, 1947).

Three levels of appeal are found in "great writers who are also popular": sentimental conceptions and use of melodrama, pervasive style and structure and narrative energy, and "meditation and concealed conflict." Critics have failed to read the prefaces cautiously, and JC has remained "a latter-day Walter Scott," read, but imperfectly understood. He seemed at times to understand that "his were triumphs not of dramatic suspense but of moral suspense: of the slow working outward of fatal deficiencies, of the spectacle of character in action." The "secret of his art" is found in subjects of moral or psychological interest. His best works came between 1897 and 1904. His "most startling loss" in the later years was "control over the elementary resources of the language," a "failure of imagination" primarily. The problem is "to define the relevance of Conrad's best, experimentally traditional as it is, to our own literary needs."

JC's world of exiles and uprooted persons is doubtless traceable to his own wanderings. There is a claustrophobia in all the Malayan books, important not for its causes but for its effects. The jungle symbolizes the "savage and the subconscious mind." "The Secret Sharer" is the only story to study the preconscious and the subconscious explicitly, and with "extensive symbolist techniques." JC was interested in "complex temptations" and "abnormal impulses which threaten the justifiably normal mind." His approach "to sexual difficulties" has seemed justifiably tepid to some reviewers. In *Chance,* however, sexual repression is a major theme; and there are fairly subtle treatments of the subject in the works of 1910-1920 (*'Twixt Land and Sea, Chance, Victory,* and *The Arrow of Gold*).

JC's plots seem designed "to exhibit our essential character in action." His is "a truly classical pessimism," but with little reliance on reason. He sees that "the lust for power and the lust for irresponsibility" ("the universal longing for peace") are identical. Against these threats to the self, JC "can throw up only the barrier of semi-military ethics . . . and as a last resort, the stoic's awareness of his own plight." His method "is to observe from as many points in space and time as possible the working out in action of fairly simple human traits. Sometimes he analyzes his characters in lucid expository paragraphs, or employs an observer with Marlow's speculative mind." More often he endows his characters "with highly individual mannerisms" and with "a more than lifelike simplicity of motive and with abnormally coherent impulses." His handling of time does not, as it does with Sterne, Proust, and Huxley, illustrate "philosophical conceptions"; his aim was "to converge on a single and isolated 'fact' from as many directions . . . as possible." For him "moral life is an exercise in progressive understanding, an adventure through ambiguous appearance." The key is "solitude"—and solitude "creates a vicious circle, within which the victim tramps: egotism isolates the individual and isolation intensifies his egotism. The deteriorating effect of isolation is visible and swift." All that "limits the 'original man'" is removed. Skepticism may remain, "the peculiarly modern malady," as JC sees it; and the stoic temperament refusing to surrender has "only two alternatives. It may elevate inaction into a principle, and look with detachment on the meaningless spectacle, or it may act as though life did matter, and construct a tentative and desperate humanism." While isolation is immoral, "intervention is certain to corrupt— or to find itself corrupted by absurd fatality." For JC, a "classical pessimism is more consoling than neutral behaviorism . . . because it posits the existence of a 'human nature'" and gives "meaning to life."

1169 Johnson, Fred Bates. "Notes on Conrad's Finance," INDIANA QUARTERLY FOR BOOKMEN, III (Jan 1947), 27-30.

Although it appears that JC, in his letters to such people as Edward Garnett, H. G. Wells, John Galsworthy, G. B. Shaw, and Richard Curle, had the unconscious thought that they might be published, in those to J. B. Pinker, his literary agent from 1899 to 1919, he displayed "the unvarnished truth of his harassed current living" of his "lean years," 1899 to 1909. Unrecognized by the public "in a substantial way," JC was in debt to Pinker for ten years, but upon recognition by the public he repaid his benefactor in full. Three letters of 1903 to Pinker, published for the first time, support this conclusion. According to an unpublished letter of Richard Curle, JC's relationship with Pinker was "always honourable and highly satisfactory to both parties."

1170 Liddell, Robert. A TREATISE ON THE NOVEL (Lond: Cape, 1947), pp. 63, 110-11, 130-32, 134.

JC recognized the need for a contemplative life for a writer, but he objected to being a mere spectator. False criticism that distinguishes between "style" and "subject-matter" has "exalted Conrad as a painter of sunsets and tropical landscapes" to the neglect of his dramatic powers. Three passages quoted from JC's writings may be considered *loci classici* for the novelist's art.

1171 Mégroz, R. L. "A Conrad Setting," TIMES LITERARY SUPPLEMENT (Lond), 15 Nov 1947, p. 591.

"Mr. Roberts is probably quite right [in that Tanjong Redeb, not Bulungan, is the original of "Sambir" in *Almayer's Folly*], though I cannot think that this kind of topography has much significance to Conrad's art." [Reply to John H. Roberts, ibid., 18 Nov 1947, p. 577.]

1172 Oliver, H. J. "A Note on Joseph Conrad," TIMES LITERARY SUPPLEMENT (Lond), 6 Sept 1947, p. 451.

Despite JC's protest that he could not remember reading it, JC employed incidents and details from "A Very Strange Bed" by Wilkie Collins in "The Inn of the Two Witches." "Only the width of his own experience prevented" JC's using this "Shakespearian method" more often.

1173 *"The Portable Conrad,"* BULLETIN FROM VIRGINIA KIRKUS'S BOOKSHOP SERVICE, XV (1 July 1947), 349.

This collection of JC's works is disappointing in omissions but a useful first volume for new readers. The introduction is excellent. [Brief note.]

1174 Redman, Ben Ray. "New Editions," SATURDAY REVIEW OF LITERATURE, XXX (15 Nov 1947), 30.

THE PORTABLE CONRAD (1947), edited by Morton Dauwen Zabel, is mainly to be commended; especially good is Zabel's introduction.

1175 Roberts, John H. "A Conrad Setting," Times Literary Supplement (Lond), 8 Nov 1947, p. 577.

Tanjong Redeb, not Bulungan, is the original of "Sambir" in *Almayer's Folly*. [See reply by R. L. Mégroz, ibid., 15 Nov 1947, p. 591.]

1176 Root, E. Merrill. Frank Harris (NY: Odyssey P, 1947), 136-37.

"Harris set Wells to reviewing novels. Thus Wells discovered Joseph Conrad, in his sympathetic and brilliant review of *Almayer's Folly*." [Purely incidental on JC.]

1177 Shklovskii, V. "Chuzhaia loshad" (Another Man's Horse), Literaturnaia Gazeta, No. 8 (1947), 2.

[A review of "The Duel."] [In Russian.]

1178 Tindall, William York. Forces in Modern British Literature (NY: Knopf, 1947), rptd (NY: Random House, Vintage Books, 1956), pp. 22, 59-61, 105, 140-42, 144, 189, 192-94, 201, 205, 209, 211, 218, 287-89, 292.

JC's political conservatism is what one might expect, although he was not, like Kipling, an imperialist. Lord Jim's enterprise in Patusan shows British imperialism at its best; Gould's silver in *Nostromo* shows it to less advantage. JC considered man's consciousness his tragedy. Indifferent or malevolent nature may, by testing men, increase their moral stature and discover courage, honor, and integrity. Morality, an illusion, Stein's "destructive element," is man's noblest "answer" to natural law. The irony of the "glorious defeats" in *Lord Jim* and *Victory* reveals JC's divided mind. Incapable of thought, moralists like Lord Jim, Lingard of *The Rescue,* and Nostromo, brood; and JC, "wisely disdaining analysis, broods over their brooding." Marlow is "a kind of detective of conscience," whose own consciousness is the scene of several important stories and novels. Marlow's impressions of reality distort it, however, before passing it on to the reader; and before Marlow receives them, they have been distorted by the temperaments and memories of persons who have reported them to him. JC has produced symbolist novels in which the burden is carried by image, pattern, and rhythm, with emergent symbols like the forest in "Heart of Darkness," the "nightmarish" city in *The Secret Agent,* the silver mine in *Nostromo,* and the island, the volcano, the "hopeless" pier, the paternal portrait, and the three intruders in *Victory*. "Essentially inexplicable," JC's vision of what confronts man gives us a way of apprehending it. [Tindall delves deeply into JC's mind and art, and carefully relates his work to that of other modern writers.]

1179 Wright, Walter F. "How Conrad Tells a Story," Prairie Schooner, XXI (Fall 1947), 290-95.

In *Lord Jim,* Marlow represents the best maritime tradition and provides a basis for evaluating Jim's conduct. Marlow's quest for truth and his interest in Jim fuse so that Marlow's search will provide the total picture of Jim's situation. Marlow's way of piecing together Jim's story and its implications makes for artistic verisimilitude and reader interest. Marlow's relationship to Jim's story provides the "necessary perspective" and focus.

1180 Zabel, Morton Dauwen. "Africa and the Congo: Editor's Note," THE PORTABLE CONRAD (NY: Viking P, 1947), pp. 455-58.
Although JC's Congo journey of 1890 cost him dearly, it gave him a subject for "Heart of Darkness," it brought about a confirmation of his imagination and temperament, and it helped him to become "a master of the tragedy of moral desolation and defeated egoism which is one of the salient themes of modern literature."

1181 Zabel, Morton Dauwen. "Editor's Introduction," THE PORTABLE CONRAD (NY: Viking P, 1947), pp. 1-47.
Except for his private letters, JC "spoke with his full voice" only as an imaginative writer. Since his talent was not instinctively dramatic, nor naturally inventive, nor highly inspired, he was driven by a compulsion to write that often tortured and baffled him. But he added to English fiction, during a time of "triumphant journalism and commercialized banalities," an "exotic force of language and a passion of moral insight." He needed the distance of irony, as in *The Secret Agent,* the distance of history, as in *Nostromo,* the distance of dramatic structure and objectification, as in *Victory,* or an intermediary voice, like Marlow, in "Heart of Darkness," *Under Western Eyes,* or *Chance,* in order to be at his best. JC's contribution to the methods of modern fiction was his imposition of "the processes and structure" of the moral experience on the form of the plot; consistent throughout his work is the figure who is caught up in circumstances which enforce self-discovery or the discovery of reality or truth, as with Razumov, Heyst, Lord Jim, and many other characters. The divided man—the soul and its shadow—becomes a metaphor of society and humanity; love, a sense of honor, or the obligation of duty forces the individual out of his isolation toward external standards of value. In his craftsmanship, JC belongs with Flaubert, James, Joyce, and Gide. His nature was poised between the world of fantasies and impossible desires and that of "brutal facts," but he refused to allow the form to falsify the situation or the psychic and moral conditions which it entailed. The principle of honor binds the private agony of a JC hero to the outer world of values and proofs. Technical devices such as the time-shift, the use of narrators, the repeated motif or incident, and the exhaustive analysis of events became for JC a method of exploring sensibility and instinct. The essential JC knew the cruelest

humiliations of the spirit and spared neither himself nor his heroes the humility of "standing alone with fate, in mortal enmity and embrace with the Self that commits us to the one destiny that is inescapable." JC's best works are *Agent, Eyes, Chance,* and *Victory* [an evaluation that is generally unacceptable today]. JC was a "poet in fiction" who takes us more deeply into the "agony of the creative process" than do most writers. [Excellent in 1947 for its overview of JC and his achievement, this essay, although somewhat dated now, is still valuable.]

1182 Zabel, Morton Dauwen. "England and the World: Editor's Note," THE PORTABLE CONRAD (NY: Viking P, 1947), pp. 111-14.

From his boyhood, JC was drawn to England, especially by his love of English literature and language. His "conscious dignity of an acquired speech" and his "idealizing reverence" for British tradition and institutions may have hidden, however, the fact that his "secret and deepest loyalties" always lay with Poland.

1183 Zabel, Morton Dauwen. "Europe, Asia, and the East: Editor's Note," THE PORTABLE CONRAD (NY: Viking P, 1947), pp. 605-8.

From *Almayer's Folly* (1895) to *The Rescue* (1920), the East remained "a recurring presence" in JC's fiction. The Eastern islands were really an exile's "transplantations" from Polish history, stories in which JC turned from society to psychology to explore "a man's intrigue with himself," as in *Lord Jim* and "The Secret Sharer."

1184 Zabel, Morton Dauwen. "On Life and Letters: Editor's Note," THE PORTABLE CONRAD (NY: Viking P, 1947), pp. 701-4.

Except for *The Mirror of the Sea* and *A Personal Record,* JC's letters contain the most intimate and revealing personal record of his personality and labors. In these and in passages of commentary in his fiction, JC states his literary ideals and includes his insistent theme, "the condition of life."

1185 Zabel, Morton Dauwen. "Poland and the East: Editor's Note," THE PORTABLE CONRAD (NY: Viking P, 1947), pp. 55-57.

[Briefly places JC and his works in relation to his Polish background.]

1186 Zabel, Morton Dauwen (ed). THE PORTABLE CONRAD (NY: Viking P, 1947, and later printings with slight changes).

[Contents, abstracted separately, all under Zabel (1947): "A Conrad Chronology, with a Bibliography of His Principal Works"; "Poland and the Past: Editor's Note"; "England and the World: Editor's Note"; "A Tale of the Sea: Editor's Note"; "Africa and the Congo: Editor's Note"; "Europe, Asia, and the East: Editor's Note"; "On Life and Letters: Editor's Note"; and "Bibliographical Note."]

1187 Zabel, Morton Dauwen. "A Tale of the Sea: Editor's Note," THE PORTABLE CONRAD (NY: Viking P, 1947), pp. 289-91.

The Nigger of the Narcissus remains, if not JC's greatest or most ambitious book, "one of his most perfectly realized and poetically conceived works."

1948

1188 Banyard, Grace. "Books on the Table: Oh to be in England —then," FORTNIGHTLY REVIEW, N.S. CLXIII (April 1948), 299-300.

JC was a contributor to the first, 1908 number, of THE ENGLISH REVIEW. [Review of Douglas Goldring's THE LAST PRE-RAPHAELITE (1948).]

1189 Erné, Nino. "Joseph Conrad und die Prosa der männlichen Einsamkeit" (Joseph Conrad and the Prose of Masculine Loneliness), GEISTIGE WELT, III (Dec 1948), 118-24.

Twentieth-century literature mainly deals with masculine loneliness. After the decline of the social order, the only choice was battle or flight. Two writers (JC and Hamsun) who could believe in neither the old nor the new order, in neither the Christian religion nor material progress, became the presagers of the "Lost Generation." They believed only in the wildness of earth and man's spirit; they believed in the power of raw danger-ridden life and placed man on the razor's edge between life and death. This allowed two possibilities: the right of might, or responsibility bought at the price of certain extinction [discussion of Hamsun's place in the light of these extreme poles]. JC in *Lord Jim,* however, reveals that he retains faith in man, if not in the community.

Jim contains the essence of JC's worldview and is a modern version of Don Quixote's tragedy, of the discrepancy between dream and reality, ideality and life. But unlike Quixote, Jim discovers his courage in death. JC's victims are victors, his victors are victims. They are true to themselves at the moment reality buries them. JC the seaman attained a yardstick and values from his experience in the small world of a ship. Despite reality, JC believed in the possibility of a dignified living and dying. [Relates JC's autobiography to such fictions as "Heart of Darkness" and *Jim.*]

JC has yet to reach the high point of his effect. Both JC and Hamsun, however different in some respects, have much in common with such Lost Generation writers as Hemingway, in their sense of isolation and at the same time their sense of the need for discipline. Thomas Wolfe and Thornton Wilder, like JC and Galsworthy, also bear the portrait of Don Quixote in their hearts. Kurt Heuser's DIE REISE DES INNERE (The Journey of the Psyche) reveals him to be a natural son of JC, as is Antoine de Saint-Exupéry in WIND, SAND AND STARS. However, the progenitors of JC find a joy and lust for life of which the turn of the century was hardly capable. For Ernst Junger the war was the pitiless testing ground, the boundary line between life and death, as for Saint-Exupéry it was the plane and for JC the ship. Junger, however, carried the theme of isolation and the view into the abyss of nothingness the furthest. [An interesting and suggestive attempt to relate JC to the post–World War I writers.] [In German.]

>**1190** Goldring, Douglas. THE LAST PRE-RAPHAELITE, A RECORD OF THE LIFE AND WRITING OF FORD MADOX FORD (Lond. MacDonald, 1948), pp. ix, 60-90, 93-95, 100, 105, 106, 112-16, 124-28, 133-35, 137-43, 148-50, 153, 160, 162, 180, 182, 186, 187, 213, 235, 240-44, 256; rptd as TRAINED FOR GENIUS (NY: Dutton, 1949).

Although Garnett introduced Ford to JC via a manuscript of *Almayer's Folly,* the two did not meet until years later. Ford's appreciation for JC's talent always came before his feeling for him, although it was warm and friendly. JC found in Ford, more than in any other man of the time, a kindred spirit. Their views of art and their appreciation of French literature were identical. H. G. Wells, who knew both JC and Ford, felt that Ford helped greatly to "English" JC and his idiom. [Goldring reviews the collaboration on *The Inheritors* and *Romance.*]

>**1191** Guerard, Albert, Jr. "The Heart of Conrad," NATION (NY), CLXVI (3 Jan 1948), 21-22.

In THE PORTABLE CONRAD (1947), Zabel's introduction is "one of the finest critical surveys yet written" and his selections are almost entirely from JC's best work. Zabel "is the first critic to have allowed Conrad's sense of moral isolation its proper importance," but "the suicides of Heyst and Decoud are . . . 'recognitions' . . . that the world and the self are no longer tolerable." Even Lord Jim "confuses innocence with honor at the last proud moment of his life," and "the dreaming isolation of Lingard, Conrad's most representative hero, remains incorrigible and uncombated." The symbolism in these stories is different from that in *Nostromo,* which is "modern, experimental, and devoted to multiple meanings." "Heart of Darkness" and "The Secret Sharer" are "voyages through the distrusted secret self." JC left his "distinguishing mark" through "the exploration of self," not through "the ironic criticism of his world." [An unusually perceptive review.]

>**1192** Halle, Louis J., Jr. "Joseph Conrad: An Enigma Decoded," SATURDAY REVIEW OF LITERATURE, XXXI (22 May 1948), 7-8, 32-33.

"Heart of Darkness" is a story which "misleads the reader [from the outset] as to his [JC's] subject." JC seems a sphinx-like author. [The enigma is a straw man, and its "decoding" hence unsatisfactory. The characteristic student misspelling "Marlowe" is used throughout.]

1193 Kettle, Arnold. "The Greatness of Joseph Conrad," MODERN QUARTERLY, N.S. III (Summer 1948), 63-81; mostly absorbed in "Joseph Conrad: *Nostromo* (1904)," AN INTRODUCTION TO THE NOVEL (Lond: Hutchinson's University Library, 1953), II, 67-81.

The greatness of JC, the finest British novelist of the past sixty years, "stems from his grappling honestly, manfully, and unneurotically with the real problem of his world, and that is inextricably bound up with . . . his awareness of the underlying social movement of his time." Greatness is seen in his descriptive power, moral interest, artistic control, and especially in his understanding of the social nature of man. His "moral discoveries" are never really defined, and he does not usually succeed when he attempts to define them. JC and Kipling were the only two major English writers to recognize and grapple with imperialism—a central theme in JC's works—when it was most rampant. "The horror! The horror!" of "Heart of Darkness" is imperialism. Imperialism is also important in *Nostromo,* the main theme of which is the corrupting influence of the mine. Nostromo's tragedy is that he has no true sense of social movement and of the overall purpose of life. JC, unlike Hemingway, succeeds in the imaginative discovery that "every man is . . . a part of the main." *The Secret Agent* and *Under Western Eyes,* concerned with anarchy and social revolution, demonstrate JC's intensity and control of the novel medium, but are limited in value, because JC does not effectively "sense" revolutionary activity. JC's nightmare of alienation and his emphasis on "guilt and betrayal, loneliness and terror" is thus a result of his sanity and his "obstinate insistence on the social nature of man." [A perceptive essay.]

1194 McDonald, P. A. "Conrad's *Otago,*" SEA BREEZES: THE SHIP LOVERS' DIGEST, N.S. V (Jan-June 1948), 303.

[A letter to the editor requesting photographs of the *Otago* as she looked fully rigged and including a photograph of the ship's hulk as it then appeared in the Derwent, Australia, ship graveyard near Hobart. For more recent news on the hull of the *Otago,* see ENGLISH LITERATURE IN TRANSITION, XIII: 1 (1970), ii-iii.]

1195 Orvis, Mary Burchard. THE ART OF WRITING FICTION (NY: Prentice-Hall, 1948), pp. 83-85.

JC successfully uses long "plateau passages" to prepare for contrasting scenes of dramatic tragedy, as in *Lord Jim.*

1196 Parton, Herwig. "Prosawerks Joseph Conrads und John Masefields. Eine Untersuchung unter Besonderer Berücksichtigung

Ihrer Kunstlerischen Gestaltung" (The Proseworks of Joseph Conrad and John Masefield. A Study with Special Emphasis on Techniques). Unpublished thesis, University of Vienna, 1948.

A comparison of Masefield and JC as persons, novelists, and thinkers reveals many differences which are explained with reference to the Polish-British dualism in JC and Masefield's Englishness. [In German.]

1197 Stallman, Robert Wooster. "Life, Art, and 'The Secret Sharer,'" FORMS OF MODERN FICTION, ed by William Van O'Connor (Minneapolis: University of Minnesota P, 1948), pp. 229-42; differently developed in "Conrad and 'The Secret Sharer,'" ACCENT, IX (Spring 1949), 131-33; and again as "Analysis," in THE ART OF MODERN FICTION, ed by Robert W. Stallman and Ray B. West, Jr. (NY: Rinehart, 1949), pp. 490-98.

Although JC wrote "The Secret Sharer" to resolve a personal crisis, that personal crisis is not at all identical with the imagined crisis confronting the captain in the story. JC's characters, settings, and incidents, however, are based to some extent on life; hence there is a personal basis for his art even if his art remains impersonal. "The Secret Sharer" is the "microcosm" of JC's imaginative work in plot, structure, and theme: the plot of a double conflict, external and internal; the structure of a moment of crisis in which the individual is put to a test of his selfhood; and the theme of lack of spiritual unity and moral or aesthetic isolation. In addition to the psychological and moral meaning of this work, the aesthetic meaning, the allegory of the spiritual disunity of the isolated artist, is important; and this theme is both impersonal, applying as it does to the artist in general, and personal, representing JC's own crisis as an artist in creating his art. Both the captain and the artist successfully pass the test imposed upon them: the captain measures up to his vision of "Ideal Selfhood" and the artist measures up to "that ideal of artistic integrity, that ideal conception of one's esthetic conscience" which every artist holds secretly for himself.

1198 Wright, Walter Francis. "Critical Discussion of Joseph Conrad's Novels." Unpublished thesis, University of Nebraska, 1948.

1949

1199 Breit, Harvey. "Talk with Christopher Morley," NEW YORK TIMES BOOK REVIEW, 31 July 1949, p. 13.

In *The Shadow-Line,* JC was "disastrously honest" with himself and the reader.

1200 Ekelof, Gunnar. "Kamratskap Mellan Man" (Comradeship Among Men), BONNIERS LITTERARA MAGASIN (Stockholm), XVIII (1949), 639-40.

The new volume of translations into Swedish, translated by Louis Renner (Stockholm: Forum, 1949), contains three novellas: *The Shadow-Line,* "Youth," and "Heart of Darkness." *Shadow-Line* is in JC's traditional style. The picture of the tropic calm followed by a storm is reminiscent of "Typhoon." In "Youth" JC shows himself a humorist in fantastic and grotesque situations. "Heart of Darkness" is reminiscent of the film TRADER HORN—the same grandiose retinue and the same bizarre encounter with a white queen (in JC she is black, but equally terrifying) which makes TRADER HORN an ethnological fantasy. In a way, JC's tale gives the same impression of sick doom; actually, Kurtz is just a Eurafrican troll. Because of JC's versatility, he is able to satisfy the simplest and most adventure-hungry and also the most fastidious reader. He gives conventional details, sometimes even in bad taste, but he can also present enormous panoramas, both oceanic and psychological, the latter best when women are omitted. *Romance,* translated by Nils Fredricson (Stockholm: Faulkrantz and Gumaelius, 1949), despite collaboration with Ford Madox Ford, bears JC's mark. The hero resembles the rather naive heroes of Trelawney, Marryat, and R. L. Stevenson. JC is at his best when he lets the strength of the weather take care of the course of events and does not try to write according to a stereotype of what can or should happen. Aristocrat and anarchist, JC considers politics dirty and turns away from them, but he has lost his sense of proportion to such a degree that his politics and intrigues become rather one-sided. [In Swedish.]

1201 Ekelof, Gunnar. "Med Stort C" (With a Capital C), BONNIERS LITTERARA MAGASIN (Stockholm), XVIII (1949), 152-53.

Only in Faulkner can one find Negro psychology comparable to that depicted in *The Nigger of the Narcissus,* in a volume including "Typhoon" now translated into Swedish by Louis Renner (Stockholm: Forum, 1948). Molière's sick man was only a cultural phenomenon, while JC's Negro, who simulates his own real sickness, is a magic, primitive man, illustrating the actual complexity of primitivism. JC is indeed something of a psychological mystic. His one-sided portrait of the beachcomber officer in "Typhoon" appears simple, but the psychology of this man lies on another plane than that of objective description. JC's novels must be understood as poems, Greek dramas of fate, and it is their action, where men are mouthpieces for the gods, which is the real psychological lesson. The convictions of his characters are often reasonable and irrational at the same time. The unyielding Captain MacWhirr in "Typhoon" must be understood as a buoy to which the author anchors the convictions that lie beneath the novel's stormy surface. JC condemns force which appears at its most unpleasant in Donkin in *Nigger* and the new mate in "Typhoon." Because JC hated the politician bitterly, he left this type of character relatively undefined, but it comes through like a Giotto fresco. The Sea and Time, Neptune and Chronos, are the strongest elements in JC's world, and he would not be the poet he is if he were not simultaneously obvious and oblique. [In Swedish.]

1202 Haugh, Robert F. "Joseph Conrad and Revolution," COLLEGE ENGLISH, X (Feb 1949), 273-77.

JC's revolutionary novels, especially *Under Western Eyes,* are clearly adapted "to an inquiry into the meaning of the sea for Conrad." There is a strong resemblance between "the currents of revolution" in this novel and "the forces of the sea" as they affect men in *Lord Jim*. Just as the sea tested "the purposes of men" in *Jim,* so did "the sea of revolutionary belief and activity" test "the moral purposes" of Razumov in *Eyes*. But there are also differences between the two novels: Jim thought that he had been untrue to "the principles of the British merchant marine as well as those romantic shades of conduct in which he moved" whereas Razumov thought that "he was being true to the only precepts that meant anything to him—the traditions of his fatherland." Razumov's dilemma was "more devious than Jim's": he had "the mature sense of being trapped by his own nature as well as by circumstance." The later novel "fulfils" the earlier one and has "greater breadth" than *Jim*.

1203 Hewitt, Douglas. "Joseph Conrad's Hero: 'Fidelity' or 'The Choice of Nightmares,'" CAMBRIDGE JOURNAL, II (Aug 1949), 684-91.

Although the concept of "Faith in Fidelity" may be the key to *Chance* or *Victory* or *The Rover,* "it is soon obscured in 'Heart of Darkness' and other early works, where he [JC] treats of ideas and themes which are far from simple and to which such naive moralizing is irrelevant." Most of JC's early works are "profoundly disturbing" because the central characters are confronted with "that side of us" which is not clearly understood and because of "a sense of inadequacy or guilt which comes from this confrontation." Good examples are found in "Heart of Darkness," "Youth," and "The End of the Tether," in the first of which Marlow at last "seems to have a choice between the 'pilgrims' and Kurtz," the "choice of nightmares."

Since JC had an equivocal attitude towards "the emotions upon which men erect systems of belief and behaviour," with "an awareness of the darkness" which exists in "the unexplored country of the mind," as well as in the Congo basin, he must have had difficulty in reposing his confidence in "fidelity" or in any other simple virtue. But after about 1909 the tension is no longer found in his work. The harm caused by this change appears most clearly in his first popular success, *Chance,* in which "the hero of tragedy has been replaced by the hero of melodrama"; and the same decline of power is clear in *Victory.* "The moment of change," somewhere between *Nostromo* and *Under Western Eyes,* is marked by "The Secret Sharer" [written 1909], a story in which "the theme of the responsible man, the centre of his own 'world,' " is most highly developed; and JC's dealing with this theme here and the "solution" at the end seem to be "an allegory of his own development." With the narrator's "other self" gone, he is probably no longer so complete a man as he had been, just as JC's "price of peace" is the giving up of "the knowledge of the compact with evil, of the sense of guilt and a reliance on the simple faiths of honesty and fidelity to one's shipmates," which the earlier works show to be "inadequate in themselves." [A good article, later developed and expanded into an important book, CONRAD: A REASSESSMENT (1952).]

1204 Klingopulos, G. D. "Arthur Koestler," SCRUTINY, XVI (June 1949), 82-92.

In *Under Western Eyes,* JC's successful aim is "trying to catch the very soul of things Russian"; DARKNESS AT NOON, Koestler's Russian book, fails in its inability to evaluate national feeling as a social positive. JC does not generalize what he cannot make implicit.

1205 Morley, Christopher. "A New Estimate of a Great Novelist," NEW YORK TIMES BOOK REVIEW, 14 Aug 1949, pp. 1, 15.

JC is "the most astonishing writer of our life-time." "Heart of Darkness" is "a stark . . . political parable." JC wrote all his stories twice: *An Outpost of Progress* was "a dry run" for the immortal "Heart of Darkness." JC was strongly moved by his personal experiences, but "he could not write his purpose until he had invented some Doppelgänger . . . to tell it to him." Fables of double meaning, as in *The Shadow-Line,* "The Secret Sharer," and "A Smile of Fortune," "were especially significant to him."

1206 Simon, Irène. FORMES DU ROMAN ANGLAIS DE DICKENS À JOYCE. (Forms of the English Novel from Dickens to Joyce) (Liège: Université de Liège, 1949), pp. 258-97.

Since to JC truth is something elusive, he tries only to suggest it by describing action very precisely so that the reader gets the same impression as the character without any explicit authorial comment. JC's style speaks to the imagination by appealing to all the senses. His heroes live adventures which reveal their true natures: integrity, a sense of duty, endurance, and courage. Usually JC's novels are narrated by a spectator who has taken part in the action in order to convince us of its truth. Sometimes several narrators give us several points of view to increase the realism, as well as to round out the impression. Confidence in the narrator is achieved by making him objective. Time-shift creates the illusion that all action takes place in the present and reveals different aspects of the action without regard to chronology. What interests JC is not what happens but how man confronts his destiny. In *Nostromo* social and individual values are woven into a complex scheme of harmonizing and conflicting relationships. The general theme of the corruption of ideals by material interests is dramatized both by the political action and by individual actions. [Original ideas, well-supported.] [In French.]

> **1207** Stallman, Robert W. "Conrad and 'The Secret Sharer,'" ACCENT, IX (Spring 1949), 131-33; based on a differently developed version in "Life, Art, and 'The Secret Sharer,'" FORMS OF MODERN FICTION, ed by William Van O'Connor (Minneapolis: University of Minnesota P, 1948), pp. 229-42; in another version, as "Analysis," in THE ART OF MODERN FICTION, ed by Ray B. West and R. W. Stallman (NY: Rinehart, 1949), pp. 490-98; and most fully rptd from the ACCENT version in THE ART OF JOSEPH CONRAD: A CRITICAL SYMPOSIUM, ed by R. W. Stallman (East Lansing: Michigan State U P, 1960), pp. 275-95.

JC's most characteristic writings are stories of action such as *Nostromo, The Secret Agent, Victory,* and *Suspense;* but in "The Secret Sharer" the external action is practically limited to the drama of the ship in "the moment of the captain's crisis and triumph." The entire story may be considered as "a prolonged analysis of a series of tensions" anticipating this culminating moment. The captain risks his ship for one particular stranger because the two men closely resemble each other and because the captain also recognizes a psychic identity in the stranger. Both men are wholly isolated, and at the end of the story "the over-confident soul of the swimmer stands in contrast to the self-questioning, Hamletlike soul of the newly appointed captain." Leggatt is "the embodiment of the captain's moral consciousness"; and in terms of the psychological allegory, Leggatt also represents "that world which lies below the surface of our conscious lives." The captain takes his ship as close as possible to the shore literally because he wants to catch the breezes from the land and allegorically because he has now attained sufficient self-confidence to risk this dangerous maneuver. This action is a test of the captain, a test in which he puts to trial his "secret conception of his ideal self." And "the transferred moral quality of Leggatt has infused itself into the captain's soul." This transaction, symbolized by the spot of white hat on the dark waters, saves him. He has displayed his fidelity to his ideal of selfhood. The trial of the captain and of the artist is resolved by "the trial he imposes upon his secret self." The artist must not betray his "creative conscience."

> **1208** Stallman, Robert W. "The Structure and Symbolism of Conrad's *Victory*," WESTERN REVIEW, XIII (Spring 1949), 146-57; rptd in revised form as *"Victory,"* in THE ART OF MODERN FICTION, ed by Ray B. West and Robert Wooster Stallman (NY: Rinehart, 1949), pp. 607-20.

In *Victory*, Heyst's meeting with Morrison initiates the chain of actions which reveal the multiple Heyst: "Hard Facts" Heyst, "Enchanted" Heyst, Creator Heyst, Utopist Heyst, Hermit Heyst. The novel is framed by a mythic ritual: Morrison's praying and Heyst's dying by fire, both purification rituals. The unnamed narrator, with McNab, "an English clerk," and Davidson, is one of "the fellows." The narrator, Davidson, and Ricardo are curious and have talents for fact finding, "a passion for truth." "The point of view in *Victory* . . . is a circle (a circle of newsmongering), at whose center of interest is Axel Heyst." The true Heyst is the product of multiple viewpoints finally adjusted by the reader. "The whole plot of *Victory* is motivated by calumny and gossip"; it is "the disembodied evil of the world" as Jones and Company are "the embodied evil of the world." Point of view, theme, structure, and action are ordered by the dominant circular pattern of the novel. Heyst's attempts to estrange himself from life sets in motion destructive gossip; his forming a tie with Lena (life) leads to his being "saved." Jones (death, Satan) hates women (Lena-life). Again fidelity and trust in life are the central values. [The explications are sometimes forced by an overly assertive amassing of images to fit the pattern.]

> **1209** Webster, H. T. "Conrad's 'Falk,' " EXPLICATOR, VII (June 1949), Item 56.

Connections appear between "Falk" and *Victory*: both deal with different aspects of Schopenhauer's "Will to Life" theme. Falk represents a principle of affirmation, Axel Heyst, one of negation.

> **1210** Wright, Walter F. ROMANCE AND TRAGEDY IN JOSEPH CONRAD (Lincoln: University of Nebraska P, 1949); rptd (NY: Russell & Russell, 1966).

JC has no one consistent attitude toward life, but his points of view can be grouped under two major divisions: romance and psychological tragedy. The romance portrays "the hope and excitement associated with life as an unreflecting acceptance of adventure for its own sake"; the psychological tragedy pictures life as "a tragic experience to him." The romance of adventure portrays men who are not aware of the greatness of their lives, like Singleton in *The Nigger of the Narcissus* and Marlow in "Youth." The interest of this romance, neither dramatic nor epic, is lyrical, expressing the "magical nature of being alive"; JC loves living for its own sake. He considers illusion, which is the form we perceive of the world, as the imaginative creation which gives meaning to facts. For him, "the exploring of the heart's dream" can lead a man to destruction, or it can be the single blessing which spares man from tragedy. Sometimes both themes are juxtaposed: Lord Jim is tragic because of his introspection whereas Stein is scarcely conscious of self. Some of JC's characters, through love of their work, like Jukes and Singleton, are at home in the order of the universe; such men as Anthony and Stein find their true nature by unwaveringly following their dream. Man may also find out where he fits by admiring the spectacle of the universe, like Stein, or by a feeling of kinship with his fellowmen, like Captain Whalley and Captain MacWhirr. Solidarity is for JC an apprehension of the mysterious nature of human personality and destiny and the finding of a dream that gives a man's world a center. Insofar as JC believes that man can become involved in the adventure of living without introspection, life can be a romance; he can achieve his destiny without doubts either about its value or about his own soul. But when he begins to question fate or to detach his personality from the universal order, he is potentially tragic. In JC's tales, there are different possible attitudes toward death: death may come as the unexpected fulfillment of one's dream; its acceptance may affirm, as in *Under Western Eyes* where the hero invites it or in *Victory* where he achieves it, the reality that one has denied; death may, as in "The End of the Tether," be the last and sufficient payment of a bargain; or, as in "The Lagoon," *The Rescue,* and "The Tale," the mastery may lie beyond the story, but with the certainty that the impulse has been identified and that the nobility of the hero will, by way of expiation, lead him toward eventual peace. In *Almayer's Folly, An Outcast of the Islands,* and *Nostromo,* the characters follow their paths to destruction, which is the descent to truth. JC's approach to criticism was psychological, with no conflict with traditional views. His hypotheses include the assumption that man's life is ultimately a search, conscious or unconscious, for his identity. If a man accepted life as an adventure and magically enjoyed being alive in a universe of wonder, he identified with universal order; or if he could, by recalling an emotion, attain to a new and purer form of it, he had a romantic experience. At the same time, in his reflective moments man perceives the tragedy inherent in his possession of mind, and when he becomes conscious of himself apart from the natural world he is subject to that tragedy. JC himself was sometimes as bewildered as any of his heroes, but to the extent to which he was an artist he could create a world in which he could believe, for him there was in the universe and in human life a magical quality for the artist to visualize—"a world in which facts lose their usual proportions and are translated into manifestations of imaginative truth."

1211 Young, Vernon. "Joseph Conrad: Outline for a Reconsideration," HUDSON REVIEW, VII (Spring 1949), 5-19.

JC's "gentry" of critics has "over-promoted the positive Elizabethan gentleman-adventurer qualities" of his life and art. JC was a master of the Symbolist novel and of the "psycho-political genre." He presented "the pathos of the incompatible 'foreigner,'" expanding "the predicament of the alien into the universal experience of spiritual isolation that has become the common property of almost all our major novelists." A fresh critical estimate of him should attempt to judge the success with which he did or did not resolve artistically "the moral problems he enunciated." JC seems to have had "neither a consistently ironic nor a consistently affirmative vision." His "was an art of contraries in which the features of bleak pessimism were barely controlled by the ill-worn masks of irony or affirmation." Despite Zabel and other critics, it is likely that JC "was congenitally incapable of real skepticism, as he was of real commitment." Some of his "compulsive hesitation" may come from the sort of quest his heroes are on: they seek "moral identity alone; they do not seek being, total function. They seek final gratification through *notions* of self, never through *expression* of self." They are "self-conscious" in an abstract sense. They lack any satisfying correlation with the "magnificently visualized world of objects" behind and around them. When they are confused "through the exclusiveness of solitude, events appear not to exist." This was JC's own experience: the flight from Poland. His women are greater failures—as credible beings. They are tiresome and JC's treatment of them facetious. He is limited severely by his inability to allow his characters any fulfillment or redemption through sex. Even though JC is classified usually as a nineteenth-century skeptic, he is closer to our contemporaries who "find the burden of consciousness too great because it is unqualified . . . by a centrally emotional adhesion to the earth, . . . to the flesh they should unite with, to the interior world of empathy and passion which is the only abiding vehicle of our identity, our assurance."

1950

1212 Altick, Richard Daniel. "The Search for Sambir," THE SCHOLAR ADVENTURERS (NY: Macmillan, 1950); rptd (NY: The Free Press, 1966), pp. 289-97.

John D. Gordan's trip to Borneo in 1939 to discover the identity of Sambir and Kaspar Almayer proved the former to be Berouw, a remote settlement on the Berouw River; the latter, Carel Olmeijer. [See Gordan, JOSEPH CONRAD: THE MAKING OF A NOVELIST (1940).]

1213 Bates, Herbert Ernest. EDWARD GARNETT (Lond: Parrish, 1950), pp. 10, 15, 19, 21, 25-26, 27 [JC's inscription of *Almayer's Folly* to Garnett], 31, 41, 46, 57, 59, 84, 86-87.
[Bates admits JC's influence on his own work, notes Garnett's objection to the obvious JC influence, and reports Garnett's and JC's meeting in connection with *Folly*. Generally slight references to JC.]

1214 Berryman, John. STEPHEN CRANE (NY: Sloane, 1950), pp. 200-2, 206-8, 238-39.
JC's remarks about Crane differ from those of Crane's friends, because Crane "never knew Conrad really, nor Conrad him." Crane was fascinated with JC's son Borys during Crane's visit to Pent Farm. [Largely miscellaneous details connecting Crane and JC, especially during 1897 and 1898.]

1215 Cornelius, Samuel Robert. "The Sea as the Core of Conrad." Unpublished thesis, University of Pittsburgh, 1949. UNIVERSITY OF PITTSBURGH BULLETIN, XLVI (June 1950), 3-9.

1216 Ford, William J. "*Lord Jim:* Conrad's Study in Depth Psychology," QUARTERLY BULLETIN OF NORTHWESTERN UNIVERSITY MEDICAL SCHOOL, XXIV (Spring 1950), 64-69.
Lord Jim depicts "a man upon whom life closed down," but while "Nature's violence, isolation, and unpredictable circumstance tested him, . . . the great conflict is internal and his character determined his fate." JC was "a great intuitive psychologist"; the perceptions of his narrator Marlow, and the circumstances of Jim's life, show JC's awareness of such fundamental concepts known in psychoanalytic psychology as the unconscious, the superego, and the death-instinct. In fact, the death-instinct is "the unconscious motivation which best explains . . . the mystery of [Jim's] compulsion to repeat experiences of self-punishment and isolation." That it is an unconscious drive explains why Jim's behavior is an enigma to himself and to others. The problem Jim faces throughout the story (as the much-quoted speech by Stein suggests) is not how to discover reality but how to live with his particular illusions about life. The course of events shows that in his struggle with that problem the life-loving forces in him are not a match for the deathward forces, and his career is a "step by step advance toward self-harm [and] self-punishment." Ultimately, in the encounter with the adventurer Brown, Jim works himself unwittingly into a position where he can die in a way that accords with his "illusion," "the exacting standard of his honor. . . . *Lord Jim,* then, is the story of one neurotic man's unsuccessful attempt to attain maturity, to effect a practical compromise between reality and his illusion of life. Conrad portrays the presence of deep

forces in the personality, non-rational and self-destructive forces impelling the neurotic yet admirable Jim to his tragic end."

1217 Harkness, Bruce. "The Handling of Time in the Novels of Joseph Conrad." Unpublished thesis, University of Chicago, 1950.

1218 Hill, Robert W., and Lewis M. Stark. "The Edward S. Harkness Collection," NEW YORK PUBLIC LIBRARY BULLETIN, LIV (Dec 1950), 585-94.

Among the books from the library of Edward S. Harkness left to the New York Public Library in 1950 were a group of fifteen first editions of works by JC and five JC pamphlets. [For JC items bequeathed by Mrs. Harkness, see Lewis M. Stark and Robert W. Hill, "The Bequest of Mary Stillman Harkness," ibid., LV (May 1951), 213-24.]

1219 Hondequin, Ghislain. "The Influence of Flaubert on Pater and Conrad." Unpublished thesis, Ghent University, 1950.

1220 "Joseph Conrad, Dichter der Männlichkeit" (Joseph Conrad, Poet of Masculinity), CHRIST UND WELT (Stuttgart), II (14 Dec 1950), 10.

[A brief introductory appreciation of JC mentioning his work, romantic themes, his influence on Faulkner and Hemingway, and listing German translations of some of his works.] [In German.]

1221 Millett, Fred B. READING FICTION (NY: Harper's, 1950), pp. 11, 28, 34-35, 36, 38, 45, 49, 52, 58, 59, 64, 75, 78, 161-77, 250.

JC often begins in the middle of a chronological sequence of plot, as in "The Lagoon," and gradually uncovers past events and the effect of the past in the story. He prepares the reader for the turning point by carefully prepared emotion and by a carefully plotted denouement. In "The Lagoon," JC creates a completely alien world. However, in interpreting the story, one must delve beyond the exotic setting, which did not concern JC for its own sake, to the moral problem on which the action turns. The meaning and theme of the story are expressed in elaborate patterns of symbols. [The slant of this book is toward helping the reader interpret fiction orally.]

1222 Morris, Robert L. "Eliot's 'Game of Chess' and Conrad's 'The Return,' " MODERN LANGUAGE NOTES, LXV (June 1950), 422-23.

The first fifty lines of Eliot's "Game of Chess" in THE WASTE LAND, often likened to the opening lines of Shakespeare's description of Cleopatra, are closely parallel to passages from JC's "The Return." "The discreet silence of closed doors, curtained windows, and feeble candle flames," in passages of "The Return," and "images of burnished gold, streaming hair, emphasis on the word *nothing* expressing a personal vacuum" are close to Eliot.

1223 Pritchett, V. S. "Books in General," NEW STATESMAN AND NATION, XL (15 July 1950), 72-73; enlgd and absorbed in "Conrad," THE LIVING NOVEL AND LATER APPRECIATIONS (1964).

Under Western Eyes and *The Secret Agent* follow in general the Conradian motif of the isolation and sense of guilt of the exile, here seen most clearly in Razumov and Verloc.

1224 Rébora, Piero. "James, Conrad, Mansfield," LETTERATURA INGLESE DEL NOVECENTO (English Literature of the Twentieth Century) (Firenze: Edizioni Lingue estere, 1950), pp. 41, 49-53.

JC, the Polishman of noble birth who became a British seaman and later an author, is unique in literature. *Lord Jim* anticipated a century of literature which emphasizes the interior man. JC has been lauded by many as the best contemporary stylist in the novel and as perhaps the best example of the quality of the modern English spirit. His artistry is marked by careful observation, precision, and a concern for universal truth. He does not deal with life's exceptions, the pathological, but rather with life's enduring experiences. In his treatment of fundamental qualities of men—fidelity, courage, loyalty—JC recollects a stoic hardness. Yet for JC these qualities must coexist with human sympathy. All JC's narrative work can be considered autobiographically. *The Nigger of the Narcissus* (1897) is the most frankly autobiographical. JC's world was spaceless and timeless, and his stories have an epic sense of inevitability and eternity, qualities which do not necessarily make an author popular. The psychological study of Jim in *Jim* is handled minutely and is one of the most significant studies in modern letters. The simultaneity of all time is not beckoned up again until T. S. Eliot. The faults of *Jim*—the minute care for particulars, the obsession for the right word, the scrupulousness of detail which sometimes becomes arid estheticism—are the limitations of a grand author. In the second period of his career JC worked with Ford Madox Hueffer (*The Inheritors*, 1901; *Romance*, 1903) and also on "Typhoon," "Youth," "Heart of Darkness." Most noted for this period of his career, ending with *Nostromo*, JC recreates with the skill of a portrait painter the storms on the coast of Malaya and boats redolent with the odors of salt and tar. With his last novels, JC departs from an autobiographical phase. *Nostromo* is realistic and romantic; *The Mirror of the Sea* (1906) is lyric; *Chance* (1914) returns to the technique of the tale within the tale. In the last novels, women, cultural facts, historical information, almost absent earlier, enter prominently. JC's early work has a profound evocative ability. He is not an easy author. [In Italian.]

1225 Schlecht, Elvine. "Mensch und Welt in den Werken Joseph Conrads" (Man and the World in Joseph Conrad's Works). Unpublished thesis, University of Wien, 1950. [In German.]

1226 Schorer, Mark. THE STORY, A CRITICAL ANTHOLOGY (Englewood Cliffs, NJ: Prentice-Hall, 1950), pp. 243-46.
[Reprinting of and slight commentary on JC's "Amy Foster."]

1227 Short, Raymond W., and R. B. Sewall. A MANUAL OF SUGGESTIONS FOR TEACHERS USING SHORT STORIES FOR STUDY, rvd ed (NY: Holt, 1950); 3rd ed (1956), pp. 58-65.
Examined in three sections, "Heart of Darkness" (1) establishes a meaningful mood through a series of "magnificent objectifications of the atmosphere, the 'haze,' moral, mental, and physical, enveloping Marlow's African experience"; (2) "establishes enormous potentialities for good that lay in Kurtz, and at the same time shows the danger he is placed in because of the manager's fear of him" and "describes the degradation to which Kurtz has actually sunk"; and (3) shows how Marlow "is forced to side with Kurtz against the manager, not by circumstance as before, but by an act of moral volition." [The explication is largely developed by means of Socratic questions.]

1228 Smith, Arthur J. M. "Joseph Conrad (1857-1924): *Victory*," AN INTRODUCTION TO LITERATURE & THE FINE ARTS (East Lansing: Michigan State College P, 1950), pp. 362-66.
[Smith gives a brief biographical sketch, outlines the plot of *Victory*, discusses JC's place among his contemporaries, and reviews his philosophy of the novel, art, and life.]

1229 Stegner, Wallace. "Variations on a Theme by Conrad," YALE REVIEW, XXXIX (March 1950), 512-23, espec 512-515, 523.
Lord Jim is at least superficially close to Hemingway's "Short Happy Life of Francis Macomber" and Fitzgerald's THE GREAT GATSBY. Macomber, like Jim, commits an act of cowardice, but when he dies, death comes treacherously. Jim's death is something he chooses. Gatsby, like Jim, is a romantic chasing an impossible vision who achieves a kind of realization in catastrophe. Gatsby romanticizes Daisy. Jim's romantic notions concern only himself and his idea of conduct. *Jim* is about conduct and the relation of an individual to ethics. The theme is supported by images of isolation. This is not a picturesque novel of the South Seas nor a sociological study, but an ethical novel.

1230 Tomlinson, H. M. THE FACE OF THE EARTH (Lond: Duckworth, 1950), pp. 91-96.

JC added to literature a "witness to an era of seamanship that otherwise would have been lost." [Mainly general reminiscences.]

> **1231** Turner, Lionel H. "The Genius of Joseph Conrad. A Study of the Neurotic Emotions that Stimulated his Imagination." Unpublished thesis, University of Southern California, 1949. UNIVERSITY OF SOUTHERN CALIFORNIA ABSTRACTS OF DISSERTATIONS (1950), 59-61.

> **1232** Ujević, Tin. "Joseph Conrad," *Mladost* (Youth) (Zagreb: Zora, 1950), pp. 61-63.

[This afterword to Ujević's Serbo-Croat translation of "Youth" insists on the romantic JC of the sea adventures, and regrets his later development which has to some extent diminished his creative drive and lyricism.] [In Serbo-Croatian.]

> **1233** Ure, Peter. "Character and Imagination in Conrad," CAMBRIDGE JOURNAL, III (Sept 1950), 727-40.

JC realized the necessity of having illusions and was often "his own hollow man," struggling to finish *The Rescue* or *Lord Jim* or *An Outcast of the Islands*. His reluctance and equivocations in the face of his "self-imposed imaginative task" sometimes help in understanding the natures of his heroes. The heroes, partly like himself, are sometimes highly imaginative men who, at the same time, can be punished by "a degeneration of the imaginative faculty"; or their imagination "in a state of decay" becomes the symbol of their loss of selfhood. JC often explored the inward lives of his characters in an attempt to demonstrate how their passions—for prestige, for honor, for a woman's love—can be transformed into a "fine-grained" imaginative activity.

MacWhirr in "Typhoon" and the narrator-hero in *The Shadow-Line* illustrate his theme of "mere, blank resistance to those potencies in and outside a man which threaten to destroy his capacity for service"; and *The Nigger of the Narcissus* is a study of "a whole crew of merchant seamen who become the victims of a disorder of heart and mind" occasioned by James Wait. *Jim*, however, is the "touchstone" of JC's attempts "to endow his heroes not only with a sense of stability threatened but with something more positive—with passions, with *raison d'être,* and with the wish to transform such passions into achievement, to realize dreams of love and power." In *Nostromo,* Gould, who is morally bound to make a success of the silver mine, becomes obsessed and is "haunted by his *idée fixe* to the point of insanity"; and Nostromo, feeling himself betrayed, turns to crime and tragedy. Thus both men are "self-betrayed by the ambiguity of their most expressive and valuable impulses."

In his later works JC places in the center of his compositions "not the ambiguity of the imaginative nature but its capacity for devotion and its response to love." In *Under Western Eyes,* for example, Razumov's love for Miss Haldin saves him from "ultimate undoing" just when he is through with life. In *Victory,* Heyst's greatest achievement is making possible the conditions for Lena's victory; here the struggle is represented "not as the fantasia of a clouded imagination but with the objectivity of the great and the little devils in DR. FAUSTUS." Thus JC's journey leads from Lord Jim, "that lofty and solitary existence," to "the creative and interacting duality, Heyst-Lena"; his is therefore "a progress from the epic to the drama."

1234 Weber, David C. "Conrad's *Lord Jim,*" COLBY LIBRARY QUARTERLY, 2nd Ser, No. 16 (Nov 1950), 266-68.

[A commemoration of the fiftieth anniversary of *Lord Jim,* this article traces the publication history from serial through many editions of the book.]

1951

1235 A., F. D. "Conrad's 'The Lagoon,' " EXPLICATOR, IX (May 1951), Item Q7.

Are there two technical errors in the opening paragraphs of "The Lagoon"? (1) "The boat is said to be moving up a river that flows eastward, but there are confusing suggestions of a downstream journey and of a westward flow"; and (2) "Do Malay boatmen change from paddling in deep water to poling in shallow, or is JC confused about the propulsion of Tuan's canoe?"

1236 Arendt, Hannah. THE ORIGINS OF TOTALITARIANISM (NY: Harcourt, Brace, 1951), pp. 172, 185, 189, 193.

"Heart of Darkness" is "the most illuminating work on actual race experience in Africa." Ruthless gold and diamond seekers of South Africa and other adventurers are similar to Kurtz, Mr. Jones, and Heyst: some were bored with everything, like Mr. Jones, or "drunk with contempt," like Heyst. These outcasts were sometimes as "incomprehensible as a madhouse." Their situation is best described in JC's own words: "The prehistoric man was cursing us."

1237 Belden, Albert D. "Joseph Conrad—Apostle of Loyalty," EXPOSITORY TIMES (Edinburgh), LXIII (Dec 1951), 77-79.

[Part of a series entitled "Vital Messages of Great British Writers" of which JC is number two. A brief biographical sketch followed by equally brief comment on loyalty as the theme of *Lord Jim, Victory,* and "Typhoon." Of no value.]

1238 D., F. A. "Conrad's 'The Lagoon,' " EXPLICATOR, IX (May 1951), Item 7.

Are there two technical errors in the opening of the story? Directions seem inconsistent, and Malays at one moment use paddles, at another poles.

1239 Gatch, Katherine Haynes. "Conrad's Axel," STUDIES IN PHILOLOGY, XLVIII (Jan 1951), 98-106.

Since JC could not have missed being familiar with the pessimism and *fin de siècle* romanticism of AXEL by Villiers de l'Isle-Adam (1890 and produced as a play in Paris, 1894), his novel, *Victory,* and its hero Axel Heyst were at least partially suggested by this drama, even though in large areas the two works have no relation to each other. Axel Auersperg, however, like JC's Axel, had received an unusual education; both Axels were supposed by certain "malevolent worldlings" to be guarding a fabulous hoard of treasure; both Axels, contrary to their desire to avoid active life, were drawn into melodramatic events; JC, like Villiers de l'Isle-Adam, personifies in an intruder "a singularly noxious brand of evil"; the women in the two books display certain similarities; and the self-immolation of the lovers adds still further to the pattern of resemblances. But JC in the tragedy of Axel Heyst, because of his "romantic feeling of reality," corrected Villiers's "hyperaesthesia."

1240 Haugh, Robert F. "The Structure of *Lord Jim,*" COLLEGE ENGLISH, XIII (Dec 1951), 137-41.

[Rejects the "old critical judgment" revived by F. R. Leavis in THE GREAT TRADITION (1948) that the later scenes of *Lord Jim* laid in Patusan have "no inevitability" and "seem decidedly thin."] Although the "dominant figure in the design is the jump from the *Patna,*" Jim really jumps three times, each of which "resembles a recurring musical figure, with minor figures in the design giving depth and complexity." Jim's first two jumps, or tests, come from the impersonal sea; the third comes in Patusan from Gentleman Brown, a test which is "offered by evil in human form." In this test JC makes "his final statement of the dominant theme: the transcendence of fidelity, honor, and nobility of soul over the moral darkness that forever assaults man from the outer darkness." JC is thus seen to be "a dualist": there is an "outer world" which "has no concern for man," and there is an "inner world" which is "preserved for us by fidelity, trust, honor, where to be 'one of us' is the only bulwark against the forces of darkness." Jewel, in love with Jim, repeats the theme presented earlier by the three renegades of the *Patna,* but in this instance Jim has had time to make his decision. Thus the Patusan material contains the elements of the major theme: "the irrational malice of the universe" is not in the sea but in Gentleman Brown, and "the temptation to yield" is not "in mistaken words of renegades but in the words of love." "The story is right; it is inevitable; it is necessary to the full statement of Conrad's theme."

1241 Hergešić, Ivo. "Joseph Conrad," *Lord Jim,* trans by Tin Ujević (Zagreb: Zora, 1951), pp. 385-90; rptd and enlgd as "Francuski firmis i egleski filtar: Joseph Conrad" (French Varnish and English Filter: Joseph Conrad), KNJIŽEVNI PORTRETI III (Literary Portraits III) (Cetinje, 1959), pp. 127-40; rptd rvd ed (Zagreb, 1967), pp. 541-54.

[This postface pleasantly and systematically surveys JC's life and work and some of the literature on JC.] [In Serbo-Croatian.]

1242 Herzfeld, Margaret. "Die ethischen Grundbegriffe und Werte im Erzählwerk Joseph Conrads" (The Ethical Terms and Moral Values in Joseph Conrad's Fiction). Unpublished thesis, University of Mainz, 1951.

JC turns away from the pessimism of such writers as Hardy and places his trust in man's ability to make moral choices and fight the dangers surrounding him. Since man is conscious of his position in the world and of the subjectivity of his ethical beliefs, his situation is a tragic one. If he succeeds in living up to his own ethical standards, he may emerge triumphant (though defeated in a superficial sense). [Several novels are analyzed under such headings as guilt and punishment, solidarity and fidelity.] [In German.]

1243 Klingopulos, G. D. "The Criticism of Novels," USE OF ENGLISH (Lond), III (Winter 1951), 85-90.

Some three or four novelists "succeeded in creating situations which present and analyse the harsh moral complexities of modern life": James, Lawrence, JC, Forster. JC's *The Secret Agent* is "one of the finest novels in the language." The macabre atmosphere is part of the whole vision. The novel is chiefly a "contemplation of the working of law" and it suggests "a loathing for . . . love of domination over our fellow-creatures." "The backward and forward timing" in this intricate novel "is brilliantly managed." It gains "organic symmetry" from the three long interviews, used like acts in Shakespeare. JC makes the reader feel the presence of the "moral jungle." In the beautiful "prose poem" "Amy Foster," JC shows his difficulty in remaining " 'sustained' by his 'illusions.' " [One of the more insightful pieces on *Agent*.]

1244 Lehmann, John. "On Re-reading *The Rover,*" WORLD REVIEW, N.S. XXVIII (June 1951), 41-45; rptd in THE OPEN NIGHT (NY: Harcourt, Brace, 1952), pp. 54-62.

In scattered passages in *The Rover,* JC develops the legendary character of Peyrol and suggests a reference to Odysseus's return to Ithaca and to some of the famous battles in THE ILIAD. Peyrol becomes a symbolic character, representing the man of action who has retired for the sake of peace but is not unwilling to respond when recalled by patriotic purposes. Sharply contrasted with him is Scevola, who likewise has a background of partly-suggested violence. For JC this contrast represented a modern theme, "the opposition of the man of heart and the man of head in a revolutionary time." The ending of the story prepares for the happy union of Arlette and Réal, but more importantly, illuminates the basic contrast between Peyrol and Scevola. In the last paragraph of the book, JC, like the chorus of a Greek drama, comments on his hero Peyrol, whom he designates "the man of dark deeds, but of large heart." [In JOSEPH CONRAD: A CRITICAL BIOGRAPHY (1959), Jocelyn Baines perceptively recognizes John Lehmann's "fascinating parallel between Peyrol and the other wanderer, Odysseus," and the "symbolic overtones" of the figure of Peyrol; but he also notes, no doubt correctly, that the contrast between the two men is implied but not developed.]

1245 Lenormand, H.-R. "Rencontre avec Joseph Conrad" (A Meeting with Joseph Conrad), GAZETTE DES LETTRES, VII (15 March 1951), 30-32.

During the winter of 1921, JC, at the age of sixty-four, had come to Ajaccio, Corsica, to work on *Chance.* Generally affable and polite, he talked with the captains of ships in port and told such anecdotes as his adventure in Malaysia, where he nearly died of thirst trying to mark a channel. But behind this heartiness lurked his fear of death and anxiety at not being able to finish his novel. He talked also of his alternate fears of having shrouded his characters in obscurity and of having explained their actions too explicitly. Ultimately he hoped to have remained objective, to have suggested only the depths of reality. [In French.]

1246 Miller, James E., Jr. *"The Nigger of the Narcissus:* A Reexamination," PMLA, LXVI (Dec 1951), 911-18.

The subject of *The Nigger of the Narcissus,* the crew passing from ignorance to knowledge, provides a dramatic structure. A dramatic tension results because of two possibilities: the crew may turn to Singleton (wisdom); the crew may turn to Donkin (ignorance). The imagery of *Nigger* supports this tension; the images are appropriately searching for meaning. The "knot" that binds the crew at the end of *Nigger* is "a sailor's knot tied with a sailor's wisdom."

1247 Pavese, Cesare. "Joseph Conrad," LA LETTERATURA AMERICANA ED ALTRI SAGGI (American Literature and Other Essays) (Torino: Einaudi, 1951), pp. 207-10.

An important technique of JC is the refraction of events by the use of a number of narrators. In spite of a gossipy format, JC reminds us that he is not recounting personal experience. There is more interest in the quality of the voice than in the event itself. However, JC, when making his best proof, relies on a foundation of memory and emotion, as in "Youth." Nothing from early in his life enters his stories without a shudder, a quake, or a feeling of a secret disclosed. The predilection for the exotic writers in JC has nothing of caprice about it. Yet of exotic writers (Hudson, Kipling), JC is less picturesque, less dedicated to rendering a rich palette of tourist color. All is disclosed in a vague, nostalgic, and introspective atmosphere, always magical. He presents a daily atmosphere, yet so intense that it seems to move in the enchantment of symbols. The sea for JC is a place of spirit, mind, and not the biblical context that it is for Melville or the historical and legendary context for Stevenson. This atmosphere, along with the tale being told through many mouths, creates another atmosphere. Because of the atmosphere of resignation, readers would wish to discern an ethnic sign of his Slavic origins. Despite his method of isolating individuals from the society and culture in which they live, JC was alien to the ethical and religious preoccupations of Tolstoi and Dostoevski, and it is not unusual that he prefers Turgenev and Chekhov and admires even more Maupassant and Flaubert. [In Italian.]

1248 Scott-James, Rolfe Arnold. "Above the Battle," FIFTY YEARS OF ENGLISH LITERATURE, 1900-1950 (Lond and NY: Longmans, Green, 1951), pp. 54-74, espec. 59-62.

Lord Jim gave scope to JC's "luxuriant imagination probing the secrets of reality." The only weakness is in prolonging the moments of highest tension beyond bearing. *The Mirror of the Sea* is perhaps his best book. JC retained his power to the end. "The mixture of French manner and Slav feeling, of classicism and mysticism, of order and unrest . . . at the last appealed to the romantic yet practical English when they had learnt to appreciate his subtle, nervous expressive style."

1249 Stark, Lewis M., and Robert W. Hill. "The Bequest of Mary Stillman Harkness," NEW YORK PUBLIC LIBRARY BULLETIN, LV (May 1951), 213-24.

The books left by Mrs. Harkness to the New York Public Library included over forty titles by JC, "all in fine condition in the original bindings," among them several rare items. [For JC items bequeathed by Edward S. Harkness, see Robert W. Hill and Lewis M. Stark, "The Edward S. Harkness Collection," ibid., LIV (Dec 1950), 585-94.]

1250 Warner, Oliver. JOSEPH CONRAD. Men and Books Series (Lond: Longmans, Green, 1951); rvd ed (1954); 3rd ed (1960).

The "greater novels" are: *Lord Jim,* with its theme of lost honor which is finally "redeemed in full"; *Nostromo,* in which Nostromo is not so much a conventional hero as a character who gives the story "unity of person"; *The Secret Agent,* where JC reaches beyond his familiar materials to shock many readers with his "actuality of the most fly-blown kind"; *Under Western Eyes,* JC's most direct and sustained political commentary, which contains continuous suspense and also expresses the author's feelings of "undisguised hatred" of Russians; *Victory,* which includes "sustained excitement," particularly in the last chapters, and intense feeling, both of which cause the reader to overlook imperfections; and *The Rover,* which, serene and practically flawless, "stands in relation to the rest of Conrad's work as THE TEMPEST does to that of Shakespeare." JC's best shorter works are closely autobiographical. Especially notable are *The Nigger of the Narcissus,* with the ship and her seamen at once the subjects and the heroes of the story; "Heart of Darkness," one of JC's "finest things" even if it contains, "excusably," a greater emotional charge than is consistent with its form; "The End of the Tether," the simple story of Captain Whalley, a noble portrait of a good man who "appeals directly to the heart"; "Typhoon," chiefly notable for the character of Captain MacWhirr, but "renowned perhaps beyond its deserts"; "The Secret Sharer" [considered outstanding, but for no reason recognized as important today]; and *The Shadow-Line,* noteworthy above all for its portrait of Ransome, the cook, who acts bravely during the trials of the ship and then requests his discharge after he has helped the captain cross the "shadow-line of trial." JC wrote his tales with more ease than he wrote his novels, and they contain more spontaneity. Of the lesser novels, only *Chance* deserves serious attention. Here, for once, one of JC's novels has, in Flora de Barral, a heroine "who may be said to be at the center rather than the circumference." But the book seems to lack central energy and to leave the impression of a display of virtuosity unjustified by the theme. JC reveals himself most closely in *A Personal Record* and *Notes on Life and Letters.* Since he placed great value in people, he believed, fundamentally, in mankind. Romance and realism fuse in him as, in his own words, "an inborn faculty." Most important to him is the impact of good and evil, both of which exist, on individual men and women. Being complex himself, as he demonstrates in his works, it is his simplicities which make him "enduring." [Warner relies too heavily on JC's often unreliable statements about himself and his works, but his comparatively early insights are perceptive and often suggestive of later criticism. He notes an idea that was to be emphasized in later years: "signs of tiredness" in JC's later works.]

1251 Warren, Robert Penn. *"Nostromo,"* SEWANEE REVIEW, LIX (Summer 1951), 363-91; rptd as the "Introduction" to the Modern

Joseph Conrad

Library Edition of *Nostromo* (1951), vii-xxxix; JOSEPH CONRAD: A CRITICAL SYMPOSIUM, ed by R. W. Stallman (East Lansing: Michigan State U P, 1960), pp. 209-27; and in SELECTED ESSAYS (NY: Random House, 1958), pp. 31-58.

Nostromo is JC's "masterwork." Because JC is not familiar with South America, he must rely on imagination. His later work is "specializations and elaborations of elements that had been in suspension" in *Nostromo*. Dr. Monygham is "an older and more twisted Lord Jim." Gould is a cousin of Kurtz. Emilia Gould sets up the sense of human solidarity. Nostromo, the natural man, has "natural grandeur unredeemed by principle, by idea." Nostromo's significance parallels Captain Brierly's experience in *Lord Jim* in that Nostromo commits a kind of suicide by killing the self by which he had lived. Decoud is the intellectually isolated man, a "dilettante of experience." JC's characteristic story is the relation of man to the human communion. His stories may be divided into three types: (1) the story of the unimaginative character who cannot see "the horror" and can cling to fidelity and the job, (2) the story of the sinner against human solidarity, (3) the story of redemption. JC's attitude toward the first is ambivalent. He admires men of natural virtue, but the character is static. The last type engages him most fully, as it is concerned with the efforts of the alienated to enter communion. All men must idealize their existences to exist. JC's "scepticism is ultimately but a 'reasonable' recognition of the fact that man is a natural creature who can rest on no revealed values and can look forward to neither individual immortality nor racial survival." "In *Nostromo* Conrad endeavored to create a great, massive, multiphase symbol that would render his total vision of the world, his sense of individual destiny, his sense of man's place in nature, his sense of history and society." The book is a complex of personal stories, "a chromatic scale of attitudes," a study of illusion. The stories are related also by the social and historical theme, dealing with main issues of JC's theme: "capitalism, imperialism, revolution, social injustice." Gould's conception of his role, bringing law, order, and prosperity to a land of poverty, is "the central fact of the social and historical theme of *Nostromo.*" The personalities of narrators function as commentary in the work. "Heart of Darkness" and *Nostromo* are analyses of capitalism in the imperialistic adventure, which necessarily involves revolution. JC analyzes revolution later in *The Secret Agent* and *Under Western Eyes*. He sees man as balanced between "the black inward abyss of himself and the black outward abyss of nature." *Nostromo* is a fable of man lost in the blankness of nature. Leavis "takes Conrad's work as too much a casual matter of temperament. For I think that even if Conrad is an 'imperfect' philosopher as esthete, he is still, in the fullest sense of the term [striving to rise from the documentation of the world to symbol], a philosophical novelist."

1951: 1252-1253

1252 Zabel, Morton Dauwen. "Introduction," *The Nigger of the Narcissus* (NY: Harper, Harper's Modern Classics, 1951), pp. vii-xxxi; rptd as "Conrad: The East and the Sea," CRAFT AND CHARACTER (1957).

The experience of fifteen years' voyaging in the East and the practical knowledge of the sea and ships gave JC the necessary material to write a novel charged with the drama of his personal and racial plight and yet controlled by his addiction to fact. In *The Nigger of the Narcissus,* JC began to learn the art of "verbal spareness, aphoristic sureness, and stylistic security" that came to fruition in "The Secret Sharer," *Under Western Eyes, Victory,* and *The Shadow-Line.* Of the *Narcissus* and her crew JC makes a world, with its "plague spots" (Donkin), its "steadfast faith" (Singleton), and its tests (represented by the storm as a test of life and Wait as a test of death). JC in *Nigger* dramatizes the instability of nature and of men and shows the need of men to share their lives with others. All men must know the secret sharer in themselves and in others and thus discover "the moral community in men."

1253 Zabel, Morton Dauwen. "Introduction," *Under Western Eyes,* New Classics (NY: New Directions, 1951), pp. xi-xxxvi; rptd as "Conrad: The Threat to the West," in CRAFT AND CHARACTER (1957); as "Introduction," *Under Western Eyes* (NY: Doubleday, Anchor Books, 1963); and as "Introduction to *Under Western Eyes,*" in CONRAD: A COLLECTION OF CRITICAL ESSAYS, ed by Marvin Mudrick (Englewood Cliffs, NJ: Prentice-Hall, Spectrum Books, 1966).

Late in 1907, during the period (1902-1912) which saw him going through "his severest tests in authorship," JC began to write *Under Western Eyes.* The personal and professional pressures bearing on him prompted JC to seek "a different subject matter, a new direction in his work, an attack on themes more closely actual and contemporary than those of his exotic or maritime tales." The books of his middle period, those dealing with "the drama of modern society and politics" (*Nostromo, The Secret Agent, Chance,* and *Eyes*), long neglected, have in the light of history taken on more importance in JC's canon. *Eyes,* in particular, is important for its "personal relevance" and "the force of prophecy." The total effect of *Eyes,* despite apparent "stretches of dramatic indirection," "brings it into the company of the most memorable books of its period and certainly of Conrad's own finest powers."

The preparatory work toward *Eyes* consisted of *Nostromo,* "Autocracy and War," *The Mirror of the Sea,* "Gaspar Ruiz," "An Anarchist," "The Informer," and *Agent.* Traces how JC conceived *Eyes* out of bits and pieces of recollection and historical events that occurred at various times and in various locations. Because of his Polish background, JC felt the force of his subject "more intimately and personally than James could have felt it" in THE PRINCESS CASAMASSIMA. JC's confessed major problem in the writing of *Eyes* was "to strike and sustain the note of scrupulous impartiality." Despite its unique features, *Eyes'* "subject and artistry are continuous with his other work"; its hero and moral drama are also evident in *Lord Jim, Nostromo,* "Heart of Darkness," "The Secret Sharer," and *Victory.* The original form of the novel underwent many changes as JC worked out a method appropriate to his material. "The prolonged attentuation and indirection of Conrad's narrative seems as if designed to put the reader's senses on the rack as much as Razumov's. . . . But the process is continuously relieved and condensed in superb moments of imagery and action—moments that mount toward the novel's shattering climax and thus toward its bitter conclusion, poised between pathos and irony."

Eyes is "pre-eminent of its kind in English fiction and calls for a rank in European fiction as well." It is descended from the type of book established by Stendhal, Turgenev, Dostoevski, and James, and it foreshadows the work of Malraux, Silone, Sartre, Koestler, Camus, Orwell, and Pasternak. It, too, "forms a judgment on modern history and on the morality of political actions." In JC's hands, *Eyes* became a political argument, a parable, and "a story of the soul of man under tyranny and rebellion, the drama of a character subjected to the most searching tests of challenge, moral probity, and self-knowledge to which the human spirit can be exposed." What finally gives the novel its strength is not the detachment JC sought but "sympathy, compassion, participation, insight." In the novel, JC discovered and dramatized the fact that "Russia too was a sharer in the moral and political destiny of mankind." It is significant that JC's aversion to Dostoevski is balanced by his high regard for another Russian—Turgenev. *Eyes* has, "at any rate, the quality of translating the Dostoevskian vision and ethos into the terms of a moral necessity which the West, whatever its compromises or failures of principle, can never forget, and which it will forget now only at its peril."

1952

1254 Aldrich, John W. (ed). CRITIQUES AND ESSAYS ON MODERN FICTION: 1920-51 (NY: Ronald P, 1952).

[Contents, abstracted separately under date of first publication: F. R.

Leavis, "Joseph Conrad: Minor Works and *Nostromo*," from "Revaluations (XIV)," SCRUTINY (1941); Morton Dauwen Zabel, "Joseph Conrad: Chance and Recognition," SEWANEE REVIEW (1945).]

1255 Ballard, E. G. "Principles of Structure in Joseph Conrad's Novels." Unpublished thesis, North Texas State Teachers College, 1952.

1256 Bigongiari, Piero. "Joseph Conrad: un universo paramente [sic] spettacolare" (Joseph Conrad: A Universe Similarly Spectacular), IL SENSO DELLA LIRICA ITALIANA (The Meaning of Italian Lyric Poetry) (Firenze: Sansoni, 1952), pp. 262-69.

JC's style, though verbose, is not overbearing; vocabulary gives the narrative a cadence of "dark facility," flowing freely into our consciousness. JC did for the South Seas what Virginia Woolf did for the English coast. Marlow has an "indefinable humor" and a "harsh objectivity" that is "equidistant from himself and the other." JC, unlike Dostoevski, relies on external rather than internal development of character, extracting the inner man and solidifying him to oppose the cosmic mystery. If men "jump," as Jim does, the external valor proves the inner worth. [In Italian.]

1257 Cronin, Edward J. "Joseph Conrad: A Moral Analysis." Unpublished thesis, University of Minnesota, 1952.

1258 Day, A. Grove. "Pattern in *Lord Jim:* One Jump After Another," COLLEGE ENGLISH, XIII (April 1952), 396-97.

The "dominant image" or symbol in *Lord Jim* is the jump, which is found throughout the novel, even at the end when Jim "makes the last great leap of his life, into the unknowable." This image unifies the work and also "harmonizes with the theme (that romantic idealism dooms one to tragedy)." The structure of the book is "saltatory; Conrad's story seems to be leaping back and forth in space and time." The "focus of narration" shifts also, and the philosophy of the work is best stated by Stein, who uses an image of "a plunge into the sea." JC used this pattern deliberately because he had "significantly . . . made several leaps in his own life which might have seemed impulsive and irremediable at the moment."

1259 Downing, Francis. "The Meaning of Victory in Joseph Conrad," COMMONWEAL, LV (28 March 1952), 613-14.

In *Victory*, JC employs his usual method of moving backward and forward in time, delaying his story to achieve suspense and to reveal men gradually, not "in a single act." Heyst, whose sin is "an in-turning, a withdrawal," is "the prototype of the political neutralist of our unhappy and agonized generation" when no one should avoid a "moral and intellectual engagement" with our enemy. Lena is an unusual woman who gives to Heyst an illusion that is necessary for all men, "the symbol of life." But to Heyst's island comes the unpredictable in the form of Mr. Jones, who "was violence," and his partner, Ricardo. They destroy "aloofness and detachment and life." This novel should encourage its generation to face bravely "what appears ugly and degrading."

1260 Gallaher, Elizabeth. "James and Conrad in France." Unpublished thesis, Radcliffe College, 1952.

1261 Gordan, John D. *"The Ghost* at Brede Place," NEW YORK PUBLIC LIBRARY BULLETIN, LVI (Dec 1952), 591-95.

Two sources, the program of the play and a review of the play, reveal the nature of the drama, "The Ghost," written by several collaborators, among them Henry James, George Gissing, H. G. Wells, Stephen Crane, and JC, and produced at Christmas time, 1899, by the house party at Brede Place, Stephen Crane's second residence in England. These sources indicate that if the lost manuscript should eventually turn up it will reveal no more than a "curiosity."

1262 Hart-Davis, Rupert. HUGH WALPOLE: A BIOGRAPHY (NY & Lond: Macmillan, 1952), pp. 31, 65, 116, 136, 158n, 168, 171, 175, 176, 186, 187, 195, 203-4, 236, 197-98, 215-16, 219, 227, 253, 282, 286, 377, 429.

Walpole planned to begin a study of JC in 1914; he completed his critical book 4 May 1915. He was thankful for JC's appreciation of his novels and cherished JC's acceptance to write a preface to an anthology of Walpole's work.

1263 Haugh, Robert F. "A Critical Study of Joseph Conrad." Unpublished thesis, University of Michigan, 1952.

1264 Haugh, Robert F. "Death and Consequences: Joseph Conrad's Attitude Toward Fate," UNIVERSITY OF KANSAS CITY REVIEW, XVIII (Spring 1952), 191-97.

The Nigger of the Narcissus contains, in its sequence of events, a dramatization of all the elements in the human solidarity of JC's world, arrayed against the forces that would destroy them. These events include the presence on the ship of Wait and Donkin, JC's "synonyms" for evil; the subsequent demoralization of the crew; the storm, in which order and discipline give stability to the precarious existence of the men; the long ordeal of endurance against the sea; the overthrow of the "overt nihilism" of Donkin and the "more insidious falsehood" of Wait; the final restoration of order to the men when Captain Allistoun confronts Donkin and forces him to obey; the release given to the men when Jim's body at last slips reluctantly into the sea; and the finding of a safe port at the end of the story.

This pattern implies what to be "one of us" in JC's world means; it is the experience offered in each of his novels, "which do not deny, but affirm human solidarities against the coldness of cosmic law." [An unusually perceptive analysis of this novel leads to testing this pattern against JC's other works.]

> **1265** Häusermann, Hans Walter. "Joseph Conrad's Literary Activities in Geneva," THE GENEVESE BACKGROUND (Lond: Routledge & Kegan Paul, 1952), pp. 199-213.

JC visited Geneva in October 1874; returned for twenty-five days in May-June 1891 for medical treatment in the aftermath of the Congo trip (writing chapter 8 of *Almayer's Folly* while he was there); visited again in 1895 when he was having difficulty with *An Outcast of the Islands* (the 1895 visit is used thirteen years later in *Under Western Eyes*); and returned again in 1907 when both of his sons were ill. The prejudicial treatment of Geneva in *Eyes* is due to the bleak circumstances of JC's 1907 trip. [Biographical details are followed by conventional comments on *Folly* and *Eyes*.]

> **1266** Hewitt, Douglas. CONRAD: A REASSESSMENT (Cambridge: Bowes & Bowes, 1952); developed from "Joseph Conrad's Hero: 'Fidelity' or 'The Choice of Nightmares,'" CAMBRIDGE JOURNAL, II (Aug 1949), 684-91; 2nd ed (Lond): Bowes & Bowes, 1969 [adds a preface which "suggests that my exuberance has become orthodox"].

The isolation of JC's characters is achieved by setting scenes so that "our eyes are never directed outwards to any other part of the human society"; the main characters are "central in the same ways as the heroes of tragedy, in that the whole of the isolated 'world' is centered on them and usually dependent, both morally and physically, on them." The characters' "inner problems are mirrored in external events and relationships" in such a way that "the facts of the external world become symbolic of the moral problems with which they are at grips, without ceasing to be facts which are perfectly convincing in naturalistic terms." *Lord Jim* and "The Secret Sharer" are clear examples of this "externalization" of psychological and moral problems.

In almost all of JC's earlier important works, "a penetrating scrutiny is directed against the simple virtues of honesty, courage, pity, and fidelity to an unquestionable ideal of conduct"; but one important situation recurs: for a man who relies on these simple virtues, they finally "become suspect" because he is "confronted by a partially apprehended sense of evil" against which he seems powerless. Often his awareness is aroused by "an obscure link between himself and a manifestation of the evil which he cannot fail to know for what it is." In "Heart of Darkness," "the voyage is both into the impenetrable darkness of Africa and into the darkness of Marlow's thoughts."

JC's characters often "find themselves in a world which offers them nothing but a 'choice of nightmares,' " like Falk; and from this world there is no escape. In *Nostromo,* JC utilizes his usual method, that of "isolation and concentration," along with "changes in tone," a juxtaposition of events which forces the reader to make judgments, the employment of symbols which are also concrete facts, and the recurrence of important themes and symbols.

"The Secret Sharer" marks the end of JC's period of work in which such characters as Marlow, Lord Jim, or Charles Gould find no solution to their problems; here the narrator finds a solution by freeing himself from "the haunting presence of his 'other self.' " In JC's later work such a sense of guilt no longer exists, nor does "this indefinable compact with the 'secret double.' " Hereafter, "the simple virtues of honesty, courage and fidelity to one's comrades" are to be "sufficient guides."

Chance, JC's first popular success, "marks . . . the decline in his art." In general, the later works show "a retreat from the degree of awareness of the complexity of human emotion found in the early ones," and the division of mankind into the good and the bad is "clearly a sign of restriction rather than a change of interest." Among JC's later works *The Shadow-Line* is less complex in its design and "markedly free from all the flaws of lush rhetoric and moralizing which disfigure the others," thus resembling "Typhoon" (completed in 1901). It is "far more a naturalistic psychological study than any other important work of Conrad." As in "Typhoon," JC considers only situations and problems "which can be perfectly dealt with in action"; the scope of the story is limited and there is no preoccupation with evil. JC is never cynical; his purpose is "constantly to reveal unexpected resemblances and to imply that the plight of his central characters is but one manifestation of the working of universal spiritual and moral laws." His work thus resembles tragedy in that the hero is "a *typical* figure in a central and responsible situation, so that he may be said to crystallize the problem of good and evil into precise and significant situations. In his fate is worked out the implications of the moral and spiritual order." [An influential and important book in the reassessment of JC's works, a part of the achievement-and-decline theory of JC's development.]

> **1267** Hoffman, Anastasia C. "Studies in the Impressionistic Novel, 1890-1914: James, Crane, Conrad, and Ford." Unpublished thesis, University of Wisconsin, 1952.

1268 Kenner, Hugh. "Conrad and Ford," SHENANDOAH, III (Summer 1952), 50-55; rptd in GNOMON: ESSAYS ON CONTEMPORARY LITERATURE (NY: McDowell, Obolensky, 1958), pp. 162-70.

In the first part of *Under Western Eyes,* the "presented fact" becomes the "economic metaphor" so that JC actually does "above all else, . . . make you see"; then the Western Eyes of the elderly language teacher are interposed between the reader and Razumov's saga in such a way that the presented fact is removed from our attention, with commentary becoming the medium through which events are seen. *Nostromo* is the most notable example of "technique," in the "detached" parts of JC's works, obscuring the fact that his mind, no longer obsessed by the reality of his subject, begins to manipulate it philosophically. Basically, JC does not know what his attitude toward his events and characters is. Ford Madox Ford, having no "philosophy," has a far greater technical virtuosity (especially in THE GOOD SOLDIER) than JC has and achieves a far greater "sense of flexible life." Whereas JC's "detachment" suggests a "symbolic" remoteness, Ford's nearness to life conveys the illusion of no more and no less order than life assumes; and the bewilderment of Ford's narrator prevents the author from having to bring his novel to a definite resolution. Both writers suffer from an excess of technique; but their achievement is great. [Without obscuring JC's achievement, Kenner convincingly suggests what may be his greatest weakness.]

1269 Kloth, Friedrich. "Das Problem der Einsamkeit bei Conrad" (The Problem of Isolation in Conrad): Unpublished thesis, Kiel University, 1952. [In German.]

1270 Mendilow, Adam Abraham. TIME AND THE NOVEL (Lond: Peter Nevil, 1952); rptd (NY: Humanities P, 1965), pp. 20, 48, 54, 75, 83, 104, 181, 185, 226; originally a thesis, University of London, 1952.

JC, like Gide, employs the "technique of multiple focussing." With F. M. Ford, JC evolved the fictional mode of "purposed *longueur*," the integration of digression with environment in the novel, "emphasizing its relation to the passage of fictional time." Ford and JC also tried the "chronological looping method" or "time shift." JC presents the "allusion of unbroken completeness" and occasionally experiments with counterpoint. "Marlow and other observers . . . [use] the device of refraction through intervening minds . . . [to form] the basis of a highly complex technique." [Cursory treatment of JC.]

1271 Neill, S. Diana. A SHORT HISTORY OF THE ENGLISH NOVEL (NY: Macmillan, 1952), pp. 205, 223-29.

Joseph Conrad

JC wrote English with richness and sonority due, perhaps, to a preference for the longer cadences of French and Latin-derived words. His novels reflect the influence of Flaubert, Maupassant, the Russian novelists, and Henry James. He aims to convey the inexplicability of life and man perplexed by fate. The atmosphere is most important to JC; by means of exotic atmosphere he represents evil (e.g., *The Nigger of the Narcissus*). There is no plot; the action in *Nigger* is psychological (the effect of a dying Negro on the crew). It is an absorbing book despite the lack of plot and feminine interest. JC creates the atmosphere of evil in his novels, not by directly presented horror but rather by suggestion. His work reflects his stoic philosophy, the inscrutability of life.

1272 Paulding, Gouverneur, Helen MacInnes, and Lyman Bryson. "Conrad's *Lord Jim*," INVITATION TO LEARNING READER, II (Fall 1952), 236-42.

[This exchange deals in a general way with these themes: JC's faith in man, Jim's cowardice, JC's "overcharged" writing, and *Lord Jim* as an adventure story.]

1273 Rogers, B. J. "The Collaboration of Conrad and Ford Madox Ford." Unpublished thesis, Geneva University, 1952.

1274 Sasse, Maria-Elisabeth. "Wesensmerkemale der Völker im Spiegel der Werke Joseph Conrads" (Characteristic Traits of People in Light of Joseph Conrad's Works). Unpublished thesis, University of Münster, 1952.

[In a survey of most of JC's writings, Sasse discusses his descriptions and views of the Poles, the Russians, the English, the Germans.] As a rule JC is not interested in those traits of his main characters which are characteristic for the nations they come from. His opinions on the various nations and their qualities must be deduced from his minor characters and his background descriptions. [In German.]

1275 Tindall, William York. "The Symbolic Novel," A.D., III (Winter 1952), 56-68; rptd in THE LITERARY SYMBOL (NY: Columbia U P, 1955), pp. 86-91.

"Heart of Darkness," Henry Green's PARTY GOING, and Joyce's PORTRAIT OF THE ARTIST, are, like Kafka's THE CASTLE, archetypal quests: symbolic, many-leveled, organized like poems. "Heart of Darkness" may be read as a politico-economic commentary, a "moral discourse," or as a "psychological investigation." Marlow's quest is moral (his obsession with integrity) and psychological (his quest for self-realization). "The exploring of Africa's interior becomes the exploring of man's interior." Three women knitting, gunboat, heaps of dead machinery, river (called "a snake") form a burden of horror, widening ripples of the forest symbol. This horror leads analogically to the unknown. The "imagistic organization of the symbols of forest and journey is that of a dream." The symbol perhaps represents the "natural, the primitive, the unconscious." "As sign, it carries all these meanings, but as symbol, it carries feelings and ideas that are suggested and limited by their meanings, their concrete embodiments, and their context. No statement is adequate for Conrad's vision of reality. Its only equivalent is his book, an elaborate analogy for conception and feeling."

1276 Tuong-Buu-Khanh, M. "Conrad et l'Orient" (Conrad and the Orient). Unpublished thesis, University of Paris, 1952. [In French.]

1277 Young, Vernon. "Trial by Water: Joseph Conrad's *The Nigger of the Narcissus*," ACCENT, XII (Spring 1952), 67-81; rptd in THE ART OF JOSEPH CONRAD: A CRITICAL SYMPOSIUM, ed by Robert Wooster Stallman (East Lansing: Michigan State U P, 1960), pp. 108-20.

The Nigger of the Narcissus is an "adventure of the soul" and therefore of a mythic aspect which JC "never openly acknowledged." The sea, "the unstable element," was to JC "the amniotic ocean of life"; like life it is "uncertain, incalculable but enchanting and worthier of men's challenge than the land." On its voyage the *Narcissus* "sails *out of* darkness" into the light, then *"into* darkness" again at the end of the novel. Wait, the Negro, is "set off against" Singleton, "the Able Seaman." Black and white dualism are moral polarities in the work, and the association of "narcissus with death" gives a "paradoxical twist to the pairing of skull and blossom, root and flower." The voyage of the *Narcissus* is a trial by water, "not so much to initiate as to chasten, to test the illusion of invulnerability which each man wears in varying proportions." The "primary agent" of the trial is James Wait, the Nigger, who is "the spirit of blackness, archetype of the unknown forces from the depths"; he is not "sensationally demonic," but rather "insidious and emanating."

The crew of the *Narcissus* "become victims of benevolent egotism," and "their sponsorship [of Wait] is betrayed." They are "modified" by Wait according to "the drift of their respective temperaments": Captain Allistoun is supremely rational, always in charge of the situation; Singleton's simple candor is "the exact countercheck to the simplicity of the Nigger's deceit"; Podmore, the religious fanatic, helps to discover "behind the mask of a dying shirker, the infra-human visage of the Satanic"; Donkin is "the eternal and omnipresent grumbler, a thing of rags and patches with no soul of his own"; and the "mercurial" Belfast perhaps suffers most from "the burden of Wait's travesty of humility." JC thus maintained a precarious balance "between the naturalistic, biographical material and its symbolic transmutation," thereby creating "a fable with many layers of interconnection."

1953

1278 Bantock, G. H. "The Two 'Moralities' of Joseph Conrad," ESSAYS IN CRITICISM, III (April 1953), 125-42.

JC's heroes are aware of two "moralities," one represented by the world of society at large and the other by the morality of the self "where there is no answering reciprocity in the sanctions of the everyday social world even when represented at its best." There is then "the morality of a certain order of public obligation . . . inadequate to cover those complexities of the inner life . . . ; and the morality of the self in isolation following its egoism, at best striving to find some coherence in itself, so often, however, the victim of its own inner compulsions." Unlike Lawrence, JC "never completely throws over the best of public morality at the behest of the private" morality.

1279 Breit, Harvey. "Repeat Performances Appraised," NEW YORK TIMES, 8 Nov 1953, p. 45.

[Comments on the contents of TALES OF LAND AND SEA (Garden City, NY: Hanover House, 1953) and the "workmanlike introduction" by William McFee.]

1280 Chillag, Charles. "The 'Others' in Conrad's *Lord Jim*," ENGLISH "A" ANALYST (Department of English, Northwestern University), No. 21 (15 Feb 1953), 1-10.

Although we see Jim mainly through Marlow, we also note other perspectives, for example, Brierly's, which assumes a major import when his suicide is juxtaposed with Jim's jump. In committing suicide, Brierly destroys himself "to forestall self-knowledge" whereas Jim "is destroyed by self-knowledge." In jumping, Jim follows the "herd" and deserts his private way of "how to live," but he loses his identity. The jump leaves the impression that the failure is the possibility of everyone who has never failed. Each person, who is for himself a "subject," is for others who see him an "object." The "Eye of Others" fixes one so that he becomes, paradoxically, an "object" for himself also, fixed and limited in his being as the "Eye of Others" places him. Jim is thus "defined and limited" in himself as the person who took the "infamous leap," and he continues to see himself as "Others" see him. His later flight, then, is not so much from disgrace or dishonor as from his "inner conviction of worthlessness." Through Marlow, Jim is constantly related to "a concrete Other" in whose eye Jim's present and future are linked to his past. Jim cannot escape from Marlow: in Jim, Marlow sees in himself his own possibility of failure. And, too, Marlow reveals the enigma of Jim's being: Jim, "under a cloud," is counterfeit and yet noble and genuine. Jim finally transcends the jump by placing himself in the hands of the natives in Patusan: he ceases to flee, that is, to try to live as if he had not jumped. But, as Jewel had feared, he yields to the call of his own race for the sake of the freedom he can enjoy in the eyes of Gentleman Brown. Then, by accepting death, Jim no longer flees from himself nor struggles for the old illusion; he shoulders the alien offense—Brown's and his own—and "the extreme affirmation of the code by which he condemns his self-deception." Although we finally see Jim "under a cloud," this Jim is "not so much the Jim who is blemished but the Jim who is left untouched by the jump, precisely because he succeeds in leaving the code, the norm and the ideal untouched. His death affirms the universality of moral value—which is pure, hard, and exalting." [A closely reasoned, perceptive analysis of an important aspect of Lord Jim. This article should be made more readily available than its original mimeographed form.]

1281 Davis, Robert Gorham. "Joseph Conrad," INSTRUCTOR'S MANUAL: TEN MODERN MASTERS: AN ANTHOLOGY OF THE SHORT STORY (NY: Harcourt, Brace, 1953), pp. 7-8, 10-11, 32-35.
[Brief commentary and suggestions for discussion dealing with "Youth" and "The Secret Sharer." Also see ibid., 2nd ed (1959).]

1282 Ekelof, Gunnar. "Exotiskt" (Exotic), BONNIERS LITTERARA MAGASIN (Stockholm), XXII (1953), 538-39.
One can criticize JC in details, but not in entirety. His ideas of women and love are idealized, but one must remember he is not of our time: the world of his novels was primitive; personal courage and initiative were necessary to life, and he must be forgiven his use of melodramatic villains. In *Almayer's Folly*, translated by Vera and Stig Dahlstedt (Stockholm: Forum, 1953), he has more strings to his psychological lyre than in his later books where he was more firmly for or against an issue. In the jealous slave girl we see JC's conception of woman as a beast or lower being; the daughter, Nina, is his idealized image of woman. He is so attracted by the good, noble, and healthy that even the books' manly hero becomes a stereotype. There is a Victorian influence behind this tendency, but it is also innate in JC. More important is the penetrating atmosphere of the book. It is made up not only of tropical beauty, flowers, birds, and sunsets, but also the ugliness of flies, filth, and decay, a blending which has the intensity of a memory from an earlier life. JC was a memory artist, and

although he concerned himself with the jungle and the sea, he in some respects resembles the salon-bred Proust. [In Swedish.]

1283 "Fiction," A. L. A. BOOKLIST, L (1 Dec 1953), 145.

TALES OF LAND AND SEA (Garden City, NY: Hanover House, 1953), with an introduction by William McFee, is a collection of short stories and short novels, some of which have been frequently anthologized. "The typography and illustrations enhance the attractiveness of a low-priced volume."

1284 Fraser, G. S. THE MODERN WRITER AND HIS WORLD (Lond: Derek Verschoyle, 1953); rvd ed (Baltimore: Penguin Books; NY: Frederick A. Praeger, 1964), pp. 29, 75, 85-88, 90, 166, 325, 397.

Is JC "really ever quite a novelist in the strict sense, and not rather a writer of romances?" He, unlike Jane Austen, George Eliot, and Henry James, does not write about any settled "worlds" but "about the dangerous edges of the earth." Instead of being concerned about manners, he is interested in codes of honor, in heroism, and disgrace. His "grandiose rhetoric" is compensated for by "an underlying irony." JC is not in the modern sense a psychologist; he presents his characters as an observer sees them. They seem to be simple men or even symbolic types. But an "ultimate mystery" about them gives many of his works a poetic quality. The irony in *The Secret Agent* is coarsely heavy, and *Victory* is little more than a first-rate melodrama.

1285 Garnett, David. THE GOLDEN ECHO (Lond: Chatto & Windus, 1953; NY: Harcourt, Brace, 1954), pp. 62-63.

[Anecdotes about acquaintance with JC.]

1286 Howe, Irving. "Order and Anarchy: The Political Novels," KENYON REVIEW, XV (Autumn 1953), 505-21; concluded as "The Political Novels (continued)," ibid., XVI (Winter 1954), 1-19; rptd in POLITICS AND THE NOVEL (NY: Horizon P, 1957), pp. 76-113.

Although JC felt "hostile to the life of politics," he turned "repeatedly" and with "a visible shudder of distaste to the world of London anarchists, Russian emigrés, Latin revolutionaries." The paradox takes its opposite points from JC's responses to Dostoevski and to James: Dostoevski he "hated with a dull fury," very likely because the Russian was able to stir in him the political past and the sufferings of his family. James was for him the ideal of the civilized writer, the gentleman writer. In the novels and stories "the Jamesian Conrad directs, the Dostoevskian Conrad erupts." His conservatism resulted in his stress upon order and responsibility; to believe, however, that his attitudes led "to a redeeming vision of human solidarity, must be sharply discounted." He reaches for such a vision, it is true, but almost never achieves it. Life for Dostoevski is "always drenched with terror, yet men turn to each other for comfort and support; in Conrad each man faces it alone and the only solidarity is a solidarity of isolated victims." He possessed the mixture of sternness and simplicity characteristic of the stoical attitude; but his "fondness for the theatrical, . . . the exotic" is romantic. "In the contrast between what Marlow says and what he tells lies the distance Conrad can allow between the stoical norm and the romantic deviation." He is anti-romantic, however, in one significant way: "he violently resists the demonic and the sensual. By straining his will, he suppresses the chaos within him; but it breaks past his guard as a free-floating anxiety. . . . Conrad is finally unable to sustain either commitment or skepticism: what remains is the honorable debris of failure."

1287 Paulding, Gouverneur, Robert Penn Warren, and Lyman Bryson. *"Nostromo,"* INVITATION TO LEARNING READER, III (1953), 247-52.

Warren: JC is "one of the big seminal writers of this century." *Nostromo* contains his characteristic theme: a man approaches a moral test and either fails or succeeds in "achieving the proper moral awareness." JC's landscape symbolizes "a kind of fundamental drama of man trying to find meaning." Man is part of the "vast indifference of nature." Nostromo and Captain Mitchell are instinctively honest men, types. The book is really of the world around Nostromo. *Paulding:* The book is "absolutely contemporary in interest and seriousness." In JC's changing society, one who departs from "the entire optimistic feeling" of the nineteenth century, may lack "the spiritual power to make" for "real" social change. *Bryson:* JC combines a healthy "romanticism . . . and wit" to form his "complex and powerful" fiction.

1288 Pritchett, V. S. "An Emigré," BOOKS IN GENERAL (NY: Harcourt, 1953), pp. 216-22; based on "Books in General," NEW STATESMAN AND NATION, N.S. XL (15 July 1950), 72-73.

The émigré, because of his isolation, becomes preeminently a conscience, JC is a reactionary; "for him the old despotism and the new Utopianism are complementary forms of moral anarchy." His weakness is "the creaking sentence, the rumble of stage scenery and some staginess of dialogue." *The Secret Agent* and *Under Western Eyes* are especially suggestive to the modern reader because the books are free from destiny, melodrama, and rhetoric. "They put a central modern question to ourselves—what is our attitude to treachery and other moral consequences of a belief in revolution?" JC shows in *Eyes* an ironical wonder at the Russian's readiness for cynicism. *Agent,* a thriller, shows the influence of Meredith and R. L.

Stevenson. JC's genius for "picturesque discussion" of characters is evident, but the tone of the book is contrived. He moves in narratives from idea to idea, not event to event. His dramas are of change of view.

1289 Russell, Bertrand. "Portraits from Memory—V. Joseph Conrad," LISTENER, L (17 Sept 1953), 462-63; trans by Zdzisław Bronal in WIADOMOŚCI, IX (14 Feb 1954), 1; rptd in PORTRAITS FROM MEMORY (Lond: Allen; NY: Simon & Schuster, 1956), pp. 86-92.

Despite his naval career, JC was an aristocratic Polish gentleman with a romantic love for the sea and England. Most admirable is JC's "Heart of Darkness," in which a weak idealist becomes crazed by the loneliness among savages and the horror of the forest—a story which reflects his philosophy of life: though man is born in chains he can be free by submitting impulse to a larger purpose. Not interested in political systems, JC had definite political feelings (he hated Russia, loved England). His concern was for the individual man against indifferent Nature. Loneliness and fear of what is strange interested JC most; both blended in "Amy Foster," in which a Slavic youth is shipwrecked in a Kentish village where he is mistreated by all except the dull, plain girl that he eventually marries and who ultimately abandons him. JC's pessimistic remarks about China had shown a deeper wisdom than Russell had shown in his book on China. [Russell and JC disagreed about most things but had a great mutual admiration.]

1290 Sherbo, Arthur. "Conrad's *Victory* and HAMLET," NOTES AND QUERIES, CXCVIII (Nov 1953), 492-93.

The verbal echoes of HAMLET found in the first seventeen pages of *Victory* are significant and may be accounted for in two ways: (1) perhaps JC deliberately echoed "to further a resemblance for which he was consciously working"; (2) perhaps he unconsciously used them. "Either interpretation reveals something about the act of composition."

1291 Stresau, Hermann. "Joseph Conrad: tragische Figuren in Konflikt mit der Wirklichkeit" (Joseph Conrad: Tragic Figures in Conflict with Reality), DEUTSCHE UNIVERSITÄTSZEITUNG, VIII (18 May 1953), 7-10.

The years that JC spent in the British merchant marine were the happiest of his life, and they provided him with a reality commensurate with his powers of imagination. JC's work can be characterized as a *recherche du temps perdu,* as an attempt to recapture a vanished reality. This reality should not be interpreted, however, as the sea itself or as his sailor's life, but as the forces that had ruptured his existence and transformed him from a sailor into an author. It was the image of man defying an inhuman power that awoke the writer in JC. What fascinated JC in his characters was a fatal flaw in their moral constitution. The sea provides merely a background against which he can examine an inner drama. His typical protagonists are tragic characters alone in the universe. His interest in such utter isolation is traceable to his change of profession: after he turned his back on that wide ocean that had seemed so real and he retired to a narrow study, he was struck more powerfully than ever before by the realization that the ocean was empty and meaningless, that the universe was empty and meaningless, and that man by his desperate and fruitless endeavors to extract some meaning from a meaningless cosmos is an isolated and tragic figure. Nature accentuates man's isolation: it offers no security, no peace, no help. The only way in which man can be himself is through defiance of the elements. And if nature offers no haven, neither does society. Like many of his generation, JC saw through the bourgeois illusions of political security. The world he deals with is a fleeting, international world on which stable forms take no hold. Out of human isolation, including his own isolation, JC created a kind of freedom that might be defined as a lack of commitment to any one point of view. He is unwilling, or unable, to come to final decisions, and his narrative techniques reflect this unwillingness or inability. Man cannot decide, because he has no certainty. Such protagonists as Heyst, Lord Jim, and Tom Lingard do not shape their own destiny: they *are* destined. What, then, is the ultimate human reality? Confronted by a meaningless universe man nevertheless is endowed with understanding, a gift that is the mark of his humanity and that enables him to recognize and love his spiritual kindred. Jim, after all, was "one of us." Such understanding is a form of power through which man, in a limited way, can overcome his tragic fate. [In German.]

> **1292** Van Ghent, Dorothy. "On *Lord Jim*," THE ENGLISH NOVEL (NY: Rinehart, 1953), pp. 229-44; rptd in THE ART OF JOSEPH CONRAD: A CRITICAL SYMPOSIUM (East Lansing: Michigan State U P, 1960), ed by Robert Wooster Stallman, pp. 142-54.

Jim, last seen by Marlow as "at the heart of a vast enigma," is not enigmatic. He is "one of us." The enigma is what we are and how to be what we are. The indirect narrative presentation of Jim "is uniquely humanizing, for we see him only as people can see each other, ambivalently and speculatively." JC implies a division between a man and his acts. Marlow provides the necessary medium of intelligent consciousness to show the relativity of Jim's case. JC "works through epiphanies, that is, through dramatic manifestations of elements hidden or implicit in the already constructed character." The major epiphanies appear to show a collusion of outer nature with the "dark power," but really are the workings out of character through circumstances. "[T]he only cases in which subjective identification with Jim does not take place are those of a man—the French lieutenant—who is above Jim's failings by virtue of his medocrity, and of men who are below Jim's problem by virtue of their psychotic maliciousness." JC's tale is in the manner of the older classical dramatists wherein law is justified to the self. "But he managed to do a tale that put both the law and the self to question, and left them there."

1293 Walcutt, Charles Child. "Interpreting the Symbol," COLLEGE ENGLISH, XIV (May 1953), 452-54.

The special quality of the symbol in literature is that "it is powerfully concrete and yet suggests more than can be logically accounted for." With one kind of symbol, the critic may define " 'symbolic' intentions which cannot really be felt by himself or anyone else." In JC's "The Secret Sharer," for example, the test which Leggatt failed could have destroyed the captain in the story. Leggatt has "absorbed the current ill fortune," and he has also "acted, symbolically, as the captain's potential other self"; his fate has thus been "a ritual—a symbolic ritual—sacrifice in which the captain has seen his tragic potentialities enacted and therefore forestalled." Just as the dance is really "a ritual incantation" so is "the symbolic action of a story the same thing." Leggatt's "ritual dance of evil" has satisfied or duped the gods and thereby given a chance to the captain "to gain control of his ship, his crew, and himself." The captain's risk in protecting Leggatt is, symbolically, "his participation in this ritual forestalling." The climax of the symbolism appears "when Leggatt's hat remains floating by the ship and enables the captain to know that he has enough sternway to come about and sail free of the rocks to which, in his part of the propitiating dance, he has brought his ship dangerously close." The critic should, however, avoid carrying this symbolism so far as to drift into allegory.

1294 Young, Vernon. "Lingard's Folly: The Lost Subject," KENYON REVIEW, XV (Autumn 1953), 522-39; rptd in THE ART OF JOSEPH CONRAD: A CRITICAL SYMPOSIUM, ed by Robert Wooster Stallman (East Lansing: Michigan State U P, 1960), pp. 96-108.

Albert Guerard, Jr., is wrong to find in *Almayer's Folly* (1895), *An Outcast of the Islands* (1896), and *The Rescue* (1920) a "moral continuity" in Tom Lingard. The works collectively show "Conrad's shifts of intention, . . . his uncertain psychological orientation and . . . his aesthetic polarities." They show "the initiation of a novelist and his anti-climax, the promise and the loss, the beginning of mastery and the collapse of it." The formally insecure *Folly* is original in its physical *atmosphere* and "the tenebrous *moral* atmosphere." This "extraordinary" first novel provides "hints" of future achievements. *Outcast* "consolidates features merely traced in *Almayer's Folly.*" As an "achieved novel" it is better than most critics have said. *Rescue,* written when JC "was beyond the force of its germinal requirements," is "a moral retrenchment, a concession to criticism of the heroic ideal while maintaining the aura of the idea."

1954

1295 Allen, Walter. THE ENGLISH NOVEL: A SHORT CRITICAL STUDY (Lond: Phoenix House, 1954), pp. 290-300; rptd (NY: Dutton, 1955), pp. 361-74.

In most of his works, JC's theme is "man against himself, the environment, whether sea or exotic place, having a double function, to isolate the character from society and the larger world of men, so that he can be put *in extremis,* and to act as the agent of his self-confrontation." In his earlier and best work, JC is greatly preoccupied with evil, but he never explains its nature. Marlow, who is sometimes a *persona* and sometimes more, "talks too much and sometimes in the wrong way"—like JC himself. From about 1910 onwards JC "gives way to rhetoric, the tragic vision having departed," as in *Chance.* His best works seem to be "Youth," "Heart of Darkness," "Typhoon," "Falk," "The Secret Sharer," *The Nigger of the Narcissus, Lord Jim, Nostromo,* and *The Secret Agent.* Of the novels, *Nostromo* is "undoubtedly the finest"; "it may stand as a picture of the modern world in microcosm." JC interprets his characters "through their ideal conception of themselves"; he persuades the reader "not only of their ordinary reality as lifelike characters but of their symbolic reality" as well.

1296 Benson, Carl. "Conrad's Two Stories of Initiation," PMLA, LXIX (March 1954), 46-56; rptd in CONRAD'S "SECRET SHARER" AND THE CRITICS, ed by Bruce Harkness (Belmont, Calif: Wadsworth, 1962), 83-93.

"The Secret Sharer" and *The Shadow-Line* are twin stories of initiation into maturity and its demands. Isolation is inherent in the commands of the two captains; both begin with an oversimplified view of their duties. *Shadow-Line* completes the passage from egocentric youth to human solidarity, while "The Secret Sharer" gives only the beginning of the initiation.

1297 Brewster, Dorothy. EAST WEST PASSAGE (Lond: George Allen & Unwin, 1954), 214-15.

[A discussion of the influence of Turgenev, Tolstoi, and Dostoevski on JC;

abstracted from Douglas Hewitt's JOSEPH CONRAD: A REASSESSMENT (1952).]

1298 Cecil, Lord David. "Joseph Conrad," LONDON MAGAZINE, I (Sept 1954), 54-71; rptd in THE FINE ART OF READING (Indianapolis: Bobbs-Merrill, 1957), pp. 179-215.

JC's unusual background and experiences led him to unusual subject matter, basically not unlike R. L. Stevenson's. His "brooding questioning intelligence was out to explore motives behind the simple violent events." His interest was in man, not men; and the "thrilling, highly colored adventures are simply a vehicle through which to express his sense of man's predicament." His view is a mixture of "pessimistic skepticism and romantic faith." JC believed that life was precarious, he disbelieved official myths, but admired courage, integrity, and self-sacrifice. His characters are of two sorts: those who are true to their ideals and those who are untrue. His wicked figures are of two types: (1) Schomberg (*Victory*), Marsey ("The End of the Tether"), Donkin (*The Nigger of the Narcissus*), who have no moral ideal, fail through vanity, cowardice, and (2) Gentleman Brown (*Lord Jim*), Mr. Jones (*Victory*), Necator (*Under Western Eyes*), the Professor (*The Secret Agent*), who deliberately reject honor, recognize but hate moral ideals. JC's idea of love is that it is a violent force, an illusion, "like everything else," sometimes for good, more often for harm. "Woman is born to love man"; her world is limited, and she does not understand the masculine world. Only two of his heroines, Miss Haldin (*Eyes*) and Antonia (*Nostromo*), "guide their lives by a more abstract idea" (both are "heroic patriots"), but their idealism is that of the unquestioning nun.

JC's themes express his philosophy: "Youth" praises a romantic sense of glory, triumphing; "Heart of Darkness" shows the other side, original sin; "Typhoon" shows stupid man rising through integrity. Most of his stories are "concerned with honor (*Jim, The Rescue,* "The End of the Tether," "The Secret Sharer"). JC's love of the adventure-story provided him with the right material to illustrate his philosophy: man alone in a storm or on a lonely island must depend on individual virtue. The "tension" in JC's novels arises from "simultaneous realization of the dignity of man's nature and the dreadfulness of his predicament." JC's ironies rise out of this disparity, incongruity. JC is one of the few who manage to reconcile realism with poetic beauty and intensity.

JC has deficiencies: his text is too glossy, too rich; he thrills but does not always touch the heart; "he never lets the characters speak for themselves"; he, the "cautious rhetorician," is always manipulating, heightening, darkening. Sometimes form is too portentous, elaborate, for his subject. *Chance* fails because the apparatus of indirect narrative and forward-backward movement is "too great." In *Eyes,* the moralist is in conflict with the artist; JC went too far in trying to show how Razumov's betrayal worked on his conscience.

1299 Collins, Harold R. "Kurtz, the Cannibals, and the Second-Rate Helmsman," WESTERN HUMANITIES REVIEW, VIII (Autumn 1954), 299-310; rptd in JOSEPH CONRAD'S "HEART OF DARKNESS": BACKGROUNDS AND CRITICISMS, ed by Leonard F. Dean (Englewood Cliffs, NJ: Prentice-Hall, Spectrum Books, 1960), pp. 149-59.

In such characters as "the slovenly prisoners' guard, the ill-conditioned manager's boy, and the second rate helmsman," JC is depicting, in "Heart of Darkness," detribalized natives, i.e., those who can no longer rely on native standards and yet are unable to fit in with the white man's social patterns.

1300 Epstein, Sir Jacob. EPSTEIN: AN AUTOBIOGRAPHY (Lond: Hulton P, 1954), pp. 73-77, 89, 288; rptd (NY: E. P. Dutton; Lond: Vista Books, 1963).

JC sat for a bronze bust in 1924, for twenty days. JC was neat, had rheumatism and neurasthenia, was crotchety and was patient during long sittings. He admitted his ignorance of the plastic arts. JC commented on Melville: "He knows nothing of the sea. Fantastic, ridiculous. . . . Mystical, my eye! My old boots are mystical."

1301 Gillon, Adam. "Isolation in the Life and Works of Joseph Conrad," DISSERTATION ABSTRACTS, XIV (1954), 1409. Unpublished thesis, Columbia University, 1954; much expanded in THE ETERNAL SOLITARY: A STUDY OF JOSEPH CONRAD (NY: Bookman Associates; Lond: Burns & MacEachern, 1960), which see for abstract.

1302 Glasgow, Ellen. "Pages from the Autobiography of Ellen Glasgow," AMERICAN SCHOLAR, XIII (Summer 1954), 284-87; rptd in THE WOMAN WITHIN (NY: Harcourt, Brace, 1954), pp. 200-204.

JC was "a brilliant talker," despite his "strong foreign accent." [Account of a visit to JC in 1914.]

1303 Harkness, Bruce. "The Epigraph of Conrad's *Chance,*" NINETEENTH-CENTURY FICTION, IX (Dec 1954), 209-22.

The title *Chance,* along with the epigraph, is ironic, but the basis of the novel is "the reverse of chance." The narrators of the story are important to the theme, and the actions of "outsiders" both cause and cure Flora's problem, "which in its simplest terms is an 'inferiority complex.' " In the ironic motto, taken from Sir Thomas Browne, "chance (accident) does not govern life"; and in the novel there is "a determinative causality at work." Both Browne and JC mean that Fortune, or Chance, does not control life; "events are always caused." In JC's novel, "psychological necessity" orders the action.

According to the standard critical interpretation of *Chance,* while we get "a portion of the story, coming through as many as five narrator-lenses, each lens is somehow distorting, untrue, in its picturing of Flora; but with Marlow's juxtaposition of the many lenses, we at last see her in the true light." But a close inspection of the work shows that the theory of lenses completely collapses: there is no change of tone for different narrators, the sequences in which narrators and re-narrators appear are obscured and distorted too much to serve as lenses, and in much of the novel Marlow is the only narrator whose presence the reader feels. The narrators make Flora's "case" probable by surrounding her life with realism. They also "directly condition" her life by acting in it. Thus, not accident or chance, but "psychological necessity" controls the plot. Marlow should not be completely identified with JC, and his insight is incomplete. His views are corrected not by another character but by JC's management of the plot. In spite of many accidental happenings, "accident is not central to the plot." The attack on Flora by her governess is not accidental: it is "completely centered" on the abnormality of the governess; and de Barral's failure in the market is inevitable, brought on by the sentimental backing of an Indian Prince. From this novel one might conclude that "in the midst of apparent chaos, coincidence, and accident, the real issues are decided by man's character." [An ingenious and convincing interpretation of *Chance.*]

> **1304** Howe, Irving. "The Political Novels (concluded)," KENYON REVIEW, XVI (Winter 1954), 1-19; concludes "Order and Anarchy: The Political Novels," ibid., XV (Autumn 1953), 505-21; rptd in POLITICS AND THE NOVEL (NY: Horizon P, 1957), pp. 76-113.

Although the conception of Mr. Verloc in *The Secret Agent* is "brilliantly original," the novel fails from an overdone style, a surfeit of a peevish irony, and evidence of "some deep distemper." JC the novelist is not required "to admire the anarchists or accept their doctrine"; but he must satisfy the reader's "sense of what 'really happens' in the kind of world that is summoned by the word 'anarchist.'" *Nostromo,* on the other hand, is "a work of the first rank." It possesses scope and personal drama; its "problems of morality and problems of politics" come to seem "very much the same." As a "fictional study of imperialism," like A PASSAGE TO INDIA, it seems like a lonely, towering peak. "It is the one novel in which Conrad handles the political theme with something very close to mastery, with a balance and poise, a sense of dispassionate justice, that can hardly be too much admired. And nowhere more so than in the ending of the book, where society appears resurgent and confident, but of community, of that which makes men human, nothing remains." Like MIDDLEMARCH, it is one of the few novels in English to command "a whole society."

1305 Lynskey, Winifred. "Conrad's *Nostromo*," EXPLICATOR, XIII (Oct 1954), Item 6.

The role of silver in *Nostromo* is central; it represents the evil of material interest, and people are defined by their relations to it.

1306 Mudrick, Marvin. "Conrad and the Terms of Criticism," HUDSON REVIEW, VII (Autumn 1954), 419-26.

Modern critics, in turning from literary gossip to literary analysis, have established terms like "myth," "symbol," "structure," and "tone." There is a danger, however, in taking these terms literally. Critics who do, select for praise writers who are "most prolific in modish clues of myth, metaphor, symbol, etc." JC is among the chosen, and his defects are frequently overlooked. He was not, for example, averse to betraying his narrative skill for some "portentous image or generalization or symbolic gesture" interesting to him. *Victory* is one of his failures, since here he reduced "almost every character to a single symbol and function." "Typhoon" and *The Nigger of the Narcissus,* on the other hand, are successes. "The Secret Sharer" and "Amy Foster" are contrived and pathetic; here JC takes "rib-cracking" nudges at us with his light-and-dark symbolism. It is easy to proclaim mystery; it is not so easy to persuade skeptical readers "to suspend our disbelief in it." In "Amy Foster" JC broods inordinately on "Mystery, tragedy, truth, imagination, fate, the Incomprehensible and the Infinite. . . . None of them is earned or penetrated during the action." Leggatt, in "The Secret Sharer," is unconvincing as a precursor of depth psychology. "The captain-patient is too conscious of the symbols . . . that the artist-doctor would like him to exhibit. Conrad might have done better . . . if he had been described by his critical partisans not as a poet in fiction, but as a man who merely tells a tale."

1307 Stallman, R. W., and R. E. Watters. THE CREATIVE READER (NY: Ronald P, 1954), pp. 326-28.

JC's "Amy Foster" is greater literature than Galsworthy's "The Black Godmother" in its superior handling of setting, complex theme and character, emotional power, integration of structure, overtones and symbolic implication. The technique of indirect narration is logical and corresponds to the theme: "the desire for and simultaneously the difficulty of understanding human nature and communicating between human beings." JC "uses parallel events to create the sense of inevitability and to enrich the emotional texture of the story." The story may be about the fundamental mystery of life, about isolation in JC's life, and about Mankind's making terms with an incomprehensible world.

1308 Whicher, George F. "Reprints, New Editions," NEW YORK HERALD TRIBUNE BOOK REVIEW, 17 Jan 1954, p. 13.

The stories of TALES OF LAND AND SEA, edited by William McFee (Garden City, NY: Hanover House, 1953) make this a "substantial volume."

1309 Wiley, Paul L. CONRAD'S MEASURE OF MAN (Madison: University of Wisconsin P, 1954); part rptd in CONRAD: A COLLECTION OF CRITICAL ESSAYS, ed by Marvin Mudrick (Englewood Cliffs, NJ: Prentice-Hall, Spectrum Books, 1966); rptd (NY: Gordian P, 1966).

A leading clue to JC's particular view of man in a natural or a social setting is his "cosmic or creational" imagery, typified by a small scene of human endeavor—a ship, a trading station, an island, a state—threatened by external disaster. The first stage of development of JC's work, "The Hermit: Man in the World," leads him to move away from depicting men who cannot become heroes to depicting heroes who are not quite men (*Almayer's Folly, An Outcast of the Islands, The Nigger of the Narcissus, Lord Jim*). In many ways Almayer is the prototype for the other "hermits": the hermit figure is "divided between mind and will, virtue and vice, morality and instinct"; he is also frequently a visionary subject to "paradisal or infernal" illusions; much more than an agent of anti-bourgeois satire, in his retreat he offers a challenge to the ruling principle of order. And closely bound to this view of the anchorite is the question of the will and its failure; because of the division between mind and instinct, the solitary cannot act even when acting is necessary for survival.

In JC's second phase, "The Incendiary: Man in Society," JC displayed notable improvement in the long novel as he turned to man's predicament as an individual in society where he should fulfill his limited task (*Nostromo, The Secret Agent, Under Western Eyes,* and the stories in *A Set of Six*). He found applicable again the familiar conception of life divided between the realm of chance and brute struggle and that of human ideals of order and values. Failure still occurs because of man's passion or instinct, and the "arena" for the contest is a scene of "violence, cruelty, and madness." In this world of strife, anarchy threatens from the spiritual laxity of members of a community who agree to tendencies which lead to their own ruin; true anarchy, for JC, is the "will for self-destruction." Whereas in JC's first period the seafaring order of *Nigger, Jim,* and "Youth" approximate, with some misgivings, a communal ideal, JC exhibits no such trust in European forms of government "with their routine systems of authority." In the middle period, the train of action is a set of circumstances set in motion by an impulsive or irrational act which moves swiftly towards a disastrous end. The short stories halt near a fatal conclusion; the novels move onward to a tragic denouement.

In JC's final phase, "The Knight: Man in Eden," the novelist utilizes a tragi-comic flavor in contrast to the tragic irony of the middle period. Here is his most characteristic theme, "the fall of the knightly rescuer," toward which he had been working since his early career as a writer. The heroine of *Chance* fits the definition of what Mario Praz called "the persecuted maiden." The enchantresses of the last phase are wholly different from the few who appear in the earlier tales; the presence of these women enlarges in JC's art "the erotic strain," the treatment of love between man and woman which is a new feature in his writings and one which "relates immediately to his firmest convictions." As a complement to this group of "distressed and distressing" heroines JC provides an array of men of "knightly appearance and lofty intentions" who are distinguished by their readiness to assume the role of rescuer or savior. They find, though, that putting their ideal into practice is rather troublesome. Their quest ends in disaster because they confuse their attempt to save a woman as a human being with their "pursuit of a phantasmal Aphrodite." This knight is a more potent figure of irony than was the hermit, but there is an essential resemblance between the two figures: "both are deviations from the norm of limited man"; the relationship between fallen idealists and erring knights is their common failure to overcome the division between mind and instinct. The major interest in *Chance* is psychological, whereas in *Victory* it is "as near philosophical" as JC ever became. *The Shadow-Line* emphasizes JC's view that man is a limited being, a conception that is central in his work. That a bond between men or a tradition like that of a seafaring order should exist to prevent division or evil which follows man's indulgence in folly or egotism is the conclusion toward which most of his writing points, but one reason he is modern is that he asserts this need while doubting its fulfillment. The power to stimulate rather than depress springs from a source untainted by despair; it derives ultimately from his fidelity to life and his resistance to death. [There is much validity in Wiley's broad divisions of JC's career, and the resistance to the idea of a "decline" in JC's later works bears further investigation.]

1955

1310 Allen, Walter Ernest. "Joseph Conrad," SIX GREAT NOVELISTS (Lond: H. Hamilton, 1955), pp. 154-82.
Until James and JC arrived on the literary scene, the novel was a simple

genre; after them it could not easily be simple again. JC "is emphatic on the all-importance of fidelity because he knows so well how easy it is to fall into its opposite"; he uses the sea as a laboratory where men are tested in extreme situations, and he shows us that the ideal conception of himself that a man holds may be an agent in his betrayal. "A very good case could be made out for claiming [*Nostromo*] as the greatest novel written in English this century." JC is the greatest English novelist of the century because of his tragic vision, a product of the whole of his experience. His only rival is Herman Melville.

1311 Bache, William B. "OTHELLO and Conrad's *Chance*," NOTES AND QUERIES, N.S. II (Nov 1955), 478-79.

There is a number of similarities between OTHELLO and *Chance:* Flora and Desdemona, Captain Anthony and Othello, Powell and Iago. "OTHELLO hovers over the novel, echoing the action, establishing the design, and ironically directing the theme."

1312 Beebe, Maurice. "Criticism of Joseph Conrad: A Selected Checklist with an Index to Studies of Separate Works," MODERN FICTION STUDIES, I (Feb 1955), 30-45.

[An important listing of general studies of JC and his works and of *"significant* critical discussions" of each of his stories and novels. It is brought up to date in, but not supplanted by, Beebe, "Criticism of Joseph Conrad: A Selected Checklist," MODERN FICTION STUDIES, X (Spring 1964), 81-106.]

1313 Brashear, Jordan L. "Joseph Conrad: Social Critic." Unpublished thesis, University of California, Berkeley, 1955. [Apparently an error in Ehrsam's listing. See item 1314.]

1314 Brotman, Jordan L. "Joseph Conrad: Social Critic." Unpublished thesis, University of California, Berkeley, 1955.

1315 Carroll, Wesley. "The Novelist as Artist," MODERN FICTION STUDIES, I (Feb 1955), 2-8.

JC's art is dominated by a purpose and direction—though he never formulated precisely his principles and techniques, believing imagination must not be encumbered by precepts. His purpose is to make the reader experience life through his senses; therefore, his works abound with sights, sounds, sensations. His imaginary world resembles something the reader can relate to by his feelings without possessing only a single meaning. The art is then humanitarian and symbolic, not systematic.

1316 Cazamian, Madeleine L. LE ROMAN ET LES IDÉES EN ANGLETERRE (The Novel and Ideas in England) (Paris: Les Belles Lettres, 1955), pp. 128-69.

JC's work might not have existed if he had not traveled in the Orient. Almayer is the prototype of a series of characters who represent the conflict between East and West. In *Almayer's Folly, An Outcast of the Islands,* and *The Rescue,* JC deals with the half-civilized man who falls victim to the temptations of the great. These mediocre anti-heroes are too weak to support their destiny. In *Under Western Eyes,* JC shows his contempt for the vain, inept, jealous revolutionary. *Nostromo* contains JC's deepest character studies. Although impartial, JC reveals his hate for the masses, and his respect for an elite, whether of birth or money. His women usually play either the role of the subjugated woman in love or that of the temptress, and are the highest or most fatal inspiration for man. The sea forces man to realize his ultimate loneliness and the indifference of natural forces to his plight. The ship symbolizes man's will as it struggles with more powerful forces. The crew is marked by devotion, unity, pride in the ship, discipline, and especially endurance. JC's technique consists in his use of first-person narrators, his time-shifts, his realism, and his romanticism as subjectivity. His Polish heritage inspired his novels dealing with political intrigue. His British temperament gave him his ideas of will power, fair play, class consciousness, and the importance of morality. JC doubts progress and utopian improvements. An anti-rationalist, he believes rather in action, imagination, and art. [Much plot summary; relies heavily on previous criticism.] [In French.]

1317 Chaikin, Milton. "Zola and Conrad's 'The Idiots,'" STUDIES IN PHILOLOGY, LII (July 1955), 502-7.

JC read at least some of Zola's novels "with a good deal of interest" and used them as literary sources. "The Idiots" is a "pastiche" of borrowings from the writings of several Frenchmen, but mainly from two of Zola's novels, LA TERRE and LA JOIE DE VIVRE. LA TERRE supplied material on the peasant spirit and LA JOIE DE VIVRE gloomy descriptions of a coast in Normandy. Furthermore, one of the characters in LA TERRE is an idiot; and Zola's pessimism, evident in both novels, is not alien to JC's temperament and to the mood of "The Idiots." Parallel passages from Zola and JC display similarities of theme.

1318 Connolly, Francis. THE TYPES OF LITERATURE (NY: Harcourt, Brace, 1955), pp. 712-15.

JC's "Typhoon" is a story that contains a theme obviously too many-sided to be communicated successfully in a short story." ["Comment" of a genre-oriented textbook; "Typhoon" is the novel with "Points for Discussion."]

1319 Curle, Richard. "Conrad's Favourite Novel," TIMES LITERARY SUPPLEMENT (Lond), 14 Oct 1955, p. 605.

Although JC regarded *Nostromo* as his greatest creative effort, his favorite novel was *The Nigger of the Narcissus,* not primarily because of its literary qualities, but because of the nostalgic memories it evoked.

1320 Feder, Lillian. "Marlow's Descent into Hell," NINETEENTH-CENTURY FICTION, IX (March 1955), 280-92; rptd in THE ART OF JOSEPH CONRAD: A CRITICAL SYMPOSIUM (East Lansing: Michigan State U P, 1960), ed by Robert Wooster Stallman.

JC in "Heart of Darkness" tells the story of Marlow's attainment of self-knowledge not in the language of psychology but in "the imagery and symbolism of the traditional voyage into Hades," thus making concrete "the hidden world of the inner self" and probing the depths of his own and his nation's conscience. By combining "the traditional imagery of the epic descent" with realistic details from his own trip to the Congo, he "created an image of hell credible to modern man." Marlow's journey most closely parallels the visit to Hades in Book VI of the AENEID.

"Heart of Darkness" has three levels of meaning: the story of a man's adventures, the account of this man's discovery of "certain political and social injustices," and a study of this man's "initiation into the mysteries of his own mind"; and these three levels are also found in Book VI of Virgil's AENEID. Marlow, in detecting "the lowest possible depths of evil in Kurtz, also discovers "the potential hell in the heart of every man," and he experiences "a kind of spiritual depth" himself in lying to the Intended.

1321 Gettmann, Royal A., and Bruce Harkness. A BOOK OF STORIES: TEACHER'S MANUAL (NY: Rinehart, 1955); rptd and expanded as "Morality and Psychology in 'The Secret Sharer,' " in CONRAD'S "SECRET SHARER" AND THE CRITICS, ed by Bruce Harkness (Belmont, Calif: Wadsworth, 1962), pp. 125-32. [See Gettman and Harkness, 1962.]

1322 Hagan, John, Jr. "The Design of Conrad's *The Secret Agent*," JOURNAL OF ENGLISH LITERARY HISTORY, XXII (June 1955), 148-64.

The problem of the organic whole is crucial to an understanding of *The Secret Agent*. The domestic tragedy of the Verlocs, the core of the plot, accounts for Mr. Vladimir, Karl Yundt, Chief Inspector Heat, Winnie, and Comrade Ossipon; but "there are other characters who are extraneous in these terms: Winnie's mother, Michaelis, the Assistant Commissioner, his wife's friend (the society hostess), and Sir Ethelred." JC knew what he was doing, however, and aimed at "a wider, multiple focus" which would provide him with "the moral atmosphere" rather than a conventional unity. This work is "made up of a series of interviews . . . confined in space . . . to no greater length than the actual time it takes to read them." Seventeen such interviews occur and gain force because of various repetitions of setting (the recurring bedroom scene) and comment (the putting out of the light). Entire moral situations are epitomized in these devices. Conrad had in mind "some of the very same issues we associate preeminently . . . with

Henry James": the hidden or buried life flows beneath conventional reality and holds the significant "inner truth"; because of fear, indolence, and self-regard, it is difficult for persons to communicate with one another; and anarchy "is a moral condition involving everyone." The world here "is a chaos of blindly driven storms never cohering, a masque of deluded, helpless, lonely, and futile lives." This "process of dissolution becomes even more headlong" as the book nears its conclusion. *Agent* is "a veritable fugue of crises. It is indeed one of the bitterest and most harrowing novels he [JC] ever wrote."

1323 Harkness, Bruce. "Conrad on Galsworthy: The Time of FRATERNITY," MODERN FICTION STUDIES, I (May 1955), 12-18. Whereas Galsworthy tries to realistically provide the reader with literal accuracy of time's passage, JC is more impressionistic and interested in the effect of time on the reader. Galsworthy's use of flashback and parallel time blocks are confusing while JC's use shows clearly that various scenes and events can happen simultaneously. JC once suggested to Galsworthy that FRATERNITY was marred by the imperfectly conceived and realized psychology of Hilary, and that a time-shift was needed for correction; it was corrected.

1324 Haugh, Robert F. "Conrad's *Chance: Progression d'effet*," MODERN FICTION STUDIES, I (Feb 1955), 9-15. JC's term—*progression d'effet*—for the selection and arrangement of narrative elements has been inadequately treated, especially in *Chance*. His best locales for narrative are the "shallows"; *Chance*'s two parts could be called "earth" and "sea." The novel embodies classic myth wherein the hero descends to nether regions, running into monsters on the way, and returns with a talisman, encountering the monsters in reverse order. Complex ethical and psychological problems are therein explored.

1325 Hollingsworth, Alan M. "Freud, Conrad, and the Future of an Illusion," LITERATURE AND PSYCHOLOGY, V (Nov 1955), 78-83. Both JC and Freud were concerned with the ills of society as reflected in the social function of religion. Religion as a unifying power hindered the private egoism necessary for man to accept reality. In *The Nigger of the Narcissus*, only Old Singleton's non-Christian attitude towards death is heroic and practical. In "Heart of Darkness," JC presents the inner and external corruption of white, Christian imperialism. In Freud and JC, psychology and literature, the common concern is "the preservation of society."

1326 Tung, Ursula. "Das Verhältnis des Menschen zum Kosmos im Werke Joseph Conrads" (The Relationship of Man to the Cosmos in the Works of Joseph Conrad). Unpublished thesis, University of Berlin, 1955. [In German.]

1327 Kohler, Dayton. "Introduction," *Lord Jim* (NY: Harper & Row, Perennial Classics, 1965), pp. xii-xix.

Since art for JC was a moral act, Jim's leap from the deck of the *Patna* figuratively plunges him into a moral universe, where his flight from his unfortunate deed becomes the "spiritual passage" of alienated man in quest of identity and the possibility of redemption. In utilizing new techniques and in bringing together most of the themes with which JC was to be concerned during the rest of his career, *Lord Jim* became the most representative of JC's novels. What the novelist did in this work was "to give shape and life to an enigma"—not Jim, but man—and to leave us "surrounded by the powers of darkness . . . lighted only by the hope of some redemptive vision." [This essay is largely a synopsis of familiar critical opinions.]

1328 Lee, Richard Eugene. "The Political and Social Ideas of Joseph Conrad," DISSERTATION ABSTRACTS, XV (1955), 1073. Unpublished thesis, New York University, 1955.

[On *Romance, Nostromo, Under Western Eyes, The Secret Agent.*]

1329 Lynskey, Winifred. "The Role of the Silver in *Nostromo,*" MODERN FICTION STUDIES, I (Feb 1955), 16-21.

In *Nostromo,* revolution is the stage on which JC puts forth his philosophical analysis of the power of evil as manifested in human conduct related to material interests. Silver is the symbol of wealth; and three men—Gould, Decoud, and Nostromo—represent three ethical attitudes about wealth: idealism, skepticism, and simple faith. The real power of evil lies in its ability to override good men; the only answer to the problem seems to be the faith, compassion, and courage of men.

1330 Moser, Thomas C. "Joseph Conrad's Surrender: Some Sources and Characteristics of the Decline of His Creative Powers." Unpublished thesis, Harvard University, 1955; pub as JOSEPH CONRAD: ACHIEVEMENT AND DECLINE (Cambridge, Mass: Harvard U P, 1957).

1331 Rapin, René. "Conrad's *Nostromo,*" EXPLICATOR, XIII (June 1955), Item 50.

Recent discussion of the role of silver in *Nostromo* overlooks the first mention of the subject by Guerard in 1946.

1332 Schwab, Arnold T. "Joseph Conrad's American Friend: Correspondence with James Huneker," MODERN PHILOLOGY, LII (May 1955), 222-32.

James Gibbons Huneker, one of JC's earliest American admirers, was influential as a critic in enlarging JC's reputation and audience in America. In a postscript of a letter (16 Oct 1912), JC writes of his dissatisfaction with a Scott-James article. JC is probably referring to an untraced article written for the PALL MALL GAZETTE, not to the piece in Scott-James's MODERNISM AND ROMANCE (1908). [The article explores their personal friendship and includes in their entirety all the known letters of their correspondence: six letters of JC to Huneker, one of Huneker to JC.]

>1333 Stallman, Robert Wooster. "Conrad and THE GREAT GATSBY," TWENTIETH-CENTURY LITERATURE, I (April 1955), 5-12; rptd in THE HOUSES THAT JAMES BUILT (East Lansing: Michigan State U P, 1961), pp. 150-58.

From JC, Fitzgerald learned themes, plot-situations, ambivalence of symbolism, the craft of the novel, the device of the perplexed narrator and turns of phrasing. "The world as spoil is the dominant idea in 'Heart of Darkness' and also in *Nostromo*. THE GREAT GATSBY transposes JC's world-as-spoil idea into the contemporary idiom." There is a number of parallels between Kurtz and Gatsby.

>1334 Thale, Jerome. "Marlow's Quest," UNIVERSITY OF TORONTO QUARTERLY, XXIV (July 1955), 351-58; rptd in THE ART OF JOSEPH CONRAD: A CRITICAL SYMPOSIUM, ed by R. W. Stallman (East Lansing: Michigan State U P, 1960), pp. 154-61; and JOSEPH CONRAD'S "HEART OF DARKNESS": BACKGROUNDS AND CRITICISMS, ed by Leonard F. Dean (Englewood Cliffs, NJ: Prentice-Hall, Spectrum Books, 1960), pp. 159-66.

"Heart of Darkness" is an archetype of the grail quest, in which Marlow meets the usual tests and obstacles of his search—to bring back a sick company agent. The grail motif is related to the light-darkness symbolism: paradoxically, Marlow has an illumination from the heart of darkness. Expecting to find a good man amidst darkness and corruption, Marlow finally sees Kurtz as the alternative to the plundering company. The causes of Kurtz's tragedy are his ambition, "rootless idealism," the mysterious jungle, and the "corruption of colonial exploitation." Kurtz has discovered himself and has thereby become completely human, and Marlow's illumination is "a similar discovery about himself and about all men." Existence is dangerous and menacing; and most people, according to JC, are saved by illusion and ignorance. For Kurtz, Africa is truth; the journey into the heart of the continent is the journey "into the depths of the self." Once in the silence and the solitude, Kurtz has no restraint. The freedom which Kurtz found allowed him to become "his own diabolical god," a radical freedom that seems both exalting and revolting to Marlow. The danger in being free is the unpredictable, "even the Kurtzian." Although Kurtz's choice is for evil, it is a human choice; and Marlow turns with relief to this humanity even though it is a nightmare. Kurtz fails horribly because he has no "inborn strength," no faithfulness, no "restraint," as Marlow says. Thus, Kurtz is the grail at the end of Marlow's quest. Though most people are unable to understand Kurtz, Marlow has had his almost incommunicable illumination. [One of the best articles on "Heart of Darkness."]

1335 Visiak, E. H. THE MIRROR OF CONRAD (Lond: Werner Laurie, 1955; NY: Philosophical Library, 1956).

In JC, imagination and memory were "virtually united"; they worked together "metabolically": JC *"saw,* he *remembered,* he *imagined."* His mnemonic material was produced by the experiences of his earlier and middle life. The contents of the mirror include his early years, his sojourn in France, and his "various voyages," from 1857 to 1883. From Poland and Russia, JC developed his conception of fatality, of inevitability, which was to become the "cardinal motif" of his novels and cause him to become eventually a "tragic writer in the old, classic signification rather than . . . a romantic realist." From an early age he cherished a love of the sea, which was for him a symbol of freedom. The loss of the *Tremolino* was a tragic event for him, just as was his loss of Doña Rita; it aroused in him a "chronic state of disturbance" which led him back to sea and eventually to a life of even greater difficulty, that of a writer. His personal knowledge of the physical and nervous fatigue of a sailor appears in his works, as in *The Nigger of the Narcissus.* His feeling of guilt because of deserting Poland appears in "Falk," *Lord Jim, Nostromo, Under Western Eyes, The Shadow-Line,* and *Victory.* His early voyages provided impressions, appearances, and aspects for *Almayer's Folly, An Outcast of the Islands,* and *The Rescue.* Through his years at sea, JC lived strenuously and "dangerously," in the Nietzschean sense; later, when he engaged in what he called "the hard slavery of writing," he profited from the experiences of his earlier life. About 1893, JC began to strengthen the bridge which was being formed between his two very different worlds. Since he began his life at sea under the compulsion of his will, love, or a "form of love," was the "efficient agent" in his maritime career. His literary career, too, may have been, in effect, a "form of love," since writing, or "true eloquence," according to Milton, is nothing but "the serious and hearty love to truth." [Visiak relies too heavily upon JC's own statements and considers *The Arrow of Gold* almost as literal autobiography. This book has little value as either biography or criticism.]

1336 Wills, John H. "Adam, Axel, and 'Il Conde,' " MODERN FICTION STUDIES, I (Feb 1955), 22-25; rptd in THE ART OF JOSEPH CONRAD: A CRITICAL SYMPOSIUM, ed by Robert Wooster Stallman (East Lansing: Michigan State U P, 1960), 254-59.

The story exhibits a complex symbolism that is almost allegorical. The two strands consist of the fall or expulsion from Eden and the ivory tower myth. The fall stresses how the order, security, and quality of the Count's world are gradually dissipated by his realization of the disharmony and evils of the real world; he is led into the wilderness of evil and learns a respect for power. The ivory tower myth indicates the attempt to avoid the pain of life, which will not be denied. The story seems to suggest that the best men to lead society are descended from the aristocratic class of emperors who are traditionally stronger than other men.

1337 Woodruff, Neal. "The Structure of Conrad's Fiction." Unpublished thesis, Yale University, 1955.
[On "Typhoon," *Lord Jim,* "Heart of Darkness," and *Nostromo.*]

1338 Worth, George J. "Conrad's Debt to Maupassant in the Preface to *The Nigger of the Narcissus,*" JOURNAL OF ENGLISH AND GERMANIC PHILOLOGY, LIV (Oct 1955), 700-4.

JC's debt to Maupassant's preface to PIERRE ET JEAN consists mainly of the codification of certain theoretical assumptions which he regarded as basic to the practice of his art: an insistence that the artist-writer must ceaselessly try to depict the truth by avoiding the fleeting and transitory surfaces of things, a strong emphasis on the seriousness of the vivid rendering of sense impressions, the importance of using "felicitous diction," an insistence that the writer-artist must be free to choose his subject, and a concern for the supreme importance of craftsmanship.

1339 Wright, Walter F. " 'The Truth of My Own Sensations,' " MODERN FICTION STUDIES, I (Feb 1955), 26-29.

JC defined the artist as a creator who tries to make people hear, see, and feel what the artist regards as the truth of his own sensations. The problem that troubled him was the antithesis between the fact that each moment in the artist's mind is unique and cannot be recaptured, but that also there is a principle of universal order. He used images and incidents as shadows of vast myths, and myths were inseparable from actual phenomena of experience.

1956

1340 Brown, Dorothy Snodgrass. "The Irony of Joseph Conrad," DISSERTATION ABSTRACTS, XVI (1956), 2148. Unpublished thesis, University of Washington, 1956.

1341 Cambon, Glauca. "Giacobbe e l'angelo in Melville e Conrad" (Jacob and the Angel in Melville and Conrad), LETTERATURA, IV (1956), 53-69.

Whatever similarities one can detect between Melville and JC are bound to seem superficial. Melville—Shakespearean, baroque—writes with a Joycean multiplicity of styles. JC, with an obliquity in point of view, is more mindful of Flaubert and not unlike Henry James. For Melville, the sea is tranquilly beautiful with the heart of a tiger; it is a character. For JC, the sea is immortal, a cosmic mystery; it is a landscape. In Melville, the sea is a measure of man from a metaphysical intuition; in JC, the sea is a measure of man from a psychological, aesthetic, and moral point of view. Melville's man struggles between God and Satan, along with the man of Milton, Blake, and Byron, in order to affirm his own reality. JC's man, a child of decadent civilization, has seen the breakdown of myths and has encountered cosmic and psychological nature from which it is possible to be saved through fidelity to oneself, to come to an understanding of one's lot. Melville, typically American, and JC, typically European, converge remarkably in the profundity of their ethical and artistic worlds. It is not unusual, according to Henry Luedeke in GESCHICHTE DER AMERIAKNISCHEN LITERATUR (History of American Literature), that the discovery of Melville in Europe and in America coincides with JC's popularity in the post-war period. Comments made by Richard Chase on the aesthetic Melvillian atmosphere in BENITO CERENO can certainly be applied to *Lord Jim, The Nigger of the Narcissus,* and "Heart of Darkness." Melville in his metaphysical and theological sphere and JC in his psychological dimension share a tragic attitude not interpretable as a moral assumption outside of their work but as an intrinsic factor in it. Tragedy in Melville rests in the desperate resolution with which his heroes throw harpoons in the ambiguous face of God. In JC, however, the God-demon dilemma which Melville perceived did not have a very direct significance. JC struggled with the angel of indifference and ambiguity. Ambiguity appears in JC in a purely psychological way—as an elusive atmosphere that nourishes characters. One is not able to mean by "art" a simple literary fact, but rather the complex totality of human experience which, facing the real, penetrates it, unveils it, and reduces it to significant form because in no other way can man situate himself in the world. For JC, the angel of defeat was also a demon, even if in theological dress. In "Heart of Darkness," Marlow says he has struggled with death and continues that it is a strife, less enthusiastic than one can imagine without spectators, voices, glory, desire for victory or even fear of defeat. Melville, more bold and less sage, wants to take the angel by the throat. Adventures in Melville expand in a colossal space, and in Melville, intoxication with space rises to metaphysical dimensions. JC's adventures waste away in an interior labyrinth of memory, as in *Lord Jim* or "Heart of Darkness."

Reality and unreality, light and shadow, identity and anonymous existence, knowledge and mystery, alternate, intensify, and blend to present us the figure of Jim as individual and as the myth of Adam. The artist, immersing himself fully in a psychological void, has here reported the victory of Jacob over the angel, because instead of violating the mystery with brutality, he has touched it with humility and courage. In man, as Stein says of Jim, there is a native flaw because the artist that has shaped him was a little mad. In "The Specksnyder" Melville explains prodigious passivity as the superiority of the Inert Divine or the contemplative. The Inert Divine recurs also in JC —Lord Jim, Kurtz, Jimmy Wait. Lord Jim is Billy Budd in a minor tone because Lord Jim does not have the explicit Christological allusions Melville gives Billy. In the end, though, Jim is a deliverer. Lord Jim is benign while Jimmy Wait is malign; yet, in both is an incorruptible foundation of primordial innocence. In Jim is the paradox of the presence of original sin (abandoning the boat) and yet an Edenic innocence. Melville, likewise, finds an innocence in the Christ-Adam figure of Billy Budd and in the primitive innocence of the Polynesian savages.

Going up the Congo in a boat, Marlow-Conrad voyaged backward toward the frontiers of his soul and civilization toward the terror of the darkness of irrationality. The black continent contaminated the contaminator. Kurtz, Jacob of evil, modified the soul of Marlow who returns from there with the wisdom of the darkness. Kurtz, after having atoned in a last moment of lucidity all the terror of the darkness, had to succumb, paying the penalty for his treason to civilization. Marlow widened the ray of his own conscience, getting the meditative serenity of the Buddha. Melville's concerns are similar. Jacob and the angel are civilization and nature; I and the unconscious, thought and existence. JC, the adventurous exile, as well as Ishmael-Melville, are in search of themselves in the seas of the world and the spirit. The mutual itinerary of these two sailors in the symbolic and real voyages is from sin to expiation and from innocence to a state beyond the vertex of evil. The pilgrimage of the Western conscience toward a sanctuary of new spiritual values is a fundamental stage in Melville's and JC's work. The closed world of the ship in WHITE JACKET and MOBY DICK as well as in *Nigger* and "Typhoon" figures as an explicit metaphor of the human universe in motion. [In Italian.]

> **1342** Davis, Harold Edmund. "Method and Form in the Novels of Joseph Conrad," DISSERTATION ABSTRACTS, XVI (1956), 1682. Unpublished thesis, Louisiana State University, 1956.
>
> **1343** Davis, Harold Edmund. "Symbolism in *The Nigger of the Narcissus*," TWENTIETH CENTURY LITERATURE, II (April 1956), 26-29.

The plot of *The Nigger of the Narcissus* is relatively simple; the texture is complex. "Color is an important symbolic force. The dominant colors . . . seem to be black and white, or shades of grey." The "pilgrimage theme" provides the basic pattern. James Wait "is equated with the devil, a 'black idol,' the prince of darkness, the tortured and dark areas of experience through which all men must pass to arrive at certainty."

1344 Evans, Robert O. "Conrad's Underworld," MODERN FICTION STUDIES, II (May 1956), 56-62; rptd in THE ART OF JOSEPH CONRAD: A CRITICAL SYMPOSIUM, ed by R. W. Stallman (East Lansing: Michigan State U P, 1960), pp. 171-81.

JC uses in his fiction symbols pertaining to a concept of the underworld, especially the Inferno; these express his concern with modern ethical and spiritual values, and the shabbiness of modern life. "Heart of Darkness" is a special form toward which JC was working to present his view of the universe; much of its moral structure resembles a skeletalized version of Dante's Hell. Marlow, who descends into a legendary, not an actual, Hell is the only character who adheres to the true purpose of life, viz., to develop ethical insight.

1345 Gullason, Thomas Arthur. "Conrad's 'The Lagoon,' " EXPLICATOR, XIV (Jan 1956), Item 23.

Arsat, purged of despair, no longer a victim of illusion, now "must return to civilization . . . to win back his full manhood." [Questions the Brooks and Warren reading.]

1346 Hackett, Francis. "Back to Conrad," NEW REPUBLIC, CXXV (6 Aug 1956), 20-21.

Nostromo is a great book. The critics who called it a failure were "torpid." The main characer is the silver mine, not the captain of the stevedores. Because of JC's supreme art, the searching of conscience in the novel is not dull.

1347 Hollingsworth, Alan. "The Destructive Element: A Study of Conrad's Tragic Vision." Unpublished thesis, University of California, Berkeley, 1956.

1348 Krżyżanowski, Ludwik. "Joseph Conrad's 'Prince Roman,' " POLISH REVIEW, I (Autumn 1956), 22-62; rptd in JOSEPH CONRAD: CENTENNIAL ESSAYS, ed by Ludwik Krżyżanowski (NY: Polish Institute of Arts and Sciences in America, 1960), pp. 29-72.

The hero of the tale, Prince Roman Sanguszko, an outstanding figure in the Polish November Insurrection of 1830-31, existed in reality, but in a somewhat different manner from his portrayal in JC's story. The immediate source of "Prince Roman" seems to be the MEMOIRS of Tadeusz Bobrowski, JC's maternal uncle and guardian. Passages from the tale and from Mickiewicz's PAN TADEUSZ and other works reveal close similarities. Characteristic of Mickiewicz is his presenting indirectly the motives of his heroes, a practice followed by JC in his story. JC's fictitious additions include a description of Roman's marriage as a love match, antedating the main event by one year, making the young princess die at an earlier age than could have been possible, describing the illness of the Princess and her attachment to her native land, characterizing Roman's father fictitiously as a foil for the hero, adding Yankel as "a fictional character," changing the circumstances of Prince Roman's capture, and extending the duration of Roman's exile by a decade. [Contains much historical and literary information, but little that is of critical value.]

1349 Lorentzen, Renate. "Interpretation der Erzählung 'Falk' von Joseph Conrad (Die Entsprechung von Gehalt und Gestalt in J. Conrads Werzählungen)" (Interpretation of the Story "Falk" by Joseph Conrad [The Correspondence between Content and Form in J. Conrad's Narratives]). Unpublished thesis, Kiel University, 1956. [In German.]

1350 McCann, Charles John. "Nature Imagery in Conrad's Novels," DISSERTATION ABSTRACTS, XVI (1956), listed only in index p. 143. Unpublished thesis, Yale University, 1956.

1351 Moser, Thomas. " 'The Rescuer' Manuscript: A Key to Conrad's Development and Decline," HARVARD LIBRARY BULLETIN, X (Autumn 1956), 325-55.
Since JC's manuscript, "The Rescuer," and its book form, *The Rescue,* span most of the author's writing life, they reveal some of his early problems in writing, indicate some of his developing interests, and illustrate the decline in the quality of his work. Like *The Sisters,* "The Rescuer" had to be shelved in 1899 because "the sympathetic treatment of love between a white man and woman is not congenial to Conrad's creativity." This early work, however, illustrates JC's emerging interests in the symbolic use of setting and in the psychology of moral failure. But the JC who "took up" part IV of "The Rescuer" in 1916 was a very different writer from the JC who had "laid it aside" in 1899. This work indicated JC's decline because it reveals his "uncritical acceptance of the association between love and death," "his simplification and emasculation of Lingard," his perversion of Lingard "by sapping him of his intense, if unacknowledged, longings for self-destruction," and the deterioration of his style. [For Moser's further development of the achievement-and-decline theory of JC's works, see his JOSEPH CONRAD: ACHIEVEMENT AND DECLINE (Cambridge, Mass: Harvard U P, 1957, rptd with minor corrections (Hamden, Conn. Archon Books, 1966); part rptd in CONRAD: A COLLECTION OF CRITICAL ESSAYS, edited by Marvin Mudrick (Englewood Cliffs, NJ: Prentice-Hall, 1966).]

Joseph Conrad

1352 Phelps, Gilbert. THE RUSSIAN NOVEL IN ENGLISH FICTION (Lond: Hutchinson's University Library, 1956), pp. 95, 115, 119, 125-32, 134-35, 137, 169, 176-79.

To "the Conrad-James-Crane school" around F. M. Ford, Turgenev was a genius and "a profound moral influence." In the correspondence between Galsworthy and JC and others, Bazarov, of Turgenev's FATHERS AND CHILDREN, is most often mentioned around 1900. The Russian influence on JC's work has been exaggerated. Edward Garnett taught JC to value Turgenev, whom JC read in Constance Garnett's English translation. What is crucial for JC is not "a Slav element or a French element or an English element, but . . . a way of looking at Life and his relation to it as an artist." On this basis, JC rejected Tolstoi and Dostoevski. At the end of Turgenev's A NEST OF GENTLEFOLK, "Lavretsky's frame of mind . . . can be seen as particularly relevant to Conrad's own view of life." JC admires Turgenev because of "the simple emotional and moral patterning of his tales and novels." Like Turgenev, JC, "as far as motivation was concerned, [was] content with a handful of basic moral generalizations." As in Turgenev, in JC, character and background are poetically fused. In *The Arrow of Gold,* the characters "are puppets set against a series of unrelated purple passages"—no fusion takes place. Turgenev's influence is most evident in *Almayer's Folly, Lord Jim, Victory,* and *Under Western Eyes.* Both writers shared a similar "deep psychological conditioning" resulting in a preoccupation with the outcast, with alienation. *Under Western Eyes* is JC's "exercise in the Dostoevskian mode." For his use of "doubles" in *Lord Jim,* "Heart of Darkness," and, most brilliantly in "The Secret Sharer," JC may have learned something from Dostoevski, but the purpose of *Eyes* "is a purely ironical, and even satirical one." JC's "own antipathy towards the Dostoevskian effects are exercises of art, felt objectively not subjectively." *Eyes* is an *"exposé* of the kind of Russian psychology that Dostoevski represented."

1353 Rahv, Philip. "Fiction and the Criticism of Fiction," KENYON REVIEW, XVIII (Spring 1956), 284-85.

Robert W. Stallman's treatment of "The Secret Sharer" as a "double allegory" is a typical example of the exaltation of symbolism in current critical practice. [Followed by a ten-page attack on the symbolist approach to literature.]

1354 Sickels, Eleanor M. "Conrad's 'The Lagoon,' " EXPLICATOR, XV (Dec 1956), Item 17.

Arsat is a tragic figure torn between two loves and two loyalties, not between loyalty and disloyalty. The notion of purge is not part of the story: Arsat will receive no consolation from his revenge; there is no possible escape from guilt, grief, or intolerable choices.

1355 Stein, W. B. "The Lotus Posture and 'The Heart of Darkness,'" MODERN FICTION STUDIES, II (Winter 1956), 235-37; rptd in THE ART OF JOSEPH CONRAD: A CRITICAL SYMPOSIUM, ed by Robert Wooster Stallman (East Lansing: Michigan State U P, 1960), pp. 179-81.

The tableaux of the lotus posture instruct the reader how to interpret Marlow's descent into the underworld. His posture indicates a readiness to engage in an exercise on intense introspection, self-mortification, and a denial of the power of physical matter. After triumphing over suffering and toil, Marlow teaches the "egoless compassion" he has learned. R. Evans, in "Conrad's Underworld," ibid. (May 1956), 56-62, has slighted JC's tone by not considering the significance of the posture.

1356 Swinnerton, Frank. BACKGROUND WITH CHORUS (NY: Farrar, Strauss, Cudahy, 1956), pp. 49, 115, 117, 125-29, 146, 177, 192.

If JC baffled his contemporary readers and now baffles sophisticates, it is because he was "an artist of hardly relieved earnestness, and a man writing in a language which was not the language in which he thought." [Some personal anecdotes.]

1357 Swinnerton, Frank. "Joseph Conrad," AUTHORS I NEVER MET (Lond: George Allen and Unwin, 1956), pp. 25-32.

JC, genuine both as artist and man, was a great writer of long short stories rather than a great novelist. He had the "continental grand manner," was afraid of being considered a fraud, and spoke broken English that H. G. Wells used to mimic. "Yet you don't find broken English in the books. What you find lies deeper, fresh beginnings, the results of a series of crises, the crises of despair that mercifully stopped short of destruction." [One of a series of talks originally given on BBC.]

1358 Unger, Leonard. "Laforgue, Conrad, and T. S. Eliot," THE MAN IN THE NAME (Minneapolis: University of Minnesota P, 1956; Lond: Oxford U P, 1957), pp 190-242.

Eliot originally intended to use "Mistah Kurtz—he dead" as an epigraph for THE WASTELAND, but was discouraged by Pound. Both THE WASTELAND and "Heart of Darkness" show glimpses of the past and have water imagery. [Compares phrases of THE WASTELAND and THE HOLLOW MEN with phrases from "Heart of Darkness."] There are similarities in images, ideas, and rhythmical patterns. Laforgue and JC show the rhythmic pattern of the Bible, which "echoes and re-echoes in Eliot's poetry." All three writers imply that "the essential quality of the moment of death is also the essential quality of the individual in all his living." JC and Eliot express the idea that the uncivilized is insecurely concealed in civilization. Both use the theme of the unbearability and timelessness of this reality. Both writers paradoxically fuse opposites. Laforgue, Eliot, and JC use the theme of isolation from ordinary living. [Also notes other similarities in phrases and situations between JC's early novels and Eliot's poetry.]

1359 Vidan, Ivo. "One Source of Conrad's *Nostromo*," REVIEW OF ENGLISH STUDIES, VII (July 1956), 287-93.

A reading of G. F. Masterman's SEVEN EVENTFUL YEARS IN PARAGUAY (Lond, 1869) "proves undoubtedly not only that this book was read by Conrad before or in the initial stages of his writing of *Nostromo,* but also that a considerable number of characters, incidents, names, and other details were drawn from it."

1360 Warner, John Riley. "The Ethics of Joseph Conrad," DISSERTATION ABSTRACTS, XVI (1956), 1458. Unpublished thesis, University of Colorado, 1955.

1361 Wasiolek, Edward. "Yanko Goorall, A Note on Name Symbolism in Conrad's 'Amy Foster,'" MODERN LANGUAGE NOTES, LXXI (June 1956), pp. 418-19.

Yanko (Polish Janku) is really the "vocative diminutive." *Jan* (John) expresses familiarity, affection. The preservation of the name *Yanko* is part of the character's pathetic attempt to recapture the village life from which he had been torn (attempt to dance, in tavern, arguing in the field, wearing a coat over his shoulder, speaking to his son in his native language). The name *Yanko* is a "badge of identity" connecting with the "concrete texture" of his former life in a Carpathian village.

1362 Wethered, H. N. "Conrad," THE CURIOUS ART OF AUTOBIOGRAPHY FROM BENVENUTO CELLINI TO RUDYARD KIPLING (NY: Philosophical Library, 1956), pp. 218-29.

Three remarkable points about JC are (1) he chose *not* to write in his native language; (2) he had a passion for the sea; (3) he had a strong political sense. Although JC never wrote full-blown autobiography, his autobiographic writings are characteristic—"he usually begins at the end and works back to the beginning." JC frequently spoke of "seeing the back of a person, not the front. He adopts it in speaking of himself, as if to avoid the possibility of being inspected straight in the eye. The phrase occurs with reference to certain characters in three of his books, definitely indicating his peculiarly individualistic method of approach. The merest hint of a gesture, a turning away of a passing glance, could open up for his extraordinary developments of construction enough to start up his mental machinery to work smoothly and continuously."

1957

1363 Bache, William B. *"Nostromo* and 'The Snows of Kilimanjaro,' " MODERN LANGUAGE NOTES, LXXII (Jan 1957), 32-34.
Parallels between *Nostromo* and "The Snows of Kilimanjaro" suggest that *Nostromo* "seems to have functioned for Hemingway as a thematic inspiration, a critical model, a source," an influence which may account for the differences between this story and the rest of Hemingway's work. The epigraph, "bulky italized thoughts, hallucinations" are not really Hemingwayesque. Nostromo and Harry are alike in character; both are forced into inactivity; both are forced to "reckon the cost," to "take stock"; both meet death ironically, away from home, isolated, at night; both are picked up and betrayed. The rising of Nostromo's name over the gulf is like Harry's hallucination that he is flying toward the snows of Kilimanjaro.

1364 Baines, Jocelyn. "The Affair in Marseilles," LONDON MAGAZINE, IV (Nov 1957), 41-46; rptd in THE ART OF JOSEPH CONRAD: A CRITICAL SYMPOSIUM, ed by R. W. Stallman (East Lansing: Michigan State U P, 1960), pp. 347-51.
Instead of fighting a duel with J. M. K. Blunt because of the mysterious "Rita," JC attempted, for unknown reasons, to commit suicide. [Baines argues further for his version of JC's wound in JOSEPH CONRAD: A CRITICAL BIOGRAPHY (Lond: Weidenfeld and Nicholson, 1959).]

1365 Baines, Jocelyn. "The Young Conrad in Marseilles," TIMES LITERARY SUPPLEMENT (Lond), 6 Dec 1957, p. 748.
A long letter from T. Bobrowski to Stephen Buszczynski, 24 March 1879, reveals JC's attempted suicide in 1878. [Material reappears in Baines's JOSEPH CONRAD: A CRITICAL BIOGRAPHY (1959).]

1366 Bentley, Eric. THE MODERN THEATRE (NY: Doubleday, Anchor Books, 1955, 1957), III, 305-7.
[Favorable comments by John Galsworthy and Max Beerbohm on JC's play *One Day More*.]

1367 Bobkowski, Andrzej. "Alma," CONRAD ŻYWY (The Living Conrad), ed by Wit Tarnawski (Lond: B. Świderski, 1957), pp. 58-68.
[In the short story, a character says Lena (or Alma in Spanish) of *Victory* is "the most beautiful and the most interesting woman among the heroines of all the novels" the character has read. Abstract based on English summary, pp. 280-81.] [In Polish.]

1368 Bradbrook, M. C. "Conrad i Tragiczna Wyobraznia" (Conrad and the Tragic Imagination), PRZEGLAD KULTURALNY, VI (5-11 Dec 1957), 1, 3; rptd as "Conrad and the Tragic Imagination," KWARTALNIK NEOFILOLOGICZNY, V (1958), 7-10; rptd JOSEPH CONRAD KORZENIOWSKI: ESSAYS AND STUDIES (Warsaw: Państwowe Wydawnictwo Naukowe, 1958), pp. 7-10.

Whoever seeks for absolute truth in JC does so in vain; JC says frankly that he does not know such truths. Furthermore, he will not admit that others are acquainted with such truths either. His vision is certainly tragic, but he bears his tragic sense with serenity and forbearance. [In Polish.]

1369 Broncel, Zdzisław. "Pokusa nadczłowieka" (Temptation of the Superman), CONRAD ŻYWY (The Living Conrad), ed by Wit Tarnawski (Lond: B. Świderski, 1957), pp. 159-68.

T. S. Eliot's "The Hollow Men" "interprets the hidden implications" of JC's "Heart of Darkness." For Eliot "the importance of an individual existence transcends the limits of earthly life"; JC, "more sceptical about the general design of the world," believed "life presents a cruel and insoluble enigma." Based on his experiences in the Congo, JC's story depicts "the surge of wild, primitive instincts, rising from the collective unconscious in man's soul and finally overcoming the moral conscience given to man by civilisation." The story "develops into a meditation on the ethics of solitude." Kurtz, lacking appropriate moral convictions and desiring to be a superman, becomes "a barbaric deity." Kurtz is a nineteenth-century "hollow man," talented, energetic but without a defined direction or purpose. In "Heart of Darkness" we can see "an exploration of the psychological sources of the fascist mind." [Abstract based on English summary, pp. 292-93.] [In Polish.]

1370 Burgess, O. N. "Joseph Conrad: The Old and the New Criticism," AUSTRALIAN QUARTERLY, XXIX (March 1957), 85-92.

The "Old Criticism" (concerned with JC's "power of presenting gripping incident" and revelation of character of "men of action") was nearer to the truth, more "instinctively well-directed" than the "New Criticism" (emphasizing revelation of the subconscious, overingenious interpretation of the symbolic). The old criticism recognized the storytelling of *The Nigger of the Narcissus* and "Typhoon" as "patently fine" and found *The Rover* the "most fascinating and authentic of historical novels" and *Nostromo* admirable for colorful and exotic detail and an "almost sociological" assessment of forces in Costaguana, that "fully envisaged South American state." *The Secret Agent* is a "beautifully sustained excursion into irony" and a "grim comedy" that attains the "true resonance of tragedy"; *Nostromo,* the reverse. The new criticism, leaving these novels largely untouched, and centering on *Victory,* "The Secret Sharer," and "Heart of Darkness," has by overfastidious interpretations found virtue in what are really flaws. To the

New Criticism, for example, *Victory* is a morality; Heyst an exponent of "indifferentism"; Jones a "living Skeleton, the Heart of Darkness"; and the novel shows a perception of psychological subtlety in the delicately depicted gradual thawing of Heyst before Lena's ministrations. The old criticism would see *Victory* (for which JC claimed "the symbolism of great art") as convincing, good-humored irony up to the point at which Heyst carries off Lena. Then the novel becomes melodramatic and ends in a melodramatic holocaust. According to the new criticism, JC throws in deeper suggestions (Jones is the Spectre, the Skeleton, the Ghost; Ricardo is "tigerish") really to titillate the interest. In "The Secret Sharer," JC has "insinuated . . . a sporadic suggestiveness that lends itself to overimaginative treatment." For the old criticism, Leggatt represents "spirited courage and maritime efficiency fallen on hard days, obedience and unfortunate disobedience" to the sea code; and JC stressed the alter ego theme simply to "endow the story with a vague aura of mystery." "Heart of Darkness" succeeds, not because of the "heavy emphasis on indescribable and occult evil" but in spite of it. JC himself has misled the critics by inserting suggestions designed to add interest rather than to create a whole new symbolic dimension. His suggestion of the supernatural in *The Shadow-Line* is wholly misleading; *Under Western Eyes* and *Chance* are "artistically invalidated by withholding until three-quarters through, vital elucidatory material in a fashion that recalls 'surprise' tricks of cheapest melodrama." JC's obliquity, his use of Marlow, is open to question. JC is at his best when straightforward.

1371 Conrad, Borys. "A Famous Father and His Son," NEW YORK TIMES BOOK REVIEW, 1 Dec 1957, pp. 7, 74.
[A brief series of anecdotal reminiscences of JC.]

1372 Conrad, John. "Garść wspomnień o moim ojcu"/"Some Reminiscences of My Father," CONRAD ŻYWY (The Living Conrad), ed by Wit Tarnawski (Lond: B. Świderski, 1957), pp. 10-31.
[Summary of subjects recounted: toy boat sailing in England, JC's concern with automobiles, boat trip to Poland (Zakopane) and return via Austria and Italy, JC's frequent sailings out to ships anchored in "the Downs." Incidentally, John Conrad confirms the fact that JC could never swim.] [In Polish, with English on facing pages.]

1373 Ć[určija]-P[rodanović], N[ada]. "Joseph Conrad," in *Crnac sa Narcisa*, trans by Nada Ćurčija-Prodanović (Belgrade: Nolit, 1957), pp. 267-70.
[An elementary post-face to the Serbian translation of *The Nigger of the Narcissus* and "Heart of Darkness."] [In Serbo-Croatian.]

Joseph Conrad

1374 Curle, Richard. "Conrad and Jean-Aubry," LONDON MAGAZINE, IV (Nov 1957), 46-49.

Aubry's VIE DE CONRAD, though performing the service of pioneering a "panorama" of JC's life, is far from definitive. To make JC live requires a different type of biographer.

1375 Curle, Richard. JOSEPH CONRAD AND HIS CHARACTERS: A STUDY OF SIX NOVELS (Lond: William Heinemann, 1957; Fairlawn, NJ: Essential Books, 1958); rptd (NY: Russell & Russell, 1968).

The book is by design a psychological study of characters in relation to setting (*Lord Jim, Nostromo, The Secret Agent, Under Western Eyes, Chance,* and *Victory*). [An introductory chapter gives the origin of most of the names to be discussed.] (1) Jim's inner existence consists of secret dreams of courage; he tries to justify the "inner vision of himself." His experience is universal. Marlow is an extension of JC's mind; he is shadowy, detached, lacking essential detail, but can "pierce to the heart of things" without really getting involved. (2) Nostromo is a man of contradictions (his love of praise and contempt for humanity), but is resolute, courageous, vigorous, and honest in his way. Vanity, the accident to the lighter, an untutored mind in a situation beyond his control (leading to his fear that his incorruptibility would be questioned), and his desire to "settle his personal account with society" eventually lead to his downfall. Charles Gould is a "self-contained" and an "extremely English" man who at heart is a Costaguanan. Idealistically attached to the mines, and possessing a high sense of duty and rare abilities, he lacks a sense of introspection in relation to the feelings of others; he lacks "imaginative insight" to make him a good husband to Emilia. Emilia, presented in "feminine and . . . human perfection," cares for everyone, and believes that in marriage the self should be swallowed up in giving. (3) Verloc is "infinitely worthless." Winnie is completely devoted to Stevie until his death, when she reverts to primitive instincts, losing her reason in the process. Stevie hovers between two worlds, seeing things in black and white, which allows Verloc (Stevie thinks him good) to work his will. The Professor is vindictive, narrow-minded, and insufferable, "conscious of his own splendid isolation." (4) Razumov is an "ordinary young man" with an unusual mind and "physical and moral courage" who becomes embroiled in betrayal. Natalia Haldin is straightforward and genuine; the enigmatic Councillor Mikulin is faithful to his code, symbolizing governmental inability to face problems; the power-loving Peter Ivanovitch is perhaps an "inspired man" but the "secret of his dominance . . . eludes us"; and Sophia Antonovna is direct and easy, selfless, and without egotism, rather like a "mediaeval saint." (5) The Governess's "shuddering intensity," propriety, exclusiveness, cruelty, and contempt for society represents the "feeling of the treachery of life, of deadly forces lying in wait . . . when least expected." The Fynes form an entity, serious and humorless. Flora de Barral demonstrates "simplicity and directness," and evolves in the final chapter "like a fine tranquil afternoon." [!] Roderick Anthony cannot understand the complexities of life away from the sea. De Barral is a megalomaniacal, "stupid nonentity." (6) Lena, whom JC keeps "enveloped in a gauzy haze," forms an instinctive bond with Heyst, and she is justified in her victory. Heyst, free from petulance and pettiness, observes rather than participates in life. Schomberg is stupid and malicious, yet he has a "slobbering sincerity" for Lena; his lies defeat Lena's sacrifice, and cause the death of five people; Plain Mr. Jones is one of JC's most depraved creatures; and Ricardo is one with Mr. Jones. [Curle did not use the apparatus of psychological study available to him; consequently he gives little of the psychological insight that he promises. Too much space is devoted to plot summary, and quotations are often substituted for critical insight. He repeatedly asks the reader to turn to the novel to "sense" what he is trying to communicate.]

>**1376** Dabrowski, J[an] P. "Conrad a 'wielka trójka' Literatury Rosyjskiej" (Conrad and "The Big Three" of Russian Literature), CONRAD ŻYWY (The Living Conrad), ed by Wit Tarnawski (Lond: B. Świderski, 1957), pp. 150-58.

JC's anti-Russian bias did not "make him hate all things Russian." He appreciated Turgenev but was blind to the positive achievements of Tolstoi and to a "great extent" Dostoevski. In his attack on Russia (*Under Western Eyes*), Dostoevski was his guide. JC is inconsistent in his attitudes toward Tolstoi, Dostoevski, and Turgenev. [Abstract based on English summary, p. 291.] [In Polish.]

>**1377** Dowden, Wilfred S. "The Light and the Dark: Imagery and Thematic Development in Conrad's 'Heart of Darkness,'" RICE INSTITUTE PAMPHLETS, XLIV (April 1957), 33-51. [Festschrift for George Wesley Whiting.]

An image JC frequently used is that "of contrasts in light and darkness, sun shine and shadow, dark night and bright day." He uses this type of imagery in "Heart of Darkness" "to develop a threefold theme, each aspect of which is inherent in the ambiguity of the title": (1) the heart of darkness on the Thames as Marlow tells his story; (2) the heart of the "Dark Continent" into which Marlow journeys; (3) "The shadowy, mysterious nature of Kurtz, and of humanity which he comes to symbolize, . . . a darkness which also deepens as Marlow approaches his destination." "There is the contrasting light and deepening darkness of the physical setting in which the narrative is told; there is the contrast of the light on the river up which the steamer moves with the darkness of the bordering jungle . . . and there is the contrast of the light in which men like Marlow move with the darkness which surrounds Kurtz and, potentially, every man, since, in the thematic development of the novel, Kurtz represents the ultimate possibility of degradation in mankind. This last aspect of the theme is the center, the heart, of Conrad's 'Heart of Darkness,' and the first two aspects form the matrix for it."

1378 Duffin, Henry C. "Conrad: A Centenary Survey," CONTEMPORARY REVIEW, CXCII (Dec 1957), 319-23.

[A brief tribute and survey of JC's main works. Slight.]

1379 Evans, Robert O. "Conrad: A Nautical Image," MODERN LANGUAGE NOTES, LXXII (Feb 1957), 98-99.

Technical nautical terms reinforce symbolism and meaning in "The Secret Sharer." At the moment of Leggatt's crime, the vessel is described as a "deep ship"—the sail must be put up or the ship will founder, a dilemma suggestive of the situation: Leggatt is an "instrument of salvation, but at the moment the balance of the universe is disturbed, and he commits a murder." The phrase "hang in stays" describes the condition of the ship (dangerously close to shore, momentarily crosswise of, unpropelled by wind, subject to sudden disaster or success) and also the condition of the captain's career—in the balance, the outcome depends not on fate, as in Hardy, nor experience, "but on skill and perhaps a little luck." The Captain's hat is also symbolic. Successfully coming out of dangerous suspensions, the captain answers his role and is free.

1380 Evans, Robert O. "Further Comment on 'Heart of Darkness,'" MODERN FICTION STUDIES, III (Winter 1957), 358-60; rptd in THE ART OF JOSEPH CONRAD: A CRITICAL SYMPOSIUM, ed by Robert Wooster Stallman (East Lansing: Michigan State U P, 1960), pp. 184-86.

The first narrator profits less from the tale than Marlow; but the main point is that the tale is really directed at the reader who may apply knowledge gained about darkness to his own experience. The Yoga posture of Marlow does not imply being a spokesman for Yoga but merely identifies him with a commonplace image of Buddha; JC did not intend to suggest in Marlow that the end of life is self-abnegation but rather the contemplation of ethical consequences of one's actions in terms of future existence. [Argues against the views of W. B. Stein in ibid., II (Winter 1956), 235-37, and S. L. Gross in ibid. (Summer 1957), 167-70.]

1381 Freislich, Richard. "Marlow's Shadow Side," LONDON MAGAZINE, IV (Nov 1957), 31-36.

JC wishes Marlow to appear before the world as a great storyteller whose "soundness of delicacy" invited the friendship of tortured people. Though

Marlow's sea records (and JC's as well) were successful, in the back of his mind Jim's failure as "one of us" shows the shadow side of Marlow the man.

1382 Fryling, Jan. "Plon mórz dalekich" (The Yield of the Oceans), CONRAD ŻYWY (The Living Conrad), ed by Wit Tarnawski (Lond: B. Świderski, 1957), pp. 74-78.

JC's "humane attitude toward the coloured races" is due to "his sympathy towards all people who, as in his own nature, were suffering from oppression." [Abstract based on English summary, p. 281.] [In Polish.]

1383 Gażdzikówna, Barbara. "Nieznana część rekopisu 'Ocalenia' " (The Strange Respect for the Manuscript of "The Rescuer"), CONRAD ŻYWY (The Living Conrad), ed by Wit Tarnawski (Lond: B. Świderski, 1957), pp. 169-80.

The first version of what became *The Rescue* is heavily corrected and shows that JC found the "poetic treatment of language" too inflexible for this work. The last part shows JC's "inability to present—and to resolve—the conflict of Lingard." The MS forecasts the themes of JC's later novels, the device of Marlow, and the "ironic mannery observation" as "an attitude of detachment." [Abstract based on English summary, p. 293.] [In Polish.]

1384 Grabowski, Zbigniew. "Po trzydziestu latach" (After Thirty Years), CONRAD ŻYWY (The Living Conrad), ed by Wit Tarnawski (Lond: B. Świderski, 1957), pp. 134-40.

[Grabowski revises the views, expressed in 1927 in his ZE STUDIÓW NAD JÓZEFEM CONRADEM (not seen), to the effect "that only in England could Conrad's curious love-hatred relationship with the sea be fully understood, and that his restraint in the presentation of emotional problems could be traced to English influences."] JC's "Polish heritage" now appears to have been more significant than even JC cared to admit. Dignity and "a strong sense of honour" were the chief components of his heritage. Polish romanticism, as in the work of Słowacki and Mickiewicz, and certain moral attitudes also derived from the Polish tradition. He shared with the Polish romantics the belief "that youth was of unique value." He was most troubled by the question of a man's "right to follow his dream *usque ad finem.*" JC's "vision was probably too gloomy for Victorian and Edwardian optimism." His lack of popularity today is due to his prose being "too ornate" and its rhythms jarring "on the ears to-day more than some twenty years ago." [Abstract based on English summary, pp. 288-90.] [In Polish.]

1385 Green-Armytage, Adrian. "The Religion of Joseph Conrad. Reflections on the Centenary," TABLET (Lond), CCX (7 Dec 1957), 501-2.

JC was a self-made man and almost an agnostic who disliked anything "institutional, abstract and . . . inherited." He insisted on trust and integrity; his moral code is that of the "medieval knight" rather than the "conventional Christian." Characters lose honor by betraying a comrade rather than an abstract idea. He may "compel us to love the sinner, . . . never . . . to condone the sin." Significant is the way of redemption of Karain, Falk, and Jim: "all these men are saved by the intervention" of one to whom each has confessed, each of whom has a "full measure of genuine charity." The typical JC theme is "the discovery of truth about one-self." The emphasis on confession is not surprising for one with a Catholic upbringing.

1386 Greenwood, Thomas. "Joseph Conrad: Un centénaire littéraire" (Joseph Conrad: A Literary Centenary), ÉTUDES SLAVES ET EST-EUROPÉENNES, II (Winter 1957-1958), 195-200.

JC's Polish background supplies the invisible framework of all his writing; his theme of isolation springs from his having left his homeland; and the source of Polish culture, as JC himself wrote, is France and Italy: it is in France and Italy that "one must search for the substructure of his personal psychology." [General survey of life and works on the 100th anniversary of JC's birth.] [In French.]

1387 Gross, Seymour L. "Conrad and ALL THE KING'S MEN," TWENTIETH CENTURY LITERATURE, III (April 1957), 27-32.

JC's "Heart of Darkness" played a significant, perhaps crucial, role "in the artistic formulation and execution of ALL THE KING'S MEN" for the following reasons: (1) Kurtz and Willie as idealists go wrong; (2) the close parallels between Marlow and Jack Burden; (3) Warren's affinity to JC and his admiration of him.

1388 Gross, Seymour L. "A Further Note on the Function of the Frame in 'Heart of Darkness,'" MODERN FICTION STUDIES, III (Summer 1957), 167-70; rptd in THE ART OF JOSEPH CONRAD: A CRITICAL SYMPOSIUM, ed by Robert Wooster Stallman (East Lansing: Michigan State U P, 1960), pp. 181-84.

The function of the frame (the four men who sit listening to Marlow) has been ignored or misconstrued. Three of them do not understand the implications of the tale and the hidden truth of the moral abyss into which they have descended; but the first narrator relates to Marlow as the latter relates to Kurtz, becoming capable of facing the darkness and accepting its black message. The first narrator is set apart from others, and thereby illustrates JC's faith in the moral efficacy of experience presented through literature.

1389 Guerard, Albert J. *"The Nigger of the Narcissus,"* KENYON REVIEW, XIX (Spring 1957), 205-32; rptd in CONRAD THE NOVEL-

IST (Cambridge, Mass: Harvard U P, 1958), pp. 67-81; and in THE ART OF JOSEPH CONRAD: A CRITICAL SYMPOSIUM, ed by Robert Wooster Stallman (East Lansing: Michigan State U P, 1960), pp. 121-39.

Besides its value as a tribute to a particular ship and as "a memorial to a masculine society," *The Nigger of the Narcissus* is "a study in collective psychology"; "a prose-poem carrying overtones of myth." Such an approach to the novel more nearly does justice to its complexity than Vernon Young's "Trial by Water," ACCENT, XII (Spring 1952), 67-81, an example of "recent sophistication" in reading JC too simply and for discrediting his achievement. The ship symbolizes "our dark human pilgrimage, a vision of disaster illumined by grace." Man is both dignified and irremediably "little"—a reading characteristic of "most great works in the Christian tradition." But JC's sky is essentially "soulless." Nature is frequently antagonistic (the sun symbolizes "inhuman Nature which Man must oppose"). Man's dignity "lies in his vast silence and endurance." This "message" resembles Faulkner's, "these good seamen are like 'good negroes.'" Authority, tradition, and obedience save us. These are "purely human" and constitute "grace." Wait serves to unify the men against "latent egoism of tenderness to suffering." He is both flesh and symbol, takes on "the largest meanings" and becomes, "as in Melville, 'the Negro.'" Our task, however, "is not to discover what Wait *precisely* means but to observe a human relationship."

1390 Haugh, Robert F. JOSEPH CONRAD: DISCOVERY IN DESIGN (Norman: University of Oklahoma P, 1957).

The Nigger of the Narcissus, the first of three tales of "the Ship," has no hero as such; but in the sense that the ship is the crew's "society" and the symbol of their solidarity, she may be considered the central character. Although the point of view shifts, JC's "polarities" move to greater and greater complexity, to "a manifold polarity." By his use of *progression d'effet,* JC demonstrates how every person on board the *Narcissus* met darkness at sea and reacted uniquely. This novel affirms JC's belief that the human spirit must be strong and maintain its faith in opposition to "the negative coldness of cosmic law." "Youth" has no suggestion of the "menace of universal evil" found in *Nigger.* "Typhoon" depicts a universe in which "the plodding ships of ordinary souls (Captain MacWhirr, Jukes, and Solomon Rout) have indeed the special regard of an ironically amused Providence." JC's imagination was "most quickened" by "the Shallows," a place where "land meets and interpenetrates with the sea." "Heart of Darkness" is an "epiphany story," in the sense used by James Joyce. Kurtz, after attempting to take seriously the impossibly idealistic notions with which he was charged when he went to the Congo, dived deep into inhuman hate and darkness. Marlow goes neither as deep nor as high as Kurtz, and therefore he is saved.

In *Lord Jim,* the hero is an exile until, by a redemptive act, he at last gains a sense of belonging to a cherished group. He dies, but in doing so "he shows the rest of us, with our surface truths, 'how to be.' " The captain in "The Secret Sharer" becomes at last satisfactorily one with his crew; but *The Shadow-Line,* with the captain's maturity a resignation instead of a heroic resolution, is a dull and wearisome story. *Chance* is a book of "puzzling *progression d'effet"* (the second part is related to the first part obversely). And in *Victory,* the "Samburan mystery" ends, with all "dark passions spent": Lena's victory is to die in faith to Heyst; and he, in his turn, finds in her "triumphant sacrifice" the "measure of love that quells his skepticism completely."

In three novels of "the State," JC also displays his imaginative power, especially when the state is in a condition of unrest or revolution. In spite of its "massive ideational strength" and its "maze" of conceptions of character and of situation, *Under Western Eyes* is a lesser achievement than *Lord Jim:* the "management of event" is slight and the preparation for Razumov's confession to Natalia is frail in relationship, in sequence of scene, and in situation. Despite the relatively light circumstances and the few characters in *The Secret Agent,* the novel contains the "amazing symmetry and counterpoint" that strengthen JC's fiction. JC expended so much energy in the writing of *Nostromo* that he had no strength left for creating the scene and the postures of his characters, but elements of his "artistic conscience" may be seen in operation. [This study of the structure and design of most of JC's major works supplies some good critical insights—along with some very inept ones—and provides a helpful introduction to JC.]

> **1391** Heilman, Robert B. "Introduction," *Lord Jim,* ed with intro and notes by Robert B. Heilman (NY: Rinehart, 1957), pp. v-xxv, xxvii-xxx, xxxi-xxxiii, 365-69.

Lord Jim, JC's fourth novel, is his first major work. It presents the first full dramatic portrait of a hero and embodies the theme of isolation and the idea that crime is a breach of faith within the community of mankind. Marlow's conversation is one of JC's main yoking devices. He gives form to both halves of Jim's life by making actions in Patusan a duplication of the *Patna* events. Another unifying device is Jim's progression toward self-knowledge. After his trial, Jim runs from stories of his guilt, yet, with Brown, Jim admits to human liability, to acquaintance with evil. Stein's interpretation of the paradox that safety and danger, glory and disgrace, while opposites, spring from a common source, helps the reader to see Jim's journey as one journey.

Jim cannot really be explained in terms of JC's literary taste. He liked Turgenev and admired Dickens whose influence on him appears in certain comic elements in *Jim*. He had some philosophical affiliation with George Eliot, Meredith, and Hardy. Both he and George Eliot recognized man's ability to save and damn himself, but JC's range is greater. It is ironic that despite its merits, JC had a low opinion of *Jim* after he had finished it. [Includes biographical note, bibliographical note, and textual note.]

1392 Hoentzsch, Alfred. "Versuch über *Lord Jim* (Essay on *Lord Jim*), ECKART, XXVI (1957), 316-23.

Jim's dream, which is to him the better part of his life, is in fact hubris, a challenge to destiny. His leap overboard starts a chain reaction which affects the other figures deeply. Brierly and Jim acknowledge the law of their native community ("Heimat"), a law that requires loyalty, and fidelity to duty, and do not return home. After pitiless self-examination, Jim demands a second chance from destiny. Having received it, he triumphs over fate in his fall. [Unscholarly; enthusiastic appreciation.] [In German.]

1393 Hopkinson, Tom. "The Short Stories," LONDON MAGAZINE, IV (Nov 1957), 36-41.

JC's best short stories are "enormously long"; they have a solidity and grandeur different from the polished works of the greatest short story writers: Chekov, Turgenev, and Maupassant. JC belongs not with these writers but with a larger group that wrote a small number of truly great short stories: Tolstoi, Lawrence, Hardy, Melville.

1394 Hostowiec, Paweł. "Bagaż z Kalinówki" (Baggage from Kalinówki), CONRAD ŻYWY (The Living Conrad), ed by Wit Tarnawski (Lond: B. Świderski, 1957), pp. 87-91.

JC's efforts to reach the "inner truth" of different nations and races derives from the Jagiellon tradition (freedom and tolerance) of his home country. [Abstract based on English summary, pp. 282-83.] [In Polish.]

1395 Hough, Graham. "Chance and Joseph Conrad," LISTENER, LVIII (26 Dec 1957), 106-65; rptd in IMAGE AND EXPERIENCE (Lond: Duckworth, 1960), pp. 211-22.

There is an important neglected truth in the commonplace notion of JC as a sea writer. JC participated in and understood only one society: the ship at sea. The first half of *Chance* is weak because it deals with a group on land; the second half is strong because it takes place on the *Ferndale*. [Useful remarks on JC's narrative method. Originally a centenary broadcast, BBC Third Programme.]

1396 Janta, Aleksander. "Pierwszy szkic *Lorda Jima* i polskie listy Conrada w zbiorach Amerykańskich" (The First Sketch of *Lord Jim* and the American Collection of Conrad's Polish Letters), CONRAD ŻYWY (The Living Conrad), ed by Wit Tarnawski (Lond: B.

Swiderski, 1957), pp. 208-28; rptd as "A Conrad Family Heirloom at Harvard," POLISH REVIEW, II (Autumn 1957), 41-64.

[JC's visit to America (May 1923) was followed by the "sensational sale" of John Quinn's Conrad Collection. Parities in American collections, for which Quinn and Keating were responsible, turned up previously unknown letters, but most important is the "28 page pencil draft, 'Tuan Jim—A Sketch,'" which is discussed in John D. Gordan's JOSEPH CONRAD: THE MAKING OF A NOVELIST (1941; see 1940). The complete transcript is given here for the first time. The title and the opening sentences belie JC's preface to *Lord Jim* (1917) stating that his first thought was " 'concerned with the pilgrim ship episode; nothing more.' "] [Abstract based on English summary, pp. 295-96.] [In Polish.]

1397 "Joseph Conrad," TIMES LITERARY SUPPLEMENT (Lond), 6 Dec 1957, p. 739.

The changed critical attitude toward JC reveals that he, as much as Joyce and James, is one of the makers of the modern novel. He took "the novel of action and [made] of it the symbolic expression of man's fate."

1398 "Joseph Conrad: A Critical Symposium," LONDON MAGAZINE, IV (Nov 1957), 21-49.

[Contents, abstracted separately under author (1957): Oliver Warner, "The Sea Writer"; John Wain, "The Test of Manliness"; W. W. Robson, "The Politics of Solitude"; Richard Freislich, "Marlow's Shadow Side"; Tom Hopkinson, "The Short Story"; Jocelyn Baines, "The Affair in Marseilles"; Richard Curle, "Conrad and Jean-Aubry."]

1399 Kagarlitskii, Iu. "O Dzhozefe Konrade" (About Joseph Conrad), INOSTRANNAIA LITERATURA, No. 12 (1957), 205-9.

[In Russian.]

1400 Karl, Frederick R. "Conrad's Debt to Dickens," NOTES AND QUERIES, N.S. IV (Sept 1957), 398-400.

Three of JC's critics—Richard Curle, JOSEPH CONRAD: A STUDY (1914), p. 173; Morton D. Zabel, "Conrad: 'The Secret Sharer,'" NEW REPUBLIC, CIV (2 April 1941), 567-74; Paul L. Wiley, CONRAD'S MEASURE OF MAN (1954), p. 142—correctly believe that Dickens influenced JC. J. H. Retinger's opinion (CONRAD AND HIS CONTEMPORARIES [1941]) that Dickens did not influence JC is wrong. *The Secret Agent* and *Chance* "owe debts to Dickens's presentation of pathetic eccentrics in a grubby but great city and to his persistent theme of the imprisoned heart which may either free itself or be broken."

1401 Karl, Frederick R. "Joseph Conrad: A Modern Victorian: A Study in Novelistic Technique," DISSERTATION ABSTRACTS, XVII (1957), 1764. Unpublished thesis, Columbia University, 1957.

1402 Kaye, Julian B. "Conrad's *Under Western Eyes* and Mann's Doctor Faustus," Comparative Literature, IX (Winter 1957), 60-65.

Under Western Eyes is an important source for Mann's Doctor Faustus. Both stories are ostensibly factual accounts compiled, after the death of the protagonist, by an elderly professor of languages. Since both Mann and JC are partisans of Western values who refrain from seeing the West without faults and its opponents as completely wrong, they give ample scope to ambiguity and irony. In both novels, the narrator is a humanist, but the hero is human. Both Razumov and Leverkühn search for a mother and desire to return to the womb. The story in both books is conceived as both political and individual, as is the hero's pact with the Devil. Both Mann and JC consider Switzerland as the world and the opposing countries, Germany and Russia, as provincial. And in both novels Switzerland, "passionless, emotionally tepid," is the scene of the love of the hero.

1403 Kirschner, Paul. "Conrad and the Film," Quarterly of Film, Radio, and Television, XI (Summer 1957), 343-53.

The fiction of JC, whose years of writing (1895-1924) coincided with the development of the cinema, contains "a conscious and expert use of many techniques strikingly analogous to those of films today." The novelist's frequent use of "cinematic" description, for example, is exemplified in the opening paragraphs of *The Arrow of Gold*. The device of editing, which demonstrates an even closer relation between JC's works and the film, is demonstrated effectively in the murder scene in *The Secret Agent*, while other forms of editing create various effects such as the simultaneous cutting in the climax of *Victory* and *The Rescue*, and at the end of *The Rover*; montage in *Rescue*; a "perfect dissolve" in the opening of *Agent*; and symbolic rendering of both emotions and events, which becomes the use of "active similes" in fiction, like those found in *Almayer's Folly*, *An Outcast of the Islands*, and "The Lagoon." In several instances JC catches, even before he could have seen anything like the modern motion picture, "the spirit of symbolic editing, the film's nearest approach to poetry." "The colorful battle scenes of the Sulaco Revolution in *Nostromo*," for example, and "the superb geography of the seaboard republic which Conrad imagined to the last grain of sand . . . could be done justice only by the film." The fact that seven English and American productions of JC's works have been made (including two versions of *Victory*) indicates that the fictional pieces are "suited uniquely to the film." [Accompanied by adequate quotations from JC's writings, the explanation of the devices of the cinema are useful in recognizing some of the novelist's techniques.]

1404 Krzyżanowski, Ludwik. "Joseph Conrad: A Bibliographical Note," Polish Review, II: 2-3 (Spring-Summer 1957), 133-40.

Joseph Conrad

Kenneth A. Lohf and Eugene P. Sheehy's JOSEPH CONRAD AT MID-CENTURY (1957) is an "impressive bibliography," but the omission of Russian material, the occasional misspellings of Polish words, the poor choice of "significant" translations of JC's works and writings about him, and the omission of some pertinent material published in English detract from its value. [Lists about five pages of Polish items not included in Lohf and Sheehy's bibliography.]

1405 Kuncewiczowa, Maria. "Odkrycie Patusanu" (Discovery of Patusan), CONRAD ŻYWY (The Living Conrad), ed by Wit Tarnawski (Lond: B. Świderski, 1957), pp. 50-57.

Lord Jim revealed "that other, private war for individual dignity." What caused people "to love and understand" JC was "his genius for capturing the very essence of solitude." [Records conversation with Desmond McCarthy and H. G. Wells; cites Bertrand Russell.] [Abstract based on English summary, p. 280.] [In Polish.]

1406 Levin, Gerald Henry. "Conrad and the 'Atmosphere of Authenticity'; An Inquiry into the Structure and Meaning of *Chance*," DISSERTATION ABSTRACTS, XVII (1957), 1340-41. Unpublished thesis, University of Michigan, 1956.

1407 Lisiewicz, Mieczysław. "Czytajac listy ojca" (On Reading Father's Letters), CONRAD ŻYWY (The Living Conrad), ed by Wit Tarnawski (Lond: B. Świderski, 1957), pp. 141-49.

[Based on Apollo Korzeniowski's letters to his friend Kaszewski, this essay reveals Apollo's concern for his son's training in moral principles and most academic subjects, including "the appreciation and technique of literary work."] [Abstract based on English summary, p. 290.] [In Polish.]

1408 Lohf, Kenneth A., and Eugene P. Sheehy. JOSEPH CONRAD AT MID-CENTURY: EDITIONS AND STUDIES, 1895-1955 (Minneapolis: University of Minnesota P, 1957).

[Published in the centennial year of JC's birth, this is the first comprehensive bibliography of writings by and about this important author. It includes 230 entries under the heading "The Writings of Joseph Conrad" and 1,045 under "Works about Joseph Conrad," in addition to which the many reviews cited bring the total number of items to approximately 3,000.] [Still indispensable.]

1409 McFee, William. "Lord Jim," NEW STATESMAN AND NATION, LVI (28 Sept 1957), 385.

Lord Jim is based on a *cause célèbre* in Malaya. "Everybody knew it." The real Lord Jim lost his ticket. The engineer who had told McFee said, on reading the novel, " 'He's idealized the fellow.' " Aubry's biography is "most inadequate," compared with biographies of Shaw. It is inaccurate in its details about the Merchant Service and the Royal Navy, and it is vague about Mrs. Conrad's family and where she lived in London. [Letter in reply to V. S. Pritchett's "The Exile," ibid. (20 Aug 1957), 229.]

1410 Marković, Vida E. "Predgover" (Preface), in *Crnac Sa Narcisa,* trans by Nada Curčija-Prodanović (Belgrade: Nolit, 1957); rptd (1964), pp. 257-58.

[A clear account aimed at readers with an elementary literary education, in tune with the purpose of the series in which this translation of *The Nigger of the Narcissus* appears.] [In Serbo-Croatian.]

1411 Maser, Frederick E. "The Philosophy of Joseph Conrad," HIBBERT JOURNAL, LVI (Oct 1957), 69-78.

While JC's stories are diverse in thought and philosophy, they do not lack "a characteristic philosophy . . . although not always clearly defined." The first of JC's "basic truths" is a "faith in the essential dignity and significance of men." He holds this faith confronted by "a dark line on the face of Life, a cloud of Evil shadowing the sunlight of the brightest day." A second truth is "solidarity," or the feeling of kinship one has with his fellow-man. A third truth is that man must depend not upon God but upon action, his own action and that of his fellows. "Providence plays no role in the affairs of men. The Universe is as unthinking as the sea, and man plays his part with no aid from God and no consolation from the Divine. Conrad was not, in the accepted sense of the word, a religious man."

1412 Maxwell, J. C. "Conrad: A Misdated Letter," NOTES AND QUERIES, N.S. IV (July 1957), 314-15.

The letter to Spiridion Kliszczewski in Aubry's JOSEPH CONRAD: LIFE AND LETTERS (1927), I, 273-74, dated "12th April [1899]" belongs to the previous year.

1413 Milivojević, D[ragoljub]. "Slava u izgnanstvu" (Famous in His Exile), POLITIKA (Belgrade), LIV (Literary Section I), 29 Dec 1957, p. 38.

[Sympathetic commonplace information marking the centenary.] [In Serbo-Croatian.]

1414 Miłosz, Czesław. "Joseph Conrad in Polish Eyes," ATLANTIC MONTHLY, CC (Nov 1957), 219-28; rptd in THE ART OF JOSEPH CONRAD: A CRITICAL SYMPOSIUM, ed by Robert Wooster Stallman (East Lansing: Michigan State U P, 1960), pp. 35-45.

JC, descended from the nobility of Poland, more importantly grew up in a literary milieu. From the unhappiness of his childhood he "derived both his deep-seated antipathy for Russia and that tragic outlook on life which is so evident in his later books." JC's guardian after the death of his father, his uncle Brobowski [sic], was completely different from the father and thus caused the boy to be "torn between two contrary influences." One newly discovered fact may have caused his uncle's unwilling acceptance of his nephew's becoming a sailor—the young student, who was already causing enough trouble, had "a scandalous love affair" with one of his cousins, Tekla Soroczynska. Then, England gave the sailor what he most needed, "an understanding of the struggle for life and an awareness of human fraternity in the face of a cruel and indifferent Nature." And she also gave him her language, but "what happened in Conrad was a perfect fusing of two literatures and two civilizations." Biographical details lead to the conclusion that "a carefully hidden complex of treason is discernible in some of his writings—a feeling that he had betrayed the cause so fanatically embraced by his compatriots and, above all, by his father." He did not believe in the future of his own country, and thus *Lord Jim* acquires new meaning if it is read as "a drama of national loyalties." Even JC's marriage to an Englishwoman failed to make his adaptation to the new country complete. When the Communist Party "proclaimed Conrad an immoral writer and a corrupter of youth" and his ethical ideals capitalistic, indirectly through some of his father's plays and new editions of his own works, JC, "the son who did not want to assume a burden that had crushed his father, had nevertheless become the defender of freedom against the blights of autocracy." [An astute scrutiny of JC. Complements Gustav Morf's and R. L. Mégroz's conclusions.]

> **1415** Miłosz, Czesław. "Stereotyp u Conrada" (Conrad's Stereotype), CONRAD ŻYWY (The Living Conrad), ed by Wit Tarnawski (Lond: B. Świderski, 1957), pp. 92-99.

JC is indebted to Polish political traditions, those of "the conservative gentry of the eastern borders": antagonism to Russia, Germans, attraction for and disillusion with France and England. [Abstract based on English summary, pp. 283-84.] [In Polish.]

> **1416** Młynarska, Maria. *"Lord Jim* w powstaniu Warszawskim" (*Lord Jim* During the Warsaw Uprising," CONRAD ŻYWY (The Living Conrad), ed by Wit Tarnawski (Lond: B. Świderski, 1957), pp. 262-66.

JC's works, especially *Lord Jim,* warned those in the uprising of what happens to "those who flee." [Abstract based on English summary, p. 298.] [In Polish.]

> **1417** Moczulski, Mariusz Hrynkiewicz. "Conrad na obszyźnie: II. Klub Miłośników Conrada" (Conrad Abroad: II. Association of Conrad Lovers), CONRAD ŻYWY (The Living Conrad), ed by Wit Tarnawski (Lond: B. Świderski, 1957), pp. 272-75.

[An account of the actions of The Polish Activities Club, founded in London in 1948.] [Abstract based on English summary, p. 300.] [In Polish.]

1418 "Monografia o Dzhozefe Konrad" (Monograph about Joseph Conrad), INNOSTRANNAIA LITERATURA, No. 7 (1957), 276. [Discusses the forthcoming publication of the book by Jocelyn Baines.] [In Russian.]

1419 Moser, Thomas. JOSEPH CONRAD: ACHIEVEMENT AND DECLINE (Cambridge, Mass: Harvard U P, 1957); based on "Joseph Conrad's Surrender: Some Sources and Characteristics of the Decline of His Creative Powers." Unpublished thesis, Harvard University, 1955; rptd with minor corrections (Hamden, Conn: Archon Books, 1966); part rptd in CONRAD: A COLLECTION OF CRITICAL ESSAYS, ed by Marvin Mudrick (Englewood Cliffs, NJ: Prentice-Hall, Spectrum Books, 1966).

"The Early Conrad's Anatomy of Moral Failure (1895-1912)" reveals four "Conrads": psychologist, political observer, artist and moralist. JC feels "pity and admiration for suffering humanity in general" and asserts loyalty and service as "the central virtues" of his creative world. The central situation of his early stories is the test which reveals whether an individual is faithful to his community. He creates three major types of character: the simple hero, the vulnerable hero, and the perceptive hero who meets his crisis successfully and thereby achieves self-knowledge; and one minor type, the man who fails but who could never be taken for a hero, the villain. Fidelity is the greatest virtue of JC's moral code, and its opposite, betrayal, is the central theme of his early period. The man who fails interests JC "more deeply" than one who succeeds: failures include Jim, all the main characters of *Nostromo,* and Razumov. JC's primary interest in his characters is psychological, why they fail.

"The Uncongenial Subject: Love's Tangled Garden (1895-1924)" finds love as the "lowest common denominator" of the early novels and stories and of the weaker parts of *Lord Jim* and *Nostromo,* and the source of "certain fundamental weaknesses" in JC's imagination. The two lovers are the weakest part of *Almayer's Folly;* JC seems to be aware of Willems's "lack of masculinity" and to equate death with woman in *An Outcast of the Islands;* the ship is the only woman of an "ideal world"; and in "Heart of Darkness" Marlow comments interestingly on women, and the scene between Marlow and Kurtz's Intended is significant. After these works, JC entered a new phase of writing which includes his "four best full-length novels," *Jim, Nostromo, The Secret Agent,* and *Under Western Eyes.* In *Jim,* JC tames the materials that had been baffling to him by eliminating a "powerful yet supposedly sympathetic female," Edith Travers of *The Rescue,* and substituting one of his most "congenial types," "the isolated, egotistic, cynical yet romantic figure with a criminal past," Gentleman Brown. Mrs. Gould in *Nostromo* is JC's "only truly successful characterization of a woman," but the novel is weakened by one of the "worst" love affairs (Nostromo and Giselle) of JC's early period. *Agent* continues JC's political explorations and depicts successfully "a memorable female character," Winnie Verloc. The love story in *Eyes* is managed well by its restriction to less than ten per cent of the pages of the novel. "A Smile of Fortune" is a "first-rate story of female sexuality and male impotence." But JC's decision at last to finish *Chance* "determined his decline" because this novel has love as its central subject. Sometimes JC's affirmation of the value of love leads him "to value love over life." Thus, in 1913, JC began to write love stories, "the intended meanings of which ran counter to the deepest impulses of his being." The villains in the later novels are "new and unusual" for JC: their actions symbolize evil, and the hero, like the villain, is "an impotent voyeur" whose destiny it is to be destroyed when he becomes involved with a woman. The failure of the lover's "masculinity," the "implicit subject" of the later novels, resembles the early JC's concern with the test of a man's "moral fitness." *The Shadow-Line,* however, suggests that JC's decline was caused basically by something more general than his choice of subject matter: his choice of love as a subject suggests a shift in his "fundamental attitude."

"The Later Conrad's 'Affirmation' (1913-1924)" contrasts JC's earlier and later views of man as they are revealed in central ideas, types of characters, and technique. Whereas JC's early period revealed the significance of test and betrayal, his later period turns from these "moral interests" to an acceptance of "chance" as the force which controls human action. This change is exemplified in *Chance, Victory, Shadow-Line,* and *Rescue,* in which "dark powers" do not so much lurk within the characters as they do in the early works but, rather, are caused by influences outside them. Thus, JC's later "affirmation" found by several eminent critics is a "very evasive affirmation," and JC no longer sees his characters as "part of the world community of suffering and damned humanity" but rather as "figures of purity afflicted by an external evil." Their greatest good is to lose themselves in a love that will "blot out all awareness of the world and bring the semblance of death." The later JC therefore has a "new attitude" toward the world, but scarcely an affirmative one. The "faithful seaman and vulnerable hero" of the early works is superseded by the "untried boy and the impeccable hero"; the "popular-magazine heroine and the unremittingly black villain" become dominant. JC's technique accordingly becomes in reality less complex and less dense, despite the apparent complexity which still exists: *Chance* is "intrinsically much less complex" than *Jim* or *Nostromo*.

JC's fatigue and his loss of creative energy in *The Arrow of Gold, The Rover,* and *Suspense* leave these novels "virtually without a redeeming feature." JC cannot dramatize the emotions and ideas of his characters, and his prose is "very faulty." [This is one of the few indispensable critical books on JC, although several more recent writers have at least partly modified Moser's assessment of JC's later creations. It contains close and illuminating analyses of most of JC's major works and makes an important contribution to the achievement-and-decline theory of JC's writing career.]

1420 Mroczkowski, Przemysław. "A Polish View of Joseph Conrad," LISTENER, LVIII (12 Dec 1957), 979-80.

JC's romanticism is perhaps dated; but his sense of the drama of life—the struggle and play of opposing principles—makes his work especially meaningful today. [Little specifically Polish in the article, which was a broadcast on BBC.]

1421 Mudrick, Marvin. "The Artist's Conscience and *The Nigger of the Narcissus*," NINETEENTH-CENTURY FICTION, XI (March 1957), 288-97.

Although JC's "power realizes itself in sustained passages of description unsurpassed in English fiction," especially in the episode of the storm in *The Nigger of the Narcissus,* and although the image of James Wait is "another triumph of disinterested observation," JC's shift of point of view away from that of an anonymous member of the crew for the "sure-fire scene" in which Donkin at last confronts Wait with the fact that he is near death is a disappointing expedient. After the midpoint of the novel, the reader becomes aware of JC's "dissatisfaction" with his own "chosen . . . limitations of vision"; this dissatisfaction and "the expedients that issue from it in the latter part of the novel, produce nothing . . . that compares with what comes before." JC's characters "so fluently blend with such abstractions as authority, skill, responsibility, duty, courage *versus* ineptness, panic, malingering, the touchy indocile solidarity of the mob," that the reader is left with "a parvenu's-eye view of things, a hand-me-down 'aristocratic' universe in which everybody in charge deserves to be and everybody else had better jump." But JC is "too taken with his metaphysics to go much beyond merely stating it," and almost all the characters in the novel are "such elementary emblems of what they are intended to demonstrate—Conrad's expressly and frequently stated 'view of life' "—that they would seem unacceptable or even sometimes ludicrous if it were not for "the magnificent descriptive passages and the sonorities that rescue us, periodically, from the responsibility of contemplating character."

In *Nigger,* there is lacking "a kind of patience" that "presents an action, not to define it, but to let it define itself and move with a certain (however illusory) freedom." JC eventually becomes impatient of everything but "philosophizing, of telling us what to think about life, death, and the rest." [Interesting, if not completely convincing.]

1422 Naglerowa, Herminia. "Wezwanie" (The Call), CONRAD ŻYWY (The Living Conrad), ed by Wit Tarnawski (Lond: B. Świderski, 1957), pp. 69-73.

Reading JC during the war recalled one "to a life of creative work after a long period of almost complete inactivity." The preface to *The Nigger of the Narcissus* stimulates one toward renewed creative activity. [Abstract based on English summary, p. 281.] [In Polish.]

1423 Najder, Zdzisław. "Conrad w Polsce w latach 1939-1957" (Conrad in Poland during the Years 1939-1957), CONRAD ŻYWY (The Living Conrad), ed by Wit Tarnawski (Lond: B. Świderski, 1957), pp. 258-61.

During the German occupation JC's works "were circulating continuously." JC became a most influential author at the time because he appeals "to people who have to face difficult moral problems demanding loyalty and courage." [Abstract based on English summary, p. 298.] [In Polish.]

1424 Najder, Zdzisław. "O 'filozofii' Conrad" (About the "Philosophy" of Conrad), PRZEGLAD KULTURALNY, No. 49 (Dec 1957), 3; rptd in NAD CONRADEM (Warsaw: Państwowy Instytut Wydawniczy, 1965), pp. 185-203.

Although JC read the books of his friend Bertrand Russell, he consistently displayed an aversion for abstract philosophical concepts in his own works. As an artist, he believed that man was the measure of all things. Vacillating between resignation and rebellion, he ultimately rejected despair. Man is a microcosm, and he alone creates values on this earth. But these values are nonetheless real and great. The quintessence of JC's philosophy of life can be stated as tragic optimism. [In Polish.]

1425 Najder, Zdzisław. "Trzy Pory Życia" (The Three Seasons of Life), Twórczość, XIII (Dec 1957), 63-69; rptd in NAD KONRADEM (Warsaw: Państwowy Instytut Wydawniczy, 1965), pp. 112-27.

In three narratives ("Youth," "Heart of Darkness," *Within the Tides*), JC has presented a wide spectrum of human experience. The experiences portrayed vary from the charming and simple picture of youth with its sensuality and blustering faith to the world of old age with its rejection of faith in the moral structure of the universe. We might ask ourselves why JC, in the preface to these collected stories, did not attempt to tie these stories together so as to present them as a unified view of life. The answer lies in the fact that conclusions which we can deduce from *Within the Tides* are not definitive conclusions of JC's view of the world. He would tell us, rather, to look for these conclusions in "Youth." For although he knew how to express the hopelessness and despair of human existence, he was, nevertheless, far from sterile pessimism. [In Polish.]

>**1426** Ostrowski, Witold. "Problem Josepha Conrada" (The Problem of Joseph Conrad), KULTURA I SPOŁECZEŃSTWO, I (Oct-Dec 1957), 50-70; rptd in O LITERATURZE ANGIELSKIEJ (Warsaw: Pax, 1958), pp. 292-96; excerpted in JOSEPH CONRAD KORZENIOWSKI, by Róża Jabłkowska (Warsaw. Państwowe Zakłady Wydawnictwo Szkolynch, 1964), pp. 320-24.

[Gives a history of Polish attempts to start a JC Institute from before World War II to date and advice on what the Poles should do in JC studies: translate all works and critical work such as Oliver Warner's (1950, 2nd ed, 1964, rptd with slight changes, 1966); bring Grzegorczyk's bibliography (1933) of Polish scholarship up to date.] [In Polish.]

>**1427** Owen, Guy, "A Note on 'Heart of Darkness,' " NINETEENTH-CENTURY FICTION, XII (Sept 1957), 168-69.

Along with two recent articles on classical allusions in JC's "Heart of Darkness," the nonclassical allusion to King Arthur and his Round Table is also important. JC's "greedy traders" are "knights" as well as "pilgrims," and their goal is ivory. This allusion is particularly important because "the ironic contrast between the grandeur and nobility of Arthur's court and the ignobility of the unheroic traders is patent. Yet Conrad also suggests that, just as Arthur's world was doomed by dissension and sin, the white man's order will not prevail in the heart of darkness."

>**1428** Peterkiewicz, Jerzy. "Conrad and Poland. For the Centenary: Patriotic Irritability," TWENTIETH CENTURY (Lond), CLXII (Dec 1957), 545-57.

Two JC legends still prevail: (1) JC is "an enigmatic fusion of writer and sailor"; (2) he keeps vigil before Fidelity and Honor as "a Quixotic Polish nobleman in the England of Kipps, Major Barbara and Pan." *A Personal Record* is "poised between autobiographical intimacy and legendary aloofness." JC is not hypocritical in this division of mind; "he was the poet of Fate." He did not want his Polish background used for sensational journalism. Cunninghame Graham prevented JC's giving up writing just in time to permit *Chance* to be published and to become popular; it is his "least inspired" novel. His puzzling strength lies in JC's self-restraint. Misunderstanding of JC's "Polishness" has underlain much inept criticism (e.g., Orzeszkowa's 1899 attack; the commentaries of English and American psychological critics). In general, JC "held moderate opinions about the solution of the Polish question." He is neither "an escapist" nor "a penitent." On the basis of similar backgrounds, JC is compared with Chopin and Norwid.

1429 Pfase [Pfabe], Teresa. "Bertrand Russell o Conradzie" (Bertrand Russell on Conrad), KULTURA I SPOŁECZEŃSTWO, No. 4 (1957), 46-47.

[In Polish.]

1430 Pritchett, V. S. "The Exile," NEW STATESMAN, LIV (24 Aug 1957), 229.

Aubry's THE SEA DREAMER (1957; see VIE DE CONRAD [1947]) is "informed but incurious and can hardly now be up to date." In his position as exile, JC had freedom in viewing society but he saw its terrors too. The exile's temperament "gave [JC] his obsession with the allusive." JC is better with the evil fact than with evil in general. "His greatness lies in the handling of a large range of moral types who suffer these evils [fear, guilt, remorse, corruption, betrayal] each in a different way, so that we feel he understands a universal condition." [See, for a reply, William McFee's "Lord Jim," ibid. (28 Sept 1957), 385.]

1431 Retinger, J. H. "Dwie narodowości Józefa Conrada" (The Dual Nationality of Joseph Conrad), CONRAD ŻYWY (The Living Conrad), ed by Wit Tarnawski (Lond: B. Świderski, 1957), pp. 129-33.

JC remained a Pole in "his way of life, his sentiments and mannerisms," but he "was a loyal English citizen." These generalizations are supported by personal knowledge of JC. JC's style "had its roots in the Polish language," yet in "Il Conde," he wrote about a Pole as a foreigner would. [Abstract based on English summary, p. 288.] [In Polish.]

1432 Robson, W. W. "The Politics of Solitude," LONDON MAGAZINE, IV (Nov 1957), 26-31.

Under Western Eyes confirms JC's preoccupation with "moral solitude," the condition of modern man. The betrayer, Razumov, is isolated and alone. There is no way he can escape his predicament. The teacher of languages, the "Western eyes," imagines Razumov's misery with the power of Dostoevski while retaining "an ultimate aloofness." JC would register no surprise at the coming of "darkness at noon."

1433 Sakowski, Juliusz. "Żyje sie tylko raz" (One Lives Only Once), CONRAD ŻYWY (The Living Conrad), ed by Wit Tarnawski (Lond: B. Świderski, 1957), pp. 79-83.

The work of JC and Proust is timeless, although it is in every other way "completely different": Proust is "a scientist of literature"; JC, like Shakespeare and the Greek tragedians, is concerned "with the essence itself of the human heart." According to JC, it is man's duty "to make of life a great thing in its earthly limits." [Abstract based on English summary, p. 282.] [In Polish.]

1434 Squire, Sir John. "Master Mariner and Novelist," ILLUSTRATED LONDON NEWS, CCXXXI (17 Aug 1957), 264.

Aubry's THE SEA DREAMER: A DEFINITIVE BIOGRAPHY (1957; see VIE DE CONRAD [1947]) is not a "definitive biography," since many of JC's letters are still missing, and since there is little publication history of JC's various works. Aubry does give an unforgettable picture of JC the passionate Pole, the "British sailor, and the unflinching artist."

1435 Stallman, Robert. "Fiction and Its Critics: A Reply to Mr. Rahv," KENYON REVIEW, XIX (Spring 1957), 290-99.

Mr. Rahv is wrong in thinking that "the proper use of language in fiction excludes the poetic. . . . This critic does not like symbolism, but then neither does he like Conrad." Abundant quotations from JC's letters demonstrate that he regarded "symbol and myth" as desirable in fiction. "Until I am persuaded otherwise, it is right that the poetic should infect the prosaic and, conversely, that the prosaic should infect the poetic. *Contra* Mr. Rahv and the Russians, I see no iron curtain between poem and novel, linguistically."

1436 Stein, William Bysshe. "Buddhism and 'Heart of Darkness,'" WESTERN HUMANITIES REVIEW, XI (Summer 1957), 281-85.

Whatever the explanation of "Marlow's sympathy for Kurtz," one should not overlook the significance of the four Buddha Postures in "Heart of Darkness." From his experience with Kurtz, Marlow has learned the renunciation of self, and Marlow thus achieves the status of a Bodhisattva. In this role Marlow uses "a parable to direct his listeners to the path of redemption." The first Buddha Posture shows "Marlow in the condition of complete withdrawal from the karmic world." In the second Buddha Posture, Marlow "breaks the rigidity of his inturned lotus position. . . . Symbolically, Marlow is seated upon the throne of an opened lotus, inhaling as it were the inspiration of the absolute." But Marlow's effort is wasted since his story is judged to be another of his "inconclusive experiences." In the third Buddha Posture, "Marlow's lean face appeared, worn, hollow, with downward folds and drooped eyelids, with an aspect of concentrated attention." Here Marlow experiences the spiritual illumination of Kurtz's suffering. Because his auditors are unable to comprehend the message, Marlow at the end is "once more in a state of self-contained meditation, enclosed in the invulnerable pose of the inturned lotus: 'Marlow ceased, and sat apart, indistinct and silent, in the pose of the meditating Buddha.'"

1437 Taborski, Roman. APOLLO KORZENIOWSKI; OSTATNI DRAMATOPISARZ ROMANTYCZNY (Apollo Korzeniowski; the Last Romantic Dramatist) (Wroclaw: Polish Academy of Science, 1957 [STUDIA HISTORY-CZNOLITERACKIE, IX (Historical-Literary Studies, IX), ed by Jan Kott].)
[This is probably the only study besides Buszczynski's devoted exclusively to JC's father. It is carried out in a biographical vein and carries Apollo Korzeniowski through his childhood and youth, devotes a chapter to his poetry, a chapter to his play KOMEDIA, a chapter to his play DLA MIEGO GROSZA, one to his translations, one to his life in Zytomierz and Warsaw, another to his decline, and a final chapter to the work of the father and the son. The bibliography contains details of the Apollo Korzeniowski manuscripts, a list of Apollo's published work, and a list of studies of Apollo Korzeniowski.] [In Polish.]

1438 [Tarnawski, Wit (ed)]. CONRAD ŻYWY (The Living Conrad) (Lond: B. Świderski, 1957). [Contents, abstracted separately under author (1957): W[it] T[arnawski], "Zamiast przedmowy"; John Conrad, "Garść wspomnień o moin ojcu" (as "Some Reminiscences of My Father" on facing pages); poems by Jan Lechoń, Zbigniew Chałko, Jan Leszcza, Józef Żywina (unlisted and not abstracted); Maria Kuncewiczowa, "Odkrycie Patusanu"; Andrzej Bobkowski, "Alma"; Herminia Naglerowa, "Wezwanie"; Jan Fryling, "Plon mórz dalekich"; Juliusz Sakowski, "Żyje się tylko raz"; Paweł Hostowiec, "Bagaż z Kalinówki"; Czesław Miłosz, "Stereotyp u Conrada"; Tymon Terlecki, "Conrad w kulturze Polskiej; Stanisław Vincenz, "Conrad a konwencje"; J. H. Retinger, "Dwie narodowości Józefa Conrada"; Zbigniew Grabowski, "Po trzydziestu latach"; Mieczysław Lisiewicz, "Czytając listy ojca"; J. P. Dabrowski, "Conrad a 'wielka trójka' literatury Rosyjskiej"; Zdzisław Broncel, "Pokusa nadczłowieka"; Barbara Gażikówna, "Nieznana część rękopisu 'Ocalenia' "; Wit Tarnawski, "Niedoceniona powieśc Conrada"; Aleksander Janta, "Pierwszy szkic *Lorda Jima* i polskie listy Conrada w zbiorach Amerykańskich"; Zdzisław Najder, "Conrad w Polsce w latach 1939-1957"; Maria Młynarska, *"Lord Jim* w powstaniu Warszawskim"; Witold Turno, "Conrad na obczyżnie: I. Od Rumunii do Wielkiej Brytanii"; Mariusz Hrynkiewicz Moczulski, "Conrad na obczyżnie: II. Klub miłowników Conrada"; "The Living Conrad: English Summary of the Polish Text," pp. 279-300. The summaries are rather free and mingled with comments on the authors and on the text. By Conrad and not abstracted: "Tuan Jim: A Sketch," transcribed by Aleksander Janta [copy of the first draft of *Lord Jim* and "an unknown play by Joseph Conrad"], pp. 195-

207; "Listy do Johna Galsworthy' ego" (Letters from Me to John Galsworthy) edited by Maria Danilewiczowa, pp. 229-57.] [In Polish.]

1439 Tarnawski, Wit. "Niedoceniona powieść Conrada" (An Underestimated Novel of Conrad), CONRAD ŻYWY (The Living Conrad), ed by Wit Tarnawski (Lond: B. Świderski, 1957), pp. 181-92.

An Outcast of the Islands "has been underestimated both as a work of art and as a reflection on Conrad's personal problems." JC's "drama of conscience" was expressed as *Outcast* long before *Lord Jim*. The "betrayal of his race" and the subsequent solitude reflect JC's own experience. Shortly after *Outcast*, "Karain" and "The Lagoon" are also based on the theme of betrayal. As in *Outcast*, however, the theme is treated objectively and even ironically because JC's "moral preoccupations were still mainly subconscious." JC probably first faced the question of betrayal consciously when he received Orzeszkowa's accusatory letter; *Jim* was in a sense a fictional reply, since "situations and peculiarities of technique" in *Outcast* were later used in JC's "more mature work." [Abstract based on English summary, pp. 294-95.] [In Polish.]

1440 Tarnawski, Wit. "Zamiast Przedmowy" (Instead of a Preface), CONRAD ŻYWY (The Living Conrad), ed by Wit Tarnawski (Lond: B. Świderski, 1957), pp. 185-89.

With the exception of a poem by Lechoń, all the selections in this volume are original, written especially for this collection. To the contributors of this volume, JC is first of all a master of life, not art: a teacher of moral and intellectual attitudes. The book is divided into three parts: (1) literature, (2) literary criticism, (3) historical documents. [In Polish.]

1441 Terlecki, Tymon. "Conrad w kulturze polskiej" (Conrad in Polish Culture), CONRAD ŻYWY (The Living Conrad), ed by Wit Tarnawski (Lond: B. Świderski, 1957), pp. 100-13.

There is no possibility or "reason to claim Conrad for Polish literature," although Polish culture "influenced and formed his mind in the first fifteen or twenty years of his life." The uprising of 1860-63 influenced JC's sensibility as it did the writers of the "Young Poland" movement. In romanticism "they found an escape in exotism and searched for new sources of spiritual energy for the fulfillment of individual and collective longings." The "flight from reality and the mastering of reality" are particularly evident in JC. According to *A Personal Record* (1912), JC may have made contact with writers of the "Young Poland" group in 1890 and 1893, when he visited his uncle. From Polish romanticism JC may have taken over "the heroic attitude towards life." [Abstract based on English summary, pp. 285-86.] [In Polish.]

1442 Thale, Jerome. "The Narrator as Hero," TWENTIETH CENTURY LITERATURE, III (July 1957), 69-73.

Nick Carraway of THE GREAT GATSBY and Marlow of "Heart of Darkness" are two classic examples of a hero who learns about himself by observing others. "Nick and Marlow stand in the same relation to the main figures that we do to the conventional hero of a novel. . . . But Gatsby and Kurtz are so grotesque that we could not possibly comprehend them on our own, could not identify ourselves in any way with them. . . . The novels are not about Kurtz or Gatsby but about people who come to know themselves through reacting to Kurtz and Gatsby. And just as the hero-narrator comes to know himself in another, so we come to know ourselves projected in the images of fiction."

1443 Turno, Witold. "Conrad na obczyźnie" I. Od Rumunii do Wielkiej Brytanii" (Conrad Abroad: I. From Rumania to Great Britain), CONRAD ŻYWY (The Living Conrad), ed by Wit Tarnawski (Lond: B. Świderski, 1957), pp. 267-72.

JC's works were much admired by Poles in exile because they "are so amazingly opposite to the exiles [sic] present situation and their problems." His hostility toward Russians also contributed to his popularity among Poles. JC's works had excellent sales among Polish Forces in Italy. Much writing on JC in the Polish Press (e.g., in WIADOMOŚCI) of England further reveals his popularity among exiles. [Abstract based on English summary, pp. 298-99.] [In Polish.]

1444 Van Slooten, Henry. "The Reception of the Writings of Joseph Conrad in England and the United States from 1895 through 1915," UNIVERSITY OF SOUTHERN CALIFORNIA ABSTRACTS OF DISSERTATIONS (1957), 103-5. Unpublished thesis, University of Southern California, 1957.

1445 Vincenz, Stanisław. "Conrad a konwencje" (Conrad and Convention) CONRAD ŻYWY (The Living Conrad), ed by Wit Tarnawski (Lond: B. Świderski, 1957), pp. 114-28.

JC "considers the ideal to be the innate actuating force of the soul." His discovery of "the brutal facts and chaotic forces of life" caused him to question and probe ideals. JC's "spiritual solitude . . . forms the basis of the interchange" between the old and the new realities. Sometimes, when these realities clash, "he is compelled to take recourse to convention." Both Bunyan's PILGRIM'S PROGRESS and some of JC's novels "show the strife between the moral pattern and the realities of life." Bunyan's pilgrim "approaches his aim and ideal"; "the dramatic wrestling in Conrad is rather that of a *faustischer Mensch.*" JC may also be compared with Freud (all people are ill) and Lord Baden Powell ("men may be healthy if they renew in active life their fellow creatures"). This comparison throws light on JC's polarities: "the breaking off of attachments and a mistrustful probing into the secrets of the human heart"; in *Lord Jim,* the hero's "boyish ideals." Douglas Hewitt (CONRAD: A REASSESSMENT [1952]) is mistaken in drawing a parallel between JC and Dostoevski. The latter is "acosmic if not anti-cosmic"; the former is "a philosophical writer in the sense that he is a tragedian who poses problems but does not give any explicit solutions." JC is loyal to "a pattern of conduct with which every man is born." [Abstract based on English summary, pp. 286-88.] [In Polish.]

1446 Vlahović, Josip. "Pustolovan i zanimljiv zivot jednog od najvećih pisaca o moru" (The Adventures and Interesting Life of One of the Greatest Writers on the Sea), GLAS ZADRA, VIII (17 Aug 1957), 320.

[A newspaper feature marking the centenary.] [In Serbo-Croatian.]

1447 Wain, John. "The Test of Manliness," LONDON MAGAZINE, IV (Nov 1957), 23-26.

JC's English contemporaries were obsessed with service to a greater good, even at the sacrifice of personal honor. JC's continental background allowed him to conceive of personal honor as a vital idea. The sea is an appropriate place for JC's independent heroes; the sea is where a man must survive on his inner resources.

1448 Warner, Oliver. "The Sea Writer," LONDON MAGAZINE, IV (Nov 1957), 21-23.

JC established a standard for judging maritime fiction. The talk of his fellow seamen, the newspapers, and Newton's GUIDE FOR MASTERS AND MATES gave JC his true education in English. The labelling of JC as a "sea writer" is inappropriate in its limitation, not in its accuracy.

1449 Werner, Harry. "Joseph Conrad, 'Freya of the Seven Isles': Eine Schulinterpretation" (Joseph Conrad, "Freya of the Seven Isles": A School Interpretation), NEUEREN SPRACHEN, N.S. VI (1957), 577-83.

The Captain at first adopts a subjective attitude towards the people of his story. From chapter IV on, his sympathetic comments are less frequent. He attempts to analyze the characters more objectively and to give a glimpse of the meaning of fate. In chapter V, he reports what he has learned from his friend's letters. Then Old Nelson himself is introduced as a narrator. His loneliness is mirrored in his style. But only the old Captain seems to comprehend Freya's misery. His sympathy makes him trustworthy to the reader. [This study, which is addressed to high school students, tries to show how the discussion of the personality and the functions of the narrator may be expanded into a comprehensive interpretation of JC's story.] [In German.]

1450 West, Rebecca. THE COURT AND THE CASTLE: SOME TREATMENTS OF A RECURRENT THEME (New Haven: Yale U P, 1957), pp. 209-12, 240.

JC "was a religious man and his life fostered religion, and he strongly believed that the courtiers would be saved by the action of grace bestowed by God." In JC, kingship was reborn; human security depends on the keeping of oaths by captain and crew. Fidelity is "the guiding principle," an idea different from and similar to Kipling's idea of loyalty. JC was "in a sense nearer Shakespeare than any other modern novelist."

1451 Zabel, Morton Dauwen. "Conrad," CRAFT AND CHARACTER: TEXTS, METHOD, AND VOCATION IN MODERN FICTION (NY: Viking P, 1957), pp. 147-227.

Contents [four articles collected, with revisions, from other sources, abstracted separately under date of first publication]: "Conrad: Chance and Recognition," from SEWANEE REVIEW (1945); "Conrad: The East and the Sea," from "Introduction," *The Nigger of the Narcissus* (1951); "Conrad: The Threat to the West," from "Introduction," *Under Western Eyes* (1951); "Conrad in His Age," here a new essay based on material in "Conrad: Nel Mezzo del Cammin," NEW REPUBLIC (1940), "Conrad: The Secret Sharer," NEW REPUBLIC (1941), and "Conrad in His Age," NEW REPUBLIC (1942). [Zabel's articles on JC in their final form, ranging from 1940 to 1957 in their development, provide one of the most stimulating general descriptions of the novelist's career. JC's conscious center may be seen as an ethical view of the universe and of man's place in it, with the growth of his art as a process of self-discovery. Zabel thus refutes to some extent the popular achievement-and-decline theory of JC's writing career.]

1958

1452 Allen, Jerry. THE THUNDER AND THE SUNSHINE: A BIOGRAPHY OF JOSEPH CONRAD (NY: Putnam's, 1958).

[Concerned largely with Rita of *The Arrow of Gold,* Allen identifies her original as Paula de Somoggy (more correctly, Somogyi), a Hungarian peasant girl; brings JC to the age of twenty; touches briefly on his later years; attempts to place him among his contemporaries; and explains social and political backgrounds of his works. No more than a poor popular biography, this book supplies no critical insight into JC's works and fails to produce convincing evidence as to the identification of Rita.]

1453 Baines, Jocelyn. "Joseph Conrad—Raw Material into Art," KWARTALNIK NEOFILOLOGICZNY, V: 1-2 (1958), 11-18; rptd in JOSEPH CONRAD KORZENIOWSKI: ESSAYS AND STUDIES (Warsaw: Państwowe Wydawnictwo Naukowe, 1958), pp. 11-18.

In *A Personal Record,* JC proclaimed, "Imagination, not invention, is the supreme master of art as of life." He utilized his imagination in transforming his life experiences into works of art and, therefore, presented vivid passages with perception and sensitivity. There are four main sources upon which JC drew material for his works: (1) his life experiences for background or framework, (2) anecdotes, (3) his reading for details of setting and character development, (4) his subjective and psychological experiences.

JC's acquaintance (although brief) with Almayer (or Olmeijer) supplied information for *Almayer's Folly*. Other specific examples of JC's use of objective experience: "Youth," a narrative involving the themes of youth and the East; "Heart of Darkness" (with some fictional alterations); and *The Shadow-Line*. The source involving anecdotes and hearsay provided information for *The Rescue, The Secret Sharer, Under Western Eyes* and "Freya of the Seven Isles." John D. Gordan's JOSEPH CONRAD: THE MAKING OF A NOVELIST (1940) accounts for how JC drew details from other novels for his characters, settings, and framework, for example, *Lord Jim, Nostromo, Rescue*. Galsworthy is incorrect in presupposing that JC "created" the world of Nostromo or recollected details from remote experiences in South America. Some of JC's works (*Folly, Jim, Eyes*) personify his own deep struggles and internal conflicts (freedom, adventure, leaving his homeland, desires, and demands). The essence of JC's art as an integrated whole is his sense of the isolation of the individual. Tragedy is oftentimes the consequence although some do surmount their alienation. Nevertheless, isolation is seen as a "necessary condition of life" existing with the inability to communicate. The dominant theme running throughout JC's works is his deep awareness of individual isolation transmuted into his work.

1454 Bantock, G. H. "Conrad and Politics," JOURNAL OF ENGLISH LITERARY HISTORY, XXV (June 1958), 122-36.

Few novelists of high caliber have found little "good to say about modern political movements or have been in any way able to identify themselves with any particular political undertaking." One reason is that the novelist is "almost inevitably bound to take the Cleopatra's nose view of human history," to observe and to present the private worlds of individual men.

He is also "the enemy of Marxist attempts to explain history in terms of social forces because he sees that 'social force' (so called) draws its sustenance only from the temporary and impermanent harmonization of particular interests working in uneasy collaboration." No one "has exposed this root truth about the nature of political activity as unerringly as Conrad." Irony saves JC from abusing what he dislikes in political man. His penetration of motives is "clear-sighted and unsentimental," and he [Conrad] positively appreciates the "truths of human existence." It is true, however, that "order" as generally thought of is "obviously absent from his work." His microcosm of the right ordering of social life is the world of the ship. The world outside is a chaos of collapsed values and crude ideals, without any coherent view of the universe. We find in JC "no support for any political or social creed." What he admires usually is not the creed but the pure motive of the person holding it. *Nostromo, The Secret Agent,* and *Under Western Eyes* deal with the dilemma of the moral personality strung between an autocratic lawlessness and the lawlessness of revolution. As the lawlessness of autocracy causes the lawlessness of revolution, "so it is true that the dynamics of revolution inevitably involve the failure of the noble and the idealist." The "expediency and inhumanity that Dr. Monygham forecast as being the concomitants of material interests are now, in various guises, always with us; and the political act based upon them contains within the conditions of its very being the possible seeds of corruption and rapacity."

1455 Baskett, Sam S. "Jack London's Heart of Darkness," AMERICAN QUARTERLY, X (Spring 1958), 66-77.

Although there are some obvious similarities in the fiction of JC and Jack London, JC's emphasis is different; JC objected to being considered "as literarily a sort of Jack London." London regarded JC with enthusiasm; at least once he borrowed directly from a story by JC ("In a Far Country" is a close parallel of "An Outpost of Progress"), and in MARTIN EDEN and JOHN BARLEYCORN he used one of JC's basic themes, the "universal thing," found especially in "Heart of Darkness" and "Youth." But in spite of the "aesthetic deficiencies of his portrayal" of the struggle to transmute his personal and private agonies into "something universal and impersonal," London, like JC, has given "a memorable portrait of the heart of darkness of a violent soul" who knows of his loss and has "subsided into the hollow man."

1456 Blackburn, William. "Conrad and William Blackwood," JOSEPH CONRAD: LETTERS TO WILLIAM BLACKWOOD AND DAVID S. MELDRUM, ed by William Blackburn (Durham, NC: Duke U P, 1958), pp. xiii-xxxiii.

JC's letters to William Blackwood, the Edinburgh publisher, extend essentially from the summer of 1897 into the winter of 1903. These are supplemented by JC's letters to David S. Meldrum, Blackwood's literary adviser in London, "whose name must now be added to that small circle of readers who were the first to recognize in [JC] a writer of enduring quality." The letters emphasize that between 1897 and 1903 JC was overextended in his work and pressed by financial difficulties. Appendix B gives the publishing history of Blackwood's editions of *Lord Jim* and "Youth"; Appendix C publishes for the first time James's recommendation of JC to the Royal Literary Fund.

1457 "Books in Brief," NEW YORK HERALD TRIBUNE BOOK REVIEW, 9 Nov 1958, p. 12.

[A one-paragraph statement about the varied collection and Zabel's lengthy introduction to TALES OF THE EAST AND WEST, edited by Morton Dauwen Zabel (1958).]

1458 Bradbrook, Frank W. "Samuel Richardson and Joseph Conrad," NOTES AND QUERIES, N.S. V (March 1958), 119.

There are similarities between Richardson's novels and *Victory:* (1) Mrs. Jewkes (PAMELA), Mrs. Sinclair (CLARISSA) and Mrs. Schomberg are "similarly described"; (2) the simple opposition of good and evil appears in both Richardson's novels and *Victory;* (3) all are treated realistically; (4) a "hot-house atmosphere" exists in both.

1459 Burton, Dwight L. "Teaching 'The Secret Sharer' to High School Students," ENGLISH JOURNAL, XLVII (May 1958), 263-66.

"The Secret Sharer" is a good choice for a high school class because its concrete plot will interest the average student, and its symbolic meanings will fascinate brighter minds.

1460 Chwalewik, Witold. "Conrad a tradycja literacka" (Conrad and the Literary Tradition), KWARTALNIK NEOFILOLOGICZNY, V: 1-2 (1958), 29-37; rptd in JOSEPH CONRAD KORZENIOWSKI: ESSAYS AND STUDIES (Warsaw: Państwowe Wydawnictwo Naukowe, 1958), pp. 29-37; and in POLSKA AKADEMIA NAUKOWYCH SPRAWOZDANIA WYDZIAŁU NAUK, I (1958), 74-77.

JC did participate in romantic, aesthetic, and realist traditions, yet remained free in originality. He even accepted Fielding's models of modernity and humanism: "Man, therefore, is the highest subject which presents itself to the pen of our historian (realistic novelist) or poet." JC attained freedom of digression in his framework of a tale-telling narrator, poet, and moralist in one. Although this device was employed by Fielding, JC asserted his originality of structure with his style of poetic diction and unlikely synthesis of elements. In his earlier phase, JC alluded to a school of Polish romantic poets. As a European romantic, he included an appreciation of nature imbued with the universal implications in the landscape. Illuminated in his art is an expression of loyalty to the past, to honor, and to glory. His work compares with such popular Polish poets as Malczeski, Mickiewicz, and Slowacki. The themes lurk over wide stretches of sea, land or forest described by adjectives suggesting infinity or another world. His romantic spirit is tempered by French naturalism (Flaubert, Maupassant, and Zola). Yet JC's view was not influenced by Zola, who regarded man as nature's plaything. Naturalism enlarged his view of human solidarity and developed his sensitive art of individual study—careful and sympathetic. He wasn't an epic writer, a creator of heroes; his characters are "morally questionable, or morally deserving, but hardly ever pretending to fabulous Homeric proportions." His art strives "to make the best of Truth, hard as it may be; and in this hardness discovers a certain aspect of beauty." His art is to make one see. [In Polish.]

1461 Cook, Albert. "Conrad's Void," NINETEENTH-CENTURY FICTION, XII (March 1958), 326-30.

JC's plots contain what Forster calls a "central obscurity." It is a circumstance in which "the protagonist is maneuvered through a tightening nexus of incident, a situation, that exacts a recognition not so much of chaos as of a void" at the heart of the plot; and "the motives, the 'dreams,' or 'illusions' . . . permute into a situation complex in its extent but simple in its tightness, to discharge a final void-revealing action." In *Nostromo,* for example, the "indispensable" central figure seems to become incorruptible, but "the void prevails" and he is eventually lost; the captain in "The Secret Sharer" is humbled by a knowledge of the void; in *The Secret Agent* "the ruthlessness of purposes that do homage to it sets up a chain reaction of murders"; Heyst in *Victory* is disillusioned by the void to the point at which he commits suicide; and Razumov in *Under Western Eyes* "cannot bear the cold embrace of the void after he has betrayed Haldin to death." Yet JC's plots have "a kind of displacement which their central object, a 'nothing,' induces, and against which the human spirit can remain indomitable in 'victory,' " as "immersion in knowledge of the void permits the first tempering of life in 'Youth.' " JC's "something hollow," his "emptiness," is "the core of [his] theme, man braving in his mortality the 'heart of darkness,' the void." The coldness of JC's "painstaking diction" "reflects the void it is his whole fictional vision to render," and his images, "especially those of the sea," are "analogues of the void." Consequently, for a "full insight of the void," loneliness is "literally and metaphorically" the price JC's characters must pay.

1462 Curle, Richard. "My Impressions of the Conrad Centenary Celebrations," KWARTALNIK NEOFILOLOGICZNY, V: 1-2 (1958),

3-5; rptd in JOSEPH CONRAD KORZENIOWSKI: ESSAYS AND STUDIES (Warsaw: Państwowe Wydawnictwo Naukowe, 1958), pp. 3-5. In Poland, the centenary was marked by "tributes affectionately . . . personal" and an "intimate touch" not possible elsewhere. [Based on but not identical with Curle's "reminiscent talk" on 3 Dec 1957.]

1463 Daiches, David. THE PRESENT AGE IN BRITISH LITERATURE (Bloomington & Lond: Indiana U P, 1958); rptd (Midland Books, 1969), pp. 112-13, 252.

The JC who has survived as a great novelist is not the JC recognized in his own time, "the romantic Conrad, the picturesque, inscrutable, polychromatic exploiter of the call of the sea and of the unknown," but the "subtler and more profound" JC of the "middle" novels and stories, from *Nostromo* to *Chance*, the "novelist of moral exploration and discovery presented through particularized detail of character and action."

1464 Davis, Harold E. "Conrad's Revision of *The Secret Agent*: A Study in Literary Impressionism," MODERN LANGUAGE QUARTERLY, XIX (Sept 1958), 244-54.

Changes in the three versions of *The Secret Agent* (the serial in RIDGEWAY'S MILITANT WEEKLY, 6 Oct 1906 to 15 Dec 1906; the expanded novel, published 1907; and the play, written 1920 and produced Nov 1922) show JC's development of impressionism. Generally, the novel is expanded, closing scenes twice as long as originally; pages of descriptive details added, and theme strengthened through greater realization of character. Most marked is JC's sharpening and deepening of atmosphere, emotional depth; his filling in and clarifying chiefly by impressionistic methods, a "rendering" rather than a "reporting." Also, in revising, JC rarely discards; he keeps similes and metaphors, but he does "add on" to create rounded, fuller perceptions of scene and character. [This conclusion amply supported with quotations.]

1465 "Fiction," A. L. A. BOOKLIST, LV (1 Oct 1958), 73.

TALES OF THE EAST AND WEST, edited by Morton Dauwen Zabel, is a companion collection to McFee's TALES OF LAND AND SEA (1953).

1466 Fricker, Robert. "Joseph Conrad," DER MODERNE ENGLISCHE ROMAN (The Modern English Novel) (Goettingen: Vandenhoeck & Ruprecht, 1958), pp. 54-75.

JC's works are to a large extent based on personal experiences and observations. The "poetry of circumstance" (Stevenson) is, however, made to serve his interest in psychology and in situations that involve a moral choice. *The Nigger of the Narcissus* illustrates his concept of solidarity and his ability to make the reader see. *Lord Jim* is a tragedy of idealism (with a highly melodramatic, opera-like ending) and a not quite successful experiment in narrative technique (in comparison with THE AMBASSADORS, JC's handling of the point of view is too obtrusive). "Heart of Darkness" is a story of evil with a nightmarish atmosphere reminiscent of MACBETH. Leavis's assertion that *Nostromo, Chance,* and *The Secret Agent* are JC's most important works is correct. For reasons of space only *Nostromo* is dealt with. JC's technique as well as his impressionistic portrayal of society are praiseworthy; in spite of his skepticism, JC advocates fidelity to moral ideas. [In German.]

1467 Friedman, Norman. "Criticism and the Novel: Hardy, Hemingway, Crane, Woolf, Conrad," ANTIOCH REVIEW, XVIII (Fall 1958), 343-70.

The usual conception of James Wait as the crew's secret sharer in *The Nigger of the Narcissus* is not exactly correct. According to the "standard interpretation," both the sea and Wait threaten the solidarity of the crew, which is regained by "meeting the successive tests of the storm and Wait's death." In this view, the storm is the "central turning point" of the plot. A close analysis of the story fails, however, to reveal the crew either in fear of death or unwilling to perform the tasks required by the sea; the crew simply do not know whether or not Wait is ill; they are faced with a dilemma: if Wait is faking, he deserves their scorn; but he acts sick enough to deserve their pity. The result is that they serve all his whims while really hating him. But when they learn that Wait is really dying and when their attitude is no longer ambivalent, they almost perversely pretend that he is well and is therefore being treated unjustly by the captain. What they are actually afraid to recognize "is not their fear of death but rather their own stupidity in allowing Jimmy to make fools of them." Now Jimmy must live not because the crew fear death but because they fear more greatly being proved wrong. The solution of the problem of the plot is this: "having been deceived by Wait and then by themselves, they are now ashamed of their self-deceit, seeing their hypocrisy in its true light." The meaning they have wrung from the sea and their sinful lives is that they are really most deeply afraid of admitting they were wrong.

1468 Gleckner, Robert F. "Conrad's 'The Lagoon,' " EXPLICATOR, XVI (March 1958), Item 33.

Arsat is not confused and deluded at the end; he sees *beyond* illusion.

1469 Grabowski, Z. A. "Joseph Conrad—Under Polish Eyes," ÉTUDES SLAVES ET EST-EUROPÉENNES, III (Spring 1958), 53-55.

From his father, JC inherited a passionate love of freedom and the gloom of the Polish liberals who in 1863 had for the second time been defeated in their attempt to throw off Russian rule. Stoic and defeated, JC's mistrust of Russia, his dislike of Dostoevski and Tolstoi, and his hatred of Pan-slavism are other aspects of this legacy from his youth. He was attracted to English discretion and reticence by their contrast to Polish emotionalism. At the same time—as shown especially in "Youth"—he shared some of the romantic ideals of the Polish romantic poets of the second half of the nineteenth century in their cult of youth and heroism. Their influence can be seen in his going to sea as a youth as well as in his writings. But the chief elements in JC's aristocratic Polish heritage are the sense of honor and loyalty which are so often the themes of his works and which form the chief positive values "illuminating the dark night of his *Weltanschauung.*" Even his style seems to mingle "the rhythm and melody of Polish and French prose."

1470 Guerard, Albert J. CONRAD THE NOVELIST (Cambridge, Mass: Harvard U P, 1958); part rptd in CONRAD: A COLLECTION OF CRITICAL ESSAYS, ed by Marvin Mudrick (1966); rptd (Cambridge, Mass: Harvard U P, 1966).

[Chapter one, "The Journey Within," is, according to the author, "both dark and difficult," and setting, as it does, the tone of the entire book, it has been frequently reprinted.] An obvious trait of JC's temperament is an "evasiveness bent on keeping distances" (evidenced in *A Personal Record* and *The Mirror of the Sea*). JC's conception of himself caused him to write in the un-English genre of the spiritual autobiography, the *"examen-de-conscience* and confession," as in five short novels based to varying degrees on personal experience and being as a rule "distinctly purer . . . works of art" than the longer books. They exemplify the archetypal myth of the night journey in which the voyager undergoes profound spiritual change and contain both realistic details and psychological symbolism. "Youth" is the least interesting because the would-be initiate learns nothing, whereas "The Secret Sharer," the "most frankly psychological" of JC's shorter works, dramatizes a human relationship and individual moral bond which is "at variance with the moral bond to the community implicit in laws and maritime tradition," and represents a situation which JC frequently dramatizes, indicating in JC the presence of a respectable and rational "seaman-self" and a "more interior outlaw-self." *The Shadow-Line* divides the soul into three parts: the irrational, represented by Burns; the rational: Ransome; and the narrator, who at the end of the story needs neither one. "Heart of Darkness" suggests and dramatizes evil as an active energy (in Kurtz and his lusts) but defines evil as vacancy, thereby creating a contradiction. "A Smile of Fortune" is the story of a "true seaman (not seaman-trader)" corrupted by his stay on land. His first three novels (including the uncompleted *The Rescue*) form a loose trilogy, the volumes being connected by Tom Lingard. In all three volumes he wrote most impressively when he allowed himself ironic or retrospective distance and exploited his temperamental evasiveness. *The Nigger of the Narcissus* is a "version of our dark human pilgrimage, a vision of disaster illumined by grace." *Lord Jim* is an "art novel" which changes with each reading: the mystery to be solved or the conclusion to be reached rests not in Jim but in ourselves. *Nostromo* is a pessimistic and skeptical meditation on politics, history, and motivation; it is a wise book with one major defect—it is too long. *The Secret Agent* is an "entertainment," a work of virtuosity, an idea which can easily be questioned. *Under Western Eyes* is a great tragic novel. After Razumov, most of JC's heroes are incapable of action (except in *Shadow-Line*), and his later works reveal a period of decline. Characteristics of JC's anticlimax are the "sentimental ethic," the narrator or central consciousness as dullard, and a failure of imaginative power and imaginative common sense. Even if the world of the early novels is a dark one, the human materials are the essential ones of human beings in crisis, facing moments which test their lives; the later works are either melodramatic or pathetic. [This psychological approach to JC and his works, with its concern with "the creative temperament in relation to subject and method," is one of the best general and critical considerations available, a seminal inquiry on its subject.]

1471 Gurko, Leo. "Joseph Conrad at the Crossroads," UNIVERSITY OF KANSAS CITY REVIEW, XXV (Dec 1958), 97-100.

At the very beginning of JC's career as a writer, the struggle between art and temperament was fought. In *Almayer's Folly,* his temperament, "enamored of lushness," resulted in remarkable painting of the physical scene, but of the physical scene detached from any significant concept. [See Gurko, "Conrad's First Battleground: *Almayer's Folly,*" ibid. (Spring 1959).]

1472 Gurko, Leo. *"The Secret Agent:* Conrad's Visions of Megalopolis," MODERN FICTION STUDIES, IV (Winter 1958-1959), 307-18.

The heart of this novel lies not in anarchism, and not in heroic strife to achieve an ideal of self, but in London and the torpid, suffocating life of man in the great city.

1473 Helsztyński, Stanisław. "Joseph Conrad—człowiek i twórca" (Joseph Conrad—the Man and the Writer), KWARTALNIK NEOFILOLOGICZNY, V: 1-2 (1958), 39-60; rptd in JOSEPH CONRAD KORZENIOWSKI: ESSAYS AND STUDIES (Warsaw: Państwowe Wydawnictwo Naukowe, 1958), pp. 39-60.

On the basis of the Bobrowski letters to JC, a case can be made for the Warsaw Positivist influence on JC's heroes through JC's uncle and guardian. [Oddly, the first and last phases of JC's work are stressed.] [In Polish.]

1474 Jabłkowska, Róża. "Polska Conradystyka za Granica" (Polish Conradiana Abroad), KWARTALNIK NEOFILOLOGICZNY, V: 1-2

(1958), 101-14; rptd in JOSEPH CONRAD KORZENIOWSKI: ESSAYS AND STUDIES (Warsaw: Państwowe Wydawnictwo Naukowe, 1958), pp. 101-14.

In an effort to present a better understanding of JC and his works, a number of Polish scholars residing in London have compiled their studies in a volume entitled THE LIVING CONRAD: AN ENGLISH SUMMARY OF THE POLISH TEXT, edited by Wit Tarnawski (Lond: B. Świderski, 1957). This is a valuable and interesting collection of JC scholarship outside of Poland. The collection is large, and the themes presented are at times curious, but the scholarship is vital and universal in approach. The importance of this research is even greater than that produced in Poland. In Polish intellectual circles abroad, JC has become the symbol of various personal and universal ideas. Polish scholarship in England, the United States, and in various parts of the world reveals new aspects in JC's works. The newest triumph of his art, as shown in this collection, is the ability to arouse a deep personal involvement in the reader. [In Polish.]

1475 Jabłkowska, Róża. "Z angielskich i amerykańskich studiów nad Conradem" (From the English and American Studies of Conrad), KWARTALNIK NEOFILOLOGICZNY, V: 1-2 (1958), 83-100; rptd in JOSEPH CONRAD KORZENIOWSKI: ESSAYS AND STUDIES (Warsaw: Państwowe Wydawnictwo Naukowe, 1958), pp. 83-100.

[A review of the major English and American scholarship in book form. Beginning with the translation of Georges Jean-Aubry into English, Jabłkowska moves to CONRAD ŻYWY, edited by Wit Tarnawski (Lond: B. Świderski, 1957), the collection of Polish émigré essays in Polish with English summaries, discusses the work of Walter F. Wright and Douglas Hewitt, gives much space to Thomas Moser's book, and then brings the reader up to the centennial collections of essays and finally to the Lohf and Sheehy bibliography and Ludwik Krzyżanowski's critique of it in POLISH REVIEW.] [In Polish.]

1476 JOSEPH CONRAD KORZENIOWSKI: ESSAYS AND STUDIES (Warsaw: Państwowe Wydawnictwo Naukowe, 1958); rptd from KWARTALNIK NEOFILOLOGICZNY, V: 1-2 (1958), [Special Number].

Contents, abstracted separately under date of first publication (1958, unless otherwise noted): Richard Curle, "My Impressions of the Conrad Centenary Celebrations"; M. C. Bradbrook, "Conrad and the Tragic Imagination," rptd from Bradbrook, "Conrad i tragiczna wyobrazbia," PRZEGLAD KULTURALNY (1957); Jocelyn Baines, "Joseph Conrad—Raw Material into Art"; Ivo Vidan, "Some Aspects of Structure in the Works of Conrad"; Witold Chwalewik, "Conrada tradycja literacka"; Stanisław Helsztyński, "Joseph Conrad—człowiek i twórca"; Wit Tarnawski, "O artystycznej osobowści i formie Conrada"; Ivo Vidan, "Conrad in Yugoslavia"; Róża

Jabłkowska, "Z angielskich i amerykańskich studiów nad Conradem"; Róża Jabłkowska, "Polska Conradystyka za Granica." [Papers read at the Conrad Centenary Celebration (Warsaw, 1957).]

1477 Jung, Ursula. "Joseph Conrad und das Problem des Selbstverständnisses" (Joseph Conrad and the Problem of Self-Knowledge), NEUEREN SPRACHEN, N.S. VII (1958), 353-66.

JC's purpose is to give man a glimpse of the mysterious transcendent reality behind the appearances of life, to make him realize his dependence upon the "eternal force" and accept consciously its constant demands on himself. Everyone, as JC exemplifies in his conception of the seaman's code, must justifiy his life under "the inscrutable eyes of the Most High." The moral problem involved is whether man conceives himself as a self-sufficient master of his own affairs or allows himself to be informed by existence in order to arrive at self-knowledge. Faulty self-knowledge stems from egotism, naive beliefs in a harmonious universe, or a complete self-satisfied trust in one's code, ideals, and defenses against life. Since it implies an unsound relationship with reality, its collision with life produces disillusionment and necessitates an act of renunciation. True wisdom is to will again and again the will of the "gods," to reject those principles which merely offer temporary security, and to dedicate oneself deliberately to an a-religious belief in reality. Even if the disenchanted person's change of heart leads to suicide, it has the moral significance which JC seeks to inculcate in his tales. JC is, however, well aware that the belief in a higher reality will continually break down because of the questionings of the intellect and the demands of everyday life. Doubts, he says, assail man from every side and give him a feeling of lostness. Man, in the final analysis, can only aspire to self-knowledge. His moments of awakening are rare. Usually man hides in his shell and trusts to the saving power of illusions. Thus JC affirms the dialectic tension between man's striving towards reality and its non-fulfillment. [A well-documented, subtle study.] [In German.]

1478 Kagarlitskii, Iu., and I. Kamarskii. "Dzh. Konrad" (Joseph Conrad), ISTORIA ANGLISSKOI LITERATURY (Academy of Science, USSR), III (1958), 76-80.

[In Russian.]

1479 Karl, Frederick R. "Conrad's Stein: The Destructive Element," TWENTIETH CENTURY LITERATURE, III (Jan 1958), 163-69.

The usual reasons given for the ineffectiveness of *Lord Jim* are the following: (1) JC failed in his attempt to stretch a short story into a novel, (2) he failed to fuse the two parts of the novel—the *Patna* incident and the Patusan episode, (3) he failed because his use of "shifting chronology" for the first part jars against the use of a straightforward narrative for the second part. But these reasons do not adequately account for the novel's thinness. Stein is really *the* destructive element of the novel. Jim is too weak to serve as a tragic protagonist and Stein, the only character capable of sustaining "a consistently tragic view," completely overshadows Jim's story.

1480 Kimpel, Ben, and T. C. Duncan Eaves. "The Geography and History in *Nostromo*," MODERN PHILOLOGY, LVI (Aug 1958), 45-54.

JC "obviously had not made a chronological outline of Costaguana history, any more than he had a detailed mental outline of the map of Costaguana." But such fiindings are not brought as a serious charge against the overall impression and impressiveness of the novel. [Explores in careful detail the accuracy—and the inaccuracies—in the geographical setting of Costaguana and in its historical chronology.]

1481 King, Carlyle. "Conrad for the Classroom," ENGLISH JOURNAL, XLVII (May 1958), 259-62.

JC's honesty and candor appeal to the young; "he tells no pretty lies about either the universe or man."

1482 Knopf, Alfred A. "Joseph Conrad: A Footnote to Publishing History," ATLANTIC MONTHLY, CCI (Feb 1958), 63-67.

JC's reputation as a novelist was established in the United States largely by Knopf who, as an apprentice with Doubleday, Page in 1913, was the first to read the manuscript of *Chance*. Knopf then appealed to several well-known writers of the time for favorable comments on JC's books, and finally wrote an article, "Joseph Conrad. The Romance of His Life and Books," for a booklet on JC which he edited, JOSEPH CONRAD (Garden City, NY: Doubleday, Page, 1913), pp. 3-19. Distributed in time, this pamphlet helped make *Chance* a success and secure a good market for his works for many years.

1483 Kreisel, Henry. "Joseph Conrad and the Dilemma of the Uprooted Man," TAMARACK REVIEW, VII (Spring 1958), 78-85.

Only after World War I did isolation, exile, and expatriation become common themes in literature. In JC's books the dilemma of the "lost generation" is plainly foreshadowed. *Almayer's Folly* and *An Outcast of the Islands,* both "wasteland novels," depict "a tragically dislocated native society and . . . the conflicts in such a society and . . . the conflicts in such a society when old tribal values have been destroyed but no new values have taken their place"; and both Almayer and Willems find themselves separated from their surroundings.

JC had a "profound understanding" of the historical and psychological factors that cause the condition of exile and the various kinds of response to it. These matters he studied most deeply in *Nostromo*. Giorgio Viola finds the traditions of his past inadequate to deal with the complex world of Costaguana, and he is condemned, "an exile in a strange land," to live only passively. Nostromo, with no roots at all, has a sense of honor centered entirely upon himself, "the one way in which a man can face the condition of exile." Martin Decoud, unlike Nostromo, has deliberately and knowingly uprooted himself, thereby becoming the "intellectual expatriate" who has become more familiar in the twentieth century than he was in 1904.

Decoud, JC's double, his "secret sharer," is resurrected later in the person of Axel Heyst in *Victory*. Heyst, unable to remain indifferent to suffering, becomes involved with Lena, who, in helping Heyst to realize himself as a human being, becomes enabled herself to resist the evil in the world. JC, however, perhaps tried too hard to reach a positive assertion here; he must have realized that none of the choices of an uprooted man can lead to a fully satisfactory resolution. Only in stories like *The Nigger of the Narcissus* and "Typhoon," where the characters are confronted with relatively simple situations, is a satisfactory resolution of conflict possible. The dilemma of the uprooted man can be mitigated by such values as loyalty, honor, and duty. [Helps to relate JC's work to the literature of the twentieth century.]

>**1484** Krzyżanowski, Ludwik. "Joseph Conrad: Some Polish Documents," POLISH REVIEW, III (Winter-Spring 1958), 59-85; rptd in JOSEPH CONRAD: CENTENNIAL ESSAYS, ed by Ludwik Krzyżanowski (NY: Polish Institute of Arts and Sciences in America, 1960), pp. 111-43.

In reference to JC's Polish identity and the charge of betrayal of Poland, JC's Polish "memories and sentiments" were a part of his "innermost soul," and Jessie Conrad was probably correct in her statement that JC seriously considered returning to Poland. Both Mme. Eliza Orzeszkowa's charge that JC betrayed Poland and Gustav Morf's conclusion about *Lord Jim* (that the *Patna* equals Poland, and Jim's jump represents JC's desertion of Poland) are questionable. JC's letters, especially to Tadeusz Bobrowski and Spiridion Kliszczewski, and visits to Poland in 1890, 1893, and 1914 demonstrate his concern for the "Polish question." Unpublished documents indicate JC's desire to convince England to accept the "idea that the Poles should have a legal recognition of their *nationality* in the defeated as well as in the victorious states" and to convince England that British self-interest dictates support for Austria's Polish policy.

>**1485** Leavis, F. R. "Joseph Conrad," SEWANEE REVIEW, LXVI (April-June, 1958), 179-200.

Relatively less important matters are JC's commitment to the English language, the lack of intelligent appreciation given to his work during his lifetime, and the charge that he oversimplified "man's problems in the world." [Leavis attempts to refute this charge by devoting most of the article to a detailed consideration of *The Shadow-Line,* a work which Leavis considers "central to his genius." Little change of view since Leavis's "Revaluations (XIV): Joseph Conrad," SCRUTINY, X (June and Oct 1941), 22-50, 157-81, which was included in THE GREAT TRADITION (1949).]

1486 Levin, Gerald H. "An Allusion to Tasso in Conrad's *Chance,*" NINETEENTH-CENTURY FICTION, XIII (Sept 1958), 145-51.

Near the end of *Chance,* Captain Anthony realizes for a moment that "in his involvement with Flora and her father he has entered 'the enchanted gardens of Armida,'" and he then compares Flora to Armida. Anthony has in mind Rinaldo's bewitchment by the enchantress Armida in Tasso's JERUSALEM DELIVERED. This single reference to Armida helps in an understanding of Anthony's motives: since Anthony fears that his motives are impure, he offers Flora "a marriage of convenience, for he must prove to himself that he is gaining nothing for himself in marrying her." Struggling to escape self-knowledge, he realizes that he has "lost control of his ship and of his own fortunes." Marlow alone realizes in Anthony "a paralysis of the will." And furthermore, the allusion to Book XIV of Tasso's work "may provide a clue to the reversals in the fortunes of Anthony in the final scene." The allusion at least suggests "that Anthony has approached the threshold of self-knowledge but has not been able to cross it." [Mostly speculative, but helpful in understanding *Chance.*]

1487 Levin, Gerald. "The Scepticism of Marlow," TWENTIETH CENTURY LITERATURE, III (Jan 1958), 177-84.

The explanation (Edward Crankshaw's JOSEPH CONRAD: SOME ASPECTS OF THE NOVEL [1936]) that JC devised Marlow as a way of moralizing without breaking the narrative framework of the story fails to account for JC's moralizing in works where Marlow does not appear, and this concept oversimplifies JC's complex view of life. JC introduces Marlow "in order to dramatize the transformation of an idealist into a sceptic," as shown in his use of Marlow in "Youth," "Heart of Darkness," *Lord Jim,* and *Chance.* Marlow remains skeptic and a disillusioned idealist; "he finds in contemplation a release from action. . . . He . . . never ceases to regard all solutions as means of escaping from reality, of pursuing an impossible dream, rather than as means to dignifying the human struggle for moral identity."

1488 Levinson, B. A. "A Conrad Letter," TIMES LITERARY SUPPLEMENT (Lond), 25 July 1958, 423.

An unpublished letter from JC to the author comments on a passage in *A Personal Record* about the *James Westoll,* the first English ship which JC had ever seen.

1489 Lukács, Georg. Die Gegenwartsbedeutung des Kritischen Realismus (Hamburg, 1958); rptd as The Meaning of Contemporary Realism, trans by John and Necke Mander (Lond: Merlin P, 1963); and as Realism in our Time: Literature and the Class Struggle (NY: Harper and Row, 1964), pp. 71, 98, 99.

JC was "firmly opposed to socialism"; his faith in capitalism is such that in his best novels "the narrative does not even touch on its social implications." JC is not a novelist but a short story writer; he does not portray "the totality of life." He excluded "the most important social problems of his time." [Refreshingly wrong-headed.] [In German.]

1490 MacShane, Frank. "Conrad on Melville," American Literature, XXIX (Jan 1958), 463-64.

JC did not want to be known as a writer of sea stories. When requested in 1907 to write a preface to Moby Dick, he replied that long ago he had been disappointed in Typee and Omoo and that recently he had found in Moby Dick "not a single sincere line in the three volumes of it."

1491 Mann, C. W. "New Books Appraised," Library Journal, LXXXIII (1 Nov 1958), 3138.

[Descriptions of contents in a review of Joseph Conrad: Letters to William Blackwood and David S. Meldrum, edited by William Blackburn (Durham, NC: Duke U P, 1958).]

1492 Marković, Vida. "Đozef Konrad" (Joseph Conrad), Savremenik (Belgrade), VII: 1 (1958), 49-62.

[Surveys most salient points of JC's life and work.] [In Serbo-Croatian.]

1493 Mayoux, Jean-Jacques. "Joseph Conrad," Lettres Nouvelles, No. 56 (Jan 1958), 15-34; no. 57 (Feb 1958), 222-36. [Two-part centennial article: I.—"L'homme et sa liberté" (Man and His Liberty); II:—"L'enfance des consciences" (The Childhood of Consciousnesses).]

JC's somber psychology is reflected in some of his fictional creations, especially in Heyst and Decoud. His major theme, found in such works as *Lord Jim, Under Western Eyes, Nostromo, Victory,* and "Heart of Darkness," "est la perte de la liberté, c'est la révélation irradiante de cette perte, ce sont les vains efforts pour la regagner, et l'issue dans le désastre." Like Faulkner later, JC "fait tenir l'essence démoniaque du personnage en une métaphore analogique, répétée avec des variations, et qui sa marque." His reserve and detachment indicate that if we want the universe to make sense, our "activité imaginaire" must create it: "Le monde est fait pour que le poète, pour que le romancier l'inventent." But this is not easy; man's life is an imprecise and confused effort to which thought and art must give form. The characteristics of JC's art are thus *"ce qui est à éclairer,"* for the writer has made a "voeu de vérité," which comes from the soul, the only reality for him. This "interiorization" in the work of creation, being an act of memory, is the beginning of the modern art of the novel, which lets us see the imagination at work. JC's impressionism, unlike that of the Impressionistic painters, is "acharné à restituer l'objet dérobe, obscur; à le révéler, à le faire surgir de l'ombre," like Rembrandt. JC's universe is an individual universe absorbed in the symbolic, where appearances are affected by a "puissante surcharge affective," where the organic resistance of things is opposed to the human organism's effort to rationalize the contact. JC's aesthetic was one of separation, stemming from his abandoning Poland, to which he professed to remain faithful. [In French.]

1494 Moore, Harry T. "Hand-Up for an Author," NEW YORK TIMES BOOK REVIEW, 30 Nov 1958, p. 62.
Although the letters in JOSEPH CONRAD: LETTERS TO WILLIAM BLACKWOOD AND DAVID S. MELDRUM, edited by William Blackburn (1958), "don't greatly increase our general knowledge of Conrad, they intensify what we know and add some important particulars about some of his finest writings ["Youth," *Lord Jim,* "Heart of Darkness"]."

1495 Moynihan, William T. "Conrad's 'The End of the Tether': A New Reading," MODERN FICTION STUDIES, IV (Summer 1958), 173-77; rptd in THE ART OF JOSEPH CONRAD: A CRITICAL SYMPOSIUM, ed by Robert Wooster Stallman (East Lansing: Michigan State U P, 1960), pp. 186-91.
The volume of stories, *Youth,* has running throughout a thematic pattern of struggle: the boy faces physical difficulties; Kurz and Captain Whalley contend with both physical difficulties and the forces of evil. Whalley, like Kurtz, is a "remarkable man" who deserves a place with other notable "ironic-tragic" heroes in JC's works. Described often in ironic terms, he is a man of physical strength, not spiritual; and when his physical strength is impaired, he is destroyed. Kurtz's "horror" overcomes "this placid and serene Victorian seaman" and he dies, like Kurtz, with guilt on his soul. Whalley's daughter and his son-in-law are the immediate causes of his difficulties and mirror ironic aspects of the story. JC consistently uses "mystical numbers" (seven, three, thirty): Massey's attempts to concoct a winning number is only one hint of the concentric design of the story and of the everpresent fate which rules men's lives. Captain Whalley's ship, the *Sofala,* supplies the best example of the symbolic and mythical background which JC created for the testing of the "conventionally holy seaman": the ship is obviously a symbol of death, and it is closely related to the myth of the "king-killing" custom in Sofala, a region in Africa. Appropriately enough, pride leads Whalley to ignore his blindness, which is an "act of

God." Having reached "the end of the tether" when Massey deflects the compass with pieces of iron, Whalley takes the iron from Massey's coat and puts it in his pockets. But Whalley, in spite of his fault, is still the "most worthy and sympathetic character in the ironic and fallen world in which he lives," and the reader feels that his punishment is too great. [Accents the rich thematic, tragic, and mythic elements in this often underrated tale.]

> **1496** Mudrick, Marvin. "The Originality of Conrad," HUDSON REVIEW, XI (Winter 1958), 545-53; rptd in CONRAD: A COLLECTION OF CRITICAL ESSAYS, ed by Marvin Mudrick (Englewood Cliffs, NJ: Prentice-Hall, Spectrum Books, 1966), pp. 37-44.

JC's works recall "everything else he wrote, in a pervasive melancholy of outlook, a persistency of theme . . . , and a conscientious manipulation of innovational method." What marks him "as a genuine innovator occurs only sporadically in his full-length novels, with discretion and sustained impulse only in several long stories or short novels: in *The Nigger of the Narcissus,* "Typhoon," Part I of *Under Western Eyes,* and—with most impressive immediacy—in "Heart of Darkness." This innovation is "the double-plot," which is neither allegory nor "catch-all symbolism" but "a developing order of actions so lucidly symbolic of a developing state of spirit . . . as to suggest the conditions of allegory without forfeiting or even subordinating the realistic 'superficial' claims of the actions and their actors." JC has two styles: "the narrative-descriptive, in which details triumphantly cohere with implicit moral moments in an accumulating point-to-point correspondence" and "the oracular-ruminative, which dotes on abstractions, exclamations, unexpressive directions, pat ironies. . . ." His symbolism is "as unallegorical as possible"—it is "severely realistic." In "Heart of Darkness," JC's imagination and technique fail: the theme is too great for him—the evil he must project "exceeds his capacity" to imagine it.

> **1497** Najder, Zdzisław. "Conrad Under Polish Eyes," POLISH PERSPECTIVES, No. 1 (May 1958), 37-42.

In Poland, *Lord Jim,* "Typhoon," and *The Rover* are most admired, *Jim* especially because of chivalrous values associated with the *szlachta* and because the style resembles the Polish literary "chat." Stein, also popular, is associated with the political émigré from post-1848 Europe. Poles wish that JC had made some of his secondary characters Polish. JC is a romanticist, "a guide in life, a comforter in misfortune, a teacher of the principles of honour, fidelity, and duty."

> **1498** Naumov, Ćićifor. "Dva dela Josepha Conrada" (Two Works by Joseph Conrad), SAVREMENIK (Belgrade), No. 2 (1958), 246-51.

[A pleasantly written account of the story in *The Nigger of the Narcissus* and "Heart of Darkness," with critical observations on the Serbian translation.] [In Serbo-Croatian.]

1499 Owen, Guy, Jr. "Crane's 'The Open Boat' and Conrad's 'Youth,'" Modern Language Notes, LXXIII (Feb 1958), 100-2.
JC, on guard against Crane's influence (as seen in his letter to Crane of 24 Dec 1897, disclaiming any intentions of imitating Crane) may nevertheless have been inspired by and/or have leaned lightly on "The Open Boat," or have subconsciously reflected it in writing up his own sinking and ensuing open-boat adventure in "Youth." JC's letter to Edward Garnett (5 Dec 1897) recounts JC's meeting Crane and a discussion of "The Open Boat." In May and June 1898, JC wrote "Youth." At least two passages in "Youth" suggest and have overtones of passages in "The Open Boat"; there is obvious similarity in theme, and in both an emphasis on the "democratization and subtle bond" felt by men who suffer and endure together.

1500 Owen, R. J. "Joseph Conrad: Two Books," Notes and Queries, N.S. V (June 1958), 260.
In relation to the question whether "Heart of Darkness" is based on an actual incident, the following passage from Lord Ernest Hamilton's The Halcyon Era (1933), pp. 90-91, is suggestive: "I once knew a young man of amiable and engaging personality. He was the scion of an old and illustrious country stock and the house where he was born is one of the oldest in the Kingdom. He went out to West Africa and settled among the natives, a solitary white man in a community of primitive savages. After a year or two so spent, he himself reverted in part to the primitive type and actually took an active part in the horrible rites which have always formed one of the hideous features of Darkest Africa. Luckily, he was murdered in the end by the natives, in revenge for some flogging atrocity for which he was responsible, so that his family were spared the shame of the exposure which must otherwise have followed." [But see C. J. Rawson, "Conrad's 'Heart of Darkness,'" Notes and Queries, N.S. VI (March 1959), 110-11.]

1501 Poznar, Walter P. "The Two Worlds of Joseph Conrad," Dissertation Abstracts, XIX (1958), 532. Unpublished thesis, Indiana University, 1957.

1502 Schwamborn, Heinrich. "Joseph Conrad—der Mann und das Werk" (Joseph Conrad—the Man and the Work), Neueren Sprachen, N.S. VII (1958), 233-42.
[A general introduction, which emphasizes the close relationship between JC's life and work, defends his originality against his detractors, and dis-

cusses briefly the meaning of fidelity and JC's attitude towards both England and Russia.] [In German.]

1503 Spector, Robert D. "Irony as Theme: Conrad's *The Secret Agent,*" NINETEENTH-CENTURY FICTION, XIII (June 1958), 69-71.

F. R. Leavis in THE GREAT TRADITION (1948) "fails to note . . . that the basic structure of the novel [*The Secret Agent*] is dependent upon its theme of irony," and JC's "failure is a result of a misconception of the terms of irony that Conrad has brought to *The Secret Agent.*" West and Stallman have explained irony in a manner appropriate to this novel: "Irony is based on contrast—between what seems to be intended and what is actually meant, between the apparent situation and the real one." Thus, in *Agent,* Mrs. Verloc does not understand why her mother leaves her house, the mother is unable to realize why her daughter marries, and both judge incorrectly the character of the secret agent. In this manner the major characters as well as most of the minor ones contribute to "the theme of fatal ignorance [that] governs the action." Leavis "has actually come close to comprehending the theme of the novel, but without perceiving the importance of it to the structure and without realizing its significance."

1504 Stevens, Arthur W. "George Orwell and Contemporary British Fiction of Burma: The Problem of 'Place,'" DISSERTATION ABSTRACTS, XVIII (1958), 1799-1800. Unpublished thesis, University of Washington, 1957.

[Pp. 121-33 of the thesis are on JC's *Victory.*]

1505 "Stoletie so dnia rozhdenia Dzhozefe Konrada (v Polshe)" (Centennial of the Day of Birth of Joseph Conrad [in Poland]), INNOSTRANNAIA LITERATURA, No. 1 (1958), 280.

[In Russian.]

1506 Swarthout, Glendon F. "The Creative Crisis," DISSERTATION ABSTRACTS, XIX (1958), 816. Unpublished thesis, Michigan State University, 1958.

[Includes comments on JC's *The Rescue.*]

1507 Tarnawski, Wit. "O artystcznej osobowości i formie Conrada" (The Creative Turn of Conrad's Mind and Work), KWARTALNIK NEOFILOLOGICZNY, V: 1-2 (1958), 60-78; rptd in JOSEPH CONRAD KORZENIOWSKI: ESSAYS AND STUDIES (Warsaw: Państwowe Wydawnictwo Naukowe, 1958), pp. 60-78; and in JOSEPH CONRAD KORZENIOWSKI, ed by Róża Jabłkowska (Warsaw: Państwowe Zakady Wydawnictwo Szkolynch, 1964), pp. 281-97.

JC's moral and intellectual interests are marked by catholicity and recall the poets and painters of the Renaissance; thus, his vision of the world has an "impervious and exotic character" difficult to approach on a reader's first exposure to his works. His work is also marked by "deep pathos," "personal rhythm and the nature of the linguistic side of his books." JC derived his "formally disruptive technique in narrative" from the Polish narrator and dramatist Aleksander Fredro. [Also provides disconnected but illuminating remarks on "the tragic feeling of loneliness visible in the mind and work of Conrad, the impact of primitive social and political stages observed by the writer in the life and tribes on the Malayan Archipelago and the importance Conrad attributed to the creative artistic symbols drawn both from antiquity and from the moderns." [Abstract and quotations drawn from English summary, p. 78 of the periodical publication.] [In Polish.]

1508 Tillyard, E. M. W. "Conrad; *Nostromo*," THE EPIC STRAIN IN THE ENGLISH NOVEL (NY: Essential Books; Lond: Chatto & Windus, 1958), pp. 126-67.

Nostromo is unique among JC's novels in its span of place and time. By combining "the closely inbred, the strictly documented domestic, with the ecumenical *Nostromo* achieves the kind of variety and amplitude propitious to the epic effect." JC uses an historical setting, but *Nostromo* is also a fairy tale. Montero is the malicious fairy at the christening feast of the infant railway; Gould, the exiled prince. Captain Mitchell is one of the great comic characters in fiction. The humorous element, although subordinate in *Nostromo,* is acutely felt. Some critics have narrowed *Nostromo* by making it too pessimistic and by emphasizing the Decoud-JC resemblance. Higuerota is a permanent symbol of ideal truth. In *Nostromo,* JC combines the theme of the heart of darkness with the theme that men are not subject to its tyranny. "It is Christian thought that is behind [JC's] conception of human destiny." Gould is the tragic hero; Nostromo, Gould's foil. Gould errs not only because of "material interests," but also because of inflexibility. "[T]here is something specious about [JC's] whole development of Nostromo's enslavement to the silver and especially about the two last chapters recounting his entanglement with Giselle and his death." The episodes in these chapters are trivial, melodramatic, and sentimental. These faults do not, however, "endanger the main constructions." The political doctrine of *Nostromo* is that of JC's essay "Autocracy and War" (1905), in which he noted a spiritual deterioration in international affairs and that democracy had put its trust in aggressive commercial competition; nations committed to this competition must precipitate wars. He expresses a "profound distrust in the ultimate benefits of material and scientific progress, the suspicion that the element of action has hopelessly preponderated over the element of thought, that man has become the slave of his own inventions." The chief difference between "Autocracy and War" and *Nostromo* is that the essay puts "material interests" in special reference to Germany; the novel, to England and America. *Nostromo* "corresponds to the wishes of a great body of people today. . . . Thus *Nostromo* fulfills the choric task that belongs properly to the epic." JC's treatment of the great themes "recalls the Homeric theme in the ILIAD of the irreconcilable virtues of heroic valour and the ordered domestic life."

> **1509** Tindall, W. Y. "Apology for Marlow," FROM JANE AUSTEN TO JOSEPH CONRAD, ed by Robert C. Rathburn and Martin Steinmann, Jr. (Minneapolis: University of Minnesota P, 1958), pp. 274-85.

JC's use of Marlow in "Heart of Darkness," *Lord Jim,* and "Youth" is wrongly attacked by critics like F. R. Leavis. Marlow is usually "a creature distinct from his creator," for Marlow is "distanced" as Joyce's Stephen is. Marlow is also a device for establishing reality, which "is in Marlow's head, not somewhere else." Whereas James interprets through his narrator, JC reports. Marlow "is an embodied point of view," anticipated by the nameless narrator of *The Nigger of the Narcissus.* Marlow emerges as "the embodiment maybe of Conrad's aspirations [the Victorian gentleman]." "Marlow shares with his creator the all but existentialist conviction that however meaningless and hopeless things are, we must cherish ideals and by their aid change necessary defeat to a kind of futile victory." Enigmas and uncertainties are also "part of the nature of things." Marlow has little humor or wit, but much irony in his attitude; he is both "cynical and sentimental." Marlow changes from "Youth" to *Chance.* In "Youth," Marlow's "periodic exclamations" are self-revealing and not JC's "cheap insistence," as Leavis has it. In the more complex "Heart" Marlow is not only a "discursive commentator" but "an imagist as well," and "he has acquired moral concerns." Marlow almost seems familiar with JC's preface to *Nigger* or Yeats's "The Symbolism of Poetry"; in "Youth" he reveals he has read Carlyle's SARTOR RESARTUS, with its chapter on symbol, and he might know Baudelaire, "as Conrad did." In "Heart" Marlow "saw his outer adventure as the archetypal embodiment of an inner adventure." Since this story is about Marlow's "response" to reality, his stated anticipations of the reader's reactions are legitimate. His comments "celebrate uncertainty," as Carlyle's symbol "conceals as it reveals." Marlow's confusion of images of dark and light allows subtle moral choices between, for example, shades of dark. The principal irony in "Heart" is "the acceptance of darkness by an apostle of light." Whatever there is of "Chivalric diminution of woman" is peculiar to Marlow rather than JC. Lord Jim objectifies fears within as Kurtz and the forest do: "Not Jim but what Marlow makes of him is the matter before us." With *Jim* Marlow also becomes more complex by winning "freedom from time." [Time-shift is briefly discussed.] Marlow "is a kind of artist," a notion JC developed in *Chance*. In *The Secret Agent* and *Nostromo,* JC returns to "earlier technique" with "emphasis on things as they are, not on what is made of them." In *Under Western Eyes* JC "turned (while writing *Chance*) to an observer, one who is too objective and impersonal, however, to have much in common with Marlow." In *Chance,* Marlow may be ill adapted to manage the "psychological muddle," but he is "excellently adapted" to his role as artist.

1510 Van Baaren, Betty Bishop. "Character and Background in Conrad," DISSERTATION ABSTRACTS, XIX (1958), 1392. Unpublished thesis, University of Wisconsin, 1958.

1511 Vidan, Ivo. "Conrad in Yugoslavia," KWARTALNIK NEOFILOLOGICZNY, V: 1-2 (1958), 79-81; rptd in JOSEPH CONRAD KORZENIOWSKI: ESSAYS AND STUDIES (Warsaw: Państwowe Wydawnictwo Naukowe, 1958), pp. 79-81.
[Survey of JC scholarship in Yugoslavia up to 1958.]

1512 Vidan, Ivo. "Joseph Conrad—Poljak i engleski pisac" (Joseph Conrad—Pole and English Writer), NARODNI LIST (Zagreb), XIV (4 Jan 1958), 4.
[A general appreciation on an elementary level with an account of the Warsaw centenary celebrations.] [In Serbo-Croatian.]

1513 Vidan, Ivo. "Majstor romana" (A Master of the Novel), OSLOBODENJE (Sarajevo), XVI (12 Feb 1958), 4.
[This appreciation stresses the moral pressures felt by JC's characters.] [In Serbo-Croatian.]

1514 Vidan, Ivo. "Poljak, pomorac, umjetnik engleske proze" (Pole, Sailor, a Master of English Fiction), ZIVOT (Sarajevo), X: 4 (1958), 254-58.
[A brief introduction to JC's narrative method and his central moral theme.] [In Serbo-Croatian.]

1515 Vidan, Ivo. "Some Aspects of Structure in the Works of Conrad," KWARTALNIK NEOFILOLOGICZNY, V: 1-2 (1958); rptd in JOSEPH CONRAD KORZENIOWSKI: ESSAYS AND STUDIES (Warsaw: Państwowe Wydawnictwo Naukowe, 1958), pp. 19-28; and trans by Zdzisław Najder, in TWÓRCZOŚĆ, XIV (July 1958), 105-15.
An appreciation of JC's literary structure will illuminate a meaningful perception on human relationships which is achieved by external and internal organization. The external structure organizes the novel's development and the internal places characters. His organization and technique can be studied in three divisions, according to distinctive features in structure. In one group of novels (*Almayer's Folly, An Outcast of the Islands, The Res-*

Joseph Conrad

cue, "The End of the Tether," "Typhoon," *Nostromo, The Secret Agent, Victory,* "An Outpost of Progress," "To-morrow," "The Tale," and *The Rover*), "the plot unfolds through an interplay of circumstances and conflicting forces" focusing on the main character. The behavior of each character reveals a variation on the moral theme. The second type consists of stories "with the theme of initiation": *The Nigger of the Narcissus,* "The Secret Sharer," "A Smile of Fortune," *The Shadow-Line, The Arrow of Gold.* This initiation illustrates a new life-style linked with moral awareness, duty, and trials, often a sea-life experience. The narration by the hero with authenticity reveals the author's experience. The characters represent a function to expand or delineate the problems faced by the hero through his process of moral awareness. The third group comprises "Heart of Darkness," *Lord Jim,* "Falk," *Under Western Eyes, Chance,* "Karain," "Amy Forster," "The Informer," "Il Conde" and other short stories. There exists an outer setting from which a narrator (not the hero) will relate the story. For example, Marlow is attracted to Kurtz and suggests a moral identity with Kurtz. In *Jim,* Marlow doesn't investigate his moral reactions, but tries to learn the circumstances of Jim's weakness. In *Chance,* JC felt the need of an outsider to understand Flora's situation. From one view, narrators are superimposed machinery blurring the autonomous inner story as well as, in another sense, means to getting nearer to the hero.

From these three parts, the importance of a subjective view is evident. Marlow is placed in *Jim* when JC feels the need to grip Jim's situation; the narrator in *Victory* is dropped when Heyst is "placed." From JC's handling of point of view, one sees the technical features of time-handling in respect to complex compositions created through active relationships. The time-sequence can rid the novel of fragments, speed suspense, and use "chronological loopings to explore the psychological moral subtleties." There are intricacies resultant from a narrative-within-narrative structure which involves three or four time levels. Many of JC's stories concern the past or involve what F. M. Ford called "progression d'effet," which covers two main movements in his novels: (1) slow; covering a long period of time in the past; (2) longer part dealing at swift pace with a shorter time period. It is a characteristic structure in his complex works—meditative and retrospective followed by the dramatic. The action finishes with a coda—the final resolution with the death of the protagonist. It is retrospective and reveals the meaning of the relationships within the novel. In "Heart of Darkness," the relationship between narrator and hero unfolds the significance of the story. Unifying themes are sometimes forecast in JC's works ("Heart of Darkness," "Youth," "Falk," "A Smile of Fortune," *The Secret Agent*). JC's works can be approached on three levels: (1) good story; (2) "Image of specific social and individual significance," and (3) "universal expression of a moral vision of life." Contrary to Edward Crankshaw's view, JC created integral wholes of theme, tone, and actions.

1516 Von Klemperer, Elizabeth Gallaher. "The Fiction of Henry James and Joseph Conrad in France: A Study in Penetration and Reception." Unpublished thesis, Radcliffe College, 1958.

[Lists French translations of JC's work in periodicals and books, pp. 397-400.]

1517 Watt, Ian. "Conrad Criticism and *The Nigger of the Narcissus*," NINETEENTH-CENTURY FICTION, XII (March 1958), 257-83.

JC is justified in this novel in shifting the viewpoints from which the story is narrated, and this shifting enables him to convey, in addition to the "immediacies of his subject," their perspective in the "whole tradition of civilization." JC's purple passages are useful because this author, "a preeminently pictorial writer," occasionally requires a set-piece. The content of JC's writing must allow him the benefit of some flexibility which is generally given to poetry.

The emphasis on symbolism in *The Nigger of the Narcissus* has been carried too far by modern criticism: at the present time the literary critic "typically functions as the romantic seer"; each critic tries to demonstrate how "he saw the book first, or at least that his reading of it is the first *real* one"; and the urge to read a literary work in a new manner has led to symbolic interpretations which are incapable of empirical proof or disproof. Symbolic interpretations are usually *heterophor, mythophor,* or *cryptophor,* but JC's work is not symbolic in these ways; it is symbolic, however, "by natural extension of the implications of the narrative content, and retains a consistent closeness to it"; thus the term *homeophor* is most appropriate to the symbolism of *Nigger*. Symbolically, JC seems to be saying that "although pitilessness is characteristic of the selfish, yet the increasing sensitiveness to the sufferings of others which civilization brings necessarily poses grave problems of control for the individual and society." *Nigger* is a "compressed drama" which can easily be, in part, "representative of society at large"; and the general values seen in the book are mainly traditional. [This assessment of a decade's criticism of *Nigger* serves as a useful corrective to some questionable interpretations.]

1518 Zabel, Morton D. "Introduction," *Lord Jim,* by Joseph Conrad (Boston: Houghton Mifflin, Riverside Editions, 1958), pp. v-xxxvii, xxxix-xlviii, 301-2.

JC's experiences with BLACKWOOD's were of great value to him because of the encouragement he received and because he was able to achieve the "basis of dramatic method and artistry" in his writings for BLACKWOOD's. Although much of his early work comments on the subject of one's secret superiority, it is *Lord Jim* that establishes "the total realization" of the drama which develops in the conflict between one's secret ideal of oneself and the harsh realities. "Conrad's central moral problem was to be most typically established and achieved" in *Jim*. In "Youth," "Heart of Darkness," and *Jim*, Marlow is more than a narrator; he is a "secret sharer" of the lives of the characters. One finds in JC's work a "double vision" or "double focus"; the self, and the "human or moral community to which the self appeals for the 'reality of its own existence.'" *Jim* is notable in that it "dramatizes an ambiguity." While one may easily dismiss JC's "minor tales and later rhetorical dramas," one cannot dismiss *Jim* and the dozen other novels and tales of his best work. *Jim* "is one of the books that establish the basis of sincerity and moral capacity on which the highest achievement in modern fiction rests." [Zabel includes a biographical sketch and selected bibliography.]

1519 Zabel, Morton Dauwen. "Introduction," TALES OF THE EAST AND WEST, ed and with an intro by M. D. Zabel (Garden City, NY: Hanover House, 1958), pp. ix-xxx.

In the typical JC hero one finds "a conflict of sympathies": on the one hand "the attraction towards standards of honor, fidelity" and on the other the "more secret or covert attraction toward primitive forms of knowledge . . . the forces of 'darkness' in nature or character that must be faced, explored, and recognized as elements of the human personality." What is vital in JC's works "lies in his profound submission to the fact of confusion or ambiguity in human affairs." Because JC is an especially consistent writer, "[h]is central subjects are few. His books and tales finally give an effect of repeating a single theme. His art is an art of tension. . . . It may seek relief in frequent evasions, rhetoric, abstraction, moral compromise, or in the desperate catastrophes that are sometimes resorted to in the conclusions of his plot." The subject of *The Secret Agent* concerns more than Winnie Verloc's fate; the subject "is the fate of Europe." *Agent* is a part of JC's "triptych of political-historical studies [the others are *Nostromo* and *Under Western Eyes*] of 'the destiny of man as determined by forces of power and anarchy.'"

1520 Zellar, Leonard Eugene. "Conrad's Use of Extra-Narrative Devices to Extend Time," DISSERTATION ABSTRACTS, XIX (1958), 1075. Unpublished thesis, University of Illinois, 1958.

[Chiefly on *Nostromo*, *Under Western Eyes*, and *The Nigger of the Narcissus*.]

1959

1521 Allott, Miriam. NOVELISTS ON THE NOVEL (NY: Columbia U P; Lond: Routledge and Kegan Paul, 1959), pp. 5, 19, 27, 30, 31, 38-39, 40, 117, 118, 120, 121, 122, 167, 188, 194-95, 196, 204, 222, 225.

JC's novels "derive some of their power from the sense of the supernatural which they evoke." JC's love of "the uncommon" results in such sentimental falsifying as in *The Arrow of Gold* and "such compelling achievements" as "Heart of Darkness," *Nostromo,* "The Secret Sharer," and *Victory*. JC, like Henry James, understood that "French Realist doctrines stultify imagination and interfere with poetic truth." JC, Hardy, and James pose the "question of the ethics of the novel" more subtly than earlier writers. In the "context of doubt and scepticism," as in JC, Hardy, and James, "the novel acquires its most potent supernatural ambience."

Coming to novel-writing in his later years, JC combines "fullness of experience with artistic fastidiousness." He was among many English writers to be haunted by "the concept of 'epic regularity' as a structural principle." He uses the frame story "to give perspective and variety as well as authenticity" to his work. Marlow, who provides artistic discipline, "more exclusively even than the Jamesian narrator, is 'the impersonal author's deputy or delegate.'" JC, like Richardson before him and like James, explores "beneath the surface appearance of things . . . to draw near to the central areas of tragic experience." [JC is frequently quoted for supporting evidence.]

1522 Andreas, Osborn. JOSEPH CONRAD: A STUDY IN NON-CONFORMITY (NY: Philosophical Library, 1959); rptd (Lond: Vision, 1962).

JC's early life caused his works to be "obsessed by the specter of the outcast, the rebel, the non-conformist, and by the themes of guilt and rejection of guilt." "Heart of Darkness" "marks Conrad's first peak of emancipation from neurotic involvement in the coils of guilt." Although he employs variations on this theme, JC's usual point of view is "that of the outcast looking with fear at society." [Although he displays some ingenuity in his analysis, Andreas strains to fit all of JC's works into the theme of non-conformity: *Under Western Eyes, The Secret Agent,* "The Informer," and "An Anarchist," for example, all "tell of men who, like the Trojan horse in Troy, are filled with deadly hostility to the groups which contain them"; and JC's "jump out of Poland is the equivalent of Falk's eating human flesh."]

Joseph Conrad

1523 Baines, Jocelyn. JOSEPH CONRAD: A CRITICAL BIOGRAPHY (Lond: Weidenfeld & Nicolson, 1959; NY: McGraw-Hill, 1960).
[Baines's biography supersedes all others and contains critical analyses which deserve the attention of anyone interested in JC. It brings extensive biographical information to bear upon analyses of the works, which contain some new and provocative arguments: JC's going to sea was an attempt to escape "psychological rather than political claustrophobia," a fact which appears in his fiction. The concise analyses of the works are usually excellent: the irony in *The Secret Agent;* JC's approval of Jim's final conduct in *Lord Jim;* the near-perfection in *Nostromo* so that this novel "transcends a particular epoch or continent and contains an element of the universal"; *Chance* as "the least profound and least satisfying" of JC's major novels; Heyst in *Victory* as "certainly the most complex character" that JC created, a judgment which places this novel among JC's best works; and *The Rover* as "a worthy swan song" which does not aim at the profundity or range of the major works.] [Baines's criticism may be somewhat too literal, but no one interested in JC or his works can ignore this indispensable biography.]

1524 Bell, Inglis F., and Donald Baird. THE ENGLISH NOVEL, 1578-1956: A CHECKLIST OF TWENTIETH-CENTURY CRITICISMS (Denver: Alan Swallow, 1959), pp. 18-29.
[*Almayer's Folly, The Arrow of Gold, Chance, Lord Jim, The Nigger of the Narcissus, Nostromo, An Outcast of the Islands, The Rescue, The Secret Agent, Under Western Eyes,* and *Victory* are listed with critical books and articles about each. A useful, highly compressed preface traces the history and reception of each novel.]

1525 Bluefarb, Sam. "The Sea—Mirror and Maker of Character in Fiction and Drama," ENGLISH JOURNAL, XLVIII (Dec 1959), 501-10.
For the sole reason that the sea is both a mirror and maker of character but never the protagonist, the genre of the sea story, whether in fiction or drama, is a definite genre. Yet JC strongly objected to being called "a writer of sea stories." The sea "molds character, yet, in setting the conditions for shipboard drama—as to some extent it inevitably must—it reveals, like a mirror, the face of character itself." In the fiction and the drama of the sea, the storms and the calms "both induce and reflect the storms and the calms within the souls and the bodies of the characters themselves" (e.g., *The Nigger of the Narcissus* and *The Shadow-Line*).

1526 Casey, Bill. "André Malraux's Heart of Darkness," TWENTIETH CENTURY LITERATURE, V (April 1959), 21-26.
Malraux's THE ROYAL WAY resembles "Heart of Darkness" in theme, basic philosophy, setting, plot, and character. Two characters in THE ROYAL

WAY, Perken and Grabot, correspond to Kurtz. Whereas JC asked, "What is true?" Malraux asks, "What is one to do in the face of truth?"

1527 Cox, Roger L. "Conrad's *Nostromo* as Boatswain," MODERN LANGUAGE NOTES, LXXIV (April 1959), 303-6.

The Italian *nostromo* means *boatswain,* derived from Spanish *nostramo, nuestramo,* meaning *our master.* It is "not correct to interpret *nostromo* or its dialect forms, *nostrommu* (Genoese) and *nostruomo* (Corsican) as *our man,* however much they look like a contraction of *nostro* and *uome.*" The interpretation of *Nostromo* as *our man* (one aspect of his character) rests on JC's elaborate "pun" (*Nostromo* [Doubleday, 1924], p. 43) suggesting that the camp master was called "Nostromo" because of Captain Mitchell's "mispronunciation." But mispronounced word or words are never mentioned and ambiguity results. The DIZIONARIO DI MARINA says that a small wind instrument generally of silver is part of a boatswain's equipment. Nostromo has such a whistle, and he is a "form of trust" (*la persona di fiducia* of the definition; "One of Nostromo's names is in fact, Fidanza, a variant of *fiducia*"). This "paradox of master and man epitomizes his dilemma in connection with the hidden silver."

1528 Curle, Richard. "Joseph Conrad as I Remember Him," CONTEMPORARY REVIEW, CXCVI (July 1959), 25-31.

[Recollections of JC, most of which are included in Curle's earlier books.]

1529 D., S. "Joseph Conrad: *Tajfun-Mladost*" (Joseph Conrad: *Typhoon-Youth*), POLITIKA (Belgrade), LVI (Literary Section III), 1 Nov 1959, p. 134.

[Slight comment on the new edition.] [In Serbo-Croatian.]

1530 Davis, Robert Gorham. "Joseph Conrad," INSTRUCTOR'S MANUAL: TEN MODERN MASTERS: AN ANTHOLOGY OF THE SHORT STORY, 2nd ed (NY: Harcourt, Brace & World, 1959), pp. 7, 8, 10, 13, 18, 27-31.

["Amy Foster" substituted for "Youth." See ibid., 1st ed (1953).]

1531 "The Dedicated Conrad," TIMES LITERARY SUPPLEMENT (Lond), 24 April 1959, p. 242.

JOSEPH CONRAD'S LETTERS TO WILLIAM BLACKWOOD AND DAVID S. MELDRUM, edited by William Blackburn (1958), reveals that JC is not a great letter writer. His letters are rewarding for mundane reasons: they show the day-to-day agonies of a temperamental writer dedicated to his art. Albert Guerard's CONRAD THE NOVELIST (1958) is "intensely stimulating," but some of its interpretations are extravagant. [Surveys JC's relationship with BLACKWOOD'S MAGAZINE.]

1532 Diakonov, N. "Predislovie" (Preface), *Lord Dzhim* (*Lord Jim*), with commentaries by I. Komarova (Moscow: Innostrannyka Iazykov, 1959).
[In Russian.]

1533 Greene, Maxine. "A Return to Heroic Man," SATURDAY REVIEW (NY), XLII (22 Aug 1959), 10-11, 35-36, espec p. 11.
Breaking from a determinist point of view, JC's hero in *Lord Jim* makes a gesture toward human dignity. Though the hero has a fatal flaw, he conceives an ideal image of himself as a man.

1534 Gross, Seymour L. "Hamlet and Heyst Again," NOTES AND QUERIES, N.S. VI (March 1959), 87-88.
There are parallels "between the two sets of fathers and sons." Hamlet's difficulty had been to act as his father commanded; Heyst's difficulty had been to be inactive. [Elaborates on Arthur Sherbo's remarks in "Conrad's *Victory* and HAMLET," ibid., CXCVIII (Nov 1953), 492-93.]

1535 Guerard, Albert J. "Introduction," "HEART OF DARKNESS" AND "THE SECRET SHARER" (NY: Signet Classics, 1959), pp. 7-15.
Both stories must be read with the narrator as the center of interest. The captain in "The Secret Sharer" and Marlow in "Heart of Darkness" undergo a process of "self-exploration, self-recognition, self-mastery."

1536 Gurko, Leo. "Conrad's First Battleground: *Almayer's Folly*," UNIVERSITY OF KANSAS CITY REVIEW, XXV (Spring 1959), 189-94.
JC's apprenticeship, which began with *Almayer's Folly,* ended with *An Outcast of the Islands*. In the latter novel, JC juxtaposed, unlike his practice in the former, the intense activity of the river and the forests and Willems's intense inactivity, thereby heightening each and employing the one to alter the other. The corrupt and corrupting jungle becomes the "perfect ecological setting" for Willems's fall; civilization and barbarism struggle within Willems precisely as life and death struggle in the jungle. [For an introductory article on this subject, see Gurko, "Joseph Conrad at the Crossroads," ibid. (Dec 1958).]

1537 Hainsworth, J. D. "An Approach to *Nostromo*," USE OF ENGLISH, X (Spring 1959), 181-86.
A description of the drawing-room of the Casa Gould is more than a mere description: the furnishings of the room "illustrate the social and economic pressures to which the province is subject" and quite properly reveal Mrs. Gould as a "tableau-vivant rather than a character, a part of the scene rather than an intrusion on it," a woman who "pits her puny idealism against the might of social and economic pressures." A second passage, a commentary on Mr. Holroyd and his building, "epitomises the novel as a

whole in the pervasiveness of the sardonic contemplation, and also in the objects towards which that contemplation is directed." The passage suggests that Charles Gould's "declared motive" of securing justice for an oppressed people by means of his pursuit of material interest "does not long remain credible to either Mrs. Gould or the reader," and that Mr. Holroyd's building "characterises the civilization of which it is a part," clearly foreshadowing early in the novel "the devouring and dehumanising effect that material interest is to have" on more important persons, especially on Charles Gould, Nostromo, and Sotillo, along with a hint of the vision finally communicated to Mrs. Gould by Dr. Monygham. The predominant note here is, however, that of "unillusion"; the evident contrast between the reader's view and the views of other people in the passage produces "an amusement not incompatible with compassion." A third passage, which describes the entry of the combined forces of Gamacho and Pedrito Montero into Sulaco, is a reminder of "the deprivations and aspirations which lie behind the popular response to Montero," and it also creates "a sympathy for the common people which the novel so consistently evokes." Certain symbols underline the implicit idea of the novel, "that idealism can exist unsullied only in dissociation from life." Charles Gould's idealism is forced "to compromise with things as they are" and at last becomes merely "a blind for his ambition," Mrs. Gould's is "thwarted and pathetic," and Dr. Monygham's is "complicated by an awareness of fallibility amounting almost to cynicism." [Explains the results of an attempt "to bring to bear upon the teaching of *Nostromo* the experience of the practical criticism class."]

1538 Halverson, John, and Ian Watt. "The Original Nostromo: Conrad's Source," REVIEW OF ENGLISH STUDIES, X (Feb 1959), 45-52.

The book JC refers to in his "Author's Note" as the suggestive basis for *Nostromo* is Frederick Benton Williams [pseudonym of Herbert Elliott Hamblen], ON MANY SEAS: THE LIFE AND EXPLOITS OF A YANKEE SAILOR, edited by his friend William Stone Booth (NY: Macmillan, 1897). JC drew on this book for the theft of silver. The character of Nicolo did not suit JC's purpose, so he drew Dominic Cervoni out of his own past. The whole story may have been invented by Hamblen or by Nicolo because of (1) the psychological implausibility, (2) the substantial loss of silver by a large American company without any confirming records or news of the loss, and (3) the "geography of the episode is quite unconvincing." Perhaps the basis of Hamblen's story and the anecdote as heard by JC is the "story of how one Captain Thompson absconded with an enormous treasure entrusted to him by citizens of Lima during an insurrection led by Bolivar in 1821." Concerning the matter of JC's "unacknowledged borrowing," it appears that in *Nostromo* and elsewhere "the weight of evidence suggests that Conrad indicated his indebtednesses in his 'Author's Notes' as well as he remembered them."

1539 Jurak, Mirko. "Joseph Conrad: *Nostromo*," NOVI RAZGLEDI (Ljubljana), VIII: 14 (1959), 341-42.

[A rapid view of the Slovene translation of the novel.] [In Slovene.]

1540 Karl, Frederick R. "The Rise and Fall of *Under Western Eyes*," NINETEENTH-CENTURY FICTION, XIII (March 1959), 313-27.

Since JC was "interested more in man's social role than in his relationship to the state," the plot of *Under Western Eyes* is concerned with "the student Razumov as an outcast from normal society rather than as an outcast from the Russian political scene." When Razumov's "self-imposed isolation" proves ineffectual, he must then choose between conquest or renunciation. Paradoxically, his choice of the latter "leads to both his destruction and acceptance, in each by the same people." In this novel, JC's greatest achievement is perhaps an irony that "is evoked through the juxtaposition of people and objects, an irony not so much of the word as of the scene." Razumov's betrayal of Haldin actually destroys himself, for his existence is never again his own; he has betrayed his double, who is really himself.

Eyes has a weak ending. JC "seriously misjudged the true climax of his story," thereby creating an "esthetic flaw." The real climax is Razumov's confession to Miss Haldin, not to the revolutionaries. After Razumov confesses to Miss Haldin, everything that follows is merely explanatory, not dramatic necessity. [Valuable. Somewhat expanded in Karl's A READER'S GUIDE TO GREAT TWENTIETH CENTURY ENGLISH NOVELS (1959).]

1541 Karl, Frederick R. "The Significance of the Revisions in the Early Versions of *Nostromo*," MODERN FICTION STUDIES, V (Summer 1959), 129-44.

The four versions of *Nostromo* [manuscript (fragmentary) in Rosenbach Library; typescript (fragmentary) in Yale University Library; serial (T. P.'s WEEKLY, 1904); and first edition (1904)] reveal JC's gradual development of natural description to support theme, character, and tone, and suggest the possible causes of the "aesthetic failure" of the novel's concluding section.

1542 Karl, Frederick R., and Marvin Magalaner. A READER'S GUIDE TO GREAT TWENTIETH CENTURY ENGLISH NOVELS (NY: Noonday P, 1959), pp. 3, 4, 5, 6, 8, 12, 16, 18, 20, 40, 42, 44, 48, 57, 63, 66, 85, 86, 94, 95, 96, 97, 98, 101, 110, 111, 118, 145, 153, 156, 159, 160, 185, 236, 237, 249, 252, 256, 269, 270, 287, 288.

JC, Joyce, and Lawrence realized that an individual gains identity by coming into conflict with both sustaining and destructive influences. JC, Joyce, and Forster helped put the hero in the grave—JC especially with his self-destructive protagonists. He does not write a typical *Bildungsroman;* he rather treats crucial aspects of a character's moral development. In the preface to *The Nigger of the Narcissus,* JC stresses the non-representational quality of the novel and naturalistic details heightened into symbols, which blend impressionism with realism. Joyce and JC are two of the greatest prose stylists.

1543 Kocmanová, Jessie. "The Revolt of the Workers in the Novels of Gissing, James, and Conrad," BRNO STUDIES IN ENGLISH, I (1959), 119-39.

JC belongs to a group of writers "of middle class or petty-bourgeois origin, unconnected with political theory or political organization, who nevertheless were obliged in the course of their artistic development to devote one or more novels to a theme related to proletarian revolt." What gives JC greater insight, greater possibility than Gissing (DEMOS, THYRZA) or James (THE PRINCESS CASAMASSIMA) of making clear his moral discovery in *The Secret Agent* "is not more knowledge of the proletarian revolutionary movement, but what he knew about the bourgeois-liberation movement and reprisals against it."

1544 Komarova, I. [Commentaries], *Lord Dzhim* (*Lord Jim*), [with preface by N. Diakonov] (Moscow: Innostrannyka Iazykov, 1959).

[In Russian.]

1545 Konjar, Viktor. "Nove knjige" (New Books), MLADA POTA (Ljubljana), VIII: 1 (1959-60), 35-36.

[Note on the Slovene edition of *Nostromo,* with stress on JC, the sea dreamer.] [In Slovene.]

1546 Krieger, Murray. "Conrad's 'Youth': A Naive Opening to Art and Life," COLLEGE ENGLISH, XX (March 1959), 275-80.

JC wanted a point of view that was "purely dramatic," and the situation of Marlow's feeling of "group understanding" as he recounts the tale of his early experience allows the reader to be "at once outside and inside our narrator, his story, and his view of it." We cannot know which Marlow is the protagonist—"the youthful or the middle-aged"—who is more worth our attention. "Pass the bottle," Marlow's repeated request, destroys the mood of the story he is telling, but JC's technique in "Youth" is only a "weak shadow" of what it was to become in later works. In JC there is no "single-dimension of meaning"; a dilemma always appears. JC's art is not "designed to give answers." In "Youth" there is a balance between the "romantic striving" that may appear aimless from a more sober view and "the sensible compromise with reality that speaks of an inglorious weariness even as it boasts of wisdom." Marlow cannot choose; neither can the reader.

1547 Las Vergnas, Raymond. JOSEPH CONRAD, ROMANCIER DE L'EXIL (Joseph Conrad, Novelist of Exile) (Lyon: E. Vitte, 1959).

JC's life is a series of exiles (from Poland, the sea), and these autobiographical factors influence his work deeply. Exiled from maternal and female influence in his childhood by his mother's early death, he married a mother figure, Jessie George. The unhappiness of this marriage, JC's persistent ill health, his lack of even average *joie de vivre,* the lack of love in his life, his strange reserve, and the fits of rage to which he was prone are all ways in which JC was an exile. Many of JC's heroes are exiles, engaged in a dialectic of honor and of dishonor; in general, there is too much contrast between the black traitors and the demigod heroes. JC's effort not to be exiled from daily life, from ordinary reality, from verisimilitude, leads to his increasing use of narrators; his refusal to use the omniscient point of view is a reflection of his atheistic refusal to adopt any attribute of God. Morf's Freudian analysis of JC is wrong; the "treason" which JC committed was not his abandonment of Poland but rather his abandonment of his vocation as sailor; in large terms, JC abandoned the idealism which had caused him to go to sea in the first place: "It was Don Quixote that he betrayed." JC's philosophy of exile envisions the sea as neither hostile nor favorable, but merely indifferent; his skepticism, which is characterized by a "lucid sadness," is made bearable only by his reliance on the idea of loyalty. [In French.]

1548 Levin, Harry. "Literature and Exile," LISTENER, LXII (1959), 613-17.

[JC is mentioned among famous writers (Ovid, Dante, Heine) who were exiles.]

1549 "Literary Relations: Joseph Conrad," THE GARNETTS: A LITERARY FAMILY: AN EXHIBITION (Austin: Humanities Research Center, University of Texas, 1959), pp. 10-11.

[This article includes editions, association items, and three holograph letters, JC to Edward Garnett.]

1550 McCann, Charles J. "Conrad's 'The Lagoon,' " EXPLICATOR, XVIII (Oct 1959), Item 3.

In putting "The Lagoon" back into a Conradian context, one sees that Arsat, like Lord Jim, is a victim of a decision based on a false alternative; he will remain isolated.

1551 Marković, Vida E. "Joseph Conrad," *Tajfun,* trans by Aleksander Vidaković (Belgrade: Rad, 1959), pp. 130-35.
[Unpretentious post-face to a re-issue of Serbian translation of "Typhoon" and "Youth."] [In Serbo-Croatian.]

1552 Morgan, Gerould. "Captain Korzeniowski's 'Prince Roman': Nautical Allusion in Conrad's Patriotic Tale," ÉTUDES SLAVES ET EST-EUROPEÉNNES, IV (Spring-Summer 1959), 49-57.
JC cannot be understood until his nautical allusions are, and "a study of Conrad revealing the seaman behind the timeless author can be extended to reveal the Pole within the seaman." In "Prince Roman" the narrator uses the simile of "a running sea" in a landlocked tale of Polish cavalry men; such nautical allusions are JC's usual way to announce a hero on trial. JC symbolizes the Polish situation, "a parable of human existence," in terms of the sea. Since his heroes are often pilgrims, metaphors are often religious.

1553 Mroczkowski, Przemysław J. "O Conradowskiej gnomice" (The Gnomic Element in Conrad), KWARTALNIK NEOFILOLOGICZNY, VI (1959), 193-209; rptd in slightly shortened form in Barbara Kocówna's WSPOMNIENIA I STUDIA CONRADZIE (MEMORIES AND CONRADIAN STUDIES) (Warsaw: Państwowy Instytut Wydawniczy, 1963), pp. 472-94.
[An interesting and objective assessment of the maxims and aphorisms in JC's work, this article is extremely worthy of translation for the English reader. This study seems to touch the heart of what has made JC popular with readers over the years, the line that stops the thoughtful reader and sets him to pondering.] [In Polish.]

1554 Mroczkowski, Przemysław. "A Glance Back at the Romantic Conrad: 'The Lagoon.' A Study in the Technique of the Short Story," POLISH REVIEW, IV (Winter-Spring 1959), 15-23; rptd in JOSEPH CONRAD: CENTENNIAL ESSAYS, ed by Ludwik Krzyżanowski (NY: Polish Institute of Arts and Sciences in America, 1960), pp. 73-83; and in WSPOMNIENIA I STUDIA O CONRADZIE, ed by Barbara Kocówna (Warsaw Państwowy Instytut Wydawniczy, 1963), 457-71.
[This commemorative essay promises a "dynamic analysis," which attempts, by "continuous commentary on the narrative," to "build up certain effects" and to ask whether "implied questions" have been answered. Actually presented is a summary of "The Lagoon" with commonplace responses and questions that arise as the narrative unfolds (e.g., "we see how distinctly Conrad enjoys the experience of exotic nature as scenery").]

1555 Rawson, C. J. "Conrad's 'Heart of Darkness,'" NOTES AND QUERIES, N.S. VI (March 1959), 110-11.

Owen's suggestion [ibid., V (June 1958), 260] that there is a similarity between the young man described by Lord Ernest Hamilton and Kurtz is mistaken.

1556 Ray, Gordon N. "H. G. Wells Tries to Be a Novelist," EDWARDIANS AND LATE VICTORIANS (ENGLISH INSTITUTE ESSAYS, 1959), ed by Richard Ellmann (NY: Columbia U P, 1960), pp. 106-59.

Contemptuous of the popular favorites of his time, Wells was "profoundly respectful" of great novelists like JC, who told him in 1898 that even in his scientific narratives he was the "Realist of the Fantastic." Wells admired JC's *An Outcast of the Islands,* but he thought the author's "visual splendor" was obscured by his "wordy" and hazy style. LOVE AND MR. LEWISHAM, a novel "of limited aims," occupies in Wells's work about the same place as *The Nigger of the Narcissus* in JC's. Wells is ranked in Edwardian literature just below James, Yeats, Shaw, and JC.

1557 S., L. A. "Shorter Reviews," NEW STATESMAN, LVIII (19 Sept 1959), 369-70.

In LETTERS TO WILLIAM BLACKWOOD AND DAVID S. MELDRUM, edited by William Blackburn (1958), the passages on JC's craft in fiction and his single-minded integrity as an artist are especially worthy of praise.

1558 Sawyer, A. E. "Joseph Conrad: A Centenary Review," CANADIAN SLAVONIC PAPERS, IV (1959), 182-98.

In 1899, JC was cited on the one hand as a talented *émigré* writer who served his native country, and on the other as one who betrayed it. Forty-five years later the controversy was resolved when JC's writing inspired the Warsaw insurrectionists. [Sawyer reviews the revolutionary careers of JC's family and the place of his uncle in his life.] The uncle, "a second father to him," intensified JC's skepticism about revolution, a skepticism present in *Nostromo, The Secret Agent,* and *Under Western Eyes.* At the same time, he had absorbed some of his father's "visionary . . . characteristics." JC's world is very much "a tragic world." His characteristic situation centers on "a catastrophic reversal of fortune." The virtues of "control and assurance" are present in the stories from the beginning. Supporting them is a clear moral and political attitude, one deeper than H. G. Wells described. JC's "fiction is informed by a powerful sense of the irrational both without and within man, against the assaults of which no one is proof and no defense certain."

1559 Spoerri-Müller, Ruth. JOSEPH CONRAD: DAS PROBLEM DER VEREINSAMUNG (Joseph Conrad: The Problem of Isolation) (Winterthur: P. G. Keller, 1959).

[In the first part of this survey of JC's oeuvre, Spoerri-Müller treats the motif of loneliness systematically. She singles out the dreamer, the hermit, and the knight for special attention and discusses the alienation of these and other character types with reference to external pressures and the experiences both of evil and anxiety. The difficulties of overcoming one's isolation are illustrated from several novels. The second part describes in detail how JC uses point of view, imagery, and irony to express human loneliness. A common-sense study, in some ways surpassed but not superseded by Gillon's monograph.] [In German.]

1560 Stallman, Robert Wooster. "Conrad Criticism Today," SEWANEE REVIEW, LXVII (Jan-March 1959), 135-45.

[Surveys the current (1958) state of JC criticism, with special reference to Thomas Moser's JOSEPH CONRAD: ACHIEVEMENT AND DECLINE (1957) and Albert J. Guerard's CONRAD THE NOVELIST (1958).] John D. Gordan's JOSEPH CONRAD: THE MAKING OF A NOVELIST (1940) remains a "landmark"; the Moser and Guerard volumes are two of the most important studies since Hewitt's JOSEPH CONRAD: A REASSESSMENT (1952). JC ranks among the greatest writers of fiction.

1561 Stallman, Robert Wooster. "Time and *The Secret Agent*," TEXAS STUDIES IN LITERATURE AND LANGUAGE, I (Spring 1959), 101-22; rptd in THE ART OF JOSEPH CONRAD: A CRITICAL SYMPOSIUM, ed by Robert Wooster Stallman (East Lansing: Michigan State U P, 1960), pp. 234-54; and THE HOUSES THAT JAMES BUILT (East Lansing: Michigan State U P, 1961), pp. 111-30.

The Secret Agent, "one of the most cryptographic works in all British fiction," has a central idea that has eluded JC's critics: "all time—legal time, civil time, astronomical time, and Universal Time—emanates from Greenwich Observatory *and* . . . Verloc's mission, in the intended bombing of Greenwich Observatory, is to destroy Time-Now, Universal Time, or life itself." It is significant that Stevie, the only artist in the world of the novel, is a half-wit. Stevie's circles, which he constantly draws, make the design of the book: every character in the work is "rendered as a circle of insularity, each insulated from another by his own self-love, by self-illusions and fixed ideas or theories, while like eccentric circles each selfhood impinges upon another by sharing some portion of its attributes, outlook, or theory." The "ironic concatenation of theories or illusions" is "shocked to zero" by the impingements of reality, of the unexpected, or of the unpredictable. All the characters have in common "an abhorrence of ideas which contradict and upset their own"; everyone is "a fragmented and frustrated anonymity." Insignificant things such as the cracked bell, the cracked wedding ring, and the lonely mechanical piano, manifest reality; and each one "signifies the unpredictable." Thus, the nature of reality in the novel is "irrational, incongruous, and incalculable." The structure of the book is confusing, with the "distorted chronology of narrated events" shaping the narrative into circular form, and thus relating it to the theme—time. JC's "diabolic irony" reduces all theories—scientific, political, sociological, economic, and psychological—to zero, leaving as a protection against life what we can devise of "superstition, myths, theories, conventional conceptions of reality, systems and creeds, codes of behavior by which society is manipulated and controlled," in other words, all that the "muddling intellect" can contrive. "Time-Now is the Unpredictable, life in all its irrational particulars"; and it is "Time the Unpredictable—agent of life and death"—that JC "cryptographically intends as *the* Secret Agent." [An important article, ingeniously and thoughtfully developed.]

1562 Waggoner, Hyatt H. WILLIAM FAULKNER: FROM JEFFERSON TO THE WORLD (Lexington: University of Kentucky P, 1959), pp. 34, 49, 216, 259.

The view expressed by Gavin Stevens in INTRUDER IN THE DUST "seems not very different from that expressed . . . by Stephen Crane in 'The Open Boat' and by Conrad in 'The Secret Sharer' and elsewhere: a naturalistic moralism in which a sense of community is stimulated by a perception of the precariousness of man's situations."

1563 Weiand, Hermann Joseph. "The Story as a Creative Medium in the Work of Joseph Conrad." Unpublished thesis, University of Edinburgh, 1959.

1564 Widmer, Kingsley. "Conrad's Pyrrhic *Victory*," TWENTIETH CENTURY LITERATURE, V (Oct 1959), 123-30.

"Conrad's essential fable has a hero isolated in an ominous nature, his will threatened or corrupted, the victim of nearly inexplicable forces of malignancy. The alien scene is variously a jungle, a deserted island, a strange land, a ship in danger, or even the purlieus of the modern metropolis." The villain in JC is frequently, as in Dostoevski, a double of the hero, e.g., Jim and Gentleman Brown in *Lord Jim,* Razumov and Haldin in *Under Western Eyes,* and Heyst and Jones in *Victory*. JC's success with this "moralist's pattern for the corruption inherent in goodness" varies from the subtlety of "The Secret Sharer" to the "sentimental machinations of the final novels." *Victory* falls in between. The love story in *Victory* is uncongenial, and Lena is "a pathetic but exalted Dickensian heroine." "Both the gross failure and the incisive strength of this fable can be accounted for" by three possible meanings of *victory:* (1) evil is not the victor since Heyst conquers his own weakness and Jones "inexplicably drops dead"; (2) "No one . . . seriously suggests that the melodramatic love sacrifice of Lena's constitutes the victory because of the stock Victorianism and the undeveloped rhetorical handling by Conrad—though recent Freudian critics would certainly suggest this as Conrad's defeat"; (3) "the moral-sentimentalist view . . . sees Heyst as undergoing a progressive redemption from skepticism to love." On the contrary, the pattern is from "skepticism to demonism to despair." The title is ironic, and Heyst kills himself in despair. T. S. Eliot's phrase "counter-romanticism" suggests "that the final Conradian irony is the victory of evil over evil, ending in the provocative by pyrrhic virtues of a homeopathic art in which the malady and the medicine are identical."

1565 Zabel, Morton Dauwen. "Conrad Writing on His Career and Craft," NEW YORK HERALD TRIBUNE BOOK REVIEW, 8 Feb 1959, p. 4.

JOSEPH CONRAD: LETTERS TO WILLIAM BLACKWOOD AND DAVID S. MELDRUM, edited by William Blackburn (1958), makes available another major part of JC's correspondence. "It was Blackwood's patronage that carried him over the most harrowing phase of his writing life, that gave him both editorial and financial encouragement when he needed it most, and that guided him out of his first phase of authorship into the decade of full maturity and ripened powers that lay ahead between 1903 and 1912." JC's letter to Blackwood, 31 May 1902, "must now be added to the major personal and defensive statements that Conrad wrote on his career, his craft, and his doctrine as an artist."

1566 Zabel, Morton D. "Introduction," THE SHADOW-LINE AND TWO OTHER TALES: "TYPHOON" / "THE SECRET SHARER" (Garden City, NY: Doubleday, Anchor Books, 1959), pp. 1-27.

JC is the master in English of the sea story, and his mastery is best seen in the three stories of this volume, in "Youth," and in *The Nigger of the Narcissus*. E. M. Forster was one of the early formulators of a basic criticism of JC's work: its " 'central obscurity' "; this obscurity resulted from the discrepancy between his emphasis on detailed actualities and his romantic philosophizings. The three stories in this volume cover the three phases of JC's career: "Typhoon," the first phase; "The Secret Sharer," the middle phase; and *The Shadow-Line,* the final phase. "Each turns on a crisis of shock, challenge, or initiation. Each centers in a trial of 'command.' And the stories range from youth to age."

1567 Zabel, Morton Dauwen. "Introduction," *Youth: a Narrative and Two Other Stories: Heart of Darkness / The End of the Tether* (Garden City, NY: Doubleday, Anchor Books, 1959), pp. 1-25.

JC's tales form a major part of his achievement. In range, theme, and style the tales "define the scope of Conrad's creation." Six of his tales are among his best work: *The Nigger of the Narcissus,* "Youth," "Heart of Darkness," "Typhoon," "The Secret Sharer," and *The Shadow-Line*. Sometimes "the art of fable" flaws his work. "But when the fable is subjected to his sense of fact, or is subdued to his skill in irony, it produces the convincing resonance of complex truth and moral ambiguity that he achieved in his greatest work—*Nostromo, The Secret Agent, The Shadow-Line,* 'Typhoon,' 'Heart of Darkness.' " The *Youth* volume possesses a conscious organic unity, and it is this volume which brings most clearly JC's first phase to a close. The three tales work to balance one another: "Youth"—the shock of "the initiation into experience"; "Heart of Darkness"—the "descent into the riddle of self-betrayal and corruption"; "The End of the Tether"—"the tragic pathos of old age."

1960

1568 Balvanoic, Vlado. "Joseph Conrad: 'Freja sa sedam ostrva' " (Joseph Conrad: "Freya of the Seven Isles"), OSLOBODENJE (Sarajevo), XVIII (31 Aug 1960), 4.

[The Serbo-Croatian translation of "Freya" and "The End of the Tether" is briefly noted.] [In Serbo-Croatian.]

1569 Bayley, John. THE CHARACTERS OF LOVE (Lond: Constable; NY: Basic Books, 1960), pp. 267-68.

JC's greatness "reposes very simply upon the person and the fact. He has no myth with a view to insight: he has scenes and he has people." "Conrad is a particularly good illustration of the dangers of 'deep' criticism because he is such a queerly portentous writer whose large intentions and resounding irony are the least satisfactory side of him."

1570 Buckler, William E., and Arnold B. Sklare (eds). STORIES FROM SIX AUTHORS (NY: McGraw-Hill, 1960), pp. 509-11.

[A biographical note, questions for discussion, an interpretation of "Youth," suggestions for writing, along with texts of "An Outpost of Progress," "The Secret Sharer," and "Youth."]

1571 Cook, Albert Spaulding. "Plot as Discovery: Conrad, Dostoevski, and Faulkner," THE MEANING OF FICTION (Detroit: Wayne State U P, 1960), pp. 202-41; based on Cook's "Conrad's Void," NINETEENTH-CENTURY FICTION, XII (March 1958), 326-30.

JC's "plots have a kind of displacement which their central object, a 'nothing,' induces. Yet against total void the human spirit can remain indomitable in victory." The " 'emptiness' is not a defect in Conrad's work, but the core of his theme, man braving in his mortality the heart of darkness. Toward this insight is directed Conrad's scrupulous construction, evidenced in the closed plot, the tightness of the pattern, and in his frequent hall-of-mirrors points of view." JC's "images, especially those of the sea, are analogs of the void."

1572 Dean, Leonard F. "Conrad and the Congo," JOSEPH CONRAD'S "HEART OF DARKNESS": BACKGROUNDS AND CRITICISMS, ed by Leonard F. Dean (Englewood Cliffs, NJ: Prentice-Hall, Spectrum Books, 1960), p. 143.
[Dean explains the relationship among JC's Congo diary, Mrs. Jessie Conrad, and Captain Otto Lütken.]

1573 Dean, Leonard F. "Conrad and His Critics," JOSEPH CONRAD'S "HEART OF DARKNESS": BACKGROUNDS AND CRITICISMS, ed by Leonard F. Dean (Englewood Cliffs, NJ: Prentice-Hall, Spectrum Books, 1960), p. 89.
[Very brief sketches of the lives and works of Sir Hugh Clifford, Edward Garnett, Harold Collins, Jerome Thale, and Albert Guerard, all of whom have made important contributions to the criticism of "Heart of Darkness."]

1574 Dean, Leonard F. "Conrad, Stanley, and the Scramble for Africa," JOSEPH CONRAD'S "HEART OF DARKNESS": BACKGROUNDS AND CRITICISMS, ed by Leonard F. Dean (Englewood Cliffs, NJ: Prentice-Hall, Spectrum Books, 1960), pp. 76-78.
Both JC and Henry Morton Stanley went to the Congo and, although there is no evidence that the two men ever met, Stanley's reactions to the outposts of Matadi and Boma provide an interesting contrast to "Heart of Darkness."

1575 Dean, Leonard F. "Conrad's Decision to Leave the Congo," JOSEPH CONRAD'S "HEART OF DARKNESS": BACKGROUNDS AND CRITICISMS, ed by Leonard F. Dean (Englewood Cliffs, NJ: Prentice-Hall, Spectrum Books, 1960), pp. 101-2.
There are some similarities and some differences between JC's leaving the Congo and certain details in "Heart of Darkness"; JC was dissatisfied with what he saw in Africa and the men he had to work with.

1576 Dean, Leonard F. (ed). JOSEPH CONRAD'S "HEART OF DARKNESS": BACKGROUNDS AND CRITICISMS (Englewood Cliffs, NJ: Prentice-Hall, Spectrum Books, 1960).
Contents, abstracted separately under date of first publication: Morton D. Zabel, "A Conrad Chronology," from THE PORTABLE CONRAD (1947); Morton D. Zabel, "Conrad's Early Life, Temperament, and Characteristic Themes," from THE PORTABLE CONRAD (1947); Leonard F. Dean, "Con-

rad, Stanley, and the Scramble for Africa" (1960); Leonard F. Dean, "Conrad and the Congo" (1960); Mrs. Jessie Conrad, "To the Editor of THE LONDON MERCURY, July, 1930," from LONDON MERCURY (1930); Captain Otto Lütken, "To the Editor of THE LONDON MERCURY, August, 1930," from LONDON MERCURY (1930); Leonard F. Dean, "Conrad's Decision to Leave the Congo" (1960); Leonard F. Dean, "Sir Roger Casement, Conrad, and the Congo" (1960); Albert J. Guerard, "Conrad's Discovery of a Fictional World," from CONRAD THE NOVELIST (1958); Ford Madox Ford, "Conrad at Work," from PORTRAITS FROM LIFE (1937; see "Conrad and the Sea" [1935]); Leonard F. Dean, "Conrad and His Critics" (1960); Hugh Clifford, "The Art of Mr. Joseph Conrad," from SPECTATOR (Lond) (1902); Edward Garnett, "Mr. Conrad's New Book: *Youth: A Narrative; and Two Other Stories,*" from ACADEMY AND LITERATURE (1902); "'*Youth*,'" from TIMES LITERARY SUPPLEMENT (Lond) (1902); John Masefield, "Deep Sea Yarns: '*Youth*, a Narrative,'" from SPEAKER (1903); Harold R. Collins, "Kurtz, the Cannibals, and the Second-Rate Helmsman," from WESTERN HUMANITIES REVIEW (1954); Jerome Thale, "Marlowe's [sic] Quest," from UNIVERSITY OF TORONTO QUARTERLY (1955); Albert J. Guerard, "The Journey Within," from CONRAD THE NOVELIST (1958); and Leonard F. Dean, "For Discussion and Writing" (1960). Works by others not on JC and not abstracted: Henry M. Stanley, "Through the Dark Continent: Arrival at Matadi," from THROUGH THE DARK CONTINENT (1878); Sir Roger Casement, "Report from His Majesty's Consul . . . ," from CORRESPONDENCE AND REPORT. . . . (nd). Works by JC not abstracted: "Heart of Darkness"; "Geography and Some Explorers: Africa," from *Last Essays;* "The Congo Diary: Book I," from JOSEPH CONRAD IN THE CONGO (1926); "A Letter to Marguerite Poradowska," from LETTERS OF JOSEPH CONRAD TO MARGUERITE PORADOWSKA, ed by John A. Gee and Paul J. Sturm (1940); and "Prefaces to *Youth* and to *The Nigger of the Narcissus*"; "Correspondence between Conrad and William Blackwood Concerning the Composition and Publication of 'Heart of Darkness,'" from JOSEPH CONRAD: LETTERS TO WILLIAM BLACKWOOD AND DAVID MELDRUM, ed by William Blackburn (1958). [Some of the titles listed above, as they appear in Dean's collection, are not those of the original authors but devised by Dean for his casebook.]

1577 Dean, Leonard F. "Sir Roger Casement, Conrad and the Congo," JOSEPH CONRAD'S "HEART OF DARKNESS": BACKGROUNDS AND CRITICISMS, ed by Leonard F. Dean (Englewood Cliffs, NJ: Prentice-Hall, Spectrum Books, 1960), pp. 104-6.

[Dean clarifies JC's relationship to Sir Roger Casement, a British consul in Africa who, in 1903, made a sensational report on atrocities in the Belgian Congo.]

1578 Dowden, Wilfred S. "The 'Illuminating Quality': Imagery and Theme in *The Secret Agent*," RICE INSTITUTE PAMPHLET, XLVII (Oct 1960), 17-33.

The tone of *The Secret Agent* is provided by "an atmosphere of sinister darkness which is penetrated spasmodically by the blood-red glare of gaslight." Mrs. Verloc's wedding ring emphasizes Mr. Verloc's isolation, for this marriage with Winnie was a mistake. "The introduction of a wife into such an existence . . . is an illustration of Verloc's depravity." The ending with Comrade Ossipon's downfall and the description of the Professor brings the reader from the "world of darkness" back to the world of normal, everyday life, much like the effect DeQuincey described in his explanation of the knocking-at-the-gate scene in MACBETH.

1579 Gillon, Adam. "Betrayal and Redemption in Joseph Conrad," POLISH REVIEW, V (Spring 1960), 18-35.

French and Polish romanticism and "moral lessons of national misfortune" perhaps "make passion and conviction the main levers" of JC's fiction. The conflict between the two usually brings about the themes of betrayal and redemption. JC's outcasts, who face a hostile and often mysterious universe, will suffer and sometimes die in "total failure or in tragic triumph," but they "uphold the principle of human solidarity." A man with a conscience cannot live alone; the supreme sin is betrayal. JC depicts three types of traitors: (1) those who exhibit self-pity (Almayer, Willems, Kayerts); (2) those who have "severe inner conflict" resulting from treachery and who often long for redemption (Lord Jim, Nostromo, Lingard); and (3) those who "have no remorse because they have no conscience." When Jim, Brierly, and Razumov (among others) realize what they are, they seek death and self-sacrifice as a redemptive act, or "final epiphany." JC, unlike the Polish Romantics, the Victorians, and Dostoevski, does not espouse the Christian practice of seeking salvation through God. JC does find Christianity "improving, softening, compassionate," but dislikes the impossible standards that cause so many human problems. Thus, JC preaches individuality while remembering ties to the human community. JC belongs to no school, but follows "the voice from inside."

1580 Gillon, Adam. "Conrad and Sartre," DALHOUSIE REVIEW, XL (Spring 1960), 61-71.

Critics have failed to "pigeonhole Conrad into a precise literary category" because of his "individualism both as a person and as a novelist." His romanticism "is not quite English nor wholly Polish. He is a realist, but his realism is different from that of other literary men of his age. He is an impressionist, yet his impressionism is but one of the many aspects of his art of fiction." Nor was he merely a spinner of sea yarns or a political novelist: "his main intention was not to grapple with tangible, contemporary problems." He belongs to no school. Since existentialism lacks "a clear-cut philosophical doctrine" and values a "perfervid individualism," an examination of Sartre and of JC would reveal "some remarkable similarities . . . as well as significant differences." "Conrad's vision of the world is more rewarding aesthetically as well as morally. He too has lost his illusions, but not a sense of human values. Sartre reveals the incongruous and the pathological in man, Conrad his moral complexity. Conrad's world is as sad as that of Sartre, but only the latter is depressing in the final count. . . . Sartre's characters cannot attain to tragedy for, by definition, they exist in a metaphysical emptiness; Conrad's heroes may suffer as much as Sartre's do—they almost invariably meet with a violent death or languish in solitude—but even in their extreme state of isolation or defeat they are an affirmation of human fidelity and compassion." JC arouses feelings of catharsis in the reader; Sartre cannot.

>**1581** Gillon, Adam. THE ETERNAL SOLITARY: A STUDY OF JOSEPH CONRAD (NY: Bookman Associates; Lond: Burns & MacEachern, 1960); much expanded from "Isolation in the Life and Works of Joseph Conrad," an unpublished thesis, Columbia University, 1954.

Isolation is a "dominant motif" in JC's life and works. JC's "isolato" is "a man incapable of living the kind of life he wishes to live, through adverse circumstances or through his own faults," one who faces "an inescapable wall" that separates him even from the people who are closest to him. JC himself was such an isolated man. He thus achieved his artistic aims at the cost of suffering throughout his life. The "Romantic Man" is "condemned to isolation by the nature of his endeavor, which is to view life through the prism of his personal illusion," but illusion makes life worthwhile for some of JC's characters (Kurtz, the Russian youth, and the Intended in "Heart of Darkness"; young Marlow in "Youth"; and Stein in *Lord Jim*). Lord Jim and Lingard of *The Rescue* exemplify the paralyzing power of the romantic dream, and George in *The Arrow of Gold* is a variation on the theme of Lingard. Most of JC's women are passive and, like their male counterparts, have one common characteristic, their isolation (Flora of *Chance*). The theme of romantic love is associated with the theme of isolation (Lord Jim and Jewel, Willems and Aissa, Alice Jacobus and the Captain). JC's treatment of sex reveals his vision of mankind: sexual love, which promises the closest union between man and woman, usually brings solitude and thus dramatizes the human condition of loneliness. JC, to whom nature was "a senseless mechanical power," uses it symbolically: both "the impenetrable, somber forests" and "the vast solitude of waters" are forces that shape human destiny. Man's struggle against the elements shows his inner worth both to others and to himself, and it finally brings self-knowledge. For JC, the sea may be a place of romance, but the jungle is "a symbol of the savage in man" and also a symbol of man's isolation. JC appears to be more concerned with the moral atmosphere of his fiction than with the "sheer exoticism" which appeals to the average reader. [A table of some length lists the various kinds of fate that befall JC's heroes, only a few of whom finally emerge from their isolation.] The "supreme sin" is failure to be loyal, which in its more extreme form is betrayal, the "crime of crimes," as fidelity is to him the "virtue of virtues." Nothing can save a man from himself: "when man is made to face the evil of the human soul and its primordial wilderness, he usually recognizes a certain degree of affinity with it." Thus the "haunted and persecuted isolatoes" cannot completely condemn the person or power responsible for their misfortunes: they may also condemn themselves and destroy themselves.

JC created two kinds of men, exemplified by the simple MacWhirr and the complex Heyst, because he himself lived a double life "as sailor and thinker." In *Victory* and *Chance* the "perfidious hand of fate" enters to make these works consist of "seemingly disconnected pictures" and "a symbolic rather than a dramatic consistency," like the worlds of James Joyce and Virginia Woolf. Although *Victory* is poorly constructed, it has a "singular symbolic felicity." The "dramatic looseness" of *Victory* and *Chance,* and of *Jim,* is an excellent device for JC to convey "the instability of the world," since life is the reverse of existence as it is planned. JC's object was "to examine man's destiny, his weakness and strength, his goodness and evil." Death does not always mean defeat; death to an "isolato" is a "welcome visitor." Such men as Kurtz, Heyst, and Decoud have the choice of a way of being; their helplessness against the forces of destiny does not prevent them from making their own decision; in fact, Heyst is JC's Faust, Jones is a nineteenth-century Mephistopheles, and Decoud is the victim of the "disillusioned weariness" which the retribution of "intellectual audacity" brings.

JC used the concept of the *Flammentod,* employed by so many Victorian writers concerned with the problem of conversion: Heyst, Razumov, Captain Anthony, the Captain in *The Shadow-Line,* and other characters are literary studies in the subject of man's spiritual re-birth, which may be accomplished by fire (Almayer) or water (Renouard and Decoud). And in each instance there is a "symbolic cleansing of the soiled self," a discovery of the real self which man does not dare to face (Charles Gould in *Nostromo*).

JC's theme of isolation is of special significance in the modern world. JC wrote of the world as he saw it and of the few virtues that "stand out in the pathos of human weakness." The result is a "strange blend of romanticism and realism" with counterparts in the novels of such authors as D. H. Lawrence, Virginia Woolf, and James Joyce. JC's treatment of the isolated man has affinities with both the romantic and the Victorian points of view and even with the existentialism of Jean-Paul Sartre. His closest psychological counterparts are William Faulkner, F. Scott Fitzgerald, and Graham Greene, along with Camus, Malraux, and François Mauriac. JC thus went further in revealing the complexities of man's spiritual life than did his contemporaries Wells and Galsworthy. [A good study of one important aspect of JC's life and works.]

> **1582** Gose, Elliott B., Jr. " 'Cruel Devourer of the World's Light': *The Secret Agent*," NINETEENTH-CENTURY FICTION, XV (June 1960), 39-51.

Like any artist, JC forced his imagination to give shape to his material, but his "means of control" was always his technique, especially images and symbolism in *The Secret Agent*. One standard for judging both mental attitudes and physical actions is derived from the Professor, whose conclusions are opposed to JC's because "he owes his allegiance to destruction." Verloc "has tried to combine the business of being a secret agent with the pleasure of belonging to the home-owning middle class" and has thus failed to be true to any kind of ideal, even that of anarchism. The "coming together" of the forces of good and evil at the center of the action has its counterpart in the imagery of light and dark and also in the confusion of personal relations. The characters are flawed by a "dissociation of the social sensibility"; they do not understand or communicate with one another. In fact, each character has a certain "mental faculty" which is lacking in the others, with the result that the Verloc family group lacks unity, like the society around them.

The images serve as "details which support the destinies and relations of the characters, while the symbolic conception provides a pattern for Conrad's statement of his theme." A contrast between light and dark is a "central symbolism" which serves as a unifying form for JC's moral vision. Whereas a "passive stagnation" is characteristic of the lives of most of the people in London, there is an "active movement toward dissolution" in the desire for destruction of Vladimir and the Professor, as well as in Stevie's activities, all of which suggest "chaos and eternity." The Verloc home is placed at the center of "both the passive and the active movement toward chaotic anarchy." JC's irony is here apparent: the expedients intended to preserve society from corruption are secret, and therefore they actually aid the disintegrative process; and because each flaw in character is secret, it is dark, "hidden from the light," much like the Verloc's home life, existing in "a shop where the sun never shone." As night had characterized Mr.

Verloc's life, "so night and its secrecy characterize his death." And the same darkness characterizes London. JC thus renders successfully his belief in the efficacy of "the symbolic conception" of a work of art.

1583 Greenberg, Robert A. "The Presence of Mr. Wang," BOSTON UNIVERSITY STUDIES IN ENGLISH, IV (Autumn 1960), 129-37. An investigation of the prominent role played by Wang in *Victory* emphasizes the contrast between Wang and Heyst, as well as Wang's character. Wang's growth and his serving of the action of the novel are illustrated. Wang is a foil to Heyst in a correcting or qualifying sense and has a victory of his own which is integral to the pattern of the book.

1584 Gregory, Michael. JOSEPH CONRAD: HIS PLACE IN THE MODERN DILEMMA. San Francisco: Hesperion House, 1960. [Not seen. Publisher reportedly out of business.]

1585 Guerard, Albert J. "Introduction," *Heart of Darkness, Almayer's Folly, The Lagoon* (NY: Dell, Laurel Series, 1960), pp. 7-23.
The decade from *Almayer's Folly* (1895) to *Nostromo* (1904) is the decade of JC's greatest work, after which occurs a marked decline. This period "offers the essential Conradian dreams and the three great segments of his fictional world": the sea, the jungle, and politics. [A strong Jungian emphasis is given to the analyses of the works. General introduction extending over the whole of JC's life.]

1586 Gurko, Leo. *"Under Western Eyes:* Conrad and the Question of 'Where To?'" COLLEGE ENGLISH, XXI (May 1960), 445-52.
[An excellent analysis of *Under Western Eyes,* but incorporated with additional material in Gurko's JOSEPH CONRAD: GIANT IN EXILE (1962), pp. 179-96.]

1587 Harkness, Bruce (ed). CONRAD'S "HEART OF DARKNESS" AND THE CRITICS (San Francisco: Wadsworth, 1960).
Contents, abstracted separately under date of first publication: G. J.-Aubry, "In the Heart of Darkness," from THE SEA DREAMER (1957, see JOSEPH CONRAD: LIFE AND LETTERS [1927]); Edward Garnett, "On Conrad's Use of Memory," from the introduction to LETTERS FROM JOSEPH CONRAD, 1895-1924 (1928); Douglas Hewitt, "Reassessment of 'Heart of Darkness,'" from JOSEPH CONRAD: A REASSESSMENT (1952); Albert J. Guerard, "The Journey Within," from CONRAD THE NOVELIST (1958); M. C. Bradbrook, "Marlow's Function," from JOSEPH CONRAD: POLAND'S ENGLISH GENIUS (1941); W. Y. Tindall, "Apology for Marlow," from FROM JANE AUSTEN TO JOSEPH CONRAD, ed by R. C. Rathburn and M.

Steinmann, Jr. (1958); Marvin Mudrick, "Marlow and Conrad," from "Conrad and the Terms of Modern Criticism," HUDSON REVIEW (1954); Robert O. Evans, "Conrad's Underworld," from MODERN FICTION STUDIES (1956); William Bysshe Stein, "The Lotus Posture and 'The Heart of Darkness,'" from MODERN FICTION STUDIES (1956); Seymour Gross, "A Further Note on the Function of the Frame in 'Heart of Darkness,'" from MODERN FICTION STUDIES (1957); Walter F. Wright, "Ingress to the Heart of Darkness," from ROMANCE AND TRAGEDY IN JOSEPH CONRAD (1949); Thomas C. Moser, "The Lie and Truth," from JOSEPH CONRAD: ACHIEVEMENT AND DECLINE (1957); Wilfred S. Dowden, "The Light and Dark Lie," from "The Light and the Dark: Imagery and Thematic Development in Conrad's *Heart of Darkness,*" RICE INSTITUTE PAMPHLET (1957); and Bruce Harkness, "Textual Note," "Study Questions, Theme and Paper Topics," and a "Bibliography of Works for Further Study" [not abstracted]. Works by JC, not abstracted: "Heart of Darkness," based on first ed collated with all important eds; "The Congo Diary," from *Last Essays.*

1588 Hay, Eloise Knapp. *"Lord Jim:* From Sketch to Novel," COMPARATIVE LITERATURE, XII (Fall 1960), 289-309.

The Harvard manuscript, "Tuan Jim: A Sketch," has "nothing of Jim's tendency to cast himself in the role of hero." Lacking also is "any mention of the dual nature of Jim's imagination." In both sketch and novel a physically crippling accident detaches Jim from "the objective necessities of life"; but in the novel the tragic dimension is enlarged when Jim, frustrated over his failure to be a hero, feels his moral lapse keenly. Perhaps this change in Jim was related to JC's own sensitivity to the criticism that he had betrayed Poland by becoming an émigré, a deserter, in a sense, of a public trust. All of this may have suggested to JC that Jim's character could be broadened, could become less of a personal Hamlet-figure and more of a Culture-figure. JC's addition of "the halo and the curse of Jim's Romantic egoism" was a theme few English readers recognized as of concern to all Poles. In his handling of Jim, JC was, finally, involved on two planes—the personal and the public. His attitude towards Poland was an ambivalent one. He felt some need to explain why he left Poland, but he probably felt more guilt over "his congenital and chronic drift toward reverie." Jim began as "a sort of Conrad." He ended by "representing Conrad and 'everyman'" as well as "the great lost Polish nation, which Conrad held in both love and fear."

1589 Herndon, Richard. "The Genesis of Conrad's 'Amy Foster,'" STUDIES IN PHILOLOGY, LVII (July 1960), 549-66.

Four possible sources of "Amy Foster" are (1) a true anecdote about the shipwreck, persecution, and tragic isolation in England of a German sailor, whose story JC learned partly from Ford Madox Ford, and much of the geography and rural atmosphere from the area of his home in Kent; (2) JC's endurance of "acute physical and moral isolation" in the Belgian Congo; (3) his recalling or rereading Flaubert's story, "Un Coeur Simple," but patterning the plot as a whole on his own earlier story, "The Idiots"; and (4) probably reflecting in the conclusion of "Amy Foster" his poor health and fear of an early death, possible dissatisfaction with his wife, and a tendency to end tragic action in his stories with the protagonist's death. These diverse sources demonstrate that this story cannot be regarded —as can "Youth," "Heart of Darkness," and *The Arrow of Gold*—as a "fictionalized chronicle" of a phase of JC's early life.

1590 Hough, Graham. *"Chance* and Joseph Conrad," IMAGE AND EXPERIENCE: STUDIES IN A LITERARY REVOLUTION (Lond: Duckworth, 1960), pp. 211-23; rptd (Lincoln: University of Nebraska P, Bison Books, 1962), pp. 211-22; much expanded from a BBC Third Programme broadcast.

The two views of JC the popular writer of romantic sea stories and the critical JC as puzzling philosopher—are not mutually exclusive. "The sea setting goes very deep into his sensibility." He is apart from the central tradition of the novel since he "writes as a foreigner in a language not his own." He never portrayed society (except ship life), the family, home life, immediately. Even *Nostromo* is not vivid reality, but a *tour de force*, "scene-painting." JC uses narrators and second-hand accounts of "big scenes" rather than scenes themselves because of a lack of "specific, intimate knowledge." But scenes aboard ships have the reality based on such knowledge missing from the land scenes. JC is "a great novelist of a whole tract of experience that no other writer of his stature has ever attempted before."

1591 Hunt, Kellog W. *"Lord Jim* and THE RETURN OF THE NATIVE: a Contrast," ENGLISH JOURNAL, XLIX (Oct 1960), 447-56. Both *Lord Jim* and THE RETURN OF THE NATIVE are "heroic masterpieces," but otherwise different; *Jim* is a moral evaluation; Hardy's THE RETURN OF THE NATIVE is an account of man's place in the cosmos. Hardy's novel is season-time-space related (one year; action related to season, summer and honeymoon of Clym and Eustacia; final dread action in November). Space is important: Egdon Heath circumscribes it all. JC's events are neither time- nor space-related except in the "most inward sense." Hardy's technique is that of the dramatist; his novel is in five parts. Out of six main persons, Hardy produces four triangles. JC does not cut up the action into discrete parts; there is a sort of "twoness" one, moral failure; two, success. "Each mirrors the other." The action breaks in the middle, a break minimized by a "non-chronological" approach. JC "splices by weaving strands of the second episode clear up to the beginning of the first." He has one central person, Hardy has six. Hardy requires a network of plot; JC produces a "Nile of moral concern" with the "stubbiest tributaries" (the interpolated events—like the little story of Bob Stanton which concerns not plot but moral concern with Jim). Hardy's hundreds of events form a chain of cause-and-effect whereas JC's novel is like a "philosophical essay about certain general moral and psychological matters," delivered via Marlow's limitless memory and speculating intelligence. JC's theme, expressed as Jim's "going away from a living woman to celebrate his pitiless wedding with a shadow of conduct," contrasts sharply with Hardy's theme expressed in Clym's words: "Instead of men aiming to advance in life with glory they should celebrate how to retreat out of it without shame." The great difference between the two novels lies in the fact that in *Jim* one subject, one theme, interpenetrates all aspects of the work whereas in THE RETURN OF THE NATIVE the theme is "overlaid upon the novel like loose veneer." Hardy involves his characters in a careful plot, but the novel does not compare in effectiveness to *Jim.*

1592 Karl, Frederick R. "Conrad's Waste Land: Moral Anarchy in *The Secret Agent,*" FOUR QUARTERS, IX (Jan 1960), 29-36.
Contrary to what some critics have maintained—Irving Howe, in particular—JC's *The Secret Agent* and *Under Western Eyes* are not aesthetic and political failures because the novelist failed to describe what "really happens in the world of anarchism." "If . . . one recognizes that the anarchists are only part of the general immorality and intellectual wasteland of the pre-World War One scene, then one can see them in a more reasonable perspective. . . . [A] more realistic presentation of anarchy, rather than adding to the aesthetic truth of the novel, might have shifted the entire theme to something that was never intended, to something more topical but less significant." "Moral anarchy is the subject and ironic humor the method" of *Agent*—as JC himself suggested in his "Note" to the work. His treatment of London as the depressing wasteland background for Winnie Verloc's story was modelled after Dickens. JC's "aim is the castigation of modern life, particularly the middle-class worship of science and materialism and the drab world it has built for itself." His ironic handling of Verloc "comes to support the major theme of the novel." In *Agent,* "the inability of Winnie and Ossipon to communicate with each other is the inability of science to come to terms with human emotions, the inability of one person to enter into another's tragedy, and, finally, the inability of human beings to be honest even in their relation to each other's feelings. Conrad is forcefully suggesting that a failure in understanding is a concomitant of a failure in morality, and that to communicate with each other, human beings must have not only minds and feelings but also a sense

of ethical conduct that can rise above immediate needs. This belief, and not the criticism of political anarchy, is the fundamental stuff of Conrad's first city novel."

1593 Karl, Frederick R. "Joseph Conrad and HUCKLEBERRY FINN," MARK TWAIN JOURNAL, XI (Summer 1960), 21-23.

The jump in artistic maturity from "Youth" to "Heart of Darkness" is like a similar leap from TOM SAWYER to HUCKLEBERRY FINN. The world of retributive and self-seeking evil in HUCKLEBERRY FINN is comparable to the denigration of humanity and regression presented by JC as Kurtz in "Heart of Darkness" and money-worshipping in nineteenth-century America; to the Congo's leading away from stagnant jungle, the evil shore, and the Mississippi's symbolizing freedom as opposed to the deceit and treachery of the shore; to the recognition by JC and Twain that society is unable to accept raw reality; and the fact that the faith of Huck, like that of Kurtz's fiancée, remains "the only light under a sky 'that seemed to lead into the heart of an immense darkness.'"

1594 Karl, Frederick R. "Joseph Conrad's Literary Theory," CRITICISM, II (Fall 1960), 317-35.

An examination of JC's letters, essays, and notes shows that when he forsook theories "he worked out with Ford" and those in the preface to *The Nigger of the Narcissus*, "his work became thin and uninteresting." His later notes "were almost frivolous for a major novelist intent on . . . his craft." His early theories, worked out with Ford, included his use of *phanopoeia*, which Pound called Imagistic. He and Ford sought "to create a semblance of actual experience." Their "planned novel" was built of steps all pointing to a predetermined end—there was "a novelistic *progression d'effet*." They hoped to suggest "the basic rhythm" of the work in the very first paragraph. The true test of these theories, however, did not come in the collaborations; *Romance* "is only a simple adventure story," although it opens with "a disjointed initial scene." JC's best use of this device was in the fragmentary scenes of *Nostromo* and *Chance*. Monotonous speech had to be livened up and broken. Flaubert and James were models for both men, and there were hints of technique derived from the French Symbolists. JC relied from the first on image and simile "to give a tone beyond a surface realism." He wanted the "clean edges and limpidity of the French." Verbal clarity provided exactitude. "He did not want his extensions of meaning to stem from verbal confusion but rather to be projections from his sense of scene and human psychology." In this "nervous concern" for the exact word he was reflecting his French background. And it is to Flaubert that we return, whose letters "reflect a spirit almost identical with Conrad's." As JC entered his middle period (1904-1914), his images became symbols, his fancy "transmuted into imagination." He realized that "the kinds of subjectivity that fail to project emotive knowledge into objective forms . . . fail to recognize the variability of experience." The result is journalism, not art.

1595 Karl, Frederick R. A READER'S GUIDE TO JOSEPH CONRAD (NY: Noonday P, 1960).
In his "working aesthetic," JC stressed the impersonality of the creator; he maintained that the writer can only suggest, that he must leave "final meanings" to imagination. After 1914, when his "power to conceptualize" and his "ability to imagine his material" had begun to wane, he relied increasingly upon the "props of strictly realistic fiction." Throughout his writing career, he utilized many techniques, several of which he and Ford Madox Ford developed: *phanopoeia, progression d'effet,* the central narrator, the evocative image, and various time-shift techniques. In the early novels, JC was concerned with the evershifting relation between the individual and society and with the role that each must play in conflict with the other: *Lord Jim* displays almost all of JC's favorite technical devices; all of "Heart of Darkness" is structured on a series of "trenchant images" whose cumulative effect provides a frame for Kurtz, whose loss of human responsibility is the center of the story; *Nostromo* is JC's "broadest and most profound" novel. "Middle Conrad" includes *The Secret Agent,* an ironic castigation of modern life; *Under Western Eyes,* in which Razumov tries to "pry himself from human solidarity" so he may go his own way, a decision that inevitably proves self-destructive; "The Secret Sharer," a major story which deals mainly with the theme of "apprenticeship-to-life"; and *Chance* which, although thematically one of JC's most "straight-forward" novels, allows the vast "scaffolding of method" to be more detrimental than constructive. Although *Victory* is the best novel of JC's middle period, it, like *Nostromo,* is aesthetically unsatisfying because of JC's lack of staying power to complete satisfactorily an intensively felt work. Even *The Shadow-Line* remains a minor work, "minor in conception and in execution." With his major works, though, JC stands with Joyce, Lawrence, Mann, Gide, Proust, Kafka, and Faulkner as "one of the significant creative novelists of the twentieth century." [Karl's book, which contained much fresh material at the time of publication, remains an excellent introduction that not only discusses JC's works individually but also provides a valuable commentary on his theory of fiction and his most characteristic methods. Karl's achievement-and-decline approach follows that of Douglas Hewitt (1952), Thomas Moser (1957), and Albert J. Guerard (1947, 1958, 1960).]

1596 Kogur, G. "Nova Suctrich z Dzhozefom Konradom" (A New Meeting with Joseph Conrad), VSE LITERATURA (Kiev), No. 4 (1960), 133-34.
[In Ukrainian.]

1597 Krieger, Murray. "Joseph Conrad: Action, Inaction, and Extremity," THE TRAGIC VISION: VARIATIONS ON A THEME IN LITERARY INTERPRETATION (NY: Holt, Rinehart, and Winston, 1960), pp. 154-194, 13, 14, 19, 129, 251, 263, 266.

(1). The Varieties of Extremity: In the contrast between Kurtz and Marlow ("Heart of Darkness"), JC schematized relations between representatives of ethical and tragic realms. Marlow has the "innate strength" and "restraint" JC speaks of. Marlow restrains himself from joining the dancing and howling natives on the bank because of practicability (he had to fix the leaky steam pipes) and subordinates all to his repair of the steamboat. His distrust of action on principle and Kurtz's abandoned embrace of principle place these two men at extremities. Yet, Marlow recognizes Kurtz's achievement of insight and ultimate victory, and he involves himself, however partially, with Kurtz's experience by lying to the woman he cherishes. In this concession to Kurtz, Marlow delineates the tragic vision, beyond which JC cannot go even in *Lord Jim*. Thus, JC detests facts because they are deceptive and because ultimately they cannot convey human experience which JC conveys by manipulating point of view. JC works out the theme of common guilt in recording Jim's effect on others. The judges at Jim's trial as well as Marlow feel guilt—recognizing that Jim is one of them. In turn, Jim, who as a romantic cannot exclude anyone from his circle, sees himself in Brown, the murderer. With this insight, Jim refuses to act. But action, even the act of refusing to act, is devil's work according to Heyst and leads not out of the dilemma, but rather toward the tragic.

(2). *Victory:* Pseudo Tragedy and the Failure of Vision: In *Victory* JC vitiates Heyst's world view (resisting human involvement). Lena's sacrifice thrusts Heyst into a new sense of dream and life, and his grasp of reality, that of his father, which transformed the world into delusion, weakens. Heyst discovers the enmity of the world his father had recognized when he has once yielded to Lena and shows this attitude when he recognizes the deluge—the jolt from secure comfort which reveals cosmic caprice—her vision above the sea. The "good-natured, lazy fellow of a volcano" in its stillness is an analogue to the inactive Heyst who threatens to "explode." Agents who contribute to the indifferent cosmos are "envoys of the outer world," like Mr. Jones, the ghost, and Wang, the Chinese, who in refusing Lena and Heyst sanctuary, show the indifference of an organized community pursuing its own welfare. The novel follows Heyst into the ranges of isolation outside the human communion and his return through self-commitment to Lena and total commitment to the warmth that destroys. We learn that commitment and the action to which it leads are fatal, but only to Heyst, who couldn't accept them totally. JC, discontented with the tragic vision, tried to create tragedy in Heyst and his sacrifice, but he had to come back to the ethical existence of his characters.

1598 Leiter, Louis H. "Echo Structures: Conrad's 'The Secret Sharer,'" TWENTIETH CENTURY LITERATURE, V (Jan 1960), 159-75; rptd in APPROACHES TO THE SHORT STORY, ed by Neil D. Isaacs and Louis H. Leiter (San Francisco: Chandler, 1963), pp. 185-208.

Although it is generally agreed that the Captain and Leggatt "are one person figuratively," it has not been noted that there are also "echo structures" of narration, parable, and metaphor. An echo structure "implies one or more structures similar to itself. The tautology which is the echo structure may be a repeated symbol, metaphor, scene, pattern of action, state of being, myth, fable, or archetype," which may be of four varieties: image cluster, parable, action, and archetype. The opening sentences and those describing the captain's attempts to raise the ladder which Leggatt is hanging on to are related. [Specific illustrations follow.]

1599 Lewis, R. W. B. "The Current of Conrad's *Victory:* Conrad, 1915," TWELVE ORIGINAL ESSAYS ON GREAT ENGLISH NOVELS, ed by Charles Shapiro (Detroit: Wayne State U P, 1960), pp. 203-31; rptd in TRIALS OF THE WORD (New Haven: Yale U P, 1965), pp. 148-69.

The basis of *Victory* is "a profound conflict rooted in opposition and likeness." JC makes "real and visible the manifold *and* unitary truth of things." Forster was right in asserting that JC "had no 'creed'—no coherent order of intellectual principles"; the main aim of the novel is to observe the human condition "in the way of art." *Victory* "is Conrad's test of the nature of fiction: in general, of the ability of drama to move towards allegory while retaining its identity as fictional form and essence; and in particular, the ability of fiction to move towards drama while retaining its identity as fictional narrative." Whereas *Nostromo* is JC's " 'most anxiously meditated work,' . . . with a greatness so complex and extensive that only belatedly and partially has it become appreciated [,] *Victory* is a triumph of a different kind, of a nearly opposite kind." *Nostromo,* like KING LEAR, is "made up of a variety of parallel plots and involve[s] several different groups of persons"; it illustrates what Fergusson calls "action by analogy." In *Victory,* "the action emerges directly from the peculiar temperaments of a few eccentric individuals." Literally accidental incidents are "symbolically inevitable and dramatically appropriate." "Each of the main figures in *Victory* has his of her private plan. . . . In human terms, the separate plans are catastrophically irreconcilable, and in their difference they provide the 'manifold' truth. . . . But artistically, they form a living pattern of parallels and contrasts, and so provide the unitary truth Conrad equally envisaged."

Jones's plan is "the least reconcilable of all the plans"; that of Lena, who "can formulate her own plot and purpose to herself with exactness," has "the most coherent" plot; and that of Heyst, who is central, reveals him in a series of complex relationships (with Lena and Ricardo, Morrison and Lena, Heyst and Jones). "The action disclosed by the effect" of Lena, Heyst, and Jones "upon each other is the gradual location" of "a dimension beyond the dimension occupied by all other persons in the book." The domain of reality and truth "lies somewhere between the . . . intellectualism of Heyst and the deathiness [sic] of Jones." "The form of *Victory* grows dramatic, and it gives forth intimations of allegory. But . . . it never fails to take account of the variable and highly unpredictable character of individual human beings."

1600 Marsh, D. R. C. "Moral Judgments in *The Secret Agent*," ENGLISH STUDIES IN AFRICA (Johannesburg), III (March 1960), 57-70.

JC condemns anarchists because they live lives of illusion, unaware that their moral judgments are contaminated by self-interest. They have no capacity for loyalty and place no value on life itself. [Analyzes character portrayals.]

1601 Martin, Sister M. "Conrad's 'Typhoon,'" EXPLICATOR, XVIII (June 1960), Item 57.

Part of Captain MacWhirr's strength comes from his ability to see things as things, to be aware of "the indifference of matter."

1602 Morey, John Hope. "Joseph Conrad and Ford Madox Ford: A Study in Collaboration," DISSERTATION ABSTRACTS, XXI (1960), 1568-69. Unpublished thesis, Cornell University, 1960.

1603 Newman, Paul B. "Joseph Conrad and the Ancient Mariner," KANSAS MAGAZINE (1960), 79-83.

Life-in-Death, defined by Erich Maria Remarque in SPARK OF LIFE as that ghostlike state into which a man is transformed on account of suffering or despair, lurks in JC's novels. In *The Shadow Line,* it is suggested by the lunatic first mate and the wasted mariners, and by the compulsion to confess. ["A Confession" is the sub-title of the novel, based on the same experience which gave birth to "The Secret Sharer."] Quitting his position on the steamship and taking a post aboard a sailing ship, JC subjects himself to a test which brings him across "the shadow-line," destroying his youthful illusions. He has, in Coleridge's terms, killed the albatross, and he "carries it around his neck like the symbol of a lapsed belief." Winning his command of a sailboat, JC leaves behind the world of his discontent; however, his ship is illfated: the malarial first mate with glittering eyes confronts JC with a vision of Life-in-Death. The former captain of the ship, who had tried to destroy it and the crew, lies buried, and like the underwater spirit in "The Ancient Mariner," he impedes the progress of the ship, at least according to the mate. JC is convinced that his difficulties are the result of evil in the mind of the insane, not chance. He blames himself for the ordeal. Being the only well man on the ship, he is tortured by guilt, taking any mention of fever by the crew as a self-reproach. His remorse increases, and he feels he is going mad. This disintegration of the man contributes to the central vision in the story, one prevalent in most of his stories: "the corruptibility and mortality of man's spirit." Ransome, the ship's cook, always kind to the crew, serves as a kind of ransom for JC and "the sanity for the human race" when insanity is prevalent aboard, helping JC to face his problem decisively. Captain Giles, instrumental in getting JC this command, summarizes the moral: a man should assert himself in the face of bad luck and conscience. In *Shadow-Line,* "an ironic re-telling of 'The Ancient Mariner,' " JC draws a picture of himself as sensitive and self-demanding in which empathy in conjunction with conscience destroys self-assertion. Redemption lies in courage —knowing weakness, facing the uncaring universe. Regeneration lies in a renewal of self-assertion that is "in balance with empathy in any active faith." [Newman talks about the narrator as if he were JC.]

1604 Owen, Guy. "Conrad's 'The Lagoon,' " EXPLICATOR, XVIII (May 1960), Item 47.

The story is "not *about* a purge or a betrayal: it is a story of love, of the conflict of love and duty." Arsat sacrifices the world to win a woman; "Conrad thought the price too great."

1605 Phillipson, John S. "Conrad's Pink Toads: The Working of the Unconscious," WESTERN HUMANITIES REVIEW, XIV (Autumn 1960), 437-38.

The hallucination of pink toads experienced by the chief engineer of the *Patna* (*Lord Jim,* Ch. 5) is "a symbol of the eight hundred pilgrims." Four speculations as to why JC used toads instead of snakes, the more usual reptile, are: (1) toads, like human beings, have legs; (2) legs suggest flight from death and the horror of the drowning pilgrims; (3) toads are ugly as the contortions of the drowning pilgrims would be ugly; (4) the easy confusion of toads and frogs makes possible the connection between frogs croaking, and *croak* means to die, a slang meaning which goes back to 1812.

1606 Rees, Richard. "The Unobscure Conrad," FOR LOVE OR MONEY: STUDIES IN PERSONALITY AND ESSENCE (Lond: Secker & Warburg; Carbondale: Southern Illinois U P, 1960), pp. 124-29.

The way in which much that is really uncomplicated about JC's writing is misconstrued, misinterpreted or overlooked by critics, is illustrated by

The Shadow-Line, its preface and motto: "Worthy of my undying regard." [Rees recounts his personal contact with the novelist, quotes from a letter JC wrote to him, and adds a few remarks on "Youth."]

1607 Robinson, E. Arthur. "Conrad's 'The Secret Sharer,'" EXPLICATOR, XVIII (Feb 1960), Item 28.
The crucial problem of both figures is to "assimilate certain qualities from each other." Leggatt learns to understand; the captain gains "courage to act despite the danger of doing evil, plus, no doubt, a lesson in self-control."

1608 Sawyer, Arthur Edward. "Tragedy in the Fiction of Joseph Conrad." Unpublished thesis, University of Toronto, 1960.

1609 Stallman, R. W. (ed). THE ART OF JOSEPH CONRAD: A CRITICAL SYMPOSIUM (East Lansing: Michigan State U P, 1960). Contents, abstracted separately under date of first publication: R. W. Stallman, "Introduction" (1960); André Gide, "Joseph Conrad," from NOUVELLE REVUE FRANÇAISE (1924); H.-R. Lenormand, "Note on a Sojourn of Conrad in Corsica," trans from "Note sur un séjour de Conrad en Corse," NOUVELLE REVUE FRANÇAISE (1924); Ramón Fernández, "The Art of Conrad," trans from "L'art de Conrad," NOUVELLE REVUE FRANÇAISE (1924); John Shand, "Some Notes on Joseph Conrad," from CRITERION, III (Oct 1924); M. D. Zabel, "Chance and Recognition," from SEWANEE REVIEW (1945); Czeslaw Miłosz, "Joseph Conrad in Polish Eyes," from ATLANTIC MONTHLY (1957); Thomas Moser, "Conrad's Voyeur-Villains," from JOSEPH CONRAD: ACHIEVEMENT AND DECLINE (1957); John D. Gordan, "The Four Sources," from JOSEPH CONRAD: THE MAKING OF A NOVELIST (1940); Vernon Young, "Lingard's Folly: The Lost Subject," from KENYON REVIEW (1953); Vernon Young, "Trial by Water: Joseph Conrad's *The Nigger of the 'Narcissus,'* " from ACCENT (1952); Albert J. Guerard, *"The Nigger of the 'Narcissus'"* from KENYON REVIEW (1957); Gustav Morf, "On Lord Jim," from THE POLISH HERITAGE OF JOSEPH CONRAD (1930); Dorothy Van Ghent, "On Lord Jim," from THE ENGLISH NOVEL (1953); Jerome Thale, "Marlow's Quest," from UNIVERSITY OF TORONTO QUARTERLY (1955); Lillian Feder, "Marlow's Descent into Hell," from NINETEENTH-CENTURY FICTION (1955); Robert O. Evans, "Conrad's Underworld," from MODERN FICTION STUDIES (1956); "Three Notes on 'Heart of Darkness' ": (1) William Bysshe Stein, "The Lotus Posture and the 'Heart of Darkness,' " from MODERN FICTION STUDIES (1956); (2) Seymour Gross, "A Further Note on the Function of the Frame in 'Heart of Darkness,' " from MODERN FICTION STUDIES (1957); and (3) Robert O. Evans, "Further Comment on 'Heart of Darkness,' " from MODERN FICTION STUDIES (1957); William Moynihan, "Conrad's 'The End of the Tether': A New Reading," from MODERN

Joseph Conrad

Fiction Studies (1958); F. R. Leavis, "On 'Typhoon' and *The Shadow-Line*," from The Great Tradition (1948; see 1941); Gustav Morf, "On *Nostromo*," from The Polish Heritage of Joseph Conrad (1930); Robert Penn Warren, "On *Nostromo*," from introduction to *Nostromo* (Modern Library, 1951; see Sewanee Review [1951]); Thomas Mann, "Conrad's *The Secret Agent*" [an excerpt], from Past Masters and Other Papers (1933); see "Vorwort," Der Geheimagent [1926]; R. W. Stallman, "Time and *The Secret Agent*," from Texas Studies in Literature and Language (1959); John Howard Wills, "Adam, Axel, and 'Il Conde,'" from Modern Fiction Studies (1955); Albert J. Guerard, *"Under Western Eyes,"* from Conrad the Novelist (1958); R. W. Stallman, "Conrad and 'The Secret Sharer,'" from Accent (1949); Douglas Hewitt, "The Secret Sharer," from Conrad: A Reassessment (1952); Edward Crankshaw, "Joseph Conrad: *Chance*," from Joseph Conrad: Some Aspects of the Art of the Novel (1936); Douglas Hewitt, "Conrad, A Reassessment: *Chance*," from Conrad: A Reassessment (1952); M. C. Bradbrook, "The Hollow Men: *Victory*," from Joseph Conrad: Poland's English Genius (1941); Paul L. Wiley, "The Knight: Man in Eden: *The Arrow of Gold*," from Conrad's Measure of Man (1954); Thomas Moser, "On *The Rescue*," from Joseph Conrad: Achievement and Decline (1957); Thomas Moser, "On *The Rover* and *Suspense*," from Conrad: Achievement and Decline (1957); Appendix I, consisting of A. J. H., "Joseph Conrad: A Biographical Note," from Collected Edition (Lond: Dent, var dates), at end of several volumes [not abstracted]; "The Works of Joseph Conrad: A Chronological List," from Collected Edition (Lond: Dent, var dates) [not abstracted]; "Bibliographies on Conrad" [not abstracted]; "Chronology of Composition" [not abstracted]; and Appendix II, consisting of Jocelyn Baines, "The Affair in Marseilles," from London Magazine (1957); "Letter of Thaddeus Bobrowski" [not abstracted]. [This collection contains many of the best statements about JC and his work through 1959.]

1610 Stallman, R. W. "Introduction," The Art of Joseph Conrad: A Critical Symposium, ed by R. W. Stallman (East Lansing: Michigan State U P, 1960), pp. ix-xxix.

That which counts for notable literary interest is the complexity of JC. *The Secret Agent* is JC's best written novel. JC is "interesting because of the contradictions in the man and in his works." Articles and works which "score very useful insights" are: John D. Gordon, Joseph Conrad: The Making of a Novelist (1940), "a landmark"; Albert J. Guerard, "The Voyages of Captain Korzeniowski," Reporter, XVI (21 March 1957), 42-44, and Conrad the Novelist (1958), "best summary of JC's achievement"; Douglas Hewitt, Conrad: A Reassessment (1952), "the best of its kind";

F. R. Leavis, "Revaluations . . . ," SCRUTINY, X (June, Oct 1941), 22-50, 157-81; and Thomas Moser, JOSEPH CONRAD: ACHIEVEMENT AND DECLINE (1957). [Critical Survey of JC's reputation, 1924-1959.]

1611 Stavrou, C. N. "Conrad, Camus, and Sisyphus," AUDIENCE, VII (Winter 1960), 80-96.

The thought of JC and Albert Camus is similar in certain ways: in *Lord Jim,* for example, a speech by Stein is "existential" in that both commitment and acting out the commitment are necessary, and Jim and Mersault (in THE STRANGER) bear out closely in their deeds and words Sartre's conceptions of being and nothingness. The starting point for JC and Camus is often the isolation of the individual, and the "moderation and temperance" expressed by Camus are considered as "virtues and right guides to conduct" in many of JC's works. Also, "the humanism of Conrad and Camus consists basically in their awareness, and poignant portrayal, of Pascalian Man," although in their fiction "man's misery is more in evidence than man's grandeur." Both writers begin with a position of pessimism and/or nihilism, then make "brilliant endeavors" to advance from this position to "another position more commensurate with their faith in man as sole arbiter of his destiny." JC never succeeded in "banishing the bugbear of a Melville universe." He is "in perfect accord with" some aspects of Camus's humanism. His cynicism "could be relegated to the limbo where Camus has consigned most of the contemporary nihilisms which tempted him, were it not the oblique expression of a deep-seated faith in man and in man's capacity for compassion, courage, loyalty, and self-appraisal." Even in his "darker works" (*Nostromo, The Secret Agent,* and *Chance*) "an implicit affirmation of life's primal glory" resides. JC expresses best in practice what he professed in theory in "Heart of Darkness": "the ambivalence Marlow experiences in regard to Kurtz is the ambivalence Conrad experienced toward man and the world he lives in." But Lord Jim is undoubtedly "the most vivid and memorable" of JC's characters; at first he overestimates his strength and fails to reckon with his weakness, but in his second attempt he is not found wanting. [Gives convincingly greater importance to *Jim* than do many critics.]

1612 Watt, Ian. "Story and Idea in Conrad's *The Shadow-Line*," CRITICAL QUARTERLY, II (Summer 1960), 133-48; rptd in revised form in MODERN BRITISH FICTION: ESSAYS IN CRITICISM, ed by Mark Schorer (NY: Oxford U P, 1961), pp. 119-36.

JC's values are neither ethical nor normative, in the usual sense, and critics who complain are misguided. Because JC has no "philosophy," his work seems to fall far short in conceptual analysis. The truth is that he pretends to no more "than partial glimpses of any universals." The vacillations of *The Shadow-Line,* frequently seen as a failure in craftsmanship, in fact "constitute a series of concrete enactments of the narrator's initial reactions to the ironic social and spiritual divisions which are Conrad's theme." The darkness and immobility symbols require little explanation: "the increment of suspense and pictorial vividness would be justified for its own sake. . . . But if one looks for larger meanings, for symbolic representations of universal elements . . . , there are several. . . . The calm before the storm, and the intensified darkness that precedes dawn, are well enough established commonplaces of human experience." The calm has a psychological parallel with the narrator's "prolonged inward lethargy." Further, the rhythm of alternating calm and storm parallels the "duality of rest and work" in the human sphere. What JC evokes through these complex symbolic designs is an "historical dimension of the theme of human solidarity; the narrator, having been deprived, first through the loneliness of command, and then through darkness, of the support of his fellows, is brought face to face with the long tradition of civilisation since the creation, and his own utter dependence on it." JC's shadow-line deals with "a host of different social and individual and historical circumstances" which is crossed whenever "youth's idealised image of the world, of itself, and its own destiny is penetrated and modified by its sense of solidarity with those who, in the past and in the present, continue man's struggle against all the powers of darkness and anarchy which pervade the natural, the historical, the social, and the personal order. And Conrad is being realistic rather than ironic . . . in presenting all the forces opposed to human solidarity so powerfully." We do not select which "solidarities with the past and present" we prefer; we "come to them—as we come into the world—involuntarily and unconsciously: are usually, indeed, dragged into them, screaming."

1613 Wilcox, Stewart C. "Conrad's 'Complicated Presentations' of Symbolic Imagery in 'Heart of Darkness,' " PHILOLOGICAL QUARTERLY, XXXIX (Jan 1960), 1-17.

"The metaphor of the whited sepulchre . . . interpenetrates both the narrative theme of economic exploitation and the archetypal theme of Marlow's exploration of himself," and achieves a combination with the motif of moral purification in the Buddha posture "so as ironically to blend Christian morality into its oriental religious implications." The source of the image (Matthew 23: 27-28) warns against the evils which make modern Christians as contemptible as the scribes and Pharisees in the time of Christ. When Marlow lies to the Intended, JC's use of whiteness is symbolic of "timeless purity and fidelity" in contrast to the word "whited" in the image of the sepulchre or to "white worsted" as a sign for "vicious capitalism." Throughout "Heart of Darkness," JC manipulates the evocation of atmosphere by means of images which become "fluid, variable, mutually interrelated," like his conception of Time. Since truth is eternal, it must be "stripped of its cloak of time"; and this is what Kurtz does when he finally exclaims with horror at the time of his self-realization. Marlow, in order to be freed from time, has to travel far back into the depths of his own and of his racial consciousness. His journey occurs on a river to time. JC's "complicated presentations" have basic functions: "the interplay of their imagery gives rise to the resonances of the recorded events—tomb, whiteness, blackness and darkness, bones, ivory, Time, nightmare, all contribute in their various meanings and overtones to a full understanding of Kurtz's tragedy and Marlow's journey in seach of himself."

JC's method seldom begins with the symbol; it creates instead the desired atmosphere from the implications of images. Kurtz, for example, ending his journey in night, is in a sepulchre of his own making; and he is Marlow's double, a double to be faced if he is to know himself. Marlow ironically lies to the Intended because of his compassion for her; and his lie affirms a moral significance beyond himself, a value which JC calls an "illusion." The tragic irony of the story is that a modern civilization of hypocrites professes to bring progress to remote regions in the name of Christ who "drove forth the Pharisees." "Heart of Darkness" is, then, "an extended parable damning man's inhumanity to man, the highest hope of mankind lying in the sort of self-purification exemplified by Marlow." Its pattern illustrated JC's view of man moving in space and in Time in a search for "the illumination of values." [With earlier scholarship as a background, Wilcox adds new and valuable insights to a story that has almost innumerable possibilities of interpretation.]

1614 Wilkening, Vjera. "Die Erzählsituation der Ich-Form in Werke Joseph Conrads" (The Narrative Situation of the I-Form in Works by Joseph Conrad). Unpublished thesis, University of Berlin, 1960.

[In German.]

1615 Wright, Elizabeth Cox. "The Defining Function of Vocabulary in Conrad's *The Rover*," SOUTH ATLANTIC QUARTERLY, LIX (Spring 1960), 265-77.

Despite the contradictory assessments of *The Rover*, "the theme is one of traditional importance, and . . . , in so far as the vocabulary defines it, it is recreated with particularity, subtlety, and power." The book is "neither a boy's adventure story nor a lurid melodrama"; the narrative uses the mythical materials of "the hero's unknown paternity, his exile . . . return . . . fall . . . victory . . . and his undocumented death."

It is the earlier novels that are guilty of JC's "repetition of long, loose polysyllables, abstract nouns with vague ethical or emotional connotations, and inflated adjectives suggesting horror, mystery, immensity." JC's vocabulary in *Rover* is less idiosyncratic and more precise. Five aspects of this vocabulary are: (1) the French words for the French background; (2) technical terms of seamanship; (3) the argot and colloquialisms that characterize Peyrol; (4) the use of single sensory details with exactness; (5) "Another kind of sensory impression [which] is quite different in character and function; it includes certain objects and colors schematically used, but at the same time, distinctly visible or solidly tactual." Although the basic character of this vocabulary does not change, "a chronological view reveals a movement from the exact and realistic words to an intermingling of fact and suggestion. Coinciding with this movement is an intensification of feeling associated with the archetypal undercurrents."

1616 Zabel, Morton Dauwen. "Introduction," THE MIRROR OF THE SEA AND A PERSONAL RECORD (Garden City, NY: Doubleday, Anchor Books, 1960), pp. ix-xlix.

JC was open and intimate about himself in his letters and at the same time reserved about himself in his literary memoirs. The antithesis of these two aspects "contributed to his radical quality as a novelist." Using JC's changing terms of *The Mirror of the Sea*—"sketches," "bosh," "a very intimate revelation"—reveals that this kind of discrepancy "between self-deprecation at the time of writing and a later high-keyed apologetic is a recurring strain in Conrad's judgment of his work." *A Personal Record* is JC's best work of non-fictional prose; in it he focuses on the three turning points of his career: (1) leaving Poland; (2) his French adventures in Marseilles and turning to the sea; (3) the adoption of literature as a profession. Two other factors that were almost of equal significance were his experience of the East and his becoming a British subject. *Almayer's Folly* is the work of a mature, "instructed craftsman."

1617 Zabel, Morton Dauwen. "Introduction," TALES OF HEROES AND HISTORY (NY: Doubleday, Anchor Books, 1960), pp. vii-xlv.

During JC's first phase as a writer he used the materials of the East and of the sea. His best work with these materials was done in the period 1895-1903. After 1902 JC turned to subjects of "modern life and politics" (*Nostromo, The Secret Agent, Under Western Eyes,* and *Chance*). The nine tales—"An Outpost of Progress," "Gaspar Ruiz," "An Anarchist," "The Informer," "The Duel," "Prince Roman," "The Inn of the Two Witches," "The Warrior's Soul" and "The Tale"—supplement the four novels. The general meaning of JC's tales of heroes and history may be something like the following: "history is a long tale of high ideas brought to degradation, of heroic purpose brought to defeat or humiliation, and of human pride subjected to doubt, grief, and mortification," and "Conrad's general view of history, past or present, hinges on a persistent and incurable doubt—an inveterate suspicion of the passions that animate it; a fear of the selfish, irrational, or predatory forces it unleashes to prey on the pride and honor of men and societies; a repugnant sense of its hostility to the truth and decency in the conscience of the hero or man of honor."

1961

1618 Adams, Robert M. "Views on Conrad," PARTISAN REVIEW, XXVIII (Jan Feb 1961), 124-30.
Jocelyn Baines, in JOSEPH CONRAD: A CRITICAL BIOGRAPHY (1959), should have explained the relation of his book to Georges Jean-Aubry's work, which it closely resembles when dealing with JC's life. Baines's biography is, however, superior to others in some strictly biographical matters of considerable importance; but it is deficient in its several "surprising oversights and obliquities," and it "strikes a hollow note as criticism." Some of JC's works are great imaginative fiction even if they are seriously flawed, but from them all the reader remembers the real poetry that is there. If JC had resolved all the problems which he raised, we would be much poorer in our perception of his stories: some of the power of his "evocation must depend on its incompleteness." [A bit severe with Baines but perceptive, within limits, of JC's achievement.]

1619 Basner, Peter. "Stephen Crane and Joseph Conrad," KLEINE BEITRAGE ZUR AMERIKANISCHEN LITERATURGESCHICHTE: ARBEITSPROBEN AUS DEUTSCHEN SEMINAREN UND INSTITUTEN (Little Contributions to American Literary History: Specimens from German Seminars and Institutes), ed by Hans Galinsky and Hans-Joachim Land (Heidelberg: Winter, 1961), pp. 34-39.
JC considered Crane his literary senior and relied on him for moral support. And yet his "philosophy of life as well as his theorizing on problems of artistic creation show a higher degree of maturity." JC emphasized the importance of intuition and the powers of suggestion in art. His insistence on fidelity to purpose led him to adopt Henry James's theory of "perfect indifference." He called Crane inspired because his delicate sense of craftsmanship and his belief in the mysterious interconnection of things came close to his own ideal. But Crane always remained to some degree prone to superficiality. "While thinking of Crane and Conrad, one is reminded of the similar friendship of Hawthorne and Melville, in which the superior man also showed a strange appreciation of the inferior's artistic capabilities." [Useful summary of well-known facts.]

1620 Bates, H. E. THE MODERN SHORT STORY: A CRITICAL SURVEY (Boston: The Writer, 1961), pp. 35, 66, 105, 119, 141-42, 182-83.

JC is outside the mainstream of the English short story because he "lacked the art of compression." Most of his stories belong to the genre of the long short story; his themes are big, and his methods are those employed in his novels.

1621 Beker, Miroslav. "Virginia Woolf's Appraisal of Joseph Conrad," STUDIA ROMANICA ET ANGLICA ZAGRABIENSIA (Zagreb), No. 12 (1961), 17-22.

Virginia Woolf's attitudes to JC in her essays and reviews provide a touchstone of her critical sensibility. However acute some of her judgments on JC's art and the shifts in his vision, her appraisal of *Nostromo* is inadequate, and she never mentions *Under Western Eyes* because these works do not square with her insistence on small matters being "reality" and "life."

1622 Bojarski, Edmund A. "Joseph Conrad's Polish Soul," THEORIA, XVI (1961), 41-46; rptd in ENGLISH STUDIES (Amsterdam), XLIV (Dec 1963), 431-37.

Published for the first time in English, a report of a young Polish journalist, Marian Dabrowski [sic], who was probably the first "foreign pressman" to interview JC (in 1914), finds JC striking in appearance: his eyes "had peered into the depths of the soul of the earth, into the depths of the sea." The two Poles realized that they shared certain qualities in common, "something incomprehensible, unfathomable, impalpable"—characteristics which marked their "Polishness." JC declared that he was, "strictly speaking," a seaman and "the last of the romantics." He admitted that there burned in him the "immortal fire" of the Polish people, but two facts filled him with pride: "that I, a Pole, am a captain in the English merchant navy, and that I don't write badly in English." [The report of the Polish journalist remains unidentified.]

1623 Booth, Wayne C. THE RHETORIC OF FICTION (Chicago: University of Chicago P, 1961), pp. 10, 40, 57, 152, 154, 189, 191, 192, 197, 274, 286, 297, 346.

Marlow, unlike the "I" of TOM JONES, THE EGOIST, and TROILUS AND CRISEYDE, is a "narrator-agent" who produces "some measurable effect on the course of events." As a narrator, Marlow is scarcely distinguishable from JC, and can therefore be taken as a reliable commentator.

1624 Brown, Douglas. "From 'Heart of Darkness' to *Nostromo:* An Approach to Conrad," THE MODERN AGE. The Pelican Guide to English Literature, Vol. 7, ed by Boris Ford (Baltimore: Penguin

Books, 1961); 2nd ed (1963); rptd (Lond: Cassell, Belle Sauvage Library, 1964), pp. 119-37, and scattered refs.

One must approach JC's fiction on its own terms. The effect of the Jungian approach is "to falsify and simplify the truth of his art, and not surprisingly the plain force of his tales often gets obscured, too." [A concise analysis of "Heart of Darkness."]

1625 Bruccoli, Matthew J., and Charles A. Rheault, Jr. "Imposition Figures and Plate Gangs in *The Rescue*," STUDIES IN BIBLIOGRAPHY: PAPERS OF THE BIBLIOGRAPHICAL SOCIETY OF THE UNIVERSITY OF VIRGINIA (Charlottesville: University Press of Virginia, 1961), XIV, 258-62.

When a second edition of *The Rescue* was published in 1920 by J. M. Dent in England (the original publication having been in America), a first impression of forty copies from standing type was distributed by the publisher for review. These copies are, in fact, proofs. In addition to textual alterations, a "curious" system of numbers was placed in the lower right corners of certain pages. These numbers are imposition keys, and the pages were ganged (i.e., "four pages were cast as a single large plate and reckoned as one plate in the imposition"). The English printer may have marked the press bed or cylinder with a key figure and then put the same figure on the gang. *Rescue* was not printed in London as originally planned; the printing was done at the Temple Press in Letchworth, where the workmen, being unfamiliar with the use of imposition figures, failed to remove them when printing the trade copies of the novel.

1626 Cassell, Richard A. FORD MADOX FORD: A STUDY OF HIS NOVELS (Baltimore: The Johns Hopkins P, 1961), pp. 20-21, 32-33, 35-36, 43-72, 206, and passim.

By 1898, when JC stated his aesthetic theory in the preface to *The Nigger of the Narcissus,* Ford "had developed similar criteria and attitudes." JC "added substance to the impressionistic novel by the demands of his artistic conscience." Both men learned much from Flaubert; both believed technique, the *how,* to be more important than the subject, the *what;* and both believed the novel must aspire to "the magic suggestiveness of music." Ford had some reservations about JC's later work, which he thought had too much the incompleteness of a de Maupassant *conte.* Both writers "had trouble toning down their language," but both tried "to achieve a nonliterary, nonpoetic vocabulary." [Contains references to *Chance,* "Heart of Darkness," *Lord Jim, Nigger, Nostromo, The Secret Agent, The Sisters, Suspense,* and *Under Western Eyes.*]

1627 Cox, Roger Lindsay. "Master and Man: A Study of Conrad's *Nostromo*," DISSERTATION ABSTRACTS, XXII (1961), 255. Unpublished thesis, Columbia University, 1961.

1628 Croft-Cooke, Rupert. "Introduction," *Nostromo: A Tale of the Seaboard* (San Francisco: ptd for the Limited Editions Club; NY: Heritage P, 1961), pp. ix-xvii.

JC, seeming to have been nagged throughout his life by a "half-conscious remorse" caused by his deserting Poland for the sea and literature, reveals implicitly the theme of betrayal and atonement in *Nostromo,* especially in the stories of Nostromo himself and of Dr. Monygham. *Nostromo* is different from JC's other works in that heretofore JC had been concerned with the individual whereas in this book he "takes a diversity of creatures, sets them against running history," and makes them part of the public life of a disturbed country. In this instance, JC comes nearer to achieving objectivity than in any other novel. If no "fully observed, deeply understood, four-dimensional character" appears in *Nostromo,* a large number of people are "shrewdly perceived and admirably portrayed."

1629 Evans, Robert O. "Dramatization of Conrad's *Victory:* And a New Letter," NOTES AND QUERIES, N.S. VIII (March 1961), 108-10.

Baines's discussion of the dramatization of *Victory* (in JOSEPH CONRAD, A CRITICAL BIOGRAPHY [Lond: Weidenfeld and Nicolson, 1959], p. 409) needs modification: "the adaptation by [Macdonald] Hastings was not 'prompted' by [H. B.] Irving, and Conrad's renewed enthusiasm for the stage dates back to midsummer of 1916." This interpretation is supported by an hitherto unpublished letter of JC to H. B. Irving, dated 19 July 1916.

1630 Foulke, Robert Dana. "Conrad's Sea World: The Voyage Fiction and the British Merchant Service, 1875-1895," DISSERTATION ABSTRACTS, XXII (1961), 1173. Unpublished thesis, University of Minnesota, 1961.

1631 Freeman, Rosemary. "Conrad's *Nostromo:* A Source and Its Use," MODERN FICTION STUDIES, VII (Winter 1961-1962), 317-26.

There are several known sources of background and incident for *Nostromo,* and JC's debt, in this novel and (more slightly) in "The End of the Tether," to the MÉMOIRES DE GARIBALDI, translated by Alexandre Dumas (Paris: Michel Lévy, 1860) is notable.

1632 Gossman, Ann M., and George W. Whiting. "The Essential Jim," NINETEENTH-CENTURY FICTION, XVI (June 1961), 75-80.

Whereas Guerard claims that chapters twenty-two to thirty-five of *Lord Jim* mark "the change from passive suffering to adventurous action" and make Jim's "introspections" seem unimportant and detract from "the moral problem and the theme," thereby causing a structural flaw, passages from the serial version of the novel help to demonstrate that Jim's romanticism, which was "potentially either good or bad," gave him his last chance, in which he displayed the characteristic success "of a romantic man who has added alertness to imagination." For this purpose "the development or manifestation of Jim's character in these chapters is essential." "The logic of the final events" proceeded from "deep-seated causes," one of which was "Jim's own nature." "By the edict of his own exalted code, his life was forfeited." But the Jim who jumped from the *Patna* and the Jim who "embraced the darkness as a bride" were "essentially one: the almost primitively youthful romantic, who in turn betrays and fulfills an egoistic but generous and valiant ideal."

> **1633** Graver, Lawrence S. "The Short Stories of Joseph Conrad," Unpublished thesis, University of California, 1961; revd and expd as CONRAD'S SHORT FICTION (Berkeley and Los Angeles, University of California P; Lond: Cambridge U P, 1969).

Contents include "Conrad's First Story," STUDIES IN SHORT FICTION, II (Winter 1965), 164-69; "Conrad's 'The Lagoon,'" EXPLICATOR, XXI (May 1963), Item 70; "Critical Confession and Conrad's 'The End of the Tether,'" MODERN FICTION STUDIES, IX (Winter 1963), 390-93; and "'Typhoon': A Profusion of Similes," COLLEGE ENGLISH, XXIV (Oct 1962), 62-64.

> **1634** Gross, Seymour L. "The Devil in Samburan: Jones and Ricardo in *Victory*," NINETEENTH-CENTURY FICTION, XVI (June 1961), 81-85.

Jones in *Victory* "reflects the familiar characteristics of the Devil as cast-out rebel" and also resembles "the Satan in Job." Heyst, "like Job, although in a different way, is to be tested by the powers of darkness and hatred and negation." Jones is "a temptation that Heyst is subjected to"; Ricardo *is* Schomberg's calumny and cowardice. Ricardo's real hatred of "tame souls" and his great need to "rip them up" are plainly derived from the biblical devil of I Peter 5:8. Lena, who is Magdalene or Alma (Soul), is the opposing force to the allegorical satanic forces. She represents to Heyst an acceptance of life "through transcendent love." JC follows the Bible closely when he depicts Lena's "victory" as that of a woman crushing the serpent's head. On a literal level *Victory* is a tragedy, but on an allegorical level there is real "victory": Lena's "beatific death" is contrasted with "the desperate and despairing suicide of Jones-Ricardo."

> **1635** Gurko, Leo. "Death Journey in *The Nigger of the Narcissus*," NINETEENTH-CENTURY FICTION, XV (March 1961), 301-11; included in Gurko's JOSEPH CONRAD: GIANT IN EXILE (NY: Macmillan, 1962), pp. 68-79.

Just as Mr. Baker, chief mate of the *Narcissus*, steps, in the opening sentence of the book, from his lighted cabin "into the darkness of the quarter-deck," and as the narrator's last view of the crew at the end of the novel "is shrouded in the invisibility of night," so is the voyage of the ship as a whole "a penetration into the tensions, powers, and mysteries of death." And the Nigger "belongs to it [the death journey] literally, just as the other men belong to it symbolically." Wait is "the incarnate symbol of death in the novel, just as Donkin is its active agent." These two men exert upon the crew a "terrifying blackmail which splits open the cosmic order of the ship and threatens to pull it down in ruins." It is as if Captain Allistoun and the officers suggest God, Wait and Donkin "the dark powers," and the crew "common humanity contended for by the two sides in the drama of the fallen angels." Only old Singleton is immune from the disease which is caused on the ship by the moral disorder; throughout the novel he plays the role of a prophet, "a special link between humanity and the cosmos." Although the men at the end of the story practically fade from the scene, "they are reborn on the last page in the memory of the narrator," and thus the death journey is rescued from the oblivion of death "by the illuminations of a novel destined to rank as Conrad's earliest masterpiece."

1636 Herndon, Richard James. "The Collaboration of Joseph Conrad and Ford Madox Ford," DISSERTATION ABSTRACTS, XXI (1961), 3098. Unpublished thesis, Stanford University, 1957.

1637 Hristić, Jovan. "Joseph Conrad, pomorac (Joseph Conrad, Sailor)," *Nostromo,* trans by Svetislav Predić (Belgrade: Prosveta, 1961), pp. 479-90.

[A post-face to the Serbian translation of *Nostromo,* surveying conventional facts of JC's life.] [In Serbo-Croatian.]

1638 Jabłkowska, Róża. "Joseph Conrad, 1857-1924" (Wrocław: Ossolinski National Institute, 1961). Published thesis, University of Warsaw [not seen].

[In Polish.]

1639 Lewis, O[live] S[taples]. AN EXPERIMENT IN CRITICISM (Lond: Cambridge U P, 1961), p. 84.

"A fault in Conrad's *Nostromo* is that we have to read so much pseudo-history before we get to the central matter, for which alone this history exists."

1640 Lordi, R. J. "The Three Emissaries of Evil: Their Psychological Relationship in Conrad's *Victory,*" COLLEGE ENGLISH, XXIII (Nov 1961), 136-40.

Jones, Ricardo, and Pedro should be regarded "as complementary aspects of a single evil and destructive force visited upon Heyst." JC frequently emphasizes "the essential unity" of the three villains, based on the subservience of Ricardo to Jones and of Pedro to both. At first, Ricardo accepts his subservient position to Jones, but Lena's presence on the island finally results in his entirely forgetting his "governor" to attack the woman in Heyst's bungalow. And gradually Ricardo's feelings have changed toward Jones until he appears to be about to kill his master. Jones's shooting Ricardo was probably not incidental, now that both his adherents—"instinctive savagery and brute force"—are dead (Wang has shot Pedro). "It seems appropriate that evil intelligence or the destructive principle, disarmed and powerless, should die. That it should die through the agency of water is of course appropriate to Jones's symbolic reference as Death."

1641 Ludwig, Richard M. "The Reputation of Ford Madox Ford," PMLA, LXXVI (Dec 1961), 544-51.

JC's meeting with Ford in 1898 helped to affirm Ford's interest in impressionism, and it also, with subsequent events, established the *persona* of Ford as collaborator and editor. Some forgotten but important facts about the JC-Ford collaboration offer "proof" of JC's debt to Ford, "both emotional and financial." There was actually no complete break in the friendship of the two men before JC's death in 1924.

1642 MacShane, Frank. "Ford Madox Ford and His Contemporaries: The Techniques of the Novel," ENGLISH FICTION IN TRANSITION, IV: 1 (1961), 2-11.

In his preface to *The Nigger of the Narcissus,* JC states more philosophically what Henry James technically writes to Hugh Walpole: "The primary appeal of art, he [JC] says, is emotional." "Intellectual persuasion is the province of exposition and oratory, but the vision of life provided in a work of fiction relies almost entirely on its emotional impact." "Writers like James, Conrad, and Ford all therefore insisted on adopting a completely aloof point of view, for they believed that the artist as creator could not take sides with his characters." "Behind Wells's irritation with technical concerns [excessive particularity of style—"the exact word and the precise turn of phrase"] lies a serious criticism of the literary methods of James, Conrad, and Ford." [Gives additional references to Ford's JOSEPH CONRAD: A PERSONAL REMEMBRANCE (1924), regarding their collaboration on *The Inheritors.*]

1643 Maksimović, Miodrag. "Joseph Conrad: Srce tame" (Joseph Conrad: "Heart of Darkness"), ILLUSTRVANA POLITIKA (Belgrade), IV: 133 (1961), 39.

[A short review.] [In Serbo-Croatian.]

1644 Masback, Fredric J. "Conrad's Jonahs," COLLEGE ENGLISH, XXII (Feb 1961), 328-33.

The Book of Jonah appealed strongly to JC's imagination because for him "a violation of trust" was extremely serious, and he found such a violation most serious when men on a ship faced destruction from their environment. In *Lord Jim* and "Typhoon," JC deals with men's responsibility to a mass of men; in "The End of the Tether," "Heart of Darkness," and "The Secret Sharer," he "portrays solidarity and trust as it exists man to man." In *The Shadow-Line* and *The Nigger of the Narcissus,* he uses "almost all of the basic ingredients of the Jonah story"; but he does not permit the crews to "forsake their Jonahs," and "without the crew's undertaking the drastic actions which Jonah's shipmates did, the fate of each ship is settled by what happens to the Jonah in the natural course of events." Jonah's shipmates were cowards, but JC knew that "the only hope for man is to act out of courage, out of a conviction of the solidarity of the human race." These books "triumphantly reaffirm a belief in the individual dignity of every human being, even the Jonah."

1645 Michel, Lois A. "The Absurd Predicament in Conrad's Political Novels," COLLEGE ENGLISH, XXIII (Nov 1961), 131-36. JC is an existentialist writer because he "recognizes that each man is subject to inescapable evils of irrational suffering or conflict, guilt, chance, folly and death," which the existentialist philosopher calls "the absurd." For the thoughtful man in JC's works, the greatest evil that can happen is "the loss of personal moral integrity." JC speaks, in his three political novels, in different ways of "the absurdity man must try to assimilate, if not to master." In the characters Gould, Decoud, and Nostromo in *Nostromo,* and in Razumov in *Under Western Eyes,* the "range of attitudes toward the absurd . . . includes a view of persons of admirable intent being wrecked by absurdity." *The Secret Agent* is "the more forceful in its demonstration of the human havoc absurdity causes" because the characters are on a level so low that "there is almost no human communication" among them; they do not realize "the significance of their most important actions." The basic value for an existentialist is "to exist": "Things are worth nothing by themselves; their only significance rests in the spiritual meaning each man discovers in his own form of activity." In *Nostromo,* "this idea is a long diffused revelation"; in *Agent,* "this concept of value is either directly apprehended . . . or it is totally missed" by the reader. Each of the political novels has, furthermore, "certain characters whose 'being-in-the-world' is pervaded by an existentialist apprehension of existence called by Heidegger the 'ecstasies of time' ": they are Mrs. Gould, Winnie Verloc, and Razumov. JC's theme in these novels is that "mind and will are potentially more powerful than the absurdity of the universe; they are capable of inventing values upon which paradoxically men can base triumphant, even though defeated, action." [Thought-provoking in general, but is the vain Nostromo "a person of admirable intent"?]

1646 Morgan, Gerould. "Conrad, Madach et Calderón" (Conrad, Madach and Calderón), ÉTUDES SLAVES ET EST-EUROPÉENNES, VI (August-Winter, 1961), 196-209.

JC's philosophy can be analyzed in terms of existentialism. His second novel, *An Outcast of the Islands,* bore an epigraph ("The greatest shortcoming of man is to be born") from Calderón's LA VIDA ES SUEÑO. Another precursor of JC who resembled him in his typical theme of illusion and in his rejection of logic is Cardinal Nicholas de Cues of the fifteenth century, who, as an anti-rationalist, had influenced Hegel and his followers in the romantic movement, especially Novalis and Schelling. JC also shares a negative philosophy with the nineteenth-century Hungarian romantic poet Madach. [In French.]

1647 Resink, G. J. "De excentrieke Lord Jim" (Eccentric Lord Jim), DE GIDS, CXXIV (March 1961), 178-80.

There are some impressive parallels between MAX HAVELAAR and *Lord Jim.* In MAX HAVELAAR, Stern, who is a partial incarnation of Multatuli, "composed" fifteen of the twenty chapters; his relation to the author and his important narrative role obviously anticipate similar aspects of Marlow in *Jim.* In MAX HAVELAAR, the end of the affair in Lebak is revealed to the reader through letters—just as it is by means of a letter that we are informed of Jim's end in Patusan. There is little difference between the names Stern and Stein, and both quote German poetry. Both Jim and Max are bachelors; both of them have gone through a shipwreck, and through a past that makes them prefer the isolation of a distant outpost; they both have a non-European girlfriend. Jim as well as Max gets involved in conflicts between local groups, and both want to promote peace and prosperity among the natives. Both are "marginal men." [MAX HAVELAAR (1860; in English, 1868) is a novel by Eduard Douwes Dekker (pseudonym, Multatuli).] [In Dutch.]

1648 Resink, G. J. "Het Juweel van Landak, Kaatje Stoltes Dochter, en Emma van Heine" (The Jewel of Landak, Kaatje Stolte's Daughter, and Heine's Emma), DE GIDS, CXXIV (1961), 183-87.

In *Lord Jim* we are told about a rumor concerning a "mysterious white man in Patusan" who owned a precious stone of immense value; the rumor was so persistent "that less than forty years ago there had been an official Dutch inquiry into the truth of it." As a matter of fact, in 1822 George Muller was sent as "agent diplomatique" to Borneo, and in 1825 he wrote an official report which includes some interesting information about that "precious stone." Muller regards the whole story as an allegory: a ruler of Landak gave his only and extremely beautiful daughter in marriage to the reigning prince of Succadana and in this way "the greatest and most precious treasure of Landak passed into the possession of Succadana."

Is it not likely that the story was the origin of Cornelius's only daughter and Jim's "Jewel"? Jewel's mother was white and her maternal grandfather was "a high official." Their appearance in a forgotten corner such as Patusan at first appears highly unlikely; however, they seem to have historical antecedents. Kaatje Stolte, daughter of a physician attached to the Dutch East Indies Company, fled into the interior of Sumatra when a French pirate attacked Padang in 1793; she married a native and a daughter was born to them. Doramin's Malayan wife also is historically identifiable. She is the Malayan princess Inche Maida from Perak who married the Buginese Nakoda Trong. Stein's only child was his daughter Emma, who died young. The most likely source of her name is Heine's NEUE GEDICHTE. [In Dutch.]

1649 Resink, G. J. "Marlow-Almayer-Havelaar," DE GIDS, CXXIV (1961), 28-35.

Marlow is a composite figure upon whom several of JC's works throw some light. There is a strong possibility that the original of Marlow in "Youth" was Max Havelaar, protagonist of one of the greatest novels in Dutch literature (MAX HAVELAAR, OR THE COFFEE AUCTIONS OF THE DUTCH TRADING COMPANY, by Eduard Douwes Dekker [pseudonym, Multatuli], 1860; English translation, 1868). One can also detect similarities between such proto-Marlows as the narrator of "Karain" and Max Havelaar's characteristics and way of life. The influence of MAX HAVELAAR is already detectable in *Almayer's Folly*. Both Almayer and Max Havelaar confront the highest Indonesian authorities; the Dutch rulers distrust both protagonists; Almayer and Max are threatened by or afraid of poison. All this seems to indicate that JC must have read MAX HAVELAAR early in his writing career. It also confirms the notion that Kaspar Almayer owed little to the real Charles Olmeijer; he owed more to Havelaar. [In Dutch.]

1650 Resink, G. J. "Stuurman Korzeniowski ontmoet Shawlman" (Steersman Korzeniowski Meets Shawlman), DE GIDS, CXXIV (1961), 107-12.

When Eduard Douwes Dekker (pseudonym, Multatuli) died in February 1887, his book MAX HAVELAAR had been available in an English translation for almost twenty years. In that same bitterly cold February, JC was aboard the *Highland Forest* in Amsterdam. He can hardly have failed to hear of the death of the great Dutch writer. To that time the inception of his literary career is perhaps traceable. It is not impossible that since in MAX HAVELAAR Drystubble "owes" his book to Shawlman (who did not wear a "respectable wintercoat," but a "shawl of plaid"—in spite of the bitter cold of wintry Amsterdam), JC may have *his* Shawlman under the stimulus of his reading MAX HAVELAAR: after all, Almayer, to whom JC "owes" his *oeuvre,* is also dressed far too lightly for that chilly, drizzly morning in Tandjong Redeb when the *Vidar* arrives there. This possibility is supported by additional parallels between MAX HAVELAAR and *Almayer's Folly*. [In Dutch.]

1651 Ryan, Alvan S. "Robert Penn Warren's NIGHT RIDER: The Nihilism of the Isolated Temperament," MODERN FICTION STUDIES, VII (Winter 1961), 338-46.

Just as JC's *The Nigger of the Narcissus* "defined the central motives of his art" (a work in which Morton Zabel found "the primary conceptions that were to be developed and given their full complexity of realization in his [JC's] future novels"), Robert Penn Warren's NIGHT RIDER can be said to define the central motives of Warren's art. In NIGHT RIDER "there is no movement from the nihilism of the 'isolated temperament' toward such a sense of solidarity as is expressed in the narrator's final words of his shipmates on the *Narcissus*." Mr. Percy Munn, the "night rider" himself, "never wins the recognition and self-knowledge that Marlow returns with." "His failure is that the solidarity he embraces is at its roots universal and absolutist, a travesty of the true solidarity that begins with 'the deep, inner certainty of self.'" [Strictly an abstraction, for purposes of analyzing NIGHT RIDER and Morton Zabel's essay on *Nigger*.]

1652 Schorer, Mark (ed). MODERN BRITISH FICTION (NY: Oxford U P, 1961), pp. vii; 65-136.

Contents, abstracted separately under date of first publication: Morton Dauwen Zabel, "Chance and Recognition," from CRAFT AND CHARACTER IN FICTION (1957; see SEWANEE REVIEW [1945]); F. R. Leavis, "Minor Works and *Nostromo*," from THE GREAT TRADITION (1948; see "Revaluations . . . ," SCRUTINY [1941]); Albert J. Guerard, "The Journey Within," from CONRAD THE NOVELIST (1958); and Ian Watt, "Story and Idea in Conrad's *The Shadow-Line*," from CRITICAL QUARTERLY (1960), slightly revised here.

1653 Tillyard, E. M. W. "*The Secret Agent* Reconsidered," ESSAYS IN CRITICISM, XI (July 1961), 309-18; rptd in ESSAYS: LITERARY AND EDUCATIONAL (NY: Barnes and Noble, 1962), pp. 144-53; and CONRAD: A COLLECTION OF CRITICAL ESSAYS ed by Marvin Mudrick (Englewood Cliffs, NJ: Prentice-Hall, Spectrum Books, 1966), pp. 103-10.

JC intended to write "a simple ironic tale" but was unable, in *The Secret Agent*, to resist the technique of the long novel. As a result, "the supporting incidents acquire an excessive consequence." Nevertheless, the parts of the work are so fine that while we are actually reading it we are not "bothered with their disproportionate scale, or with their relation to the whole." Only when we reflect do we have doubts, despite the skillful handling of several unifying ironies and contrasts. *Agent* "hovers a little uneasily between a novel in the grand manner and the long short story."

1654 Trilling, Lionel. "On the Modern Element in Modern Literature," PARTISAN REVIEW, XXVIII (Jan-Feb 1961), 25-26.

For Marlow, in "Heart of Darkness," Kurtz dies "a hero of the spirit" —the essence of the modern belief about the nature of the artist, the man who goes down into that hell which is the historical beginning of the human soul, a beginning not outgrown but established in humanity as we know it now, preferring the reality of this hell to the bland lies of the civilization that has overlaid it."

1655 Van Ghent, Dorothy. "Introduction," *Nostromo* (NY: Holt, Rinehart and Winston, Rinehart Editions, 1961), pp. vii-xxv.

JC's "most fertile invention" in *Nostromo* is his adaptation of the legendary idea of the mysterious potency of a treasure to the conditions of a frontier country in a time of modern colonial imperialism. The ambiguity of the treasure is illustrated by the differing reactions of major characters to it. According to the legend, the "stranger knight" comes to a "waste land," rehabilitates it, and rules happily ever after; but Charles Gould misinterprets the use of the treasure and therefore fails to reign happily. And the fairy princess, whose union with the stranger knight brings union and communion between people, is another variation on the legend. Before the hero, who starts out pure of heart, can command the treasure and become the "good king," he must confront wisely and courageously the ordeal of three phases: (1) bravely facing the destructive forces of nature, represented by Nostromo, whose greatest achievements lie in the natural world; (2) confronting the evil in other people, exemplified by Charles Gould, who fails to realize that the "treasure" has no value without the "fairy princess"; and (3) recognizing the evil in himself, portrayed in Dr. Monygham who, with proper humility, offers his life for Mrs. Gould, the "fairy princess." The setting of *Nostromo* combines the "ordeal," the dramatized action, which is correlated with the cosmic law, with the spiritual law, which operates in the human heart. JC's method of narrative leaves the effect of a cyclical review which is in conformity with the "impressionistic" technique of the book. His modulations from vast space to intensely immediate visual detail, as in the early description of Giorgio Viola in his house, illustrate what he meant in trying to "make you *see.*" Of all the characters in the novel, only Nostromo is a tragic figure: he is thrown forcefully on a personal destiny in which the basic chance of his manhood is enacted in opposition to a mysterious historical necessity which he is unable to understand. But in spite of the tragic view of life portrayed, *Nostromo* is a comedy in the Dantean and the Balzacian sense. [Although the archetypal interpretation is worked for all it is worth, it presents the novel in a fresh light.]

1656 Vidan, Ivo. "Rehearsal for *Nostromo*," STUDIA ROMANICA ET ANGLICA ZAGRABIENSIA (Zagreb), No. 12 (Dec 1961), 9-16. Though the idea for *Romance* and the early [as well as the last] parts of the novel come from F. M. Ford, JC's contribution to it makes it a rehearsal of his next few books, first of all of *Nostromo,* showing a total involvement of man in a modern set-up of political forces. Where JC takes over the conduct of the story, it deviates from the early Fordian synopsis. The introduction of O'Brien brings the political background closer to the core of the action, subordinating the more conventional pirate story to a more significant narrative. Politics affect the whole being of the main character, John Kemp. Whereas in an adventure story like Stevenson's KIDNAPPED the political set up provides just a brilliantly picturesque background, the heroes of *Romance,* because of their manifold involvement, are not allowed unthinkingly to adapt themselves to any new occurrence and to look for the shortest way out of an unpleasant situation. The effect of the story is cumulative, with its two highpoints [Kemp's collision with O'Brien and the cave episode] suggesting the archetypal Conradian image of lonely beings in an isolated spot, betrayed and endangered by intruders. The later one, in particular, reduces this situation to a rough, unhumanized, and unadorned natural setting, and intensifies it by uncertainty. *Romance,* nevertheless, is not a great novel, because the trapped hero ought to have been a more consistent and more profoundly envisaged character, such as the later Razumov. This is also why O'Brien, a much more worthy opponent than Mr. Jones from *Victory,* does not leave the impact of which he would have been capable. Yet the atmosphere of tension, the wonderful narrative rhythm *potentially* embrace almost such a wide and ramified world of significant action as does *Nostromo* or, in a different key, *The Secret Agent. Romance* is a rehearsal for *Nostromo* not only in the compelling effect of its masterly narration, but also because it contains the historically imagined Latin American setting, the somewhat crude method of providing local color, the thoughtful massing of political forces in a sinister atmosphere which enfolds the scene and the characters.

1657 Wills, John Howard. "Conrad's 'The Secret Sharer,'" UNIVERSITY OF KANSAS CITY REVIEW, XXVIII (Dec 1961), 115-26. The world of "The Secret Sharer" is an immense world in which man must struggle constantly to complete his life, and often his free will is strictly limited. Furthermore, JC's strongly satirical view of society in the story points out the fact that few men understand the world in which they must strive. The novelist's portrayal of the bourgeoisie makes this class caricatures, not characterizations; and his treatment of the aristocrats makes Leggatt a fugitive, "the only just man in a world of injustice." Leggatt, as conscientious and responsible as JC can make any of his characters, makes no attempt to find justification for having killed a man, but because he needs understanding and because the narrator responds favorably, the relationship between the two men seems wonderful to the runaway. At the same time, the narrator equally admires Leggatt. The world of "The Secret Sharer" is therefore a threatened society with no leader. The narrator recounts precisely how it acquires a leader and thereby its hope of "temporary salvation." It is easy for him to become like Leggatt in acting as his convictions indicate because his "secret self" and Leggatt are identical. He therefore makes every possible effort to protect his "double" from Archbold and his officers, and he learns thereby to give commands himself, to be more capable as a leader than anyone else on his ship. Then he gains the respect and obedience of his men so that he can take his ship dangerously close to the rocks in order to put Leggatt ashore. Soon after the fugitive has left, the narrator realizes that he has achieved "salvation," which is symbolized by the hat on the water, "a symbol of his and Leggatt's 'secret partnership.' " He thus becomes a man of wisdom who can direct the lives of his fellow men.

1658 Wohlfarth, Paul. "Joseph Conrad als Geschichtserzähler" (Joseph Conrad as Historical Writer), SCHWEIZER RUNDSCHAU, LX (July-Aug 1961), 978-84.

JC does not choose great men of history as the heroes of his novels, but he often introduces historical events and references to historical figures in order to lend atmospheric authenticity to his stories. He deals with the Napoleonic era, Russian anarchism, the Carlists in Spain, the Polish insurrection, the first World War, and South American civil wars. His personal experiences color his writings a great deal. His Polish patriotism lies behind "Gaspar Ruiz" and *Nostromo,* Sulaco standing for Poland, Costaguana for Russia, Hirsch being only plausible within a Polish context. [Sketchy, too brief.] [In German.]

1659 Zabel, Morton Dauwen. "Introduction," TALES OF THE EAST (NY: Doubleday, Anchor Books, 1961), pp. 9-39.

The sea and the East were essential and decisive elements in JC's life and art. The five tales—"The Lagoon," "Karain: A Memory," "A Smile of Fortune," "The Planter of Malata," and "Because of the Dollars"—provide five examples of his use of Eastern material during the years 1897-1914, although these five are not the best of his work. One must accept with serious reservations the basic findings of Morf's Polish-guilt theory. "The Lagoon" and "Karain" are "exercises on themes that foreshadow *Lord Jim* and the books of his finest years between 1897 and 1911." "A Smile of Fortune" is another of his exercises dealing with the "uncongenial subject." Both "The Planter of Malata" and "Because of the Dollars" foreshadow *Victory*. JC's later tales of the East are usually tales of disenchantment.

1962

1660 Adams, Richard P. "The Apprenticeship of William Faulkner," TULANE STUDIES IN ENGLISH, XII (1962), 113-56.
JC had some importance for Faulkner while he was learning to write: Faulkner is reported as having told a friend that he ranked Sherwood Anderson's "I'm a Fool" with "Heart of Darkness" as "the two finest stories" he had ever read; he also suggested that since America has no tradition one must look to exceptions from other countries: he was indebted to JC's writings and their "impressionistic" methods; and his use of "scrambled chronology," his twice and three times removed narrators, and other devices of "gradual revelation" are easily traceable to JC. JC's influence upon Faulkner is the strongest and "most pervasive" that came from any writer of fiction. LIGHT IN AUGUST probably contains the greatest number of links with JC's works.

1661 Allen, Jerry. "Conrad's River," COLUMBIA UNIVERSITY FORUM, V (Winter 1962), 29-35.
Little has been known about the influential twenty years JC spent at sea. Almayer, a Borneo trader, has provided the clue of an "Eastern River" with a Malay settlement on it which appears in several novels and stories. This river, the Pantai, named accurately in *Almayer's Folly* and *An Outcast of the Islands,* has now been "located conclusively." JC called the village "Patusan" in *Lord Jim,* "Sambir" in *Folly* and *Outcast,* "Samburan" in *Victory,* and "Darat-es-Salam" in *The Rescue,* and included it in several stories. The river and the village, Berau, were identified decisively by the Dutch manager of a coal mine, Mr. R. Haverschmidt. Mrs. C. C. Oehlers, the daughter of Jim Lingard, whom JC had used in *Jim,* described the Borneo settlement as her birthplace and identified the village; Mr. Haverschmidt, in correspondence with Dr. J. C. Reed, gave a "detailed portrait" of the village while he read JC's novels and recognized many descriptions of local places in them. Then he learned several more details from old residents of Berau. JC, long thought of as a "romancer," is now seen as a realistic writer, so much so that during World War II American troops used his novels as guides. "With the art of which he was a great master, Conrad built a universal place from a wilderness settlement." [Scarcely proves JC to be a realistic writer and lacks sufficient evidence to establish Berau as his "universal place."]

1662 Bojarski, Edmund A. "Joseph Conrad, Alias 'Polish Joe,'" ENGLISH STUDIES IN AFRICA (Johannesburg), V (March 1962), 59-60.

Dr. Wit Tarnawski, the "foremost Conradian scholar" now writing in Polish, has brought to light in a Polish daily the fact that after JC landed at Lowestoft in 1878 and soon afterwards became a seaman on the coastal coaler *Skimmer of the Sea,* the crew called him "Polish Joe" and remembered for many years stories about him and his friend, William Munning, and their "successes in the port dives of the time." From these seamen and others met in the taverns of Lowestoft, JC gained his first knowledge of English.

1663 Brady, Emily Kuempel. "The Literary Faulkner: His Indebtedness to Conrad, Hemingway, and Other Novelists," DISSERTATION ABSTRACTS, XXIII (1962), 2131-32. Unpublished thesis, Brown University, 1962.

1664 Brady, Marion B. "Conrad's Whited Sepulcher," COLLEGE ENGLISH, XXIV (Oct 1962), 24-29.

"The whited sepulcher" is a basic image for the two analogous themes of "Heart of Darkness": "a journey into the unconscious self" and an indictment of the "vilest scramble for loot that ever disfigured the history of human conscience and geographical exploration"—"a fusion of personal and public themes—a consideration of man and of society in their relationship to evil." These two themes are "informed by 'deception' at the public level and 'self-deception' at the personal level." At first Marlow sees the whited sepulcher "only as an image of the Company itself," but by the end of his experiences in Africa he sees it "as a symbol of all those who suffer self-deception as well as a symbol of all those who practice deception," a symbol of "all kinds of delusion or self-delusion that may keep a man or a company or a nation from understanding or living the truth." Both Marlow and the reader see "the parallels between the image of Brussels and the image of Kurtz," and see that the darkness and the ivory are "merely two components of the same entity." After Marlow meets the world of evil in the two classical Fates, he constantly finds "variations upon the theme of hypocrisy and delusion" until, upon his return from Africa to Brussels, he sees the city "as the heart of darkness in all its variations." And Marlow recognizes the inadequancy of the Intended's response, which is "symbolized by the ever-diminishing light in her room." He at last reaches the conclusion that man must take positive action or he "compounds his guilt by using hypocrisy—the hypocrisy of the whited sepulcher—to disguise the hollowness, the moral desolation, within him." [An excellent analysis of the symbolic meaning of "Heart of Darkness." See Thomas C. Kishler, "Reality in 'Heart of Darkness,'" COLLEGE ENGLISH, XXIV (April 1963), 561-62 for a rebuttal; Marion B. Brady, "Reply," COLLEGE ENGLISH, XXIV (April 1963), 562-63.]

1665 Curley, Daniel. "Legate of the Ideal," CONRAD'S "SECRET SHARER" AND THE CRITICS, ed by Bruce Harkness (Belmont, Calif: Wadsworth, 1962), pp. 75-82; rptd in CONRAD: A COLLECTION OF CRITICAL ESSAYS, ed by Marvin Mudrick (Englewood Cliffs, NY: Prentice-Hall, Spectrum Books, 1966), pp. 75-82.

In "The Secret Sharer," three kinds of evidence seem to exclude Guerard's interpretation of Leggatt as "criminally impulsive": (1) in a letter to Galsworthy (1913), JC stated that Leggatt is not "a murderous ruffian"; and in the preface to *The Shorter Tales,* he seems to exclude the possibility of the swimmer's being violent or evil. (2) The changes JC made in converting the historical material of the *Cutty Sark* into the fictional material of the story support the identification between Leggatt and the Captain and therefore rule out the likelihood of a secret bond of criminal impulsiveness. (3) Most convincing, the evidence of the story itself, in which both the Captain and Leggatt must rely upon their basic moral strength to make a responsible choice in a situation which is not clear-cut, carries the Captain through his unique moral test by means of his "ideal conception of himself made manifest in Leggatt," who is not a criminal but "one of us" by birth, by training, and by his own acts. [Convincing.]

1666 Daiches, David. "Experience and the Imagination: The Background of 'Heart of Darkness,'" WHITE MAN IN THE TROPICS: TWO MORAL TALES, ed by David Daiches (NY: Harcourt, Brace & World, 1962), pp. 3-16.

JC elaborates in "Heart of Darkness" the theme of the fate of the individual who faces something alien to his experience with no deep inward moral resources. Civilization provides external checks for persons living in the western world, and without some deep inner check one would succumb completely to the "Heart of Darkness" in man if exposed to it. Kurtz did not completely succumb: his dying words of revulsion are evidence of some moral conviction that resisted moral nihilism. Part of Marlow's fascination by Kurtz derives from man's tendency in moments of great crisis to see his own real self in a person who is his moral opposite. On another level, "Heart of Darkness" indicates that man cannot bear too much reality and that the innocent idealism of the ignorant should not be destroyed: therefore Marlow lies to Kurtz's Intended. The truth would have revealed the "desperate paradox" at the heart of civilization and of moral life in general—"that only a truly moral man is capable of real depravity and that most men have not principle enough to be damned." This makes nonsense of the principles which are supposed to govern civilization. At the most profound level, then, "Heart of Darkness" is about the nature of man and the nature of civilization. JC, a "deep pessimist," saw that society, which is a "commitment to our fellows," is an essential need of man, but that it "inevitably corrupts"; "loneliness, the integrity of the isolated individual, is desirable, but it either maddens or destroys."

1667 Dike, Donald A. "The Tempest of Axel Heyst," NINE-TEENTH-CENTURY FICTION, XVII (Sept 1962), 95-113.

Victory is "curiously unnovelistic"; the scene of action is "significant in the measure of its abstraction from history"; life in Sourabaya and on the island of Samburan exists "virtually in empty space," and "neither of these places has identity." The leading characters are "outcasts not merely from one or another society but from history." In Samburan, "evil claims to be free from any contingency, an absolute," opposed to which is its adversary, "an enlightened and righteous skepticism"; and "their conflict has necessarily to result in theatrical melodrama." Heyst is "disabled for living by a bequest from the dead" so that when he loses the sense of Lena's existence his doom is certain. His skepticism reduces him to "somnambulant futility," but even his skepticism contains "the supreme illusion of sanctuary." Heyst's deficient sense of the outer world, however, is not the only deficient attitude in the novel: Morrison, Schomberg, Jones, and Ricardo all fail to *realize* Heyst. Heyst's island, then, "the insularity of pure self," is in danger from several outer worlds. Each world, though, fails to understand chance; the action of the novel is "impelled by misinformation; almost every developing moment of the plot turns on missing or faulty knowledge." But chance is not a mere accident; each character is incapable of recognizing it because it would challenge or discredit his purposes and assumptions. Heyst fails to know Lena; his skepticism fails when his situation needs belief.

Victory, a "moral melodrama," often presses toward allegory, but JC does not attempt "to draw a systematic theological analogy," although his story of corruption and redemption "regularly alludes to or invokes the Judaic-Christian myth." He generalizes his people into "a connection with prototypes": *Victory* gives Lena the name of Magdalen but also presents her as a sort of Eve; and Heyst fulfills his role in the dedication "of his sonhood," but he cannot accomplish his father's will that he be an "independent spectator," uninvolved in human affairs. His skepticism is governed by feelings so that at last his involvement with men leads him into action in such a way that he is "lost," but also, in a way that he understands too late, is saved. Thus Heyst "fails as a savior out of unsuspected hubris"; the purity of his motives contains "a refusal to accept the terrible responsibility of being human." JC demonstrates that avoiding the contamination of the world is impossible, but the idea behind the attempt is a necessary one, however vulnerable it may be. The theme of *Victory* is "as old as the third chapter of Genesis," and its most striking antecedent is to be found in THE TEMPEST. Less ostensibly it is related to THE TURN OF THE SCREW and to Blake's SONGS OF INNOCENCE AND EXPERIENCE. These works "compose a fantasy way of seeing the duality of illusion and reality in ambiguous, inseparable connection with the duality of innocence and guilt, so that in this way of looking, the two problems, moral and epistemological, fuse and become one."

1668 Gale, Bell. "Conrad and the Romantic Hero." Unpublished thesis, Yale University, 1962.
[Examines "Heart of Darkness," *Lord Jim, Nostromo, Under Western Eyes, Chance,* and *Victory.*]

1669 Gettmann, Royal A., and Bruce Harkness. "Morality and Psychology in 'The Secret Sharer,'" CONRAD'S "SECRET SHARER" AND THE CRITICS, ed by Bruce Harkness (Belmont, Calif: Wadsworth, 1962), pp. 125-32; rptd and expd from Royal A. Gettmann and Bruce Harkness, TEACHER'S MANUAL: A BOOK OF SHORT STORIES (NY: Rinehart, 1955).
To Basil Lubbock's account of the incident on the *Cutty Sark* in THE LOG OF THE *Cutty Sark,* which is a source of or an analogue to "The Secret Sharer," JC adds the psychological and the moral elements of his tale, especially the latter, which give "the shape and drive of the story." JC portrays Leggatt as having "a streak of violence within him," thus symbolizing, through the same criminal instinct in the Captain, this instinct in every man. From Leggatt, the Captain, by sharing his "climactic experience," gains self-knowledge, that is, knowledge of inner savagery. He must, therefore, "pay" Leggatt by going closer than necessary to Koh-ring. The hat symbolizes both the impulsive Leggatt and the impulsive Captain, and thereby becomes a symbol of integration which sets up "a kind of amoral spectrum." The "management" of this spectrum is for JC the "art of life" —a matter of morality. [An important perception which relates the moral problem to that of Marlow and Kurtz in "Heart of Darkness."]

1670 Gold, Joseph. "Two Romantics: Jim and Stein," CEA CRITIC, XXIV (May 1962), 11-12.
"Conrad intends the reader to link Stein and Jim in his mind." This "sad and pathetic or perhaps . . . ironic figure," Stein, is "what Jim would have become had he run away from Patusan. One can be only a Stein or a Jim, one must suffer either a spiritual or a physical death, because unlike the butterflies, it is given to man to make choices and with every choice there is also rejection."

1671 Graver, Lawrence. "'Typhoon': A Profusion of Similes," COLLEGE ENGLISH, XXIV (Oct 1962), 62-64; based on material

in a 1961 dissertation and absorbed in CONRAD'S SHORT FICTION (Berkeley and Los Angeles: University of California P, 1969).
Although JC usually uses "metaphors which are generally contrifugal" because they "start from a sharply observed fact and then tend to move toward something larger, more abstract, less clearly defined," in "Typhoon" he "is interested primarily in the triumph of a naive, unimaginative hero"; he therefore uses "specific detail and . . . simile rather than metaphor to reinforce the crucial thematic contrast of the story," the contrast between Captain MacWhirr, "an absolute literalist," and Jukes, the first mate, who is "a high-spirited, reasonably imaginative man." JC's "clear and definite language" is eminently suitable to describe the storm. "The need for tenacity in the face of severe outward obstacles is reinforced by many strands of imagery in 'Typhoon' which are so often mechanistic and have a kind of surface, metallic hardness." The numerous images employed are "especially effective because of their immediate link with the world of direct sensation." When JC sketches a minor character briefly, he always relies on simile, mostly visual, but often aural because much of the story happens in complete darkness. The letters from the three major characters to people back home are a perfect device "for a story in which facts speak so insistently for themselves." Thus "Typhoon" gains some of its unity from JC's "manipulation of pure fact." It is "more artful or unified; but obviously less ambitious and profound than, say, *The Nigger of the Narcissus* or *Lord Jim.*"

1672 Green, Jesse D. "Diabolism, Pessimism, and Democracy: Notes on Melville and Conrad," MODERN FICTION STUDIES, VIII (Autumn 1962), 287-305.

Comparison of the works of Melville and JC shows many similarities and differences. Among the former are their uses of myth, symbolism, and depth psychology as well as the structural frame consisting of a dream or nightmare, a ship's captain in strange waters, and a threat by unseen forces. A major difference centers upon their use of contrasting roles for black men. JC's fiction has no ambiguity about the symbolic role and value of blackness; its truth is ugly and its power is evil. Blackness is rarely embodied preeminently in persons of black skin; no intimacy or democratic quality of brotherhood is possible between the European and the savage. Melville allows the savage credit for being basically equal, rejects the notion of unbridgeable dichotomy between blacks and whites, and presents situations showing human solidarity as "a priceless good." Whereas JC emphasized the test of enduring truth, not pursuing it, and thus is pessimistic, Melville is disposed to submit to inner forces of passion and intuition and the tide of the unconscious and thus to present volatile, changing conflicting attitudes.

1673 Gross, Harvey. "Aschenbach and Kurtz: The Cost of Civilization," CENTENNIAL REVIEW, VI (Spring 1962), 131-43.

Freud has explained the dilemma of modern man as "one of impossible alternatives: man cannot live at peace in his culture; he dies without it." "Heart of Darkness" and Mann's DEATH IN VENICE present men who collapse trying to maintain barriers "against the dark powers." The heroes of these short novels "are representative men of their civilization; they are the best that Europe can offer in cultivation and high-minded humanity. Both disastrously succumb to their instincts." These stories are, therefore, allegories of culture. The final degradation of both men "is bitterly ironic." They become what they have deplored. Neither man's dissolution and death, however, is meaningless. Men struggling are unequal to the effort and end "spiritually and emotionally exhausted." Mann and JC attempt to bring this world under formal control "through an attitude which avoids commitment." They "neither affirm nor deny: they have uncomfortable loyalties." Such writers find salvation in a style "which holds before the reader's mind mutually contradictory points of view. Irony can do these things, and Mann and Conrad discourse in the ironic mode." If we do not understand these stories we "miss a chance for survival. They are arguments to persuade the Erinyes to serve as Eumenides; they are parables of instruction from which we can learn to transform and transfigure the powers which seem, at this anguished moment in history, destined to destroy us."

1674 Gurko, Leo. JOSEPH CONRAD: GIANT IN EXILE (NY: Macmillan; Galt, Ontario: Brett-Macmillan, 1962).

Philosophically, JC accepted as the most durable attitude a sophisticated pessimism. In his writings, he emphasized technique more than content. His exile from his native country resulted in his being obscurely inhibited from participating in life even while longing to be more active; consequently, he created characters who suffer from paralysis of will, from the inability to release themselves into action and thereby into life. His avoidance of any close relationships with others, his life's being filled with experiences instead of relationships, resulted in a feeling of insecurity as the foundation of his art. Since he was acutely aware that life might be rich but that it is also dangerous, his pessimism avoids morbidity and hollowness; it contains effective dramatic tension. The two novels of his apprenticeship are bound by the theme of inertia, and in them JC succeeded in drawing together his vision of man and his vision of nature. Six sea tales in which a ship transmits the "pulsations of the sea" to the men aboard are *The Nigger of the Narcissus,* in which the death journey is dominant; "Youth"; "The End of the Tether"; "Typhoon," which portrays both a struggle for material survival and a "psychic penetration" into MacWhirr, one of JC's "most deceptive figures"; "The Secret Sharer"; and *The*

Shadow-Line, which follows the hero from a descent into an abyss of emptiness across the shadow-line to an emergence from sterility by responding to the challenges and responsibilities of the outer life. *Lord Jim* is a good example of JC's desire for his readers to understand his protagonists but not to love them. Whereas Jim fails at first because he is alone and succeeds later when he enters the human community, Nostromo is drawn into the human community at first to find later that it fails him. JC's abnormal awareness of place, his "ecology of art," is best demonstrated in *The Mirror of the Sea,* "Heart of Darkness," and *A Personal Record.* His "dark vision of megalopolis" is *The Secret Agent;* and here the city of London is a symbol of his life of failure, of JC's own feeling of failure. *Under Western Eyes* is JC's double vision of the "Russian colossus," and Razumov is his greatest achievement in the use of the unfulfilled man. JC's later works, with the exception of *Shadow-Line,* are inferior. JC's task was to "peel life down to the essential core" to find out whether it made sense; his conclusion was one of affirmation, "the affirmation of existence as a self-producing, self-nourishing, and self-sustaining process that carried its own reason for being." [This combination of biography and criticism offers no new biographical information; but it supplies several original and impressive interpretations of JC's works, especially of "Typhoon," *Shadow-Line, Jim, Personal Record, Eyes,* and *Victory,* as well as some of the shorter works. Generalizations on JC's struggle with nature, his ecology of art, and the concept of the "Conradian centaur" are provocative and rewarding.]

1675 Harkness, Bruce (ed). Conrad's "Secret Sharer" and the Critics (Belmont, Calif: Wadsworth, 1962).
Contents, abstracted separately under date of first publication: B. Harkness, "Textual Note," "Study Questions, Theme and Paper Topics," and "Bibliography of Works for Further Study" [not abstracted]; Albert J. Guerard, "The Journey Within," from Conrad the Novelist (1958); Daniel Curley, "Legate of the Ideal" (1962); Carl Benson, "Conrad's Two Stories of Initiation," PMLA (1954); R. W. Stallman, "Conrad and 'The Secret Sharer,'" Accent (1949); Marvin Mudrick, "Conrad and the Terms of Modern Criticism," Hudson Review (1954); Jocelyn Baines, "Conrad's Biography and 'The Secret Sharer,'" Joseph Conrad: A Critical Biography (1959); Walter F. Wright, "'The Secret Sharer' and Human Pity," Romance and Tragedy in Joseph Conrad (1949); Royal A. Gettman and Bruce Harkness, "Morality and Psychology in 'The Secret Sharer'" (1962); and Louis H. Leiter, "Echo Structures: Conrad's 'The Secret Sharer,'" Twentieth Century Literature (1960). Items by others not about JC and not abstracted: Basil Lubbock, "A Hell-Ship Voyage," The Log of the *Cutty Sark* (1960 ed); "Arrest and Trial of Sidney Smith," Times (Lond), 5 July 1882, p. 6; items by JC, not ab-

stracted; "The Secret Sharer"; "Author's Note," from 'TWIXT LAND AND SEA. [This casebook is important for the text of the story reprinted. The critical selections include most of the significant current interpretations of the story.]

1676 Hartley, L. P. "The Novelist's Responsibility," ESSAYS AND STUDIES, N.S. XV (1962), 88-100.

A novelist should choose as his subject something he "feels" about rather than something he "knows" about; he should have a certain sensibility about his subject. JC, for example, was especially concerned about honor; he saw life "in terms of faithfulness, as a trust." He believed a man should be faithful to himself and to his employers, that he must maintain his self-respect. For him, the chief virtue was "some form of faithfulness."

1677 Hodges, Robert. "The Death of Stefan Bobrowski: A Conrad Discovery," NOTES AND QUERIES, N.S. IX (March 1962), 109-10.

The obscurity surrounding Stefan Bobrowski's death "can be explained by the fact that the incident was 'regarded as a family disgrace.' " Both Tadeusz Bobrowski and JC concealed the fact that "Stefan Bobrowski's enthusiastic participation in radical politics and his irrational desire to find a scapegoat for one of the setbacks of the revolution [caused] an obsession so strong that it led to a duel and thus his death." The story can be found in THE PRIVATE HISTORY OF A POLISH INSURRECTION (Lond: Saunders, Otley, 1865) by H. Sutherland Edwards, a reporter for *The Times* who had "spent some months in Poland during the January Insurrection [of 1863]."

1678 Hodges, Robert. "Joseph Conrad's Dual Heritage," DISSERTATION ABSTRACTS, XXIV (1962), 1160-61. Unpublished thesis, Stanford University, 1962; later published as THE DUAL HERITAGE OF JOSEPH CONRAD (The Hague: Mouton, 1967).

When JC's mind was divided because of the contrasting influences of his father, Apollo Korzeniowski, poet and patriot, and his uncle, Tadeusz Bobrowski, who "taught JC to fear the instability, impracticality, and egoism of his father, and encouraged him to control these by settling in a definite profession," his fiction was great; when the conflict of influences diminished, when JC tended toward his father's view, his fiction lost its richness. Apollo, too, was a man divided [yet his life seems unified by his devotion to the cause of Polish independence]. Apollo, too, was an egoist because he was ready to give himself and his family up to a national cause [but his wife also supported the cause outright and was co-accused with her husband]. Tadeusz Bobrowski was a positive influence on JC [but Zdzisław Najder describes Bobrowski as cold and "tormented by ambition"]. In his letters to his nephew, Bobrowski encouraged "reason, sober self-knowledge, and duty." A father-son relationship detrimental to the son is shown in *Chance, Nostromo,* and *Victory,* reflecting JC's relationship to Apollo. In *The Shadow-Line, Lord Jim,* and *Nostromo* "the steadying moral influence" of Tadeusz Bobrowski is evident. The reconciliation between contrasting influences of Apollo and Tadeusz, first manifest in JC's acceptance of his father's romantic nationalism, proved to be the reason for the decline of JC's artistic powers in 1912. [Hodges does not make use of all available material in Polish or English in explaining details like Polish Messianism and the 1863 Polish Rising. He carelessly dates JC's works. His book is poorly proofed, and "utter confusion reigns in the application of Polish diacritical signs." The main defect of Hodges's book, however, is its attempt to see JC exclusively in the light of his Polish background.] [The abstract is based on the book and on Andrew Busza's review in ENGLISH LITERATURE IN TRANSITION, XI: 4 (1968), 222-26.]

1679 Hoffman, Charles G. "Point of View in 'The Secret Sharer,'" COLLEGE ENGLISH, XXIII (May 1962), 651-54.

The three aspects of point of view in "The Secret Sharer" "correspond to the thematic structure of the story." The first fourth of the story establishes "the subjective point of view" in which the captain is "a stranger to himself," with his thoughts "land-bound." His "land-consciousness is created by the subjective point of view," in which the significance of the descriptive details is "the subjective *impression* they make on the captain's consciousness." The long middle section of the tale "creates the objectification of self through identification with Leggatt which leads to self-recognition." Here the point of view is "at the crux of the captain's identification with Leggatt and his personal crisis." Leggatt's crisis "tests the narrator's conscience as a man" and he is, like Leggatt previously on the *Sephora,* not found wanting. The final fourth of the tale "provides an actual test of the captain's mastery of his ship and his self." As the narrator gains the mastery which he has desired, Leggatt, the "double," no longer needed, lowers himself into the sea, to disappear. The white hat on the water "marks the spot and the moment of self-knowledge." Thus "the externalization of point of view through the device of the second self . . . enabled Conrad to show the development of the captain from self-doubt to self-realization, from self-ignorance to self-knowledge." [A closely reasoned and convincing psychological interpretation which clarifies JC's technical problem in this story.]

1680 Koc, Barbara. "Conrad a Polska" (Conrad and Poland). Unpublished thesis, University of Warsaw, 1962. [In Polish.]

1681 Lohf, Kenneth A. (comp). COLLECTION OF BOOKS, MANUSCRIPTS & AUTOGRAPH LETTERS IN THE LIBRARY OF JEAN AND DONALD STRALEM (NY: Athoensen P, 1962), pp. 18-19.

[Lists first and special editions of five works, including first edition of *Youth* with four-page A. L. from JC to Edward Garnett, 27 Nov 1902.]

1682 McConnell, Daniel J. " 'The Heart of Darkness' in T. S. Eliot's 'The Hollow Men,' " TEXAS STUDIES IN LITERATURE AND LANGUAGE, IV (Summer 1962), 141-53.

T. S. Eliot in "The Hollow Men" (and also in THE WASTE LAND) and JC in "Heart of Darkness" saw something similar "at the heart of the crisis besetting western civilization": both writers suggest that back of every civilization that ventures into a "heart of darkness" must be "an intellectual purpose," and both use symbols (Kurtz for JC) of the "hollowness" of "international greed and false concepts of European 'progress.' " Kurtz represents the illusion of progress, "the false rational principle," which both Eliot and JC believe exists at the "heart of darkness" of the modern world. JC's assessment of the destiny of Europe appears, however, to be less hopeful than Eliot's: after Kurtz's death the world becomes continually darker until light is finally extinguished, and it is not necessarily only the Congo but *Europe* that is the "heart of darkness." "The evil spawned by finance capital in the heart of the Congo, the evil that Kurtz through his vision at last *understood,* is now invading Europe, coming like the plague on all the rivers of the world." [An important interpretation of "Heart of Darkness."]

1683 McIntyre, Allan Ormsby. "Joseph Conrad and the Philosophy of Illusion," DISSERTATION ABSTRACTS, XXII (1962), 3659. Unpublished thesis, University of Texas, 1961.

1684 Meixner, John A. *"Romance:* Collaborating with Conrad," FORD MADOX FORD'S NOVELS: A CRITICAL STUDY (Minneapolis: University of Minnesota P, 1962), pp. 27-39, and passim; derived from "The Novels of Ford Madox Ford: A Critical Study," unpublished thesis, Brown University, 1957.

Romance, the best of the three collaborative works, is "much more Conradian than Fordian." Ford's role was to tone down JC's penchant for seeking "highly dramatic effects." JC in part contributed the "political imagination," particularly in relation to such characters as Kemp. JC was mainly responsible for part III and entirely for part IV. JC's "world is rendered with extreme physical clarity and vividness"; Ford's "is much more indistinct and subjective." JC also tends to develop his material more fully than Ford. Stylistically, there is often disharmony because of the distinctively different ways in which the collaborators imagined and rendered, evident in the flawed handling of tone, pace, and point of view. Ford's work is at its best when he can treat "the interplay of society," a subject almost wholly lacking in JC. In the collaboration, JC had the advantage of maturity and a toughening experience behind him. These Ford only gained about 1914-18.

1685 Mizener, Arthur. "Part One: Introduction," MODERN SHORT STORIES: THE USES OF IMAGINATION, ed by Arthur Mizener (NY: Norton, 1962); rvd (1966), pp. 2-3.

JC's "Heart of Darkness" combines objective reality and subjective responses to the reality. JC manages this by making the realistically described scene "ultimately metaphorical." [Also see Mizener, A HANDBOOK OF ANALYSES, QUESTIONS, AND A DISCUSSION OF TECHNIQUE FOR USE WITH MODERN SHORT STORIES: THE USES OF IMAGINATION (1966).]

1686 Morgan, Gerould. "Sea Symbol and Myth in the Works of Joseph Conrad." Unpublished thesis, University of Montreal, 1962.

1687 Moseley, Edwin M. "Christ as Tragic Hero: Conrad's *Lord Jim*," PSEUDONYMS OF CHRIST IN THE MODERN NOVEL (Pittsburgh: University of Pittsburgh P, 1962), pp. 15-35.

In JC's rejection of naturalism and in Hemingway's embrace of it are represented two separate worlds of thinking. In "Heart of Darkness" JC, however, describes Marlow's journey in terms as biological and psychological as a naturalist. JC, though admitting animalism in man, does not lose faith in human nature, for he believes man has a moral sense as inborn as the flesh and passions (Marlow is surprised that the natives, though hungry, do not eat men although their mores do not forbid this practice). Man, JC also asserts, can cope with and rise above anything he encounters; and, fallen, he can re-exercise his moral capacity. For the strict naturalist there is only the dualism between what man pretends to do and what he does; and for the behaviorist, who believes man is what he does, even this dualism does not exist. Without even an implicit dualism, tragedy is impossible, and the hero may be regarded as a foolish idealist. JC wrote tragedy well in *Lord Jim,* and he emphasizes Jim's being a type for every man and for Christ. JC suggests levels beyond the literal by using the artistic pun, related to metaphor and irony, as well as the complexity of ideas that symbolism brings: in "Heart of Darkness" he plays upon the words "civilization" and "jungle"; in *Jim,* "Western" and "Eastern," "white" and "black" enter into this complex pun. Jim is a white Western man with a white Western crew, who is responsible for pilgrims, colored and oriental; he jumps ship, and is associated with the fallen angel and "descent into hades" imagery; Jim is also a Christ-figure who reminds us of man's dualistic nature.

1688 Rosenfield, Claire. "An Archetypal Analysis of Conrad's *Nostromo*," TEXAS STUDIES IN LITERATURE AND LANGUAGE, III (Winter 1962), 510-34; derived from "Paradise of Snakes: Archetypal Patterns in Two Novels by Conrad," unpublished thesis, Radcliffe College, 1960; included in PARADISE OF SNAKES: AN ARCHETYPAL ANALYSIS OF CONRAD'S POLITICAL NOVELS (Chicago: University of Chicago P, 1967).

Nostromo is an "astonishing failure" because it is "essentially two imperfectly integrated stories": first, the historical story which includes the past of Costaguana, the Montero rebellion, and the attempts of the republic of Sulaco to separate itself from the rest of Costaguana, with Nostromo as the traditional or romantic hero; and, second, the story of the mine and the silver, with Decoud as the historical hero. The novel thus has a "composite" hero, but neither Nostromo nor Decoud really confronts the "possibilities of his own nature" until the two are on the lighter with its cargo of silver. Then JC "unconsciously blurred" the boundary between the actual voyage and the "interior journey of the psyche," thus making the irrationality of the situation an outstanding example of man's fate in an irrational world. Both men symbolize the theme of the *bateau ivre*. Sulaco suggests Eden, but it is undoubtedly a part of the fallen world, a parody of the Eden of Genesis, and it is also a prophecy of the future which displays the threat of corruption. Mr. and Mrs. Gould are the Adam and Eve who first yield to the "temptations of power." By using the "conventional imagery of myth," JC reveals how materialism can be equated with the "orderly but unknown cosmos" of Greek or Shakespearean tragedy. Mr. Holroyd is a kind of "God figure," motifs from fairy tales or Märchen are associated with the mine, Charles Gould's idealism takes the form of a "moral romance," and Mrs. Gould is frequently described as fairy-like. The influence of the mine is destructive to nature and "dehumanizing" to its owner. The collision of the two boats in the darkness of the gulf is equated for Nostromo with the mythic journey to the underworld; but the "reborn" Nostromo, unlike the usual hero, is not equipped to meet the world he once knew. Only at the time of his death does he admit that he cannot "transcend the limitations of his own ego." Decoud, too, after making the mythic voyage into darkness, is destroyed by his own ego. Even Charles Gould, whose silver mine becomes a substitute for a woman, is also isolated from the traditional hero's reward—the woman he loves. The "obsessive sense of isolation and fragmentation" of Nostromo and Decoud indicate that the composite hero of the novel is a "tragedy of modern man's loss of identity," and even JC's community of Sulaco is unlike that of the traditional myths in that the treasure merely supports the decay "already apparent in the timed world of historical events." Unlike the magic sword of the traditional hero, the silver—and material interests in general—is a double-edged weapon displaying "the cupidity and misery of mankind." [An important but somewhat strained interpretation of *Nostromo*.]

1689 Sister Estelle, S. P. "Thematic and Formal Function of Gentleman Brown," NOTRE DAME ENGLISH JOURNAL, I (Spring 1962), 26-28.

Throughout *Lord Jim,* "the spectre of Jim's cowardly desertion of the supposedly floundering *Patna* has obsessed the man-boy"; and his pride, combined with his emotional immaturity, finally exiles him to Patusan, where JC introduces "his final foil," Gentleman Brown. Brown's question, "What made you come here?" shatters the "comfortable image" of the "white god saviour" which Jim has created for himself. Knowing that he can find no other refuge, Jim is actually "the trapped rat of which Brown so ironically speaks," although Brown, unlike the reader, is ignorant of Jim's past. Brown is employed functionally as "a multiple foil" for Jim: physiologically, sociologically, and psychologically. Unaware of Jim's two earlier unwise choices, his remarks, unknown to him, "imply the tragic flaw which had caused Jim's first leap"; and he forces decision upon Jim, a decision which ironically brings death. Jim has risen only to "a pseudo-heroic stature because he fell short in prudence and good judgment"; his was "the romantic decision of an idealist." He has an "exaggerated revulsion" for his connection with the *Patna* whereas Brown, an extrovert, "glories in his universal reputation for evil." Thus Gentleman Brown "fulfills an important thematic and formal function" in JC's novel.

1690 Smith, David R. *"Nostromo* and the Three Sisters," STUDIES IN ENGLISH LITERATURE 1500-1900 (Rice University), II (Autumn 1962), 497-508.

Silver produces moral isolation, it produces death, and it *is* death. Nostromo, whose reward for saving the silver is the treasure itself, along with death, supplies "a general symbolic underpinning" for the entire book, and he comes closer than anyone else in defining the structure of the work.

In his description of the Isabels in the first chapter, JC, no doubt unconsciously, utilizes the archetypal concept of the three sisters found in folklore, mythology, and literature. The three islands, the Great Isabel, the Little Isabel, and Hermosa, have as their human counterparts Teresa Viola and her daughters, Linda and Giselle. In the two sequences of names, the third name is markedly different from the others. Teresa Viola is not only the mother of the two girls but also in some measure of Nostromo, and Linda, apparently destined to be Nostromo's wife, is very much like her mother; but Giselle, whose very name indicates her role, is death. Teresa Viola and the Great Isabel are as closely associated with death as are Giselle and Hermosa, so that "birth is death and death is birth." The silver, the symbol of death, is transferred to the island: the lighthouse is built there and the stage is gradually set for the main characters to gather on the mother island "to play out the inexorable drama of life, desire, deceit, and death." Nostromo is killed there by Giorgio Viola, the surrogate father, because of Giselle, while Linda, also in love with Nostromo, tends the lighthouse. In this manner the titles of the second and third parts of the novel are as significant as JC claimed the title of the first part to be.

Nostromo dies in part from seeking out Giselle and in part from seeking out the silver, which is also death. Giselle and the silver are, in fact, linked in other ways, just as JC links Nostromo and the silver to Decoud and to the rest of the book. As for Charles Gould, his fate was that of a marriage which became a wasteland. When, toward the end of the novel, Mrs. Gould, "the unravished bride" of a barren marriage, unknowingly becomes involved in Nostromo's death as well as in his relations with both Giselle and the silver, the book "goes full circle." At the very end, when the dying Nostromo offers Mrs. Gould the secret of the silver, she replies, "No, capataz, . . . no one misses it now. Let it be lost forever." But ironically it is not lost forever, because at the end of the book Giselle knows of its existence. Thus, "Death does not die." [An important archetypal approach to *Nostromo*.]

>**1691** Spinner, Kaspar. "Embracing the Universe: Some Annotations to Joseph Conrad's 'Heart of Darkness,'" ENGLISH STUDIES (Amsterdam), XLIII (Oct 1962), 420-23.

A letter from JC to Cunninghame Graham in 1897 anticipates the knitter of "Heart of Darkness" and Kurtz's dying cry, "The horror! The horror!" Kurtz's "summing-up whisper signifies, among other things, his ultimate recognition of the black needlework of the universe." Kurtz is also reminiscent of Orpheus, the "civilising hero." But Kurtz does not return from death; he is, however, praised as an artist, musician, poet, and painter. There is also in his final experience "more than just a trace" of *angoisse Pascalienne*.

>**1692** Tanner, Tony. "Mountains and Depths—An Approach to Nineteenth-Century Dualism," REVIEW OF ENGLISH LITERATURE, III (Oct 1962), 51-61.

It was a "characteristic Victorian syndrome" to use the "conventional metaphor" of mountains to describe the spiritual, ideal, and unphysical and of depths to describe the carnal, unpleasant, and seamy. "The fall from a realm of pure unsullied ideals into a foul muddy world of material impulses—fear, selfishness, appetite—is often repeated in Conrad," for example, in Jim's jump. In *Victory,* "Once Heyst has surrendered his inviolability by acting on a fleshly sexual impulse (no matter how chivalrously rationalised) 'life had him fairly by the throat.' "

>**1693** Tanner, Tony. "Nightmare and Complacency: Razumov and the Western Eye," CRITICAL QUARTERLY, IV (Autumn 1962), 197-214.

Readers who see *Under Western Eyes* "as an anti-Russian polemic have not learned to respond to the full range of Conrad's wide-ranging irony and scepticism, nor to the depths of his insight into the human mind." Not only does the narrator disclaim any comprehension of the Russian character, but the work's "complex shifting structure" depicts "a distant Russian experience which then draws suddenly closer until finally it bulks so large that it . . . has taken on the quality of artificiality." Razumov's "experience" is the "reality" of the book. His responses to Haldin and his eventual betrayal of him are the main substance. Razumov, "a disowned bastard," is "perpetually" in the "alienated state which Conrad found the critical testing time for man." Razumov has two desires: he needs to keep hold of a "normal, practical, everyday life"; and he hopes to win the Ministry of Education prize, the silver medal. Into his "precariously maintained existence erupts the most dangerous, extreme opposite type": a fanatic holder of a creed supported by a loyal group. Razumov's intelligence is not a sufficient defense against "an unintelligible world." His "aloneness" opens him to claims on his allegiance, which he submits to. His imagination leads him to betray Haldin: "Imagination always represents a threat to orderly conduct in Conrad because it causes the mind to slide away from the 'saving facts' of life and indulge in graphic, immobilising fantasies of terror and glory." *Eyes* "is the tragedy of 'a man with a mind.'"

1694 Theimer, Helen Agnes Prentice. "Conrad and Impressionism," DISSERTATION ABSTRACTS, XXIII (1962), 1024. Unpublished thesis, Stanford University, 1962.

1695 Toliver, Harold F. "Conrad's *Arrow of Gold* and Pastoral Tradition," MODERN FICTION STUDIES, VIII (Summer 1962), 148-58.

Negative reactions to *The Arrow of Gold* are due primarily to stylistic failure, not to a common view that JC had become a tired writer who no longer believed in the "heart of darkness." He had difficulty correlating the language of the sophisticated drawing room with a rhetoric of passion. In advocating the liberating simplicity of Arcadian love in a corrupt and complex society, he was trying to find defenses against crumbling institutions and to reaffirm the sacred core of life. Opposed ways of defining "how to be" are represented by Mills, Blunt, and George. George's initiation into spiritual and sexual love is both a transcendence of historical conditions and a submergence into the darkness of the pastoral love-dream.

1696 Tomlinson, Maggie. "Conrad's Integrity: *Nostromo*, 'Typhoon,' *The Shadow-Line*," MELBOURNE CRITICAL REVIEW, IV (1962), 40-53.

D. H. Lawrence's comment, "I can't forgive Conrad for being so sad and for giving in" is not wholly justified. Although JC was on the "edge of being defeated" by loneliness, isolation, and frustration, charges against modern life in *Nostromo* are just, firm, and right; JC's irony conditions our response to the positive elements in the novel; ideals are "seen and judged in terms of the practical results in action." Decoud's fate is a negative statement of the truth *Victory* tries to grasp fully. In *Nostromo,* JC is the "unwilling victim of his own skepticism." MacWhirr in "Typhoon" is not only a triumph of the unimaginative: he becomes a "considerable moral achievement." In *The Shadow-Line,* the captain resists the despair of acquiescence caused by his overly sensitive reaction to the suffering of his crew by relying on his "seaman's instinct" and his "habit of command."

1697 Vidan, Ivor. "Conradov *Lord Jim,* Ogled o strukturi" (Conrad's *Lord Jim,* An Essay in Structure), FILOLOGIJA (Zagreb), No. 3 (1962), 175-99.

JC may have used Marlow because he had failed to create a dramatic situation through the impersonal procedure in *The Rescue.* Marlow's relationship to Jim is ambiguous [he is "one of us," yet he has betrayed the code]. Technically, Marlow's personal reactions are an interpretation of Jim's story, or rather a universe of possible interpretations. The subsidiary characters do not really serve as "lens" as is often suggested, but produce a wider and livelier microcosm, of which Jim's story is also a part. Brierley's suicide, e.g., should not be thought to be in any direct connection with Jim. It only incites Marlow to think of the inscrutable powers of disintegration behind the facade of a man's apparent behavior. As a "story in two parts," as JC called it at a certain stage of its composition, *Lord Jim* is not a homogeneous work. The method applied in the first part has no sufficient justification in the second, and in trying to come to terms with the melodramatic action Conrad intensified his "indirections" and encumbered them with much technical complication. The intricate time-scheme is not an expression of a metaphysical insight, but is produced by the simultaneous aperception of several time layers, of which at least three are constantly present. It is only in the middle one—in Marlow's mind—that the action runs forward and backward. This too contributes to the unique, yet characteristic shape of the novel which both affirms and negates the epic tradition. *Jim,* in fact, can be envisaged both as a gradually progressing narrative action and as a constant yet expanding situation growing out of a central focal event. [An attempt to approach the inner life of the work as a whole by examining its external organization (the order in which the narrative material exists) and its inner organization (the mutual relationships between the characters)—the narrator thus being of key significance because of his importance for both aspects of structure.] [In Serbo-Croatian.]

1698 Vidan, Ivo. "Perspective of *Nostromo,*" STUDIA ROMANICA ET ANGLICA ZAGRABIENSIA (Zagreb), 13-14 (1962), pp. 43-54; expanded [in Serbo-Croatian] as "Politicki roman Vremena (Konradov *Nostromo*)" (The Political Novel of the Time [Conrad's *Nostromo*]), ZIVOT (Sarajevo), XI: 9 (1962), 695-712.

In a letter to R. Curle, JC said that his art was "fluid, depending on grouping [sequence] which shifts, and on the changing lights giving varied effects of perspective." This phenomenon may be studied through different aspects of the structure of *Nostromo,* in order to arrive at a fuller appreciation of the novel's unity. (1) A parallel could be drawn between each one of the characters and almost any other. The differences which exist within each of such pairs indicate polarities of human behavior which are absorbed in the total whole. This unidentified number of internally juxtaposed pairs testifies that all the psychological and moral possibilities confronting the characters form together a unique and integrated experience evolving from a situation repeatedly realized in history. (2) The image of the social set-up of Costaguana is achieved through an interaction of characters suggested through a selection of functional, not simply illustrative details (as, in Balzac's LES PAYSANS). The motive force of each character's relation to the silver is different and is entirely personal. United on a public level, they are all isolated from each other by their private interests. The particular isolation of every member of this delimited group creates in its turn a division within each of the characters. In each individual it produces a split which divides the public man from the private man. (3) *Nostromo* is essentially a multicentric work of art which could be symbolized by a complex graphic design: a number of superimposed polygons each representing the pattern of human relationships as experienced by one participant in the action. Their attitudes together amount to a complex interpretation of the events in the novel; there is no fixed point of view from which any beholder might self-assuredly evaluate and interpret them. In spite of its nineteenth-century solidity, *Nostromo* belongs to the twentieth century. (4) The perfect balance of political and private *motifs* does not persist to the end of the book. The political implications reach their culminating point in the last chapters, yet at the same time the political issues are not rendered in this part of the novel; they are pushed into the background by the personal history of one character, Nostromo. He is really outside the circle of the main characters of the novel, and not in its center; the only major figure symbolic of the people. At the end, however, the theme of the novel can be defined only by bringing the people into the story. *Nostromo* is a novel about history in progress, and at its close its subject transcends itself without adequately achieving presentation. Yet even as an anticlimax the final episode suggests the open continuity of history: the public aspect continues potentially to develop and to affect new lives, and eventually also the private aspect of these lives.

1699 Wills, John Howard. "Conrad's Organic Artistry," DISSERTATION ABSTRACTS, XXII (1962), 4356. Unpublished thesis, Washington University, 1961.

1963

1700 Barker, Dudley. THE MAN OF PRINCIPLE: A VIEW OF JOHN GALSWORTHY (NY: London House & Maxwell, 1963); rptd (NY: Stein & Day, 1969), pp. 39-41, 62, 72, 76-77, 79, 82, 83, 85, 86, 91, 95, 97, 98, 102, 103, 114, 117, 118, 127, 129, 131, 146, 162, 201, 204.

In 1892, Galsworthy sailed on the clipper *Torrens,* where the first mate was JC, who had completed *Almayer's Folly* but had not had the courage to show it to a publisher. Neither man made any special impression on the other; only later, in England, did the enduring friendship begin. Galsworthy sought JC's opinions of his productions and helped him financially. JC usually had "exaggerated praise" for his friend's works. The two men remained close friends until JC's death in 1924.

1701 Beebe, Maurice. "The Masks of Conrad," BUCKNELL REVIEW, XI (Dec 1963), 35-53.

JC is at least three persons: Josef Korzeniowski, the biographical JC; the literary JC who evolved from the former; and the "very Genuine Conrad," the daemon. JC's fiction reflects the obsession of English writers of the 1890s for the artist's frequent use of doubles, secret sharers, and nonparticipant narrators. "Heart of Darkness" is a "bitter indictment of life and an affirmation of art." In realizing his boyhood dream to go to the Congo, JC was bitterly disillusioned by his loneliness and loss of faith in the power of common beliefs to bind civilized men together. The novel shows the "profound, transforming effect" the Congo experience had on him. The last scene shows the new Marlow, who chooses to look on the darkness of life "with sympathetic but horrified detachment." In *Victory,* Heyst's error is in not remaining detached from life. He cannot, as Marlow did, "retreat before the evil incarnate in . . . Jones." *Victory,* then, should be read as a "tragedy of inadequate detachment."

1702 Bennett, Carl D. "A Choice of Nightmares. A Study of Conrad's Ethical Vision," DISSERTATION ABSTRACTS, XXIV (1963), 293-94. Unpublished thesis, Emory University, 1962.

1703 Bernard, Kenneth. "Marlow's Lie," ENGLISH RECORD, XIII (April 1963), 47-48.

Near the end of "Heart of Darkness," Marlow lies to Kurtz's Intended for two reasons: (1) having identified himself with Kurtz who has found "The horror!" in human life, he realizes that man's nature, unchanged through the ages, contains "an ineradicable component" of evil; and (2) believing that women, "with their ideals, their beliefs in man's essential goodness, however wrong, are a haven for men from the uncompromising, dismal truth they live with," understands at last that "it is better to live with a lie than to die with the truth." For these reasons the last section of the story is relevant to the whole.

1704 Billiar, Donald E. "The Philosophic Romance in Nineteenth-Century England," DISSERTATION ABSTRACTS, XXIV (1963), 2472-73. Unpublished thesis, University of Michigan, 1963.

1705 Boyle, Ted Eugene. "Symbol and Meaning in the Writings of Joseph Conrad," DISSERTATION ABSTRACTS, XXIII (1963), 3894. Unpublished thesis, University of Nebraska, 1962; pub as SYMBOL AND MEANING IN THE FICTION OF JOSEPH CONRAD (The Hague: Mouton; NY: Humanities P, 1965).

1706 Brady, Marion B. "Reply," COLLEGE ENGLISH, XXIV (April 1963), 562-63.
Thomas C. Kishler, "Reality in 'Heart of Darkness,'" ibid., pp. 561-62, "impressively echoes the views of various well-known critics of Conrad's work." (1) "Mr. Kishler's 'mysterious Russian' is simply another illustration of blindness and delusion"; (2) the book on seamanship is "another example of Marlow's reliance on 'efficiency,' on the rivets, on his work"; (3) Marlow does search "for positive values" and finds the truth "when he reaches the 'heart of darkness'"; and (4) "Marlow, notwithstanding his new knowledge and his new understanding, ultimately returns to a 'sepulchral city,'" and by the end of the story "he is aware of a darkness which covers the whole world." [Demonstrates the importance of relating one's critical work to previous scholarship.]

1707 Burgess, C. F. "Conrad's Pesky Russian," NINETEENTH-CENTURY FICTION, XVIII (Sept 1963), 189-93.
The presence of the Russian in "Heart of Darkness" seems to cause Marlow —and also the critics of the work—some difficulty; but Marlow's bewilderment, intermixed with something like disgust, appears to reflect the attitude of the Polish patriot Teodor Korzeniowski. The Russian is used to bring Marlow up to date on what has happened to Kurtz since he has been out of contact with the trading company; in fact, for a time he assumes the role of narrator and helps in preparing for the climactic meeting with Kurtz. But, more importantly, he is also "perfectly drawn in the trappings of the Fool, the royal jester," who in this instance has previously played his role of Fool in Kurtz's court without being completely aware of the full implications of the "sordid saga" which he reveals to Marlow. Marlow's "commingling of disgust and awe" toward Kurtz's treatment of the Russian "prefigures" Marlow's final judgment of Kurtz, who was, according to JC, both "an atrocious phantom" and "a remarkable man."

1708 Burkhart, Charles. "Conrad the Victorian," ENGLISH LITERATURE IN TRANSITION, VI:1 (1963), 1-8.

JC belongs with such Victorian novelists as Dickens, Thackeray, and Charlotte Brontë instead of D. H. Lawrence, Joyce, and Virginia Woolf, because (1) he was the product of a "backward and provincial" culture, the land-owning gentry of Poland; (2) he was a conservative in his views of politics, class, women's rights, and revolution; (3) his concept of England was "curiously atavistic," somewhat like that of Dickens and Collins; (4) his treatment of character and his moral outlook were Victorian; and (5) his technical innovations do not place him among the modern novelists with whom he is usually classified. Characters of Victorian novelists can be classified as the good, the bad, and the silly or grotesque. The Victorian and the Conradian concepts of character are opposed to the modern practice by asking whether one thinks of Mrs. Dalloway as basically good, bad, or silly; whether Leopold Bloom is an allegory of any virtue or vice; whether Gerald and Rupert of WOMEN IN LOVE fit Thackeray's concept of the good, the bad, and the silly. Whereas JC conceived of character "in primarily moral terms," the modern novelist does not. Typical also of both the Victorian novelist and JC is the lack of development of character; in fact, JC, failing to understand his characters, leaves them mysterious or inscrutable: he is unable "to reconcile static externals of characters with the fluid interests of psychological exploration," as modern novelists do. In JC, as in Charlotte Brontë and Thackeray, "moralizing is omnipresent"; and JC also shares the sexual morality of the Victorians. JC's technical innovations seldom lead to "authorial aloofness"; his "intricate organization of time" is largely a "suspense device," a "melodramatic jangling"; and his use of point of view is typically "more a contrivance than an organic, an essential, an inevitable means of telling the tale." JC, though, is not entirely Victorian; he is "a transitional novelist who embodies an older concept of character and morality in an art whose techniques, if only at times, and if only faintly, foreshadowed the modern." [Seems to be a bit of special pleading—thoughtfully done, however—in which the major ideas developed are qualified at the end of the article.]

1709 Cross, D. C. "Replies," NOTES AND QUERIES, N.S. X (Dec 1963), 467.

Three references to JC's use of the MEMOIRS OF THE COUNTESS DE BOIGNE are important. [Refers to Manfred Mackenzie, "Fenimore Cooper and Conrad's *Suspense*," ibid. (Oct 1963), 373-75.]

1710 Dale, Patricia. "Conrad: A Borrowing from Hazlitt's Father," NOTES AND QUERIES, N.S. X (April 1963), 146.

In a letter from Jim's father in *Lord Jim,* JC "echoes . . . word for word" a letter of March, 1790, from the Rev. William Hazlitt to his son.

1711 Day, Robert A. "The Rebirth of Leggatt," LITERATURE AND PSYCHOLOGY, XIII (Summer 1963), 74-81.

The plot of "The Secret Sharer" "surrounds Leggatt rather than the captain" —a new approach—and thus reveals JC's "double narrative" in which the maturation of the captain is "paralleled and complemented by a symbolic presentation of the archetype or rebirth." JC emphasizes Leggatt's part as outcast, suggesting the Ancient Mariner and also Job. Critics have generally disregarded many significant details about Leggatt, but these details contribute to JC's "intended effect": Leggatt is saved by "blind chance"; the captain, who plays the part of the female element, is responsible for the "saving factors"; Leggatt enters "a fetus-like state" on the ship; eventually he escapes from "his imprisonment into liberty"; and this entire experience, "like the agony of birth," gives the captain a new maturity. According to this interpretation, the captain and the ship play the "feminine role"; Leggatt plays that of the fetus; the "womb-imagery" is applied to Leggatt's food; Leggatt's identification with the captain, usual in all cultures as linking mother and child, is significant; when Leggatt's release comes, both he and the captain are "reluctant" but realize that the "birth" is necessary; and the last lines of the story are about the release and "baptism" of the "reborn" Leggatt, not about the captain. The "rebirth archetype" and the imagery of birth, both somewhat realigned from their usual elements, are organically present in the story. JC thus wrote, perhaps unconsciously, "a double narrative of rebirth and initiation," the latter element of which is the more obvious of the two. [A well developed new interpretation of JC's story, but marred by a bit of special pleading.]

1712 Drew, Elizabeth. "Joseph Conrad: *Lord Jim*," THE NOVEL: A MODERN GUIDE TO FIFTEEN ENGLISH MASTERPIECES (NY: Norton, 1963), pp. 156-72.

Jim is the ethical and emotional center of *Lord Jim*. The other characters exist simply to reveal facets of his situation. "The whole range of reaction to Jim comes into focus." After Jim's trial, he is faced for the first time with the problem of his selfhood. Stein sees that Jim's true existence is in a dream world that has proved destructive. "Therefore, in order to *be,* he must turn the dream, the illusion, into fact. He must live in action." JC was a forerunner of twentieth-century novelists in abandoning chronological sequence and in his "careful creation of symbolic significance" of external details. His life led him to write of exiles, lonely sea captains, someone in a solitary struggle. Man's moral and emotional responses to "the malignant irony of external events" is JC's theme.

1713 Eschbacher, Robert L. *"Lord Jim,* Classical Rhetoric, and the Freshman Dilemma," COLLEGE ENGLISH, XXV (Oct 1963), 22-25.

One can teach *Lord Jim* to freshman classes by fusing "solid composition with a solid introduction to literature." The Patusan section is not a falling off from the *Patna* affair. [Concentrates mainly on methods of teaching the novel.]

1714 Fleishmann, Avrom Hirsch. "Conrad's Politics: Community and Anarchy in the Fiction of Joseph Conrad." Unpublished thesis, Johns Hopkins University, 1963; pub as CONRAD'S POLITICS: COMMUNITY AND ANARCHY IN THE FICTION OF JOSEPH CONRAD (Baltimore: The Johns Hopkins P, 1967).

1715 Foulke, Robert Dana. "Life in the Dying World of Sail, 1870-1910," JOURNAL OF BRITISH STUDIES, III (Nov 1963), 105-36.

There is an historical correlative to JC's "nostalgic and romantic" rendering of the professional sailor's life at sea up to the end of sailing ships. [Lists the real dangers faced by seamen on these ships as crews were reduced in size and tonnage per ship increased in order to compete with steamships.] JC's viewpoint was that of an officer rather than that of a sailor who endured the terrible hardships with less devotion.

1716 Gillon, Adam. "The Jews in Joseph Conrad's Fiction," CHICAGO JEWISH FORUM, XXII (Fall 1963), 34-40.

Since JC's anti-Jewish feelings were probably caused by his background, in which Jews were social inferiors who "did not belong," his attitude toward Jewish characters in his fiction assumes significance.

Of his two Jewish characters, Yankel, the innkeeper in "Prince Roman," is an idealized and sympathetic figure who seems to be drawn from PAN TADEUSZ by Mickiewicz and is therefore sustained almost entirely by a literary tradition. In the character of Hirsch in *Nostromo,* JC creates a more compelling figure. Hirsch's function on the lighter is clear: his fear endangers all three men aboard. JC needed Hirsch for the sake of melodramatic contrast, since all three men, each destroyed by the corrupting evil of the silver mine and the revolution it engenders, come to a violent end. Hirsch's archetypal cowardice contrasts with Nostromo's reputation of fearlessness and with Decoud's "ostensible self-control." Furthermore, Hirsch's cowardice dramatizes Nostromo's eventual spiritual collapse when he becomes a cringing coward, and it also forces the hand of Sotillo and actually causes his downfall. In the scene on the lighter Decoud is identified with Hirsch, as he is again at the end of the novel. In addition, JC uses Hirsch as a foil to Nostromo and also to Captain Mitchell, Sotillo, and Dr. Monygham. But JC perhaps intended Hirsch to be a more significant symbol than a stock figure of the archetypal Jew. Hirsch, indeed, exemplifies the chaotic conditions in Costaguana, becoming a "symbol of a profound social disintegration." Finally, in the scene of Hirsch's torture, the villain is not the Jew, but actually his tormentor Sotillo. Hirsch no longer appears comic or despicable: he remains alive in the minds of other characters, and he also suggests Christ on the cross. His death is perhaps more poignant than that of Decoud or Nostromo. [An excellent analysis of Hirsch's role in *Nostromo*—marred by a consistent misspelling of the word *Costaguana*.]

1717 Glicksberg, Charles I. THE SELF IN MODERN LITERATURE (University Park, Pa: Pennsylvania State U P, 1963), pp. xv, 95.
JC, like Hardy, Malraux, and Sartre, interpreted "Nature" as "nonmoral and totally indifferent to human weal or woe." The "destructive element" which JC refers to in *Lord Jim* is seen, in the light of later relativistic writers, to be "the river of time" with each point of view being justified "in its own right."

1718 Goetsch, Paul. "Joseph Conrad: *The Secret Agent*," NEUEREN SPRACHEN, XII (1963), 97-110.
In *The Secret Agent,* JC clothes a basically melodramatic subject in heavy irony. Thus, he distances the reader from the pathetic fate of the figures and forces him to adopt his own critical attitude toward them. No character, not even Stevie, Winnie, or the Assistant Commissioner, escapes JC's criticism. The pattern of events brings out the egotism and the blindness of the people and a fundamental lack of communication which is due to their illusions and *idées fixes*. Far from leading to the emotional involvement of tragic irony, JC's ironic treatment has an alienating effect and, in various scenes, results in grotesqueness. Many of the characters are confronted with the absurd (in Camus's sense), an experience irreconcilable with their illusions; but in refusing to accept this, they behave in a grotesque manner. Verloc, for example, believes himself to be on safe ground again after Stevie's death, and Winnie tries desperately to cling to security when she joins Ossipon. The grotesque scenes are prepared for by JC's technique of characterization. The anarchists, the Verlocs, and the police are conceived as figures whose attitudes, words, and actions contrast sharply with their inclinations. Their inner distintegration is reflected in their eccentric appearance and movements and in many images which suggest the inhuman, the inorganic, and the machine-like. The novel reveals the anarchy and chaos underlying a society of egocentric persons, who are deficient in self-knowledge and thus act as secret agents undermining the society. In contrast with *Nostromo* and "Heart of Darkness," JC's vision has so darkened here that no figure in the novel has that "resignation open-eyed, conscious, and informed by love," that critical and pragmatic attitude toward the ideal which acknowledges the solidarity of man. It is only the

omniscient narrator who is aware of the pity and horror of the human condition. [In German.]

1719 Gordon, Robert (ed). THE EXPANDED MOMENT: A SHORT STORY ANTHOLOGY (Boston: Heath, 1963), pp. 23-24, 62-76, 297. [In addition to brief commentary and questions for discussion, the editor prints the text of JC's "The Tale," the printing based upon the Dent edition of TALES OF HEARSAY AND LAST ESSAYS (1955).]

1720 Graver, Lawrence. "Conrad's 'The Lagoon,'" EXPLICATOR, XXI (May 1963), Item 70; based on material in a 1961 dissertation and absorbed in CONRAD'S SHORT FICTION (Berkeley and Los Angeles: University of California P, 1969).

JC revised the CORNHILL version of "The Lagoon" when it was to be printed in *Tales of Unrest* so he could strengthen the "thematic unity" of the five stories by making the theme of destructive illusions crucial in at least four of them. In the book version he added the word "illusions" because he wanted to suggest that Arsat, like the other principal characters in the collection of stories, "had been a victim of defective vision in the past and will continue to be so in the future." "Illusions" thus becomes the last word of both the story and the book, "both of which are preoccupied with the crippling and ultimately destructive nature of moral blindness."

1721 Graver, Lawrence. "Critical Confusion and Conrad's 'The End of the Tether,'" MODERN FICTION STUDIES, IX (Winter 1963-64), 390-93; based on material in a 1961 dissertation and absorbed in CONRAD'S SHORT FICTION (Berkeley and Los Angeles: University of California P, 1969).

JC was primarily interested not in Captain Whalley's fortitude or bad luck but in "the flaw which motivated his life, the weakness which led so inexorably to his criminal act." Vulnerable because of his overwhelming love for his daughter, he makes a disastrous agreement with Massy; and his religious point of view is "too ingenuous, too idyllic," for the evil which at last engulfs him. The old man's single failure was for JC "more provocative than all of his many earlier successes" because it exposed frailty and the weakness of a view of life "based on illusion and simple-minded piety." The last pages of the tale are therefore especially important: Whalley "has a vision [of the horror of life] and stubbornly denies its validity"; everyone— the authorities, Van Wyck, and the Captain's daughter—has an image of Whalley which is "woefully incomplete." Some of the critical confusion is caused by failure to emphasize the ending properly, but some is caused by JC himself, who spent too much energy in making Whalley appear an heroic figure.

1722 Gross, Seymour L. "Conrad's Revision of 'Amy Foster,'" NOTES AND QUERIES, N.S. X (April 1963), 144-46.

After the publication of "Amy Foster" in THE ILLUSTRATED LONDON NEWS in 1901, JC made several revisions before including it in *Typhoon and Other Stories* in 1903. Many of these changes are slight, but some indicate that JC's aim was to revise largely, though not "dramatically," in order to make the reader "see." Certain additions seem to help achieve this end, but others afford some evidence of JC's weakness for the rhetorically "high-sounding."

1723 Harper, George Mills. "Conrad's Knitters and Homer's Cave of the Nymphs," ENGLISH LANGUAGE NOTES, I (Sept 1963), 53-57.

JC intended his knitters in "Heart of Darkness" to convey more than a simple parallel with the fates. They were conceived as guardians of the two gates of Homer's cave of the world and share in the complexity of the originals. It is "likely that Conrad was remembering either a well-known passage on the cave of the nymphs from the ODYSSEY, or Porphyry's explanation of Homer's symbolism."

1724 Hay, Eloise Knapp. THE POLITICAL NOVELS OF JOSEPH CONRAD: A CRITICAL STUDY (Chicago and Lond: University of Chicago P, 1963).

Accidents "of national origin and family background compelled him [JC] from earliest childhood to see in life a political dimension that strongly affected his perspective of all human affairs." For JC, every individual is related to the political dilemma: "politics is implicit in the ego," and for JC "man is a political animal" with "a dual nature, empowered with titanic good and titanic evil, as a result of which he is at war with himself and with his fellow men." JC's achievement was to turn politics from action to art.

JC's first political novel (*The Rescue*) was intended to be a contrast not between Malay and Westerner but between two kinds of Westerner, Martin Travers, with his "shallow pride" in his cultural superiority, and Tom Lingard, an unconvincing but complex English figure whose basic characteristics are "the paragon of a pure politician" and a "pure" lover. Since JC, in completing the novel after writing "Heart of Darkness," had to maintain Lingard's "primal purity" even if he no longer believed in it, he portrays his hero as "so detached from his homeland and so personally disinterested" that his motives are obscure. He excised from the manuscript a character, Wyndham, who linked all the other characters together. Having promised his publishers a love story, the best JC could do was to develop Edith Travers as "a *femme fatale,* a woman who could maintain her heady appeal for Lingard in spite of her part in the disastrous intrusion of the

Western civilizers"; since she must either be spared or become a villainess, the entire point of the "political fable" almost vanishes.

"Heart of Darkness" shows how Marlow, while claiming concern above all with self-knowledge and truth, "progresses toward deception and denial." Marlow as the narrator on the *Nellie,* supposing himself freed of Kurtz's influence, misses the point that his talk of method and efficiency is in itself despicable. Kurtz's characteristics are seen "in diluted solution" in all the other Europeans, including Marlow, who behaves consistently as a "punctilious, well-meaning British conservative." Marlow rejects what he has seen in Kurtz—"civilization's superman" who had not conquered but had surrendered to the savage customs he hated. Marlow lies for Kurtz to the Intended, whose house is "a good image for the 'house' of all Europe," which had contributed to the making of Kurtz. Thus "Heart of Darkness" appears as "an extraordinary example of political fiction, conveying its most important meanings through the evasions and self-contradictions of the narrator."

In *Nostromo* Charles Gould is an imperfect model of the real capitalist, Holroyd; everything in the book illustrates JC's theory of history. *Nostromo* is typical of the modern political novel, which is "on the whole a foil to the modern novel centering on private experience" (*Lord Jim* is probably the best example). Charles Gould is both Nostromo's double and the initiator of his fall.

The Secret Agent is one of JC's "master works" because of its dramatization of London. This book, in which Russian politics become part of JC's subject for the first time, is "very un-Russian." In spite of its serious content, this novel is "as frolicsome as any melodrama ever composed," but also "profoundly disturbing." JC's irony "turns corrosive not on the political or structural aspects of society but on the more homely features of city life and modern thought"; he wants "to make you *see*" modern city life as "hygienically sterile," with man scarcely existing or existing only in a dream. The central theme of the novel is the "contrast between what is fully human and affirmative toward life and what is wretchedly less than human and revolted by life." *Agent* is JC's only novel in which England appears as what Poland had previously been to the author—"the highest example of political rectitude." Winnie Verloc becomes a central character as she changes from "a woman who carefully avoids 'the inwardness of things' to one for whom there is no longer any external or objective substance to cling to"; Ossipon too changes "from one with little or no insight into his own life to one who sees too much," until he is the only person in the story who reaches a state of real madness and despair. Ironically, the unity of the novel evolves from Winnie's progress from "the English woman's basic soundness" to "a kind of madness" unknown either to Vladimir or to the Professor.

Under Western Eyes is JC's last important political work in fiction. In it the subject of politics, and particularly the novelist's opinions about socialism and democracy, about revolution and Russia, is closely related both geographically and emotionally to his Polish inheritance. Razumov's response to the betrayal of Haldin raises complex moral issues: "I am independent—and therefore perdition is my lot" signifies more than excommunication from the world. The tragic situation is the result of a terrible independence which is man's final responsibility for his actions. In *Eyes*, JC's final word on politics "seems to be that political institutions form the national character of a people." Razumov's subjection on the one hand to "autocratic despotism" and on the other to "revolutionary despair" makes his tragedy "peculiarly Russian." [For a commentary on Mrs. Hay's treatment of *Nostromo*, see T. A. Hanzo's review, "The Politics of Loyalty," ENGLISH LITERATURE IN TRANSITION, VII:2 (1964), 125-27. Mrs. Hay finds much more in JC's political novels than her thesis of a "political dimension" calls for or accounts for. She writes well about issues which lead beyond political implications, and many of her suggestions point to further conclusions. However valuable her insights may be, Mrs. Hay's book does not sharpen sufficiently the blurred image of JC that we receive from his previous and less exhaustive critics.]

> **1725** Hoffman, Stanton de Voren. "Comedy and Form in the Fiction of Joseph Conrad," DISSERTATION ABSTRACTS, XXIII (1963), 3898-99. Unpublished thesis, Pennsylvania State University, 1962.

> **1726** Johnson, Bruce M. "Conrad's 'Karain' and *Lord Jim*," MODERN LANGUAGE QUARTERLY, XXIV (March 1963), 13-20.

In "Karain," begun sometime in 1897, JC introduces characters and a motif which anticipate "some of the more basic involutions" of *Lord Jim*. Karain, like Jim, believes that he can leave the "ghost" of his past behind; he assembles a band of natives and rules his kingdom much as Jim does in Patusan; both men feel a sense of great guilt and seem able to avoid it by "the sheer success of their governing enterprise"; and both, revered by their subjects, appear "clothed in the illusion of unavoidable success," but act as if they were on a stage. In both men there is the "intuition" that guilt may be overcome "by passing a cultural or racial barrier." JC, however, is puzzled by the attempts of these two men "to leave behind or metamorphose their guilt via some cultural barrier," and thus both stories are somewhat ambiguous. Deep resemblances between the short story and the novel appear in the manner in which Karain and Jim contribute to the "main theme of illusion": both receive aid from a man who "recognizes that dreams are 'cured' with dreams"—Hollis and Stein. Hollis is a "proto-Stein, an anticipation of the theme which is full-blown in the later character." Both the narrator of "Karain" and Marlow of *Jim* must separate illusion from reality continually because they fear the consequences of failing to do so; they cannot "play the game" engaged in by Hollis or Stein, that is, "therapeutically manipulate illusion." "Karain" thus resembles *Jim* in its analysis of illusion. [A well-supported thesis.]

1727 Johnson, Bruce. "Joseph Conrad and Crane's RED BADGE OF COURAGE," PAPERS OF THE MICHIGAN ACADEMY OF SCIENCE, ARTS, AND LETTERS, XLVIII (1963), 649-55.

JC seemed to be unusually annoyed by any suggestion that his friend's THE RED BADGE OF COURAGE had even slightly influenced his *The Nigger of the Narcissus*. He carefully intimated that he could not have been affected by Crane's work because he had not read it until after he had finished his own and sold it to the NEW REVIEW. Some of his comments (LAST ESSAYS), however, indicate that he could not have followed the critical stir caused by THE RED BADGE without reading it while he was at work on *Nigger* or even earlier. From the evidence available it appears that JC was too sensitive to Crane's alleged influence because he felt that his book, unlike Crane's, "had gone much beyond the psychologically revealing visual metaphors he thought were the essence of Crane's impressionism, and that Crane's attention to the outside of things never quite revealed an inside." The reviewers of the two books were right in detecting a relationship between them; both writers had realized "the moral problem of their novels partly through visual technique," and JC, largely at fault in failing to recognize the "concert of technique and moral depth" in Crane, therefore "reacted so peevishly" to the reviewers, who had "touched a sore spot." Crane's novel may have served as "a goad" to JC's thinking about his art, and possibly the early reviewers of Crane partially caused JC to append his preface (first called an "Author's Note") to the last installment of *Nigger,* so he might announce publicly that *"his* technique promised much more—promised, in fact, the shifting lights of moral consciousness" that were to become evident in *Lord Jim.*

1728 Joseph, Edward D. "Identity and Joseph Conrad," PSYCHOANALYTIC QUARTERLY, XXXII (Oct 1963), 549-72.

An analysis of JC's life and major literary creations indicates that "in the totality of his work" JC "achieved an identity and mental harmony that was lacking in his nonliterary life." He was isolated from other people; he had a "depressive disposition"; he was constantly concerned with bodily illness; he continually deprecated his work, was "testy, yet friendly" toward strangers, and was almost unable to choose a career; and he seemed to lack a natural relationship with women. These characteristics, all related to his childhood experiences and to his "severe superego," prevented him from achieving the harmony necessary for his own identity. In his artistic works, however, JC created a new world which gave him "an 'identity' beyond his own actual experience." A major theme in the novels and stories is "man's attempt to find his place in a hostile world." Although the characters may develop in different ways, JC's sympathies are with those "who find redemption through recognition of the forces against which they struggle and rise above them, even at the expense of happiness or of life." Tuan Jim [*Lord Jim*] is triumphant and happy at the moment of his death: "his superego is appeased." Razumov [*Under Western Eyes*] finally "atones for his murderous betrayal and achieves, through his confession and punishment, a state of harmony between his ego and punitive superego." In *Victory,* Heyst, the isolated man, achieves "an awareness of himself, an identity, through his relationship with a woman." The "reality aspect of identity" is the theme of *Nostromo:* the main struggle centers about the silver and the silver mine; and "through the acceptance of the existence of this reality each of the various characters achieves his place and his inner peace, thus finding an aspect of his identity in his relationship to reality."

In most of his work JC's characters "achieve an identity, a place in the hostile world created by him, through a relationship to different aspects of the psychic apparatus," and "the working out of the identity evolves through establishing a state of harmony between disparate elements of the mind." Apparently, JC's personal life was "bound around an intense sense of guilt, no doubt related to his early relationships, deprivations, and losses"; and he appears to have found a personal identity of his own "through establishing a state of relative harmony between various structures of the psychic apparatus" in the characters he created. [Intriguing, but scarcely adequate. Who, for example, found "inner peace" in *Nostromo?* Too facile.]

> **1729** Kerf, René. *"The Nigger of the Narcissus* and the MS. Version of *The Rescue,"* ENGLISH STUDIES (Amsterdam), XLIV (Dec 1963), 437-43.

In tracing the development of a writer's art, one must consider the order and date of composition. *The Rescue,* partially written between 1896 and 1899 but not published until 1920, is chronologically very close to the period of composition of *The Nigger of the Narcissus;* and various elements in part I of the former novel are further developed in *Nigger.* Similarities in common are the nautical setting; the imagery used to describe this setting; and the direct relationship between a character like Shaw, the first mate of

Lingard's brig, and the portraits of the sailors in *Nigger*. Thus several elements of part I of *Rescue* foreshadow *Nigger*.

1730 Killinger, John. THE FAILURE OF THEOLOGY IN MODERN LITERATURE (NY and Nashville: Abingdon P, 1963), pp. 27, 178. In "Heart of Darkness," the jungle is "some kind of demonic region that has the power of completely demoralizing the European mind," a conception which parallels Dante's vision of damned souls.

1731 Kimbrough, Robert (ed). "HEART OF DARKNESS": AN AUTHORITATIVE TEXT, BACKGROUNDS AND SOURCES, ESSAYS IN CRITICISM (NY: Norton, Norton Critical Editions, 1963). Contents, abstracted under date of first publication: Kimbrough, "Preface" (1963); Kimbrough, "Notes on the Text" (1963); Muriel C. Bradbrook, ["Conrad: A Sketch"], from JOSEPH CONRAD: POLAND'S ENGLISH GENIUS (1941); Albert J. Guerard, "From Life to Art," CONRAD THE NOVELIST (1958); G. J.-Aubry, ["From Sailor to Novelist"], from JOSEPH CONRAD: LIFE AND LETTERS (1927); Edward Garnett, ["Art Drawn from Memory"], from "Introduction," LETTERS FROM JOSEPH CONRAD 1895-1924 (1928); Richard Curle, ["His Piercing Memory"], from THE LAST TWELVE YEARS OF JOSEPH CONRAD (1928); Ford Madox Ford, ["The Setting"], from "'Heart of Darkness,'" PORTRAITS FROM LIFE (1936; 1937; see "Conrad and the Sea" [1945]); Ford Madox Ford, ["The Ending"], "'Heart of Darkness,'" PORTRAITS FROM LIFE (1936; 1937; see "Conrad and the Sea" [1945]); Max Beerbohm, *"The Feast* by J*s*ph C*nr*d," A CHRISTMAS GARLAND (1912); H. L. Mencken, "Joseph Conrad," A BOOK OF PREFACES (1917; see 1924); Robert F. Haugh, ["'Heart of Darkness': Problem for Critics"], from JOSEPH CONRAD: DISCOVERY IN DESIGN (1957); Albert J. Guerard, "The Journey Within," CONRAD THE NOVELIST (1958); Alan M. Hollingsworth, "Freud, Conrad, and the Future of an Illusion," LITERATURE AND PSYCHOLOGY (1955); Jerome Thale, "Marlow's Quest," UNIVERSITY OF TORONTO QUARTERLY (1955); Lillian Feder, "Marlow's Descent into Hell," NINETEENTH-CENTURY FICTION (1955); Robert O. Evans, "Conrad's Underworld," MODERN FICTION STUDIES (1956); Guy Owens, Jr., ["An Arthurian Allusion"], "A Note on 'Heart of Darkness,'" from NINETEENTH-CENTURY FICTION (1957); Albert J. Guerard, ["Allusion and Overtones"], from CONRAD THE NOVELIST (1958); William Bysshe Stein, "The Lotus Posture and 'Heart of Darkness,'" MODERN FICTION STUDIES (1956); Seymour Gross, ["The Frame"], "A Further Note on the Function of the Frame in 'Heart of Darkness,'" from MODERN FICTION STUDIES (1957); George Williams, "The Turn of the Tide in 'Heart of Darkness,'" MODERN FICTION STUDIES (1963); Marvin Mudrick, "The Originality of Conrad," HUDSON REVIEW (1958); Stewart C. Wilcox, "Conrad's 'Complicated Presentations' of Symbolic Imagery,"

JOSEPH CONRAD

PHILOLOGICAL QUARTERLY (1960); Leo Gurko, ["Conrad's Ecological Art"], from JOSEPH CONRAD: GIANT IN EXILE (1962); and Paul L. Wiley, "Conrad's Skein of Ironies" (1963).

By others, not about JC and not abstracted: "A Map of the Congo Free State, 1890," p. 85; "The Congo," containing three brief quotations by King Leopold II, of Belgium, H. M. Stanley, and Mark Twain, p. 86; ["The Congo: A Brief History, 1876-1908"], from Sir Harry Joynston, GEORGE GRENFELL AND THE CONGO (1910); ["The Visionary King"], from John De Courcy MacDonnell, KING LEOPOLD II: HIS RULE IN BELGIUM AND THE CONGO (1905); ["His Brother's Keeper"], from Richard Harding Davis, THE CONGO AND THE COASTS OF AFRICA (1907); ["The Sacred Mission of Civilization"], from King Leopold II, in Guy Burrows, THE LAND OF PIGMIES (1898); ["New Forms of Slavery"], from H. R. Fox-Bourne, CIVILIZATION IN CONGOLAND (1903); and ["The Testimony of the Kodak"], from E. D. Morel, KING LEOPOLD'S RULE IN AFRICA (1904).

By JC and not abstracted: an "authoritative" text of "Heart of Darkness"; "Geography and Some Explorers," from LAST ESSAYS, ed by Curle (1926); "When I Grow Up I Shall Go *There,*" from *A Personal Record* (1912); ["Extracts from Correspondence, January 16-June 18, 1890"], from LETTERS OF JOSEPH CONRAD TO MARGUERITE PORADOWSKA, ed by Gee and Sturm (1940) and Aubry's JOSEPH CONRAD: LIFE AND LETTERS (1927); "The Congo Diary," from LAST ESSAYS, ed by Curle (1926); ["Extracts from Correspondence, September 6-December 27, 1890"], from Aubry's JOSEPH CONRAD IN THE CONGO (1926), Aubry's JOSEPH CONRAD: LIFE AND LETTERS (1927), and LETTERS OF JOSEPH CONRAD TO MARGUERITE PORADOWSKA, ed by Gee and Sturm (1940); "Two Final Notes," from *A Personal Record* (1912); ["Extracts from Correspondence, December 13, 1898-February 12, 1899"], from Aubry's JOSEPH CONRAD: LIFE AND LETTERS (1927), JOSEPH CONRAD: LETTERS TO WILLIAM BLACKWOOD AND DAVID S. MELDRUM, ed by William Blackburn (1958), LETTERS FROM JOSEPH CONRAD 1895-1924, ed by Edward Garnett (1928), and from LETTRES FRANÇAISES, ed by Aubry (1929).

> **1732** Kimbrough, Robert. "Note on the Text," HEART OF DARKNESS: AN AUTHORITATIVE TEXT, BACKGROUNDS AND SOURCES, ESSAYS IN CRITICISM, ed by Robert Kimbrough (NY: Norton, Norton Critical Editions, 1963), pp. 80-81.

A survey of the publishing history of "Heart of Darkness" reveals that of the many versions of this story the one published by Heinemann (1921) is the best copy-text because it seems to be the last edition which JC had a chance to correct or revise.

1733 Kimbrough, Robert. "Preface," HEART OF DARKNESS: AN AUTHORITATIVE TEXT, BACKGROUNDS AND SOURCES, ESSAYS IN CRITICISM, ed by Robert Kimbrough (NY: Norton, Norton Critical Editions, 1963), pp. vii-viii.

When JC began to write "Heart of Darkness" in 1898, he was well established as a literary figure, having made a rapid transition from "a life of isolation to one of fellowship, . . . from captain to writer"; and by this time he was ready to experiment artistically with material which was very personal to him. His earlier narratives are mainly "objective, descriptive, and thematically clear," whereas "Heart of Darkness" tends to be "interior, suggestively analytic, and highly psychological," thereby introducing into his fiction a "new mode," the symbolic

1734 Kishler, Thomas C. "Reality in 'Heart of Darkness,'" COLLEGE ENGLISH, XXIV (April 1963), 561-62.

Marion B. Brady ["Conrad's Whited Sepulcher," ibid. (Oct 1962), 24-29] "presses too hard to convey a tidy and consistent impression of a complex fictional situation which many readers have found considerably more involved than his analysis of the interrelated themes of personal and public deception would suggest." Brady underestimates "Marlow's evaluation of the chief accountant," the book on seamanship, the young Russian, and "something real in Kurtz himself." "Marlow not only needs and seeks substance and reality in his African experience, he occasionally finds them."

1735 Kumar, Shiv K. BERGSON AND THE STREAM OF CONSCIOUSNESS NOVEL (NY: New York U P, 1963), p. 19.

According to Bergson, one may know reality either by adopting a point of view in relation to an object and stopping at the relative, or one may seek an intuitive identification with the object in an attempt to "possess the original." The stream of consciousness novel purports to achieve this realization of the original. Novelists like JC and Henry James, "in spite of their extremely subjective techniques of treating character and scene," fail to measure up to the "new ideal" in that they arrange their material from a specific point of view. James's observer and JC's Marlow are thus considered as remnants of the "traditional" novel.

1736 Laskowski, Irmina Teresa. "Conrad's Settings: A Study of Descriptive Style." Unpublished thesis, Harvard University, 1963.

1737 Lee, Robert Francis. "Conrad's Colonialism," DISSERTATION ABSTRACTS, XXIV (1963), 1172. Unpublished thesis, University of Minnesota, 1962, based on "Joseph Conrad and the White Man's Burden," an M.A. thesis abstracted in VANDERBILT UNIVERSITY BULLETIN, II (Sept 1953), 40.

1738 Mackenzie, Manfred. "Fenimore Cooper and Conrad's *Suspense*," NOTES AND QUERIES, N.S. X (Oct 1963), 373-75.

JC's puzzling passages at the beginning of *Suspense* and the reference to these pages just before the novel breaks off, in which Attilio tells Cosmo Latham about his meeting with a hermit on the coast of South America, seem to be related to Cooper's THE PRAIRIE, in which there are several resemblances to JC's work, such as the reverie or expectation of death and the similar descriptions of the prairie and the sea.

1739 Marković, Vida. "Joseph Conrad," ENGLESKI ROMAN XX VEKA (The English Novel of the Twentieth Century) (Belgrade: 1963), pp. 53-64, 135-38.

[Marković surveys the most striking characters and situations in JC's main works, with a glance at his personality.] [In Serbo-Croatian.]

1740 Martin, W. R. "The Captain of the *Narcissus*," ENGLISH STUDIES IN AFRICA (Johannesburg), VI (Sept 1963), 191-97.

The pattern of *The Nigger of the Narcissus* is simply that of the Fall, and it recalls that of PARADISE LOST as well as that of Genesis. James Wait is associated with Satan, the crew with fallen Man, and the cook with the Church. Wait's release is seen as the birth of evil; his cabin corresponds to Hell. Five members of the crew, including the narrator, deliver Satan into the world. Wait is the source of evil, and Donkin "manipulates the evil force that is released." Another important term in JC's pattern is Captain Allistoun, who is—or "is *like*"—God, or Jehovah. JC's tone is ironical at the expense of the Captain, who is "unlike Zeus." Since the ship is the world, Allistoun obviously corresponds to God in the storm; but JC merely gives certain hints of this interpretation and allows the reader to enjoy tracing the rest of the pattern. For the Captain, the mutiny is a greater test than the storm is; he pities Wait while understanding completely his situation. This is his reason for confining Wait to his cabin. JC contrives a situation in which Allistoun, seemingly harsh, is really wise, compassionate, and just. And he completes the myth by a suggestion of the redemption. Thus the novel "embodies a vision of the divided and paradoxical nature of man," an insight which "informs every part of the work."

1741 Matlaw, Ralph E. "Dostoevskij and Conrad's Political Novels," AMERICAN CONTRIBUTIONS TO THE FIFTH INTERNATIONAL CONGRESS OF SLAVISTS, SOFIA, SEPT. 1963. (The Hague: Mouton, 1963), II, 213-230.

Dostoevski's CRIME AND PUNISHMENT and THE DEVILS influenced JC's *Under Western Eyes* and *The Secret Agent,* respectively. Perhaps JC's novels are polemic replies to Dostoevski's work. Despite significant differences, the plots of CRIME AND PUNISHMENT and *Eyes* are similar. *Eyes* attempts to show "in rational and moral terms" what is depicted in CRIME AND PUNISHMENT in "the frenzied struggle and religious solution." Some of the similarities between Raskolnikov and Razumov are "their ambition and pride, their susceptibility to abstract ideas, their impulsiveness." "The difference between CRIME AND PUNISHMENT and [*Eyes*] lies to a considerable extent in the interposition between the characters and the reader of a narrator who eliminates the sense of immediacy Dostoevskij was so anxious to preserve." As regards the similarities between THE DEVILS and *Agent,* "both novels imaginatively reconstruct an actual event—the attempt to blow up Greenwich in 1895, and the murder of the student Ivanov by Nechaev's cell." These two JC novels "resemble Dostoevskij's novels, . . . a curious coincidence." At another level, however, they may be a response to very deep forces stirring within Conrad, which is found abhorrent and controlled by his ordered existence and searing irony. If these issues—both moral and political—had to be dealt with, this could be done without the uncivilized eruptions he apparently considered Dostoevskij's work. They could also be handled without the religious fervor and extremes of behavior everywhere noted in the Russian writer."

1742 Maxwell, J. C. "Conrad and Turgenev: A Minor Source for *Victory*," NOTES AND QUERIES, N.S. X (Oct 1963), 372-73.

There are significant resemblances between Lavretsky in A HOUSE OF GENTLEFOLK and Heyst in *Victory*. Both men had developed a "disabling scepticism" because of the "eccentric and doctrinaire" education imposed by their fathers, and there are several "verbal parallels."

1743 Meyer, Bernard C. "Conrad's Duel," POLISH REVIEW, VIII (Summer 1963), 46-60; absorbed in JOSEPH CONRAD: A PSYCHO-ANALYTIC BIOGRAPHY (Princeton, NJ: Princeton U P, 1967).

JC's bullet wound in the chest (1878) was sustained not in a duel, as JC himself indicated, but was self-inflicted. A letter written by Thaddeus Bobrowski presents an account very different from JC's romantic version in *The Arrow of Gold*. Because duelling enjoyed an honorable status, where a suicide was regarded as disgraceful, sinful, and criminal, it is unlikely that a Polish gentleman would have concealed a duel behind a false confession of an attempt at suicide. Jerry Allen in THE THUNDER AND THE SUNSHINE (1958), gives a rather romantic explanation of JC's refusal to disclose the identity of Doña Rita. JC sometimes turned to fiction as a means of "effecting a corrective revision of a painful reality" and therefore the love affair in *The Arrow of Gold* is a "triumphant fictional revision of an unhappy real experience with a woman from which Conrad emerged in humiliation and defeat"—thus the reason for his attempt at suicide. In Rita (*The Sisters*) JC was "confiding his secret yearnings for his dead mother," and the general outline of this Rita's history is "almost identical" with that of the Rita of *Arrow.* Rita, then, must have been a "school girl sweetheart," not a contemporary of JC's when he was in Marseilles. Also, the man who is M. George's rival for her love, Mr. J. M. K. Blunt, is JC's father; thus M. George's rivalry with Blunt contains "a pattern of competition between father and son for the same woman." JC never recovered from his mother's death. The suicidal gesture of his youth appears eighteen times in his fictional world; in fact, his self-destructive impulses appeared many times in his adult life, but "only within the confines of his heartsick soul." [A good example of literary detection and psychological analysis. Meyer's psychoanalytic approach to JC is more fully developed in his JOSEPH CONRAD: A PSYCHOANALYTIC BIOGRAPHY (1967).]

1744 Mitchell, Sidney H. "Conrad and His Critics: 1895-1914," DISSERTATION ABSTRACTS, XXIII (1963), 2917. Unpublished thesis, University of Virginia, 1962.

1745 Moore, Carlisle. "Conrad and the Novel as Ordeal," PHILOLOGICAL QUARTERLY, XLII (Jan 1963), 55-74.

JC frequently combined in his works the literal and the symbolic in severe ordeals which test and almost break his protagonists. A relationship between JC's painful efforts to be a good writer and the themes of trial and failure is seen in *Almayer's Folly, An Outcast of the Islands,* and the other Malayan stories, which deal with treachery, cowardice, and corruption and disintegration of personality; and such characters as Kurtz, Lord Jim, Nostromo, Razumov, and Heyst are subjected in various ways to ordeals and broken by them. The survivors, like Marlow in "Youth," the young captain of "The Secret Sharer" and *The Shadow-Line,* Captain MacWhirr, and the captain and crew of *The Nigger of the Narcissus,* endure at least partly by holding fast to an ideal code of conduct and partly by meeting "relenting circumstance."

JC's difficulties were both temperamental and financial. He identified himself with his protagonists and experienced in completing a work of art an ordeal similar to those about which he wrote. In seeking for a kind of involvement which JC was particularly careful to conceal in his works, one must look for indirect evidence which appears beneath his "objective, post-Jamesian technique." Even Marlow, not a writer but a teller of tales, is unlike JC in that his purpose of presenting "the sublime spectacle of men in fateful contest with the Dark Powers" is not JC's problem of presenting this sublime spectacle in a work of art. In *Lord Jim,* Marlow is both an asset and a liability: on the one hand he helps JC avoid direct narrative and subjective commentary; he provides an objective point of view; he acts as a scapegoat, carrying his creator's limitations, doubts, and uncertainties; but on the other hand, he allows JC to avoid difficulties, to disarm the reader, and to regain confidence. In the way he vicariously shares the tests undergone by other characters, Marlow is a sort of "vicar": Kurtz's tragic fall in "Heart of Darkness" becomes Marlow's ordeal, and in *Jim* his attraction becomes a personal involvement. But on another level, JC's interest in Jim's ordeal is the abstract interest of the artist, not at all like Marlow's interest in Jim. Marlow thus reflects JC's personal involvement in Jim's ordeal only to a limited extent because his concern is not aesthetic but psychological.

The complexity of the narrative method of *Jim*, with its scrambled chronology of events and its multiple point of view, was a test for the author, to be passed only by using the most difficult way. But JC, by having Marlow enter the story late, faced the difficulty of recounting Jim's later life by means of a packet of letters, thus causing a hiatus and some awkwardness. There are also other relatively unimportant inconsistencies, all of which provide evidence that JC's method of narration was almost too much for him. The novel as a whole, though, shows the method more than justified. With *Jim*, then, JC may be said "to have won his master's papers as a writer," and his change of profession was justified. Perhaps his artistic strength lay in his "constitutional weakness," for when he later acquired both confidence and financial success, the quality of his work declined. [A biographical approach combined with a close textual analysis of one novel clarifies some important aspects of JC's works and adds considerably to an understanding of *Jim*.]

1746 Nelson, Harland S. "Eden and Golgotha: Conrad's Use of the Bible in *The Nigger of the Narcissus*," IOWA ENGLISH YEARBOOK, No. 8 (Fall 1963), 63-67.

The Nigger of the Narcissus is JC's "myth of the human predicament" and his "prophetic vision" of how men should bear their condition. In that symbolic dimension, the crew's relations with Wait embody mankind's struggle to come to terms with "the awareness all men have that they must die." JC uses echoes of Eden and the fall of man to suggest this part of his theme, in the scene aboard ship where the reader first learns how Wait's presence thrusts the consciousness of death on the unwilling crew. Later, in the storm, JC evokes a parallel between the ship's ordeal and the crucifixion and resurrection of Christ, but for ironic effect, to point the spiritual pride the crew falls into when they take the credit for saving the ship which really belongs to the captain. In their fatal self-confidence they make an alliance of wills with Wait, in effect denying his mortal illness in futile opposition to the wisdom of the captain. Put explicitly, JC's point is that the "weight" of contemplating their own mortality steadily is beyond men's capacity to bear. Life is possible for men only on condition that they do not let the consciousness of death distract them from "the web of mutual responsibilities and duties, the enclosing and mutually received discipline that defines human brotherhood."

1747 Ordoñez, Elmer Alindogan. "The Early Development of Joseph Conrad: Revisions and Style," DISSERTATION ABSTRACTS, XXIII (1963), 4362. Unpublished thesis, University of Wisconsin, 1963; pub as THE EARLY JOSEPH CONRAD: REVISIONS AND STYLE (Quezon City: University of Philippines P, 1969).

1748 Palmer, John Alfred. "Joseph Conrad's Fiction," DISSERTATION ABSTRACTS, XXIII (1963), 3383. Unpublished thesis, Cornell University, 1962.

1749 Reid, Stephen A. "The 'Unspeakable Rites' in 'Heart of Darkness,'" MODERN FICTION STUDIES, IX (Winter 1963-64), 347-56; rptd in CONRAD: A COLLECTION OF CRITICAL ESSAYS, ed by Marvin Mudrick (Englewood Cliffs, NJ: Prentice-Hall, Spectrum Books, 1966), pp. 45-54.

An understanding of Kurtz's rites and secrets throws important light on Kurtz's life and Marlow's reactions. Established to help perpetuate Kurtz's position as "man-god" among the natives, these rites concern human sacrifice and Kurtz's "consuming a portion of the sacrificial victim." The deep concern of the natives about the possible death or departure of Kurtz, described by Sir George James Frazer, is "one of the most striking things" in the story. But Kurtz, unlike the usual man-god described by Frazer, has come from the outside and is unwilling to consent to his death when his strength fails; thus Kurtz must have been trying to allay the anxieties of the natives by having a young and more vigorous man sacrificed and must have consumed a portion of his body, therefore dying himself by "proxy," but still retaining his high position among the natives. The heads on the poles were no doubt the victims of this procedure.

This explanation of Kurtz's rites indicates that the Russian was considered by the natives as an eventual successor to the failing Kurtz. Marlow, dimly sensing the real situation when the steamer arrives—that the natives now demand Kurtz's death—is morally shocked to think that Kurtz would voluntarily attend the rites. Kurtz's "immense plans" were "dominion over the world," with the ivory as the means to this end, just as the sacrifices were the means to the continued collection of ivory. And Kurtz hoped to exercise a "benevolent tyranny." Ironically, both he and the natives wanted his "domination" to continue, but only he considered the sacrifices "morally reprehensible." He therefore has become a prisoner of the natives, but believes his tyranny over them to be of a morally high purpose. His essential problem had been not to gain ascendancy but to maintain it, and thus he had descended into bestiality. Marlow does not know exactly what the rites are, and he does not find out; he dares not learn the truth because he may find an "echo" of the bestiality in himself. Even JC only "peeped over the edge," and we must reconstruct what he saw there. [An ingenious and well-argued speculation, worth serious consideration.]

>1750 Resink, G. J. "Axel Heyst and the Second King of the Cocos Islands," ENGLISH STUDIES (Amsterdam), XLIV (Dec 1963), 443-47.

A little known book, HEROES OF EXILE, by one of JC's closest friends, Hugh Clifford, may have provided the prototype from real life for Axel Heyst in *Victory*. There are resemblances between both Heyst and his father in the second "King of the Cocos" (from about 1839 to 1854), a member of the well-known Ross dynasty of the Cocos or Keeling Islands, an archipelago south of Sumatra. Clifford's description of the second Ross fits Heyst "in every detail." Lena also, as well as Jewel in *Lord Jim,* seems to have been drawn from a regal original described by Clifford; and Schomberg's and Davidson's names are the same as real-life figures in the history of the Ross family.

>1751 R[ice], H[oward] C., Jr. "Additions to the Doubleday Collection," PRINCETON UNIVERSITY LIBRARY CHRONICLE, XXIV (Spring 1963), 191-96.

Some forty newly acquired letters written by JC to F. N. Doubleday are a reminder of "the warm personal friendships that grew out of the business dealings" of the American publisher with "his" English authors. The letters, which extend from 1914 through 1924, cover the years in which JC was writing *The Arrow of Gold, The Rescue* and *The Rover,* and the period when he was also preparing new prefaces for the collected edition of his works for Doubleday. Included, too, is JC's visit to the United States. Only a few of these letters have been previously published. Also acquired are a set of corrected galley proofs of *Victory* and the original typescript, with many additions and corrections, of JC's prefatory note to *A Personal Record* as he prepared it for his collected works.

>1752 Ridley, Florence H. "The Ultimate Meaning of 'Heart of Darkness,'" NINETEENTH-CENTURY FICTION, XVIII (June 1963), 43-53.

Kurtz is Marlow's opposite rather than his double: "Both men are subjected to a moral test" in which Kurtz "succumbs completely" whereas Marlow "does precisely the opposite." It is this difference, "later emphasized by the two men's reaction to Kurtz's Intended," that constitutes "the heart of the novel." Throughout "Heart of Darkness," evil for white men as well as for black is "lack of restraint," which "arises from the lack of an inner core of faith" embodied in terms of light, in this instance by Kurtz's Intended. There are two kinds of men in the book, the hollow men, best represented by Kurtz, and "those who have some kind of inner strength, of faith in something," like Marlow. JC seems to have considered work as having great significance, and it is mainly work that keeps Marlow steady. The two women are also opposites; one is "the embodiment of primitive darkness," the other, "the embodiment of light." Both represent the "two opposing forces which control Kurtz," who turns away from the Belgian girl to surrender to the native one. Marlow, however, remains faithful to the Intended and "protects her from . . . the darkness into which Kurtz would have plunged her," even if he must tell her a lie; the lie is necessary because illusion, unreal as it is, is essential to preserve one from contact with reality. This is why the Belgian girl's faith in Kurtz must be protected. Ironically, the Intended's faith in illusion was for JC "the irony of the universal human condition"; from illusion alone "comes light which can be opposed to the world's darkness." [A searching and original analysis.]

1753 Rosenfield, Claire. "The Shadow Within: The Conscious and Unconscious Use of the Double," DAEDALUS, XCII (Spring 1963), 333.

"In JC's 'The Secret Sharer' and 'Heart of Darkness,' a bodily double is present whose outlaw freedom is evidence for the narrator and the reader that no man is above the threat of the irrational." Here the "double novel" reveals "not a disintegration of personality but a reintegration, a recognition of the necessary balance between order and freedom."

1754 Saveson, J. E. "Masterman as a Source of *Nostromo*," NOTES AND QUERIES, N.S. X (Oct 1963), 368-70.

JC evidently used G. F. Masterman's SEVEN EVENTFUL YEARS IN PARAGUAY (Lond, 1869) as a source of *Nostromo* by borrowing certain names, by using some details of character and incident, by writing at least one near-paraphrase, by developing his political parties from the Paraguayan parties, by describing the rooms and the patio of the Casa Gould after some descriptions by Masterman, and by summarizing to some extent the history of Paraguay. [Adds new parallels to those found in Ivo Vidan, "One Source of Conrad's *Nostromo*," REVIEW OF ENGLISH STUDIES, VII (July 1956), 287-93.]

1755 Sherry, Norman. "Conrad and the S. S. *Vidar*," REVIEW OF ENGLISH STUDIES, N.S. XIV (May 1963), 157-63.

Some of JC's experiences of the period 22 Aug 1887 to 4 Jan 1888, when the young man was first mate on S. S. *Vidar*, are found in his works, especially in *The Shadow-Line* and "The End of the Tether." A history of the

1963: 1753-1759

ship and of JC's relation to it suggests that JC did not alter details from his past when he included them in his novels unless he had "a dramatic reason" for making changes. Such biographers as Jean-Aubry and even Jocelyn Baines are sometimes incorrect in relating JC's life to his works. Whenever JC's factual material is of no dramatic or symbolic significance, the writer "kept exactly to his own experience and observation."

1756 Sherry, Norman. "Conrad's Eastern World." Unpublished thesis, University of Singapore, 1963; basis for CONRAD'S EASTERN WORLD (Cambridge: Cambridge U P, 1966).

1757 Sherry, Norman. "Conrad's *Otago:* A Case of Mistaken Identity," NOTES AND QUERIES, N.S. X (Oct 1963), 370-72.

The photograph of the *Otago,* JC's first command, in Jocelyn Baines's biography of JC is really that of another ship of the same name, not of the *Otago* that JC commanded. The novelist was inspired by his experiences on this ship and by some of the people he knew there.

1758 Sherwin, Jane King. "The Literary Epiphany in Some Early Fiction of Flaubert, Conrad, Proust, and Joyce," DISSERTATION ABSTRACTS, XXIII (1963), 3902. Unpublished thesis, University of Michigan, 1962. [Deals with "Heart of Darkness" and *Lord Jim.*]

1759 Smith, J. Oates. "The Existential Comedy of Conrad's 'Youth,'" RENASCENCE, XVI (Fall 1963), 22-28.

"Youth," a tale about "latently tragic and ostensibly brutal material," is basically comic: it has "the grace of existential comedy" which is able to "transform all suffering into acceptance" and even more. The young hero therefore survives with his "youth (or illusion) destroyed and yet intact." The only "organically mutable" element is the human condition; "the order of nature is . . . inviolate." In this story only does JC create "so icily brittle a vision . . . of the sky and sea as immense jewels upon whose brilliant surface man moves in a 'pestiferous cloud'" as he struggles for life. For JC the land, not the sea, endangers one's innocence. In "Youth" even the last, devastating explosion has no power to destroy young Marlow's faith, and a certain communion among the men is also born: JC's greatest praise is really for the crew. What matters is the "spirited, blind egotism of youth," but Marlow realizes the meaning of the loss of the ship: "the art of youth approaches narrative *as* lyric." JC here reveals the "spoils" of the voyage: Marlow's victory is also man's because this young man "shapes out of the grotesque voyage of life the triumph of the human spirit." Notable in "Youth" is a "skillful fusion of the absurd and the traditionally heroic, the grotesque and the touching, the bitter and the comic"; but its "vision—that man must heroically and necessarily struggle against the indifference of nature"—is constantly present. [An excellent existentialist interpretation.]

> **1760** Stewart, J. I. M. "Conrad," EIGHT MODERN WRITERS. Oxford History of English Literature, XII (Oxford: Clarendon P, 1963), pp. 184-222, 656-65.

JC is one of eight modern writers no longer living who seem "of unchallengeable importance in the period." He is "undoubtedly an artist in whose creations the echo of some deep inner conflict is constantly heard." "The possible eruption of a subliminal self" is a theme for which JC "finds symbolical expression." JC is never afraid of rhetoric or of prose approaching poetry, but he is "a very notable, if an obstinately uncertain" stylist. In some of his early works (*Almayer's Folly* and *An Outcast of the Islands*), although the characters are not wholly convincing, JC learns to command the spirit of place. In "Heart of Darkness" he "marshals all his developed resources of atmospheric writing, and achieves a masterpiece which is at once overpowering and enigmatical." *The Nigger of the Narcissus* is largely "heroic in kind," although "not without symbolic implications." To an English reader of *Lord Jim,* the "concept of honour upon which it turns" may seem somewhat excessive, "even obsessed." More than he realized, JC may have remained a man banished from his native soil, but his power over the reader does not arise simply from "an underlying special situation"; "it is the grand characteristic of Conrad's art that, wherever it takes us, the scene universalizes itself even as that art begins to speak"—the deck of the *Narcissus,* the upper reaches of the Congo, Jim's Patusan, the republic of Costaguana, the little kitchen behind Verloc's shop, "all take larger dimension while we watch." In *Nostromo,* a somber book concerned with self-betrayal and self-distrust, JC's genius achieves its "most vigorous and abundant, if not perhaps its most subtle, expression." Beneath the artistic detachment, JC shows his passionate self, which makes the characters of the novel so convincing. His use of description in sustained drama, his interbalance of characters, and the movement of time evidence the book's deep artistic consideration. In *The Secret Agent,* JC's "impressionism—his power to create in terms of the immediate reports of the senses—is supreme"; but this book stands apart from most of his writing because it contains no prominent character in "a typically Conradian situation." Whereas *Under Western Eyes* displays a loss of much of JC's complex and subtle art and appeals only to "a cultivated literary intelligence," *Chance* is "the first mature work in which his grip of his theme is less assured than his command over his craft." But *Chance* "lacks the dispassionateness, the ubiquitously impartial penetrations" of *Nostromo. Victory* is "a stronger, deeper, and simpler novel" than *Chance.* The last novels (*The Arrow of Gold, The Rescue, Suspense*) display a decline in JC's power. Henry James and JC, unlike Thomas Hardy, write in their greatest books "about the horror of betrayal," of "a new sense of guilt never quite to be localized or pinned down," and thus are perhaps the products of "a specifically modern society" which is largely controlled by the " 'material interests' so distrusted by Dr. Monygham" in *Nostromo*. [An excellent survey of JC's works; contains a valuable bibliography.]

1761 Swinnerton, Frank. FIGURES IN THE FOREGROUND (Lond: Hutchinson, 1963), pp. 21, 24, 26, 29, 32, 44, 106, 154, 166, 190. [Casual reminiscences and simple references to JC.]

1762 Tanner, Tony. "Butterflies and Beetles—Conrad's Two Truths," CHICAGO REVIEW, XVI (Winter-Spring 1963), 123-40.

Stein, as a collector of butterflies and beetles in *Lord Jim*, seems to have "an uncanny knowledge of the qualitative extremes of humanity: man as butterfly, man as beetle," and he is thus especially well qualified to understand Jim and to help him. There is an analogy between Jim and Stein's butterflies: Jim is "a creature of 'light' threatened by the forces of darkness"; he is the "creature of purity who stands above the dirty crowd," the beetles. He finds himself at the time of his jump from the *Patna* a fallen butterfly "sprawling ingloriously" among the beetles. In *Jim,* there are several beetles, men who are unscrupulous enough to live on any terms— the skipper of the *Patna,* Chester, Cornelius, and Brown—and Jim flees continually in an attempt to escape from "the beetles of mankind." JC created Jim in an effort to find out whether he embodies some kind of real value, no matter how deeply involved it is with "the mud of the world." Jim becomes JC's "regretful farewell to the butterflies"; so far as JC was concerned, Jim was "the last of a dying species"—he was "not good enough," and, in fact, "nobody is good enough." *Jim* is a "prelude to profound pessimism" in JC.

JC's conclusions in this novel throw some light on two recurring themes of his work, the experience of total darkness and the special significance of "steering." At crucial moments JC invests physical darkness with philosophical darkness, and his answer as to how one should behave in the dark is a firm one—"you steer," like old Singleton in *The Nigger of the Narcissus*. Haunted by the impossibility of knowing, JC could not accept the beetle (Donkin's view of things), and he renounced the "fallible, if beautiful, butterfly—Jim's conception of life." [Incorporated in a full critique, CONRAD: LORD JIM, Studies in English Literature, 12 (Lond: Edward Arnold, 1963).]

1763 Tanner, Tony. CONRAD: *Lord Jim,* Studies in English Literature, No. 12, Barron's Educational Series (Lond: Edward Arnold; Great Neck, NY, 1963).

JC's distorted narrative method in *Lord Jim* indicates that although Jim may be a simple person, the whole truth about him and the problems he raises are not simple. After Jim has jumped from the *Patna,* he fixes his mind on only the glory he might have secured for himself; he has no sense of honor irrevocably lost. The romantic Stein, who exists at the exact center of the novel, makes a central but not definitive assessment of Jim: Stein, a collector of both butterflies and beetles, affords a metaphor for the two extremes of human conduct and values in the novel [see Tanner, "Butterflies and Beetles—Conrad's Two Truths," CHICAGO REVIEW, XVI (Winter-Spring 1963), 123-40]. At the time of his final test in Patusan, Jim becomes a martyr who takes the evil acts of others upon his head: he dies "with dignity and glamour to vindicate his honor." For Marlow, Jim remains forever a mystery; but for the reader, Jim is "egotistic" to the end. His allegiance is always to "the Abstract, the Ideal"; but he is never equal to the demands of the actual. As for a final judgment of Jim's character, JC dissuades us from performing such an unwise act. [This book, intended for both "the advanced Sixth former and the university student," contains a lengthy synopsis of the plot of *Jim* and many perceptive insights into the work; but the detailed retelling of the story becomes monotonous.]

1764 Tanner, Tony. "Conrad's Politics," NEW YORK REVIEW OF BOOKS, 14 Nov 1963, pp. 18-19.

In Eloise Knapp Hay's THE POLITICAL NOVELS OF JOSEPH CONRAD, some of JC's major novels appear in a new way, supported by new material on the author's Polish origins and his "contradictory heritage." *The Rescue* is falsified into a love story JC had promised his publishers because he was uncertain as to what he wanted to say to his English readers "about progress, civilization, and the suppression of primal instincts." In "Heart of Darkness" he was more sure but also more evasive; he totally indicts all Western ideals, even "efficiency," and "the white man's 'light' . . . is the true darkness." The horror that Kurtz sees at last is both in himself and "in the Europe that made him." In *Nostromo* each character acts under "the illusion of some sort of idea," and "the futility and chaos are vast"; in spite of idealism "a vicious squabble for booty develops: pity and justice die underfoot," and men desirous of conquest and others who are victims emerge. In *The Secret Agent* both despots and revolutionaries are "grotesquely comic"; but real, human victims still exist. In *Under Western Eyes* "the absurdity of things" is treated even more profoundly so that this novel is JC's "deepest inquiry into the helplessness of Intelligence in an absurd world." JC was really a pessimist, but "one of the greatest." [Review-article.]

1765 Tick, Stanley. "Conrad's 'Heart of Darkness,' " EXPLICATOR, XXI (April 1963), Item 67.

The imagery of a serpent as applied to the Congo River is symbolic of "the tempter offering access to the primitive wilderness, that 'prehistoric earth,' as Marlow calls the jungle." It tempts first the boy, then the young man Marlow, "from afar," luring him like a snake attracting a bird. The "river-serpent" makes of Kurtz a kind of Eve in the primitive "gardens" along the banks of the river, causing him to fall and thereby be placed "outside the community of men." The river also apparently led the corruptible white men, the "pilgrims," to consider their "evil exploitation"; and it makes it possible for Marlow to learn about "good and evil," thus leaving him a better man because of his experience. [Considers the image of the serpent-river somewhat differently from Norman Farmer, Jr., ibid., XXII (March 1964), Item 51.]

1766 West, Paul. THE MODERN NOVEL. Two Volumes (Lond: Hutchinson University Library, 1963), I, pp. 17-18, 27, 40, 76, 84, 152; Vol. II, pp. 244, 280.

JC pretends that his fiction is life and acts "as if he has not created his own fiction," thus wrongly making fiction "as baffling as life." We want to know more about Kurtz than Marlow reveals in "Heart of Darkness," just as Jim in *Lord Jim* is "too deep for Marlow." JC makes inquiries "into the metaphysical region," but "he just inquires"; he fails even to understand men's actions and pretends that his characters are unfathomable. He never takes the reader to the "point" of a theme. *Chance* is "a dossier on frustration and abnormality." In such works as "Heart of Darkness," *Nostromo*, *The Secret Agent*, "The Secret Sharer," and *Victory*, JC uses elementary images in a sophisticated manner for his symbolism, mainly "to awaken a vague sense of insecurity."

1767 Whittemore, Reed. "The Fascination of the Abomination—Wells, Shaw, Ford, Conrad," THE FASCINATION OF THE ABOMINATION (NY: Macmillan, 1963), pp. 129-66.

"For Wells and Shaw a fact was an idea or an ideal; for Conrad it was something which could be made to stand for something." Wells and Shaw are "weak on the here-and-now of 'experienced' reality, Conrad, . . . in the world of ideas." JC was incapable of "getting out of himself"—hence he could not let his characters speak for themselves. Yet he still is considered a realist, despite his "rather conspicuous artistry." He is deeply involved in his characters, and reveals himself in his fiction, as in "Heart of Darkness." Here, Marlow acts as "recording angel," but "he is playing the part, vicariously of the man he is recording." The story traces Marlow's progress from detachment to commitment.

1768 Wiley, Paul L. "Conrad's Skein of Ironies," "HEART OF DARKNESS": AN AUTHORITATIVE TEXT, BACKGROUNDS AND SOURCES, ESSAYS IN CRITICISM, ed by Robert Kimbrough (NY: W. W. Norton, 1963), pp. 223-27.

"Heart of Darkness" represents "a very modern blend of comic absurdity, tragedy, and satire almost Swiftian in manner," bound together by "a controlling play of irony." JC's purpose in the story is to demonstrate satirically how the "fraudulent philanthropy" of the trading company is completely routed. His "sequence of ironies," Marlow's gradual discoveries of the real nature of the colonial situation, arises from the dilemma created by the fact that ethics or restraint is "pure deceit" whereas primitive nature, which has no moral checks, is by contrast "visibly true even in its frank destructiveness." The truth at last drives Fresleven to an "ironical accord" with nature as it exists, and this truth finally justifies Kurtz and explains his superiority to the weaker agents at the lower stations. Marlow, a norm of integrity, moves from uneasiness to a sense of unreality and hallucination, but at last he sees Kurtz just as he is and chooses the "nightmare" of being at one with nature. He realizes that Kurtz's vision of "the horror" is "a true expression of belief" which may be true in itself. The trading companies and the sepulchral cities have nothing to offer in its place. [Published in this "casebook" for the first time.]

1769 Williams, George Walton. "The Turn of the Tide in 'Heart of Darkness,'" MODERN FICTION STUDIES, IX (Summer 1963), 171-73.

The reader of "Heart of Darkness," through his association with the first narrator, "suffers a moral transformation" caused largely by the turn of the tide in the Thames River. During Marlow's recital, the *Nellie,* whose bow is at first pointing eastward, away from London, makes a swing of 180° because of the turn of the tide so that at the end of the story the bow is pointing westward, toward London. The result is that the narrator's vision has also changed from the bright eastward view of the beginning of "an interminable waterway" which is "luminous" to a gloomy westward view, where "the offing was barred by a black bank of clouds, and the tranquil waterway leading to the uttermost ends of the earth flowed sombre under an overcast sky." The contrast scarcely needs to be pointed out: the river leads no longer "inward to the particular . . . but now outward to the universal," from brightness and hope to what is the general tone of the story—darkness.

1770 Wills, John Howard. "A Neglected Masterpiece: Conrad's 'Youth,'" TEXAS STUDIES IN LITERATURE AND LANGUAGE, IV (Spring 1963), 591-601.

The theme of "Youth" is that man in order to experience the brief happiness of life must hold the illusion that he is strong and important as he grows older. JC's use of Marlow "as a narrator within a narrator" is an improvement over the point of view in *The Nigger of the Narcissus* because Marlow's narrative provides a "double perspective" in which the same events are seen "from the vantage point of both youth and age, illusion and reality, hope and fatality." Three kinds of romance are found in "Youth": (1) the romance of adventure—the young man's heroics; (2) the romance of wonder—the East; (3) the romance of nostalgia—"a hymn to the vanished past." The language is not overwrought except where it should be, "toward the conclusion of the narrative, where Marlow is hopelessly involved in his vision." The symbolic overtones of the voyage of the *Judea* are symbolic of the life of ancient and modern man; the allegory functions not merely "to glorify human endurance." The religious overtones of "the sinking of the *Judea,* the spiritual death of her aged officers, and crew" may suggest "the waning influence of Christianity" upon JC's own generation. The greatness of "Youth" lies in the fact that "it is an abiding vision of modern man."

> **1771** Wohlfarth, Paul. "Joseph Conrad and Germany," GERMAN LIFE AND LETTERS, N.S. XVI (Jan 1963), 81-87.

JC naturally held an attitude of enmity to Germany, an attitude expressed in the first preface to *Victory*. But in "Falk" he treats the German family "with evident fondness"; and two more "good Germans" appear in "The End of the Tether" and *Lord Jim*. The outbreak of World War I accounts for JC's change towards Germans. Among all of his friends, there was not one Russian, but there were at least two Germans. JC also had some knowledge of German literature and civilization; he refers at least once to Goethe's FAUST, to Grimm's fairy tales, and to Novalis In chapter XX of *Jim* he includes a quotation from Goethe. And this novel reveals the deepest conflict in JC's life. JC was, in fact, a traitor to his own country. Jim is, "without doubt," JC himself and the name *Patna* is "a thin disguise" for "Patria," fatherland. In *Nostromo,* JC expresses his faith in Poland's future. His need to use confessional materials in his works is similar to that of German novelists, but in general unlike that of English novelists. JC's early impressions of German literature undoubtedly left their influence on his productions. [Tries too hard to verify a somewhat tenuous idea.]

> **1772** Yelton, Donald Charles. "Symbol and Metaphor in Conrad's Fiction," DISSERTATION ABSTRACTS, XXIV (Aug 1963), 752-53. Unpublished thesis, Columbia University, 1962; revised and published as MIMESIS AND METAPHOR: AN INQUIRY INTO THE GENESIS AND SCOPE OF CONRAD'S SYMBOLIC IMAGERY (The Hague: Mouton, 1967).

[An examination of the symbolic and metaphoric aspects of JC's fiction, his relation to the French *Symboliste* movement, and the influence of his literary predecessors—Turgenev, Dickens, Flaubert—as reflected in the general themes of his novels. The final section contains analyses of "The Secret Sharer" and *The Shadow-Line*.]

JOSEPH CONRAD

1773 Zabel, Morton Dauwen. "Introduction to *Under Western Eyes*," *Under Western Eyes* (Garden City, NY: Doubleday, Anchor Books, 1963), pp. ix-lviii; rptd in CONRAD: A COLLECTION OF CRITICAL ESSAYS, ed by Marvin Mudrick (Englewood Cliffs, NJ: Prentice-Hall, Spectrum Books, 1966), pp. 111-44.

Under Western Eyes, with *Nostromo* and *The Secret Agent,* gives JC "his major rank among the political novelists of the twentieth century"; the subject is "Russian character, despotism, and revolution"; this novel and *Agent,* both "written well in advance of the wars and crises of the twentieth century, have become appallingly corroborated by the events of contemporary history." The assassination of Viatscheslav Konstantinovitch Plehve and the experiences of the notorious police spy and double agent Azeff provided the historical sources and JC's own personal relationship with the Russians, "his divided allegiance between East and West, between the Slavic world and the European or English, remains basic to his tale."

Eyes has a subject and an artistry which are continuous with JC's other works. In the composition of the book, JC changed several of his original plans, including the title and the plot, again making isolation and conscience the dominant motifs. Razumov enacts a drama that had already been played in *Lord Jim,* by both Kurtz and Marlow in "Heart of Darkness," by Decoud, Dr. Monygham, and Nostromo in *Nostromo,* by the young captain in "The Secret Sharer"; and this drama was to be enacted again by Flora de Barral and Captain Anthony in *Chance,* by Axel Heyst in *Victory* and by Tom Lingard in *The Rescue.* Razumov, a Conradian solitary, is condemned and saved by Natalia, whose "pure and credulous spirit" drives him to self-condemnation and confession, "to the test of honor that at last breaks and redeems him."

As a political novel, *Eyes* is descended from the type established by Stendahl, Turgenev, Dostoevski, and James; and it is prophetic of the forthcoming novels by Malraux, Silone, Sartre, Koestler, Camus, Orwell, and Pasternak. JC's Polish temper is displayed in this book in the form of "mystical dedication and realistic caution, the elation of a sacred martyrdom and the mortifications of political and military defeat." This work shows JC "writing in the strength of his sincerity and despair, his lacerating irony and his passionate humanism." [One of the best analyses hitherto available of a somewhat neglected but very important novel in the JC canon.]

1774 Zuckerman, Jerome. "The Theme of Rule in Joseph Conrad," DISSERTATION ABSTRACTS, XXIII (1963), 4367. Unpublished thesis, University of Wisconsin, 1963.

1964

1775 Beachcroft, T. O. The English Short Story (Lond: Longmans, Green, 1964), pp. 14-18.

JC is at his best "when the brooding intensity of his visual scenes moves on for page after page." The tendency in his shorter stories is for "the skeleton of melodrama to stick out too clearly." JC's "use of the narrator is sometimes an embarrassment."

1776 Beebe, Maurice. "Criticism of Joseph Conrad: A Selected Checklist," Modern Fiction Studies, X (Spring 1964), 81-106. [Brings up to date the checklist published by Beebe in Modern Fiction Studies, I (Feb 1955), 30-45. Discards some of the items in the earlier list. Contains items on individual works as well as the most important general studies of JC. An invaluable guide for "the modern student" of JC.]

1777 Beebe, Maurice. Ivory Towers and Sacred Founts: The Artist as Hero in Fiction from Goethe to Joyce (NY: New York U P, 1964), pp. 9, 165-71, 204, 300-303, 307.

"'Heart of Darkness' is . . . a bitter indictment of life." Heyst, in *Victory,* is a "detached man forced to commit himself in action" in standard interpretations, but *Victory* actually is a "tragedy of inadequate detachment." One difficulty in interpreting this novel is its inconsistent point of view: "the novel seems to exist between poles of nothingness and victory, and is therefore more complex, ironic, and ambivalent than is generally assumed." The victory is in seeing evil at the heart of life, in achieving complete detachment from life through death. It is the victory of the artist. "Awareness of [JC's] persona forces us to recognize a strongly nihilistic strain in the novel, a contrary moral which affirms that life is expendable for the artist, who finds *his* victory in the destruction of life that it may be transformed into art." *Victory* is a good example of the split between the man's and the artist's values.

1778 Bernard, Kenneth. "The Significance of the Roman Parallel in Joseph Conrad's 'Heart of Darkness,'" Ball State Teachers College Forum, V (Spring 1964), 29-31.

The political meaning in "Heart of Darkness," significantly exemplified by means of a parallel between ancient and modern colonizing, displays JC's pessimism about the nature of man. Marlow's recollection early in the story of another "inconclusive experience," the earliest Roman colonizers of England, appears implicitly to indicate that modern colonizers, unlike the Romans, possess efficiency; but any notion of efficiency is "overwhelmingly destroyed" in what follows. All that Marlow sees is an "atmosphere of inefficiency," which he speaks of sarcastically and ironically. Even the "pilgrims" are merely "greedy exploiters." And Kurtz, the Chief of the Inner Station, representing civilization, fails. There simply is no saving "idea" to the modern colonizing. In JC's portrait of Kurtz the criticism of the "idea" is most explicit. The modern colonizers are only more hypocritical than the ancient. JC does not believe that men have improved: man's evil nature is permanent. Here the political level of the narrative meets the moral level.

> **1779** Bojarski, Edmund A. "Josph Conrad's Sentimental Journey: A Fiftieth-Anniversary Review," TEXAS QUARTERLY, VII (Winter 1964), 156-65.

As soon as *Chance* and *Victory* achieved profitable sales, JC returned to Poland, arriving in Cracow on the very day when Germany declared war on Russia, August 1, 1914. Then, unable to return to England because of illness in his immediate family, he visited a relative by marriage, Mrs. Karol Zagorski, who was living in a villa in Zakopane. Although JC, in "Poland Revisited," gave this sojourn only a paragraph or two, the daughter of the house and his cousin, Aniela Zagorska, published, among more than sixty books and articles about JC and his work, two reminiscences of his visit to Zakopane. Now, for the first time, "Western Conradists" are given, not an English translation of these pieces, but a "portrait" of the "enigmatic Polish-Englishman" based on a collation of them.

In Zakopane, JC was known principally for his charms, since only two of his books had appeared in Polish at that time. Despite the war, JC was exceptionally calm and cheerful, and "nearly always" friendly and loquacious. Even he and his wife were "a happy and united couple," and his relationship with his two sons was "very pleasant." According to his cousin, JC's patriotism was for him "a continuing source of spiritually worrisome discord" because of his being torn between "loyalty to England and love for Poland with obvious weight in favor of his adopted country." In Poland, JC met several notable persons, among them Stefan Zeromski, the novelist, who later wrote a "splendid" preface to a Polish edition of JC's works. There he also found himself surrounded by preparations for an insurrection against Russia, and he was disturbed because he did not believe in Poland's regaining independence. He avidly read the works of the contemporary Polish novelists and dramatists. Once Aniela elicited from her cousin a comment on a duel which he said he had fought, and a few years later she read the description of that duel in *The Arrow of Gold,* which she considered one of JC's "most autobiographical" novels. She also understood later, after she had read "Heart of Darkness," that all the mystery of Africa had become personified in JC's description to her of a "wild, splendid woman" who stood on the bank of the Congo, passionately stretching out her arms toward the steamer that was carrying away "her deity, her lover." Although JC fully expected and planned to return again to Poland, this occasion was his last visit there. [Indicative of the existence of a great amount of Polish writing about JC which has not yet been examined.]

1780 Bojarski, Edmund A., and Henry T. Bojarski (comps). JOSEPH CONRAD: A BIBLIOGRAPHY OF MASTERS' THESES AND DOCTORAL DISSERTATIONS (Lexington: University of Kentucky Libraries, Occasional Contribution No. 157, 1964); rptd in POLISH AMERICAN STUDIES, XXII (1965), 30-46; and in BULLETIN OF BIBLIOGRAPHY, XXVI (July- Sept 1969), 61-66, 79-83.

[Unpublished theses at all levels completed at universities in Australia, Canada, England, France, Germany, Ireland, New Zealand, Poland, Scotland, South Africa, the United States, and Wales are listed with references to published abstracts. Some of the 336 "unpublished papers" listed by the Bojarskis have, in fact, been published in various forms. Useful because doctoral dissertations only are listed in the present bibliography.]

1781 Bojarski, Edmund A. "A Window on Joseph Conrad's Polish Soul," ENGLISH LITERATURE IN TRANSITION, VII: 4 (1964), 234-38.

Containing only an estimated one-fourth of JC's Polish letters (the others presumably having been lost or destroyed), CONRAD'S POLISH BACKGROUND: LETTERS TO AND FROM POLISH FRIENDS, ed by Zdzisław Najder (1964) makes available to readers of English "a solid contribution toward an understanding of the Polish facet of Conrad's life, mind and work." The seventy-eight communications from JC's uncle and guardian, Tadeusz Bobrowski, provide most of our knowledge of JC's first thirty years, especially of those between his leaving Poland in 1874 and the publication of his first novel in 1895. Bobrowski's two long letters to Stefan Buszczynski relate JC's adventures in France, including his "suicide attempt" in 1878; other papers contain important materials about JC's political views; and one hundred four Polish letters from JC to various correspondents help to compensate for the loss of the novelist's other writings to Bobrowski. Important also are the biographical and psychological details, many of which appear in print here for the first time and nearly all of which are newly translated into English. The logical conclusion reached from these materials is that JC at the age of forty was still misunderstood and underestimated. "The plight of the outcast, the solitary" therefore naturally becomes evident in his works.

1782 Boyle, Ted E. "Marlow's 'Lie' in 'Heart of Darkness,'" STUDIES IN SHORT FICTION, I (Winter 1964), 159-63.

Marlow's lie to Kurtz's Intended is Marlow's acceptance of the "trust of carrying the torch of . . . a truth that neither Kurtz nor the uninitiated

Marlow could understand." A key to the higher kind of truth which Marlow can comprehend after his Congo voyage is found in Kurtz's painting of "justice"; Marlow finally realizes that Kurtz, as well as all mankind, wants not merely justice but "a complex kind of truth—a truth which is a mixture of illusion and love." Furthermore, the mythic journey which is the framework of the story demands that the hero descend to the lower world to gain knowledge and that he communicate this knowledge after his return. Marlow then lies to the Intended in order to save his own soul, to complete the salvation of Kurtz's soul, and to save the soul of the Intended; he thus "keeps back the darkness for an entire community of souls." His lie preserves "the small, frail truth inherent in Kurtz's dying exclamation." [For a fuller development of these concepts, see Ted E. Boyle, SYMBOL AND MEANING IN THE FICTION OF JOSEPH CONRAD (1965).]

1783 Broderick, Lillian Negueloua. "A Study of Conrad's Prose Style." Unpublished thesis, Harvard University, 1964.

1784 Bruffee, Kenneth A. "The Lesser Nightmare: Marlow's 'Lie' in 'Heart of Darkness,'" MODERN LANGUAGE QUARTERLY, XXV (Sept 1964), 322-29.

Two paradoxes seem fundamental to "Heart of Darkness": (1) Marlow participates in Kurtz's self-revelation and both men profit by the experience, and (2) the "profit" is ironic in that Kurtz's original insight is "both a reward of life and a terrible penalty for it" and that Marlow's further insight, engendered by Kurtz's, is "at the same time illuminating and apparently corrupting." The two paradoxes then resolve themselves into one paradoxical action, telling a lie, which "establishes a condition of truth" and can be resolved in several ways, one of which is "a peculiarly twentieth-century kind of Faustian experience." JC seems to depart from the earlier Faustian tradition in that in his story the pursuit of forbidden knowledge remains evil and ultimately degrades man instead of ennobling him and in that he maintains the original assumptions that such things as forbidden power and knowledge exist. But he alters the outcome of the experience "by extending its effect": through Marlow, the "saving virtue" acquired by the experience he shares with Kurtz is extended to "their whole civilization."

The saving virtue that results from the experience is restraint, the virtue which Kurtz lacks but which becomes in Marlow the "most important, conscious, and compelling force in his character." Kurtz's Intended deserves not to hear the truth; Marlow therefore lies to her, first, to alleviate her immediate grief, and second, to "relieve the suffering that she does not know she suffers"; although she represents a hollow or dead civilization, Marlow believes that she is "worthy" enough to deserve not to be forced to confront the truth about Kurtz. This conviction indicates how thoroughly

Marlow has become identified with Kurtz: the girl represents the best of Kurtz's ideals; and by lying, Marlow, in protecting Kurtz's good intentions, thereby "reaffirms his fellowship with Kurtz" and achieves vicariously through self-revelation the same wholeness which Kurtz had achieved. But Marlow, unlike Kurtz, lives on to act upon what he has learned. Marlow discovers a "larger standard of truth," according to which "the ethically repulsive, dishonorable act" proves to be a kind of "honorable restraint." Unlike Kurtz, whose "excessive aspiration" fails, Marlow, both by recognizing the existence of the light and the dark and by affirming that they must be carefully distinguished, represents "his, the girl's and all society's only salvation." [An ingeniously developed and impressive interpretation of a perplexing matter in "Heart of Darkness."]

1785 Carpenter, Richard C. THOMAS HARDY. Twayne's English Authors Series (NY: Twayne, 1964), pp. 16, 30, 91, 106.

Hardy, like JC, is an "anti-realist," more nearly like Gide than Howells or Gissing; JC's Sulaco is a "symbolic microcosm" like Hardy's Wessex; the Golfo Placido, like Egdon Heath, is "one of the great *places* of fiction"; and Michael Henchard is "kin to" characters like Lord Jim in that both are "rigidly obsessive minds which can find no peace this side of the grave."

1786 Curle, Richard. "Son of Poland," CONTEMPORARY REVIEW, CCV (Oct 1964), 552.

CONRAD'S POLISH BACKGROUND: LETTERS TO AND FROM POLISH FRIENDS, ed by Zdzisław Najder (1964), contains letters from JC's guardian, Thaddeus Bobrowski, which are "full of sound advice and sensible reflections," but "decidedly tedious." Although they are of unique value in portraying JC through the eyes of his guardian and are practically our only source of information for a long period of his life, it is too bad to use so much space for such "dull prolixity." It is also tragic that JC's part of the correspondence was destroyed during World War 1. [Najder's book is much more important than Curle indicates it to be.]

1787 Farmer, Norman, Jr. "Conrad's 'Heart of Darkness,'" EXPLICATOR, XXII (March 1964), Item 51.

In "Heart of Darkness" JC uses the serpent as an ancient symbol of evil to indicate that Marlow is first charmed, then "completely swallowed," by the serpent-river as he travels toward the very center of evil. Aware of the possible horrors, he is unable to turn back. "The snake has charmed me," he says; and this charm leads to increasingly great evils, which finally culminate in Kurtz, who represents "the epitome of degradation." JC blends his symbol of temptation with the way Marlow must go in his exploration of evil so that he achieves "an unbroken narrative line from the map on the wall to the very heart of darkness." [Supplements Stanley Tick's discussion of the river-serpent image in ibid., XXI (April 1963), Item 67.]

1788 Fuchs, Carolyn. "Words, Action, and the Modern Novel," KERYGMA, IV (Winter 1964), 3-11.

The nature of man in the universe, a "tension between the realm of the idea and the realm of the act"—the "great concern" of the novel as of all literature—is illustrated in three modern novels: Faulkner's AS I LAY DYING, Robert Penn Warren's ALL THE KING'S MEN, and JC's *Nostromo*. It is not Decoud nor Nostromo nor Charles Gould who finally realizes that his ideals are merely words; only Emilia Gould, in her "wisdom of the heart," is able, in Addie Bundren's words, "to straddle" the line between words and deeds, to understand fully the ultimate meaning and implications of the events in the world of Costaguana.

1789 Gillon, Adam. "The Merchant of Esmeralda—Conrad's Archetypal Jew," POLISH REVIEW, IX (Autumn 1964), 3-20.

Hirsch, the only Jewish character in *Nostromo,* looked down on by everyone else in the novel, helps to create an atmosphere of the macabre and a "poignantly symbolic" situation: Decoud, Nostromo, and Hirsch are aliens and all three will meet a violent end; and all three are linked by one common experience—fear. Hirsch's cowardice, too, dramatizes the later spiritual collapse of Nostromo when he, the fearless man, becomes a coward himself. Although both Decoud and Nostromo want to kill Hirsch, they cannot do so because they have identified themselves with the Jew as a hunted figure. Closed in by the symbolic darkness of the gulf, Decoud loses his only weapon, his intelligence, and Nostromo in effect identifies Decoud with Hirsch. JC sometimes displayed evidence of anti-Jewish prejudice; he may have been affected by the general attitudes and prejudices of his time; or he may have been influenced by the character Yankel in Mickiewicz's PAN TADEUSZ.

JC in *Nostromo* transforms Hirsch from a largely comic archetype into a symbolic character with a trace of tragic dimensions. Captain Mitchell is a foil to Hirsch, whose difficulty is not only his inferior position as an alien but also his possession of imagination, which "apparently makes him more aware of his existence than Captain Mitchell could ever be!" Hirsch evokes not laughter but compassion and indignation in Nostromo when he sees the Jew's tortured body hanging from the roof; the dead Jew, suspended in a posture of crucifixion, is a symbolic warning to Nostromo. Now both Nostromo and Dr. Monygham, like Decoud before them, identify themselves with Hirsch's direful fate. But Hirsch, in addition, now symbolizes the chaotic conditions of Costaguana; he no longer performs his archetypal role—he becomes a symbol of "profound social disintegration." Then he becomes the scapegoat to Sotillo, who includes Hirsch with the "rogues" who have "hidden" the silver, Charles Gould, Captain Mitchell, Nostromo, and Holroyd. The scene of torture is significant because Hirsch changes from an abject coward to a man brave enough to spit in his torturer's face. In death, the alien Jew attains a new dignity.

Finally, Hirsch's name appears much later, in JC's description of the background against which Nostromo returns to Giorgio Viola's house, with that of Decoud: the alien Jew is at last an equal of Decoud and Nostromo—his death is as tragic and poignant as theirs, or perhaps more so. [The close textual analysis of this article reveals Hirsch, hitherto a somewhat ambiguous figure, as a major character in *Nostromo*.]

> **1790** Gose, Elliott B., Jr. "Pure Exercise of the Imagination: Archetypal Symbolism in *Lord Jim*," PMLA, LXXIX (March 1964), 137-47.

In *Lord Jim*, the opposed halves of the book contain two different conceptions: the *Patna* episode is "informed by the assumption that the beliefs men share govern their fate" whereas the Patusan sequence is "informed by the possibility that one man's imagination can determine his fate." The Western world of the *Patna* is dominated by Marlow's moral principles; the Eastern world of Patusan functions "according to Jim's application of Stein's romantic prescription." Marlow believes in " 'the craft of the sea,' " a concept implying that a good sailor must "reshape his unconscious life in the image of his consciousness of the outside," whereas Stein advises "living from the dream, *submitting* to the destructive element."

The major pattern of images in *Jim* is probably based on the opposition of light and dark. Jim jumps "into an everlastingly deep hole" in the scene set by the "Dark Powers"; the problem of the second half of the novel is Jim's ability to climb back out to the sunlight. Jim turns his allegiance from the temporal world of day alternating with night to "a timeless world." He feels a need "to jump off the mundane world on which he can never escape his guilt." The pattern of action is familiar: according to Otto Rank, it is "The Myth of the Birth of the Hero," and as analyzed by Carl Jung, it is based on the rising, setting, and reappearance of the sun. Also, the maternal aspect of water is like the nature of the unconscious. Stein treats water philosophically as the dream, the unconscious. "On the passage westward toward Mecca, the strength of the sun is emphasized. Then after plunging into darkness, Jim moves always to the east," as JC clearly indicates. When he goes to Patusan, he plunges even further into Stein's "destructive element." Symbolically Jim must withdraw when he reaches the point where he is unable to cope with the outside world.

That JC in *Jim* was able to go as far as he did in sympathizing with the claims of the "romantic ego-ideal" is a triumph of the imagination. The Patusan section is "purposefully romantic, highlighted, archetypal," and on that level is successful. Realistically, however, it is not so successful as the first section is. JC constructed Patusan on principles like those used later by Jung to analyze the structure of the collective unconscious. Jim achieves a kind of "psychic harmony" with Jewel as the mate, with the father-mother figures as Doramin and his wife, and with Jim himself as the hero, "the white god upon whom depends the stability and order of the chaotic land he has invaded." But after conquering the hostile archetypes (the four murderers sent by the Rajah), the hero still faces an equally subtle danger, that of being "simply caught," of accepting the role of savior. Jim can gain psychic unity only by making, like the sun, a complete circle. Jim does not face squarely the moral implications of Gentleman Brown, who corresponds closely to Jung's description of the shadow, the "lower level" of personality "with its uncontrolled . . . emotions."

Within the Jungian framework of the sun myth, rebirth is achieved by a journey in darkness (Jonah's journey in the whale and the resurrection of Lazarus and Christ). Jim follows a similar pattern. Jim, in choosing to become a victim, "disdains destructiveness and cannot accept vicarious immortality; he assumes the role of the unworthy son whose early sacrifices redeem him and returns to the mother, undifferentiated nature." "By sacrificing his physical body to his concept of himself," Jim finally frees himself from "the mud and filth of the temporal world"; he mounts "to the height of the stars, become[s] the high light he longed to be." And if that light has no heat, it is at least eternal, "an archetype of this slightly inhuman son of nature." [An excellent analysis of Jim as a Jungian archetype.]

>   **1791** Hagopian, John V. "Il Conde," INSIGHT II: ANALYSES OF MODERN BRITISH LITERATURE, ed by John V. Hagopian and Martin Dolch (Frankfurt Am Main: Hirschgraben-Verlag, 1964), pp. 62-70; rptd, with slight differences, as "The Pathos of 'Il Conde,'" STUDIES IN SHORT FICTION, III (Fall 1965), 31-38.

Previous interpretations of "Il Conde"—the Count as a tragic figure, the Camorra as the Count's "secret sharer"—are excesses of mythic criticism, and the Ivory Tower myth of the fin de siècle. This "slight work" is not a bad story within its limits. It is well worth study as "an ironic, though sympathetic, account of an ineffectual, innocent old aristocrat" who is not tragic at all but a "pathetic victim." [Followed by questions and discussions for students.]

>   **1792** Hagopian, John V. "The Informer," INSIGHT II: ANALYSES OF MODERN BRITISH LITERATURE, ed by John V. Hagopian and Martin Dolch (Frankfurt Am Main: Hirschgraben-Verlag, 1964), 58-62.

Contrary to earlier criticism, "The Informer" is "remarkably complex":

two stories by two narrators who are in an unusual manner doubles, with a third figure behind them, the Parisian collector of curious personalities, who may be manipulating both narrators. Mr. X's "little joke" is the inner story of the tale as distinguished from the frame story. "The Informer" is an ironic tale, and the joke is really on both narrators, but not on the careful reader. [Followed by questions and explanations for students.]

> **1793** Hagopian, John V., and Martin Dolch (eds). INSIGHT II: ANALYSES OF MODERN BRITISH LITERATURE (Frankfurt Am Main: Hirschgraben-Verlag, 1964), pp. 47-76.

[Analyses of four of JC's shorter tales all abstracted separately under authors' names (1964): Hermann Weiand, "Typhoon," John V. Hagopian, "The Informer" and "Il Conde," and Alvan S. Ryan, "The Secret Sharer."]

> **1794** Hardy, John Edward. " 'Heart of Darkness': The Russian in Motley," MAN IN THE MODERN NOVEL (Seattle: University of Washington P, 1964), pp. 17-33.

Marlow creates two problems in "Heart of Darkness," his identity as hero of the story and his identity as narrator of the same story. If there is any fusion of Marlow and Kurtz, who is the object of Marlow's expedition, it is Kurtz who becomes Marlow because the latter "retains moral control" and also retains control as storyteller. The Russian has neither significance nor identity except in his "function" in relation to Kurtz and the savages; and JC makes Marlow's references to the Russian contain a quality of the unreal, the symbolic, but more specifically "the mimetic, the aspect of a clown." Kurtz probably needed the sympathy or at least a partial understanding of a white man, but in holding the Russian in contempt, Kurtz came "perilously close to allowing the fool to perform his highest service, that of showing him his own absurdity." Marlow is reassured by the apparition of the Russian that the moral world is not entirely reducible to the opposition of Kurtz and the pilgrims, and Marlow's admiration of the Russian extends itself into a new respect for Kurtz. Marlow forms his loyalty to Kurtz as a matter of choice but, unlike the Russian, he wakes up and meditates about his choice. By recognizing the flaw in the Russian's "moral equipment," Marlow is prepared to insist upon his right to a choice. From the Russian, Marlow "receives his commission of loyalty to Kurtz," with the Russian acting as Kurtz's "agent"; thus beyond the consciousness of either Marlow or Kurtz the Russian is JC's agent. The Russian is part of "an extended pattern of absurdities, of unrealities," and his role as fool finally opposes him ("divine simplicity, innocence, restoring sanity") to the diabolical "folly" of the world of the pilgrims. "Heart of Darkness" remains the "basic mystery of human existence," but a new understanding of the Russian in the story lessens its obscurity. [This is a convincing and important explication of the place of the Russian in "Heart of Darkness."]

1795 Harrington, David V., and Carol Estness. "Aesthetic Criteria and Conrad's 'The Tale,'" DISCOURSE, VII (Autumn 1964), 437-45.

A minimal criterion for a short story is "an organic unity embracing the total characterization, action, dialogue, and tone," with an expression of "subjective human feeling" as a part of the unity. At the end of "The Tale," the Commanding Officer's predicament in regard to the neutral ship is ambiguous, and JC leaves us with the "dramatic portrait" of a sensitive man embarrassed also by uncertainty in the presence of the woman he loves. Significant parallels between the character of the woman (no doubt the narrator's mistress) and that of the Northman of the neutral ship contribute both to coherence and to organic form in the story. The Commanding Officer, aware of his mistress's "capriciousness," realizes also an apparent "deterioration" in their relationship and in his attitude toward the Northman—he must be suspicious of both people. The introductory part of "The Tale" and the short conclusion add to the organic nature of the work: the Commanding Officer is "embarrassed at having revealed to his mistress his own duplicity," and he is also "increasingly uncertain about the loyalty of the woman." His last statement, that he "shall never know," refers, therefore, both to his uncertainty about his treatment of the Northman and to his suspicions of the woman, with only the first meaning clear to his mistress. The conclusion of the story is the Commanding Officer's recognition of his own "tragic inability to cope with uncertainties"; it includes the "introductory dramatic presentation" of the relationship between the officer and the woman and the "tale" itself. Thus this story has a "truly organic unity."

1796 Heimer, Jackson W. "Patterns of Betrayal in the Novels of Joseph Conrad," DISSERTATION ABSTRACTS, XXIV (June 1964), 5408-9. Unpublished thesis, University of Cincinnati, 1963.

[Portions of the dissertation have been published in various journals during 1967.]

1797 Hicks, John H. "Conrad's *Almayer's Folly:* Structure, Theme, and Critics," NINETEENTH-CENTURY FICTION, XIX (June 1964), 17-31.

The significance of the themes of fidelity and illusion is established by both external and internal evidence. The follies of Lingard and in part those of Almayer lead, in each case, to a perversion of fidelity; and the structure of the novel contrasts the perversions of fidelity in the main plot with a valid affirmation of love and loyalty in the Nina-Dain relationship of the subplot. Almayer is born a victim of the illusion of the importance of material values alone, and he also inherits his racial prejudice, thus being a kind of "cultural orphan" who must find any loyalties he can to live by. The major plot of the novel is the "ruinous result" of his "grandiose and divided allegiances" which are created by Lingard's "moral pretensions and false assumptions."

Almayer's reliance on Lingard eventually leaves him a permanent resident of Sambir with a wife who is not absorbed into the western community into which she has been thrust. The resentful Mrs. Almayer informs against Lingard and Almayer in order to help Lakamba; she is "suspended between white and Malay worlds." But in Nina Almayer's escape from such a destiny lies "the moral significance and the aesthetic purpose" of the subplot of the novel. Dain Maroola's entrance into Sambir is the plot necessary for testing the loyalties of both Almayer and Nina: Nina now has her first opportunity to choose her ultimate allegiances, and Almayer must clearly expose the inadequacy of his "professed altruism." The Nina-Dain relationship moves toward an ethical relation as well as a physical one; Nina must turn from Almayer's selfish claims upon her to her natural role of queen and that of wife or mistress. Her subsequent life indicates that she has attained personal and social fulfillment, but Almayer cannot relinquish his conceptions of fidelity to himself and to his race. He therefore sends his daughter away unforgiven and tries to expunge her memory from his mind; he destroys in the name of duty whatever there may have been of the loyal parent in himself. His destruction of fidelity becomes his death. at the end of the novel he is merely "the Infidel." [A reasonable argument for a new view of *Almayer's Folly,* but too vague in its references to other critics.]

1798 Hodges, Robert R. "The Four Fathers of Lord Jim," UNIVERSITY REVIEW, XXXI (Dec 1964), 103-10.

In addition to romantic egoism, the hero of *Lord Jim* "exhibits a long-lasting attachment to a father he feels certain can never approve of him and a desire for the approval of men as ready to be a father to him as he is to appeal to them as a son," thus revealing Jim's character as more understandable, less "inscrutable" or mysterious, than a close follower of Marlow's comments finds it to be. It is thus that he turns to Marlow, to Denver, and finally to Stein as father surrogates, each of whom he ultimately deserts to continue his quest for personal honor. Marlow, Jim's second "father," has a dual attitude toward the young man: he instinctively considers him as one of the many young men he has trained for the sea, but at the same time he realizes that Jim's defection from his duty on the *Patna* has made him unworthy of his calling and that therefore he and Jim are not bound by a common profession. His first arrangement is for Jim to work for Denver (Jim's third "father"); but when the second engineer of the *Patna* comes to work with Jim, he is unable to confess to Denver, who has soon become "more like a father" to him, and he therefore leaves without explanation.

Marlow then takes Jim's problem to Stein, who has "paternal motives" for being willing to help Jim. He sends Jim to Patusan to restore Doramin and his people to prosperity, hoping thereby to make some reparation for his own earlier failure in Celebes. Jim, re-enacting Stein's jungle adventure a generation later, at last fails, for a second time, to protect people in his charge and virtually takes his own life. One important fact is clear: Jim has "profoundly disappointed" his three surrogate fathers, and he leaves Stein to care for his widow, "another victim of his desertion." [A valid reading of *Jim,* but it must be supplemented by a consideration of JC's sources; for this purpose Norman Sherry's "Conrad's Source for *Lord Jim,*" MODERN LANGUAGE REVIEW, LIX (Oct 1964), 545-57, is the best available.]

1799 Hoffman, Frederick J. THE MORTAL NO: DEATH AND THE MODERN IMAGINATION (Princeton: Princeton U P, 1964), pp. 40, 42, 50-57, 57-64, 89, 90.

If the novel of manners is not dead, it has been forced to come to terms with a violence which is opposed to some kind of decorum. In two of JC's novels, violence and decorum exist "in an uneasy imbalance": in *The Secret Agent,* Stevie is literally blown to bits, and in *Nostromo* the silver mine becomes increasingly an abstractly materialistic symbol.

When *Agent* is seen in terms of a novel of violence, JC's use of irony to condemn the irresponsibility, the narrowness, and the idleness of anarchism is notable. His depiction of two kinds of death—Verloc's murder and Winnie's suicide, which fit into the pattern of the *crime passionnel,* and Stevie's completely irrational death—is the "major contribution" of this novel to a study of modern violence. In *Nostromo,* JC examines much more subtly the problems of violence and supplies "a geography, an anthropology, even a geo-metaphysics of violence." The silver mine is at once a natural resource, a "buried treasure," and the focus of both political and economic organization; it makes men and women what they are. As a center of the technological genius of man, it separates Emilia and Charles Gould, making Mrs. Gould's "conquest" of the community a moral conquest even in her defeat; and it causes Charles to become "an inflexible technological materialist whose rationality is rhetorically supported by an idealism of ends." As a moral focus, the mine forces three main characters into the act of self-definition. Only Mrs. Gould achieves it. Decoud commits suicide because he cannot bear isolation, but fundamentally because he has no ideology to enable him to endure it. Nostromo, "a romantic of deeds," is equally inadequate to himself. The country of Costaguana, isolated from specific historical reality because it is an imaginery land, is almost a perfect symbol of "the way in which nature and man both attract and need ideological definition." The history of Costaguana has been a succession of irrational acts, all leading to Charles Gould's "orderly universe." Above all, this novel is an analysis of the relationship of rhetorics to forces: many rhetorical systems are evoked to explain or exact approval of political or moral positions. More clearly than *Agent, Nostromo* is "a record of the conflict of violence with forms of decorum, manners, moral convention."

> **1800** Hoffman, Stanton de Voren. "Conrad's Menagerie: Animal Imagery and Theme," BUCKNELL REVIEW, XII (Dec 1964), 59-71; incorporated in COMEDY AND FORM IN THE FICTION OF JOSEPH CONRAD (The Hague: Mouton, 1969).

JC's villains, frequently puzzling in their contexts, have a common trait, irresponsibility, and they represent the anarchy and chaos which is related to the themes of the works in which they appear. De Barral in *Chance* and Donkin in *The Nigger of the Narcissus* seem to belong to "an underworld of bestial life"; in books like *Lord Jim* and *Victory* there are recurring images of "the animal and the irrationally bestial." The animals (birds, amphibians, serpents) represent "a regression into a meaningless chaos which is made clear through a series of 'burlesque' and slapstick actions" asociated with characters who regress into the irrational or animal state, as Jim does in his plunge from the *Patna*. In *Victory* the emphasis on animal imagery serves different purposes: basically, it provides dehumanization, which is required for allegorical characters like Ricardo and his companions. But the animal imagery applied to Heyst does not seem relevant to his kind of fall. *Jim* and *Victory*, written fifteen years apart, represent two different uses of JC's menagerie.

After Powell in *Chance* falls from innocence through his "cavernous journey" to Saint Katherine's Dock House, he begins to see mankind in a new light: JC's description of the street by the docks is "the city of night and the grave," the "slimy" city of *The Secret Agent,* the "prison-house" city of "The Return," the "dead and sepulchral" city of "Heart of Darkness." When the voyage in *Nigger* is completed, the city and the land become a place of confusion, of clamor, and of "bestial shapes"; and Donkin, a product of the land and the animal symbol of the fall, is the only person in this book who seems to belong there. This novel, in fact, presents several persons "in various stances and poses upon a death journey" and contains notable images of a disorderly world, of doubt, pride, and complacency. Thus the corrupt land and city are the analogues to the disorder on the ship, and the problem is to exist somehow, "even in this nightmare." The nightmare in *Agent,* the world of anarchy, is also presented through images of disorder.

Generally, then, in JC's bestial imagery, the animals of this menagerie define an "underworld of desires and actions" into which one may fall; and for JC the fallen man becomes "abstract, dehumanized, an image, . . . a caricature, and a beast." The collection of animals is always part of "a vision of evil, part of a theme which explores man's relationship to dirt." [This kind of interpretation is applied particularly to *Jim* in Hoffman, " 'Scenes of Low Comedy': the Comic in *Lord Jim*," BALL STATE TEACHERS COLLEGE FORUM, V (Spring 1964), 19-27.]

1801 Hoffman, Stanton de Voren. " 'Scenes of Low Comedy': the Comic in *Lord Jim*," BALL STATE TEACHERS COLLEGE FORUM, V (Spring 1964), 19-27; incorporated in COMEDY AND FORM IN THE FICTION OF JOSEPH CONRAD (The Hague: Mouton, 1969).

The comic aspect of Jim's fall in leaping from the *Patna* contains mainly "knockabout clowning and slapstick," which Bergson defined as mechanical and dehumanized. In the lifeboat the officers of the ship are mechanized and puppet-like as they comport themselves like animals. In a sense Jim jumps into a boat which soon becomes a "ship of fools." Stein unites the two major parts of the novel, those of the *Patna* and of Patusan, and provides a commentary on both. Stein sees in the *Patna* affair "a question of how to be," and he maintains that man's task (Jim's task) is to force a sea which is both a dream and a destructive element to maintain him. The low comedy that JC employs suggests a rebellion against normal order; and the violence, the sweating, and the cursing imply a basic disorder or formlessness: "knockabout clowning" is the objective depiction of the disorder implicit in the "animal regression." Jim fails "to be" and thereby closely approaches the irrational and the bestial, but the implication is that man is "poised" at some point between angel and animal and that his greatest danger is a "lapse into formlessness."

Lord Jim is also about Marlow and the conflict within his being; and low comedy, which helps to explain Jim, is a part of Marlow's reaction to Jim as well as a part of his attempt to see himself clearly. Marlow, too, is constantly in danger of falling. In prolonging and dwelling upon the "burlesque" elements in various situations (the words of the alcoholic chief engineer and Brierly's suicide), Marlow parallels Jim's "desire" to approach the disorder represented by the low comic. Marlow the intellectual and Jim the acting man are thus similar, with low comedy, farce, or "burlesque" essential for an understanding of the novel. Marlow's inability to reach a decision about Jim is, in fact, his own particular kind of disorder. [An intriguing concept which is applied to several other works by JC in Hoffman, "Conrad's Menagerie: Animal Imagery and Theme," BUCKNELL REVIEW, XII (Dec 1964), 59-71, and "The Hole in the Bottom of the Pail: Comedy and Theme in 'Heart of Darkness,' " STUDIES IN SHORT FICTION, II (Winter 1965), 113-23.]

1802 Kaehele, Sharon, and Howard German. "Conrad's *Victory:* A Reassessment," MODERN FICTION STUDIES, X (Spring 1964), 55-72.

JC's treatment of character and episode in *Victory* is far too complex for the charge of sentimentality to be valid, and JC's usual concern with the "old preoccupations" is too apparent to be ignored. Heyst and Jones play analogous roles; Heyst and Schomberg are doubles because of their similar physiques and experiences; and Heyst, Sr., is linked to Jones by means of numerous details, one of which is their ethical concepts. Heyst deviates in two important ways from the precepts of his father's injunction merely to "look on"—his ties with Morrison and with Lena—and thus reveals both the "impact of sceptical detachment as an ideal" and the serious consequences of infidelity to any ideal.

Much of the detail in *Victory* shows that JC is concerned with loyalty between individuals as well as with loyalty to the community or to one's self: the four rescue scenes and the relationship between Heyst and Morrison. By means of various details JC also links Morrison with another of Heyst's trials, the arrival of Jones on the island. This linkage functions like the character doubles: it leads the reader to see that Heyst's behavior towards Morrison is "only a polite version of Jones's treatment of Heyst." Another major element in the novel is JC's concept of the importance of illusion, "a possible antidote for a Heystian scepticism." For JC *illusion,* meaning "a sense of purpose, or something or someone to believe in," is ambivalent even if necessary in life; and for Lena, if not for Heyst or Schomberg, having a cause, an illusion, makes a difference in her behavior and gives her strength and a new feeling of significance. The most elaborate study of illusion is found in Lena herself, who is a double of Ricardo. The most informative similarity in the doubles, though difficult to define, lies in their behavior, in "their comparable courses of betrayal." Heyst and Lena, though, do not contain only flaws; both have courage, Heyst has integrity, and Lena has devotion to a noble purpose. *Victory* seems to be a pessimistic novel; it portrays "the rarity of loyalty" and emphasizes "the difficulty of achieving a mature balance of scepticism and illusion." [A penetrating and convincing analysis of *Victory.*]

1803 Kiely, Robert. ROBERT LOUIS STEVENSON AND THE FICTION OF ADVENTURE (Cambridge, Mass: Harvard U P, 1964), pp. 3, 14, 25, 27, 77, 102-5, 132-33, 167, 185, 236, 250, 264.

The difference between R. L. Stevenson and JC is displayed in KIDNAPPED and DAVID BALFOUR. Stevenson, beginning to be aware of "dissatisfaction and bewilderment over his vision of a 'pure dispassionate adventure,'" still shares the fault with his characters and "clings almost apologetically to a dream in which he has already begun to disbelieve." JC understood better than Stevenson "the temptations which beset the romantic dreamer." Stevenson, in one episode in THE DYNAMITER, anticipates JC's "satiric masterpiece on a similar theme," *The Secret Agent,* although this episode has a most "un-Conradian conclusion." Like JC, Stevenson objected to sudden or violent social change, and he used the same kind of "rhythmic and insane rambling" for his "rebellious characters" that JC was to use twenty-two years later in the "passionate and obscure dialogues" of his conspirators. The atmosphere and several details of THE EBB TIDE remind one of JC, especially in *Victory,* and in WEIR OF HERMISTON Stevenson started what JC was "to fulfill with genius" in his writing career, beginning with *Almayer's Folly.*

1804 Kirschner, Paul. "Conrad's Strong Man," MODERN FICTION STUDIES, X (Spring 1964), 31-36.

JC's creative imagination served the needs of the creator while also serving the cause of art by developing the titular character in "Gaspar Ruiz" from the source of this character, a bandit named Benavides; and by utilizing Monsieur George of *The Arrow of Gold* as a counterpart. Gaspar Ruiz, unlike Benavides in EXTRACTS FROM A JOURNAL WRITTEN ON THE COASTS OF CHILE, PERU, AND MEXICO IN THE YEARS 1820, '21, '22, by Captain Basil Hall, R. N., is "a simple, good-hearted man, acting out of loyalty and passion." Ruiz and Erminia have their counterparts in the later and somewhat autobiographical novel (*Arrow*) in Monsieur George and Rita de Lastaola. However, according to recent evidence, the young JC did not fight a duel over Rita but rather attempted to kill himself. JC was pursued throughout his life by a feeling of guilt because he had left Poland and deserted the cause of his patriotic father. In writing "Gaspar Ruiz," JC exorcised the guilt of desertion and of attempted suicide by creating a chivalrous arrangement greatly unlike the events of his own life. When writing in *Arrow* about his experience in Marseilles, he relied on a similar arrangement, creating what appears to be a romantic and chivalrous portrayal of Monsieur George and Doña Rita, with the duel being another chivalrous disguise which helped to exorcise the memory of an excess of pessimism which once had overwhelmed him. The same "imaginative mechanism" was editing JC's part in "Gaspar Ruiz," "guiding him to discover a passionate and loyal strong man behind the unflattering descriptions of the traitor Benavides."

1805 Levine, Paul. "Joseph Conrad's Blackness," SOUTH ATLANTIC QUARTERLY, LXIII (Spring 1964), 198-206.

James Wait in JC's *The Nigger of the Narcissus* partically masters the ship, however briefly, before his death by arousing the "irrational sentiments" of the crew because symbolically he suggests "the blackness of evil and of man as well as the shadow of death and the unconscious." Since Wait is seen almost entirely through his mates' reactions to him, the "Nigger" and the *Narcissus* represent "the two extremities of narcissism: one legitimate and the other false." The sailors fight with both the elements and themselves in a psychological conflict lying "between the *super ego* (duty) and the *id* (self-gratification)." Only after Wait is dead and buried in the ocean is the *id* at last submerged, but then the common bond of a "sentimental lie," which is contrasted with the bond of the natural loyalty of the men to the ship, is gone. Only old Singleton seems exempt from "the community of the sentimental lie and its potential blackness." Considered as an account of initiation like "Heart of Darkness" and "The Secret Sharer," this novel contains initiation on two levels: in his struggle with the "external elements," Singleton finds "the physical truth of his own morality," but the others find in their encounter with Wait "the psychological fallacy of their own egoism," "the primitive and impenetrable blackness of man," which first attracts and then repels them. They can understand Donkin's "malevolent hypocrisy" but are thwarted by Jimmy's "sham existence."

"The impenetrability of blackness" is likewise the "major fact" of "Heart of Darkness." Marlow's voyage may be called "a journey into the dark night of the soul." The Congo is both "the river of life" and a river in Africa. Marlow, having been previously committed to belief in "a surface truth," slowly realizes that he himself "responds to the primitive" and recapitulates Kurtz's experience. Kurtz, in descending into the dark night of the soul, had "crossed the frontier into blackness, insanity, and death" and, apparently finding nothing there, had "gone mad." Thus, the evil black men like Wait and Kurtz, not the good seamen, intrigue us as they no doubt did Marlow and JC. In the preface to *The Nigger of the Narcissus,* JC deals with the artist who "descends within himself, and in that lonely region of stress and strife, if he is deserving and fortunate, he finds the terms of his appeal." If, then, the novelist's descent is represented by Kurtz's and Marlow's, and if, as Stein said, "The way is to the destructive element submit yourself," "Kurtz succumbed to it, Marlow endured, but only Conrad prevailed." [One of the best interpretations of *The Nigger of the Narcissus* and "Heart of Darkness." A closely reasoned concept.]

1806 Levy, Milton A. "Conrad's 'The Lagoon,'" EXPLICATOR, XXIII (Dec 1964), Item 35.

To some extent, his brother's love for Arsat is "ironically responsible for Arsat's very disloyalty to him and for Arsat's disloyalty to himself," Arsat implicitly asserts that there is "a fundamental ambiguity in the nature of things," that the "world of illusions" is "manifold," reaching beyond the world of the lagoon. [For another interpretation, see George Walton Williams, ibid. (Sept 1964), Item I, and ibid. (March 1965), Item 51.]

1807 Lid, R. W. FORD MADOX FORD: THE ESSENCE OF HIS ART (Berkeley and Los Angeles: University of California P, 1964), pp. 10-15 and passim; derived from "Time in the Novels of Ford Madox Ford," an unpublished thesis, University of Michigan, 1959.

While Ford may have paid a high price for the collaborative experience, JC "turned Ford into a serious novelist" and "in effect 'talked' him into the mainstream of twentieth-century literature." Out of their talk "grew a theory of the 'Impressionist novel.'" Both were "beguiled by technique," both "would have been better writers if they had not had to rely so heavily on it," and both, as aliens to England, used their fictional strategy as a mask, "a 'persona' behind which to hide when necessary." Despite JC's help in getting Ford underway, it was Henry James "who played the larger role in the development" of Ford's art.

1808 Lodge, David. "Conrad's *Victory* and THE TEMPEST: An Amplification," MODERN LANGUAGE REVIEW, LIX (April 1964), 195-99.

Parallels between *Victory* and THE TEMPEST are not fortuitous. Wang is identified with Ariel by his "apparent ability to transcend the laws of physics"; the basic situations in the two works are "strikingly similar" in that the representatives of a corrupt civilization come out of the sea to threaten the "idyllic peace" of a man and a woman on a remote island, although in THE TEMPEST power is justified by its use whereas in *Victory* power corrupts; the hierarchies of guilty people are alike in the two works; in Heyst's relationship with Lena the Prospero-Miranda and Ferdinand-Miranda relationships are "fused and transmuted"; JC manipulates in *Victory* many elements of THE TEMPEST "to form a pattern which is the opposite" of that in Shakespeare's play—"not a tragicomedy, but a tragedy of the absurd"; and both Heyst and Prospero, hermits dwelling on desert islands, have libraries. The echoes from Shakespeare contribute to the unity of "spatial form" in JC's novel and help the author to "magnify and universalize" the significance of his characters and their actions.

1809 Lorch, Thomas M. "The Barrier Between Youth and Maturity in the Works of Joseph Conrad," MODERN FICTION STUDIES, X (Spring 1964), 73-80.

Although JC's characters undergo tests at every stage of life, their confrontation of the barrier between youth and maturity is especially important. Such tests have certain characteristics in common: the unexpected always happens (*Lord Jim*), the character is "taken unawares" (*Jim* and *Under*

Western Eyes), it appears that one's very existence is undermined "in some mysterious manner" (*Eyes*), an unpleasant fact presents itself and the conception of one's own existence is shattered (*Chance*), one's illusions are destroyed (*Eyes*), a sense of security is gone (*Chance*), and the character feels that he is losing control of both himself and the situation. The test always involves a conflict between the character's "romantic conception of himself" and a recognition of the "hard facts of existence" which he shares with mankind and reveals the true nature of each character. The barrier between youth and maturity is the moment when each character first becomes aware of "the destructive element" and decides about his relation to it. In all instances the character's usual routine is violated, and the test demands "a decision, an action, a positive reply"; in a naked state the youth "assumes the moral responsibility for his actions for the first time" and irrevocably determines the future course of his life.

The Shadow-Line provides the best example of the barrier between youth and maturity: after many complications of the unexpected command, the hero breaks the barrier and succeeds because of his "instinctive adherence to the inflexible seaman's code of duty and responsibility." Those characters who fail to surmount the barrier (Jim, Razumov, and Flora de Barral) reject reality and do not live up to this code because they are handicapped by "a combination of selfish illusions, personal inadequacy, and adverse circumstances." Thus JC's young characters succeed if they "repudiate selfish egotism and escape, face reality with 'faith' and 'courage,' and accept their responsibilities to their fellow men."

1810 Luecke, Sister Jane Marie, O.S.B. "Conrad's Secret and Its Agent," MODERN FICTION STUDIES, X (Spring 1964), 37-48.

The truth in *The Secret Agent* is "an affirmation of positive values," revealed through the artistic structure of the novel and caught by the reader only in glimpses. In the structure of the work as a whole, chapter VIII, placed in the middle of the book, produces the aesthetic effect: here JC forces the reader to note what the novel is really about—"the inner story of human reactions rather than the outer frame of action." The address sewn in Stevie's coat "ties the chapter physically . . . to those around it" and thereby gives the reader "a heightened apprehension of the Winnie-Stevie-Mother-Verloc relationships." The aesthetic effect of the position and the relation of this chapter in and to the novel is rhythmic.

JC uses three obvious comic techniques. First, there is his use of "single words (and then synonyms and metaphors for these words) that ordinarily signify 'something' to signify 'nothingness,'" such as "circle," "silence," and "secret," with associated words. The word "secret" naturally creates its most complex reference to Verloc as the secret agent. Verloc as "a non-agent of a no-secret" originates rhythmic patterns which remove the experience of the Verloc household from a physical to an aesthetic level and then suggests that the disorder is in this particular situation, not in the universal order, thus exemplifying ironic or comic detachment. The second comic technique is "the use of verbal patterns to indicate what should be regarded by the reader with scorn or laughter," such as the prevalence of animal imagery. The third and subtlest comic technique derives from "the presence of an approved standard that acts as a frame of reference for judging the situation portrayed."

The only character in the world of the novel who is not shown to be either stupid or perverted is the Assistant Commissioner. Thus, the world of the police is not supposed to be "perfectly integrated" with that of the Verlocs, a fact which suggests that "civilized human society has the power to survive, to surmount its inferior and destructive elements." In addition, civilized society, or "mankind in general," is also seen in the novel as "a positive force for order," for which the sun is the symbol. The movement in *Agent* is not from light to darkness; it is, instead, "the small circular movement of a group of dark figures grasping after their own tails in darkness within the large circle of an 'Empire on which the sun never sets.' " [An able critic displays convincingly that JC is at least not entirely pessimistic.]

1811 McIntyre, Allan O. "Conrad on Conscience and the Passions," UNIVERSITY REVIEW, XXXI (Oct 1964), 69-74.

In his novels, JC included "an extensive treatment of the passions," especially of fear and courage, which he considered universal. He clearly developed certain conclusions about them: (1) Most of the passions are inherent, not acquired; (2) in themselves they have no moral significance; (3) they are associated with morality only in extremity or when unchecked; and (4) although inherent and essentially nonmoral, they serve the mind in "its muddy though irremeable quest for happiness and feeling." JC knew that the "fullest passions" are always wisely restrained by "conscience, resignation, or renunciation" and that the remedy for unbridled passion could take several forms, such as curiosity, resignation, dignity, timidity, faithfulness, and renunciation, with "unremitting labor and suffering" the most effective of all. Neither "inevitable failure" nor "worthless despair," but the endurance of suffering or tribulation, is the "mark of manhood"; without a "steadfastness of soul" and the "restraint of faithfulness," passion "leads its votary astray." JC considered passion as almost synonymous with suffering, with a release sometimes obtained through the "dignity of honest labor" and sometimes through forgetfulness, the latter "an illusion common to Christians, sailors, and children." Only the "elect," a few, "see life for what it is: a dumb show of illusions, passions, suffering, and torment." [This argument is well supported by several references to JC's writings. Also see McIntyre's "Joseph Conrad and the Philosophy of Illusion," unpublished thesis, University of Texas, 1961, and other related articles.]

1812 McIntyre, Allan O. "Conrad on the Functions of the Mind," MODERN LANGUAGE QUARTERLY, XXV (June 1964), 187-97.
JC, who found the mind "the most complex of human functions," formed a lucid and unvarying epistemology, consistent in all his fiction, his prefaces, and his letters. In practically all of his fiction, the story is interrupted by the narrator, frequently Marlow, or by the author himself; and this speaker reveals a basic and consistent philosophy. Fundamental in JC's epistemology is his conception of the "fact," that facts are one of the many mysteries of the world. Inside the mind is another important element, memory, "a subtle commentator upon events of the past"—memory which becomes more sharply personal as the mind more consciously transforms experience. Allied to memory is conscience, not the "diminutive voice" of the Victorians but "the romantic guardian of past traditions." Whereas memory colors the facts and events of experience, conscience selects the memorable and useful part of it and recommends this part for use in the future. A "gloomy realist," JC realized that a miserable and ignoble environment cannot produce a man of "high conscience"; a noble conscience is the result of a culture with traditions.

For JC, then, the human mind may rely upon conscience, facts, memory, and tradition, but not upon ideas, reason, logic, books, and reflection. For him, most of man's conduct is based not upon ideas but upon passions, upon "so-called fixed ideas," which are the most dangerous of all because they contain too much personal emotion. For JC, an "anarchy" of the emotions is axiomatic and the result is always that "instinct prompts, impulse misrules." But the emotions shield the mind from almost unbearable insights it might perceive by means of reflection. The best way to avoid indolence, or even idiocy, is "to be concerned with and involved in the ordinary business of the world." JC's anti-intellectual views go well with his opinion of books ("Books are nothing") and words ("The great foes of reality"). JC's main purpose as an artist is to make his readers see and feel, to know the power of conscience and memory, and to have them avoid the barren and lifeless activity of the intellect. The happiest man simply works hard, knows his work well, and "follows the dream." Education is dangerous primarily because it enhances thought, which usually destroys the illusory dreams that make life bearable. [Although JC was an artist first and a philosopher afterwards, his basic epistemology, as explained here and supported by pertinent quotations from his writings, provides a necessary background for understanding his works.]

1813 McIntyre, Allan O. "Conrad on Writing and Critics," FORUM (Houston), IV (Fall 1964), 37-42.

Because JC believed [illustrative citations given] that criticism, either his own or that of professional critics or journalists, was "wrong-headed, absurd, and annoying—or simply barren and useless," the opinion of other people made little difference to him. His own attempts at criticism are "remarkably unenlightening." Fidelity to past impressions is the nearest he came to a creed, his purpose in writing was moral "in the loosest sense of that term," and his method was that of recollection. Essentially, JC is unclassifiable. He felt a deep sense of moral obligation to his art, as he made clear in his prefaces.

1814 Maclennan, D. A. C. "Conrad's Vision," ENGLISH STUDIES IN AFRICA (Johannesburg), VII (Sept 1964), 195-201.

An analysis of several of JC's works, with emphasis on *Nostromo,* reveals that JC finds "at the centre of things" only "disorder, bland, neutral. Life and death, good and evil, moral qualities and moral judgments are all gratuitous. Chance is the most powerful agent in the world, and it reveals a world where the value imposed by men are [sic] seen as entirely relativist, and where the only permanence is a ghostly, abstract indifference." JC's vision is "an extreme form of humanism seen against a background of indifference," a "philosophical romanticism," which goes easily with nihilism. In one way, JC tries to impose on us "the extreme value of humanity without understanding that extreme humanism only destroys its own version of the dignity of man." This great value placed upon man must be seen "in terms of man's apparent valuelessness and frailty." The paradox at the center of JC's "philosophical melodramas" is that "man is as weak as water and as strong as steel." Some interesting points about *Nostromo* arise from the fact that its profundity lies in its defects: the novel is too long for the author's purpose, Nostromo appears entirely too late in the story, and too many characters are "integrated" in theory and not in practice in the book. Martin Decoud is the "real hero." JC implicates both "hordes and heroes" in what Decoud would have called *"une bonne blague, a big-scale tragic farce,"* by means of the "ironic principle of fidelity"— Charles Gould, Mrs. Gould, Dr. Monygham. JC's characters are most nearly alive when we understand their motives the least, "where they are involved completely and yet remain inscrutable." JC, unable to write comedy or tragedy, wrote only drama in which the "fidelity principle" prevents him from being deeply involved or committed—like Decoud, whose problem is his commitment. [A thought-provoking article which might have been more fully developed.]

1815 Meyer, Bernard C. "Death Was the Fate of His Heroes," COLUMBIA UNIVERSITY FORUM, VII (Summer 1964), 14-19; absorbed in JOSEPH CONRAD: A PSYCHOANALYTICAL BIOGRAPHY (Princeton, NJ: Princeton U P, 1967).

Though his works are not literal autobiography, JC drew heavily upon his own varied experiences, one outcome of which is "an impressionistic disclosure of himself." Like many of the author's works, *The Arrow of Gold* has certain elements in common with JC's personal experiences and would appear to act as a catharsis, absolving his own sense of humiliating failure. In setting, action, character, and their heroes' unfulfilled love for an already betrothed woman, "A Smile of Fortune" and "The Planter of Malata" reflect strong overtones of JC's poignant infatuation in Mauritius with Mlle Eugénie Renouf. Likewise, JC's difficulty in writing the name Renouard instead of Renouf, as well as the English-to-French language switch in "Planter," make this work the more "accurate psychological reflection" of the author's own experience in Mauritius. Furthermore, JC's behavior upon proposing marriage to his wife, his behavior with Mlle. Renouf, and some of the letters he wrote to Marguerite Poradowska (whom he addressed as "Aunt," though she was no relative) suggest that he was "terrified of intimate relations with women" and wished to avoid their intimacy in both his fiction and real life. No fewer than eight of his heroes, like Renouard, are ruined as a result of their "romantic involvements." Similarly, both JC and Renouard left home young in life and wandered the earth, indicating further that the melancholy Geoffrey Renouard is a self-portrait of the author.

Some of JC's characters and episodes are derived also from his reading. Leopold von Sacher-Masoch's VENUS IN FURS, read by JC, and JC's *Arrow* and "Planter" are similar in both characterization and action particularly in that they all present a "symbolic reversal" of sexual roles which can be traced psychologically to JC's own longing for the past and his yearning to be embraced by his mother who died when he was only seven. "Falk," "A Smile of Fortune," and one of the letters written to Mme. Poradowska also express psychologically this longing for maternal reunion. [A reasonably argued psychoanalytic interpretation of JC's works.]

1816 Moody, William Vaughan, and Robert Morss Lovett. A HISTORY OF ENGLISH LITERATURE, 5th ed, rvd by R. M. Lovett (NY: Scribner's, 1935); 6th ed, ed and rvd by Fred B. Millett (1943); 7th ed (1956); 8th ed (1964), pp. 377, 382-83, 425, 501.

JC, with R. L. Stevenson, Barrie, and Kipling, illustrates "the desire to restore the spirit of romance to the novel." JC's fiction, like Meredith's and James's, has a tendency "to postpone the crisis and defeat expectation." He "concentrates the force of the situation in a total effect of explosive intensity" and "handles scene with wonderful effect." *Victory* and "Heart of Darkness" best illustrate JC's use of "prolonged tension" and unity of effect.

1817 Morgan, Gerould. "The Future of Welsh Literature," ANGLO-WELSH REVIEW, XIV (Winter 1964-65), 47-51.

Although pedantic insistence on linguistic accuracy is "a Welsh trademark," it appears that no critic has inspected JC's work and found that, because of some "slight (hypothetical) inaccuracies," his novels have no literary value. A confusion of linguistic and literary standards is one sign of the immaturity of Welsh criticism; yet English was for JC his *third* language, and not many other writers have used a second language successfully.

1818 Morgan, Gerould. "Narcissus Afloat," HUMANITIES ASSOCIATION OF CANADA BULLETIN, XV (Autumn 1964), 45-57.

In *The Nigger of the Narcissus*, JC's method, "to descend within the unknown self and there find some truth of the universe," results in symbolism. In his art he "begins with visible fact, vividly described, assumed to be illusion; he descends to the inner selfhood of persons affected by their pictures of visible fact and of themselves; he emerges with a vision of man in the universe voyaging through the visible toward the inscrutable, while peering within his unknown depths through the barely expressible toward the unspeakable." Thus the symbolic name of the ship, the *Narcissus*. Important symbols for him are the dream and the mirror, both equivocal but assisting in the projection of a man's ideal conception of himself. When one of JC's heroes loses this ideal conception of himself, he often commits suicide, or a "moral harakiri," like Willems, Kurtz, Jim, Brierly, Falk, Nostromo, Decoud, Razumov, and many more. JC represents the sea as a mirror "both physically and metaphysically" until the sea as a mirror becomes invisible and, no longer solid, changes to "pure space." The ship becomes symbolically comparable to a planet. Eventually, experience is one of "almost perfect isolation of the spirit from the senses," analogous to the moral isolation of a man from his fellows. Creative genius as he is, JC uses myth "to set Narcissus on the open sea, as a double of Aphrodite in Neptune's domain," thereby being the first modern author "to identify Aphrodite's mirror with the sea itself, as a universal analogue resolving the dichotomy between world and soul, between reality and illusion." JC's heroes are not good at loving: a failure in treating sexual themes seems, however, to be less in JC than in the characters he creates, because his women generally take lightly the "complicated masculine game of self-deception." The ship *Narcissus*, though, means more than self-absorption: the "Narcissus-figures who flicker in and out of the Conradian mirror" also search for solidarity and "fellowship with all creation." But since modern man is deprived not only of selfhood but also of a meaningful cosmos, JC's Narcissus "doubles

Ulysses wandering among physical and psychic dimensions." His well-known technique of using timeshifts, his "ranging on moving entities or personalities," emphasizes his pronouncement that "the meaning of an event lies outside the event." Thus JC's art is "a science of relativity, open to all the implications of a cosmology without absolutes; a literature as well devised to represent our world as Narcissus is to symbolize it." This concept of Narcissus as a vessel does, nevertheless, seem to suggest that if, like the chastened crew of the *Narcissus,* one begins unselfconsciously his voyage upon "the immortal sea," the "mirror of the infinite," he may possess "at least the universe," which brings him close to a statement by the existentialist Gabriel Marcel in REFLECTION AND MYSTERY. [An excellent use of myth for the elucidation of JC's works.]

1819 Mukerji, N. "*The Secret Agent:* Anarchy and Anarchists," CALCUTTA REVIEW, CLXXII (Aug 1964), 139-48.
The Secret Agent is a melodrama seen through the "emotionally detached" perspective of irony. "Essentially melodramatic and blood-curdling ingredients are woven into a beautifully sustained and complex ironic pattern." "Conrad's hatred of these so-called anarchists, the sham revolutionaries, is conveyed through the general contemptuous tone and a refrain-like emphasis on the ridiculousness of their physical appearance which is comical in effect." A man's exterior suggests the morbidity of his mind. A tone of "amicable contempt" characterizes JC's attitude towards these "professed prophets of people." All JC's revolutionaries are not open shams like Ossipon. "But even at their best they are victims of an illusion; they are under a curse." Personal impulses disguised into creeds become the basis for revolution. JC is scornful of the madness, nihilism, and fanaticism which spring from the anarchists in the novel. *Agent* is "an exploration of madness, despair, and suffering" which conveys "a sense of criminal futility and unfathomable insanity." [Analyzes the criminal futility of pseudo-revolutionaries, "the failure of moral vision, and the exploitation of the eager half-witted humanity by selfish monsters like Ossipon and Karl Yundt."]

1820 Najder, Zdzisław. "Conrad i Bobrowski" (Conrad and Bobrowski), PRZEGLĄD HUMANISTYCZNY, VIII: 5 (1964), 13-24; combines "Polskiłata Conrada," TWÓRCZOŚĆ, XII (Nov 1956), 137-52, and "Conrad w Marsylli," ŻYCIE LITERACKIE, No. 40 (1957), 298, and rptd in NAD CONRADEM (Warsaw: Państwowy Instytut Wydawniczy, 1965), pp. 46-69.
Parallel texts reveal JC's borrowings from his uncle's memoirs. [Since the memoirs themselves are not available in English, nor in Polish in the U.S., this article is extremely valuable to anyone engaged in the study of JC's sources in that it indicates what a considerable percentage of JC's auto-

biographical material is indebted to the careful notations of his uncle rather than to his own memory.] [In Polish.]

> **1821** Najder, Zdzisław. "Introduction," CONRAD'S POLISH BACK-GROUND: LETTERS TO AND FROM POLISH FRIENDS, ed by Zdzisław Nadjer and trans by Halina Carroll (Lond: Oxford U P, 1964), pp. 1-31.

It is important to know as much as possible about JC's national and social background and to discard some of the "mask of Polishness" found by several critics of the novelist. A strong internal conflict in the young man, caused largely by his father's heritage, at last resulted in his finding himself at the age of sixteen in Marseilles, "alone and free, and reasonably well equipped with money." The reasons for JC's leaving Poland and going to sea are readily seen in the fact that going abroad was a natural thing for a young exile to do; that dreaming about adventures and a more than ordinary life is natural for all young men; that JC felt "misunderstood and superior, and out of tune with his environment"; that his ill health seemed to require sea air and physical exercise; that he was lazy and egocentric; and that his guardian could not care for his nephew without the risk of bringing him back into Russia.

JC's cultural background for his journey seems to have consisted mainly of the leaders of Polish romantic literature of the time, especially the works of Mickiewicz, Slowacki, and Krasiński, the basic reading of all educated Poles. Two of JC's letters "prove beyond any doubt that the 'duel' described by Conrad in the pseudo-autobiographical *The Arrow of Gold* was in fact an attempted suicide." The death of Bobrowski, JC's uncle, in 1894 caused a "serious loosening" of JC's associations with Poland. Important, though, was the attack on him by Maria Orzeszkowa, a well-known Polish novelist, who in 1899 severely castigated her fellow-countryman for deserting his national duties and for writing in English, branding him a "shameless careerist," betraying for money his country and his language. Also important is JC's visit in Poland in 1914, one result of which was his "Political Memorandum" of the same year [included in this book].

JC's attitude towards Poland was very complex, and we have no way of knowing whether he at first believed his country could regain its independence; but certainly he was in despair for many years. While in Poland in 1914, however, he came to believe possible the political revival of his country and, wanting to help in some way, lost his reticence in writing about the matter. But to the end of his life he never lost an "uncomfortable attitude of mixed pride and shame, yearning and guilty conscience." The unusual uses of English in his style may be attributed to Polish syntax and literary conventions, but the peculiarities of his imagination and his outlook upon the world reflect the "peculiarly Polish romantic tradition" which he knew and cherished. The influence of this tradition can also be clearly seen in his "treatment of moral responsibility: his moral awareness is stated in social, not individual terms; in terms of duties and obligations, not in terms of conscience and self-perfection." Because of the isolation which resulted, JC was disinherited and lonely, and "(for a Western writer of that time) exceptionally conscious of the sinister brutalities hidden behind the richly ornate facade of *bourgeois* political optimism [JC's outlook was that of an uprooted nobleman]. And these characteristics are precisely what makes Conrad our contemporary." [A basic contribution to an understanding of JC's origins. Both Edmund A. Bojarski, "A Window on Joseph Conrad's Polish Soul," in ENGLISH LITERATURE IN TRANSITION, VII: 4 (1964), 234-38, and his "Conrad's Polish Background," in ENGLISH STUDIES IN AFRICA (Johannesburg), VIII (March 1965), 81-85, assess reliably the value of this book.]

1822 Ohmann, Carol. FORD MADOX FORD: FROM APPRENTICE TO CRAFTSMAN (Middletown, Conn: Wesleyan U P, 1964), pp. 8, 10, 13, 14, 18, 31, 59, 67, 166-69, 171, 173, 176-77.

Of the two novels JC wrote with Ford, *Romance* is the better book; but in certain ways *The Inheritors* is more profound, and certain "striking parallels" may be drawn between this work and JC's independent novels. When Katya in Ford's A CALL rejects Grimshaw as a suitor, the picture is close to JC's usual portrayal of meetings between men and women, "a symbolic one of sexual failure—of inadequacy on the part of the man and contempt on the part of the woman." Love had no place in JC's "true moral world," unlike that of Ford; and JC, unlike Ford, was willing to close his novels with "unsolved, and perhaps insoluble, problems of judgment." But JC's characters, in comparison with Ford's, have "a fairly firm relationship with their world." JC's use of "nonobjective words and phrases that accumulate meanings from context and serve . . . to convey moral evaluations" is less prominent than Ford's.

1823 Perry, John Oliver. "Action, Vision, or Voice: The Moral Dilemmas in Conrad's Tale-Telling." MODERN FICTION STUDIES, X (Spring 1964), 3-14.

JC constantly reiterates that in a universe which has no objective meaning, purposeful action requires some illusion, private or shared; no accurate record of the meaning and value of a man's actions can ever be formulated. In his letters and novels after *The Nigger of the Narcissus* (1897) and before *Nostromo* (1904) are found his "most profound and gloomy thoughts" about man's creating a communicable meaning for his life. Both *Lord Jim* and "Heart of Darkness" show Marlow, the tale-teller, including his dilemmas of "creating, comprehending, and communicating" meaning as a part of the action. For JC, "meaning is a private affair, truth subjective and relative, and morality a feeling created in particular circumstances." Thus, the artist's meaning is created in him by "an effort of sympathetic imagination" which must be re-created in language and then created a third time by the reader's imagination, with each reader eventually finding his own meaning in each story. For some years JC's conception of "the involved process of seeing, understanding, and communicating" meaning in human beings produced a generally pessimistic outlook. Usually, JC's heroes fail "either to produce or to communicate" the meaning they picture to themselves, and the reader may question the value of "both their heroism and the illusion on which it was based," as in *Jim,* "Karain," and JC's letters of the time. Although Marlow is deeply concerned with the fate of Jim and Kurtz, the meaning of their experiences lies in their own imaginations. But JC is not a cynic even if each character can be judged only "within the frame of reference he himself provides for that purpose."

As we see the "impressionist esthetic" at work, the mists into which Marlow's ruminations fade become "the only truth, the only ascertainable facts, an evanescent memory." But we can see JC affirmatively in Marlow's experience as narrator or story-teller: Marlow could "set himself to face and pursue and feel through his moral bones the chill of absolute doubt." "Heart of Darkness" makes the same point in a slightly different manner: Marlow has prepared himself to look "into the nothingness that is the final and only truth of a heartless universe." His greatest vision implies "not only an irremediable isolation and subjectivity in morality but also a recognition of the hollowness of all pretensions to meaning." Nowhere else did JC later touch so deeply "the roots of meaninglessness lying in the limited minds and words of men." [Good in showing Marlow's importance, but perhaps too strongly influenced by recent pessimistic attitudes towards life.]

> **1824** Pritchett, V. S. "Conrad," THE LIVING NOVEL AND LATER APPRECIATIONS (NY: Random House, 1964), pp. 114, 190-99, 252, 254, 261-62; rptd and greatly enlarged from two earlier articles, "Books in General," NEW STATESMAN AND NATION, XXIII (31 Jan 1942), 78; ibid., XL (15 July 1950), 72-73; and "A Pole in the Far East," THE LIVING NOVEL (Lond: Chatto & Windus, 1946; NY: Reynal and Hitchcock, 1947), pp. 143-48.

JC "exists" in English literature, but he is "a harsh exotic" who cannot quite be "assimilated to our modes." Even in *Nostromo,* where his "powers of concretion" are united to a great subject, "we shall not exactly know where we stand" because JC, with his "special and tragic brilliance" of an exile, is always conscious of his "defensive and histrionic irony." *Nostromo* is the "most strikingly modern" of his novels, including every issue of the economic exploitation of a backward country; and it is pervaded by "a profound, even morbid sense of insecurity which is the very spirit of our age." His later books are "simply the early rhetoric expanded." Mr. and Mrs. Gould are not fully realized characters: they are "states of mind," even as Decoud and Heyst are "attitudes, not people." Important characters in the major novels demonstrate the fact that JC's pessimism, his lack of "a positive scheme of spiritual values," left him, as a Romantic artist, in an unbearable situation, because he was an exile and therefore "uncommitted." In spite of his active life, his real heritage was political and literary. An active man with a strong imagination, he saw the "relativeness of experience." Evil in his works becomes "diffused and generalized." His special contribution to the English novel is "the sense of an atmosphere of evil which is notoriously lacking." Even Kurtz is not fully explained; JC gives us only the "distorting illusion." His greatness lies in his handling "a large range of moral types" who suffer fear, guilt, remorse, and "the tincture of corruption in good things" so well that he seems to understand "a universal condition." As a prophet, he anticipated a time "when exile has become, to our sense, a general experience." [Thoughtful and perceptive, developing the prophetic nature of JC's works, but marred by some careless and annoying errors.]

1825 Pritchett, V. S. "Conrad the Pole," NEW STATESMAN, LXVII (29 May 1964), 846.

In CONRAD'S POLISH BACKGROUND, edited by Zdzisław Najder (1964), the letters of Tadeusz Bobrowski, JC's uncle and guardian, written to his nephew, and the few surviving letters of JC to Polish friends, reveal what influenced the young JC's mind and character. The uncle seems to be the source of some of the youth's pessimism; Mickiewicz, who represents "the important influence of the Polish Romantics," appears to have been the source of Lord Jim; and JC's attitude to life was seemingly colored by the Polish Romantics. Although JC may have been an expatriate, he was not a "cosmopolitan."

1826 Ryan, Alvan S. "The Secret Sharer," INSIGHT II: ANALYSES OF MODERN BRITISH LITERATURE, ed by John V. Hagopian and Martin Dolch (Frankfurt Am Main: Hirschgraben-Verlag, 1964), pp. 70-76.

The theme of "The Secret Sharer" concerns the captain's emergence from his "romantic isolation" into "a sense of community, first with Leggatt and then, symbolically, with other men." Although the captain's sense that Leggatt is his "double" or alter ego is stressed, the similarity is between Leggatt and what the captain might become, not what he is early in the story. Leggatt, unlike the captain, is self-possessed, "A strong soul"; he is "the committed man, the engaged man." If he is the captain's submerged nature, the latter is still restricted by the "romantic solitary" who wants security and freedom from responsibility. The last two paragraphs indicate a separation of Leggatt from the captain which is paradoxically a union. The "new" self has been called forth by the "secret sharer," and the young captain is now prepared to submit himself to his command as he moves toward "a new destiny." [Followed by questions and discussions for students.]

1827 Ryf, Robert S. "Conrad's Stage *Victory,*" MODERN DRAMA, VII (Sept 1964), 148-60.

In 1916, H. B. Irving, the well-known actor-producer, became interested in the dramatic possibilities of *Victory* and suggested that Basil Macdonald Hastings dramatize it. After much difficulty as to the dialogue and the shape of the play, in addition to obtaining actors and actresses, the drama was produced on 26 March 1919 at the Globe Theatre, and ran until June 14. The reviews were "mildly favorable," but the play was never published. A summary of the plot reveals that much of the quality of the novel was necessarily lost, especially JC's handling of time; but more serious was the loss in understanding the characters of Jones and Heyst, whose motivations are "extremely murky" in the play. The greatest weakness, however, is the concept of Heyst's character: little of Heyst's opportunity, through Lena's presence on the island, to grapple with life and to realize eventually that one must commit himself to life emerges in the stage version. Many of JC's special elements of the story, such as atmosphere, philosophical overtone, and manner, were lost in the stage version, leaving only melodrama. This dramatization, the only one of JC's works to succeed in the theater, was a venture in which the novelist played only a small part, but undoubtedly it rekindled his interest in the drama and encouraged him to turn *The Secret Agent* into dramatic form, a play which was to be a failure.

1828 Said, Edward W. "Joseph Conrad and the Fiction of Autobiography," Unpublished thesis, Harvard University (1964); developed into JOSEPH CONRAD AND THE FICTION OF AUTOBIOGRAPHY (Cambridge, Mass: Harvard U P, 1966).

JC's letters "present a slowly unfolding discovery of his mind, his temperament, his character," and display the major periods of his "dramatic comprehension of his role in existence." These periods correspond to stages in his "developing sense of himself as a man and a writer." Interestingly, the intellectual and spiritual climax of the letters "coincided not only with the fulfillment of his desire for self-discovery, but also with the climax of an important phase of European history," the period of World War I, at which time a "radical transformation in outlook occurred" and influenced his "spiritual and artistic activity" until his death. And since JC always believed that "artistic distinction" was more forcefully demonstrated in shorter than in longer works, a study of the letters and the shorter fiction together provides the outline for an "integral reading" of JC's "total *oeuvre.*"

JC's life seen in relation to his shorter works reveals his desire to "rescue meaning for the present out of the obscure past," an attempt best noted in the following groups of shorter works: (1) the earliest short stories, beginning in 1896 with "The Idiots" and ending in 1902 with "The End of the Tether," in which JC "repeatedly manipulates the tale with philosophic ingenuity" to discover that "quite simply nothing" can finally be rescued from the past; (2) the second group, comprising the stories up to and including "The Secret Sharer" (1910), in which the conclusion is "more hopeful, if contrived"; (3) the works that end with "The Planter of Malata" (1914), where there is again a "falling off into despair"; and (4) the final period, in which JC, by returning to the "sounds and sights" of his earlier years was able to recapture his "native inspiration" and restore "his vision and his pen" to "healthy fluency" in *The Shadow-Line*. His works after this major achievement, consisting of episodes out of his past and of completing stories he had once begun, "now to idealize, almost always to elegize" the past, indicate that ironically JC "could not finally transmute all his own suffering into an earned peace."

Notable in the progress of JC's life and works is the basic significance of "The Planter of Malata" of 1914 which, contrasted with the earlier story "The Secret Sharer," represents a "fall into grievous despair"; but it cannot be said that JC's creativity at this time fell off in quality and force; it is more accurate to recognize that he had arrived at an impasse, that "his ability to harmonize past and present, action and thought, objective and subjective, failed him at just the moment that Europe failed him." But because of the war, he was to recapture much in *Shadow-Line*. [Said refutes to some extent the Moser-Guerard thesis of achievement and decline.] In "The Secret Sharer," the young captain "contains truth" in his determination to free himself by mastery of his trade, to prove himself a good sailor, just as JC at this time analogously altered the course of his own work to enter a new phase which includes his "most pessimistic" story, "The Planter of Malata." This story is, nevertheless, a masterpiece: each of the avenues toward salvation that Renouard takes leads him back to the "dull impasse" in JC's own mind where he could no longer cope with truth or any of its "deceiving ideas and images." And, finally, *Shadow-Line* is not only a reworking of a single past experience of JC's but also of the whole experience contained in his other works.

The "special beauty and courage" of this last major work is that it begins with an admission of failure, like JC's own realization that all his youthful hopes had been exhausted in a continual search for new truths—a failure that is not easy to admit. But the young captain's eventual satisfactory union with his ship is similar to that between a practicing artist and his art, "surely the deepest reality and truth" of JC's own experience. The "humble reality" that the captain sees in his relation with his fellow men is that "life is a blessing; any life, even the sick, hard one, is worth living." A man must resort to a "protection larger than himself," as shown by Ransome in the story and in JC's "belief in Europeanism." A view of the body of JC's fiction from the vantage point of *Shadow-Line* (the shadow line being the "edge of darkness that one crosses over to create character") displays JC's "evolving mastery of this passage": the darkness in which Marlow in "Heart of Darkness" has "so stark and personal an experience" yields place to the "intellectual fabrications" of "The Secret Sharer," then to the "full harmony between experience and understanding" gained in *Shadow-Line*. JC's achievement is thus seen as his ordering the "chaos of his existence" into a "highly patterned art that accurately reflected and controlled the realities with which it dealt." [Said's method of approaching JC's life and shorter works appreciably enriches one's understanding of both and also presents several stories in a fresh manner.]

1829 Sherry, Norman. "Conrad's Source for Lord Jim," MODERN LANGUAGE REVIEW, LIX (Oct 1964), 545-57; incorporated in CONRAD'S EASTERN WORLD (Cambridge: Cambridge U P, 1966).

It has long been accepted that JC based the desertion of the *Patna* in *Lord Jim* on an actual happening, the desertion of the pilgrim ship *Jeddah* by her European captain and officers, and it has also been thought that JC found his inspiration for Jim's character in one of the *Jeddah*'s officers. This theory is now specifically shown, by both external and internal evidence, to be accurate: Augustine Podmore Williams, the first mate of the *Jeddah* at the time of the desertion, seems to have been JC's source for the entire first part of the novel. Williams's background is identical with Jim's, but JC has the *Patna* deserted under circumstances totally different from those on the *Jeddah*. He changed the details of the desertion of the *Jeddah* "radically" in writing *Jim* because he did not want Jim's desertion of the *Patna* to be in any way justified. Parallels between the attitudes assumed by Williams and Jim indicate that the latter felt the necessity of "sticking it out" because he could not return home where his father, who cared deeply for his son, would have read of the scandal in the newspapers, just as Williams may have remained in Singapore because of his father. Williams's later life has several similarities with Jim's. When Williams died in 1916, an obituary contained a reference to the desertion of the *Jeddah*;

Williams "faced" his disgrace—unlike Jim—but he never "lived it down." JC's inspiration "depended upon a much closer contact with his source than he indicates in the 'Author's Note' to *Lord Jim.*" His intimate knowledge of Williams's life and character led JC "to seek fit words for his meaning" "with all the sympathy of which he was capable." [Such an overwhelming collection of evidence leaves no doubt that the conclusions are valid.]

1830 Sherry, Norman. " 'Exact Biography' and *The Shadow-Line,*" PMLA, LXXIX (Dec 1964), 620-25; incorporated in CONRAD'S EASTERN WORLD (Cambridge: Cambridge U P, 1966).

In spite of the fact that JC stated in two letters that the story of *The Shadow-Line* is "exact biography," more reliable evidence reveals that the conflicting versions of JC's taking command of the *Otago* in January 1888 and arriving in Bangkok in February—those of *Shadow-Line,* "Falk," and "The End of the Tether"—cannot be completely resolved. Apparently, JC deliberately altered the facts to achieve dramatic effect in *Shadow-Line,* substituting an excised passage from his manuscript of "Falk." He also exaggerated, for the same purpose, the account of losing his entire crew. Since the facts of JC's first command are not completely available, it seems best not to be too definite about the amount of exact biographical detail in *Shadow-Line.*

1831 Sherry, Norman. " 'Rajah Laut'—A Quest for Conrad's Source," MODERN PHILOLOGY, LXII (Aug 1964), 22-41; incorporated in CONRAD'S EASTERN WORLD (Cambridge: Cambridge U P, 1966).

Captain William Lingard, whom JC probably did not know, is the original of Captain Tom Lingard, the "Rajah Laut" in *Almayer's Folly, An Outcast of the Islands,* and *The Rescue.* A reconstruction of the life of William Lingard, trader in the East, based on such evidence as Singapore newspaper accounts, the Shipping in Harbour columns of several newspapers of Singapore, THE WHITE RAJAHS OF SARAWAK by Robert Payne (1960), one of JC's letters, and Lingard's marriage certificate, indicates clearly that the character and reputation of Tom Lingard in JC's Malayan novels corresponds closely to those of William Lingard.

JC relied upon a "prototype" for his "successful portraits"; without one, he failed as a novelist. *Rescue* fails because JC did not know the history of young William Lingard. Lingard's disappearance in JC's novels is startling when contrasted with his earlier position "as benevolent despot and father figure." His generosity is constantly related to his misfortune, and it seems to bring disaster both to his protégés and to himself, perhaps because of its "strong aspect of possessiveness." The disappearance of the actual William Lingard seems to have impressed JC so strongly that he portrays his fictional Lingard's mysterious end in his first two novels, although it is unlikely that he came into contact with the real man. When JC joined the *Vidar* in 1887, however, he must have learned about Lingard's story from many sources, and he was undoubtedly able then to see the result of Lingard's actions. William Lingard must have fascinated JC as "the type of adventurer and protective father figure" which appears frequently in the Malayan novels. Furthermore, the close parallels between the actual Lingard and the fictional trader support JC's own claim that "one's literary life must turn frequently for sustenance to memories and seek discourse with the shades." [Filled, as it is, with evidence—and with some speculation—this "quest" for JC's source may be more useful to a biographer of JC than to a critic of his works; but some of the explanation of the novelist's methods of developing his characters is valuable.]

1832 Solomon, Eric. STEPHEN CRANE IN ENGLAND: A PORTRAIT OF THE ARTIST (Columbus: Ohio State U P, 1964), pp. 4, 5, 10, 11, 12, 13, 24, 27, 35, 36, 37, 38, 39, 46, 48, 50, 51, 52, 54-56, 58, 62-65, 75, 88, 89, 91-118.

[Most references to JC are about his relationships with Stephen Crane and other literary men, like Henry James, Ford Madox Ford, H. G. Wells, and Edward Garnett.] In their works, both Crane and JC "were looking for the figure in the carpet," and like James, they "shared the same literary method": for them, disillusionment appears everywhere in life. Crane and JC shared a mutual respect which was "obviously based on art as well as personality." [The account on pp. 91-118 of their friendship and work is excellent, as is the clear explanation of their "similarities in style and content."]

1833 Stein, William Bysshe. "'The Heart of Darkness': Bodhisattva Scenario," ORIENT/WEST, IX (Sept 1964), 37-46.

Marlow, JC's "alter ego" in "Heart of Darkness," symbolizes the "mercy and pity in the creative imagination" that produced the fictional tale after the author's "African catharsis," and JC utilizes the "Buddha postures" of the *yogi*, the Bodhisattva, to convey a "kind of intuitive aspiration" through Marlow, who speaks as a *guru* in an attempt to lead his listeners through the "deceptions of *maya* (the impermanent forms of time and history)." Significantly, the narrator describes Marlow in the first of the two tableaux in part I as sitting in what is obviously the "ascetic" lotus posture (*padmasana*). Although Marlow insists that verbal communication among human beings is futile, he desires his auditors to evaluate the transformation he has undergone in his "voyage to the edge of the abyss" with Kurtz and to share with him his new outlook on life. His failure to communicate with them means that he—and consequently JC in his fiction—

"like the Bodhisattva, will continue to carry the burden of conscience disavowed by his culture."

JC's use of a second Buddha posture, which depicts the act of teaching, indicates that Marlow allows the steamboat in the story to serve as the Buddhist ferryboat of redemption on which he journeys to "The Heart of the Wisdom of the Other Shore." He thus learns to pity others, in this specific instance "the criminally barbaric Kurtz." Marlow's self-control, suppression of fear, and defiance of death in his voyage of initiation generate his sense of a deeper reality as the old world recedes while he regresses symbolically into the timeless past; JC thus prepares the reader for the "paradox of enlightenment," the primeval darkness where Marlow's wisdom arises from a direct encounter with the "primitive energies of archetypal *maya*." Marlow's vision of "The Heart of Wisdom of the Other Shore" in part III shows Marlow confronted by "an unconquerable and sublime warrior maiden, the incarnation of . . . the externalization of the vital energy (*maya*) which he pours into the universe" and from which man creates his dream of the world. As she appears now, Maya-Shakti is the destroyer goddess, Kali, the Black One, "the personification of the destructive principle of time." This "materialization of Maya-Shakti–Kali into an anthropomorphic woman . . . anticipates the extension of her identity with the heart of darkness," because in her mystic antecedents she is *"materia prima,* the earth, the universal womb." For Marlow she reveals both "the alternating life-death rhythm of the universe" and "the *yogic* peace in which death and birth are brought into equipoise." Thus Marlow tries to communicate to his audience that man is like "the twofold nature of the universe which materializes out of the womb of Maya-Shakti" and is consequently "hopelessly split into components of good and evil." Destined to carry this tension in his soul, he is lost unless someone is willing to share his "transmigrative agonies," just as he is willing to do this for Kurtz. Sublimating all concern with himself, as with Kurtz "he challenges the powers of darkness," Marlow "transcends the delusions of physical self-interest." At last JC portrays him "in the act of achieving the all-encompassing sympathies of the Bodhisattva, the ability to commiserate with the agonies of human depravity in all of its forms" and reiterates once again 'The Heart of the Wisdom of the Other Shore' as it was summed up in the cry "The horror! The horror!"

In the account that follows, JC depicts Marlow as he acquires the enlightenment that "reconciles the finite with the infinite," a union which "symbolizes the marriage of the human with the divine, the role of the Bodhisattva in his eternal round of redemption." Marlow's auditors, unable to detect the suffering in Marlow's despair, are unready "to ride the Buddhist ferryboat of redemption to 'The Heart of the Wisdom of the Other Shore.' " At the end of the story, JC leaves a last glimpse of his hero in the "inturned" lotus posture, the tableau "bringing the *mystery* of the Bodhisattva full circle" with Marlow once again in "serene, self-contained introversion in the timelessness of eternity." Marlow's experience has transformed his heart "into a universal vessel of mercy." [A serious and valid consideration of Marlow and the meaning of his voyage up the Congo.]

>**1834** Sullivan, Sister Mary Petrus, R.S.M. "The Descriptive Style of Joseph Conrad," DISSERTATION ABSTRACTS, XXV (July 1964), 486-87. Unpublished thesis, University of Notre Dame, 1964.

>**1835** Sweetser, Wesley D. ARTHUR MACHEN. Twayne's English Authors Series (NY: Twayne, 1964), pp. 62, 116.

Machen, who "writes of life in terms of enigmas and inscrutable mysteries," should have found JC especially congenial; but apparently he read only *Victory,* and that because of financial pressure to write a commentary for George T. Keating's A CONRAD MEMORIAL LIBRARY (1929). In many tales written in the 1890s, Machen included a symbol that signified "a dark, fearful, awesome elemental force of nature outside society and beneath the veneer of civilization"—not unlike what one finds at the center of "Heart of Darkness."

>**1836** Tanner, Jimmie Eugene. "The Twentieth-Century Impressionistic Novel: Conrad and Faulkner," DISSERTATION ABSTRACTS, XXV (Sept 1964), 1927-28. Unpublished thesis, University of Oklahoma, 1964.

>**1837** Tanner, Tony. "Conrad the Great," SPECTATOR (Lond), CCXII (8 May 1964), 636.

In Zdzisław Najder's CONRAD'S POLISH BACKGROUND (1964), the most important letters, those from JC's uncle, reveal that Tadeusz Bobrowski is a major source of several of JC's "most cherished values," although JC's temperament was much more complex than his uncle's. The letters enlarge especially the picture of the young JC: they show him as "an idler, a spendthrift, a victim of impulse who beyond all doubt did attempt suicide in Marseilles." But JC later learned what life is like, after he had "experienced the danger of the indulged imagination." JC's "Polishness" consists of tensions between "individual romantic impulse and commitment to group endeavor," between "betrayal and fidelity," and between "idealism and work." Out of the ambiguities and paradoxes of life JC, however, "made himself a good citizen," and a great one, "an embellishment to the race."

>**1838** [Tanner, Tony]. "The Rover's Uncle," TIMES LITERARY SUPPLEMENT (Lond), 4 June 1964, p. 488.

1964: 1834-1839

Zdzisław Najder's CONRAD'S POLISH BACKGROUND (1964) shows that JC must have carried within him all his life "a haunting mental image of Poland," with his maternal uncle, Tadeusz Bobrowski, prominent in that image. The letters of JC's guardian are well edited and annotated. They leave the impression that Bobrowski allowed his nephew to go his own way. Part of our curiosity about JC's uncle comes from the thought that he was corresponding intimately with a genius without ever realizing the fact, but he commands our interest and sympathy in his own right.

1839 Tick, Stanley. "The Gods of *Nostromo*," MODERN FICTION STUDIES, X (Spring 1964), 15-26.

JC was either generally indifferent to the subject of Christian assumptions or he refused to explore the subject because he was aware of "the artistic perils of his own ambiguous attitude." He probably had no adequate language for discussing matters of faith. In *Nostromo,* the religious controversy is merely one part of a deep discord which defies resolution. The history of the established Catholic Church of Costaguana is at best inconclusive. Just as institutional religion is an indecisive part of the main story, so is the concept of "belief" treated only in the minor story of Nostromo and Viola. It does not seem that JC uses these two strands of religious implication in any balanced or contrasted manner. JC did, however, work hard with the Nostromo-Viola substory, making it his most elaborate and sympathetic study of supernatural—rather than psychological—forces, a carefully contrived account of "religious faith and superstition that is brought to a conclusion with the inevitability of Divine Justice." JC makes Nostromo's story parallel that of the legend of the ghosts that haunt Azuera. He has carefully prepared for this situation by making the principal characters in the substory "simple believers," as opposed to the sophisticated "realists" in the main plot. The major dramatic impulse for the substory comes from Nostromo's refusal to obtain a priest for the dying Teresa Viola and her fearful prophecy about him. The great Capataz de Cargadores can credit both the legend of Azuera and a solemn curse. In order to overcome the curse, he determines to marry one of the Viola girls. And at the end of the novel he seems to have avoided Teresa's prophecy, only to die under a greater curse attached to stolen treasure. Thus the affront to Christian belief, it seems, could be reconciled in a manner that the evil spirits could not. The substory of Nostromo and the Violas is made to work itself out according to the legend of Azuera, and therefore it seems pagan rather than Christian. But here also JC's ambiguity seems to be intended. The moral ends of this story, like those of the main plot, are not closed, and again the "spectacle" is everything; it is even more impressive than the ethic. The only explicit credo offered anywhere in the novel is this: "In our activity alone do we find the sustaining illusion of an independent existence as against the whole scheme of things of which we form a helpless part."

1840 Wagner, Geoffrey. "John Bull's Other Empire," MODERN AGE, VIII (Summer 1964), 284-90.

The titular concept "loosely connoted" by the British Empire was first brought to the United States through "fictive literature" rather than through sociology: the general public in this country read Kipling, JC, E. M. Forster, Cary, Orwell, and other lesser writers.

The hero of *Lord Jim,* in floundering out of the mud at Patusan, is not separating himself from "black humanity"; he is "learning the settler's loneliness at being compelled to create, and maintain, his values out of nothing." And Wait in *The Nigger of the Narcissus* is not "the NAACP stereotype of the New York City classroom, rather simply another human being." His "Malaysian construct" is "fairly typical" and contains the following "hierarchy": (1) the good "white" man, "the man of duty and integrity, a superior individual who can be of any color," like Tamb' Itam, Jim's servant; (2) the remainder of the majority population—Malays, Tamils, Chinese, Arabs; and (3) the bad white man, like "Gentleman" Brown or Donkin or even Kurtz. In *The Rescue* "King Tom" Lingard is impelled by the color of his skin to assist Travers, who is "everything Conrad dislikes"; and his tragic flaw is "the fissure in his code created by passion." But in this novel JC has injected an ambivalence—"what to do when you have to defend a bounder because he happens to be of your race." Implicitly, "the reply is that loyalty to skin color cannot make such demands. Humanity comes first." For JC, men are "oddly equal." His entirely good man, Captain Whalley or Tom Lingard, is "responsible, dutiful, kind to natives." JC, who held "an ultra-romantic suspicion of the machine age in general," created the British colonialist-adventurer far different from the exploiter of the present time. [An interesting approach to JC's works, which might be developed further.]

1841 Watt, Ian. "Joseph Conrad: Alienation and Commitment," THE ENGLISH MIND: STUDIES IN THE ENGLISH MORALISTS PRESENTED TO BASIL WILLEY, ed by Hugh Sykes Davies and George Watson (Cambridge: Cambridge U P, 1964), pp. 257-78.

E. M. Forster's detection of a "continual contradiction" in JC's works between his "further vision," which is very similar to that of the other great writers of his time, and his "nearer vision," or his own range of experience, which was dissimilar, seems to offer a "key" to the three respects in which he is unique. JC's further vision was that of the late Victorian worldview: in a meaningless universe there is no apparent reason for any concern with people's lives, consciousness is really a curse, and Nature is permanently alien to man. In various ways JC shared the rejection of traditional Victorian views on religion, the social and intellectual order, and also rejected with Yeats, Pound, Eliot, Joyce, D. H. Lawrence, and Thomas Mann the "religion of progress" of the Edwardians. Although JC appeared to be totally estranged from the natural world, from other people, from the process of writing, and from the self, he leaves a sense of a much wider commitment to the main ethical, social, and literary attitudes than do any of the other great authors of his time.

The cause of this seeming paradox is probably present in JC's life: his being an orphan, his belonging to a country which in fact no longer existed, and his failure in France from 1874 to 1878; but what JC meant by solidarity is made clear in his preface to *The Nigger of the Narcissus*. Solidarity supplies both the individual and the collective life some little pattern of meaning, as in *Nigger,* "Typhoon," *The Shadow-Line,* "Heart of Darkness," *Lord Jim, Chance,* and *Victory,* which depict the movement of the protagonist toward another human being. JC considered "the master of the process of moral self-discovery leading to human commitment" as an approach to Existentialism, but his consideration of solidarity as "an eventual consequence of corporate activity" draws him closer to Marx's philosophical materialism. His view of commitment, having strong affinities with three contradictory ideologies—the conservative, the existentialist, and the Marxist—helps to explain his current appeal to many readers; the discrepancies between JC's nearer and his further vision suggest that JC's obscurity may result from his failure to establish any real connection between the alienation which he felt and the commitment which he desired. Although he could not resolve the irrationality of his dual perspective, in "The Ascending Effort" (*Notes on Life and Letters*) he justified it on the basis that it "reflected the facts of common human experience": his view of solidarity was "the way people actually react to the circumstance of their lives." Thus JC appears to accept an impasse; at the age of twenty, when he became an English sailor, his sense of total alienation began to change. His success as a seaman became extremely important for his career as a writer, largely because it added to his earlier alienation a foreground of personal and social commitment: to his career, to his fellow-seamen, and to his adopted country. He reveals the conflict in his views of his audience: although he scorned the mass reading public, he realized that the object of his scorn could "weep and suffer," and he retained sufficient faith in a "direct appeal to mankind" to write for readers as different as his former shipmates and his later literary friends. He also reveals the conflict in his views of his art: escaping the accepted literary modes of his early writing career, he relied on the basic facts of experience which he shared with mankind in general; his nearer vision (ultimate commitment) allowed him to bypass his intellectual sense of alienation and, unlike his contemporaries, to make a broad appeal to "the basic feelings and elementary convictions which make life possible to the mass of mankind" ("Author's Note," *Chance*). The alienation, however, is still present in such elements as the "defeated cadences of his rhetoric" or the "tendency of the narrative progress to seem under the constant threat of enveloping torpor," even if the negative undertones of alienation are largely overcome by the possibilities of commitment, or, of solidarity. The seaman could not allow the seer to leap out of the chaos of immediate reality which must precede the formation of a system. In order to concentrate on the achievements of men rather than on the illogicalities, JC seems to believe that one must not question too seriously the intellectual foundations of human needs: Marlow speaks of Jim's need for a truth, or an illusion of truth, to live by; Marlow in "Heart of Darkness" lies to the Intended because sometimes truth should be sacrificed to fidelity; and Emilia Gould in *Nostromo* feels that in some way both the past and the future are a part of oneself. In an essay (1905) on Henry James (*Notes on Life and Letters*), JC's further vision sees disaster in spite of the appeal of the nearer vision: after the "last utterance," mankind "will sleep on the battlefield among its own dead. . . . It will not know when it is beaten." This passage William Faulkner, JC's "greatest literary descendant," seems to have had in mind when he stated in his Nobel Prize Address that "I believe that man will not merely endure: he will prevail"; but JC's terms are so qualified by "the ironic distance of the seer" that Faulkner seems to protest too much. [Placing JC in his intellectual milieu and considering him and his work as a whole, this article is one of the most impressive achievements of its kind.]

1842 Watts, C. T. "Joseph Conrad and the Ranee of Sarawak," REVIEW OF ENGLISH STUDIES, XV (Nov 1964), 404-7.

Two letters, published here in complete form for the first time, one from JC to R. B. Cunninghame Graham and one from JC to the Ranee of Sarawak, complete the account of JC's borrowing from the Ranee Margaret's autobiography, MY LIFE IN SARAWAK, for such works as *Lord Jim* and *The Rescue*. This external evidence supplements the internal evidence cited in John D. Gordan's articles: "The Rajah Brooke and Joseph Conrad," STUDIES IN PHILOLOGY, XXXV (Oct 1938), 613-34; and "The Ranee Brooke and Joseph Conrad," ibid., XXXVII (Jan 1940), 130-32.

1843 Weiand, Hermann. " 'Typhoon,' " INSIGHT II: ANALYSES OF MODERN BRITISH LITERATURE, ed by John V. Hagopian and Martin Dolch (Frankfurt Am Main: Hirschgraben-Verlag, 1964), pp. 49-58.

Captain MacWhirr, the "ponderous centre" of "Typhoon," is revealed to the reader by various secondary characters, including Jukes, the first mate, who is used as a contrast to the Captain, often with a comic effect. Jukes is typical of all JC's young heroes "with artists' minds" who generally perish. The story has "a unity of place, action and time" and "constant insistence on the notion of order." The ship is a symbol "for individual man as well as for a community," both of which require order for survival. And part of the necessary order requires that one be both efficient in his craft and ready to meet the unexpected. JC seems convinced that it is the "simple, prosaic, down-to-earth fellow" who finally survives. [Followed by useful questions and discussions for students.]

1844 Williams, George Walton. "Conrad's 'The Lagoon,'" Explicator, XXIII (Sept 1964), Item 1.

Two "intrusions" of the landscape in "The Lagoon" represent Arsat's two tasks: "he must overcome his immobility (the lagoon must ripple), and he must see through his illusions (the mist must rise)." These two themes are related to the third intrusion of the landscape, that at the end of Arsat's narrative. Then the last picture of Arsat reveals him as "a man free of illusions." The last sentence is the key to the story, which releases at least two meanings: (1) As Arsat stares at the sun, he looks beyond the present into the future with its illusions, and (2) as he stares at the sun, Arsat sees beyond his own illusions and "frees himself from [his] past and purifies himself for activity in the sunburnt world of reality." [For a different interpretation, see Milton A. Levy, ibid. (Dec 1964), Item 35.]

1845 Williams, Porter, Jr. "The Brand of Cain in 'The Secret Sharer,'" Modern Fiction Studies, X (Spring 1964), 27-30.

Early in "The Secret Sharer," Leggatt makes an allusion to the "'Brand of Cain' business," a reference that becomes more important in part II of the tale when Leggatt persuades the captain to maroon him. The story of Cain in the Book of Genesis seems to become "a precise symbol of Leggatt's predicament": the traditional brand on Cain's forehead was actually not merely a stigma but a mask of God's compassion. Thus both murderers, Cain and Leggatt, asked for protection and received it. The captain's white hat suggests the moral significance of the ending of the story: the captain's pity for Leggatt, which had at first endangered the ship, finally saves it from destruction when Leggatt, knowing just how close under the rocks of Koh-ring the captain could safely take his ship, placed his floppy hat on the water as a marker. Just as Cain went to meet his punishment knowing that something had been done for him to make that punishment endurable, so Leggatt sets out in the same way, but with the additional confidence that he has done something in return for his own redemption. Although the captain carries the heavier burden of compassion, Leggatt also for a moment becomes "his brother's keeper." Now both sharers strike out "for new destinies which both seem to have deserved."

1846 Williams, Porter, Jr. "The Matter of Conscience in Conrad's 'The Secret Sharer,'" PMLA, LXXIX (Dec 1964), 626-30.

The captain in "The Secret Sharer" realized that Leggatt's dependence upon the emotional bond between the two men must be broken for Leggatt, even at the risk of losing the ship. "It was a matter of conscience, ultimately," to give Leggatt "a compelling demonstration of absolute understanding and sympathy by indulging in an act of supreme daring," rash enough to convince the hesitant Leggatt of "the sincerity of the captain's moral support." Through the captain's feelings of identity, the reader is brought to understand how Leggatt's heroism easily turns into unnecessary violence, and "the necessity of compelling Leggatt to leave becomes crucial" only when it is clear "how desperately the captain needed to establish his authority"—the discovery of Leggatt's presence would have been fatal to the captain's career. The nautical details are important because "more than anything else they record the exact moral significance of what the captain thought he was doing," but unfortunately they occurred at a moment during which the captain had "lost touch," when the ship was nearly wrecked. At the most dangerous point, the captain recalls that he did not know what his ship could do. Now, therefore, he must compensate for his lack of an earlier alertness. Both sharers, "the exiled murderer and the lucky navigator," are given a second chance. But JC refuses to judge: he creates "an ambivalent realm where guilt and innocence, selfishness and compassion, inexperience and skill," overlap, thereby hinting at a central theme of "Heart of Darkness." The captain remained loyal to his fugitive, but in spite of his worthy motives he had "all but stepped over the threshold of disaster"; and now he understood "the precarious terms upon which success is won." [An unusually perceptive analysis which reveals JC's concept of relativity.]

1847 Wolfe, Peter. "Conrad's *The Mirror of the Sea:* An Assessment," McNeese Review, XV (1964), 36-45.

The Mirror of the Sea is a work of art with major themes which indicate that the attitude of the sea toward the sailor is one of "pure cosmic indifference"; JC, unable to comprehend the sea's power and mystery, conveys the impression of "human insignificance juxtaposed against a cynical, compassionless force" and declares his faith in "an unstable, yet truly sovereign element." With such an enemy as the sea, JC glorifies the struggle of the sailor and acutely feels "the long historical drama of seamanship." Thus the sea operates concurrently in this book at two levels: it is at the same time a "sphere of vigorous action" and a "challenge to the individual's devotion and fidelity." In JC's comparisons of the past with the present, the latter is seen at a disadvantage; the "accumulated effort of generations" in faithful service to the sailor's craft is given a "mythical grandeur." Among the themes of the book, the advent of the steamship is perhaps the major one: "the fine art [of sailing] is lost," JC laments, and the bonds of fellowship and tradition that "link the man of masts and sails" to his forebears and shipmates are broken by modern travel by sea. Although *Mirror* has a thematic organization, the presentation of the material without a Marlow "acting as a screen" restricts JC somewhat in certain ways: there is, for instance, little irony here. A basic structural principle is the use of language to "render" the work more dramatic and spontaneous; but the "author-as-narrator" technique calls too much attention to himself, and JC's "platitudinous discourses" detract from the possibility of "greater dramatic interest and uninterrupted force." The common source of the strengths and weaknesses lies in the Impressionistic method [an idea that has been convincingly refuted]. Here, however, JC has no "reflector of his personality" like Jim, Kurtz, or Captain Beard, and "the light given off by Conrad's generalizations is refracted only weakly, most of it being absorbed by the immortal, rolling sea"; but as a mirror "the sea cannot reflect the many facets of the individual personality." [Leaves *Mirror* almost as elusive and nebulous as other critics have found it to be.]

1848 Wright, Walter F. "Introduction: Conrad's Critical Perspectives," JOSEPH CONRAD ON FICTION, ed by Walter F. Wright, Regents Critics Series (Lincoln: University of Nebraska P, 1964), pp. ix-xiv.

Although the writer of fiction must deal with reality, this reality must be created by the disciplined imagination; and JC believed that every novelist must begin by creating for himself some world in which he can sincerely believe. For him, reality was always "a romance of adventure, potentially of epic proportions; it was most often a tragic one." For him, too, the nature of the adventure of writing was an important subject for criticism. His critical writings reveal hints of truth from his own experience, thereby inevitably containing a subjective aspect which must, however, resemble something already familiar to the reader. JC thus believed that the author must first see distinctly and then "render" objectively and that communication with a reader takes place through art as symbol.

1849 Yates, Norris W. "Social Comment in *The Nigger of the Narcissus*," PMLA, LXXIX (March 1964), 183-85.

The Nigger of the Narcissus contains, in addition to symbolism and allegory, "socio-historical criticsm" of attempts made by reformers to improve the working conditions of British seamen in the latter part of the nineteenth century. Knowles's reference to "that 'ere Plimsoll man," Samuel Plimsoll, a Radical in the House of Commons from 1868 to 1880, is a direct attack upon one kind of "do-gooder" like Donkin; in fact, JC's main attack on maritime reforms in this novel is his depiction of Donkin, who may represent "any unscrupulous self-seeker who has a divisive effect." At times, JC displays his dislike of "shore-going reformers" in direct commentary; at other times, Wait, Belfast, and the cook are criticized "by association with the meddling of landbound reformers." JC thus by means of direct statement and of character included in his novel "a social commentary on one phase of late Victorian reform agitation."

 1850 Zukerman, Jerome. "Contrapuntal Structure in Conrad's *Chance*," MODERN FICTION STUDIES, X (Spring 1964), 49-54.

Chance is a strong novel. This book demonstrates a structure as firm as any other by JC in that the use of material on rule or command as a subplot counterpoints the main plot of self-discovery. The main love theme (Roderick Anthony and Flora) and the subordinate rule theme (Captain Anthony and the crew of the *Ferndale*) are "worked out fully and convincingly through the two-part division on land and sea." Anthony's troubles as ruler of the ship parallel his troubles as lover and husband; when he resolves his "marital dilemma," he also resolves his situation as captain. Anthony, lacking knowledge of women and influenced by his father, is impotent both in his marriage and in his role as ship's ruler. Thus the love and rule plots "parallel and reinforce each other." The love and rule plots are fused in several ways: the "new régime" under the married captain is symbolized by the description of the renovated saloon; and the eccentricities of Anthony's marriage cause him to violate maritime tradition, his false role as husband making him dangerous as captain. Young Powell untangles the knot and illustrates, perhaps too melodramatically, the part played by chance. When de Barral's attempt at murder is exposed, Flora, who then realizes fully her love for her husband and speaks the words that show her love, breaks the spell; and the captain, now with a real marriage, is able to resume his command of the ship. The love and rule themes merge again. But Anthony must also come to terms with himself, and the scene of self-conquest resolves the two themes, with the contrapuntal structure suggesting that the rule theme evolves from and dramatizes the love theme. JC displays in *Chance* no lack of ability in creating "a harmonious and unified artistic structure." [An unusual and important interpretation of *Chance*.]

 1851 Zukerman, Jerome. " 'A Smile of Fortune': Conrad's Interesting Failure," STUDIES IN SHORT FICTION, I (Winter 1964), 99-102.

"A Smile of Fortune" is a failure because JC's sense of form was faulty: he juxtaposed unequally two themes, that of love involving the protagonist-captain and Alice Jacobus, and a "subordinate rule theme" concerning the protagonist-captain and his crew, with the latter only sketchily developed. The captain's failure on land (in love) leads to a failure at sea. Jacobus represents the corruption of life on land, and erotic feelings weaken the narrator—as they had done for Jacobus—and lead him almost to shirk his duty. Indeed, the sea-land antithesis perhaps too neatly symbolizes the contrast between the ideal world of illusions and the actual world. Some of JC's difficulty in treating the rule theme adequately may have arisen from his idealization of life at sea.

1965

1852 Allen, Jerry. THE SEA YEARS OF JOSEPH CONRAD (NY: Doubleday, 1965); continues the account of findings in "preserved records" of JC's years at sea begun in THE THUNDER AND THE SUNSHINE (1958).

[Investigation of JC's adventures in the West Indies, Australia, South America, and Africa, provides useful information for an interpretation of *A Personal Record, The Mirror of the Sea, The Nigger of the Narcissus, Nostromo, Victory,* "Heart of Darkness," "Typhoon," and some of the shorter tales. Some of Allen's conclusions seem to be based on inadequate evidence: her version of JC's life in Marseilles, according to which M. George's duel in *The Arrow of Gold* is accepted as autobiography which was obscured by an invented story of an attempt at suicide, was current before the publication of Jocelyn Baines's JOSEPH CONRAD: A CRITICAL BIOGRAPHY (1960) and Zdzisław Najder's CONRAD'S POLISH BACKGROUND (1964). Also questionable is Miss Allen's contention that JC and Paula de Somoggy, mistress of Don Carlos, the Spanish pretender, were lovers; both Baines and Bernard C. Meyer in JOSEPH CONRAD: A PSYCHOANALYTIC BIOGRAPHY (1967) disagree with her. Illuminating, though, are the facts about Carlist activity in France and Spain in the 1870s and those which seem to prove that Blunt and his mother in *Arrow* were based on people whom JC knew in Marseilles. Important also is the apparently proved fact that JC used the factual version of the abandoning of the pilgrim ship *Jeddah* in his own special manner for *Lord Jim,* that Jim in the first part of the novel was patterned on Augustine Podmore Williams of the *Jeddah,* and that Tuan Jim of the latter part of the novel was based on Jim Lingard, a resident of Berau, in Borneo. A scandal of 1880, the incident of the *Cutty Sark,* is the source of "The Secret Sharer," and JC's experience in Bangkok furnished the basis for *The Shadow-Line.* Allen's history of JC's East and her accounts of related subjects like piracy in the East Indies are interesting and informative. Although anticipated by John D. Gordan's JOSEPH CONRAD: THE MAKING OF A NOVELIST (1940) and complemented by Norman Sherry's CONRAD'S EASTERN WORLD (1966), this search for sources is undoubtedly fascinating and it adds greatly to our knowledge of

JC and his life; but it fails, largely, in displaying the process by which "experience is transposed into spiritual terms," a procedure which JC, in a letter of February 1917 to Disney Colvin, claimed to have done in *Shadow-Line*. "By his art," Allen states in her preface, "Conrad transmuted actual events into enduring fiction"; her greatest weakness is that she fails almost completely to demonstrate this vital process.]

      1853 Andreach, Robert J. "The Two Narrators of 'Amy Foster,'" STUDIES IN SHORT FICTION, II (Spring 1965), 262-69.

Since there are two narrators in "Amy Foster," a combination of their conclusions supplies the meaning of the narrative. The first narrator, Doctor Kennedy, suggests two answers, one of which offers a hypothetical explanation which reason can grasp and another which eliminates the need for explanation by ascribing supernatural qualities to the events. But with each question Kennedy fails to find a natural cause, and he cannot accept the supernatural cause.

The second narrator links Amy to the "wreckage of this world" and to the doctor's wasteland imagery, and he realizes that man cannot see "beyond his own disaster." The nameless narrator also can find no purpose to existence, and in failing to find any possibility of an intelligible supernatural reason for life, he places the responsibility for Yanko's tragedy in its proper place, in man himself. Seen in this manner, "Amy Foster" is extremely important among JC's works. As to form, it is related to his other first-person tales and to the experiments with limited narration by such writers as James and Ford; and as to content, it depicts the universe in which JC "insists on the values and virtues that must be preserved in a darkened world and on the prerequisites for moral knowledge." [Supported and well developed as it is, this interpretation requires at least serious reconsideration of "Amy Foster."]

      1854 Bass, Eben. "The Verbal Failure of *Lord Jim*," COLLEGE ENGLISH, XXVI (March 1965), 438-44.

In *Lord Jim,* JC has certain difficulties in making figures of speech sound true; but if Jim's words sound unreal when the young man is under stress, they suggest "the subtle unsoundness" of the man himself. Several incidents in the novel illustrate Jim's verbal confusion, one of them, his jumping from the *Patna,* being at least partially a verbal error. And Jim's auditory errors are "in keeping with his halting, boyish manner of speech." Jim's emotions are too extreme to allow clear verbal expression; gratitude, humiliation, and love are some of the feelings which display his ineptness. When Jim leaves Patusan, the captain of the ship uses a "verbal hodgepodge" which is in keeping with the social and political disorder Jim meets in the Eastern country; the real effect of the language is to show the failure of the white man in the Far East. In Patusan, Jim uses his own language as well as that of the natives; and verbal error still accompanies him although his few verbal successes occur there "when he acts upon his own concept of chivalry, courage, and honor": in his attack upon Cornelius for his mistreatment of Jewel and in his organization of one of the Patusan factions against its own enemy. But Jim fails in the encounter with Brown because of Brown's "lucky verbal hits," and Jim's inarticulate message written on the day of his disaster confirms the return of his old inarticulateness. No doubt JC's choice of a verbal dilemma as an aspect of Jim's failure as a man is associated with JC's own sense of alienation in a foreign country.

1855 Bojarski, Edmund A. "Conrad's Polish Background," ENGLISH STUDIES IN AFRICA (Johannesburg), VIII (March 1965), 81-85.

CONRAD'S POLISH BACKGROUND: LETTERS TO AND FROM POLISH FRIENDS, edited by Zdzisław Najder (1964) makes available to English readers much information that helps to dispel the mysteries, the "Polishness," the "incomprehensible" something, that has long been associated with JC. The young Pole's sense of being out of place in his early environment can now be understood: going abroad was an obvious move for a young man in Poland; the normal dreams of an adventurous life must have been reinforced by the tension between him and his surroundings, including his conflict with his father; and important "health reasons" indicated the advantages of going to sea (JC was apparently an early subject of something like epilepsy). In removing the usual "mask of Polishness," this book provides a standard work for the future study of JC's Polish heritage and invalidates the accusation of "betrayal" of his country and the guilt that he later felt. Two letters relate JC's adventures in France, including his attempt in 1878 to commit suicide. [Many writers differ, of course, as to whether JC fought a duel or attempted suicide.] Dispelled, too, is the commonly accepted theory that JC's first love and the prototype for Rita in *The Arrow of Gold* was Janina Taube, later Baroness de Brunnow, and strengthened is another theory that JC's "original puppy love" was Tekla Syroczynska, his distant cousin. All these matters are "integrated" in Najder's preface into an analysis of their influence on JC's work and his treatment of "moral responsibility, the formation of his own code of honour." Undoubtedly this book will become a *sine qua non* for every serious student of JC. [An accurate appraisal of Najder's book.]

1856 Bojarski, Edmund A. "Poland Looks at Conrad," BOOKS ABROAD, XXXIX (Winter 1965), 29-32.

Several important conclusions can be drawn from Barbara Kocówna's collection of hitherto scattered Polish pieces on JC, WSPOMNIENIA I STUDIA O CONRADZIE (Warsaw: Państwowy Instytut Wydawniczy, 1963 [not seen]): JC apparently did fight a duel "à la *The Arrow of Gold"* in Marseilles in 1878; it is "fairly certain" that JC's references to his "first love" in the author's note to *Nostromo* and to his "second love" in the cancelled opening to *Arrow* are not to Janina Taube, as some of the "most meticulous" scholars have assumed, but to JC's third cousin, Tekla Syroczynska; Eliza Orzeszkowa, a popular Polish "lady novelist," because of an early tirade in a St. Petersburg literary magazine about JC's deserting his native country, influenced the theme of his most widely read book, *Lord Jim:* in 1903 and 1904 very little was known about JC in his own country, "a situation which has completely reversed itself" in the past sixty years; Róża Jabłkowska's JOZEF CONRAD, 1857-1924 (Wrocław: Ossolinski National Institute, 1961 [not seen]) is so "complete, detailed, penetrating, and profound" that it should be translated into English; "penetrating" Polish criticism of JC began in the mid-thirties and has not yet reached its peak. Although Kocówna's anthology of Polish Conradiana is far from exhaustive, it offers "a representative sampling of the valuable material scattered throughout various Polish literary journals" and makes accessible "a veritable gold mine" of previously unavailable Polish materials on JC. [Indicates the importance of Polish scholarship about JC, much of which has not yet been recognized.]

1857 Boyle, Ted E. SYMBOL AND MEANING IN THE FICTION OF JOSEPH CONRAD. Studies in English Literature, VI (The Hague: Mouton; NY: Humanities P, 1965).

JC's "use of symbolism comprises one of the major facets of his art." Mythic patterns, symbolism, irony, "double" imagery like that in "The Secret Sharer," symbolic relationships among characters and certain opening and closing frames aid in the explication of JC's works. JC is less pessimistic than many commentators consider him to be: in *Lord Jim,* Jim finally rids himself of "his hollow romanticism, but has not forsaken his dream"; in "Heart of Darkness," Marlow brings back from the African jungle a light hitherto unpossessed by London; in *Nostromo,* JC "assiduously avoided" drawing a moral; and in *Victory,* in spite of the great "welter of blood" at the end, "Good has triumphed and evil has consumed itself in perfect consistency" with JC's fictional world.

[The chapter on *Nostromo* discusses in detail its four seekers "after the truth of life," Charles Gould, Decoud, Monygham, and Nostromo, the last of whom "unites the various private histories of the novel."] Gould is the "knight-saviour" who finds life to be corrupt and illogical but who refuses to doff his shining armor and deal with the problems of Costaguana "with his bare hands." The skeptical Decoud, who finally doubts the reality of the sensational world in which he had placed his trust, cannot ignore the monsters which "fly at him out of the dark hell of his own solitude" and therefore takes his life. The cynical Dr. Monygham's lack of self-confidence is contrasted with Nostromo's trust in his own capabilities. Having failed to withstand the tortures of Guzman Bento, Monygham has "completely lost faith in the nobility of the human spirit," and he therefore cannot believe in himself; he fails to realize that "man need not be a flawless being for life to be worthwhile." Like a vulture, Monygham uses the corruption of others to feed his own ego, and he is a symbol of the arrogant depravity of the declared "pessimist." Nostromo, the boatswain, combines the private histories of other characters and achieves a victory over the cynicism of which Monygham is a symbol. As a boatswain is indispensable to the captain of a merchant ship, so is Nostromo indispensable to the Europeans of Sulaco: he saves Ribiera, he is a body-guard for the wealthy Englishman who visits the country to invest in railroading, he organizes the force of "cargadores" in a kind of proletarian counterpart of the great force for order represented by the San Tomé mine, he helps to quell riots, he takes the lighter-load of silver out of Sulaco into the gulf, and he makes the famous ride to Cayta. In his story are united the various threads of moral failure which appear throughout the novel: Gould places his faith in "material interests," Decoud relies upon idealized sensual love, and Monygham's "ruling passion" is his distrust of himself. Before Nostromo dies, he has fallen prey to each of these destructive passions; but he salvages something which the other three fail to do. Desiring recognition from the European community and feeling resentful when he fails to receive it, he changes from the poor, trustworthy Capataz de Cargadores into the rich, deceitful Captain Fidanza. He betrays himself, but JC brings him to the threshold of discovery and thus ironically demonstrates the truth of the values which he does not allow his hero to discover. Although JC avoids drawing a moral in *Nostromo,* the novel represents the "reality of human experience—a mine from which one cannot help but discover at least a small fragment of knowledge about 'how to be.' " [An important addition to the understanding of eleven of JC's novels and tales.]

1858 Chatterjee, Sisir. "Joseph Conrad: The Power of the Written Word," PROBLEMS IN MODERN ENGLISH FICTION (Calcutta: Bookland Private, 1965), pp. 112-22.

[The author discusses a number of JC's works in terms of his experimentation in novelistic technique, his impressionistic style, and his unique method of characterization.]

1859 Cross, D. C. *"Nostromo:* Further Sources," NOTES AND QUERIES, N.S. XII (July 1965), 265-66.

There are several additional sources for *Nostromo* in George Masterman's SEVEN EVENTFUL YEARS IN PARAGUAY (1869) and E. B. Eastwick's VENEZUELA: LIFE IN A SOUTH AMERICAN REPUBLIC (1868).

1860 Cross, Donald. "On Many Seas," Times Literary Supplement (Lond), 2 Sept 1965, p. 761.

JC used Frederick Benton Williams's On Many Seas: The Life and Exploits of a Yankee Sailor (1897) not only as a source for *Nostromo* but also for *The Nigger of the Narcissus* and possibly for "Typhoon." Williams, who must have offended JC with his "devil-may-care attitude towards authority, work and the normal decencies," provided an admirable model for the malingerer, Donkin. In writing "Typhoon," JC probably obtained from Williams's book the idea of having confined Chinese coolies struggling below deck, and whereas Captain MacWhirr deliberately steers his ship into a typhoon, a captain in the book must sail his ship between two icebergs after stubbornly driving it "dead before a live gale in a blinding snowstorm."

1861 Dale, James. " 'One of Us': Craft and Caste in *Lord Jim*," English Record, XV (April 1965), 5-7.

The "us," the group to which Jim belongs in *Lord Jim,* is only in part the British mercantile marine; he belongs also to a larger group, "the English upper-middle class," because of his parentage and upbringing. His caste is, furthermore, "the elite produced by . . . the English public school," including "the ideal of the Christian gentleman"; but more especially he comes from a line of explorers, soldiers, and administrators, with a sense of responsibility. He is, in fact, "a type of the virtuous paternalistic administrator." Part of the "essential irony" of the novel is that "the values and standards of Jim's class are inadequate when there is a failure of nerve, because there is precious little room for failure in the public-school ethos." The rigidity of Jim's moral code therefore "doomed" him to defeat by Gentleman Brown, who was no gentleman and, of course, not at all "one of us."

1862 Deutsch, Helene. *"Lord Jim* and Depression," Neuroses and Character Types: Clinical Psychoanalytic Studies (NY: International Universities P, 1965), pp. 353-57.

[*Lord Jim* is used as a clinical case to support a theoretical discussion of Dr. Edward Bibring's paper on "The Mechanism of Depression." Although some significant points made by JC are passed over and three errors of fact appear, Deutsch gives an explanation of Jim's behavior, of the role of other characters, and of the setting—all in psychoanalytical terms. The interest of the study lies in what psychoanalysis can get from literature, not in what literary scholars can learn from this report.]

1863 Dowden, Wilfred S. *"Almayer's Folly* and *Lord Jim:* A Study in the Development of Conrad's Imagery," Rice University Studies, LI (Winter 1965), 13-27.

JC's use of imagery in *Almayer's Folly,* which is representative of his practice in his early works, lacks subtlety and displays a "trite conventionality," just as his attempt to develop an ironic theme is not sustained. At best, this novel illustrates the author's interest in imagery without his using it as a structural device or for maintenance of tone. *Lord Jim,* though, is the best example of JC's use of visual imagery in portraying character. Here the author considers Jim as a man, not in an abstract sense but "as he lives and breathes in everyday life." In order to represent Jim sympathetically, JC chose words that express the gloom which surrounds him but also included enough light to illuminate his human qualities. The meaning of Stein's speech about the "destructive element," is that Jim is an ordinary human being, and Jim's tragedy is not his jump from the *Patna* but his failure to submit himself to this element "which is life itself." The imagery of the novel, including fog, mist, moonlight, and shadow, which confirms "the shifting, unreal quality of Jim's dream, supports this viewpoint and also helps to establish the idea that Jim and all men are complex and can be understood only in part, "as if seen through the rents in the mist." Jim's isolation on Patusan "identifies him with Western Man," even if his position among the natives is ambiguous. Finally, wanting to be one of the natives, Jim identifies himself with Brown, partly because he sees in the intruder some of the evil in himself and partly because Brown is, "in spite of his isolation in evil, one of Jim's own kind." In order to understand the mystery of Jim, one must perceive the mystery of man himself. In *Jim,* then, JC developed to the fullest extent his use of imagery and thereby made the novels of this period notably better than his early works, not so much in his choice of plot and character as in his method.

1864 Eastman, Richard M. A GUIDE TO THE NOVEL (San Francisco: Chandler, 1965), pp. 24, 43, 60-66, 138, 182-83.

Some novels, like *Lord Jim,* show background influences of a character: JC, in tracing Jim's early years, develops his character's "soft streak into a ruinous flaw" [a statement which has been questioned]. In one short passage of *The Nigger of the Narcissus,* JC uses both literal and figurative language to describe a moment in a terrible storm. Sometimes two characters in a novel serve as a chorus to "editorialize to opposite effect" (Donkin and Captain Allistoun); the reader is to believe the latter person, especially since his position is supported by the anonymous narrator. JC, like Hemingway, seems to utilize the aesthetic principle that courage is "almost equivalent to good manners and cowardice to a breach of poise or taste" to determine virtue. He shows that lapses of nerve are so "ugly" that they lead to social ostracism: after Jim abandons his ship, he is no longer a proper gentleman; but by devoting his life to protecting the natives of Patusan, he "keeps in touch" with the gentleman's world which had ejected him. For JC virtue works through "positive thrust, through transformation of one's surroundings": Jim always advances, looks for changes, and "charges without reserve into his climactic acts." Heroism for JC is "a rigid reality, . . . the very condition of his civilization." In JC's unusual management of time, Marlow "unfolds" Jim's story by the order in which he acquires information and by the order of his own changing evaluations of Jim, a device which "draws the reader into Marlow's growing fascination, bafflement, and quest for the meaning of Jim's life." [Contrasts JC in *Lord Jim* and Hemingway in A FAREWELL TO ARMS.]

1865 Echeruo, M. J. C. "James Wait and *The Nigger of the Narcissus*," ENGLISH STUDIES IN AFRICA (Johannesburg), VIII (Sept 1965), 166-80.

JC's unique treatment of James Wait in *The Nigger of the Narcissus* does not make the repulsive Negro represent an abstract idea but instead causes him to correspond to the traditional expectation from the black man: Wait's impact on the crew arises from the anticipations of the men when confronted by a combination of negroid features and the terror assumed to accompany them. Thus the symbolic power of Wait's blackness is not a "metaphorical construct" but a kind of "brutal fact" which is a part not of his illness but of his racial appearance; the Negro is an "incongruous opposite" to the other men on the ship, a tyrant over them and, because of his color and his inscrutability, "the antithesis of light." JC equates physical with moral blackness: he makes no distinctions between literal description of Wait and symbolic applications of his repugnant and demoralizing personality. Furthermore, the limitation in point of view in the story—assuming that JC is the impersonal narrator—greatly limits the reader's view of the hero. Two implications, then, seem inevitable: JC found in Wait, the "outsider," the antithesis of all he expected of a sailor, and he relied completely upon the general concept of "spontaneous revulsion" usually found in a Negro face.

1866 Fleishman, Avrom. "The Symbolic World of *The Secret Agent*," JOURNAL OF ENGLISH LITERARY HISTORY, XXXII (June 1965), 196-219; rptd with slight revision in COMMUNITY AND ANARCHY IN THE FICTION OF JOSEPH CONRAD (Baltimore: The Johns Hopkins P, 1967), pp. 185-214.

A study of the imagery in *The Secret Agent* reveals that the symbolic world of the novel is London itself, a city which displays the social fragmentation characteristic of urban life, and that JC uses the "language of secrecy" to express the fragmented condition of the world. The furtive activities of Verloc and Winnie are generalized to apply to all human institutions, but particularly to the political, and since secrecy exists also among politically allied nations, the basis of social order is seen to be very unstable. The opposite of secrecy, *knowledge,* supplies resolution and partial community, being on the political level a system of mutual expectations among men that stabilizes their conduct, like the relationship between Heat and the Professor. In *Agent,* such words as *ignorance, fool,* and *madness* are used as terms for distortion of perception. JC's tragic view of the participation of his characters in the human condition allows him to make the anarchists an extreme example of the decay of the social order through ignorance, secrecy, and madness, mental deficiencies found not only in the underground world but also in the bureaucratic structure. The theme of madness in the public world has its parallel in the domestic world of Stevie's madness, and Stevie's imbecility (the word *fool* is most salient for him) has moral possibilities of both the most destructive and the most exalted kinds. Stevie's circles suggest an "awesome perfection, an irrational harmony," just as the ideal is traditionally accompanied by a certain fear. The circle thus becomes in the novel the emblem of moral freedom with all its dangers Physical fragmentation in *Agent* is represented in JC's emphasis on private life and private property, in the environment of stone surrounding the characters, and in the insularity prized in all realms of life. The safety of physical isolation is only temporary; it is subject to physical disorders, decay, and explosion. The human being is ultimately reduced to fragments of matter, and man is "imaginatively—and literally—annihilated" in this novel. The irrationality of the social order, represented in the irrationality of London streets and house numbers, is "crystallized" in the confusion of the landscape of the city and related to the greater absurdities of society by Verloc's acceptance of it. And the animal world and its presence as physical animality in man is represented at the extreme by gross fatness. Eventually, man is totally annihilated as Verloc's death leads him to *nothing.* In *Agent,* the themes of isolation, secrecy, and ignorance achieve a special form in images of insularity, such as islands and walls, which make this book a novel of London like OUR MUTUAL FRIEND and THE PRINCESS CASAMASSIMA. London is established as the spatial expression of the moral universe of *Agent.* As for the use of time in the novel, the fictional world is rendered by indirection and out of sequence to create the temporal structure of events as they are experienced, that is, subjectively by the characters. And abstract time also is present, implicitly affirming "the potency of man's consciousness of historical time." Time is a moral reward and also a political weapon. Then, too, the shortness of time and man's frailty are displayed against eternity, the time of the universe. *Agent* is, then, a novel about social anarchy, a dramatic portrayal of "radical disorder in the social structure and consequent personal dislocation," containing important implications for conduct. It suggests an ideal of social order by its representation of a world with no order, and it propounds the value of human anonymity. Instead of being a virulent attack on revolutionists, as it has been seen to be, the novel "makes an explicit appeal for restraint in public policy towards them." [This detailed and convincing analysis of the symbolic world of *Agent* places this work in an entirely new light. One of the best commentaries available on this novel, it is indispensable for the student of JC's works.]

1867 Ford, George H. DOUBLE MEASURE: A STUDY OF THE NOVELS AND STORIES OF D. H. LAWRENCE (NY: Holt, Rinehart & Winston, 1965, pp. 3, 21, 154, 182, 188, 197, 206, 218-19, 233n.
Marlow ("Heart of Darkness") had to confront the fact that "his forerunner, the idealistic Mr. Kurtz, a fellow 'emissary of light,' had ended his report on his humanitarian mission in the Congo with the exclamation: 'Exterminate all the brutes!' " This is what D. H. Lawrence meant in his introduction to the Magnus memoir about the need for "realization" of the war, and also in WOMEN IN LOVE. Lawrence admired JC's early writings, but expressed exasperation over his pessimism; writing WOMEN IN LOVE during the tensions of war, Lawrence, without "giving in, . . . certainly experienced what it was like to feel as Conrad had felt."

1868 Friedman, Alan Howard. "The Turn of the Novel: Changes in the Pattern of English Fiction since 1890 in Hardy, Conrad, Forster, and Lawrence," DISSERTATION ABSTRACTS, XXV (May 1965), 622, Unpublished thesis, University of California, Berkeley, 1964; pub as "Joseph Conrad: 'The End, Such As It Is,' " in THE TURN OF THE NOVEL (Lond: Oxford U P, 1966), pp. 75-105.
A shift took place from the "traditionally well-tapered shape of experience in the English novel" to a "radically untapered shape of experience," a shift which is "the complication and intensification, event by event, of the moral and emotional relation of the inward self to the outward world." JC's first two novels reveal a "formal impulse to provide a well-contained ending and an explicit antagonism toward such an ending." *Nostromo,* "a novel in which experience is conceived as an explosive and irreversible process, . . . may be taken as rendering the central structural process for experience" in JC's works.

1869 Geller, Robert. "The Search for Redemption: A Comparison of *Lord Jim* and THE FALL," EXERCISE EXCHANGE, XIII (Nov 1965), 24-25.
Lord Jim and THE FALL were used in a "tutorial" for high school seniors enrolled in an elective course in the modern novel. Noted there was the fact that both JC and Camus dealt with "an act of cowardice based on omission" and with the effect of the omission on the central characters. Both Jim and Clamence "search for redemption, and their pitiful search leads to a tragic waste of human potential."

1870 George, Gerald A. "Conrad's 'The Lagoon,' " EXPLICATOR, XXIV (Nov 1965), Item 23.
The important symbolic value of the sun in "The Lagoon" is evident in

the story no less than nineteen times. The white man, leaving the world of reality, enters Arsat's lagoon; and Diamelen, by dying, introduces the world of reality to the lagoon: both events are accompanied by images of the sun. At last, Arsat must confront reality; and as the sun rises, Diamelen dies. Arsat then retains his dreams and looks beyond the sunlight "into the darkness of a world of illusions."

> **1871** Goetsch, Paul. "Joseph Conrad: *Nostromo,*" DER MODERNE ENGLISCHE ROMAN: INTERPRETATIONEN (The Modern English Novel: Interpretations), ed by Horst Oppel (Berlin: Eric Schmidt, 1965), pp. 49-77.

In *Nostromo,* neither Decoud nor Mitchell is a reliable narrator, for, in a sense, JC is more skeptical than Decoud and more of a believer than Mitchell. He conceives of politics and history as expressions of irrational reality and realizes the "immense indifference of things." At the same time he calls human action consolatory and does not entirely discard man's illusions as futile. What he is chiefly interested in is suggested by the title of the novel. He wishes to investigate whether man is "master" or "slave" of reality and of his illusions, whether he accepts the meaninglessness of reality or tries to follow a moral principle. Accordingly, he distinguishes among four groups of persons. The first consists of politicians and others who pretend to have ideals but think chiefly of the silver and their personal advantage. The second group includes Viola and Don José, who are idealists characterized by immobility, and thus incapable of adapting themselves to changing reality. Gould and Nostromo, the members of a third group, are gradually corrupted by the silver, Gould's idealism giving way to fanaticism. As members of a fourth group, Decoud and Monygham are skeptics. While Decoud is defeated by his own insights, Monygham is saved by his devotion to Emilia Gould. Mrs. Gould is the only main character who remains master of herself and her ideals. This is due to her "mobility" and her "ironic eye," "her resignation open-eyed, conscious, and informed by love." Though disillusioned, she attempts to live up to the ideal of solidarity. So do Don Pépé and Father Romàn, but their instinctive rather than critical acceptance of the JC code might prove disastrous when tested, or even ridiculous, as Mitchell's naiveté indicates. JC is ironically aware of how questionable and necessary beliefs and illusions are at one and the same time. *Nostromo* is his most daring experiment with the novel form, but his central moral argument and other aspects of the novel make it the work of a transitional period in the history of English fiction, a period in which Victorian tendencies were gradually being replaced by modern ones.

> **1872** Gordan, John D. "An Anniversary Exhibition . . . (Part II: Conclusion)," BULLETIN OF THE NEW YORK PUBLIC LIBRARY, LXIX (June 1965), 398.

[Comments on the "heavily corrected" typescript of *The Rover:* title page dated Oct 1921–July 1922; three "typed copies of this first draft were made."]

1873 Gordan, John D. "An Anniversary Exhibition . . . (Part II)," BULLETIN OF THE NEW YORK PUBLIC LIBRARY, LXIX (Nov 1965), 603.

[A brief sketch of JC's career is followed by a summary of the Berg Collection holdings: nearly one dozen MSS of works by JC and about 75 letters. A 140-page MS and 12-page typescript of "A Smile of Fortune" are described.]

1874 Graver, Lawrence. "Conrad's First Story," STUDIES IN SHORT FICTION, II (Winter 1965), 164-69; based on material in an unpublished thesis, 1961, and absorbed in CONRAD'S SHORT FICTION (Berkeley and Los Angeles: University of California P, 1969).

Written in an early form in 1886, three years before JC began *Almayer's Folly,* "The Black Mate" was rejected by TIT-BITS, rewritten and published in 1908 in LONDON MAGAZINE, and remained uncollected until the posthumous publication of *Tales of Hearsay* (1925). This "extraneous phenomenon," as it was labeled by JC, this "anecdotal tale with little significance," was apparently intended only for popular audiences. In revising the story when he was struggling with Razumov and the Russian conspirators, JC seems to have been looking back to a comparatively untroubled time of his life; and perhaps significantly, he returned to the direct narrative method of an early favorite writer of his, Alphonse Daudet. Like Daudet's anecdotal tales, "The Black Mate" employs "anecdotal reminiscence" as a framework for the narrative and uses deception and trickery to reach a happy ending. It relies heavily on "sentimental irony, a steady suspense, mechanically developed characters, a colloquial style, a whimsical plot, and a surprise ending"—traits found frequently in Daudet, TIT-BITS, and THE LONDON MAGAZINE, but very seldom in JC's best work. [A much needed accounting for this unusual story in the JC canon.]

1875 Guetti, James Lawrence, Jr. "The Failure of the Imagination: A Study of Melville, Conrad, and Faulkner," DISSERTATION ABSTRACTS, XXV (1965), 4145-46. Unpublished thesis, Cornell University, 1964; the JC section pub as " 'Heart of Darkness' and the Failure of the Imagination," SEWANEE REVIEW, LXXIII (Summer 1965), 488-504; rptd in THE LIMITS OF METAPHOR: A STUDY OF MELVILLE, CONRAD AND FAULKNER (Ithaca, NY: Cornell U P, 1967).

"Heart of Darkness," apparently a story in which the difficult journey will lead to a meaningful disclosure and in which the "degeneration" will take its place in a moral framework, actually denies the relevance of a moral framework and questions generally the possibility of meaning for the journey. The paradox implied in the title is most obvious at what seems to be the center of the story, Kurtz's cry, "The horror! The horror!" in response to which Marlow insists that this moment is one of "complete knowledge." Kurtz's faith was in himself, "not as a moral being, but as a being who could use or discard morality." Marlow is perhaps as "morally rootless" as Kurtz himself; he suggests that man can scarcely see any real connection between moral "rights" and his experience; a man encounters his most severe challenges in an "atmosphere of tepid skepticism." For this reason Marlow refuses to condemn Kurtz "in a moral way." Marlow journeys into the heart of darkness, declares his allegiance to Kurtz, watches Kurtz die, and journeys out again; but he ends where he began; he does not even approach a central reality. Marlow then reveals a general condition of human experience. In "Heart of Darkness," language has meaning only in terms of the "exteriors of experience"; with the intimation that something exists beyond the verbal comes the realization that language is fiction. Thus, although Marlow uses the term "reality" in two ways, the reality which he actually discovers "exists in the realization that 'surface' and 'heart' are inevitably separate matters, and that mind can have ordered awareness only of the former." Marlow's final reality is "a state of suspension between the disciplined world of mind and language and the world of essences at the center of experience—whatever these may be—which mind attempts to apprehend but cannot, a dream-state of suggestions and futilities." The literary experience of "Heart of Darkness," "The horror," has only one meaning—all hearts are in darkness: "the reality of experience lies beyond language and the processes of the human imagination." The ultimate reality in this story is analogous to Stein's "destructive element"; and the conflict between this "element" and man's illusory creeds and beliefs is what JC frequently dramatizes, thereby "suggesting that there is more to life than language." [Displays original and convincing insight into the meaning of "Heart of Darkness."]

1876 Gurko, Leo. THE TWO LIVES OF JOSEPH CONRAD (NY: Crowell, 1965).

[A good children's book about JC. Gurko made his scholarly contribution on this subject in JOSEPH CONRAD: GIANT IN EXILE (1962).]

1877 Harkness, Bruce. "The Secret of 'The Secret Sharer' Bared," COLLEGE ENGLISH, XXVII (Oct 1965), 55-61.

The "true archetype" of "The Secret Sharer" is "Hyacinthine" and its secret can be stated in one word: "homosexuality." Although JC may not have been consciously aware of his actual achievement, the name Leggatt (*Leg-it*) is slang for the sexual organ and the sexual act, the word *queer* is used repeatedly, physical contacts of the narrator and Leggatt are frequently referred to, phallic symbols are clearly apparent in several instances, and Archbold, the chief mate, and the steward are developed in a manner that emphasizes their "masculinity and acceptance of the normal sexual and/or social order." As for the Hyacinthine archetype, "in so far as the Captain *is* everyman and Leggatt *is* his double, in these mythic terms, the Captain *is* Apollo and Leggatt *is* Hyacinth," even if JC could not follow the archetype in all respects. And only this archetype can explain the last paragraph of the story; while the narrator seems to be thinking of his secret sharer as a "free man . . . striking out for a new destiny," what he really feels is: "Come back to the ship ag'in, Leggatt Honey!" [In part a parody of psychoanalytic criticism taken seriously by several respondents, e.g., in ibid. (March 1966), 504-5.]

1878 Harvey, William John. CHARACTER AND THE NOVEL (Ithaca, NY: Cornell U P, 1965), pp. 57, 75, 88, 116-17, 133, 148, 194, 197-98.

Lord Jim "manoeuvres us into the task, not merely of exploring the character in greater depth, but also of exploring ourselves." JC draws parallels between the *Patna* situation and Patusan, "but . . . the situations are quite different." Jim's self-sacrifice is "a fine but useless gesture, an act of immature romanticism." For a definition of "immature" and "romanticism" "we can only turn to ourselves." The subordinate characters in the novel create a "penumbra of possibilities around the protagonist": Jim has become surrounded by men he might have become. [Mostly brief references to JC's novels.]

1879 Herget, Winfried. "Untersuchungen zur Wirklichkeitsdarstellung im Frühwerk Joseph Conrads (mit besonderer Berücksichtung des Romanes *Lord Jim*)" (Examinations of Realistic Representation in Joseph Conrad's Early Work [with Particular Consideration of the Novel *Lord Jim*]). Unpublished thesis, University of Frankfurt (am Main), 1965.

[In German.]

1880 Hoffman, Stanton de Voren. "The Hole in the Bottom of the Pail: Comedy and Theme in 'Heart of Darkness,' " STUDIES IN SHORT FICTION, II (Winter 1965), 113-23; derived from "Comedy and Form in the Fiction of Joseph Conrad," Unpublished thesis, Pennsylvania State University, 1962; abstracted in DISSERTATION ABSTRACTS, XXIII (1963), 3898-99; incorporated in COMEDY AND FORM IN THE FICTION OF JOSEPH CONRAD (The Hague: Mouton, 1969).

At the center of "Heart of Darkness" is the scene of the fire at the central station in which a stout man with black mustaches tries to extinguish the fire by using a small tin pail that has a hole in the bottom—an element of farce which is seen in several other incidents. Among many things, "Heart of Darkness" seems to be a journey toward a kind of selfhood, and Marlow, who makes the journey and lives to tell about it, is apparently at all times in danger of a fall; but he maintains control and sanity by means of the comic images which he sees or creates. His use of the comic image provides him with a traditional knowledge so he can first encounter darkness and himself safely and later communicate his knowledge to his auditors; that is, the comic, like Marlow himself, is a part of Western European culture which is examined in this story.

Marlow has two styles, one of which frequently breaks down because Marlow as "narrator-artist-arranger" is able to utilize "farce," clear images, and a smooth movement of the narrative as he approaches Kurtz; but a closer proximity to Kurtz results in "something beyond control, an enchantment, or unconscious pull," and a corresponding loss of the use of irony and comic images which indicates, as does the final scene with the Intended, the power of the unconscious with its connotation of a fall. The use of a comic image in an attempt to maintain control over an experience like Marlow's with Kurtz reveals the fact that all is a deception or an illusion. The irony in one's employing something to save himself only to fall may therefore be basic to JC's "dark intention" and may also be the theme of the story.

When Marlow encounters darkness, he fails; as a civilized European, a "child of light," he first recognizes failure and limitation (or the reader does) when he finds a light burning in Kurtz's cabin but the occupant gone. "Heart of Darkness" is concerned with Marlow's crisis in his encounter with Kurtz, with Kurtz's encounter with the dark forest, and with the "condition of hollowness," with a "crisis of Western civilization." JC's ironical use of Marlow is part of a broader theme in "Heart of Darkness": it is the crisis of a self related to the crisis of the civilization of that self, and "a pessimism which sees an inescapable two-sidedness in a saving grace which does not save." [A serious and original interpretation of "Heart of Darkness."]

1881 Hynes, Samuel. "Two Rye Revolutionists," Sewanee Review, LXXIII (Winter 1965), 151-58.

A loosely related group of writers scattered about near Rye, where Henry James lived, included such experimenters as Stephen Crane, Ford Madox Ford, and JC, who agreed that a novel should be "rendered action" from which the author attempted to exclude himself and that writing fiction could be "a high and noble calling" made so not by morality in the content but by a technique developed into art. Most of JC's critical writing is either appreciative, reminiscent, or "pale imitation" of Henry James. According to his own statement in a letter to Cunninghame Graham, we are conscious only of ourselves, and therefore fiction can include only consciousness and the sensations recorded by consciousness. Thus, his statement in the preface to *The Nigger of the Narcissus,* which contains his entire aesthetic, informs us that to hear, to feel, to see is all there is in "a world of isolated consciousness." For JC, the artist has no special wisdom; like everyone else, the artist has only what he perceives by means of his senses, and his one moral imperative is to be true to "his own sensations." JC concludes that the accurate rendering of one's perceptions requires a rigorous method of including only elements of sensation. The voice of the author and an account of events in chronological order must therefore be avoided. The result for JC is that the forms of his novels are intentionally obscure. In his thinking about fiction, he allowed his forms to evolve from his vision of things, not from theories.

Whether Ford Madox Ford shared to any great extent in the composition of some of JC's novels, he certainly contributed more than anyone else to JC's reputation as a "Conscious Artist." The facts of their collaboration and their individual contribution to the Rye Revolution have probably been obscured forever by JC's reticence and Ford's "romancing," but it seems likely that JC provided the conception of the artist and the concern with form while Ford, among other things, eventually provided the critical formulations of their ideas. Ford, then, is responsible for the theory of Impressionism which, for JC, means "the right rendering of experience." Walter F. Wright as editor of JOSEPH CONRAD ON FICTION (1964) has failed to choose wisely from JC's statements about other writers, and he has done almost no editing of his book, leaving, as a result, several unanswered questions. [An unusually concise statement of JC's aesthetic. Ostensibly a review-article on Walter F. Wright (ed), JOSEPH CONRAD ON FICTION (1964) and Frank MacShane (ed), CRITICAL WRITINGS OF FORD MADOX FORD (1964).]

> **1882** Jacobs, Robert G. "Comrade Ossipon's Favorite Saint: Lombroso and Conrad," NINETEENTH-CENTURY FICTION, XXIII (June 1968), 74-84.

The physiognomic theories of Cesare Lombroso, an Italian criminologist, discover a pattern in JC's abundant use of detail. Comrade Ossipon, himself a Lombrosoian type, explains other characters in terms of their departure from physical and emotional norms: Stevie and Winnie are murdering types; the large and protruding ears mark the Professor as an extreme type of criminal mind. *The Secret Agent* makes overt use of the theories, but all of JC's fiction reflects Lombroso's definition of the genius and the criminal as men departing from the typical.

[Listed in error as published in 1965, by Ehrsam.]

    1883 Jacobson, Dan. "Commonwealth Literature: Out of Empire," NEW STATESMAN, LXIX (29 Jan 1965), 153-54.

Most gifted English literary men have displayed no interest in the theme of British imperialism; but JC, himself not a native Englishman, is "the greatest exception." Typical British attitudes toward colonialism carried to their extremes produce "Mistah Kurtz" of "Heart of Darkness," who loses his early idealism in Africa to be driven "so mad by his power and isolation that he makes a depraved god of himself." JC's two most important studies of imperialism, "Heart of Darkness" and *Nostromo,* however, are not set in British territories. [Develops an important concept and contains pertinent references to Defoe, E. M. Forster, Disraeli, and Kipling and to their methods of dealing with the problem of colonialism.]

    1884 Johnson, Bruce. "Conrad's 'Falk': Manuscript and Meaning," MODERN LANGUAGE QUARTERLY, XXVI (June 1965), 267-84.

A comparison of the MS of "Falk" with the published version of the story indicates that the work imperfectly assimilates the experience upon which it is based, that is, the horror of JC's first command on the *Otago* in Bangkok early in 1888. Ill-suited for the "intellectual and emotional burden it simultaneously carries and avoids," this tale seems to contain a confusion between what a man like Falk may have meant to the narrator, presumably JC, who had not hitherto understood the East as he had imagined it to be and what he thought it safe to make it mean to his narrator.

For JC, man cannot live satisfactorily in "fidelity to nature" because he is conscious of his mind in an indifferent universe, conscious that there is no morality in nature. Darwin is obviously back of this concept; thus one of JC's seemingly existential ideas is truly Victorian. The story of Falk, then, is that of a "sport" among human beings. In associating a Buddha posture with Hermann in an unpublished passage of the MS, JC suggests that both Hermann's middle-class propriety and Buddhism, each in its own way, "sought to deny the uncomfortable supremacy of the will to live." Hermann takes this attitude because cannibalism appears indecent; Buddhism, because "desire is 'fire,' and must be overcome in the search for Nirvana." Falk is "refreshing" in contrast both to Hermann and Buddhism, for he "intuitively accepts the ugly basis of life." In his narration of the story of cannibalism on the *Borgmester Dahl,* JC, trying to control his reader's response to Falk, insists on associating the "toughest" and the "best," unsavoury though they are usually thought to be. JC's complex reasons for his failure to make "comfortable readers" accept Falk's importance are more interesting than many successful stories. Both JC's "heroic acceptance of the tragedy inherent in consciousness" and his "taste for the perfectly egoistic . . . personality" which is at peace with the universe, like Falk in loving Hermann's niece, are pertinent for an understanding of his analysis of human ego. [This examination of "Falk" may suggest some changes in the criticism of JC by noting the superficiality of the generally accepted differences between his monolithic men like Falk and his imaginative characters like Lord Jim.]

1885 Jones, Bernard. "Conrad the Historian," LISTENER, LXXIII (6 May 1965), 674.

[Letter noting Laurence Lerner's misinterpretation of the last paragraph of VANITY FAIR as the starting point in a discussion of JC (ibid. [15 April 1965], 554-56).]

1886 Kerf, René. "Ethics *versus* Aesthetics: A Clue to the Deterioration of Conrad's Art," REVUE DES LANGUES VIVANTES (Brussells), XXXI (1965), 240-49.

An analysis of JC's conception of art as he reveals it in articles about literature and in his author's notes accounts, in part, for the deterioration of his art from *Chance* onward. His pessimistic view of life as it is revealed by the problem he explored in his early works, namely, "the conflict between facts and illusions" (author's note, *Almayer's Folly,* 1895) is changed to a new degree of optimism when he attempts to find a practical solution in a "romantic feeling of reality" ("Author's Note," *Within the Tides,* 1920). In his well-known preface to *The Nigger of the Narcissus,* JC suggests that the artist's vision of life has very little influence on our practical existence; what he does, in fact, is to dissociate ethics from aesthetics and to declare that he himself is first of all an artist. In the author's note to *Chance,* however, there is a change in his conception of the relations between art and life: he becomes preoccupied with the "practical, moral value" revealed by the artist in his works. Three articles of 1898 contain several references to what may be called the "dualism of life and art or of ethics and aesthetics" and demonstrate that an important problem for JC was the relationship between the artist's view of life and the practical view man takes of existence. In articles written in 1904, he attempts to reconcile the two views but admits, in fact, that "a moral judgment may be passed on the artist's view of life and—more directly—that this view should not be a negation of the beliefs on which mankind has founded its existence," thus indicating that the artist has a moral responsibility towards his readers. In other articles of 1904 and 1905, a new idea appears: writing a book is an act which belongs to the realm of active and practical life. JC thus solves his problem of dualism posed by the concept of art versus life and stresses the claims of life at the expense of the claims of art. His quest for truth in his early works, having brought him near the verge of "moral nihilism" from which he temperamentally recoiled, he tends in his later works to accept "illusion" at face value and to allow doubt to be replaced by what critics have called his later "affirmation." This simplified outlook is clear in "A Familiar Preface" to *A Personal Record* (1912). It appears that "the claims of life" gradually became more important to JC than the freedom of the artist to question them.

In the series of author's notes written from 1917 to 1920 for the first collected edition of his works, JC objects to the charges against him of morbidness, of "social surrounding" and of "moral squalor" and definitely affirms that his vision of life, as reflected in his works, does not contradict "the views mankind takes of it in the conduct of its practical existence." No doubt his attempt to reconcile ethics and aesthetics is one cause of "the simplification of his outlook and the consequent deterioration of his art in the later works." [An impressive argument despite the fact that JC's own statements have been frequently doubted and that Samuel Hynes in "Two Rye Revolutionists" (Sewanee Review, LXXIII (Winter 1965), 151-58) claims that the "intellectually simple" JC possessed only "few and plain" aesthetic principles.]

1887 Killam, C. D. "Kurtz's Country," CBCL Newsletter, No. 7 (April 1965), 1-2; pub in full in Lock Haven Review, No. 7 (1965), 31-42 [not seen].

Literature concerning Africa, such as "Heart of Darkness," shows the European's actions being overcome by the savage background of the country. JC is effective in showing the setting as "a special dimension of the action of the novel" in which moral considerations are primary. [Abstract from a paper first delivered before Conference on Commonwealth Literature, New York, December 1964.]

1888 Kinney, Arthur F. "Jimmy Wait: Joseph Conrad's Kaleidoscope," College English, XXVI (March 1965), 475-78.

In *The Nigger of the Narcissus*, Jimmy Wait serves the other members of the crew as a kind of kaleidoscope. In the formal introductions to each chapter, JC indicates his "allegorical superstructure": he likens the *Narcissus* to struggling humanity; the sea to cosmic forces; and Jimmy Wait to the "dark side of human nature which brings about decay, disorder, and death," and which "must be sliced like a tumor from the body to allow life to triumph once again." Within this context JC develops Jimmy as what Henry James might have called a "reflector" of consciousness. Like a kaleidoscope, Jimmy is passive. Twice he acts as a "group kaleidoscope," at the moment of his rescue and at the time when his death is imminent; and in both instances "the group impression is not what Jimmy does but what the viewers see of themselves as reflected in what Jimmy does or does not do." JC uses the technique of character as kaleidoscope in his purpose of probing multiple consciousness. Jimmy thus functions as the "control factor" around which JC explores "the multiple reactions of men trapped on a ship (life), caught up in a single event (living)." So ultimately the reader, too, looks at Jimmy Wait and sees—himself.

1889 Kirschner, Paul. "Conrad and Maupassant," REVIEW OF ENGLISH LITERATURE, VI (Oct 1965), 37-51.

Maupassant's influence on JC indicates that the two writers shared a similar "conception of life and human nature." The French author's effect on JC's idea of sexual love is illustrated in a comparison of FORT COMME LA MORT and *Victory,* and his fear of death as expressed in BEL-AMI similarly reappears in the latter's *An Outcast of the Islands* and *The Nigger of the Narcissus.* It seems clear that JC "made conscious use" of Maupassant's "descriptions and insights" and that he unjustifiably "borrowed" from the writer whom he greatly admired. Apparently Maupassant's "intellectual influence" on JC as well as JC's "borrowings" reveal "a deep temperamental and philosophical accord" in the two men which was lasting and not all limited to literary technique.

1890 Lerner, Laurence. "Conrad the Historian," LISTENER, LXXIII (15 April 1965), 554-56.

Unlike Thackeray, who reminds his readers that the characters in VANITY FAIR are his puppets and that he understands and controls them, JC seems not to understand his characters but to be desperately trying to comprehend their actions. Thus, JC is the novelist as historian. He is skeptical about people's motives and feelings. In *Lord Jim,* the reader cannot determine whether Lord Jim finally learns the truth about himself or runs away from it; it is notable that the reader is given very little direct access to Jim's own consciousness.

That JC makes the writing of fiction difficult for himself by his employment of indirect narration is obvious in *Chance,* which is successful in technique but not in artistry; this novel is "a *tour de force,* as barren in the end as all merely technical skill." In this book, JC uses the device of "extra distancing," the inserting of another narrator between Marlow and the reader: Flora (like Lena in *Victory*) can be seen in two ways. In all his works, JC has two conceptions of woman: (1) "the simple and chivalrous idealization of the sailor" (Jewel in *Lord Jim,* Kurtz's Intended in "Heart of Darkness," Hermann's niece in "Falk") and (2) "the 'cynical' view of woman as strong, shrewd, even unscrupulous, cunning in protecting herself and her loved ones in a hostile world" (Mrs. Verloc in *The Secret Agent*). It is difficult to know whether Flora has gained from her experience "the charm of virtue" or has been "stung . . . to shrewdness." The indirect narration also makes it possible for the reader to experience "the process of misunderstanding Flora" instead of merely being told about her.

With its social analysis "perhaps the most profound and perceptive in modern history," *Nostromo* is "the finest Marxist novel ever written" [a dangerous generalization; some degree of modesty would avoid the claim of omniscience]. The order in which the reader learns things has little relation to the order in which they happen. Like Henry James, JC searches for the truth, but he never completely finds it. [A good attempt to understand JC's technique in writing novels.]

1891 *Lord Jim.* Gold Key [comic book] (NY: K. K. Publications, 1965), "Based on the novel by Joseph Conrad" [but more accurately based on the Columbia Pictures movie version of the novel]. [Of the thirty-two pages, only four deal with the *Patna* incident, one with Stein, and twenty-seven with the melodramatic Patusan episode. Such distortions of JC's book are typical here: after Jim has jumped from the *Patna*, he communes with himself, "She's—she's still afloat! With no officer aboard! Dear Heaven, what have I done?"; the Inquiry is merely mentioned once; and the guns, when "Gentleman" Brown and his "bully boys" shoot up the Bugi village, sound their "Bam! Crang! Bang!" A distortion of JC's work, leaving practically nothing of *Lord Jim* as it is.]

1892 Lyngstad, Sverre. "English Literature," BOOKS ABROAD, XXXIX (Summer 1965), 349.
JOSEPH CONRAD ON FICTION, edited by Walter F. Wright (1964), a collection of JC's "critical" writings, is "merely a compilation." The editor's scheme of organization has produced "an unreadable book" which, with no index, "falls short even for reference purposes." As for JC's theory of fiction, the preface to *The Nigger of the Narcissus* is "by far the most comprehensive, lucid and authoritative exposition of his literary principles." And however interesting, JC's comments on fiction other than his own "seem merely to express an individual temperament rather than to illustrate an artistic creed." [Perhaps too severe on JC's pronouncements on other writers.]

1893 McCann, Charles. "Lord Jim vs. The Darkness: The Saving Power of Human Involvement," COLLEGE ENGLISH, XXVII (Dec 1965), 240-43.
Unlike some of JC's works, *Lord Jim* affords a basis for hope instead of pessimism, although it is a "delicate, tentative" hope, tentative because the

trope that might have been the most pessimistic is limited to Marlow's perception: "the dark background of the story resides in Marlow's awareness of Jim"; *"the relation of Jim to the darkness is not static—it varies."* The variation between Jim and his background "always results from an action of Jim's." Several scenes in the novel indicate that "man preserves his dignity by responsible actions which are occasioned by ties to other men," and in the Patusan section JC develops "an apparent growth in Jim's human involvement." The sense of what might have been is present in the novel, fragile though it is: "by the trope of Jim and the dark world waiting to engulf him," JC sets aside all inhuman demands; by the artistry of confining the impressions to Marlow, JC expresses the ideal. "Jim's relation to other human beings causes the waxing and waning of the darkness in Marlow's impression of him." In Patusan, especially by his marriage to Jewel, Jim appears to join humanity. The conclusion is that *Lord Jim* is "no single-minded expression of stoicism or of pessimism, but great tragedy complicated by a sense of the promise of human involvement, felt despite the fact that our destinies are 'graven in imperishable characters upon the face of a rock.' "

1894 MacShane, Frank. THE LIFE AND WORK OF FORD MADOX FORD (NY: Horizon P, 1965), pp. 29, 31, 32-33, 36-54, 56, 57, 58, 59, 60, 62, 63, 69, 72, 74, 77, 79, 82, 83-84, 99, 101, 116, 119, 122, 130, 131-32, 133, 156, 157, 163, 165-66, 186, 192, 203, 204, 218, 222, 248, 268.

JC wanted to collaborate with Ford Madox Ford because he needed the opportunity to work with another English writer on a book about which he would care relatively little and because he needed money. Their collaboration (1898-1909) was practical because the two men were united by intellectual and artistic agreement. THE INHERITORS now seems trivial: it is dated and, being a *roman à clef,* much of its interest depends upon identifying the politicians and public figures on whom the characters were based. Apparently Ford suggested the idea for the novel and also did most of the writing while JC completed many passages and made them more definite. One value in writing this book was that it imposed practical limits to experimentation, and by working with it JC also became more flexible and fluent. More important to both writers was their work on *Romance;* with his greater experience, JC seems to have been more conscious than Ford of the necessity to tighten the plot and to fill in the background of smuggling on the Kentish coast; he was largely responsible for the third and fourth sections, and he made serious alterations in the final section. His concept of the novel as a "dramatic rendering of life" was his guiding principle for the changes and simplifications which he made. Through the years, "both alone and with Conrad," Ford developed the method he called Impressionism. [Some critics have presumably shown that Ford alone developed the theories of their writing.] But the tradition of the French novel of the nineteenth century was important to both men: both considered the *mot juste* of the French tradition insufficient because they believed that the first function of style was to make the subject interesting. [This book contains much about JC's relationship with Ford and gives an excellent account of the collaboration.]

>**1895** Malbone, Raymond Gates. " 'How to Be': Marlow's Quest in *Lord Jim*," TWENTIETH CENTURY LITERATURE, X (Jan 1965), 172-80.

In *Lord Jim*, Marlow is the main character, and the theme of the novel "rests in what Jim's story means to Marlow rather than in what happens to Jim." His first narrative of Jim leads him to consider Jim's jump from the *Patna* as both a betrayal of "Marlow's personal conception of his craft" and a breach of faith with a community of men, and he wants to find some mitigating circumstances that will explain away Jim's "treachery to mankind." But this part of Jim's story brings him no answer. Marlow's second stage of exploration of the implications of Jim's story leads him only to a question about Jim's career in Patusan: Did Jim redeem himself there? Here JC's use of point of view is important: most of Marlow's tale is told before all the facts are available; therefore Marlow's attitude toward Jim in his oral narrative might reasonably differ from that of the letter which he later writes. Furthermore, the opening four chapters of the novel, written from the author's point of view, characterize Jim in a way that is little altered or developed in the remainder of the book. Thus the novel is primarily concerned not with Jim but with Marlow. Marlow's letter and narrative written to a privileged man mark the third major stage of Marlows' explorations of Jim's story. JC partially juxtaposes the two antithetical views of life held by the privileged man and Jim, responsibility to the group and individual idealism.

The safest conclusion to make is that *Jim* provides no answers but simply poses the antithesis and examines several of its aspects, but the conclusion may be reached from this impressionistic novel that Marlow encounters three major concerns in his quest: (1) his concern about Jim's jump from the *Patna* as a breach of faith which casts doubt on a fixed standard of conduct; (2) his concern about Jim's later redemption in Patusan, judged by the same fixed standard; and (3) his concern for Jim's life as perhaps "higher" than the fixed standard. The book gives a sort of answer to Marlow's quest for "how to be"; Marlow becomes aware that "Jim's life poses a view antithetical to the whole social standard by which Marlow has tried to judge him" and concludes that "the best life is somewhere in an active (rather than static) middle ground between the antitheses." This reading of *Jim* removes several points of critical difference and indicates that neither Marlow nor JC is so "muddled" as some commentators have supposed; indeed, this interpretation may help us "to live with that doubt which is the inseparable part of our knowledge." [An original thesis ingeniously developed and supported, but somewhat weakened by the special pleading of the conclusion.]

>**1896** Michael, Marion Cicero. "Joseph Conrad: A Textual and Literary Study of Four Stories," DISSERTATION ABSTRACTS, XXVI (1965), 2756. Unpublished thesis, University of Georgia, 1963. [Concerns *Almayer's Folly, The Nigger of the Narcissus,* "Heart of Darkness," and *The Secret Agent*.]

>**1897** Miller, J. Hillis. "Joseph Conrad," POETS OF REALITY: SIX TWENTIETH-CENTURY WRITERS (Cambridge, Mass: Belknap Press of Harvard U P, 1965), pp. 13-67.

[This chapter is preceded by some necessary comments on "The Poetry of Reality," pp. 1-13, which indicate JC's place in the literature which preceded and followed him. In the twentieth century, many modern poets begin with an experience of the "nihilism which is one of the possible consequences of romanticism"; JC follows this nihilism into its darkness and "so prepares a way beyond it," thereby beginning a "journey beyond nihilism toward a poetry of reality," a new art which emerges gradually in the poetry of Yeats, Eliot, Dylan Thomas, and Wallace Stevens, and reaches "full development" in the poetry of William Carlos Williams.]

JC's darkness, his universe, and his aesthetic result from the two sides of civilization, devotion to work and "the idea." The idea is civilized man's protection against the "anarchic power of atavistic ways of life." But all human ideals are fabrications of human beings so that "what remains within the human realm is illusory and insubstantial." JC's pessimism arises from his recognition that ethical terms have no meaning because they do not refer to something outside man which informs him as to what he ought to do and from his realization that the "tragedy of man's existence" lies in the fact that he is "cut off irrevocably from the truth of the universe." JC therefore aims in his fiction to give the reader a glimpse of the truth, "however dark and disquieting that truth may be." His detachment leads the reader to discover that he is an outcast, to note the "detachment of things from one another and from man," by expressing precisely what there is to be seen or heard to make the "truth of life," which for JC is darkness, "momentarily visible." This darkness is several things: a sensible experience, the "original chaos," and the "end toward which all things hurry to return." JC's universe is the "process of the birth of things out of a genetic darkness and their return to that darkness," which is the "basic stuff of the universe." Any of the forms of darkness which appear in JC's works causes the collapse of the rational forms by which civilized man lives; and the darkness is the "present nature" of man, too, for no man has outgrown his beginning; sex is "descent into the darkness of irrational emotion"; and religious experience is a loss of rationality. Throughout his career, JC realized that there is no way to evade the "tragic contradictions of the human situation," but he learned that writing gives a form to the "indefinable." Words can name the darkness "by describing a double motion of descent into the darkness and return from it," and the writer must "structure the experience of some surrogate" in such a way as to reveal its truth. This truth will either destroy that other self, as Kurtz and Decoud are destroyed, or will be hidden from them, as it is hidden from Lord Jim or from Flora de Barral in *Chance*. Writing is a "dangerous hovering between two realms that are incompatible," but through literature the author both brings them together and yet keeps at a distance. The only authentic kind of action is writing. JC's aesthetic is based on the momentary glimpse of truth grasped by the writer, the glimpse which is the "highest human accomplishment" and the aim of all "authentic writing." True art, for JC, must "shift the gaze of the reader from the unreal dream of the future to the immediate moment of sensation" so that a "meticulous description" of that moment will lead to a brief glimpse of the "truth behind appearance"; and that glimpse is the goal of art. The return from this brief vision, however, is to an "eternal rest," to the darkness in the "flux at the heart of things," and the return of man to the "forgetful sleep of everyday life."

In *The Secret Agent* JC's own voice and the "voice of darkness most nearly become one." Mr. Verloc is a perfect example of the "sinister connectedness" of all levels of society, of society which JC sees as "rotten at the core." His symbol for this "web of secret connections" is the city of London, and for him civilization is "an arbitrary creation, resting on no source of value outside humanity." The purpose of the novel is to liberate the reader from his "fatuous complacency" by effecting it for the chief characters of the novel. JC uses two ways of separating his readers from the "dark city": the point of view of the narrator and his stance of ironic detachment, and the plot as a "chain reaction," a sequence of disenchantments started by M. Vladimir's demand that Verloc create a sensational anarchist demonstration. One by one the characters are shaken out of their complacency and placed in a situation outside their previous knowledge. The theme of *Agent* seems to be the "disjunction between matter and spirit"; JC's vision seems to culminate in the recognition of an "irreconcilable dualism": man, in the human condition, is the meeting place of matter and spirit, and he is "riven apart" by their contradictions. Stevie's circles represent the "inconceivable": if what lies behind time and space is not nothingness but this contradictory present, and if this "inconceivable something" is the "secret ground" of every man's consciousness, the new meaning which the novel now takes on does not so much deny the first as transcend it. The three deaths in the story suggest the horror of being impossible to die and yet unable to return to life: to be in Verloc's state or Winnie's is "to persist in an interminable moment of freedom, irresponsibility, and leisure," a moment with no content, free of everything; yet it is not nothing: it is a "positive awareness of nothing," a living death—in JC's words, "madness or despair." Comrade Ossipon, the last survivor of the chain reaction, survives to enter a state of living death symbolized by walking and insomnia, two important motifs of the novel. The last paragraphs of *Agent* juxtapose two walkers, Comrade Ossipon moving toward madness and despair and the Professor in his impasse of being unable to destory men's beliefs without actually killing them, thus indicating that "all the living deaths in the novel are the same death" and that the theme is "the universal death which underlies life" (but death is not the obliteration of everything; it is "that which cannot end"). Though the characters of *Agent* go toward death in different ways, most of them ultimately reach the same state, a state like that approached by the protagonists of JC's other novels, Kurtz, Marlow, Decoud, Flora de Barral, or Mrs. Travers. [An unusually perceptive view of JC's place in literature and one of the best analyses of *Agent*.]

1898 Newman, Paul B. "The Drama of Conscience and Recognition in *Lord Jim*," MIDWEST QUARTERLY, VI (July 1965), 351-66. In many of his works, JC portrays the obsessions of his characters first in moments of crisis which yield to self-recognition only after painful ordeals of conscience (the incident in *Lord Jim* when, disabled by a falling spar, Jim lies in his cabin filled with fear without self-recognition). Jim's great desire for heroism is the basis of all his weakness; the lofty nature of his dreams may plunge him at any moment into the muck, as it literally does when he escapes from the stockade at Patusan and plunges into the slime of the creek. Brierly commits suicide because he is an "unhealthy idealist" who carries to an ultimate extreme the concept of "fastidious honor" as he recognizes himself in Jim. For the heroic man, the moment of commitment is often that which leads swiftly to his death. Marlow desires to save Jim for a hero's death; he intuitively realizes that Jim will achieve self-recognition if he does not first destroy himself through romantic despair. His unsoundness is his habit of living "among the shadows of imagined ideals without the force of character to back them up." When Jim goes to meet certain death at the hands of Doramin, "his act is a symbolic celebration of his devotion to the heroic ideal, at the same time that it is as much a suicide as the death of Brierly." He recognizes not only that he is betrayed but also that he has "an undiminished devotion to the ideal to which he has proved so false." But his death proves him not completely unworthy: Jim is an ordinary man who dies betrayed, but he is a hero in his power "to provoke the image of the ideal in all its innocence"; he is therefore a "commonplace hero," like Theodore Dreiser's heroes. JC's emphasis upon acts of individual decision expresses the nature of the European character in that even if Jim "stands marooned in the darkness of the jungle," he must act alone, and herein lies the significance of his death and his final recognition. [A good psychological analysis.]

1899 Ober, Warren U. " 'Heart of Darkness': 'The Ancient Mariner' a Hundred Years Later," DALHOUSIE REVIEW, XLV (Autumn 1965), 333-37.

Whereas Coleridge's criminal Mariner, although "spiritually scarred" by his deed, is at last readmitted into "the fellowship of The One Life" and achieves unity with a "beneficent Nature" through a "wise passiveness," Kurtz's union with Nature "brings madness rather than peace"; and unlike the Mariner, Kurtz represents a "powerfully ironic post-Darwinian and pre Golding parody" of Coleridge's theme. Furthermore, at one level Kurtz is JC's Mariner, but Marlow too is JC's Mariner: Marlow casually approaches his "moment of awareness of the meaning of existence" but finally learns Kurtz's "bitter lesson." Then "the dice are thrown, Death wins Kurtz, and Marlow recovers from his illness to become the prize of Life-in-Death"; like Coleridge's Mariner JC's Marlow is "condemned to tell his story—and Kurtz's story—to an uncomprehending audience." Marlow's first wedding guest is Kurtz's Intended, to whom he gives a message of love instead of the truth because he realizes that she could not survive the truth as he has learned it from Kurtz. Marlow as Mariner, however, "entrusts" his genuine message not to the Intended but to his audience on the yawl *Nellie,* thereby reinforcing the frame device and making the story more than a monologue; but his physical appearance transfixes at least one person in his audience who must leave the *Nellie* "a sadder and a wiser man." Thus JC's statement about man, about man's place in nature, and about the meaning of existence is a reversal of Coleridge's theme in "The Rime of the Ancient Mariner"; JC's tale, marked as it is by a greater degree of sophistication, subtlety, and complexity, is, in effect, " 'The Rime of the Ancient Mariner' one hundred years later."

1900 O'Grady, Walter. "On Plot in Modern Fiction: Hardy, James, and Conrad," MODERN FICTION STUDIES, XI (Summer 1965), 107-15.

E. M. Forster's distinction between story and plot implies the existence of five things: an external situation, an internal situation, an external event, an internal event, and change; and defines an incident as an external event and an event as an internal event. The first four aspects of a plot work upon each other to produce the fifth aspect—change. Therefore, the term *struc-*

ture applied to the novel, implying as it does a static relationship, is misleading. Whereas the "direction of flow" of James's THE AMBASSADORS is forward and inward and the flow of Hardy's TESS OF THE D'URBERVILLES is outward and backward, JC in *The Secret Agent* "orders and directs all situations and incidents to one climactic incident, an attempt to blow up the Greenwich Observatory and the consequent destruction of Stevie." In James and Hardy, incident is "generally formative as well as indicative"; in *Agent,* "incident is generally indicative only"; and in this sense, this novel is the "most uncharacteristic" of JC's works. Here JC directs "the given interior situation, the exterior situation, the incidents which their combination produces, to a complete destruction of the exterior situation." The flow of his plot, like Hardy's, is therefore backwards and outwards.

1901 O'Hara, J. D. "Unlearned Lessons in 'The Secret Sharer,'" COLLEGE ENGLISH, XXVI (March 1965), 444-50.

Leggatt is really a criminal and Captain Archbold is the "moral center" of "The Secret Sharer." In Leggatt's description of the storm, if anyone is mad it is Leggatt himself. Archbold's description of the storm contradicts Leggatt's, and the narrator realizes this fact. Though the narrator is basically hostile, he reveals no doubt of Archbold's honesty; the Captain and Leggatt are the poles between which the narrator "fluctuates," and the narrator finally sides with Archbold, just barely saving himself from Leggatt's fate. The narrator's initiation into life is a specific test—"an initiation into the fullest responsibility," that of command. Readers are warned in various ways early in the story not to accept the narrator's point of view. The narrator is slowly dislodged from his "position of identification" with Leggatt until at last he is forced to admit that he really suspects Leggatt of being "a murdering brute," and he displays "a new maturity" in his handling of the events in which Leggatt leaves the ship. JC, indeed, "makes the narrator's shedding of his secret sharer as foolishly romantic and irresponsible as his reception of him." Such accidents as the floating hat contain no deep understanding of life; they merely save the narrator's ship and his career. But the narrator does not learn from his experience: Leggatt's freedom is an illusion and the narrator is still overconfident. JC "is working less profoundly and more cheerfully in this story than many critics believe"; the tale appears "to have interested Conrad primarily as a technical exercise, a stylistic experiment in communicating through an unsympathetic point of view." [Removes from "The Secret Sharer" most of the seriousness and profundity found by preceding critics.]

1902 Pilecki, Gerard A. "Conrad's *Victory*," EXPLICATOR, XXIII (Jan 1965), Item 36.

In chapter XI of *Victory,* when Heyst confronts Jones in the bungalow, he suffers from a kind of "moral paralysis" and fails to act because Jones has many of the characteristics of the man who has much power over Heyst—his father. Both Jones and the elder Heyst are "Satanic figures who have rebelled against society and against all law," both lived only for themselves, both became "bored," and both have "strangely lifeless voices"; but their singular dress links them still more closely. Heyst remembers his father in a blue dressing-gown; and when he sees Jones, the desperado too is "tightly enfolded" in a blue dressing-gown. Jones then is the "spectre" of the elder Heyst; he is, in fact, "the terrifying embodiment of 'the absolute moral and intellectual liberty' which the elder Heyst had claimed."

> **1903** Resink, G. J. "Conradiaanse interraciale vriendshappen" (Interracial Friendships in Conrad), FORUM DER LETTEREN, VI (Feb 1965), 35-44.

In his "Indonesian" narratives JC addressed himself frequently and intensely to the problems of interracial friendship. Surprisingly this significant aspect of works such as *Almayer's Folly, An Outcast of the Islands, Lord Jim,* "The End of the Tether," and *The Rescue* has not yet received the critical attention it deserves. In JC's work, interracial friendships are characterized by a sense of equality that is particularly striking in view of their colonial or semi-colonial settings. A closer examination usually reveals that this equality derives from two kinds of superiority that tend to cancel each other: the Asian partners in the friendship usually belong to a significantly higher social class than their white counterparts; offsetting this is the whites' belief in racial superiority.

A second characteristic of these relationships is that the men are either unmarried or unhappily married or widowers. Widowhood and marital unhappiness are universal afflictions, but more significant is the number of bachelors in the Indonesian works. Less convincing is the single state of so many prominent natives. JC's only possible justification here is that most of his Malayans are almost as much colonists and "outcasts" as their European counterparts, in other words, people for whom marriage and its responsibilities had little appeal. Most of JC's Malayans are indeed Buginese, Makassarians, or Mandarese, and ethnographical maps of Borneo and Celebes indicate that it was precisely these population groups that showed most migratory propensities.

A third characteristic belongs to psychology rather than sociology, namely, erotic ambivalence. Dain Marola has an "almost feminine eye"; Aissa (*An Outcast of the Islands*) is proud of her man-like valor; Arsat is told by his brother that he is only half a man and that the other half has been absorbed by his valorous love Diamelen, who therefore is "bisexual." Jim is repeatedly spoken of in feminine terms. Hassim, in *The Rescue,* with his delicate face and smile and his "negligent elegance," is juxtaposed to his sister Immada, who has "the fearlessness of a great fighter" and is "dressed practically in man's clothes." Through his reading in the journals of James Brooke and through personal observation, JC knew that institutionalized bisexuality played a very important part in the cultures of Borneo and Celebes, and probably he wanted to show that such cultures were free of the excesses and tragedies to which social taboos often drove Europeans such as the lesbian Mrs. Fyne in *Chance* and the misogynous, murderous homosexual, Mr. Jones, in *Victory*. The friendship between Jim and Dain Waris was "one of those strange, profound, rare friendships between brown and white, in which the very difference of race seems to draw two human beings closer by some mystic element of sympathy."

Perhaps young Josef Korzeniowski had been as much "captivated" by a Dain of Daeng as Jim. Jocelyn Baines has suggested that JC's "deepest impulses could find disguised expression through a portrayal of the father-daughter relationship"—a kind of travesty of his own relationship as an only son to his father. Something else may also have been involved here: Jozef Korzeniowski may have been so charmed by the real Daeng Marola in Berau that JC needed the travesty of Nina Almayer in Sambir in order to be able to paint the idealized portrait of Dain Marola as lovingly as he did. In this view, Nina's many half-sisters in the archipelago—all of them only daughters and unhappy in love, such as Omar's Aissa, Cornelius's Jewel, Whalley's Ivy, Nielsen's Freya of Pulau Tudjuh, Lena in *Victory*, and Edith Travers in *The Rescue*—are indeed creations through which the author expressed some disturbing personal feelings and at the same time freed himself from them through objectification. [In Dutch.]

1904 Said, Edward W. "Conrad: *Nostromo:* Record and Reality," APPROACHES TO THE TWENTIETH-CENTURY NOVEL, ed by John Unterecker (NY: Crowell, 1965), pp. 108-52.

As every individual in *Nostromo* appears interested in keeping a "record" of his thought and action, JC, in his letters, also kept a record of his struggles in the composition of the novel, a record which reveals him as an *homo duplex,* a man obsessed by the dichotomy of his actual struggles in his work and the public image which he felt was a compromise between two conflicting modes of existence. In *Nostromo* the two modes are the conflict between immersion in action and the retrospective definition, or record, of that action. A reconciliation between action and record appears only in Emilia Gould, the one character in the novel who possesses accurate vision. During the course of the narrative, silver gradually becomes the *raison d'être* of everyone (except Mrs. Gould) and of the independent Republic of Sulaco. The craze for "material interests" makes *Nostromo* a record of public, political history that is eventually reduced to a condition of mind; but this novel possesses both the "objective personality" and the very "subjective personality" which undermines the objective edifice. *Nostromo,* appearing to be an ordinary political or historical novel, has as its *real* action man's overambitious intention to create his own world in opposition to the intolerable actual world which he finds. The horror appears in the gradual, prolonged discovery that man's created world is just as intolerable as the world he has tried to supersede. Higuerota, the tall mountain which dominates Sulaco, is a transcendent, abiding power which contrasts with Sulaco's "atomized" political life, where man is weak and untidy. JC's letters reveal a despairing search in his own life for the qualities possessed by Higuerota—consistency, power, and unity; and his personal predicament appears especially in the central episode of *Nostromo,* the night on the lighter. Neither Nostromo nor Decoud is working for himself there, but rather for the silver; and each in his own way represents one of the two strains in JC's life. According to the novel, each man believes himself free and is believed by others to be free; but from the reader's point of view in the light of the entire work, exactly the opposite is true. A man's life (e.g., Gould's) is remarkably similar to the process of history—neither one is free: "the very fabric of life is manufactured by some devilish process whose purpose and logic is profoundly anti-human." There is no disgust in JC's conclusion; JC is simply "coldly realistic." He learned from life the lesson of self-abnegation; and from the imprisonment of the human condition he utilized the condition of art to allow others "to know life for what it is." [Said's method of using JC's letters a a means of understanding his mind in relation to his work is impressive in this penetrating analysis.]

1905 Sanders, Charles. "Conrad's 'Heart of Darkness,'" EXPLICATOR, XXIV (Sept 1965), Item 2.

JC, in his "method of suggestion" discussed by M. C. Bradbrook, indicates that two of "the queer knitting women" in the office in Belgium obviously connote at least Clotho and Lachesis. Atropos, who cuts the thread of life, is missing because Marlow does not die. Marlow's life will be long, in contrast to that of Kurtz, whose name signifies *short.*

1906 Schwab, Arnold T. "Conrad's American Speeches and His Reading from *Victory,*" MODERN PHILOLOGY, LXII (May 1965), 342-47.

In the spring of 1923, JC prepared notes for speeches to be delivered in the United States: on May 5, he spoke at Garden City, New York, to the staff of Doubleday, Page, his American publisher; on May 10, he gave a lecture and a reading from *Victory* at the home of Arthur Curtiss James. [Since no exact records of what he said and read were kept, the first publication in this article of his "Notes for Speeches in America" and a description of the markings in his reading copy of *Victory* are of value to everyone interested in JC.] For the lectures JC chose seven passages from the novel and apparently read them, with small cuts intended to heighten the dramatic effect. His own description of the "Notes" (now in the possession of an anonymous collector) provides at least a fairly accurate account of his remarks. [Informative; important also in understanding JC's artistic principles. Documented with citations from JC.]

1907 Scrimgeour, Cecil. "Jimmy Wait and the Dance of Death: Conrad's *Nigger of the Narcissus*," CRITICAL QUARTERLY, VII (Winter 1965), 339-52.

JC struggled to find himself in writing *The Nigger of the Narcissus,* which became "a means of dominating the fears that rose obsessively in him." His fatalistic resignation about the book is illustrated through letters he wrote to Cunninghame Graham. JC's discomfort of spirit sprang from a common contemporary condition—"from a subversion of belief, from doubt about the purposefulness of the world of nature and about the place of man, moral man, within it." [Examines the major imagery and symbolism: light and darkness, the sea and death.] The Cockney seaman Donkin is representative of a new generation of seamen, whose fidelity lies with the corrupt earth (land) rather than with captain and ship. The unstable crew contrasts with the only three figures who live by the principle of loyalty—Captain Allistoun, the chief mate Mr. Barker, and the ordinary seaman Old Singleton. In Jimmy Wait, JC "creates one of those ambiguous figures in which contradictory worlds of feeling and moral value converge." For JC, "moral courage, a stoic firmness in facing evil and dissolution, was the highest good that man can wrest from life." JC "was dedicated to the proposition that in embracing the sea and wrestling with its mystery men could undergo a healthful purgation of spirit and learn to discover themselves." Yet in the final analysis, "Those who sail in ships . . . will find . . . only disillusion." JC has couched his story in the form of a Dance of Death.

1908 Sherry, Norman. "Conrad and the BANGKOK TIMES," NINETEENTH-CENTURY FICTION, XX (Dec 1965), 255-66; incorporated in CONRAD'S EASTERN WORLD (Cambridge: Cambridge U P, 1966).

A study of the BANGKOK TIMES "gives an accurate account of certain events which Conrad made use of in his stories" and reveals that "these events cannot be taken as facts of Conrad's biography" as has been done. For instance, the Chinese thief in "Falk" is not based on a real thief who existed, but a report in the BANGKOK TIMES shows that he robbed a member of JC's crew. Also, the fictional character Schomberg and the hotel that he managed find their source or inspiriation in two Bangkok hotels, the Universal and the Oriental (which advertised a table d'hôte similar to Schomberg's in *Victory*) and in a "German broker living in Singapore named

Schomburgk." It is interesting to note that JC obtained numerous suggestions "for his later stories from only two weeks' stay at Bangkok."

1909 Sherry, Norman. "Conrad's Eastern Port: The Setting of the Inquiry in *Lord Jim,*" REVIEW OF ENGLISH LITERATURE, VI (Oct 1965), 52-61; incorporated in CONRAD'S EASTERN WORLD (Cambridge: Cambridge U P, 1966).

An abundance of evidence, including such records as newspaper reports and photographs, strongly indicates that JC set the Inquiry into the desertion of the pilgrim ship, *Patna,* in Singapore. Simply called an "Eastern port" in *Lord Jim,* Singapore was the place of one inquiry into the desertion of the pilgrim ship, *Jeddah,* on which JC based his fictional account, even though he had no experience of this inquiry. He had, however, his own knowledge of an Inquiry in Singapore into the desertion of the ship *Palestine,* on which he was first mate. On his own Inquiry, then, JC based the account of Jim's desertion, making suitable changes so that the atmosphere of his experience, though not the outcome, serves as a basis for the Inquiry in *Jim.*

1910 Sherry, Norman. *"Lord Jim* and 'The Secret Sharer,' " REVIEW OF ENGLISH STUDIES, XVI (Nov 1965), 378-92; incorporated in CONRAD'S EASTERN WORLD (Cambridge: Cambridge U P, 1966).

Newspaper accounts, photographs, and letters; such internal evidence as the fact that both stories contain a culpable action, that a desecration of the accepted code by a man who is "one of us" leads to the man's becoming a wanderer, and that a suggestion is made that the narrator might have acted in a similar manner—indicate that JC used the same sources for both works. These are the *Jeddah* case, with the chief officer being A. P. Williams, on which JC based the *Patna* incident in *Lord Jim;* an occurrence on the *Cutty Sark* in which the chief officer struck a seaman a deadly blow and then made his escape; and JC's own experience on the *Otago.*

Jim includes the first conception of the relationship between the narrator and Leggatt in "The Secret Sharer" and uses Williams as the "inspiration" for Jim. JC probably combined the two incidents of the *Jeddah* and the *Cutty Sark* so that in *Jim* he included his knowledge of Williams with only slight changes whereas in "The Secret Sharer" he employed Captain Clark of the *Jeddah* as the original of Captain Archbold of the *Sephora.* The story of Brierly in *Jim,* an inset piece of sailor's gossip, is taken from the account of the suicide of the master of the *Cutty Sark,* Captain Wallace. JC also drew upon his own experience on the *Otago,* in which the chief mate, Charles Born, may have wanted the command himself; and Born thus appears as Burns in *The Shadow-Line* and as Jones in *Jim.* Certainly, Born's scare among the islands of the Gulf of Siam becomes the basis of JC's incident in "The Secret Sharer" in which the narrator takes his ship close enough to the islands to allow Leggatt to escape. [Supplies new biographical facts about JC and also demonstrates some of his narrative methods.]

1911 Sherry, Norman. "The Pilgrim Ship in *Lord Jim:* Conrad's Two Sources," PHILOLOGICAL QUARTERLY, XLIV (Jan 1965), 88-99; incorporated in CONRAD'S EASTERN WORLD (Cambridge: Cambridge U P, 1966).

Since Sir Frank Swettenham wrote ["The Story of *Lord Jim*," TLS, 6 Sept 1923, p. 588] that JC based his story of the *Patna* in *Lord Jim* on the desertion of the pilgrim ship *Jeddah* by her European officers, his account has been accepted with little question. There is evidence, however, that JC did not rely entirely upon the *Jeddah* incident but also upon his own experience on the barque *Palestine,* which he included in "Youth" and re-worked for *Jim*. He "was likely to have met" A. P. Williams, who was serving as a ship chandler's water clerk and was Chief Officer of the *Jeddah* at the time of the desertion. Williams became JC's "inspiration" for Jim in his story. Of the *Jeddah* incident, JC used only "the framework"; but for "the interpretation of motive, feeling, and individual situation" he "looked in part" to his own experiences in the abandonment of the *Palestine*. He departed somewhat from both incidents, since he wanted to remove all possible excuse for Jim's leaving the *Patna* and to isolate him from the other deserters. [Copious evidence, both internal and external, makes the main points of this article seem reasonable.]

1912 Simmons, J. L. "The Dual Morality in 'The Secret Sharer,'" STUDIES IN SHORT FICTION, II (Spring 1965), 209-20.

"The Secret Sharer" is about the narrator-captain who tries to live up to his ideal and then immediately finds this ideal dramatized in Leggatt. At sea, any acts to the end of keeping the ship afloat are moral. The captain of the *Sephora* dramatizes duality of land-sea morality further by rationalizing the idea that Leggatt must be returned to the law of the land, thus trying to justify his own failure and to obscure his own immorality in terms of the sea. He fails because he is not fully committed to his present life, whereas Leggatt is "instinctively a saint" in relation to life on a ship.

From this point on, the story leads to the test for the narrator, and for him the ideal must be embodied in terms of action. Knowing that he must act without his "secret sharer," that he must see whether the ideal self is truly a part of him, the narrator commits himself totally to the morality of the sea and sails close to the "black mass of Koh-ring" even if his first command should meet disaster. In the closing paragraphs of the story, human solidarity is quickly portrayed as the narrator-captain, comprehending the fusion of the literal and the symbolic, is for the first time actually the captain of his ship. The reader then recognizes a clear instance of symbolic re-enactment. [Convincingly refutes several other critics and effectively develops the concept of the dual morality in the story.]

1913 Smith, Curtis C. "Conrad's *Chance:* A Dialectical Novel," THOTH, VI (Spring 1965), 16-24.

The tensions in *Chance* are functional, for it is a dialectical novel in which JC resolves the tension between several sets of opposites to produce in each instance a synthesis which is "higher and better" than either member of the set. The tension between Flora's belief that her story is a tragedy and Marlow's "sardonic assumption" that it is a farce is resolved by a transition to romance. Although Flora has missed her youth, she finds both youth and laughter in Powell. This laughter is, in turn, the most important synthesis of the novel, because it supplies an alternative to "the Fynes' ridiculous seriousness and Marlow's sardonic laughter—and also to Anthony's empty laughter."

The triple narration is an illustration of JC's use of "configurations" of three in this book. Three, an unstable figure in human relationships, is a tension resolved finally in the expected marriage of Powell and Flora, where the stable figure two is substituted for the various triangular relationships. Configurations of three characters dominate most of *Chance:* the narrator, Powell, and Marlow; young Powell, shipmaster Powell, and Captain Anthony; Marlow and the Fynes; the Fynes and Flora; the governess, her lover, and Flora; and even the Fynes's dog, Marlow and Flora. On the *Ferndale,* the triangles become more unstable and more nearly tragic: Franklin, Anthony, and Flora; de Barral, Flora, and Anthony; and Powell, Flora, and Anthony. The anticipated marriage of Powell and Flora resolves not only the unstable triangular configurations but also the important tension between the demands of life at sea and those of life on land. Powell and Anthony represent the sea as opposed to Fyne, a landlubber. Land and sea values ultimately mix in Flora, whose experience is the synthesis of land and sea, which transcends both: Flora returns to the land with her experience of the sea to make life richer than it could otherwise have been. The marriage of Powell and Flora also resolves the tension between good and bad luck, since at the end of the novel Flora has character and thus no longer needs luck. And the marriage eliminates still another set of opposites, the lonely (Powell) and the encumbered (Flora). The dialectic in *Chance,* however, is not too neat: Flora is capable of working out her own destiny, but her story is not over. She may also need to work out the destiny of the "curiously shadowy" Powell. In this novel, the dialectic moves not toward an end but toward the beginning of a higher cycle. [A good explication of an important concept in *Chance.*]

1914 Souvage, Jacques. An Introduction to the Study of the Novel (Gent: Wetenschapplijke Uitgeverij E. Story—Scientia P.V.B.A., 1965) (Imported, NY: Humanities P, 1965), pp. 21, 45, 53, 94.

In such novels as *Lord Jim,* "Youth," and *Chance,* JC achieves "dramatic presentation" of his content by utilizing Marlow, a "permanently involved spectator," who is able to objectify the material of the narrative while the author, at one further remove, controls him. Marlow in *Jim* provides, as noted by Norman Friedman, the "I" as witness point of view, i.e., the novel is written from the view-point of a narrator who is not the main character, a narrator who sees the story from the "wandering periphery." In an attempt at a typology of the novel, Irène Simon distinguishes the "epic form," represented by Dickens and Thackeray; the "dramatic form," represented by Emily Brontë, George Meredith, George Eliot, Thomas Hardy, Henry James, and JC; and the "lyric form," represented by D. H. Lawrence, Virginia Woolf, and James Joyce, while Edwin Muir considers the dramatic form a kind of structure in which the end of the novel is inevitable, resulting either in an equilibrium or a catastrophe "which cannot be pursued farther."

1915 Stein, William Bysshe. "Conrad's East: Time, History, Action, and *Maya,*" Texas Studies in Literature and Language, VII (Autumn 1965), 265-83.

Instead of making the backgrounds of his Malayan novels re-creations of tropical realities, JC places his heroes in psychological environments, where he then anatomizes them. Long before Heidegger and Sartre, he perceived man as basically a historical being whose participation in history immerses the individual in the flux of impermanence which inevitably produces despair and uncertainty. This perverted vision of man's role in time and history—the product of centuries of conditioning—always takes the form of a quest for some kind of success, and in such works as *Lord Jim* and "Heart of Darkness," JC asserts that nothing will ever change the "aggressive self-destructive urges of Western man." The only certain knowledge accessible to man is the discovery of self-delusion, a discovery which causes the disintegration of the structure of time. Opposed to this concept is the Eastern evaluation which we find in JC's fiction of the East. Whereas Western man is unable to reconcile his personal aspirations to the strict limitations of a temporal existence and therefore lapses into baffled cynicism and despair (similar to the surrender of Amiel in his *Journal Intime*), JC, at least once in each Eastern tale, uses an image of the abyss to mediate some encounter with nothingness. This awareness of nothingness that underlies "every moment of self-doubt" is always converted to the operation of *maya,* "the wheel of universal illusion," which manifests itself objectively on the human level in time and history as "the unappeasable truth of impermanence." In order to recover this awareness dramatically, JC employs in his fiction the abyss, the concomitant experience of absurdity, and the symbols and images of the Indian scriptures. He thus found in Eastern concepts a solution of the Western problem of the absurdity of man's egoist desires. Whether he genuinely believed in this "redemptive formula" is unimportant, but his reading and his travels indicate that in *yoga* he discovered the "salvational character of action," especially that in *karma-yoga,* the discipline of action leading to liberation from the spell of *maya.* [Contains convincing support for the premise of a strong impact of the East upon JC. It should be considered with other similar inquiries by Stein, such as his " 'The Heart of Darkness': Bodhisattva Scenario," ORIENT/WEST, IX (Sept-Oct 1964), 37-46.]

1916 Sterba, Richard F. "Remarks on Joseph Conrad's 'Heart of Darkness,' " JOURNAL OF THE AMERICAN PSYCHOANALYTIC ASSOCIATION, XIII (July 1965), 570-83.

Elements of JC's description of Marlow's journey through the primitive wilderness on his voyage up the Congo are an unconscious psychological expression of a common boyhood experience, "the sight of the female genital with its consequent reaction of horror and fright."

1917 Stravinsky, Igor. "Memories of T. S. Eliot," ESQUIRE, LXIV (Aug 1965), 92-93.

[Stravinsky, in his last meeting with Eliot, discussed, among other topics, JC.] Eliot described JC as "a Grand Seigneur, the greatest I have ever met, though it was a shock after reading him to hear him talk. He had a very gutteral accent." Eliot declared "Youth" and "The End of the Tether" to be "the finest stories of the kind that I know."

1918 Triller, A. "Joseph Conrad (Korzeniowski) in polnischer Sicht" (Joseph Conrad [Korzeniowski] in Polish Eyes), ZEITSCHRIFT FÜR SLAVISCHE PHILOLOGIE, XXXII (1965), 46-60.

It is to England's credit that since the days of Voltaire London has welcomed famed exiles of all kinds and from all countries. Yet, in Polish eyes, JC's case presents some special problems. Even before JC was generally recognized in Poland, his name was drawn into a controversy which had in fact begun as early as 1837, when Bronisław Trentowski explained why he wrote in German rather than in Polish. The question of the advantage or perniciousness of a Pole's writing in a language other than his own was raised with particular reference to JC by Wincenty Lutosawski's "Emigracja zdolności" (Emigration of Talents), KRAJ (St. Petersburg), No. 12 (31 March 1899). In 1925, the same writer, who had earlier met JC through Henry James, again represented JC's rationale for writing in English: to earn a living and because England had provided a refuge. Lutosawski defended the right of talented persons to emigrate and argued that Poland benefited from the fact that talented persons wrote in a major foreign language, because they gained a wider and more sympathetic hearing for the Polish voice. JC's works are the fruit of the Polish spirit. Lutosawski made big waves with his article, and many critics soon became involved in the controversy. Eliza Orzeszkowa, particularly, attacked JC for his act of "desertion" and even wrote him a private letter whose content can only be guessed from JC's violent reaction in later years to the mention of Orzeszkowa's name. These charges of desertion had a deep and lasting effect on JC [evidence from letters and other works is cited]. Even after World War I (1923), when JC's "spiritual homecoming" began, the debate about his "Polishness" continued. Not all criticism was anti-JC, for some critics attempted to analyze JC's works objectively using a psychoanalytic method, and others suggested that the basic question was whether an artist might give his allegiance to his own country or to the larger world of humanity. Today most writers on JC would regard him as essentially belonging to English literary history. JC himself might well have come to regard himself as a Polish-French-English personality. The correspondence with his uncle Tadeusz Bobrowski probably extended his "Polish years" into his "English period." Even in later years, JC remained admirably fluent in Polish. He abhorred earlier poor Polish translations, but later translations have been outstanding and help to mark JC's "homecoming" among Poles. It is believed that there is little Polishness to be found in JC's early works but more in those written toward the end of his life, perhaps because he had no knowledge of Polish maritime terminology but did have the necessary technical English vocabulary. English thus served him best for particular subjects.

In the course of the controversy, JC's journalism dealing with Poland was often overlooked (e.g., "Autocracy and War" and "The Crime of Partition"). Today these writings are used as evidence to show how deeply JC stood in the nationalist Polish tradition, for which both his parents had suffered severely. JC was never more popular in Poland than during World War II, but, during the reign of Stalinist powers, he was regarded as a propagandist for an irrational hero-cult, his ethical ideals serving only the world of the wealthy shipowners. Even this episode passed, for the centenary celebration (1957) took place openly; today JC has again found official sanction, and his work is recognized as part of the spiritual life of Poles. The newest Polish emigration finds a powerful bond with JC's work. He is now also viewed as spokesman for the whole cultured world and is analyzed by many critics without false ambitions and emotions. [An interesting attempt to place Polish criticism of JC and JC himself in the context of Polish history.] [In German.]

1919 Wang, Joan Parsons. "Joseph Conrad, Proto-Existentialist: A Comparative Study of Conrad, Camus and Sartre," DISSERTATION ABSTRACTS, XXVI (1965), 1051-52. Unpublished thesis, Indiana University, 1964.

1920 Watts, C. T. "Joseph Conrad, R. B. Cunninghame Graham, and the *Tourmaline*," NOTES AND QUERIES, N.S. XII (July 1965), 262-65.

Two letters to Cunninghame Graham are important for their biographical information as well as for their references to the *"Tourmaline* Venture." JC may have tried to conceal the name of the vessel on which he had done his own gun-running by "borrowing" the name *Tourmaline* and altering the vowels to *Tremolino*.

1921 Watts, C. T. "A Minor Source for *Nostromo*," REVIEW OF ENGLISH STUDIES, XVI (May 1965), 182-84.

Both external and internal evidence strongly suggest that Ramón Paez's WILD SCENES IN SOUTH AMERICA; OR LIFE IN THE LLANOS OF VENEZUELA (Lond, 1863) provided JC with some specific details of natural description and of political activity.

1922 Weingart, Seymour Leonard. "The Form and Meaning of the Impressionist Novel," DISSERTATION ABSTRACTS, XXVI (1965), 1656-57. Unpublished thesis, University of California, Davis, 1965.

1923 Welsh, Alexander. "The Allegory of Truth in English Fiction," VICTORIAN STUDIES, IX (Sept 1965), 7-28.

The concept of "the allegory of truth," the contest of truth and falsehood, stated in Locke's ESSAY CONCERNING HUMAN UNDERSTANDING but descending from Spenser's THE FAERIE QUEENE and appearing in the "century of fiction" from Scott's THE HEART OF MIDLOTHIAN to James's THE GOLDEN BOWL, is a convention adapted by JC in "Heart of Darkness." Marlow, who detests a lie, finds the truth in Kurtz's famous last words, "The horror! the horror!"; but in telling the Intended that her lover's last word was her name, he is guilty "only of irony." He is "content with a simple irony about truth," thereby displaying that his impressionistic method, which requires that meaning "should be only partly articulated," can usually be understood if the reader is "prepared to meet traditional allegories in an ironic context."

1924 Whitehead, Lee M. "Alma Renamed Lena in Conrad's *Victory*," ENGLISH LANGUAGE NOTES, III (Sept 1965), 55-57.

The usual understanding that the name *Alma* signifies *spirit* or *soul* seems strange if Alma (so-called for almost half the book) wants to forget her frightful earlier existence as Alma. But this word is an Arabic term for "hetaera" or dancing girl, with a morally licentious connotation, which JC may have heard in his travels or may have come across in his reading. At the climax of *Victory,* interestingly enough, Lena, in playing the part of a courtesan to Ricardo, deludes Heyst into thinking her genuinely a licentious *Alma,* but he realizes his error at the time of her death. The name *Lena,* which came to Heyst with no connotations, is the diminutive of *Helen,* the eternal woman, and of *Magdalen,* one of Helen's old names as well as that of the harlot whose love for Christ became "spiritual," as Lena's does for Heyst. Thus Alma and Lena are the same woman, but her "sensuous, physical nature"—to which Ricardo falls prey—is changed into "a genuine, spiritual love for Heyst"; in fact, "the frail, defeated little performer for Zangiacomo has become a woman capable of the ultimate sacrifice and victory." [Although well documented, this ingenious and logical interpretation depends entirely upon the possibility that JC *may have known* the word *Alma* as it was used by Egyptians and Arabs of his time.]

1966

1925 Allen, Jerry. "Introduction," GREAT SHORT WORKS OF JOSEPH CONRAD (NY: Harper and Row, Perennial Classics, 1966), pp. 1-9.

[The introduction (to "An Outpost of Progress," "Youth," "Heart of Darkness," "Typhoon," "The Lagoon," and "The Secret Sharer") has a biographical sketch and brief comments on JC's style (which has the "cadence of the sea"), on his use of characters from real life, on the "ideal conception of one's personality" in "The Secret Sharer," and on JC's hatred of bigotry, his concern for "inner isolation," his rambling storytelling technique, and the "atmospheric depth of setting." Biographical information comes largely from THE SEA YEARS OF JOSEPH CONRAD (1965).]

1926 Allen, Jerry. "Lord Jim's Line," TIMES LITERARY SUPPLEMENT (Lond), 10 Nov 1966, p. 1032.

In reply to the reviewer of THE SEA YEARS OF JOSEPH CONRAD (1965), and Norman Sherry's CONRAD'S EASTERN WORLD (1966), the present writer made certain discoveries about Williams, about the village of Berau, and about Captain William Lingard in 1960 whereas Norman Sherry first appeared in 1962 "at the locale he gives for his research, the STRAITS TIMES library." Furthermore, Sherry once undertook some minor research for Miss Allen in Singapore and left it incomplete. Her purpose in writing biography is the same as the reviewer's. [For the origin of the controversy in 1923, see references listed under "The History of Mr. Conrad's Books,"

TLS, 30 Aug 1923, p. 670; for the controversy revived in 1966, see references listed under "Lord Jim's Line," TLS, 3 Nov 1966, pp. 993-94.]

1927 Allen, Jerry. "Lord Jim's Line," TIMES LITERARY SUPPLEMENT (Lond), 15 Dec 1966, p. 1175.

In reply to A. Van Marle, the material in THE SEA YEARS OF JOSEPH CONRAD (1965) "has been painstakingly attributed" "as is clear from the 787 reference notes" and was ten years in the writing, without subsidy. [For the origin of the controversy in 1923, see references listed under "The History of Mr. Conrad's Books," TLS, 30 Aug 1923, p. 670; for the controversy revived in 1966, see references listed under "Lord Jim's Line," TLS, 3 Nov 1966, pp. 993-94.]

1928 Bentley, Thomas R. (comp). STUDENT SOURCES FOR SHAKESPEARE'S HAMLET, SHAW'S SAINT JOAN, CONRAD'S "Heart of Darkness" (Agincourt, Ont: The Book-Society of Canada, 1966), pp. 1-2.

[Lists five articles on JC's "Heart of Darkness," as follows: Albert J. Guerard, "The Journey Within," CONRAD THE NOVELIST (1958); Richard Curle, "Introduction to 'The Congo Diary,'" *Last Essays of Joseph Conrad* (1926; see Curle, 1925); Jerome Thale, "Marlow's Quest," UNIVERSITY OF TORONTO QUARTERLY (1955); Seymour Gross, "A Further Note on the Function of the Frame in 'Heart of Darkness,'" MODERN FICTION STUDIES (1957); and Marion B. Brady, "Conrad's Whited Sepulcher," COLLEGE ENGLISH (1962), all abstracted in the present bibliography.]

1929 Bojarski, Edmund A. "Joseph Conrad: Original Ugliness," POLISH AMERICAN STUDIES, XXIII (Jan-June 1966), 8-11.

JC's first love, Tekla Wojakowska (née Syroczynska), tells in a letter written three years after JC's death of her first acquaintance with him. The letter contains some inaccuracies (e.g., JC saw Tekla often for thirteen months, not eight, between Jan 1868-Feb 1869). Tekla comments on JC's desire to become a seaman and on his unhappiness at the gymnasium at Cracow. [The physical description of JC is the basis for the title: "His ugliness was original and complete."]

1930 Buckley, Jerome Hamilton. THE TRIUMPH OF TIME: A STUDY OF THE VICTORIAN CONCEPTS OF TIME, HISTORY, PROGRESS, AND DECADENCE (Cambridge, Mass: Harvard U P, 1966), pp. 13, 59, 67, 151, 178.

In much of his early work, especially in "Heart of Darkness" and *Nostromo*, JC was concerned with "the moral ambiguities of a progress linked to self-interest and the imperialistic exploitation of uncivilized peoples." "Progress," for him, is an enterprise in which the victims do not matter, like the attitude of Travers in *The Rescue;* and JC and other such men came to think of progress with "profound distrust." Many alert Victorians would have understood JC's lament that "if you believe in improvement you must weep," and his perception of a doomed humanity is closely related to the idea of decadence.

> **1931** Busza, Andrezej. CONRAD'S POLISH LITERARY BACKGROUND AND SOME ILLUSTRATIONS OF THE INFLUENCE OF POLISH LITERATURE ON HIS WORK (Rome and Lond: Institutum Historicum Polonicum/Societas Polonica Scientiarum et Litterarum in Exteris, 1966), pp. 109-255 [separately bound monograph].

Apollo Korzeniowski, JC's father, is noteworthy for the early and pervasive effect of his "intensely patriotic literary efforts." JC's father was not just a gentleman inclined to literary pursuits, but rather "an important literary figure in his own time." Apollo probably did not influence JC's writing directly, for no one knows how much of his father's writing JC read. However, Apollo imbued his son with his own Polish patriotism and acquainted JC early with literature and creative writing. This is supported by JC's disinclination toward all things Russian and his early determination, based on *A Personal Record,* to "become a great writer."

JC's uncle, Tadeusz Bobrowski, had a realist influence on JC as opposed to the romantic influence of Apollo; Bobrowski's urging JC to learn English, refine his Polish, write travel essays for Polish newspapers; and JC's borrowing from Bobrowski's MEMOIRS. One of the effects of being subjected to both realistic and romantic influences was JC's "unwillingness to make literary capital of his Polish experiences." However, "things Polish" are an important latent element in JC's work. Polish literature had some influence on JC. "Karain" uses the plot of a ballad by Mickiewicz and includes echoes of DZIEJE GRZECHU (The History of a Sin) by Stefan Zromksi. "Amy Foster" is much like popular Polish fiction at the time, and "Prince Roman" is reminiscent of Polish romantic literature. It "is unlikely that his borrowings were often deliberate"; they were "probably unconscious reminiscences of reading." Zdzisław Najder's theory that JC's claim that he had been educated at St. Anne's was spurious is in error.

> **1932** Crämer, Tordis. "Der Stil im Frühwerk Joseph Conrads" (Style in Joseph Conrad's Early Work). Unpublished thesis, Hamburg University, 1966. [In German.]

> **1933** DeLaura, David J. "Echoes of Butler, Browning, Conrad, and Pater in the Poetry of T. S. Eliot," ENGLISH LANGUAGE NOTES, III (March 1966), 211-21.

Although T. S. Eliot's interest in JC's tales has been demonstrated frequently, it appears that no one has detected a group of three "consciously depressing" descriptions of empty streets in "On the Pavement," (*Chance,* part I, chapter 7), which may have "influenced" Eliot in writing about the streaming "dead" crowd in THE WASTE LAND, in composing such scenes as the passage about the "thousand sordid images" of "Preludes," and in describing the empty streets of London in "Burnt Norton." [The quotations in this article clearly indicate the close parallels suggested by the author.]

1934 Donoghue, Denis. "Conrad's Facts," NEW STATESMAN, LXXXII (26 Aug 1966), 291.

The first merit of Mr. Sherry's "excellent book is that on many issues it puts an end to speculation." JC did not take pains to "get his facts right"; but contrary to Norman Sherry [CONRAD'S EASTERN WORLD (1966)], JC "was unable to trust them, right or wrong." *Chance* was "grossly overwritten" because JC "thought the facts were not enough." There are many stories in which JC "does not commit himself to action [the vehicle of facts in other stories]: in which the meaning is largely a matter of metaphysical assertions, comment, critique, the narrator's essays, verbal hubbub."

1935 Donoghue, Denis. "Magic Defeated," NEW YORK REVIEW OF BOOKS, 17 Nov 1966, pp. 22-25.

Rebecca West's novel, THE BIRDS FALL DOWN, is "a Conradian novel in the sense that Conrad is the only writer who could have written it." It says interesting things, but "it badly needs Conrad to make it a novel." As in JC's works, an impression of determinism hangs over the book, but JC is needed to relate idea to action convincingly and to strengthen the dramatic sense. "To think of *Under Western Eyes* and *The Secret Agent* is to see that what Miss West lacks is the power of invention, the narrative and dramatic gift."

1936 Eigner, Edwin M. ROBERT LOUIS STEVENSON AND ROMANTIC TRADITION (Princeton, NJ: Princeton U P, 1966), pp. 6, 14, 20, 33, 76, 142, 143n, 144, 216-17, 229, 239-43.

Stevenson influenced the use of uninvolved or seemingly uninvolved narrators like JC's Marlow. "The Beach of Falesá" has been suggested as a source of "Heart of Darkness," and the savagery in THE EBB-TIDE is closer to Kurtz's darkness than to anything in "The Beach of Falesá." Stevenson's greatest contribution to JC was psychological: *Under Western Eyes,* a tale of double identity, is Stevensonian in theme, as is Axel Heyst reminiscent of Stevenson's unfortunate Will o' the Mill. Also, JC's conception of the violent, hollow man, like Kurtz, may have been derived from THE MASTER OF BALLANTRAE. Unlike the protagonists of THE EBB-TIDE, the narrator-hero in JC's "The Secret Sharer" and in "Heart of Darkness" is able, momentarily, to accept his double with all his savagery. On the other hand, Charles Darnaway of "The Merry Men" draws back from

Marlow's identical vision, expressed in the same words, "the horror—the horror," and piously rejects his uncle as an enemy of God.

1937 Galsworthy, John. "Deux lettres inédites de J. Galsworthy à André Chevrillon" (Two Letters Written by J. Galsworthy to André Chevrillon), ÉTUDES ANGLAISES, XIX (Oct-Dec 1966), 404-6.

"Conrad's death was a great grief to us. I have been looking through his letters. Two hundred and fifty of them. He was so affectionate. I wish, indeed, you had known him. He liked the French, you know, from his youth. He respected *them* and shared your feeling about the people of 'God's own Country.' " "A great artist, and a great friend!" [In French.]

1938 Gillon, Adam. "Cosmopolitanism in Conrad's Work," PROCEEDINGS OF THE IVTH CONGRESS OF THE INTERNATIONAL COMPARATIVE LITERATURE ASSOCIATION. Two Volumes (Fribourg, 1964), ed by François Jost (The Hague: Mouton, 1966), I, 94-99.

Ironically, JC's cosmopolitanism stems from his Polish background: he had no opportunity to develop a sentimental attachment for any part of his native country, his dreams of a seafaring career were unreconcilable with the ideals of Polish patriotism and could not be realized in his own land, and as a child he was lonely and discontented. As a novelist, JC was a "civilized, ironic commentator on mankind" whose protagonists are of many nationalities and races and whose heroes and villains are bound by no national boundaries. JC's vision of man, his "world," is that of "the universal values of fidelity, courage, perseverance in the face of adversity, above all, the virtue of human solidarity." His many international locales represent microcosms which foreshadow the "universal human condition" with its "divided human soul" and man's search for ideal values. His art is a humanism in which man, despite all his absurdity and isolation, has a "profound affinity" for man—"a brotherhood that goes beyond economic, political, national, social or racial differences."

1939 Gillon, Adam. "Some Polish Literary Motifs in the Works of Joseph Conrad," SLAVIC AND EAST EUROPEAN JOURNAL, X (Winter 1966), 424-39.

JC shunned Poland as the central theme in his works, unlike writers such as Mickiewicz and Sowacki (only *A Personal Record* and "Prince Roman" deal directly with Polish themes). Roman, one of the few to triumph over his predicament, alone in all of JC's fiction speaks openly of Poland's troubles. Yanko Gooral ("Amy Foster") resembles Sienkiewicz's depiction of the Polish émigrés who seek a better life. From the Polish-Ukrainian school of early Romantics, JC was influenced by the "concepts of fidelity and honor, and the association of great spaces with great silences" (cf. Mickiewicz's STEPY AKERMANSKIE, Sowacki's LAMBRO, and Malczewski's MARIA.) Other Polish themes are moral transformations; destruction of the soul by evil external forces (cf. Mickiewicz's KONRAD WALLENROD); the sense of individual mission, self-sacrifice, and dreams of leadership; battles against destiny; and the conflict between despair and hope. JC's romantic heroes differ from those of Mickiewicz, Sowacki, and Krasiński because JC differentiates between illusion and reality. [In this revealing and compact study, Gillon illustrates JC's indebtedness by citing several passages from the Polish; but he fails to remind the reader that many of the Polish themes are also common elsewhere.]

> **1940** Gordan, John D. "Lord Jim's Line," TIMES LITERARY SUPPLEMENT (Lond), 15 Dec 1966, p. 1175.

In Jerry Allen's article "Conrad's River," COLUMBIA UNIVERSITY FORUM, V (Winter 1962), 29-35, she had noted Gordan's finding the first "accurate facts" about the Almayer known to JC, but in her TLS letter "even this vague admission is conspicuously lacking." Gordan's JOSEPH CONRAD: THE MAKING OF A NOVELIST (1940) has "much of interest . . . that has been underestimated or disregarded by Miss Allen and Dr. Sherry." [For the origin of the controversy in 1923, see references listed under "The History of Mr. Conrad's Books," TLS, 30 Aug 1923, p. 670; for the controversy revived in 1966, see references listed under "Lord Jim's Line," TLS, 3 Nov 1966, pp. 993-94.]

> **1941** Hanson, Paul Edward. "Character Motivation in the Novels of Joseph Conrad," DISSERTATION ABSTRACTS, XXVI (1966), 3953. Unpublished thesis, New York University, 1964.

> **1942** Hoffman, Frederick J. "The Religious Crisis in Modern Literature," COMPARATIVE LITERATURE STUDIES, III (Oct 1966), 263-72.

In modern literature, the serious writer must, in most instances, confront the problem of re-creating God as best he can. This necessity involves a consideration of how the eternal can be made real and how some kind of Incarnation will allow the particular to converge upon the universal. In *The Secret Agent,* JC, according to J. Hillis Miller in POETS OF REALITY (1965), makes Stevie Verloc's "mad art" of drawing "inane circles and spirals" represent the "inconceivable, . . . a swarming multiplicity of identical forms which cancel one another out and yet by this mutual destruction leave the same chaos, unchanged and eternal." In this world, JC thus finds no God and no purpose; he sees "only darkness, fatness, conspiracies, anti-conspiracies, and violent destruction." Like other British writers, he approaches an Incarnation only by making a negative gesture.

1943 Holland, Norman N. "Style as Character: *The Secret Agent*," MODERN FICTION STUDIES, XII (Summer 1966), 221-31.

By means of a psychological concept of style, *The Secret Agent* can be seen to have as an "informing principle" the unsuspected, "a sense throughout the book that each character has a doubleness or a tripleness, a secret self": Verloc, for example, has been designated a triangle, one side of which is the anarchist, one the bourgeois family man dealing in pornography, and a third the protector of property and servant of embassies. Also, the characters bisect and trisect one another, each touching only a part of the others in such a manner that the novel "fairly bristles with geometric images" as if JC were attempting to form some sort of order out of the chaos, which is denoted first by Stevie's circles. Key images in the novel are light and dark; and London, which serves as "inner madness rendered as outer setting," is in the deepest sense "the engulfing sea or maze of irrationality." Among other things, *Agent* is a study in sloth. Stevie's circles suggest the "chaos and eternity" he and the anarchists find in human relationships, and opposed to this moral and emotional anarchy are the police and the other forces of government. The theme of the novel is thus anarchy "masked over" by control or indolence; the "secret agent" in human affairs is the "potential" for violence in all people, including JC himself. Since JC seems to be preoccupied in general with the dualism of controller and controlled, *Agent* deals with the control of the impulse to sink into the "swamp or sea" of "madness or despair" depicted in it; but JC's dry, ironic style, his shifting of focus from one character to another, and his flashbacks extricate and distance the reader from "that tempting sea." Thus "drive and defense, content and form," unite as the style and theme of the whole work, thereby making the style "Conradian" indeed. This style performs the moral function of literature, "to bring back to light . . . a character and style of life buried in our own dark, anarchic past."

1944 Hudspeth, Robert N. "Conrad's Use of Time in *Chance*," NINETEENTH-CENTURY FICTION, XXI (Dec 1966), 283-89.

Chance has seven different time levels in seven characters; Marlow the "central intelligence" unifies the time levels. JC uses past time not as a basis from which to evaluate future time, but as a body of detached events constantly demanding their own reconsideration. Marlow maintains a distance from the confusing past time, yet bridges the past with a current sympathy.

1945 Jacobs, Robert Glenn. "Psychology, Setting and Impressionism in the Major Novels of Joseph Conrad," DISSERTATION ABSTRACTS, XXVI (1966), 6022. Unpublished thesis, University of Iowa, 1965.

1946 Kaplan, Harold. "Character as Reality: Joseph Conrad," THE PASSIVE VOICE: AN APPROACH TO MODERN FICTION (Athens: Ohio U P, 1966), pp. 131-57, 17, 21, 162, 208-9.

"Heart of Darkness," which is central to an understanding of JC's works, establishes the concept that human values can depend only upon themselves; but when a man reaches ultimate reality, as Kurtz did, a choice remains: one can either yield or choose loyalty. Marlow is necessary in this story because he "plays the crucial role of consciousness in a field of action which resists meaning": he finds out what Kurtz has learned and thereby comes to know himself. The darkness which he confronts is a metaphysical and moral incoherence, a darkness which Heyst and Lena in *Victory* try to avoid by means of a "shared habitation" in the indifferent universe. In a world deserted by metaphysical meaning, a moral meaning takes its place, and faith is a substitute for knowledge. In JC's world, reality, "the mutual need of men huddling together in the universe, is the moral fact which is the basis for the intelligible structure of life." *Lord Jim* is JC's clearest effort to relate a kind of metaphysical reassurance with the achievement of moral character. He returns to an essentially classic definition of character as opposed to nature rather than a part of it; and for him nature represents a darkness in which consciousness and purpose are lost. The theme of the novel is man's struggle for his coherent existence in opposition to an essentially incoherent order in nature. Jim's final success in Patusan consists of his accepting death and judgment from Doramin and thereby proving that in the face of all denials he is able to remain faithful to the idea of himself and to the people for whose good opinion he has lived. His sacrifice is a pure act of will, because nature cannot be affected by moral questions. The conclusion of Jim's final act is that a man cannot run away from the commitment which is his character. There is no reality other than character, which has a profoundly moral base; nothing exists other than what we do ourselves, or have had done for us by our human ancestors. [A clear and logically developed statement of JC's conception of reality.]

1947 Kirschner, Paul. "Conrad and Maupassant: Moral Solitude and 'A Smile of Fortune,'" REVIEW OF ENGLISH LITERATURE (Leeds), VII (July 1966), 67-77.

Maupassant had considerable influence on JC's concept of human nature; JC's characters experience acute isolation, a distinction they share with Maupassant's characters. Alice in "A Smile of Fortune" is an "uneasy hybrid" of JC's autobiography and Maupassant's Francesca in LES SOEURS RONDOLI.

1948 Kramer, Dale. "Marlow, Myth, and Structure in *Lord Jim*," CRITICISM, VIII (Summer 1966), 263-79.

In *Lord Jim,* Marlow's early recognition of Jim's egoism prepares us for Jim's destruction. Both men, though essentially romantics, adhere to mutually contradictory codes of ethics. Marlow defends a code of ego-abnegation based on a fixed standard of conduct. Jim, who desires approval, defines himself as the only standard of behavior.

Two primary episodes continue the dichotomy in codes of ethics. In the *Patna* episode, Marlow attempts to verbalize the significance of Jim's act; the act is a static myth. In the Patusan episode, however, the myth is active. Marlow suggests that Jim's river journey "goes into the self." In describing Jim's increased social importance in Patusan, Marlow cannot help noticing that there is little change in Jim himself; he is still the boyish romanticizer. Though on taking leave of Patusan, Marlow seems pleased with Jim's success, he leaves us with the tentative view of Jim standing "at the heart of a vast enigma."

Brown exploits what Marlow acknowledges in Jim. The "enigma" came for Marlow because he could not understand Jim's romantic egoism. When Brown meets Jim, he flays his self-justification and self-centeredness. Jim's destruction is retribution for his egotistic, "cavalier attitude toward the community." His death concludes his concept of self-idealization. Marlow's conclusion is that Jim fought "a personal enemy, not a signifying enemy." Though Jim does "to the tragic element submit" (himself), he ignores the larger knowledge of group wisdom, a knowledge Marlow has.

1949 Long, Robert Emmet. "THE GREAT GATSBY and the Tradition of Joseph Conrad, Part I," TEXAS STUDIES IN LITERATURE AND LANGUAGE, VIII (Summer 1966), 257-76.

References to JC in Fitzgerald's letters are particularly frequent during the period in which THE GREAT GATSBY was written. The craftsmanship in THE GREAT GATSBY is related to Fitzgerald's developing adherence to JC's aesthetic ideas. The affinity between the plot and theme of *Almayer's Folly* and THE GREAT GATSBY is striking; Gatsby's and Almayer's "futuristic dreams are even described with the same vocabulary, both heroes' illusions are embodied in their houses." In *Lord Jim,* there is a second parallel. The careers of Jim and Gatsby are Icarian. Their flight towards the ideal was foredoomed "by the human limitations their imaginations could not accept." [For part II, see ibid. (Fall 1966), 407-22.]

1950 Long, Robert Emmet. "THE GREAT GATSBY and the Tradition of Joseph Conrad, Part II," TEXAS STUDIES IN LITERATURE AND LANGUAGE, VIII (Fall 1966), 407-22.

The two themes of "Heart of Darkness" and THE GREAT GATSBY are the drama of "a spiritually alienated hero" and the exposure of a society which caused his alienation. In describing a confused society, JC uses broad, striking images; Fitzgerald uses less obtrusive, visual images. Both create an unreal real world. There is a "dream sensation" about Kurtz's life in the Congo and Gatsby's life at West Egg. There is a similarity in the narrator-hero relationship in the two works. Both narrators disapprove of the heroes and are forced to compromise themselves: Carraway has an affair with Jordan Baker; Marlow lies to Kurtz's Intended. At the conclusion of the works, both narrators are left as spokesmen for the heroes. The career of Kurtz and Gatsby condemns inadequate societies. Both heroes loom larger than the shabby members of society. Fitzgerald consciously adapted from JC's works in structuring THE GREAT GATSBY. *Almayer's Folly* sets up "a framework for an illusionist hero." *Lord Jim* contributes an emphasis on the past in order "to reinstate a Platonic identity." "Heart of Darkness" adds a social reference and theme. [Part I, ibid. (Summer 1966), 257-76. Long, thought-provoking comparison between these authors' works.]

1951 "Lord Jim's Line," TIMES LITERARY SUPPLEMENT (Lond), 3 Nov 1966, pp. 993-94.

In a letter to TLS, 6 Sept 1923, p. 588, Sir Frank Swettenham identified the desertion by captain and crew of the pilgrim ship *Jeddah* with Jim's desertion of the *Patna* in *Lord Jim*. Only recently has anyone taken Swettenham seriously, but his account was "the beginning of a scent" followed by Jerry Allen in THE SEA YEARS OF JOSEPH CONRAD (1965) and in Norman Sherry's CONRAD'S EASTERN WORLD (1966). Both established that JC drew to some extent for Jim on his knowledge of the chief officer of the *Jeddah*, A. P. Williams. Allen's book follows her earlier biography of JC, THE THUNDER AND THE SUNSHINE (1958), but Sherry's is "of an altogether more academic nature." In spite of Sherry's admirable industry in showing in what measure JC's fiction is based on personal experience, he tends to lose JC the writer in the process. Allen allows JC (in *The Shadow-Line,* for instance) to exist in his own right as a creative artist. As far as Jim is concerned, we know that Williams's way was not Jim's in the novel. Then the matter of a prototype for Lord Jim on Patusan arises: Sherry finds only an "amalgam" of the Lingard uncle and nephew and Rajah Brooke whereas Allen accepts, as others have done, Jim Lingard as Jim's "continuation," plus "a dash of Brooke and Uncle William." Both critics agree upon Berau as the site of *Almayer's Folly*. Such research, however interesting it may be, finally reveals the "essential deadness" of this kind of "literary goose chase," and neither account adds nor detracts from the character of Jim in JC's novel. Allen does more than Sherry: in a "general biographical way" she examines all the seafaring backgrounds that JC used. But since neither Sherry nor Allen appreciably examines the artist's creative process, the value of these books may be to aid future biographers to look more closely at JC; and for this purpose Allen is the more successful. [For the origin of the controversy in 1923, see references listed under "The History of Mr. Conrad's Books," TLS, 30 Aug 1923, p. 670; for the controversy initiated by the present review of the Allen and Sherry books, see the following, all in TLS and all letters to the editor under title "Lord Jim's Line": Jerry Allen, 10 Nov 1966, p. 1032; F. T. Prince, 10 Nov 1966, p. 1032; A. Van Marle, 8 Dec 1966, p. 1149; Michael Thorpe, 15 Dec 1966, p. 1175; Jerry Allen, 15 Dec 1966, p. 1175; John D. Gordan, 15 Dec 1966, p. 1175; and A. Van Marle, 12 Jan 1967, p. 32. The controversy often descends to mere bickering over trivia, and some personal vituperation. On the whole, Miss Allen seems to have the worst of it at the hands of other JC scholars.]

1952 Lyngstad, Sverre. "Time in the Modern British Novel: Conrad, Woolf, Joyce, and Huxley," DISSERTATION ABSRACTS, XXVII (Nov 1966), 1374A-1375A. Unpublished thesis, New York University, 1960.

1953 Madden, William A. "The Search for Forgiveness in Some Nineteenth-Century English Novels," COMPARATIVE LITERATURE STUDIES (University of Maryland), III (1966), 139-53; espec 149-51.

With JC and Thomas Hardy, the nineteenth-century search for forgiveness concludes despairingly. Their novels focus upon individual consciousness from which implications of cosmic meaning may be adduced. In *Lord Jim,* the hero alone, "a puzzled Ancient Mariner," is unable to rationalize his sense of guilt. Jim's self-sacrificing attempts to settle the question of whether or not he is actually guilty. In Jim's mind his leap into Patusan was to expiate the guilt of his leap from the *Patna*. In reality, the second leap was more destructive. Jewel finds it impossible to forgive him; Marlow can give her but small reason to do so—"We all need to be forgiven." Jim, an incurable romantic, could neither ignore the problem of guilt nor accept forgiveness from his fellowman. In *Jim,* JC anticipates Kafka's twentieth-century paradox: "The state in which we find ourselves is sinful, quite independent of guilt."

1954 Mizener, Arthur. "Joseph Conrad: 'Heart of Darkness,'" A HANDBOOK OF ANALYSES, QUESTIONS, AND A DISCUSSION OF TECHNIQUE. . . . [For use with MODERN SHORT STORIES: THE USES OF IMAGINATION]; rvd ed (NY: Norton, 1966), pp. 1-9.

"Heart of Darkness" is perhaps the greatest of all the stories written by the greatest twentieth-century romantics. JC's central conception of human experience "is that there is an organic relation between the outward, objective experience of men and their inner subjective life . . ."; man to save himself must seek the "support of the civilization that surrounds him." This image of the world is supported by all facets of JC's art. Marlow is a self-revealing and world-discovering narrator; England and the Congo are related images of the "heart of darkness"; primitive savagery is no worse than civilized inefficiency. True civilization is difficult to achieve in the face of "complacent greed." Marlow's faith in civilization is severely tested in the Congo as he sees civilization at its worst and feels the powerful pull of the mysterious jungle. Kurtz, Kurtz's Intended, and the native girl dramatize the struggle between different aspects of savagery and of civilization. [Also see Mizener, ibid. (1962).]

1955 Mudrick, Marvin (ed). CONRAD: A COLLECTION OF CRITICAL ESSAYS (Englewood Cliffs, NJ: Prentice-Hall, Spectrum Books, 1966).

Contents, abstracted under year of first publication: Marvin Mudrick, "Introduction" (1966); Max Beerbohm, "The Feast," from A CHRISTMAS GARLAND (1912, 1950); Albert Guerard, "On *The Nigger of the Narcissus*," from CONRAD THE NOVELIST (1958); Marvin Mudrick, "The Originality of Conrad," from HUDSON REVIEW (1958); Stephen A. Reid, "The 'Unspeakable Rites' in 'Heart of Darkness,'" from MODERN FICTION STUDIES (1963); Douglas Hewitt, "*Lord Jim:* Conrad and the 'Few Simple Notions,'" from CONRAD: A REASSESSMENT (1952); Paul L. Wiley, "Conrad's Solitaries," from CONRAD'S MEASURE OF MAN (1954); Daniel Curley, "Legate of the Ideal," from CONRAD'S "SECRET SHARER" AND THE CRITICS, ed by Bruce Harkness (1962); Jocelyn Baines, "*Nostromo:* Politics, Fiction, and the Uneasy Expatriate," from JOSEPH CONRAD: A CRITICAL BIOGRAPHY (1959, 1960); E. M. W. Tillyard, "*The Secret Agent* Reconsidered," from ESSAYS IN CRITICISM (1961); Morton Dauwen Zabel, "Introduction to *Under Western Eyes*," from *Under Western Eyes* (NY: Doubleday, Anchor Books, 1963); Thomas Moser, "Conrad's Later 'Affirmation,'" from JOSEPH CONRAD: ACHIEVEMENT AND DECLINE (1957); Ford Madox Ford, "Conrad on the Theory of Fiction," from JOSEPH CONRAD: A PERSONAL REMEMBRANCE (1924); a "Chronology of Important Dates" and a "Selected Bibliography." [The "Selected Bibliography" is practically worthless; most excerpts and articles are readily accessible; a dated and "weary" assemblage of comments on JC.]

1956 Mudrick, Marvin. "Introduction," CONRAD: A COLLECTION OF CRITICAL ESSAYS, ed by Marvin Mudrick (Englewood Cliffs, NJ: Prentice-Hall, Spectrum Books, 1966), pp. 1-11.

JC wrote his "great and unprecedented works" within a period of six years, 1896 to 1902; JC is a puzzle for both the critic and biographer; what is called "the primary fact about Conrad criticism" is "the insensitivity with which it has performed its task of discrimination among the tales and novels of the most uneven of fiction-writers in English." [Commonplace truisms.]

1957 Newhouse, Neville H. JOSEPH CONRAD (Lond: Evans Brothers, 1966); rptd (NY: Arco, 1969).

A common theme in JC's works is the concept that "a man is what his life has made him, rather than the captain of his fate and master of his soul." Since man is "the illusion of a dream," JC's characters, when they realize their loneliness, often struggle to maintain their integrity and their basic dignity as human beings. When his perspective broadened to include whole societies, as in *Nostromo,* the theme became the difficulties and dangers which harass men who pursue political and economic ends. In his later books new themes appeared: salvation through devotion to a person and the exercise of compassion, like Razumov in *Under Western Eyes,* Heyst in *Victory,* and Peyrol in *The Rover.* In addition to his themes, JC's techniques are notable: many of his plots are melodramatic and he tends toward theatrical exaggeration, his "rendering" of character in action fails to produce fully rounded persons, his main characters are generally blurred because he refrains from making completely clear judgments, in some instances Marlow helps to reflect the fact that external appearance is not full reality, the breaking of the normal time-sequence is an effective method of conditioning the reader's attitude to the novels, JC's vigorously idiomatic dialogue suggests conflicting points of view in his characters and reveals the basic moral issues in his works, and his use of symbolism is often very effective. Dealing with man in society produces some of JC's best compositions: in *Nostromo,* both theme and treatment are fully united; as a work of art *The Secret Agent* presents a grim picture of a world completely devoted to the worship of materialistic values; and *Eyes* and *Victory* have heroes who try to avoid involvement with others, fail to do so, and thereby learn to exercise compassion. JC's attempts to explore the depths and uncertainties of life which he could not fully understand often led him to verbosity and to the over-elaboration of an already elaborate technique, but his "extraordinarily vivid art" is a search for greater awareness. [Intended as a brief introduction to JC and his works, this small book is extremely perceptive, and the author's analyses of many of JC's works are original and convincing. Its greatest weakness is that a tyro in the study of JC could not recognize that real value of the new contributions.]

1958 O'Leary, Sister Jeanine. "The Function of City as Setting in Dickens' OUR MUTUAL FRIEND, Trollope's THE WAY WE LIVE NOW, James' THE PRINCESS CASAMASSIMA, and Conrad's *The Secret Agent,*" DISSERTATION ABSTRACTS, XXVI (1966), 6048-49. Unpublished thesis, University of Notre Dame, 1966.

1959 Parrill, Anna Sue. "The Theme of Revolution in the English Novel from Disraeli to Conrad," DISSERTATION ABSTRACTS, XXVI (1966), 4669. Unpublished thesis, University of Tennessee, 1965.

1960 Pendexter, Hugh, III. "Techniques of Suspense in Conrad," CEA CRITIC, XXVIII (Feb 1966), 9-11.

In *The Rescue,* JC may appear to be telling a mere adventure tale. He uses traditional suspense devices such as suggesting unknown peril by treating Lingard's relationship with the natives mysteriously and foreshadowing disaster by introducing Jorgenson, who prefigures Lingard. However, JC succeeds in directing the reader's attention away from the plot to the characters and their internal struggles. He plays down the suspenseful scenes in the plot. For instance, he does not relate the tense scene which precedes the explosion of Emma. Instead, he focuses on the character's recollection of that event rather than the explosion itself. The reader never has to await the outcome of the plot; he waits for the resolution of the effects of the happenings on the characters.

1961 Prince, F. T. "Lord Jim's Line," TIMES LITERARY SUPPLEMENT (Lond), 10 Nov 1966, p. 1032.

Has any critic or researcher even connected the character of Kurtz in "Heart of Darkness" with what JC may have "known and thought of Roger Casement?" [For the origin of the controversy in 1923, see references listed under "The History of Mr. Conrad's Books," TLS, 30 Aug 1923, p. 670; for the controversy revived in 1966, see references listed under "Lord Jim's Line," TLS, 3 Nov 1966, pp. 993-94.]

1962 "The Re-baring of 'The Secret Sharer': Leg Pull?" COLLEGE ENGLISH, XXVII (March 1966), 504-5.

[Readers respond to Bruce Harkness's pseudo-serious article, "The Secret of 'The Secret Sharer' Bared," COLLEGE ENGLISH, XXVII (Oct 1965), 55-61.]

1963 Reinecke, George F. "Conrad's *Victory:* Psychomachy, Christian Symbols, and Theme," EXPLORATIONS OF LITERATURE, ed by Rima Drell Reck (Baton Rouge: Louisiana State U P, 1966), pp. 70-80.

[In a discussion designed as a reply to certain points made by Albert J. Guerard, the author presents an analysis of the systematic symbolism in the structure of *Victory,* also offering some very illuminating comments on JC's meaning in his choice of names for his characters.]

1964 Rose, Alan Manuel. "Joseph Conrad and the Eighteen Nineties," DISSERTATION ABSTRACTS, XXVII (1966), 485A. Unpublished thesis, Columbia University, 1965.

1965 Schneider, Daniel J. "Symbolism in Conrad's *Lord Jim:* The Total Pattern," MODERN FICTION STUDIES, XII (Winter 1966-67), 427-38.

In *Lord Jim,* the central conflict is that between dream and reality, and from this conflict the symbolism arises. JC deals with the paradox that "the real is unreal and dead, whereas the unreal is alone real and alive." One large family of contrasting symbols is that of heights and depressions: from his "lofty ideality" Jim jumps into an "everlasting deep hole." Another major group of symbols points the contrast between animality and spirituality: there is the irony in the division between "Lord" and "Jim," and Stein's collection of beetles and butterflies symbolizes man's real difficulty in remaining romantic—that is, human. Color is the central device for a third family of contrasting symbols: Jim's leap from the *Patna* is a leap into the heart of darkness, gaudy and violent colors are strongly associated with jungle animality, and yellow indicates cowardice. Finally, the contrast between straightness and crookedness also derives from the antithesis between dream and reality: Jim bends or wavers, follows a crooked or uneven course, when, untrue to his dream, he departs from the "fixed" path by jumping from the *Patna;* and several fat people in the novel represent not the straight, permanent, flawless dream but crooked, impermanent reality. This "basic pattern" of JC's symbolism in *Jim* should permit other critics to apply "external schemes," alternative symbolic readings, to the novel. [Too pretentious in claiming to have found "*the* (italics added) total pattern of the symbolism" in *Jim.*]

1966 Scrimgeour, Gary J. "Against THE GREAT GATSBY," CRITICISM, VIII (Winter 1966), 75-86.

THE GREAT GATSBY and "Heart of Darkness" similarly have a first-person narration in an adventure-story tale. Both narrators encounter the heroes by chance and are "unwittingly intrigued" by them. Marlow is "a man who cannot deny reality" while Carraway is "a man who cannot face it." A close comparison of Marlow and Carraway suggests the superiority of "Heart of Darkness" and the sentimentality of THE GREAT GATSBY.

1967 Sherry, Norman. CONRAD'S EASTERN WORLD (Cambridge: Cambridge U P, 1966); based on unpublished thesis, University of Singapore, 1963.

Between the years 1883 and 1888, JC, a British merchant seaman, sailed for a time in Eastern waters; and the influences of his experiences there appear in many of his works: from *Almayer's Folly* (1895) through "Youth" and "The End of the Tether" (1902) and "The Secret Sharer" (1912) to the later novels, *Victory* (1915), *The Shadow-Line* (1917), and *The Rescue* (1920), as well as in several other works of these years. An examination of JC's source materials reveals how the writer "brought out the deeper significance of the original," what changes he considered necessary, what "leading motives" arose from his reflections upon the source material, and how "his creative intelligence went to work."

Illustrative examples of JC's use of his sources appear in many instances. The first part of *Lord Jim,* for example, is based on the case of the pilgrim ship, *Jeddah.* JC found his inspiration for Jim in Augustine Podmore Williams who, like Jim, was the last officer to leave the *Jeddah.* Then, too, Captain Tom Lingard, the "Rajah-Laut," who plays a progressively important role in *Folly, An Outcast of the Islands,* and *Rescue,* was apparently based on William Lingard's life as a trader in the East. As for settings, an Eastern river, with a native settlement and a European trading post on its banks, provides the scenes for *Folly, Outcast,* and the second part of *Jim;* the fictional river is based on JC's limited knowledge of the river Berau in Dutch East Borneo, and in the second part of *Jim,* JC's source for Jim changed from A. P. Williams to Jim Lingard, about whom JC knew very little. In addition to using Malayan people and Malayan settings in his works, JC also used several "dull, wise books"; for example, Wallace's THE MALAY ARCHIPELAGO, a favorite source, supplied materials for the character of Stein; and McNair's PERAK AND THE MALAYS provided much information for *Jim,* which JC, in his typical manner, blended with information from other sources. And under the guise of "an Eastern port," Singapore affords at least a part of the setting for such works as *Jim, Shadow-Line,* and "The End of the Tether." Captain Henry Ellis, the Master-Attendant at Singapore, who gave JC his first command, remains in the background of some works as a "prime mover": he results in Captain Whalley's friend in "The End of the Tether," in Captain Elliott in *Jim,* and in Ellis in *Shadow-Line. Shadow-Line* contains JC's predecessor on the *Otago,* Captain John Snadden, whose death was surrounded with some mystery; but JC's portrayal of this man is not "exact biography."

In his selection of source material, JC kept in mind two major influences: (1) his conception of the nature of his art, in which we note that he was lacking in inventive faculty and his interest in the importance of truth; and (2) his conception of life's predicaments, his recognition of the curious workings of fate or destiny or chance. [This book, excellent on its subject, reveals many new sources of JC's works; but, more importantly, it clarifies significantly JC's creative process. Many parts of this book were published in various periodicals between 1963 and 1966 and are separately abstracted under dates of first appearance.]

1968 Sims, George. "Copies of Conrad's *Chance,* Dated 1913," BOOK COLLECTOR, XV (Summer 1966), 213-14.
In reply to David Randall's query [ibid., XV (Spring 1966), 68] in regard to the whereabouts of a copy of *Chance* with a 1913 title page, an edition is

listed in Everard Meynell's Catalogue No. 5 (1921), which is inscribed by JC, and corresponds to the description given by Wise in his bibliography of JC.

1969 Stone, Wilfred. THE CAVE AND THE MOUNTAIN: A STUDY OF E. M. FORSTER (Stanford: Stanford U P, 1966), pp. 118, 381.
According to E. M. Forster, JC cannot be prophetic. For Forster, the prophetic author with his "bardic influence" does not necessarily "say" anything about the universe; instead, he sings and "the strangeness of song arising in the halls of fiction is bound to give us a shock," the "sensation of a song or of sound." The prophetic vision is "literature turned to music." JC is not prophetic because Marlow's voice "is too full of experience to sing." But perhaps only JC, Hardy, and—less certainly—Meredith can share with Forster and Lawrence what might be called the "vision of the cave," the "encounter with the chthonic underworld of human experience."

1970 Thorpe, Michael. "Lord Jim's Line," TIMES LITERARY SUPPLEMENT (Lond), 15 Dec 1966, p. 1175.
In reply to F. T. Prince, JC knew Roger Casement and wrote favorably of his "active idealism." [For the origin of the controversy in 1923, see references listed under "The History of Mr. Conrad's Books," TLS, 30 Aug 1923, p. 670; for the controversy revived in 1966, see references listed under "Lord Jim's Line," TLS, 3 Nov 1966, pp. 993-94.]

1971 Turner, Michael L. "Conrad and T. J. Wise," BOOK COLLECTOR, XV (Autumn 1966), 350-51.
JC's dealings with T. J. Wise in the area of privately printed pamphlets and the sale of MS are highlighted in connection with a new acquisition of the Bodleian Library: a notebook of 209 leaves (a quarter of which is in the hand of Miss Hallowes, JC's secretary) giving details of agreements with publishers, payments received for stories and novels, and other business matters.

1972 Van Marle, A. "Lord Jim's Line," TIMES LITERARY SUPPLEMENT (Lond), 8 Dec 1966, p. 1149.
Jerry Allen in "her remarkably swift reaction" to the review of her THE SEA YEARS OF JOSEPH CONRAD (1965), and of Norman Sherry's CONRAD'S EASTERN WORLD (1966), is wrong in positing that a discovery can be made only once and that "various people, independently of each other," had preceded her in identifying Berau as the setting of *Almayer's Folly*. Marle had lectured on JC in Indonesia early in 1961 at the University of Münster, had included several previously unpublished details in NOTES AND QUERIES in 1960, and had begun research in 1959, having thereby discovered independently several facts that Allen had others find for her and which Sherry had found for himself. Allen had acted in a manner which "must

disqualify her as a champion of the protection of research." [For the origin of the controversy in 1923, see references listed under "The History of Mr. Conrad's Books," TLS, 30 Aug 1923, p. 670; for the controversy revived in 1966, see references listed under "Lord Jim's Line," TLS, 3 Nov 1966, pp. 993-94.]

1973 Vidan, Ivo. "Kusnje pripovjedaceve svemoci" (The Temptations of the Narrator's Omnipotence), FORUM (Zagreb), Nos. 3-4 (1966), espec pp. 514-19.

JC's main artistic problem was how to keep the original freshness of his first-hand experience, while at the same time objectifying it, detaching himself from it, and opening it to the reader. The theme resides less in the narrated events than in their subjective interpretation. Marlow's mood oscillates between sarcasm and a moralist's indignation, remaining always this side of pathos and sentimentality, and affecting his audience in a manner which makes it accept different possibilities of meaning. Marlow is incapable of defining and assessing straightforwardly any observation: the metaphorical language of the story has reference to an ambiguous set of values. Even the narrative frame, apparently undramatic and remote from the facts of the story itself depends on Marlow's vision and suggests to the reader an interpretation from Marlow's perspective within the story. The inner center of meaning shifts according to whether Marlow or Kurtz is taken to be the pivot of the story. The story is either about Marlow or about Kurtz—it is an interpreted experience or an experienced set of real circumstances. As Umberto Eco, the theoretician of the poetics of "indeterminability," has put it in a different context, each aspect contains the whole work and reveals it in one of the possible perspectives; center and periphery can exchange their position—which is a feature characteristic of all modern "open" works of art. [In this part of a longer study, ambiguities of Marlow's voice and imagery in "Heart of Darkness" are discussed and compared to Ivo Andrić's procedure in DEVIL'S YARD.] [In Serbo-Croatian.]

1974 Vidan, Ivo. "THE PRINCESS CASAMASSIMA Between Balzac and Conrad," STUDIA ROMANICA ET ANGLICA ZAGRABIENSIA (Zagreb), Nos. 21-22 (1966), 259-76, espec pp. 271-76.

A passage on the first page of *The Secret Agent* seems to be full of ironic echoes from the first paragraph of THE PRINCESS CASAMASSIMA. There is irony also in James's novel, as part of his self-defensive tactics, until the point at which he allows his apprehensions to take over. His humane sympathy softens the absoluteness of his convictions in a permanent interplay with his social ease. JC, on his part, acute and narrow, remains consistent in a savage belligerence. Though both books occasionally have a Dickensian flavor, several situations in *Agent,* particularly in the cab-ride chapter, may be leading more immediately back to passages in James. The analogies in the two stories are fairly numerous, but not all of them are necessarily indications of a literary connection. In order to have significance they ought to color the works as wholes. Thus, the central situation in James's plot is that of a great lady patronizing an anarchist. JC uses the same motif to give a decisive ironic twist to his story, a most representative sample of the method which he applies throughout the book on the levels of both style and story. James's Princess leads to the young heiress in JC's "The Informer," a story dealing not only with the millionaire-anarchist type, but also with the connection between political nihilism and a wholesale cultivation of aesthetic sensibility to which moral consideration is entirely irrelevant—a leading theme in James's THE PORTRAIT OF A LADY.

1975 Walton, James Hackett. "The Background of *The Secret Agent:* A Biographical and Critical Study." Unpublished thesis, Northwestern University, 1966.

1976 Warger, Howard Nicholas. "The Unity of Conrad's *Nostromo:* Irony as Vision and Instrument," DISSERTATION ABSTRACTS, XXVI (1966), 3931. Unpublished thesis, Fordham University, 1965.

1967

1977 Van Marle, A. "Lord Jim's Line," TIMES LITERARY SUPPLEMENT (Lond), 12 Jan 1967, p. 32.
"It is time for Miss [Jerry] Allen either to provide us with the evidence [that her own researches predated those of Van Marle and of Norman Sherry] that is genuinely indisputable or to retract her charge"; she "should put up or shut up." [For the origin of the controversy in 1923, see references listed under Richard Curle, "The History of Mr. Conrad's Books," TLS, 30 Aug 1923, p. 670; for the controversy revived in 1966, see references listed under "Lord Jim's Line," TLS, 3 Nov 1966, pp. 993-94. With the present item, this literary quarrel has apparently reached its conclusion.]

Index

AUTHORS

Included here are authors of articles and books on Conrad, editors and compilers of works in which criticism on Conrad appears. Editors and translators are identified parenthetically: (ed), (trans). Numbers after each name refer to the item(s) in the bibliography where the name occurs.

A., C. E. [Aiken, Conrad?]: 454
A., F. D.: 1235
Abbot, L. F.: 396
Adams, Elbridge Lapham: 397, 576, 669
Adams, J. Donald: 917
Adams, Richard P.: 1660
Adams, Robert M.: 1618
Adelgiem, E.: 900
Affable Hawk: 812
Aiken, Conrad [A., C. E. (?)]: 454
Aksenov, I. A.: 398
Al, F.: 780
Alden, William L.: 31, 35, 36, 37, 49, 66
Aldington, Richard: 455
Aldrich, John W. (ed): 1254
Allen, C. K.: 456
Allen, Jerry: 1452, 1661, 1852, 1925, 1926, 1927
Allen, Walter Ernest: 1295, 1310
Allott, Miriam: 1521
Altick, Richard Daniel: 1212
American Art Association: 781, 1031
Ames, Van Meter: 782
Anderson Galleries, Inc.: 783, 1031
Andreach, Robert J.: 1853
Andreas, Osborn: 1522
Anglin, Norman: 316
Anisimov, I. I. [Also Hagen]: 618
Anthony, Irwin: 940
Arendt, Hannah: 1236
Armstrong, Martin: 399, 457
Arns, Karl: 670, 745
Aronsberg, E.: 458
Aseev, N.: 672

Ashton-Gwatkin, W. H. T.: 673
Atkinson, Brooks: 1112
Atkinson, Mildred: 674
Atteridge, A. H.: 577
Aubry, Georges Jean-: 355, 400, 401, 459, 460, 461, 462, 463, 464, 578, 579, 675, 676, 746, 747, 784, 839, 840, 841, 941, 1149, 1158, 1159; (trans): 896, 1149
Austin, H. P.: 785
Austin, Mary: 842, 942
Aynard, Joseph: 172, 381, 465
B., H. I.: 403
Babb, James T.: 843
Bache, William B.: 1314, 1363
Baines, Jocelyn: 1364, 1365, 1453, 1523
Baird, Donald: 1524
Baker, Ernest A.: 1075; (ed): 943
Ballard, E. G.: 1255
Balvanovic, Vlado: 1568
Bancroft, William Wallace: 918
Bantock, G. H.: 1278, 1454
Banyard, Grace: 1188
Barker, Dudley: 1700
Bartoszewic, Kazimierz: 677
Baskett, Sam S.: 1455
Basner, Peter: 1619
Bass, Eben: 1854
Bates, Herbert Ernest: 1032, 1213, 1620
Batho, Edith C.: 1058
Baum, Paul Franklin: 273
Bayley, John: 1569
Beach, Joseph Warren: 944
Beachroft, T. O.: 1775

Joseph Conrad

Becker, May Lamberton: 1049, 1160
Beebe, Maurice: 1312, 1701, 1776, 1777
Beerbohm, Max: 78, 130
Beker, Miroslav: 1621
Belden, Albert D.: 1237
Bell, Inglis F.: 1524
Bellessort, André: 317
Bendz, Ernst: 274, 403
Bennett, Arnold: 104, 678, 901
Bennett, Carl D.: 1702
Benson, Carl: 1296
Bentley, Eric: 1366
Bentley, Thomas R. (comp): 1928
Berkovic, Josip: 919
Bernard, Kenneth: 1703, 1778
Berryman, John: 1214
Bigongiari, Piero: 1256
Billiar, Donald E.: 1704
Binsse, Harry Lorin: 1145
Björkman, Edwin: 131
Blackburn, William: 1456; (ed): 1456
Blair, Eric [See Orwell, George]
Bluefarb, Sam: 1525
Blunden, Edmund: 748
Blüth, Raphael [also Rafał]: 920
Bobkowski, Andrzej: 1367
Bohneberger, Carl (ed): 844
Bojarski, Edmund A.: 1622, 1662, 1779, 1780, 1781, 1855, 1856, 1929
Bojarski, Henry T.: 1780
Bolander, Louis H.: 945
Bolles, Edwin Courtlandt: 1130
Bone, David: 580, 845
Bone, Muirhead: 466, 467
Booth, Wayne C.: 1623
Borie, Edith: 201
Bork-o, Božidar: 968
Bowen, Elizabeth: 1033
Boyle, Ted Eugene: 1705, 1782, 1857
Boynton, H. W.: 174, 247, 248, 321
Bradbrook, Frank W.: 1458
Bradbrook, M. C.: 1102, 1368
Brady, Emily Kuempel: 1663
Brady, Marion B.: 1664, 1706
Brashear, Jordan L.: 1313
Braudo, E.: 681
Braybrooke, Patrick: 921, 946
Breit, Harvey: 1199, 1279
Brewster, Dorothy: 468, 1297
Brickell, Herschel: 583, 749
Bridges, Horace James: 469, 584
Britten, Lew: 1050
Broch, H. I.: 404, 405, 470
Broderick, Lillian Negueloua: 1783
Bronal, Zdzisław (trans): 1289
Broncel, Zdzisław: 1369
Brotman, Jordan L.: 1314

Brown, A. J. C.: 382
Brown, Bob: 1059
Brown, Dorothy Snodgrass: 1340
Brown, Douglas: 1624
Brown, E. K.: 1145
Bruccoli, Matthew J.: 1625
Bruffee, Kenneth A.: 1784
Bryson, Lyman: 1272, 1287
Buckler, William E. (ed): 1570
Buckley, Jerome Hamilton: 1930
Budnev, V.: 586
Buenzod, Emmanuel: 750, 846
Bullett, Gerald William: 682
Bullis, Helen: 175
Burgess, C. F.: 1707
Burgess, O. N.: 1370
Burkhardt, Johanna: 1003
Burkhart, Charles: 1708
Burrell, Angus: 468
Burt, H. T.: 471
Burt, Struthers: 847
Burton, Dwight L.: 1459
Busza, Andrezej: 1931
By "A Conrad Collector": 357
By An Occasional Contributor: 358
C., C.: 406
C., G.: 848
Cadby, Carine: 472
Cadot, Raoul: 947, 969
Cambon, Glauca: 1341
Canby, Henry Seidel: 383, 849
Capes, M. Harriet M. (comp): 202
Carpenter, Richard C.: 1785
Carroll, Halina (trans): 1821
Carroll, Sydney Wentworth: 408
Carroll, Welsey Barnett: 987, 1315
Casey, Bill: 1526
Cassell, Richard A.: 1626
Cazamian, Madeleine L.: 1316
Cecchi, Emilio: 473, 474
Cecil, David [Lord]: 1004, 1298
Chadbourne, Marc: 581
Chaikin, Milton: 1317
Chamberlain, J.: 1005
Chatterjee, Sisir: 1858
Chevalley, Abel: 359
Chevrillon, André: 475
Chevrillon, Pierre: 788
Chew, Samuel C.: 588
Childs, Mary: 683
Chillag, Charles: 1280
Chubb, Edwin Watts: 684
Church, Richard: 751, 789, 1131
Churchill, R. C.: 1161
Chwalewik, Witold: 1460
Clarke, David Waldo: 1162
Clarke, George Herbert: 384, 385

Index of Authors

Clarke, Joseph I. C.: 322
Clemens, Cyril: 948, 950
Clemens, Florence: 1051, 1076, 1090, 1103
Clifford, Sir Hugh Charles: 47, 71, 79, 476, 752, 790, 850
Cobley, W. D.: 685
Colbron, Grace Isabel: 177, 204
Colby, Elbridge: 409
Coleman, A. P.: 922
Colenutt, Richard: 1034
Colin, Betty (trans): 531
Collins, Harold R.: 1299
Colvin, Sir Sidney: 290, 386
Connolly, Francis: 1318
Connolly, James E.: 477
Connolly, Myles: 478
Conrad, Borys: 1371
Conrad, Jessie (Mrs. Joseph): 480, 481, 482, 592, 593, 686, 687, 754, 755, 851, 852, 902, 903, 923, 924, 950, 1007
Conrad, John: 1372
Constant Reader: 414
Cook, Albert Spaulding: 1461, 1571
Cooper, F. G.: 1091
Cooper, Frederic Taber: 54, 73, 105, 122, 134, 135, 161, 178, 179, 292
Cornelius, Samuel Robert: 1215
Cornish, W. Lorne: 1092
Cox, Roger L.: 1527
Cox, Roger Lindsay: 1627
Cox, Sidney: 904
Crämer, Tordis: 1932
Crane, Stephen: 13, 691
Cranfield, Lionel: 1150
Crankshaw, Edward: 1035, 1163
Croft-Cooke, Rupert: 1628
Cronin, Edward J.: 1257
Cross, Donald C.: 1709, 1859, 1860
Cross, Wilbur Lucius: 361, 692, 791, 905
Crudgington & Company: 323
Cunliffe, John William: 970, 971, 988
Cuppy, Will: 693
Ćurčija-Prodanović, Nada: 1373; (trans): 1373, 1410
Curle, Richard: 108, 136, 137, 180, 205, 415, 416, 485, 486, 596, 597, 686, 694, 695, 792, 793, 794, 853, 906, 907, 951, 989, 1139, 1319, 1374, 1375, 1462, 1528, 1786
Curley, Daniel: 1665
Curran, Edward T.: 123
Cushwa, Frank W.: 972
Cutler, Frances Wentworth: 277, 908
D., E.: 854
D., F. A.: 1238
D., S.: 1529

D., W.: 233, 250
Dabrowski, Jan P.: 1376
Dabrowski, Marian: 181
Daiches, David: 1077, 1463, 1666; (ed): 1666
Dale, James: 1861
Dale, Patricia: 1710
Dataller, Roger [Pseudonym of A. E. Eagleston]: 1093
Davray, Henry D.: 487, 757
David, Maurice: 855
Davidson, Donald: 598, 599
Davies, Hugh Sykes (ed): 1841
Davis, Harold Edmund: 1342, 1343, 1464
Davis, Robert Gorham: 1281, 1530
Dawson, Ernest: 795
Dawson, Warrington: 163
Day, A. Grove: 1258
Day, Robert A.: 1711
Dean, Leonard F.: 1140, 1572, 1573, 1574, 1575, 1577; (ed): 48, 53, 58, 911, 1010, 1299, 1334, 1572, 1573, 1574, 1575, 1576, 1577
De Gruyter, J.: 600
De la Mare, Walter: 208
DeLaura, David J.: 1933
De Ternant, Andrew: 796
Deutsch, Helene: 1862
Diakonov, N.: 1532
Diego, Juan Mateos De (trans): 605
Dierlamm, G.: 856
Dike, Donald A.: 1667
Dinamov, S.: 7, 488, 489, 601, 696, 697, 857
Dobrée, Bonamy: 1058
Dodd, Lee Wilson: 490
Dolch, Martin (ed): 1791, 1792, 1826, 1843
Donoghue, Denis: 1934, 1935
Doran, George Henry: 1008
Doubleday, F. N.: 797
Doubleday, Page and Company: 294, 699
Dowden, Wilfred S.: 1377, 1578, 1863
Downing, Francis: 1259
Drew, Elizabeth: 698, 1712
Droz, Juliette: 278
Duffin, Henry C.: 1378
Douglas, Robin: 858
Dukes, T. Arch.: 798
Dunbar, O. H.: 80
Dyboski, Roman: 1104
Eagleston, A. E. [See Dataller, Roger]
Eastman, Richard M.: 1864
Eaves, T. C. Duncan: 1480
Echeruo, M. J. C.: 1865
Edgar, Pelham: 973

Edgett, Edwin Francis: 164, 182, 209, 210, 234, 251, 295, 296, 325, 417
Egart, M.: 1036
Ehrentreich, Alfred: 1078
Eigner, Edwin M.: 1936
Ekelof, Gunnar: 1200, 1201, 1282
Ellman, Richard (ed): 1556
Ellis, Havelock: 297, 952
Elphinstone, Petronella: 953
Eno, Sara W.: 252
Epstein, Sir Jacob: 1300
Erné, Nino: 1189
Eschbacher, Robert L.: 1713
Estaunié, Edouard: 492, 603
Estelrich, Juan: 604, 605, 606
Estness, Carol: 1795
Evans, C. S.: 387
Evans, Robert O.: 1344, 1379, 1380, 1629
F., G. G.: 326
F., J. H.: 211
F., W. A. [Wilson Follett?]: 212
Fabes, Gilbert Henry: 859, 954
Fairley, Barker: 327
Farmer, Norman, Jr.: 1787
Farrelly, John: 1165
Feder, Lillian: 1320
Feider, V.: 799
Ferguson, J. De Lancy: 607, 1009
Fernández, Ramón: 418, 493, 860
Ficke, Arthur Davison: 166
Field, Louise Maunsell: 329, 362
Fisher, Rev. Ernest E.: 861
Fleishmann, Avrom Hirsh: 1714, 1866
Fletcher, James V.: 1094
Follett, Helen Thomas: 255
Follett, Wilson: 212 [F., W. A.] 217, 255, 800, 1165
Ford, Boris (ed): 1624
Ford, Ford Madox: 127, 332, 365, 494, 758, 801, 802, 803, 804, 862, 863, 864, 925, 926, 1010, 1011
Ford, George H.: 1867
Ford, William J.: 1216
Forster, E. M.: 363
Foulke, Robert Dana: 1630, 1715
Françillon, Robert: 495
Franklin, John: 496
Franzen, Erich: 990
Fraser, G. S.: 1284
Freeman, John: 236
Freeman, Rosemary: 1631
Freislich, Richard: 1381
Freund, Philip: 1167
Fricker, Robert: 1466
Frid, Ia: 610
Friedman, Alan Howard: 1868
Friedman, Norman: 1467

Fryer, Benjamin N.: 1060
Fryling, Jan: 1382
Fuchs, Carolyn: 1788
Gale, Bell: 1668
Galinsky, Hans (ed): 1619
Gallaher, Elizabeth: 1260
Galsworthy, John: 108, 497, 498, 700, 759, 865, 1937
Gardner, Monica M.: 611
Garnett, Constance: 701
Garnett, David: 1012, 1285
Garnett, Edward: 15, 48, 499, 612, 613, 614, 702, 805, 806, 866, 1052
Garrett, George: 1037
Gatch, Katherine Haynes: 1239
Gates, Barrington: 807
Gaździkówna, Barbara: 1383
Gee, John Archer: 1061, 1095, 1113
Geller, Robert: 1869
George, Gerald A.: 1870
Georgin, B.: 615
Gerlach, Richard: 1062
German, Howard: 1802
Gerould, Gordon Hall: 1114
Gerould, Katherine Fullerton: 299, 760
Gettman, Royal A.: 1321, 1669; (ed): 1669
Gibbon, Perceval: 126, 141
Gide, André: 500
Gillet, Louis: 300, 616
Gillon, Adam: 1301, 1579, 1580, 1581, 1716, 1789, 1938, 1939
Gissing, George: 704
Glasgow, Ellen: 1302
Glaenzer, Richard Butler: 256
Gleckner, Robert F.: 1468
Glicksberg, Charles I.: 1717
Goetsch, Paul: 1718, 1871
Gold, Joseph: 1670
Golding, Henry J.: 761
Goldring, Douglas: 1132, 1190
Gomulicki, Wiktor: 81
Gordan, John Dozier: 1063, 1096, 1097, 1261, 1872, 1873, 1940
Gordon, Robert (ed): 1719
Gorman, Herbert: 762
Gose, Elliott B., Jr.: 1582, 1790
Gossman, Ann M.: 1632
Gould, Gerald: 502, 617
Grabo, Carl H.: 808, 809
Grabowski, Zbigniew A.: 1384, 1469
Graham, Robert B. Cunninghame: 503
Graham, Stephen: 504
G[raher] I[re]: 927
Graver, Lawrence S.: 1633, 1671, 1720, 1721, 1874
Gray, Hugh: 1098

Index of Authors

Green-Armytage, Adrian: 1385
Green, Jessie D.: 1672
Greene, Graham: 706, 1013, 1053
Greenberg, Robert A.: 1583
Greene, Maxine: 1533
Greenwood, Thomas: 1386
Gregory, Michael: 1584
Grein, James Thomas: 506
Groom, Bernard: 867
Gross, Harvey: 1673
Gross, Seymour L.: 1387, 1388, 1534, 1634, 1722
Grzegorczyk, Piotr: 955
Guedalla, Philip: 388
Guerard, Albert J., Jr.: 1168, 1191, 1389, 1470, 1535, 1585
Guetti, James Lawrence, Jr.: 1875
Gullason, Thomas Arthur: 1345
Gurko, Leo: 1471, 1472, 1536, 1586, 1635, 1674, 1876
Gwynn, Stephen: 331
Hackett, Francis: 1346
Hagan, John, Jr.: 1322
Hagen [See Anisimov, I. I.]
Hagopian, John V.: 1791, 1792, 1793; (ed): 1791, 1792, 1826, 1843
Hainsworth, J. D.: 1537
Hale, Edward E.: 237
Hall, James Norman: 1114, 1115
Hall, Leland: 257
Halle, Louis J., Jr.: 1192
Halverson, John: 1538
Hamilton, Cosmo: 975
Hanley, James: 1133
Hansen, Harry: 763, 810
Hanson, Paul Edward: 1941
Hardy, John Edward: 1794
Harkness, Bruce: 1217, 1303, 1321, 1323, 1669, 1877, (ed). 1296, 1321, 1587, 1665, 1669, 1675
Harper, George Mills: 1923
Harrington, David V.: 1795
Harris, G. W.: 811
Hart-Davis, Rupert: 1262
Hartley, L. P.: 619, 1676
Hartman, Captain Howard: 1014
Harvey, William John: 1878
Haugh, Robert F.: 1202, 1240, 1263, 1264, 1324, 1390
Häusermann, Hans Walter: 1265
Hay, Eloise Knapp: 1588, 1724
Haycraft, Howard (ed): 1117
Heilman, Robert B.: 1391; (ed): 1391
Heimer, Jackson W.: 1796
Heine, Herta: 956
Helsztyński, Stanisław: 1473
Hemingway, Ernest: 507

Herget, Winfried: 1879
Hergešić, Ivo: 1241
Herndon, Richard James: 1589, 1636
Herrick, Robert: 419
Herzfeld, Margaret: 1242
Hewitt, Douglas: 1203, 1266
Hicks, Granville: 909
Hicks, John H.: 1797
Hill, Norman H. (ed): 844
Hill, Robert W.: 1218, 1249
Hind, Charles Lewis: 364
Hoare, Dorothy M.: 1064
Hodges, Robert: 1677, 1678, 1798
Hodgson & Company, Auctioneers: 620
Hoentzsch, Alfred: 1392
Hoffman, Anastasia C.: 1267
Hoffman, Charles G.: 1679
Hoffman, Frederick J.: 1799, 1942
Hoffman, Stanton de Voren: 1725, 1800, 1801, 1880
Hoffmann, Richard: 508
Hohoff, Curt: 1079
Holder, Alfred: 976
Holland, Norman N.: 1943
Hollingsworth, Alan M.: 1325, 1347
Holt, Alfred & Company: 420
Hondequin, Ghislain: 1219
Hopkins, Frederick M.: 764
Hopkinson, Tom: 1393
Hoppé, A. J.: 1151, 1152
Horvath, Josip: 621
Hostowiec, Paweł: 1394
Hough, Graham: 1395, 1590
Hourcade, Pierre: 977
Howe, Irving: 1286, 1304
Hristić, Jovan: 1637
Hudspeth, Robert N.: 1944
Hueffer, Ford Madox [See Ford, Ford Madox]
Hughes, Helen Sard: 959
Huneker, James Gibbons: 142, 186, 187, 188, 707
Hunt, Kellog W.: 1591
Hunt, Violet: 708
Hutchison, Percy Adams: 421, 422, 510, 622, 623, 709, 765, 1016
Hynes, Samuel: 1881
Inge, W. R.: 978
Isaacs, Neil D. (ed): 1598
J., H.: 573
J., T. E.: 333
Jabłkowska, Roża: 1426, 1474, 1475, 1637; (ed): 1507
Jacobs, Robert Glenn: 1882, 1945
Jacobson, Dan: 1883
Jaloux, Edmond: 514
James, Henry: 189, 710

619

JOSEPH CONRAD

Janta, Aleksander: 1396
Jarc, Miran: 928
Jesse, F. Tennyson: 978
Jézéquel, Roger: 813
Johnson, Bruce M.: 1726, 1727, 1884
Johnson, Fred Bates: 1153, 1169
Johnson, James: 1060
Jones, Bernard: 1885
Joseph, Edward D.: 1728
Jost, François (ed): 1938
Journeyman, The: 522
Jung, Ursula: 1326, 1477
Jurak, Mirko: 1539
K., E. E.: 815
K., H. F.: 868
K., Q.: 258
Kaehele, Sharon: 1802
Kagarlitskii, Iu.: 1399, 1478
Kalinovich, M. A.: 713, 766
Kamarskii, I.: 1478
Kaplan, Harold: 1946
Karl, Frederick R.: 1400, 1401, 1479, 1540, 1541, 1542, 1592, 1593, 1594, 1595
Kashkin, Iv.: 714, 816
Kaye, Julian B.: 1402
Keating, George T.: 870, 871, 872, 873, 874, 875; (ed): 869
Kellett, Ernest Edward: 715
Kennedy, P. C.: 627
Kenner, Hugh: 1268
Kerby-Miller, Charles: 1105
Kerf, René: 1729, 1886
Kessel, J.: 523
Kettle, Arnold: 1193
Kiely, Robert: 1803
Killam, C. D.: 1887
Killinger, John: 1730
Kimbrough, Robert: 1732, 1733; (ed): 1731, 1732, 1733, 1768
Kimpel, Ben: 1480
King, Carlyle: 1481
Kinney, Arthur F.: 1888
Kinninmont, Kenneth: 301
Kipling, Rudyard: 716
Kirschner, Paul: 1403, 1804, 1889, 1947
Kishler, Thomas C.: 1734
Kleczkowski, Paul: 425
Klingopulos, G. D.: 1204, 1243
Kloth, Friedrich: 1269
Knight, Grant C.: 929
Knopf, Alfred A.: 142, 1482
Koc, Barbara: 1680
Koch[karev], N. A.: 426
Kociemski, Leonardo: 876
Kocmanová, Jessie: 1543
Kocówna, Barbara: 1553; (ed): 1554

Kogur, G.: 1596
Kohler, Dayton: 1327
Komarova, I.: 1544
Konjar, Viktor: 1545
Kott, Jan (ed): 1437
Kovarna, Fr.: 957
Kramer, Dale: 1948
Kranedonk, A. G. van: 335
Krasilnikov, V.: 628
Kreemers, Raph.: 877
Kreisel, Henry: 1483
Krieger, Murray: 1546, 1597
Krżyżanowski, Ludwik: 1348, 1404, 1484; (ed): 1348, 1484, 1554
Kumar, Shiv K.: 1735
Kuncewiczowa, Maria: 1405
Kunitz, Stanley J. (ed): 1117
L., G. A.: 979
L., P.: 302, 366, 427
L., T.: 524
Lalou, René: 717
Lambuth, David: 629
Lamont, William Hayes Fogg: 980
Land, Eugeniusz [see Lann, E.]
Land, Hans-Joachim (ed): 1619
Lann, E. [Also Land, Eugeniusz]: 878, 991, 1080
Larbaud, Valéry: 367
Laskowski, Irmina Teresa: 1736
Las Vergnas, Raymond: 1081, 1547
Latcham, Ricardo A.: 1118
Latorre, Mariano: 630
Leavis, Frank Raymond: 1106, 1485
Leavis, Q. D.: 958, 992
Lee, Richard Eugene: 1328
Lee, Robert Francis: 1737
Lehmann, John: 1244
Leiteizen, M.: 631
Leiter, Louis H.: 1598; (ed): 1598
Leites, A.: 879
Lenormand, H.-R.: 525, 526, 1245
Lerner, Laurence: 1890
Leslie, Shane: 993
Levin, Gerald Henry: 1406, 1486, 1487
Levin, Harry: 1548
Levine, Paul: 1805
Levinson, André: 818, 819
Levinson, B. A.: 1488
Levy, Milton A.: 1806
Lewis, Olive Staples: 1639
Lewis, R. W. B.: 1599
Lewis, Sinclair: 632
Lid, R. W.: 1807
Liddell, Robert: 1170
Lisichenko, M. (trans): 875
Lisiewicz, Mieczysław: 1407
Littell, Robert: 429, 633, 634, 820

Index of Authors

Little, James Stanley: 3
Lloyd, C. F.: 930
Lodge, David: 1808
Lohf, Kenneth A.: 1408
Lohf, Kenneth (comp): 1681
Loks, K.: 635, 719, 720, 767
Long, Robert Emmet: 1949, 1950
Lorch, Thomas M.: 1809
Lordi, R. J.: 1640
Lorentzen, Renate: 1349
Lovett, Robert Morss: 430, 959, 1816
Lowe-Porter, H. T. (trans): 723
Lubbock, Basil: 768
Lucas, E. V.: 721
Ludwig, Richard M.: 1641
Luecke, Sister Jane Marie, O.S.B.: 1810
Lukács, Georg: 1489
Lukić, Berislav: 1019
Lunn, Arnold: 303
Lütken, Otto: 910, 911
Lynd, Robert: 221, 238, 304, 369
Lyngstad, Sverre: 1892, 1952
Lynskey, Winifred: 1305, 1329
M., A.: 431
M., C. S.: 336
M., N.: 981
MacCarthy, Desmond: 112, 389, 531, 931
MacInnes, Helen: 1272
MacLennan, D. A. C.: 1814
MacShane, Frank: 1490, 1642, 1894
Machen, Arthur: 881
Mackay, W. MacDonald: 769
Mackenzie, Compton: 982
Mackenzie, Manfred: 1738
Macy, John: 89, 259, 372, 824
Madden, William A.: 1953
Magalaner, Marvin: 1542
Maksimović, Miodrag: 1643
Malbone, Raymond Gates: 1895
Malone, Andrew E.: 533
Mander, John (trans): 1489
Mander, Necke (trans): 1489
Manly, John Matthews: 1020
Mann, C. W.: 1491
Mann, Thomas: 723
Mansfield, Katherine: 305, 337, 912
Marble, Annie Russell: 825
Marković, Vida E.: 1410, 1492, 1551, 1739
Marquet, Jean: 1039
Marsh, D. R. C.: 1600
Martin, Dorothy: 433
Martin, Sister M.: 1601
Martin, W. R.: 1740
Masback, Frederic J.: 1644
Masefield, John: 58
Maser, Frederick E.: 1411

Mason, John Edward: 1066
Matlaw, Ralph E.: 1741
Maurice, Furnley: 113
Maurois, André: 535, 1021, 1022
Maxwell, J. C.: 1412, 1742
Mayne, Ethel Colburn: 536
Mayoux, Jean-Jacques: 1493
McAlmon, Robert: 530
McAlpin, Edwin A.: 821
McCann, Charles John: 1350, 1550, 1893
McConnell, Daniel J.: 1682
McCullough, Bruce: 1154
McDonald, Evelyn: 932
McDonald, P. A.: 1194
McFee, William: 370, 371, 390, 532, 636, 722, 822, 823, 880, 1065, 1107, 1118, 1409
McGoldrich, Rita C.: 432
McIntyre, Allan Ormsby: 1683, 1811, 1812, 1813
Medanić, Lav: 1067
Mégroz, Rodolphe Louis: 434, 724, 933, 934, 1171
Meixner, John A.: 1684
Mélisson-Dubreil, M.-R.: 1134, 1135
Meldrum, D. S.: 307
Mencken, Henry Louis: 260, 538, 735, 1023
Mendilow, Adam Abraham: 1270
Meredith, Mark: 261
Meyer, Bernard C.: 1743, 1815
Michael, George: 1141
Michael, Marion Cicero: 1896
Michel, Lois A.: 1645
Middleton, George: 190
Milivojević, D[ragoljub]: 1413
Miłosz, Czesław: 1414, 1415
Mille, Pierre: 637, 882
Miller, James E., Jr.: 1246
Miller, J. Hillis: 1897
Millett, Fred B.: 1020, 1221; (ed): 1816
Mirande, R.: 1024
Mitchell, Sidney H.: 1744
Mizener, Arthur: 1685, 1954; (ed): 1685
Młynarska, Maria: 1416
Moczulski, Mariusz Hrynkiewscz: 1417
Mogilianskii, M.: 638
Monroe, N. Elizabeth: 1108
Morey, John Hope: 1602
Moore, Harry T.: 1494
Morf, Gustav: 913
Morgan, Gerould: 1552, 1646, 1686
Morley, Christopher D.: 281, 436, 639, 640, 770, 827, 883, 884, 960, 983, 1205; (selector): 883
Moody, William Vaughan: 1816
Moore, Carlisle: 1745

Morgan, Gerould: 1817, 1818
Morris, Lawrence J.: 726
Morris, Robert L.: 1155, 1222
Mortimer, Raymond: 437
Moseley, Edwin M.: 1687
Moser, Thomas C.: 1330, 1351, 1419
Moss, Mary: 92
Moult, Thomas: 374, 539, 540, 641
Mouradian, Jacques: 914
Moynihan, William T.: 1495
Mroczkowski, Przemysław J.: 1420, 1553, 1554
Muddiman, Bernard: 338
Mudrick, Marvin: 1306, 1421, 1496, 1956; (ed): 1253, 1309, 1419, 1470, 1496, 1665, 1773, 1955, 1956
Muir, Edwin: 541
Mukerji, N.: 1819
Müller, Erich: 1054
Muller, Herbert J.: 1055
Munro, Neil: 885
Murdoch, Walter: 1068, 1069
Naglerowa, Herminia: 1422
Najder, Zdzisław: 1423, 1424, 1425, 1497, 1820, 1821; (ed): 1821
Naumov, Cićifor: 1498
Neill, S. Diana: 1271
Nelson, Harland S.: 1746
Nemerouska, O.: 828
Neri, Fernando: 1040
Newbolt, Sir Henry John: 961
Newhouse, Neville H.: 1957
Newman, Paul B.: 1603, 1898
Nikolskii, A.: 886
Noble, Edward: 645
Noble, James Ashcraft: 2
Novorusskii, M.: 151
Nusinov, I.: 646, 648
Oates, David W.: 935
Ober, Warren U.: 1899
O'Connor, William Van: 1197; (ed): 1207
O'Flaherty, Liam: 887, 915
O'Grady, Walter: 1900
O'Hara, J. D.: 1901
Ohmann, Carol: 1822
O'Leary, Sister Jeanine: 1958
Oliver, H. J.: 1172
Onofrio, Lilia D': 1121
Oppel, Horst (ed): 1871
Ordoñez, Elmer Alindogan: 1747
Orvis, Mary Burchard: 1195
Orwell, George [Eric Blair]: 1041
Osbourne, Maitland LeRoy: 438
Ostrowski, Witold: 1426
Ould, Herman: 439
Overton, Grant: 440, 829, 916

Owen, Charles (trans): 500
Owen, Guy: 1427, 1499, 1604
Owen, Lyman B.: 1025
Owen, R. J.: 1500
Packman, James (ed): 943
Page, R. Edison: 543
Palffy, Eleanor: 888
Palmer, John Alfred: 1748
Parker, W. M.: 984
Parrill, Anna Sue: 1959
Partington, Wilfred: 771, 1082
Parton, Ethel: 728
Parton, Herwig: 1196
Paulding, Gouverneur: 1272, 1287
Pavese, Cesare: 1247
Payn, James: 20
Payne, William Morton: 21, 76, 83, 102, 120, 223
Pearson, Edmund: 647
Pearson, Hesketh: 376
Pease, Frank: 282
Pell, Elsie (trans): 500
Pendexter, Hugh, III: 1960
Perry, F. M.: 729
Perry, John Oliver: 1823
Peterkiewicz, Jerzy: 1428
Pfase [Pfabe], Teresa: 1429
Phelps, Gilbert: 1352
Phelps, William Lyon: 241
Phillipson, John S.: 1605
Pierrefeu, Jean de: 391
Pilecki, Gerard A.: 1902
Platt, Rutherford H., Jr.: 648
Potocki, Antoni: 545
Potter, Norris W.: 1142
Powys, John Cowper: 441, 889
Powys, Llewelyn: 891
Powys, T. F.: 890
Poznar, Walter P.: 1501
Preston, John Hyde: 649
Prezelj, Jeske: 962
Price, Arthur J.: 935, 936
Pridorogin, A.: 650
Priestly, J. B.: 651
Prieur, François: 652
Prince, F. T.: 1961
Pritchett, V. S.: 1026, 1122, 1223, 1288, 1430, 1824, 1825
Putnam, George Palmer: 50, 340
Quiller-Couch, A. T.: 61
Quinn, John: 443
R.: 1099
R., A.: 653
R., C. M.: 341
Rahv, Philip: 1353
Raimondi, Giuseppe: 1123
Randall, John Herman: 730

Index of Authors

Rang, Bernhard: 830
Raphael, Alice: 963
Rapin, René: 1331
Rascoe, Burton: 546
Rathburn, Robert C. (ed): 1509
Rawson, C. J.: 1555
Ray, Gordan N.: 1556
Read, Herbert: 731
Rébora, Piero: 1224
Redman, Ben Ray: 378, 1174
Rees, Richard: 1606
Reid, Forrest: 547
Reid, Stephen A.: 1749
Reilly, Joseph J.: 311
Reinecke, George F.: 1963
Renner, Louis (trans). 1200, 1201
Resink, G. J.: 1647, 1648, 1649, 1650, 1750, 1903
Retinger, Joseph Hieronim: 1109, 1431
Reynolds, Stephen: 155
Rheault, Charles A., Jr.: 1625
Rhys, Ernest: 392
Rice, Howard C., Jr.: 1751
Rickert, Edith: 1020
Richards, Grant: 343
Rider, Fremont: 226
Ridley, Florence H.: 1752
Riesenberg, Felix: 892
Rihtersic, Boris: 985
Rinz, Arthur Friedrich: 832
Roberts, Cecil: 654
Roberts, Giuseppe De (comp): 1123
Roberts, John H.: 1175
Roberts, R. Ellis: 344
Robertson, J. M.: 283
Robinson, E. Arthur: 1607
Robson, W. W.: 1432
Rockwood, Stanley W.: 893
Roditi, Edouard. 1143
Rogers, B. J.: 1273
Roman, F. Vinci: 548
Root, E. Merrill: 1176
Rops, H. Daniel: 833
Roquette de Fonvielle: 772
Rose, Alan Manuel: 1964
Rosenfield, Claire: 1688, 1753
Ross, Ernest Carson: 550
Rothenstein, William: 345, 937, 964, 965
Roughead, William: 834
Routh, Harold Victor: 1056, 1156
Ruch, Gertrud: 733
Russell, Bertrand: 1289
Ryan, Alvan S.: 1651, 1826
Ryan, John K.: 551
Ryf, Robert S.: 1827
S., G.: 379
S., L. A.: 1557

Safroni-Middleton, A.: 773
Said, Edward W.: 1828, 1904
St. John, William E.: 1042
Sakowski, Juliusz: 1433
Salmon, Arthur L.: 284
Sanders, Charles: 1905
Sanger, Vincent: 157
Sargent, G. H.: 552
Sasse, Maria-Elisabeth: 1274
Saueson, J. E.: 1754
Saugère, Albert: 553
Sawyer, Arthur Edward: 1558, 1608
Saxton, Eugene P.: 197
Schelling, Felix Emmanuel: 393
Schieszlová, Olga: 1043
Schlecht, Elvine. 1225
Schneider, Daniel J.: 1965
Schorer, Mark: 1226; (ed): 1612, 1652
Schriftgiesser, Karl: 655, 734, 774, 835
Schunk, Karl: 1124
Schwab, Arnold T.: 1332, 1906
Schwamborn, Heinrich: 1502
Schwartz, Jacob: 938
Scott-James, Rolfe Arnold: 117, 1248
Scrimgeour, Cecil: 1907
Scrimgeour, Gary J.: 1966
Sealey, Ethel: 1044
Sebba, Helen (trans): 1159
Sée, Ida R.: 554
Seldes, Gilbert: 348, 836
Seligmann, Herbert J.: 555
Selle, Cäcilie: 1144
Sewall, R. B.: 1227
Shand, John: 556
Shanks, Edward: 313, 445, 557, 775
Shannon, Homer S.: 837
Shapiro, Charles (ed): 1599
Shaw, Roger: 894
Sheehy, Eugene P.: 1408
Sherbo, Arthur: 1290
Sherman, Stuart P.: 558
Sherry, Norman: 1755, 1756, 1757, 1829, 1830, 1831, 1908, 1909, 1910, 1911, 1967
Sherwin, Jane King: 1758
Shklovskii, V.: 1177
Sholl, Anna McClure: 559
Short, Raymond W.: 1227
Sickels, Eleanor M.: 1354
Simmons, J. L.: 1912
Simon, Irène: 1206
Sims, George: 1968
Sinha, Dr. Murari Shri: 1136
Sire, P.: 966
Sister Estelle, S. P.: 1689
Skarzewski, Tadeusz Żuk: 736
Sklare, Arnold B. (ed): 1570

Smalc, Matevz: 776
Smith, Arthur J. M.: 1228
Smith, Curtis C.: 1913
Smith, David R.: 1690
Smith, J. Oates: 1759
Smet, Joseph De: 158
Solomon Eagle [See Squire, John C.]
Soloman, Eric: 1832
Souvage, Jacques: 1914
Spector, Robert D.: 1503
Sper, Felix: 777
Spicer-Simson, Theodore: 558
Spinner, Kaspar: 1691
Spoerri-Müller, Ruth: 1559
Squire, Sir John C. [Solomon Eagle]: 268, 314, 1434
Stallman, Robert Wooster: 1610; (ed): 1609, 1610
Staral, Margarete: 1137
Stark, Lewis M.: 1218, 1249
Stauffer, Ruth M.: 394
Stavrou, C. N.: 1611
Stawell, F. Melian: 350
Steegmuller, Francis: 1110
Stegner, Wallace: 1229
Stein, William Bysshe: 1355, 1436, 1833, 1915
Steinmann, Martin (ed): 1509
Sterba, Richard F.: 1916
Stevens, Arthur W.: 1504
Stewart, J. I. M.: 1760
Stiles, Villa: 908
Stillman, Clara Arvening: 1027
Stone, Wilfred: 1969
Stravinsky, Igor: 1917
Strawson, H.: 995
Stresau, Hermann: 1291
Sturm, Paul J.: 1095
Strunsky, Simeon: 560
Sufflay, Milan: 737
Sullivan, Sister Mary Petrus, R. S. M.: 1834
Sullivan, T. R.: 29
Süskind, W. E.: 986, 1045, 1070, 1071, 1072, 1083
Sutherland, J. G.: 243
Swarthout, Glendon F.: 1506
Sweetser, Wesley D.: 1835
Swettenham, Sir Frank: 446, 447
Swinnerton, Frank: 996, 1356, 1357, 1761
Symons, Arthur: 230, 561, 658, 895
T., R.: 1157
Taborski, Roman: 1437
Talbot, Francis X.: 562
Tanner, Jimmie Eugene: 1836
Tanner, Tony: 1692, 1693, 1762, 1763, 1764, 1837, 1838

Tarnawski, Wit: 1439, 1440, 1507; (ed): 1367, 1369, 1372, 1376, 1382, 1383, 1384, 1394, 1396, 1405, 1407, 1415, 1416, 1417, 1422, 1423, 1431, 1438, 1439, 1440, 1441, 1443, 1445
Taylor, W. D.: 351
Teincey, Jean: 34
Temple, Phillips: 1125
Terlecki, Tymon: 1441
Tetauer, Frank: 997
Thale, Jerome: 1334, 1442
Theimer, Helen Agnes Prentice: 1694
Thiébaut, Marcel: 896
Thompson, Alan Reynolds: 897
Thompson, J. C.: 352
Thorpe, Michael: 1970
Tick, Stanley: 1765, 1839
Tillyard, E. M. W.: 1508, 1653
Tindall, William York: 1178, 1275, 1509
Tittle, Walter: 448, 564, 661
Toliver, Harold F.: 1695
Tomlinson, Maggie: 1696
Tomlinson, H. M.: 778, 898, 1230
Tonquédec, Joseph de: 939
Townsend, R. D.: 565
Tretiak, Andrzej: 998
Triller, A.: 1918
Trilling, Lionel: 1654
Tuong-Buu-Khanh, M.: 1276
Turno, Witold: 1443
Turner, Lionel H.: 1231
Turner, Michael L.: 1971
Ujević, Tin: 1232; (trans): 1241
Unger, Leonard: 1358
Unterecker, John (ed): 1904
Ure, Peter: 1233
Vaisbrod, A.: 662
Valéry, Paul: 566
Van Baaren, Betty Bishop: 1510
Van Ghent, Dorothy: 1292, 1655
Van Marle, A.: 1972, 1977
Van Slooten, Henry: 1444
Vengerova, Z.: 159
Verschoyle, Derek (ed): 1032
Vestdijk, S.: 1126
Vidaković, Aleksandar: 567, 738; (trans): 1551
Vidan, Ivo: 1359, 1511, 1512, 1513, 1514, 1515, 1656, 1697, 1698, 1973, 1974
Villard, Léonie: 739, 740
Vinaver, Stanislav: 568
Vincenz, Stanisław: 1445
Visiak, Edward Harold: 1084, 1085, 1086, 1087, 1088, 1100, 1335
Vlahović, Josip: 1446
Voisins, Gilbert de: 285
Von Klemperer, Elizabeth Gallaher: 1516

INDEX OF AUTHORS

Vorse, M. H.: 65
W., G.: 569, 570
Wadell, Helen: 315
Wagenknecht, Edward: 1127, 1138
Waggoner, Hyatt H.: 1562
Wagner, Geoffrey: 1840
Wain, John: 1447
Walcutt, Charles Child: 1293
Waldman, Milton: 663, 664, 741
Waliszewski, Kazimir [Kazimierz(?)]: 84
Walpole, Hugh: 244, 899
Walsh, James J.: 271
Walton, James Hackett: 1975
Wang, Joan Parsons: 1919
Ward, Alfred Charles: 571, 838
Ward, Laura A.: 272
Warger, Howard Nicholas: 1976
Warner, John Riley: 1360
Warner, Oliver: 1250, 1448
Warren, C. Henry: 665
Warren, Robert Penn: 1251, 1287
Wasiolek, Edward: 1361
Watson, George (ed): 1841
Watt, Ian: 1517, 1538, 1612, 1841
Watters, R. E.: 1307
Watts, C. T.: 1842, 1920, 1921
Weber, David C.: 1234
Webster, H. T.: 1147, 1209
Weiand, Hermann Joseph: 1563, 1843
Weingart, Seymour Leonard: 1920
Wellek, René: 967
Wells, Carolyn: 286
Wells, Herbert George: 742
Welsh, Alexander: 1923
Werner, Harry: 1449
West, Paul: 1766
West, Ray B. (ed): 1207, 1208
West, H. F.: 572
West, Rebecca: 1450
Wethered, H. N.: 1362
Weygandt, Cornelius: 450
Whicher, George F.: 1308
White, Stewart Edward: 119
Whitehead, Lee M.: 1924
Whitford, Robert Calvin: 395

Whiting, George Wesley: 451, 999, 1057, 1632
Whittemore, Reed: 1767
Widmer, Kingsley: 1564
Wilcox Stewart C.: 1613
Wiley, Paul L.: 1309, 1768
Wilkening, Vjera: 1614
Willard, Grace: 666, 743, 744
Williams, George Walton: 1769, 1844
Williams, Michael: 231
Williams, Porter, Jr.: 1845, 1846
Williamson, Claude C. H.: 352
Wills, John Howard: 1336, 1657, 1699, 1770
Wimsatt, W. K., Jr.: 1128
Wise, Thomas J.: 354, 380, 1046
Wittig, Kurt: 1074
Wohlfarth, Paul: 1000, 1028, 1047, 1048, 1658, 1771
Wolfe, Peter: 1847
Wollnick, Ludwig: 1001
Wood, Miriam H.: 1029
Woodruff, Neal: 1337
Woolf, Leonard: 573, 667
Woolf, Virginia: 287, 452, 574
Worth, George J.: 1338
Wright, Elisabeth Cox: 1615
Wright, Walter Francis: 1179, 1198, 1210, 1339, 1848; (ed): 1848
Writer of the Article, The: 453
Wyzewa, T. de: 198
Yates, Norris W.: 1849
Yelton, Donald Charles: 1772
Young, Filson: 575
Young, Vernon: 1211, 1277, 1294
Zabel, Morton Dauwen: 1030, 1101, 1111, 1129, 1148, 1180, 1181, 1182, 1183, 1184, 1185, 1187, 1252, 1253, 1451, 1518, 1519, 1565, 1566, 1567, 1616, 1617, 1659, 1773; (ed): 1186, 1519
Zelie, John Sheridan: 576, 668
Zellar, Leonard Eugene: 1520
Zeromski, Stefan: 779
Zuckerman, Jerome: 1774, 1850, 1851

Index

TITLES OF SECONDARY WORKS

Titles of articles in periodicals and chapters in books are in quotation marks; book titles are in upper case; translations of article titles originally appearing in a foreign language are in parentheses, without quotation marks, and in lower case; translations of book titles originally appearing in a foreign language are in parentheses and in upper case. Numbers after each title refer to the item in the bibliography where the title appears.

"About Books, More or Less: Complex or Complicated": 560
(About Joseph Conrad): 1399
(About the "Philosophy" of Conrad): 1424
"Above the Battle": 1248
"The Absurd Predicament in Conrad's Political Novels": 1645
"The Accustomed Manner and Some Recent Novels": 178
"Action, Vision, or Voice: The Moral Dilemmas in Conrad's Tale-Telling": 1823
"Adam, Axel, and 'Il Conde' ": 1336
"Additions to the Doubleday Collection": 1751
(The Adventures and Interesting Life of One of the Greatest Writers on the Sea): 1446
"Adventuring with Joseph Conrad": 1025
"Aesthetic Criteria and Conrad's 'The Tale' ": 1795
AESTHETICS OF THE NOVEL: 782
"The Affair in Marseilles": 1364
"Africa and the Congo: Editor's Note": 1180

(After Thirty Years): 1384
"Against THE GREAT GATSBY": 1966
(Agent Jackobus): 489
THE ADVANCE OF THE ENGLISH NOVEL: 241
"The Allegory of Truth in English Fiction": 1923
"Alma": 1367
"An Allusion to Tasso in Conrad's *Chance*": 1486
"Alma Renamed Lena in Conrad's *Victory*": 1924
(*Almayer's Folly*): 7
"*Almayer's Folly*: A Story of an Eastern River": 1
"*Almayer's Folly* and *Lord Jim*: A Study in the Development of Conrad's Imagery": 1863
"*Almayer's Folly*: The Prelude": 898
ALTES UND NEUES: 723
AMERICAN CONTRIBUTIONS TO THE FIFTH INTERNATIONAL CONGRESS OF SLAVISTS, SOFIA, SEPT. 1963: 1741
(AMERICAN LITERATURE AND OTHER ESSAYS): 1247
AMERICAN NIGHTS ENTERTAINMENT: 440

Joseph Conrad

(The American Novel and *The Nigger of the Narcissus*): 34
"Analysis": 1197, 1207
"Anarchists": 389
"André Malraux's Heart of Darkness": 1526
"An Anniversary Exhibition . . . (Part II)": 1873
"An Anniversary Exhibition . . . (Part II: Conclusion)": 1872
"Another Look at the Collaboration of Joseph Conrad with Ford Madox Hueffer": 581
(Another Man's Horse): 1177
(Apollo Korzeniowski; the Last Romantic Dramatist): 1437
Apollo Korzeniowski; Ostatni Dramatopisarz Romantyczny: 1437
"Apology for Marlow": 1509
Appraisements and Asperites as to Some Contemporary Writers: 393
An Appreciation of Joseph Conrad: 935, 936
"The Apprenticeship of William Faulkner": 1660
"An Approach to *Nostromo*": 1537
Approaches to the Short Story: 1598
Approaches to the Twentieth-Century Novel: 1904
"An Archetypal Analysis of Conrad's *Nostromo*": 1688
"Arbeit und Kunst: Anmerkungen zu Joseph Conrads *Spiegel und See*": 1083
"L'Aristocratisme slave de Conrad": 406
"An Armful of Fiction": 583
Arnold Bennett to Joseph Conrad: 678
Around Theaters: 78
"Arriving with Joseph Conrad": 429
"*Arrow of Gold*": 288
"The Arrow of Gold": 290, 893
(*The Arrow of Gold*): 300
"L'art de Conrad": 493
(The Art of Conrad): 493
"The Art of Joseph Conrad": 136, 450
The Art of Joseph Conrad: A Critical Symposium: 493, 500, 526, 556, 723, 1102, 1106, 1148, 1207, 1251, 1277, 1344, 1292, 1294, 1320, 1334, 1336, 1355, 1364, 1380, 1388, 1389, 1414, 1495, 1561, 1609, 1610
The Art of Modern Fiction: 1197, 1207, 1208
"The Art of Mr. Joseph Conrad": 47
The Art of Reading the Novel: 1167
The Art of the Novel: 973
The Art of Writing Fiction: 1195

"Arthur Koestler": 1204
Arthur Machen: 1835
"The Artist Philosopher": 370
"The Artist's Conscience and *The Nigger of the Narcissus*": 1421
"As Joseph Conrad Appeared to His Wife/Jessie Conrad's Memoir of Her Husband Gives a Lively Picture of Genius in Shirtsleeves": 671
"Aschenbach and Kurtz: The Cost of Civilization": 1673
The Ashley Library: A Catalogue of Printed Books, Manuscripts and Autograph Letters Collected by Thomas J. Wise: 1046
Aspects of the Modern Short Story: English and American: 571
At Sea with Joseph Conrad: 243
"At the World's End": 208
Authors and I: 364
Authors I Never Met: 1357
Authors of the Day: 440
Autumn Leaves: 500
"Avanpost Progressy": 638
"Axel Heyst and the Second King of the Cocos Islands": 1750
"Back to Conrad": 1346
Background with Chorus: 1356
"The Backgrounds of *The Secret Agent*: A Biographical and Critical Study": 1975
"A Backward Glance": 305
"Bagaż z Kalinówki": 1394
(Baggage from Kalinówki): 1394
"The Balfour-Conrad Question": 1068
"The Barrier Between Youth and Maturity in the Works of Joseph Conrad": 1809
"Die Behandlung des Meeres bei Joseph Conrad": 1137
Beiträge zur Ästhetik des Romans der Ausgehenden Viktorianischen und nach Viktorianischen Periode: 976
"The Bequest of Mary Stillman Harkness": 1249
Bergson and the Stream of Consciousness Novel: 1735
"Bertrand Russell o Conradzie": 1429
(Bertrand Russell on Conrad): 1429
"The Best Recent Novels": 67
"Betrayal and Redemption in Joseph Conrad": 1579
"Better than Ecstasy": 836
(Between Life and Books): 604, 606
"Betwixt and Between": 728
"Beyond Idolatry": 822

Index of Titles of Secondary Works

(Bibliographical Chronicle: *'Twixt Land and Sea,* by Joseph Conrad, trans by G. J.-Aubry): 896
"Bibliographical Notes: Joseph Conrad. *Suspense*": 1153
"Bibliographie": 848, 854
"Bibliographies of Modern Authors: Joseph Conrad": 318
"Bibliographies of Young Republicans: Joseph Conrad (Korzeniowski)": 157
(Bibliography): 848, 854
"The Bibliography of Joseph Conrad": 769
A BIBLIOGRAPHY OF THE WRITINGS OF JOSEPH CONRAD: 380
THE BIG FIVE: 1141
"Biographical and Autobiographical. Novels and Stories": 180
"Biography": 679, 786, 1002
"A Blessing in Disguise": 480
(A Book about Joseph Conrad): 1018
A BOOK OF PREFACES: 260
A BOOK OF STORIES: TEACHER'S MANUAL: 1321
"A Book of Substance and Dignity": 80
"Book Reviews": 10, 384, 395
"Book Selection Department": 199
"The Book Table": 565, 647
"The Book Table: Devoted to Books and Their Makers": 319
"The Book World: The First Reader; Jean-Aubry's 2-Volume Study Shows Life Was Conrad's Source": 763
"The Book World: The First Reader; Richard Curle's Reminiscences of Joseph Conrad Describe 'The Anguish of the Creative Mind'": 810
"The Book World: What Britain Is Reading; Huntsman's Book, Hewlett's Letters, Conrad's Essays and 'Rough Justice'": 741
"Books": 787, 1089
"Books and Authors": 9, 581
BOOKS AND AUTHORS: 369
"Books and Things": 302, 366
"Books: Fiction": 132, 173, 200, 246, 289, 320
"Books in Brief": 582, 680, 1030, 1457
"Books in General": 812, 824, 1122, 1150, 1223, 1288
BOOKS IN GENERAL: 1288
BOOKS IN GENERAL, BY SOLOMON EAGLE: 314
"Books: Novels": 68, 96
"Books on the Table. Oh to be in England—then": 1188
"Books Reviewed—Fact and Fiction": 65

"Books That Hold the Harsh Salt of the Sea": 1112
(Books: *The End of the Tether,* by Joseph Conrad [N.R.F.]): 966
"The Brand of Cain in 'The Secret Sharer'": 1845
"Brewed From the French Revolution by Conrad": 404
"Briefer Mention": 356, 585
"Briefs on New Books": 133
BRITISH AUTHORS: 1131
"Brown Humanity": 11
BRUCE ROGERS AND THE FIGUREHEAD OF THE *Joseph Conrad*: 1060
"Buddhism and 'Heart of Darkness'": 1436
"The Burdens of Restless Lives": 29
"A Burial in Kent": 576
"Butterflies and Beetles—Conrad's Two Truths": 1762
(The Call): 1422
CANDELABRA: 498
"Capitano Conrad": 1123
"Captain Conrad": 407
"Captain Korzeniowski's 'Prince Roman': Nautical Allusion in Conrad's Patriotic Tale": 1552
"The Captain of the *Narcissus*": 1740
THE CAPTAIN'S DEATH BED: 452
"Un Caràcter": 604
CARAVANSARY AND CONVERSATION: MEMORIES OF PLACES AND PERSONS: 907
CARTE D'EUROPE: 833
"Le cas de Joseph Conrad": 545
"Un cas de naturalisation littéraire: Joseph Conrad": 84
(The Case of Joseph Conrad): 545
(A Case of Literary Naturalism: Joseph Conrad): 84
CASTLES IN SPAIN AND OTHER SCREEDS: 497, 498, 759
A CATALOGUE OF BOOKS, MANUSCRIPTS, AND COLLECTED TYPESCRIPTS FROM THE LIBRARY OF THE LATE JOSEPH CONRAD. TO BE SOLD . . . MARCH 13, 1925 . . . : 620
CAVALCADE OF THE ENGLISH NOVEL. 1138
THE CAVE AND THE MOUNTAIN: A STUDY OF E. M. FORSTER: 1969
(Centennial of the Day of Birth of Joseph Conrad [in Poland]): 1505
"C'est toi qui dors dans l'ombre . . .": 494
(THE CHALLENGE OF THE DAY): 723
"*Chance*": 889
"Chance and Her Victims": 176

629

Joseph Conrad

"Chance and Joseph Conrad": 1395, 1590
"Character and Background in Conrad": 1510
"Character and Imagination in Conrad": 1233
CHARACTER AND THE NOVEL: 1878
"Character as Reality: Joseph Conrad": 1946
"Character Motivation in the Novels of Joseph Conrad": 1941
(Characteristic Traits of People in Light of Joseph Conrad's Works): 1274
THE CHARACTERS OF LOVE: 1569
"A Check List of Additions to A Conrad Memorial Library": 843
(The Childhood of Consciousness): 1493
"A Choice of Nightmares: A Study of Conrad's Ethical Vision": 1702
"Christ as Tragic Hero: Conrad's *Lord Jim*": 1687
A CHRISTMAS GARLAND: 130
"Chronicle and Comment": 12, 69, 70, 160, 203, 286
CHRONICLES OF BARABBAS: 1008
"Chronique Bibliographique: *Entre Terre et Mer*, par Joseph Conrad, traduit par G. J.-Aubry": 896
"Chuzhaia loshad": 1177
(A Classic of Our Century): 991
"The Classical Reference in Conrad's Fiction": 1155
"The Clothing of Thoughts and Some Recent Novels": 122
(Coincidence in Joseph Conrad): 1124
"The Collaboration of Conrad and Ford Madox Ford": 1273
"The Collaboration of Joseph Conrad and Ford Madox Ford": 1636
COLLECTED ESSAYS: 452, 574, 1069
COLLECTED ESSAYS OF PHILIP GUEDALLA: 388
COLLECTED IMPRESSIONS: 1033
COLLECTION OF BOOKS, MANUSCRIPTS, AND AUTOGRAPH LETTERS IN THE LIBRARY OF JEAN AND DONALD STRALEM: 1681
"Collector's Luck": 1059
COLUMBIA UNIVERSITY COURSE IN LITERATURE, BASED ON THE WORLD'S BEST LITERATURE: 257
"Comedy and Form in the Fiction of Joseph Conrad": 1725
COMEDY AND FORM IN THE FICTION OF JOSEPH CONRAD: 1800, 1880
"The Coming of Joseph Conrad": 432
"Comment on Current Books": 85, 97

[Commentaries]: 1544
THE COMMON READER: 574
"Commonwealth Literature: Out of Empire": 1883
COMMUNITY AND ANARCHY IN THE FICTION OF JOSEPH CONRAD: 1866
"A Comparative Study of the Works of Pierre Loti and Joseph Conrad": 893
"Complementary": 1105
"Comrade Ossipon's Favorite Saint: Lombroso and Conrad": 1882
(Comradeship Among Men): 1200
"The Conception of the Novel as Presented by the Leading English and American Novelists Since 1800": 1042
(Concerning a Book by Mr. Joseph Conrad): 278
"Concerning Conrad and his Work": 790
"Concerning the English 'Academy' ": 13
" 'Il Conde' ": 1791
"Une conférence sur Joseph Conrad": 615
"Conrad": 141, 230, 350, 475, 931, 1033, 1050, 1760, 1824, 1362, 1451
"Conrad: A Borrowing from Hazlitt's Father": 1710
"Conrad: A Centenary Survey": 1378
CONRAD: A COLLECTION OF CRITICAL ESSAYS: 1253, 1309, 1419, 1470, 1496, 1653, 1665, 1749, 1955, 1956
"Conrad: A Misdated Letter": 1412
"Conrad: A Nautical Image": 1379
CONRAD: A REASSESSMENT: 1266
"Conrad à Marseille": 784
"Conrad a konwencje": 1445
"Conrad a Polska": 1680
"Conrad a tradycja literacka": 1460
"Conrad a 'wielka trójka' Literatury Rosyjskiej": 1376
(Conrad Abroad: II. Association of Conrad Lovers): 1417
(Conrad Abroad: I. From Rumania to Great Britain): 1443
"Conrad After Five Years": 909
"Conrad After Fourteen Years": 1065
"Conrad and ALL THE KING'S MEN": 1387
"Conrad and Anatole France": 914
(Conrad and Bobrowski): 1820
(Conrad and Convention): 1445
"Conrad and Cowes": 522
"Conrad and Ford": 1268
"Conrad and Galsworthy": 970
"Conrad and Hardy": 455
"Conrad and his Circle": 1006
CONRAD AND HIS CONTEMPORARIES: SOUVENIRS: 1109

630

Index of Titles of Secondary Works

"Conrad and His Critics": 1572
"Conrad and His Critics: 1895–1914": 1744
"Conrad and His Fame": 479
"Conrad and Impressionism": 1694
"Conrad and Jean-Aubry": 1374
"Conrad and Maupassant": 1889
"Conrad and Maupassant: Moral Solitude and 'A Smile of Fortune' ": 1947
"Conrad and Melville": 383
(Conrad and Poland): 772, 1680
"Conrad and Poland. For the Centenary: Patriotic Irritability": 1428
"Conrad and Politics": 1454
"Conrad and Sartre": 1580
"Conrad and T. J. Wise". 1971
"Conrad and the 'Atmosphere of Authenticity': An Inquiry into the Structure and Meaning of *Chance*": 1406
"Conrad and the BANGKOK TIMES": 1908
(Conrad and "The Big Three" of Russian Literature): 1376
"Conrad and the Congo": 1573
"Conrad and the Critics": 408
"Conrad and the Film": 1403
"Conrad and THE GREAT GATSBY": 1333
(Conrad and the Literary Tradition): 1460
(Conrad and the Navy): 947
"Conrad and the Novel as Ordeal": 1745
(Conrad and the Orient): 1276
CONRAD AND THE REPORTERS: 436
"Conrad and the Reporters": 436
"Conrad and the Romantic Hero": 1668
"Conrad and the S. S. *Vidar*": 1755
"Conrad and the Sea": 1010
"Conrad and 'The Secret Sharer' ": 1197, 1207
"Conrad and the Terms of Criticism": 1306
"Conrad and the Tragic Imagination": 1368
(Conrad and the Tragic Imagination): 1368
"Conrad and the Younger Generation": 906
"Conrad and Trafalgar": 961
"Conrad and Turgenev: A Minor Source for *Victory*": 1742
"Conrad and William Blackwood": 1456
A CONRAD ARGOSY: 1119
(Conrad at Marseilles): 784
"Conrad at Thirty-one": 949
"Conrad at Work". 1010
"Conrad Books and Manuscripts": 589
"Conrad by Chance": 1059

"Conrad, Camus, and Sisyphus": 1611
"A Conrad Collection": 753
THE CONRAD COMPANION: 1151
"Conrad Compared with Dostoevsky and Other Masters": 291
"Conrad Criticism and *The Nigger of the Narcissus*": 1517
"Conrad Criticism Today": 1560
"Conrad et l'Orient": 1276
"Conrad et la Pologne": 772
"Conrad et le Navire": 947
"Conrad For 'Movies' But Can't Sell One": 410
"Conrad for the Classroom": 1481
"Conrad Fought Death to Finish His Book, Author's Widow Tells of Last Vain Efforts": 590
"Conrad: From Life to Literature": 316
"Conrad, Galsworthy and Others": 241
"A Conrad 'Genesis'; How He Harks Back to His Youth in His Novel *The Arrow of Gold*": 301
"A Conrad Heroine in Real Life": 739
"A Conrad Hero's Quest for the Truth": 249
"Conrad i Bobrowski": 1820
"Conrad i Tragiczna Wyobraznia": 1368
"Conrad in a New Field": 72
"Conrad in Cracow": 340
"Conrad in Excelsis": 666
"Conrad in His Age": 1101, 1111, 1129
"Conrad in Poland": 275
(Conrad in Poland during the Years 1939–1957): 1423
(Conrad in Polish Culture): 1441
"Conrad in School": 1161
"Conrad in the East": 415
"Conrad in Yugoslavia": 1511
"Conrad is 'Gripping' ": 411
"Conrad, Joseph: *Jugend. Der Geheimagent. Spiel des Zufalls. Die Schattenlinie.* Romane. S. Fischer, Berlin 1926": 670
"Conrad, Joseph: *Mit den Augen des Westens*. Übertragen von E. W. Freissler, Berlin 1933": 979
"Conrad, Joseph. *Taifun*, Stuttgart, 1927, *Sieg*, *Nostromo*, Berlin 1927": 745
(Conrad, Joseph: *Typhoon,* Stuttgart, 1927; *Victory*; *Nostromo*, Berlin 1927): 745
(Conrad, Joseph: *Under Western Eyes*, trans by E. W. Freissler, Berlin 1933): 979
(Conrad, Joseph. *Youth. The Secret Agent. Chance. The Shadow-Line.* Novels. S. Fischer, Berlin 1926): 670

Joseph Conrad

"A Conrad Letter": 1488
"Conrad Letters": 756
A Conrad Library; A Catalog of Printed Books, Manuscripts and Autograph Letters by Joseph Conrad: 792
Conrad: *Lord Jim*: 1763
"Conrad, Madach et Calderón": 1646
(Conrad, Madach and Calderón): 1646
"Conrad Manuscripts in America": 552
"Conrad Manuscripts. Notes on Sales": 412
"Conrad: Master on Sea and Land": 824
"A Conrad Memorial": 673
A Conrad Memorial Library: The Collection of George T. Keating: 840, 841, 842, 845, 847, 849, 850, 852, 853, 862, 865, 866, 869, 870, 871, 872, 873, 874, 875, 880, 881, 884, 885, 887, 889, 890, 891, 892, 895, 898, 899, 1061
"Conrad Memories": 591
"A Conrad Miscellany": 372
"Conrad na obczyźnie: I. Od Rumunii do Wielkiej Brytanii": 1443
"Conrad na obszyżnie: II. Klub Miłośników Conrada": 1417
"Conrad: Nel Mezzo de Cammin": 1101
"Conrad; *Nostromo*": 1508
"Conrad: *Nostromo*: Record and Reality": 1904
"Conrad on Conscience and the Passions": 1811
"Conrad on Crime: A Note of Admiration": 834
"Conrad on Galsworthy: The Time of Fraternity": 1323
"Conrad on Melville": 1490
"Conrad on the Functions of the Mind": 1812
"Conrad on Writing and Critics": 1813
"Conrad Pays Tribute to Mark Twain": 483
(Conrad, Psychologist of the Imagination): 495
"Conrad, psychologue de l'imagination": 495
The Conrad Reader: 1151
"A Conrad Repository": 748
"Conrad Reveals his Literary Loves and Antipathies": 560
"Conrad, Seas and Men": 562
"A Conrad Setting": 1171, 1175
"Conrad Slave": 523
"Conrad Spinning Sea Yarns with Bone": 466

"Conrad, Stanley, and the Scramble for Africa": 1574
"A Conrad Story": 547
"Conrad Supplement": 484, 507, 530, 536
"Conrad the Catholic": 577
"Conrad: The East and the Sea": 1252
"Conrad the Great": 321, 1837
"Conrad the Historian": 1885, 1890
"Conrad, the Man": 569
Conrad: The Man. With a Burial in Kent: 397, 576
Conrad the Novelist: 1389, 1470
"Conrad the Pole": 1825
"Conrad, the Pole Famous in English Letters": 688
"Conrad: The Secret Sharer": 1111
(Conrad the Slav): 523
"Conrad the Statesman": 379
"Conrad: The Threat to the West": 1253
"Conrad the Victorian": 1708
"Conrad the Writer": 477
Conrad to a Friend: 793
"Conrad Under Polish Eyes": 1497
"Conrad w Kulturze polskiej": 1441
"Conrad w Marsylli": 1820
"Conrad w Polsce w latach 1939–1957": 1423
"The Conrad Who Sat for Me": 661
"Conrad Writing on His Career and Craft": 1565
Conrad Żywy: 1367, 1369, 1372, 1376, 1382, 1383, 1384, 1394, 1396, 1405, 1407, 1415, 1416, 1417, 1422, 1423, 1431, 1433, 1438, 1439, 1440, 1441, 1443, 1445
"Conradiaanse interraciale vriendshappen": 1903
"Conradiana": 736, 1110
"Conradova *Nahoda*": 957
"Conrad's *Almayer's Folly*: Structure, Theme, and Critics": 1797
"Conrad's American Speeches and His Reading from *Victory*": 1906
"Conrad's Arrow of Gold and Pastoral Tradition": 1695
"Conrad's Art Spans Two Decades": 329
"Conrad's Axel": 1239
"Conrad's Catholicism Questioned": 551
"Conrad's *Chance*": 354
(Conrad's *Chance*): 957
"Conrad's *Chance*: A Dialectical Novel": 1913
"Conrad's *Chance: Progression d'éffet*": 1324
"Conrad's *Chance*. The Real First Edition and the 'Fakes' ": 352

632

Index of Titles of Secondary Works

"Conrad's Colonialism": 1737
"Conrad's 'Complicated Presentations' of Symbolic Imagery in 'Heart of Darkness' ": 1613
"Conrad's Craftsmanship": 933
"Conrad's Debt to Dickens": 1400
"Conrad's Debt to Maupassant in the Preface to *The Nigger of the Narcissus*": 1338
"Conrad's Decision to Leave the Congo": 1575
"Conrad's Diary": 596
"Conrad's Dislike of the Camera, and How it was Conquered by Will Cadby": 472
"Conrad's Duel": 1713
"Conrad's East: Time, History, Action, and *Maya*": 1915
"Conrad's Eastern Port: The Setting of the Inquiry in *Lord Jim*": 1909
"Conrad's Eastern World": 1756
CONRAD'S EASTERN WORLD: 1756, 1829, 1831, 1908, 1909, 1910, 1911, 1967
"Conrad's Facts": 1934
"Conrad's 'Falk' ": 1209
"Conrad's 'Falk': Manuscript and Meaning": 1884
(Conrad's Father): 677
"Conrad's Favorite Bedside Book": 1076
"Conrad's Favourite Novel": 1319
"Conrad's First Battleground *Almayer's Folly*": 1536
(Conrad's First Novel): 317
"Conrad's First Story": 1874
"Conrad's Greatest Romance—Himself": 510
"Conrad's 'Heart of Darkness' ": 1555, 1765, 1787, 1905
CONRAD'S "HEART OF DARKNESS" AND THE CRITICS: 1587
"Conrad's Implacable Comprehension Interpreted by Arthur Symons": 276
"Conrad's Integrity: *Nostromo*, 'Typhoon,' *The Shadow-Line*": 1696
"Conrad's Jonahs": 1644
"Conrad's 'Karain' and *Lord Jim*": 1726
"Conrad's Knitters and Homer's Cave of the Nymphs": 1723
"Conrad's Last Essays": 689, 690
"Conrad's Last Novel": 394
(Conrad's Last Novel): 616
"Conrad's Last Words": 692
"Conrad's Latest Novel": 121, 665
"Conrad's Letters to a Literary Relative": 1107
"Conrad's Letters to Edward Garnett": 820

"Conrad's Life Was a Romance/In His Tales He Transmuted Much of His Own Experience": 765
"Conrad's *Lord Jim*": 1234, 1272
(Conrad's *Lord Jim*, An Essay in Structure): 1697
"Conrad's Malaysia": 1103
"Conrad's Malaysian Fiction. A New Study in Sources with an Analysis of Factual Material Involved": 1051
"Conrad's Management of the Point of View": 808
CONRAD'S MEASURE OF MAN: 1309
(Conrad's Men): 977
"Conrad's Menagerie: Animal Imagery and Theme": 1800
(Conrad's Message): 939
"Conrad's New Book": 86
"Conrad's New Story": 258
"Conrad's *Nostromo*": 1305, 1331
"Conrad's *Nostromo*: A Source and Its Use": 1631
"Conrad's *Nostromo* as Boatswain": 1527
"Conrad's Organic Artistry": 1699
"Conrad's '*Otago*' ": 1194
"Conrad's *Otago*: A Case of Mistaken Identity": 1757
"Conrad's Pesky Russian": 1707
"Conrad's Pink Toads: The Working of the Unconscious": 1605
"Conrad's Place in English Literature": 1052
"Conrad's Polish Background": 1855
CONRAD'S POLISH BACKGROUND: LETTERS TO AND FROM POLISH FRIENDS: 1821
CONRAD'S POLISH LITERARY BACKGROUNDS AND SOME ILLUSTRATIONS OF THE INFLUENCE OF POLISH LITERATURE ON HIS WORK: 1931
"Conrad's Political Prophecies": 1098
"Conrad's Politics": 1764
"Conrad's Politics: Community and Anarchy in the Fiction of Joseph Conrad": 1714
CONRAD'S POLITICS: COMMUNITY AND ANARCHY IN THE FICTION OF JOSEPH CONRAD: 1714
CONRAD'S PREFACES TO HIS WORKS: 1052
"Conrad's Pyrrhic *Victory*": 1564
"Conrad's Revision of 'Amy Foster' ": 1722
"Conrad's Revision of *Lord Jim*": 999
"Conrad's Revision of Six of His Short Stories": 451
"Conrad's Revision of 'The Lighthouse' in *Nostromo*": 1057

"Conrad's Revision of *The Secret Agent*: A Study in Literary Impressionism": 1464
"Conrad's River": 1661
"Conrad's Sea World: The Voyage Fiction and the British Merchant Service, 1875-1895": 1630
"Conrad's Secret and Its Agent": 1810
CONRAD'S "SECRET SHARER" AND THE CRITICS: 1296, 1321, 1665, 1669, 1675
"Conrad's Settings: A Study of Descriptive Style": 1736
"Conrad's Share in *The Nature of a Crime* and His Congo Diary": 592
CONRAD'S SHORT FICTION: 1633, 1671, 1721, 1874
"Conrad's Skein of Ironies": 1768
"Conrad's Source for Lord Jim": 1829
"Conrad's Stage *Victory*": 1827
"Conrad's Stein: The Destructive Element": 1479
(Conrad's Stereotype): 1415
"Conrad's Strong Man": 1804
"Conrad's *Suspense*": 595, 672
"Conrad's 'The End of the Tether': A New Reading": 1495
"Conrad's 'The Lagoon'": 1235, 1238, 1345, 1354, 1468, 1550, 1604, 1720, 1806, 1844, 1870
"Conrad's *The Mirror of the Sea*: An Assessment": 1847
"Conrad's *The Nigger of the Narcissus*": 1037
"Conrad's *The Rover* and Its Structural Method": 809
"Conrad's *The Secret Agent*": 723
"Conrad's 'The Secret Sharer'": 1607, 1657
"Conrad's Treasure Chest of Experience": 413
"Conrad's Two Stories of Initiation": 1296
"Conrad's 'Typhoon'": 1601
"Conrad's *Under Western Eyes* and Mann's DOCTOR FAUSTUS": 1402
"Conrad's Underworld": 1344
"Conrad's Unfinished Novel Resembles His *Nostromo*": 622
"Conrad's Use of Extra-Narrative Devices to Extend Time": 1520
"Conrad's Use of Time in *Chance*": 1944
"Conrad's *Victory*": 1902
"Conrad's *Victory*: A Reassessment": 1802
"Conrad's *Victory* and HAMLET": 1290
"Conrad's *Victory* and THE TEMPEST: An Amplification": 1808

"Conrad's *Victory*: Psychomachy, Christian Symbols, and Theme": 1963
"Conrad's Vision": 1814
"Conrad's Void": 1461, 1571
"Conrad's Waste Land: Moral Anarchy in *The Secret Agent*": 1592
"Conrad's Whited Sepulcher": 1664
"Conrad's 'Youth': A Naive Opening to Art and Life": 1546
(Conrad's Youth): 1158
"Conradov *Lord Jim,* Ogled o strukturi": 1697
CONSTANCE GARNETT TO JOSEPH CONRAD: 701
CONTEMPORARY BRITISH LITERATURE: 1020
(Contemporary English Writers): 1021
"Contemporary Reminiscences. A Remembered Interview with Conrad on the Occasion of His First Visit to America": 546
"Un conteur anglais: M. Joseph Conrad": 198
"Contrapuntal Structure in Conrad's *Chance*": 1850
(CONTRIBUTIONS TO THE AESTHETIC OF THE NOVEL OF THE LATE VICTORIAN AND POST-VICTORIAN PERIOD): 976
"Contributions to Martyrology": 1023
"Copies of Conrad's *Chance,* Dated 1913": 1968
"Cosmopolitanism in Conrad's Work": 1938
THE COUNTRY LIFE PRESS: 197, 294
THE COURT AND THE CASTLE: SOME TREATMENTS OF A RECURRENT THEME: 1450
CRAFT AND CHARACTER: TEXTS, METHOD AND VOCATION IN MODERN FICTION: 1101, 1111, 1129, 1148, 1252, 1253, 1451
"The Craft of Joseph Conrad as a Novelist": 1136
"Crane's 'The Open Boat' and Conrad's 'Youth'": 1499
"The Cream of Conrad": 777
"The Creative Crisis": 1506
"Creative Memory. (A Note on Joseph Conrad)": 1084
THE CREATIVE READER: 1307
(The Creative Turn of Conrad's Mind and Work): 1507
"Creators as Critics": 378
(The Criminal in Dostoevski and Joseph Conrad): 1028
"Critical Confusion and Conrad's 'The End of the Tether'": 1721

Index of Titles of Secondary Works

"Critical Discussion of Joseph Conrad's Novels": 1198
The Critical Game: 89, 372
"A Critical Study of Joseph Conrad": 1263
"A Critical Symposium": 1398
"The Critical Theory and Literary Practice of Joseph Conrad": 1142
"Criticism and the Novel: Hardy, Hemingway, Crane, Woolf, Conrad": 1467
"Criticism of Joseph Conrad: A Selected Checklist with an Index to Studies of Separate Works": 1312, 1776
"The Criticism of Novels": 1243
Critiques and Essays on Modern Fiction 1920-1951: 1148, 1254
"'Cruel Devourer of the World's Light': *The Secret Agent*": 1582
The Curious Art of Autobiography from Bevenuto Cellini to Rudyard Kipling: 1362
"Curle Sale of Conradiana": 764
"Current Fiction": 98, 106, 138, 162, 206, 207, 232
"Current Literature: Books in General": 1012
"Current Literature: New Novels": 627
"The Current of Conrad's *Victory*: Conrad, 1915": 1599
"Czytajac listy ojca": 1407
"The Danger of Idols": 612, 617
"Dark Blue and Rose": 293
"Dat Ole Davil Sea": 504
"David Copperfield and *Lord Jim* in the Upper School": 932
Dead Reckonings in Fiction: 468
"Death and Consequences: Joseph Conrad's Attitude Toward Fate": 1264
"The Design of Conrad's *The Secret Agent*": 1322
"Death Journey in *The Nigger of the Narcissus*": 1635
(The Death of Joseph Conrad): 568
The Death of Yesterday: 504
"The Death of Stefan Bobrowski: A Conrad Discovery": 1677
"Death Was the Fate of His Heroes": 1815
"Decennial (It is ten years on the day of writing since the last book of Joseph Conrad's writing was posthumously published in New York): 1011
"The Dedicated Conrad": 1531
"Deep Sea Yarns": 58
"The Defeated Hermit": 213
"The Defining Function of Vocabulary in Conrad's *The Rover*": 1615

Definitions: Essays in Contemporary Criticism: 383
"Le dernier roman de Conrad": 616
"The Descriptive Style of Joseph Conrad": 1834
"The Destructive Element: A Study of Conrad's Tragic Vision": 1347
"Deux lettres inédites de J. Galsworthy à André Chevrillon": 1937
"The Development of the English Sea Novel from Defoe to Conrad": 550
"The Devil in Samburan: Jones and Ricardo in *Victory*": 1634
"Diabolism, Pessimism, and Democracy: Notes on Melville and Conrad": 1672
Did Joseph Conrad Return as a Spirit?: 948, 950
(Discovery of Patusan): 1405
"A Disillusioned Romantic": 324
"Dlia pishchevarenia": 426
"The Domestic Background": 706, 1013
"Dostoevskij and Conrad's Political Novels": 1741
Double Measure: A Study of the Novels and Stories of D. H. Lawrence: 1867
"Dozef Konrad": 1492
"The Drama of Conscience and Recognition in *Lord Jim*": 1898
Dramatis Personae: 230
"Dramatization of Conrad's *Victory*: And a New Letter": 1629
"Drunk on Conrad": 888
"Du Nouveau sur la collaboration de Joseph Conrad avec Ford Madox Hueffer": 587
The Dual Heritage of Joseph Conrad: 1678
"The Dual Morality in 'The Secret Sharer'": 1912
(The Dual Nationality of Joseph Conrad): 1431
"Dva angleska romana": 962
"Dva dela Josepha Conrada": 1498
"Dva zapadnykh khudozhnika upadka": 857
"Dwie narodowośći Józefa Conrada": 1431
"Dzh. Konrad": 1478
"Dzhozef Konrad": 524, 653, 672, 713, 886
"Dzhozef Konrad *Na Vzgliad Zapada*": 628
"Dzhozef Konrad: Snpoba literaturnovo portretu": 828
"Dzhozef Konrad (Vmesto Nekrologa)": 602

Joseph Conrad

"Dzozef Konrad. Pomorac i pisac 'Tajfuna' ": 1019
E. V. Lucas to Joseph Conrad: 721
"Earlier and Later Days": 754
"Early Conrad First Editions": 358
"The Early Development of Joseph Conrad: Revisions and Style": 1747
The Early Joseph Conrad: Revisions and Style: 1747
Early Victorian Novelists: 1004
Earth Horizon: Autobiography: 942
East-West Passage: 1297
(*Ebbs and Flows*): 442
(Eccentric Lord Jim): 1647
"Echo Structures: Conrad's 'The Secret Sharer' ": 1598
"Echoes of Butler, Browning, Conrad, and Pater in the Poetry of T. S. Eliot": 1933
"Les écrivains anglais contemporains": 1021
"Eden and Golgotha: Conrad's Use of the Bible in *The Nigger of the Narcissus*": 1746
"Editorial Notes": 491
"Editor's Introduction": 1148, 1181
Edward Garnett: 1213
"The Edward S. Harkness Collection": 1218
Edwardians and Late Victorians: 1556
"Eenige proefjes zout water": 1126
"Eidolons of Ulysses": 229
Eight Modern Writers: 1760
"Eliot's 'Game of Chess' and Conrad's *The Return*": 1222
"Embracing The Universe: Some Annotations to Joseph Conrad's 'Heart of Darkness' ": 1691
"An Emigré": 1288
"En marge des marées": 535
"L'enfance des consciences": 1493
"England and the World: Editor's Note": 1182
Engleski Roman XX Veka: 1739
(English and American Writers): 473, 474
"English Literature": 1892
English Literature and Ideas in the Twentieth Century: 1156
English Literature During the Last Half Century: 257
English Literature in the Twentieth Century: 971
(English Literature of the Twentieth Century): 1224
The English Mind: Studies in the English Moralists Presented to Basil Willey: 1841
The English Novel: 651, 1292
The English Novel, 1578-1956: A Checklist of Twentieth-Century Criticisms: 1524
The English Novel: A Short Critical Study: 1295
The English Novel, From the Earliest Days to the Death of Joseph Conrad: 863
(The English Novel of Our Time): 359
(The English Novel of the Twentieth Century): 1739
The English Novel Today: 502
The English Novelists: 1032
The English Short Story: 1775
(An English Story-Teller: Mr. Joseph Conrad): 198
Entre la Vida i els Llibres: 604, 606
"Das Erlebnis der Wirklichkeit und Seine Künstlerische Gestaltung in Joseph Conrads Werk": 1003
The Epic Strain in the English Novel: 1508
The Epigraph of Conrad's *Chance*": 1303
Epstein: An Autobiography: 1300
"Die Erzählsituation der Ich-Form in Werke Joseph Conrads": 1614
"Escaped into Print": 960
(Essay about a Great Romantic): 1080
(Essay on *Lord Jim*): 1392
Essays: 639
Essays: Literary and Educational: 1653
"Essays on Conrad's Suspense": 598, 607
Essays on Joseph Conrad and Oscar Wilde: 441
Essays on Literature, History, Politics . . . : 573
"Essays on *Suspense*. I": 588
"Essays on *Suspense* (II)": 629
"Esse o velikom romantike": 1080
"The Essential Conrad": 731
"The Essential Jim": 1632
The Eternal Solitary: A Study of Joseph Conrad: 1301, 1581
"Ethical Symbolism in Conrad": 1094
(The Ethical Terms and Moral Values in Joseph Conrad's Fiction): 1242
"The Ethics of Joseph Conrad": 1360
"Ethics *versus* Aesthetics: A Clue to the Deterioration of Conrad's Art": 1886
"Die ethischen Grundbegriffe und Werte im Erzählwerk Joseph Conrads": 1242

Index of Titles of Secondary Works

"Europe, Asia, and the East: Editor's Note": 1183
"An Evening with Joseph Conrad": 668
Ex Libris Carissimis: 960
"'Exact Biography' and *The Shadow-Line*": 1830
(Examinations of Realistic Representation in Joseph Conrad's Early Work [with Particular Consideration of the Novel *Lord Jim*]): 1879
"De excentrieke Lord Jim": 1647
"Exertions in the Deep": 1164
(Exhibition Dedicated to Joseph Conrad in the Library at Yale University): 1073
"The Exile": 1430
"The Existential Comedy of Conrad's 'Youth' ": 1759
(Exotic): 1282
(The Exoticism of Joseph Conrad in *Lord Jim*): 381
"Exotiskt": 1282
"Experience and the Imagination: The Background of 'Heart of Darkness' ": 1666
Explorations of Literature: 1963
"Explorers of the Inner Life": 1114
"L'exotisme de Joseph Conrad à propos de *Lord Jim*": 381
The Expanded Moment: A Short Story Anthology: 1719
(The Experience of Reality and its Artistic Representation in Joseph Conrad's Work): 1003
An Experiment in Criticism: 1639
The Face of the Earth: 1230
"The Failure of the Imagination: A Study of Melville, Conrad, and Faulkner": 1875
The Failure of Theology in Modern Literature: 1730
"A Famous Father and His Son": 1371
(Famous in His Exile): 1413
"The Fascination of the Abomination—Wells, Shaw, Ford, Conrad": 1767
The Fascination of the Abomination: 1767
"The Fatalism of Joseph Conrad": 1125
"The Feast. By J*S*PH C*NR*D": 130
"Fenimore Cooper and Conrad's *Suspense*": 1738
Feuillets d'Automne: 500
"A Few of the Season's Novels": 165
(A Few Sips of Salt Water): 1126
"Fiction": 38, 41, 55, 56, 107, 124, 125, 139, 167, 183, 184, 213, 214, 215, 216, 235, 253, 254, 298, 328, 608, 609, 663, 664, 1283, 1465
"Fiction and Its Critics: A Reply to Mr. Rahv": 1435
"Fiction and the Criticism of Fiction": 1353
Fiction and the Reading Public: 958
"Fiction (Division III)/Books by English Novelists": 99
"The Fiction of Henry James and Joseph Conrad in France: A Study in Penetration and Reception": 1516
"The Fiction of Joseph Conrad": 987
"Fifty-Year Rule": 287
Fifty Years of English Literature 1900 1950: 1248
Figures Étrangères: 514
Figures in the Foreground: 1761
"La fin de Conrad": 485
"The Final Typescript of Book III of Conrad's *Nostromo*": 1113
The Fine Art of Reading: 1298
"The First Edition of *Chance*": 323, 330, 332, 336, 343
First Essays on Literature: 445
(The First Sketch of *Lord Jim* and the American Collection of Conrad's Polish Letters): 1396
"Five Hundred New and Recent Books": 185
Five Letters by Joseph Conrad Written to Edward Noble in 1895: 645
"Five Novels": 57
"Fleet Street and Pierian Roses": 992
The Flurried Years: 708
"The Folder": 983
(For Digestion): 426
For Love or Money: Studies in Personality and Essence: 1606
Forces in Modern British Literature: 1178
Ford Madox Ford 1873-1939, A Bibliography of Works and Criticism: 332
Ford Madox Ford: A Study of His Novels: 1626
"Ford Madox Ford and His Contemporaries: The Techniques of the Novel": 1642
Ford Madox Ford: From Apprentice to Craftsman: 1822
Ford Madox Ford: The Essence of His Art: 1807
Die Forderung des Tages: 723
(Foreign Letters: English Letters): 367
(Foreign Literature in Italy): 876
(Foreign Personages): 514
"Foreword": 645, 870

637

Joseph Conrad

(Foreword): 766, 879
Forging Ahead: The True Story of Thomas James Wise: 1081
"The Form and Meaning of the Impressionist Novel": 1922
Forms of Modern Fiction: 1197, 1207
(Forms of the English Novel from Dickens to Joyce): 1206
Formes du Roman Anglais de Dickens à Joyce: 1206
Forsytes, Pendyces and Others: 497
Four Contemporary Novelists: 905
"The Four Fathers of Lord Jim": 1798
Four Letters from Edward Garnett to Joseph Conrad: 702
"Four Tales by Mr. Conrad": 61
(Four Years in Corsica with Joseph Conrad, the Sea Rover): 525
"Francuski firmis i egleski filtar: Joseph Conrad": 1241
(Fragments): 462
Frank Harris: 1176
"Freia semi ostrovov": 488, 1036
(French Letters of Joseph Conrad): 839
" 'French Literature' in England": 575
(French Varnish and English Filter: Joseph Conrad): 1241
"Freud, Conrad, and the Future of an Illusion": 1325
(Freya of the Seven Isles): 488, 1036
Friday Nights: 15
"From a Wife's Point of View": 1027
"From Departure to Landfall": 87
(From the English and American Studies of Conrad): 1475
"From 'Heart of Darkness' to *Nostromo*: An Approach to Conrad": 1624
From Jane Austen to Joseph Conrad: 1509
"From Outlying Stations": 14
(From Recent English Literature. Joseph Conrad): 382
"The Function of City as Setting in Dickens' Our Mutual Friend, Trollope's The Way We Live Now, James' The Princess Casamassima, and Conrad's *The Secret Agent*": 1958
"Further Comment on 'Heart of Darkness' ": 1380
"A Further Note on the Function of the Frame in 'Heart of Darkness' ": 1388
"Further Thoughts on Joseph Conrad": 789
"The Future of Welsh Literature": 1817
A Gallery: 388
The Garnetts: A Literary Family: An Exhibition: 1549

Garść wspomnień o moim ojcu": 1372
"Der Gattenmord in *Der Geheimagent* von Joseph Conrad": 1047
Die Gegenwartsbedeutung des Kritischen Realismus: 1489
"General Gossip of Authors and Writers": 42
"General Literature": 140
"The Genesis of Conrad's 'Amy Foster' ": 1589
The Genevese Background: 1265
"Genius at the Turn of the Century": 964
"The Genius by the Hearth": 703
"The Genius of Joseph Conrad": 186, 584
"The Genius of Joseph Conrad. A Study of the Neurotic Emotions that Stimulated his Imagination": 1231
"The Genius of Mr. Joseph Conrad": 71
"Gentlest of Deep-Sea Skippers": 402
"The Geography and History in *Nostromo*": 1480
"George Orwell and Contemporary British Fiction of Burma: The Problem of 'Place' ": 1504
The Georgian Scene: 996
"*Geschichten vom Hörensagen*. Von Joseph Conrad. Deutsch von Richard Kraushaar und Hans Reisiger. Berlin 1938, S. Fischer": 1070
"*The Ghost* at Brede Place": 1261
"Giacobbe e l'angelo in Melville e Conrad": 1341
Giornale Ossia Taccuino 1925-30: 1123
"A Glance Back at the Romantic Conrad: 'The Lagoon.' A Study in the Technique of the Short Story": 1554
"Glimpses of Conrad": 761
Gnomon: Essays on Contemporary Literature: 1268
(The Gnomic Element in Conrad): 1553
The God of Fundamentalism and Other Stories: 584
"The Gods of *Nostromo*": 1839
Goethe the Challenger: 963
The Golden Echo: 1285
"The Gossip Shop": 322, 326, 501
"Granules from an Hour-glass: The Longest Parenthesis": 883
"A Great Adventure": 705
"The Great Gatsby and the Tradition of Joseph Conrad. Part I": 1949
"The Great Gatsby and the Tradition of Joseph Conrad. Part II": 1950
Great Men and Women of Poland: 1104
Great Short Works of Joseph Conrad: 1925

Index of Titles of Secondary Works

"Great Tales of a Great Victorian": 390
THE GREAT TRADITION: 1106
"The Greatest of Sea Writers: Newspaper Tributes to Joseph Conrad": 505
"The Greatness of Joseph Conrad": 1193
A GUIDE TO THE BEST FICTION: 943
"A Guide to the New Books": 88
A GUIDE TO THE NOVEL: 1864
"Hamlet and Heyst Again": 1534
A HANDBOOK OF ANALYSES, QUESTIONS, AND A DISCUSSION OF TECHNIQUE. . . .": 1954
"The Handling of Time in the Novels of Joseph Conrad": 1217
A HANDLIST OF THE VARIOUS BOOKS, PAMPHLETS, NOTES, ARTICLES, PREFACES, REVIEWS AND LETTERS WRITTEN ABOUT JOSEPH CONRAD BY RICHARD CURLE 1911-1931: 951
"Hand-up for an Author": 1495
HARBOURS OF MEMORY: 370
(Heart of Darkness): 767
"HEART OF DARKNESS": AN AUTHORITATIVE TEXT, BACKGROUNDS AND SOURCES, ESSAYS IN CRITICISM: 1731, 1732, 1733, 1768
"'Heart of Darkness' and the Failure of the Imagination": 1875
"'Heart of Darkness': Bodhisattva Scenario": 1833
"'Heart of Darkness': 'The Ancient Mariner' a Hundred Years Later": 1899
"'Heart of Darkness': The Russian in Motley": 1794
"'The Heart of Darkness' in T. S. Eliot's 'The Hollow Men'": 1682
"The Heart of Joseph Conrad": 1191
"Here are Essays": 693
"A Hero of the Old Guard": 109
"A Hero-Worshipper": 815
"H. G. Wells Tries to Be A Novelist": 1556
THE HISTORIC EDWARD GARNETT CONRAD-HUDSON COLLECTION. TO BE SOLD THE EVENINGS OF APRIL 24 & 25, AT 8:15: 781
A HISTORY OF ENGLISH LITERATURE: 1816
"The History of Mr. Conrad's Books": 416
"The History of My Conrad Collection": 694
THE HISTORY OF THE ENGLISH NOVEL: 1075
THE HISTORY OF THE NOVEL IN ENGLAND: 959

"The Hole in the Bottom of the Pail: Comedy and Theme in 'Heart of Darkness'": 1880
"The Hollow Men: Victory": 1102
(Homage): 492
(Homage to Joseph Conrad): 509
"El hombre y el mar en la novela de José Conrad": 1121
"Hommage": 492
"Hommage à Joseph Conrad": 509
"L'homme dans le roman marin de Conrad": 788
"Les hommes de Conrad": 977
"L'homme et sa liberté": 1493
THE HOUSES THAT JAMES BUILT: 1333, 1561
"How Conrad Came to Write": 648
"How Conrad Tells A Story": 1179
"How I 'Broke Into Print,' III. Joseph Conrad": 218
"'How to Be': Marlow's Quest in *Lord Jim*". 1895
HOW TO BECOME A LITERARY CRITIC: 1167
"How's Your Wild Man?": 1015
"Hudson, Conrad, and the Simple Style": 478
HUGH WALPOLE: A BIOGRAPHY: 1262
"The Humanism of Joseph Conrad": 897
I HAVE THIS TO SAY: 708
"I Meet Joseph Conrad": 1014
"Identity and Joseph Conrad": 1728
(An Idyll of Conrad on the Island of Mauritius): 941
"Une idylle de Conrad à l'Ile Maurice": 941
"Il y a quatre ans, en Corse avec Joseph Conrad, coureur de mers": 525
"The 'Illuminating Quality': Imagery and Theme in *The Secret Agent*": 1578
"The Illusion of Joseph Conrad": 940
"The Illusions of Joseph Conrad": 791
IMAGE AND EXPERIENCE: STUDIES IN A LITERARY REVOLUTION: 1395, 1590
"Imposition Figures and Plate Gangs in *The Rescue*": 1625
"Impressionism: Conrad": 944
"The Impressionist Novel": 1154
"In Conrad's *Last Essays* Is the Key to His Character/Spiritually He belonged to 'the Company of the Great Navigators'": 709
"In Memory of Joseph Conrad": 669
"In Praise of Devotion": 726
(In the Footsteps of Conrad): 1039
"In the Kingdom of Conrad": 440
"In the Last Quarter of a Century": 863

Joseph Conrad

(In the Shallows): 618
(In the Shallows, *Tales of Unrest*): 635
(Indiscretions on Joseph Conrad [1924]): 473
"Indiscrezioni su J. Conrad (1924)": 473
"The Influence of Flaubert on Pater and Conrad": 1219
" 'The Informer' ": 1792
"The Inheritors": 43, 44, 862
"The Inner History of Conrad's *Suspense*: Notes and Extracts From Letters": 578
INSIGHT II: ANALYSES OF MODERN BRITISH LITERATURE: 1791, 1792, 1793, 1826, 1843
"The Inspirations of Joseph Conrad: A Literary Journey in Pictures": 511
(Instead of a Preface): 1440
INSTRUCTOR'S MANUAL: TEN MODERN MASTERS: AN ANTHOLOGY OF THE SHORT STORY [1953]: 1281
INSTRUCTOR'S MANUAL: TEN MODERN MASTERS: AN ANTHOLOGY OF THE SHORT STORY [1959]: 1530
INTERNAL REVENUE: 770
"Interpretation der Erzählung 'Falk' von Joseph Conrad (Die Entsprechung von Gehalt und Gestalt in J. Conrads Erzählungen): 1349
(Interpretation of the Story "Falk" by Joseph Conrad [The Correspondence between Content and Form in J. Conrad's Narratives]): 1349
"Interpreting the Symbol": 1293
(Interracial Friendships in Conrad): 1903
(Interview with J. Conrad): 181
"An Interview with Joseph Conrad": 181, 392
"Introduction": 497, 596, 675, 792, 793, 801, 805, 839, 917, 935, 948, 1095, 1119, 1149, 1151, 1251, 1252, 1253, 1327, 1391, 1518, 1519, 1535, 1566, 1567, 1585, 1610, 1616, 1617, 1628, 1655, 1659, 1821, 1925, 1956
"Introduction: Conrad's Critical Perspectives": 1848
(Introduction, *The Mirror of the Sea*): 1149
AN INTRODUCTION TO CONRAD: 972
AN INTRODUCTION TO LITERATURE AND THE FINE ARTS: 1228
AN INTRODUCTION TO THE NOVEL [Vol II]: 1193
AN INTRODUCTION TO THE STUDY OF THE NOVEL: 1914

"Introduction to *Under Western Eyes*": 1253, 1773
"Inveni Portum; Joseph Conrad": 503
"Irony as Theme: Conrad's *The Secret Agent*": 1503
"The Irony of Joseph Conrad": 1340
(Is the Novel in Danger?): 603
"Isolation in the Life and Works of Joseph Conrad": 1301
(It is You Who Sleeps in the Shadow): 294
IT WAS THE NIGHTINGALE: 974
IVORY APES AND PEACOCKS: 186
IVORY TOWERS AND SACRED FOUNTS: THE ARTIST AS HERO IN FICTION FROM GOETHE TO JOYCE: 1777
"Iz nove engleske literature. Joseph Conrad": 382
"Izdanja Tiskovne zadruge u Ljubljani za 1931. god": 919
"Jack London's Heart of Darkness": 1455
(Jacob and the Angel in Melville and Conrad): 1341
"The J. B. Pinker Collection of Conradiana": 572
"James and Conrad": 1146
"James and Conrad in France": 1260
"James, Conrad, Mansfield": 1224
"James Wait and *The Nigger of the Narcissus*": 1865
"La jeunesse de Conrad": 1158
(The Jewel of Landak, Kaatje Stolte's Daughter, and Heine's Emma): 1648
"The Jews in Joseph Conrad's Fiction": 1716
"Jimmy Wait and the Dance of Death: Conrad's *Nigger of the Narcissus*": 1907
"Jimmy Wait: Joseph Conrad's Kaleidoscope": 1888
"John Bull's Other Empire": 1840
"José Conrad": 630, 698
"José Conrad (1857-1924), El autor y su obra": 605
"Josef Conrad": 985
"Josef Conrad: La Novella": 606
"Joseph Conrad": 89, 127, 134, 137, 143, 158, 164, 166, 174, 201, 236, 258, 260, 261, 282, 285, 335, 344, 364, 387, 487, 500, 515, 516, 517, 518, 519, 538, 539, 540, 559, 573, 574, 651, 682, 685, 711, 712, 725, 775, 776, 778, 779, 806, 825, 830, 832, 856, 868, 905, 929, 930, 967, 971, 973, 978, 981, 982, 996, 1049, 1055, 1077, 1085, 1104, 1148, 1162, 1168, 1232, 1241, 1247, 1281, 1298,

Index of Titles of Secondary Works

1310, 1357, 1373, 1397, 1466, 1485, 1493, 1530, 1551, 1739, 1897
(Joseph Conrad): 524, 567, 653, 672, 713, 886, 985, 1478, 1492
JOSEPH CONRAD: 197, 244, 500, 1066, 1081, 1250, 1957
"Joseph Conrad, I.": 1021
"Joseph Conrad: 1857-1924": 533, 908, 1638
(Joseph Conrad. A Bibliographical Argument): 877
"Joseph Conrad: A Bibliographical Note": 1404
JOSEPH CONRAD: A BIBLIOGRAPHY OF MASTERS' THESES AND DOCTORAL DISSERTATIONS: 1780
"Joseph Conrad: A Biographical Note": 1152
"Joseph Conrad: A Centenary Review": 1558
"Joseph Conrad: A Contribution Toward a Bibliography": 252
JOSEPH CONRAD: A CRITICAL BIOGRAPHY: 1523
(Joseph Conrad. A Critical Study): 1001
"Joseph Conrad, A Disquisition": 108
"Joseph Conrad, A Disquisition: 1910": 108
"Joseph Conrad: A Footnote to Publishing History": 1482
(Joseph Conrad: A Literary Centenary): 1386
"Joseph Conrad, A Master of Literary Color": 131
"Joseph Conrad: A Memorial Tribute": 469
"Joseph Conrad—A Modern Ulysses": 467
"Joseph Conrad: A Modern Victorian (A Study in Novelistic Technique)": 1401
"Joseph Conrad: A Moral Analysis": 1257
"Joseph Conrad: A Note": 363
"Joseph Conrad: A Pen Portrait": 142
"Joseph Conrad: A Personal Impression": 561
"Joseph Conrad: A Personal Remembrance": 481
JOSEPH CONRAD: A PERSONAL REMEMBRANCE: 494
"Joseph Conrad: A Portrait": 294
JOSEPH CONRAD: A PSYCHOANALYTIC BIOGRAPHY: 1743, 1819
"Joseph Conrad: A Reinterpretation of Five Novels": 1147
"Joseph Conrad: A Reminiscence": 654
JOSEPH CONRAD: A SHORT STUDY: 217

JOSEPH CONRAD: A STUDY: 180
JOSEPH CONRAD: A STUDY IN NON-CONFORMITY: 1522
"Joseph Conrad: A Textual and Literary Study of Four Stories": 1896
(Joseph Conrad: A Universe Similarly Spectacular): 1256
"Joseph Conrad à Montpellier": 554
"Joseph Conrad, Able Seaman": 470
JOSEPH CONRAD: ACHIEVEMENT AND DECLINE: 1330, 1419
"Joseph Conrad: Action, Inaction, and Extremity": 1597
"Joseph Conrad—Alchemist of the Sea": 510
"Joseph Conrad, Alias 'Polish Joe'": 1662
"Joseph Conrad: Alienation and Commitment": 1841
"Joseph Conrad als Dichter des Meeres": 956
"Joseph Conrad als Geschichtserzähler": 1658
"Joseph Conrad: An Appreciation": 126, 471, 921
JOSEPH CONRAD: AN APPRECIATION: 403, 915
"Joseph Conrad, an Eccentric but Loveable Genius—Described by His Wife": 851
"Joseph Conrad: An Enigma Decoded": 1192
"Joseph Conrad and Crane's RED BADGE OF COURAGE": 1727
(Joseph Conrad and Dostoevski: The Problem of Crime and Punishment): 920
"Joseph Conrad and Ford Madox Ford": 803, 814, 837
"Joseph Conrad and Ford Madox Ford: A Study in Collaboration": 1602
(Joseph Conrad and France): 401
"Joseph Conrad and Germany": 1771
"Joseph Conrad and His Art": 385
JOSEPH CONRAD AND HIS CHARACTERS: A STUDY OF SIX NOVELS: 1375
"JOSEPH CONRAD AND HIS CIRCLE": 1017
JOSEPH CONRAD AND HIS CIRCLE: 1007
"Joseph Conrad and His Idolaters": 417
"Joseph Conrad and HUCKLEBERRY FINN": 1593
(Joseph Conrad and Latin America): 400
"Joseph Conrad and Revolution": 1202
"Joseph Conrad and Sea Fiction": 155
"Joseph Conrad and the Ancient Mariner": 1603

Joseph Conrad

"Joseph Conrad and the Athenaeum": 104
"Joseph Conrad and the Congo": 902
"Joseph Conrad and the Dilemma of the Uprooted Man": 1483
"Joseph Conrad and the Eighteen Nineties": 1964
(Joseph Conrad and the English Adventure Novel): 514
"Joseph Conrad and the Fiction of Autobiography": 1828
(Joseph Conrad and the Frame Tale): 1000
"Joseph Conrad and the Ironic Attitude": 785
(Joseph Conrad and the Memorialists [With Reference to *Suspense*]): 740
"Joseph Conrad and the Philosophy of Illusion": 1683
(Joseph Conrad and the Pilots of Marseilles): 652
(Joseph Conrad and the Poles): 968
(Joseph Conrad and the Problem of Self-Knowledge): 1477
(Joseph Conrad and the Prose of Masculine Loneliness): 1189
"Joseph Conrad and the Ranee of Sarawak": 1842
(Joseph Conrad and the Tragedy of the West): 1054
"Joseph Conrad and To-day": 1163
"Joseph Conrad—Apostle of Loyalty": 1237
"Joseph Conrad as a Friend: His Publisher's Memories of the Novelist, Who Was as Shy as He Was Brilliant": 797
"Joseph Conrad as a Geographer": 1090
"Joseph Conrad as a Pole": 611
"Joseph Conrad as He Knew Himself": 774
(Joseph Conrad as Historical Writer): 1658
Joseph Conrad as I Knew Him: 686
"Joseph Conrad as I Remember Him": 1528
"Joseph Conrad as Novelist": 861
"Joseph Conrad as Playwright": 374
(Joseph Conrad as Writer of the Sea): 956
Joseph Conrad at Mid-Century: Editions and Studies: 1408
(Joseph Conrad at Montpellier): 554
"Joseph Conrad at the Crossroads": 1471
"Joseph Conrad au Congo: d'après des documents inédits": 579
"Joseph Conrad Behind the Scenes: Unpublished Notes on His Dramatisations": 771
"Joseph Conrad: Blown Sand and Foam": 975
Joseph Conrad: Centennial Essays: 1348, 1484, 1554
"Joseph Conrad: Chance and Recognition": 1148
"Joseph Conrad. Concluding Remarks": 1100
"Joseph Conrad Critic and Prophet": 362
"Joseph Conrad, curieux homme": 1024
"Joseph Conrad—człowick i twórca": 1473
Joseph Conrad: Das Problem der Vereinsamung: 1559
"Joseph Conrad—der Mann und das Werk": 1502
"Joseph Conrad, Dichter der Männlichkeit": 1220
Joseph Conrad: Discovery in Design: 1390
"Joseph Conrad. Een bibliographisch argument": 877
(Joseph Conrad [1857–1924]. The Writer of the Sea): 605
"Joseph Conrad. En kritisk studie": 1001
"Joseph Contre: *Entre terre et mer* (N. R. F.)": 846
"Joseph Conrad, est-il un écrivain français?": 818
"Joseph Conrad, est-il un écrivain polonais?": 819
"Joseph Conrad et Dostoevski: le problème du crime et du châtiment": 920
"Joseph Conrad et l'Amérique Latine": 400
"Joseph Conrad et la France": 401
"Joseph Conrad et le roman d'aventure anglais": 514
"Joseph Conrad et les mémorialistes (À propos de *Suspense*)": 740
"Joseph Conrad et les pilotes de Marseille": 652
"Joseph Conrad: 'Freja sa sedam ostrva' ": 1568
(Joseph Conrad: "Freya of the Seven Isles"): 1568
(Joseph Conrad, "Freya of the Seven Isles": A School Interpretation): 1449
"Joseph Conrad, 'Freya of the Seven Isles': Eine Schulinterpretation": 1449
Joseph Conrad: Giant in Exile: 1635, 1674

Index of Titles of Secondary Works

"Joseph Conrad/Hardy, Meredith and Conrad the Great Triumvirate": 163
"Joseph Conrad: 'Heart of Darkness' ": 1954
(Joseph Conrad: "Heart of Darkness"): 1643
"Joseph Conrad, Hip-Pocket Size": 1166
"Joseph Conrad: His Development as a Novelist from Amateur to Professional": 1095
"Joseph Conrad—His Outlook on Life": 730
Joseph Conrad: His Outlook on Life: 730
Joseph Conrad: His Philosophy of Life: 918
Joseph Conrad: His Place in the Modern Dilemma: 1584
Joseph Conrad: His Romantic-Realism: 391
(Joseph Conrad in Poland. Bibliographic Materials): 955
"Joseph Conrad in Polish Eyes": 1414
"Joseph Conrad in Poljaki": 968
"Joseph Conrad in the Congo": 910, 911
Joseph Conrad in the Congo: 579
"Joseph Conrad in the Heart of Darkness": 676
"Joseph Conrad in the Role of Essayist": 734
"Joseph Conrad in the South Seas": 209
Joseph Conrad: Including an Approach to His Writings: 416, 699
(Joseph Conrad [Instead of an Obituary]): 602
"Joseph Conrad—Interpreter of the Sea": 438
(Joseph Conrad: Is He a French Writer?): 818
(Joseph Conrad: Is He a Polish Writer?): 819
Joseph Conrad Korzeniowski: 1426
Joseph Conrad Korzeniowski: Essays and Studies: 1368, 1453, 1460, 1462, 1473, 1474, 1475, 1476, 1507, 1511, 1515
(Joseph Conrad [Korzeniowski] in Polish Eyes): 1918
"Joseph Conrad (Korzeniowski) in polnischer Sicht": 1918
Joseph Conrad: L'Homme et l'Oeuvre: 855
"Joseph Conrad: La Flèche d'or": 300
Joseph Conrad: Letters to William Blackwood and David S. Meldrum: 1456
Joseph Conrad: Life and Letters: 746

"Joseph Conrad: *Lord Jim*": 1712
"Joseph Conrad: Man and Artist": 724
"Joseph Conrad, 'Master in Sail for All Oceans' ": 421
"Joseph Conrad—Master Mariner and Master Novelist": 995
"Joseph Conrad: Master Novelist": 946
"Joseph Conrad—Master of the Interaction of Nature and Moral Forces": 729
"Joseph Conrad: Master Seaman and Master Writer": 624
"Joseph Conrad, 1907—: a Humble Apology": 800
"Joseph Conrad: *Nostromo*": 1539, 1871
"Joseph Conrad: *Nostromo* (1904)": 1193
(Joseph Conrad, Novelist of Exile): 1547
Joseph Conrad on Fiction: 1848
"Joseph Conrad on Life and Letters": 393
(Joseph Conrad. On Our New Novel): 513
"Joseph Conrad on Sea and Shore": 234
"Joseph Conrad: Original Ugliness": 1929
"Joseph Conrad: Outline for a Reconsideration": 1211
"Joseph Conrad, Personal Memories": 625
"Joseph Conrad, Playwright": 497
(Joseph Conrad, Poet of Masculinity): 1220
Joseph Conrad: Poland's English Genius: 1102
(Joseph Conrad—Pole and English Writer): 1512
"Joseph Conrad—Poljak i engleski pisac": 1512
"Joseph Conrad. Poljak koji je postao glavni engleski moderni knjizevnik": 1099
"Joseph Conrad, pomorac": 1637
"Joseph Conrad, Proto-Existentialist: A Comparative Study of Conrad, Camus and Sartre": 1919
"Joseph Conrad, R. B. Cunninghame Graham, and the *Tourmaline*": 1920
"Joseph Conrad—Raw Material into Art": 1453
(Joseph Conrad: Recollections of a Literary Portrait): 828
"Joseph Conrad Revisits the South Seas": 325
Joseph Conrad, Romancier de l'Exil: 1547

Joseph Conrad

"Joseph Conrad: Russian Pole, British Seaman, English Novelist": 284
(Joseph Conrad, Sailor): 1637
"Joseph Conrad: Sailor and Novelist": 353
"Joseph Conrad, Sculptor of Words": 405
(Joseph Conrad, Seaman and Author of "Typhoon"): 1019
"Joseph Conrad, Seaman and Novelist": 520
"Joseph Conrad: Senčna črta": 927, 928
"Joseph Conrad, Sexagenarian": 274
"Joseph Conrad (6th December, 1857–3rd August, 1924)": 459
"Joseph Conrad: Social Critic": 1313, 1314
JOSEPH CONRAD: SOME ASPECTS OF THE ART OF THE NOVEL: 1035
"Joseph Conrad: Some Polish Documents": 1484
"Joseph Conrad: Some Scattered Memories": 476
"Joseph Conrad: Srce tame": 1643
"Joseph Conrad: *Tajfun-Mladost*": 1529
"Joseph Conrad Tells a New Tale": 341
"Joseph Conrad: Ten Years After": 989
"Joseph Conrad, The Evolution of Love": 1086
"Joseph Conrad: the Gift of Tongues": 424
JOSEPH CONRAD: THE HISTORY OF HIS BOOKS: 416
JOSEPH CONRAD: THE MAKING OF A NOVELIST: 1095
"Joseph Conrad—the Man": 397
(Joseph Conrad—The Man and the Work): 855, 1502
(Joseph Conrad—the Man and the Writer): 1473
(Joseph Conrad: The Novel): 606
"Joseph Conrad: the Old and the New Criticism": 1370
(Joseph Conrad. The Pole Who Became the Chief Modern English Writer): 1099
(JOSEPH CONRAD: THE PROBLEM OF ISOLATION): 1559
"Joseph Conrad: The Power of the Written Word": 1858
JOSEPH CONRAD: THE ROMANCE OF HIS LIFE AND OF HIS BOOKS: 142
"Joseph Conrad: *The Secret Agent*": 1718
(Joseph Conrad: *The Shadow-Line*): 927, 928

"Joseph Conrad the Supreme Analyst": 251
"Joseph Conrad: The Teacher as Artist": 904
"Joseph Conrad the Versatile": 210
"Joseph Conrad. Tragedy: Sublimity": 1087
(Joseph Conrad: Tragic Figures in Conflict with Reality): 1291
"Joseph Conrad; tragische Figuren in Konflikt mit der Wirklichkeit": 1291
"Joseph Conrad—Twelve Years After": 1034
(Joseph Conrad: *'Twixt Land and Sea* [N. R. F.]): 846
"Joseph Conrad: Two Books": 1500
"Joseph Conrad: 'Typhoon' ": 571
(Joseph Conrad: *Typhoon—Youth*): 1529
"Joseph Conrad: Un centénaire littéraire": 1386
"Joseph Conrad: un universo paramente [sic] spectacolare": 1256
"Joseph Conrad und das Problem des Selbstverständnisses": 1477
"Joseph Conrad und die Prosa der männlichen Einsamkeit": 1189
"Joseph Conrad und die Rahmenerzählung": 1000
"Joseph Conrad und die Tragik des Westens": 1054
"Joseph Conrad—Under Polish Eyes": 1469
(Joseph Conrad, Unusual Man): 1024
"Joseph Conrad. Uz nas novi roman": 513
"Joseph Conrad (1857–1924): *Victory*": 1228
"Joseph Conrad [with selections]": 257
"Joseph Conrad, *Within the Tides*": 1074
(Joseph Conrad, *Within the Tides*. Trans by E. McCalman): 1062
"Joseph Conrad, *Zwischen Ebbe und Flut*. Übertragen von E. McCalman": 1062
"Joseph Conrad's American Friend; Correspondence with James Huneker": 1332
"Joseph Conrad's Blackness": 1805
"Joseph Conrad's Confessions": 355
JOSEPH CONRAD'S DIARY OF HIS JOURNEY UP THE VALLEY OF THE CONGO IN 1890: 596
"Joseph Conrad's Directed Indirections": 599
"Joseph Conrad's Dual Heritage": 1678
"Joseph Conrad's Faust": 963

Index of Titles of Secondary Works

"Joseph Conrad's Fiction": 1748
"Joseph Conrad's First Play": 439
"Joseph Conrad's Funeral": 572
JOSEPH CONRAD'S "HEART OF DARKNESS": BACKGROUND AND CRITICISMS: 48, 53, 58, 911, 1010, 1299, 1334, 1572, 1573, 1574, 1575, 1576, 1577
"Joseph Conrad's Hero: 'Fidelity' or 'The Choice of Nightmares' ": 1203, 1266
"Joseph Conrad's Heroic Pessimism: What Life Meant to the Author of 'Youth' and 'Typhoon' ": 521
"Joseph Conrad's Last Day": 486
JOSEPH CONRAD'S LAST DAY: 486, 794
"Joseph Conrad's Last Ship": 945
"Joseph Conrad's Latest and Best": 100
"Joseph Conrad's Latest Novel": 182
"Joseph Conrad's Latest Romance": 219
JOSEPH CONRAD'S LETTERS TO HIS WIFE: 755
"Joseph Conrad's Literary Activities in Geneva": 1265
"Joseph Conrad's Literary Theory": 1594
"Joseph Conrad's *Lord Jim*": 39
JOSEPH CONRAD'S MIND AND METHOD: A STUDY OF PERSONALITY IN ART: 934
Joseph Conrad's Polish Soul": 1622
"Joseph Conrad's 'Prince Roman' ": 1348
"Joseph Conrad's Profession of Artistic Faith": 144
"Joseph Conrad's Sentimental Journey: A Fiftieth-Anniversary Review": 1779
"Joseph Conrad's Surrender: Some Sources and Characteristics of the Decline of His Creative Powers": 1330, 1419
"Joseph Conrad's Tales": 626
"Joseph Conrad's *The Nigger of the Narcissus*": 190
(Joseph Conrad's Treatment of the Sea): 1137
"Joseph Conrad's Tribute to Stephen Crane": 334
(Joseph Conrad's *Under Western Eyes*): 628
(Joseph Conrad's Use of Leitmotifs): 1078
"Joseph Conrad's War Service": 923
"Joseph Conrad's War-time Thoughts of Ships and Sea": 279
"Joseph Conrad's Women": 177
"Josif Conrad": 567
THE JOURNAL OF ARNOLD BENNETT: 901
(JOURNAL OR NOTEBOOK [1925–30]): 1123

"Journeys with Joseph Conrad: Poland in the Great War": 924
"Jozef Conrad w Polsce. Material bibliograficzne": 955
(Jump Overboard): 696, 719
"Het Juweel van Landak, Kaatje Stoltes Dochter, en Emma van Heine": 1648
"Kamratskap Mellan Man": 1200
"*Kapriz Olmeira*": 7
"Kipling and Conrad": 259
(Kipling and Conrad): 1038
"Kipling et Conrad": 1038
"Klassik nashevo veka": 991
KLEINE BEITRAGE ZUR AMERIKANISCHEN LITERATURGESCHICHTE: ARBEITSPROBEN AUS DEUTSCHEN SEMINAREN UND INSTITUTEN: 1619
"Kniga o Dzhozefe Konrade": 1018
KNJIŽEVNI PORTRETI III: 1241
"Komissioner Dzhekobus": 489
"Kurtz, the Cannibals, and the Second-Rate Helmsman": 1299
"Kurtz's Country": 1887
"Kusnje pripovjedaceve svemoci": 1973
"Laforgue, Conrad, and T. S. Eliot": 1358
"The Last Conrad": 667
"The Last of Conrad": 486
"Last Essays": 871
THE LAST OF THE WINDJAMMERS: 768
THE LAST PRE-RAPHAELITE, A RECORD OF THE LIFE AND WRITING OF FORD MADOX FORD: 1190
THE LAST TWELVE YEARS OF JOSEPH CONRAD: 486, 597, 794
"Late Victorian Novelists": 988
LAUGHING ANNE & ONE DAY MORE: TWO PLAYS BY JOSEPH CONRAD: 497
LEADERS OF THE VICTORIAN REVOLUTION: 988
(A Lecture Delivered to the Ceylon Branch of the English Association): 752
(A Lecture on Joseph Conrad): 615
LECTURES ÉTRANGÈRES. 300
"Legate of the Ideal": 1665
"The Lesser Nightmare: Marlow's 'Lie' in 'Heart of Darkness' ": 1784
"Let This Be a Warning to Wives": 1026
A LETTER FROM JAMES GIBBONS HUNEKER TO JOSEPH CONRAD: 707
A LETTER FROM JOHN GALSWORTHY TO JOSEPH CONRAD: 700
A LETTER FROM RUDYARD KIPLING TO JOSEPH CONRAD: 716
LA LETTERATURA AMERICANA ED ALTRI SAGGI: 1247

Joseph Conrad

Letteratura Inglese del Novecento: 1224
"Letters and Art: Joseph Conrad": 527
"Letters and Art: Meeting Conrad at the Ship": 428
"Letters From Joseph Conrad": 817
Letters from Joseph Conrad, 1895–1924: 805
"The Letters of Joseph Conrad to Stephen and Cora Crane": 844
Letters of Joseph Conrad to Marguerite Poradowska 1890–1920: 1095
Letters to the Colvins: 783
"Letters Written by the Novelist to Edward Garnett": 835
"Lettres Anglaises": 757
"Lettres étrangères": 418
"Les lettres étrangères: lettres Anglaises": 367
Lettres Françaises de Joseph Conrad: 839
Library of John Quinn: Part One [A-C]: 443
The Library of the Late Elbridge L. Adams . . . [including] The Extraordinary Adams Collection of Books Inscribed by Joseph Conrad. To Be Sold 29 January at 8:15: 1031
The Life and Work of Ford Madox Ford: 1894
"The Life and Work of Joseph Conrad": 641
"Life, Art, and 'The Secret Sharer'": 1197, 1207
"Life in the Dying World of Sail, 1870–1910": 1715
"Life, Letters, and the Arts: Tributes to Joseph Conrad": 528
(The Life of Conrad): 1159
"The Life of Joseph Conrad": 751
"The Light and the Dark: Imagery and Thematic Development in Conrad's 'Heart of Darkness'": 1377
The Limits of Metaphor: A Study of Melville, Conrad and Faulkner: 1875
"Lingard's Folly: The Lost Subject": 1294
"Literary Causerie: To a Distant Friend (VIII)": 531
"The Literary Circle": 529
"The Literary Epiphany in Some Early Fiction of Flaubert, Conrad, Proust, and Joyce": 1758
"The Literary Faulkner: His Indebtedness to Conrad, Hemingway, and Other Novelists": 1663

A Literary History of England: 867
"The Literary Landscape": 749
(Literary Portraits III): 1241
"Literary Relations: Joseph Conrad": 1549
"The Literary Review: Conrad to Garnett; Conrad as a Letter Writer, The Jean-Aubry 'Life' Is Supplemented, Admirably, with Everything He Wrote to Edward Garnett": 811
"The Literary Review: Jean-Aubry's Conrad: Life and Letters; Conrad's Earlier Years and His Later Letters; in the Former, He Lived the Gist of His Romances": 762
The Literary Symbol: 1275
(Literary West Today: Joseph Conrad): 878
"Literature": 82, 110, 111, 145, 169, 368, 718
"Literature and Art": 220
"Literature and Exile": 1548
"Literature and Twaddle": 271
Literature in My Time: 982
The Literature of Sea Travel since the Introduction of Steam, 1830–1930: 1130
"Literature: *Tales of Unrest*": 16
"Literature: XIII—Joseph Conrad": 231
"Litteratura straniere in Italia": 876
"Literaturnii zapad sevodnia: Dzhozef Konrad": 878
(Little Contributions to American Literary History: Specimens from German Seminars and Institutes): 1619
(The Living Conrad): 1367, 1369, 1372, 1376, 1382, 1383, 1384, 1394, 1396, 1405, 1407, 1415, 1416, 1417, 1422, 1423, 1431, 1433, 1438, 1439, 1440, 1441, 1443, 1445
The Living Novel [1946]: 1122, 1824
The Living Novel and Later Appreciations [1964]: 1824
"Les Livres: '*Au bout du rouleau,*' par Joseph Conrad (N. R. F.)": 966
"London, February 20": 313
"London Literary Letter": 31, 35, 36, 37
"Looking Backward: Joseph Conrad": 414
Loose Ends: 303
"*Lord Dhim*": 681
"*Lord Jim*": 890, 1409
(*Lord Jim*): 681
"*Lord Jim*—A Story of a Guilty Conscience": 821

Index of Titles of Secondary Works

"*Lord Jim* and Depression": 1862
"*Lord Jim* and THE RETURN OF THE NATIVE: a Contrast": 1591
"*Lord Jim* and 'The Secret Sharer' ": 1910
"*Lord Jim,* Classical Rhetoric and the Freshman Dilemma": 1713
"*Lord Jim*: Conrad's Study in Depth Psychology": 1216
"*Lord Jim*: Do You Remember It?": 916
(*Lord Jim* During the Warsaw Uprising): 1416
"*Lord Jim* w powstaniu Warszawskim": 1416
"*Lord Jim*: From Sketch to Novel": 1588
"*Lord Jim* vs. The Darkness: The Saving Power of Human Involvement": 1893
"Lord Jim's Line": 1926, 1927, 1940, 1951, 1961, 1970, 1972, 1977
THE LOST CHILDHOOD AND OTHER ESSAYS: 706, 1053
"The Lotus Posture and 'The Heart of Darkness' ": 1355
"Magic Defeated": 1935
MAGICIENS ET LOGICIENS: 1022
"Majstor romana": 1513
MALICE DOMESTIC: 834
(The Man and His Liberty): 1493
(Man and the Sea in Joseph Conrad's Novels): 1121
(Man and the World in Joseph Conrad's Works): 1225
(Man in Conrad's Sea Novels): 788
THE MAN IN THE NAME: 1358
THE MAN OF PRINCIPLE: A VIEW OF JOHN GALSWORTHY: 1700
"The Man's Novels and Some Recent Books": 73
A MANUAL OF SUGGESTIONS FOR TEACHERS USING SHORT STORIES FOR STUDY: 1227
"The Manuscript of *Almayer's Folly*": 903
(Map of Europe): 833
(The Marital Murder in Joseph Conrad's *The Secret Agent*): 1047
"Le Marin Moraliste, II.": 1021
(THE MARITIME VOCABULARY OF JOSEPH CONRAD): 1135
"Marlow Almayer-Havelaar": 1649
"Marlow, Myth, and Structure in *Lord Jim*": 1948
"Marlow's Descent into Hell": 1320
"Marlow's Lie": 1703
"Marlow's 'Lie' in 'Heart of Darkness' ": 1782

"Marlow's Quest": 1334
"Marlow's Shadow Side": 1381
"The Masks of Conrad": 1701
"Mass-penny": 315
"Master and Man: A Study of Conrad's *Nostromo*": 1627
"A Master Dies": 534
"Master Mariner and Novelist": 1434
"A Master of English": 600
"A Master of Language": 123
"A Master of the Ironic": 239
(A Master of the Novel): 1513
"A Master Makes Mistakes": 306
"Masterman as a Source of *Nostromo*": 1754
"The Matter of Conscience in Conrad's 'The Secret Sharer' ": 1846
THE MEANING OF CONTEMPORARY REALISM: 1489
"The Meaning of Conrad": 537
THE MEANING OF FICTION: 1571
(THE MEANING OF ITALIAN LYRIC POETRY): 1256
"The Meaning of Victory in Joseph Conrad": 1259
"Med Stort C": 1201
(Meeting with Joseph Conrad): 1245
(MEMORIES AND CONRADIAN STUDIES): 1553, 1554
MEMORIES & NOTES OF PERSONS & PLACES: 386
"Memories of Conrad": 580
"Memories of Joseph Conrad": 798
"Memories of T. S. Eliot": 1917
MEN AND MEMORIES: 937, 965
MEN AND MEMORIES, 1872–1900: 937
MEN AND MEMORIES [1900–1922]: 965
MEN OF LETTERS: 388
MEN OF LETTERS OF THE BRITISH ISLES: PORTRAIT MEDALLIONS FROM LIFE: 558
THE MEN OF THE NINETIES: 338
A MENCKEN CHRESTOMATHY: 725
"Mensch und Welt in den Werken Joseph Conrads": 1225
"The Merchant of Esmeralda—Conrad's Archetypal Jew": 1789
"Le message de Conrad": 939
MESSAGES: 493
MESSAGES, PREMIÈRE SÈRIE: 493
"Method and Form in the Novels of Joseph Conrad": 1342
"Methods in Fiction": 280
MIMESIS AND METAPHOR: AN INQUIRY INTO THE GENESIS AND SCOPE OF CONRAD'S SYMBOLIC IMAGERY: 1772
"*The Mirror of the Sea*": 90, 91, 892
MIGHTIER THAN THE SWORD: 1010

Joseph Conrad

"A Minor Source for *Nostromo*": 1921
"Minority Report": 1133
THE MIRROR OF CONRAD: 1335
"Miscellany: Tuan Jim": 953
Mit den Augen des Westens. Roman. Von Joseph Conrad. Deutsch von Ernst W. Freissler. Berlin 1933, S. Fischer": 986
THE MODERN AGE: 1624
MODERN BRITISH AUTHORS: THEIR FIRST EDITIONS: 908
MODERN BRITISH FICTION: ESSAYS IN CRITICISM: 1612, 1652
MODERN ENGLISH FICTION: A PERSONAL VIEW: 682
THE MODERN ENGLISH NOVEL: 359, 1466
(THE MODERN ENGLISH NOVEL: INTERPRETATIONS): 1871
MODERN ENGLISH WRITERS: 1162
MODERN ESSAYS: 383
MODERN FICTION: A STUDY OF VALUES: 1055
MODERN FIRST EDITIONS: POINTS AND VALUES: 859, 954
MODERN MEN AND MUMMERS: 376
THE MODERN NOVEL: 698, 1766
THE MODERN SHORT STORY: A CRITICAL SURVEY: 1620
MODERN SHORT STORIES: THE USES OF IMAGINATION: 1685, 1954
THE MODERN THEATRE: 1366
THE MODERN WRITER AND HIS WORLD: 1284
DER MODERNE ENGLISCHE ROMAN: 1466
DER MODERNE ENGLISCHE ROMAN: INTERPRETATIONEN: 1871
MODERNISM AND ROMANCE: 117
THE MODERNS: 236
"Monografia o Dzhozefe Konrad": 1418
(Monograph about Joseph Conrad): 1418
"Moral Judgments in *The Secret Agent*": 1600
(The Moral Traits of the Sea in Joseph Conrad's Work): 969
"Morality and Psychology in 'The Secret Sharer' ": 1321, 1669
"More About Conrad": 570
"More about *The Nigger of the Narcissus*": 461
"More Conrad Letters": 826
THE MORTAL NO: DEATH AND THE MODERN IMAGINATION: 1799
MORLEY'S VARIETY: 639
"Mountains and Depths—An Approach to Nineteenth-Century Dualism": 1692
"Mr. Alden's Views": 66

"Mr. [William L.] Alden's Views": 49
"Mr. Conrad: A Conversation": 452
"Mr. Conrad and Romance": 419
"Mr. Conrad at His Best": 146
"Mr. Conrad at Home": 369
"Mr. Conrad's Crisis": 287
"Mr. Conrad's Latest Story": 17
"Mr. Conrad's Masterpiece": 268
"Mr. Conrad's Miscellanea": 373
"Mr. Conrad's New Book: *Youth: A Narrative; and Two Other Stories*": 48
"Mr. Conrad's New Field": 175
"Mr. Conrad's New Novel": 308, 337, 435
"Mr. Conrad's New Stories": 114
"Mr. Conrad's Own Story": 147
"Mr. Conrad's Play": 78
"Mr. Conrad's *The Secret Agent*": 119
"Mr. Conrad's Way": 59
"Mr. Conrad's World": 297
"Mr. Joseph Conrad": 15, 304, 388, 557
"Mr. Joseph Conrad and *Victory*": 205
"Mrs. Conrad Speaks": 722
"Mrs. Conrad's Book About Her Husband: 'Conrad Was an Amateur Husband but Always Remained Great Lover' ": 743
"My Boyhood with Conrad": 858
"My Conrad": 1115
"My Impressions of the Conrad Centenary Celebrations": 1462
MY WORLD AS IN MY TIME: MEMOIRS OF SIR HENRY NEWBOLT, 1862–1932: 961
"Na Otmeliakh": 618
" 'Na Otmeliakh,' *Rasskazy o Nepokoe*": 635
"NA VZGLIAD ZAPADA": 148, 151
"*Na Vzgliad Zapada*": 586, 610, 631, 642
"*Na Vzgliad Zapada* (Angliiskii Roman Iz Ruskoi Zhizni)": 159
NAD CONRADEM: 1424, 1425, 1820
"Najnovija dela engleske knijizevnosti": 738
"Narcissus Afloat": 1818
"Národnostni bloudění Josefa Conrada": 1043
"The Narrator as Hero": 1442
(The Narrative Situation of the I-Form in Works by Joseph Conrad): 1614
(The National Gropings of Joseph Conrad): 1043
"Nature Imagery in Conrad's Novels": 1350
The Nature of a Crime: 649, 872
(The Nature of the Power of Fate According to the Work of Joseph Conrad

Index of Titles of Secondary Works

and its Significance for His World View)": 1144
"A Neglected Masterpiece: Conrad's 'Youth' ": 1770
"*Negr s Nartsissa*": 662
Neuroses and Character Types: Clinical Psychoanalytic Studies: 1862
"New Books": 149, 339
(New Books): 1545
"New Books Appraised": 1491
"The New Books": 170, 191, 222, 262, 309, 375
"New Books Reviewed": 128, 150, 263
"The New Conrad—and the Old": 327
"New Discoveries in the Bibliography of *Chance*": 357
"New Editions": 1174
"The New Editions": 1120
"A New Estimate of a Great Novelist": 1205
"New Fiction: *Suspense*": 643
"The New Flamboyance and Some Recent Fiction": 161
(A New Meeting with Joseph Conrad): 1596
"The New Novel": 189
(The New Novel by Mr. Conrad): 300
"New Novels": 2, 3, 60, 74, 101, 129, 437, 496, 542, 644
"New Publications . . .": 4
"The New Romance": 117
The New World of the Theatre, 1923–1924: 506
"New Writer: Joseph Conrad": 45
"New Writers: Mr. Joseph Conrad": 5
"The Newest Fiction": 240
"Niedoceniona powieść Conrada": 1439
"Nieznana część rekopisu 'Ocalenia' ": 1383
"*The Nigger of the Narcissus*": 18, 32, 1389
(*The Nigger of the Narcissus*): 662, 884
"*The Nigger of the Narcissus*: A Re-examination": 1246
"*The Nigger of the Narcissus* and the MS. Version of *The Rescue*": 1729
"Nightmare and Complacency: Razumov and the Western Eye": 1693
(Nine Essays in Literary Criticism): 1121
"Nineteen Notable New Novels": 192
"Nostr'Omo": 454
"*Nostromo*": 75, 780, 799, 865, 1251, 1287
"*Nostromo* and 'The Snows of Kilimanjaro' ": 1363
"*Nostromo* and the Three Sisters": 1690

"*Nostromo*: Further Sources": 1859
"*Nostromo*: Thirty Years After": 468
"*Nostromo*: Twenty Years After": 468
"Notable Novels to Suit Many Tastes/ Woman: An Amazing Study": 292
"A Note on Conrad": 827, 952
(A Note on Conrad's Sojourn in Corsica): 526
"A Note on 'Heart of Darkness' ": 1427
"A Note on Joseph Conrad": 715, 998, 1172
"A Note on Mr. Conrad": 541
"Note on the Text": 1732
"Note sur un séjour de Conrad en Corse": 526
"Notes": 860
"Notes and Discussions: Joseph Conrad: 'A Dedicated Soul' ": 1092
"Notes on Conrad's Finance": 1169
"Notes on Joseph Conrad": 1157
Notes on Joseph Conrad with Some Unpublished Letters: 658
"*Notes on Life and Letters*": 873
"Note on New Novels": 92
Notes on Novelists with Some Other Notes: 189
"Le nouveau roman de M. Conrad": 300
"Nova Suctrich z Dzhozefom Konradom": 1596
"Nove knjige": 1545
"The Novel": 867
The Novel: A Modern Guide to Fifteen English Masterpieces: 1712
(The Novel and Ideas in England): 1316
The Novel and Society: 1108
The Novel and the Modern World: 1077
The Novel in English: 929
"Novel Notes": 19, 46
(The Novel of Chance by Joseph Conrad): 172
"The Novelist as Artist": 1315
(A Novelist of Adventure: Joseph Conrad): 391
"A Novelist of Courage": 348
Novelists on the Novel: 1521
"The Novelist's Responsibility": 1676
Novels and Novelists: 305, 337, 912
"Novels by Joseph Conrad and Ibañez": 310
"Novels of Joseph Conrad": 331
"The Novels of Joseph Conrad": 283, 351
"The Novels of Mr. Conrad": 193
"Novels too Good to Miss. . . . *A Set of Six*": 226

Joseph Conrad

"Novoe O Konrade": 816
Nueve Ensayos de Critica Literaria: 1121
"O artystcznej osobowości i formie Conrada": 1507
"O Conradowskiej gnomice": 1553
"O Dzhozefe Konrade": 1399
"O 'filozofii' Conrad": 1424
"O Josephu Conradu": 1067
"O Joseph Conradu. Polksa i ruska umjetnicka krv": 737
O Literaturze Angielskiej: 1426
"Objection and Reproof": 695
"Odkrycie Patusanu": 1405
"La obra novelesca de Joseph Conrad": 1118
Of Books and Men: 311
"Ojciec Conrada": 677
Old and New Books as Life Teachers: 821
Old and New Masters: 304
"Old Ships": 113
"On Conrad's Vocabulary": 802
(On Joseph Conrad): 882, 990, 1067, 1079
(On Joseph Conrad. Polish and Russian Artistic Blood): 737
"On Life and Letters: Editor's Note": 1184
"On *Lord Jim*": 1292
"On Many Seas": 1860
"On Plot in Modern Fiction: Hardy, James, and Conrad": 1900
(On Reading Father's Letters): 1407
"On Re-reading *The Rover*": 1244
"On 'Typhoon' and *The Shadow-Line*": 1106
(On the Death of Joseph Conrad): 463
(On the Edge of the Tides): 535
"On the Modern Element in Modern Literature": 1654
"On Unbending Over A Novel": 115
(One Lives Only Once): 1433
"One of the Masters": 490
"'One of Us': Craft and Caste in *Lord Jim*": 1861
"One Source of Conrad's *Nostromo*": 1359
1100 Obscure Points: The Bibliographies of Twenty-Five English and Twenty-One American Authors: 938
The Open Night: 1244
"Order and Anarchy: The Political Novels": 1286, 1304
"The Original Nostromo: Conrad's Source": 1538

"The Originality of Conrad": 1496
The Origins of Totalitarianism: 1236
"Othello and Conrad's *Chance*": 1311
"The Other House": 758
"Other People's Books": 314
"The 'Other' in Conrad's *Lord Jim*": 1280
"Our Awards for 1898: Mr. Joseph Conrad and *Tales of Unrest*": 33
"Our Own Bookshelf": 727
"Our Library Table": 93, 152
"Our Note Book": 20
(An Outcast of Progress): 638
"*An Outcast of the Islands*": 6, 850
"Outstanding Novels of the Year": 247
"*Ozhidanie*": 714
"Pages from the Autobiography of Ellen Glasgow": 1302
Panorama de la Littérature Anglaise Contemporaine: 717
(Panorama of Contemporary English Literature): 717
"Paradise of Snakes: Archetypal Patterns in Two Novels by Conrad": 1688
Paradise of Snakes: An Archetypal Analysis of Conrad's Political Novels: 1688
"Part One: Introduction": 1685
The Passing Chapter: 993
The Passive Voice: An Approach to Modern Fiction: 1946
Past Masters and Other Papers: 723
"Pattern in *Lord Jim*: One Jump After Another": 1258
"Patterns of Betrayal in the Novels of Joseph Conrad": 1796
The Patterns of English and American Fiction: 1114
People Worth Talking About: 975
"Perdmova": 766
"Peredmova": 879
"La Persona Velata": 1040
'Personal Documents, Works Biographical, Critical, and Bibliographical, Letters, Etc.": 874
Personal Recollections of Joseph Conrad: 482, 686
"*A Personal Record*": 153
"Personalities: Joseph Conrad": 77
La Personnalité de Joseph Conrad: 1134
(The Personality of Joseph Conrad): 1134
"The Personality of Joseph Conrad": 434, 597
Persons: Being Comments on a Past Epoch: 104

Index of Titles of Secondary Works

"Perspective of *Nostromo*": 1698
"'Pessimism' in Hardy and Conrad": 1127
"The Philosophic Romance in Nineteenth-Century England": 1704
The Philosophy of Fiction: 829
"The Philosophy of Joseph Conrad": 1411
"Pictorial Survey of the Literary Life of Joseph Conrad": 544
"Pierwszy szkic *Lorda Jima* i polskie listy Conrada w zbiorach Amerykańskich": 1396
"The Piligrim Ship in *Lord Jim*: Conrad's Two Sources": 1911
"Pilgrims' Scrip". 94
The Plain Man and the Novel: 1093
"Plon mórz dalekich": 1382
"Plot as Discovery: Conrad, Dostoevsky, and Faulkner": 1571
"The Plot of Conrad's 'The Duel' ": 1009
"Po trzydziestu latach": 1384
"*Pobeda*": 646
Poets of Reality: Six Twentieth-Century Writers: 1897
"Point of View in 'The Secret Sharer' ": 1679
"Pokusa nadczłowieka": 1369
"Polak czy Anglik?": 81
"Poland and the East: Editor's Note": 1185
"Poland Looks at Conrad": 1856
"A Pole in the Far East": 1122, 1824
(Poland in the Life and Work of Joseph Conrad): 747
(Pole or Englishman?): 81
(Pole, Sailor, a Master of English Fiction): 1514
(Polish Conradiana Abroad): 1474
The Polish Heritage of Joseph Conrad: 913
"Polish Picture": 1145
(A Polish Translation of the Works of Joseph Conrad): 425
"A Polish View of Joseph Conrad". 1420
"The Political and Social Ideas of Joseph Conrad": 1328
(The Political Novel of the Time [Conrad's *Nostromo*]): 1698
"The Political Novels (continued)": 1286
"The Political Novels (concluded)": 1304
The Political Novels of Joseph Conrad: A Critical Study: 1724
"Politički roman Vremena (Konradov *Nostromo*)": 1698
Politics and the Novel: 1286, 1304

"The Politics of Solitude": 1432
"Polska Conradystyka za Granicą": 1474
"Poljak, pomorac, umjetnik engleske proze": 1514
"La Pologne dans la vie et l'oeuvre de Joseph Conrad": 747
"Polonisms in the English of Conrad's *Chance*": 922
"Polska w zyciv dzielach Josepha Conrada": 747
"Polskilata Conrada": 1820
"Popular Fiction and Publishers' Notes: Early Conrad; *The Nature of a Crime* in Format Much Too Flattering": 548
The Portable Conrad: 1148, 1173, 1180, 1181, 1182, 1183, 1184, 1185, 1187
(A Portrait): 604
"A Portrait of Conrad As a Husband/His Wife's Book About Him Is a Domestic Rather than a Literary View of Him". 1016
Portraits: 931
Portraits from Life: 1010
Portraits from Memory: 1289
"Portraits from Memory—Joseph Conrad": 1289
"Portraits in Pencil and Pen": 448
"Portraits in Pencil and Pen II": 564
"Ports of the Conrad Country": 894
"Pourquoi Conrad n'a pas écrit en français?": 637
Post Victorians: 978
"Predgovor": 621, 1410
"Predislovie": 1532
"Preface": 380, 755, 1733
(Preface): 621, 723, 1410, 1532
"Preface to Conrad's Plays": 497
"Preface to Conrad's Plays: 1924": 497
(Preface to Joseph Conrad's *The Secret Agent*): 723
Prejudices: Fifth Series: 725
"Le premier roman de Conrad": 317
"The Presence of Mr. Wang": 1583
The Present Age in British Literature: 1463
"The Pride of Mr. Conrad": 363
"*Prilivy I Otlivy*": 398, 431, 442
"A Prince of Prose": 377
The Princess Casamassima Between Balzac and Conrad": 1974
"Principles of Structure in Joseph Conrad's Novels": 1255
Private View: 208
"Das Problem der Einsamkeit bei Conrad": 1269
"Problem Josepha Conrada": 1426

651

Joseph Conrad

(The Problem of Isolation in Conrad): 1269
(The Problem of Joseph Conrad): 1426
PROBLEMS IN MODERN ENGLISH FICTION: 1858
PROCEEDINGS OF THE IVTH CONGRESS OF THE INTERNATIONAL COMPARATIVE LITERATURE ASSOCIATION: 1938
PROPHETS AND POETS: 1022
"Proportion and Incident in Joseph Conrad and Arnold Bennett": 508
"A propos d'un livre de M. Joseph Conrad": 278
"Prosawerks Joseph Conrads und John Masefield. Eine Untersuchung unter Besonderer Berücksichtigung Ihrer Kunstlerischen Gestaltung": 1196
(The Proseworks of Joseph Conrad and John Masefield. A Study with Special Emphasis on Techniques): 1196
"Pryzhok za Bort": 696, 719
PSEUDONYMS OF CHRIST IN THE MODERN NOVEL: 1687
"La psychologie et la morale de Conrad": 855
(The Psychology and Moral Principles of Conrad): 855
"Psychology, Setting and Impressionism in the Major Novels of Joseph Conrad": 1945
(Publications of the Printing Co-operative in Ljubljana for 1931): 919
"Pure Exercise of the Imagination: Archetypal Symbolism in *Lord Jim*": 1790
"Pustolovah i zanimljiv zivot jednog od najvećih pisaca o moru": 1446
"Quelques recherches dans la conscience des héros de Conrad": 553
"The Quiet Captain": 51
"The Rajah Brooke and Joseph Conrad": 1063
" 'Rajah Laut'—A Quest for Conrad's Source": 1831
"The Rambler": 22
"The Ranee Brooke and Joseph Conrad": 1097
"Rasskazy o Nepokoe": 650
READ AMERICA FIRST: 429
"Read This One First": 1160
A READER'S GUIDE TO GREAT TWENTIETH CENTURY ENGLISH NOVELS: 1542
A READER'S GUIDE TO JOSEPH CONRAD: 1595
READING FICTION: 1221
REALISM IN OUR TIME: LITERATURE AND THE CLASS STRUGGLE: 1489

"Reality in 'Heart of Darkness' ": 1734
"The Realm of Conrad": 430
"The Re-baring of 'The Secret Sharer': Leg Pull?": 1962
"The Rebirth of Leggatt: 1711
"Recent Additions: Essays: 732
"Recent English Novels: 543
"Recent Fiction: 21, 23, 24, 25, 26, 62, 76, 83, 95, 102, 120, 223, 237, 633
"Recent Fiction and the Critics": 116, 154
(A Recent Interview with the Great English Novelist, Joseph Conrad): 464
"Recent Novels": 8, 1041
"Recent Reflections of a Novel-Reader": 194, 224
"Recent Short Stories": 27
(Recent Works of English Literature): 738
"Un récent entretien avec le grand romancier anglais, Joseph Conrad": 464
"The Reception of the Writings of Joseph Conrad in England and the United States from 1895 through 1915": 1444
"Recollections of Stephen Crane": 687
RECONSIDERATIONS; LITERARY ESSAYS": 715
REDEEMED AND OTHER SKETCHES: 503
"Rehearsal for *Nostromo*": 1656
(The Relationship of Man to the Cosmos in the Works of Joseph Conrad): 1326
"The Religion of Joseph Conrad: Reflections on the Centenary": 1385
"The Religious Crisis in Modern Literature": 1942
"Remarks on Joseph Conrad's 'Heart of Darkness' ": 1916
"Remembering Mr. Jones": 1053
(Reminiscences of Conrad): 498
"Reminiscences of Conrad: 1924": 108
"Rencontre avec Joseph Conrad": 1245
"Repeat Performances Appraised": 1279
"Replies": 1709
"Reply": 1706
REPRESENTATIVE ENGLISH NOVELISTS: DEFOE TO CONRAD: 1154
"Representative English Story Tellers: Joseph Conrad": 135
"Reprints, New Editions": 1308
"The Reputation of Ford Madox Ford": 1641
"The Rescue": 342, 885
" 'The Rescuer' Manuscript: A Key to Conrad's Development and Decline": 1351
"A Return to Heroic Man": 1533
RETURN TO YESTERDAY: 864, 925

Index of Titles of Secondary Works

"Revaluations (XIV): Joseph Conrad": 1106
"Revealing the Soul of a Sea-Rover": 422
"Review": 264
[Review of *Tales of Hearsay*]: 619
"Reviews": 211, 233, 250
"Reviews: Conrad's Last Tales": 613
"Reviews: More News of Conrad": 807
"Reviews of New Books": 195, 225, 265
"The Revolt of the Workers in the Novels of Gissing, James, and Conrad": 1543
THE RHETORIC OF FICTION: 1623
THE RICHARD CURLE CONRAD COLLECTION. TO BE SOLD THURSDAY APRIL 28, AT 8:15: 694
"Richard Curle Recalls Conrad in His Later Years": 831
"The Rise and Fall of *Under Western Eyes*": 1540
ROBERT LOUIS STEVENSON AND THE FICTION OF ADVENTURE: 1803
ROBERT LOUIS STEVENSON AND ROMANTIC TRADITION: 1936
"Robert Penn Warren's NIGHT RIDER: The Nihilism of the Isolated Temperament": 1651
"The Role of the Silver in *Nostromo*": 1329
"Rolling Home": 532
"Le roman américain et *'Le Négre du Narcisse'* ": 34
LE ROMAN DE NOTRE TEMPS: 359
"Le roman du hasard par Joseph Conrad": 172
"Le roman est-il en danger?": 603
LE ROMAN ET LES IDÉES EN ANGLETERRE: 1316
"*Romance*": 880
"*Romance*: Collaborating with Conrad": 1684
"*Romance*: An Analysis. (I)": 549
ROMANCE AND TRAGEDY IN JOSEPH CONRAD: 1210
"A Romance of Chance": 196
"The Romance of Conrad": 684
"The Romance of Mr. Conrad. How His Genius Has Found Us and How We Have Absorbed It": 307
"The Romance of *The Rescue*": 593
"Un romancier d'aventures: Joseph Conrad": 391
(Romantic Adventure of John Kemp). 697, 720
"Romantic Biography": 499
"The Romantic Circle and Some Recent Books": 105
"A Romantic Realist": 399

"The Romantic Story of Joseph Conrad": 197
"Romanticheskie prikliuchenia Dzhona Kempa": 697, 720
ROMANY STAIN: 639
"Rosmowa z J. Conradem": 181
"*The Rover*": 427, 840
"The Rover's Uncle": 1838
"The Run of the Shelves": 346
THE RUSSIAN NOVEL IN ENGLISH FICTION: 1352
SAGGI DI LETTERATURA: 1040
"Sailor and Author, Too": 156
(The Sailor-Moralist): 1021
"A Sale of Conrad Letters": 994
"A Sample of Bibliographical Method": 409
"Samuel Richardson and Joseph Conrad": 1458
" 'Scenes of Low Comedy': the Comic in *Lord Jim*": 1801
"The Scepticism of Marlow": 1487
THE SCHOLAR ADVENTURERS: 1212
SCRITTORI INGLESI E AMERICANI: 473, 474
"The Sea—and Conrad": 371
"The Sea—and Conrad: Revelation and Inspiration in the New Volume *Notes on My Books*": 371
"The Sea as the Core of Conrad": 1215
"Sea Captain and Novelist": 823
"Sea Captain and Novelist: Memories of Joseph Conrad": 1139
THE SEA DREAMER: A DEFINITIVE BIOGRAPHY OF JOSEPH CONRAD: 1159
"The Sea in English Fiction from 1918-1930": 272
"The Sea—Mirror and Maker of Character in Fiction and Drama": 1525
"Sea Symbol and Myth in the Works of Joseph Conrad": 1686
"The Sea Writer": 1448
THE SEA YEARS OF JOSEPH CONRAD: 1852
"The Search for Forgiveness in Some Nineteenth-Century English Novels": 1953
"The Search for Redemption: A Comparison of *Lord Jim* and *The Fall*": 1869
"The Search for Sambir": 1212
THE SEAS WERE MINE: 1014
SECOND ESSAYS ON LITERATURE: 557
"*The Secret Agent*": 103, 112, 899
"*The Secret Agent*: Anarchy and Anarchists": 1819
"*The Secret Agent*: Conrad's Visions of Megalopolis": 1472

"*The Secret Agent*—The Late Alfred Capus, November 18, 1922": 506
"*The Secret Agent* Reconsidered": 1653
"The Secret of Conrad's Unfinished Romance": 636
"The Secret of Joseph Conrad": 347
"The Secret of Joseph Conrad's Appeal": 444
"The Secret of 'The Secret Sharer' Bared": 1877
" 'The Secret Sharer' ": 1826
"Seeing Conrad Plain": 735
"Die Seele des Kriegers: Anmerkungen zu Joseph Conrad": 1071
SELECTED ESSAYS: 1251
"A Selected List of Current Books": 312
"A Selected List of New Novels and Children's Books": 349
SELECTED PREJUDICES: 725
THE SELF IN MODERN LITERATURE: 1717
(The Sense of Destiny in Joseph Conrad): 813
IL SENSO DELLA LIRICA ITALIANA: 1256
"Le sentiment de la destinée chez Joseph Conrad": 813
"Serdtse Tmy": 767
"*A Set of Six*": 227, 228, 895
"The Seven Arts": 187, 188
"Seven Books of the Month": 204
"*The Shadow-Line*": 265, 845
"The Shadow Within: The Conscious and Unconscious Use of the Double": 1753
"Shadows of Conrad": 634
A SHORT HISTORY OF THE ENGLISH NOVEL: 1271
"Short Stories": 28, 52, 118
"The Short Stories": 1393
"The Short Stories of Joseph Conrad": 311, 1633
"Shorter Reviews": 1557
"The Significance of the Revisions in the Early Versions of *Nostromo*": 1541
"The Significance of the Roman Parallel in Joseph Conrad's 'Heart of Darkness' ": 1778
"A Sinister Voyage": 267
"Sir Roger Casement, Conrad and the Congo": 1577
SIX GREAT NOVELISTS: 1310
"Six Novelists in Profile: An Address": 759
"Sketch of Joseph Conrad': 79
"The Skipper (Conrad)": 281
(The Slav Aristocracy of Conrad): 406
(Slav, English Story-Teller. Joseph Conrad [Korzeniowski]): 656
"Slava u izgnanstvu": 1413

"Slaven, engleski pripovjedac Joseph Conrad (Korzeniowski)": 656
" 'A Smile of Fortune': Conrad's Interesting Failure": 1851
"Smrt Josepha Conrada": 568
"Snap-Shots of English Authors. Conrad": 256
"Snapshots of the Literary World: Last Essays of Joseph Conrad": 683
"Social Comment in *The Nigger of the Narcissus*": 1849
"Some Aspects of Joseph Conrad": 1091
"Some Aspects of Structure in the Works of Conrad": 1515
SOME DRAMATIC OPINIONS: 408
SOME ENGLISH STORY TELLERS: 134
(Some Investigations into the Conscience of Conrad's Heroes): 553
"Some Notes on Joseph Conrad": 556
"Some Novels of 1920": 361
"Some of the Fiction That is Being Read this Spring": 221
SOME MODERN NOVELISTS: APPRECIATIONS AND ESTIMATES: 258
"Some Personal Reflections . . . III—Robert Louis Stevenson": 386
"Some Polish Literary Motifs in the Works of Joseph Conrad": 1939
"Some Recollections of Joseph Conrad": 795
"Some Reminiscences": 852
"Some Reminiscences of My Father": 1372
"Some Stories of the Month": 248
SOME STUDIES IN THE MODERN NOVEL: 1064
SOME VICTORIAN AND GEORGIAN CATHOLICS: THEIR ART AND OUTLOOK: 946
(Something New about Conrad): 816
"Son of Poland": 1786
"A Source": 273
"A Source of Conrad's *Suspense*": 1029
SOUTH LODGE: REMINISCENCES OF VIOLET HUNT, FORD MADOX FORD AND THE ENGLISH CIRCLE: 1132
"A South Sea Hamlet": 229
"Souvenirs": 462
"Souvenirs sur Conrad": 108, 498
"*Spannung*. Roman. Von Joseph Conrad. Deutsch von E. McCalman. Berlin 1936, S. Fischer": 1045
"The Spiritual Fall (A Note on Joseph Conrad's Philosophy)": 1088
(Steersman Korzeniowski Meets Shawlman): 1650
STEPHEN CRANE: 1214

Index of Titles of Secondary Works

"Stephen Crane and Joseph Conrad": 1619
STEPHEN CRANE IN ENGLAND: A PORTRAIT OF THE ARTIST: 1832
"Stereotyp u Conrada": 1415
"Der Stil im Frühwerk Joseph Conrads": 1932
"Stoletie so dnia rozhdenia Dzhozefe Konrada (v Polshe)": 1505
STORIES FROM SIX AUTHORS: 1570
STORIES OF AUTHORS, BRITISH AND AMERICAN: 684
"Stories by Conrad": 63
"Stories of Men and the Sea": 242
"Storms and Calms": 639
"The Story of a Remarkable Friendship": 108, 907
THE STORY, A CRITICAL ANTHOLOGY: 1226
"Story and Idea in Conrad's *The Shadow-Line*": 1612
"The Story as a Creative Medium in the Work of Joseph Conrad": 1563
"The Story of a Storm": 50
"The Story of *Lord Jim*": 420, 446, 447, 453
STORY WRITING: LESSONS FROM THE MASTERS: 729
"The Strange Case of Joseph Conrad": 295
(The Strange Respect for the Manuscript of "The Rescuer"): 1383
"Stream of Consciousness": 760
"The Structure and Symbolism of Conrad's *Victory*": 1208
"The Structure of Conrad's Fiction": 1337
"The Structure of *Lord Jim*": 1240
STUDENT SOURCES FOR SHAKESPEARE'S HAMLET, SHAW'S SAINT JOAN, CONRAD'S "HEART OF DARKNESS": 1928
"Studies in the Impressionistic Novel, 1890-1914": 1267
"A Study of Conrad's Prose Style": 1783
"A Study of Isolation in the Life of Joseph Conrad": 980
A STUDY OF THE MODERN NOVEL BRITISH AND AMERICAN SINCE 1900: 825
"Stuurman Korzeniowski ontmoet Shawlman": 1650
"Style as Character: *The Secret Agent*": 1943
(Style in Joseph Conrad's Early Work): 1932
(Subject of a Conversation with Conrad): 566

"Sujet d'une conversation avec Conrad": 566
"Sur Joseph Conrad": 882
"Sur la mort de Joseph Conrad": 463
"Sur le traces de Conrad": 1039
SUSPENDED JUDGMENTS: ESSAYS ON BOOKS AND SENSATIONS: 441
"*Suspense*": 657, 841
"*Suspense*: A Napoleonic Chronicle": 655
(*Suspense*. By Joseph Conrad. German by E. McCalman. Berlin 1936, S. Fischer): 1045
(*Suspense*): 714
"The Sustained Effort and Some Recent Novels": 54
"Suavity and Color": 555
"Svět Josepha Conrada": 997
SWALLOWING THE ANCHOR: 532
"Symbol and Meaning in the Writings of Joseph Conrad": 1705
SYMBOL AND MEANING IN THE FICTION OF JOSEPH CONRAD: 1705, 1857
"Symbol and Metaphor in Conrad's Fiction": 1772
"Swan Song of Joseph Conrad": 632
"The Symbolic Novels": 1275
"The Symbolic World of *The Secret Agent*": 1866
"Symbolism in Conrad's *Lord Jim*: The Total Pattern": 1965
"Symbolism in *The Nigger of the Narcissus*": 1343
"*Taifun*": 601, 900
"A Tale of the Sea: Editor's Note": 1187
"Tales of Adventure": 40
"*Tales of Hearsay*": 614, 623, 659, 875
(*Tales of Hearsay*. By Joseph Conrad German by Richard Kraushaar and Hans Reisiger. Berlin 1938, S. Fischer): 1070
"*Tales of Unrest*": 30, 866
(*Tales of Unrest*): 650
A TALK ON JOSEPH CONRAD AND HIS WORK: 752
"Talk with Christopher Morley": 1199
TEACHER'S MANUAL: A BOOK OF SHORT STORIES: 1669
"Teaching 'The Secret Sharer' to High School Students": 1459
"The Technique of the Novel": 782
THE TECHNIQUE OF THE NOVEL: 808, 809
"Techniques of Suspense in Conrad": 1960
"Temperamental Writing": 770
"The Tempest of Axel Heyst": 1667
(Temptation of the Superman): 1369

Joseph Conrad

(The Temptations of the Narrator's Omnipotence): 1973
"The Test of Manliness": 1447
"Thematic and Formal Function of Gentleman Brown": 1689
"The Theme of Revolution in the English Novel from Disraeli to Conrad": 1959
"The Theme of Rule in Joseph Conrad": 1774
"This Week's Books": 563, 660
THOMAS HARDY: 1785
"Thomas Hardy and Joseph Conrad": 1032
THOMAS WISE IN ORIGINAL CLOTH: 1081
"Three Ages of Youth": 269
"Three Americans and a Pole": 926
"The Three Emissaries of Evil: Their Psychological Relationship in Conrad's *Victory*": 1640
THREE LETTERS FROM HENRY JAMES TO JOSEPH CONRAD: 710
(The Three Seasons of Life): 1425
"Three Tombstones": 1069
THE THUNDER AND THE SUNSHINE: A BIOGRAPHY OF JOSEPH CONRAD: 1452, 1852
"Thus to Revisit . . .": 332
THUS TO REVISIT: SOME REMINISCENCES: 332, 365
"Tiger, Tiger: Being a Commentary on Conrad's *The Sisters*": 804
(Time and Angle of Narration in Joseph Conrad's Novels): 733
TIME AND THE NOVEL: 1270
"Time and *The Secret Agent*": 1561
"Time in the Modern British Novel: Conrad, Woolf, Joyce, and Huxley": 1952
"Title is Like a Knell: Conrad's *Last Essays*, Swan Song of Master": 744
"To the Editor of the LONDON MERCURY, August 1930": 911
TOWARDS THE TWENTIETH CENTURY: ESSAYS IN THE SPIRITUAL HISTORY OF THE NINETEENTH: 1056
"Une traduction polonaise des oeuvres de Joseph Conrad": 425
"Traductions: Joseph Conrad: 'Gaspar Ruiz' (N. R. F.)": 750
"Tragedy in the Fiction of Joseph Conrad": 1608
"The Tragic in Hardy and Conrad": 1064
"Tragic Pattern in Conrad's 'The Heart of Darkness'": 1140
THE TRAGIC VISION: VARIATIONS ON A THEME IN LITERARY INTERPRETATION: 1597

"Les traits moraux de la mer dans l'oeuvre de Joseph Conrad": 969
(Translations: Joseph Conrad: "Gaspar Ruiz" [N. R. F.]): 750
A TREATISE ON THE NOVEL: 1170
"Trial by Water: Joseph Conrad's *The Nigger of the Narcissus*": 1277
TRIALS OF THE WORD: 1599
"Trick Perspectives": 1143
THE TRIUMPH OF TIME: A STUDY OF THE VICTORIAN CONCEPTS OF TIME, HISTORY, PROGRESS, AND DECADENCE: 1930
TROPIC SHADOWS: MEMORIES OF THE SOUTH SEAS, TOGETHER WITH REMINISCENCES OF THE AUTHOR'S SEA MEETINGS WITH JOSEPH CONRAD: 773
"'The Truth of My Own Sensations'": 1339
"Trzy Pory Życia": 1425
"Tunnelled Pages": 1115
"The Turn of the Novel: Changes in the Pattern of English Fiction since 1890 in Hardy, Conrad, Forster, and Lawrence": 1868
"The Turn of the Tide in 'Heart of Darkness'": 1769
TWENTY-FOUR PORTRAITS, WITH CRITICAL APPRECIATIONS BY VARIOUS HANDS: 345
TWELVE ORIGINAL ESSAYS ON GREAT ENGLISH NOVELS: 1599
TWENTIETH CENTURY AUTHORS: 1117
"The Twentieth-Century Impressionistic Novel: Conrad and Faulkner": 1836
TWENTIETH-CENTURY LITERATURE: 838
THE TWENTIETH CENTURY NOVELISTS: STUDIES IN TECHNIQUE: 944
TWENTY LETTERS TO CONRAD: 675
"Twenty or More of the Latest Novels": 179
"'Twixt Land and Sea": 171, 887
"Two Aspects of Conrad": 433
(Two English Novels): 962
TWO ESSAYS ON CONRAD: 907
TWO ESSAYS ON CONRAD. WITH THE STORY OF A REMARKABLE FRIENDSHIP BY RICHARD CURLE: 108, 498
TWO LETTERS FROM GEORGE GISSING TO JOSEPH CONRAD: 704
TWO LETTERS FROM H. G. WELLS TO JOSEPH CONRAD: 742
TWO LETTERS FROM STEPHEN CRANE TO JOSEPH CONRAD: 691
(Two Letters Written by J. Galsworthy to André Chevrillon): 1937
THE TWO LIVES OF JOSEPH CONRAD: 1876

Index of Titles of Secondary Works

"The Two 'Moralities' of Joseph Conrad": 1278
"The Two Narrators of 'Amy Foster'": 1853
"Two Novels of Distinction": 270
"Two Romantics: Jim and Stein": 1670
"Two Rye Revolutionists": 1881
(Two Western Writers of Decadence): 857
(Two Works by Joseph Conrad): 1498
"The Two Worlds of Joseph Conrad": 1501
The Types of Literature: 1318
"Typhoon": 64, 842, 1044, 1943
(Typhoon): 601, 900
"'Typhoon': A Profusion of Similes": 1671
"Über Joseph Conrad": 990, 1079
"The Ultimate Meaning of 'Heart of Darkness'": 1752
"Under the Knife IV—Mr. Joseph Conrad": 388
Under A Thatched Roof: 1115
"Under Western Eyes": 849
(Under Western Eyes): 148, 151, 586, 610, 631, 642
(Under Western Eyes [An English Novel From Russian Life]): 159
"Under Western Eyes: Conrad and the Question of 'Where To?'": 1586
(Under Western Eyes. Novel. By Joseph Conrad. German by Ernst W. Freissler. Berlin 1933, S. Fischer): 986
(An Underestimated Novel of Conrad): 1439
"The Unity of Conrad's Nostromo: Irony as Vision and Instrument": 1976
"An Unknown Episode of Conrad's Life": 796
"Unlearned Lessons in 'The Secret Sharer'": 1901
"The Unobscure Conrad": 1606
"The 'Unspeakable Rites' in 'Heart of Darkness'": 1749
"Untersuchungen zur Wirklichkeitsdarstellung im Frühwerk Joseph Conrads (mit besonderer Berücksichtigung des Romanes Lord Jim)": 1879
"An Unusual Modern": 449
"Values and Joseph Conrad": 1138
"Variations on a Theme by Conrad": 1229
(The Veiled Person): 1040
"The Verbal Failure of Lord Jim": 1854
The Verbal Icon: Studies in the Meaning of Poetry: 1128

"Das Verhältnis des Menschen zum Kosmos im Werke Joseph Conrads": 1326
"Die verbrecherische Persönlichkeit bei Dostojewski und Joseph Conrad": 1028
"Versuch über Lord Jim": 1392
"Verwendung von Leitmotiven bei Joseph Conrad": 1078
Victorian Novelists: Essays in Revaluation: 1004
The Victorians and After: 1058
"Victory": 881, 1208
(Victory): 646
Vie de Conrad: 1159
Views and Reviews: A Selection of Uncollected Articles, 1884-1932: 952
"Views on Conrad": 1618
"Virginia Woolf's Appraisal of Joseph Conrad": 1621
"A Visit to Joseph Conrad, The Mirror of the Sea": 142
Le Vocabulaire Maritime de Joseph Conrad: 1135
"Vorwort": 723
"Vorwort zu Joseph Conrads Roman Der Geheimagent": 723
"Vystavka, posviashchannaia Dzhozefu Konradu v B-ke Ielskovo Un-ta v S. Sh. A": 1073
"War Joseph Conrad ein englischer Dichter?": 1048
The Warner Library: 257
(The Warrior's Soul: Notes on Joseph Conrad): 1071
(Was Joseph Conrad an English Writer?): 1048
"Das Wesen der Schicksalsmacht nach dem Werk Joseph Conrads und ihre Bedeutung für seine Weltbetrachtung": 1144
"Wesenmerkmale der Völker im Spiegel der Werke Joseph Conrads": 1274
"Wezwanie": 1422
"When is Variation 'Elegant?'": 1128
White Man in the Tropics: Two Moral Tales: 1666
"Why Conrad Did Not Write in French": 637
(Why Did Conrad Not Write in French?): 637
"Why Marlow?": 274
William Faulkner: From Jefferson to The World: 1562
"A Window on Joseph Conrad's Polish Soul": 1701
Wisdom and Beauty from Conrad: An Anthology: 202

Joseph Conrad

(With a Capital C): 1201
"With Joseph Conrad on the High Seas": 984
"Within the Tides": 238, 245, 847
(*Within the Tides*): 398, 431
(*Within the Tides*. By Joseph Conrad. German by E. McCalman. Berlin 1937): 1072
THE WOMAN WITHIN: 1302
"A Word About Joseph Conrad": 640
"Words, Action, and the Modern Novel": 1788
(Work and Art: Notes on Joseph Conrad's *The Mirror of the Sea*): 1083
"Working with Conrad": 864, 925
"The World in Books": 1005
(The World of Joseph Conrad): 997
"Worth Reprinting": 1165
"Writers and Books": 296
WRITERS OF THREE CENTURIES, 1789-1914: 353

WSPOMNIENIA I STUDIA CONRADZIE: 1553, 1554
"Wspomnienie o Conradzie": 498
"Yanko Goorall, A Note On Name Symbolism in Conrad's 'Amy Foster' ": 1361
(The Yield of the Oceans): 1382
"The Young Conrad in Marseilles": 1365
"The Younger Generation": 189
"Youth": 53, 891
"Z angielskich i amerykańskich studiów nad Conradem": 1475
"Zamiast Przedmowy": 1440
"Zeitverlauf und Erzählerstandpunkt in Joseph Conrads Romanen": 733
"Zola and Conrad's 'The Idiots' ": 1317
"Der Zufall bei Joseph Conrad": 1124
"Zwischen Ebbe und Flut von Joseph Conrad. Deutsch von E. McCalman. Berlin 1937": 1072
"Żyje sie tylko raz": 1433

Index

PERIODICALS AND NEWSPAPERS

Included here are periodicals and newspapers for which entries occur in the bibliography. Numbers after each title refer to the number(s) of the item in the bibliography where the title appears.

ACADEMY: 2, 3, 10, 15, 33, 38, 41, 48, 55, 59, 77, 90, 115, 124, 176
ACCENT: 1197, 1207, 1277
A.D.: 1275
ADELPHI: 522, 1037
A.L.A. BOOKLIST: 107, 125, 140, 167, 183, 213, 214, 235, 253, 298, 328, 368, 608, 609, 679, 718, 786, 1002, 1283, 1465
ASIA: 430
ALBANY REVIEW (Lond): 112
ALMANAKH: 602
AMERICA: 169, 211, 231, 233, 250, 271, 432, 449, 478, 529, 551, 562, 581, 1125
AMERICAN LITERATURE: 1490
AMERICAN MERCURY: 1010
AMERICAN QUARTERLY: 1455
AMERICAN SCHOLAR: 181, 1302
ANGLO-WELSH REVIEW: 1817
LES ANNALES POLITIQUES ET LITTÉRAIRES: 772, 1024
ANTIOCH REVIEW: 1467
ARTS AND DECORATION: 546
ATENEA (Santiago de Chile): 630
ATHENAEUM: 1, 6, 28, 40, 43, 52, 60, 64, 74, 93, 101, 118, 129, 139, 152, 184, 215, 216, 254, 305, 337
ATLANTIC MONTHLY: 89, 92, 194, 224, 255, 964, 1115, 1414, 1482
AUDIENCE: 1611
AUSTRALIAN QUARTERLY: 1370
BALL STATE TEACHERS' COLLEGE FORUM: 1778, 1801
BIBLIOTHÈQUE UNIVERSELLE ET REVUE DE GENÈVE: 750, 813, 846

BLUE PETER: 596, 923, 984
BOEKZAAL: 877
BONNIERS LITTERARA MAGASIN: 1200, 1201, 1282
BOOK BUYER (NY): 22, 29
BOOK COLLECTOR: 1968, 1971
BOOK MONTHLY (Lond): 301, 307
BOOK NEWS MONTHLY (Phila): 261, 284
BOOKMAN (Lond): 5, 19, 45, 61, 126, 141, 146, 212, 264, 379, 457, 539, 619, 654, 665, 724
BOOKMAN (NY): 12, 13, 46, 54, 69, 70, 73, 105, 119, 122, 135, 157, 160, 161, 168, 177, 178, 180, 190, 203, 204, 241, 248, 256, 275, 286, 299, 322, 326, 344, 371, 392, 439, 440, 480, 501, 583, 654, 676, 687, 693, 800, 802, 803, 804, 814, 820, 824, 837, 844, 863, 940
BOOKMAN'S JOURNAL AND PRINT COLLECTOR: 323, 330, 333, 336, 343, 352, 354, 357, 358, 374, 461, 476, 512, 552, 578, 592, 593, 769, 771, 903
BOOKS ABROAD: 1856, 1892
BOSTON EVENING TRANSCRIPT: 164, 182, 209, 210, 234, 251, 295, 296, 325, 417, 1105
BOSTON EVENING TRANSCRIPT BOOK SECTION: 655, 734, 774, 835
BOSTON UNIVERSITY STUDIES IN ENGLISH: 1583
BRNO STUDIES IN ENGLISH: 1543
BUCKNELL REVIEW: 1701, 1800
BULLETIN FROM VIRGINIA KIRKUS' BOOKSHOP: 1173

JOSEPH CONRAD

BULLETIN OF BIBLIOGRAPHY (Bryn Mawr College): 252
BULLETIN OF THE NEW YORK PUBLIC LIBRARY: 1872, 1873
CBCL NEWSLETTER: 1887
CAHIERS DU SUD: 966, 977
CALCUTTA REVIEW: 1819
CAMBRIDGE JOURNAL: 1203, 1233, 1266
CANADIAN BOOKMAN: 327, 930
CANADIAN SLAVONIC PAPERS: 1558
ČASOPIS PRO MODERNÍ FILOLOGII (Prague): 1043
CATHOLIC MIND: 477, 577
CATHOLIC WORLD: 123, 149, 153, 227, 311, 339, 559, 817, 960
CEA CRITIC: 1670, 1960
CENTENNIAL REVIEW: 1673
CENTURY MAGAZINE: 448, 564, 806
CHAMBER'S JOURNAL: 924
CHERVONII SHLIAKH: 828
CHICAGO EVENING POST: 166
CHICAGO JEWISH FORUM: 1716
CHICAGO REVIEW: 1762
CHRIST UND WELT (Stuttgart): 1220
CHRISTIAN CENTURY: 576, 668, 787, 1089
CHRISTIAN SCIENCE MONITOR: 641, 1026 (Weekly Magazine Section)
CHRONIQUE DES LETTRES FRANÇAISES: 401, 406, 423, 487, 615
COLBY LIBRARY QUARTERLY: 1234
COLLEGE ENGLISH: 1094, 1103, 1127, 1128, 1140, 1147, 1155, 1202, 1240, 1258, 1293, 1546, 1586, 1640, 1644, 1645, 1664, 1671, 1679, 1706, 1713, 1734, 1854, 1877, 1888, 1893, 1901, 1962
COLUMBIA: 477, 577
COLUMBIA UNIVERSITY FORUM: 1661, 1815
COMMONWEAL: 1145, 1259
COMPARATIVE LITERATURE: 1402, 1588
COMPARATIVE LITERATURE STUDIES: 1942, 1953
CONTEMPORARY REVIEW: 456, 1378, 1528, 1786
CORNHILL MAGAZINE: 858, 1034
CORONET: 1059
CRITERION: 556
CRITIC: 16, 65, 80
CRITERIUM (Amsterdam): 1126
CRITICAL QUARTERLY: 1612, 1693, 1907
CRITICISM: 1594, 1948, 1966
CUBA CONTEMPORÁNEA: 605
CURRENT HISTORY: 1005
CURRENT LITERATURE: 42, 89, 116, 144, 154
CURRENT OPINION: 220, 276, 279, 291, 334, 360, 444, 505, 521
DAEDALUS: 1753
DAILY TELEGRAM (Lond): 290
DALHOUSIE REVIEW: 1580, 1899
DE GIDS: 1647, 1648, 1649, 1650
DIAL (Chicago): 21, 76, 83, 102, 120, 133, 223, 237, 259, 313, 348, 356, 585, 836
DISCOURSE: 1795
DIRECTION: 1168
DOM IN SVET (Ljubljana): 928
DROGA: 747
DUBLIN REVIEW: 921
DEUTSCHE UNIVERSITÄTSZEITUNG: 1291
ECKART: 1392
EDDA (Oslo): 1001
EDINBURGH REVIEW: 331, 597
EMPIRE REVIEW: 531, 790
ENGLISH "A" ANALYST (Northwestern University): 1280
ENGLISH FICTION IN TRANSITION [Later ENGLISH LITERATURE IN TRANSITION]: 1642, 1708 (ELT), 1781 (ELT)
ENGLISH JOURNAL: 651, 904, 999, 1025, 1459, 1481, 1525, 1591
ENGLISH LANGUAGE NOTES: 1723, 1924, 1933
ENGLISH LITERATURE IN TRANSITION [See ENGLISH FICTION IN TRANSITION]
ENGLISH RECORD: 1703, 1861
ENGLISH REVIEW: 127, 332
ENGLISCHE STUDIEN: 274, 1074
ENGLISH STUDIES (Amsterdam): 335, 610, 1622, 1691, 1729, 1750
ENGLISH STUDIES IN AFRICA: 1600, 1662, 1740, 1814, 1855, 1865
ESQUIRE: 1917
ESSAYS IN CRITICISM: 1278, 1653
ESSAYS AND STUDIES BY THE ENGLISH ASSOCIATION: 350, 1676
ÉTUDES ANGLAISES: 1937
ÉTUDES, REVUE CATHOLIQUE D'INTÉRÊT GÉNÉRAL (Paris): 939
ÉTUDES SLAVES ET EST-EUROPÉENNES: 1386, 1469, 1552, 1646
EUROPAISCHE REVUE: 868
EVERYMAN: 136
EXERCISE EXCHANGE: 1869
EXPLICATOR: 1209, 1235, 1238, 1305, 1331, 1345, 1354, 1468, 1550, 1601, 1604, 1607, 1720, 1765, 1787, 1806, 1844, 1870, 1902, 1905
EXPOSITORY TIMES (Edinburgh): 1237
LE FIGARO: 401, 406, 941
FILOLOGIJA: 1697

Index of Periodicals and Newspapers

Fortnightly Review: 108, 205, 355, 459, 785, 795, 888, 989, 1133, 1188
Forum (Houston): 56, 230, 1830
Forum (Zagreb): 1973
Forum der Letteren: 1903
Four Quarters: 1592
Freeman: 341, 433
Gazette des Lettres: 1245
Geistige Welt: 1189
German Life and Letters: 1771
Germano-Slavica: 1048
Glas Zadra: 1446
Golden Book Magazine: 894
Gral (Munich): 670, 745, 979
Graphic: 472
Greensborough (N.C.) Daily News: 411
Harper's Weekly: 50, 79
Harvard Library Bulletin: 1351
Hefte für Büchereiwesen: 830
Hibbert Journal: 471, 1411
Hochland (Munich): 1079
Holborn Review: 861
Hrvatska Revija (Zagreb): 919
Hrvatska Straža: 1099
Hudson Review: 1211, 1306, 1496
Humanities Association of Canada Bulletin: 1818
Il Convegno: 474
Illustrated London News: 20, 23, 388, 1434
Illustrvana Politika (Belgrade): 1643
Independent: 82, 110, 111, 156, 171, 196, 242, 267, 511, 515, 534
Indiana Quarterly for Bookmen: 1169
Innostranaaia Literatura: 1399, 1418, 1505
Internationatiosional'naia Literatura: 1073
Invitation to Learning Reader: 1272, 1287
Iowa English Studies: 1746
Istoria Anglisskoi Literatury (Academy of Science, USSR): 1478
Italia Che Scrive: 876
Jadranska Straza (Split): 1019
John O'London's Weekly: 486, 625
Le Journal des Débats: 172, 381, 391, 465
Journal of the American Psychoanalytic Association: 1916
Journal of British Studies: 1715
Journal of Education (Lond): 1161
Journal of English Literary History: 1322, 1888
Journal of English and Germanic Philology: 1338

Juridical Review (Edinburgh): 834
Jutro (Ljubljana): 968
Kansas Magazine: 1603
Kenyon Review: 1286, 1294, 1304, 1353, 1389, 1435
Kerygma: 1788
Knica I Profsoiuzy: 642, 780
Knignosha: 7, 431, 488, 489, 586, 601, 618, 646, 650, 696, 697
Kölnische Zeitung: 1071, 1083
Kraj: 81
Krasnaia Niua: 442, 524, 878
Kultura I Społeczeństwo: 1426, 1429
Kwartalnik Neofilologiczny: 1453, 1460, 1462, 1473, 1474, 1475, 1476, 1507, 1511, 1515, 1553
Land and Water: 268
Latitudes: 541
Leningrad: 653
Lese Zirkel (Zurich): 498
Letopis Matice Srpske (Novi Sad): 738
Letteratura: 1341
Lettres Nouvelles: 1493
Library Journal: 1491
Life and Letters Today: 1098
Listener: 1139, 1289, 1395, 1420, 1548, 1885, 1890
Literarische Welt: 514
Literary Digest: 71, 88, 195, 225, 265, 428, 466, 510, 527, 637, 1059
Literary Digest International Book Review: 422, 510, 623, 636, 649, 683
Literary World (Lond): 14
Literatur: 498, 986, 1000, 1045, 1054, 1070, 1072
Literature and Psychology: 1325, 1711
Literaturanaia Gazeta: 991, 1018, 1177
Living Age: 47, 108, 290, 369, 400, 457, 528, 637, 654, 727, 739, 949
Ljubljanski Zvon (Ljubljana): 776, 962
London Magazine: 1298, 1364, 1374, 1381, 1393, 1398, 1432, 1447, 1448
London Mercury: 318, 491, 557, 663, 664, 715, 748, 902, 910, 911, 1010, 1011
Lookout (NY): 810
Magdeburgische Zeitung: 1062
Manchester Guardian: 467
Mariner's Mirror: 1091
Mark Twain Journal: 1593
McNeese Review: 1847
Melbourne Critical Review: 1696
Mentor: 483, 486, 591, 624, 625, 640, 648, 916
Le Mercure de France: 158, 487, 579, 757, 1038, 1039
Mermaid (Detroit): 694

MIDWEST QUARTERLY: 1898
MLADA POTA (Ljubljana): 1545
MODERN AGE: 1840
MODERN DRAMA: 1827
MODERN FICTION STUDIES: 1312, 1315, 1323, 1324, 1329, 1336, 1339, 1344, 1355, 1380, 1388, 1472, 1495, 1541, 1631, 1651, 1672, 1695, 1721, 1749, 1769, 1776, 1802, 1804, 1809, 1810, 1823, 1839, 1845, 1850, 1900, 1943, 1965
MODERN LANGUAGE NOTES: 273, 922, 1009, 1029, 1222, 1361, 1363, 1379, 1499, 1527
MODERN LANGUAGE QUARTERLY: 1464, 1726, 1784, 1812, 1884
MODERN LANGUAGE REVIEW: 1808, 1829
MODERN PHILOLOGY: 1332, 1480, 1831, 1906
MODERN QUARTERLY: 1193
MODRA PTICA (Ljubljana): 927
MOLODAIA GVARDIA: 662
MONATSSCHRIFT FÜR KRIMINALPSYCHOLOGIE: 1028, 1047
MUSIC TEACHER: 387
NARODNI LIST (Zagreb): 1512
NATION (NY): 24, 25, 26, 57, 95, 98, 106, 138, 145, 162, 174, 206, 207, 232, 247, 269, 282, 293, 344, 378, 424, 479, 538, 582, 669, 680, 1023, 1191
NATION AND THE ATHENAEUM: 363, 452, 499, 547, 573, 613, 667, 705, 731, 807
NATIONAL EDUCATION: 1157
NATIONAL MAGAZINE: 438
NATIONAL REVIEW: 1163
DIE NEUEREN SPRACHEN: 1449, 1477, 1502, 1718
NEUE RUNDSCHAU (Frankfurt): 990
NEUPHILOLOGISCHE MONATSSCHRIFT: 1078
NEW AGE: 104
NEW ENGLISH WEEKLY: 1041
NEW REPUBLIC: 201, 258, 302, 366, 427, 429, 454, 537, 614, 633, 634, 726, 909, 1030, 1101, 1111, 1129, 1165, 1346
NEW STATESMAN: 369, 437, 496, 689, 812, 815, 1430, 1557, 1825, 1883, 1934
NEW STATESMAN AND NATION: 315, 389, 617, 627, 796, 953, 1012, 1122, 1150, 1223, 1288, 1409
NEW YORK EVENING POST: 436, 555, 762, 811
NEW YORK EVENING POST LITERARY REVIEW: 372, 383, 414, 419, 455, 458, 569, 570, 632, 666, 743, 744
NEW YORK HERALD TRIBUNE BOOKS: 497, 722, 758, 822, 823, 1027, 1110, 1308, 1457, 1565

NEW YORK PUBLIC LIBRARY BULLETIN: 1218, 1249, 1261
NEW YORK REVIEW OF BOOKS: 1764, 1935
NEW YORK TIMES: 4, 185, 306, 410, 970, 1279
NEW YORK TIMES AUTUMN BOOK NUMBER: 99
NEW YORK TIMES MAGAZINE: 142, 402, 945
NEW YORK TIMES SATURDAY REVIEW OF BOOKS AND ART: 18, 31, 32, 35, 36, 37, 39, 44, 49, 51, 62, 63, 66, 72, 75, 86, 100, 109, 121
NEW YORK TIMES SUNDAY REVIEW OF BOOKS: 147, 163, 175, 228, 229, 239, 249, 280, 310, 329, 362, 390, 404, 405, 413, 416, 421, 470, 560, 575, 590, 622, 671, 695, 709, 765, 831, 1016, 1112, 1120, 1166, 1199, 1205, 1371, 1494
NEW YORK WORLD: 548, 741 (Education Section), 763 (Education Section)
NEW YORK WORLD-TELEGRAM: 810 (Education Section)
NINETEENTH CENTURY AND AFTER: 779, 906
NINETEENTH-CENTURY FICTION: 1303, 1320, 1421, 1427, 1461, 1486, 1503, 1517, 1540, 1571, 1582, 1632, 1634, 1635, 1667, 1707, 1752, 1797, 1882, 1908, 1944
NORTH AMERICAN REVIEW: 71, 128, 150, 186, 263, 283, 749
NOSOTROS: 605, 1118
NOTES AND QUERIES: 1084, 1085, 1086, 1087, 1088, 1100, 1290, 1311, 1400, 1412, 1458, 1500, 1534, 1555, 1629, 1677, 1709, 1710, 1722, 1738, 1742, 1754, 1757, 1859, 1920
NOTRE DAME ENGLISH JOURNAL: 1689
LES NOUVELLES LITTÉRAIRES: 401, 464, 587, 637, 784, 818, 819, 882
NOUVELLE REVUE CRITIQUE: 855
NOUVELLE REVUE FRANÇAISE: 108, 418, 462, 474, 475, 485, 492, 493, 495, 498, 500, 503, 509, 514, 516, 523, 526, 535, 553, 566, 621, 860
NOVII MIR: 610, 681, 1036
NOVI RAZGLEDI (Ljubljana): 1539
NOVYI ZHURNAL DLIA VSEKH: 151
NOWA REFORMA (Cracow): 677
OBZOR (Zagreb): 513, 656, 737
OPEN SHELF (Cleveland): 245, 288, 342, 659, 1017
ORIENT/WEST: 1833
ORIGENES (Havana): 1148
ORPLID (Augsburg): 832

Index of Periodicals and Newspapers

Oslobodenje (Sarajevo): 1513, 1568
Outlook (Lond): 11, 87, 417
Outlook (NY): 9, 67, 85, 97, 170, 191, 222, 262, 309, 319, 340, 375, 396, 397, 407, 520, 565, 647, 657, 661, 728
PMLA: 451, 1057, 1246, 1296, 1641, 1790, 1830, 1846, 1849
Papers of the Bibliographical Society of America: 409, 1153
Papers of the Manchester Literary Club: 316, 685
Papers of the Michigan Academy of Science, Arts, and Letters: 1727
Partisan Review: 1618, 1654
Pechat i Revolutsia: 398, 631, 635, 719, 720, 767
Petit Meridional: 554
Petit Provençal: 652
Philological Quarterly: 1613, 1745, 1911
Poet Lore: 777
Poland: 438, 448, 677, 736
Polish American Studies: 181, 1929
Polish Perspectives: 1497
Polish Review: 1348, 1396, 1404, 1484, 1554, 1579, 1743, 1789
Politica (Belgrade): 1413, 1529
Pologna (Paris): 425
Pologne Littéraire: 747
Polska Akademia Naukowych Sprawozdania Wydziału Nauk: 1460
Prairie Schooner: 1179
Prijatelj (Zagreb): 981
Princeton University Library Chronicle: 1751
Prosveshchenie: 799
Przeglad Humanistyczny: 1820
Przeglad Kulturalny: 1368, 1424
Psychoanalytic Quarterly: 1728
Public Ledger Literary Review (Phila): 455
Publishers' Weekly: 179, 221, 226, 238, 292, 764
Puck: 187, 188
Quarterly Bulletin of Northwestern University Medical School: 1216
Quarterly of Film, Radio, and Television: 1403
Quarterly Review (Lond): 155, 540, 995, 1092
Queen: 561
Queen's Quarterly: 351
Rabochii Zhurnal: 628
Reading and Collecting: 1050
Rechi Bulletenin Lit. I Zhizni: 159
Renascence: 1759
Revi (Belgrade): 382

Review of English Literature: 1692, 1889, 1909, 1947
Review of English Studies: 1359, 1538, 1755, 1842, 1910, 1921
Review of Reviews (NY): 30, 131, 165, 192, 219, 240, 270
Review of Reviews (Lond): 434
Revolutsia i Kultura: 857
La Revue Anglo-Americaine: 740, 788, 998
Revue Britannique: 34
La Revue de France: 367, 463
Revue de L'Amérique Latine: 400
Revue de L'Enseignement des Langues Vivantes: 848, 854, 947, 969
La Revue de Paris: 285, 896, 1158
Revue des Deux Mondes: 198, 300, 616
Revue des Langues Vivantes: 1886
Revues des Revues [Revue Mondiale]: 84
Revue Hebdomadaire: 278, 460, 603, 1021
Revue Mensuelle: 531
Revue Politique et Littérataire [Formerly Revue Bleue]: 317
Rhythm: 137
Rice Institute Pamphlets: 1377, 1578
Rice University Studies: 1863
Rozhledy Po Literature a Umeni (Prague): 957, 964, 997
Russkow Bogatstvo: 148
Saturday Evening Post: 754
Saturday Review (Lond): 17, 78, 503, 518, 612, 617, 643, 735, 775
Saturday Review of Literature (NY): 490, 504, 532, 544, 572, 580, 588, 595, 598, 607, 629, 639, 674, 760, 778, 827, 883, 983, 994, 1015, 1174, 1192, 1533
Savremenik: 1067 (Zagreb), 1492 (Belgrade), 1498 (Belgrade)
Scholastic: 1049, 1160
School (Toronto): 932, 1044
Schweitzer Rundschau: 1658
Scientific Monthly: 1090
Scribner's Magazine (Lond): 386, 498, 926
Scrutiny: 992, 1106, 1204
Sea Breezes: The Ship Lovers' Digest: 1194
Sewanee Review: 277, 384, 385, 508, 599, 897, 1148, 1251, 1485, 1560, 1881
Shenandoah: 1268
Slavic and East European Journal: 1937
South Atlantic Quarterly: 395, 1076, 1615, 1805
Speaker: 58

SPECTATOR (Lond): 8, 27, 47, 68, 94, 96, 113, 114, 132, 143, 173, 200, 246, 289, 320, 373, 399, 563, 611, 626, 660, 703, 706, 711, 751, 789, 798, 1013, 1033, 1053, 1837
SPRSKI KNSIZEVNI GLASNIK (Belgrade): 567
ST. LOUIS PUBLIC LIBRARY MONTHLY BULLETIN: 732
STANDARD: 469, 761
STRAND (NY): 218
STRAND (Lond): 218, 448
STUDIA ROMANTICA ET ANGLICA ZAGRABIENSIA: 1621, 1656, 1698, 1974
STUDIES: 533
STUDIES IN BIBLIOGRAPHY (PAPERS OF THE BIBLIOGRAPHICAL SOCIETY OF THE UNIVERSITY OF VIRGINIA): 1625
STUDIES IN ENGLISH LITERATURE: 1500-1900: 1690
STUDIES IN PHILOLOGY: 1063, 1097, 1239, 1317, 1589
STUDIES IN SHORT FICTION: 1782, 1851, 1853, 1874, 1880, 1912
SYDNEY BULLETIN: 770
T. P.'S AND CASSELL'S WEEKLY: 739
TABLET (Lond): 1385
TAMARACK REVIEW: 1483
TEXAS QUARTERLY: 1779
TEXAS STUDIES IN LITERATURE AND LANGUAGE: 1561, 1682, 1688, 1770, 1915, 1949, 1950
THEORIA: 1622
30 DNEI: 672, 1080
THIS QUARTER (Paris): 933
THOTH: 1913
TIME: 1164
TIMES LITERARY SUPPLEMENT (Lond): 53, 91, 103, 189, 193, 208, 266, 287, 308, 324, 377, 412, 416, 420, 435, 446, 447, 453, 481, 542, 574, 589, 594, 644, 673, 674, 690, 712, 753, 756, 826, 914, 1006, 1171, 1172, 1175, 1319, 1365, 1397, 1488, 1531, 1838, 1860, 1926, 1927, 1940, 1951, 1961, 1970, 1972, 1977

TRANSATLANTIC REVIEW: 484, 494, 507, 525, 530, 536, 543, 545, 549
TWENTIETH CENTURY (Lond): 1428
TWENTIETH CENTURY LITERATURE: 1333, 1343, 1387, 1442, 1479, 1487, 1526, 1564, 1598, 1895
TULANE STUDIES IN ENGLISH: 1660
TWÓRCZOŚĆ: 498, 1425
TYGODNIK ILLUSTROWANY: 181
UNITY (Chicago): 730
UNIVERSITY REVIEW: 1798, 1811
UNIVERSITY OF KANSAS CITY REVIEW: 1264, 1471, 1536, 1657
UNIVERSITY OF TORONTO QUARTERLY: 1334
UREME: 568
USE OF ENGLISH (Lond): 1243, 1537
VESTI INNOSTRANNI LITERATURY: 816
VICTORIAN STUDIES: 1923
LA VIE INTELLECTUELLE: 920
VIRGINIA QUARTERLY REVIEW: 989, 1143
VSE LITERATURA (Kiev): 1596
WEEKLY REVIEW (NY): 321, 343
WEST AND EAST (Moscow): 714
WESTERN HUMANITIES REVIEW: 1299, 1436, 1605
WESTERN REVIEW: 1208
WIADOMOŚCI: 1289
WISCONSIN LIBRARY BULLETIN: 199, 312, 349
WORLD REVIEW (Chicago): 688, 1244
WORLD TODAY (Lond): 797, 851
WORLD'S WORK: 371, 519
YALE REVIEW: 361, 415, 596, 641, 692, 791, 864, 925, 1107, 1146, 1229
YALE UNIVERSITY LIBRARY GAZETTE: 843, 1061, 1065, 1113
ZEITSCHRIFT FÜR FRANZÖSISCHEN UND ENGLISCHEN UNTERRICHT: 856
ZEITSCHRIFT FÜR SLAVISCHE PHILOLOGIE: 1918
ZENA IN DOM (Ljubljana): 985
ZH ITTIA REVOLUTSIA: 638
ZIVOT (Sarajevo): 1514
ZORI: 426
ŻYCIE I SZTUKA: 81

Index

FOREIGN LANGUAGES

Included here are the languages in which articles and books listed in the bibliography originally appeared. Numbers under each language refer to items in the bibliography where the foreign-language title is given. English language items are not listed.

Czechoslovakian: 957, 967, 997, 1043, 1159
Dutch: 877, 1125, 1647, 1648, 1649, 1650, 1903
French: 34, 84, 158, 172, 198, 278, 285, 300, 317, 359, 367, 381, 391, 400, 401, 406, 418, 423, 425, 460, 462, 463, 464, 465, 475, 485, 487, 492, 493, 495, 498, 500, 509, 514, 523, 525, 526, 535, 545, 553, 554, 566, 579, 587, 603, 615, 616, 637, 652, 717, 740, 747, 750, 757, 772, 784, 788, 813, 818, 819, 833, 839, 846, 848, 854, 855, 860, 882, 896, 914, 920, 939, 941, 947, 966, 969, 977, 1021, 1022, 1024, 1038, 1039, 1081, 1134, 1135, 1158, 1206, 1245, 1276, 1316, 1386, 1493, 1547, 1646, 1937
German: 670, 723, 733, 745, 830, 832, 856, 868, 956, 976, 979, 986, 990, 1000, 1003, 1028, 1045, 1047, 1048, 1054, 1062, 1070, 1071, 1072, 1078, 1079, 1083, 1124, 1137, 1144, 1189, 1196, 1220, 1225, 1242, 1269, 1274, 1291, 1326, 1349, 1392, 1449, 1466, 1477, 1489, 1502, 1559, 1614, 1658, 1718, 1871, 1879, 1918, 1932
Italian: 473, 474, 876, 1040, 1123, 1224, 1247, 1256, 1341

Norwegian: 1001
Polish: 81, 181, 677, 747, 955, 1367, 1368, 1369, 1372, 1376, 1382, 1383, 1384, 1394, 1396, 1405, 1407, 1415, 1416, 1417, 1422, 1423, 1424, 1425, 1426, 1429, 1431, 1433, 1437, 1438, 1439, 1440, 1441, 1443, 1445, 1460, 1473, 1474, 1475, 1507, 1553, 1638, 1680, 1820
Russian: 7, 148, 151, 159, 398, 426, 431, 442, 488, 489, 524, 586, 601, 602, 610, 618, 628, 631, 635, 638, 642, 646, 650, 653, 662, 672, 681, 696, 697, 714, 719, 720, 767, 780, 799, 816, 857, 878, 991, 1018, 1036, 1073, 1080, 1099, 1177, 1399, 1418, 1478, 1505, 1532, 1544
Serbo-Croatian: 382, 513, 567, 568, 621, 656, 737, 738, 919, 962, 981, 985, 1019, 1067, 1232, 1241, 1373, 1410, 1413, 1446, 1492, 1498, 1512, 1513, 1514, 1529, 1551, 1568, 1637, 1643, 1697, 1739, 1973
Slovene: 776, 927, 928, 968, 1539, 1545
Spanish: 516, 604, 605, 606, 630, 1118, 1121
Swedish: 1200, 1201, 1282
Ukrainian: 713, 766, 828, 879, 886, 900, 1596

Index

PRIMARY TITLES

Included here are all titles by Conrad which occur in titles of articles or books or in the abstracts. Numbers after each title refer to the item in the bibliography where the title appears.

Almayer's Folly: 1, 2, 5, 6, 7, 79, 89, 108, 123, 126, 134, 136, 137, 158, 160, 177, 178, 201, 203, 217, 218, 236, 261, 274, 285, 314, 317, 327, 331, 350, 358, 391, 403, 407, 415, 425, 450, 457, 460, 469, 476, 526, 533, 539, 603, 621, 645, 648, 656, 685, 733, 752, 769, 771, 782, 790, 805, 806, 823, 825, 804, 879, 898, 903, 909, 925, 945, 959, 970, 971, 983, 1011, 1021, 1032, 1041, 1048, 1063, 1096, 1102, 1118, 1138, 1152, 1165, 1171, 1175, 1176, 1183, 1190, 1210, 1213, 1265, 1282, 1294, 1309, 1316, 1335, 1352, 1403, 1419, 1453, 1471, 1483, 1515, 1524, 1536, 1585, 1616, 1649, 1650, 1661, 1700, 1745, 1760, 1797, 1803, 1831, 1863, 1874, 1886, 1896, 1903, 1949, 1950, 1951, 1967, 1972

"Amy Foster": 54, 59, 61, 63, 311, 747, 839, 854, 1048, 1226, 1243, 1289, 1306, 1307, 1361, 1515, 1530, 1589, 1722, 1853, 1931, 1939

"An Anarchist": 114, 895, 934, 1253, 1522, 1617

Arrow of Gold: 288, 289, 290, 292, 293, 295, 296, 298, 299, 300, 301, 302, 305, 306, 307, 308, 309, 310, 312, 344, 401, 403, 450, 452, 459, 464, 551, 557, 578, 594, 636, 666, 698, 784, 803, 814, 837, 853, 859, 869, 889, 912, 914, 944, 959, 986, 1000, 1035, 1045, 1048, 1088, 1106, 1138, 1147, 1152, 1159, 1168, 1335, 1352, 1403, 1419, 1452, 1515, 1521, 1524, 1581, 1589, 1695, 1743, 1751, 1760, 1779, 1804, 1815, 1821, 1852, 1855, 1856

"The Ascending Effort": 1841

"Autocracy and War": 425, 1098, 1253, 1918

"Because of the Dollars": 215, 238, 374, 450, 1062, 1072, 1167

"The Black Mate": 613, 614, 623, 626, 666, 1048, 1071, 1874

"The Brute": 123, 206, 227

Chance: 172, 173, 174, 175, 176, 178, 179, 180, 182, 183, 184, 185, 187, 189, 191, 192, 193, 194, 195, 196, 198, 201, 220, 229, 241, 255, 257, 261, 264, 283, 284, 313, 323, 327, 330, 333, 336, 339, 343, 354, 357, 367, 378, 380, 385, 388, 403, 450, 452, 533, 536, 539, 578, 599, 670, 682, 733, 769, 770, 804, 808, 829, 830, 832, 849, 856, 859, 869, 883, 889, 894, 901, 918, 922, 944, 957, 959, 967, 971, 988, 996, 997, 1000, 1028, 1035, 1048, 1059, 1064, 1082, 1115, 1126, 1129, 1131, 1138, 1147, 1148, 1152, 1154, 1163, 1168, 1181, 1203, 1224, 1245, 1250, 1253, 1295, 1298, 1303, 1309, 1311, 1324, 1370, 1375, 1390, 1395, 1400, 1406, 1419, 1428, 1463, 1466, 1482, 1486, 1487, 1509, 1515, 1523, 1524, 1581, 1594, 1611, 1617, 1626, 1668, 1678, 1760, 1766, 1773, 1779, 1800, 1809, 1841, 1850, 1886, 1890, 1897, 1903, 1913, 1914, 1933, 1934, 1944, 1968

667

Joseph Conrad

Children of the Sea (N.Y. ed. of *The Nigger of the Narcissus*): 9, 12, 18, 21, 22, 23, 26, 29, 32, 122, 190, 407
"Il Conde": 206, 210, 895, 1336, 1431, 1515, 1791, 1793
"The Crime of Partition": 1098, 1918
"The Duel" (In America as "Point of Honor: A Military Tale"): 114, 118, 120, 201, 206, 227, 388, 401, 578, 750, 806, 895, 1009, 1177, 1617, 1967
"The End of the Tether": 48, 53, 57, 58, 62, 137, 264, 284, 415, 450, 451, 460, 680, 725, 766, 791, 830, 862, 864, 876, 903, 966, 974, 1039, 1123, 1138, 1152, 1203, 1210, 1250, 1298, 1495, 1515, 1567, 1568, 1631, 1633, 1644, 1674, 1721, 1755, 1771, 1828, 1830, 1903, 1917
"Falk": 54, 59, 61, 63, 84, 260, 415, 450, 480, 854, 941, 996, 1039, 1048, 1088, 1209, 1295, 1335, 1349, 1515, 1771, 1815, 1830, 1884, 1890, 1908
"The Feast": 130
"Freya of the Seven Isles": 132, 169, 311, 415, 450, 488, 894, 896, 918, 947, 1000, 1028, 1036, 1449, 1453, 1568
"Gaspar Ruiz": 114, 226, 227, 400, 469, 750, 895, 1048, 1072, 1253, 1617, 1658, 1804
"Geography and Some Explorers": 709
"A Glance at Two Books": 620
"Heart of Darkness": 31, 35, 48, 52, 53, 57, 58, 84, 122, 134, 155, 217, 244, 260, 282, 284, 327, 332, 451, 483, 533, 596, 636, 639, 676, 680, 682, 698, 717, 725, 767, 791, 804, 827, 830, 832, 856, 865, 877, 891, 910, 911, 958, 992, 996, 1011, 1021, 1035, 1064, 1088, 1095, 1101, 1128, 1129, 1138, 1140, 1147, 1152, 1155, 1163, 1167, 1178, 1180, 1181, 1189, 1191, 1192, 1200, 1203, 1205, 1224, 1227, 1236, 1250, 1251, 1253, 1266, 1275, 1289, 1295, 1298, 1299, 1320, 1325, 1334, 1337, 1341, 1344, 1352, 1355, 1358, 1369, 1370, 1373, 1377, 1380, 1387, 1388, 1390, 1419, 1425, 1427, 1436, 1442, 1453, 1455, 1466, 1470, 1487, 1493, 1494, 1496, 1498, 1500, 1509, 1515, 1518, 1521, 1522, 1526, 1535, 1555, 1567, 1572, 1574, 1575, 1576, 1577, 1581, 1585, 1587, 1589, 1593, 1595, 1597, 1611, 1613, 1624, 1626, 1644, 1654, 1660, 1664, 1666, 1668, 1669, 1673, 1682, 1685, 1687, 1691, 1701, 1703, 1706, 1707, 1718, 1723, 1724, 1730, 1731, 1732, 1733, 1734, 1745, 1749, 1752, 1753, 1758, 1760, 1764, 1765, 1766, 1767, 1768, 1769, 1773, 1777, 1778, 1779, 1782, 1784, 1787, 1794, 1800, 1801, 1805, 1816, 1823, 1833, 1835, 1841, 1846, 1852, 1857, 1867, 1875, 1880, 1883, 1887, 1890, 1896, 1899, 1905, 1915, 1916, 1923, 1925, 1928, 1930, 1936, 1946, 1950, 1954, 1961, 1966, 1973
"The Idiots": 24, 30, 338, 372, 866, 1317, 1589, 1828
"The Informer": 114, 895, 918, 1048, 1253, 1515, 1522, 1617, 1792, 1793
The Inheritors (With Ford Madox Hueffer): 41, 43, 44, 494, 599, 862, 864, 869, 1190, 1224, 1642, 1822, 1894
"The Inn of the Two Witches": 215, 234, 238, 273, 1062, 1072, 1172, 1617
"Karain": 11, 27, 311, 403, 415, 450, 451, 866, 1439, 1515, 1659, 1726, 1823, 1931
"The Lagoon": 27, 28, 311, 415, 450, 451, 776, 866, 1210, 1221, 1235, 1238, 1345, 1354, 1403, 1439, 1468, 1550, 1554, 1585, 1604, 1633, 1659, 1720, 1806, 1844, 1870, 1925
Last Essays: 680, 683, 689, 690, 692, 693, 709, 711, 718, 726, 727, 728, 731, 732, 734, 741, 744, 757, 869, 871, 1727
Laughing Anne, A Play (Adaptation of "Because of the Dollars"): 215, 374, 497, 771, 1082
Lord Jim: 36, 37, 38, 39, 40, 42, 44, 46, 66, 71, 89, 122, 123, 126, 129, 135, 136, 137, 158, 179, 180, 203, 212, 230, 236, 255, 261, 268, 278, 280, 283, 285, 292, 327, 331, 332, 347, 350, 353, 358, 370, 378, 381, 385, 403, 406, 407, 415, 416, 418, 419, 420, 446, 447, 450, 452, 453, 457, 459, 477, 504, 533, 536, 539, 561, 565, 627, 664, 667, 681, 682, 684, 696, 698, 733, 791, 808, 821, 825, 830, 838, 855, 856, 869, 877, 890, 913, 916, 917, 918, 920, 929, 932, 944, 953, 959, 971, 973, 982, 988, 996, 997, 999, 1000, 1004, 1014, 1021, 1022, 1028, 1035, 1048, 1064, 1075, 1077, 1093, 1094, 1096, 1102, 1105, 1106, 1108, 1115, 1138, 1146, 1148, 1152, 1154, 1155, 1160, 1167, 1178, 1179, 1183, 1189, 1195, 1202, 1216, 1224, 1229, 1233, 1234, 1237, 1240, 1241, 1248, 1250, 1251, 1258, 1266, 1272, 1280, 1292, 1295, 1298, 1309, 1327, 1335, 1337, 1341, 1352, 1375, 1390, 1391, 1392, 1396, 1405, 1409, 1414, 1416, 1419, 1439, 1445, 1453, 1456, 1466,

Index of Primary Titles

1470, 1479, 1484, 1487, 1493, 1494, 1497, 1509, 1515, 1518, 1523, 1524, 1532, 1533, 1544, 1564, 1581, 1588, 1591, 1595, 1597, 1605, 1611, 1626, 1632, 1644, 1647, 1648, 1659, 1661, 1668, 1670, 1674, 1678, 1687, 1689, 1697, 1710, 1712, 1713, 1717, 1724, 1726, 1727, 1728, 1745, 1750, 1758, 1760, 1762, 1763, 1766, 1771, 1790, 1798, 1800, 1801, 1809, 1823, 1829, 1840, 1841, 1842, 1854, 1856, 1857, 1861, 1862, 1863, 1864, 1869, 1878, 1879, 1890, 1891, 1893, 1895, 1898, 1903, 1909, 1910, 1911, 1914, 1915, 1946, 1948, 1949, 1950, 1951, 1953, 1965, 1967

The Mirror of the Sea: 85, 86, 87, 88, 90, 91, 93, 94, 95, 117, 158, 203, 301, 434, 457, 533, 557, 761, 779, 794, 805, 869, 892, 934, 947, 961, 969, 996, 1011, 1021, 1038, 1083, 1112, 1125, 1149, 1184, 1224, 1248, 1253, 1470, 1616, 1674, 1847, 1852

The Nature of a Crime (With Ford Madox Hueffer): 496, 542, 547, 548, 555, 563, 592, 634, 649, 864, 869, 871

The Nigger of the Narcissus: 8, 9, 10, 12, 13, 17, 18, 19, 20, 21, 22, 23, 25, 26, 29, 31, 32, 34, 40, 71, 89, 123, 126, 129, 134, 135, 137, 155, 158, 190, 217, 231, 241, 282, 327, 351, 358, 361, 370, 371, 378, 380, 385, 391, 392, 401, 403, 407, 432, 450, 452, 460, 461, 464, 487, 533, 565, 599, 606, 662, 699, 770, 781, 782, 791, 794, 806, 807, 825, 830, 856, 859, 865, 869, 884, 918, 929, 944, 947, 971, 973, 990, 996, 1010, 1011, 1021, 1035, 1037, 1040, 1052, 1083, 1091, 1093, 1096, 1102, 1115, 1119, 1122, 1123, 1125, 1138, 1147, 1152, 1161, 1167, 1187, 1201, 1206, 1210, 1224, 1233, 1246, 1250, 1252, 1264, 1271, 1277, 1295, 1298, 1309, 1319, 1325, 1335, 1338, 1341, 1343, 1370, 1373, 1389, 1390, 1410, 1419, 1422, 1466, 1467, 1470, 1483, 1496, 1498, 1509, 1515, 1517, 1520, 1524, 1525, 1542, 1556, 1566, 1567, 1594, 1626, 1635, 1642, 1644, 1651, 1670, 1674, 1727, 1729, 1740, 1745, 1746, 1760, 1762, 1770, 1800, 1805, 1818, 1823, 1840, 1841, 1849, 1852, 1860, 1864, 1865, 1881, 1886, 1888, 1889, 1892, 1896, 1907

Nostromo: 66, 68, 73, 74, 75, 79, 80, 82, 83, 89, 92, 98, 103, 106, 123, 135, 136, 137, 158, 179, 180, 188, 217, 236, 244, 255, 257, 260, 283, 287, 327, 367, 371, 378, 385, 403, 421, 422, 427, 450, 459, 460, 468, 533, 551, 597, 622, 717, 733, 745, 748, 757, 780, 785, 791, 794, 799, 829, 830, 849, 855, 862, 864, 865, 869, 901, 913, 918, 934, 959, 967, 971, 973, 990, 992, 995, 996, 1000, 1001, 1011, 1021, 1035, 1040, 1048, 1055, 1057, 1075, 1102, 1106, 1113, 1115, 1123, 1129, 1138, 1146, 1147, 1148, 1160, 1163, 1167, 1178, 1181, 1191, 1193, 1203, 1206, 1207, 1210, 1224, 1233, 1250, 1251, 1253, 1254, 1266, 1268, 1287, 1295, 1298, 1304, 1305, 1309, 1310, 1316, 1319, 1328, 1329, 1331, 1333, 1335, 1337, 1346, 1359, 1363, 1370, 1375, 1390, 1403, 1419, 1453, 1454, 1461, 1463, 1466, 1470, 1480, 1483, 1493, 1508, 1509, 1515, 1519, 1520, 1521, 1523, 1524, 1527, 1537, 1538, 1539, 1541, 1545, 1558, 1567, 1581, 1585, 1590, 1594, 1595, 1599, 1611, 1617, 1621, 1624, 1626, 1627, 1628, 1631, 1637, 1639, 1645, 1655, 1656, 1658, 1668, 1678, 1688, 1690, 1696, 1698, 1716, 1718, 1724, 1728, 1754, 1760, 1764, 1766, 1771, 1773, 1788, 1789, 1799, 1814, 1823, 1824, 1839, 1841, 1852, 1856, 1857, 1859, 1860, 1868, 1871, 1883, 1890, 1904, 1921, 1930, 1957, 1976

Notes On Life and Letters: 356, 360, 362, 363, 366, 368, 369, 372, 373, 375, 377, 378, 379, 384, 393, 395, 531, 734, 859, 869, 873, 1152, 1250, 1841

"A Note on the Polish Problem": 1098

Notes On My Books: 367, 371

One Day More, A Play in One Act (Adaptation of "To-morrow"): 78, 155, 374, 497, 1366

An Outcast of the Islands: 3, 4, 5, 6, 137, 178, 274, 285, 327, 331, 358, 403, 415, 450, 533, 539, 685, 769, 850, 866, 869, 903, 959, 971, 1048, 1063, 1122, 1125, 1138, 1210, 1233, 1265, 1294, 1309, 1316, 1335, 1403, 1419, 1439, 1483, 1515, 1524, 1536, 1556, 1646, 1661, 1745, 1760, 1831, 1889, 1903, 1967

"An Outpost of Progress": 11, 30, 311, 451, 464, 638, 713, 809, 866, 911, 996, 1205, 1455, 1515, 1570, 1617, 1925

"The Partner": 215, 238, 239, 1062, 1070, 1072, 1074

A Personal Record (Also as *Some Reminiscences*): 133, 140, 144, 145, 147, 153, 156, 255, 281, 285, 369, 531, 668, 751, 852, 869, 924, 973, 1083, 1098,

1112, 1145, 1184, 1250, 1428, 1441, 1453, 1470, 1488, 1616, 1674, 1751, 1852, 1886, 1931, 1939

"The Planter of Malata": 215, 232, 238, 1062, 1072, 1074, 1659, 1815, 1828

"Point of Honor: A Military Tale" (American title of "The Duel"): 106, 107, 109, 111, 120, 168, 206

"Poland Revisited": 375, 1779

"Political Memorandum": 1821

"Prince Roman": 613, 614, 623, 626, 666, 747, 1048, 1071, 1348, 1552, 1617, 1716, 1931, 1939

The Rescue: 22, 319, 320, 321, 324, 325, 327, 328, 329, 337, 339, 341, 342, 344, 346, 348, 349, 385, 405, 407, 415, 450, 452, 464, 593, 636, 788, 805, 825, 829, 839, 862, 869, 885, 894, 912, 971, 1000, 1001, 1014, 1039, 1048, 1063, 1086, 1097, 1106, 1138, 1152, 1178, 1183, 1210, 1233, 1294, 1298, 1316, 1335, 1351, 1383, 1403, 1419, 1453, 1470, 1506, 1515, 1524, 1581, 1625, 1661, 1697, 1724, 1729, 1751, 1760, 1764, 1773, 1831, 1840, 1842, 1903, 1930, 1960, 1967

"The Return": 11, 28, 29, 372, 557, 804, 866, 1048, 1222, 1800

Romance, A Novel (With Ford Madox Hueffer): 55, 60, 67, 70, 72, 76, 84, 400, 456, 478, 494, 549, 578, 587, 599, 697, 801, 862, 864, 869, 880, 936, 1028, 1040, 1102, 1224, 1328, 1594, 1656, 1684, 1822, 1894

The Rover: 399, 404, 406, 411, 417, 422, 427, 435, 437, 513, 533, 539, 543, 562, 565, 578, 588, 627, 636, 715, 809, 840, 869, 913, 934, 967, 997, 1035, 1040, 1067, 1138, 1203, 1244, 1250, 1370, 1403, 1419, 1497, 1515, 1523, 1615, 1751, 1872, 1957

The Secret Agent: 96, 97, 98, 99, 100, 101, 102, 103, 105, 106, 108, 110, 112, 115, 116, 119, 123, 126, 132, 155, 180, 201, 367, 374, 389, 401, 403, 408, 439, 454, 506, 533, 611, 627, 670, 685, 723, 724, 805, 830, 832, 839, 859, 864, 869, 895, 899, 901, 934, 958, 967, 971, 986, 997, 1000, 1011, 1028, 1035, 1047, 1048, 1075, 1138, 1148, 1152, 1178, 1181, 1193, 1207, 1243, 1250, 1251, 1253, 1284, 1288, 1295, 1298, 1304, 1309, 1322, 1328, 1370, 1375, 1390, 1400, 1403, 1419, 1454, 1461, 1464, 1466, 1470, 1472, 1503, 1509, 1515, 1519, 1522, 1523, 1524, 1543, 1558, 1561, 1567, 1578, 1582, 1592, 1595, 1600, 1610, 1611, 1617, 1626, 1645, 1653, 1656, 1674, 1718, 1724, 1741, 1760, 1764, 1766, 1773, 1799, 1800, 1803, 1810, 1819, 1827, 1866, 1882, 1890, 1896, 1897, 1900, 1935, 1942, 1943, 1957, 1958, 1974, 1975

"The Secret Sharer": 169, 203, 311, 415, 450, 457, 639, 771, 838, 846, 856, 860, 896, 918, 941, 960, 967, 1028, 1122, 1129, 1154, 1163, 1183, 1191, 1197, 1203, 1205, 1207, 1223, 1250, 1252, 1253, 1266, 1281, 1293, 1295, 1296, 1298, 1306, 1321, 1353, 1370, 1379, 1390, 1400, 1419, 1453, 1459, 1461, 1470, 1515, 1521, 1535, 1562, 1566, 1567, 1570, 1595, 1598, 1603, 1607, 1644, 1657, 1665, 1669, 1674, 1675, 1679, 1711, 1745, 1753, 1766, 1772, 1773, 1793, 1805, 1826, 1828, 1845, 1846, 1852, 1857, 1877, 1901, 1910, 1912, 1925, 1936, 1962, 1967

A Set of Six: 104, 114, 118, 197, 198, 199, 202, 206, 210, 213, 226, 227, 228, 869, 895, 947, 998, 1009, 1123, 1309

The Shadow-Line: 246, 247, 248, 249, 250, 251, 253, 254, 257, 258, 259, 262, 263, 264, 265, 266, 267, 269, 270, 283, 285, 406, 415, 450, 459, 599, 639, 670, 830, 845, 848, 869, 919, 927, 928, 941, 947, 959, 962, 968, 1000, 1035, 1039, 1079, 1102, 1106, 1138, 1150, 1199, 1200, 1205, 1233, 1250, 1252, 1266, 1296, 1309, 1335, 1370, 1390, 1419, 1453, 1470, 1485, 1515, 1525, 1566, 1567, 1581, 1595, 1603, 1606, 1612, 1644, 1674, 1678, 1696, 1745, 1755, 1772, 1809, 1828, 1830, 1841, 1852, 1910, 1951, 1967

The Sisters: 770, 801, 802, 803, 804, 814, 837, 1351, 1626, 1743

"Skimmer of the Sea": 406

"A Smile of Fortune": 132, 161, 169, 311, 639, 846, 896, 941, 1126, 1167, 1205, 1470, 1515, 1659, 1815, 1851, 1873, 1947

Some Reminiscences (Also as *A Personal Record*): 137, 141, 143, 152, 284, 397, 457, 652, 852, 869, 1040

Suspense: 578, 581, 582, 583, 588, 590, 594, 595, 598, 600, 607, 609, 612, 616, 617, 622, 627, 629, 632, 633, 636, 643, 647, 655, 657, 664, 665, 667, 674, 714, 738, 739, 740, 757, 841, 869, 909, 1028, 1029, 1040, 1045, 1048, 1102, 1138, 1153, 1207, 1419, 1626, 1709, 1738, 1760

"The Tale": 613, 614, 620, 623, 626,

Index of Primary Titles

666, 923, 1048, 1070, 1071, 1078, 1210, 1515, 1617, 1719, 1795

Tales of Hearsay: 585, 608, 613, 614, 619, 623, 626, 644, 659, 660, 666, 869, 875, 1070, 1071, 1102, 1719, 1874

Tales of Unrest: 11, 14, 16, 24, 27, 28, 29, 30, 33, 358, 533, 635, 650, 859, 869, 954, 1123, 1138, 1152, 1720

"To-morrow": 54, 61, 63, 137, 311, 839, 854, 1515

"Tremolino": 1048

'Twixt Land and Sea: 132, 139, 146, 161, 162, 163, 164, 165, 166, 167, 169, 170, 171, 450, 639, 846, 859, 860, 869, 887, 896, 941, 1152, 1168

"Typhoon": 50, 51, 56, 59, 61, 64, 71, 89, 123, 135, 158, 217, 241, 244, 253, 260, 311, 327, 347, 358, 407, 415, 425, 450, 472, 477, 521, 533, 535, 536, 539, 571, 599, 639, 699, 788, 791, 839, 842, 854, 856, 869, 900, 973, 996, 1001, 1019, 1021, 1040, 1044, 1079, 1085, 1093, 1106, 1115, 1119, 1122, 1123, 1138, 1152, 1161, 1167, 1200, 1201, 1224, 1233, 1237, 1250, 1266, 1295, 1306, 1318, 1337, 1341, 1370, 1390, 1483, 1496, 1515, 1551, 1566, 1567, 1601, 1633, 1644, 1670, 1674, 1696, 1793, 1841, 1843, 1852, 1860, 1925

Typhoon, and Other Stories: 45, 52, 54, 56, 59, 61, 64, 255, 601, 745, 854, 1529, 1722

Under Western Eyes: 121, 122, 124, 125, 126, 128, 129, 136, 137, 138, 148, 149, 151, 154, 155, 159, 217, 236, 297, 310, 350, 385, 450, 504, 523, 533, 586, 610, 611, 628, 631, 642, 829, 839, 849, 855, 869, 918, 920, 934, 944, 952, 971, 979, 986, 990, 1000, 1011, 1028, 1035, 1048, 1075, 1101, 1111, 1115, 1116, 1129, 1138, 1148, 1152, 1163, 1167, 1181, 1193, 1202, 1203, 1204, 1210, 1223, 1233, 1250, 1251, 1252, 1253, 1265, 1266, 1268, 1288, 1298, 1309, 1316, 1328, 1335, 1352, 1370, 1375, 1376, 1390, 1402, 1419, 1432, 1453, 1454, 1461, 1470, 1493, 1496, 1509, 1515, 1519, 1520, 1522, 1524, 1540, 1558, 1564, 1586, 1592, 1595, 1617, 1621, 1626, 1645, 1668, 1674, 1693, 1724, 1728, 1741, 1760, 1764, 1773, 1809, 1935, 1936, 1957

"The Unlightened Coast": 620, 923

Victory: 186, 201, 204, 205, 207, 208, 209, 211, 212, 214, 216, 217, 219, 220, 221, 222, 223, 224, 225, 229, 241, 244, 255, 257, 261, 283, 284, 322, 326, 327, 344, 367, 374, 403, 415, 422, 430, 450, 533, 535, 646, 698, 745, 760, 830, 839, 869, 881, 888, 929, 936, 959, 963, 967, 978, 997, 1001, 1028, 1077, 1101, 1102, 1115, 1119, 1123, 1125, 1129, 1138, 1146, 1147, 1148, 1152, 1154, 1155, 1163, 1165, 1167, 1168, 1178, 1181, 1203, 1207, 1208, 1209, 1210, 1228, 1233, 1237, 1239, 1250, 1252, 1253, 1259, 1284, 1290, 1298, 1306, 1309, 1335, 1352, 1367, 1370, 1375, 1390, 1419, 1458, 1461, 1483, 1493, 1504, 1515, 1521, 1523, 1524, 1534, 1564, 1581, 1583, 1595, 1597, 1599, 1629, 1634, 1640, 1656, 1659, 1661, 1667, 1668, 1674, 1678, 1692, 1696, 1701, 1728, 1742, 1750, 1751, 1760, 1766, 1771, 1773, 1777, 1779, 1800, 1802, 1803, 1808, 1816, 1827, 1835, 1841, 1852, 1857, 1889, 1890, 1902, 1903, 1906, 1908, 1924, 1946, 1957, 1963, 1967

"The Warrior's Soul": 613, 614, 623, 626, 644, 666 ["The Warrior's Song" (sic)], 1048, 1070, 1071, 1617

Within the Tides: 200, 215, 232, 233, 234, 235, 237, 238, 239, 240, 241, 242, 245, 273, 391, 398, 431, 442, 847, 859, 869, 954, 1062, 1070, 1072, 1074, 1425, 1886

The Works of Joseph Conrad: 390, 490

Youth, A Narrative, and Two Other Stories: 47, 48, 62, 63, 370, 670, 830, 1461, 1495, 1529, 1567, 1681

"Youth": 48, 49, 52, 53, 57, 58, 71, 137, 158, 168, 244, 253, 260, 332, 347, 358, 448, 450, 452, 459, 521, 533, 636, 639, 699, 717, 725, 791, 827, 839, 849, 856, 866, 869, 891, 973, 996, 1011, 1021, 1078, 1079, 1083, 1093, 1115, 1122, 1138, 1152, 1161, 1167, 1200, 1203, 1210, 1224, 1232, 1247, 1281, 1295, 1298, 1309, 1390, 1419, 1425, 1453, 1455, 1456, 1469, 1470, 1487, 1494, 1499, 1509, 1518, 1530, 1546, 1551, 1566, 1567, 1570, 1589, 1593, 1606, 1649, 1674, 1759, 1770, 1911, 1914, 1917, 1925, 1967